D0429907

ROGET'S THESAURUS OF THE ENGLISH LANGUAGE IN DICTIONARY FORM

Being a Presentation of Roget's Thesaurus of English Words and Phrases in a Modernized, More Complete, and More Convenient Dictionary Form, Together with Briefer Synonymies for the Busy Writer, the Whole Comprised in One Alphabetical Arrangement

WITH AN APPENDIX OF

FOREIGN WORDS AND EXPRESSIONS

BY

C. O. SYLVESTER MAWSON

Litt.D., Ph.D.

GARDEN CITY BOOKS

Garden City, New York

Both the plan of this book and the application of the dictionary idea to Roget's Thesaurus are original and must not be imitated.

Patent Applied For

Garden City Books Reprint Edition, 1940, by special arrangement with G. P. Putnam's Sons

Revised Edition, 1936

Printed in the United States
At the Country Life Press, Garden City, N.Y.

PREFACE

Roget's Thesaurus has been the stand-by of writers for almost three generations. Edition after edition has been published; revisions and enlargements have enhanced its usefulness: but the form has remained the same: classification according to ideas, followed by a colossal index.

A Roget dictionary is an innovation. Users of the Thesaurus well know that the excellence of the book is heavily discounted by the time required to find a word. As in any other academic treatise, it is always necessary to look in two places: the index and the chapter or category. From the viewpoint of the actual user, the strength of the Thesaurus constitutes its essential weakness. Separation into watertight compartments makes neither for speed nor convenience. In substance, the arrangement is: one word, one sense. Thus, under *greenness*, the color alone is treated (and rightly so according to the original plan); for other senses, the index refers us to nine different categories. *Softness* (including *soften* and *soft*) likewise deals only with the literal meaning; for others. the index sends us hunting through no less than twenty categories. And so it goes. We do not mean that a man must necessarily consult this number to find the particular word he has in mind, for the index does briefly suggest the general character of the references. But if a reader is not very clear as to the meaning; if, as frequently happens, the senses of a word shade off into each other; above all, if he is in a hurry; then his search will be a tedious one.

Imagine a dictionary built on these lines. Suppose you turned to a common word and found only one meaning given, obliging you to look under several generalized headings for the other senses. However logically such a system might be worked out, it would be unwieldy, unworkmanlike, and unalluring.

The present volume retains the practical advantages of the standardized Thesaurus without the disadvantages. It was fashioned with a two-fold aim: to provide ready synonyms for the time-pressed worker and to give a richer list—thought-expressing and thought-provoking—to the more leisured writer, the scholar, and the stylist. There is an abundance of plain fare for the plain man; there is besides a discriminate and bounteous provision—a Lucullan feast—for the literary epicure.

About 1910, I made my first revision of Roget and twelve years later, a still more elaborate version. This was the *International Thesaurus*. But though various improvements in arrangement and format were devised, the general plan was the same. Increasing the size but added to the complexity. Further progress could be made only by cutting loose from tradition.

The severance has at last been made and this dictionary is the result. Virtually, it is a dictionary within a dictionary. The old Roget lists are here, modernized, refurbished, and rearranged; but there is one striking difference: *every meaning is covered under one head.* The categories are no longer mere exemplifications of a philosophical treatment but are self-contained lists of classified synonyms, reflecting every phase of meaning and every shade of thought. It is a true dictionary, not of words and their meanings but of words and their synonyms.

Simplicity is the keynote, the convenience of the consulter being always kept in mind. The hyphen-and-dash devices, adopted by Roget for saving space, have been abolished. They were a source of confusion to the uninitiated and often threw into juxtaposition words in no way allied. Clarity was sacrificed to formula. Space has now been gained by other methods, typographical and editorial.

The outstanding characteristics of this volume may be briefly summarized:

1. The dictionary method is followed throughout, all entries being listed in alphabetical order and in one vocabulary.

2. Synonyms, grouped according to meaning, immediately follow each entry, so that reference to other parts of the book is not absolutely essential.

3. The reconstructed Roget categories are incorporated in the general alphabet. All senses—and not one alone—are covered under each main heading, thus making each category complete in itself.

4. The Roget plan of giving nouns, verbs, adjectives, adverbs, and interjections under each main head has been retained; but whereas Roget made his "adverbs" an olla-podrida of adverbs, prepositions, conjunctions, and sometimes of nonadverbial phrases, such terms are now separately classified.

5. Under these main heads, each meaning of a synonymized word is clearly distinguished, a keyword giving the general sense of each subdivision.

6. Reference to the major subjects is made from the ordinary entries in the vocabulary, which entries take the place of the former index.

7. All special words have been characterized, so that the writer may select his synonyms with greater sureness. If he wishes to use a scientific or technical term, a colloquial or slang expression, an Americanism or a Briticism, or some word peculiar to another country, he can do so knowingly and with precision. All foreign literary terms are italicized and labeled; a translation of every one of them is given in the appendix.

8. Plurals are recorded in every case of irregularity and wherever the consulter might be in doubt.

9. Phrases are given freely. This was one of Roget's most valuable contributions to the subject. It is just as important, and as difficult, to find a substitute phrase as a synonymous word; moreover, a phrase is often the only alternative for a word that has no true synonym. Yet most books of synonyms omit phrases entirely.

10. Obsolete words have been discarded. This is a dictionary of living words only.

11. New words have been added—thousands of them—to bring the work abreast of modern scholarship and usage. Our language has been enriched in recent years with many terms contributed by aëronautics, radio, the moving-picture industry, meteorology, psychology—in fact, by practically every branch of knowledge and every technical calling. Side by side with these recruited terms are many older words that have taken to themselves new meanings. The synonym book, like the ordinary dictionary, must keep pace with these additions and changes.

12. The ROGET DICTIONARY is at once a vade-mecum for the busy man and a complete thesaurus for the exacting writer who lives with words and by them.

In these days, when worth is often measured by magnitude, it may be pointed out that this book not only contains more synonyms than any previous edition of Roget, but is more comprehensive than any other book of synonyms whatever. Size alone, however, is a poor criterion of merit. A work of reference must stand or fall by its accuracy and authority.

The authority of this work rests on almost a lifetime of practical experience in the making of dictionaries. This experience included association with great lexicographers such as Sir James Murray of the Oxford Dictionary and Benjamin E. Smith of the Century, while several years were spent on the permanent staff of Webster. Those years were an invaluable preparation for this undertaking, for on such dictionaries accuracy and scholarship are appraised at their full value. This book has been made under the stimulus of that great tradition. Three years have been spent in its actual construction, but behind this period is the accumulated store of a quarter of a century.

C. O. S. M.

WELLESLEY, MASSACHUSETTS

HOW TO USE THE BOOK

1. If you are in a hurry. Use this book as you would any other dictionary. A choice of good synonyms will be at your disposal as soon as you have found the entry. You need look no further in the book. There is only one alphabet, and you are not sent from pillar to post in pursuit of a fugitive term. You will find your synonym where you first look for it.

Now a word or two in explanation of these entries. You will notice that when a word has more than one well-defined meaning, these meanings are grouped and are separated from each other by semicolons. Thus the synonyms are presented to you in an orderly manner instead of in a jumble. Let us illustrate this. Suppose you want a synonym for the word "raw." You turn to the letter R and find the entry thus recorded:

> **raw,** *adj.* chilly, piercing, cutting; immature, crude, unripe, uncooked, unprepared; excoriated, galled, chafed; unskilled, untrained, green, inexperienced; wind-swept, exposed, bleak. See COLD, NONPREPARATION, PAIN, UNSKILLFULNESS, WIND.

Here are five distinct senses of the word "raw." A glance will show you the particular sense you have in mind and provide you with a usable synonym. You need not trouble about the references at the end of each entry. Those are for your more leisurely and discriminating brother.

Should you, however, require synonyms for such words as *aëronautics, benevolence, conduct, exertion, music, thought, world,* or *zoölogy*, a greater wealth will be spread before you. These words and more than a thousand like them are the backbone of the book. They represent the Roget idea in their major divisions into nouns, verbs, adjectives, adverbs, etc. But there is a great difference. In the old Roget, only one general sense is covered by each main heading. In this book, each is self-contained; that is, every shade of meaning is given. Hence, you need not look further for your word. The synonyms under each part of speech are grouped according to meaning. The keyword at the beginning of each subdivision indicates the general significance of that particular group.

In using this dictionary, if you do not find the particular word you have in mind, take the word that most nearly suggests it. Thus, if you wanted a synonym for "abandonment," you would find only "abandon" in the vocabulary, but the reference to RELINQUISHMENT would give you the synonyms of the noun. Derivatives are commonly omitted to save space.

2. If you have more leisure. Suppose you are a writer seeking not a mere synonym but an exact expression of your thought. In that case, the subjects referred to at the end of the ordinary entries will best serve your turn. The order of the references, as a rule, follows that of the listed groups. For example, under the word "raw," the first reference (COLD) is associated with the first group, "chilly, piercing, cutting"; while the last reference (WIND) carries on the idea of the last group, "wind-swept, exposed, bleak." When you have referred to the subject you want, you will note—with satisfaction, we trust—that every meaning is adequately covered and that you need not turn elsewhere to find some omitted sense. The labeling of all foreign words and the characterization of all scientific, technical, colloquial, dialectic, and slang expressions will prove of value. The references at the foot of the major entries may be ignored, unless you desire to explore these related bypaths. Lovers of words who have leisure for linguistic adventuring will find these ramifications of absorbing interest, suggesting not synonyms alone but new ideas and alluring fields of thought. The hard-pressed writer, however, will do well to resist the temptation.

A WORD OF CAUTION

Synonyms are good servants but bad masters; therefore select them with care. Theoretically, a synonym is a word identical in meaning with another of the same language. If this were literally true, the choice of a substitute word would be child's play. It is doubtful, however, whether any two words are identical in all their senses and connotations; which is another way of saying that there are no perfect synonyms. For this reason, synonyms should not be chosen at random. This book, by its groupings, reduces the difficulty to a minimum; nevertheless, great care must be exercised by the writer who wishes to fit the exact word to his thought.

Another point to remember is that words which are broadly synonymous with one particular entry are not necessarily interchangeable with one another. Thus, while *uncooked* may be substituted for *raw* in referring to vegetables, we should not employ it in reference to silk or recruits, much less to describe the weather or the state of an open wound.

We should like to close this comment by quoting the words of the well known scholar and lexicographer, H. W. Fowler, joint author of *The Concise Oxford Dictionary* and author of *Modern English Usage:*

"No one who does not expend a good deal of care upon points of synonymy is likely to write well. A writer's concern with synonyms is twofold. He requires first the power of calling up the various names under which the idea he has to express can go. Everyone has this in some degree; everyone can develop his gift by exercise; but copiousness in this direction varies, and to those who are deficient in it, ready-made lists of synonyms are a blessed refuge. . . . Such lists, to be of much use, should be voluminous, and those who need them should try ROGET'S THESAURUS or some other work devoted to that side of synonymy. Secondly, he requires the power of choosing rightly out of the group at his command, a power which depends on his realizing the differences between its items."

ABBREVIATIONS USED IN THIS BOOK

abbr....abbreviation
adj....adjective
adv....adverb
aëro....aëronautics
Am. or *Amer*....America, American
anat....anatomy
antiq....antiquities
anthropol....anthropology
Ar....Arabic
arch....architecture
archæol....archæology
arith....arithmetic
astrol....astrology
astron....astronomy
Bib....Biblical
biol....biology
bot....botany
Brit....British
cap....capital (initial)
cf....confer (L., compare)
Ch....Church
chem....chemistry
Ch. of Eng....Church of England
colloq....colloquial
comp....comparative
conj....conjunction
derog....derogatory
dial....dialect, dialectal
dim....diminutive
E....East
eccl....ecclesiastical
econ....economics
elec....electricity
embryol....embryology
Eng....English, England
entom....entomology
esp....especially
ethnol....ethnology
F....French
fem....feminine
fig....figurative, figuratively
G. or *Ger*....German
geol....geology
geom....geometry
Gr....Greek
gram....grammar
Gr. Brit....Great Britain
Heb....Hebrew
Hind....Hindustani
hist....history, historical
hort....horticulture
interj....interjection
It....Italian
Jap....Japanese
L....Latin
l. c.....lower case
lit....literal, literally
LL....Low Latin
masc....masculine
math....mathematics
mech....mechanics
med....medicine
metal....metallurgy
meteorol....meteorology
Meth....Methodist
mil....military
Moham....Mohammedan
mus....music
myth....mythology
N....North
n....noun
naut....nautical
NL....New Latin
Per....Persian
Pg....Portuguese
pharm....pharmacy
philol....philology
philos....philosophy
physiol....physiology
pl....plural
polit....political
p. p.....participle past
prep....preposition
pros....prosody
psychol....psychology
R.C.Ch....Roman Catholic Church
relig....religion
rhet....rhetoric, rhetorical
Russ....Russian
S....South
Scot....Scottish
sculp....sculpture
sing....singular
Skr....Sanskrit
Sp....Spanish
superl....superlative
tech....technical
theat....theatrical
theol....theology
theos....theosophy
typog....typography
Univ....University
U. S.....United States
v....verb
W....West
zoöl....zoölogy

THE ROGET DICTIONARY
OF
SYNONYMS AND ANTONYMS

A

abandon, *v.* desert, forsake, renounce, leave, quit, relinquish. See RELINQUISHMENT.
abandoned, *adj.* deserted, vacant; homeless, desolate, friendless, lonely, forsaken; depraved, shameless, reprobate, profligate. See ABSENCE, EXCLUSION, VICE.
abase, *v.* humble, degrade, humiliate, dishonor, shame. See HUMILITY.
abasement, *n.* debasement, degradation, disgrace. See DISREPUTE.
abash, *v.* disconcert, mortify, confuse, confound, bewilder. See HUMILITY.
abate, *v.* lessen, moderate, diminish, mitigate, subside. See DECREASE.
abbreviate, *v.* abridge, contract, shorten, curtail, condense. See SHORTNESS.
abdicate, *v.* relinquish, abandon, renounce, resign, surrender. See RESIGNATION.
abdomen, *n.* belly, paunch, epigastrium. See CONVEXITY.
abdominal, *adj.* ventral, stomachic, cœliac *or* celiac. See INTERIORITY.
abduct, *v.* kidnap, carry away, transport, shanghai. See STEALING.
abet, *v.* assist, sanction, incite, instigate, encourage, support, uphold. See AID.
abhor, *v.* loathe, hate, abominate, detest, despise. See HATE.
abhorrence, *n.* repugnance, antipathy, aversion, hatred. See DISLIKE.
abide, *v.* remain, stay, rest; endure, tolerate; dwell, reside, live. See EXISTENCE, INEXCITABILITY, INHABITANT.
ability, *n.* talent, capacity, faculty, aptitude, expertness, efficiency, capability. See POWER, SKILL.
abject, *adj.* degraded, despicable, vile; servile, base, slavish, beggarly. See DISREPUTE, SERVILITY.
abjure, *v.* recant, retract, forswear, repudiate. See APOSTASY, NEGATION.
able, *adj.* capable, efficient, competent, skillful, clever, gifted, proficient. See POWER, SKILL.
able-bodied, *adj.* strong, muscular, athletic. See STRENGTH.
abnormal, *adj.* unusual, unnatural, irregular, anomalous, erratic. See UNCONFORMITY.
abode, *n.* dwelling, lodging, residence, quarters. See HABITATION.
abolish, *v.* destroy, annihilate; nullify, annul, abrogate, repeal, rescind, revoke. See ANNULMENT.
abominable, *adj.* base, villainous; offensive, odious, detestable, loathsome, abhorrent. See BADNESS, HATE.
abominate, *v.* detest, abhor, loathe, dislike. See HATE.
abortion, *n.* abortiveness, miscarriage, prematurity, immaturity. See NONPREPARATION.
abound, *v.* teem, swarm, overflow, be plentiful, flourish. See SUFFICIENCY.
about, *adv.* around, surrounding; approximately, nearly; regarding, respecting, anent, touching, concerning. See ENVIRONMENT, NEARNESS, SMALLNESS; RELATION.

above, *adv.* overhead, on high, up, aloft; earlier, before. See HEIGHT, PRECESSION.
abrade, *v.* rub, scrape, scour, erase, grate, grind. See FRICTION, POWDERINESS.
abrasive, *adj.* abradant, fricative (*phonetics*), anatriptic (*med.*). See FRICTION.
abridge, *v.* shorten, condense, epitomize; curtail, lessen, reduce, diminish. See COMPENDIUM, SHORTNESS.
abridgment, *n.* summary, abstract, synopsis, epitome, digest; contraction, reduction. See COMPENDIUM, DECREASE, SHORTNESS.
abroad, *adv.* away, elsewhere, afar, overseas, wandering, adrift. See DISTANCE, EXTRANEOUSNESS.
abrupt, *adj.* brusque, curt, unceremonious; sudden, hasty, unexpected; steep, precipitous, sheer. See BLUNTNESS, INSTANTANEITY, OBLIQUITY.
abscond, *v.* depart, disappear, fly, withdraw, decamp. See AVOIDANCE.

ABSENCE.—I. *Nouns.* **absence,** nullibicity *or* nullibiety (*rare*), inexistence, nonexistence; nonattendance, nonappearance, cut (*colloq.*); alibi; nonresidence, absenteeism.
preoccupation, absorption, abstraction, inattention, heedlessness, absentmindedness, absence of mind, woolgathering, daydreaming, reverie, brown study (*colloq.*).
want, lack, need, requirement, deficiency, scarcity.
emptiness, void, vacuum, vacuity, vacuousness, voidness (*rare*), hollowness, vacancy.
interval, hiatus, interruption, pause, recess, interlude, interim, space; interregnum.
truant, absentee; shirk, slacker (*colloq.*), quitter.
II. *Verbs.* **be absent,** keep away, keep out of the way, play truant, absent oneself, stay away, hold aloof; shirk, evade; abscond, decamp.
withdraw, retreat, retire, quit, vacate; make oneself scarce (*colloq.*), go away.
III. *Adjectives.* **absent,** not present, away, A. W. O. L. (absent without leave), nonattendant, nonresident, gone, from home; missing, lost, wanting, omitted; abroad, oversea; on vacation, on tour, on the road.
empty, void, vacant, vacuous, blank, clear; deserted, abandoned, desert (*archaic*), forsaken, desolate, waste, untenanted, unoccupied, uninhabitated, tenantless; uninhabitable.
absent-minded, abstracted, inattentive, heedless, listless, thoughtless, distracted, preoccupied, engrossed, removed, far-away, dreamy, musing, woolgathering.
IV. *Adverbs.* **absently,** distractedly, absent-mindedly, inattentively, heedlessly; elsewhere, elsewhither, neither here nor there.
V. *Prepositions.* **without,** in the absence of, in default of, beyond, sans (*esp. in reference to the line from As You Like It: "sans teeth, sans eyes, sans taste, sans everything"*), deprived of, free from, in want of, less; outside of.
See also AVOIDANCE, DEPARTURE, INATTENTION.—*Antonyms.* See PRESENCE.

---

absolute, *adj.* unrestricted, unqualified, unconditional; complete, perfect, entire; despotic, autocratic, supreme. See CERTAINTY, COMPLETENESS, GREATNESS.
absolutely, *adv.* positively, decidedly, wholly, unconditionally. See GREATNESS.
absolution, *n.* forgiveness, acquittal, dispensation, intercession, exoneration See FORGIVENESS.
absolve, *v.* forgive, pardon, excuse, overlook, condone. See FORGIVENESS.
absorb, *v.* imbibe, assimilate; engulf, merge, overwhelm; occupy, engross, enwrap. See COMBINATION, RECEPTION, THOUGHT.
absorbed, *adj.* engrossed, occupied, intent. See THOUGHT.
absorbent, *adj.* absorptive, receptive, sorbefacient (*med.*); spongy. See RECEPTION.

abstain, *v.* refrain, forbear, desist; fast. See AVOIDANCE, TEMPERANCE.
abstainer, *n.* ascetic, teetotaler. See TEMPERANCE.
abstemious, *adj.* sober, temperate, abstinent, self-controlled, austere. See SOBRIETY.
abstention, *n.* abstinence, forbearance. See AVOIDANCE.
abstinence, *n.* temperance, self-denial, abstemiousness. See TEMPERANCE.
abstract, *adj.* difficult, abstruse, recondite; ideal, transcendental; theoretic, pure (*as mathematics*). See DIFFICULTY, IMAGINATION, PURITY.
abstract, *n.* epitome, summary, abridgment, précis, brief. See COMPENDIUM.
abstracted, *adj.* inattentive, preoccupied, thoughtful, removed. See INATTENTION.
abstraction, *n.* absent-mindedness, preoccupation; removal. See ABSENCE, INATTENTION, THOUGHT; TAKING.
abstruse, *adj.* dark, enigmatical, profound, hidden, obscure, difficult, recondite, deep. See DARKNESS, UNINTELLIGIBILITY.
abstruseness, *n.* obscurity, reconditeness, profundity, unintelligibility. See DARKNESS.

ABSURDITY.—I. *Nouns.* **absurdity,** absurdness, comicality, nonsense, *bêtise* (*F.*), paradox, inconsistency, fallacy, nugacity, futility, stultiloquy (*rare*), imbecility, stupidity, foolishness.
blunder, muddle, bungle, bull, Hibernicism; anticlimax, bathos.
farce, burlesque, travesty, parody, caricature, amphigory, farrago, extravagance.
pun, *calembour* (*F.*), play upon words, sell (*colloq.*), catch (*colloq.*), quillet (*archaic*), *double-entendre* (*F.*), joke, paronomasia.
jargon, gibberish, galimatias, balderdash, bombast, twaddle, moonshine, stuff, claptrap, bunk (*slang*), hot air (*slang*), bull (*slang*).
tomfoolery, mummery, buffoonery, fooling, *boutade* (*F.*), monkey trick, practical joke, escapade.
II. *Verbs.* **be absurd,** play the fool, frisk, caper, joke, fool, tomfool (*colloq.*), play practical jokes, talk nonsense; blunder, bungle, muddle.
III. *Adjectives.* **absurd,** nonsensical, preposterous, unreasonable, egregious, senseless, inconsistent, ridiculous, extravagant, self-contradictory, paradoxical; foolish, ludicrous, laughable, asinine, silly, stupid, inane, stultiloquent (*rare*), amphigoric, meaningless, fantastic, bombastic, stilted, high-flown; farcical, burlesque; incredible, incongruous, irrational; without rime or reason.
See also IMBECILITY, IMPOSSIBILITY, UNMEANINGNESS.—*Antonyms.* See INTELLIGENCE, MAXIM, REASONING.

---

abundance, *n.* plenty, fullness, profusion, wealth. See SUFFICIENCY.
abundant, *adj.* ample, plentiful, copious, teeming, profuse. See SUFFICIENCY, WEALTH.
abuse, *v.* maltreat, ill-use, mistreat; revile, disparage, vilify, malign, traduce, reproach, slander, defame; misapply, pervert. See BADNESS, DISAPPROBATION, MISUSE.
abuse, *n.* injury, maltreatment; vituperation, invective, opprobrium, insult; cursing, scurrility; desecration. See BADNESS, DISAPPROBATION, MALEDICTION, MISUSE.
abusive, *adj.* condemnatory, vituperative, defamatory, slanderous. See DISAPPROBATION.
abyss, *n.* chasm, gulf, pit, gorge, depth. See INTERVAL, PITFALL.
academic, *adj.* scholarly, erudite; scholastic. See SCHOLAR, TEACHING.
accede, *v.* acquiesce, comply, agree, concur; conform, yield. See ASSENT, CONSENT.
accelerate, *v.* speed, hurry, hasten, quicken, expedite, facilitate. See EARLINESS, HASTE, VELOCITY.

accent, *n.* tone, inflection, pronunciation; stress, emphasis, beat. See [1]SOUND, VOICE.
accentuate, *v.* stress, emphasis, accent. See IMPORTANCE.
accept, *v.* admit, approve, adopt, recognize; receive, take. See ASSENT, RECEIVING.
acceptable, *adj.* expedient, desirable, wise, convenient; welcome. See EXPEDIENCE, PLEASURABLENESS.
acceptance, *n.* acknowledgment, reception, approval; guarantee, indorsement. See ASSENT, SECURITY.
access, *n.* accessibility, admittance; path, way. See APPROACH.
accessible, *adj.* approachable; attainable, obtainable. See APPROACH, OPENING, POSSIBILITY.
accession, *n.* acquiescence, agreement; addition, growth, accretion. See ASSENT, INCREASE.
accessory, *adj.* additional, supplementary, contributory, auxiliary. See ADDITION, OBJECTIVENESS.
accessory, *n.* addition, accompaniment, appendage; abettor, accomplice See ADJUNCT, AUXILIARY.
accident, *n.* mishap, casualty, mischance, disaster, calamity; contingency. See ADVERSITY, CHANCE.
accidental, *adj.* fortuitous, casual, incidental, unforeseen. See ATTRIBUTION.
acclimatize, *v.* habituate, accustom, naturalize, inure, season. See HABIT.
acclivity, *n.* incline, rise, ascent, pitch, grade. See OBLIQUITY.
acclivous, *adj.* rising, uphill, ascending, steep, abrupt. See OBLIQUITY.
accommodate, *v.* adapt, adjust, conform, fit, suit; oblige, furnish, supply. See AGREEMENT, AID.

ACCOMPANIMENT.—I. *Nouns.* **accompaniment,** adjunct, concomitant, accessory; appendage, appanage, appurtenance, attribute; context; concomitance *or* concomitancy, coexistence.
[*in music*] subsidiary part, supplementary part, instrumental part; obbligato.
company, association, partnership; companionship.
companion, associate, colleague, partner, side kick (*slang*), buddy (*U. S. colloq.*), mate, chum, pal (*colloq.*), *fidus Achates* (*L.*); consort, spouse; satellite, hanger-on, shadow; escort, attendant, *cortège* (*F.*), suite, train, retinue, convoy, follower, adherent.
II. *Verbs.* **accompany, attend, escort, guard, conduct, usher, company** (*archaic*), convoy, chaperon; associate with, couple with.
III. *Adjectives.* **accompanying,** concomitant, fellow, twin, joint; associated with, coupled with; accessory, attendant.
IV. *Adverbs.* **in company with,** withal (*archaic*); **together with, along with,** therewith, herewith, also, moreover, likewise; hand in hand, side by side, cheek by jowl.
together, conjointly, mutually, in a body, in conjunction, collectively.
See also ADJUNCT, SIMULTANEOUSNESS.—*Antonyms.* See RELINQUISHMENT, UNITY.

---

accomplice, *n.* accessory, ally, abettor, confederate, assistant, colleague. See AUXILIARY.
accomplish, *v.* perform, do, achieve, effect, execute, attain, fulfill. See COMPLETION.
accomplished, *adj.* cultivated, learned, skillful, proficient, finished. See LEARNING, SKILL.
accomplishment, *n.* achievement, realization, performance, fulfillment; feat, acquirement. See COMPLETION, SKILL.
accord, *v.* harmonize, conform, tally; concur, acquiesce; grant, bestow. See AGREEMENT, ASSENT, GIVING.

accordance, *n.* agreement, accord, conformity, concurrence, uniformity. See CORRESPONDENCE.

accordingly, *adv.* hence, therefore, in that case, thus. See CIRCUMSTANCE, REASONING.

accost, *v.* greet, address, hail, salute, speak. See SPEECH.

account, *n.* reckoning, score, record, bill; narrative, narration, report, recital. See CREDIT, DESCRIPTION.

accountable, *adj.* explicable; responsible, liable, answerable. See ATTRIBUTION, LIABILITY.

ACCOUNTS.—I. *Nouns.* **accounts,** accompts (*archaic*), money matters, finance, budget, bill, score, tally, reckoning, account.

bookkeeping, accountancy; audit, single entry, double entry; daybook, cashbook, ledger, journal; balance sheet; receipts, assets, accounts receivable; expenditure, liabilities, accounts payable; profit and loss account (*or* statement).

accountant, bookkeeper; cashier, teller; auditor, actuary, expert accountant, certified accountant, chartered accountant (*Eng.*).

II. *Verbs.* **keep accounts,** enter, post, post up, book, credit, debit, balance; cast up accounts, add, add up, tot up (*colloq.*); square accounts.

---

accretion, *n.* adhesion, concretion; accumulation, growth, increment. See COHERENCE, INCREASE.

accrue, *v.* fall (from *or* to), arise, result; yield, bring in. See ACQUISITION, EFFECT, RECEIVING.

accumulate, *v.* collect, gather, hoard, amass, assemble, increase. See ASSEMBLAGE, STORE.

accumulation, *n.* amassment, aggregation, cumulation, store, stock. See ASSEMBLAGE, INCREASE.

accuracy, *n.* exactness, verity, correctness, precision, preciseness. See CARE, TRUTH.

accurate, *adj.* exact, correct, true, precise, proper, just. See TRUTH.

accursed, *adj.* execrable, detestable, damnable, diabolic; doomed, ill-fated. See BADNESS, PAIN.

ACCUSATION.—I. *Nouns.* **accusation,** charge, imputation, slur, incrimination, recrimination; blame, censure, denunciation, crimination, inculpation, delation (*esp. by an informer*), plaint (*law*), complaint.

libel, challenge, citation, arraignment, impeachment, indictment; true bill; lawsuit; condemnation, conviction, sentence.

accused, defendant, prisoner, respondent, litigant.

accuser, prosecutor, plaintiff, complainant, informant, informer, delator; libelant.

II. *Verbs.* **accuse,** charge, tax, impute, twit, taunt, upbraid, reproach, blame, stigmatize, slur; criminate, incriminate, inculpate, implicate.

inform against, indict, denounce, impeach, arraign; charge with, saddle with, lodge a complaint; challenge, cite, prosecute; blow upon (*colloq.*), squeal (*slang*), show up (*colloq.*).

III. *Adjectives.* **accusatory,** denunciatory, criminatory, recriminatory, accusing, threatening.

inexcusable, indefensible, unpardonable, unjustifiable, unallowable.

See also CONDEMNATION, DISAPPROBATION, LAWSUIT.—*Antonyms.* See APPROBATION, VINDICATION.

---

accustom, *v.* habituate, familiarize, season, inure. See HABIT.

ache, *v.* hurt, twinge, shoot, smart. See PAIN.

achievement, *n.* fulfillment, execution; accomplishment, exploit, feat, performance. See COMPLETION, COURAGE.

acknowledge, *v.* own, admit, confess, concede, grant. See ASSENT, DISCLOSURE.

acknowledgment, *n.* avowal, confession, admission; voucher. See DISCLOSURE, PAYMENT, RECEIPT.
acquaint, *v.* inform, tell, apprise, notify, familiarize. See INFORMATION.
acquaintance, *n.* intimate, associate; familiarity, insight, information. See FRIEND, KNOWLEDGE.
acquiesce, *v.* agree, concur, accede, comply. See ASSENT, CONSENT.

ACQUISITION.—I. *Nouns.* **acquisition,** acquirement, obtainment, attainment, procuration, procurement; purchase; heritage, patrimony, inheritance; gift, donation, benefaction, grant.
recovery, retrieval, replevin, redemption, salvage, find.
gain, thrift, money-making, money-grubbing; lucre, filthy lucre, pelf, loaves and fishes, fleshpots of Egypt; the main chance.
profit, earnings, wages, salary, income, emolument, remuneration; winnings, pickings, perquisite, graft, velvet (*slang*); proceeds, avails, produce, product; outcome, output; return, fruit, crop, harvest; benefit; prize, reward, award.
II. *Verbs.* **acquire,** get, gain, win, earn, obtain, procure, gather, collect, pick, pick up, glean, find, light upon, come across, come at, scrape up (*or* together), get in, net, bag, capture, secure; derive, draw, get in the harvest; increase, accrue
profit, advantage, benefit, turn to profit (*or* account), make capital out of, make money by, obtain a return, reap, reap the fruits of; gain an advantage; make (coin, *or* raise) money, raise funds, raise the wind (*slang*), realize, clear, produce, take, receive, come by, inherit, succeed to.
regain, recover, get back, retrieve, redeem, repossess, recapture, retake.
III. *Adjectives.* **acquisitive,** acquiring, grasping, griping, grabbing, avaricious, rapacious, covetous.
profitable, productive, advantageous, gainful, remunerative, paying, lucrative, beneficial.
IV. *Adverbs.* **acquisitively,** graspingly, etc. (see *adjectives*); in the way of gain; for money; at interest.

See also RECEIPT, REWARD, SECURITY (*obtain*), WEALTH.—*Antonyms.* See EXPENDITURE, LOSS, PENALTY.

ACQUITTAL.—I. *Nouns.* **acquittal,** exculpation, clearance, clearing, exoneration, discharge, release, absolution, quietus, reprieve, respite, pardon.
[*freedom from punishment*] **impunity,** immunity, privilege, prerogative, exemption.
II. *Verbs.* **acquit,** exculpate, exonerate, clear, absolve, extenuate, whitewash, discharge, release, liberate, free, emancipate, remit, reprieve, respite, pardon.
exempt, immunize, privilege.
III. *Adjectives.* **acquitted,** exonerated; released, discharged; uncondemned, unpunished.

See also EXEMPTION, LIBERATION, FORGIVENESS.—*Antonyms.* See CONDEMNATION, RESTRAINT.

---

acrid, *adj.* acrimonious, caustic, biting, keen, severe, tart, pungent, bitter. See PUNGENCY, SOURNESS, UNSAVORINESS.
acrimony, *n.* bitterness, spleen, asperity, acerbity, virulence. See RESENTMENT.
across, *adv.* crosswise, athwart. See CROSSING.
act, *n.* deed, exploit, action, step; statute, law, edict, decree, ordinance; scene, curtain. See ACTION, COMMAND, DRAMA.
act, *v.* perform, do, make, operate; behave; personate, play, impersonate; simulate, feign, dissemble. See ACTION, CONDUCT, DRAMA, FALSEHOOD.—**act a part,** act, play; dissemble, feign, simulate; help, aid, assist. See DRAMA, FALSEHOOD, UTILITY.
acta, *n. pl.* official acts, transactions, minutes. See ACTION.
actable, *adj.* performable, doable, practicable, possible. See POSSIBILITY.
acting, *adj.* working, functioning; officiating, delegated. See ACTION, DEPUTY.
acting, *n.* rendition (*U. S.*), performance, playing. See DRAMA.
actinoid, *adj.* radiated, raylike, actiniform. See SYMMETRY.

ACTION.—I. *Nouns.* **action,** performance, perpetration, exercise, movement, operation, work, labor, task, exertion, execution; response, reaction; process, mechanism, working; procedure, conduct, behavior, deportment; handicraft; business, occupation, employment, pursuit, agency.
deed, act, effort, transaction, job, doings, dealings, proceeding, acta (*pl.*), measure, step, maneuver, bout, passage, move, enterprise, *coup* (*F.*), *coup de main* (*F.*), stroke, blow; feat, stunt (*colloq.*), exploit, achievement; handiwork, craftsmanship, workmanship; manufacture; stroke of policy.
[*in law*] **lawsuit,** legal proceeding, suit, legal process, proceedings.
battle, fight, engagement, combat, conflict, encounter.
doer, performer, perpetrator, worker, agent, actor, operator.
II. *Verbs.* **act,** operate, function, take action, take steps, take in hand, put in practice, carry into execution, make good.
do, perform, execute, achieve, transact, enact; commit, perpetrate, inflict; exercise, prosecute, carry on, labor, work, practice, employ oneself, ply one's task, have in hand, shape one's course; officiate, preside.
feign, pretend, make believe, simulate, counterfeit, dissemble, dissimulate.
play (*on the stage*), personate, impersonate, represent, perform, enact, take (*or* act) the part of.
behave, conduct oneself, bear oneself, comport oneself, demean oneself, acquit oneself.
III. *Adjectives.* **acting,** performing, officiating, in harness, on duty, at work, in action; operating, operative.
IV. *Adverbs.* **in the act,** in the midst of; red-handed, *in flagrante delicto* (*L.*).

See also COMPLETION, CONDUCT, CONTENTION, DRAMA, EXERTION, LAWSUIT.—*Antonyms* See INACTION, NONCOMPLETION, REPOSE.

ACTIVITY.—I. *Nouns.* **activity,** energy, enterprise, vigor, vim (*colloq.*), snap (*colloq.*), go (*colloq.*), briskness, liveliness, animation, life, vivacity, spirit, dash.
quickness, alertness, smartness, nimbleness, agility, alacrity, dispatch, expedition, haste, speed, celerity, velocity; promptitude, punctuality.
eagerness, zeal, ardor, *empressement* (*F.*), enthusiasm, keenness, earnestness, intentness, devotedness, devotion, exertion.
industry, assiduity, assiduousness, sedulousness, laboriousness, drudgery, diligence, perseverance, persistence, application.
vigilance, watchfulness; wakefulness, sleeplessness, insomnia, restlessness.
bustle, stir, fuss, ado, bother, hustle (*colloq.*), rustle (*slang*), movement, flurry, turmoil; press of business; no sinecure.
officiousness, dabbling, meddling, interference, intermeddling, meddlesomeness, inquisitiveness; intrigue.
enthusiast, zealot, fanatic, devotee; live wire (*colloq.*), human dynamo, hustler (*colloq.*), rustler (*slang*), go-getter (*U. S. slang*), man of action.
busybody, meddler, intriguer, intrigant (*fem.* intrigante); tattler, gossip, talebearer; Paul Pry, snoop (*colloq.*), snooper (*colloq.*).
II. *Verbs.* **be active,** busy oneself in; stir, stir about, bestir oneself; speed, hasten, bustle, fuss; push, go ahead, push forward; make progress; toil, moil, fag, drudge, plod, persist, persevere, hustle (*colloq.*), rustle (*slang*), push (*colloq.*), keep moving, seize the opportunity, lose no time, dash off, make haste.
have a hand in, take an active part, put in one's oar, have a finger in the pie, dabble, intrigue; agitate.
meddle, interfere, interpose, intermeddle, tamper with; obtrude, butt in, horn in (*both slang*), poke one's nose in.
III. *Adjectives.* **active,** brisk, lively, animated, vivacious, alive, frisky, spirited; nimble, agile, light-footed, nimble-footed; watchful, vigilant, wakeful.
quick, prompt, instant, ready, alert, spry (*colloq.*), sharp, smart; fast, swift, speedy, rapid, fleet; expeditious, awake, snappy (*colloq.*), up and coming (*colloq.*), live (*colloq.*), go-ahead (*colloq.*), wide-awake.
eager, ardent, strenuous, zealous, enterprising, keen, intent, pushing, aggressive, resolute.
industrious, assiduous, diligent, sedulous, painstaking, indefatigable, pertinacious, persevering, unwearied, busy, occupied; plodding, hard-working, businesslike.

bustling, hurried, rushing; restless, unquiet, agitated, fussy, fidgety, pottering.
meddlesome, interfering, officious, busy, intrusive, obtrusive, forward.
sleepless, slumberless, insomnious (*rare*), insomnolent (*rare*), wakeful.
IV. *Adverbs.* **actively,** briskly, etc. (see *adjectives*); with life and spirit, with might and main, with all one's might, full tilt.
astir, in motion, afoot, on foot, out of bed, up, in full swing; on the alert, on the *qui vive* (*F.*).

See also ENERGY, EXERTION, HASTE.—*Antonyms.* See INACTIVITY, LEISURE, REPOSE.

---

actor, *n.* doer, worker; player, tragedian, comedian. See AGENT, DRAMA.
actual, *adj.* real, veritable, positive, absolute, genuine. See EXISTENCE, TRUTH.
actuality, *n.* reality, fact, verity, certainty, realness. See EXISTENCE, TRUTH.
actually, *adv.* truly, really, in fact, veritably, indeed. See EXISTENCE.
actuate, *v.* persuade, induce, move, impel. See INFLUENCE.
acumen, *n.* acuteness, discernment, sagacity, shrewdness. See INTELLIGENCE.
acute, *adj.* sagacious, astute, shrewd, discerning; poignant, severe, keen, piercing; pointed, sharp. See INTELLIGENCE, PAINFULNESS, SENSITIVENESS, SHARPNESS.
adage, *n.* proverb, motto, aphorism, precept, saw. See MAXIM.
adapt, *v.* suit, conform, regulate, adjust, fit, accommodate, reconcile. See AGREEMENT.
adaptable, *adj.* conformable, tractable, compliant, adaptive; utilizable. See CONFORMITY, UTILITY.
adaptation, *n.* adjustment, accommodation, conformity. See AGREEMENT.
add, *v.* affix, join, compute, reckon; increase, amplify, enlarge. See ADDITION, INCREASE.
addicted, *adj.* habituated, accustomed, given. See HABIT.

ADDITION.—I. *Nouns.* **addition,** annexation, accession, reënforcement; increase, increment; adding (*arithmetic: opposite of* subtraction).
affix, adjunct, prefix, postfix, suffix, subscript, appendage, postscript, attachment, tab, pendant, tag, rider, codicil, addendum (*pl.* addenda), supplement; accompaniment; insertion, interpolation; extension, ell, wing, annex.
II. *Verbs.* **add,** annex, affix, prefix; subjoin, amplify, enlarge; superpose, superimpose; tack to, tag, append, attach, join; interpose, interpolate, introduce, insert.
reckon, compute, enumerate, numerate, number, calculate, total, cast (sum, *or* count) up, figure, cipher (*U. S. colloq.*).
reënforce, strengthen, augment, buttress, fortify.
III. *Adjectives.* **additional,** supplemental, supplementary; extra, spare, further, fresh, new, other, contributory, accessory, auxiliary.
IV. *Adverbs.* **additionally,** in addition, *au reste* (*F.*), more, and, also, likewise, too, furthermore, further, besides, to boot; over and above, moreover, withal (*archaic*); as well as, together with, along with, in conjunction with, conjointly, *cum multis aliis* (*L.*).

See also ACCOMPANIMENT, INCREASE, NUMERATION.—*Antonyms.* See DECREASE, DEDUCTION.

---

address, *v.* superscribe, direct; court, woo; accost, salute, hail, greet, approach. See DIRECTION, ENDEARMENT, SPEECH.
address, *n.* superscription; abode, house, residence; cleverness, dexterity; discourse, oration, talk. See DIRECTION, HABITATION, SKILL, SPEECH.
adduce, *v.* bring forward, present, offer, allege, cite. See EVIDENCE.
adept, *n.* master, veteran, connoisseur. See EXPERT.
adequate, *adj.* sufficient, enough; effectual, competent, able. See SUFFICIENCY, USE.

adhere, *v.* stick, cleave, attach, join, cling, hold, cohere. See COHERENCE.
adherent, *n.* supporter, follower, advocate, partisan. See AUXILIARY.
adhesive, *adj.* sticky, gummy, glutinous, viscous. See COHERENCE.
adieu, *n.* farewell, parting, good-by. See DEPARTURE.
adjacent, *adj.* bordering, near, close, neighboring. See NEARNESS.
adjoin, *v.* border, touch, neighbor, meet, abut. See CONTACT.
adjourn, *v.* prorogue, defer, postpone. See LATENESS.
adjudge, *v.* adjudicate, decide, settle, award, decree; condemn. See JUDGE.

ADJUNCT.—I. *Nouns.* **adjunct,** addition, affix, suffix, appendage, attachment, annex, augmentation, increment, reënforcement, accessory, appurtenance, accompaniment; addendum (*pl.* addenda), appendix (*L. pl.* appendices), complement, supplement, sequel, continuation.
rider, allonge, offshoot, episode, corollary, codicil.
flap, lug, lappet, lap, leaf, tab, fly, skirt, apron, tuck, pocket cover; valve.
II. *Adjectives.* **adjunct,** added, conjoined, additional, annexed.
See also ACCOMPANIMENT, ADDITION.—*Antonyms.* See DECREMENT, DEDUCTION.

---

adjust, *v.* arrange, regulate, settle, reconcile; sort, grade, classify. See ARRANGEMENT, ORDER, SIZE.
administer, *v.* govern, lead, control; furnish, dispense. See AUTHORITY, GIVING.
admirable, *adj.* excellent, commendable, estimable, praiseworthy. See GOOD.
admiration, *n.* approval, esteem, appreciation; astonishment. See RESPECT, WONDER.
admire, *v.* esteem, value, honor; marvel. See RESPECT, WONDER.
admission, *n.* acknowledgment, concession; inclusion, admittance. See CONSENT, DISCLOSURE, RECEPTION.
admit, *v.* acknowledge, own, concede, confess; receive. See DISCLOSURE, INCLUSION.
admonition, *n.* warning, caution, exhortation, reprehension. See VOICE.

ADOLESCENCE.—I. *Nouns.* **adolescence,** youth, juvenescence, youthfulness, pubescence, adolescency; immaturity, nonage, minority.
manhood, virility, adulthood (*rare*), full age, majority; womanhood; flower of age; full bloom.
middle age, maturity, prime of life, meridian of life.
II. *Verbs.* **come of age,** come to man's estate, come to years of discretion; attain majority, assume the *toga virilis* (*L.*); come out (*colloq.*), make one's *début* (*F.*), début (*colloq.*), be presented (*as in society or on the stage*).
III. *Adjectives.* **adolescent,** pubescent, of age, of full age, of ripe age; out of one's teens, grown up, full-grown, manly, manlike, virile, adult; womanly; marriageable, nubile, marriable (*rare*).
middle-aged, mature, in one's prime, *entre deux âges* (*F.*); matronly (*fem.*).
See also YOUTH.—*Antonyms.* See AGE.

---

adopt, *v.* appropriate, use, take; choose, embrace. See BORROWING, CHOICE.
adore, *v.* idolize, hold dear; revere, reverence, glorify. See LOVE, WORSHIP.
adorn, *v.* deck, garnish, beautify, decorate. See ORNAMENT.
adrift, *adv.* lost, perplexed, at sea, astray. See UNCERTAINTY.
adulterate, *v.* corrupt, contaminate, debase, alloy. See DETERIORATION, SOPHISTRY.
advance, *v.* allege, propose; mount, rise; proceed, go. See AFFIRMATION, INCREASE, PROGRESSION.
advantage, *n.* profit, benefit, gain; purchase, leverage; power, authority, prestige, precedence. See INCREASE, INFLUENCE, SUPERIORITY.
advantageous, *adj.* helpful, useful, profitable, favorable, beneficial. See USE.

adventure, *n.* risk, hazard, venture; occurrence, happening. See DANGER, EVENT.

adventurer, *n.* free lance, soldier of fortune; pretender, impostor; gambler, speculator; wanderer, voyager. See COMBATANT, DECEIVER, RASHNESS, TRAVELER.

ADVERSITY.—I. *Nouns.* **adversity,** bad (ill, evil, adverse, *or* hard) fortune *or* luck, frowns of fortune; broken fortunes; slough of despond; evil day, hard times, rainy day, cloud, gathering clouds, ill wind; affliction, trouble, hardship, curse, blight, load, pressure, humiliation; evil, harm.

misfortune, mishap, mischance, misadventure, disaster, calamity, catastrophe; accident, casualty, blow, trial, sorrow, visitation, scourge, infliction, reverse, check, setback, comedown (*colloq.*), *contretemps* (*F.*).

ruin, downfall, fall, overthrow, failure, crash, wreck; losing game; undoing, extremity.

II. *Verbs.* **come to grief,** go downhill, be up against it (*colloq.*), go to rack and ruin, go to the dogs (*colloq.*); decay, sink, decline, fall, go down in the world; have seen better days; be all up with (*colloq.*); be on the rocks (*colloq.*).

III. *Adjectives.* **adverse,** untoward, opposed, opposite, contrary, conflicting, opposing; disastrous, calamitous, ruinous, dire, deplorable.

unfortunate, unblest, unhappy, unlucky, unprosperous, unsuccessful, luckless, hapless, out of luck, in a bad way; under a cloud, badly off, in adverse circumstances, poor, penniless, destitute; decayed, undone, on the road to ruin, on its last legs.

inauspicious, ill-fated, ill-starred, ill-omened; devoted, doomed; ominous, sinister, unfavorable, unpropitious, hostile.

IV. *Adverbs.* **adversely,** unluckily, disastrously, unfavorably; from bad to worse, out of the frying pan into the fire.

See also CONTRARIETY, EVIL, FAILURE, OPPOSITION, PAINFULNESS.—*Antonyms.* See PROSPERITY, SUCCESS.

---

advertisement, *n.* announcement, notice, bill, placard, circular. See PUBLICATION.

ADVICE.—I. *Nouns.* **advice,** counsel, word to the wise, *verbum sapienti* (*L.*), *verbum sap.* (*abbr.*), suggestion, recommendation, advocacy; exhortation, persuasion, expostulation, dissuasion, admonition, caution; guidance.

information, intelligence, news, notification, notice, announcement, communication, intimation: *usually in plural.*

instruction, charge, injunction, message, bidding, dictate, mandate, commission, writ, precept.

consultation, conference, parley, *pourparler* (*F.*), interview, powwow (*chiefly U. S.*), council.

adviser, prompter, director, guide, counsel, counselor, monitor, mentor, Nestor, sage, wise man, Solon; teacher, instructor, tutor; physician; arbiter, judge, referee.

II. *Verbs.* **advise,** counsel, suggest, prompt, recommend, urge, move, prescribe, advocate, exhort, persuade, guide.

enjoin, enforce, charge, instruct, call, call upon, request, dictate.

expostulate, remonstrate, dissuade, admonish, warn, caution.

confer, consult, discuss, palaver, powwow (*chiefly U. S.*); refer to, call in; follow, take (*or* follow) advice; be advised by, have at one's elbow, take one's cue from.

notify, inform, apprise, tell, acquaint, enlighten, edify.

III. *Adjectives.* **advisable,** desirable, recommendable, commendable, expedient advantageous, fitting, proper, suitable, meet.

advisory, consultative, consultatory (*as, an* advisory *board*).

See also DIRECTION, DISSUASION, INFORMATION, WARNING.—*Antonyms.* See PLEA. PROHIBITION.

advocacy, *n.* assistance, favor, countenance, championship, intercession See SUPPORT.
advocate, *v.* recommend, prescribe, suggest, counsel. See ADVICE, SUPPORT.

AËRONAUT.—*Nouns.* **aëronaut,** aviator, airman, birdman (*colloq.*), aëroplanist, eagle, flyer; airwoman, birdwoman (*colloq.*), aviatress *or* aviatrix; pilot, navigator, observer, scout, spotter (*mil.*); ace; balloonist; Icarus; parachutist, aërialist.

AËRONAUTICS.—I. *Nouns.* **aëronautics,** aërial navigation, avigation (*cant*), aviation, flying, flight, wing, volation, volitation, airmanship; ballooning, ballooning, balloonery.
[*allied sciences*] aërodonetics, aërodynamics, aërostatics, aërography; aëromechanics, pneumatics.
aircraft, aëroplane, airplane, *avion* (*F.*), *aviatik* (*Ger.; with twin propellers*), bus (*slang*), crate (*slang*), aëro (*colloq.*), ship (*colloq.*); monoplane, biplane, triplane, tripe (*slang*), quadruplane, multiplane; landplane, plane, monocoupe, *monocoque* (*F.; lit.*, single shell), jenny (Curtis J. N. 4: *slang*), shipplane (*a landplane designed to rise and land on the deck of a ship*); tractor (*propeller in front*), pusher (*propeller in rear*), canard (*kind of pusher*); helicopter, ornithopter; penguin (*for ground practice*).
[*seaplanes*] **seaplane,** waterplane, hydromonoplane, hydro-airplane (*erroneously*, hydroplane), hydro-aëroplane, aëro-hydroplane, flying boat, aëroboat, aëroyacht; amphibian.
[*motorless planes*] **glider,** sailplane; *aviette* (*self-propelled*).
[*aërostats or lighter-than-air craft*] **airship** (*rigid, nonrigid, or semirigid*), dirigible, zeppelin, air liner, air cruiser, blimp (*cant*); balloon, free balloon, captive balloon, observation balloon, kite balloon, sausage balloon, sausage, kite sausage, pilot balloon; kite, box kite; parachute.
airdrome, aërodrome, seadrome, drome (*colloq.*), nest (*slang*), aviation field, flying field, landing field, landing, airport, air base; hangar, shed; runway.
[*technical terms*] wing, aileron, aërofoil *or* airfoil, wing rib, false rib *or* former rib, drag strut *or* compression rib, wing skid, stay, strut, truss; drag wire, drift wire, stagger wire, brace wire, lift wire, control wires, antidrag wire, landing (*or* antilift) wire; leading edge, entering edge, trailing edge; cabane, fuselage *or* body, *longéron* (*F.; longitudinal member of a fuselage*); cockpit, office (*slang*), cabin; gondola, nacelle (*of a balloon or of the pusher type of aircraft*); horn (*small lever*), controls, control stick, Joyce stick (*after its inventor, a British officer*), joy stick (*slang*), stick (*colloq.*); propeller, prop (*slang*), spinner; tail unit, tail assembly, tail group, rudder, tail, empennage; elevator, flipper (*slang*), diving rudder; stabilizer, horizontal tail fin, fin; landing gear, undercarriage, tail skid; mooring mast (*for large airships*); airway, air route.
line of flight (*or* thrust), longitudinal axis *or* fore-and-aft axis, lateral axis *or* transverse axis, *décalage* (*F.*), longitudinal dihedral angle, angle of attack, dihedral angle, center of mass, center of pressure, impact pressure, torque, sweepback, head resistance, back wash *or* slip stream, skin friction, drag, drift, gliding angle, landing angle, ground angle; revolutions per minute (*abbr.* R. P. M.), rev (*slang*).
[*instruments*] air-speed indicator, altimeter, anemometer, barograph, climb indicator, compass, drift meter (*or* indicator), flight indicator *or* turn and bank indicator, gasoline (*or* gas) gauge, inclinometer, oil-pressure gauge, oil thermometer, Pitot tube, tachometer, tac (*slang*).
[*maneuvers*] take-off, zoom, banking; loop, inside loop, outside loop, inverted flight, reverse turn, Immelmann turn (*named after the German war ace*); roll, barrel roll; spiral, whip stall, tail slide, spin, tail spin, power spin; sideslip (*opposite of* skidding); dive, nose dive, power dive, falling leaf; glide, volplane, fish-tailing, hedge-hopping (*colloq.*); landing, pancake (*abrupt landing*), three-point landing; circus, flying circus.
II. *Verbs.* **fly,** aviate, take the air, take off, hop; zoom, soar, climb; drift, hover; glide, volplane, plane (*colloq.*); pilot.
flatten off (*or* out), level off (*or* out), redress; loop, loop the loop (*obsolescent term*), roll; bank, skid, sideslip, spiral, spin, dive, nose-dive, pique; pancake,

land; taxi; give her the gun (*i. e., open up the throttle: slang*), rev (*i. e., speed the motor intermittently: slang*).
III. *Adjectives.* **aëronautical,** aëronautic, flying; aërial; airworthy; air-minded, air-conscious.
IV. *Interjections.* switch off! contact! let her go!
See also AËRONAUT, COMBATANT, HEIGHT (*ceiling*).

---

aëroplane, *n.* aircraft, flying machine, plane, airplane. See AËRONAUTICS.
æsthetic, *adj.* artistic; cultured, cultivated, refined. See BEAUTY, TASTE.
ætiology, *n.* ontogeny, phylogeny, evolution. See ZOÖLOGY.
afar, *adv.* far, away, abroad, aloof. See DISTANCE.
affable, *adj.* amiable, bland, gracious, friendly, sociable, approachable. See COURTESY, FACILITY.
affair, *n.* event, occurrence, matter, concern, question: *often in plural.* See BUSINESS, EVENT.
affect, *v.* touch, influence, move; concern, regard. See EXCITEMENT, RELATION.

AFFECTATION.—I. *Nouns.* **affectation,** affectedness, artificiality, insincerity pretense, pretension, airs, pedantry, formality, stiffness, mannerism, modishness, frill, side (*slang*), dog (*slang*); charlatanism, quackery.
primness, prudery, stiffness, coyness, demureness; *minauderie* (*F.*), mock modesty *mauvaise honte* (*F.*), false shame.
foppery, dandyism, coxcombry, puppyism, conceit.
pedant, pedagogue, doctrinaire, purist, euphuist, formalist, mannerist, poser, *poseur* (*F.; fem. poseuse*); blue stocking, *bas bleu* (*F.*), *précieuse ridicule* (*F.*), prig, charlatan; prude (*usually a woman*), puritan, precisian.
II. *Verbs.* **affect,** act a part, give oneself airs, boast, simper, mince, attitudinize, pose, posture, overact, overdo.
III. *Adjectives.* **affected,** pretentious, pedantic, stilted, stagy, theatrical, canting, insincere, unnatural, self-conscious, artificial, *maniéré* (*F.*), mannered awkward; overdone, overacted.
stiff, formal, starchy, up-stage (*slang*), high-hat (*slang*), precise, prim, smug, complacent; demure, puritanical, prudish.
priggish, conceited, vain, egotistic, self-satisfied, self-sufficient, intellectually foppish; finical, finicking, mincing, simpering, namby-pamby, sentimental, languishing, lackadaisical.
See also BOASTING, FOP, INELEGANCE, INSOLENCE, OSTENTATION, VANITY.—*Antonyms.* See ARTLESSNESS, MODESTY.

---

affection, *n.* malady, ailment; fondness, tenderness, devotion; quality, property, attribute; disposition, bent. See DISEASE, LOVE, POWER, TENDENCY.
affectionate, *adj.* loving, tender, fond, doting. See LOVE.
affectionate regard, esteem, estimation, honor, devotion. See DEARNESS.

AFFIRMATION.—I. *Nouns.* **affirmation,** confirmation, ratification, corroboration; allegation, profession, acknowledgment, assertion, declaration; predication, avowal, avouchment, asseveration, swearing, oath, affidavit, deposition; assurance, protest, protestation, averment, emphasis, positiveness, peremptoriness, dogmatism, cocksureness, weight.
vote, voice, say, ballot, plebiscite; suffrage, franchise.
remark, observation, assertion, expression, utterance, statement, communication; saying, dictum, sentence.
II. *Verbs.* **affirm,** assert, say, declare, state, protest, profess, acknowledge; put forward, advance, predicate, announce, pose, lay down, allege, propose, propound, enunciate, broach, set forth, maintain, claim, insist, contend, pronounce.
depose, aver, avow, avouch, asseverate, swear, affirm; take one's oath, testify, depone; make an affidavit; vow, vouch, warrant, certify, assure; attest.
emphasize, stress, insist upon, lay stress on; accentuate, enforce, lay down the law, dogmatize: repeat, reassert, reaffirm.

III. *Adjectives.* **affirmative,** positive, emphatic, decided, clear, certain, express, explicit, absolute, insistent, dogmatic, formal, solemn, categorical, peremptory, declaratory, unmistakable; complying, concurring.
IV. *Adverbs.* **affirmatively,** positively, emphatically, etc. (see *adjectives*); with emphasis, ex-cathedra, without fear of contradiction.

See also CERTAINTY, EVIDENCE.—*Antonyms.* See NEGATION, UNCERTAINTY.

---

affix, *n.* adjunct, appendage, supplement. See ADDITION.
afflict, *v.* trouble, distress, grieve, hurt, torment, wound. See PAIN.
afford, *v.* yield, produce, supply; command money. See GIVING, WEALTH.
afloat, *adv.* adrift, floating, aboard, at sea. See SHIP.
aforesaid, *adj.* preceding, above-mentioned, foregoing, former. See REPETITION.
afraid, *adj.* frightened, timorous, fearful, cowardly, alarmed, apprehensive, terrified. See FEAR.
after, *adv.* behind, aft, astern, in the rear, back, in the wake; subsequently, afterwards, later. See REAR, SEQUENCE.
aftermath, *n.* outcome, issue; rowen, fog, aftergrass. See EFFECT, VEGETABLE.
afternoon, *n. post meridiem* (*L.*), *p. m.* See EVENING.
after-part, *n.* tail, tailpiece, stern. See REAR.
again, *adv.* repeatedly, once more, anew, afresh. See REPETITION.
against, *prep.* opposite, counter, contrariwise. See OPPOSITION.

AGE.—I. *Nouns.* **age,** oldness, agedness, old age, advanced age, senility, years, gray hairs, grand climacteric, declining years, decrepitude, superannuation, second childhood, dotage; vale of years, decline of life, senescence, "sear and yellow leaf" (*Macbeth*); green old age, ripe age; longevity.
period, era, æon *or* eon, kalpa (*Hindu*), yuga (*Hindu*), epoch, century; duration, generation, lifetime; a long time: *in this sense,* age *is colloquial.*
seniority, eldership, primogeniture; elder, *doyen* (*F.*), dean; father; veteran.
II. *Verbs.* **age,** grow old, decline, wane, senesce (*rare*).
III. *Adjectives.* **aged,** old, elderly, eldern (*archaic*), senile; ripe, mellow, declining, senescent, waning, past one's prime; gray, grayheaded, hoar, hoary, venerable, ancient, patriarchal, time-worn, *passé* (*F.; fem. passée*), antiquated, effete, decrepit, superannuated; advanced in life (*or* years); stricken in years; having one foot in the grave.
senior (*abbr.* Sr.), elder, older, superior (*as in rank or standing*): *opposite of* junior.
eldest, oldest, firstborn; primogenitary.

See also DURABILITY, LAPSE, OLDNESS, PERIOD, VETERAN.—*Antonyms.* See NEWNESS, YOUTH.

AGENCY.—I. *Nouns.* **agency,** force, function, office, maintenance, exercise, work, swing, play; action, operation, procedure, method; causation, impelling force, causality.
mediation, intervention, intercession, interposition; instrumentality, medium, means; influence, pull (*colloq.*), drag (*colloq.*).
[*in commerce*] **office,** bureau, business, place of business, establishment.
II. *Verbs.* **function,** act, operate, work; perform, play, support, sustain, maintain, take effect, go, quicken, strike; have play, have free play; bring to bear upon.
III. *Adjectives.* **agential,** official, acting, operative, operant (*rare*); in operation, at work, in force, in action, in play, on foot; effective, efficient, practical, effectual, efficacious, exertive, conative (*tech.*).

See also ACTION, INFLUENCE, MEANS.—*Antonyms.* See INACTION, POWERLESSNESS.

AGENT.—*Nouns.* **agent,** doer, actor, performer, perpetrator, operator, executor, executrix (*fem.*), practitioner, worker; representative, deputy, substitute, emissary, proxy, minister, broker, attorney, go-between, mediary; factor, steward; servant, factotum.

workman, artisan, craftsman, handicraftsman, mechanic, operative; workingman, laboring man; handworker, handworkman, hewers of wood and drawers of water; laborer, navvy (*Eng.*); hand, man, hired man, day laborer, journeyman, hack, drudge.
maker, artificer, artist, wright, manufacturer, architect, contractor, *padrone* (*It.*), builder, smith; carpenter, joiner.
machinist, mechanician, engineer, electrician.
workwoman, female operative; dressmaker, *modiste* (*F.*), needlewoman, seamstress, milliner; laundress, washerwoman; charwoman, cleaning woman, accommodator, maid, hired girl.
coworker, fellow worker, associate, colleague, *confrère* (*F.*), coöperator.
staff, force, help, helpers, hands, crew; assistants, personnel; faculty.
[*of things*] **cause,** active power, natural force; factor, instrument, means.
See also DEPUTY, INSTRUMENTALITY, REPRESENTATIVE, SERVANT.

---

aggrandize, *v.* enrich, augment, enlarge, elevate. See INCREASE.

AGGRAVATION.—I. *Nouns.* **aggravation,** heightening, intensification, exacerbation; overestimation, exaggeration.
provocation, irritation, exasperation, annoyance, vexation, acridity: *in this sense,* aggravation *is colloquial.*
II. *Verbs.* **aggravate,** render worse, worsen, heighten, embitter, sour, envenom; intensify, enhance.
provoke, irritate, exasperate, annoy, vex, nettle, anger, fret, ruffle, roil, rile (*colloq.*): *in this sense,* aggravate *is colloquial.*
III. *Adjectives.* **aggravated,** worse, unrelieved, aggravative, intensified.
aggravating, exasperating, annoying, irritating: *in this sense,* aggravating *is colloquial.*
IV. *Adverbs.* from bad to worse, worse and worse.
See also EXAGGERATION, INCREASE, OVERESTIMATION.—*Antonyms.* See RELIEF, UNDERESTIMATION.

---

aggregate, *n.* aggregation; all, total, sum, sum total. See ASSEMBLAGE, WHOLE.
aggression, *n.* inroad, offense, encroachment, invasion. See ATTACK.
aggressive, *adj.* pushing (*as in business*), energetic; combative, offensive, pugnacious, invasive. See ACTIVITY, ATTACK.
agile, *adj.* nimble, spry, brisk, active, lithe, quick. See VELOCITY.

AGITATION.—I. *Nouns.* **agitation,** stir, tremor, shake, ripple, jog, jolt, jar, jerk, hitch, shock, trepidation, flurry, flutter, fluster; quiver, quaver, dance; twitter, flicker, flutter, pitapat, pulsation.
disquiet, perturbation, discomposure, disconcertion, confusion, commotion, excitement, turmoil, turbulence; tumult, hubbub, rout, bustle, fuss, racket.
spasm, throe, throb, palpitation, convulsion, seizure, paroxysm, cramp, gripes.
disturbance (*mental or physical*), disorder, derangement, restlessness, jactitation *or* jactation (*med.*), floccillation (*med.*), vellication, twitching, subsultus (*med.*), jumps (*slang*); changeableness, instability.
ferment, fermentation, ebullition, effervescence, hurly-burly.
whirlwind, cyclone, tornado, waterspout, dust spout, dust whirl, twister (*U. S.*), typhoon; tempest, storm.
discussion (*esp. of controversial matters*), debate, ventilation, consideration, deliberation, argument, inquiry, examination.
II. *Verbs.* agitate, shake, convulse, toss, tumble, wield, brandish, wave, flap, flourish, whisk, switch, swish, swing, sweep; jerk, hitch, jolt, jog, joggle, disturb, stir, shake up, churn.
jostle, buffet, hustle, elbow, push.
discuss, debate, ventilate, argue, consider, inquire, deliberate, examine.
be agitated, shake, tremble, flutter, fly, flicker, quiver, quaver, quake, shiver, writhe, toss; shuffle, tumble, stagger, bob, reel, sway, waver; wag, waggle,

wriggle; stumble, shamble, flounder, totter, flounce, flop; dance, tread (*as a minuet*), curvet, prance, caper, cavort (*colloq.*); squirm; vellicate, twitch.
flurry, fluster, excite, confuse, perturb, trouble, rattle (*colloq.*), disconcert, bewilder, alarm.
throb, pulsate, beat, palpitate, pitapat.
ferment, effervesce, work, foam, boil, boil over, bubble, bubble up; simmer.
III. *Adjectives.* **agitated,** shaking, tremulous; convulsive, spasmodic, successive, jerky, saltant, saltatorial, saltatoric *or* saltatory; effervescent, bubbly, bubbling; unquiet, restless, vellicative.
IV. *Adverbs.* by fits and starts; *per saltum* (*L.*); in convulsions, in fits; in a flurry, in a flutter.

See also CHANGEABLENESS, DISORDER, EXCITEMENT, WIND.—*Antonyms.* See ORDER, [1]REST, STABILITY.

---

agitator, *n.* ringleader; malcontent, demagogue. See DIRECTOR, OPPONENT.
agnostic, *n.* disbeliever, skeptic, unbeliever. See INCREDULITY.
ago, *adv.* since, gone, past. See PAST.
agony, *n.* torture, torment, suffering, anguish. See PAIN.
agree, *v.* correspond, fit, accord, tally; acquiesce, concur. See AGREEMENT, ASSENT.
agreeable, *adj.* suitable, compatible; pleasant, congenial. See CONFORMITY, PLEASURE.

AGREEMENT.—I. *Nouns.* **agreement,** accord, accordance, coincidence, keeping, unison, consonancy, consonance, harmony, concord, union, unity, unanimity, reunion, reconcilement; conjunction, coherence; combination, understanding, consort, concert (*as, the* concert *of Europe*), *entente* (*F.*), *entente cordiale* (*F.*); compact, contract.
conformity, uniformity, consistency; congruence, congruity; correspondence, parallelism, apposition.
fitness, aptness, relevancy, pertinence, pertinency, appositeness, aptitude, propriety, applicability, admissibility, compatibility.
adaptation, adjustment, accommodation; assimilation, reconcilement, reconciliation, appeasement, pacification.
consent, acquiescence, concurrence, consensus; coöperation.
II. *Verbs.* **agree,** accord, harmonize, correspond, tally; consent, acquiesce, respond, meet, fall in with; concur, coincide.
adapt, accommodate, graduate, calibrate (*tech.*), rectify (*elec.*), adjust, correct, suit, conform, fit, square, befit, match, equal, dovetail, resemble, parallel; regulate, reconcile.
III. *Adjectives.* **agreeing,** accordant, correspondent, congenial; coherent; harmonious, reconcilable, conformable; consistent, compatible, consonant, congruous; commensurate, proportionate; in accordance with, in harmony with, in keeping with.
apt, apposite, pertinent, pat, neat, happy, felicitous, germane, *ad rem* (*L.*), in point, to the point, applicable, relevant, admissible.
appropriate, suitable, becoming, proper, timely, meet, expedient, fit, fitting, adapted, apropos, opportune, seasonable.

See also ASSENT, COMPOSITION, CONCORD, CONCURRENCE, CONFORMITY, EQUALITY, HARMONY.—*Antonyms.* See DISAGREEMENT, DISSENT, INEQUALITY, UNCONFORMITY

---

agricultural, *adj.* rural, agrarian, predial, farming. See HUSBANDRY.
agriculture, *n.* farming, gardening, cultivation, tillage. See HUSBANDRY.
ahead, *adv.* in front, before, forward, onward, in advance. See OVERRUNNING.

AID.—I. *Nouns.* **aid,** assistance, help, succor, support, lift, advance, advancement, furtherance, promotion, coöperation, coadjuvancy.
patronage, countenance, favor, interest, advocacy, championship, defense; auspices.

sustenance, nutrition, nourishment, manna in the wilderness, food, alimentation, maintenance, supplies, stores; means, subsidy, bounty, subvention, premium.
relief, alleviation, mitigation, ministration, ministry, deliverance, rescue; supernatural aid, *deus ex machina* (*L.*).
reënforcements *or* reinforcements, additional troops (*or* ships, etc.), supports, contingents, auxiliaries, allies, recruits.
II. *Verbs.* **aid**, assist, help, succor, lend a hand; contribute, subscribe to; take by the hand, take in tow; relieve, rescue, free, deliver; set up, set on one's legs give new life to, be the making of; reënforce, recruit; promote, further, forward, advance; speed, expedite, quicken, hasten.
support, sustain, uphold, prop, hold up, bolster.
nourish, nurture, nurse, cradle, foster, cherish, feed.
serve, do service to, tender to, pander to, minister to; tend, attend, wait on; take care of; regale, entertain, gratify, refresh.
oblige, accommodate, favor, consult the wishes of; humor, cheer, encourage.
second, stand by, back, back up; abet, work for, stick up for (*colloq.*), stick by, take up (*or* espouse) the cause of; advocate, countenance, patronize, smile upon, befriend, side with.
III. *Adjectives.* **aiding**, auxiliary, adjuvant, assisting, helping, helpful, subservient, accessary, accessory, subsidiary.
friendly, amicable, favorable, propitious, well-disposed, benevolent, neighborly, obliging, at one's beck.
IV. *Adverbs.* **in aid of**, on (*or* in) behalf of, in favor of, in the name of, in furtherance of, on account of, for the sake of, on the part of.
V. *Interjections.* **help!** save us! to the rescue! *au secours!* (*F.*), *à moi!* (*F.*).
See also BENEVOLENCE, CARE, COÖPERATION.—*Antonyms.* See HINDRANCE, NEGLECT, OPPOSITION.

---

aider, *n.* assistant, helper, coöperator; ally, friend. See AUXILIARY.
ail, *v.* be sick, suffer, sicken. See DISEASE.
ailment, *n.* illness, malady, infirmity, disorder, affection. See DISEASE.
aim, *v.* direct, point, level, train (*as a gun*), steer for; try, endeavor; aspire to, labor for. See DIRECTION, ESSAY, INTENTION.
aim, *n.* course, drift, bearing; object, goal, purpose, end. See DIRECTION, INTENTION.
aimless, *adj.* erratic, wandering, capricious. See CAPRICE.

AIR.—I. *Nouns.* **air**, atmosphere; ventilation; the open, open air, sky, welkin (*archaic*), blue sky.
[*in meteorology*] troposphere (*lower atmospheric layer*), stratosphere (*upper layer*), tropopause (*boundary or transition region between the two layers*); ozone layer *or* ozone blanket (*effective in cutting off ultra-violet rays*); Heaviside layer (*an atmospheric region in which, on account of its high electric conductivity, radio signals are bent downward, thus making long-distance radio transmission possible*).
[*air in motion*] breath, wind, breeze, draft *or* draught, light wind.
weather, climate, clime; rise and fall of the barometer (*or* mercury).
science of air: aërology, aëroscopy, aërography; meteorology, climatology, climatography; pneumatics, aërometry; aëronautics.
barometer, baroscope, aneroid, weatherglass, weathergauge; airometer, air meter.
weathervane, weathercock, cock, vane.
ventilator, funnel, air shaft, flue, transom, louver; fan, punkah, electric fan.
mien, bearing, action, gesture, carriage, demeanor, deportment, attitude; outward appearance, style, manner, behavior, semblance, look, aspect.
publicity, outlet, utterance, vent, currency, exposure, publication.
[*in music*] tune, melody, aria; predominant part, soprano.
[*in plural*] airs, affected manner, affectation, affectedness, swagger, side (*slang*) pretense, pretension (*as*, airs *and graces*).
II. *Verbs.* **air**, ventilate, fan, winnow; **aërate**, **aërify**; **arterialize** (*physiol.*); **purify**, **oxygenate**.

fly, soar, drift, hover, hang, poise; aviate, take the air, go by air (*or* plane).
parade, display, exhibit, show off, flaunt; vent, ventilate, publish (*as, to* air *one's learning;* air *a grievance*).
III. *Adjectives.* **airy,** atmospheric, aërial, aëriform, aëry, pneumatic; gaseous, effervescent; windy, breezy, exposed, lofty (*as a room*), roomy, light.
meteorological, climatic, atmospherical, barometric *or* barometrical, aërographic, aëroscopic, baroscopic; weatherwise.
[*resembling air*] **airlike,** thin, tenuous, unsubstantial, immaterial, ethereal, delicate, graceful, elastic.
vivacious, sprightly, animated, lively, gay, brisk; flippant, superficial.
IV. *Adverbs.* **in the open air,** in the open, out of doors, outdoors; *al fresco* (*It.*), under the stars, *à la belle étoile* (*F.*).
See also AËRONAUT, AËRONAUTICS, APPEARANCE, GASEITY, MELODY, MUSIC, OSTENTATION, WIND.

---

aircraft, *n.* airplane, aëroplane, plane, airship. See AËRONAUTICS, COMBATANT.
airdrome, *n.* aviation, field, flying field, airport; hangar. See AËRONAUTICS.
airily, *adv.* breezily, vivaciously, gayly. See CHEERFULNESS.

AIR PIPE.—*Nouns.* **air pipe,** air hole, blowhole, breathing hole, vent, spile hole, vent hole, bung, bunghole; shaft, moulin (*in glacier*), air shaft, air trunk; smokeshaft, chimney, flue, funnel, ventilator, louver; air port (*naut.*); air passage, air space.
nostril, nozzle, throat; trachea, windpipe, weasand (*archaic*).
blowpipe, blowtube, blowgun.
See also OPENING.

---

air service, air force, fourth arm (*colloq.*). See AËRONAUTICS, COMBATANT.
airship, *n.* dirigible, zeppelin, aërostat. See AËRONAUTICS.
akin, *adj.* kindred, allied, related, consanguineous. See RELATION.
alacrity, *n.* promptness, briskness, quickness, readiness. See ACTIVITY.

ALARM.—I. *Nouns.* **alarm,** fear of danger, fear, dread, scare, fright, panic, apprehension.
[*indication of danger*] **warning,** signal, summons, call to arms, alarm signal; alarum, alarm bell, tocsin, beat of drum, sound of trumpet; war whoop, war cry; hue and cry; signal of distress, SOS; fog alarm, fog horn, fog signal, siren; yellow flag, yellow jack; danger signal, red light, red flag; fire alarm, fire flag, still alarm; burglar alarm; police whistle; hooter, buzzer; fire cross, fiery cross.
false alarm, cry of wolf, bugbear, bugaboo, bogy, hoax.
II. *Verbs.* **alarm,** give (raise, *or* sound) an alarm, warn, ring the tocsin, beat the general (*mil.*), *battre la générale* (*F.*).
frighten, scare, startle, arouse, disturb, agitate, excite, affright, terrify, appall.
See also FEAR.

---

alarmist, *n.* panic-monger, pessimist. See COWARDICE.
alas! *interj.* alack! woe is me! See LAMENTATION.
alcoholic, *adj.* ardent, strong, hard, spirituous. See DRUNKENNESS.
alert, *adj.* quick, prompt, spry; vigilant, watchful. See ACTIVITY, CARE.
alien, *n.* foreigner, stranger, emigrant, immigrant. See EXTRANEOUSNESS.
alienate, *v.* estrange, turn, set against. See HATE.
alight, *v.* arrive, come, stop; descend, dismount. See ARRIVAL, DESCENT.
align, *v.* range, line, line up, collimate (*tech.*). See ARRANGEMENT.
alike, *adj.* like, resembling, akin, analogous, identical. See SIMILARITY.
alive, *adj.* brisk, spry, animated; keen, quick-witted; living, breathing. See ACTIVITY, INTELLIGENCE, LIFE.
all, *n.* total, aggregate, sum, entirety. See WHOLE.
allay, *v.* mitigate, lessen, slacken, assuage, ease. See MODERATION.
allegiance, *n.* loyalty, obedience, homage, fealty, duty. See OBEDIENCE.

alleviation, *n.* lessening, mitigation, abatement, relief. See MODERATION.
alley, *n.* passage, lane, walk. See OPENING.
alliance, *n.* league, federation, compact; affinity, connection. See COÖPERATION, RELATION.
allied, *adj.* related, connected, associated, united, joined, leagued. See COMBINATION.
allot, *v.* assign, distribute, share, divide. See APPORTIONMENT.
allow, *v.* concede, admit, grant; tolerate, let, suffer. See DISCLOSURE, PERMISSION.
allowance, *n.* concession; contribution; grant, stipend, remittance, salary, pay. See DISCOUNT, GIVING, REWARD.
alloy, *n.* mixture, combine, compound. See COMBINATION.
allude, *v.* suggest, infer, imply, connote. See LATENCY.
allure, *v.* draw, attract, tempt. See DESIRE.
allusion, *n.* quotation, reference, implication, suggestion, hint. See LATENCY
ally, *n.* associate, coworker, friend. See AUXILIARY.
almanac, *n.* calendar, ephemeris (*astron.*), Whitaker (*Eng.*). See CHRONOMETRY.
almighty, *adj.* omnipotent, all-powerful. See DEITY.
almost, *adv.* nearly, all but, approximately. See NEARNESS, SMALLNESS.
alms, *n.* charity, dole, gratuity. See GIVING.
aloft, *adv.* up, above, overhead, on high. See HEIGHT.
alone, *adj.* solitary, apart, lone. See UNITY.
alongside, *adv.* abreast, beside, side by side, broadside on, neck and neck, on a level. See PARALLELISM, SIDE.
aloof, *adj.* remote, distant, reserved, unneighborly. See DISTANCE, SECLUSION.
aloof, *adv.* away, apart, aside. See DISTANCE.
aloud, *adv.* audibly, loudly, vociferously. See LOUDNESS.
already, *adv.* by now, previously. See PRESENT.
also, *adv.* likewise, too, furthermore, besides. See ADDITION.
alter, *v.* modify, vary, qualify, shift, convert, transform. See CHANGE.
alternate, *v.* change, take turns, vacillate. See DISCONTINUITY, OSCILLATION.
alternation, *n.* recurrence, succession, periodicity, taking of turns. See OSCILLATION.
alternative, *n.* option, preference, horn (*of a dilemma*). See CHOICE.
although, *conj.* though, notwithstanding, albeit. See COUNTERACTION.
altitude, *n.* elevation, perpendicular distance, loftiness, tallness. See HEIGHT.
altogether, *adv.* totally, entirely, all, collectively, completely. See WHOLE.
altruism, *n.* benevolence, generosity, humanitarianism, unselfishness, liberality: *opposite of* egoism. See PHILANTHROPY.
altruist, *n.* philanthropist, humanitarian: *opposite of* egoist. See PHILANTHROPY.
always, *adv.* constantly, continually, at all times, ever, uniformly, perpetually, regularly, invariably. See UNIFORMITY.
amateur, *n.* dilettante; volunteer, nonprofessional, novice. See TASTE, WILLINGNESS.
amatory, *adj.* loving, amorous, ardent, erotic. See LOVE.
ambiguous, *adj.* vague, equivocal, undefined, obscure. See UNCERTAINTY.
ambition, *n.* aspiration, longing, zeal; design, resolve. See DESIRE, INTENTION.
ambitious, *adj.* aspiring, soaring, zealous, desirous; bold, pretentious. See DESIRE, OSTENTATION.

AMBUSH [means of concealment].—I. *Nouns.* **ambush,** ambuscade, ambushment, lurking place, trap, snare, pitfall; secret way, secret path, retreat.
hiding place, hiding, secret place, recess, hole, closet, cubbyhole, crypt; safe, secret drawer, safe-deposit box, safety-deposit box; cache.

screen, cover, shade, blinker; veil, curtain, blind, cloak, shroud, camouflage, cloud.
mask, visor, disguise, masquerade, domino.
II. *Verbs.* **ambush,** ambuscade, waylay, lie in ambush, lie in wait for; trap, set a trap for, ensnare, entrap.
hide, conceal, ensconce, secrete, cache, bury, cover, screen, shelter, shroud, cloak, veil, camouflage.
See also CONCEALMENT, DECEPTION, PITFALL.—*Antonyms.* See DISCLOSURE, INFORMATION.

---

amenable, *adj.* responsible, liable, answerable, accountable; submissive, pliant, yielding. See DUTY, WILLINGNESS.
amend, *v.* change, rectify, correct. See IMPROVEMENT.
amiable, *adj.* agreeable, pleasant, affable, kindly. See COURTESY.
amidst, *prep.* amid, mid (*poetic*), midst, among. See MIXTURE.
amiss, *adv.* untowardly, badly, ill. See EVIL.
ammunition, *n.* shot, powder, charge, bullets. See ARMS.
amnesty, *n.* general pardon. See OBLIVION.
among, *adv.* amid, in the midst, amidst, with, in the middle. See MIXTURE.
amount, *n.* sum, total, aggregate. See QUANTITY.
ample, *adj.* large, abundant, considerable; spacious, roomy. See GREATNESS, SPACE.
amputate, *v.* cut off, cut away, sever. See DEDUCTION.
amulet, *n.* talisman, charm, phylactery. See [1]SPELL.

AMUSEMENT.—I. *Nouns.* **amusement,** entertainment, diversion, distraction, reaction, relaxation, solace; pastime, sport, recreation, merriment; avocation, labor of love; pleasure.
fun, frolic, merriment, jollity, joviality, laughter, pleasantry, jocoseness; drollery, buffoonery, tomfoolery, mummery.
play, game, gambol, romp, prank, antic, lark (*colloq.*), spree, skylarking, vagary, monkey trick, escapade, practical joke.
dance, hop (*colloq.*), shindig (*U. S. slang*), ball; masquerade, ballet; gavot, minuet, quadrille, lancers, cotillion; waltz, polka, mazurka, schottische, one-step, two-step, fox-trot; cakewalk, black bottom; tango, maxixe; reel, hornpipe, Highland fling, sword dance, step dance; folk dance, morris dance.
festivity, fête, festival, merrymaking; party, excursion, outing; revels, revelry, reveling, carnival, Saturnalia, jollification (*colloq.*), junket, picnic, bat (*U. S. slang*), whoopee (*slang*), high jinks (*colloq.*).
holiday, gala, gala day, red-letter day, play day; high days and holidays; high holiday.
place of amusement, theater *or* theatre; concert hall, ballroom, dance hall, assembly room, arena, auditorium; moving-picture theater, movies (*colloq.*), cinema (*Brit. colloq.*); music hall; vaudeville theater; circus, hippodrome; park, common, public gardens; country club, golf links, tennis courts, ball ground, gymkhana (*East Indian*), gymnasium, playing fields.
athletics, agonistics, athletic sports, track events, gymnastics; tournament.
toy, plaything, doll, puppet, bauble, gewgaw, whirligig, teetotum, kickshaw, teddy bear.
sportsman, sportswoman (*fem.*), hunter, Nimrod; shikari (*East Indian*).
gamester, sport, gambler; dicer, plunger, punter.
devotee, votary, enthusiast, follower, fan (*U. S. slang*).
II. *Verbs.* **amuse,** entertain, divert, beguile, charm, occupy, enliven, raise a smile, excite (*or* convulse with) laughter; cheer, rejoice, solace, please, interest, regale.
amuse oneself, sport, disport, revel, junket, feast, carouse, banquet, make merry; frolic, gambol, frisk, romp, caper, dance; have one's fling; play, toy, trifle, dally, kill time, while away the time.
III. *Adjectives.* **amusing,** entertaining, diverting, recreative, pleasant, laughable, ludicrous, side-splitting (*colloq.*), comic, comical, witty, jocose, festive, festal, jovial, jolly, roguish, arch, playful, sportive.
IV. *Adverbs.* in joke, in jest, at play, in sport.
See also PLEASURE, PLEASURABLENESS, WIT.—*Antonyms.* See DULLNESS, PAIN, WEARINESS.

ANACHRONISM.—I. *Nouns.* **anachronism,** error in time, error in chronology, antichronism (*rare*), misdate; prolepsis, anticipation, prochronism (*before the real date*), metachronism (*after the real date*), parachronism, disregard (neglect, *or* oblivion) of time.
II. *Verbs.* **anachronize** (*rare*), misdate, mistime; antedate, postdate, overdate, anticipate; take no note of time.
III. *Adjectives.* **anachronistic,** anachronous, misdated; antedated, postdated, overdated; undated; overdue; out of date, behind time, ahead of time.
See also ERROR.

---

anæmia, *n.* lack of blood, bloodlessness. See WEAKNESS.
anæsthetic, *n.* drug, gas, opiate, sedative. See INSENSIBILITY.
analogous, *adj.* correspondent, parallel; similar, related, associated, like, resembling. See PARALLELISM, SIMILARITY.
analysis, *n.* disintegration, break-up; investigation, study, consideration. See DECOMPOSITION, INQUIRY.
analyze, *v.* disintegrate, resolve, separate; examine, dissect. See DECOMPOSITION, INQUIRY.
anarchical, *adj.* lawless, anarchistic, nihilistic, red. See LAXITY.
anarchy, *n.* terrorism, lawlessness, disorder, turmoil, confusion, chaos, disorganization, rebellion. See LAXITY.
anatomy, *n.* analysis, dissection; anatomical structure; framework; zoötomy. See INQUIRY, ORGANIZATION, STRUCTURE, ZOÖLOGY.
ancestor, *n.* forefather, progenitor, forbear *or* forebear. See PATERNITY.
ancestry, *n.* descent, lineage, race, family, family tree, line. See PAST.
anchor, *n.* safeguard, protection, mainstay, hold, stay; grapnel, kedge, killick. See HOPE, REFUGE.
anchorage, *n.* roadstead, mooring; safety, harbor. See HABITATION, LOCATION, REFUGE.
ancient, *adj.* antique, archaic, antiquated, venerable, hoary, aged. See OLDNESS.
anecdote, *n.* tale, story, narrative, sketch, account. See DESCRIPTION.

ANGEL [beneficent spirits].—I. *Nouns.* **angel,** divine messenger, archangel, Messenger of God, guardian angel; ministering spirits, invisible helpers, Choir Invisible, host of heaven, heavenly host, sons of God; Seraphim (*sing.* seraph, *Eng. pl.* seraphs), Cherubim (*sing.* cherub, *Eng. pl.* cherubs; cherubim *or* cherubin *are often treated as sing.*); thrones, principalities, powers, dominions; saints.
Madonna, Our Lady, *Notre Dame* (*F.*), The Virgin, The Blessed Virgin, The Virgin Mary, Holy Mary, Queen of Heaven, *Regina Cœli* (*L.*).
II. *Adjectives.* **angelic** *or* angelical, seraphic, cherubic, archangelic, celestial, heavenly, divine, saintly, adorable.
See also DEATH (*angel of*).—*Antonyms.* See SATAN.

---

anger, *v.* arouse, inflame, irritate, annoy, incense, exasperate, enrage, provoke, offend, infuriate. See RESENTMENT.
angle, *n.* crook, fork, obliquity; phase, aspect, guise. See ANGULARITY, APPEARANCE.
angry, *adj.* enraged, irritated, incensed, annoyed, infuriate, furious, wrathful, indignant, irate. See RESENTMENT.
anguish, *n.* agony, torture, torment, distress, suffering. See PAIN.

ANGULARITY.—I. *Nouns.* **angularity,** angulation, divarication, dichotomy (*biol.*), bifurcation; fork, notch, crotch, branch, Y, angle, bend, elbow, knee, shoulder, cusp, knuckle; zigzag; right angle, acute angle, obtuse angle; fold, crease, corrugation, obliquity.
corner, nook, recess, niche, coign (*chiefly in* coign of vantage), cantle.

[*measurement of angles*] goniometry, trigonometry; goniometer, clinometer, sextant, quadrant, theodolite, transit *or* transit theodolite.
[*of persons*] **lankness,** leanness, boniness, etc. (see *adjectives*); ungainliness, uncouthness; stiffness, sharpness.
II. *Verbs.* **fork,** branch, ramify, bifurcate, bend, elbow, hook, diverge, divaricate.
III. *Adjectives.* **angular,** bent, crooked, jagged, serrated; forked, bifurcate, bifid, biforked, divaricate, dichotomous (*biol.*), dichotomal, dichotomic, Y-shaped, V-shaped, sharp-cornered, crotched, akimbo; oblique, zigzag, staggered; sharp-cornered, pointed; triangular, triagonal, trilateral; rectangular, right-angled, quadrilateral, foursquare.
aquiline, eaglelike, hooked, beaked, curved; Roman-nosed.
[*of persons*] **lank,** lean, bony, spare, gaunt, scrawny, scraggy; awkward, uncouth, ungainly, ungraceful; stiff (*in character*), sharp.

See also NOTCH, OBLIQUITY.—*Antonyms.* See CURVATURE, STRAIGHTNESS.

---

anile, *adj.* childish, foolish, simple. See IMBECILITY.

ANIMAL.—I. *Nouns.* **animal kingdom,** fauna, brute creation.
animal, creature, created being, living thing; dumb animal, dumb creature; brute, beast, zoön (*zoöl.*), vertebrate, invertebrate.
mammal, quadruped, bird, reptile, fish, crustacean, shellfish, mollusk, worm, insect, zoöphyte; animalcule.
beasts of the field, fowls of the air; flocks and herds, live stock, domestic animals, wild animals, game, wild fowl.

DOMESTIC ANIMALS: **horse,** steed, mount, charger, war horse, cavalry horse, bayard (*as, a bold* bayard), Waler (*originally from New South Wales*), hunter; race horse, racer, courser (*poetic*), steeplechaser, plater, pacer, trotter, goer, ambler; Arab, barb, jennet *or* genet; blood horse, thoroughbred; galloway, cob, palfrey; nag, jade, hack; pony, broncho, cayuse (*Western U. S.*), mustang, cow pony; stallion, entire horse, entire; brood mare (*fem.*), mare; filly (*fem.*), colt (*often restricted to the male*), gelding, foal.
cattle, stock, kine, ox; bull, bullock; cow, milch cow, Alderney, Jersey, Holstein, calf, heifer, shorthorn, redpoll, red polled cattle; yearling, steer.
sheep, mutton (*humorous*), lamb, lambkin, ewe, ram.
pig, swine, boar, hog, sow (*fem.*), shote, shoat, porker, razorback.
dog, hound, canine; pup, puppy; whelp, cur (*contemptuous*), mongrel; *feminines:* bitch, slut, lady, brach, brachet.
cat, feline, puss, pussy, grimalkin, tabby, tomcat, tom; Angora, Persian, Maltese, Manx, tortoiseshell, mouser; kitten, kitty.

WILD ANIMALS: **deer,** buck, fawn, stag, hart, roe, caribou, roebuck, moose, elk, reindeer, wapiti *or* American elk, fallow deer, red deer; doe (*fem.*), hind (*fem.*).
antelope, gazelle, pronghorn, chamois.
ape, monkey, simian, gorilla, chimpanzee, marmoset, baboon, orang-utan, lemur.
fox, reynard, Reynard, tod, Charley *or* Charlie, vixen (*fem.*); varmint (*cant*).
lion, lioness (*fem.*), Leo, cat; cub, whelp; lioncel (*heraldry*); king of beasts.
tiger, tigress (*fem.*), stripes (*colloq.*), bagh (*East Indian*), cat; cub, whelp.

BIRDS: feathered tribes, singing bird, warbler, dickybird (*colloq.*); nestling, fledgling.
bird of prey, eagle, *aquila* (*L.*), eaglet, bald eagle (*emblem of U. S.*), golden eagle, ringtail, harpy eagle, sea eagle, ern *or* erne; vulture, hawk, falcon, owl.
game, grouse, blackcock, pheasant, duck, plover, rail, snipe.
poultry, fowl, cock, rooster, chanticleer, barndoor fowl, barnyard fowl, hen, Partlet, chicken, chick; peafowl, peacock, peahen; guinea fowl, guinea hen.

INSECTS: bee, honeybee, queen bee, drone; wasp; ant, white ant, termite, red ant; locust, grasshopper, cricket; beetle; butterfly, moth; fly, weevil, earwig.
vermin, lice, cooties (*slang*), fleas, flies, cockroaches *or* roaches, bugs, bedbugs, water bugs, mosquitoes; rats, mice.

REPTILES: **reptile,** reptilian, saurian, lacertian, lizard, gecko, Gila monster, dragon, chameleon, newt, iguana, dinosaur (*extinct*), ichthyosaur (*extinct*), pterosaur (*extinct*), pterodactyl (*extinct*).
snake, serpent, ophidian, viper; asp, adder, cobra, cobra de capello, king cobra; rattlesnake, rattler, boa constrictor, boa, python.
crocodilian, crocodile, mugger *or* magar (*India*), gavial, alligator, cayman (*pl.* caymans), jacare *or* yacare (*Amazon*).

CETACEANS: **whale,** cete (*rare*), finback, finner, rorqual, sulphur-bottom (*largest of all*), right whale, whalebone whale, humpback, sperm whale, blackfish, grampus, zeuglodont (*extinct*).
dolphin, delphinoid (*zoöl.*), porpoise, beluga, killer, narwhal.

ELASMOBRANCHS (*or* Elasmobranchii): **elasmobranch,** placoid, placoidean (*rare*), selachian: *all zoöl.*
shark, carchariid *or* carcharioid (*zoöl*), man-eater, tiger of the sea, blue shark, hammerhead, shovelhead, porbeagle, basking shark (*harmless*), dogfish.
ray, batoid (*zoöl.*), sting ray, sawfish, skate, barn-door skate.
chimæra, chimærid *or* chimæroid (*zoöl.*), Holocephali (*pl.*).

GAME AND FOOD FISHES: **salmon,** shad, alewife, striped bass, sea perch, sea trout, salmon trout, sturgeon (*all anadromous, that is, ascending rivers to spawn*); tarpon, tuna *or* tunny, jewfish, black sea bass, swordfish; trout, grayling, oquassa, char; pike, muskellunge (*Great Lakes*), pickerel; carp, chub, roach, mahseer (*India*), bream, tench, sucker, dace, shiner, barbel, schnapper (*Australia*); flounder, turbot, bluefish, mackerel, etc.
II. *Adjectives.* **animal,** zoölogical, zoic (*zoöl.*), zooid (*biol.*); mammalian; equine; bovine, vaccine (*tech.*); canine; feline; fishy, piscatorial; ophidian, reptilian, snakelike.
animalistic, animalized, animalian, animalic (*rare*); carnal, fleshly, bodily, corporeal, human.
See also CARRIER, EVILDOER (*wild beast*), ZOÖLOGY.—*Antonym.* See VEGETABLE.

---

animalcule, *n.* microscopic animal, protozoan, amœba, paramecium. See LITTLENESS.

ANIMAL LIFE.—I. *Nouns.* **animal life,** animality, animal existence, animal nature, animalization, animalness (*rare*), animalism.
flesh, flesh and blood; physique, animal force, muscular energy, strength, power, vigor, force; spring, elasticity, tone.
II. *Verbs.* **animalize** (*fig.*), reduce to animalism, carnalize, sensualize.
incarnate, embody, incorporate; vitalize, animate.

---

animal physiology, zoöphysiology, biodynamics. See ZOÖLOGY.
animate, *v.* cheer, enliven, encourage; inspire, actuate. See CHEERFULNESS, EXCITEMENT.
animation, *n.* liveliness, vivacity, spirit. See ACTIVITY.
annalist, *n.* historian, compiler, chronicler. See RECORDER.
annex, *v.* attach, join, affix. See ADDITION.
annihilate, *v.* destroy, wreck, demolish, end, eradicate, exterminate. See DESTRUCTION, NONEXISTENCE.
annihilation, *n.* extermination, end, demolishment. See DESTRUCTION, NONEXISTENCE.
anniversary, *n.* commemoration, jubilee, festival. See CELEBRATION, REGULARITY.
annotate, *v.* expound, commentate (*rare*), gloss, margin, make notes on. See INTERPRETATION.
annotator, *n.* commentator, scholiast. See INTERPRETER.
announce, *v.* tell, inform, proclaim, assert, publish, broadcast, report, declare; predict, foretell. See INFORMATION, PREDICTION.

announcement, *n.* notice, proclamation; declaration, notification. See INFORMATION, PREDICTION.

annoy, *v.* vex, harass, molest, disturb, irritate, worry, tantalize, bother, trouble. See PAIN, TOUCH (*irritate*).

annoyance, *n.* vexation, irritation, worry, nuisance, trouble, uneasiness. See PAINFULNESS.

annular, *adj.* ringlike, ring-shaped, rounded, circular. See CIRCULARITY.

ANNULMENT.—I. *Nouns.* **annulment,** nullification, cancellation, vacatur (*law*), *nolle prosequi* (*L.*), defeasance, abrogation, revocation, rescission, recall, repeal, countermand, counterorder, retractation, recantation, repudiation; abolition, abolishment, invalidation, vacation.

dismissal, discharge, removal, bounce (*U. S. slang*), *congé* (*F.*), sack (*slang*); expulsion, degradation; deposition, dethronement; disestablishment, disendowment; dissolution.

II. *Verbs.* **annul,** cancel, vacate, abrogate, revoke, repeal, rescind, reverse, withdraw, retract, recall; overrule, override, set aside, invalidate, disannul, dissolve, quash, nullify, nol-pros (*law, short for* nolle prosequi), declare null and void, disestablish; countermand, counterorder, throw overboard, destroy, abolish.

disclaim, deny, ignore, repudiate; recant, break off.

dismiss, discard; turn out, cast off (adrift, aside, *or* away); send off, send away, discharge, get rid of, sack (*slang*), fire (*slang*), bounce (*U. S. slang*); cashier, displace, expel; depose, dethrone, uncrown; unseat, unfrock (*a priest*), disbar (*law*), strike off the roll, break (*colloq.*), oust.

See also EJECTION, NEGATION.—*Antonyms.* See COMMISSION, RECEPTION.

---

anoint, *v.* oil, salve, lubricate, rub. See UNCTUOUSNESS.

anonymous, *adj.* nameless, unnamed, unknown, unacknowledged. See MISNOMER.

another, *adj.* other, different. See DIFFERENCE.

ANSWER.—I. *Nouns.* **answer,** response, reply, acknowledgment, respondence, respondency, return, rejoinder, rebuttal; retort, repartee; password, counterstatement, counterblast, countercharge, contradiction; echo, return, reverberation; antiphon, antiphony.

[*in law*] **defense,** plea, reply, rejoinder, rebutter, surrebutter, surrejoinder, counterclaim.

solution, explanation, interpretation, *dénouement* (*F.*), elucidation; discovery, disclosure; cause; clew *or* clue, key.

II. *Verbs.* **answer,** respond, reply, say, rebut, retort, return, rejoin, give answer, acknowledge; echo.

[*in law*] defend, plead, reply, rebut, surrejoin, surrebut, counterclaim.

explain, interpret; solve; fathom, elucidate, disclose, discover, hunt out, inquire; satisfy, set at rest, determine.

III. *Adjectives.* **answerable,** accountable, responsible, liable, amenable.

answering, responsive, respondent, responsorial (*rare*), antiphonal; oracular; conclusive.

See also DISCOVERY, INTERPRETATION, VINDICATION.—*Antonyms.* See INQUIRY, REQUEST.

---

antagonism, *n.* hostility, opposition, antipathy, animosity. See ENMITY.

antagonistic, *adj.* opposed, adverse, opposing, hostile. See COUNTERACTION.

antecede, *v.* go before, precede, preëxist. See PRIORITY.

antedate, *v.* predate, misdate: *opposite of* postdate. See ANACHRONISM.

antelope, *n.* deer, gazelle, gnu. See ANIMAL.

anteroom, *n.* antechamber, lobby, hall. See RECEPTACLE.

anticipate, *v.* forestall, be early, precede; surmise, predict; await, expect, hope for. See EARLINESS, FORESIGHT, FUTURE.

anticipation, *n.* prevenience, forestallment, prematurity; expectation, outlook, hope. See EARLINESS, FUTURE.

antidote, *n.* counterpoison, antipoison, emetic. See COUNTERACTION, REMEDY.
antipathy, *n.* clashing, opposition, incompatibility; abhorrence, detestation, repugnance. See CONTRARIETY, DISLIKE.
antipodes, *n.* opposite poles. See OPPOSITE.
antiquary, *n.* antiquarian, archaist, archæologist. See PAST.
antiquated, *adj.* old-fashioned, obsolete, bygone, ancient. See OLDNESS.
antiquities, *n.* ancient relics, remains. See OLDNESS.
antiquity, *n.* ancientness, age; the past, ancient times. See OLDNESS, PAST.
antonym, *n.* opposite, counterterm: *opposite of* synonym. See CONTRARIETY.
anxiety, *n.* solicitude, concern; fearfulness, apprehension; trouble, trial. See CARE, FEAR, PAIN.
anxious, *adj.* desirous, solicitous; apprehensive, fearful, troubled. See DESIRE, FEAR.
anyhow, *adv.* anywise, anyway; at any rate, nevertheless. See WAY.
apart, *adv.* asunder, alone; aloof, away; separately, independently, singly. See DISJUNCTION, DISTANCE, UNITY.
apathetic, *adj.* indifferent, cold, unfeeling, impassive, insensible. See INDIFFERENCE, INSENSITIVENESS.
apathy, *n.* impassivity, unconcern, indifference, dullness. See INSENSITIVENESS.
ape, *n.* simian, monkey, gorilla. See ANIMAL.
ape, *v.* mimic, mock, simulate. See IMITATION.
aphoristic, *adj.* proverbial, axiomatic. See MAXIM.
apiece, *adv.* each, one by one, severally, respectively. See SPECIALTY.
apologetic, *adj.* excusatory, justificative. See ATONEMENT.
apologist, *n.* defender, pleader. See VINDICATION.
apologize, *v.* ask pardon, make amends. See ATONEMENT.
apology, *n.* excuse, regret; makeshift, stopgap. See ATONEMENT, SUBSTITUTION.

APOSTASY.—I. *Nouns.* **apostasy,** recantation, renunciation, abjuration, defection, retraction, withdrawal, disavowal, revocation, tergiversation, perversion, recreancy, reversal; backsliding, recession, abandonment, relapse, lapse.
apostate, renegade, turncoat, pervert, deserter, recreant, backslider.
[*trade-unionist cant*] **strike breaker,** scab, rat, knobstick (*Eng.*), snob (*Eng.*), blackleg.
timeserver, timepleaser, Vicar of Bray, trimmer, double dealer, temporizer, opportunist; weathercock.
II. *Verbs.* **apostatize,** secede, lapse, relapse, veer round, change sides, go over, shift one's ground, turn, turn round, change one's mind, abjure, renounce, relinquish, back down, swallow one's words, recant, retract, revoke, rescind, forswear.
trim, hedge, temporize, dodge, shuffle, blow hot and cold, be on the fence, straddle (*colloq.*), wait to see how the cat jumps (*or* how the wind blows), hold with the hare but run with the hounds.
III. *Adjectives.* **apostate,** recreant, renegade, apostatic *or* apostatical, false, unfaithful.
changeful, irresolute, ductile, slippery; trimming, timeserving, opportunistic; reactionary, revulsive, revulsionary; capricious, coquettish, unreliable.
See also CHANGEABLENESS, IMPIETY, IRRESOLUTION.—*Antonyms.* See OBSTINACY, STABILITY.

---

appall, *v.* terrify, petrify, horrify; disgust, revolt, nauseate. See FEAR, PAIN.
apparatus, *n.* equipment, outfit; contrivance, machine; machinery. See INSTRUMENT.
apparent, *adj.* seeming, probable; clear, obvious, plain, patent, manifest, evident, certain; visible, appearing, perceptible. See APPEARANCE, MANIFESTATION, VISIBILITY.

apparition, *n.* ghost, phantom, spirit. See APPEARANCE, SPECTER, VISION.
appeal, *n.* petition, prayer, entreaty, invocation. See REQUEST.

APPEARANCE.—I. *Nouns.* **appearance,** phenomenon, sight, show, scene, view, *coup d'œil* (*F.*); lookout, outlook, prospect, vista, perspective, bird's-eye view, scenery, landscape, seascape, picture, tableau, representation, display, exposure, rising of the curtain; stage setting, *mise en scène* (*F.*).
spectacle, pageant; peep show, magic lantern, biograph, cinematograph, cinema (*Brit. colloq.*), moving pictures, movies (*colloq.*), films *or* film (*collective*), screen (*cant*), photoplay, photodrama; panorama, diorama; exhibition, exposition, review, *revue* (*F.*), *coup de théâtre* (*F.*); parade, procession.
aspect, phase, angle, shape, form, guise, likeness, semblance, look, complexion, color, image, mien, air, cast, carriage, port, demeanor; presence, expression, effect, impression, point of view, light.
lineament, feature, trait, lines; outline, outside; contour, *tournure* (*F.*), silhouette, face, countenance, visage, profile; physiognomy; cut of one's jib (*colloq.*).
phantom, apparition, specter, ghost, vision, phantasm, illusion.
II. *Verbs.* **appear,** be visible, seem, look, show; cut a figure, figure; present to the view; become manifest, come in sight, emerge, issue, arrive, loom, rise; look like, resemble.
III. *Adjectives.* **apparent,** seeming, ostensible; on view, manifest, in sight, clear, distinct.
IV. *Adverbs.* **apparently,** seemingly, clearly, manifestly, ostensibly, on the face of it, at the first blush, at first sight, to the eye.
See also LIGHT, MANIFESTATION, [1]SOUND (*seem*), SPECTER, VISIBILITY.—*Antonyms.* See DISAPPEARANCE, INVISIBILITY.

---

appease, *v.* pacify, placate, quiet, soothe, mollify, allay, moderate; satisfy (*as the appetite*). See INEXCITABILITY, MODERATION, PLEASURABLENESS.
append, *v.* attach, affix, annex, supplement, add, subjoin. See ADDITION, SEQUENCE.
appendage, *n.* addition, accompaniment, attachment, appurtenance, tag. See ADJUNCT, SEQUEL.
appetite, *n.* want, hunger, longing, craving, passion. See DESIRE.
appetizer, *n.* relish. See SAVORINESS.
applause, *n.* praise, plaudit, acclaim, clapping, acclamation. See APPROBATION.
applicable, *adj.* pertinent, suitable, appropriate, relevant, fitting, convenient. See UTILITY.
application, *n.* diligence, assiduity, devotion; relevancy, pertinency; appeal, petition, entreaty. See ATTENTION, RELATION, REQUEST.
apply, *v.* canvass, solicit, ask; employ, adopt, take. See REQUEST, USE.
appoint, *v.* prescribe, establish, assign, ordain; nominate. See APPORTIONMENT, COMMISSION, PLACE.
appointment, *n.* position, place, office; nomination, ordination; meeting, interview, arrangement, engagement, date (*colloq.*). See BUSINESS, COMMISSION, SOCIALITY.

APPORTIONMENT.—I. *Nouns.* **apportionment,** allotment, consignment, assignment, appropriation, allocation, distribution, division, deal; partition, administration, dispensation.
portion, dividend, share, allotment, lot, measure, dose, dole, meed, pittance, ration; ratio, proportion, quota, quantum, modicum, allowance.
II. *Verbs.* **apportion,** divide, distribute, administer, dispense, allot, allow, allocate, detail, cast, share, mete, portion (parcel, *or* dole) out; dole, award, grant, deal, carve; partition, assign, appropriate, appoint.
III. *Adjectives.* **apportionable,** divisible, distributable, dispensable, severable. **respective,** particular, several, individual, proportionate, proportional, commensurate.
IV. *Adverbs.* **respectively,** severally, each to each; by lot; in equal shares.
See also PARTICIPATION.

appraise, *v.* estimate, assess, value, rate. See JUDGE.
appreciate, *v.* esteem, value, prize; note, realize, mark, comprehend. See APPROBATION, KNOWLEDGE.
apprehend, *v.* dread, distrust; perceive, see, understand; arrest, seize, imprison. See FEAR, KNOWLEDGE, LAWSUIT.
apprenticeship, *n.* probation, novitiate. See LEARNING.

APPROACH.—I. *Nouns.* **approach,** approximation, hearing, drawing near, advance, access, accessibility, admittance, admission, advent; convergence.
pursuit, chase, hunt, quest, search.
access, path, passage, passageway, means of approach, opportunity.
[*in plural*] **approaches,** advances, overtures, proposals, tenders.
II. *Verbs.* **approach,** near, get (*or* draw) near; move towards, drift; gain upon; advance, come, converge; make land.
III. *Adjectives.* **approachable,** accessible, get-at-able (*colloq.*), come-at-able (*colloq.*), attainable; open, affable, sociable, democratic.
approaching, nearing, advancing, coming; approximate, imminent, impending; converging, convergent.
See also FUTURE, NEARNESS, PURSUIT, WAY.—*Antonyms.* See AVOIDANCE, RECESSION.

APPROBATION.—I. *Nouns.* **approbation,** approval, sanction, advocacy; esteem, estimation, good opinion, favor, admiration; appreciation, regard, affection, love; account, popularity, credit, repute, renown, kudos (*colloq.*).
commendation, compliment, congratulation, praise, laudation; good word; encomium, eulogy, eulogium, homage, hero worship; panegyric, blurb (*slang*); benediction, blessing, benison.
recommendation, letter of recommendation, testimonial, certificate, reference (*U. S. in this sense*), chit (*Anglo-Indian*).
applause, plaudit, clap, handclap, clapping, acclaim, acclamation; cheer, hurrah, huzza; pæan, shout (peal, chorus, *or* thunders) of applause.
II. *Verbs.* **approve,** esteem, value, prize, set great store by, honor, hold in esteem, look up to, admire, like, appreciate; think well of, think highly of; stand up for, stick up for (*colloq.*), uphold, countenance, sanction, sanctify, justify, indorse, recommend.
commend, praise, laud, compliment, congratulate, applaud, clap, cheer, acclaim, encore; eulogize, cry up, puff, extol, magnify, glorify, exalt, sing the praises of; root for (*U. S. slang*), boost (*U. S. colloq.*).
III. *Adjectives.* **approbative,** approbatory, commendatory, laudatory, complimentary, praiseful, encomiastic, encomiastical, panegyrical, eulogistic, lavish of praise, uncritical.
approved, praised, popular, in good odor; in high esteem, in favor, in high favor.
praiseworthy, commendable, laudable, worthy of praise, good, meritorious, estimable, creditable, unimpeachable.
IV. *Adverbs.* with credit, to admiration; with three times three.
See also FLATTERY, REPUTE.—*Antonyms.* See DETRACTION, DISAPPROBATION, DISREPUTE.

---

appropriate, *adj.* suitable, fit, timely, proper, adapted, becoming. See AGREEMENT.
appropriate, *v.* take, steal, borrow; allot, assign, set apart. See BORROWING, TAKING.
approval, *n.* sanction, advocacy; ratification, indorsement. See APPROBATION, ASSENT.
approve, *v.* like, commend, be pleased, praise, admire; sanction, authorize, support, ratify. See APPROBATION, ASSENT.
approved, *adj.* praised, admired, fashionable, correct, popular. See APPROBATION.
approximate, *adj.* near, close, comparative. See RELATION, SIMILARITY.
approximately, *adv.* comparatively, incompletely, roughly. See ROUGHNESS.

apt, *adj.* suitable, qualified, appropriate, adapted; clever, quick, dexterous, skillful. See AGREEMENT, SKILL.
aquatic, *adj.* water, watery. See NAVIGATION.
aquiline, *adj.* eaglelike, hooked, curved, beaked, Roman-nosed. See ANGULARITY.
arable, *adj.* fertile, tillable, fruitful, productive. See HUSBANDRY.
arbitrary, *adj.* imperious, harsh, despotic, tyrannical, dictatorial, peremptory, domineering, overbearing. See ILLEGALITY, OBSTINACY.
arbitration, *n.* intercession, settlement, intervention. See MEDIATION.
arbitrator, *n.* umpire, arbiter, referee. See JUDGE.
[1]**arbor,** *n.* bower, shady retreat, pergola. See RECEPTACLE.
[2]**arbor,** *n.* axle, spindle, shaft, mandrel. See ROTATION.
arboreal, *adj.* arboreous, silvan, treelike. See VEGETABLE.
arch, *n.* curve, bend, arc, vault. See CONVEXITY, SUPPORT.
archaic, *adj.* antiquated, primitive. See OLDNESS.
archer, *n.* bowman, toxophilite, Sagittarius. See COMBATANT, PROPULSION.
archetype, *n.* ideal, prototype. See IDEA.
architect, *n.* builder, designer, originator, creator. See AGENT, PRODUCER.
architecture, *n.* construction, architectonics. See FINE ARTS.
archive, *n.* register, chronicle, entry. See RECORD.
ardent, *adj.* zealous, enterprising, eager; passionate, devoted. See ACTIVITY, LOVE.
ardor, *n.* warmth, fervor, enthusiasm, zeal, eagerness. See FEELING, HEAT, VIGOR.
area, *n.* stretch, expanse, space, tract, arena, clearing. See PLAIN, REGION.

ARENA.—I. *Nouns.* **arena,** field, theater *or* theatre, walk, course; hustings, platform; stage, boards, amphitheater, Coliseum, Colosseum; hippodrome, circus, race course, turf, cockpit, bear garden, gymnasium, ring, lists; campus (*U. S.*), playing field, playground, court.
battlefield, battle ground, field of battle, scene of action, Aceldama, theater (*or* seat) of war; the enemy's camp.
See also SPACE.

---

argument, *n.* discussion, debate; evidence, case, data. See REASONING.
argumentation, *n.* debating, discussion, disputation, debate, dialectics. See REASONING.
aright, *adv.* well, satisfactorily, rightly, properly. See GOOD.
arise, *v.* rise, get up, mount; commence, originate; happen, occur. See ASCENT, BEGINNING, EVENT.
aristocracy, *n.* four hundred (*colloq.*), upper classes. See NOBILITY.
aristocrat, *n.* noble, nobleman, peer, lord, patrician. See NOBILITY.
arm, *n.* limb, member, wing, branch; might, strength. See PART, POWER.
armed, *adj.* equipped, accoutered, girded, arrayed, outfitted; protected, prepared. See COMBATANT, WARFARE.
armed force, troops, military, army. See COMBATANT, SAFETY.
armistice, *n.* truce, peace, interval, respite. See CESSATION.
armor, *n.* mail, panoply, protective covering. See DEFENSE.
armored, *adj.* mailed, iron-clad, bullet-proof. See DEFENSE.

ARMS.—*Nouns.* **arms,** weapons, deadly weapons, armament, armor *or* armour.
sword, *arme blanche* (*F.*), saber, cutlass, scimitar, machete, bolo, kukri; blade, brand (*archaic*); broadsword, claymore, glaive (*archaic*), rapier, foil, dagger, creese *or* kris, poniard, stiletto, dirk, bowie knife, bayonet; cold steel, naked steel.
ax *or* **axe,** battle ax, poleax, halberd, partisan, bill, tomahawk.
spear, lance, pike, assagai (*South Africa*), javelin, dart, harpoon, boomerang.

arrow, missile, shaft, cloth-yard shaft (*hist.*); quarrel (*for crossbow*), bolt, **vire** (*hist.*); flight (*volley*).
club, war club, mace, truncheon, staff, bludgeon, cudgel, shillalah, stick, quarterstaff; billy, life-preserver, blackjack, sandbag.
bow, long bow, crossbow, sling, catapult.
firearms, gun, piece; artillery, ordnance, siege artillery, field artillery, coast artillery, mountain artillery, field battery; park, battery; cannon, fieldpiece, field gun, siege gun, big Bertha (*slang*), Krupp gun, mortar, howitzer, pompom, "seventy-five" (*French rapid-fire 75 mm. field gun*); antiaircraft gun, aërogun, Archibald *or* Archie (*World War slang for German antiaircraft gun*); machine gun, Gatling gun, Lewis gun.
tank, armored car; whippet, land ship (*Brit.*).
small arms, musket, firelock, fowling piece, rifle, carbine, blunderbuss, matchlock, harquebus, shotgun, breechloader, muzzle-loader, magazine rifle; revolver, repeater, automatic pistol, automatic; shooting iron (*U. S. slang*), six-gun (*U. S.*), six-shooter (*U. S.*), gun (*colloq. for revolver or pistol*), pistol, rod (*U. S. slang*).
missile, bolt, projectile, shot, ball, slug; grape, shrapnel; grenade, shell, bomb, black Maria (*slang*), smoke bomb, gas bomb, depth bomb, bullet; dumdum (explosive, *or* expanding) bullet; torpedo.
ammunition, tear shell, explosive; cartridge; powder, powder and shot, gunpowder, "villanous saltpetre" (*Henry IV*); dynamite, cordite, lyddite, high explosive, smokeless powder, guncotton, nitrocotton, melinite, T.N.T. *or* TNT, trinitrotoluene, trinitrotoluol, trotyl; picric acid, trinitrocresol; poison gas, asphyxiating gas, chlorine gas, mustard gas, tear gas.
military service, war, military exploits, military profession.
heraldic devices, armorial ensigns, heraldic bearings, armorial bearings, **blazonry,** emblazonry, emblazonment; coat of arms.

See also ATTACK, COMBATANT, DEFENSE, INDICATION (*heraldry*), WARFARE.

---

army, *n.* troops, soldiers, soldiery, military forces; host. See COMBATANT, MULTITUDE.

around, *adv.* surrounding, about, encircling, encompassing, **near, round-about,** without, neighboring. See ENVIRONMENT.

arouse, *v.* stir, kindle, rouse, stimulate, whet. See EXCITEMENT.

arraignment, *n.* accusation, charge, indictment, summons, censure. **See** LAWSUIT.

ARRANGEMENT.—I. *Nouns.* **arrangement,** preparation, provision; disposal, disposition, array; distribution, allocation, sorting, assortment, allotment, apportionment; gradation, organization, grouping; analysis, classification, collocation, division, systematization, orderliness.
method, plan, design, system, scheme, rule, form, organism; process, procedure.
[*result of arrangement*] digest, synopsis, compendium, *résumé* (*F.*), report, table; register, record; card index, filing system; file, letter file; reminder, jogger (*colloq.*).
settlement (*as of a dispute*), adjustment, reconciliation, agreement, compromise, stipulation.
II. *Verbs.* **arrange,** dispose, fix, place, form; order, set in order, set out, prepare, marshal, array, rank, group, range, size, align *or* aline, line up, collimate (*tech.*); parcel out, allot, allocate, apportion, distribute, assign the parts, assign places to, dispose of, assort, sort, sift; tidy (*colloq.*), trim.
classify, class, file, list, register, catalogue, tabulate, index, alphabetize, grade, graduate, range; codify, digest.
methodize, regulate, systematize, coördinate, organize; unravel, disentangle, card.
settle (*as a disagreement*), adjust, reconcile, compromise, adapt; contrive, determine, stipulate.
III. *Adjectives.* **arranged,** classified; arrayed, embattled, in battle array; **cut** and dried; on file; tabular.
methodical, orderly, regular, systematic, businesslike; neat, tidy.

See also COMPOSITION, COMPROMISE, DISPOSITION, ORDER, PLAN, RECORD.—*Antonyms.* See DERANGEMENT, DISORDER.

array, *n.* apparel, finery; host, army; arrangement, system. See CLOTHING, MULTITUDE, ORDER.
arrears, *n.* liability, obligation. See DEBT.
arrest, *v.* stop, end; imprison, seize, apprehend, capture, detain. See CESSATION, LAWSUIT, RESTRAINT.
arrest, *n.* stoppage, check; apprehension, seizure, imprisonment. See CESSATION, LAWSUIT.

ARRIVAL.—I. *Nouns.* **arrival,** advent, coming; alighting, dismounting; landing; debarkation, disembarkation; home-coming, homecome (*rare*).
destination, goal; harbor, haven, port, landing place, landing stage; terminus, terminal; home, journey's end; halting place, bourn; anchorage, refuge.
meeting, joining, encounter, junction, rejoining; return, reëntry; reception, welcome.
[*person or thing arriving*] **visitant,** incomer, passenger, visitor, guest, new-born child (*colloq.*), newcomer, transient.
II. *Verbs.* **arrive,** get to, come to, come, reach, approach, attain (*archaic*), gain, hit, make, fetch; overtake, join, rejoin; return; appear, enter, drop in, **visit.**
alight, light, dismount, detrain.
land, cast anchor, put in, debark, disembark, go ashore.
meet, encounter, come across; come (*or* light) upon; come in contact; **unite,** connect, join.
[*of events*] **come about,** happen, occur, come to pass, result.
III. *Adjectives.* **arriving,** approaching, entering, incoming, homeward, homeward-bound; inward bound, inbound.
IV. *Adverbs.* **here,** hither, hitherward *or* hitherwards (*archaic*).
See also COMPLETION, EVENT, INGRESS, REFUGE, VISIBILITY.—*Antonyms.* See DEPARTURE, EGRESS.

---

arrogance, *n.* haughtiness, pretension, ostentation, swagger, airs. See INSOLENCE, SIDE.
arrogate, *v.* demand, assume, usurp, appropriate, seize, claim, take. See SEVERITY, TAKING.
arrow, *n.* shaft, bolt, quarrel (*for crossbow*), missile. See ARMS.
arsenal, *n.* magazine, storehouse, depot, armory. See STORE, WORKSHOP.
art, *n.* artifice, trickery; depiction, illustration, designing; science. See CUNNING, REPRESENTATION, SKILL.
artful, *adj.* crafty, designing, sly, tricky, shrewd; dexterous, skillful, adroit. See CUNNING, SKILL.
article, *n.* review, commentary, essay; thing, object. See DISSERTATION, SUBSTANTIALITY.
artifice, *n.* stratagem, ruse, wile, trick, deceit, fraud; device, contrivance. See CUNNING, PLAN.
artificial, *adj.* unnatural, affected, constrained; false, counterfeit, spurious, sham. See AFFECTATION, DECEPTION.
artillery, *n.* ordnance, battery, cannon, guns. See ARMS.
artisan, *n.* craftsman, artificer, workman, mechanic. See AGENT.

ARTIST.—*Nouns.* **artist,** *artiste* (*F.*), painter, brush, depictor, drawer, sketcher, designer, engraver, graver, etcher, draftsman *or* draughtsman; copyist; enameler, enamelist; cartoonist, caricaturist; dabbler, dilettante, dauber (*derogatory*).
historical (landscape, marine, flower, portrait, genre, miniature, *or* scene) painter; water-colorist, pastellist, colorist; portraitist, landscapist, miniaturist; impressionist, futurist, cubist; Raphael, Titian; Royal Academician, R.A.
sculptor, sculptress (*fem.*), statuary; molder, modeler, carver; Phidias, Praxiteles, Michelangelo.

---

artistic, *adj.* beautiful, graceful, exquisite, elegant, accomplished, talented, æsthetic, cultured. See BEAUTY, TASTE.

ARTLESSNESS.—I. *Nouns.* **artlessness,** unskillfulness, awkwardness, etc. (see *adjectives*); want of skill (*or* training).
guilelessness, innocence, frankness, *naïveté* (*F.*), ingenuousness, *épanchement* (*F.*), unsophistication, simplicity, candor, sincerity, singleness of purpose, honesty. rough diamond, matter-of-fact man; *enfant terrible* (*F.*).
II. *Verbs.* **be artless,** be natural, etc. (see *adjectives*); think aloud; speak one's mind; be free with one; call a spade a spade; wear one's heart upon one's sleeve, lack reserve.
III. *Adjectives.* **artless,** unskillful, awkward, clumsy; untalented, uncultured, uncultivated.
guileless, innocent, frank, open, ingenuous, unselfconscious, candid, *ingénu F.; fem. ingénue*), sincere, pure, simple, plain, unsophisticated, unaffected, naïve; confiding, unreserved, natural, simple-minded, unsuspicious, honest, genuine; childlike, straightforward, aboveboard; single-minded, single-hearted, simple-hearted.
blunt, downright direct, matter-of-fact, outspoken, plain-spoken, bluff, brusque, abrupt, plump, unqualified, unflattering, unvarnished.
IV. *Adverbs.* **artlessly,** frankly, openly, downright, bluntly, in plain terms (words, *or* English); without ceremony; without mincing the matter.

See also INNOCENCE, PROBITY, UNSKILLFULNESS.—*Antonyms.* See AFFECTATION, CUNNING.

ASCENT.—I. *Nouns.* **ascent,** ascension, ascendance *or* ascendence, rising, rise, upgrowth, upward flight; upgrade; slope, ramp, grade (*U. S.*), gradient (*Eng.*), acclivity, hill, climb; leap, jump; buoyancy, buoyantness.
stairway, staircase, stairs; flight of steps *or* stairs; companion (*naut.*), companionway (*naut.*); escalator, elevator, lift (*esp. Eng.*); ladder, scaling ladder; stepladder, steps (*colloq.*).
II. *Verbs.* **ascend,** rise, lift, mount, arise, uprise; go up, get up, work one's way up, start up, spring up, shoot up; aspire.
climb, swarm (*colloq.*), shin (*colloq.*), clamber, scramble, scrabble; escalade, surmount, scale, top.
tower, soar, spire, overtop, go aloft, fly aloft; surge; leap.
III. *Adjectives.* **ascendant** *or* ascendent, rising, climbing, towering, ascending, ascensional, mounting, scandent (*as, a* scandent *plant*), scansorial (*zoöl.*).
buoyant, floating, supernatant, superfluitant (*rare*), floaty (*colloq.*), light.
upturned, turned up, *retroussé* (*F.*), elevated, raised, uplifted.
IV. *Adverbs.* **up,** upward, upwards, aloft, heavenward, skyward; uphill, upstairs; upstream; uptown (*colloq.*).

See also LEAP, OBLIQUITY, PROGRESSION.—*Antonyms.* See DESCENT, REGRESSION.

---

ascertain, *v.* determine, find, discover. See JUDGE.

ASCETICISM.—I. *Nouns.* **asceticism,** austerity, puritanism, abstemiousness, total abstinence; mortification, sackcloth and ashes, penance, fasting; scourging, flagellation, flagellantism, self-mortification; hair shirt; martyrdom.
ascetic, anchoret *or* anchorite, hermit, recluse, monk, solitary, solitaire (*rare*), puritan, yogi (*Hindu*), sannyasi (*Hindu*), calender (*Persian*), fakir (*Moham.*), dervish (*Moham.*), Heauton Timoroumenos (*Gr.*), self-tormentor; martyr.
II. *Adjectives.* **ascetic,** austere, abstemious; puritanical, flagellant, flagellatory.

See also ATONEMENT, FASTING, SECLUSION.—*Antonyms* See INTEMPERANCE, GLUTTONY, SENSUALIST.

---

ascribe, *v.* attribute, impute, refer; assign. See ATTRIBUTION.
asexual, *adj.* sexless, neuter. See NEUTRALITY.
ashamed, *adj.* abashed, crestfallen, conscience-stricken. See HUMILITY.
ashen, *adj.* ashy, cinereous, ashen-gray, pale, ghastly. See COLORLESSNESS.
ashore, *adv.* on land, to the shore, on shore. See LAND.
as if, as though, as it were. See SIMILARITY.
ask, *v.* inquire, interrogate, question; beg, entreat, beseech, implore. See INQUIRY, REQUEST.

askew, *adj.* awry, distorted, crooked, oblique. See DISTORTION, OBLIQUITY.
aspect, *n.* view, look, semblance, expression, air, mien, phase, side. See APPEARANCE, SUBJECTIVENESS.
aspirant, *n.* aspirer, candidate, bidder, suitor, applicant. See PETITIONER.
aspire, *v.* seek, desire, hope for. See HOPE.
ass, *n.* donkey, moke (*slang*), jackass; dolt, booby. See CARRIER, FOOL.
assail, *v.* assault, set upon, charge, encounter, overwhelm. See ATTACK.
assailant, *n.* adversary, foe, invader, aggressor, antagonist, opponent, accuser, plaintiff. See ATTACK.
assassin, *n.* killer, slayer, murderer, cutthroat. See KILLING.
assassinate, *v.* kill, slay, murder, bump off (*slang*). See KILLING.

ASSEMBLAGE.—I. *Nouns.* **assemblage,** collection, levy, conflux, concourse, gathering, ingathering, mobilization, meet, concentration, convergence, forgathering, muster, congregation.
assembly, meeting, levee, reunion, drawing room, at home, *conversazione* (*It.*); congress, senate, house, legislature, convocation, caucus, convention, council, committee, lodge, society, company, association, union, club; suite, audience; set, *cénacle* (*F.*), coterie, clique, faction; watch; caravan.
miscellany, medley, miscellanea, collectanea, ana, compilation; symposium; library, museum, menagerie.
crowd, throng; flood, rush, deluge; rabble, mob, host, multitude, press, crush, horde, body, tribe; gang, knot, troop, troupe, corps, posse, team, crew, squad, force, band, party; swarm, shoal, covey, flock, herd, round-up (*U. S.*), drove, drive, bunch, bevy, array, galaxy.
clan, brotherhood, association, league, guild, fraternity, tribe, sept, caste.
group, cluster, sorus (*pl.* sori: *bot.*), Pleiades, series, nest (*as of boxes*), set, tissue (*as of lies*), batch, lot, pack; budget, assortment, bunch; parcel, bundle, packet, package, bale, fagot, wisp, truss, tuft, tussock, pompon, shock, clump, thicket; rick, stack, sheaf, swath; volley, shower, flight (*as of arrows*).
accumulation, amassment, conglomeration, cumulation, store, stock, aggregation, aggregate, congestion, heap, lump, pile, litter, mass, pyramid; drift, snowball, snowdrift; quantity.
II. *Verbs.* **assemble,** come together, collect, muster; meet, unite, join, rejoin; cluster, flock, swarm, rush, surge, stream, herd, mass, crowd, throng, huddle, associate; congregate, concentrate, resort, forgather.
muster, bring together, gather together, fit together (*as parts of a machine*), collect, gather, round up; hold a meeting, call, convene, convoke; rake up, dredge, heap, mass, pile; pack, bunch, huddle, bundle, cram, lump together; compile, group, concentrate, unite, amass, agglomerate, accumulate, hoard, store; heap Ossa upon Pelion.
III. *Adjectives.* **dense,** compact, solid, close, tight, crowded, thick, thickset, serried, teeming, swarming, populous.

See also COMBINATION, CONVERGENCE, COUNCIL, PARTY, STORE.—*Antonyms.* See DISJUNCTION, DISPERSION, DIVERGENCE.

---

assembly room, hall, auditorium, chapel. See HABITATION.

ASSENT.—I. *Nouns.* **assent,** acquiescence, accession, admission; consent, compliance, concession, agreement, understanding; affirmation, nod, recognition, acknowledgment, avowal, confession.
unanimity, unison, accord, common consent, consensus, acclamation, chorus; public opinion; concurrence, accordance, like-mindedness, unanimousness, consentience; coöperation.
ratification, confirmation, corroboration, approval, sanction, support, indorsement, visé, acceptance; verification.
II. *Verbs.* **assent,** give assent, acquiesce, agree, comply, accept, accede, accord, concur, consent, coincide, echo, reciprocate, go with; recognize; subscribe to, conform to, defer to; go (*or* swim) with the stream; be in the fashion; join in the chorus.

acknowledge, own, admit, allow, avow, testify, confess; concede, yield; abide by; permit.
confirm, ratify, approve, indorse, visé, seal, countersign; validate, corroborate, verify, accredit, sustain, substantiate, clinch (*colloq.*).
III. *Adjectives.* **assenting,** acquiescing, etc. (see *verbs*); assentive, agreed, acquiescent.
unanimous, agreeing, consentient, concurrent, solid (*U. S. polit. cant*), accordant, consentaneous, like-minded, of one accord (*or* mind), of the same mind, at one; uncontradicted, unchallenged, unquestioned.
IV. *Adverbs.* **yes,** yea, aye *or* ay, true, granted, even so, just so, to be sure, as you say, surely, assuredly, exactly, precisely, certainly, certes (*archaic*), of course, unquestionably, no doubt, doubtless.
unanimously, by common consent, to a man, as one man; with one consent (voice, *or* accord), *nem. con.* (*L. nemine contradicente*), one and all.

See also AGREEMENT, CONCURRENCE, CONSENT, PERMISSION, WILLINGNESS.—*Antonyms.* See DISAGREEMENT, DISSENT, PROHIBITION, REFUSAL.

---

assert, *v.* affirm, declare, maintain, avow, state, claim, allege. See AFFIRMATION.
assess, *v.* estimate, value, appraise; charge, exact, ask. See JUDGE, PRICE.
assets, *n.* goods, goods and chattels, effects, possessions. See PROPERTY.
assign, *v.* allot, distribute; delegate, commit; deliver, hand over. See APPORTIONMENT, COMMISSION, GIVING.
assimilate, *v.* absorb, digest; transform, incorporate; harmonize. See COMBINATION, CONVERSION, UNIFORMITY.
assist, *v.* help, succor, support, relieve. See AID.
associate, *v.* accompany; combine (with), join, unite, fraternize, club, federate; link, connect, correlate. See ACCOMPANIMENT, COMBINATION, RELATION.
associate, *n.* companion, comrade, fellow, mate, colleague, partner. See FRIEND.
association, *n.* alliance, federation, league, club, fellowship, fraternity, partnership, combine, trust; similarity, homogeneity, analogy. See COMBINATION, COÖPERATION, RELATION.
assort, *v.* separate, classify, sort. See ARRANGEMENT.
assume, *v.* suppose, presuppose, understand, presume; appropriate, undertake, take, affect. See SUPPOSITION, TAKING.
assumed, *adj.* adopted, fictitious, false, make-believe, pretended, hypocritical; given, granted. See DECEPTION, GIVING.
assuming, *adj.* forward, insolent, arrogant, presuming, presumptuous. See INSOLENCE.
assumption, *n.* arrogance, presumption, impudence, seizure; theory, postulate, axiom. See RIGHTLESSNESS, SUPPOSITION.
assurance, *n.* sureness; confidence, belief; impudence, boldness; guarantee, pledge, security. See CERTAINTY, EXPECTATION, INSOLENCE, PROMISE.
assure, *v.* convince; make certain, certify; insure; promise, vow. See BELIEF, CERTAINTY, PROMISE.
assured, *adj.* certain, sure, settled, guaranteed; self-possessed, confident. See CERTAINTY, VANITY.
astern, *adv.* aft, abaft; backward. See REAR.
astir, *adv.* afoot, on foot, up, in motion. See ACTIVITY.
astonish, *v.* amaze, surprise, startle, astound, perplex. See WONDER.
astray, *adv.* adrift, at fault, wandering, lost. See UNCERTAINTY.
astringent, *adj.* binding, styptic, contractive, constringent; sour, tart, austere. See CONTRACTION, ROUGHNESS.
astrologer, *n.* soothsayer, Chaldean, astromancer. See WORLD.
astronomer, *n.* stargazer (*jocose*), astrophysicist, astrochemist. See WORLD
astute, *adj.* shrewd, quick, bright, acute. See INTELLIGENCE.

asylum, *n.* sanctuary, retreat, shelter, home; insane asylum. See REFUGE.
asymmetric, *adj.* unsymmetrical, irregular, formless. See DISTORTION, FORMLESSNESS.
atheist, *n.* unbeliever, heretic, agnostic. See IRRELIGION.
athlete, *n.* gymnast. See STRENGTH.
athletic, *adj.* gymnastic, acrobatic; muscular, strong, robust, powerful. See CONTENTION, STRENGTH.
athletics, *n.* sports, gymnastics. See AMUSEMENT, STRENGTH.
at large, free, unconfined, unrestrained. See LIBERATION.
atmospheric, *adj.* aërial, airy. See AIR.
atom, *n.* iota, particle, mote, jot, speck. See LITTLENESS.
atomize, *v.* vaporize, spray. See VAPORIZATION.
atomizer, *n.* vaporizer, spray, sprayer. See VAPORIZATION.

ATONEMENT.—I. *Nouns.* **atonement,** reparation, *amende honorable* (*F.*), expiation, redemption, reclamation, conciliation, propitiation; indemnification, redress, amends, recompense, compensation; peace offering, sacrifice; compromise, composition.
apology, explanation, satisfaction, admission, regret, self-reproach, self-condemnation, justification, vindication, defense, extenuation, excuse.
penance, fasting, sackcloth and ashes, shrift, flagellation, self-mortification, purgation, purgatory.
II. *Verbs.* **atone,** atone for, expiate, propitiate, appease, make amends; reclaim, redeem, repair, ransom, absolve, purge, shrive, do penance, pay the penalty; sacrifice, immolate.
apologize, make an apology, express regret, beg pardon, give satisfaction, *faire l'amende honorable* (*F.*).
III. *Adjectives.* **atoning,** piacular, propitiatory, expiatory, expiational; sacrificial, sacrific (*rare*).
apologetic, apologetical, excusatory, excusative (*rare*); sorry, regretful; justificative, justificatory, vindicatory, vindicative, extenuating, extenuatory, extenuative, palliatory, palliative.
See also COMPENSATION, DEITY, VINDICATION.—*Antonyms.* See IMPENITENCE.

---

atrocity, *n.* enormity, outrage, brutality. See MALEVOLENCE.
attach, *v.* connect, fasten; join, add, affix. See JUNCTION.
attachment, *n.* addition, annex; connection; annexation, legal seizure; affection, devotion, fidelity. See ADJUNCT, JUNCTION, LAWSUIT, LOVE.

ATTACK.—I. *Nouns.* **attack,** assault, encounter, aggression, intrusion, encroachment, offense, injury; onset, onslaught, *coup de main* (*F.*), charge, incursion, inroad, invasion, irruption, outbreak, sally, sortie, raid, air raid, forced entrance (*as by the police*), surprisal, foray; storm, storming, zero hour; boarding, escalade.
siege, investment, blockade, beleaguerment, besiegement, encompassment; bombardment, cannonade.
seizure, fit, spell, stroke, sudden attack (*as of apoplexy*).
firing, shooting, discharge, burst, volley, fusillade; sharpshooting, broadside, cross fire, enfilade; *rafale* (*F.*), barrage, curtain fire, curtain of fire.
thrust, lunge, pass, home thrust, jab (*colloq.*), carte and tierce (*fencing*); bayonet; cut.
attacker, assailant, assailer, assaulter, antagonist, aggressor, invader.
sharpshooter, dead shot, crack shot, marksman, rifleman; sniper.
II. *Verbs.* **attack,** assault, assail, encounter, set upon, pounce upon, fall upon, rush, charge; enter the lists, show fight, take the offensive; strike at, thrust at, aim (*or* deal) a blow at; be the aggressor, strike the first blow, fire the first shot; advance (*or* march) against, march upon, invade, raid, harry.
close with, come to close quarters, bring to bay, come to blows; cut and thrust, bayonet, saber, stab; butt, kick, strike; horsewhip, whip.
fire upon, fire at, shoot at, pop at, snipe at, draw a bead on (*U. S.*), level at, open fire, pepper, fusillade, torpedo, submarine (*colloq.*), bomb, bombard, shell, fire a volley, enfilade, rake; hit, plug (*slang*).

besiege, beset, beleaguer, invest, encompass, blockade; sap, mine; storm, board, scale the walls, go over the top.
III. *Adjectives.* **attacking,** aggressive, offensive, combative, pugnacious; incursive, invasive; up in arms.
IV. *Adverbs.* on the warpath; on the offensive; over the top.
See also AGITATION, IMPULSE, PUNISHMENT, WARFARE.—*Antonyms.* See DEFENSE, RECOIL.

---

attain, *v.* reach, make, come to; gain, earn, win, get. See ARRIVAL, SUCCESS.
attempt, *n.* trial, endeavor, effort. See ESSAY.
attend, *v.* accompany, escort, tend; heed, listen. See ACCOMPANIMENT, ATTENTION.
attendant, *n.* helper, domestic, waiter, retainer, companion. See ACCOMPANIMENT, SERVANT.

ATTENTION.—I. *Nouns.* **attention,** intentness, alertness, ear, thought, observance, observation; consideration, avizandum (*Scots law*), reflection; heed, advertence, advertency, heedfulness, notice, recognition, note, regard; circumspection, care, application, devotion, study, scrutiny; inspection, revision, revisal.
minuteness, circumstantiality, meticulousness, particularity, exactness, exactitude, attention to detail.
II. *Verbs.* **attend,** watch, observe, look, see, view, notice, regard, take notice, mark, pay attention to, heed, mind, listen, give heed to, advert to; occupy oneself with; contemplate, look to, see to; take cognizance of, entertain, recognize; make (*or* take) note of, note.
examine, scan, scrutinize, inspect, review, explore, ransack, probe, sift, test, search, try, survey, investigate, consider (*archaic in this sense*); take stock of; overhaul, revise, pore over.
revert, return, recur, hark back, come to the point.
meet with attention, attract notice, fall under one's notice; be under consideration; catch (*or* strike) the eye.
call attention to, bring under one's notice; point out (to, *or* at), indicate, exhibit display, reveal, demonstrate, show, direct attention to; bring forward.
III. *Adjectives.* **attentive,** mindful, heedful, observant, regardful; alive to, awake to, alert, wide-awake, taken up with, occupied with; engrossed in, wrapped in; intent, tense, absorbed, rapt; circumspect, watchful; concentrated, undistracted, interested, intent on, open-eyed; on the watch.
IV. *Interjections.* **attend!** attention! mind! look out! see! observe! look! hark! listen! hear! hear ye! oyez! (*used by court criers*); *nota bene* (*L.*), N. B.
See also CARE, THOUGHT.—*Antonyms.* See INATTENTION, NEGLECT.

---

attenuate, *v.* weaken, enfeeble, lessen; rarefy, thin. See DECREASE, RARITY.
attic, *n.* garret, loft. See RECEPTACLE, SUMMIT.
attire, *n.* dress, costume, garb, array. See CLOTHING.
attitude, *n.* position, stand, pose. See SITUATION.
attorney, *n.* barrister, advocate, solicitor. See LAWYER.

ATTRACTION.—I. *Nouns.* **attraction,** attractiveness; pull, drawing power, affinity, magnetism, gravity; allurement, inveiglement, seduction, glamour, appeal, enticement.
loadstone, lodestar, polestar, magnet.
lure, bait, charm, decoy.
II. *Verbs.* **attract,** pull, drag, draw, magnetize; bait, trap, decoy, charm, lure, allure, entice, inveigle, tempt, seduce, fascinate.
III. *Adjectives.* **attractive,** attracting, drawing, alluring, charming, prepossessing, engaging, winning, fascinating, seductive.
See also CUNNING, DESIRE, PLEASURABLENESS, TAKING (*charm*).—*Antonyms.* See REPULSION.

ATTRIBUTION.—I. *Nouns.* **attribution,** theory, assignment, reference to, accounting for; ascription, arrogation, imputation, derivation.
explanation, interpretation, elucidation, explication, key, secret, cause, reason why.
II. *Verbs.* **attribute to,** ascribe to, impute to, father upon, refer to, lay to, trace to, blame, saddle; account for, derive from; theorize.
III. *Adjectives.* **attributable,** imputable, assignable, traceable, ascribable, referrible, referable, accountable, explicable; due to, owing to.
IV. *Adverbs.* **hence,** therefore, consequently, for that reason, thence (*rare in this sense*), whence.
why? wherefore? whence? how comes it? how is it? how so?
V. *Conjunctions.* **since,** seeing that, because, for, on account of, owing to, inasmuch as, whereas.

See also CAUSE, INTERPRETATION.—*Antonyms.* See CHANCE, MISINTERPRETATION.

---

audacity, *n.* dash, confidence; impudence, gall; temerity, overconfidence. See COURAGE, INSOLENCE, RASHNESS.
audience, *n.* interview, hearing; hearers, assembly. See CONVERSATION, DRAMA.
auditorium, *n.* auditory, hall. See DRAMA.
august, *adj.* majestic, grand, dignified, venerable, stately, imposing, eminent, noble. See GREATNESS.
auspicious, *adj.* favorable, propitious, promising; fortunate, opportune, expedient, successful. See HOPE, OMEN, PROSPERITY.
austere, *adj.* ascetic, abstemious; harsh, stern, strict, severe; sour, astringent. See ASCETICISM, SEVERITY, SOURNESS.
authentic, *adj.* real, genuine, true, sure, trustworthy, authoritative. See BELIEF, CERTAINTY.
authentication, *n.* verification, confirmation, establishment. See SECURITY.
author, *n.* writer, originator, creator, maker, inventor, father. See BOOK, PLAN.
authoritative, *adj.* imperative, peremptory; official, decisive, conclusive. See AUTHORITY, CERTAINTY.
authorities, *n. pl.* officials, powers that be. See MASTER.

AUTHORITY.—I. *Nouns.* **authority,** power, authorization, warrant, right, dominion, domination, dictation, command, control, bidding, hold, grasp, grip; influence, prestige; prerogative, divine right; patronage; protectorate.
leadership, headship, mastership; kingship, dictatorship, presidentship, magistracy, consulship, lordship; supremacy, primacy, suzerainty, sovereignty, royalty, iron sway, rod of empire.
government, rule, administration, lease of power, jurisdiction, sway, reign, dynasty; presidency, republic, republicanism, federalism; raj (*Anglo-Indian*), empire, monarchy; limited (*or* constitutional) monarchy; aristocracy; oligarchy; democracy; representative government, constitutional government, home rule, dominion rule (*Brit.*), colonial government; autonomy, self-government, self-determination, popular sovereignty.
socialism, social democracy, collectivism, nationalism, communism, communalism, Marxism, Fascism, Bolshevism.
mob law, mobocracy, demagogy, demagogism, ochlocracy, mob rule, lynch law, anarchy, nihilism.
government by women, gynecocracy, gynocracy (*rare*), gynarchy; metrocracy, matriarchy; petticoat rule, petticoat government.
officialism, bureaucracy, bureaucratism, bureau system, red tape, red-tapism, red-tapery, red-tapedom, beadledom, Bumbledom, officialdom, departmentalism.
martial law, military rule, military government, rule of the sword, militarism, stratocracy (*rare*).
despotism, absolutism, czarism, Cæsarism, autocracy, kaiserism, imperialism, tyranny.
feudalism, feudal system, vassalage. feudalization.

state, realm, commonwealth, country, power, polity (*tech.*), body politic.
ruler, chief, governor, head, regent, president, director, commander, commandant, sovereign, sultan, potentate, emperor, king, lord; seat of government, headquarters.
expert, specialist, adept, proficient, master hand, crackajack (*slang*); authoritative textbook (*or* reference book), court of final appeal.
II. *Verbs.* **authorize,** empower, license, sanction, enable, warrant, entitle, permit, dictate.
rule, sway, command, control, administer, govern, direct, lead, preside over, be at the head of, reign.
dominate, have the upper (*or* whip) hand; prevail, preponderate, boss (*colloq.*); override, overrule, overawe; lord it over, domineer, tyrannize, keep under, bend to one's will, have it all one's own way, be master of the situation, take the lead, lay down the law; "ride in the whirlwind and direct the storm" (*adapted from* Addison); rule with a rod of iron.
III. *Adjectives.* **authoritative,** paramount, supreme, ruling, commanding, regnant, dominant, predominant, preponderant, in the ascendant, influential; imperious, dictatorial, peremptory; executive, administrative, official, gubernatorial, bureaucratic, departmental.
regal, royal, monarchical, sovereign, kingly; dynastic, imperial, royalist; autocratic, despotic.
democratic, Jeffersonian (*U. S.*), democratical, popular; ultrademocratic, radical, Jacobinic, Jacobinical.
IV. *Adverbs.* in the name of, by the authority of, in virtue of, under the auspices of, in the hands of.
See also CERTAINTY, COMMAND, COUNCIL, EVIDENCE, EXPERT, MASTER, PERMISSION, POWER, SAGE, SCEPTER, SEVERITY.—*Antonyms.* See LAXITY, OBEDIENCE, SERVANT, SUBMISSION.

---

authorization, *n.* sanction, authority, warrant. See RIGHTFULNESS.
authorship, *n.* writing, creation. See PRODUCTION.
autocrat, *n.* absolute monarch, dictator, despot. See MASTER, SEVERITY.
autocratic, *adj.* ruling, absolute, despotic, dictatorial. See AUTHORITY.
autograph, *n.* signature, hand. See EVIDENCE.
automatic, *adj.* instinctive, mechanical. See NECESSITY.
automatism, *n.* self-motion, self-regulation. See PSYCHICAL RESEARCH.
automobile, *adj.* self-propelling, automotive, locomobile. See JOURNEY.
automobile, *n.* motor car, car (*colloq.*), machine (*colloq.*), auto (*colloq.*). See VEHICLE.
autonomy, *n.* self-government, independence. See FREEDOM.
autopsy, *n.* post-mortem, inspection, examination. See INTERMENT.
autumn, *n.* fall, harvest time. See EVENING.

AUXILIARY.—I. *Nouns.* **auxiliary,** assistant, aider, help, helper, helpmate, helping hand; colleague, partner, confrère, coöperator, coadjutor, coadjutress (*fem.*), coadjutrix (*fem.*), collaborator, recruit, copartner, right-hand man, right hand.
ally, associate, coworker; confederate, accomplice, abettor, accessory; promoter, friend, sympathiser; confidant (*fem.* confidante), *alter ego* (*L.*), pal (*slang*), comrade, companion, mate, buddy (*U. S. colloq.*), chum (*colloq.*).
upholder, seconder, backer, second (*as in a duel*), supporter, abettor, advocate, adherent, partisan, champion, patron; friend at court, mediator.
friend in need, special providence, guardian angel, fairy godmother, tutelary genius, *deus ex machina* (*L.*), lady from Philadelphia (*Peterkin Papers*).
puppet, cat's-paw, creature, tool; satellite, parasite, dependent, hanger-on, jackal, jackstraw, man of straw.
II. *Adjectives.* **auxiliary,** adjuvant, assistant, helping, aiding, ministrant, ancillary; subsidiary, subservient, subordinate.
See also AID, COÖPERATION, FRIEND.—*Antonyms.* See ENEMY, OPPONENT.

avail, *v.* serve, succeed, suffice; help, profit, benefit. See SUCCESS, UTILITY.
available, *adj.* ready, convenient, handy, usable. See PREPARATION, UTILITY.
avalanche, *n.* landslide, snowslide. See DESCENT.
avenger, *n.* revenger, requiter. See REVENGE.
average, *n.* normal, rule, standard. See MEAN.
average, *adj.* ordinary, medium, passable, mediocre, fair; medial, median. See IMPERFECTION, MEAN.
average, *v.* divide, equalize. See MEAN.
averse, *adj.* opposed, counter, conflicting; loath, reluctant. See CONTRARIETY, DISLIKE, UNWILLINGNESS.
aversion, *n.* repugnance, antipathy, loathing. See DISLIKE.
avert, *v.* keep off, ward off, turn aside, prevent. See HINDRANCE.
aviation, *n.* flying, aërial navigation, flight. See AËRONAUTICS.
aviator, *n.* aviatrix (*fem.*), aviatress (*fem.*), airman, flyer. See AËRONAUT.
avidity, *n.* eagerness, longing; greed, avarice. See DESIRE, PARSIMONY.
avocation, *n.* occupation, calling, hobby. See BUSINESS.

AVOIDANCE.—I. *Nouns.* **avoidance,** evasion, elusion, flight; escape, retreat recoil, recession, departure.
vacancy (*as of office*), vacating, voiding, annulment, dismissal; unoccupied position, opening, opportunity.
abstention, abstinence, abstaining, refraining, temperance, self-restraint, forbearance; inaction, neutrality.
shirker, slacker (*colloq.*), shirk, quitter, truant, skulker.
fugitive, refugee, runaway, deserter, renegade, runagate; exile, outcast; backslider.
II. *Verbs.* **avoid,** shun, steer (*or* keep) clear of; fight shy of, evade, elude, shirk, malinger.
abstain, refrain, spare; eschew, keep from, let alone, not do, not attempt; desist.
shrink, hang (hold, *or* draw) back; recoil, wince, funk (*slang*), start, cringe, blench, quail, flinch, shy, dodge, parry.
retreat, withdraw, recede, retire, depart, turn tail, take to one's heels; run, run away, cut and run (*colloq.*); fly, flee, take flight; make off, sneak off, sheer off; part company; slip, play truant, decamp, take French leave, levant (*Eng. slang*), make oneself scarce (*slang*), flit, bolt, abscond; escape; abandon, desert.
III. *Adjectives.* **avoidable,** escapable, evadable, eludible; preventable *or* preventible.
elusive, evasive; fugitive, runaway; shy, shifty, slippery, tricky, baffling; deceptive, illusive, misleading, tricksy (*rare*).
See also DEPARTURE, ESCAPE, RECOIL, RECESSION.—*Antonyms.* See APPROACH, ARRIVAL, PURSUIT.

---

await, *v.* anticipate, contemplate, wait for; approach, impend; be kept waiting. See EXPECTATION, FUTURE, LATENESS.
awake, *adj.* heeding, observant; keen, astute. See ATTENTION, INTELLIGENCE.
award, *n.* compensation, bestowal, conferment; decision, adjudication. See GIVING, JUDGMENT.
aware, *adj.* conscious, cognizant, apprised, informed: *with* of *or* that. See KNOWLEDGE.
away, *adv.* absent, elsewhere, out, afar. See DISTANCE.
awe, *n.* reverence, veneration, dread. See FEAR, WONDER.
awful, *adj.* terrific, tremendous, horrible, dreadful. See FEAR.
awkward, *adj.* clumsy, ungainly, ungraceful, unskillful, *gauche* (*F.*). See UNSKILLFULNESS.
ax *or* **axe,** *n.* battle-ax, tomahawk; hatchet, adz, mattock. See ARMS, SHARPNESS.
axiom, *n.* postulate, rule, proposition, truism, aphorism. See MAXIM.
axis, *n.* shaft, pivot, stem (*bot.*), axle. See CENTRALITY, ROTATION.
axle, *n.* axis, spindle, pivot, arbor. See ROTATION.
azure, *adj.* sky-blue, cerulean, sky-colored. See BLUE.

B

babble, *v.* chatter, prattle, gossip; gurgle, murmur; gibber, rave. See LOQUACITY, RIVER, UNMEANINGNESS.
baby, *n.* child, babe, tot, nursling. See INFANT.
babyish, *adj.* infantile, simple, childish. See IMBECILITY, INFANT.
bachelor, *n.* celibate, unmarried man. See CELIBACY.
back, *n.* reverse, hinder part, stern. See REAR.
back, *v.* stand by, second, help, boost; return, reverse. See AID, REGRESSION.
backbone, *n.* firmness, courage, pluck; spine, spinal column. See RESOLUTION, SUPPORT.
background, *n.* offing; back, setting; obscurity, retirement. See DISTANCE, REAR, SECLUSION.
backsliding, *n.* apostasy, perversion; retrogression, countermovement; lapse. See IMPIETY, REGRESSION, RELAPSE.
backward, *adj.* stagnant, dull; delayed, tardy; retrograde, reverse; loath, disinclined, reluctant, remiss. See DETERIORATION, LATENESS, REGRESSION, UNWILLINGNESS.
bad, *adj.* wicked, sinful; imperfect, unsuitable; rancid, tainted. See BADNESS, IMPERFECTION, FETOR.
badge, *n.* mark, sign, emblem. See INDICATION.

BAD MAN.—*Nouns.* **bad man,** wrongdoer, worker of iniquity, evildoer, sinner, transgressor, profligate, scapegallows; libertine, debauchee, wanton (*usually fem.*); bad example.
rascal, reprobate, scoundrel, villain, knave, hound, cur, rogue, blackguard, vagabond, miscreant, caitiff, wretch, reptile, viper, serpent, shyster (*U. S. slang*), trickster, sneak, snitch (*slang*), snitcher (*slang*), squealer (*slang*), traitor; swindler, sharper, thief, forger, crook (*colloq.*), hellhound, hellion (*colloq.*), monster, devil, demon, devil incarnate; fallen angel, lost sheep, black sheep, castaway.
ruffian, rowdy, bully, terrorist, rough, rough-neck (*slang*), thug, apache (*colloq.*), gangster, gunman, guerrilla, tough (*U. S. colloq.*), hoodlum (*colloq.*), hooligan (*slang*).
culprit, delinquent, criminal, malefactor, malfeasant, recidivist (*incorrigible criminal*), jailbird, felon, convict, murderer, outlaw.
scamp, scapegrace, ne'er-do-well, rotter (*Eng. slang*), good for naught, good for nothing, scalawag (*colloq.*), limp (*colloq.*), rapscallion, wretch: *scamp and its synonyms are often applied playfully.*
prodigal, spendthrift, waster, wastrel, spender, squanderer, lavisher.
riffraff, rabble, mob, scum, scum of the earth, ragtag (*colloq.*), ragtag and bobtail (*colloq.*), *canaille* (*F.*), ruck, raff; poor whites, poor white trash, white trash (*these three terms are used contemptuously by negroes in the southern U. S.*); squaw man.
See also EVILDOER, KNAVE, THIEF, VICE.—*Antonyms.* See GOOD MAN, VIRTUE.

BADNESS.—I. *Nouns.* **badness,** hurtfulness, virulence, malignancy, abomination, perniciousness, disease, pestilence, guilt, depravity, vice, wickedness; malignity, malevolence.
curse, bane, torment; imprecation, malediction, anathema, anathema maranatha; plague spot, evil star, ill wind; hoodoo (*colloq.*), Jonah, jinx (*slang*), snake in the grass, skeleton in the closet; thorn in the flesh, thorn in the side.
ill-treatment, annoyance, molestation, abuse, oppression, persecution, *Judenhetze* (*Ger.*), tyranny, outrage, misusage, injury, harm, scathe (*rare except in* without scathe), damage.
imperfection, defectiveness, poorness, inferiority, mediocrity, indifference.
II. *Verbs.* **hurt,** harm, scathe (*rare except as participle*), injure, pain, wound.
wrong, aggrieve, oppress, persecute, trample upon; overburden, weigh down; victimize.
maltreat, abuse, ill-use, illtreat, buffet, batter, contuse, bruise, scratch, maul, **smite,** molest, do violence: stab, pierce, outrage, violate.

III. *Adjectives.* **bad,** ill, dreadful, horrid, horrible, dire; rank, foul, rotten, decayed, decomposed, tainted, putrid.
unsatisfactory, indifferent, deteriorated, below par, defective, faulty, poor, imperfect, ill-conditioned, inferior, unsuitable; invalid, unsound (*as, a* bad *claim*).
lamentable, deplorable, wretched, sad, unfortunate, grievous, pitiful, pitiable, pathetic, sad, piteous, woeful.
evil, wrong, sinful, depraved, wicked, corrupt, vicious; iniquitous, shocking, reprehensible.
hateful, abominable, repugnant, abhorrent, revolting, repulsive, repellent, forbidding, disgusting, detestable, execrable, odious, vile, base, villainous, cursed, accursed, *or* accurst, damnable, diabolic, devilish.
hurtful, harmful, baneful, baleful, malefic, injurious, deleterious, detrimental, dysgenic (*opposite of* eugenic), pernicious, mischievous, mischief-making, malignant, prejudicial; oppressive, burdensome, onerous; malign, sinister, unlucky, inauspicious.
poisonous, venomous, virulent, toxic, septic; pestilent, pestilential, noxious, mephitic; deadly, destructive.
IV. *Adverbs.* **badly,** evilly, hurtfully, etc. (see *adjectives*); ill, wrong, amiss; to one's cost; where the shoe pinches.

See also DETERIORATION, DISEASE, INFERIORITY, MALEVOLENCE, UNHEALTHINESS.
—*Antonyms.* See GOODNESS, HEALTH, IMPROVEMENT, SUPERIORITY.

---

bad temper, ill temper, surliness, irritability. See DISCOURTESY, IRASCIBILITY.
bad-tempered, *adj.* ill-tempered, crabbed, surly. See DISCOURTESY, IRASCIBILITY.

BAD WOMAN.—*Nouns.* **bad woman,** Jezebel, hell-cat, hellhag, witch, hag, harridan, strumpet, jade, drab, trull, trollop, harlot, wanton, Cyprian, adulteress, courtesan; procuress, bawd; Delilah, Messalina; hussy (*sometimes playful*), minx (*usually playful*).

See also LIBERTINE.—*Antonyms.* See GOOD WOMAN.

---

baffle, *v.* check, frustrate, balk, foil; confound, outwit, nonplus. See HINDRANCE, SUCCESS.
bag, *n.* pouch, sack, container, sac (*tech.*). See RECEPTACLE.
bag, *v.* protrude, sag, bulge; capture, entrap, catch, get. See CONVEXITY, TAKING.
baggage, *n.* paraphernalia, luggage, dunnage. See PROPERTY.
bail, *n.* bond, pledge, guarantee, surety. See SECURITY.
bait, *v.* trap, decoy, lure; harass, plague, badger, worry. See ATTRACTION, PAIN.
bake, *v.* roast, cook; dry, harden. See CALEFACTION, HARDNESS.
balance, *n.* evenness, equilibrium; scales, steelyard; average; surplus, excess; mental poise, steadiness. See EQUALITY, GRAVITY, MEAN, REMAINDER, WISDOM.
balance, *v.* estimate, parallel, compare; offset, square, pay for; match, come up to; hesitate, waver; audit, check. See COMPARISON, COMPENSATION, EQUALITY, IRRESOLUTION, NUMBER.
bald, *adj.* hairless, bare; monotonous, meager; plain, undisguised. See DIVESTMENT, DULLNESS, MANIFESTATION.
baldness, *n.* hairlessness, bareness; poverty, enervation. See DIVESTMENT, FEEBLENESS.
baleful, *adj.* injurious, harmful, detrimental. See BADNESS.
balk, *v.* thwart, disappoint, foil, frustrate; back, stop, shy. See HINDRANCE, REGRESSION.
ball, *n.* dance, hop (*colloq.*), party; shot, projectile; globe, sphere. See AMUSEMENT, ARMS, ROTUNDITY.

ballet girl, *danseuse* (*F.*), figurante (*operatic*), *ballerina* (*It.*). See DRAMA.
balloon, *n.* dirigible, blimp (*cant.*). See AËRONAUTICS, COMBATANT.
ballot, *n.* poll, vote, voice. See CHOICE.
balm, *n.* sedative, anodyne, assuasive; balsam, ointment. See MODERATION, REMEDY.
ban, *n.* proscription, curse; restriction, interdict. See MALEDICTION, PROHIBITION.
[1]band, *n.* strip, tape; strap, belt. See FILAMENT, VINCULUM.
[2]band, *n.* group, crowd; brass band, military band; sect, followers, disciples. See ASSEMBLAGE, MUSICAL INSTRUMENTS, SCHOOL.
banded, *adj.* striped, barred, belted, brindled. See VARIEGATION.
bandit, *n.* brigand, outlaw, highwayman. See THIEF.
bandy, *v.* exchange, give and take, toss; discuss. See INTERCHANGE.

BANE.—I. *Nouns.* **bane,** ruin, woe, harm, fatal mischief, injury, destruction, damage, waste; curse, thorn in the flesh, thorn (*fig.*), annoyance; *bête noir* (*F.*), bugbear; evil, scourge, plague, white plague, cancer, disease, pest, moth and rust (*Bible*), fungus, mildew; dry rot; canker.
poison, venom, virus, toxin *or* toxine, ptomaine, toxicant, drug; carbon dioxide, carbonic acid, carbonic-acid gas, choke damp, black damp, mephitic air; carbon monoxide, carbonic oxide; miasma, malaria; poison gas; upas, upas tree; blood poisoning, septicæmia.
stench, malodor, stink, fetor, fetidity (*rare*), fetidness, odor, smell, fume, reek, effluvium, mofette, empyreuma; mephitis, sewer gas.
sting, fang, thorn, prick, bramble, brier *or* briar, nettle.
science of poisons: toxicology.
II. *Adjectives.* **baneful,** harmful, hurtful, dire, noxious, pernicious, noisome, unwholesome, deleterious, insalubrious, injurious, destructive.
poisonous, venomous, toxic, toxicant, toxiferous, mephitic; virulent, deadly, malignant.
See also BADNESS, EVIL, SCOURGE, UNHEALTHINESS.—*Antonyms.* See GOOD, REMEDY.

---

bang, *v.* beat, pound, batter; slam, crash. See IMPULSE, SNAP.
banish, *v.* expel, dismiss; exile, expatriate. See EJECTION, EXCLUSION, PUNISHMENT.
bank, *n.* ridge, pile, mound; shore, beach; hill, ascent, slope. See DEFENSE, LAND, OBLIQUITY.
bankrupt, *adj.* insolvent, impoverished, ruined. See NONPAYMENT.
bankruptcy, *n.* insolvency, ruin. See FAILURE.
banner, *n.* flag, pennant, standard. See INDICATION.
banquet, *n.* feast, entertainment, repast. See FOOD.
banter, *v.* rally, chaff, jolly (*colloq.*). See WIT.
banter, *n.* raillery, chaff, jesting, badinage, pleasantry. See RIDICULE, WIT.
baptism, *n.* consecration, immersion. See RITE.
baptize, *v.* purify; christen, name; sprinkle, dip, immerse. See CLEANNESS, NOMENCLATURE, WATER.
bar, *n.* legal profession; rail, barrier, rod, bolt, line; court, bench. See LAWYER, PRISON, TRIBUNAL.
bar, *v.* bolt, shut, fasten; reject, ostracize, exclude; debar, restrain, restrict. See CLOSURE, EXCLUSION, PROHIBITION.
barbarian, *n.* savage, ruffian; alien, foreigner, outsider. See EVILDOER, EXTRANEOUSNESS.
barbarism, *n.* ill-breeding, ignorance, vulgarity; solecism. See DISCOURTESY, INELEGANCE.
barbarous, *adj.* inhuman, savage, brutal; uncivilized, rude, uncultured. See MALEVOLENCE, PEOPLE.

bare, *adj.* nude, naked, undraped; empty, unfurnished, destitute; mere, simple. See DIVESTMENT, INSUFFICIENCY, SMALLNESS.
bare, *v.* disclose, expose, uncover, reveal, lay bare. See DISCLOSURE.
barefaced, *adj.* undisguised, brazen, shameless, impudent. See MANIFESTATION.
barefoot, *adj.* barefooted, unshod, discalceate (*as a friar*). See DIVESTMENT.
bargain, *n.* inexpensiveness; deal, trade, transaction, agreement. See CHEAPNESS, COMPACT.
bargain, *v.* negotiate, haggle, stipulate, contract. See BARTER.
[1]**bark,** *n.* shell, cortex, rind, skin. See COVERING.
[2]**bark,** *n.* yelp, yap, bay, howl. See ULULATION.
barometer, *n.* aneroid, gauge. See AIR.
barrage, *n.* bombardment, volley, cannonade. See ATTACK.
barred, *adj.* striped, lined, banded, streaked. See VARIEGATION.
barren, *adj.* fruitless, unprofitable, worthless; sterile, arid, unfertile. See INUTILITY, UNPRODUCTIVENESS.
barricade, *n.* stockade, fortification; barrier, obstruction. See DEFENSE, INCLOSURE.
barrier, *n.* obstacle, impediment; fence, stockade. See HINDRANCE, INCLOSURE, PRISON.

BARTER.—I. *Nouns.* **barter,** exchange, truck, trade, traffic, bargaining, marketing, interchange, swap *or* swop (*colloq.*), *quid pro quo* (*L.*).
commerce, business intercourse, commercial enterprise, exchange of commodities (*or* merchandise), mercantile business, merchantry, trading, dealing, business, trade, intercourse, buying and selling, custom; supply and demand; commercialism, mercantilism.
brokerage; jobbing, stockjobbing, stockbroking, agiotage.
free trade (*opposed to* protection).
II. *Verbs.* **barter,** exchange, truck, trade, traffic, swap *or* swop (*colloq.*), interchange, buy and sell, market, give and take, carry on (*or* ply) a trade; deal in.
bargain, drive (make, *or* strike) a bargain, negotiate, bid for; haggle, stickle, higgle, chaffer, dicker (*U. S.*), cheapen, beat down, underbid; outbid.
III. *Adjectives.* **commercial,** mercantile, mercatorial (*rare*), trading; marketable, staple, in the market, for sale; retail; wholesale.
IV. *Adverbs.* across the counter; in the way of trade; in the marts of trade; in (*or* on) the market; on 'change.
See also COMPACT, INTERCHANGE.

BASE.—I. *Nouns.* **base,** foundation, ground, earth, groundwork, *fond* (*F.*), basis, footing, foothold; bedplate, bed piece, groundsel *or* groundsill, sill; substructure, substruction, underbuilding, understructure, basement; substratum, bed rock, hardpan.
baseboard, washboard, mopboard (*U. S.*); dado, wainscot; plinth, sub-base.
floor, flooring, pavement, paving; parquet; deck; surface.
bottom (*lowest part or point*), nadir (*opposite of* zenith); keel, keelson *or* kelson, hold, bilge, sump; bed (*of a stream*), channel, coulee (*U. S.*), basin.
foot, extremity, terminal, pes (*pl.* pedes: *tech.*), hoof, paw, pad (*as of the hare, fox, wolf, etc.*), *pied* (*F.*), *patte* (*F.: heraldry*), hand (*as of an ape or a hawk*); sole, heel, toe.
[*slang terms for feet*] trotters, tootsies, understandings, dogs (*U. S.*), beetle-crushers, dew-beaters, hoofs, kickers, trampers.
root, fundamental, radical, radicle (*tech.*), rootlet, rhizoid (*bot.*), taproot; source, spring, origin, rise, commencement.
II. *Adjectives.* **basal,** basic, fundamental; bottom, undermost, nethermost, lowest, under; founded on, based on, grounded on, built on (*or* upon).
See also SUPPORT.—*Antonyms.* See SUMMIT.

---

base, *adj.* impure, debased, counterfeit, spurious; vile, low, mean, ignoble, unworthy. See DECEPTION, DISREPUTE, PEOPLE, VICE.

baseboard, *n.* washboard, scrubboard, mopboard (*U. S.*). See BASE.
basement, *n.* cellar, vault. See LOWNESS.
bashful, *adj.* timid, shy, diffident, constrained, sheepish. See MODESTY.
basin, *n.* valley, hollow, depression; vessel, bowl. See CONCAVITY, RECEPTACLE.
basis, *n.* foundation, base, groundwork. See SUPPORT.
basket, *n.* hamper, crate, pannier, skep. See RECEPTACLE.
bass, *adj.* deep-toned, deep, low. See RESONANCE.
bat, *v.* strike, hit, beat, pound, batter. See IMPULSE.
bath, *n.* shower, Turkish bath; washing, wash, cleansing, dip, plunge. See CLEANNESS, FURNACE, WATER.
bathe, *v.* immerse, dip, wet, soak, douse, wash, lave. See WATER.
batter, *v.* shatter, smash, destroy; beat, pommel, bruise. See DESTRUCTION, IMPULSE.
battery, *n.* guns, artillery. See COMBATANT.
battle, *n.* combat, fight, struggle, contest, engagement, conflict, encounter See ACTION, CONTENTION, WARFARE.
battlefield, *n.* battle ground, scene of action. See ARENA.
battleship, *n.* warship, cruiser, dreadnought, superdreadnought, destroyer, man-of-war. See COMBATANT.
bay, *n.* estuary, bayou, fiord, sound. See GULF.
be, *v.* exist, breathe, be alive, occur, take place. See EXISTENCE.
beak, *n.* neb, bill, nose; *Slang*: magistrate. See CONVEXITY, JUDGE.
beam, *n.* ray, gleam, streak; timber, joist. See LIGHT, MATERIALS, SUPPORT.
bear, *v.* suffer, feel; tolerate, endure; produce, render, yield; hold, sustain; carry, transport, convey. See FEELING, INEXCITABILITY, PRODUCTION, SUPPORT, TRANSFER.
beard, *n.* whiskers; awn. See ROUGHNESS.
bearded, *adj.* barbate, awned, tufted, hirsute, hairy. See ROUGHNESS.
beardless, *adj.* hairless, shaven, smooth-faced. See DIVESTMENT.
bearing, *n.* course, trend, drift; carriage, port, manner, demeanor; significance, import; connection, reference, association. See DIRECTION, FRONT, PRESENCE; MEANING, RELATION.
bearings, *n. pl.* whereabouts, location, position. See SITUATION.
beast, *n.* brute, quadruped; cattle (*collective*), horse; blackguard, grouch. See ANIMAL, CARRIER, DISCOURTESY.—**beast of burden,** pack animal. See CARRIER.
beat, *v.* pulsate, throb; hit, strike, batter, bruise; overcome, conquer, defeat. See OSCILLATION, PUNISHMENT, SUPERIORITY.
beat, *n.* accent, rhythm; pulse, throb; track, course, path. See POETRY, REGULARITY, WAY.
beatify, *v.* sanctify, hallow, consecrate, bless. See PIETY.
beau, *n.* dude, swell, dandy; wooer, lover. See FOP, LOVE.

BEAUTY.—I. *Nouns.* **beauty,** loveliness, the beautiful, beau ideal, pulchritude (*rare*), attractiveness, charm; form (*archaic*), elegance, grace, symmetry, comeliness, beauty unadorned; fairness, bloom, delicacy, refinement, style, polish, gloss; good effect, good looks; Apollo, Adonis.

beautiful woman, charmer (*archaic or jocose*), reigning beauty, belle, fascinator, witch, enchantress, *charmeuse* (*F.*); goddess, Venus, Hebe, Helen of Troy, "the face that launch'd a thousand ships" (Marlowe's *Faustus*).

brilliancy, splendor, gorgeousness, magnificence, radiance, luster, grandeur, glory, sublimity.

beautifying, decoration, ornamentation, adornment, embellishment.

II. *Verbs.* **beautify,** grace; embellish, adorn, deck, bedeck, trim, ornament, decorate, set off.

III. *Adjectives.* **beautiful,** beauteous, handsome, pretty, lovely, graceful, elegant, exquisite, delicate, dainty, charming.

comely, fair, pleasing, good-looking, goodly, bonny, well-favored, well-made, well-formed, well-proportioned, shapely, symmetrical, harmonious.
bright, bright-eyed; rosy-cheeked, rosy, ruddy, blooming, in full bloom.
trim, tidy, trig, neat, spruce, smart, jaunty, dapper, stylish, *chic* (*F.*), natty (*colloq.*).
brilliant, shining, beaming, sparkling, radiant, splendid, resplendent, splendorous *or* splendrous, dazzling, glowing; glossy, sleek; rich, gorgeous, superb, magnificent, grand, fine.
artistic, artistical, æsthetic, picturesque, pictorial, enchanting, attractive, becoming, ornamental; well-composed, well-grouped, well-balanced.
spotless, immaculate, unspotted, stainless; undeformed, undefaced, unsullied; perfect.
passable, presentable, tolerable, mediocre, moderate, ordinary, so-so (*colloq.*), not amiss.

See also ORNAMENT, SYMMETRY.—*Antonyms.* See UGLINESS.

---

because, *adv.* by reason of, owing to, due to. See MOTIVE.
because, *conj.* since, for, as, forasmuch as. See MOTIVE.
become, *v.* turn to, change to; befit, behoove, accord with. See CONVERSION, DUTY.
becoming, *adj.* attractive, ornamental; fit, seemly, decorous, proper. See BEAUTY, RIGHTFULNESS.
beckon, *v.* signal, call, motion, sign. See INDICATION.
bed, *n.* cot, resting place, couch; foundation, base. See SUPPORT.
bedcover, *n.* coverlet, counterpane, quilt, blanket, spread. See COVERING.
bedding, *n.* bedclothes, sheets, blankets, etc.; straw, litter. See COVERING, SUPPORT.
bedroom, *n.* bedchamber, chamber, cubicle. See RECEPTACLE.
befit, *v.* suit, fit, harmonize with; behoove, become. See AGREEMENT, DUTY.
before, *adv.* forward; foremost, ahead; sooner, earlier, previously, hitherto, heretofore. See FRONT, PRECEDENCE, PRIORITY.
beforehand, *adv.* early, in advance, first, precipitately. See EARLINESS.
befriend, *v.* assist, help, stand by, relieve, rescue. See AID.
beg, *v.* ask alms; implore, beseech, crave, ask, petition, plead. See POVERTY, REQUEST.
beget, *v.* generate, engender, procreate, reproduce. See PRODUCTION.
beggar, *n.* solicitor, suppliant; mendicant, pauper. See PETITIONER, POVERTY.
beggary, *n.* destitution, mendicancy, beggars (*collectively*). See POVERTY.
begin, *v.* commence, start, originate, initiate. See BEGINNING.
beginner, *n.* novice, tyro, recruit, probationer. See LEARNER.

BEGINNING.—I. *Nouns.* **beginning,** commencement, start, starting-point, dawn, opening, outset, incipience, inception; introduction, prelude, prologue, preamble, preface, foreword; initial; inauguration, installation; *début* (*F.*), coming out (*colloq.*); embarkation; rising of the curtain; curtain raiser, maiden speech; exordium; outbreak, onset, brunt; initiative, first move; thin end of the wedge; fresh start, new departure.
origin, cause, fountain, source, rise; bud, germ, egg, embryo, rudiment; genesis, birth, nativity, cradle, infancy.
head, heading, caption; title, title-page; front, van, forefront, foreground.
entrance, entry, ingress; inlet, orifice, mouth; portal, portico, door; gate, gateway, *porte-cochère* (*F.*); postern, wicket, threshold, vestibule, hallway (*U. S.*), entrance hall, lobby, porch; border, frontier.
rudiments, elements, outlines, grammar, alphabet, ABC; first principles, first steps.
II. *Verbs.* **begin,** commence; rise, arise; originate, conceive, introduce, inaugurate, initiate, open, start; dawn, set in, take its rise, enter upon; set out, embark in; make one's *début* (*F.*); institute; set about, set to work; make a start, open fire, open the ball, break ground, lay the first stone, cross the Rubicon; undertake.
usher in, lead the way, precede, forerun, take the lead (*or* initiative); head;

lay the foundations, found, set up, set on foot, launch, broach; open up, open the door to.
come into existence, take birth; burst forth, break out; spring up, crop up.
recommence, resume, continue, begin at the beginning, begin again, start afresh, begin *de novo* (*L.*), make a fresh start.
III. *Adjectives.* **initial**, prime, initiatory, introductory, prefatory, initiative, incipient; inaugural; embryonic, rudimentary; primal, primary, primeval, pristine, primordial, primitive, original, aboriginal; natal.
first, foremost, front, head, chief, principal, leading; maiden.
IV. *Adverbs.* **first**, firstly (*in enumerations*), *imprimis* (*L.*), in the first place, in the bud, in embryo, from the beginning, formerly, heretofore.

See also CAUSE, FRONT, OPENING, PRECURSOR, PREPARATION.—*Antonyms.* See END, REAR, SEQUEL.

---

begone! *interj.* away! go! off with you! See EJECTION.
behalf, *n.* interest, advantage, benefit, behoof. See DEPUTY (*in behalf of*), GOOD.
behave, *v.* act, conduct oneself, bear oneself. See ACTION, CONDUCT.
behavior, *n.* deportment, demeanor, manners. See CONDUCT.
behead, *v.* decapitate, guillotine, decollate. See KILLING, PUNISHMENT.
behind, *adv.* after, subsequently; backward, aft, rearward. See FOLLOWING, REAR.
being, *n.* life, subsistence, actuality; person, creature. See EXISTENCE, SUBSTANTIALITY.

BELIEF.—I. *Nouns.* **belief**, credence, assurance, faith, credit, trust, confidence, reliance, trustworthiness, hope, dependence, sheet anchor, mainstay.
conviction, persuasion, certainty; opinion, view, conception, impression, surmise; conclusion, judgment.
doctrine, teaching, tenet, dogma, maxim, rule, theory, principle, opinion, creed; articles, canons; gospel; article (declaration, *or* profession) of faith; position, assent, avowal, confession; propaganda.
credibility, believableness, believability, presumption, likelihood, probability; plausibility.
II. *Verbs.* **believe**, credit, give faith (credit, *or* credence) to; trust, realize; assume, swallow (*colloq.*), accept, take it, consider; count (depend, rely, *or* build) upon; take for granted.
confide in, believe in, put one's trust in, place reliance on, trust, rely upon, swear by.
think, hold, opine, conceive, trow (*archaic*), ween (*archaic*), judge, fancy, apprehend, surmise, presume, suppose, imagine; have (hold, entertain, adopt, embrace, foster, *or* cherish) a belief *or* an opinion.
convince, persuade, assure, satisfy, bring to reason, convert, indoctrinate; wean, bring round, bring (*or* win) over; carry conviction.
believable, credible, reliable, trustworthy, dependable, satisfactory; probable.
believed, trusted, accredited, unsuspected, undoubted.
III. *Adjectives.* **certain**, sure, assured, positive, cocksure (*colloq.*), satisfied, confident, undoubting, unhesitating, convinced, indubitable, undeniable, indisputable, undoubted, incontrovertible, unquestionable, plain, true; fixed, stated, predetermined, settled, determinate; reliable, trustworthy, unfailing, infallible, secure, established, stable, enduring.
confiding, trustful, unsuspecting, unsuspicious; credulous, gullible.
canonical, orthodox, authoritative, standard, accepted, received, approved; doctrinal.

See also CERTAINTY, CREDULITY, HOPE, IDEA, JUDGMENT, PIETY, RECEIVING, SUPPOSITION.—*Antonyms.* See DOUBT, UNBELIEF, UNCERTAINTY.

---

believer, *n.* Christian, convert. See PIETY.
belittle, *v.* disparage, run down, decry, depreciate; dwarf, underestimate, slight. See DETRACTION, UNDERESTIMATION.
bell, *n.* alarm, call. See INDICATION.

belle, *n.* reigning beauty, beautiful woman; coquette, flirt. See BEAUTY.
belligerent, *adj.* quarrelsome, pugnacious, warlike, disputatious. See CONTENTION.
bellow, *v.* bawl, shout, roar, reverberate (*as cannon*). See CRY.
bell-shaped, *adj.* campanulate, campaniform. See CURVATURE, ROTUNDITY.
belly, *n.* maw, stomach, paunch. See CONVEXITY.
belong, *v.* form part of, merge; be in one's possession; relate to, concern: *with* to. See COMPONENT, POSSESSION, RELATION.
below, *adv.* inferior, subordinate; beneath, under, underneath, lower. See INFERIORITY, LOWNESS.
belt, *n.* girdle, band, strip, zone, circuit. See CIRCULARITY.
bench, *n.* settee; seat, stool; court, board, bar. See FORM, SUPPORT, TRIBUNAL.
bend, *v.* turn, curve, double; give, yield. See CIRCUITY, SOFTNESS.
bend, *n.* fork, angle, notch; curve, turn. See ANGULARITY, CURVATURE.
beneath, *adv.* under, below, down, underfoot. See LOWNESS.

BENEFACTOR.— *Nouns.* **benefactor,** savior, protector, patron, Mæcenas, guardian, fairy godmother, good genius, tutelary genius, tutelary saint, guardian angel, good Samaritan, friend in need, "a very present help in time of trouble" (*Bible*); salt of the earth; altruist, philanthropist, supporter, angel (*slang*).

See also AUXILIARY.—*Antonyms.* See EVILDOER, OPPONENT.

---

beneficial, *adj.* valuable, helpful, salutary, useful, advantageous. See GOOD, USE.
beneficiary, *n.* receiver, donee, pensioner, legatee. See RECEIVING.
benefit, *n.* gain, profit, advantage, behalf, avail. See GOOD, USE.
benefit, *v.* assist, aid; improve, profit; avail, serve. See BENEVOLENCE, GOOD, UTILITY.

BENEVOLENCE.—I. *Nouns* **benevolence,** Christian charity; God's grace; good will, philanthropy, unselfishness, kindness, kindliness, loving-kindness, benignity, brotherly love, charity, humanity, fellow-feeling, sympathy, goodness of heart, warm-heartedness, kind-heartedness, bonhomie *or* bonhommie, good nature, amiability, tenderness, love, friendship; tolerance, consideration, mercy.

charitableness, bounty, almsgiving; good works, beneficence, liberality, generosity, a good turn; "the luxury of doing good" (Goldsmith).

philanthropist, "one who loves his fellow-men" (Hunt), salt of the earth; good Samaritan, sympathizer, well-wisher, altruist, humanitarian.

II. *Verbs.* **bear good will,** wish well, take (*or* feel) an interest in; be interested in, sympathize with, feel for; treat well, give comfort, do good, do a good turn, benefit, assist, be of use, render a service, render assistance, aid, philanthropize; enter into the feelings of others, practice the Golden Rule, do as you would be done by.

III. *Adjectives.* **benevolent,** kind, kindly, good-natured, well-meaning, amiable, genial, bland, cordial, obliging, accommodating, helpful, indulgent, gracious, tender, considerate, warm-hearted, kind-hearted, tender-hearted, large-hearted, soft-hearted, merciful; sympathizing, sympathetic, benign, benignant, salutary; lenient, forgiving, favorable.

full of natural affection; fatherly, paternal; motherly, maternal; brotherly, fraternal; sisterly, sororal; friendly.

charitable, beneficent, philanthropic, philanthropical, liberal, generous, humane, unselfish, altruistic, bountiful.

IV. *Adverbs.* **benevolently,** kind-heartedly, with the best intentions; with all one's heart.

See also AID, FRIENDSHIP, GOODNESS, PHILANTHROPY, PITY.—*Antonyms.* See MALEVOLENCE, MISANTHROPY.

---

bent, *n.* liking, fondness; bias, trend, nature, propensity, proclivity. See DESIRE, DISPOSITION, TENDENCY, WILLINGNESS.

benumb, *v.* drug, paralyze, blunt, stupefy, deaden. See INSENSIBILITY.
bequest, *n.* legacy, gift. See GIVING.
bereavement, *n.* loss, affliction; deprivation, destitution. See DEATH, LOSS.
bereft, *adj.* bereaved, deprived of, denuded. See LOSS.
berth, *n.* position, office; lodging, quarters; bunk, compartment. See BUSINESS, HABITATION, SUPPORT.
beside, *prep.* by, alongside, near, abreast. See NEARNESS.
besides, *adv.* further, also, moreover, furthermore. See ADDITION.
besiege, *v.* storm, beleaguer; surround, hedge, circumscribe. See ATTACK, ENVIRONMENT.
bespeak, *v.* engage, reserve, secure, arrange for. See ORDER.
best, *adj.* choice, rare, exquisite, precious; standard, unparalleled. See GOOD, PERFECTION.
bestow, *v.* donate, present, confer. See GIVING.
bet, *v.* wager, gamble, punt, play. See PLUNGE.
betray, *v.* insnare, play false, trick; divulge, let slip, reveal; sell. See DECEPTION, DISCLOSURE, SALE.
betrothal, *n.* affiance, engagement, espousal. See PROMISE.
betrothed, *adj.* affianced, engaged. See MARRIAGE, PROMISE.
better, *v.* mend, relieve, correct, repair. See IMPROVEMENT.
between, *adv.* among, amid, in the thick. See INTERJACENCE.
beverage, *n.* drink, liquor. See FOOD.
beware, *v.* be wary, keep on one's guard, look out. See WARNING.
beware! *interj.* ware! take care! look out! See WARNING.
bewilder, *v.* perplex, confuse, mystify, confound, puzzle; stagger, daze, dazzle. See INATTENTION, UNCERTAINTY, WONDER.
bewildered, *adj.* dazed, confused, perplexed. See MISINTERPRETATION, UNCERTAINTY.
bewitch, *v.* fascinate, charm, inveigle; enchant, hypnotize. See MOTIVE, SORCERY.
beyond, *adv.* far, farther, yonder; over, more. See DISTANCE, SUPERIORITY.
bias, *n.* warp, prepossession; slope, diagonal; inclination, bent, prejudice, partiality. See MISJUDGMENT, OBLIQUITY, TENDENCY.
bias, *v.* influence, dispose, sway, prejudice. See MISJUDGMENT, MOTIVE.
biased, *adj.* one-sided, prejudiced, unfair, inequitable. See MISJUDGMENT, PART.
Bible, *n.* Gospel, the Word, the Good Book. See SCRIPTURES.
bid, *v.* direct, order, enjoin, instruct; tender, proffer; invite, ask, call, summon. See COMMAND, OFFER, REQUEST.
bier, *n.* litter, barrow, catafalque. See INTERMENT.
big, *adj.* considerable, important; large, bulky, huge, massive, gross, immense. See GREATNESS, HEIGHT, SIZE.
bigot, *n.* dogmatist, fanatic, iconoclast; Pharisee, formalist. See CERTAINTY, HETERODOXY, IMPIETY, OBSTINACY.
bigoted, *adj.* dogmatic, intolerant, fanatical, prejudiced, narrow; arbitrary, obstinate. See HETERODOXY, IMPIETY, OBSTINACY.
bigotry, *n.* dogmatism, positiveness; fanaticism; sanctimony, pharisaism, hypocrisy; intolerance. See CERTAINTY, HETERODOXY, IMPIETY, OBSTINACY.
bill, *n.* score, reckoning; bank note, note, greenback. See ACCOUNTS, MONEY.
billet, *v.* lodge, quarter, saddle with, install: *with* on, in, *or* at. See LOCATION.
billow, *n.* undulation, surge, swell, wave. See OCEAN, RIVER.
bind, *v.* restrain, force, oblige; fasten, tighten, secure. See COMPULSION, JUNCTION.
biography, *n.* life history. See DESCRIPTION.
biology, *n.* science of life. See ORGANIZATION.
bionomics. *n.* ecology, thremmatology, zoötechnics. See ZOÖLOGY.

bird, *n.* warbler, nestling, cageling, fledgling; fowl. See ANIMAL (*birds*).
bird of prey, eagle, vulture. See ANIMAL.
birth, *n.* origin, genesis; creation. See BEGINNING, PRODUCTION.—**give birth to,** bear, produce, bring forth, originate. See LIFE, PRODUCTION.
birthmark, *n.* patch, blotch, disfigurement, mole, nævus (*med.*). See BLEMISH.
biscuit, *n.* cracker, pretzel, rusk, cracknel, hard-tack, ship bread. See FOOD.

BISECTION.—I. *Nouns.* **bisection,** bifidity, bipartition; bifurcation, forking, furcation, branching, ramification, divarication, dichotomy, divergence; halving, dimidiation (*rare*); fork, Y, cleft, crotch, prong, wishbone, furculum, furcula (*anat.*); fold.
half, moiety, mediety (*law*); hemisphere, semisphere (*rare*); fifty per cent.
II. *Verbs.* **bisect,** halve, divide, separate, split, cut in two, cleave; dimidiate (*rare*), dichotomize, middle (*naut.*).
fork, bifurcate, furcate, branch off (*or* out), ramify, divaricate.
straddle, bestride, bestraddle, cross (*colloq.*), fork (*a horse: slang*).
III. *Adjectives.* **bisected,** cloven, cleft, bipartient, bipartible, dichotomal, dichotomic, dimidiate (*rare*); bipartile, bipartite, bifid, bifurcate, two-pronged, bifurcated, bicuspid, bicuspidate, furcate, furciform (*rare*), furcular (*rare*), semi-, demi-, hemi-.
Antonyms. See DUPLICATION.

---

bishop, *n.* prelate, diocesan, suffragan, metropolitan, archbishop. See CLERGY.
bishopric, *n.* diocese, see. See CHURCHDOM.
bit, *n.* piece, slice; curb; fragment, mite. See PART, PRISON, SMALLNESS.
bite, *v.* munch, chew, snap, nip. See FOOD.
biting, *adj.* piercing, nipping, keen; piquant, pungent, hot, sharp; telling, forceful, forcible. See COLD, PUNGENCY, VIGOR.
bitter, *adj.* stinging, cutting; caustic, malignant, spiteful; inclement, rigorous; acrid, pungent, unpalatable. See COLD, MALEVOLENCE, SEVERITY, UNSAVORINESS.
blacken, *v.* blot, smudge, besmirch; malign, slander, defame. See BLACKNESS, DETRACTION.

BLACKNESS.—I. *Nouns.* **blackness,** darkness, obscurity; swarthiness, swartness; lividness, sootiness, fuliginosity, inkiness, duskiness, denigration. nigrescence, nigritude.
[*comparisons*] ink, jet, ebony, ebon (*poetic*), coal, charcoal, soot, pitch, raven, crow, night.
negro, negress, colored man, colored woman, nigger (*colloq., usually contemptuous*), darky *or* darkey (*colloq.*), black, Ethiop, Ethiopian, African, blackfellow, blackamoor, man of color.
black, blacken, denigrate, nigrify; blot, blotch, smut, smudge, smirch, smutch, sully, begrime, soot, besoot, besmut, besmutch, besmudge; ink, ebonize; darken, becloud, cloud, obscure.
III. *Adjectives.* **black,** sable, somber *or* sombre, livid, dark, inky, atramental, atramentous; ebony, ebon (*poetic*), nigrescent, coal-black, jet, jet-black, raven, pitchy, sooty; swart, swarthy, dusky, dingy, murky; blotchy, smudgy; low-toned; of the deepest dye; Negro, Negroid, Ethiopic, Ethiopian, African; Cimmerian.
[*expressing menace*] **threatening,** frowning, sullen, forbidding, foreboding, ill-boding, sinister, minatory, baneful, dismal, thundery (*as,* black *looks*).
[*expressing dishonor or evil*] evil, wicked, malignant, deadly, dishonorable, disgraceful, atrocious (*as.* black *deeds,* black *list*).
[*expressing uncleanness*] **unclean,** soiled, dirty, grimy, unwashed, muddy, grubby, foul (*as,* black *hands or linen*).
See also DARKNESS.—*Antonyms.* See WHITENESS.

---

bladder, *n.* vesicle, vesica, cyst, sound (*of a fish*), blister. See RECEPTACLE.

blade, *n.* dandy, buck, dasher (*colloq.*); cutter, edge tool, knife, sword; leaf (*of a grass*). See FOP, SHARPNESS, VEGETABLE.
blame, *v.* ascribe to, lay to, saddle; reproach, criticize, censure, reprove, condemn. See ATTRIBUTION, DISAPPROBATION.
blameless, *adj.* guiltless, clear, irreproachable. See INNOCENCE.
blameworthy, *adj.* guilty, culpable, blamable. See DISAPPROBATION.
bland, *adj.* affable, obsequious, gracious, unctuous. See COURTESY.
blank, *adj.* empty, void, unfilled; vacant, vacuous, expressionless; confused, confounded, disconcerted. See NONEXISTENCE, UNSUBSTANTIALITY, WONDER.
blanket, *n.* cover, quilt, coverlet. See COVERING.
blare, *n.* blast, peal, fanfare. See LOUDNESS.
blasphemy, *n.* profanity, irreverence. See IMPIETY.
blast, *n.* explosion, eruption; breeze, gust. See VIOLENCE, WIND.
blast, *v.* devastate, shatter, wreck, ruin, annihilate. See DESTRUCTION.
blaze, *n.* fire, flame; mark, spot. See HEAT, INDICATION.
blazon, *v.* spread, proclaim, advertise; embellish, decorate. See ORNAMENT, PUBLICATION.
bleach, *v.* whiten, blanch. See COLORLESSNESS.
bleak, *adj.* cutting, piercing, raw, windy, desolate, unsheltered. See COLD.
blear, *adj.* dim, filmy, indistinct; dim-sighted. See DIMNESS, DIM-SIGHTEDNESS.
bleed, *v.* overcharge, extort, fleece; suffer, smart, ache. See DEARNESS, PAIN.

BLEMISH.—I. *Nouns.* **blemish,** disfigurement, defacement, deformity, taint, flaw, injury; want, lack, fault, deficiency, failing, defect, imperfection, eyesore, stain, blot, spot, speck, speckle, blur, freckle, patch, blotch, macula, macule, smudge, birthmark, nævus (*med.*), cicatrice, scar, seam, cicatrix (*pl.* cicatrices), mole, pimple, blister, pustule, crack, fissure, rift.

II. *Verbs.* **blemish,** mar, disfigure, injure, impair, sully, spoil, damage, deform, deface, mutilate, maim, scar, distort, garble, mangle, pervert, wrench, twist, blur, tarnish, taint.

III. *Adjectives.* **blemished,** marred, disfigured, injured, etc. (see *verbs*); defective, imperfect, faulty, unsound; discolored, specked, speckled, freckled, pitted, pock-marked, bruised.

See also DETERIORATION, IMPERFECTION.—*Antonyms.* See IMPROVEMENT, ORNAMENT, PERFECTION.

---

blend, *v.* mix, combine, fuse, merge, amalgamate, compound; interbreed, cross; accord, shade, merge. See COMBINATION, CROSSING, HARMONY.
bless, *v.* hallow, glorify, consecrate. See DEITY.
blessing, *n.* benediction, benison, commendation; godsend, boon, benefit. See APPROBATION, GOOD.
blight, *v.* rot, corrupt, blast; thwart, foil. See DETERIORATION, DISAPPOINTMENT.
blight, *n.* decay, impairment, corruption, rot. See DETERIORATION.
blind, *adj.* sightless, unseeing; undiscerning, unmindful. See BLINDNESS, INATTENTION.
blind, *n.* screen, shade, shutter; wile, artifice, subterfuge, ruse, pretext. See AMBUSH, DECEPTION, PLEA.

BLINDNESS.—I. *Nouns.* **blindness,** sightlessness, anopsia (*med.*), cecity (*rare*); amaurosis (gutta serena *or* "drop serene" *of Milton*); cataract, benightedness.

[*aids for the blind*] braille, interpoint braille type, Moon's type, New York point, American braille; noctograph, writing frame; visagraph.

II. *Verbs.* **be blind,** not see; lose one's sight; grope in the dark.

blind, darken, benight, obscure, eclipse, hide; put one's eyes out, gouge; blindfold, hoodwink, throw dust in one's eyes; screen, dazzle, outshine.

III. *Adjectives.* **blind,** eyeless, sightless, visionless, unseeing, rayless, amaurotic (*med.*), dark; stone-blind, stark-blind; **blindfold, blindfolded; undiscerning,**

unseeing, unperceiving, purblind, dimsighted; blind as a bat (a buzzard, a beetle, a mole, *or* an owl).
blank (*as, a* blind *wall or window*); closed at one end, impassable (*as, a* blind *alley*); cæcal (*as, a* blind *gut*); hidden, unmarked, concealed (*as, a* blind *path*).
IV. *Adverbs.* **blindly,** sightlessly, unseeingly, gropingly; darkly.
See also DIM-SIGHTEDNESS.—*Antonyms.* See VISION.

---

blinker, *n.* blinder, blind, cover, shield: *usually in plural.* See DIM-SIGHTEDNESS, SHADE.
bliss, *n.* happiness, ecstasy, rapture, felicity. See PLEASURE.
blister, *n.* vesicle, bleb. See RECEPTACLE (*sac*).
blithe, *adj.* joyous, gay, lighthearted, merry. See CHEERFULNESS.
blizzard, *n.* gale, storm, windstorm, northeaster. See WIND.
bloat, *v.* expand, dilate, swell, distend, puff up. See EXPANSION.
block, *n.* row, terrace, street; mass, lump. See HABITATION, SIZE.
block, *v.* impede, hinder, check, bar, obstruct. See HINDRANCE.
blockade, *v.* obstruct, barricade; besiege, beset; isolate. See CLOSURE, ENVIRONMENT, EXCLUSION.
blockhead, *n.* dolt, simpleton, bonehead (*slang*). See FOOL.
blond, *adj.* light-colored, fair-skinned, fair, light-complexioned. See COLORLESSNESS, WHITENESS.
blood, *n.* relationship, kinship, kindred; gore, cruor (*tech.*), sap. See CONSANGUINITY, FLUID.
bloodless, *adj.* pale, anæmic; inhuman, unfeeling; peaceable, without bloodshed. See COLORLESSNESS, MALEVOLENCE, PEACE.
bloodthirsty, *adj.* murderous, bloody-minded; inhuman. See KILLING, MALEVOLENCE.
blood vessel, artery, vein, aorta, capillary. See CHANNEL.
bloody, *adj.* gory, sanguinary, murderous. See KILLING.
bloom, *v.* glow, flourish, be in health; thrive, prosper; blossom, flower. See HEALTH, PROSPERITY, VEGETATION.
blooming, *adj.* florid, rosy-cheeked; bloomy, blossoming; fresh, vigorous. See HEALTHINESS, VEGETATION, YOUTH.
blossom, *n.* flower, bud, bloom. See VEGETATION.
blot, *v.* stain, blemish, spot, tarnish, sully; erase, efface. See BLACKNESS, DISREPUTE, OBLITERATION.
blotch, *n.* blot, spot, stain, smudge; pustule (*med.*). See BLEMISH.
blouse, *n.* waist, shirt, shirt waist, smock. See CLOTHING.
blow, *v.* boast, brag; gasp, pant, puff; sound (*as a trumpet*); breeze, bluster, whiff, waft. See BOAST, FATIGUE, [1]SOUND, WIND.
blow, *n.* disillusion, blighted hope; wound, disaster; hit, knock, thwack, slap, stroke. See DISAPPOINTMENT, EVIL, IMPULSE.
blowpipe, *n.* blowgun. See AIR PIPE.

BLUE.—I. *Nouns.* **blue,** azure, etc. (see *adjectives*); bice, indigo, lapis lazuli, sapphire; blueness, bluishness; the sky (*poetic*), the sea (*poetic*).
[*comparisons*] turquoise, sapphire; smoke, haze, distant hills, moonlight; bruise.
[*pigments*] ultramarine, smalt, cobalt, Prussian blue, syenite blue, bice, indigo, zaffer.
[*in plural*] **blues** (*colloq.*), melancholy, depression, dejection, low spirits, megrims, blue devils, gloom, despondency, sadness.
II. *Verbs.* **blue,** make blue, turn blue.
III. *Adjectives.* **blue,** azure, cerulean, sky-blue, sky-colored, navy blue, ultramarine, aquamarine, cerulescent, bluish; atmospheric; cold.
[*expressing low spirits*] **melancholy,** low-spirited, dejected, depressed, despondent, sad, dispirited, downhearted, discouraged (*as, to feel* blue); gloomy, dismal, unpromising (*as, things look* blue: *colloq. in this sense*).
[*expressing moral strictness*] **puritanical,** overstrict, severe, strict, precise, scrupulous, intolerant, illiberal, narrow, narrow-minded, bigoted (*as,* blue *laws*).

[*expressing learning*] literary, bookish, learned, scholarly, well-read, bluestockingish, high-brow (*slang*), pedantic: *in this sense,* blue *is colloq. and is used only of women, or "bluestockings."*
See also KNOWLEDGE, DEJECTION.

---

bluff, *adj.* abrupt, ungracious, unceremonious, brusque. See BLUNTNESS.
bluff, *n.* cliff, headland, bank. See HEIGHT.
bluff, *v.* brag, puff; hoodwink, mislead, hoax. See BOASTING, DECEPTION.
blunder, *v.* fail, mismanage, botch, flounder, bungle. See FAILURE.
blunder, *n.* bull, Hibernicism, solecism; mistake, slip; bungle, botch, mess, fiasco. See ABSURDITY, ERROR, FAILURE, UNSKILLFULNESS.
blunt, *v.* stupefy, deaden, numb. See INSENSIBILITY.

BLUNTNESS.—I. *Nouns.* **bluntness,** dullness, etc. (see *adjectives*); obtundity.
II. *Verbs.* **be** (*or* **render**) **blunt,** dull, take off the point (*or* edge), blunt, obtund, turn.
III. *Adjectives.* **blunt,** dull, dullish, obtuse, pointless, unpointed, edgeless, unsharpened.
bluff, brusque, unceremonious, abrupt, curt, short, blunt, ungracious, unpolished, rude, rough, uncivil, impolite; downright, outspoken, direct, unflattering, matter-of-fact.
See also ARTLESSNESS, DISCOURTESY, INSENSIBILITY.—*Antonyms.* See COURTESY, SHARPNESS.

---

blur, *v.* swim, be indistinct. See DIM-SIGHTEDNESS.
blush, *v.* glow, flush, color. See RED.
bluster, *v.* rage, bully; threaten, defy. See RESENTMENT, THREAT.

BLUSTERER.—*Nouns.* **blusterer,** swaggerer, braggart, boaster, pretender swasher (*rare*), vaporer, braggadocio, blower (*slang*), ranter, bluffer, roisterer, brawler, bully, swashbuckler; desperado, dare-devil, fire eater (*colloq.*), jingo, jingoist, chauvinist, berserk, berserker; Gascon, Drawcansir, Thraso.
dogmatist, doctrinaire, bigot; zealot, fanatic, enthusiast, spellbinder, hot-air artist (*slang*), Sir Oracle, stump orator.
See also BOASTING, LOQUACITY, SPEECH.—*Antonyms.* See SERVILITY (*sycophant*).

---

blustering, *adj.* overbearing, noisy, swaggering. See INSOLENCE.
board, *n.* cabinet, committee; provisions, fare. See COUNCIL, FOOD.
boast, *v.* brag, vaunt. See BOASTING.
boaster, *n.* egoist, braggadocio, swaggerer, pretender. See BLUSTERER.

BOASTING.—I. *Nouns.* **boasting,** boast, vaunting, vaunt, pretensions, braggadocio, puff (*colloq.*), flourish, bluff, highfaluting, fanfaronade, gasconade, dog (*slang*), side (*slang*), swagger, brag, *blague* (*F.*), bounce, bluster, bravado, bunk (*colloq. or slang*), buncombe *or* bunkum (*colloq.*), claptrap, humbug, blah (*slang*); toploftiness (*colloq.*), rodomontade, bombast, hot air (*slang*), tall talk (*colloq.*), exaggeration, magniloquence, grandiloquence, heroics; jingoism, chauvinism, Nietzscheism, spread-eagleism (*U. S.*).
II. *Verbs.* **boast,** brag, vaunt, puff, show off, flourish, strut, swagger, bluster, gasconade, vapor, bluff; blow one's own trumpet, talk big (*colloq.*), blow (*colloq.*), exaggerate, draw the long bow; give oneself airs, put on side *or* dog (*slang*).
exult, crow (*colloq.*), triumph, glory, rejoice, joy, cheer; gloat, gloat over, chuckle.
III. *Adjectives.* **boastful,** braggart, vainglorious, pretentious, highfaluting, bombastic, pompous, grandiloquent, magniloquent, tall (*colloq.*), extravagant, toplofty (*colloq.*), high-flown, swollen, inflated, turgid, ostentatious, tumid, plethoric, heroic, grandiose, thrasonic, self-praising, vaunting, windy (*colloq.*); jingo, jingoish, jingoistic, chauvinistic, Nietzschean, spread-eagle (*colloq. and humorous*).
elated, elate (*poetic*), exultant, jubilant, triumphant, joyful, excited, flushed, animated; cock-a-hoop, flushed with victory, on stilts (*colloq.*), in high feather.
IV. *Adverbs.* **boastfully,** bombastically, etc. (see *adjectives*); with flying colors.
See also EXAGGERATION, VANITY.—*Antonyms.* See MODESTY.

boat, *n.* bark (*poetic*), craft, vessel, skiff, dinghy, liner, steamer. See SHIP.
boatman, *n.* rower, ferryman, waterman, lighterman, gondolier. See MARINER.
boat-shaped, *adj.* navicular, scaphoid (*anat.*). See CURVATURE.
bodily, *adj.* corporeal, physical, substantial, material. See SUBSTANTIALITY.
bodily, *adv.* wholly, completely, entirely, *en masse* (*F.*); substantially. See WHOLE.
body, *n.* throng, multitude; person, figure, being, thing; aggregate, lump. See ASSEMBLAGE, FORM, SUBSTANTIALITY, WHOLE.
body politic, commonwealth, nation, polity, government. See STATE.
bog, *n.* swamp, morass, fen, quagmire. See MARSH.
bogus, *adj.* sham, counterfeit, spurious, false, pretended, fraudulent. See DECEPTION.
boil, *v.* prepare, cook; bubble, effervesce; storm, fume, rage. See CALEFACTION, FOAM, VIOLENCE.
boiling, *n.* ebullition, ebullience; decoction. See CALEFACTION.
boisterous, *adj.* clamorous, noisy, uproarious; stormy, violent, rough. See EXCITABILITY, WIND.
bold, *adj.* courageous, fearless, daring, intrepid, dauntless, brave; forward, familiar, free; insolent, impudent; prominent, conspicuous. See COURAGE, FREEDOM, INSOLENCE, MANIFESTATION.
boldness, *n.* daring, bravery, valor; vigorousness (*as of conception*), strikingness; assurance, effrontery. See COURAGE, FREEDOM, INSOLENCE.
bolt, *v.* dash, run; bar, stop, lock; attach, fasten; sift, winnow. See AVOIDANCE, CLOSURE, JUNCTION, SIMPLENESS.
bombast, *n.* exaggeration, bluster, magniloquence, braggadocio. See GASEITY, ORNAMENT.
bombastic, *adj.* grandiloquent, pompous, tumid, turgid. See ORNAMENT, OVERESTIMATION.
bond, *n.* similarity, relationship; pledge, guaranty; stock, obligation; cord, rope. See RELATION, SECURITY, TREASURY, VINCULUM.
bondage, *n.* slavery, serfdom, servitude, yoke, confinement. See SUBJECTION.
bondman, *n.* serf, slave, vassal, thrall. See SERVANT.
bonus, *n.* donation, gift; premium, dividend. See GIVING, RECEIPT.
bony, *adj.* inflexible, stiff, osseous. See HARDNESS.

BOOK.—I. *Nouns.* **book,** volume, tome, writing, work, publication, production, lucubration; codex, treatise, monograph, brochure, pamphlet, booklet, tract, tractate, essay, dissertation; libretto; handbook, manual, textbook; novel; folio, quarto, octavo, duodecimo; magazine, periodical.

rare books, first editions, early editions, incunabula (*books printed in the 15th century*).

part, issue, number, *livraison* (*F.*), serial; album, portfolio.

chapter, division, section, article, paragraph, passage, clause.

reference book, work of reference; encyclopedia *or* encyclopædia, cyclopedia *or* cyclopædia; dictionary, wordbook, lexicon, glossary, thesaurus; concordance, anthology, gazetteer, yearbook, almanac, compilation.

writer, authoress (*fem.*), *littérateur* (*F.*), scribe, scrivener, quill driver (*jocose*), pen, penman, penwoman; essayist, novelist, story writer, short-story writer, playwright, dramatist, poet; contributor, columnist, paragraphist, paragrapher, editorial writer, leader writer (*Eng.*); editor, subeditor; lexicographer, annotator, commentator; critic, reviewer, publicist, reporter, correspondent, journalist, gentleman of the press, newspaper man, newspaper woman, magazinist; hackwriter, hack, penny-a-liner (*contemptuous*), potboiler (*colloq.*), free lance; reader (*for publisher*), literary adviser; librettist, composer.

bookseller, bookman (*colloq.*), bibliopole, publisher; the trade (*collective*).

bookshop, bookstore, bookseller's shop, *librairie* (*F.*), publishing house.

librarian, bibliothecary, bibliothec (*rare*), *bibliothécaire* (*F.*), curator; American Library Association, A.L.A.

library, public library, lending library, athenæum, book club, circulating library, bibliotheca, *bibliothèque* (*F.*).
II. *Verbs.* **book,** enter, inscribe, list, register; engage, reserve.
See also DRAMA, POETRY, PRINTING, PUBLICATION, SCHOLAR.

---

bookkeeping, *n.* accountancy, auditing, reckoning. See ACCOUNTS.
bookseller, *n.* publisher, bookman. See BOOK.
bookshop, *n.* bookstore, publishing house. See BOOK.
bookworm, *n.* student, pedant, bluestocking (*colloq.*). See SCHOLAR.
boom, *v.* push, boost, back; thunder, peal; drum, rumble. See IMPULSE, LOUDNESS, ROLL.
boor, *n.* peasant, clown, lout, churl, rustic. See PEOPLE.
boorish, *adj.* ill-mannered, rude, rustic, clownish, provincial. See VULGARITY.
boost, *v.* back, recommend, cry up, indorse. See APPROBATION.

BOOTY.—*Nouns.* **booty,** spoil, plunder, rapine; *spolia opima* (*L.*), the richest spoils; melon (*as, to cut a* melon), prize, prey, loot, swag (*cant*); perquisite, graft (*colloq.*), boodle (*cant*), pickings, pork barrel (*U. S. polit. cant*), *chantage* (*F.*), blackmail, protection money, hush money, bribe, tribute, garnish (*slang or hist.*), hand-out (*slang*), shell-out (*slang*); stolen goods.
See also STEALING.

---

border, *n.* margin, rim, brink, brim; frontier, boundary. See EDGE, LIMIT.
borderland, *n.* vicinity, frontier, boundary, meeting. See CONTACT.
bore, *v.* drill, pierce; tire, cloy, annoy. See OPENING, WEARINESS.
bore, *n.* diameter, caliber; bother, annoyance; pest, dullard, proser. See BREADTH, PAINFULNESS, WEARINESS.
born, be, *v.* come, see the light, arrive. See LIFE.

BORROWING.—I. *Nouns.* **borrowing,** raising money, getting, acquiring; appropriation, commandeering, confiscation; pledging, pawning.
II. *Verbs.* **borrow,** get, acquire, raise money, raise the wind (*slang*), touch (*slang*); see (*or* patronize) one's uncle (*slang*), pledge, pawn, put up the spout (*slang*); run into debt.
hire, engage, employ, charter, rent, farm; lease, take a lease. (*The use of "hire" for "let" in the sense "he hired me a house" is incorrect.*)
appropriate, make use of, take, claim, arrogate, usurp, confiscate, condemn, commandeer, pocket, adopt, seize, sequester (*law*), grab, misappropriate, embezzle, convert, pirate, plagiarize; allot, assign, devote, apply, misapply.
See also DEBT.—*Antonyms.* See LENDING, RESTITUTION.

---

bosom, *n.* affections; heart, breast. See DISPOSITION, INTERIORITY.
boss, *n.* knob, stud; manager, foreman; *Slang:* politician. See CONVEXITY, DIRECTOR.

BOTANY.—I. *Nouns.* **botany** (*correlative of* zoölogy), science of plants, phytology; descriptive botany, taxonomic botany, phytography; phytobiology (*life history of plants*), phytogenesis *or* phytogeny (*plant origin and history*), phytotomy (*vegetable anatomy*), phytochemistry (*chemistry of plants*); phytogeography, floristics; dendrography (*description of trees*), dendrology (*study of trees*), zylology (*wood structure*); pomology (*fruits*), horticulture, flora; Flora, Pomona; botanic garden, arboretum, herbarium.
botanist, phytologist, phytobiologist, dendrologist, pomologist, horticulturist, herborist, herbalist, herbist, herbarian; phytographer, taxonomist.
II. *Verbs.* **botanize,** study plants, herborize.
III. *Adjectives.* **botanic** *or* botanical, phytologic *or* phytological; phytoid, dendroid, dendriform, herby, herbous (*rare*), herbal; horticultural, pomological.
See also HUSBANDRY, VEGETABLE.

---

botch, *v.* bungle, blunder, mar, spoil, mismanage. See DISORDER, UNSKILLFULNESS.

bother, *n.* annoyance, perplexity, disturbance, worry, irritation. See PAINFULNESS.
bottle, *n.* flask, flagon, carafe, decanter, phial. See RECEPTACLE.
bottom, *n.* groundwork, foundation, support, foot, footing. See BASE.
bottomless, *adj.* abysmal, unfathomable, unending. See DEPTH.
boudoir, *n.* dressing room. See RECEPTACLE.
bough, *n.* offshoot, limb, branch. See PART, VEGETABLE.
bounce, *v.* jump, bound, spring. See LEAP.
bound, *v.* limit, confine, circumscribe, restrain; jump, spring, vault. See CIRCUMSCRIPTION, LEAP.
boundary, *n.* termination, border, confine, bounds. See LIMIT.
boundless, *adj.* unlimited, limitless, endless, vast. See INFINITY.
bounds, *n. pl.* border, extent, confine, pale, range. See LIMIT.
bounty, *n.* grant, subsidy, premium; generosity, liberality, munificence. See AID, BENEVOLENCE.
bouquet, *n.* perfume, redolence; garland, nosegay. See FRAGRANCE, ORNAMENT.
bourgeois, *adj.* commonplace, ordinary, middle-class. See MEAN.
bout, *n.* contest, match; turn, round. See CONTENTION, REGULARITY.
[1]bow, *n.* inclination (*of head or body*), nod, obeisance. See COURTESY, DEPRESSION.
bow, *v.* nod, greet, salaam, bend, curtsy; yield, capitulate. See COURTESY, DEPRESSION, SUBMISSION.
[2]bow, *n.* prow, jib, stem. See FRONT.
[3]bow, *n.* sling, catapult; curve, arc, crescent, loop. See ARMS, CURVATURE.
bower, *n.* retreat, nook, summerhouse, grotto. See HABITATION, RECEPTACLE.
bowl, *n.* basin, vessel, dish. See RECEPTACLE.
bow-shaped, *adj.* arcuate, arciform, bowed. See CURVATURE.
box, *n.* case, chest, carton, casket. See RECEPTACLE.
boy, *n.* lad, youth; servant, menial. See INFANT, KNAVE.
boycott, *v.* ostracize, blackball; reject, discard; oppose, withstand. See DISAPPROBATION, EJECTION, RESISTANCE.
brace, *v.* revive, refresh, nerve, sustain, restore, stimulate. See STRENGTH.
bracing, *adj.* invigorating, stimulating, tonic. See HEALTHINESS.
bracket, *n.* pair, couple; shelf, ledge, console; race, tie. See DUALITY, SUPPORT, VINCULUM.
brag, *v.* vaunt, swagger, bluster. See BOASTING.
braid, *v.* interlace, intertwine, interweave, plait. See CROSSING.
brain, *n.* mentality, capacity, intelligence, mind. See INTELLECT.
brainless, *adj.* unreasoning, weak-minded, senseless. See IMBECILITY.
brake, *v.* retard, slacken, check, curb. See SLOWNESS.
branch, *n.* member, arm, wing, ramification; descendant, offshoot; shoot, limb, bough, twig. See PART, POSTERITY, VEGETABLE.
branch, *v.* fork, divide, ramify, furcate, bifurcate; diverge, radiate. See ANGULARITY, BISECTION, DIVERGENCE.
brand, *n.* sort, kind, grade, stamp; stigma, stain; ember, coal; torch, flambeau, firebrand See CLASS, DISREPUTE, FUEL, LUMINARY.
bravado, *n.* bluster, vaunting, braggadocio. See BOASTING.
brave, *adj.* courageous, daring, valiant, fearless, gallant, bold, dauntless. See COURAGE.—**brave man,** man of courage, hero, paladin. See COURAGE.—**brave woman,** heroine. See COURAGE.
brave, *v.* defy, oppose, face; endure, bear, stand, suffer. See FRONT, INEXCITABILITY.
brazen, *adj.* shameless, impudent, bold. See INSOLENCE.
breach, *n.* schism, rupture, difference; gap, opening, crack; violation, encroachment. See DISCORD, DISJUNCTION, INTERVAL, RIGHTLESSNESS.

BREADTH.—I. *Nouns.* **breadth,** width, broadness, wideness, extent, spaciousness, roominess, expanse, latitude (*rare or jocose*), amplitude; stretch, compass, beam (*of a vessel*), tread, span, measure, reach, scope, area.
diameter, bore, caliber, module (*numismatics*); radius.
liberality, broad-mindedness, catholicity, universality, open-mindedness, tolerance, generosity.
II. *Verbs.* **broaden,** widen, expand, spread, mushroom, open, enlarge, outstretch, stretch, distend, dilate, amplify, outspread, deploy (*mil.*), unfold, unfurl.
III. *Adjectives.* **broad,** wide, ample, extended, outspread, outstretched, "wide as a church-door" (*Romeo and Juliet*); vast, spacious, immense, vasty (*archaic*), large, roomy, capacious, beamy (*naut.*); extensive, comprehensive, general.
[*of language*] **unrestrained,** outspoken, unreserved, unchecked, unbridled, coarse, unrefined, indelicate, free.
liberal, tolerant, generous, broad-minded, open-minded, catholic, liberalistic, unbigoted.
See also EXPANSION, SIZE, SPACE, THICKNESS.—*Antonyms.* See NARROWNESS.

---

break, *v.* sever, fracture, rend, shatter, rupture; violate, transgress, infringe; gentle, tame, subdue. See BRITTLENESS, SNAP; DERELICTION, DOMESTICATION.
break, *n.* interruption, disconnection; fracture, split, crack, slit, gap, interval; blunder, *faux pas* (*F.*), indiscretion. See DISCONTINUITY, DISJUNCTION, ERROR, GUILT.
breakwater, *n.* mole, sea wall, jetty. See REFUGE.
breast, *n.* bosom, heart, spirit. See INTELLECT.
breath, *n.* respiration; whiff, zephyr, breeze. See LIFE, WIND.
breathe, *v.* utter, whisper, disclose, divulge; exist, be, live; respire, inhale, exhale. See DISCLOSURE, EXISTENCE, WIND.
breathing, *n.* respiration, exhalation, blowing. See WIND.
breathless, *adj.* puffing, panting, out of breath; astonished, thunderstruck, aghast. See FATIGUE, WONDER.
breeches, *n.* smallclothes (*archaic*), smalls (*colloq.*), knee breeches, buckskins, breeks (*dial. or Scot.*), knickerbockers; trousers, pantaloons, pants (*colloq.*). See CLOTHING.
breed, *n.* strain, stock, race. See CONSANGUINITY.
breeding, *n.* refinement, culture, gentility. See COURTESY.
breeze, *n.* zephyr, stir, gust. See WIND.
brevity, *n.* shortness, terseness, succinctness, briefness. See CONCISENESS.
bribe, *n.* boodle (*cant*), hush-money, price, graft; perquisite, emolument; allurement, seduction, bait. See BOOTY, GIVING, MOTIVE.
bribe, *v.* tip, recompense, fee, square (*slang*); corrupt, suborn, tempt. See GIVING, MOTIVE, OIL.
bric-a-brac, *n.* knickknacks, curiosities, curios. See ORNAMENT.
bridal, *adj.* nuptial, connubial. See MARRIAGE.
bride, *n.* newly wedded wife. See MARRIAGE.
bridegroom, *n.* groom, husband, benedick, benedict. See MARRIAGE.
bridge, *v.* connect, span, link, get across, cross. See JUNCTION.
bridle, *v.* harness up; curb, check. See DEPARTURE, RESTRAINT.
brief, *adj.* short, succinct, terse, condensed; momentary, quick, fleeting. See CONCISENESS, TRANSIENCE.
brigand, *n.* bandit, thug, freebooter, highwayman, robber, footpad. See THIEF.
bright, *adj.* deep, intense, vivid; intelligent, apt, clever; lustrous, luminous, glistening, radiant, glowing, flashing, sparkling, brilliant. See COLOR, INTELLIGENCE, LIGHT.
brighten, *v.* cheer, enliven; lighten, illumine, illuminate. See CHEERFULNESS, LIGHT.
brilliancy, *n.* splendor, radiance, luster, glitter. See BEAUTY, LIGHT.
brilliant, *adj.* magnificent, resplendent, radiant; luminous, bright; distinguished, illustrious; clever, sparkling, keen. See BEAUTY, LIGHT, REPUTE, WIT.

brim, *n.* margin, brink, border, rim, upper edge (*as of a dish*). See EDGE.
brimful, *adj.* full, replete, chock-full, saturated. See COMPLETENESS.
brindled, *adj.* brindle, banded, brinded, tabby. See VARIEGATION.
bring, *v.* occasion, create, entail; fetch, convey, bear, transport. See CAUSE, TRANSFER.
brisk, *adj.* quick, nimble, alert, lively, swift, animated. See ACTIVITY.
bristle, *n.* hair, seta (*tech.*). See ROUGHNESS.
bristling, *adj.* perverse, sullen, angry; thorny, spiny, spiked. See DISCOURTESY, SHARPNESS.
bristly, *adj.* rough, prickly, setose. See ROUGHNESS.

BRITTLENESS.—I. *Nouns.* **brittleness,** fragility, frangibleness, frangibility, breakableness, frailness, frailty; cold-shortness, hot-shortness, red-shortness; crispness, shortness, delicateness; crumbliness, friability.
II. *Verbs.* **be brittle,** break, crack, snap, split, shiver, splinter, fracture, tear, rive, rend, shatter, dash, crash, crush; fly, burst; give way, rupture; crumble, disintegrate, crumble to dust, fall to pieces.
III. *Adjectives.* **brittle,** breakable, fragile, frangible, brash, frail, delicate, shivery, splintery; cold-short, hot-short, red-short; crumbly, friable, crisp, short (*as pastry*).
See also WEAKNESS.—*Antonyms.* See TENACITY.

---

broach, *v.* launch, usher in; tap, pierce. See BEGINNING, EJECTION.
broad, *adj.* wide, extensive, vast, ample; comprehensive, inclusive, sweeping. See BREADTH, GENERALITY.
broadcast, *v.* scatter, diffuse, disseminate; spread, utter, radiocast. See DISPERSION, PUBLICATION.
broad-minded, *adj.* tolerant, catholic, broad. See LIBERALITY.
broil, *n.* brawl, riot, disturbance, scuffle, fracas. See DISCORD.
broil, *v.* cook, heat. See CALEFACTION.
broken, *adj.* interrupted, disconnected; divided, shattered; docile, gentle; infirm, decrepit. See DISCONTINUITY, DISJUNCTION, DOMESTICATION, WEAKNESS.
brokerage, *n.* jobbing, stockbroking. See BARTER.
brood, *n.* offspring, breed, progeny. See POSTERITY.
brook, *n.* rivulet, stream, burn, creek. See RIVER.
brothel, *n.* bagnio, house of ill fame. See VICE.
brother, *n.* friar; *frater* (*L.*), cadet (*younger son*), kinsman; associate, companion, fellow member; mate, fellow, twin, counterpart. See CLERGY, CONSANGUINITY, FRIEND, SIMILARITY.
brotherhood, *n.* kinship, family; association, fraternity, fellowship; likeness, correspondence. See CONSANGUINITY, FRIENDSHIP, SIMILARITY.
brow, *n.* forehead, countenance; top, crest. See FRONT, SUMMIT.

BROWN.—I. *Nouns.* **brown,** etc. (see *adjectives*); bister *or* bistre, sepia, brown, ocher *or* ochre, Vandyke brown, mummy brown, mummy; brownness.
II. *Verbs.* **render brown,** brown, embrown *or* imbrown, tan, sunburn, bronze.
III. *Adjectives.* **brown,** brunet, nut-brown, cinnamon, puce, chocolate; fawn, fawn-colored, fuscous, musteline, écru, tawny; tan, snuff-colored, liver-colored; brownish, browny, beige, dust-colored, khaki; brown as a berry.
reddish brown, bay, chestnut, castaneous, sorrel, roan, foxy, carroty, russet, henna, hazel, auburn, terra cotta, mahogany, maroon; rust-colored, ferruginous; bronze, bronzy, copper, copperish, coppery, cupreous.
sunburnt *or* sunburned, bronzed, browned, tanned.

---

bruise, *v.* batter, contuse, injure; pound, break, pestle. See BADNESS (*maltreat*), POWDERINESS.
brunet, *adj.* brownish, dark-complexioned, dark. See BROWN.
brush, *v.* sweep, cleanse; graze, rub. See CLEANNESS, TOUCH.

brushwood, *n.* brush, underbrush, scrub, undergrowth, thicket, chaparral. See VEGETABLE.
brusque, *adj.* gruff, bluff, curt, abrupt, blunt, unrefined. See DISCOURTESY, ROUGHNESS.
brutal, *adj.* cruel, savage, barbarous, unfeeling. See MALEVOLENCE.
brutalize, *v.* brutify, sensualize, debase, demoralize. See DETERIORATION, VICE.
brute, *n.* beast, dumb animal; blackguard, scoundrel, ruffian. See ANIMAL, EVILDOER.
brutish, *adj.* bestial, sensual, gross, swinish; cruel, barbarous, inhuman. See INTEMPERANCE, MALEVOLENCE.
bubble, *n.* globule, bleb. See FOAM.
bubble, *v.* effervesce, sparkle, foam, boil, gurgle. See AGITATION.
bubbling, *adj.* effervescent, bubbly, ebullient. See AGITATION.
buckle, *n.* warp, bend, twist; fastener, fastening, clasp. See DISTORTION, VINCULUM.
bud, *v.* sprout, germinate, swell, propagate. See EXPANSION.
buddy, *n.* comrade, pal (*slang*), chum: *colloq*. See FRIEND.
buffer, *n.* fender, bumper, cowcatcher (*U. S.*). See DEFENSE.
buffoon, *n.* mummer, pantomimist; jester, clown; comedian, mountebank. See DRAMA, FOOL, HUMORIST.
buffoonery, *n.* horseplay, comedy; farce, tomfoolery. See RIDICULE, WIT.
bug, *n.* insect, anthropod (*tech.*), mite, nit. See LITTLENESS.
bugbear, *n.* bogy, goblin, bugaboo. See FEAR, MYTHICAL BEINGS.
build, *v.* fashion, carve, model; erect, raise, construct, rear, establish. See FORM, PRODUCTION.
builder, *n.* architect, contractor; carpenter, mason, master builder. See AGENT.
building, *n.* house, edifice, pile, erection. See STRUCTURE.
bulb, *n.* knob, bulge, expansion; tuber, corm. See CONVEXITY, ROTUNDITY. VEGETABLE.
bulge, *v.* protrude, bag, project, swell out. See CONVEXITY.
bulk, *n.* measure, amount, volume; largeness, expanse; mass, greater part. See QUANTITY, SIZE, WHOLE.
bulletin, *n.* report, statement, information, journal. See NEWS.
bully, *n.* swaggerer, roisterer, brawler, tyrant. See BLUSTERER, EVILDOER.
bully, *v.* browbeat, threaten, bluster, domineer. See FEAR.
bulwark, *n.* fortification, rampart, barrier, safeguard. See DEFENSE.
bump, *v.* collide, knock, strike, hit. See IMPULSE.
bunch, *n.* crowd, group; lump, hump, protuberance. See ASSEMBLAGE, CONVEXITY.
buncombe, *n.* claptrap, bombast, blah (*slang*). See BOASTING.
bundle, *n.* package, parcel, packet. See ASSEMBLAGE.
bungle, *v.* spoil, botch, blunder. See UNSKILLFULNESS.

BUNGLER.—*Nouns.* **bungler,** blunderer, muddler, tinker, botcher, blunderhead; fumbler, lubber, lout, clown, duffer (*colloq.*); butter-fingers, muff, muffer, slow coach (*all colloq.*); awkward squad; novice, greenhorn.
landlubber, fresh-water sailor, fair-weather sailor, horse marine.
Antonyms. See EXPERT.

---

bunk, *n.* buncombe (*both colloq. or slang*), humbug. See BOASTING.
buoyant, *adj.* floating, light; resilient, springy; sanguine, confident; volatile, foamy. See ASCENT, ELASTICITY, HOPE, LEVITY.
burden, *n.* load, weight, encumbrance, impediment. See HINDRANCE.
burdensome, *adj.* oppressive, onerous; weighty, heavy, cumbersome; troublesome, tiresome. See BADNESS, GRAVITY, PAINFULNESS.
bureau, *n.* department, office; chest, dresser. See JURISDICTION, RECEPTACLE.

bureaucracy, *n.* officialism, red tape, departmentalism. See AUTHORITY, SEVERITY.

burglar, *n.* yegg (*slang*), bandit, housebreaker, robber. See THIEF.

burglary, *n.* housebreaking, robbery. See STEALING.

burial, *n.* entombment, sepulture. See INTERMENT.

burlesque, *n.* farce, parody, take-off; comedy, buffoonery, drollery. See MISREPRESENTATION, RIDICULE.

burlesque, *v.* satirize, take off, parody, mimic, caricature. See IMITATION, MISREPRESENTATION, RIDICULE.

burn, *v.* sear, char, parch, destroy; glow, blaze, flame. See CALEFACTION, HEAT.

burning, *adj.* flaming, raging, blazing, ablaze; ardent, passionate. See HEAT, VIGOR.

burrow, *v.* dig, tunnel, mine, excavate, penetrate. See CONCAVITY.

burst, *v.* blow up, explode, shatter. See VIOLENCE.

bury, *v.* infold, inclose, incase; entomb. See CIRCUMSCRIPTION.

bush, *n.* shrub, clump; brushwood, woodland. See VEGETABLE.

bushy, *adj.* hairy, shaggy, dense, clumpy, bushlike. See ROUGHNESS.

BUSINESS.—I. *Nouns.* **business,** occupation, employment, undertaking, pursuit, avocations (*usually in the plural when used in this sense; it is better, however, to avoid the use of* avocation *altogether in the sense of "subordinate occupation"*); venture, financial activities; affair, concern, interest, matter, case.

task, work, job, stint, chore (*U. S.*), errand, commission, assignment, mission, charge, duty; lesson, exercise, imposition; avocation, hobby.

sphere, province, kingdom, realm, bailiwick, department, station, compass, field, scope, arena, circle, orb, range, beat, walk, round, routine, race, career; function, part, rôle, capacity.

office, place, position, post, incumbency, living; situation, job (*colloq.*), berth, billet, appointment, engagement; undertaking, enterprise.

vocation, calling, profession, cloth, faculty; art, craft, handicraft, *métier* (*F.*), line, trade, commerce, industry.

II. *Verbs.* **busy** (*or* **occupy**) **oneself with,** employ oneself in (*or* upon); undertake, covenant, contract, set about, attempt; turn one's hand to; be engaged in, be occupied with, be at work on, have in hand; ply one's trade.

officiate, serve, act, perform, function, do duty; discharge (*or* perform) the duties of; hold (*or* fill) an office; hold a portfolio; preside, direct, regulate, control, guide, occupy the chair.

III. *Adjectives.* **businesslike,** practical, thorough, orderly, well-ordered, systematic, methodical, prompt, efficient; professional (*opposed to* amateur), official, authoritative; vocational, functional, occupational; laboring, workaday, prosaic; busy, active; in hand, on hand, afoot, on foot, going on; acting.

See also ACTIVITY, UNDERTAKING.—*Antonyms.* See INACTION, INACTIVITY, LEISURE.

---

bustle, *n.* stir, rustle, flurry, ado; commotion, perturbation, turbulence. See ACTIVITY, AGITATION.

bustling, *adj.* agitated, restless, turbulent, fussy. See ACTIVITY.

busy, *adj.* employed, occupied, engrossed, engaged; industrious, diligent, active; meddlesome, officious. See ACTIVITY.

busybody, *n.* gossip, meddler, talebearer. See ACTIVITY, CURIOSITY.

but, *conj.* still, yet, however. See COMPENSATION.

butt, *n.* target, goat (*slang*). See LAUGHINGSTOCK.

buttocks, *n. pl.* rump, seat, hind quarters. See REAR.

button, *v.* fasten, loop, close. See JUNCTION.

buttress, *n.* abutment, counterfort; prop, truss, brace. See DEFENSE, SUPPORT.

buy, *v.* procure, shop, market, invest. See PURCHASE.

buyer, *n.* client, purchaser, customer. See PURCHASER.

by, *adv.* beside, alongside. See INSTRUMENTALITY, SIDE.

bygone, *adj.* former, old, gone by, departed; antiquated, obsolete. See PAST.
bystander, *n.* witness, observer, neighbor, onlooker. See NEARNESS, SPECTATOR.
by the way, by the by, in passing, *à propos* (*F.*), for example, parenthetically. See TIMELINESS.
byword, *n.* object of scorn; saying, proverb, pet expression; nickname, by-name. See DISREPUTE, MAXIM, NEOLOGY.

C

cab, *n.* hack, hackney carriage, hackney, hansom, taxicab. See VEHICLE.
cabinet, *n.* ministry, board; room, closet; repository, case. See COUNCIL, RECEPTACLE.
cackle, *v.* gabble, clack; chuckle, giggle; cluck. See LOQUACITY, REJOICING, ULULATION.
cacography, *n.* scrawling, scribble, illegible hand. See WRITING.
cage, *v.* imprison, confine, pen, incarcerate. See RESTRAINT.
cajole, *v.* wheedle, coax, deceive, delude, flatter. See DECEPTION.
cake, *v.* consolidate, agglomerate; thicken, condense, harden. See COHERENCE, DENSITY.
calamity, *n.* disaster, affliction, casualty, catastrophe. See ADVERSITY.
calculate, *v.* reckon, compute, count, estimate. See NUMERATION.

CALEFACTION.—I. *Nouns.* **calefaction,** warming, heating, torrefaction, melting, fusion, liquefaction, scorification, volcanization, combustion; cremation; calcination; incineration; carbonization, carburization, carburetion; cauterization.
ignition, kindling, firing, lighting, conflagration, fire; incendiarism, arson.
auto-da-fé (*Pg.; pl. autos-da-fé*), *auto-de-fe* (*Sp.; pl. autos-de-fe*), the stake, burning at the stake; suttee, self-cremation, self-immolation.
incendiary, arsonist (*rare*), pyromaniac, fire bug (*U. S.*), *pétroleur* (*F.; fem. pétroleuse*).
boiling, ebullition, ebullience, decoction; hot spring, hot well, geyser.
wrap, blanket, coverlet, quilt, bedquilt, puff, comfortable (*U. S.*), comfort (*U. S.*), comforter (*U. S.*); flannel, wool, fur, shawl, sweater, jersey, mackinaw, overcoat; padding, wadding, lining, interlining.
pottery, ceramics, ceramic ware, crockery, porcelain, china, chinaware, Satsuma ware, gombroon, Sèvres ware *or* Sèvres, faïence, majolica, delftware *or* delft, crouch ware, salt-glazed ware; jasper ware, Wedgwood ware, Toft ware, queen's ware, Castleford ware, crown Derby, spode, Worcester ware, old Worcester, Staffordshire ware, Rockingham ware, Lowestoft ware, Leeds pottery; Dresden ware, Meissen ware; Palissy ware, Limoges ware; eggshell porcelain, crackle (*as, Chinese or Bohemian* crackle), luster (*or* lustre) ware; biscuit, bisque; white ware; basalt *or* basaltes, black ware; ironstone ware (*or* china) cottage china, flatware, earthenware, stoneware; willow pattern, portrait pieces printed wares, Allervale pottery; terra cotta; enamel, *cloisonné* (*F.*).
[*products of combustion*] ash, cinder, coal, embers, scoriæ, lava, slag, clinker; coke, carbon, charcoal.
II. *Verbs.* **calefy,** heat, warm, chafe, foment; make hot, tepefy, mull (*as, to* mull *wine*), superheat, overheat; make white-hot, incandesce.
fire, set fire to, set on fire; kindle, inflame (*now rare in the literal sense*), enkindle, light, ignite; rekindle.
melt, thaw, fuse, flux; liquefy, dissolve; smelt, liquate (*metal.*), eliquate (*metal.*), scorify.
burn, scorch, torrefy, toast, singe, parch, brand, cauterize, sear, burn in; corrode, char, carbonize, carburize, carburet, calcine, decrepitate, incinerate, cremate, reduce to ashes.
cook, prepare; boil, stew, seethe, scald, parboil, simmer, steam, curry; fry, frizzle, devil, fricassee, griddle, grill, broil, roast, bake, braise, pan.
III. *Adjectives.* **calefactive,** calefactory, calefacient (*med.*), heating, warming, warmth-producing.

heated, warmed, baked, fried, *sauté* (*F.*), toasted, adust, scorched, burnt.
molten, melted, fused, liquated, smelted, fluxed, vitrified, volcanic.
inflammable, burnable, ignitible *or* ignitable, combustible, inflammatory.
See also FURNACE, HEAT, LIQUEFACTION.—*Antonyms.* See REFRIGERATION.

---

calendar, *n.* almanac; register, schedule, catalogue. See LIST.
calender, *v.* tabby, cloud, moiré. See WATER.
caliber, *n.* gauge, bore, diameter; capacity, ability, power, force. See BREADTH, WISDOM.
call, *v.* convene, convoke, muster, assemble; appoint, elect; bid, summon, invite; shout, yell; name, designate, entitle; visit. See ASSEMBLAGE, CHURCHDOM, COMMAND, CRY, NOMENCLATURE, SOCIALITY.
call, *n.* summons, notice, demand, claim; shout, yell, animal note; signal; impulse, urge; invitation, offer; visit. See COMMAND, CRY, INDICATION, MOTIVE, REQUEST, SOCIALITY.
calligraphy, *n.* flowing hand, elegant penmanship. See WRITING.
calling, *n.* vocation, profession; call, outcry, yell, shout; notice, notification summons. See BUSINESS, CRY, WARNING.
callous, *adj.* horny, stiff; unfeeling, hardened, obdurate. See HARDNESS INSENSITIVENESS.
calm, *adj.* impassive, placid, serene, peaceful, cool-headed, composed; tranquil, still, motionless, unruffled; quiet, soundless. See INEXCITABILITY [1]REST, SILENCE.
calmness, *n.* coolness, tranquillity, composure, steadiness. See INEXCITABILITY.
camera, *n.* photographing apparatus. See OPTICAL INSTRUMENTS.
camouflage, *v.* disguise, screen, cloak. See CONCEALMENT.
camp, *n.* tent, shack, quarters, encampment. See HABITATION.
camp, *v.* lodge, tent, encamp, locate, quarter. See LOCATION.
campestral, *adj.* campestrian; flat, open. See PLAIN
can, *n.* jar, tin, case. See RECEPTACLE.
cancel, *v.* revoke, overrule, abolish, repeal; efface, delete, dele, strike out. See ANNULMENT, DESTRUCTION.
candid, *adj.* artless, unaffected, frank, sincere, outspoken, blunt. See PLAINNESS.
candidate, *n.* contestant, nominee, office-seeker, aspirant. See PETITIONER.
candle, *n.* taper, *cierge* (*F.*), dip. See LUMINARY.
candor, *n.* candidness, frankness, openness, sincerity. See PLAINNESS.
cannibal, *n.* man-eater, anthropophagite, savage. See EVILDOER.
canon, *n.* rule, code, law, charge. See ORTHODOXY, PRECEPT.
canonical, *adj.* approved, orthodox, accepted. See BELIEF.
canopy, *n.* overhanging shelter, tester, awning; dome, vault, sky. See COVERING, WORLD.
cant, *n.* insincerity, hypocrisy; jargon, lingo, slang. See FALSEHOOD, NEOLOGY.
canvas, *n.* sailcloth, tarpaulin, tent; painting, picture; sail. See COVERING, FINE ARTS, NAVIGATION.
canvass, *v.* examine, discuss, consider; solicit, seek. See INQUIRY, REQUEST
cap, *n.* headdress, headpiece, fez, skullcap, biretta, kepi, tam-o'-shanter. See CLOTHING.
capable, *adj.* proficient, competent, qualified, able. See GOOD, SKILL.
capacity, *n.* space, room, size, volume; talent, parts, intelligence; ability, capability. See [1]CONTENT, INTELLECT, POWER.
[1]cape, *n.* mantle, capote, cloak. See CLOTHING.
[2]cape, *n.* point, headland, promontory. See CONVEXITY.
caper, *n.* skip, spring, prance, hop, gambol. See LEAP.
capital, *adj.* excellent, admirable, first-class, unequaled; primary, chief, vital, principal. See GOOD, IMPORTANCE.

capital, *n.* funds, stock, assets, resources; opulence, riches. See MONEY, WEALTH.
capital punishment, execution, electrocution, hanging, decapitation. See PUNISHMENT.

CAPRICE.—I. *Nouns.* **caprice,** fancy, humor, notion, quip, conceit, whim, whimsey *or* whimsy, fit, crotchet, kink, quirk, freak, *capriccio* (*It.*), fad, vagary, prank, trick, escapade; capriciousness, whimsicality, eccentricity, variableness, variability, inconstancy.
II. *Verbs.* **be capricious,** etc. (see *adjectives*); take it into one's head, blow hot and cold, play fast and loose.
III. *Adjectives.* **capricious,** erratic, eccentric, fitful, inconsistent, fanciful whimsical, crotchety, freakish, wayward, wanton; contrary, captious, unreasonable, indecisive, irresolute, variable, changeable, mutable, inconstant, arbitrary; fickle, frivolous, giddy, flighty, volatile, notional, moody, humorsome.
IV. *Adverbs.* **capriciously,** erratically, etc. (see *adjectives*); out of mere caprice. by fits, by fits and starts, without rime or reason.
See also CHANGE, CHANGEABLENESS, IRREGULARITY, IRRESOLUTION.—*Antonyms.* See PERMANENCE, STABILITY.

---

captain, *n.* commander, chief, leader. See MASTER.
captious, *adj.* faultfinding, carping, hypercritical; sophistical, specious. See IRASCIBILITY, SOPHISTRY.
captivate, *v.* fascinate, delight, enchant, charm. See PLEASURABLENESS.
captive, *n.* *détenu* (*F.*), convict, slave, thrall. See PRISONER.
capture, *v.* seize, catch, arrest, secure, apprehend. See TAKING.
car, *n.* automobile, motor car; trolley, coach, Pullman; chariot (*poetic or hist.*); nacelle (*of a balloon*), cage (*of an elevator*). See VEHICLE.

CARE.—I. *Nouns.* **care,** solicitude, anxiety, responsibility, concern, interest, regard, concernment, apprehension, worry, trouble.
vigilance, watchfulness, heedfulness, heed, pains, caution, attention, guardedness, precaution, alertness, prudence, circumspection, forethought, providence, wariness, surveillance, watch, vigil, lookout, watch and ward; espionage, reconnoitering; watching.
accuracy, exactness, precision, minuteness, attention to detail.
charge, supervision, superintendence, oversight, ward, custody, control, direction, management, keeping, keep, safe-keeping, protection.
watcher, watchman, lookout, observer, spy, scout, picket; spotter, detective; watchdog.
II. *Verbs.* **be careful,** take care, be cautious, take precautions; pay attention to, take care of, look (*or* see) to, look after, keep an eye upon, chaperon, keep watch, mount guard, watch, eye, keep in view (*or* sight), mind, tend.
care, heed, reck (*poetic*), mind, notice, think, consider; feel inclined, wish, desire.
care for, feel affection for, be fond of, prize, value, hold dear, like; take an interest in, be interested in.
III. *Adjectives.* **careful,** regardful, heedful, prudent, discreet, cautious; considerate, thoughtful; judicious, circumspect; guarded, chary, alert, awake, observant, wide-awake, wary, precautious; provident, frugal, thrifty, sparing, on one's guard; on the alert (watch, *or* lookout); vigilant, sleepless, watchful, wakeful, Argus-eyed, lynx-eyed; sure-footed.
scrupulous, strict, precise, minute, punctilious, conscientious; tidy, neat, methodical, orderly; clean; accurate, exact, correct.
IV. *Adverbs.* **carefully,** heedfully, etc. (see *adjectives*); with care, gingerly.
See also ATTENTION, CAUTION, ECONOMY, FORESIGHT, PAIN.—*Antonyms.* See INATTENTION, NEGLECT.

---

career, *n.* course, path, progress, passage, success, history. See CONDUCT.
careless, *adj.* easy-going, nonchalant; heedless, negligent, slack, thoughtless; reckless, impulsive, indiscreet. See INDIFFERENCE, NEGLECT, RASHNESS.
caress, *v.* hug, cling to, fondle, pet, embrace, clasp. See ENDEARMENT.

cargo, *n.* lading, shipment, load, burden, freight, freightage. See [1]CONTENT.
caricature, *v.* satirize, ridicule, parody, exaggerate, take off. See MISREPRESENTATION.
carnage, *n.* bloodshed, slaughter, massacre, butchery. See KILLING.
carnal, *adj.* bodily, fleshly; material, mundane. See ANIMAL, IRRELIGION.
carnivorous, *adj.* flesh-eating, omophagic, predaceous. See FOOD.
carom, *n.* cannon (*Brit.*), shot: *billiards*. See IMPULSE.
carouse, *v.* revel, feast, make merry; run riot, debauch. See AMUSEMENT, INTEMPERANCE.
carriage, *n.* bearing, mien, demeanor; conveyance, wagon. See APPEARANCE, VEHICLE.

CARRIER.—*Nouns.* **carrier,** conveyer, transporter, transferrer, bearer, porter, messenger, courier, runner; teamster, wagoner, expressman, freighter, shipper, stevedore; coolie; conductor, chauffeur, motorman, truck driver; letter carrier, postman; mail, air mail; pigeon post, *Tauben-post* (*Ger.*), carrier pigeon.

BEASTS OF BURDEN: **horse,** steed, charger, hunter; race horse, roadster, hack, hackney, saddler, saddle horse; carriage horse, shaft horse, thill horse, thiller, wheeler, wheel horse, leader; pack horse, cart horse, dray horse, draft (*or* draught) horse, shire horse.

broken-winded horse, roarer, whistler.

famous horses: Pegasus (*winged horse of Greek fable*), Bucephalus (*war horse of Alexander the Great*), Grani *or* Granē (*magic steed given to Sigurd by Odin*), Sleipnir (*Odin's eight-legged steed*), Alborak (*winged milk-white animal, said to have borne Mohammed on his midnight journey to the seventh heaven*), Raksh *or* Ruksh (*steed of Rustam, the Persian Achilles*), Incitatus (*horse of Caligula, Roman emperor*), Rosinante (*Don Quixote's horse, all skin and bone*), Vegliantino *or* Veillantif (*Orlando's steed*), Roan Barbary (*favorite horse of Richard II*), White Surrey (*favorite horse of Richard III*), Black Saladin (*Warwick's coal-black steed*), Marengo (*white horse of Napoleon at Waterloo*), Copenhagen (*Wellington's charger at Waterloo*), Black Bess (*Dick Turpin's fleet mare*).

pony, Shetland, shelty *or* sheltie, broncho *or* bronco, cayuse (*Western U. S.*), cow pony, mustang, tat *or* tattoo (*Anglo-Indian*), polo pony (*not over 14½ hands*).

ass, donkey, jackass, jack, jenny (*fem.*), moke (*slang*), cuddy (*slang*), neddy (*pet name or slang*), Jerusalem pony; burro (*Southwestern U. S.*).

mule, hybrid, sumpter mule, hinny (*cross between a stallion and an ass*).

[*various*] ox, buffalo; dog, sledge dog, husky; sheep (*used in parts of Europe*); reindeer; camel, ship of the desert, "the commissariat cam-u-el" (*to quote Kipling:* " 'E's a devil an' a ostrich an' a orphan-child in one"), oont *or* unt (*Anglo-Indian*), dromedary, llama; elephant.

See also ANIMAL, SHIP, VEHICLE.

---

carry, *v.* sustain, uphold; bear, convey, transport. See SUPPORT, TRANSFER.
cart, *n.* dray, wagon, tumbrel, tipcart, pushcart. See VEHICLE.
carve, *v.* slice, quarter, dissect; mold, hew, fashion, cut. See DISJUNCTION, FORM.
case, *n.* event, contingency, situation; sheath, wrapper; suit, trial, litigation; box, chest, casket; argument, proposition. See BUSINESS, COVERING, LAWSUIT, RECEPTACLE, TOPIC.
cash, *n.* currency, coin, specie, ready money. See MONEY.
cask, *n.* barrel, hogshead, tun, keg. See RECEPTACLE.
casket, *n.* coffin; box, case, chest. See INTERMENT, RECEPTACLE.
cast, *v.* fashion, mold, sculpture; throw, pitch, hurl. See FORM, PROPULSION.
cast, *n.* aspect, phase, air; company, actors; statue, sculpture; mold, stamp. See APPEARANCE, DRAMA, FINE ARTS, FORM.
caste, *n.* rank, clan, set, degree. See CLASS.
castrate, *v.* emasculate, geld, spay (*female animal*). See IMPOTENCE.
casual, *adj.* accidental, occasional, random; incidental, external, contingent, conditional, fortuitous. See CHANCE, OBJECTIVENESS.

casualty, *n.* disaster, mishap, accident, calamity, misfortune. See ADVERSITY.
cat, *n.* feline, tabby, pussy, tomcat. See ANIMAL.
catalogue, *n.* schedule, register, index, record. See LIST.
catarrh, *n.* coryza (*med.*), rheum. See COLD.
catastrophe, *n.* calamity, cataclysm, disaster, ruin; *dénouement* (*F.*), ending. See ADVERSITY, END.
catch, *v.* detect, see through; grasp, seize, take, capture, apprehend. See DISCOVERY, INTELLIGIBILITY, LAND, TAKING.
catching, *adj.* alluring, captivating, prepossessing; infectious, contagious, epidemic. See TAKING, UNHEALTHINESS.
category, *n.* group, division, classification. See ORDER.
cater, *v.* supply, provide, feed, purvey. See PROVISION.
caterer, *n.* purveyor, steward. See PROVISION.
cathartic, *n.* laxative, purgative. See CLEANNESS.
catholic, *adj.* broad-minded, tolerant; world-wide, universal. See BREADTH, GENERALITY.
cattle, *n.* stock, live stock, kine. See ANIMAL.
caudate, *adj.* caudal, tailed, tail-like. See PENDENCY.

CAUSE.—I. *Nouns.* **cause,** origin, birth, commencement, rise beginning, prime, principle, element; prime mover, ultimate cause, Great First Cause; author, producer, generator, creator, determinant; parent, ancestor; mainspring, agent; leaven; causality, causation; origination, inception, production, creation; determining condition, parameter (*math.*), variable (*math.*), factor, moment (*of force*).
spring, source, fountain, well, fountainhead, reservoir, wellspring (*archaic*), springhead, source, font, *fons et origo* (*L.*), genesis, derivation; remote cause; influence, impulse.
pivot, hinge, axis, turning point; heart, hub, focus.
reason, purpose, reason why, occasion, motive, root, basis, foundation, ground, support, wherefore (*colloq.*), rationale; undercurrents.
rudiment, egg, germ, embryo, root, radix, radical, anlage (*Ger. pl.* anlagen: *biol.*), nucleus, seed, sperm, semen, milt (*of fishes*), roe, spat (*as of oysters*), spawn; stirps.
nest, cradle, nursery, nidus, womb, venter (*of wife or mother: law*), birthplace, hotbed.
II. *Verbs.* **cause,** originate, give rise to, occasion, sow the seeds of; bring to pass, bring about, make, produce, create, develop; set on foot, entail; found, institute, establish, constitute.
procure, induce, bring, obtain, get, acquire, gain, win; contrive, effect, draw down, superinduce, evoke, elicit, provoke.
contribute, advance, forward, influence, subserve, redound to, conduce to, have a hand in, determine, decide, turn the scale.
III. *Adjectives.* **causal,** causative, generative, creative, formative, productive, originative, original, primary, primal, primitive, primordial, primeval, germinal, embryonic, in embryo, *in ovo* (*L.*); radical, basic.
See also AGENT, PRODUCTION, TENDENCY.—*Antonyms.* See EFFECT.

---

caustic, *adj.* biting, sarcastic, pungent, acrimonious; corroding, mordant, burning. See DISCOURTESY, ENERGY, PUNGENCY.

CAUTION.—I. *Nouns.* **caution,** cautiousness, discretion, worldly wisdom, prudence, heed, circumspection, wariness, care, forethought, calculation, deliberation, foresight, vigilance, watchfulness, advice, counsel, admonition, warning. safety first, Fabian policy, masterly inactivity, "watchful waiting."
coolness, self-assurance, self-confidence, nerve (*slang*), *aplomb* (*F.*), assurance, calmness, self-possession, self-command; presence of mind, *sang-froid* (*F.*).
II. *Verbs.* **be cautious,** take care, take heed, mind, be on one's guard, "make assurance double sure" (*Macbeth*); think twice, look before one leaps, count the cost, feel one's way, see how the land lies; pussy-foot (*colloq.*), keep out of harm's way, keep at a respectful distance, stand aloof; keep (*or* be) on the safe side; husband one's resources.

caution, warn, admonish, notify, prewarn, forewarn, put on one's guard, tip (*colloq.*).
IV. *Adjectives.* **cautious,** wary, shy, guarded, suspicious, on one's guard, vigilant, watchful, careful, heedful, chary, sure-footed, scrupulous, circumspect, prudent, noncommittal, canny (*Scot.*), discreet, politic, strategic, Fabian overcautious, unenterprising, unadventurous; cool, steady, self-confident, self-possessed.
See also CARE, FORESIGHT, PREPARATION, SLOWNESS, WARNING.—*Antonyms.* See RASHNESS.

---

cavalry, *n.* horse soldiers, horse, light horse, dragoons. See COMBATANT.
cave, *n.* grot, grotto, cavern; lair, den, hole. See CONCAVITY, HABITATION.
cavil, *v.* carp, mangle, quibble, haggle. See DISSENT.
cavity, *n.* hole, opening, depression, dent, excavation, hollow. See CONCAVITY.
cease, *v.* stop, discontinue, halt, end, desist, terminate, refrain, pause, break off. See CESSATION.
cede, *v.* concede, yield; surrender, give up. See GIVING, RELINQUISHMENT.
ceiling, *n.* overhead covering (*or* lining); maximum altitude (*meteorol. and aëro.*). See COVERING, HEIGHT.

CELEBRATION.—I. *Nouns.* **celebration,** solemnization, observance, commemoration; jubilation, ovation, triumph; inauguration, installation, presentation; coronation; *début* (*F.*), coming out (*colloq.*).
red-letter day, lucky day, memorable occasion, festival, fête, holiday, outing, banquet; birthday, anniversary, biennial, triennial, quadrennial, quinquennial, sextennial, septennial, octennial, decennial; "the day we celebrate"; silver wedding (*25 years*), golden wedding (*50 years*), diamond wedding (*60 years*); jubilee, 50th anniversary; diamond jubilee, 60th anniversary; centenary, centennial; sesquicentennial; bicentenary, bicentennial; tercentenary, tercentennial, etc.
triumphal arch; salute, salvo, salvo of artillery; flourish of trumpets, fanfare; colors flying; illuminations, *feu de joie* (*F.*), pœan, *Te Deum* (*L.*).
II. *Verbs.* **celebrate,** keep, observe, signalize, do honor to, lionize, honor, extol, magnify, laud, applaud, glorify, commemorate, solemnize; rejoice; paint the town red (*colloq.*).
toast, pledge, drink to, propose, name, honor, compliment, bumper (*rare*).
inaugurate, install, instate, invest, induct, chair.
III. *Adjectives.* **celebrated,** renowned, famous, famed, honored, far-famed, illustrious, eminent, distinguished.
memorial, commemorative, kept in remembrance, time-honored, immortalized, immortal; monumental.
IV. *Adverbs.* **in honor of,** in commemoration of, in celebration of, in memory of, *in memoriam* (*L.*).
V. *Interjections.* **hail!** all hail! *ave!* (*L.*), banzai! (*Jap.*), hurrah! huzza! *vivat!* (*F.*), *evviva!* (*It.*); "See the conquering hero comes!" "Hail! hail! the gang's all here!" (*occasionally mistaken abroad, especially during the war, for the American national anthem.*)
See also AMUSEMENT, OSTENTATION, REGULARITY, REJOICING, WORSHIP.—*Antonyms.* See LAMENTATION.

---

celebrity, *n.* star, hero, lion; fame, renown, glory. See NOBILITY, REPUTE.
celestial, *adj.* divine, holy; unearthly, beatific, Elysian, heavenly; solar, empyreal, starry. See DEITY, HEAVEN, WORLD.

CELIBACY.—I. *Nouns.* **celibacy,** singleness, single blessedness; bachelorhood, bachelorship; misogyny, misogamy.
virginity, maidenhood, maidenhead, purity.
unmarried man, bachelor, celibate, Cœlebs, old bachelor, old stager; misogamist, misogynist; monk, priest, religious.
unmarried woman, maid, maiden, virgin, celibate, bachelor-girl, spinster, old maid; nun, sister, *religieuse* (*F.*), vestal, vestal virgin; Diana, St. Agnes.
II. *Adjectives.* **celibate,** unmarried, unwedded; wifeless, spouseless; virgin.
Antonyms. See MARRIAGE.

cell, *n.* protoplasmic body; compartment. See ORGANIZATION, RECEPTACLE.
cellular, *adj.* cell-like, porous, honeycombed, favose, locular (*tech.*). See CONCAVITY.
cement, *n.* gum, paste, glue, adhesive, lute. See VINCULUM.
cemetery, *n.* graveyard, burial ground, necropolis. See INTERMENT.
censorious, *adj.* carping, faultfinding, hypercritical, condemnatory. See JUDGE, SEVERITY.
censure, *n.* reproach, blame, reproof, criticism, disapproval. See DISAPPROBATION.
census, *n.* poll, count. See NUMERATION.

CENTRALITY.—I. *Nouns.* **centrality,** centralness, centralism, centralization, centricality, centricalness; focalization, concentration, convergence *or* convergency; centripetence *or* centripetency, centripetalism; center of attraction, cynosure; center of gravity.
center *or* **centre,** middle, midst; centrum, centroid; focus, focoid (*math.*); core, kernel, nucleus; marrow, pith; heart, pole, axis, radiant, pivot, bull's-eye, nave, hub; metropolis.
[*European politics*] **Center,** moderates (*as in France*), Roman Catholic party (*as in Germany*): *those seated in the center of the chamber, distinguished from* Right (*monarchists and conservatives*) *and* Left (*radicals and democrats*).
II. *Verbs.* **centralize,** concentrate, center *or* centre, focus, focalize, bring to a focus, converge; consolidate, federate, unite, incorporate.
III. *Adjectives.* **central,** middle, axial, pivotal, nuclear, focal, umbilical, centrolineal, centrical, centric, convergent, concentric; median, medial, mid, equidistant, intermediate, middlemost, midmost; metropolitan.
[*figuratively*] **chief,** principal, leading, dominant, predominant.
See also COMBINATION, CONVERGENCE, FOCUS, MIDDLE.—*Antonyms.* See DIVERGENCE, EDGE.

---

centuple, *adj.* centennial, centenary, hundredth. See HUNDRED.
ceremonial, *adj.* pompous, formal, ritualistic, solemn. See OSTENTATION, STATE.
ceremony, *n.* ritual, formality, etiquette; form, ceremonial, observance. See OSTENTATION, RITE.

CERTAINTY.—I. *Nouns.* **certainty,** certitude, sureness, assurance, confidence, assuredness, indubitableness; security, safety, reassurance; infallibility, reliability, inevitableness; gospel, fact; positive fact, matter of fact, *fait accompli* (*F.*); certification, verification.
[*in law*] **lucidity,** clearness, clarity, unambiguity, unambiguousness.
bigotry, positiveness, dogmatism, dogmatization; *ipse dixit* (*L.*); zealotry, fanaticism.
bigot, dogmatist, opinionist, doctrinaire, Sir Oracle; zealot, fanatic, enthusiast.
II. *Verbs.* **render certain,** insure *or* ensure, assure; clinch, make sure; determine, decide, "make assurance double sure" (*Macbeth*); reassure, certify; know, know for certain.
III. *Adjectives.* **certain,** sure, convinced, confident, unhesitating, inevitable, unavoidable, assured, solid, fixed, settled, well-founded, true, absolute, positive, definite, clear, unequivocal, categorical, unmistakable, unqualified, actual.
conclusive, undeniable, unquestionable; indisputable, incontrovertible, irrefragable, incontestable, indubitable, irrefutable, undoubted, unquestioned, undisputed, convincing; final, ultimate, determinative, decisive.
authoritative, authentic, official, orthodox, canonical, received, standard; *ex cathedra* (*L.*), cathedral.
evident, manifest, plain, apparent, clear, obvious, palpable, visible, self-evident, axiomatic.
infallible, unerring, inerrable, inerrant, unchangeable; trustworthy, reliable, dependable, unfailing.
dictatorial, dogmatic, magisterial, doctrinaire, opinionated, bigoted, conceited, oracular, overbearing, domineering, imperious, pompous, autocratic, peremptory, arrogant, lordly; ultra, unreasonable, fanatical, fanatic.

IV. *Adverbs.* **certainly,** undoubtedly, indubitably, definitely, infallibly, unquestionably, positively, admittedly, yes, true, just so, precisely, for certain, certes (*archaic*), surely, no doubt, *sans doute* (*F.*), doubtless, to be sure, of course, as a matter of course, in truth, truly, without fail, come what may, *coûte que coûte* (*F.*).

See also ASSENT, BELIEF, MANIFESTATION, NECESSITY, STABILITY.—*Antonyms.* See UNBELIEF, UNCERTAINTY.

---

certificate, *n.* voucher, warrant, testimonial. See EVIDENCE, SECURITY.

CESSATION.—I. *Nouns.* **cessation,** cease (*obsolete except in* without cease), discontinuance, discontinuation, interruption, hitch, intermission, respite, interval, break, recess; suspense, stop, stay, arrest, pause, block, check, delay, impediment, stoppage, halt, rest, lull, truce, Truce of God, armistice; abeyance, suspension, suppression; interregnum; remission, discharge, relinquishment, annulment, cancellation.

[*in debate*] closure, cloture.

deadlock, checkmate, standstill, dead stand, dead stop; end.

punctuation: stop, point; comma, semicolon, colon, period, full stop, note of exclamation, note of interrogation, dash, points of suspension; cæsura.

II. *Verbs.* **cease,** discontinue, stay, break off, leave off, desist, refrain, quit, hold, stop, check, pull up, stop short, stall (*as a motor*), stick, hang fire; halt, pause, rest, come to a stand; arrive; go out, die away, wear away, pass away, lapse; be at an end, end.

interrupt, interfere with, suspend, intermit, remit; obstruct, check, punctuate (*fig.*), break, divide, intersect, separate; stop, cut short, arrest, bring to a stand (*or* standstill), put an end to.

punctuate, point, interpoint (*rare*), interpunctuate.

III. *Interjections.* **stop!** hold! soft! (*archaic*), enough! avast! (*naut.*), stay! cease! leave off! have done! cut it out! (*slang*), stow it! (*slang*).

See also DEATH, END, RELINQUISHMENT.—*Antonyms.* See CONTINUANCE.

---

cetacean, *n.* whale, dolphin, etc. See ANIMAL.

chafe, *v.* warm, rub; vex, fret, annoy, gall. See CALEFACTION, PAIN.

chaff, *n.* husks, refuse; banter, persiflage, raillery. See WASTE, WIT.

chagrin, *n.* mortification, vexation, annoyance. See PAINFULNESS.

chain, *n.* series, succession, course; bond, fetter. See CONTINUITY, VINCULUM.

chair, *n.* chairman, moderator, president; seat, bench, stool; professorship, fellowship. See DIRECTOR, SUPPORT, TEACHER.

chairman, *n.* president, speaker, chair. See DIRECTOR.

challenge, *v.* charge, tax, denounce; question, doubt, dispute. See ACCUSATION, UNBELIEF.

chamber, *n.* room, apartment. See RECEPTACLE.

chameleon, *n.* lizard; turncoat, inconstant person, Proteus. See ANIMAL (*reptiles*), CHANGEABLENESS.

champion, *n.* defender, supporter, backer; conqueror, victor. See AUXILIARY, SUCCESS.

CHANCE.—I. *Nouns.* [*absence of assignable cause*] **chance,** unforeseen occurrence, accident, casualty; lot, fate, destiny, fortune, luck, hap (*rare*), happening, chance-medley, fortuity; mishap (*in this sense,* chance *is archaic*).

possibility, probability (*esp. in pl., as, the* chances *are against it*), likelihood, likeliness, presumption, contingency, odds, run of luck; opportunity; main chance.

[*absence of design*] **gamble,** uncertainty, risk, jeopardy, hazard, toss-up (*colloq.*), even chance, throw of the dice, heads or tails; wheel of fortune; wager, stake, *pari mutuel* (*F.*), bet, speculation, venture, plunge (*slang*), flyer (*slang*), pyramid, flutter (*slang*); gaming, gambling, betting, wagering, game of chance; drawing lots, sweepstakes, sweep, Calcutta sweep, lottery, pool; random shot, fluke (*sporting cant*); leap in the dark, blind bargain, pig in a poke (*or* bag).

gambler, gamester, speculator, plunger, punter, dicer; bookmaker, man of the turf, bookie (*colloq.*).

II. *Verbs.* **chance,** happen, arrive, come, befall; turn up; fall to one's lot; be one's fate; stumble on, light upon, blunder on (*or* upon), hit upon, hit.
risk, venture, stake, hazard; wager, bet, back, gamble, game; toss up, draw (*or* cast) lots; tempt fortune, speculate; plunge (*slang*), punt, take a flyer (*slang*), take a chance, go it blind (*slang*), chance (*colloq., as to* chance *it.*).
III. *Adjectives.* **chance,** casual, fortuitous, accidental, haphazard, random, unintentional, unpremeditated, unforeseen, contingent, unexpected, undesigned; off-hand, unconcerned, nonchalant; incidental, irregular, occasional.
IV. *Adverbs.* **by chance,** by accident, at a venture, at random, casually, fortuitously, incidentally, accidentally, unexpectedly.

See also DANGER, POSSIBILITY, PROBABILITY.—*Antonyms.* See ATTRIBUTION, INTENTION.

---

chandelier, *n.* candelabra, sconce. See PENDENCY.

CHANGE.—I. *Nouns.* **change,** alteration, mutation, permutation, variation, modification, substitution transposition; modulation, inflection, mood, qualification, innovation, deviation, shift; metastasis, metabolism, transition; diversion, variety, break.
conversion, resolution, reduction; revolution, overturn, overthrow; vicissitude, rotation, turn; inversion, reversal; displacement, transposition, removal, transference.
[*of money*] loose money, small coin, small change; silver, copper; balance, excess.
transformation, metamorphosis, transfiguration, transfigurement, transmutation; transubstantiation; transmigration, metempsychosis; avatar.
II. *Verbs.* **change,** alter, vary, qualify, temper, moderate, modulate, inflect, diversify, tamper with; turn, shift, shuffle, veer, gybe *or* jibe, jib, tack, wear (*naut.*), chop, warp, swerve, deviate, diverge from, dodge, turn aside, deflect, take a turn, turn the corner; chop and change.
modify, work a change, patch, piece, transform, translate, transfigure, transmute, convert, reduce, resolve, revolutionize; metamorphose, transmogrify (*colloq. or jocose*), ring the changes, alternate; innovate, introduce new blood; shuffle the cards, shift the scene, turn over a new leaf
recast, remold, reconstruct, remodel; reverse, overturn, upset, invert, transpose, exchange; convert into, resolve into; reform, reorganize.
III. *Adjectives.* **changed,** altered, etc. (see *verbs*); changeable, changeful, variable, devious, transitional; newfangled, novel.

See also CHANGEABLENESS, CONVERSION, DIFFERENCE, REVOLUTION.—*Antonyms.* See PERMANENCE.

CHANGEABLENESS.—I. *Nouns.* **changeableness,** changeability, alterableness, alterability, modifiability, mutability, versatility, mobility; instability, vacillation, irresolution, indecision, fluctuation, vicissitude; alternation, oscillation; inconstancy, changefulness, fickleness, uncertainty.
[*comparisons*] moon, Proteus, chameleon, kaleidoscope, quicksilver, shifting sands, weathercock, vane, weathervane, harlequin, turncoat, Vicar of Bray, April showers; wheel of fortune.
restlessness, disquiet, disquietude, unrest, uneasiness, anxiety, inquietude, unquietness, fidgets, dysphoria (*med.*), fidgetiness, agitation.
II. *Verbs.* **be changeable,** etc. (see *adjectives*); fluctuate, wave, undulate, vary, waver, flicker, flutter, shift, shuffle, shake, totter, stagger, tremble, vacillate, sway, shift to and fro; oscillate, pulsate, vibrate; alternate.
III. *Adjectives.* **changeable,** alterable, modifiable, mutable, variable, many-sided, kaleidoscopic, protean, versatile; mobile, movable, plastic.
inconstant, changeful, uncertain, unsteady, unstable, unfixed, fluctuating, wavering, vibratory, restless, tremulous; erratic, fickle, changing, irresolute, indecisive; capricious, volatile, skittish, mercurial, spasmodic, desultory, fitful, rambling, roving, irregular, immethodical, unmethodical, cursory; vagrant, wayward; unsettled, transient.
[*of colors*] **iridescent,** nacreous, prismatic, shot (*as silk*), rainbowlike, iridian, opalescent, chatoyant (*as a cat's eye in the dark*).

See also APOSTASY, CAPRICE, CHANGE, OSCILLATION, TRANSIENCE.—*Antonyms.* See STABILITY.

changeful, *adj.* variable, changeable, plastic, timeserving, opportunistic. See APOSTASY, CHANGE.
changeling, *n.* elf-child. See MYTHICAL BEINGS.

CHANNEL.—*Nouns.* **channel,** conduit, duct, watercourse, race, run; raceway, fishway, fish ladder; cañon *or* canyon, coulee *or coulée* (*F.*), gorge, *couloir* (*F., as in the Swiss Alps*), flume, ravine, chasm; aqueduct, canal; adit, stulm (*mining*); gully, arroyo, gulch (*U. S.*); moat, ditch, dike, gutter, drain, sewer, main, cloaca, culvert; scupper (*naut.*); funnel, trough, siphon, pump, hose; pipe, tube, waterspout, spout, gargoyle; weir, floodgate, water gate, sluice, lock, valve, sound, strait, neck, fairway, tideway.
[*in anatomy*] artery, aorta, blood vessel, capillary, pore; intestines, bowels; esophagus, gullet; throat, jugulum (*pl.* jugula: *zoöl.*).
vein, vena (*L. pl.* venæ: *tech.*), nervure (*bot. and zoöl.*), nerve (*bot.*), venule (*esp. zoöl.*), veinlet.

See also OPENING, WAY.

---

chant, *n.* song, melody; psalm, canticle, hymn. See MUSIC, WORSHIP.
chaos, *n.* confusion, tumult, disorganization. See DISORDER.
chapter, *n.* section, part, division, passage; group, branch. See BOOK, COUNCIL.
char, *v.* scorch, burn, parch, sear, carbonize. See CALEFACTION.
character, *n.* type, sort; temperament, nature; sign, mark, figure; tenor, stamp. See CLASS, DISPOSITION, LETTER, STATE.
characteristic, *adj.* typical, representative; innate, fixed. See SPECIALTY, SUBJECTIVENESS.
characteristic, *n.* trait, peculiarity, quality, attribute, essential. See INDICATION, PROPERTY, SPECIALTY.
charge, *v.* admonish, instruct; assail, strike; fill, load. See ADVICE, ATTACK, COMPLETENESS.
charge, *n.* allegation, complaint, indictment, arraignment; onset, onslaught; supervision, custody, ward, trust; command, order, mandate. See ACCUSATION, ATTACK, CARE, REQUIREMENT.
charitable, *adj.* generous, unselfish, liberal, altruistic, kind; donative, eleemosynary, gratis. See BENEVOLENCE, GIVING.
charity, *n.* liberality, alms; kindness, good will; tolerance, leniency. See GIVING, LOVE, PITY.
charlatan, *n.* quack, humbug, fraud, cheat, impostor. See DECEIVER.
charlatanry, *n.* quackery, pretension. See IGNORANCE.
charm, *n.* attractiveness, personality, fascination; amulet, talisman, incantation. See LOVE, PLEASURABLENESS, [1]SPELL.
charm, *v.* draw, lure, seduce; soothe, allay; conjure, hypnotize; fascinate, bewitch, enchant, captivate. See ATTRACTION, RELIEF, SORCERY; LOVE, TAKING.
chart, *n.* map, plan, guide. See INFORMATION.
chase, *v.* follow, hunt, hound, pursue; dispel, repel. See PURSUIT, REPULSION.
chase, *n.* hunt, race, steeplechase; hunting, coursing. See PURSUIT.
chasm, *n.* abyss, pit, gap, fissure, cleft. See GULF.
chaste, *adj.* simple, unaffected; classic, severe; virtuous, undefiled. See SIMPLENESS, SYMMETRY, VIRTUE.
chat, *n.* talk, gossip, *causerie* (*F.*). See CONVERSATION.
chatter, *n.* prattle, jabber, gabble, twaddle. See LOQUACITY.

CHEAPNESS.—I. *Nouns.* **cheapness,** inexpensiveness, moderateness, reasonableness; nominal price, low price, *bon marché* (*F.*), bargain, bargain sale, sale; depreciation, unsalableness, drug in the market; seconds.
insignificance, unimportance, meanness, pettiness, triviality, paltriness, contemptibleness, vileness, trashiness, worthlessness; tawdriness, flashiness, frippery.

[*absence of charge*] **gratuity,** gift, present, bonus, bequest, scholarship, fellowship; free admission, free seats; free lunch (*a reminder of pre-war days*), free meal; labor of love.
II. *Verbs.* **be cheap,** etc. (see *adjectives*); cost little; come down (*or* fall) in price, be marked down.
buy at a bargain, buy dirt-cheap, have one's money's worth.
cheapen, beat down (*in price*), lower, stale, depreciate, undervalue.
III. *Adjectives.* **cheap,** low-priced, popular-priced, popular, low, moderate, reasonable, economical, inexpensive, cheap at the price; dirt-cheap, catchpenny.
reduced, cheapened, staled, marked down, half-price, depreciated; shopworn, shop-soiled; unfashionable, unseasonable, mediocre, inferior, unsalable.
gratuitous, gratis, free, for nothing; costless, free of cost (*or* expense), expenseless, without charge, for love; complimentary, honorary.
contemptible, mean, base, paltry, trivial, vile, worthless, inferior, sorry, trashy, scurvy, tawdry, flashy, flimsy, gaudy, gimcrack, two-by-four (*U. S. colloq.*), small, insignificant, one-horse (*U. S. colloq.*), second-rate, third-rate.
IV. *Adverbs.* **cheaply,** inexpensively, at a bargain, *à bon marché* (*F.*), for a mere song; at a reduction, at cost price, at prime cost.

See also ECONOMY, GIVING, LOWNESS, UNIMPORTANCE.—*Antonyms.* See DEARNESS, IMPORTANCE.

---

cheat, *v.* defraud, swindle, trick, dupe, beguile, delude, deceive. See DECEPTION.
check, *n.* setback, reverse, misfortune; encumbrance, drag, burden; ticket, counter, stub; draft, money order, note; plaid, tartan, checkerwork. See ADVERSITY, HINDRANCE, INDICATION, MONEY, VARIEGATION.
check, *v.* audit, balance, tally, count, verify; restrain, repress, curb, impede, stop. See NUMBER, RESTRAINT.
checkered, *adj.* uneven, varied, irregular, alternating; checked, barred, plaid. See DIVERSITY, VARIEGATION.
cheek, *n.* impertinence, effrontery, nerve (*slang*); jowl. See INSOLENCE, SIDE.
cheer, *n.* shout, yell, college yell; festivity, hospitality. See REJOICING, SOCIALITY.
cheer, *v.* applaud, acclaim, encore; enliven, inspirit, inspire; hurrah, yell, shout; encourage, hearten, reassure. See APPROBATION, CHEERFULNESS, CRY, HOPE, RELIEF.

CHEERFULNESS.—I. *Nouns.* **cheerfulness,** geniality, gayety, happiness, gladness, gladsomeness, joy, joyousness, sunniness, light-heartedness, buoyancy, hopefulness, optimism (*opposite of* pessimism); cheer, good humor, spirits; high spirits, animal spirits, glee, high glee, light heart.
liveliness, life, alacrity, vivacity, animation, sprightliness, airiness, briskness, skittishness, levity.
mirth, merriment, hilarity, exhilaration, laughter, merrymaking, rejoicing, jollity, joviality, jocularity, playfulness, sportiveness, fun, blithesomeness, glee.
II. *Verbs.* **be cheerful,** etc. (see *adjectives*); have the mind at ease, smile, keep up one's spirits, cheer up, take heart, cast away care, look on the sunny side, perk up; rejoice, carol, chirp, chirrup.
cheer, enliven, elate, exhilarate, delight, gladden, inspirit, animate, inspire, invigorate, encourage, hearten, brighten, refresh, console, comfort; applaud.
III. *Adjectives.* **cheerful,** happy, cheery, genial, heartsome (*Scot.*), sunny, smiling, optimistic; hearty, bonny, winsome, blithe, in good spirits, gay, debonair, light, lightsome, lighthearted; buoyant, bright, airy, jaunty, saucy, sprightly, spry (*colloq.*), chipper (*U. S. colloq.*), lively, dashing, dapper, racy; convivial, social, mirthful, merry, joyful, joyous, jocund, jovial, jolly, gleeful, hilarious; spirited, animated, vivacious, sparkling.
playful, tricksy, frisky, frolicsome, jocose, jocular, waggish, sportive, skittish, larky (*colloq.*), rollicking; mischievous, roguish, impish.
elated, elate (*poetic*), exultant, exalted, exulting, jubilant, flushed, rejoicing, cock-a-hoop.
cheering, inspiriting, exhilarating, pleasing, encouraging, animating.

IV. *Adverbs.* **cheerfully**, cheerily, briskly, airily, with alacrity, with relish, with zest.

See also ²CONTENT, LIGHTNESS, PLEASURABLENESS, REJOICING.—*Antonyms.* See DEJECTION.

---

cheerless, *adj.* dreary, dismal, somber, gloomy, depressing; melancholy, downcast, despondent, depressed, unhappy. See DARKNESS, DEJECTION, PAINFULNESS.

cherish, *v.* nurture, foster; prize, treasure, revere. See AID, LOVE.

chest, *n.* breast, thorax; case, box, casket; coffer. See CONVEXITY, RECEPTACLE, TREASURY.

chestnut, *adj.* reddish brown, bay. See BROWN.

chew, *v.* masticate, crunch, grind, eat. See FOOD.

chicken, *n.* hen, fowl, pullet. See ANIMAL.

chief, *n.* head, leader, chieftain, captain, commander, superior. See DIRECTOR, MASTER.

chief, *adj.* principal, first, foremost, leading, main, supreme, cardinal. See CENTRALITY, IMPORTANCE.

child, *n.* tot, brat, baby, offspring. See INFANT, POSTERITY.

childbirth, *n.* travail, labor, delivery. See PAIN.

childish, *adj.* simple-minded, credulous, trustful; infantile, puerile, senile, weak, foolish, silly. See CREDULITY, IMBECILITY, SIMPLENESS.

chill, *n.* frigidity, chilliness; shivering. See COLD.

chimæra, *n.* chimærid (*zoöl.*). See ANIMAL (*elasmobranchs*).

chimera *or* **chimæra,** *n.* fantasy, wild fancy; fabulous monster. See IMAGINATION, UNCONFORMITY.

chimney, *n.* cleft (*mountaineering*), fissure; flue, smokestack. See OPENING.

china, *n.* porcelain, crockery. See CALEFACTION.

chip, *n.* piece, bit, fragment, cut, slice, flake. See PART.

chivalrous, *adj.* gallant, brave, knightly, chivalric. See COURTESY, PROBITY.

CHOICE.—I. *Nouns.* **choice,** option, determination, election, selection; discrimination, discretion, preference, preferment, volition, adoption, decision, judgment, coöptation, coöption; alternative, dilemma, *embarras de choix* (*F.*).
[*that which is chosen*] **pick,** preference; flower, *élite* (*F.*), choicest, best.
election, poll, ballot, ticket (*U. S.*), vote, voice, suffrage, plebiscite, *vox populi* (*L.*); primary election, direct primary; primary; general election; referendum; electioneering; Australian ballot, voting, elective franchise.
voter, elector, suffragist (*rare in the general sense*), constituent, balloter; floater, repeater (*both slang and becoming rarer*); electorate, constituency.
II. *Verbs.* **choose,** elect, make one's choice, make choice of, fix upon, settle, decide, determine, make up one's mind; adopt, take up, embrace, espouse; cross the Rubicon.
select, pick, cull, glean, winnow; pitch upon, indulge one's fancy; prefer, fancy, have rather, had (*or* would) as lief; reserve, set apart, mark out for; draft *or* draught, draw off, detach (*for service*), enlist.
vote, poll, ballot; plump (*Eng.; record an unsplit vote*); hold up one's hand, give a (*or* the) voting sign; divide.
III. *Adjectives.* **choice,** select, chosen, picked out, selected, popular, preferential, preferred; conscript; elect (*theol.*).
optional, elective, discretional *or* discretionary, voluntary, not obligatory; at choice, on approval.
IV. *Adverbs.* **by choice,** by preference; in preference, first, sooner, rather, before.
optionally, at pleasure, at the option of, whether or not.
See also DESIRE, FAVORITE, GOOD, JUDGMENT, TAKING, VOICE, WILL.—*Antonyms.* See COMPULSION, NECESSITY, NEUTRALITY, REJECTION.

---

choke, *v.* clog, congest, plug; stifle, strangle, suffocate. See CLOSURE, KILLING.

choose, *v.* select, take, prefer, elect, pick. See CHOICE, TAKING.

chop, *v.* cut, cleave, split, chip, hack, hew. See DISJUNCTION.

chorus, *n.* choir, choristers; refrain, burden, bob. See MUSICIAN, POETRY.
chosen, *adj.* picked, select, elect. See CHOICE.
christen, *v.* baptize, name. See NOMENCLATURE.
Christendom, *n.* the Church, Christians, Christian countries. See CHURCHDOM, ORTHODOXY.
Christian, *n.* Christian believer, Nazarene (*in Jewish and Moham. use*), giaour (*Turkish*); churchman, Episcopalian, Methodist, Baptist, etc. See CLERGY, ORTHODOXY, PIETY.
Christmas, *n.* yule, yuletide, *Noël* (*F.*). See REGULARITY.
chronic, *adj.* persistent, unceasing, inveterate, constant. See CONTINUANCE.
chronicle, *n.* annals, account, archives, history, register. See RECORD.

CHRONOMETRY.—I. *Nouns.* **chronometry** (*measurement of time*), chronology, horology, horometry, horography, chronoscopy (*measurement of minute intervals of time*), chronography.
almanac, calendar, ephemeris (*astron.*), astronomical almanac (*or* table), *fasti* (*L.; pl.*), Whitaker, register, registry; chronicle, annals, journal, diary.
standard time, zone time, civil time, Greenwich time, mean time; solar time, sidereal time, apparent time; local time.
[*in U. S. and Canada*] Eastern time, Central time, Mountain time, Pacific time; Atlantic time (*also called* Intercolonial, Colonial, *or* Provincial time: *used in New Brunswick and Nova Scotia*).
daylight-saving time, daylight time, fast time (*distinguished from* slow time), summer time (*so called in Great Britain*).
timekeeper, timepiece, horologe (*tech.*), clock, watch, repeater; chronometer, journeyman, electric clock, chronoscope, chronograph, stop watch; dial, sundial; hourglass, clepsydra, water clock; time ball, time signal, chronopher (*for distributing electric time signals*).
II. *Verbs.* **fix the time,** register, record, date, chronicle, chronologize, measure time, beat time, mark time.
III. *Adjectives.* **chronometric** *or* chronometrical, chronoscopic, chronographic *or* chronographical, chronologic *or* chronological.

---

church, *n.* ministry, clericalism, sacerdotalism; Christendom, Holy Church, Church of Christ; chapel, cathedral. See CHURCHDOM, ORTHODOXY, TEMPLE.

CHURCHDOM.—I. *Nouns.* **churchdom,** Christendom, pale of the church; church, ministry, priesthood, prelacy, hierarchy, episcopacy, church government; clericalism, sacerdotalism, episcopalianism.
monasticism, monkhood, monkery, friarhood, monachism; cloistered life, monastic (*or* conventual) life; celibacy.
[*ecclesiastical offices and dignities*] cardinalate, cardinalship; primacy, archbishopric, archiepiscopacy; prelacy, bishopric, episcopate, episcopacy, see, diocese; benefice, incumbency, living, cure, charge, cure of souls; rectorship, vicariate, vicarship; pastorate, pastorship, pastoral charge; deaconry, deaconship, curacy; chaplaincy, chaplainship, presbytery.
holy orders, ordination, institution, consecration, induction, installation, preferment, translation (*transfer of a bishop*), presentation.
papacy, papal system, pontificate, See of Rome, the Vatican, the apostolic see.
II. *Verbs.* **call** (*as a minister*), invite, nominate, appoint, elect; present, bestow; frock, ordain, induct, install, translate, consecrate; canonize, saint, beatify.
III. *Adjectives.* **ecclesiastical,** clerical, religious, sacerdotal, priestly, pastoral, ministerial, hierarchical, episcopal, canonical; pontifical, papal, popish (*opprobrious*), papistic *or* papistical (*opprobrious*); apostolic.
See also CLERGY, COUNCIL (*ecclesiastical*), TEMPLE.

---

churchly, *adj.* monastic, cloistered. See TEMPLE.
cinematograph, *n.* moving-picture machine, kinetoscope. See OPTICAL INSTRUMENTS.
cipher, *n.* code, cryptogram, cryptograph; monogram; naught, zero. See CONCEALMENT, LETTER, UNSUBSTANTIALITY.

circle, *n.* ring, orb, globe, circlet, disk; set. See CIRCULARITY, PARTY.
circle, *v.* encircle, circumnavigate, circumscribe; gird, surround, compass, inclose. See CIRCULARITY, ENVIRONMENT.

CIRCUIT.—I. *Nouns.* **circuit,** circumference, compass, bound (*usually in pl.*), boundary, zone, circle, periphery, perimeter (*geom.*), area, contour, outline.
round, revolution, orbit, complete path (*elec.*), ambit, turn, wheel, whirl, circulation; course, lap, ring, cycle.
detour, *détour* (*F.*), roundabout way, turning, winding, loop; deviation, digression, circumlocution, periphrase, ambages.
II. *Verbs.* **circuit,** compass, circulate, go around, circle, encircle, girdle, loop, make a circuit; make a detour, go round about, detour, deviate, meander.
III. *Adjectives.* **circuitous,** indirect, roundabout, circular, devious, sinuous, serpentine, winding; intricate, tortuous, flexuous, twisted, helical, labyrinthine, mazy, zigzag.
wandering, rambling, vagrant, deviating, roving, circumlocutory, circumlocutional, circumlocutionary, periphrastic, ambagious; digressive, discursive.
IV. *Adverbs.* **circuitously,** indirectly, in a roundabout way; by an indirect course.

See also CIRCUITY, CIRCULARITY, CONVOLUTION, DEVIATION, OUTLINE.—*Antonyms.* See MIDCOURSE.

CIRCUITY.—I. *Nouns.* **circuity,** roundabout way, circumflexion, turn, excursion, circumambulation, circumnavigation; wheel, turning, evolution; coil, spiral (*as in aviation*).
II. *Verbs.* **circuit,** circle, compass, encircle, circumscribe, describe a circle, circumnavigate, "put a girdle round about the earth" (*Midsummer Night's Dream*); go the round; beat the bounds (*to walk around the boundary of a parish and strike certain landmarks with a rod: an old English custom*).
turn, bend, sway, flex, circumflex, bend round; spiral (*aëro.*), wheel, go about, put about (*both naut.*); go (*or* turn) round, veer, round, turn a corner; double a point (*naut.*); tack, warp, slue *or* slew, swing, jibe, haul, maneuver; deviate, detour, make a detour.
wind, whisk, twirl, twist, coil, twine, wreathe, reel, curl, worm, roll, crank, swivel; entwine, entwist, infold, surround; meander, sinuate, serpentine (*rare*).

See also CIRCULARITY, CONVOLUTION.

CIRCULARITY.—I. *Nouns.* **circularity,** roundness, sphericity, sphericality, orbicularity, globosity, cylindricity, rotundity.
circle, circlet, ring, annulus (*tech.*), annulet, hoop, loop, eyelet, eye, grommet *or* grummet; roller, drum, caster, trolley, wheel, cycle, orb, orbit, disk *or* disc, circuit, zone, belt, zonule, zonula, zonulet, band, cordon, hub, nave; sash, girdle, cestus, cincture, baldric, wreath, garland; crown, coronet, chaplet, snood, fillet; necklace, collar; bracelet, armlet; noose, lasso, bight, coil; meridian, ecliptic, equator, colure; halo, corona; areola (*anat.*).
ellipse, oval, ovoid, ovum (*arch.*), ellipsoid, cycloid, epicycle, epicycloid.
semicircle, half circle, hemicycle; quadrant, sextant, sector.
II. *Verbs.* **circle,** surround, encircle, ring, inclose, environ, encompass, girdle, round; wheel, revolve, rotate, pivot, turn.
III. *Adjectives.* **circular,** round, rounded, ringlike, orbed, orbicular, annular, spherical, globular, globose, cylindric *or* cylindrical, rotund, rotundate, discoid; oval, ovate, ovoid, elliptic, elliptical, egg-shaped.
[*of a letter*] encyclic *or* encyclical (*used esp. of an* encyclical letter *of the Pope*), cyclic, general.
circuitous, indirect, roundabout; circumlocutory.

See also ENVIRONMENT, ROTUNDITY.—*Antonyms.* See CONVOLUTION.

---

circulate, *v.* pass, change hands; spread, report, propagate; revolve, circle. See MONEY, PASSAGE, PUBLICATION, ROTATION.
circumference, *n.* perimeter, periphery, circuit, girth. See OUTLINE.
circumlocution, *n.* periphrasis, verbosity, wordiness, verbiage. See DIFFUSENESS.

CIRCUMSCRIPTION.—I. *Nouns.* **circumscription,** limitation, confinement; limit, bound, boundary, restraint, restriction; envelope, case, inclosure, encircling, encompassing.
[*a circumscribed space*] district, territory, political division.
II. *Verbs.* **circumscribe,** limit, bound, inclose *or* enclose, encyst (*tech.*), park; hedge in, rail in, fence round, hedge round; hem in, mark off, demarcate, delimit, delimitate, define, determine, encompass, encircle, surround, picket; corral; imprison, restrain, restrict, confine.
infold, envelop, inclose, inwrap, involve, embrace, inclasp, embosom; wrap, clothe, invest, pack, shroud, bury, incase, enshrine.
III. *Adjectives.* **circumscribed,** limited, confined, bounded, etc. (see *verbs*); begirt, girt; lapt; buried in, immersed in; embosomed, imbedded, mewed up; landlocked.
See also CIRCUITY, CONTRACTION, ENVIRONMENT, INCLOSURE, RESTRAINT.

CIRCUMSTANCE.—I. *Nouns.* **circumstance,** condition, situation; environment, surroundings, material welfare (*in pl.; as, in easy* circumstances); phase, position, time, place, cause; footing, standing, status.
[*in sing. only*] full detail, formality, ceremony, fuss, punctilio (*as, pomp and* circumstance).
occurrence, event, occasion, incident, fact, item, detail, matter, particular, instance, happening, eventuality, episode, scene.
predicament, quandary, fix, dilemma, emergency, crisis, pinch, pass, plight, hole (*colloq.*), *impasse* (*F.*), extremity, juncture, conjuncture, contingency, exigency, corner.
II. *Adjectives.* **circumstantial,** conditional, provisional; contingent, incidental, adventitious, nonessential; inferential, probable, possible, presumptive.
detailed, minute, exact, full, particular, precise, fussy.
III. *Adverbs.* **accordingly,** that being the case, therefore, consequently, so, hence, wherefore, then.
conditionally, provided, if, in case; if so, unless, in the event of; in such a case (event, *or* contingency); provisionally.
thus, in such wise, in this (*or* that) manner, in this way, so, consequently; to this degree (*as,* thus *bold*), so far; in *or* under the circumstances (*or* conditions).
See also EVIDENCE, GENERALITY, STATE.

---

circumvent, *v.* frustrate, thwart, outwit, baffle, elude. See DECEPTION, HINDRANCE.
cite, *v.* summon, arraign; illustrate, quote; allege, bring forward, adduce. See COMMAND, CONFORMITY, EVIDENCE.
citizen, *n.* resident, native, townsman. See INHABITANT.
city, *n.* town, municipality, metropolis. See HABITATION.
civil, *adj.* mannerly, urbane, well-bred, respectful; secular, lay; political, state. See COURTESY, LAITY, MANKIND.
civilize, *v.* cultivate, polish, refine, humanize. See IMPROVEMENT.
claim, *v.* assert, contend; demand, require; lay claim to (*of things*), deserve. See AFFIRMATION, COMMAND, RIGHTFULNESS.
claim, *n.* demand, requirement; plea, counterclaim; title; pretension, pretense, prerogative. See COMMAND, LAWSUIT, PROPERTY, RIGHT.
claimant, *n.* prosecutor, accuser; pretender, claimer, heir. See ACCUSATION, RIGHTFULNESS.
clamor, *n.* uproar, hubbub, outcry, noise, racket, tumult, din; contention, agitation, complaining. See CRY, LOUDNESS, DISAPPROBATION.
clamorous, *adj.* uproarious, tumultuous, vociferous, obstreperous, riotous. See CRY, LOUDNESS.
clamp, *n.* fastening, fastener, clasp; brace, band. See VINCULUM.
clan, *n.* brotherhood, faction, set, association; breed, caste, sort; family stock, tribe. See ASSEMBLAGE, CLASS, CONSANGUINITY.
clang, *v.* clangor, resound, peal, ring. See LOUDNESS, RESONANCE.
clap, *v.* applaud, cheer, acclaim. See APPROBATION.

clash, *v.* collide, conflict; dispute, contend. See COUNTERACTION, DISAGREEMENT.
clash, *n.* collision, concussion, shock, encounter, impact. See IMPULSE.
clasp, *v.* grasp, hold; hug, embrace; hook, fasten. See COHERENCE, ENDEARMENT, JUNCTION.

CLASS.—*Nouns.* **class,** division, subdivision, category, predicament (*logic*), section, department, province, domain, sphere; grouping, head, caste, clan, sept; clique, coterie, set; estate, rank, grade, rate, race, tribe, party, sect, faction; breed, feather, kidney, strain, brand, stamp; make, cast, form, mold *or* mould.
classification, systematization, phylum (*biol.*), order, family, genus (*pl.* genera), species, subspecies, variety; subgenus, subgroup, suborder, subfamily, superfamily.
kind, sort, manner, nature, type, character, *genre* (*F.*), gender (*gram.*), sex, color; description; style, denomination, persuasion (*jocose; as, the feminine* persuasion), designation, temperament, connection, selection, specification.

See also LEARNER, SCHOOL.

---

classic, *adj.* restrained, chaste, simple. See SYMMETRY.
classification, *n.* sorting, grouping, allocation; systematization, order. See ARRANGEMENT, CLASS.
classify, *v.* systematize, group, tabulate, index, file. See ARRANGEMENT.
classmate, *n.* fellow student, schoolmate. See LEARNER.
classroom, *n.* schoolroom, lecture room, lecture hall. See SCHOOL.
clatter, *n.* rattle, noise, commotion. See LOUDNESS.
claw, *n.* talon, nail, ungula (*tech.*), pincer, tentacle. See RETENTION.
clay, *n.* earth, argil, potter's clay, kaolin; mud. See LAND.

CLEANNESS.—I. *Nouns.* **cleanness,** purity, pureness, cleanliness, clearness, neatness, immaculateness, immaculacy, whiteness, spotlessness; purification, purgation; elution (*chem.*), elutriation (*tech.*), detersion (*med.*), depuration (*tech.*), lustration (*jocose in the sense of* ablution), ablution, lavation; disinfection, sanitation; drainage, sewerage.
bath, washing, bathing, immersion, tubbing; sponge bath, tub; shower, shower bath; sitz bath, hip bath; bathroom, swimming pool, swimming bath, public bath, baths, bathhouse, Turkish bath, hot-air bath, sudatorium; vapor bath, Russian bath, vaporarium; lavatory; laundry, washhouse.
cathartic, purgative, aperient, laxative, evacuant, deobstruent (*med.*), physic.
cleaner, washerwoman, laundress, laundryman, washerman, dhobi (*Anglo-Indian*); scavenger, sweeper; crossing (*or* street) sweeper, white wings (*U. S. local*); dustman; sweep.
brush, broom, besom, wisp, whisk; vacuum cleaner, carpet sweeper; mop, swab, hose.
II. *Verbs.* **clean,** cleanse, rinse, flush, mop, sponge, scour, swab, scrub; rub, wipe, clear; wash, lave, launder, purify, baptize; purge, expurgate, clarify, try, refine, elutriate, depurate.
sift, winnow, sieve, bolt, screen, riddle; pick, weed.
strain, separate, filter, filtrate, drain; percolate.
comb, rake, scrape, rasp; card, hackle, heckle, hatchel.
sweep, brush, whisk, brush up, rout out; clean house, vacuum (*colloq.*), tidy (*colloq.*), trim, neaten (*rare*), spruce up (*colloq.*).
disinfect, fumigate, ventilate, deodorize, sanitate; asepticize, antisepticize, aseptify (*rare*), Listerize, sterilize, Tyndallize, Pasteurize; cauterize; whitewash.
III. *Adjectives.* **clean,** cleanly, pure, immaculate, spotless, stainless, unspotted, unblemished, untarnished, unpolluted, unsoiled, unsullied, untainted, sweet, fair, clear, unadulterated; continent, moral, decent.
neat, spruce, tidy, trim, cleaned, orderly, shipshape, kempt (*archaic*), trig, well-groomed.
shapely, well-proportioned, well-made, clean-cut, well-formed, symmetrical, clean-limbed, trim.

smart, adroit, clever, skillful, dexterous, not bungling (*as, a* clean *catch*).
complete, entire, even; unobstructed, unimpeded, perfect, clear-cut, distinct (*as, a* clean *sweep;* clean *timber*).
cleansing, purifying, purificative, purificatory, abstergent, detersive, detergent, depurative, cathartic.
See also PURITY, WATER.—*Antonyms.* See UNCLEANNESS.

---

clear, *adj.* plain, distinct, intelligible; bright, fair, unclouded; open, patent; transparent, limpid, lucid. See INTELLIGIBILITY, LIGHT, MANIFESTATION, TRANSPARENCY.
clear-sighted, *adj.* eagle-eyed, far-sighted. See VISION.
[1]cleave, *v.* stick, adhere, cling. See COHERENCE.
[2]cleave, *v.* sever, split, rend, rive, divide. See DISJUNCTION.
cleft, *n.* gap, fissure, break, opening, crack, crevice. See INTERVAL.

CLERGY.—I. *Nouns.* **clergy,** clerical order, clergymen, clericals, ministry, priesthood, presbytery, the cloth, the pulpit, the desk.
clergyman, divine, ecclesiastic, priest, churchman, cleric, pastor, shepherd, minister, preacher, clerk in holy orders, parson, sky pilot (*slang*); father, padre, *abbé* (*F.*), *curé* (*F.*); reverend (*rare*).
[*dignitaries of the church*] Pope, pontiff, Holy Father, pontifex, prince of the Church, cardinal, primate, metropolitan, archbishop, bishop, prelate, suffragan, bishop suffragan, suffragan bishop, bishop coadjutor, diocesan; episcopate, episcopacy (*both collective*); dean, archdeacon, prebendary, canon, rector, vicar, beneficiary, incumbent, chaplain, curate; missionary, missionary apostolic (*R. C. Ch.*), missioner, revivalist; reader, lay reader, Bible reader, anagnost *or* anagnostes; elder, deacon, churchwarden, warden.
[*Jewish*] prophet, high priest, priest, rabbi.
[*Hindu*] Brahman *or* Brahmin, pundit *or* pandit, pujari, purohit, guru; yogi, sannyasi *or* sanyasi.
[*Buddhist*] poonghie (*Burma*), bonze (*Far East*), talapoin (*Indo-China and Ceylon*); lama, Dalai Lama *or* Grand Lama (*Tibet*).
[*Moslem*] imam, murshid, mullah, mufti; dervish, fakir *or* faquir, santon (*Turkey*), abdal (*pl.* abdali).
monk, cenobite, religious, conventual, caloyer (*Eastern Ch.*), monastic; stylite, pillarist, pillar saint; friar, beadsman *or* bedesman (*archaic*), abbot, prior; lay brother; begging friar, mendicant; palmer, pilgrim, Hospitaler, Templar; hermit, recluse, anchoret *or* anchorite.
Jesuits, Loyolites; Franciscans, Friars, Minor, Gray Friars, Minorites, Observantines, Recollects *or* Recollets, Conventuals, Capuchins; Dominicans, Black Friars, preaching friars; Carmelites, White Friars; Augustinians, Augustinian hermits, Austin friars, begging hermits; Benedictines, Black Monks; Carthusians; Cistercians; Trappists.
nun, sister, *religieuse* (*F.*), conventual; priestess, abbess, prioress; canoness; mother superior, the reverend mother; novice, postulant.
Clare, Minoress, Franciscan nun, Poor Clare, Urbanist, Carmelite nun; Sister of Charity; Lorettine, Sister of Loretto; Little Sisters of the Poor.
II. *Adjectives.* **clerical,** churchly, priestly, ministerial, pastoral, episcopal, sacerdotal, ecclesiastical.
ordained, in orders, in holy orders, called to the ministry.
See also CHURCHDOM.—*Antonyms.* See LAITY.

---

clerk, *n.* retail salesman (*or* saleswoman), counterjumper; registrar, secretary, scribe; typist, copyist, writer. See CONSIGNEE, RECORDER, WRITING.
clever, *adj.* adroit, dexterous; talented, able, gifted. See SKILL.
clew *or* **clue,** *n.* solution, intimation, hint, key. See ANSWER, INDICATION.
client, *n.* buyer, customer, patron. See PURCHASE.
cliff, *n.* precipice, crag, bluff. See VERTICALITY.
climax, *n.* acme, zenith, pinnacle, crest, culmination. See SUMMIT.
climb, *v.* mount, scale, rise, go up. See ASCENT.

clime, *n.* climate, atmosphere; latitude, zone, tract: *poetic.* See REGION.
clinch, *v.* settle (*as an argument*), confirm, end, close; fasten, secure, clench, rivet, clamp, grapple. See COMPLETION, JUNCTION.
cling, *v.* stick, adhere; grasp, hug; persist, continue. See COHERENCE, LOVE, PERSEVERANCE.
clip, *v.* cut, snip, shear, trim, mow, shorten. See SHORTNESS.
clique, *n.* set, circle, coterie, crowd (*colloq.*). See COMBINATION, PARTY.
cloak, *n.* cape, mantle, dolman. See CLOTHING.
clog, *v.* obstruct, choke up; hamper, encumber, impede. See HINDRANCE.
cloister, *n.* arcade; abbey, convent, hermitage, monastery. See HABITATION, SECLUSION.
cloistered, *adj.* cloistral, monastic, conventual. See TEMPLE.
close, *adj.* compact, dense, solid, firm; oppressive, muggy; firm, taut; near, intimate; stingy, niggardly; secretive, reserved. See DENSITY, HEAT, JUNCTION, NEARNESS, PARSIMONY, TACITURNITY.
close, *v.* shut, stop, plug, seal; finish, conclude, terminate. See CLOSURE, END.
close, *n.* termination, conclusion, finish. See END.
closet, *n.* cupboard, cabinet, locker, wardrobe, buffet. See RECEPTACLE.

CLOSURE.—I. *Nouns.* **closure,** closing, shutting, blockade, shutting up, sealing, obstruction, infarct (*med.*), embolus (*med.*), embolism, occlusion, imperforation; contraction; constipation; imperviousness; impermeability; blind alley, *cul-de-sac* (*F.*).

[*in debate*] cloture, *clôture* (*F.*): *similar in effect to* the previous question.

II. *Verbs.* **close,** plug, block up, stop up, fill up, cork up, button up, stuff up, dam up; blockade, barricade; obstruct, occlude, lock, padlock, bar, bolt, stop, seal, lute; choke, throttle; ram, ram down, dam, silt, cram; clinch; shut, slam, snap, clap.

inclose, encompass, confine, envelop, cover in, environ, gather around, rail, park, impark, rope, box, wall, inwall.

III. *Adjectives.* **closed,** shut, unopened; unpierced, impervious, impermeable; impenetrable; impassable, pathless, wayless; untrodden.

tight, impervious, impassable, impenetrable, snug, compact, stanch, firm, close; unventilated, air-tight, water-tight, waterproof, hermetically sealed.

See also CESSATION, CIRCUMSCRIPTION. END, HINDRANCE, STOPPER.—*Antonyms.* See OPENING.

CLOTHING.—I. *Nouns.* **clothing,** dress, covering, raiment, costume, attire, toilet *or* toilette, habiliment, robes, vesture, vestments, garments, garb, wardrobe, apparel, wearing apparel, wardrobe, clothes, finery, array.

outfit, equipment, trousseau; uniform, khaki, olive-drab, regimentals; livery, gear, harness, rigging (*colloq.*), turn-out, accouterment, caparison, suit, trappings; things (*colloq.*), togs (*slang*), duds (*slang*); outer garments, overclothes.

dishabille, undress, tea gown, wrapper, negligee, *négligé* (*F.*), *peignoir* (*F.*), dressing gown, kimono; smoking jacket; mufti, civies (*slang*), civilian dress; rags, tatters, old clothes.

loincloth, dhoti (*Hindu*), lungi (*Burmese*), moocha (*Kafir*), *pagne* (*F.*), G string.

dress suit, dress clothes, evening dress, swallowtail (*colloq.*), dinner coat, dinner jacket, tuxedo, tux (*colloq.*); glad rags (*slang*).

cloak, mantle, robe, burnoose *or* burnous, capote, cope; pelerine, cardinal, shawl. cape, plaid (*Scot.*), wraprascal (*archaic*); oilskins, slicker (*U. S.*), mackintosh, waterproof, poncho.

robe, gown, dress, suit, costume, frock, caftan, cassock; habit, riding habit, joseph (18*th century*); dolman, dolmatic, toga; cymar, simar (*archaic*), chimer *or* chimere (*upper robe of a bishop*), sari (*Hindu*)

blouse, waist, shirt waist; basque; smock, smock frock, tunic, garibaldi, camise, camisa (*Sp.*).

coat, outer garment, jacket, sack, tunic, cutaway; frock coat, Prince Albert (*colloq.*); overcoat, greatcoat, raglan, redingote; dreadnaught, fearnaught, spencer, pea-coat, pea-jacket, Inverness, surtout, ulster, tabard, paletot,

Mackinaw coat *or* Mackinaw, cardigan *or* cardigan jacket; sweater, pullover (*Brit.*), blazer, Jersey; jerkin (*hist.*), doublet, gaberdine, vest, waistcoat; vestee. **skirt,** overskirt; petticoat, hoop skirt, farthingale, crinoline; jupon, jupe, kilt. **trousers,** breeches, pantaloons, pants (*colloq.*), galligaskins (*jocose*), unmentionables (*jocose*), kicks (*slang*), trews (*worn by Highlanders*); overalls; shorts; tights; drawers; knickerbockers, knickers (*colloq.*), plus-fours, bloomers.
headdress, headgear, coiffure, hat, beaver, bonnet, cap, tam-o'-shanter, sombrero, wide-awake, straw hat, straw, panama, leghorn, derby (*U. S.*), bowler (*Eng.*), billycock (*Eng.*); nightcap, skullcap; hood, coif, cowl, capuchin, capuche, calash (*hist.*); wimple, snood, fillet; crown; turban, fez, tarboosh, shako, busby, bearskin; kepi, forage cap, service cap, service hat, overseas cap; opera hat, gibus, crush hat; mask, domino.
wig, peruke, periwig, jasey (*esp. of worsted: familiar*), Ramillie, pigtail, Gregorian (*hist.*), Brutus *or* Brutus wig.
helmet, helm (*archaic*), casque (*hist.*), headpiece, *Pickelhaube* (*German spiked helmet*); sallet *or* salade, skullcap, basinet, armet, crest, morion, burgonet, heaume (*all hist.*); trench helmet, tin hat (*slang*); sun helmet, sola topee *or* topi (*Anglo-Indian*), topee *or* topi.
underclothing, undies (*slang*), body clothes, *lingerie* (*F.*), undergarments, underclothes; linen; shirt, sark (*archaic or dial.*), shift, chemise; nightgown. nightshirt, pyjamas *or* pajamas, bedgown, camisole, slip; union suit, combination, B. V. D.'s; brassière, bandeau.
tie, neckerchief, neckcloth, necktie; ruff, collar, boa; cravat, stock, handkerchief, scarf, muffler, tippet; guimpe, chemisette; bib, tucker; girdle, cummerbund (*Anglo-Indian*).
shoe, boot, half-boot, bootee (*trade name*), high-low, bootikin; brogan, brogue, Balmoral, Blucher, stogy; top-boot, jack-boot; Wellington boot, Hessian, riding boot; buskin, cothurnus (*symbolic of tragedy*), sock (*low shoe, symbolic of comedy*); Oxford, Oxford shoe, Oxford tie, pump, sneakers (*U. S.*); slipper, moccasin, sandal, galosh *or* galoshe, arctic, overshoe, rubber; patten, clog, chopine, *sabot* (*F.*), *geta* (*Jap.*); snowshoes, ski (*pl.* ski *or* skis).
leggings, puttees, gaiters, spatterdashes, spats, gamashes (*archaic or dial.*), gambadoes, *chaparajos or chapareras* (*Mexican Sp.*), chaps (*colloq.*), shaps (*Western U. S.*); greaves (*leg armor*).
stocking, hose; half-hose, sock; trunk hose; hosiery.
glove, gauntlet, mousquetaire, mousquetaire glove; kids, suèdes; mitten, mitt.
[*garment makers*] **tailor,** tailoress (*fem.*), *tailleur* (*F.*), clothier, sartor (*jocose*), snip (*slang*), whip-cat (*itinerant tailor: dial.*), whiplouse (*contemptuous: old slang*), durzee *or* darzi (*Hindu*), busheler *or* bushelman (*U. S.*).
dressmaker, *modiste* (*F.*), *couturière* (*F.; masc. couturier*), mantuamaker (*archaic*), habit-maker; seamstress *or* sempstress.
shoemaker, cordwainer (*archaic*), Crispin (*from St. Crispin, patron saint of shoemakers*), cobbler, snob (*Scot. and dial.*), souter (*Scot. and dial.*), bootmaker.
[*various suppliers*] costumer, costumier; milliner, hatter, glover, hosier, draper, linen draper, haberdasher, mercer; outfitter.
II. *Verbs.* **clothe,** dress, fit out, rig out, deck, drape, robe, enrobe, gown, attire, apparel, costume, garb, invest, endue, indue (*as with spiritual gifts*), enclothe, dight (*archaic*), bedight (*archaic*), accouter *or* accoutre (*as for military service*), array, equip, harness, caparison; cover, muffle, wrap, shroud, swathe, swaddle.
don (*opposite of* doff,) put on, slip on, get on, dress in, wear, assume.
III. *Adjectives.* **clothed,** clad, vested (*esp. in ceremonial robes*), robed, invested, habited, costumed, dight (*archaic*).

See also COVERING, ORNAMENT, OSTENTATION, VESTMENTS.—*Antonyms.* See DIVESTMENT.

CLOUD.—I. *Nouns.* **cloud,** vapor, fog, smog (*portmanteau wood* = smoke fog), mist, haze, steam, film, haziness; scud, rack; cumulus, woolpack, alto-cumulus, cirrus, mare's-tail, curl cloud; cirro-cumulus, mackerel sky; stratus, cirro-stratus, cumulo-stratus; nimbus, rain cloud, thunderhead, thunder cloud, dirty sky.
science of clouds: nephology, nephelology (*rare*), meteorology.
II. *Verbs.* **cloud,** overcast, becloud, shadow, overshadow, darken, obscure; **fog, befog, mist, envelop.**

III. *Adjectives.* **cloudy,** clouded, overcast; vaporous, steamy, nebulous, misty, foggy, hazy, filmy, smoky, dull, thick, lowering, murky, dirty, lurid; dim, dark, shadowy, dusky, indistinct, obscure.

See also DARKNESS, DIMNESS, SEMITRANSPARENCY, THICKNESS.—*Antonyms.* See LIGHT.

---

clown, *n.* buffoon, jester, boor, rustic. See DRAMA, HUMORIST, PEOPLE.
cloy, *v.* glut, surfeit, pall; bore. See SATIETY.
club, *n.* cudgel, stick; society, fraternity, association; resort, rendezvous. See ARMS, COMBINATION, FOCUS.
clubfooted, *adj.* taliped, splayfooted, deformed. See DISTORTION.
clue, *n.* solution, intimation, key, hint. See ANSWER, INDICATION.
clump, *n.* cluster, group, bunch. See ASSEMBLAGE.
clumsy, *adj.* unwieldy, awkward; bungling, stupid, incompetent, unskilled. See INEXPERIENCE, UNSKILLFULNESS.
clutch, *v.* hold fast, keep, secure, clench; seize, grasp, collar, grip. See RETENTION, TAKING.
coach, *n.* trainer, director; tallyho, stage, car, carriage (*Brit.*), Pullman. See TEACHER, VEHICLE.
coach, *v.* teach, cram, tutor, train. See TEACHING.
coagulate, *v.* clot, thicken, curdle, congeal. See DENSITY.
coal, *n.* ember, cinder; cannel coal, anthracite, charcoal, lignite. See CALEFACTION, FUEL.
coarse, *adj.* rough, coarse-grained, homespun; uncouth, unpolished, rude, crude, vulgar. See TEXTURE; LOWNESS, UGLINESS, VULGARITY.
coarseness, *n.* grossness, indelicacy, vulgarity. See LOWNESS.
coast, *n.* shore, margin, edge, bank, beach. See LAND.
coat, *n.* jacket, cloak, ulster; tegument, envelope, surface. See CLOTHING, COVERING.
coat, *v.* cover, overlay, plaster, crust, paint, varnish; plate. See COVERING.
coax, *v.* cajole, entice, wheedle, persuade. See MOTIVE.
cock, *n.* rooster, chanticleer. See ANIMAL.
code, *n.* cipher, cryptogram; law, principle, constitution. See CONCEALMENT, LEGALITY.
coerce, *v.* force, drive, restrain, impel, make. See COMPULSION.
coexist, *v.* coincide, concur, accompany. See SIMULTANEOUSNESS.
coffin, *n.* casket, shell, box. See INTERMENT.
cogent, *adj.* potent, forcible, convincing, weighty, strong. See POWER.
cogitate, *v.* reflect, muse, ponder, consider, meditate. See THOUGHT.
cognizant, *adj.* sensible, aware, conscious, observant. See SENSIBILITY.

COHERENCE.—I. *Nouns.* **coherence** *or* coherency, cohesion, cohesiveness, adherence, adhesion, conglomeration, aggregation, consolidation, solidification, combination, cementation, concretion, accretion.

[*of argument or narration*] congruity, connection, consistency, congruence, harmony, conformity.

tenacity, adhesiveness, glutinousness, tenaciousness, viscidity, stickiness, viscosity, toughness; inseparability.

II. *Verbs.* **cohere,** adhere, stick, cling, cleave, hold, stick together, hold fast; hang together, agree, be consistent; close with, clasp, hug.

stick like a leech, stick like wax, cling like ivy, cling like a bur, adhere like a remora, adhere like Deianira's shirt (*the poisoned shirt that accidentally caused the death of her husband, Hercules*).

glue, agglutinate, cement, paste, lute, gum; solder, weld; cake, consolidate, solidify, agglomerate.

III. *Adjectives.* **cohesive,** adhesive, adhering, tenacious, sticky, clinging, glutinous, viscous, viscid, mucilaginous, tacky,

united, combined, undivided, unseparated, joined, consolidated, solidified, compact, conjunct (*chiefly Scot.*), connate (*esp. biol.*); inseparable, inextricable, infrangible, sessile (*tech.*); allied, federal, federate, leagued, confederate.

See also AGREEMENT, COMBINATION, DENSITY.—*Antonyms.* See DECOMPOSITION, DISPERSION.

---

coil, *n.* spiral, roll, ring, circle. See CONVOLUTION.
coin, *n.* currency, specie, gold, silver, copper, change. See MONEY.
coin, *v.* stamp, mint, strike, mold; invent (*as a new word*), fashion, make, fabricate. See FORM, PRODUCTION.
coincidence, *n.* correspondence, agreement. See CONCURRENCE.

COLD.—I. *Nouns.* **cold,** coldness, chilliness, coolness, chill, iciness, gelidity, gelidness, frozenness, algidity, frigidity, inclemency, bleakness.
winter, depth of winter; hard winter; zero weather; Arctic, Antarctic; polar front (*meteorol.*).
ice, sleet, glaze *or* glazed frost (*meteorol.*), graupel (*meteorol.*), soft hail, hail, hailstone; frost, rime, hoarfrost; icicle, thick-ribbed ice; iceberg, floe, berg, snow mountain, jökul *or* jökull (*Iceland*), calf (*small floating mass of ice*); ice field, ice pack, glacier; *sérac* (*F.*), ground ice, anchor ice, frazil (*Canada and Northern U. S.*).
snow, flurry, snowflake, snowball, snowdrift, snowslip, snowslide, snow avalanche; snow ice, *névé* (*F.*), firn; snowfall, snowstorm, blizzard.
[*cold in the head*] **catarrh,** coryza (*med.*), nasal catarrh, gravedo (*rare: med.*), rheum; cough, tussis (*med.*), hack.
II. *Verbs.* **be cold,** shiver, quake, shake, tremble, shudder, chill, freeze, perish with cold, starve (*Eng.*).
III. *Adjectives.* **cold,** cool, chill, chilly, frigid, algid, fresh, keen, bleak, raw, inclement, bitter, biting, cutting, nipping, piercing, pinching; shivering, aguish; frostbitten; wintry, hiemal, boreal, arctic, snow-bound.
icy, glacial, frosty, freezing, frozen, frore (*archaic*), gelid; ice-bound, frost-bound.
indifferent, reserved, undemonstrative, unsympathetic, unresponsive, unemotional, apathetic, spiritless, phlegmatic, passionless, unimpassioned.

See also INDIFFERENCE, INSENSITIVENESS, REFRIGERATION.—*Antonyms.* See HEAT.

---

cold-blooded, *adj.* ruthless, unfeeling, heartless, merciless. See MALEVOLENCE.
coldness, *n.* chill, frigidity; unresponsiveness, inattention; coolness, apathy, callousness. See COLD, INDIFFERENCE, INSENSITIVENESS.
collapse, *v.* break down, slump, fail. See SHORTCOMING.
collapse, *n.* smash, ruin, downfall; prostration, exhaustion. See FAILURE, IMPOTENCE.
colleague, *n.* associate, ally, partner, companion. See FRIEND.
collect, *v.* meet, throng, flock; gather, amass, compile; demand, exact. See ASSEMBLAGE, COMPENDIUM, TAKING.
collide, *v.* foul, bump, meet, crash, clash, conflict. See IMPULSE.
collision, *n.* encounter, skirmish; clashing, interference; concussion, shock, impact; conflict, discord. See CONTENTION, COUNTERACTION, IMPULSE, OPPOSITION.
colloquial, *adj.* conversational, chatty, informal. See CONVERSATION.
colonize, *v.* settle, found, people, establish. See LOCATION.

COLOR.—I. *Nouns.* **color,** hue, tinct (*archaic*), color tone; tint, shade, tinge, tincture, dye, complexion, glow, flush; value, luminosity; tone, key; chroma, purity, intensity; coloration, coloring, pigmentation; chromatism *or* chromism (*bot., abnormal coloration*).
primary colors, fundamental colors, complementary colors, spectral colors, saturated colors.
[*in music*] timbre, quality, tone color, clang tint, clang, variety of expression.

[*in literature*] picturesqueness, ornate style, vivid descriptiveness, pictorial quality, imagery, word painting; vividness, graphicness, force, effectiveness.
[*general*] tone, character, quality, mood, shade of meaning.
[*outward show or semblance*] appearance, aspect, guise, semblance; pretext, show, pretense.
pigment, coloring matter, tinction, paint, dye, wash, distemper, stain; medium.
II. *Verbs.* **color,** dye, tinge, stain, tint, hue (*poetic*), tone; paint, wash, crayon, distemper, ingrain, grain, illuminate, emblazon.
III. *Adjectives.* **colored,** dyed, etc. (see *verbs*); hued (*usually in combination*); colorific, tinctorial, colory (*colloq.*), chromatic, prismatic; double-dyed.
bright, vivid, intense, deep; fresh, rich, gorgeous, bright-colored, gay, brilliant, glowing, splendid, lustrous.
gaudy, florid; garish, showy, flaunting, flashy, glaring, flaring, meretricious, tawdry; many-colored, party-colored *or* parti-colored, variegated; raw, crude.
mellow, harmonious, pearly, sweet, soft, full, pure, tender, subtle, delicate, subdued, softened.
dull, sad, sober, grave, somber *or* sombre, sad-colored, deadened, obscure, plain, flat, dark, lifeless, leaden, gray, muddy.

See also BLUE, BROWN, FINE ARTS, GRAY, GREEN, ORANGE, PURPLE, RED, YELLOW. —*Antonyms.* See COLORLESSNESS.

COLORLESSNESS.—I. *Nouns.* **colorlessness,** decoloration, decolorization, etiolation, achromatization, achromatism; discoloration; pallor, paleness, pallidity, sallowness.
neutral tint, monochrome; black and white, *chiaroscuro* (*It.*), sepia.
II. *Verbs.* **deprive of color,** decolor, decolorize, whiten, bleach, blanch, etiolate, achromatize, wash out, tone down.
lose color, fade, become colorless, turn pale, pale, fade out, fly, go, vanish.
III. *Adjectives.* **colorless,** uncolored, hueless, achromatic, etiolated, dull-hued; pasty, blanched, pale, pallid, pale-faced, anæmic, bloodless, leucocytic (*med.*); faint, dull, cold, muddy, leaden, dun, wan, sallow, dingy, ashy, ashen, cinereous (*esp. of plumage*), ghastly, cadaverous, glassy, lackluster; discolored.
pale as death, pale as ashes, pale as a witch, pale as a ghost, pale as a corpse.
[*general*] without distinction, wishy-washy (*colloq.*), neutral, indifferent, impartial.
light-colored, fair, blond, light, pale, white, creamy, whitish.

See also WHITENESS.—*Antonyms.* See COLOR.

---

colossus, *n.* giant, monster, prodigy. See SIZE.
column, *n.* pillar, shaft, post. See HEIGHT.
comb, *v.* scrape, heckle, dress, cleanse. See CLEANNESS.

COMBATANT.—*Nouns.* **combatant,** fighter, fighting man, contender, contestant, assailant, belligerent; adventurer, free lance, soldier of fortune; swashbuckler, duelist, swordsman, spadassin (*rare*); gladiator; competitor, rival.
pugilist, pug (*slang*), prize fighter, bruiser; boxer, sparrer.
army, host (*archaic*), array; regular army, active army, reserves; army corps, division, column, wing, horn (*archaic*), detachment, garrison, flying column, brigade, regiment, battalion, squadron, company, battery, section, platoon, squad; detail, patrol, picket, guard, legion, phalanx, cohort.
soldier, warrior, brave, man at arms, military man; knight; mercenary, free lance, franc-tireur; private, Tommy Atkins *or* Tommy (*Brit.*), doughboy (*U. S.*), Sammy (*slang*), *Poilu* (*F.: slang*), Fritz (*World War slang for German soldier*), rank and file, sepoy (*India*); spearman, pikeman; archer, bowman; musketeer, rifleman, sharpshooter, *bersagliere* (*It.; pl. bersaglieri*), skirmisher; guardsman, grenadier, fusileer, infantryman, foot soldier, zouave, chasseur, artilleryman, gunner, cannoneer, engineer; cavalryman, trooper, dragoon; cuirassier, hussar, lancer; volunteer, recruit, rookie (*U. S. slang*), conscript, drafted man, enlisted man; campaigner, veteran, vet (*colloq.*).
commanding officer, officer, subaltern, ensign, standard bearer.
horse and foot; cavalry, horse, light horse; infantry, foot, rifles; artillery, horse artillery, field artillery, gunners; military train.

armed force, troops, soldiery, military, forces, the army, standing army, regulars, the line; militia, national guard, state guard (*U. S.*), yeomanry, volunteers, minutemen (*Am. hist.*); posse; guards, yeomen of the guard (*Eng.*), beefeaters (*Eng.*), life guards, household troops, bodyguard.
levy, levy in mass, draft *or* draught, Landwehr, Landsturm; raw levies, awkward squad.
navy, first line of defense, wooden walls (*hist.*), naval forces, fleet, flotilla, armada, squadron; man-of-war's man; marines, leather-necks (*U. S. slang*), devil dogs (*U. S. slang*), jollies (*Brit. slang*).
man-of-war, line-of-battle ship, ship of the line, battleship, warship, ironclad, war vessel, superdreadnought, dreadnought, cruiser, armored cruiser, protected cruiser; gunboat, torpedo-boat, destroyer, submarine, submersible, U-boat (*Ger.*); submarine chaser, monitor; frigate, sloop of war, corvet, flagship; privateer; troopship, transport, tender.
air service, aviation (*or* aëronautical) service, air force, flying corps, fourth arm (*distinguished from the* infantry, cavalry, *and* artillery: *colloq.*).
aircraft, aëroplane, airplane, aëro (*colloq.*), *avion* (*F.*), Handley Page superaëroplane (*Brit.*), Fokker, Farman, Wright, Spad (*Société Pour les Appareils Deperdussin*), Gotha (*Ger.*), Taube (*Ger.*, "dove"), Sopwith (*Brit.*), Caproni (*It.*); bomber, bombing plane, battleplane, fighter, fighting plane, warplane, battle cruiser, spotter, scout *or* speed scout, chaser, pursuit plane, torpedo plane; seaplane, hydro-aëroplane; airship, military balloon, dirigible balloon, dirigible, blimp (*cant*); zeppelin; airplane carrier, aircraft carrier.
squadron, *escadrille* (*F.*), flight (*Brit.*; *one third of a squadron*), division; air fleet.

See also AËRONAUT, AËRONAUTICS, ATTACK, DEFENSE, ENEMY, MARINER, OPPONENT, SAFETY, WARFARE.

COMBINATION.—I. *Nouns.* **combination,** union, aggregation, aggregate, composite, mixture, junction, unification, coadunation, synthesis, incorporation, consolidation, centralization, conjuncture, inosculation, anastomosis (*biol.*), synechia, synizesis (*gram.*), amalgamation, coalescence, fusion, blend, blending, brew.
[*combination of persons*] **association,** union, alliance, league, order, coalition, federation, confederacy, federacy, guild, club, trade-union *or* trades-union, clique, gang, coterie, set, pool, trust, combine, camarilla.
alloy, compound, admixture, amalgam, composition, resultant.
II. *Verbs.* **combine,** unite, join, link, incorporate, embody, alloy, intermix, interfuse, interlard, compound, amalgamate, absorb, assimilate, blend, merge, fuse, concentrate, centralize, center, cement, agglutinate, solidify, lump, lump together, consolidate, coalesce, impregnate.
[*relating to persons*] **associate,** amalgamate, club, fraternize, unionize, federate, federalize, league, confederate, band together, herd, mass; pair, couple, marry.
III. *Adjectives.* **combined,** united, etc. (see *verbs*); coadunate, conjoint; ingrained, imbued, inherent; coalescent.
allied, amalgamated, leagued, corporate, incorporated, federate, confederate.

See also COMPONENT, COÖPERATION, JUNCTION, MIXTURE.—*Antonyms.* See DECOMPOSITION, DISJUNCTION.

---

combustible, *adj.* inflammable, tindery. See FUEL.
come, *v.* move towards, near; arrive, reach; befall, occur. See APPROACH, ARRIVAL, EVENT.—**come about,** happen, come to pass. See ARRIVAL.—**come after,** follow, succeed, ensue. See POSTERIORITY, SEQUENCE.—**come between,** intervene, interpose, interfere. See INTERJACENCE.—**come by,** obtain, acquire, gain, get. See ACQUISITION.—**come down,** descend, alight, fall. See DESCENT.—**come forth,** emerge, issue; appear, stand forth. See EGRESS, VISIBILITY.—**come of age,** attain majority. See ADOLESCENCE.—**come out,** make one's *début* (*F.*); be disclosed, leak out, transpire; appear, come into view. See ADOLESCENCE, DISCLOSURE, VISIBILITY.—**come to,** reach, arrive at; recover, revive; amount to, aggregate. See ARRIVAL, RESTORATION, WHOLE.—**come to grief,** flounder, fall, break down, fail. See ADVERSITY, FAILURE.—**come to nothing,** collapse, fall through. See FAILURE.

—come upon, meet with, stumble upon, find; recognize, identify. See DISCOVERY.

comely, *adj.* fair, pleasing, good-looking. See BEAUTY.

comfort, *n.* ease, luxury, enjoyment; solace, consolation. See PLEASURE, RELIEF.

comfortable, *adj.* at ease, restful, snug, luxurious. See PLEASURE.

comic, *adj.* ludicrous, funny, laughable, droll. See RIDICULOUSNESS.

COMMAND.—I. *Nouns.* **command,** order, regulation, ordinance, act, fiat, bidding, word, call, beck, nod; direction, injunction, hest (*archaic*), behest (*archaic*), precept, commandment, ruling, dictation, charge, instructions; dispatch, message; appointment, fixture.

control, authority, power, leadership, sway, domination, dominion, sovereignty, rule; coercion, compulsion, restraint.

demand, exaction, imposition, requisition, claim, ultimatum; request, requirement, reclamation.

decree, dictate, mandate, caveat, rescript, prescript, writ, ordination, bull, edict, decretal (*eccl.*), dispensation, prescription, ukase, firman (*Oriental*), enactment, law, act; warrant, passport, summons, subpœna, citation; word of command, order of the day, *l'ordre du jour* (*F.*).

II. *Verbs.* **command,** order, decree, enact, ordain, dictate, enjoin, bid, charge, instruct, prescribe, set, appoint, mark out, lay out, set (impose, *or* prescribe) a task, set to work, direct, give orders, issue a command; call to order; assume the command; require, demand, exact, inflict, lay, impose, tax.

claim, demand, require, lay claim to, reclaim, counterclaim.

cite, summon, summons (*colloq.*), call for, send for; subpœna; beckon.

III. *Adjectives.* **commanding,** authoritative, decretory, imperative, dictatorial, magisterial, imperious; conclusive, final, irrevocable, decisive.

IV. *Adverbs.* **commandingly,** etc. (see *adjectives*); in a commanding tone; by a stroke (*or* dash) of the pen; by order.

See also AUTHORITY, COMPULSION, DIRECTION, LEGALITY, ORDER, PRECEPT, REQUIREMENT, WORD.—*Antonyms.* See OBEDIENCE, REQUEST, SUBMISSION.

---

commander, *n.* captain, commodore; commandant, chief, chieftain. See MARINER, MASTER.

commemorate, *v.* solemnize, keep, observe. See CELEBRATION, RECORD.

commemoration, *n.* remembrance, memorial, glorification. See REPUTE.

commence, *v.* start, begin, enter upon. See BEGINNING.

commend, *v.* praise, acclaim, recommend, approve. See APPROBATION.

comment, *n.* annotation, observation, remark, criticism. See INTERPRETATION.

commentary, *n.* explanation, criticism, exposition. See DISSERTATION, INTERPRETATION.

commentator, *n.* reviewer, critic, essayist, editor. See DISSERTATION.

commerce, *n.* trading, business, mercantilism. See BARTER.

commercial, *adj.* mercantile, trading, mercatorial (*rare*). See BARTER.

COMMISSION.—I. *Nouns.* **commission,** authorization, warrant, charge, instruction, authority, mandate, trust, brevet; permit, certificate, diploma; delegation; consignment, task, errand, office, assignment; proxy, power of attorney, deputation, legation, mission, embassy; agency.

[*in a bad sense*] committing, doing, perpetration, performance, performing (*as, the* commission *of a crime*).

appointment, nomination, charter; ordination; installation, inauguration, investiture; accession, coronation, enthronement.

percentage, allowance, fee, pay, bonus, rake-off (*slang*), compensation, discount, factorage.

II. *Verbs.* **commission,** delegate, depute; consign, commit, assign, charge, confide to, intrust, authorize, empower, accredit, engage, employ, hire, bespeak, appoint, name, nominate, return; constitute, elect, ordain, install, induct, inaugurate, invest, crown; enroll, enlist; put in commission (*as a ship*).

III. *Adverbs.* instead of, in lieu of, in place of, in one's stead, in one's place, as proxy for, as a substitute for, as an alternative.

See also BUSINESS, DEPUTY, PERMISSION.—*Antonyms.* See ANNULMENT, PROHIBITION.

---

commit, *v.* perform, perpetrate; consign, intrust; take in custody. See ACTION, COMMISSION, LAWSUIT.
commodious, *adj.* roomy; serviceable, convenient, adaptable. See SPACE, USE.
commodity, *n.* article, ware, product. See MERCHANDISE.
common, *adj.* usual, conventional; prevalent, current; customary, regular; vulgar, ill-bred. See CONFORMITY, GENERALITY, HABIT, PEOPLE.
commoner, *n.* plebeian, *bourgeois* (*F.*). See PEOPLE.
commonly, *adv.* generally, usually; equally, in common. See GENERALITY, PARTICIPATION.
commonplace, *adj.* prosy, tedious, monotonous; ordinary, usual. See DULLNESS, HABIT.
commonwealth, *n.* state, government, body politic. See AUTHORITY.
commotion, *n.* turmoil, tumult, disorder, disturbance, turbulence. See AGITATION, EXCITEMENT.
communicate, *v.* impart, make known, tell, transmit. See INFORMATION.
communication, *n.* message, intimation, announcement. See INFORMATION.
communion, *n.* talk, converse, intercourse; partnership, association. See CONVERSATION, PARTICIPATION.
Communion, *n.* Mass, Lord's Supper, Eucharist. See RITE.
communist, *n.* socialist, communalist. See PARTICIPATION.
community, *n.* body, group, neighborhood, district. See PARTY.
communize, *v.* make common, have in common, sovietize. See PARTICIPATION.

COMPACT.—I. *Nouns.* **compact,** contract, deal (*colloq.*), arrangement, understanding, gentlemen's agreement, engagement, bundobast (*Anglo-Indian*), stipulation, settlement, agreement, bargain, pact, bond, covenant, indenture (*law*); compromise, negotiation.
[*in diplomacy*] treaty, convention, league, alliance, *entente* (*F.*), *entente cordiale* (*F.*), agreement (*between nations*); protocol, charter, Magna Charta *or* Magna Carta, concordat, pragmatic sanction; *Zollverein* (*Ger.*), customs union.
ratification, confirmation, sanction, completion, signature, seal, bond.
II. *Verbs.* **negotiate,** treat, stipulate, make terms; bargain, dicker (*U. S.*), contract, covenant, engage, agree; conclude, close, close with, complete, strike a bargain; come to terms (*or* an understanding); compromise, settle, adjust.
ratify, confirm, sanction, authorize, approve, establish, fix, clinch; subscribe, underwrite, indorse; sign, seal.
III. *Adjectives.* **ratified,** confirmed, etc. (see *verbs*); complete, final, agreed; signed, sealed, and delivered.

See also BARTER, COMPROMISE, MEDIATION, PROMISE.—*Antonyms.* See CONTENTION, DISAGREEMENT.

---

compact, *adj.* terse, condensed; constricted, compressed; thick, close. See CONCISENESS, CONTRACTION, DENSITY.
compact, *v.* press together, join, knit, condense, consolidate. See DENSITY.
companion, *n.* associate, partner, colleague, chum. See ACCOMPANIMENT, FRIEND.
company, *n.* association, partnership; group, crowd, party; troop; cast, troupe; corporation, syndicate, firm; companionship. See ACCOMPANIMENT, ASSEMBLAGE, COMBATANT, DRAMA, MERCHANT, SOCIALITY.

COMPARISON.—I. *Nouns.* **comparison,** likening, comparing, collating, collation, parallelism, confrontation, contrast, identification, balance; illustration, likeness, similarity, resemblance, analogy, semblance, simile, similitude.

II. *Verbs.* compare, collate, confront, contrast, balance, parallel, similize (*rare*), liken; match, vie.
III. *Adjectives.* **comparative,** relative, contrastive, collative (*rare*), **parallelistic;** connective, analogous, corresponding; metaphorical.
IV. *Adverbs.* **comparatively,** relatively, as compared with.
See also RELATION.

---

compartment, *n.* inclosure, niche; division, section, part. See PLACE, RECEPTACLE.
compass, *n.* guide; scope, area, extent, range. See DIRECTION, SPACE.
compass, *v.* accomplish, effect, attain; beset, surround, besiege; bound, define, encircle. See COMPLETION, ENVIRONMENT, LIMIT.
compassion, *n.* sympathy, condolence, tenderness, mercy. See PITY.
compatible, *adj.* harmonious, consistent, congruous, suitable. See AGREEMENT.
compatriot, *n.* countryman, fellow countryman. See FRIEND.
compel, *v.* force, oblige, constrain, coerce, impel, drive. See COMPULSION.

COMPENDIUM.—I. *Nouns.* **compendium,** abstract, compend, *précis* (*F.*), epitome, review, bulletin, analysis, digest, brief, condensation, abridgment, abbreviation, recapitulation, *résumé* (*F.*), summary, *multum in parvo* (*L.*), sum, substance, draft, minute, note; excerpt, extract; synopsis, textbook, outline, syllabus, contents, heads, prospectus; conspectus, sketch, *aperçu* (*F.*).
extracts, excerpts, fragments, cuttings, clippings, *excerpta* (*L.*), citations, quotations; collectanea, miscellany, analects *or* analecta, symposium, fugitive pieces, anthology, compilation.
scrapbook, album, commonplace book, notebook, memorandum book.
II. *Verbs.* **abridge,** abstract, epitomize, summarize, digest, condense, compress, contract, curtail, shorten, abbreviate, diminish, lessen.
compile, collect, compose, amass; note down, edit.
recapitulate, review, sum up, summarize, reiterate, restate (*or* repeat) briefly, skim, run over.
III. *Adjectives.* **compendious,** synoptic, abridged, summarized, succinct, condensed, comprehensive, brief, concise, short, *abrégé* (*F.*), summary.
IV. *Adverbs.* **in short,** in brief, briefly, in epitome, in substance, in few words, in a nutshell.

See also ASSEMBLAGE, CONTRACTION, SHORTNESS.—*Antonyms.* See EXPANSION, LENGTH, WORD (*verbosity*).

COMPENSATION.—I. *Nouns.* **compensation,** amends, equivalent, set-off, offset, counterpoise, makeweight, balance, counterbalance, counterclaim, equivalent, *quid pro quo* (*L.*), indemnity, indemnification, satisfaction, equalization, ballast, equation; compromise, measure for measure, retaliation, recoupment.
recompense, repayment, remuneration, pay, payment, requital, reward, honorarium, solatium; bribe, hush money.
II. *Verbs.* **compensate,** offset, equalize, balance, counterpoise, counterbalance, square, make up for, recoup, redeem.
recompense, pay, reward, repay, requite, remunerate, indemnify.
III. *Adjectives.* **compensating,** compensatory, compensative, amendatory, reparative, indemnificatory; equivalent, equal.
IV. *Adverbs.* **notwithstanding,** however, yet, still, nevertheless, for all that, though; howbeit, at all events, at any rate, after all, all the same; on the other hand, at the same time.
V. *Prepositions.* **notwithstanding,** in spite of, despite, with, not the less for, without regard to.

See also COMPROMISE, COUNTERACTION, EQUALITY, RETALIATION, REWARD.—*Antonyms.* See LOSS.

---

compete, *v.* vie, rival, cope with, strive. See CONTENTION, OPPOSITION.
competence, *n.* ability, proficiency, capability; means, income, sufficiency. See SKILL, WEALTH.

competent, *adj.* qualified, able, fit, efficient, capable. See POWER, SUFFICIENCY.
competition, *n.* match, contest, trial; rivalry, emulation. See CONTENTION, OPPOSITION.
competitive, *adj.* emulous, rival, competitory. See OPPOSITION.
competitor, *n.* rival, contestant, entrant; claimant, aspirant. See OPPONENT, PETITIONER.
compile, *v.* amass, collect, arrange; write, make. See COMPENDIUM, COMPOSITION.
complain, *v.* grumble, murmur, bewail, whine, fret. See LAMENTATION.
complaint, *n.* plaint (*law*), charge; ailment, indisposition; lament, grumble. See ACCUSATION, DISEASE, LAMENTATION.

COMPLETENESS.—I. *Nouns.* **completeness,** intactness, plenitude, abundance, copiousness, fullness; fill, saturation, entirety, totality, integrity, wholeness, entireness, all, unity, solidarity; perfection, finish, ripeness, maturity; high tide, flood de, spring tide.
II. *Verbs.* **render complete,** etc. (see *adjectives*); complete, conclude, fulfill, realize, mature, consummate, cap, crown, round out; fill, saturate, charge, load, replenish; make up, eke out, supply deficiencies; fill up, fill in, satiate; go the limit (*colloq.*), go the whole hog (*colloq.*).
III. *Adjectives.* **complete,** entire, whole, all, total, universal, intact, unabridged, perfect, full, plenary, absolute, thorough, exhaustive, radical, sweeping, thoroughgoing; solid, undivided, self-contained.
brimful, brimming, chock-full; saturated, crammed, replete, fraught, laden.
consummate, perfect; regular (*colloq.*), unmitigated, sheer, unqualified, unconditional, free, abundant.
completing, completive, completory; adscititious, additional, supplemental, supplementary.
IV. *Adverbs.* **completely,** altogether, outright, wholly, totally, *in toto* (*L.*), fully, entirely, at all points, utterly, quite; effectually, in all respects, in every respect; out and out, positively; throughout, from first to last, from head to foot, cap-a-pie, from top to toe, every whit, every inch; heart and soul, root and branch; lock, stock, and barrel; bait, hook, and sinker.

See also COMPLETION, DEATH, PERFECTION, SUFFICIENCY.—*Antonyms.* See INCOMPLETENESS.

COMPLETION.—I. *Nouns.* **completion,** accomplishment, attainment, achievement, fulfillment, performance, execution; dispatch, consummation, culmination realization, perfecting, perfection, integration, finish, conclusion, limit, close, *finale* (*It.*), *dénouement* (*F.*), issue, upshot, result; crowning of the edifice, copestone, crown, finishing touch, *fait accompli* (*F.*).
II. *Verbs.* **complete,** perfect, accomplish, effectuate, effect, fulfill, achieve, compass, consummate, bring to maturity (*or* perfection); elaborate, refine, improve, develop.
do, perform, execute, make, work out, enact, dispatch, knock off (*colloq.*), dispose of, discharge, realize; carry out, carry into effect (*or* execution).
do thoroughly, not do by halves, exhaust, drive home; carry through, deliver the goods (*U. S. colloq.*), make good, fill the bill (*colloq.*), win out (*colloq.*).
finish, end, terminate, conclude, close, bring to a close, wind up, clinch, seal, put the last (*or* finishing) touch to; crown, cap, round out, bring to a happy issue.
III. *Adjectives.* **final,** conclusive, ultimate, eventual, concluding, determinate, crowning; exhaustive, complete, thorough, mature, consummate, perfect.
IV. *Adverbs.* **finally,** conclusively, etc. (see *adjectives*); to crown all; out of hand, forthwith.

See also ARRIVAL, COMPLETENESS, END, SUCCESS.—*Antonyms.* See NONCOMPLETION.

---

complex, *adj.* intricate, involved, complicated, confused. See DISORDER.
complexion, *n.* aspect, guise; hue, tinge, tint. See APPEARANCE, COLOR.

complexity, *n.* complication, entanglement, intricacy, perplexity; compositeness. See DISORDER, MIXTURE.
complicate, *v.* involve, tangle, snarl, confuse. See DERANGEMENT.
complicity, *n.* collusion, connivance, conspiracy, confederacy. See COÖPERATION.
complimentary, *adj.* commendatory, flattering. See APPROBATION.
comply, *v.* agree, assent, acquiesce; yield, submit, obey. See CONSENT, OBEDIENCE.

COMPONENT.—I. *Nouns.* **component,** component part, integral part, element, constituent, ingredient, contents; feature; member, subdivision, radicle.
II. *Verbs.* **be a component,** be (*or* form) part of, enter into, interpenetrate, share, merge, participate; belong to, appertain to; combine, unite.
form, make, make up, constitute, compose, compound.
III. *Adjectives.* **inherent,** intrinsic, indwelling, immanent, subsistent, essential, infixed, inwrought, innate, inbred, native, inborn, ingrained.
inclusive (*opposite of* exclusive), including, comprising, comprehensive, extensive, full, broad, wide, encircling, all-embracing, wide-reaching.
See also PART, PARTICIPATION.—*Antonyms.* See EXTRANEOUSNESS, WHOLE.

---

compose, *v.* constitute, make up; construct, form, fashion; calm, assuage; improvise, create; set (type); write. See COMPONENT, COMPOSITION, INEXCITABILITY, MUSICIAN, PRINTING, WRITING.
composed, *adj.* calm, serene, unruffled, tranquil, collected. See INEXCITABILITY.

COMPOSITION.—I. *Nouns.* **composition,** constitution, formation, compounding, structure, texture, nature, construction, make, make-up; combination, adjustment, conjunction, **synthesis** (*tech.*); blending, mixture, mass, aggregate, compound, composite.
[*in writing or music*] **production,** inditement (*rare*), writing, invention, imagination, literary (*or* musical) effort, opus, work, compilation; art (*or* act) of composing; art (*or* practice) of writing, authorship, pencraft.
[*in art*] arrangement, harmony, symmetry, balance; painting, design, etching, relief, sculpture.
typesetting, typography.
agreement, arrangement, compromise, settlement (*as, to make a* composition *with creditors*).
II. *Verbs.* **be composed of,** be made of, be formed of, consist of.
include, contain, comprise, embrace, embody, incorporate, hold, comprehend, admit, implicate, involve.
compose, constitute, form, make, fabricate, weave, construct; compile, scribble, draw, write.
See also COMBINATION, COMPROMISE, FINE ARTS, INEXCITABILITY (*compose*), MUSIC, PRINTING, STYLE, WRITING.—*Antonyms.* See DECOMPOSITION, EXCLUSION.

---

composure, *n.* calmness, placidity, serenity. See INEXCITABILITY, REPOSE.
compound, *v.* join, mix, unite, fuse, amalgamate. See COMBINATION.
comprehend, *v.* comprise, contain; grasp, conceive, understand. See INCLUSION, KNOWLEDGE.
comprehensive, *adj.* full, extensive, inclusive, synoptic; sweeping, widespread, wholesale. See COMPONENT, GENERALITY.
compress, *v.* reduce, abridge, condense; thicken, squeeze, compact. See CONTRACTION, DENSITY.
compression, *n,* condensation, compactness, abridgment. See CONTRACTION.
comprise, *v.* contain, embrace, comprehend, embody, cover. See INCLUSION, NUMBER.

COMPROMISE.—I. *Nouns.* **compromise,** adjustment, settlement, arrangement, mutual concession, agreement, composition, compensation, middle term (*logic*).
II. *Verbs.* **compromise,** commute, compound, split the difference, meet one halfway, give and take, come to terms, submit to arbitration, patch up, bridge over, arrange, straighten out, adjust, agree, settle; make the best of, make a virtue of necessity, take the will for the deed.
endanger, imperil, jeopardize, jeopard, hazard, put in jeopardy, bring under suspicion.

See also MID-COURSE.

COMPULSION.—I. *Nouns.* **compulsion,** coercion, pressure, constraint, necessity, *force majeure* (*F.*), Hobson's choice, necessitation, obligation; enforcement, draft, conscription; eminent domain.
force, brute (main, *or* physical) force; the sword, *ultima ratio* (*L.*); lynch law, mob law; martial law.
II. *Verbs.* **compel,** force, make, drive, impel, press, dragoon, coerce, constrain, enforce, necessitate, oblige; overpower, subjugate, restrain.
extort, exact, wrest, screw, squeeze, wring from, force upon, drag into; bind, pin down, insist upon, require; tax, put in force, take by force, commandeer, draft *or* draught, conscript, press, impress.
III. *Adjectives.* **compulsory,** obligatory, enforced, imperative, binding, peremptory, stringent, necessitative, impelling, compelling, compulsive, coercive, inexorable, unavoidable.
IV. *Adverbs.* **compulsorily,** forcibly, by force, by force of arms; on compulsion, perforce, necessarily, under protest, in spite of, in one's teeth; against one's will. *nolens volens* (*L.*), willy-nilly.

See also NECESSITY, RESTRAINT.—*Antonyms.* See OFFER, WILLINGNESS.

---

compute, *v.* calculate, reckon, count, estimate. See FIGURE, NUMERATION.
comrade, *n.* companion, associate, mate. See FRIEND.

CONCAVITY.—I. *Nouns.* **concavity,** depression, dip, hollow, hollowness, pocket, air pocket (*aëro.*), indentation, intaglio, dent, dint, dimple; sinus, cavity, antrum; follicle (*anat.*), crypt (*anat.*); honeycomb.
excavation, hole, pit, cutting, trough, furrow, ditch, drift, stope, sap, mine, shaft, quarry.
cup, basin, bowl, crater; cell, socket.
valley, vale (*poetic*), dale, dell, dingle, glen, coomb *or* combe, nullah (*Anglo-Indian*), gully, ravine, gorge, donga (*South Africa*), coulee, *coulée* (*F.*), *couloir* (*F.; as in the Swiss Alps*), bottom, intervale, strath (*Scot.*), gill *or* ghyll (*Scot. and dial. Eng.*).
cave, cavern, cove; grot (*poetic*), grotto; hole, burrow, tunnel, kennel.
excavator, sapper, miner, driller; steam shovel, dredger, dredging machine.
II. *Verbs.* **concave,** hollow, hollow out, excavate, scoop, scoop out, gouge, dig, delve (*archaic*), mine, sap, drive, sink, burrow, tunnel, undermine; dent, depress, indent, pit, dint, perforate.
III. *Adjectives.* **concave,** hollow, depressed, sunken, retreating, cavernous; arched, vaulted; funnel-shaped, infundibular *or* infundibulate (*tech.*); bell-shaped, campaniform.
cellular, loculate (*tech.*), loculose (*rare*), locular (*tech.*), favose, honeycombed, faveolate, alveolate *or* alveolated, holey, vuggy (*mining*); porous, spongy, spongiose *or* spongious, spongiform; cytoid (*tech.*), cell-like.
cup-shaped, calathiform, cyathiform, poculiform, cupped, cupular, cupulate, cotyloid (*tech.*), cotyliform (*zoöl.*).
pitted, foveate, foveolate (*bot. and zoöl.*), cuppy, punctate; pock-marked, variolous (*med.*), variolate (*med.*).

See also FURROW, INTERVAL.—*Antonyms.* See CONVEXITY.

CONCEALMENT.—I. *Nouns.* **concealment,** concealing, hiding, etc. (see *verbs*); secretion, latency; cover, disguise, masquerade, mask, camouflage, screen, smoke screen (*mil.*), cloak, veil, shroud, shelter; secrecy, privacy, secretness; ambush, ambuscade, hiding place, blind baggage (*slang*); stowaway.

reticence, reticency, taciturnity, secretiveness, closeness, silence, mystery, mystification, reserve, reservation; mental reservation, aside; suppression, evasion, white lie.
cipher, cryptogram, cryptograph, code; sympathetic ink.
stealth, stealthiness, furtiveness, slyness, caution, cunning.
masquerader, masker, mask, domino, mummer, mime, guiser (*Scot. and Eng. dial.*); incognito (*fem.* incognita).
[*in anatomy*] **secreting organ,** secretory, secretive gland, gland, gland cell, glandular organ, endocrine organ; parotid, salivary gland; thyroid, thyroid gland (*or* body), thymus gland (*called* sweetbread *in a lamb or calf*); pituitary body, sweat gland, adrenal *or* suprarenal, adrenal gland (body, *or* capsule), kidney, liver.
II. *Verbs.* **conceal,** hide, secrete; lock up; cover, screen, cloak, veil, mask, camouflage, disguise, ensconce, shelter, shroud, curtain; bury, sink, suppress, dissmeble; keep from, keep to oneself, keep secret, keep in the background; stifle, hush up, withhold, reserve, retain.
hoodwink, blind, blindfold; mystify, puzzle, perplex, nonplus, hoax, bamboozle (*colloq.*), deceive.
be concealed, hide oneself, couch; lie in ambush, lurk, sneak, skulk, slink, prowl; gumshoe (*U. S. slang*), shadow.
III. *Adjectives.* **concealed,** hidden, perdu (*fem.* perdue), secret, private, privy, *in petto* (*It.*), clandestine; recondite, mystic, mystical, esoteric, cabalistic, occult, dark, cryptic; in secret, tortuous; close, inviolate, confidential, behind a screen, under cover, in ambush, in hiding, in disguise, in a fog, in a haze, in a mist, in a cloud; undisclosed, untold, covert, latent; buried, cached, underground, mysterious.
furtive, stealthy, skulking, surreptitious, underhand, sly, cunning, evasive; secretive, clandestine; reserved, reticent, uncommunicative, close, taciturn.
[*in anatomy*] **secretory,** secreting, secretive; glandular, glandulous.
IV. *Adverbs.* **concealedly,** secretly, privately, in secret, in private; incognito.
behind closed doors, under the rose, *sub rosa* (*L.*); on the sly (*colloq.*); in a whisper, *sotto voce* (*It.*).
confidentially, between ourselves, between you and me, *entre nous* (*F.*), in strict confidence.
underhand, underhandedly, by stealth, like a thief in the night; stealthily, surreptitiously, slyly; unfairly.

See also AMBUSH, CUNNING, LATENCY, SECLUSION.—*Antonyms.* See DISCLOSURE, INFORMATION.

---

concede, *v.* yield, assent, accede; grant, acknowledge, confess; cede, surrender. See CONSENT, DISCLOSURE, GIVING.
conceit, *n.* pride, egoism, self-esteem; epigram, quip, whim, fancy. See VANITY, WIT.
conceited, *adj.* vain, puffed up, opinionated, egotistic, boastful. See VANITY.
conceive, *v.* fancy, devise, visualize, image; grasp, realize, comprehend; form, produce, become pregnant; experience. See IMAGINATION, KNOWLEDGE, PRODUCTION, TAKING (*feel*).
concentrate, *v.* collect, gather; converge, center; fix, focus. See ASSEMBLAGE, CENTRALITY.
concern, *v.* regard, relate to, pertain to, bear upon, refer to. See TOUCH.
concern, *n.* affair, matter; solicitude, regard, anxiety; import, significance; firm, house, company. See BUSINESS, CARE, IMPORTANCE, MERCHANT.
concerning, *prep.* respecting, regarding, pertaining to. See RELATION.
concert, *n.* harmony, accord; recital, musicale. See AGREEMENT, MUSIC.
concession, *n.* admission, acknowledgment, permission; reduction, allowance; grant, gift. See CONSENT, DISCOUNT, GIVING.
conciliate, *v.* reconcile, disarm, satisfy; placate, propitiate, mollify, appease. See [2]CONTENT, FORGIVENESS, PACIFICATION.
conciliation, *n.* appeasement, reconciliation. See FORGIVENESS.

CONCISENESS.—I. *Nouns.* **conciseness,** brevity, terseness, succinctness, laconicism, abridgment, compression, condensation, epitome; portmanteau word (*as Lewis Carroll's* brunch, *from* breakfast *and* lunch; slithy *from* lithe *and* slimy).
II. *Verbs.* **be concise,** compress, condense, abridge, abbreviate, telescope, abstract; come to the point.
III. *Adjectives.* **concise,** brief, commatic (*as sentences*), short, laconic, succinct, curt, terse, to the point, compact, comprehensive, summary, compendious, compressed, condensed, pointed; pithy, neat, pregnant, crisp, trenchant, sententious, epigrammatic.
IV. *Adverbs.* **concisely,** briefly, etc. (see *adjectives*); summarily; in brief, in short, in a word.

See also COMPENDIUM, SHORTNESS, TACITURNITY.—*Antonyms.* See DIFFUSENESS.

---

conclude, *v.* settle, arrange; finish, terminate, end; infer, deduce; resolve, decide. See COMPACT, COMPLETION, JUDGE, RESOLUTION.
conclusive, *adj.* convincing, unanswerable, indisputable; final, ultimate, concluding. See CERTAINTY, COMPLETION.
concoct, *v.* invent, contrive, hatch; cook, make. See PLAN, PREPARATION.

CONCORD.—I. *Nouns.* **concord,** agreement, accord, symphony, harmony consonance, unison, homology (*tech.*), correspondence, congruence, sympathy response; union, unity, peace, unanimity; amity, friendship, alliance, *entente cordiale* (*F.*), good understanding, conciliation, mediation, arbitration, reunion; happy family.
peacemaker, intercessor, interceder, mediator, pacificator.
II. *Verbs.* **agree,** accord, harmonize with, fraternize, go hand in hand, run parallel, concur, coöperate, pull together, sing in chorus; match, coincide, correspond.
side with, sympathize with; go with, chime in with, fall in with; assent, reciprocate.
mediate, intercede, intervene, interpose, appease, mollify, pacify, placate, conciliate, smooth, pour oil on the troubled waters, keep in good humor, meet half way.
III. *Adjectives.* **concordant,** agreeing, agreeable, undiscordant, consonant, sympathetic, congenial, in accord, harmonious, united, cemented, allied, kindred friendly, fraternal, conciliatory, of one mind, unanimous, solid (*political cant*), individual.
IV. *Adverbs.* **concordantly,** unitedly, unanimously, as one man, consentiently, nem. con. (*L., nemine contradicente*), *una voce* (*L.*), with one voice, with one accord; in concert with, hand in hand.

See also AGREEMENT, ASSENT, FRIENDSHIP, HARMONY, PEACE, UNITY.—*Antonyms.* See DISCORD.

---

concrete, *adj.* hard, solid, substantial; definite, exact, specific. See DENSITY, TRUTH.

CONCURRENCE.—I. *Nouns.* **concurrence,** agreement, accord, consent, assent, correspondence, uniformity, coöperation, collaboration; conformity, coincidence, concourse, conflux, confluence, conjunction, junction, union, partnership, alliance; complicity, connivance, collusion.
II. *Verbs.* **concur,** coincide, correspond, accord, join, unite, combine, agree, harmonize; acquiesce, approve, consent, assent, coöperate, conduce, conspire, contribute; hang (*or* pull) together, keep pace with, run parallel.
III. *Adjectives.* **concurrent,** conjoined, associate, joint, concomitant, united, coincident, correspondent, accompanying, meeting, conformable, confluent, concordant, harmonious, coöperating, coöperative, in alliance with, of one mind at one with.

See also AGREEMENT, ASSENT, COÖPERATION, HARMONY.—*Antonyms.* See COUNTERACTION, OPPOSITION.

CONDEMNATION.—I. *Nouns.* **condemnation,** censure, blame, disapprobation, execration, reprobation, disapproval, stricture, ban.
[*judicial*] conviction, judgment, sentence, penalty; death warrant, death penalty.
II. *Verbs.* **condemn,** censure, blame, reprehend, reprove, denounce, disapprove, discountenance, upbraid, reproach, rebuke.
[*to condemn judicially*] **convict,** find guilty, doom, damn (*archaic*), adjudge, sentence, pass sentence on; confiscate, sequestrate, sequester.
proscribe, interdict, disapprove, prohibit, veto, ban, outlaw.
III. *Adjectives.* **condemnatory,** denunciatory, damnatory, threatening, minatory.
See also ACCUSATION, DISAPPROBATION.—*Antonyms.* See ACQUITTAL, APPROBATION.

---

condensation, *n.* coagulation, thickening, solidification, abridgment, curtailment. See DENSITY, SHORTNESS.
condescend, *v.* deign, descend, stoop, vouchsafe. See HUMILITY.

CONDIMENT.—*Nouns.* **condiment,** flavoring, seasoning, sauce, spice, relish. curry, pickle, chutney; appetizer; salt, pepper, mustard, horse radish, allspice, etc.
See also PUNGENCY.

---

condition, *n.* fitness; modification, stipulation, proviso; rank, birth; situation, plight; assumption, postulate. See FORM, QUALIFICATION, REPUTE, STATE, SUPPOSITION.

CONDITIONS.—I. *Nouns.* **conditions,** terms, articles, propositions, articles of agreement; clauses, memoranda, provisions, requisites, provisos, postulates. prerequisites, stipulations, obligations, *sine qua non* (*L.*), covenant.
II. *Verbs.* **condition,** stipulate, provide, insist upon, make a point of; bind, tie up; fence in, hem in, hedge in, make (*or* come to) terms.
III. *Adjectives.* **conditional,** provisional, provisory, provisionary, conditioned, subject, dependent, contingent, limited, restricted; guarded, fenced, hedged in.
IV. *Adverbs.* **conditionally,** provisionally, *pro re nata* (*L.*); on condition, with a string to it (*colloq.*), limitedly, with a limitation (*or* reservation).
See also CIRCUMSTANCE, COMPACT, QUALIFICATION, SUBJECTION.

CONDOLENCE.—I. *Nouns.* **condolence,** sympathy, pity, commiseration, compassion, consolation, comfort, solace.
II. *Verbs.* **condole with,** console, solace, comfort, soothe, sympathize, express pity; afford consolation; lament with, express sympathy for, commiserate, compassionate, pity, grieve with, feel for, send one's condolences, express one's sorrow, share another's sorrow.
See also PITY.

---

conduce, *v.* contribute, lead, advance. See TENDENCY.

CONDUCT.—I. *Nouns.* **conduct,** behavior, deportment, carriage, comportment, address, demeanor, guise, bearing, manner, *prestance* (*F.*), presence; course of conduct, line of action; rôle; process, ways, practice, execution, procedure, method, proceeding, treating, dealing, transaction, business.
policy, management, guidance, administration, regimen, régime, government; tactics, strategy, generalship, leadership, statesmanship, plan, game; stewardship, husbandry, ménage, housekeeping, economy, organization.
worldly wisdom, knowingness, sagacity, shrewdness, ingenuity, expediency, advisability.
career, course, walk, province, race, campaign, record, life, manner of life, course (*or* line) of conduct.
II. *Verbs.* **conduct,** direct, manage, operate, work, keep, guide, govern, rule. regulate, superintend, supervise, execute, perform, do, transact, administer, carry on (out, through, *or* into effect), dispatch, proceed with, discharge, work out, go through, get through, enact, negotiate, deal.

adopt a course, shape one's course, play one's part; shift for oneself, paddle one's own canoe.
behave, act, conduct (acquit, carry, comport, bear, *or* demean) oneself.
guide, escort, conduct, lead, attend, accompany.
III. *Adjectives*. **conducting**, conductory (*rare*), directive, executive, managerial, administrative, gubernatorial, governmental; businesslike, methodical, practical, economic, strategic *or* strategical.
See also ACTION, DIRECTION, MUSICIAN.

---

conductor, *n*. guard; manager, supervisor; leader, choirmaster, drum major. See CARRIER, DIRECTOR, MUSICIAN.
cone-shaped, *adj*. conical, conic, pyramidal. See SHARPNESS.
confederacy, *n*. league, alliance, federation, union. See COMBINATION, PARTY.
confederate, *n*. companion, associate, ally, accomplice. See AUXILIARY.
confer, *v*. consult, deliberate; discuss, converse; bestow, grant. See ADVICE, CONVERSATION, GIVING.
conference, *n*. consultation, parley, interview; meeting. See ADVICE, CONVERSATION, COUNCIL.
confess, *v*. divulge, reveal; admit, own, acknowledge. See DISCLOSURE, PENITENCE.
confidant, *n*. confidante (*fem.*), intimate, bosom friend. See FRIEND.
confide in, trust, rely upon, believe in. See BELIEF.—**confide to**, intrust, commit; divulge, tell. See COMMISSION, DISCLOSURE, INFORMATION.
confidence, *n*. credit, certainty; self-reliance,boldness, spirit; trust, reliance, faith; assurance; cocksureness. See BELIEF, COURAGE, HOPE, SECURITY.
confident, *adj*. hopeful, expectant, optimistic; certain, sure, positive, assured, self-sufficient. See HOPE, SECURITY.
confidentially, *adv*. in strict confidence, *entre nous* (*F.*). See CONCEALMENT.
confiding, *adj*. open, candid, naïve; unsuspecting, gullible. See ARTLESSNESS, BELIEF.
confine, *v*. limit, bound; cage, imprison. See CIRCUMSCRIPTION, RESTRAINT.
confinement, *n*. childbirth; detention, imprisonment, bondage, servitude. See PAIN (*childbirth*), RESTRAINT.
confirm, *v*. indorse, approve; corroborate, substantiate, uphold. See ASSENT, EVIDENCE.
confirmation, *n*. ratification, corroboration, verification, evidence; Christian ceremony. See ASSENT, RITE.
confiscate, *v*. sequester, sequestrate; take, seize, appropriate. See CONDEMNATION, TAKING.
conflict, *n*. encounter, battle, combat; discord, dissension, antagonism. See CONTENTION, DISAGREEMENT, OPPOSITION.

CONFORMITY.—I. *Nouns*. **conformity**, correspondence, agreement, accord, harmony, resemblance, likeness, congruity; observance, compliance, acquiescence, assent, submission, consent, obedience, concession, performance; conventionality.
example, instance, exemplification, exemplar, representative; illustration, specimen, sample.
conventionalist, formalist, methodologist, precisian, pedant, Philistine.
II. *Verbs*. **conform to**, adapt oneself to, harmonize, fit, suit, agree with, comply with, fall in with, be guided by, obey rules, adapt to, adjust to, reconcile.
conventionalize, be regular, travel in a rut, follow the fashion; do at Rome as the Romans do; swim with the stream.
exemplify, illustrate, elucidate, explain, instance, cite, quote.
III. *Adjectives*. **conformable**, adaptable, tractable, compliant, agreeable, obedient; regular, according to rule, well regulated, orderly, uniform, symmetric.
[*usually with* to] similar, like, adapted, proper, suitable; harmonious, consistent.
conventional, customary, traditional, habitual, usual, ordinary, common; cut-and-dried (*colloq.*), formal, stiff, strict, rigid, uncompromising, Procrustean, positive, academic, canonical, orthodox, standard; contractual, stipulated.

typical, normal, exemplary, illustrative, in point, representative, model, ideal; emblematic, prefigurative, figurative, symbolic.
IV. *Adverbs.* **conformably,** by rule; in accordance with, in keeping with; according to; as usual, as a matter of course, invariably.
See also AGREEMENT, HABIT, HARMONY, PROTOTYPE, REGULARITY, RULE.—*Antonyms.* See UNCONFORMITY.

---

confound, *v.* rout, overthrow; confuse, jumble, mix; perplex, bewilder. See CONFUTATION, INDISCRIMINATION, UNCERTAINTY.
confront, *v.* defy, brave, face, front, resist. See OPPOSITION.
confuse, *v.* disturb, misplace, muddle; disconcert, fluster, bewilder; mistake, jumble. See DERANGEMENT, INATTENTION, INDISCRIMINATION.
confusion, *n.* discomfiture, embarrassment, jumble; tumult, turmoil. See DERANGEMENT, DISORDER.

CONFUTATION.—I. *Nouns* **confutation,** refutation, refutal, disproof, disproval, conviction, invalidation; exposure, *exposé* (*F.*), retort, answer, rebutter, rebuttal, clincher (*colloq.*).
II. *Verbs.* **confute,** refute, parry, negative, disprove, expose, show up; rebut, defeat, vanquish, demolish, upset, subvert, overthrow, overturn, set aside, oppugn, get the better of, squelch, disconcert, silence, confound (*archaic*), explode, invalidate, clinch an argument.
III. *Adjectives.* **confutable,** refutable, disprovable, defeasible; "hoist with his own petar" (*Hamlet*).
See also COUNTEREVIDENCE.—*Antonyms.* See DEMONSTRATION, EVIDENCE.

---

congeal, *v.* set, condense, thicken, coagulate, harden, stiffen. See DENSITY.
congenial, *adj.* harmonious, adapted, compatible, sympathetic. See AGREEMENT.

CONGRATULATION.—I. *Nouns.* **congratulation,** felicitation, gratulation (*archaic*), compliment; compliments of the season; good wishes, best wishes.
II. *Verbs.* **congratulate,** felicitate, gratulate (*archaic*), rejoice with, wish one joy, compliment, tender (*or* offer) one's congratulations; wish many happy returns of the day.
[*congratulate oneself*] rejoice, pride oneself, plume oneself, hug oneself, gratulate oneself, flatter oneself.
III. *Adjectives.* **congratulatory,** gratulatory, complimentary; congratulant.
See also COURTESY, REJOICING.—*Antonyms.* See PITY.

---

congregation, *n.* gathering, aggregation; flock, fold, brethren. See ASSEMBLAGE, LAITY.
congress, *n.* legislature, parliament, convention, assembly. See COUNCIL.
conjecture, *n.* guess, speculation, inference, surmise. See SUPPOSITION.
conjugate, *adj.* united, coupled, mated, bijugate (*bot.*); paronymous, related, coderived. See DUALITY, WORD.
connect, *v.* link, unite, attach; associate, correlate. See JUNCTION, RELATION.
connecting, *adj.* joining, binding, linking; unitive, unifying. See JUNCTION, UNITY (*uniting*).
connection, *n.* consistency, congruity, harmony; relevancy, correlation, applicability, relationship, consanguinity; bearing, reference. See COHERENCE, RELATION, RESPECT.
connivance, *n.* complicity, collusion; allowance, sufferance, toleration. See COÖPERATION, PERMISSION.
connoisseur, *n.* expert, adept, critic. See JUDGE, TASTE.
conquer, *v.* defeat, vanquish, subdue, overcome, prevail. See SUCCESS.
conqueror, *n.* victor, winner, vanquisher. See MASTER.

CONSANGUINITY.—I. *Nouns.* **consanguinity,** relationship, kinship, kindred, sib (*rare or dial.*); blood; parentage, paternity; connection, propinquity, alliance, affiliation, filiation; ties of blood, affinity.

kinsman, kinswoman (*fem.*), relative, relation, blood relation, connection, next of kin, near relation, distant relation; kinsfolk, kith and kin; father, mother, brother, *frater* (*L.*), sister, uncle, aunt, etc.; affine (*relation by marriage*).

family, kin, lineage, line, house; fraternity, brotherhood, sisterhood; household.

race, stock, strain, breed; issue, offspring, progeny, stirps; clan, tribe, generation.

II. *Verbs.* **be related to,** be akin to, claim kinship with.

III. *Adjectives.* **consanguineous,** related, kindred, akin, allied, agnate (*on the father's side*), cognate (*on the mother's side*), affiliated, sib (*rare or dial.*).

See also PATERNITY.

---

conscientious, *adj.* scrupulous, exact, painstaking; faithful, trusty, upright. See CARE, PROBITY.

conscious, *adj.* keen, understanding; aware, sensible, cognizant. See INTELLECT, KNOWLEDGE.

conscription, *n.* compulsory enlistment, draft, impressment. See COMPULSION.

consecrate, *v.* dedicate, devote, hallow. See PIETY.

consecutive, *adj.* successive, following. See CONTINUITY.

CONSENT.—I. *Nouns.* **consent,** acquiescence, approval, compliance, assent, concurrence, promise; agreement, concession, permission, permit, accession, acknowledgment, acceptance.

settlement, adjustment, arrangement, ratification, confirmation.

II. *Verbs.* **consent,** acquiesce, accede, comply, comply with, yield, concur, assent, accept, yield assent, admit, allow, concede, grant, acknowledge, give consent, agree to, close with, satisfy, settle, come to terms; deign, vouchsafe, promise.

III. *Adjectives.* **consenting,** acquiescing, etc. (see *verbs*); assentive, acquiescent, willing, compliant, agreeable (*colloq.*).

See also AGREEMENT, ASSENT, PROMISE, WILLINGNESS.—*Antonyms.* See DISSENT, REFUSAL.

---

consequence, *n.* result, outcome, termination, proceeding; decision, settlement; moment, prominence, mark, self-importance, self-consequence. See EFFECT, END, EVENT, IMPORTANCE.

consequential, *adj.* deducible, derivable, inferable, sequential; secondary, resultant, indirect; self-important, supercilious, pompous. See DEMONSTRATION, EFFECT, PRIDE.

consequently, *adv.* accordingly, therefore. See CIRCUMSTANCE, EFFECT.

conservation, *n.* maintenance, keeping. See PRESERVATION.

conservative, *adj.* stable, unprogressive, unchanging. See PERMANENCE.

conserve, *v.* preserve, keep, store. See PROVISION.

consider, *v.* heed, regard, notice; believe, think, adjudge; reflect, deliberate, ponder. See ATTENTION, JUDGE, THOUGHT.

considerable, *adj.* intense, extraordinary; notable, weighty; big, massive; sizable, substantial. See GREATNESS, IMPORTANCE, SIZE, SUBSTANTIALITY.

considerate, *adj.* solicitous, thoughtful, kind. See THOUGHT.

consideration, *n.* notice, observation; kindliness, regard; consequence, moment; reason, inducement; deference, esteem; gratuity, fee, perquisite; deliberation, reflection. See ATTENTION, BENEVOLENCE, IMPORTANCE, MOTIVE, RESPECT, REWARD, THOUGHT.—**under consideration,** in the mind, under advisement. See TOPIC.

consign, *v.* commit, assign, delegate, authorize; send, deliver, ship, dispatch. See COMMISSION, TRANSFER.

consignment, *n.* allotment, assignment; task, charge. See APPORTIONMENT, COMMISSION.

consistent, *adj.* accordant, compatible, harmonious, conformable; homogeneous, regular. See AGREEMENT, UNIFORMITY.
consist in, inhere in, lie in, be comprised in. See EXISTENCE.
consist of, be composed of, comprise, include. See COMPOSITION.
consolation, *n.* solace, comfort, sympathy; assuagement, encouragement. See CONDOLENCE, RELIEF.
consolidate, *v.* merge, federate, incorporate; compress, solidify, compact. See COMBINATION, DENSITY.
consonance, *n.* accordance, accord, concord, tunefulness. See AGREEMENT, HARMONY.
conspicuous, *adj.* famous, renowned, eminent, prominent, notable; obvious, glaring, salient, striking, flagrant. See REPUTE, VISIBILITY.
conspiracy, *n.* intrigue, plot, confederacy. See PLAN.
conspirator, *n.* conspiratress (*fem.*), plotter, complotter, accomplice, confederate, traitor. See KNAVE.
conspire, *v.* concur, combine; scheme, intrigue, plot. See CONCURRENCE PLAN.
constant, *adj.* continual, incessant; unflagging, steadfast; stanch, loyal; unchangeable, permanent; regular, even. See FREQUENCY, PERSEVERANCE, PROBITY, STABILITY, UNIFORMITY.
constitute, *v.* found, set up, establish; appoint, elect; form, frame, make up, compose. See CAUSE, COMMISSION, COMPONENT.
constitution, *n.* make-up, structure, construction; state, condition; code, law, charter; temperament, disposition, nature. See COMPOSITION, HABIT, LEGALITY, SUBJECTIVENESS.
constraint, *n.* coercion, necessity; repression, unnaturalness; confinement. See COMPULSION, RESTRAINT.
constrict, *v.* contract, bind, squeeze, compress. See CONTRACTION.
constriction, *n.* compression, astringency, stricture (*med.*). See CONTRACTION, NARROWNESS.
construction, *n.* formation, build, structure; translation, explanation; erection, creation. See FORM, INTERPRETATION, PRODUCTION.
consult, *v.* confer, discuss, consider. See ADVICE, THOUGHT.
consultation, *n.* conference, interview, deliberation, council. See ADVICE.
consume, *v.* demolish, annihilate, burn; devour, use up; exhaust, drain, expend. See DESTRUCTION, USE, WASTE.
consummate, *adj.* sheer, unmitigated; perfect, finished; profound, intense. See COMPLETENESS, COMPLETION, GREATNESS.
consumption, *n.* phthisis, tuberculosis; destruction, use. See DISEASE, WASTE.

CONTACT.—I. *Nouns.* **contact,** touching, meeting, union, conjunction, adhesion; adjacency, contiguity, contiguousness, proximity (*esp. mil.*), appulse (*tech.*), apposition, abuttal, abutment, juxtaposition; borderland, border, frontier.
II. *Verbs.* **contact,** touch, bring into contact, meet, adhere, attach, append, adjoin, join, abut upon (*or* on), be contiguous, graze, neighbor, border, march with; coincide, coexist.
III. *Adjectives.* **contactual** (*rare*), touching, in contact, contiguous, conterminous, bordering, abutting, adjacent, close, near.
See also COHERENCE, NEARNESS.—*Antonyms.* See DISTANCE, INTERVAL.

---

contagion, *n.* epidemic, pestilence, virus; transmission (*by contact*), communication, transference; poisonousness, toxicity. See DISEASE, TRANSFER, UNHEALTHINESS.
contagious, *adj.* communicable, transmittable, catching, infectious (*fig.*): *a* contagious *disease is one communicable by contact.* Cf. INFECTIOUS. See TRANSFER, UNHEALTHINESS.
contain, *v.* include, comprise, embody, incorporate, hold. See COMPOSITION.
container, *n.* utensil, vessel, vase, jar, bottle, bag, box, etc. See RECEPTACLE.

contaminate, *v.* taint, corrupt, pollute, foul, defile. See DETERIORATION, UNCLEANNESS.
contemplate, *v.* purpose, consider, design, ponder, reflect, muse; view, look on, behold. See INTENTION, THOUGHT, VISION.
contemporary, *adj.* contemporaneous, concomitant, coincident. See SIMULTANEOUSNESS.

CONTEMPT.—I. *Nouns.* **contempt,** disdain, scorn, detestation, abhorrence, despisal (*rare*), disrepute, disfavor, disesteem, contemptuousness, derision, mockery, contumely; slight, sneer, spurn, byword; shame, disgrace, humiliation.
II. *Verbs.* **contemn,** scorn, disdain, abhor, detest, despise, disregard, scout, slight, pass by, turn one's back upon, spurn, ridicule, laugh at, sneer at, look down upon, curl up one's lip, think nothing of, make light of, underestimate, esteem slightly, care nothing for, set no store by; pooh-pooh, deride, "damn with faint praise" (Pope); trample under foot, kick, fling to the winds, repudiate.
III. *Adjectives.* **contemptible,** despicable, despised, pitiable, pitiful, vile, mean, abject, low, base, worthless, trashy, trivial, paltry; corrupt, infamous, dishonest, downtrodden.
contemptuous, disdainful, scornful, withering, contumelious, supercilious, cynical, haughty, arrogant, bumptious, pompous, toplofty (*colloq.*), up-stage, (*colloq.*), cavalier; derisive; with nose in air.
See also CHEAPNESS, DEFIANCE, DISRESPECT, LITTLENESS, YELLOW.—*Antonyms.* See RESPECT.

---

contend, *v.* maintain, hold, allege; strive, struggle; dispute, debate. See AFFIRMATION, CONTENTION, REASONING.

---

[1]CONTENT.—*Nouns.* [*that which is contained*] **content,** meaning, real meaning, significance, intent, implication, connotation, signification, significant part, substance, essence, gist, subject matter (*as of a discourse*).
[*power of containing*] **capacity,** holding-power; burden (*naut.*), volume, extent, space, size.
[*all that is contained*] **contents** (*pl.*), filling, lading, packing, stuffing, inside, furnishing, furniture; cargo, freight, shipment, load, bale, pack (*as, the* contents *of a box or vessel*).
[*matters treated*] **matter,** subject matter, topics, subjects, themes, text (*as, the* contents *of a book*).

[2]CONTENT.—I. *Nouns.* **content,** contentment, contentedness; complacency, satisfaction, ease, peace of mind, serenity, happiness, gladness, cheerfulness; comfort, pleasure, gratification.
patience, fortitude, moderation, endurance, constancy, perseverance, conciliation, reconciliation; resignation, long-suffering, submission.
II. *Verbs.* **be content,** rest satisfied, let well enough alone; take in good part; be reconciled to, take heart, take comfort, put up with.
content, satisfy, appease, gratify, comfort, quiet, set at ease, conciliate, reconcile, win over, propitiate, disarm, beguile.
III. *Adjectives.* **content,** contented, satisfied, well pleased, easy, tranquil, carefree, unconcerned, unworried, untroubled, at ease, at one's ease, easy-going, not particular; conciliatory, unrepining, resigned, cheerful, serene, at rest; snug, comfortable.
willing, assenting, favorable. (*In the British House of Lords,* content *or* not content *is used as the equivalent of* aye *or* no.)
satisfactory, adequate, commensurate, proportionate, sufficient, ample, equal, full; gratifying, satisfying.
See also CHEERFULNESS, PLEASURABLENESS, WILLINGNESS.—*Antonyms.* See DISCONTENT.

CONTENTION.—I. *Nouns.* **contention,** strife, contest, struggle; altercation, quarrel, litigation, feud; controversy, variance, disagreement, dissension; debate, dispute, wrangling, polemics, war of words, paper war, high words; logomachy; belligerency, pugnacity, opposition; vehemence, ardor (*a rare sense*).

competition, rivalry, emulation, game, match, race, handicap, trial; **athletics** athletic sports; games of skill.
conflict, skirmish, encounter, rencounter, rencontre, collision, affair, brush, scrimmage, fracas, *mêlée* (*F.*), battle royal, clash of arms, tussle, scuffle, bout, broil, fray, affray, dog fight (*aviation slang*), fight, battle, combat, action, engagement, justs *or* jousts, tournament, tourney; pitched battle; guerrilla (guerilla, *or* irregular) warfare; death struggle, Armageddon.
[*Rugby football*] scrimmage *or* scrummage, scrum, pack.
duel, single combat, satisfaction, passage of arms, affair of honor; hostile meeting, appeal to arms.
pugilism, boxing, sparring, fisticuffs, bout, event, set-to (*colloq.*), mill (*cant*), round; prize fighting, the ring, the squared circle, cauliflower industry (*jocose*), modified murder (*journalistic cant*).
wrestling, grappling; Greco-Roman, catch-as-catch-can, Lancashire, Cumberland and Westmorland *or* North Country, Cornwall and Devon *or* West Country styles; jujutsu *or* jujitsu, *sumo* (*Jap.*), *kushti* (*Hind.*), glima (*Iceland*).
II. *Verbs.* **contend,** contest, strive, wrangle, oppose, antagonize, struggle, scramble, wrestle, grapple; spar, exchange blows, come to blows, tussle, tilt, box, fence; skirmish, fight, battle, join issue, exchange shots, measure swords, enter the lists, couch one's lance, take up the gauntlet.
compete (cope, vie, *or* race) with, emulate, rival; run a race.
III. *Adjectives.* **contentious,** quarrelsome, pugnacious, dissentious, litigious, wrangling, perverse, disputatious, combative, bellicose, belligerent, warlike.
athletic, gymnastic, acrobatic, agonistic *or* agonistical, palæstral *or* palestral (rare); competitive, competitory, rival.
See also COMBATANT, DISCORD, OPPOSITION, WARFARE.—*Antonyms.* See CONCORD, PEACE.

---

contents, *n.* ingredients, constituents; filling, cargo; text, matter. See COMPONENT, [1]CONTENT.
contest, *n.* struggle, opposition, race, strife, conflict. See CONTENTION.
contiguity, *n.* nearness, adjacency, union, meeting. See CONTACT.
contingency, *n.* likelihood, prospect; situation, case, predicament. See CHANCE, CIRCUMSTANCE, POSSIBILITY.
contingent, *adj.* casual, incidental, accidental, conditional, provisional. See CHANCE, LIABILITY.
continual, *adj.* repeated, incessant; constant, unceasing. See FREQUENCY, PERPETUITY.

CONTINUANCE.—I. *Nouns.* **continuance,** continuation; pursuance, maintenance, extension, permanence, stay, duration, perpetuation, prolongation; persistence, perseverance; repetition.
II. *Verbs.* **continue,** persist, go on, keep on, hold on, abide, stay, remain; pursue, stick to; maintain its course; drag on, stick (*colloq.*), persevere, endure, carry on, keep up, keep the field.
sustain, uphold, support, bear up, hold up, follow up, perpetuate, prolong, protract, maintain; preserve.
III. *Adjectives.* **continuing,** uninterrupted, unvarying, persistent, enduring, unceasing, unvaried, sustained, chronic; undying, deathless, immortal, perpetual, endless.
See also PERMANENCE, PERSEVERANCE, TIME.—*Antonyms.* See CESSATION.

---

continuation, *n.* extension, prolongation; addition, supplement, installment; succession, line. See CONTINUANCE, SEQUEL, SEQUENCE.

CONTINUITY.—I. *Nouns.* **continuity,** continuousness, succession, sequence, unbrokenness, round, suite, progression, series, train, catena, chain; scale; gradation, course; perpetuity, constancy; continuum (*pl.* continua: *math.*).
procession, *cortège* (*F.*), cavalcade, parade; column (*mil.*), train, retinue.
pedigree, descent, ancestry, genealogy, lineage, race, history, family tree, family house, line, strain, birth.
rank, file, line, row, series, chain, string, queue, range, tier.

II. *Verbs.* **arrange in continuity,** file, list, enter, record, arrange, tabulate, string, thread, inventory, catalogue.
III. *Adjectives.* **continuous,** continued; consecutive, progressive, gradual, serial, successive; uninterrupted, endless, unbroken, entire; linear; perennial, constant, incessant.
IV. *Adverbs* **continuously,** in a line, in succession, in a series, *seriatim* (*L.*), serially, in turn, running, gradually, step by step, gradation, in file, in single file, in Indian file.
Antonyms. See DISCONTINUITY.

---

contortion, *n* twist, deformation, grimace. See DISTORTION.
contour, *n.* shape, form, outline, figure. See APPEARANCE.
contraband, *adj.* illicit, forbidden, illegal, smuggled. See PROHIBITION.
contract, *n.* agreement, bargain, arrangement, covenant. See COMPACT.

CONTRACTION.—I. *Nouns.* **contraction,** reduction, diminution, decrease, lessening, shrinking, coalescence (*philol.*), constriction; atrophy, emaciation, attenuation.
compression, condensation, contractility, compressibility, compactness; compendium, abstract, epitome; strangulation (*med.*), stricture (*med.*), contracture (*med. and arch.*), astringency.
II. *Verbs.* **contract,** decrease, lessen, grow less, dwindle, narrow; wrinkle, knit; shrivel, shrink, collapse, wither, sear; decline, abate, subside, fall off, fall away, waste, wane, ebb.
diminish, reduce, curtail, dwarf, shorten, epitomize, abridge, condense, boil down, compress; constrict, squeeze, crush, pinch, strangle, tighten, cramp; deflate, exhaust, empty.
circumscribe, limit, bound, restrict, restrain, confine, inclose.
incur, bring on (*or* upon), fall into, expose oneself to, lie under, be liable, acquire, enter into; form, develop, beget, engender; assume, acquire.
covenant, bargain, undertake, agree, stipulate; affiance, betroth.
pare, cut off (*or* away), shave, skive (*as a hide*), shear, slice, chip, scrape, rub down, file, grind.
III. *Adjectives.* **contracted,** shrunk, shrunken, wizened, tabetic (*med.*); stunted, waning, compact, shortened, constricted; wrinkled, wrinkly, strangulated.
contractile, contractive, astringent, binding, constrictive, constringent, compressive, marcescent (*bot.*).
See also DECREASE, FORM, SHORTNESS.—*Antonyms.* See EXPANSION.

---

contractor, *n.* builder, architect, constructor, *padrone* (*It.*). See AGENT.
contradict, *v.* dissent, deny, gainsay; refute, disprove, overthrow. See CONTRARIETY, COUNTEREVIDENCE.
contradictory, *adj.* conflicting, refutatory, contrary. See COUNTEREVIDENCE

CONTRARIETY.—I. *Nouns.* **contrariety,** opposition, oppositeness, antagonism, repugnance, clashing, disagreement, antipathy; discrepancy, inconsistency; contrast, foil, set-off, antithesis; counterpart, complement.
inversion, subversion, reversal, antistrophe, the opposite, the reverse, the inverse, the converse, antipodes, the other extreme.
antonym, opposite, counterterm, *antonyme* (*F.*) : *opposite of* synonym.
II. *Verbs.* **be contrary,** contrast with, differ from, contradict, gainsay, impugn, contravene, thwart, oppose, antagonize.
invert, reverse, turn topsy-turvy, turn upside down, transpose; pervert.
III. *Adjectives.* **contrary,** opposite, counter, adverse, averse, converse, reverse; opposed, antithetical, contrasted, antipodean, diametrically opposite; antagonistic, conflicting, inconsistent, contradictory, contradictive, negatory, at cross purposes; perverse, self-willed, wayward, froward, cross-grained, untoward (*as, a* contrary *child*).
[*of the wind or weather*] **unfavorable,** ill, inclement, foul, inauspicious, prejudicial.
See also CAPRICE, INVERSION, OPPOSITION.—*Antonyms.* See AGREEMENT, IDENTITY.

contrariwise, *adj.* conversely, on the contrary. See COUNTEREVIDENCE.
contrary, *adj.* opposite, opposed, adverse, perverse; antagonistic, hostile. See CONTRARIETY, OPPOSITION.
contrast, *n.* foil, antithesis; dissimilarity, unlikeness, disparity, opposition. See CONTRARIETY, DIFFERENCE.
contribute, *v.* advance, conduce, tend; subscribe, donate. See CAUSE, GIVING.
contributor, *n.* correspondent, columnist, reviewer; donor, subscriber. See BOOK, GIVING.
contrivance, *n.* apparatus, gear, device; scheme, trick, stratagem. See INSTRUMENT, PLAN.
control, *v.* direct, master, dominate, subdue, restrain. See INFLUENCE.
control, *n.* power, sway, dominion, direction, regulation. See COMMAND.
controversy, *n.* argument, dispute, debate, quarrel, altercation. See CONTENTION.
controvert, *v.* deny, oppose; dispute, contradict, counter. See DEFENSE, NEGATION.
conundrum, *n.* enigma, puzzle, riddle. See EQUIVOCALNESS, SECRET.
convalesce, *v.* recover, improve, rally, revive. See HEALTH.
convene, *v.* meet, assemble, collect; convoke. See ASSEMBLAGE.
convenience, *n.* opportunity, accommodation, ease; suitability, adaptability. See LEISURE, USE.
convenient, *adj.* suitable, serviceable, opportune, advantageous, adaptable. See EXPEDIENCE.
convent, *n.* cloister, nunnery, abbey. See TEMPLE.
convention, *n.* meeting, caucus, council, assembly; propriety, conventionality; usage, custom, practice. See ASSEMBLAGE, FASHION, RULE.
conventional, *adj.* customary, habitual, usual; formal. See CONFORMITY.
conventionalist, *n.* formalist, methodologist, precisian. See CONFORMITY.
conventionality, *n.* compliance, adherence; formality, convention. See CONFORMITY, FASHION.

CONVERGENCE.—I. *Nouns.* **convergence** *or* convergency, conflux, confluence, concourse, concurrence, concentration, focalization; assemblage, meeting.
II. *Verbs.* **converge,** concur; come together, unite, meet, close in upon; center *or* centre, focalize, focus, concentrate, enter in, pour in, assemble, rally.
III. *Adjectives.* **convergent,** converging, confluent, concurrent; centripetal.
See also ASSEMBLAGE, FOCUS.—*Antonyms.* See DISPERSION, DIVERGENCE.

CONVERSATION.—I. *Nouns.* **conversation,** colloquy, converse, speech, talk discourse, intercourse, communion, interlocution (*rare*), commerce, familiarity; chat, gossip, chit-chat, tattle, tittle-tattle, babble; dialogue, duologue.
conference, parley, consultation, discussion, *tête-à-tête* (*F.*), interview, audience, reception, *conversazione* (*It.*), powwow (*U. S.*), palaver; debate, controversy, war of words, logomachy, paper warfare, *guerre de plume* (*F.*), newspaper war.
talker, speaker, conversationalist, converser, conversationist; orator, lecturer, elocutionist; spouter (*colloq.*), speechifier (*derisive*), blatherskite (*dial.*), gasbag (*slang*), windbag (*slang*); gossip, chatterer, magpie, tattler; interlocutor, questioner, interpreter.
II. *Verbs.* **converse,** talk together, hold (carry on, join in, *or* engage in) a conversation; speak, colloquize (*rare*), discourse with, commune with, confer with, confabulate, talk over, discuss, consult, reason, collogue (*colloq.*); parley, palaver; chat, gossip, tattle, prate, chatter.
III. *Adjectives.* **conversational,** chatty, colloquial, confabulatory; interlocutory, discoursive, communicative, conversable; unstudied, familiar, informal.
See also LOQUACITY, SPEECH.—*Antonyms.* See SOLILOQUY, TACITURNITY.

CONVERSION.—I. *Nouns.* **conversion,** change, transmutation, change of heart (*theol.*), transformation, metamorphosis, regeneration, growth, progress; reduction, deoxidization (*chem.*), resolution, assumption, assimilation; chemistry, alchemy; naturalization; transposition, inversion.

transition, passage, passing, change, metastasis (*tech.*), metabolism (*biol.*), metabasis (*rhet.*), transmigration; rise, fall, shifting, flux; phase.
convert, neophyte, proselyte, disciple; pervert, renegade, apostate, turncoat.
II. *Verbs.* **convert,** change, turn, alter, vary, transmute, resolve; metamorphose, transfigure, translate, transform, metabolize (*physiol.*), transmogrify (*colloq.*); exchange.
[*in law*] appropriate, embezzle, misapply, peculate, defalcate, steal.
be converted into, become, get, turn to (*or* into); turn out, lapse, shift; pass into, grow into, merge into, melt, blend; grow, wax, mature, mellow, undergo a change.
convert into, resolve into; make, render, mold, form, remodel, reform, reorganize; bring to, reduce to; digest, assimilate, transform, incorporate, absorb, appropriate.
III. *Adjectives.* **convertible,** transmutable, transformable; exchangeable, interchangeable, reciprocal, mutual, equivalent, synonymous.
See also CHANGE, INTERCHANGE.—*Antonyms.* See PERMANENCE.

CONVEXITY.—I. *Nouns.* **convexity,** swelling, swell, bulge, protuberance, prominence, projection, protrusion, excrescency, gibbosity.
excrescence, outgrowth, outshoot, superfluity, excess, exuberance, abnormal increase; appendage, growth, intumescence, tumor; pimple, papule (*med.*), pustule, wart, wen, fungus, blister, bleb, boil; nipple, mammilla, teat, dug (*no longer used of women except in contempt*), breast, chest, thorax (*anat. and zoöl.*); hump, bow, clump, bunch, bulb, bump, knob, knot, boss, tooth, peg; stump, snag, peak.
proboscis, nose, beak, neb, snout, nozzle, trunk (*esp. of an elephant*), antlia (*L. pl.* antliæ: *zoöl.*).
belly, paunch, corporation (*colloq.*), epigastrium, abdomen.
arch, span, cupola, dome, vault, ogive (*arch.*).
relief, cameo, relievo; low relief, bas-relief, basso-relievo, *basso-rilievo* (*It.; pl. -rilievi*), half relief; mezzo-relievo, *mezzo-rilievo* (*It.*); high relief, alto-relievo, *alto-rilievo* (*It.*).
ridge, raised rim, fillet, seam, inion (*craniology*), rib, ridgelet.
[*ridge of land*] crest, kame *or* kam (*Scot. and North of Eng.*), ledge, comb, spine, chine, hogback, horseback, esker (*geol.*), saddle, *arête* (*F.*).
headland, cape, promontory, mull, foreland, head, cliff, tongue, bluff, hook, peak, tor, ness (*chiefly used as a suffix in place names*), spur.
hill, elevation, rise, ascent, mound, barrow, knoll, hammock, mount, butte (*Western U. S.*), highland, kopje (*South Africa*), alp, mountain; hillside, brae (*chiefly Scot.*), slope, bank.
II. *Verbs.* **be convex,** project, bulge, protrude, bag, belly, swell, protuberate, round, bunch, pout, jut out, stand out, stick out, stick up; hang over, overhang, beetle.
raise, emboss, boss, knot, ornament; arch, embow.
III. *Adjectives.* **convex,** protuberant, prominent, swelling, bulging, bloated, swollen, tumid. distended, bellied, gibbous; bold, projecting, bossed, bossy, bunchy, hummocky, bulbous; bowed, arched, embowed, hemispheric *or* hemispherical; club-shaped, hubbly (*U. S.*), knobby, gnarled; salient, in relief, raised, *repoussé* (*F.*).
See also EXPANSION, HEIGHT.—*Antonyms.* See CONCAVITY, FLATNESS.

---

convey, *v.* carry, bear, transport, grant, cede, will. See TRANSFER.
conveyance, *n.* assignment, disposal, sale, legacy; wagon, carriage, car, van. See TRANSFER, VEHICLE.
convict, *v.* find guilty, doom, sentence. See CONDEMNATION.
convict, *n.* prisoner, captive, criminal. See BAD MAN.
conviction, *n.* opinion, view; sentence, penalty. See BELIEF, CONDEMNATION.
convince, *v.* assure, convert, satisfy, persuade. See BELIEF.
conviviality, *n.* jollity, festivity, merrymaking. See SOCIALITY.
convoke, *v.* muster, collect, gather, summon, convene. See ASSEMBLAGE.

CONVOLUTION.—I. *Nouns.* **convolution,** winding, tortuosity, involution, wave, undulation, sinuosity, sinuousness, meandering, circuit, ambages (*esp. of speech*), circumbendibus (*jocose*), twist, twirl; contortion.

coil, roll, curl, spiral, helix, corkscrew, worm, volute, scroll, tendril, scallop, kink; serpent, snake, eel; maze, labyrinth.
II. *Verbs.* **convolve,** wind, twine, twirl, loop, lap, fold, wreathe, entwine; wave, undulate, meander, zigzag, twist, coil, belay (*naut.*), roll; wrinkle; curl, friz, indent, scallop; wring, contort.
III. *Adjectives.* **convolute,** convoluted, winding, twisted, circling, snaky, serpentine, curved, sinuous, tortuous.
involved, intricate, mazy, labyrinthine; ambagious, circuitous, kinky, curly, vermicular, vermiculate, vermiform, peristaltic; turbinal, turbinate, scroll-like.
spiral, coiled, helical, cochlear, cochleate, screw-shaped.
wavy, undulating, undulant, undulate (*bot.*), undulatory, undulated, undulative, undate (*esp. bot.*), undé *or* undée (*heraldry*), sinuate (*esp. bot.*), undose (*entom.*), repand (*bot. and zoöl.*), flexuose (*bot.*), gyrose (*bot.*); ripply.
IV. *Adverbs.* **convolutely,** windingly, etc. (see *adjectives*); in and out, round and round.
See also CROSSING.—*Antonyms.* See CIRCULARITY, STRAIGHTNESS.

---

convoy, *v.* attend, escort, conduct, guard, watch, support. See ACCOMPANIMENT.
convulse, *v.* shake, stir, disturb, rend; wring, hurt. See AGITATION, PAIN.
convulsive, *adj.* spasmodic, explosive, volcanic. See VIOLENCE.
cook, *v.* prepare, concoct, make, fix. See CALEFACTION.
cool, *adj.* self-possessed, wary; chilly, frigid; unfriendly, lukewarm; easy-going, placid. See CAUTION, COLD, ENMITY, INEXCITABILITY.
cool, *v.* compose, calm; freeze, chill, harden. See MODERATION, REFRIGERATION.
coolness, *n.* self-assurance, self-possession; chilliness; calmness, *sang-froid* (*F.*); apathy, disdain, coldness. See CAUTION, COLD, EXPECTANCY, INDIFFERENCE.

COÖPERATION.—I. *Nouns.* **coöperation,** joint operation, combination, participation, collaboration, concert, coadjuvancy, union, concurrence; logrolling (*chiefly U. S.*).
[*in guilt*] **complicity,** collusion; connivance, guiltiness, guilt; conspiracy, confederacy.
association, alliance, society, company, joint stock, partnership, pool, gentlemen's agreement; confederation, coalition, fusion, federation, trust, combine; fellowship, comradeship, fraternization, fraternity, freemasonry.
unanimity, agreement, accordance, concord, harmony, consentaneity; morale, *esprit de corps* (*F.*), party spirit, school spirit; clanship, partisanship.
II. *Verbs.* **coöperate,** concur, conduce, combine, pool, unite one's efforts, pull together, stand shoulder to shoulder, act in concert, join forces, fraternize; conspire, concert.
side with, take sides with, go along with, join hands with, uphold, make common cause with, unite with, join with, take part with, cast in one's lot with; rally round, follow the lead of.
participate, take part, share, be a party to, partake of, lend oneself to; chip in (*colloq.*), contribute, bear part in, second, espouse a cause.
III. *Adjectives.* **coöperative,** coöperating, in league, hand in glove with; favorable to, coadjuvant, coactive.
IV. *Adverbs.* **coöperatively,** coactively, unanimously, as one man, shoulder to shoulder.
See also AID, COMBINATION, CONCORD, JUNCTION.—*Antonyms.* See OPPOSITION.

---

coördinate, *v.* adjust, organize, harmonize. See ARRANGEMENT.
copious, *adj.* abundant, profuse, plentiful, full, ample. See SUFFICIENCY.
coppery, *adj.* cupreous, copper, copperish. See BROWN.

COPY.—I. *Nouns.* [*result of imitation*] **copy,** facsimile, counterpart, effigy, likeness, similitude, semblance, morbidezza (*painting*), cast, tracing, imitation, model, representation, study; "counterfeit presentment" (*Hamlet*), portrait; duplicate, tenor (*law*), estreat (*law*), engrossment, transcript, transcription, fair copy, revise; adumbration, outline, reflection, shadow, echo; reprint, replica, transfer, reproduction, repetition.

servile copy *or* imitation, counterfeit, forgery; paste, strass; fake (*slang*).
[*thing to be copied*] **model,** pattern, example, plan, standard, precedent, original archetype; paragon.
II. *Verbs.* **copy,** imitate, follow, duplicate, reproduce, repeat, mirror, reflect; rewrite, engross, transcribe, etch, electrotype.
parody, caricature, burlesque, travesty, mimicry, paraphrase; cartoon.
III. *Adjectives.* **faithful,** lifelike, similar, close, accurate, exact, speaking (*as, a* speaking *likeness*).

See also FOLLOWING, IMITATION, REPETITION, REPRESENTATION, REPRODUCTION. —*Antonyms.* See NOMINATION, PROTOTYPE.

---

cord, *n.* twine, string, rope; bond, tie. See FILAMENT, VINCULUM.
cordage, *n.* rigging, tackle, ropework. See VINCULUM.
cordial, *adj.* genial, hearty, friendly, warm, sincere. See COURTESY.
core, *n.* heart, nucleus, kernel; gist, pith, substance. See CENTRALITY, IMPORTANCE.
corner, *n.* niche, nook; monopoly, control. See ANGULARITY, POSSESSION.
corporation, *n.* company, partnership, trust, pool, merger. See PARTY.

CORPSE.—I. *Nouns.* **corpse,** dead body (*of a human being*), corse (*archaic*), carcass *or* carcase (*now contemptuous when referring to a human body*), skeleton, relics, remains, body, cadaver (*as for dissection*), dust, ashes, earth, clay; mummy; carrion; tenement of clay, "this mortal coil" (*Hamlet*).
ghost, apparition, shade, spirit, sprite, wraith, phantom, specter *or* spectre, appearance, phantasm, phantasma, revenant, spook (*colloq.*); manes (*Roman relig.*), lemures (*Roman relig.*), spirits of the dead.
II. *Adjectives.* **corpselike,** deathlike, pale, ghastly, cadaverous, cadaveric.
ghostlike, ghostly, spectral, phantasmal, shadowy, illusive, phantom; spookish (*colloq.*), spooky (*colloq.*), haunted.

See also DEATH.—*Antonyms.* See LIFE.

---

corpulence, *n.* portliness, fleshiness, obesity, fatness, bulk. See SIZE.
correct, *adj.* accurate, strict, perfect, true, unerring. See RIGHT.
correct, *v.* punish, reprove, chastise, discipline; remedy, rectify, mend, amend, repair; set right, undeceive. See DISAPPROBATION, IMPROVEMENT, INFORMATION.
correction, *n.* discipline, chastisement; redress, amends, reparation, repair, remedy. See PUNISHMENT, RELIEF.

CORRELATION.—I. *Nouns.* **correlation,** interdependence, reciprocity, reciprocation, mutuality, correspondence; interchange, exchange, barter.
II. *Verbs.* **correlate,** interact, correspond, alternate, reciprocate, interchange, exchange; return, requite.
III. *Adjectives.* **correlative,** reciprocal, mutual, correspondent, corresponding, analogous, equivalent, complementary; interchangeable, alternate.

See also INTERCHANGE.

CORRESPONDENCE.—I. *Nouns.* **correspondence,** epistolary intercourse, communication; letters, writings.
letter, epistle, missive, favor (*old-fashioned commercial style*), note, line (*colloq.*), billet; love letter, *billet doux* (*F.; often used jocosely*); form letter, circular letter, circular; drop letter, dispatch *or* despatch, bulletin, bull (*papal*), pastoral (*episcopal*), monitory *or* monitory letter (*as from the Pope*), post card *or* postcard, postal (*U. S.*), postal card.
[*mutual adaptation*] **accordance,** agreement, accord, conformity, congruity, coincidence, concurrence, uniformity, reciprocity.
correspondent, writer, letter writer, epistolarian (*rare*); contributor, reporter.
II. *Verbs.* **correspond,** write to, send a letter to, communicate with, keep up a correspondence, epistolize (*rare*); reply, answer.
tally, agree, harmonize, answer, fit, suit, square, match, conform, concur, comport with, correlate, reciprocate.

III. *Adjectives.* **correspondent,** corresponding to (*or* with), agreeing, answering, conformable, suitable, fit, adapted, congruous, complementary, reciprocal, corresponsive.
[*of letters*] epistolary, epistolarian.
See also AGREEMENT, CORRELATION, LETTER, SIMILARITY.

---

corrigible, *adj.* amenable, tractable, docile, submissive. See IMPROVEMENT.
corrode, *v.* decay, rust, wear, waste. See DETERIORATION.
corrugate, *v.* flute, groove, wrinkle. See FURROW, [1]FOLD, ROUGHNESS.
corrupt, *adj.* dishonest, base; tainted, spoiled, rotten; profligate, dissolute, immoral. See IMPROBITY, UNCLEANNESS, VICE.
corrupt, *v.* taint, infect, pervert, demoralize, debase. See DETERIORATION.
corruption, *n.* decay, rot, putridity, putrefaction. See DECOMPOSITION, UNCLEANNESS.
cosmic, *adj.* terrestrial, heavenly, universal. See WORLD.
cosmologist, *n.* cosmogonist, cosmographer. See WORLD.
cosmology, *n.* cosmography; cosmism. See WORLD.
cost, *n.* charge, expense, outlay, disbursement, expenditure. See PRICE.
costly, *adj.* expensive, dear, high-priced, extravagant. See EXPENDITURE, HEIGHT.
costume, *n.* dress, attire, apparel. See CLOTHING.
[1]cot, *n.* cabin, cottage, hut. See HABITATION.
[2]cot, *n.* couch, bed. See SUPPORT.
couch, *n.* cot, bed, pallet, litter; lounge, settee. See SUPPORT.
cough, *n.* tussis (*med.*), hack. See COLD.

COUNCIL.—I. *Nouns.* **council,** committee, chapter, divan (*Oriental*), privy council, court, plenum, chamber, cabinet, board. directorate, syndicate, bench, staff.
assembly, meeting, muster, gathering, concourse, sitting, séance, salon, conference, convention, hearing, session, durbar (*India*), rada (*Ukraine*), palaver, powwow (*U. S.*), council fire (*North Amer.*); caucus, clique.
[*ecclesiastical*] convocation, synod, congregation, church, chapter, vestry, consistory, conventicle, conclave, convention.
legislature, parliament, congress, national congress, national assembly, general assembly, general council, General Court (*as of Massachusetts*), national council, cortes, states-general, diet, duma, soviet (*Russ.*); witenagemot (*Anglo-Saxon hist.*): *the specific names of legislative bodies are usually capitalized.*
upper house, upper chamber, first chamber, senate, legislative council, House of Lords, House of Peers, federal council, legislative council.
lower house, lower chamber, second chamber, house of representatives, House of Commons, the house, legislative assembly, chamber of deputies, chamber of representatives.
[*representatives*] congressman, congresswoman, M. C., senator, representative; member, member of parliament, M. P.; assemblyman, councilor; minister, delegate.

---

count, *v.* consider, estimate, esteem; figure, reckon, enumerate, compute. See JUDGE, NUMERATION.
countenance, *n.* favor, patronage; expression, aspect; visage, features. See AID, APPEARANCE, FRONT.
counter, *adj.* opposite, opposed, against. See CONTRARIETY.

COUNTERACTION.—I. *Nouns.* **counteraction,** opposition; contrariety, contradiction; antagonism, polarity; clashing, collision, interference, frustration, resistance, head (structural, *or* parasite) resistance (*aëro.*), friction; reaction, recoil; counterblast, neutralization, nullification, check, hindrance; repression, restraint.

antidote, counteractant, counteragent, counteractive, preventive, counterpoison, countervenom, alexipharmic (*med.*), alexiteric (*med.*), mithridate (*hist.*), theriac *or* theriaca (*old med.*); remedy, corrective.
II. *Verbs.* **counteract,** clash, cross, interfere with, conflict with, contravene; militate against, stultify, defeat, antagonize, frustrate, oppose, overcome, overpower, withstand, resist, impede, jostle, hinder, repress, restrain; recoil, react.
neutralize, annul, nullify, negative, offset, undo, cancel; counterpoise, counterbalance, countervail.
III. *Adjectives.* **counteractive,** antagonistic *or* antagonistical, opposing, combating, conflicting, reactionary; contrary, renitent, recalcitrant.
IV. *Adverbs.* **although,** notwithstanding, though, albeit, even though, supposing that, despite, in spite of, maugre (*archaic*), against.
See also CONTRARIETY, HINDRANCE, OPPOSITION.—*Antonyms.* See CONCURRENCE.

COUNTEREVIDENCE.—I. *Nouns.* **counterevidence,** disproof, refutation, confutation, rejoinder, rebuttal, rebutter (*law*), negation, denial; plea, vindication.
II. *Verbs.* **refute,** disprove, rebut, oppose, confute, overthrow, subvert; destroy, check, weaken; contravene, contradict, deny, negative, alter the case; turn the tables; prove a negative.
III. *Adjectives.* **contradictory,** conflicting, refutative, refutatory, countervailing, contrary, negatory; unattested, unauthenticated, unsupported, supposititious, trumped up.
IV. *Adverbs.* **contrariwise,** *per contra* (*L.*), on the contrary, on the other side (*or* hand), as an offset; oppositely, contrarily, in opposition, conversely; in rebuttal.
See also CONFUTATION, NEGATION, PLEA.—*Antonyms.* See EVIDENCE.

---

counterfeit, *adj.* bogus, fictitious, sham, spurious, false. See DECEPTION, FALSEHOOD, IMITATION.
counterfeit, *n.* sham, pretense, fake; forgery. See IMITATION.
counterfeit, *v.* forge, coin, swindle. See STEALING.
counterpart, *n.* complement; duplicate, facsimile, replica; match, mate, brother. See CONTRARIETY, COPY, SIMILARITY.
counterpoise, *n.* counterweight, counterbalance, balance, equipoise. See COMPENSATION.
countersign, *n.* authentication, seal; password, watchword, identification. See EVIDENCE, INDICATION.
countless, *adj.* numberless, innumerable, incalculable, illimitable. See INFINITY.
country, *n.* state, power, nation; fatherland, home; territory, tract, district; rural regions. See AUTHORITY, LAND, REGION, SPACE.
countryman, *n.* compatriot; rustic, farmer. See FRIEND, PEOPLE.
couple, *v.* pair, yoke; join, unite, link, tie. See DUALITY, JUNCTION.
coupled, *adj.* paired, matched, conjugate, united, mated. See DUALITY.

COURAGE.—I. *Nouns.* **courage,** fearlessness, bravery, valor, resoluteness, resolution, boldness, heart, spirit, daring, derring-do (*pseudo-archaic*), dash, *élan* (*F.*), gallantry, intrepidity, heroism, prowess, chivalry, audacity, rashness, defiance, confidence, self-reliance; manhood, manliness, nerve, mettle, grit, pluck (*colloq.*), sand (*slang*), virtue, hardihood, fortitude, firmness, backbone, spunk (*colloq.*), bulldog courage, resolution, tenacity.
exploit, feat, deed, act (*esp. an heroic act*), achievement.
brave man, man of courage, a man, hero, lion, tiger, paladin, ace (*aviation*), demigod; Hercules, Achilles, Hector, Bayard, Lancelot, Sir Galahad.
brave woman, heroine; demigoddess; Amazon, Joan of Arc.
II. *Verbs.* **be courageous,** dare, venture, make bold; face (front, confront, brave, defy, *or* despise) danger; face; meet, brave, beard, defy.
nerve oneself, summon up (*or* pluck up) courage, take heart, stand to one's guns, bear up, hold out; present a bold front show fight, face the music, run the gauntlet.

hearten, inspire courage, reassure, encourage, embolden, stimulate, inspirit, cheer, nerve, rally.

III. *Adjectives.* **courageous,** brave, valiant, valorous, gallant, intrepid, spirited, high-spirited, mettlesome, plucky; manly, manful, stalwart, stout-hearted, lion-hearted, bold, daring, audacious, fearless, dauntless, undaunted, unafraid, undismayed, unflinching, unshrinking, hard, stout, confident, self-reliant, bold as a lion.

enterprising, adventurous, venturous, venturesome, hazardous; dashing, chivalrous, warlike, soldierly, heroic.

fierce, ferocious, fell (*poetical or rhetorical*), savage, cruel, pitiless, implacable, bloody, sanguinary, bloodthirsty, relentless, ruthless, merciless, inhuman; pugnacious, bellicose; vehement, impetuous, impulsive, passionate.

strong-minded, strong-willed, hardy, doughty (*archaic or jocose*); firm, resolute, determined, dogged, indomitable.

See also DEFIANCE, GOOD, RASHNESS, WARFARE.—*Antonyms.* See COWARDICE.

---

courier, *n.* express messenger, runner. See MESSENGER, TRAVELER.

course, *n.* behavior, procedure; succession, round; path, channel, drift, trend; progress, flight; row, line; system, routine; passage, lapse (*of time*); study, subject; duration, period. See CONDUCT, CONTINUITY, DIRECTION, LAPSE, LAYER, ORDER, PROGRESSION, TEACHING, TIME.

court, *n.* addresses, attention; palace, castle, hall; courtyard, quadrangle; staff, retinue, train; bench, bar, session. See ENDEARMENT, HABITATION, PLACE, SERVANT, TRIBUNAL.

court, *v.* woo, make love; praise, cajole, curry favor; invite, solicit. See ENDEARMENT, FLATTERY, MOTIVE.

COURTESY.—I. *Nouns.* **courtesy,** politeness, *bienséance* (*F.*), urbanity, gentility, refinement, breeding, gentle breeding, cultivation, culture, polish, elegance, civility, amenity; suavity, good temper, good humor, amiability, complacency, affability, complaisance, *prevénance* (*F.*), compliance; gallantry, chivalry, courtliness, good manners, good behavior, good breeding, manners, courteousness, respect; pink of courtesy, pink of politeness.

flower of knighthood; *chevalier sans peur et sans reproche* (*F.*), Bayard, Sidney, "a verray parfit gentil knight" (Chaucer), Chesterfield, Launcelot, Gawaine.

greeting, welcome, salutation, reception, *accueil* (*F.*), presentation, introduction, ceremonial; respects, *devoirs* (*F.*), regards, remembrances; deference, love.

[*forms of greeting*] bow, curtsy *or* curtsey, salaam (*Oriental*), kotow (*China*), obeisance, bowing and scraping; kneeling, genuflection; capping, pulling the forelock, nod, shaking hands; embrace, hug, squeeze, kiss; salute.

II. *Verbs.* **be courteous,** etc. (see *adjectives*); show courtesy; behave oneself, conciliate, speak one fair, take in good part.

greet, welcome, hail, receive, bid welcome, accost, address, do the honors, usher usher in.

salute, nod to; smile upon; uncover, touch (*or* raise) the hat, doff the cap, bow, make one's bow, curtsy *or* curtsey, bob a curtsy, kneel, bow (*or* bend) the knee; salaam (*Oriental*), kotow (*China*), prostrate oneself, honor, present arms, make way for.

III. *Adjectives.* **courteous,** polite, civil, mannerly, obliging, complaisant, gentle, kindly, urbane; well-behaved, well-mannered, well-bred, gently bred, of gentle breeding; polished, cultivated, refined; gallant, chivalrous, chivalric, knightly.

ingratiating, ingratiatory, winning, good-humored, good-natured, good-tempered. cordial, gracious, amiable, familiar, sociable, affable, neighborly; tactful, diplomatic, conciliatory.

bland, suave, mild, fair-spoken, smooth, honey-tongued, oily, unctuous, plausible, smug, obsequious.

IV. *Adverbs.* **courteously,** politely, etc. (see *adjectives*); with a good grace; with open arms, *à bras ouverts* (*F.*), cordially, with outstretched arms, in good humor.

V. *Interjections.* **hail!** welcome! *ave!* (*L.*); hello! well met! all hail! hail, fellow! (*archaic, whence the phrase* hail fellow well met); good morning! good afternoon! good evening! good night!

See also RESPECT, SOCIALITY, UNCTUOUSNESS.—*Antonyms.* See DISCOURTESY.

courtship, *n.* courting, suit, wooing, flirtation, amour. See ENDEARMENT.
cove, *n.* inlet, lagoon, bay. See GULF.
covenant, *n.* pact, agreement, bargain. See COMPACT.
covenant, *v.* stipulate, undertake, agree. See COMPACT, CONTRACTION.

COVERING.—I. *Nouns.* **covering,** cover, shelter, screen, coverture, shield protection, carapace (*zoöl.*); shamianah (*India*), canopy, tester (*as over a bed or pulpit*), awning, tent, marquee, canvas, kibitka (*Kirghiz*) *tente d'abri* (*F.*), wigwam, tepee; clapboarding, weatherboarding; umbrella, parasol, *en-tout-cas* (*F.*), sunshade; veil.
[*hoodlike covering*] hood, cowl, chimneypot; capote (*as of a cabriolet*), calash (*carriage hood*), top.
roof, ceiling, thatch, tiles, slates, leads, shingles; dome, cupola; mansard, gambrel curb roof, deck (*U. S.*).
coverlet, counterpane, sheet, quilt, blanket, rug, drugget; linoleum, oilcloth; tarpaulin; eiderdown quilt, bedcover, comforter *or* comfortable (*U. S.*); pillowcase, slip, pillowslip; bedding, bedclothes.
integument, investment, coat, clothing; skin, pellicle, fleece, fur, leather, lambskin, sable, beaver, ermine, hide, coat, buff, fell, pelt, peltry (*collective noun*); cuticle, cutis, epidermis, derma, corium (*anat.*).
crust, coating, incrustation, incrustment (*rare*), efflorescence (*chem.*); scale, scab, slough (*med.*), eschar (*med.*).
peel, rind, bark, husk, shell, hull, cortex (*tech.*).
sheath, sheathing, capsule, pod, casing, case, involucrum (*zoöl.*), ocrea (*L. pl.* ocreæ: *bot. and zoöl.*), wrapping, wrapper, jacket, envelope.
veneer, facing, leaf, layer; paint, stain, varnish, gloss, enamel, wash, washing, whitewash, plaster, stucco.
II. *Verbs.* **cover,** superimpose, overlay, overspread, envelop, clothe, invest, wrap, incase; face, case, veneer, paper; clapboard, weatherboard; shingle; conceal hide, cloak, hood, shelter, shield, screen, protect.
coat, paint, stain, varnish, incrust, crust, cement, stucco, plaster; smear, daub, besmear, bedaub; gild, plate, japan, lacquer, enamel; whitewash, calcimine, white.
III. *Adjectives.* **covered,** protected, screened, shielded, loricated, hooded cowled, armored, armor-plated, ironclad.
scaly, squamous, squamate, scalelike, squamosal (*tech.*), ramentaceous *or* ramental (*bot.*); laminate.
overlapping, shingled, equitant (*bot.*), imbricate *or* imbricated, lapstreak (*said of boats*), clinker-built (*opposite of* carvel-built).
[*of the skin*] **cutaneous,** cuticular, epidermal *or* epidermic, epidermoid *or* epidermoidal, dermal; hypodermal, subcutaneous (*all tech.*).
See also CLOTHING, CONCEALMENT.—*Antonyms.* See DIVESTMENT, LINING.

---

covet, *v.* long for, want, crave, envy, wish. See DESIRE.
cow, *n.* bovine, heifer. See ANIMAL.

COWARDICE.—I. *Nouns.* **cowardice,** pusillanimity, cowardliness, cravenness, timorousness, timidity, effeminacy, faint-heartedness, baseness, abject fear, funkiness (*colloq.*), funk (*colloq.*), fear, white feather, cold feet (*U. S. slang*), yellow streak (*slang*).
coward, poltroon, dastard, sneak, recreant, cur (*contemptuous*), funk, craven, caitiff; mollycoddle, milksop; shirker, shirk, slacker (*colloq.*), deserter, quitter (*U. S.*).
alarmist, terrorist, pessimist, panic-monger.
II. *Verbs.* **be cowardly,** quail, funk (*colloq.*), cower, skulk, sneak; flinch, shy, fight shy, slink, run away; show the white feather.
III. *Adjectives.* **cowardly,** coward, fearful, shy, timid, timorous, spiritless, soft effeminate, unmanly, faint-hearted, white-livered, yellow (*slang*), funky (*colloq.*), frightened, dastard, dastardly, base, craven, sneaking, recreant; unwarlike, unsoldierlike, unsoldierly.
See also FEAR, YELLOW.—*Antonyms.* See COURAGE.

cower, *v.* quail, shrink, crouch; fawn, grovel. See COWARDICE, SERVILITY.
coworker, *n.* associate, colleague. See AGENT.
coy, *adj.* shy, retiring, bashful, shrinking, demure. See MODESTY.
crabbed, *adj.* surly, ill-tempered, perverse, cross, peevish; illegible, intricate, squeezed. See DISCOURTESY, UNINTELLIGIBILITY.
crack, *v.* split, crush, break, burst, fracture; bang, pop. See DISJUNCTION, SNAP.
crack, *n.* slit, rut, seam; cleft, crevice, fissure, rift; pop, crash, clap, crackle. See FURROW, INTERVAL, SNAP.
crackle, *v.* crack, crepitate. See SNAP.
craft, *n.* trade, handicraft; artfulness, deceit, trickery; vessel, boat; expertness, art. See BUSINESS, CUNNING, SHIP, SKILL.
cram, *v.* stuff, crowd, jam, pack, choke; gorge, guzzle. See CLOSURE, GLUTTONY.
cramp, *v.* restrain, hamper, handicap; cripple, paralyze, incapacitate. See HINDRANCE, IMPOTENCE.
crash, *n.* smash, shattering, downfall, failure; clash, collision; burst, blast. See DESTRUCTION, IMPULSE, LOUDNESS.
crass, *adj.* gross, raw, crude, stupid. See DENSITY.
crave, *v.* long for, yearn for; beseech, beg, ask, pray, petition. See DESIRE, REQUEST.
craving, *adj.* hungry, ravening, famished, desirous. See DESIRE.
crawl, *v.* fawn, cower, grovel; lag, creep, drag. See SERVILITY, SLOWNESS.
craze, *v.* madden, unsettle, unbalance. See DERANGEMENT.
crazy, *adj.* lunatic, mad, crack-brained; shaky, rickety. See INSANITY, WEAKNESS.
creak, *v.* grate, squeak, stridulate. See STRIDENCY.
cream, *n.* pick, *élite* (*F.*); gist, kernel; rich milk, *crème* (*F.*). See GOODNESS, IMPORTANCE, OIL.
create, *v.* originate, occasion; make, form, bring into being; devise, conceive, invent; propagate, breed; visualize, envisage. See CAUSE, DEITY, IMAGINATION, PRODUCTION, VISION.
creation, *n.* creature (*created thing*), product; invention, conception; formation, origination, causation, constitution, establishment; cosmos, universe. See EFFECT, IMAGINATION, PRODUCTION, WORLD.
creator, *n.* author, originator, maker. See CAUSE, PRODUCER.
Creator, *n.* God, Supreme Being. See DEITY.
creature, *n.* beast, lower animal; individual, mortal; dependent, slave; being, thing. See ANIMAL, MANKIND, SERVANT, SUBSTANTIALITY.
credence, *n.* assurance, credit, trust, reliance; acceptance, acknowledgment, recognition. See BELIEF, RECEPTION.
credibility, *n.* believableness, likelihood, trustworthiness. See BELIEF, PROBABILITY.
credible, *adj.* trustworthy, reliable; conceivable, thinkable; probable. See BELIEF, POSSIBILITY, PROBABILITY.

CREDIT.—I. *Nouns.* **credit,** belief, faith, trust, confidence, reliance; trustworthiness, credibility; good name, repute, reputation, honor, merit, esteem; prestige, influence; source of honor (*as,* a credit *to his family*).
[*in commerce*] trust, tick (*colloq.*), strap (*Eng. slang*), score, tally, account, loan. letter of credit, circular note; traveler's check (*or* cheque); draft; paper credit; mortgage, lien, securities, stocks, bonds, debentures, bank balance.
creditor, lender, lessor (*law*), mortgagee; dun; usurer.
II. *Verbs.* **credit,** believe, rely upon, put trust in; accept, receive, swallow (*colloq.*); accredit.
[*in commerce*] keep (*or* run up) an account with; place to one's credit (*or* account); give (*or* take) credit.

III. *Adjectives.* **credited,** of good credit, vouched for, accredited, in good standing, well rated.
creditable, estimable, honorable, reputable, worthy, fitting, seemly.
IV. *Adverbs.* **on credit,** to the account of, to the credit of.

See also BELIEF, REPUTE.—*Antonyms.* See DEBT, DISREPUTE, UNBELIEF.

CREDULITY.—I. *Nouns.* **credulity,** credulousness, belief, belieffulness (*rare*), gullibility, easiness (*colloq.*); infatuation, self-delusion, self-deception; superstition, *Aberglaube* (*Ger.*); bigotry.
II. *Verbs.* **be credulous;** follow implicitly; swallow (*colloq.*), swallow whole, gulp down; take on faith, take for granted.
III. *Adjectives.* **credulous,** gullible, confiding, easily deceived (*or* convinced), green, soft, simple, silly, childish, confiding, trustful, unsuspicious, unsophisticated; infatuated, superstitious.

See also BELIEF, DECEPTION, DUPE, SIMPLENESS.—*Antonyms.* See INCREDULITY

---

creed, *n.* dogma, doctrine, faith, formula. See BELIEF.
creep, *v.* crawl, dawdle, loiter, steal. See SLOWNESS, STEALING.
cremation, *n.* incineration, burning; suttee, *auto-da-fé* (*Pg.*). See CALEFACTION, INTERMENT.
crematory, *n.* crematorium, incinerator. See FURNACE, INTERMENT.
crescent, *n.* new moon, bow, lune (*geom.*). See CURVATURE.
crescent-shaped, *adj.* crescent, moon-shaped, lunate, luniform. See CURVATURE.
crest, *n.* ridge, comb; device, seal; tuft, plume; tip, top, height; culmination, peak, climax. See CONVEXITY, INDICATION, ROUGHNESS, SUMMIT, SUPERIORITY.
crew, *n.* throng, mob, company, gang, squad; sailors. See ASSEMBLAGE, MARINER.
crib, *n.* hovel, hut; key, translation, trot (*school cant*); bin, manger, rack; plagiarism, steal (*colloq.*); child's bed. See HABITATION, INTERPRETATION, RECEPTACLE, STEALING, SUPPORT.
crime, *n.* felony, outrage, wrongdoing, sin. See GUILT.
criminal, *n.* culprit, malefactor, felon, convict. See BAD MAN.
crimson, *adj.* blood-red, deep-red. See RED.
cringe, *v.* wince, shrink, flinch; fawn, grovel, truckle. See AVOIDANCE, SERVILITY.
cripple, *v.* incapacitate, disable, unfit; hurt, cramp, enfeeble. See IMPOTENCE, WEAKNESS.
crisis, *n.* emergency, extremity, pinch, trial, crux, exigency; turning point. See CIRCUMSTANCE, DIFFICULTY, TIMELINESS.
crisp, *adj.* brittle, friable; short, crumbly. See BRITTLENESS, SHORTNESS.
criterion, *n.* measure, touchstone, test, rule, norm, standard. See PROTOTYPE.
critic, *n.* censor, censurer; commentator, reviewer; judge, connoisseur, expert. See DETRACTOR, DISSERTATION, TASTE.
critical, *adj.* faultfinding, disparaging; analytical, nice; urgent, crucial; judicious. See DISAPPROBATION, DISCRIMINATION, IMPORTANCE, JUDGE.
criticize, *v.* censure, reprove, flay; examine, analyze. See DISAPPROBATION, JUDGE.
crocodilian *n.* crocodile, mugger (*India*), alligator. See ANIMAL.
crooked, *adj.* fraudulent, deceptive, sneaking; warped, askew, awry, twisted. See CUNNING, DISTORTION.
crop, *n.* fruit, product, harvest. See STORE.

CROSSING.—I. *Nouns.* **crossing,** intersection, decussation (*tech.*); crossway, crosswalk, crossroad; level crossing (*Eng.*), grade crossing (*U. S.*); traversing, passage; hybridization, interbreeding; opposition, obstruction.

network, interlacement, complexity, ramification, complex system (*as of railroads or radio stations*), interconnection, reticulation; net, web, mesh, netting, lace, plait; sieve, screen; wicker; mat, matting; trellis, lattice, grating, grille, gridiron, tracery, fretwork, fret, filigree; entanglement, plexus (*tech.*).
cross, rood (*archaic*), crucifix (*improperly used for cross without image of Christ*), gibbet, crux (*as in heraldry*), crosslet; crisscross, christcross, sign, mark.
II. *Verbs.* **cross,** intersect, decussate (*tech.*), interlace, intertwine, intertwist, interweave, interlink, lace, crisscross; twine, entwine, weave, twist, wattle, wreathe; dovetail, mortise, splice, link; plait, pleat, plat, braid; tangle, entangle, mat, ravel; net, knot.
[*to move across*] **pass,** traverse, ford, cut across; recross, repass; carry across, transport.
[*to run counter to*] **oppose,** thwart, obstruct, face, antagonize; foil, baffle, frustrate.
[*to mix the breed of*] **blend,** mix, interbreed, intercross, crossbreed, hybridize, cross-pollinate (*bot.*), cross-fertilize.
cross out (*or* **off**), cancel, strike out, erase, delete, dele (*printing*), remove, obliterate.
III. *Adjectives.* **cross,** intersecting, transverse, oblique, thwart (*archaic*); adverse, contrary, perverse, mutually opposed.
[*of persons*] **petulant,** peevish, fretful, fractious, ill-humored, querulous, touchy, irritable, ill-natured, crabbed.
crossed, matted, transverse, intersected, decussate *or* decussated (*esp. tech.*); chiasmal (*anat.*), x-shaped, cross; pleached (*esp. poetic*), intertwined, interlaced; cross-shaped, cruciate, cruciform; netlike, retiform, reticular, cancellate, latticed. grated, barred, streaked.
IV. *Adverbs.* **crosswise,** across, athwart, thwartly, thwart, cross, contrariwise, transversely; unfavorably, contrarily, perversely.
See also IRASCIBILITY, MIXTURE, OPPOSITION, PASSAGE.

---

cross-shaped, *adj.* cruciate, cruciform, decussate (*bot.*). See CROSSING.
crouch, *v.* stoop, bend; cringe, cower, fawn. See DEPRESSION, SERVILITY.
crowd, *n.* throng, multitude; populace, rabble, *hoi polloi* (*Gr.*). See ASSEMBLAGE, PEOPLE.
crown, *n.* coronet, diadem; top, crest; garland, reward, prize. See ORNAMENT, SUMMIT, TROPHY.
crown, *v.* invest, install; round out, finish; cap, top, crest. See COMMISSION, COMPLETION, SUMMIT.
crucial, *adj.* determining, decisive, supreme, final. See IMPORTANCE.
crude, *adj.* sketchy, unfinished; vulgar, uncouth, rude; raw, unprepared; unwrought, incomplete. See INCOMPLETENESS, INELEGANCE, NONPREPARATION, ROUGHNESS.
cruel, *adj.* unkind, savage, inhuman, barbarous, merciless, ruthless, brutal; acute, severe, painful. See MALEVOLENCE, PAINFULNESS.
cruelty, *n.* brutality, barbarity, persecution, torture. See MALEVOLENCE.
crumble, *v.* break up, perish, fall to pieces; decay, degenerate. See DESTRUCTION, DETERIORATION.
crush, *v.* squeeze, press; overwhelm, suppress, blot out; shame, disconcert; bruise, mash. See CONTRACTION, DESTRUCTION, HUMILITY, POWDERINESS.
crust, *n.* incrustation, hull, shell, rind, coat, coating. See COVERING.

CRY.—I. *Nouns.* **cry,** shout, outcry, clamor, exclamation, ejaculation, utterance, vociferation, call, calling, shriek, howl, bark, hoot, scream, yell, screech, skirl (*Scot.*), squawk, squall, squeak, yelp, bellow, roar; hubbub, hullabaloo, chorus, hue and cry; yoicks (*hunting*), view halloo (*hunting*), tallyho (*hunting*); cooey *or* cooee (*Australia*).
entreaty, appeal, supplication, request, prayer, plea.
crying, sob, sobbing, weeping, tears, lamentation, plaint, wail, whimper, mewl, squall, whimpering, boohoo.
II. *Verbs.* **cry,** shout, vociferate, roar, bawl, bellow, yell, halloo, halloa, yo-ho, cooey *or* cooee (*Australia*), yoick, whoop; hoot, boo; snort, snore, grunt; yelp,

howl, scream, screech, shriek; shrill, squeak, squeal, squall; cheer, huzza, hurrah raise (*or* lift) the voice; yell out, call out, proclaim, sing out, cry out; exclaim, give cry, clamor; rend the air; make the welkin ring; shout at the top of one's voice. lament, wail, moan, groan, bewail, bemoan, regret, greet (*Scot.*), keen (*Ireland*), sob, weep, whimper, pipe the eye (*colloq., of nautical origin*).

III. *Adjectives.* **crying,** flagrant, notorious, glaring, heinous, outrageous, monstrous, atrocious (*as, a* crying *evil*).

clamorous, noisy, turbulent, vociferous, clamant, boisterous, uproarious, blatant, stentorian, open-mouthed, full-mouthed.

See also LAMENTATION, LOUDNESS, ULULATION (*animal sounds*).—*Antonyms.* See REJOICING, SILENCE.

---

cryptography, *n.* cipher, code, steganography. See WRITING.

crystal, *adj.* clear, transparent, crystal-like, crystalline. See TRANSPARENCY.

cub, *n.* pup, puppy, whelp; awkward (*or* unpolished) youth. See ANIMAL, INFANT, VULGARITY.

cudgel, *n.* club, stick, bludgeon, See ARMS.

cue, *n.* catchword, password; hint, intimation. See INDICATION, INFORMATION.

culprit, *n.* criminal, offender, victim, felon, evildoer. See BAD MAN.

cultivate, *v.* till, develop, work; foster, advance, cherish. See HUSBANDRY, IMPROVEMENT.

cultivation, *n.* breeding, refinement; tillage, agriculture; civilization, elevation; learning, education. See COURTESY, HUSBANDRY, IMPROVEMENT, KNOWLEDGE.

culture, *n.* breeding, refinement, cultivation, polish; civilization; education, learning. See COURTESY, IMPROVEMENT, KNOWLEDGE.

cumbrous, *adj.* unwieldy, ponderous; burdensome; oppressive. See GRAVITY, PAINFULNESS.

CUNNING.—I. *Nouns.* **cunning,** craft, subtlety, craftiness, deceit, strategy, maneuvering, temporization; circumvention; chicane, chicanery, sharp practice knavery, jugglery, concealment, a nigger in the woodpile (*colloq.*), guile, duplicity foul play.

skill, dexterity, adroitness, deftness: *in this sense,* cunning *is archaic.*

diplomacy, address, *savoir-faire* (*F.*), skill; artful management, indirection, main chance, politics, Machiavellianism; gerrymander, jobbery, back-stairs influence, lobbyism.

artifice, art, device, machination; plot, maneuver, stratagem, dodge, wile, trick trickery, hoax, shift, ruse, finesse, subterfuge, evasion, white lie, flimflam, bunco, swindle, confidence game, gold brick (*U. S. colloq.*), imposture, deception, net, trap, sell (*colloq.*).

schemer, trickster, grifter (*slang*), shifter, sly boots (*jocose*), fox, reynard; plotter, intriguer, man of cunning.

II. *Verbs.* **be cunning,** scheme, plot, intrigue, live by one's wits; maneuver, gerrymander, finesse, double, temporize, circumvent, outdo, get the better of, throw off one's guard; surprise, waylay, undermine, flatter; have an ax to grind, play a deep game.

III. *Adjectives.* **cunning,** crafty, artful, deep, deep-laid, profound, designing, timeserving, tricky, foxy, *rusé* (*F.*), wily, sly, subtle, insidious, feline, stealthy, underhand, double-faced, shifty, deceptive, deceitful, crooked; shrewd, acute, sharp, canny *or* cannie, astute, knowing; intriguing, scheming, strategic, diplomatic, politic, Machiavellian; cunning as a fox (*or* serpent).

[*of children and small things generally*] interesting, quaint, attractive, pleasing, pretty, dainty, cute (*U. S. colloq.*): *in this sense,* cunning *is an Americanism.*

dexterous, skillful, adept, deft, masterly, ingenious: *in this sense,* cunning *is archaic.*

See also CONCEALMENT, DECEPTION.—*Antonyms.* See ARTLESSNESS.

---

cup, *n.* excavation, crater, hollow; mug, glass, goblet. See CONCAVITY, RECEPTACLE.

cupboard, *n.* closet, locker, storeroom. See RECEPTACLE.

cup-shaped, *adj.* calathiform, poculiform, cupular, cupped. See CONCAVITY.
curb, *v.* control, check, restrain, repress; slacken, retard. See RESTRAINT, SLOWNESS.
curb, *n.* check, control, restraint; brim, margin; curb market. See DISSUASION, EDGE, MART.
cure, *v.* restore, relieve, heal. See REMEDY, RESTORATION.

CURIOSITY.—I. *Nouns.* **curiosity,** inquisitiveness, research, interest, thirst for knowledge, mental acquisitiveness; inquiring mind.
[*in a bad sense*] **meddlesomeness,** prying, officiousness, intrusiveness, inquisitiveness.
[*that which is curious*] rarity, phenomenon, sight, wonder, marvel; curio, knickknack, article of virtu, bric-a-brac (*collective*), objects of art.
busybody, meddler, quidnunc, gossip, newsmonger; Peeping Tom, Paul Pry, eavesdropper, snoop (*U. S.*), snooper (*U. S.*).
II. *Verbs.* **be curious,** scrutinize, inspect, examine, scan, explore, take an interest in, investigate; stare, gape; rubberneck, rubber (*both U. S. slang*); see the sights.
pry, peep, peer, nose, search, ferret out, be inquisitive, snoop (*U. S.*).
III. *Adjectives.* **curious,** inquiring, inquisitive, burning with curiosity, overcurious, prying, meddling, meddlesome, mousing; inquisitorial; agape, expectant.
elaborate, complicated, labored, finely wrought, elegant, skillful, finished.
strange, rare, unique surprising, baffling, extraordinary (*as, a* curious *coincidence*).
See also INQUIRY, RARITY, UNCONFORMITY (*unusual*).—*Antonyms.* See INCURIOSITY.

---

curl, *v.* twist, coil, wave. See CONVOLUTION.
currency, *n.* coin, specie, cash; publicity, circulation. See MONEY, PUBLICATION.
current, *adj.* prevalent, common; rumored, published, circulating; existing, instant. See GENERALITY, NEWS, PRESENCE.
current, *n.* stream, flow, draft, circulation. See RIVER, WIND.
curse, *v.* swear, blaspheme, denounce, damn. See MALEDICTION.
curse, *n.* bane, plague; imprecation, anathema. See BADNESS, MALEDICTION.
curt, *adj.* brusque, blunt, abrupt, rude; brief, short, concise, succinct. See BLUNTNESS, CONCISENESS, SHORTNESS.
curtail, *v.* reduce, lessen, abridge, cut, abbreviate. See SHORTNESS.
curtain, *n.* screen, veil, blind; hanging, drapery. See AMBUSH, SHADE.

CURVATURE.—I. *Nouns.* **curvature,** curvedness, incurvature, incurvation, curving, bending, curvation; flexure, crook, hook, aduncity, deflexion, deviation, detour; sweep, curl; sinuosity.
curve, arc, arch, arcade, vault, bow, crescent, meniscus (*L. pl.* menisci), lune (*geom.*), lunule (*geom.*), half-moon, horseshoe, loop, festoon; turn, bend, incurve (*as in baseball*), fold; parabola, hyperbola; tracery.
II. *Verbs.* **be curved,** sweep, sag; deviate, turn; reënter.
curve, bend, crook, hook, turn, round, bow, arch, arch over, coil, curl, incurve, recurve; deflect, inflect.
III. *Adjectives.* **curved,** curvate, arched, vaulted; bowed, bow-shaped, embowed, arcuate, arclike, arciform; horned; heart-shaped, cordiform, cordate; hook-shaped, hooked, hooklike, uncinate (*tech.*), uncate, unciform; adunc, aduncal, *or* aduncate (*as a parrot's bill*); incurved, incurvate, incurvated; luniform, moon-shaped, lunar, sickle-shaped, falcate, falciform; bell-shaped, campanulate, campaniform; boat-shaped, navicular; naviform, scaphoid (*anat.*), cymbiform; helmet-shaped, galeiform, galeate *or* galeated, cassideous (*bot.*); devious, recurved, circular, oblique.
crescent-shaped, crescentiform, crescentic, crescent, meniscal, lunate, lunated, lunular, lunulate, sigmoid, convexo-concave, semilunar, crescentlike, bicorn, bicornuous (*rare*).
See also CIRCULARITY, CONVOLUTION, DEVIATION.—*Antonyms.* See STRAIGHTNESS.

cushion, *n.* pillow, bolster, pad, pillion (*of a saddle*). See SUPPORT.
custody, *n.* imprisonment, bondage; charge, protection, care, keeping. See RESTRAINT, SAFETY.
custom, *n.* patronage, trade; usage, practice, fashion, precedent, rule. See BARTER, HABIT.
customary, *adj.* habitual, normal, regular, usual. See RULE.
cut, *v.* snub, ignore; divide, sever, split; carve, shape; reap, gather; curtail, abridge. See DISCOURTESY, DISJUNCTION, FORM, HUSBANDRY, SHORTNESS.
cutaneous, *adj.* subcutaneous; tegumentary. See COVERING.
cutting, *adj.* bitter, nipping, raw; sarcastic, caustic, tart; keen-edged, sharpened. See COLD, DISAPPROBATION, SHARPNESS.
cutting-edge, *n.* knife-edge, blade. See SHARPNESS.
cycle, *n.* period, epoch; velocipede, bicycle. See TIME, VEHICLE.
cylinder, *n.* barrel, roller. See ROTUNDITY.
cynic, *n.* misanthrope, pessimist, sneerer. See MISANTHROPY.
cynical, *adj.* sardonic, cutting, surly, disdainful, satirical, sneering, contemptuous, censorious, misanthropic. See CONTEMPT, DISAPPROBATION.

D

dabble, *v.* potter, trifle; dip, moisten, paddle, splash. See INACTIVITY, WATER.
dabbler, *n.* potterer, smatterer, sciolist. See IGNORAMUS.
dactylogram, *n.* fingerprint. See INDICATION.
dagger, *n.* poniard, dirk, stiletto. See ARMS.
dainty, *adj.* pretty, exquisite, delicate, elegant; nice, particular, meticulous; delicious, appetizing, tasty. See BEAUTY, FASTIDIOUSNESS, SAVORINESS.
dally, *v.* flirt, philander; idle, dawdle; prolong, protract. See ENDEARMENT, INACTIVITY, LATENESS.
damage, *v.* harm, injure, impair, mutilate, hurt. See DETERIORATION.
damp, *adj.* moist, humid, foggy, watery. See MOISTURE, SOFTNESS.
damper, *n.* muffler, silencer; wet blanket, kill-joy. See FAINTNESS, HINDRANCE.
dance, *v.* move, flutter; trip, glide, prance, perform. See AGITATION, LEAP.
dance, *n.* party, ball, hop (*colloq.*). See AMUSEMENT.
dancer, *n.* *danseuse* (*F.*, *fem.*), figurant, figurante (*fem.*), ballet girl. See DRAMA.
dandy, *n.* beau, coxcomb, dude (*colloq.*). See FOP.

DANGER.—I. *Nouns.* **danger,** peril, insecurity, jeopardy, risk, hazard, venture, endangerment, precariousness, instability; exposure, vulnerability, vulnerable point, heel of Achilles; forlorn hope, hair-breadth escape; breakers ahead, storm brewing, clouds gathering, clouds on the horizon.

II. *Verbs.* **endanger,** expose to danger, imperil, jeopardize, put to hazard, sail too near the wind; compromise.

risk, hazard, venture, adventure, dare, stake, set at hazard; run the gauntlet, undertake.

III. *Adjectives.* **dangerous,** hazardous, risky, perilous, parlous (*archaic*), unsafe, unprotected, insecure.

defenseless, guardless, unsheltered, unshielded; vulnerable, exposed; on the rocks.

uncertain, dubious, unsteady, unstable, problematical, in question, at stake, under fire; critical, ticklish, slippery, shaky, tottery, tottering, precarious (*not good usage in sense of dangerous*), insecure, top-heavy, tumble-down, ramshackle, crumbling, helpless, trembling in the balance; nodding to its fall; between two fires (*or* perils); between Scylla and Charybdis; between the devil and the deep blue sea.

threatening, ominous, alarming, menacing, dire, thundery, black, dark, lowering, minatory, sinister, ill-omened.

See also FEAR.—*Antonyms.* See SAFETY.

dangle, *v.* swing, wave; hang, be suspended, droop. See OSCILLATION, PENDENCY.

dare, *v.* venture, face; brave, challenge. See COURAGE, DEFIANCE.

DARKNESS.—I. *Nouns.* **darkness,** duskiness, blackness, swarthiness, obscurity, gloom, murk, murkiness, dusk, dark, dimness, dinginess, gloominess, dullness, lightlessness, tenebrosity, opacity; sightlessness, blindness.

[*mental or moral blindness*] ignorance; iniquity, wickedness, sinfulness, depravity, (*as the* darkness *of the Middle Ages*).

[*want of clearness*] **abstruseness,** obscurity, unintelligibleness; reconditeness, profundity; privacy, secrecy, mystery (*as, the* darkness *of a discourse*).

dark, darkness, night; secrecy, mystery; ignorance, unenlightenment (*as, to be in the* dark).

night, nightfall, nighttime; midnight, witching hour, "the very witching time of night" (*Hamlet*), noon of night (*poetic*), dead of night; intense darkness, Cimmerian darkness, Stygian darkness, Egyptian darkness; "darkness visible" (*Paradise Lost*), darkness that can be felt; "the palpable obscure" (*Paradise Lost*); Erebus.

shadow, shade, umbra, penumbra (*as in an eclipse*); obscuration, adumbration, eclipse; skiagraph, skiagram, shadowgram; shadowgraph, radiogram, radiograph; silhouette.

II. *Verbs.* **darken,** obscure, shade, dim; lower, overcast, eclipse, overshadow, cloud, becloud, bedim; tone down.

extinguish, put out, blow out, snuff out, stifle, smother, douse (*slang; as, to* douse *the glim*).

III. *Adjectives.* **dark,** darkling, darksome, obscure, black, lightless, sunless, tenebrous, unilluminated, rayless, inky, atramentous, pitchy, swarthy, swart, coaly, sooty, ebony, funereal, opaque, dead, nocturnal.

somber, dusky, dingy, lurid, gloomy, murky; shady, shadowy, umbrageous; overcast, dull, dim, foggy, cloudy.

[*morally dark*] **evil,** wicked, atrocious, infamous, nefarious, vile (*as,* dark *deeds*).

[*intellectually dark*] **ignorant,** unlettered, untaught, benighted, unenlightened, unrefined, rude (*as, in* darkest *ignorance*).

[*not clear*] **enigmatical,** mysterious, obscure, incomprehensible, abstruse, occult, cabalistic, hidden, secret, esoteric, recondite; faint, indistinct (*as, a* dark *problem or saying*).

[*not cheerful*] **cheerless,** gloomy, sad, dismal, frowning, somber, sullen (*as, the* dark *side of things*).

[*of a race horse or contestant*] **unknown,** unheralded, little known, not recognized by the public, not expected to win, ignored (*as, a* dark *horse*).

---

darling, *n.* love, pet, sweetheart. See FAVORITE.

dart, *v.* hurl, throw, direct; shoot, spurt, scud. See PROPULSION, VELOCITY.

dash, *v.* shatter, crush, break; discourage, depress; blight, frustrate; imbue, season, blend; cast, hurl, fling; speed, rush, sprint. See BRITTLENESS DEJECTION, DISAPPOINTMENT, MIXTURE, PROPULSION, VELOCITY.

dash, *n.* spirit, verve, *élan* (*F.*); line, mark, stroke, score; trace, tinge, hint, grain, sprinkling; rush, spurt, sprint, race. See COURAGE, INDICATION, TOUCH, VELOCITY.

data, *n. pl.* facts, premises (*logic*), memoranda. See MATERIALS.

daunt, *v.* alarm, cow, frighten, discourage. See FEAR.

dauntless, *adj.* undaunted, brave, fearless, courageous. See COURAGE.

dawn, *v.* commence, set in, originate, take its rise. See BEGINNING.

daydream, *n.* air castle; reverie, musing. See HOPE, IMAGINATION.

daylight-saving time, daylight time, fast time. See CHRONOMETRY.

day of rest, Sabbath, Sunday; holiday. See REPOSE.

daze, *v.* dazzle, blind; dumfound, stupefy, bewilder. See LIGHT, WONDER.

dazzle, *v.* dim, daze, confuse; blind, bedazzle; awe, impress, confound. See DIM-SIGHTEDNESS, LIGHT, RESPECT.

dead, *adj.* defunct, lifeless, deceased, extinct, late, departed, inanimate; obsolete. See DEATH.

deaden, *v.* muffle, subdue; incapacitate, unfit; paralyze, numb. See FAINTNESS, IMPOTENCE, INSENSIBILITY.
deadlock, *n.* standstill, halt. See CESSATION.
deadly, *adj.* mortal, fatal; destructive, murderous. See DEATH, KILLING.

DEAFNESS.—I. *Nouns.* **deafness,** hardness of hearing, inaudibility, inaudibleness.
deaf-and-dumb alphabet, dactylology; lip reading, oral method; deaf mute.
II. *Verbs.* **deafen,** render deaf, make deaf, stun, split the ears (*or* eardrum).
make inaudible, drown (*said of sounds*); make soundproof, render impervious to sound (*as a floor or partition*).
III. *Adjectives.* **deaf,** hard (*or* dull) of hearing, earless, stone deaf; stunned, deafened; inattentive, regardless (*as,* deaf *to reason*).
inaudible, unhearable, out of earshot (*or* hearing); silent, mute, noiseless.
Antonyms. See HEARING.

---

deal, *v.* distribute, allot, dispense; deliver, inflict; trade; give, administer, bestow. See APPORTIONMENT, ATTACK, BARTER, GIVING.

DEARNESS.—I. *Nouns.* **dearness,** expensiveness, costliness, high price; overcharge, surcharge; extravagance, exorbitance, extortion, profiteering.
affectionate regard, esteem, value, preciousness; earnestness, sincerity, estimation, honor, devotion.
II. *Verbs.* **overcharge,** bleed (*colloq.*), skin (*slang*), fleece, extort, profiteer, gouge (*colloq.*), overreach, overtax, surcharge.
pay too much, pay dearly, pay through the nose (*colloq.*).
III. *Adjectives.* **dear,** high, high-priced, expensive, costly, sumptuous, valuable precious; extravagant, unreasonable, exorbitant, extortionate.
at a premium, beyond price, above price; priceless, of priceless value.
[*highly esteemed*] loved, beloved, cherished, precious, prized, estimable (*used also as a polite form of address; as,* dear *sir,* dear *Mrs. Green*).
heartfelt, sincere, earnest, heartful, hearty (*as, my* dearest *wish*).
IV. *Adverbs.* **dear, dearly;** at great cost, at heavy cost, at a high price; affectionately, fondly, earnestly.
See also EXPENDITURE, LOVE.—*Antonyms.* See CHEAPNESS, DISLIKE, HATE.

DEATH.—I. *Nouns.* **death,** decease, demise, dying, dissolution, departure, release, debt of nature, rest, eternal rest; cessation (loss, *or* extinction) of life; loss, bereavement; river of death; Jordan, Jordan's bank, Stygian shore; "crossing the bar" (Tennyson); the great adventure.
angel of death, death's bright angel, Azrael; Death, doom, fate, destiny.
death song, dirge, funeral hymn, coronach, requiem, elegy, threnody; swan song *chant du cygne* (*F.*).
necrology, obituary, death notice, obituary notice, register of deaths; mortality, death rate.
II. *Verbs.* **die,** expire, perish; breathe one's last; lose (*or* lay down) one's life; give (*or* yield) up the ghost, take one's last sleep, go off (*colloq.*), pop off (*slang*), pass away, shuffle off this mortal coil, pay the debt to nature, join the choir invisible; go West (*a euphemism reminiscent of the World War*); die for one's country, make the supreme sacrifice.
III. *Adjectives.* **dead,** lifeless, deceased, late, departed, defunct, gone, no more, bereft of life; inanimate, extinct, extinguished, obsolete, past.
deadly, mortal, fatal, lethal, deathly; implacable.
[*resembling death*] motionless, still, immovable, immotile, stagnant, inert, inactive, idle, inoperative (*as, a* dead *law;* dead *center*); quiet, dull, tame, tedious (*as a social season*); unprofitable, ungainful, unproductive, unsalable (*as,* dead *capital;* dead *stock*); out of play, out of the game (*as a ball*); false, blind (*as, a* dead *window*).
[*sure as death*] positive, inescapable, sure, certain; exact, direct (*as, a* dead *shot*).
complete, entire, absolute, total, sheer, thorough, unqualified (*as, a* dead *loss*).
uniform, even, unbroken, undiversified, unrelieved, regular, unvarying, monotonous (*as, a* dead *level*).
dying, moribund, at the point of death, at death's door, at the last gasp, mortal
See also INSENSIBILITY.—*Antonyms.* See LIFE.

deathblow, *n.* end, finishing stroke, *coup de grâce* (*F.*). See KILLING.
debar, *v.* check, obstruct, hinder; forbid, exclude, deny. See HINDRANCE, PROHIBITION.
debase, *v.* depreciate, lower; deprave, degrade; dishonor, disgrace. See DEPRESSION, DETERIORATION, DISREPUTE.
debased, *adj.* adulterated, mixed, deteriorated. See IMPURITY.
debasement, *n.* degradation, disgrace; deterioration, corruption, adulteration. See DISREPUTE, IMPURITY.
debate, *n.* argument, discussion, controversy, contention. See CONVERSATION.

DEBT.—I. *Nouns.* **debt,** obligation, liability, debit, score, claim, due, account, indebtedness.
arrears, outstandings, deferred payment, deficit, default; insolvency; bad debt.
interest; premium, discount, usury (*esp., excessive interest*).
debtor, ower; mortgagor, borrower, defaulter.
II. *Verbs.* **be in debt,** owe; incur (*or* contract) a debt, run up a bill (*or* an account); borrow, run into debt, outrun the constable, be in difficulties.
vouch for, answer for, be surety for, guarantee, go bail for; back one's note.
III. *Adjectives.* **indebted,** in debt, out of pocket; in embarrassed circumstances, in difficulties, encumbered, involved; insolvent.
liable, accountable, responsible, chargeable, answerable for.
unpaid, owing, due, unsettled, unliquidated, unsatisfied, in arrear, outstanding; unrequited, unrewarded.
See also NONPAYMENT.—*Antonyms.* See CREDIT.

---

decay, *v.* rot, putrefy; crumble, fall to pieces, wither. See DECOMPOSITION, DETERIORATION.
decay, *n.* putrefaction, rottenness, corruption; dilapidation, impairment, ruin. See DECOMPOSITION, DETERIORATION.
decayed, *adj.* crumbling, dilapidated, moldering, rotten. See DETERIORATION, WEAKNESS.
decease, *n.* demise, departure, dying. See DEATH.
deceit, *n.* fraud, falsehood, trickery, treachery, sham, double dealing. See DECEPTION.
deceive, *v.* delude, mislead, trick, outwit, cheat. See DECEPTION, TAKING (*take in*).

DECEIVER.—*Nouns.* **deceiver,** deluder, dissimulator, dissembler, hypocrite, Pharisee; sophist; serpent, snake in the grass, Judas, wolf in sheep's clothing; cheater, sharper, trickster, rogue, knave, swindler, cheat, cozener, fraud, faker (*slang*), four-flusher (*slang*); decoy, stool pigeon; perjurer, false witness.
liar, story-teller, prevaricator, equivocator, romancer, fibber, fibster; Ananias.
impostor, pretender, malingerer, humbug; adventurer, adventuress (*fem.*); quack, charlatan, empiric, mountebank.
magician, conjurer, necromancer, sorcerer, sorceress (*fem.*), wizard; enchanter, medicine man, witch doctor, shaman; juggler, prestidigitator.
Antonyms. See DUPE.

---

decent, *adj.* ordinary, passable, mediocre; clean, virtuous, modest. See IMPERFECTION, PURITY.

DECEPTION.—I. *Nouns.* **deception,** duplicity, deceit, wiliness, insidiousness, sophistry, quibbling, mockery, dissimulation, cunning, subtlety, falseness, untruth, imposition, imposture, fraud, guile, fraudulence, misrepresentation, bluff; trickery, hocus-pocus, hanky-panky (*colloq.*), knavery, sharp practice, collusion, chicanery; treachery, double dealing, intrigue.
delusion, jugglery, prestidigitation, sleight of hand, legerdemain, conjuring, magic.
trick, cheat, wile, blind, feint, chicane, juggle, swindle; stratagem, artifice; hoax, plant (*slang*), bunko *or* bunco, gold brick (*U. S. colloq.*), fake (*colloq.*).
snare, trap, pitfall, gin, springe; bait, decoy duck, stool pigeon; cobweb, net, meshes, toils; ambush, ambuscade.

disguise, false colors, camouflage, masquerade, mask, cloak, veil; mummery, borrowed plumes.
sham, imitation, copy, counterfeit, make-believe, forgery, fraud, untruth, lie, hollow mockery; whited sepulcher, fair outside, speciousness, gloss, tinsel, paste, brummagem, scagliola.
illusion, deceptive appearance, apparition, phantasm, myth, *ignis fatuus* (*L.*), mirage, chimera, dream, fallacy.
II. *Verbs.* **deceive,** mislead, lead astray, take in, outwit, circumvent, overreach, outreach, steal a march on; throw dust into the eyes; impose upon, practice upon, palm off on, take advantage of.
cheat, defraud, trick, swindle, gull, hoax, bamboozle (*colloq.*), chouse, cozen, victimize; beguile.
insnare *or* ensnare, entrap, catch, decoy, waylay, lure, inveigle, seduce, allure, entangle; betray, play false.
delude, fool, befool, mystify, blind, hoodwink, bluff, hoax, humbug, stuff (*slang*), sell (*slang*); trifle with, cajole, flatter; dissemble, dissimulate, lie, sham, counterfeit, practice chicanery, live by one's wits, juggle, conjure; play off, palm off, foist off.
III. *Adjectives.* **deceptive,** misleading, deceitful, tricky, cunning, elusive, insidious, delusive, illusory.
sham, make-believe, feigned, pretended, mock, glossy, specious, counterfeit, pseudo, spurious, alloyed, base (*as a coin*), snide (*slang*), assumed, so-called. bogus (*colloq.*), fraudulent, insincere, unreal, surreptitious, illegitimate, contraband; adulterated, disguised; unsound, meretricious, jerry-built; tinsel, catchpenny, brummagem, artificial, factitious.
See also CUNNING, ERROR, FALSEHOOD, SOPHISTRY, UNTRUTH.—*Antonyms.* See PROBITY, VERACITY.

---

decide, *v.* choose, fix upon; arbitrate, decree; resolve, determine, settle. See CHOICE, JUDGE, RESOLUTION, RULE.
decipher, *v.* explain, make out, translate; decode, discover. See INTERPRETATION, MANIFESTATION.
decision, *n.* purpose, resolve; decree, verdict; firmness, will. See INTENTION, JUDGMENT, RESOLUTION.
declaim, *v.* recite, hold forth, harangue. See SPEECH.
declaration, *n.* avowal, assertion; announcement, proclamation, bulletin, notice. See AFFIRMATION, PREDICTION.
declaratory, *adj.* expository, explanatory, affirmative. See INFORMATION.
declare, *v.* assert, state, aver, profess, acknowledge. See AFFIRMATION.
decline, *v.* decay, waste, age, die; refuse, repel, spurn, shun. See DETERIORATION, REJECTION.
decline, *n.* slope, declivity; decay, decadence; dotage, senility. See DESCENT, DETERIORATION, OLDNESS.
declivity, *n.* dip, pitch, slope. See DESCENT, OBLIQUITY.
declivous, *adj.* descending, declivitous, downhill. See OBLIQUITY.

DECOMPOSITION.—I. *Nouns.* **decomposition,** analysis, dissection, dissolution, resolution, break-up; disjunction, disintegration, proteolysis (*physiol. chem.*), hydrolysis (*chem.*), catalysis (*chem.*), electrolysis, electrolization.
decay, rot, putrefaction, putrescence, putridity, corruption; cariosity, caries (*med.*).
II. *Verbs.* **decompose,** dissolve, resolve into its elements, dissect, disintegrate, decentralize, break up, analyze *or* analyse, separate, disperse; crumble into dust; hydrolize (*chem.*), electrolyze (*tech.*).
rot, decay, consume, putrefy, putresce, spoil.
III. *Adjectives.* **decomposed,** dissolved, disintegrated, decompounded, analyzed, hydrolized (*chem.*); analytical, separative, solvent; corrupt, rotten, decayed, carious (*as a tooth*), putrid, tainted, infected.
See also DETERIORATION, DISJUNCTION, UNCLEANNESS.—*Antonyms.* See CLEANNESS, COMBINATION.

---

decoration, *n.* adornment, trimming, embellishment; laurel, medal, ribbon. See ORNAMENT, TITLE.

decorative design, decorative art, decoration, design. See ORNAMENT.
decoy *v.* ensnare, lure, inveigle, entice, entrap. See DECEPTION.

DECREASE.—I. *Nouns.* **decrease,** diminution, lessening, mitigation, subtraction, reduction, abatement, declension, deterioration, decay; decrement, waste, loss, shrinkage, contraction, curtailment, abridgment.
subsidence, wane, ebb, decline, reflux; ebb tide, neap tide, ebbing.
II. *Verbs.* **decrease,** diminish, lessen; abridge, shorten, shrink, contract; dwindle, fall away, waste, wear; wane, ebb, decline, subside, abate, languish, decay, crumble.
reduce, shorten, abbreviate, subtract, dwarf; ease, mitigate, moderate, lower, weaken, attenuate, discount, extenuate; minimize, belittle, depreciate.
See also CONTRACTION, DEDUCTION, MODERATION.—*Antonyms.* See INCREASE.

---

decree, *n.* mandate, edict, ordinance; verdict, decision; regulation, institution. See COMMAND, JUDGMENT, LEGALITY.

DECREMENT.—*Nouns.* **decrement,** decrease, diminution, deduction, attenuation, abatement, decrescence, diminishment, shrinkage, waste, loss, defect, decline, waning (*of the moon*), rebate, discount.
Antonyms. See ADDITION, ADJUNCT.

---

decry, *v.* belittle, disparage, underestimate; slander, censure, degrade. See DETRACTION, DISAPPROBATION.
dedicate, *v.* consecrate, devote, inscribe, offer. See REPUTE, USE.
deduce, *v.* infer, gather, derive. See JUDGE, TAKING.
deducible, *adj.* inferential, sequent, consequential, derivable. See DEMONSTRATION.

DEDUCTION.—I. *Nouns.* [*deducting*] **deduction,** subtraction, removal, excision, abstraction, mutilation, amputation, curtailment, abbreviation; retrenchment.
[*deducing*] **inference** (*from the general to the particular*), *a priori* reasoning, conclusion, consequence, illation, implication, derivation, corollary: *contrasted with* induction.
rebate, remission, abatement; discount, offtake, allowance, tare; minuend, subtrahend; decrease.
II. *Verbs.* **deduct,** subtract, take from, take away, remove, withdraw, abstract, rebate, bate, allow; detract, reduce, decimate, eliminate, diminish, curtail, shorten; deprive of, weaken; retrench.
mutilate, amputate, cut off, cut away, excise, detruncate.
pare, thin, prune, scrape, file, shave, skive (*as a hide*).
III. *Adjectives.* **deductive,** deducible, inferable, inferential, *a priori* (*L.*): *contrasted with* inductive.
minus, less, negative (*math.*), lacking, deficient, short of, devoid of, diminished, smaller.
IV. *Adverbs.* **less,** to a smaller extent, in a lower degree, not so much.
See also REASONING.—*Antonyms.* See ADDITION.

---

deed, *n.* performance, feat, exploit; document. See ACTION, SECURITY.
deep, *adj.* profound, bottomless; abstruse, unfathomable; astute, cunning, designing. See DEPTH.
deer, *n.* elk, reindeer, roe. See ANIMAL.
deface, *v.* mutilate, injure; disfigure, distort, blemish, mar. See DETERIORATION, FORMLESSNESS, UGLINESS.
defame, *v.* abuse, slander, disparage, revile; taint, smirch, sully. See DISAPPROBATION, DISREPUTE.
default, *v.* fail to pay, embezzle. See NONPAYMENT.
defaulting, *adj.* in arrear, in debt. See NONPAYMENT.
defeat, *v.* refute, rebut, silence; vanquish, overcome, subdue, conquer. See CONFUTATION, SUCCESS.
defect, *n.* fault, flaw, imperfection; deficiency, omission, shortcoming, lack; weakness, error, failing. See BLEMISH, INCOMPLETENESS, VICE.

defective, *adj.* faulty, bruised; deficient, out of order; wanting, unfinished; unsound, illogical. See BLEMISH, IMPERFECTION, INCOMPLETENESS, VICE.

DEFENSE.—I. *Nouns.* **defense** *or* defence, protection, security, preservation, guard, care, ward, guardianship; self-defense, self-preservation; resistance; *tutamen* (*L.; pl. tutamina: anat.*), protective part.

justification, vindication, support, advocacy, espousal, apologia, apology, plea, excuse.

safeguard, screen, fortification, bulwark, fosse, moat, ditch, intrenchment, trench, mine, dugout; rampart, dike *or* dyke, levee, parapet, embankment, mound, bank, breastwork, earthwork, fieldwork; battlement, bastion, redoubt, buttress, counterfort, abutment, fence, wall, paling, palisade, stockade, abatis *or* abattis, barrier, barricade, boom; portcullis, *chevaux-de-frise* (*F.; pl.*), barbed-wire entanglements, wire-fence obstacle.

[*protective devices*] buffer, fender, cowcatcher (*U. S.*), bumper, armor *or* armour; mail, shield, ægis, buckler, cuirass, helmet, steel helmet, trench helmet, tin hat (*World War slang*); bullet-proof vest.

stronghold, hold, fastness, asylum, refuge, keep, donjon, citadel, capitol, castle, tower, martello tower, fortress, fort, blockhouse, pill box (*World War slang*), post, barrack.

defender, protector, guardian, bodyguard, champion; knight-errant, Paladin; garrison, picket.

II. *Verbs.* **defend,** guard, secure, watch, protect, keep, save, fend (*archaic or poetic, except in the sense "ward off"*), shield, screen, cover, shroud; garrison, man; fence, intrench, arm, harness (*archaic*), accouter *or* accoutre.

repel, repulse, put to flight; hold (*or* keep) at bay; resist invasion, stand siege, stand (*or* act) on the defensive, parry, show fight, stand one's ground, hold stand in the gap.

uphold, maintain, support, advocate, sustain, vindicate, espouse, plead, champion.

[*in law*] controvert, deny, oppose, contest (*as a suit*).

III. *Adjectives.* **defensive;** armed, armed at all points (cap-a-pie, *or* to the teeth); panoplied, accoutered, "in complete steel" (*Hamlet*); armored, mailed, ironplated, ironclad; bullet-proof, bomb-proof; protective; loopholed, castellated casemated: *opposite of* offensive.

IV. *Adverbs.* **defensively,** on the defensive, in defense, in self-defense; at bay with one's back to the wall.

See also ANSWER, REFUGE, RESISTANCE, SAFETY, VINDICATION.—*Antonyms.* See ATTACK.

---

defenseless, *adj.* exposed, unshielded; powerless, unarmed, helpless. See DANGER, IMPOTENCE.

defensible, *adj.* invulnerable, impregnable; maintainable, supportable; excusable, justifiable. See SAFETY, SUPPORT, VINDICATION.

defensive, *adj.* armed, protected, protective. See DEFENSE.

[1]**defer,** *v.* postpone, retard, delay, procrastinate, adjourn. See LATENESS.

[2]**defer,** *v.* yield, comply, give in, capitulate. See SUBMISSION.

DEFIANCE.—I. *Nouns.* **defiance,** dare, defial, defy (*colloq.*), stump (*U. S. colloq.*), challenge, threat, provocation, opposition, disobedience, insurgency, insubordination, revolt, rebellion; war cry, war whoop.

II. *Verbs.* **defy,** dare, beard, brave, set at defiance, set at naught, hurl defiance at, mock, spurn, scorn, flout, laugh to scorn, bite the thumb at, threaten, challenge, throw (*or* fling) down the gauntlet, assume a fighting attitude, square off *or* up (*colloq.*); disobey, revolt, mutiny, secede.

III. *Adjectives.* **defiant,** resistant, insubmissive, recalcitrant, contumelious, bold, insolent, reckless, contemptuous, mutinous, rebellious, refractory, bellicose, greatly daring, regardless of consequences.

IV. *Adverbs.* **defiantly,** resistantly, etc. (see *adjectives*); in the teeth of; in open rebellion.

See also COURAGE, DISOBEDIENCE, THREAT.—*Antonyms.* See OBEDIENCE, SUBMISSION.

deficient, *adj.* wanting, short, lacking, insufficient, inadequate. See INCOMPLETENESS, SHORTCOMING.

define, *v.* explain, construe, expound; bound, circumscribe. See INTERPRETATION, LIMIT.

definite, *adj.* positive, clear, plain; specific, particular, limited; precise, concrete. See CERTAINTY, LIMIT, TRUTH.

definition, *n.* meaning, explanation, description; distinctness (*of outline*). See INTERPRETATION, VISIBILITY.

deflate, *v.* empty, exhaust. See CONTRACTION.

deflect, *v.* bend, curve, swerve, turn, diverge. See DEVIATION.

deformity, *n.* malformation, crookedness, misproportion, disfigurement. See DISTORTION, UGLINESS.

defraud, *v.* cheat, swindle, hoax, trick, dupe. See DECEPTION.

defray, *v.* pay, discharge, meet, settle, liquidate. See PAYMENT.

defy, *v.* confront, face, brave; oppose, challenge, threaten. See COURAGE, DEFIANCE.

degeneracy, *n.* lowness, demoralization, debasement. See DETERIORATION.

degradation, *n.* fall, humiliation; dishonor, shame, baseness, abasement. See DEPRESSION, DISREPUTE.

degrade, *v.* disgrace, debase, shame, humiliate. See DISREPUTE, LOWNESS.

DEGREE.—I. *Nouns.* **degree,** grade, step, gradation (*usually in pl.*), extent, measure, amount, point, mark, stage, rate, scale, ratio, standard, height, pitch, plane; reach, range, scope, caliber; tenor, compass; division, interval, space (*music*), line (*music*); shade, intensity, strength.

rank, grade, station, sphere, estate, standing, order, class.

II. *Verbs.* **graduate,** grade, calibrate, measure; classify, range.

III. *Adjectives.* **gradual,** by degrees, progressive, regular, graduated, gradational.

IV. *Adverbs.* **gradually,** by degrees, regularly, step by step, little by little, inch by inch, drop by drop; to some extent; slowly, gently.

Antonyms. See INSTANTANEITY, QUANTITY.

---

deify, *v.* canonize, idolize; venerate, immortalize, exalt. See IDOLATRY, REPUTE.

deities, *n.* gods, pantheon. See MYTHICAL BEINGS.

DEITY.—I. *Nouns.* **Deity,** Divinity, Godhead, Omnipotence, Omniscience, Providence.

GOD, Lord, Jehovah, The Almighty, The Supreme Being, The Absolute, The First Cause, I AM, The All-Father, Author of all things, Creator of all things, The King of Kings, The Lord of Lords, The Infinite, The Eternal, The All-powerful, The Omnipotent, The All-wise, The All-merciful, The All-knowing, The Omniscient.

THE TRINITY, The Holy Trinity, The Trinity in Unity, The Triune God, Triunity, Threefold Unity, "Three in One and One in Three."

I. GOD THE FATHER, The Maker, The Creator, The Preserver.

[*functions*] creation, preservation, divine government, divine sovereignty, thearchy.

II. GOD THE SON, Jesus Christ; The Messiah, The Anointed, The Savior *or* Saviour, The Redeemer, The Mediator, The Intercessor, The Advocate, The Judge; The Son of God, The Son of Man; The Only-Begotten, The Lamb of God, The Word, Logos; The Man of Sorrows; Jesus of Nazareth, King of the Jews, The Son of Mary, The Risen, Immanuel, The King of Kings and Lord of Lords, The King of Glory, The Prince of Peace, The Good Shepherd, The Way, The Door, The Truth, The Life, The Bread of Life, The Light of the World, The Vine, The True Vine, The Sun of Righteousness.

The Incarnation, The Word made Flesh, the hypostatic union (*theol.*).

[*functions*] salvation, redemption, atonement, propitiation, mediation, intercession, judgment.

III. GOD THE HOLY GHOST, The Holy Spirit, Paraclete, The Comforter, The Consoler, The Intercessor, The Spirit of God, The Spirit of Truth, The Dove.

[*functions*] inspiration, regeneration, sanctification, consolation, grace.

[*The Deity in other religions*] **Brahmanism** *or* **Hinduism:** Brahm *or* Brahmā (*neuter*), the Supreme Soul *or* Essence of the Universe; Trimurti *or* Hindu trinity *or* Hindu triad: (1) Brahmā (*masc.*), the Creator; (2) Vishnu, the Preserver; (3) Siva *or* Shiva, the Destroyer and Regenerator.
Buddhism: the Protestantism of the East; Buddha, the Blessed One, the Teacher.
Zoroastrianism: Zerâna-Akerana, the Infinite Being; Ahuramazda *or* Ormazd, the Creator, the Lord of Wisdom, the King of Light (*opposed by* Ahriman, the King of Darkness).
Islam *or* **Mohammedanism:** Allah.
II. *Verbs.* **create,** fashion, make, mold *or* mould, manifest, produce, originate, bring into being.
preserve, uphold, keep, maintain, support, conserve, protect; perpetuate, immortalize.
atone, redeem, save, propitiate, expiate; intercede, mediate.
predestinate, predestine, foreordain, preordain, predetermine, preëlect (*theol.*), elect, call, ordain.
bless, sanctify, hallow, consecrate, dedicate, glorify, beatify; justify, absolve.
III. *Adjectives.* **almighty,** all-powerful, omnipotent; omnipresent, ubiquitous; all-wise, omnispective (*rare*), all-seeing, all-knowing, omniscient, supreme, omnific.
divine, godlike, godly, deific, heavenly, celestial; holy, hallowed, sacred, sainted, blessed *or* blest.
supernatural, superhuman, spiritual, ghostly, unearthly, hyperphysical, supramundane.
IV. *Adverbs.* **by God's will** (*or* help), *Deo volente* (*L.*), D. V., God willing.

DEJECTION.—I. *Nouns.* **dejection,** depression, dejectedness, despondency, melancholy, melancholia (*med.*), blues (*colloq.*), blue devils (*colloq.*), hypochondria, hypo (*colloq.*), pessimism, hopelessness, despair, sorrow, sadness, dolefulness, dolor, distress, grief, gloom, mopishness, dumps (*chiefly jocose*), doldrums, horrors, low (*or* depressed) spirits, heaviness, weariness, disgust of life, prostration, broken heart; slough of Despond; disconsolateness, hope deferred.
demureness, soberness, sobriety, gravity, seriousness, solemnity; long face, grave face.
hypochondriac, *malade imaginaire* (*F.*), self-tormentor, croaker, pessimist, damper, kill-joy, crape hanger (*slang*), wet blanket.
II. *Verbs.* **be dejected,** grieve, mourn, lament, sorrow, give way, lose heart, despond, droop, sink, despair, lay to heart, take to heart.
mope, brood over, fret, sulk, lower, scowl, frown, pout; pine, pine away, yearn, repine.
depress, discourage, dishearten, dispirit, damp, dull, deject, sink, dash, unman, prostrate, break one's heart; sadden, dash one's hopes, prey on the mind, damp (*or* depress) the spirits.
III. *Adjectives.* **dejected,** downcast, dispirited, disheartened, despondent, low-spirited, crestfallen, cowed, discouraged, heavy-hearted, sick, sick at heart, out of heart (*or* spirits), down in the mouth (*colloq.*), down on one's luck (*colloq.*), weary, downhearted (*with memories of Tommy Atkins in the black months of the World War: "Are we downhearted?"—NO!*).
cheerless, joyless, spiritless, unhappy, melancholy, disconsolate, forlorn, comfortless, desolate, heartsick, dismal, dreary, depressing, somber, dark, gloomy, lowering, frowning, funereal, mournful, lamentable, dreadful.
sad, pensive, doleful, woebegone, woeful, melancholic, hypochondriacal, hypped (*colloq.*), depressed, sorrowful, lachrymose, splenetic, bilious, jaundiced, saturnine, lackadaisical.
serious, sedate, staid, earnest, grave, sober, solemn, demure, grim, grim-faced, grim-visaged, rueful, wan, long-faced.
overcome, broken-down, prostrate, cut up (*colloq.*), careworn, unnerved, unmanned, downfallen, downtrodden, broken-hearted, crushed, defeated, knocked out, vanquished.
sullen, glum, sulky, mopish, moody, morose, gruff, crusty, ill-humored, sour; heavy, cloudy, dark.
See also DEPRESSION, HOPELESSNESS, PAIN, REGRET, WEARINESS.—*Antonyms.* See CHEERFULNESS.

delay, *v.* impede, retard, obstruct; linger; defer, postpone, procrastinate. See HINDRANCE, LATENESS, NEGLECT.
delectable, *adj.* delightful, pleasant: *archaic or ironical.* See PLEASURABLENESS.
delegate, *n.* envoy, agent, substitute, proxy. See DEPUTY, REPRESENTATIVE.
delegate, *v.* intrust, assign, consign; depute, authorize, empower. See COMMISSION, DEPUTY.
delegation, *n.* deputation; authorization, mandate. See COMMISSION.
delete, *v.* erase, expunge, dele (*printing*), cancel. See OBLITERATION.
deliberate, *adj.* well-considered, voluntary; leisurely, moderate, gradual. See PREDETERMINATION, SLOWNESS.
deliberate, *v.* meditate, reflect, consider, ponder, reason. See THOUGHT.
deliberation, *n.* caution, coolness, deliberateness, prudence. See SLOWNESS.
delicacy, *n.* elegance, daintiness; titbit, luxury; discrimination, tact, culture, sensitiveness; frailty, infirmity. See BEAUTY, SAVORINESS, TASTE, WEAKNESS.
delicious, *adj.* pleasing, dainty, delectable, luscious, palatable. See SAVORINESS.
delight, *v.* charm, please, gratify, enchant. See PLEASURABLENESS.
delightful, *adj.* pleasing, charming, enjoyable, attractive, delicious. See PLEASURABLENESS.
delights, *n. pl.* pleasures, joys, sweets. See SWEETNESS.
delineate, *v.* sketch, block; depict, portray, set forth. See OUTLINE, REPRESENTATION.
delinquent, *adj.* neglectful, remiss. See DERELICTION.
delirious, *adj.* raving, crazed, mad, light-headed. See INSANITY.
delirium tremens, œnomania (*med.*), D. T.'s (*colloq.*). See INSANITY.

DELIVERANCE.—I. *Nouns.* **deliverance,** rescue, release, liberation, extrication, emancipation, redemption, salvation, ransom, reprieve, respite; armistice, truce.
II. *Verbs.* **deliver,** rescue, save, free, liberate, set free, release, emancipate, redeem, ransom, extricate, come to the rescue; rid.
transfer, hand over, surrender, resign, give, commit, pass over, relinquish.
utter, speak, enunciate, express, pronounce, communicate, impart.
discharge, put forth, project, emit, expel, eject, throw, fire, shoot (*as, to* deliver *a ball or broadside*).

See also ESCAPE, GIVING, LIBERATION, TRANSFER, VOICE.—*Antonyms.* See RESTRAINT, RETENTION.

---

delude, *v.* trick, fool, dupe, bluff, hoodwink. See DECEPTION.
deluge, *n.* flood, downpour, inundation. See RIVER.
delusion, *n.* conjuring, magic; illusion, fallacy, misconception, hallucination. See DECEPTION, ERROR.
demand, *v.* exact, order, impose; ask, question; sue, make application; claim, require. See COMMAND, INQUIRY, REQUEST, REQUIREMENT, RIGHTFULNESS.
demand, *n.* requisition, claim, ultimatum; request, call (for), sale, run, market. See COMMAND, REQUIREMENT.
dematerialize, *v.* disembody. See IMMATERIALITY.
democratic, *adj.* Jeffersonian (*U. S.*), popular; neighborly, accessible. See AUTHORITY, SOCIALITY.
demolish, *v.* wreck, crush, shatter, devastate, ruin, overthrow. See DESTRUCTION.
demoniac, *adj.* fiendish, devilish, hellish. See MYTHICAL BEINGS.
demonize, *v.* bewitch, possess. See SATAN.

DEMONSTRATION.—I. *Nouns.* **demonstration,** proof, substantiation, verification, apodeixis (*tech.*), conclusiveness, evidence, testimony.
manifestation, show, exposition, exhibition, display, exhibit, spread, **layout;** exhibition of force (*mil.*); procession, mass meeting.

II. *Verbs.* demonstrate, prove, establish, make good, show, evince, verify, substantiate, sustain, manifest, attest, settle the question; exhibit, show publicly. stand to reason, hold good, hold water (*colloq.*), follow, result.
III. *Adjectives.* demonstrated, proved, proven (*archaic and Scot.*), unconfuted, unanswered, unrefuted; evident, self-evident, axiomatic.
deducible, consequential, derivable, sequent, sequential, consequent, inferable, inferential, following.
demonstrative, proving, probative, probationary, conclusive, decisive, convincing; irresistible, irrefutable, undeniable, unanswerable, demonstrable.
[*given to display of feeling*] unreserved, unrestrained, emotional, ingenuous, cordial, gushing (*colloq.*); communicative, expressive.
IV. *Adverbs.* of course, consequently, as a matter of course, naturally.

See also EVIDENCE, EXPERIMENT, MANIFESTATION, OSTENTATION.—*Antonyms.* See CONFUTATION, INSENSITIVENESS.

---

demoralize, *v.* unnerve, incapacitate, undermine; deprave, corrupt, pervert. See IMPOTENCE. VICE.
demur, *v.* cavil, protest, wrangle; object, scruple, stick at. See DISSENT, UNBELIEF, UNWILLINGNESS.
demur, *n.* objection, remonstrance, scruple. See DIFFICULTY.
demure, *adj.* priggish, precise; solemn, sad; staid, sedate, grave; shy, bashful, retiring. See AFFECTATION, DEJECTION, INEXCITABILITY, MODESTY.
den, *n.* lair, cave; sanctum, study; retreat, cell; haunt, resort, dive (*U. S.*). See HABITATION, RECEPTACLE, SECLUSION, VICE.—**den of thieves,** nest of thieves (*or* robbers), Alsatia. See STEALING.
denial, *n.* contradiction; disallowance, repudiation, negation, disbelief. See DISSENT, REFUSAL.
denomination, *n.* designation, specification, name, title; side, kind, persuasion, cause, sect. See CLASS, NOMENCLATURE, PARTY.
denote, *v.* signify, betoken, stand for, represent; express, imply, convey; designate, specify. See INDICATION, MEANING, SPECIALTY.
denounce, *v.* charge, arraign; censure, blame, rebuke; curse, damn. See ACCUSATION, DISAPPROBATION, MALEDICTION.

DENSITY.—I. *Nouns.* **density,** solidity, solidness, compactness, body, closeness, impenetrability, impermeability, incompressibility, imporosity; crowdedness, thickness; costiveness, constipation.
condensation, solidification, consolidation, concretion, coagulation, congelation, cohesion, petrifaction, inspissation, thickening, crystallization, precipitation.
solid body, solid mass, block lump; concretion, concrete, conglomerate; stone, rock, cake; bone, gristle, cartilage.
stone (*of a fruit*), nucule (*bot.*), nutlet, pyrene (*bot.*), pit (*U. S.*), endocarp (*bot.*), pip, seed.
dregs, sediment, lees, settlings, grounds, bottoms, residuum, deposit, precipitate (*chem.*), precipitation (*chem.*).
stupidity, crassness, thick-headness, ignorance, ineptitude, opacity, dullness, thickness, obtuseness.
II. *Verbs.* be dense, compress, squeeze, ram down, compact, consolidate, solidify, cement, set, condense, congeal, coagulate, curd, curdle, fix, clot, thicken, inspissate, incrassate, cohere, cake, candy; precipitate, deposit; crystallize; petrify, harden, stiffen.
III. *Adjectives.* dense, solid, pucka *or pakka* (*Anglo-Indian*); solidified, coherent, cohesive, compact, thick, close, serried, thickset; substantial, massive, impenetrable, impermeable, imporous, concrete, hard, grumous, clotted.
[*of ignorance or the like*] crass, intense, profound, absolute.
stupid, thick-headed, ignorant, inept, thick, obtuse, inert, heavy, dull.
undissolved, unmelted, unliquefied, unthawed.
indivisible, indiscerptible, infrangible, infusible, indissoluble, insoluble, impartible, inseparable.

See also ASSEMBLAGE, COHERENCE, HARDNESS, HEAVINESS, IGNORANCE, THICKNESS.—*Antonyms.* See INTELLIGENCE, RARITY.

dent, *n.* hollow, indentation, depression, cavity. See CONCAVITY.
denunciation, *n.* arraignment, condemnation; curse, imprecation; menace defiance. See ACCUSATION, MALEDICTION, THREAT.
deny, *v.* protest, differ; contradict, gainsay; reject, withhold; doubt, discredit See DISSENT, NEGATION, REFUSAL, UNBELIEF.
deodorization, *n.* disinfection, fumigation. See INODOROUSNESS.
department, *n.* bureau, office, division. See JURISDICTION.

DEPARTURE.—I. *Nouns.* **departure,** going, setting out, *congé* (*F.*), leaving, exit, start, outset, embarkation, sailing, exodus, hegira, flight; deviation, abandonment; removal, death, decease.
leave-taking, leave, parting, adieu, farewell, good-by, Godspeed, valediction, valedictory (*farewell oration*).
II. *Verbs.* **depart,** go, go away, go off, take one's departure, set out, start, issue, march out, debouch, sally forth, sally, go forth; take flight, take wing, fly, flit, disappear, abscond; strike tents, decamp, break camp, take leave; entrain; saddle, bridle, harness up, hitch up (*colloq.*).
leave, quit, vacate, evacuate, abandon, withdraw, retire, remove, cut (*colloq. or slang*).
embark, go on board, take ship, go aboard; set sail, put to sea, sail, hoist the blue Peter; get under way, weigh anchor.
III. *Adverbs.* **hence,** away, from here (*in this sense,* **hence** *is archaic or poetic*), whence, thence.
IV. *Interjections.* **farewell!** good-by *or* good-bye! fare you well! adieu! Godspeed! *addio!* (*It.*), *adios!* (*Sp.*), *adeus!* (*Pg.*), *au revoir!* (*F.*), *auf wiedersehen!* (*Ger.*), *a rivederci!* (*It.*), sayonara! (*Jap.*), *bon voyage!* (*F.*), *glückliche Reise!* (*Ger.*), *lebewohl!* (*Ger.*), *vale* (*L.*), *vive valeque* (*L.*), bye-bye! (*colloq.*), so long! (*slang*).
See also DISAPPEARANCE, EGRESS, PART, PASSAGE.—*Antonyms.* See ARRIVAL.

---

depend, *v.* credit, trust; dangle, hang; rely, lean upon; be contingent. See BELIEF, PENDENCY, [1]REST, UNCERTAINTY.
dependent, *n.* satellite, parasite, slave, *protégé* (*F.*). See SERVANT.
depict, *v.* represent, delineate, portray, picture. See DESCRIPTION.
depletion, *n.* emptiness, exhaustion. See INSUFFICIENCY.
deplorable, *adj.* pitiable, lamentable, grievous, sad. See BADNESS.
deplore, *v.* mourn, bewail, lament, regret, complain. See LAMENTATION.
deport, *v.* exile, banish, transport, remove. See PUNISHMENT.
depose, *v.* swear, take oath, testify; dethrone, remove. See AFFIRMATION, ANNULMENT.
deposit, *n.* payment, installment; pledge, guarantee; sediment, alluvium. See EXPENDITURE, SECURITY, TRANSFER (*things transferred*).
deposition, *n.* dethronement, expulsion; allegation, sworn evidence, affidavit. See ANNULMENT, RECORD.
depository, *n.* storehouse, warehouse, safe-deposit vault, repository. See STORE.
depravity, *n.* corruption, badness, perversion, degeneracy, wickedness. See VICE.

DEPRECATION.—I. *Nouns.* **deprecation,** disapprobation, disapproval, remonstrance, protest, expostulation; intercession, mediation.
II. *Verbs.* **deprecate,** disapprove of, remonstrate, protest, expostulate, enter a protest.
III. *Adjectives.* **deprecatory,** expostulatory, intercessory, mediatory, mediatorial, apologetic.
Antonyms. See REQUEST.

---

depreciate, *v.* disparage, slander; lessen, fall, drop; slight, affront; undervalue, underrate. See DISAPPROBATION, DISCOUNT, DISRESPECT, UNDERESTIMATION.
depreciative, *adj.* depreciatory, derogatory, disparaging. See UNDERESTIMATION.

DEPRESSION.—I. *Nouns.* **depression,** lowering, sinking, cavity, hollow, dip, diminution.
degradation, humiliation, abasement, reduction, fall, prostration; subversion, upset, overthrow, overturn.
dejection, melancholy, dispiritedness, despondency, discouragement, gloom, sadness, down-heartedness.
bow, curtsy, dip (*colloq.*), bob, duck, kotow (*Chinese*), obeisance, salaam, genuflexion.
II. *Verbs.* **depress,** lower, cast down, let drop, let fall; sink, debase, bring low, humble, degrade, abase, reduce, precipitate; depreciate, weaken, diminish (*as trade or values*); flatten (*as the voice*).
overthrow, overturn, overset, upset, prostrate, level, fell, down (*archaic or colloq.*), cast (throw, fling, dash, pull, knock, *or* hew) down, raze, upturn, desolate.
sit, sit down, squat, couch, recline, sprawl, perch.
crouch, stoop, bend, cower, droop, incline.
bow, curtsy, kotow (*Chinese*), duck, bob, dip, incline, make obeisance, salaam, prostrate oneself, bow down, kneel, genuflect.
deject, dispirit, sadden, discourage, damp, dishearten, cast down, cow.
III. *Adjectives.* **depressed,** lowered, sunk, deadened, dulled, at a low ebb (*as trade*); prostrate (*bot.*).
dejected, dispirited, downcast, despondent, sad, forlorn, heartsick.
See also CONCAVITY, DEJECTION, DEPTH, DULLNESS, HEAVINESS.—*Antonyms.* See CHEERFULNESS, ELEVATION.

---

deprive, *v.* dispossess, bereave, strip, despoil, rob. See TAKING.

DEPTH.—I. *Nouns.* **depth,** deepness, profoundness, profundity; intensity, completeness, abundance; extent, measure.
pit, shaft, well, crater, depression, hollow, chasm, crevasse, deep, abyss, bowels of the earth, bottomless pit.
sounding (*naut.*), depth of water, water; plummet, lead, plumb, bob, plumb line, sounding lead (line, bottle, *or* machine); probe (*surgery*).
draft *or* draught (*naut.*), submergence, submersion, sinkage; displacement.
science of sounding: bathometry; bathometer.
discernment, astuteness, sagacity, penetration, acumen.
II. *Verbs.* **deepen,** sink, dig, burrow, excavate, mine, sap; intensify, strengthen, increase; make graver, lower (*as in tone*).
sound, fathom, heave the lead, take soundings, plumb, plumb-line.
III. *Adjectives.* **deep,** deep-seated, profound, buried; sunk, submerged, subaqueous, submarine, subterranean, underground.
bottomless, fathomless, soundless, unfathomed, unfathomable, abysmal, yawning, immeasurable.
[*hard to penetrate*] **obscure,** abstruse, mysterious, intricate, knotty, dark, esoteric, recondite (*as, a* deep *subject*).
[*of emotions*] **heartfelt,** sincere, profound, thorough, complete, extreme, intense (*as,* deep *sorrow*).
[*of sleep*] **profound,** fast, heavy, undisturbed, sound.
[*of tones*] **sonorous,** resonant, full-toned, grave, full, rumbling (*as thunder*).
[*of colors*] **intense,** intensified, dense, rich, strong, dark (*as,* deep *blue*).
sagacious, discerning, penetrating, shrewd, astute, cunning, skilled.
excessive, absorbing, extreme, heavy, immoderate (*as study or drinking*).
engrossed, absorbed, involved, rapt, immersed (*as in reading*).
IV. *Adverbs.* **out of one's depth,** beyond one's depth; over head and ears.
See also CONCAVITY, CUNNING, INTELLIGENCE.—*Antonyms.* See SHALLOWNESS.

DEPUTY.—I. *Nouns.* **deputy,** substitute, surrogate, proxy, *locum tenens* (*L.*), delegate, representative, agent, attorney, alternate; vice-president, vice-chairman.
regent, vicegerent, viceroy, minister, vicar, prime minister, premier, chancellor provost, warden, lieutenant, consul, ambassador, plenipotentiary.
II. *Verbs.* **depute,** delegate, deputize (*U. S.*), commission, empower, accredit, authorize, substitute.

represent, stand for, appear for, answer for, hold a brief for, stand in the shoes of, stand in the stead of.
III. *Adjectives.* acting, officiating, substituting, vice, vicegerent, vicegeral, delegated, representative, accredited.
IV. *Adverbs.* in behalf of, for, instead of, in the place of, on account of, by proxy, *per pro.* (*L., per procurationem*).
See also COMMISSION, REPRESENTATIVE.—*Antonyms.* See DIRECTOR (*head*).

DERANGEMENT.—I. *Nouns.* **derangement,** disarrangement, disorder, confusion, disturbance, static (*radio*), irregularity, discomposure, disorganization; dislocation, embarrassment, mess, muss (*U. S. colloq.*), litter, jumble, tangle, inversion; insanity, mania, madness.
II. *Verbs.* **derange,** disarrange, discompose, disturb, start (*as a bolt*), loosen, displace, misplace; mislay, disorder, disorganize; embroil, convulse, unsettle, trouble, disconcert, perturb, upset, unbalance, unhinge, dislocate, put out of joint, throw out of gear; muddle, jumble, confuse; complicate, involve, perplex, embarrass, confound; tangle, entangle, tousle (*colloq.*), dishevel, ruffle, rumple, turn topsy-turvy, turn upside down, litter, scatter, mix.
[*render insane*] **craze,** dement (*rare*), madden, unsettle, unhinge, unbalance.
III. *Adjectives.* **deranged** (*in mind*), disordered, crazy, mad, demented, insane.
See also DISORDER, INSANITY.—*Antonyms.* See ARRANGEMENT, SANITY.

DERELICTION.—I. *Nouns.* **dereliction,** abandonment, neglect, relinquishment, desertion, omission, failure, fault, delinquency, negligence, nonobservance, nonperformance, noncoöperation; indolence, faithlessness; infraction, violation, transgression, evasion, dead letter.
slacker, loafer, lounger, idler, *flâneur* (*F.*), potterer, dawdler, dallier, time-killer, time-waster, eyeservant; striker.
II. *Verbs.* **violate,** break, break through, break in upon, abuse, infringe, set aside, set at naught, encroach upon, trench upon, trample on, contravene, disregard, slight, neglect, evade, escape, transgress, fail.
III. *Adjectives.* **derelict,** abandoned, deserted, relinquished (*as, a* derelict *ship*).
delinquent, negligent, neglectful, faithless, unfaithful: *in this sense,* derelict *is chiefly U. S.*
See also GUILT, NEGLECT, RELINQUISHMENT.—*Antonyms.* See DUTY.

---

deride, *v.* scorn, disdain; mock, jeer, scoff, ridicule. See CONTEMPT, DISRESPECT.
derisive, *adj.* sarcastic, contemptuous, scornful, disdainful, mocking. See RIDICULE.
derive, *v.* gain, get, secure; trace, account for; deduce, infer; etymologize. See ACQUISITION, ATTRIBUTION, JUDGE, WORD.
derogatory, *adj.* discreditable, ignoble, scandalous, unbefitting. See IMPROBITY.
descend, *v.* go down, slide, dismount, tumble. See DESCENT.
descendant, *n.* offspring, scion, heir. See POSTERITY.

DESCENT.—I. *Nouns.* **descent,** declension, declination, drop, fall, cadence, sinking, droop, plunge, slump (*colloq.*), settlement, subsidence, lapse, downcome, comedown, setback, downfall, tumble, debacle, downrush, stumble, slip, tilt, trip, lurch; fate of Icarus (Phaëthon, *or* Lucifer).
avalanche, landslide (*U. S.*), landslip (*Eng.*), slide, snowslide, glissade.
declivity, slope, dip, decline, pitch, drop, down-grade.
incursion, attack, assault, invasion, raid (*as, a* descent *upon our shores*).
lineage, ancestry, birth, extraction, parentage, pedigree.
II. *Verbs.* **descend,** go (drop, *or* come) down, fall, gravitate, drop, slip, sideslip (*aëro.*), skid, slide, settle; decline, sink, set, dip, subside, droop, slump (*colloq.*).
get down, dismount, alight, light; swoop, pounce; crouch, stoop; fall prostrate, precipitate oneself; let fall.
tumble, trip, stumble, founder, lurch, pitch, plunge, topple; tilt, sprawl, come a cropper (*colloq.*).
raid, invade, assault, fall upon, make a descent.
originate, take rise, be derived, arise, spring, issue, come.

III. *Adjectives.* **descending,** falling, descendent; downward, down; deciduous decursive, decurrent (*bot.*).
steep, sloping, declivitous, precipitous; declivous; beetling, overhanging.

See also CONTINUITY, DEPRESSION, EXTRACTION, PATERNITY, POSTERITY.—*Antonyms.* See ASCENT.

DESCRIPTION.—I. *Nouns.* **description,** account, statement, report, record, brief, summary, outline, specification, definition, portraiture, delineation, sketch, representation, depiction, monograph; narration, recital, rehearsal, relation, explanation; kind, sort.
narrative, history, memoir, annals, journal, letters, biography, autobiography, life, adventures, experiences, ana; historic Muse, Clio.
fiction, novel, romance, story, tale, short story, anecdote, yarn, mystery story, thriller (*slang*), detective story, "grue" (Stevenson), fairy tale, myth, legend, fable, parable, allegory, epic.
narrator, recorder, relator *or* relater, teller, describer, chronicler, interviewer; historian, biographer, novelist, story-teller, romancer, anecdotist, *raconteur* (*F.*), writer, author.
II. *Verbs.* **describe,** set forth, picture, portray, depict, paint, sketch, represent, characterize, delineate, narrate, relate, recite, recount, romance, tell, report, record, chronicle, explain, define, detail, particularize, epitomize; repeat, recapitulate.
III. *Adjectives.* **descriptive,** depictive, delineatory, picaresque, narrative, epic, romantic, historic *or* historical, biographical, autobiographical; traditional, legendary, mythical, fabulous; anecdotic, storied, artistic, idealistic; realistic, vivid, graphic, true to life, lifelike.

See also COMPENDIUM, INFORMATION, RECORD, REPRESENTATION.

---

[1]**desert,** *n.* due, recompense, meed, worth. See RIGHTFULNESS.
[2]**desert,** *n.* waste, wild, wilderness, Sahara. See PLAIN, UNPRODUCTIVENESS.
desert, *v.* leave, run away, decamp, abscond; forsake, abandon. See AVOIDANCE, RELINQUISHMENT.
deserter, *n.* truant, runaway, fugitive, apostate. See AVOIDANCE.
deserve *v.* merit, be worthy of, earn. See RIGHTFULNESS.
design, *n.* make-up, arrangement; treatment, depiction, drawing; object, aim, intent; project, purpose; model, pattern. See COMPOSITION, FINE ARTS, INTENTION, PLAN, PROTOTYPE.
designate, *v.* call, name, term; show, specify, indicate. See NOMENCLATURE, SPECIALTY.

DESIRE.—I. *Nouns.* desire, wish, fancy, notion, inclination, leaning, bent, mind, whim, partiality, predilection, propensity, liking, love, fondness, relish; request, requirement, need, want, exigency, urgency, necessity.
longing, hankering, hunger, yearning, aspiration, ambition, eagerness, zeal, ardor, solicitude, anxiety, craving, itch, appetency; concupiscence, sexual desire, libido (*psychol.*), biological urge, carnal passion, lust.
appetite, keenness, hunger, stomach, twist (*dial. Eng. or slang*), thirst, polydipsia (*med.*), dipsomania (*med.*); drought; torment of Tantalus.
avidity, greed, greediness, ravenousness, grasping, rapaciousness, rapacity, voracity, covetousness, itching palm, cupidity.
frenzy, mania, passion, rage, furor; œstrus (*esp. physiol.*), heat, rut, must (*said of elephants*); craze; monomania.
desirer, aspirant, lover, votary, devotee, zealot, enthusiast; parasite, sycophant.
[*object of desire*] attraction, magnet, loadstone, lure, allurement, bait, decoy, fancy, temptation, fascination, charm; hobby, pursuit.
II. *Verbs.* **desire,** wish, wish for, care for, want, affect, like, take to, cling to, fancy; prefer, have an eye to, have a mind to; have a fancy for, have at heart, be bent upon, set one's heart (*or* mind) upon, covet, crave, hanker after, pine for (*or* after), long for, hope for, sigh for, yearn for; need, miss, lack; ask, request, solicit.
woo, court, ogle; fish for.
attract, allure, lure, bait, charm, tempt, entice, pull, draw, intrigue, whet the appetite, appetize, take one's fancy, tantalize; make one's mouth water.

III. *Adjectives.* **desirable,** agreeable, pleasing, covetable, appetizing, desired, in demand, popular, preferable, advantageous.
desirous, desiring, appetitive, inclined, fain, partial to, wishful, longing, wistful, anxious, solicitous, sedulous; eager, keen, burning, fervent, ardent, avid, agog, breathless, impatient; ambitious, aspiring, vaulting.
craving, hungry, sharp-set, peckish (*colloq.*), ravening, famished; thirsty, athirst, dry (*colloq. when meaning* thirsty), droughty.
greedy, voracious, ravenous, omnivorous, covetous, avaricious, rapacious, grasping, extortionate, exacting, sordid, insatiable, insatiate, unsatisfied, unsated.
See also DISPOSITION, EXCITABILITY, GLUTTONY, HOPE, ITCHING, RIGHT.—*Antonyms.* See DISLIKE, INDIFFERENCE, SATIETY.

---

desist, *v.* discontinue, halt, cease, stop, quit, abstain, forbear. See CESSATION.
desk, *n.* stand, pulpit, reading desk. See SCHOOL.
desolate, *adj.* deserted, uninhabited, waste; forlorn, miserable, bereaved, melancholy; forsaken, solitary, lonely. See ABSENCE, DEJECTION, EXCLUSION.
despair, *n.* despondency, dejection; misery, wretchedness, anguish. See HOPELESSNESS, PAIN.
desperado, *n.* ruffian, adventurer, dare-devil. See RASHNESS.
desperate, *adj.* despairing, incurable; reckless, headlong, wild; frantic, raging, frenzied. See HOPELESSNESS, RASHNESS, VIOLENCE.
despise, *v.* scorn, disdain, disregard, spurn, contemn. See CONTEMPT.
despite, *prep.* in spite of, notwithstanding, in the face of. See OPPOSITION.
despond, *v.* mourn, lament, sink; despair, falter, give up. See DEJECTION, HOPELESSNESS.
despotism, *n.* autocracy, imperialism; tyranny, oppression. See AUTHORITY, SEVERITY.
destination, *n.* goal, port, halting place; object, mark, point. See ARRIVAL, END.

DESTINY.—I. *Nouns.* **destiny,** fate, lot, portion, doom, fortune, fatality, fatalism; future, future state, future existence, hereafter, next world, world to come, life to come; prospect, expectation.
II. *Verbs.* **destine,** foreordain, preordain, predetermine, predestine, predestinate, doom, ordain, decree, consecrate, devote, intend, determine; reserve, bespeak.
impend, hang over, threaten, menace, hover, loom, await, approach.
III. *Adjectives.* **destined,** foreordained, etc. (see *verbs*); fated, predestinate.
impending, threatening, menacing, forthcoming, brewing, looming, coming, in store, to come, instant, at hand, near, imminent; in the wind, in prospect; on the knees (*or* lap) of the gods.
reserved, set aside, set apart, booked, engaged, bespoken, in reserve.
See also EXPECTATION, INTENTION, NECESSITY.—*Antonyms.* See EVENT.

---

destitute, *adj.* lacking, bereft; poor, needy, penniless. See INSUFFICIENCY, POVERTY.
destroy, *v.* demolish, ruin, annihilate, raze, efface, eradicate. See DESTRUCTION, LOSS.

DESTROYER.—*Nouns.* **destroyer,** demolisher, wrecker, annihilator; iconoclast, vandal, Hun, nihilist; killer, slayer, assassin, executioner; torpedo-boat destroyer.
See also BANE, EVILDOER, KILLING, SCOURGE.—*Antonyms.* See PRODUCER.

DESTRUCTION.—I. *Nouns.* **destruction,** demolition, ruin, ruination, overthrow, subversion, havoc, waste, dissolution, breaking up, disruption, disorganization, suppression, abolition, sacrifice, ravage, ravaging, devastation, incendiarism, revolution, sabotage, rattening (*Eng. trade-union cant*).
fall, downfall, crash, smash, crack-up (*esp. of an airplane: colloq.*), breakdown, break-up, cave-in (*colloq.*); wreck, shipwreck, cataclysm, debacle, perdition.
extinction, extermination, extirpation, extinguishment, annihilation, slaying killing; doom, crack of doom.

II. *Verbs.* **destroy,** unbuild, do (*or* make) away with, waste; nullify, annul, sacrifice, demolish, overturn, vitiate (*as a contract*), invalidate, overthrow, overwhelm, upset, subvert, put an end to, do for (*colloq.*), undo, break down, cut down, pull down, dismantle, mow down, blow down; suppress, quash, put down, crush, blot out, obliterate, efface, cancel, erase, strike out, expunge, delete, dele (*printing*), dispel, dissipate, dissolve, consume; smash, crash, quell, squash (*colloq.*), shatter, shiver, batter; tear (pull, *or* crush) to pieces, ruin, fell.
sink, swamp, scuttle, wreck, shipwreck, engulf, submerge; lay in ruins, raze, level; deal destruction, lay waste, ravage, gut; devour, desolate, devastate, blast, extirpate, extinguish, quench, exterminate, eradicate, annihilate.
perish, fall, fall to the ground, tumble, topple; fall to pieces, break up, crumble, go to wrack and ruin; go by the board, be all over with, go to pieces, totter to its fall; wither, waste away, die, decay, disintegrate.
III. *Adjectives.* **destructive,** ruinous, fatal, deadly, mortal, suicidal; pernicious, baleful, mischievous, extirpatory, annihilative, all-destroying, all-devouring, subversive, subversionary, demolitionary, incendiary, conflagrative (*rare*), cataclysmic *or* cataclysmal.
See also ANNULMENT, DETERIORATION, KILLING, REVOLUTION, WASTE.—*Antonyms.* See PRESERVATION, PRODUCTION.

---

desultory, *adj.* fitful, aimless, erratic; digressive, rambling; disconnected, broken; spasmodic, unmethodical. See CHANGEABLENESS, DEVIATION, DISCONTINUITY, IRREGULARITY.
detach, *v.* loosen, disconnect, sever, unfasten, separate. See DISJUNCTION.
detachment, *n.* division, squad, detail, separation, segregation; preoccupation, absentmindedness; portion. See COMBATANT, DISJUNCTION, INATTENTION, PART.
detail, *n.* detachment (*mil.*), party, patrol; minute account; item, particular, feature. See COMBATANT, SPECIALTY, WAY (*respect*).
detailed, *adj.* itemized, exact, particular. See CIRCUMSTANCE.
details, *n. pl.* minutiæ, trivialities, niceties, fine points; particulars, specifications. See SMALLNESS, SPECIALTY.
detain, *v.* delay, retard; keep in custody; secure, keep, withhold. See HINDRANCE, RESTRAINT, RETENTION.
detect, *v.* perceive, discern, reveal, expose, unearth. See DISCOVERY.
detector, *n.* discoverer; detecting device, detectograph. See DISCOVERY.
deter, *v.* restrain, hold back, discourage, hinder. See DISSUASION.

DETERIORATION.—I. *Nouns.* **deterioration,** impairment, damage, loss, detriment, injury, harm, debasement; wane, ebb, recession, retrogradation, decrease; outrage, havoc, inroad, ravage, vitiation, discoloration, pollution, poisoning, contamination, canker, corruption, adulteration, alloy.
degeneracy, degeneration, degradation, depravation, depravity, demoralization.
decline, declension, declination; decadence, decadency, depreciation, derogation, falling off; senility, decrepitude.
decay, dilapidation, disintegration, decomposition, disrepair, wear and tear, erosion, corrosion, rottenness; moth and rust, dry rot, blight, atrophy.
II. *Verbs.* **deteriorate,** degenerate, fall off, wane, ebb, retrograde, decline, droop, run to seed (*or* waste), lapse, break down, crack, shrivel, fade, go off, wither, molder, rot, rankle, decay, go bad; corrode, rust, oxidize, wear away, consume, gnaw, eat, erode, disintegrate; fall "into the sere, the yellow leaf" (*Macbeth*); rust, crumble, shake, totter, perish, die.
corrupt, taint, infect, contaminate, poison, envenom, canker, blight, rot, pollute, defile, vitiate, debase, deprave, degrade; alloy, adulterate, tamper with, doctor (*colloq.*); prejudice, subvert, pervert, demoralize, brutalize.
embitter, exasperate, irritate, exacerbate, anger, nettle, inflame.
injure, impair, damage, harm, hurt, scathe (*archaic*), spoil, mar, despoil, waste; overrun, ravage, harry, pillage.
wound, stab, pierce, maim, lame, cripple, hock, hamstring, mangle, mutilate, lacerate, disfigure, blemish, deface, warp.
III. *Adjectives.* **deteriorated,** unimproved, injured, degenerate, imperfect;

battered, weathered, weather-beaten, stale, wilted, gone by (*colloq.*), *passé* (*F.; fem. passée*), faded, antiquated, time-worn, rusty, secondhand, worn, wasted, shabby, seedy (*colloq.*), threadbare, frayed.
decayed, moth-eaten, worm-eaten, mildewed, moldy, effete, crumbling, moldering, rotten, cankered, blighted, tainted; decrepit, broken-down, dilapidated, ruinous, useless, worn-out, used up (*colloq.*).
stagnant, standing, inactive, idle, dormant, backward, unprogressive, dead, lifeless, motionless, inanimate, sluggish, effortless, inert.
See also DESTRUCTION, INUTILITY, RECESSION, REGRESSION, UNCLEANNESS, VICE, WASTE.—*Antonyms.* See IMPROVEMENT.

---

determination, *n.* resoluteness, decision, firmness, resolve, conclusion, judgment, decree. See RESOLUTION, WILL.
determine, *v.* influence, effect, impel; insure, clinch; solve, fathom, understand; ascertain, settle, conclude; limit, bound, define; decree, pass upon; specify, designate, ordain; resolve, decide. See CAUSE, CERTAINTY, DISCOVERY, JUDGE, LOCATION, RESOLUTION, SPECIALTY, WILL.
determined, *adj.* resolute, resolve, decided, firm, indomitable, set, arbitrary. See RESOLUTION, WILL.
detest, *v.* loathe, abhor, abominate, despise. See HATE.
dethrone, *v.* depose. See ANNULMENT, LAXITY.
dethronement, *n.* deposition, overthrow. See LAXITY.
detour, *n.* deviation, turning. See CIRCUIT.

DETRACTION.—I. *Nouns.* **detraction,** disparagement, depreciation, vilification, obloquy, scandal, derogation, roorback (*U. S.*), defamation, slander, calumny, evil-speaking, back-biting; sarcasm, cynicism, criticism, censure, Zoilism, invective; personalities, libel, lampoon, skit (*Scot. and dial.*), squib.
II. *Verbs.* **detract,** derogate, decry, depreciate, disparage, "damn with faint praise" (Pope), run down, cry down, belittle, criticize, pull to pieces, asperse, bespatter, spatter, blacken, vilify, brand, malign, backbite, libel, lampoon, traduce, slander, defame, calumniate, anathematize.
III. *Adjectives.* **detracting,** defamatory, detractory, derogatory, disparaging, libelous; scurrilous, abusive, foul-mouthed; slanderous, calumnious, calumniatory; sarcastic, biting, acrimonious, satirical, cynical.
See also CONTEMPT, DISAPPROBATION, UNDERESTIMATION.—*Antonyms.* See APPROBATION, FLATTERY.

DETRACTOR.—*Nouns.* **detractor,** defamer, derogator, censor, censurer, cynic, Zoilist, critic, caviler, carper, knocker (*U. S. colloq.*), backbiter, slanderer, lampooner, satirist, traducer, libeler, calumniator, reviler, vituperator, vilifier. *Antonyms.* See FLATTERER.

---

devastate, *v.* lay waste, ravage, pillage, sack, ruin. See DESTRUCTION, WASTE.
develop, *v.* grow, enlarge; promote, build; evolve, unravel. See EXPANSION, PRODUCTION, UNFOLDMENT.
development, *n.* outgrowth, consequence; growth, expansion, evolution. See EFFECT, INCREASE.

DEVIATION.—I. *Nouns.* **deviation,** digression, divagation, divergence, aberration, wandering, variation, alteration, departure, deflection, diversion, declination, swerve, sheer, sweep, drift, warp; ramification, divarication, forking; detour, switch, shunt (*chiefly Brit.*), by-pass (*elec.*).
transgression, error, offense, iniquity, sin, misdeed, misdemeanor, delinquency, fault, moral obliquity.
[*oblique motion*] tack, yaw (*both naut.*), echelon (*mil.*), zigzag, *boyau* (*F.; zigzag trench*), dancette (*arch.*), sidling, knight's move (*chess*).
II. *Verbs.* **deviate,** alter one's course, vary, turn, bend, curve, swerve, heel, bear off; gybe (*or* jibe), yaw, wear, go about, sheer, tack (*all six naut.*); sidle, edge, veer, diverge; wind, twist, slue *or* slew, turn aside, wheel, steer clear of; dodge, step aside, shy, jib; glance off; deflect, divert, shift, switch (*U. S.*), shunt (*Brit.*); sidetrack; fork, divaricate.

stray, straggle, digress, wander, meander; go astray, ramble, rove, drift; err transgress.
III. *Adjectives.* **deviating,** aberrant, wandering, errant, excursive, discursive, devious, desultory, rambling; stray, vagrant, erratic, undirected, circuitous, roundabout, sidelong, indirect, crooked, zigzag, crablike, askew, oblique.

See also CHANGE, CIRCUIT, DIVERGENCE.—*Antonyms.* See CONTINUANCE, DIRECTION, STRAIGHTNESS.

---

device, *n.* trick, stratagem; design, emblem; contrivance, appliance. See CUNNING, INDICATION, INSTRUMENT.
devil, *n.* fiend, demon; Lucifer. See MYTHICAL BEINGS, SATAN.
devious, *adj.* rambling, circuitous, indirect; erring. See DEVIATION.
devise, *v.* bequeath, will; originate, create, contrive, scheme. See GIVING, IMAGINATION, PLAN.
devoid, *adj.* wanting, destitute, void, lacking: *with* of. See EXEMPTION, INNOCENCE, INSUFFICIENCY.
devote, *v.* addict, give oneself up to; destine, preordain; consecrate, dedicate; apply, utilize. See GIVING, NECESSITY, REPUTE, USE.
devoted, *adj.* ardent, eager; loyal, faithful. See LOVE, OBEDIENCE.
devotee, *n.* zealot, fanatic; enthusiast, fan (*colloq.*); believer, religionist. See ACTIVITY, AMUSEMENT, PIETY.
devotion, *n.* affection, passion; loyalty, constancy; fidelity; consecration, worship; homage, service. See LOVE, OBEDIENCE, PIETY, WORSHIP.
devour, *v.* annihilate, consume; eat, swallow; cram. See DESTRUCTION, FOOD, GLUTTONY.
devout, *adj.* reverent, religious, sincere. See PIETY.
dexterous, *adj.* adroit, clever; expert, proficient, handy. See CUNNING, SKILL.
dextral, *adj.* dexter. See RIGHT.
diabolic, *adj.* devilish, impious, infernal, satanic, fiendish. See VICE.
diabolism, *n.* devil worship, witchcraft. See SATAN.
diagram, *n.* chart, plan, design. See REPRESENTATION.
dialect, *n.* speech, tongue; brogue, cant, idiom, vernacular. See LANGUAGE, NEOLOGY.
diameter, *n.* bore, caliber. See BREADTH.
dictate, *v.* prescribe, suggest; direct, charge, order; compose, draw up. See ADVICE, COMMAND, WRITING.
dictatorial, *adj.* autocratic, peremptory, domineering, overbearing. See CERTAINTY.
dictionary, *n.* lexicon, wordbook, vocabulary. See LIST, WORD.
die, *v.* expire, perish, depart; fade, decay; kill oneself. See DEATH, DETERIORATION, KILLING.
die, *n.* mold, matrix, seal, punch, stamp. See PROTOTYPE.
diet, *n.* victuals, fare; regimen. See FOOD, REMEDY.
dietetic, *adj.* dietary, nutritious, alimental. See REMEDY.

DIFFERENCE.—I. *Nouns.* **difference,** dissimilarity, unlikeness, variance, variation, variety, diversity, divergence, heterogeneity, antithesis; dissonance disagreement, disparity, inequality, distinction, contradiction, contrariety, incongruity, incongruousness, contrariness, incompatibility, oppositeness, contrast, adverseness, opposition.
nice (fine, *or* subtle) distinction, discrimination; modification.
dissension, quarrel, controversy, disagreement, altercation, dispute, contention, wrangle, discord.
II. *Verbs.* **differ, vary, disagree with, mismatch, contrast; diverge from, depart** from, deviate from; modify, change, alter.
quarrel, dispute, contend, wrangle, altercate, disagree, bicker, squabble, spat (*colloq.*), brawl.
III. *Adjectives.* **different,** diverse, heterogeneous, varied, variant, divergent, incongruous, modified, diversified, various, divers (*archaic*), several, sundry

manifold, many; unlike, dissimilar, contrastive, distinct; dissonant, discordant, antagonistic, adverse, hostile, irreconcilable, inharmonious.
other, another, not the same, separate, distinct, unidentical; unmatched, unequal.
distinctive, distinguishing, characteristic, peculiar, discriminative; diagnostic.
See also CHANGE, DISAGREEMENT, DISCORD, DISCRIMINATION, INEQUALITY.—*Antonyms*. See IDENTITY, SIMILARITY.

---

differentiate, *v.* discriminate, distinguish, separate; adapt, set apart. See DISCRIMINATION, SPECIALTY (*in biology*).

DIFFICULTY.—I. *Nouns.* **difficulty**, hardness, laboriousness, arduousness, impracticability, uphill work, Herculean task, Augean task, Sisyphean labor, tough job (*colloq.*), teaser (*colloq.*); dead weight, dead lift.
predicament, fix (*colloq.*), quandary, dilemma, embarrassment, matter, trouble.
perplexity, intricacy, entanglement, knot, Gordian knot, maze, coil, poser, puzzle, knotty point, paradox; hard nut to crack, vexed question; strait, pass, pinch, rub, critical situation, exigency, crisis, push, crux, trial, emergency; scrape, hot water (*colloq.*), hornet's nest, pickle, stew, imbroglio, mess, muddle, botch.
obstacle, hindrance, impediment, barrier, bar, stumblingblock, obstruction, snag, block, check, clog, hitch, bafflement, frustration; slough, quagmire.
demur, objection, cavil, kick (*colloq.*), remonstrance, protest, scruple.
II. *Verbs.* **be difficult**, be hard, etc. (see *adjectives*); go against the grain, try one's patience, go hard with one, pose, perplex, bother, nonplus.
meet with difficulty, flounder, boggle (*U. S. local*), struggle, stick fast, stall, stick in the mud, bear the brunt, lose one's way, come to a deadlock.
render difficult, encumber, hamper, complicate, embarrass, entangle, enmesh; spike one's guns.
III. *Adjectives.* **difficult, hard**, tough (*colloq.*), troublesome, uphill, toilsome, irksome, laborious, onerous, arduous, Herculean, formidable.
unwieldy, unmanageable, unaccommodating, intractable, stubborn, obstinate, perverse, refractory, knotted, knotty, thorny; pathless, trackless, intricate, labyrinthine, puzzling, obscure, abstruse, abstract.
embarrassing, perplexing, delicate, ticklish, critical, thorny, crabbed, trying, awkward, disconcerting.
in difficulty, in hot water (*colloq.*), in a fix (*colloq.*), in a scrape, between Scylla and Charybdis; between the Devil and the deep blue sea; on the horns of a dilemma; on the rocks; reduced to straits, hard pressed, run hard, pinched, straitened, hard up (*slang*); puzzled, at a loss, at one's wits' end, at a standstill; nonplused, stranded, aground, stuck fast.
IV. *Adverbs.* **with difficulty**, laboriously, arduously, onerously, with much ado; uphill, upstream, against the stream; in the teeth of; *invita Minerva* (*L.*).
See also CONVOLUTION, DISORDER, HARDNESS, IMPOSSIBILITY, UNCERTAINTY, UNTIMELINESS.—*Antonyms*. See FACILITY.

DIFFUSENESS.—I. *Nouns.* **diffuseness**, profuseness, amplification, verbosity, wordiness, verbiage, flow of words, loquacity, circumlocution, periphrasis, periphrase, ambages (*pl.*), indirection, roundaboutness, looseness; tautology, battology, exuberance, redundance, prolixity; expletive, padding (*editor's cant*); drivel, twaddle, balderdash, flapdoodle (*colloq.*).
II. *Verbs.* **be diffuse**, expatiate, enlarge, dilate, amplify, descant, expand, inflate, pad (*editor's cant*), rant, maunder, prose; harp upon, dwell on, insist upon.
digress, ramble, wander, beat about the bush, protract.
III. *Adjectives.* **diffuse**, profuse, wordy, verbose, copious, exuberant, lengthy, long, long-winded, protracted, prolix, diffusive, roundabout, maundering, pleonastic, circumlocutory, periphrastic, episodic, digressive, discursive, loose, rambling, frothy, turgid.
See also LOQUACITY, ORNAMENT, WEAKNESS.—*Antonyms*. See CONCISENESS.

---

dig, *v.* excavate, sink, mine, scoop, cast up. See CONCAVITY.
digest, *v.* arrange, classify; summarize; assimilate, transform, absorb; brook, endure; think out, settle, weigh. See ARRANGEMENT. COMPENDIUM, CONVERSION, INEXCITABILITY, THOUGHT.
digest, *n.* compilation, summary, review. See COMPENDIUM.

dignified, *adj.* stately, lofty, august, portly, noble, majestic. See PRIDE.
dignity, *n.* distinction, honor; stateliness, decorum; nobility, eminence. See GREATNESS, PRIDE, REPUTE.
digress, *v.* swerve, diverge; ramble, wander. See DEVIATION, DIFFUSENESS.
dike, *or* **dyke,** *n.* bank, levee, embankment; ditch, moat; causeway *or* causey. See DEFENSE, INCLOSURE, WAY.
dilapidated, *adj.* decayed, crumbling, worn-out, ruined. See DETERIORATION.
dilate, *v.* expatiate, amplify; enlarge, stretch. See DIFFUSENESS, EXPANSION.
dilemma, *n.* difficulty, perplexity, pickle (*colloq.*), mess, strait. See STATE.
diligence, *n.* industry, application, zeal, perseverance, care. See ACTIVITY.
dilute, *v.* reduce, weaken, thin. See WATER, WEAKNESS.
diluted, *adj.* weak, thin, watery. See SMALLNESS, WEAKNESS.
dim, *adj.* vague, obscure, dull, hazy, cloudy, faint. See DIMNESS.
dimension, *n.* measurement, extent, area, expanse. See SIZE.
diminish, *v.* reduce, curtail, decrease; abase, weaken. See CONTRACTION, SMALLNESS.
diminutive, *adj.* slight, small, insignificant. See LITTLENESS.

DIMNESS.—I. *Nouns.* **dimness,** paleness, dullness, haziness, cloudiness, nebulosity, nebulousness, duskiness, mistiness, fogginess, indistinctness, obscurity, gloom, darkness.
dusk, twilight, crepuscle *or* crepuscule, nightfall, gloaming, blind man's holiday, *entre chien et loup* (*F.*); dawn, daybreak, break of day, Aurora; moonlight, moonshine (*rare or poetic*), starlight, firelight, candlelight, rushlight.
II. *Verbs.* **dim,** bedim, obscure, cloud, becloud, shade, shadow, darken, cloud over, gloom, obscure, lower; fade, pale, grow dim.
glimmer, flicker, blink, twinkle, waver, flutter.
III. *Adjectives.* **dim,** dull, dingy, lackluster; cloudy, nebular, nebulous, *sfumato* (*It.; said of a painting*), misty, hazy, vague, filmy, bleary, obscure, indistinct, pale, faint, shadowy, blurred, darkish, dusky; tarnished, sullied, smudgy, smirchy.
lurid, dun, leaden, overcast, dirty, lowering, murky, muddy, gloomy, threatening.
See also DARKNESS, DULLNESS.—*Antonyms.* See LIGHT.

DIM-SIGHTEDNESS.—I. *Nouns.* [*imperfect vision*] **dim-sightedness,** nearsightedness, shortsightedness, myopia, astigmatism; purblindness, blearedness, lippitude; myopia, presbyopia; cataract, ophthalmia (*med.*); color blindness, chromato-dysopia (*med.*); red blindness, Daltonism; snow blindness, niphablepsia (*med.*); day blindness, hemeralopia (*med.*); night blindness, nyctalopia (*med.*), moon blindness, moonblink.
squint, strabismus (*med.*), strabism (*med.*), cross-eye, cast in the eye, swivel eye (*slang*), cockeye, goggle-eyes.
[*limitation of vision*] blinker, blinder; screen, curtain, veil; dark glasses (*or* spectacles).
[*fallacies of vision*] refraction, distortion, illusion, mirage, phantasm, phantom; vision; specter, apparition, ghost; *ignis fatuus* (*L.*), will-o'-the-wisp.
II. *Verbs.* **be dim-sighted,** see double; have a mist before the eyes, have a film over the eyes; "see men as trees walking" (*Bible*); "see through a glass darkly" (*Bible*); wink, nictitate, nictate, blink, squint, look askance, screw up the eyes, glare, glower.
dazzle, glare, blind, daze, blur, confuse, dim, bedazzle; swim.
III. *Adjectives.* **dim-sighted,** myopic, nearsighted, shortsighted; astigmatic; blear-eyed, goggle-eyed, one-eyed, boss-eyed (*Eng. dial.*), monocular, monoculate, monoculous; half-blind, purblind; cockeyed (*colloq.*), dim-eyed, mole-eyed, blind as a bat.
See also BLINDNESS.—*Antonyms.* See VISION.

---

dine, *v.* eat, banquet, feast. See FOOD.
dingy, *adj.* dirty, grimy, soiled. See DIMNESS.
diocese, *n.* bishopric, episcopate, see. See CHURCHDOM.
dip, *n.* decline, slope, declivity, inclination. See DESCENT.

diplomacy, *n.* negotiation; tact, address, skill, dexterity. See CUNNING.
diplomatist, *n.* strategist, tactician; diplomat, consul, ambassador. See EXPERT, REPRESENTATIVE.
dire, *adj.* horrible, dreadful, shocking, calamitous, deplorable, fearful, ominous. See ADVERSITY, PAINFULNESS.

DIRECTION.—I. *Nouns.* **direction,** guidance, management, government, administration, stewardship, ministry, agency, supervision, superintendence, surveillance, oversight, control, order, command, charge, eye of the master; conduct, legislation, regulation; seat, chair, portfolio.
steerage, pilotage, orientation, helm, rudder, needle, compass; reins; guiding star, lodestar, polestar, cynosure.
statesmanship, statecraft, state management, kingcraft, reins of government.
course, bearing, trend, aim, drift, run, set, tendency, tenor, tack, dip; points of the compass, cardinal points.
line, path, road, track, range, quarter, line of march, route, air line, bee line; alignment; trajectory.
address, superscription (*as, the direction of a letter*).
II. *Verbs.* **direct,** manage, govern, rule, boss (*slang*), preside, instruct, engineer, maneuver, manipulate, handle, control, command, dispose, conduct; order, prescribe, head, lead, regulate, guide, find (*or* get) the bearings of, orient, orientate, steer, pilot, take the helm, be at the helm; hold the reins, drive.
superintend, supervise; overlook, oversee, look after, see to, administer, patronize; hold office.
trend, aim, set, drift, tend toward, go to, conduct to, make for, steer for, gravitate, bend, verge, incline, dip; aim at, point to, level at, take aim, hold a course, be bound for, make a bee line for.
address, superscribe, destine, direct (*as a letter*).
III. *Adjectives.* **direct,** straight, undeviating, unswerving, straightforward, straightaway.
directing, directive, executive, gubernatorial, supervisory, managerial; statesmanlike.
dirigible, guidable, navigable, steerable, leadable.
IV. *Adverbs.* **directly,** straight, straightforward, in a direct course, in a bee line to, in a direct line to, as the crow flies, point-blank, full tilt at, straight as an arrow; on the road to, thither; hither; whither.
in charge of, in control of, at the helm, at the head of; under the auspices of.
See also AUTHORITY, COMMAND, NEARNESS, TENDENCY.—*Antonyms.* See DEVIATION, OBEDIENCE.

DIRECTOR.—*Nouns.* **director,** manager, administrator, executive, governor, controller, organizer, *entrepreneur* (*F.*), enterpriser, projector, impresario (*of an opera or concert company*); superintendent, supervisor, overseer, supercargo, ship's husband (*naut.*), inspector, surveyor, taskmaster, master; ringleader, agitator, demagogue; dean, leader, coryphæus, conductor, precentor, bellwether, fugleman.
guide, pilot; helmsman, steersman, steerer; cicerone; adviser.
driver, whip, jehu (*jocose*), charioteer; coachman, carman, cabman; postilion, muleteer, teamster; chauffeur, motorman, engine-driver.
head, headman, head center, chief, principal, burra sahib (*Anglo-Indian*), paterfamilias (*at any rate, he should be*), president, speaker, chair, chairman; captain, superior, mother superior (*of a convent*).
officer, officeholder, office bearer, functionary, official, minister, bureaucrat.
statesman, strategist, legislator, lawgiver; Solon, Minos, Draco; politician, boss (*slang*), political dictator, wire-puller (*colloq.*), power behind the throne, kingmaker.
steward, factor, agent, bailiff, middleman; foreman, factotum, major-domo, seneschal; housekeeper, matron; proctor, curator, librarian.
See also MASTER.—*Antonyms.* See DEPUTY, SERVANT.

---

dirge, *n.* requiem, threnody, coronach. See LAMENTATION.
dirigible, *adj.* steerable, navigable. See DIRECTION.
dirt, *n.* filth, mud, foulness, muck. See UNCLEANNESS.

dirty, *adj.* murky, threatening, leaden; despicable, mean, vile; soiled, sullied, filthy; stormy. See DIMNESS, IMPROBITY, UNCLEANNESS, WIND.
disable, *v.* incapacitate, impair, cripple, maim, disqualify. See IMPOTENCE.
disadvantage, *n.* drawback, hindrance, detriment; harm, injury. See EVIL.

DISAGREEMENT.—I. *Nouns.* **disagreement,** dissimilitude, difference, nonconformity, dissonance, discrepancy, unconformity, incongruity, diversity, unlikeness, disparity, inequality, disproportion, variance, divergence; disunion, discord, dispute, misunderstanding, wrangle, quarrel, dissent, dissidence, dissension, conflict, controversy, division, opposition, antagonism.
unfitness, inaptitude, impropriety, inapplicability, unsuitability, disability; incompatability, incongruity, irrelevancy.
II. *Verbs.* **disagree,** differ, dissent, vary; contradict, diverge, oppose, interfere, discommode, clash, conflict, dispute, quarrel, jar.
III. *Adjectives.* **disagreeable,** unpleasant, repugnant, offensive, repulsive, distasteful; bad-tempered, unamiable, ill-natured, grouchy (*slang*).
disagreeing, discordant, inharmonious; repugnant, clashing, jarring, factious, dissentient, hostile, antagonistic, irreconcilable, inconsistent with, incongruous; inaccordant, inconsonant.
inapt, inept, inappropriate, improper, unsuited, unsuitable, inapplicable; unfit, unbefitting, unbecoming; ill-timed, unseasonable, *mal à propos* (*F.*), ill-adapted, infelicitous, irrelevant.
uncongenial, unsympathetic, ill-assorted, mismatched, incompatible, repugnant to, displeasing, unaccommodating.
IV. *Adverbs.* in defiance of, in contempt of, in spite of.

See also DIFFERENCE, DISCORD, DISSENT, IRRELATION, OPPOSITION.—*Antonyms.* See AGREEMENT.

DISAPPEARANCE.—I. *Nouns.* **disappearance,** vanishing, fading, evanescence, dissolution, departure, withdrawal, exit; vanishing point; eclipse, occultation.
II. *Verbs.* **disappear,** vanish, dissolve, fade, melt away, pass, go, depart, withdraw, be gone, leave no trace, "leave not a rack behind" (*Tempest*), pass on, pass away, be lost to view (*or* sight), pass out of sight, perish, cease.
III. *Adjectives.* **disappearing,** vanishing, evanescent; missing, lost, lost to sight, gone.

See also DEPARTURE, NONEXISTENCE, RESOLUTION.—*Antonyms.* See APPEARANCE.

DISAPPOINTMENT.—I. *Nouns.* **disappointment,** failure, nonsuccess, frustration, check, bafflement, foil, balk, slip 'twixt cup and lip, blighted hope, chagrin, disillusion, blow, false (*or* vain) expectation, miscalculation; fool's paradise; much cry and little wool.
II. *Verbs.* **be disappointed;** look blank, look blue, look (*or* stand) aghast; find to one's cost.
disappoint, balk, defeat, frustrate, foil, baffle, crush (dash, *or* blight) one's hope, balk (*or* disappoint) one's expectation, tantalize, tease, torment; dumfounder, dumfound, delude, disconcert, disillusion, disillusionize, dissatisfy, disgruntle; fail, neglect.
III. *Adjectives.* **disappointed,** balked, etc. (see *verbs*); aghast; out of one's reckoning.

See also DISCONTENT, FAILURE, MISJUDGMENT.—*Antonyms.* See EXPECTATION, SUCCESS.

DISAPPROBATION.—I. *Nouns.* **disapprobation,** disapproval, dislike, displeasure, disfavor, disesteem, odium; depreciation, dispraise, disvaluation, derogation, disparagement, detraction, denunciation, condemnation, stricture, objection, exception, criticism; obloquy, sarcasm, satire, insinuation, innuendo, sneer, taunt; black ball, ostracism, boycott, black list.
rebuke, admonition, chiding, reproof, reprimand, lecture, curtain lecture (*or did it pass with the curtains?*), jobation (*colloq.*), wigging, dressing down (*both colloq.*), rating, scolding, trimming (*colloq.*), correction, rebuff, home thrust, hit; reprehension, remonstrance, censure, blame, reproach, castigation, objurgation, expostulation, reprobation, frown, scowl, black look.

abuse, vituperation, scurrility; revilement, reviling, vilification, invective, diatribe, tirade, philippic; contumely, malediction; hard words, personalities, bad language, ribaldry, billingsgate.

clamor, outcry, hue and cry; hiss, hissing, catcall; execration.

II. *Verbs.* **disapprove,** dislike, object to, take exception to, think ill of, view with disfavor, frown upon, look askance, look black upon, set one's face against, disallow, reject, refuse, veto, negative; expostulate, remonstrate.

blame, censure, criticize, reproach, reprobate, impugn, impeach, accuse, denounce, expose, brand, gibbet, stigmatize; show up (*colloq.*).

rebuke, reprehend, chide, admonish, reprove, berate, take to task, overhaul, lecture, blow up (*colloq.*), correct, reprimand, snub; chastise, castigate, lash, trounce, trim (*colloq.*), dress *or* dress down.

abuse, scold, rate, upbraid, fall foul of; rail, rail at, call names, execrate, revile, vilify, denounce, accuse, recriminate.

decry, cry down, run down, backbite; insinuate, "damn with faint praise" (Pope); dispraise, depreciate, slander, malign, traduce, asperse; discredit, belittle, disparage, underrate, defame, knock (*U. S. colloq.*), deprecate, speak ill of, condemn, scoff at, sneer at, satirize, lampoon; hiss, hoot, catcall; blackball, blacklist, boycott, ostracize.

incur blame, scandalize, shock, revolt; get a bad name, be under a cloud, forfeit one's good opinion.

III. *Adjectives.* **disapprobatory,** disapproving, censorious, faultfinding, critical, captious, hypercritical, caviling, carping.

disparaging, condemnatory, denunciatory, reproachful, vituperative, defamatory, derogatory, calumniatory, depreciatory, abusive, libelous, slanderous.

satirical, sarcastic, sardonic, cynical, dry, sharp, cutting, biting, severe, withering, trenchant, dyslogistic.

blameworthy, reprehensible, blamable, answerable, uncommendable, censurable, reprovable, culpable, delinquent, bad, wicked, vicious.

See also CONDEMNATION, DETRACTION, DISLIKE.—*Antonyms.* See APPROBATION.

---

disarrange, *v.* disorder, disturb, derange. displace, disorganize. See DERANGEMENT.

disaster, *n.* trouble, affliction; accident, casualty, blow, cataclysm, calamity. See ADVERSITY, EVIL.

disastrous, *adj.* hurtful, harmful, injurious, calamitous, destructive, ruinous. See EVIL, PAINFULNESS.

disbelieve, *v.* lack faith; discredit, doubt, challenge. See IRRELIGION, UNBELIEF.

discard, *v.* cancel, abolish, reject; throw away, shelve; repudiate, nullify. See ANNULMENT, DISUSE, NONOBSERVANCE.

discern, *v.* comprehend, appreciate, perceive, experience; detect, discriminate, distinguish. See KNOWLEDGE, VISION.

discerning, *adj.* discriminating, clever, keen, subtle. See FASTIDIOUSNESS, SHARPNESS.

discernment, *n.* astuteness, penetration; perception, taste; shrewdness, insight, sagacity, acumen. See DEPTH, DISCRIMINATION, FASTIDIOUSNESS, INTELLIGENCE, JUDGMENT.

discharge, *v.* absolve, release; abolish, discard; perform, execute, transact; project, shoot; leak, exude; dismiss, oust; disband, demobilize; settle, pay; explode, burst. See ACQUITTAL, ANNULMENT, CONDUCT, DELIVERANCE, EGRESS, EJECTION, LIBERATION, PAYMENT, VIOLENCE.

discharge, *n.* explosion, firing, report. See SNAP.

disciple, *n.* adherent, follower; pupil, student. See FOLLOWING, LEARNER.

discipline, *n.* orderliness, subordination, obedience; correction, chastisement, control, compulsion; development, training. See ORDER, PUNISHMENT, RESTRAINT, TEACHING.

disclaim, *v.* deny, repudiate; disown, renounce. See ANNULMENT. NEGATION

DISCLOSURE.—I. *Nouns.* **disclosure,** revelation, divulgence, vent (*fig.*), utterance, expression, exposure, publication, *exposé* (*F.*), exposition.
acknowledgment, admission, declaration, avowal, confession, confessional.
II. *Verbs.* **disclose,** discover, unmask, unveil, unfold, uncover, unseal, lay bare, expose, bare, bring to light, open, open up.
divulge, reveal, let into the secret, confide to, tell, blab, breathe, utter; peach (*slang*), betray, squeal (*slang*), squeak (*slang*), blurt out, vent, whisper about, let slip, let fall, speak out, break the news, communicate, make known, publish, broadcast.
acknowledge, allow, declare, concede, grant, admit, own, confess, avow, make a clean breast, spill (*slang*), come clean (*slang*), unbosom oneself, "own the soft impeachment" (Sheridan).
be disclosed, come to light, become known, escape the lips, ooze out, leak out, transpire (*correct meaning of* transpire: *incorrect in the sense of "happen or come to pass"*), come to one's ears.
See also DESCRIPTION, DISCOVERY, INFORMATION, NEWS.—*Antonyms.* See AMBUSH, CONCEALMENT.

---

discomfort, *n.* soreness, suffering; disquiet, uneasiness, discontent. See PAIN, PAINFULNESS.
disconcert, *v.* trouble, upset; embarrass, abash; frustrate, balk; bewilder, perplex. See DERANGEMENT, DISREPUTE, HINDRANCE, INATTENTION.
disconnection, *n.* break, interruption; separation, cleavage; dissociation, irrelevancy. See DISCONTINUITY, DISJUNCTION, IRRELATION.
disconsolate, *adj.* melancholy, sorrowful, hopeless, forlorn, desolate. See DEJECTION.

DISCONTENT.—I. *Nouns.* **discontent,** dissatisfaction, disappointment, discontentment, inquietude, uneasiness, mortification, regret, repining, querulousness, vexation of spirit, soreness, heartburning, cold comfort.
malcontent, grumbler, growler, grouch (*slang*), croaker, faultfinder, irreconcilable.
II. *Verbs.* **be discontented,** repine, regret, take to heart, make a wry face, shrug the shoulders, look blue, look black, look glum.
grumble, take ill, fret, chafe, growl, snarl, complain, whine, croak, lament.
dissatisfy, displease, disappoint, mortify, put out (*colloq.*), disconcert, disgruntle (*colloq.*), offend, annoy, dishearten.
III. *Adjectives.* **discontented,** dissatisfied, unsatisfied, discontent, faultfinding, displeased; depressed, dispirited, despondent, disconsolate, downhearted, crestfallen, discouraged, downcast, regretful, dejected, dissentient, exacting, malcontent.
sullen, morose, glum, sulky, in high dudgeon, in a fume, in the sulks (*or* dumps), in bad humor; sour, soured, sore, ill-tempered, grumpy, grouchy (*colloq.*), irritable, out of humor, out of temper.
See also DISSENT, REGRET.—*Antonyms.* See ²CONTENT.

DISCONTINUITY.—I. *Nouns.* **discontinuity,** disconnectedness, disconnection, interruption, break, fracture, flaw, fault, crack, cut, gap, opening; broken thread, cessation, intermission, disunion, discontinuance, discontinuation, disruption, disjunction, alternation.
II. *Verbs.* **discontinue,** pause, interrupt, break, part, break off, stop, drop, cease, suspend, intervene, interpose, disconnect, dissever, disjoin, separate, disunite.
III. *Adjectives.* **discontinuous,** disconnected, broken, gaping, broken off, interrupted, fitful, irregular, spasmodic, desultory; intermittent, alternate, recurrent, periodic.
alternate, interchange, intermit, vary, reciprocate.
IV. *Adverbs.* **at intervals,** by snatches, by jerks, by fits and starts.
See also DISJUNCTION, INTERJACENCE.—*Antonyms.* See CONTINUITY.

DISCORD.—I. *Nouns.* **discord,** disagreement, dissidence, dissension, difference, variance, incompatibility; contention, clashing, jar, clash, misunderstanding, cross-purposes, odds, division, split, break, shock, rupture, disruption, "rift within the lute" (Tennyson), **disunion, breach, schism, feud, faction.**

[*in music*] **dissonance**, want of harmony, discordance, disharmony, harshness, cacophony, jar, jangle, wolf (*tech.*); charivari, racket, pandemonium, Babel.
inconsistency, incongruity, impropriety, incoherence, inconsonance, inharmony.
quarrel, dispute, tiff, bicker, squabble, altercation, words, high words, family jars; controversy, polemics (*esp. religious controversy*), friction, strife, litigation, open rupture, outbreak, warfare, declaration of war.
broil, brawl, row (*colloq.*); racket, hubbub, imbroglio, fracas, breach of the peace, scrimmage, rumpus (*colloq.*), squall, riot, disturbance, commotion, tumult, bear garden, Donnybrook Fair.
subject of dispute, ground of quarrel, battle ground, disputed point, bone of contention, apple of discord, *casus belli* (*L.*), question at issue, vexed question, brand of discord.
II. *Verbs.* **disagree**, differ, dissent, misunderstand, conflict, clash, jar, quarrel, fall out, dispute, litigate; controvert, squabble, altercate, row (*colloq.*), wrangle, bicker, nag, spar, brawl.
sow dissension, embroil, entangle, disunite, widen the breach, set (*or* pit) against, set at odds; split, break with; declare war, try conclusions, join issue, pick a quarrel.
III. *Adjectives.* **discordant**, dissident, contradictory, incompatible, inconsistent, incongruous, disagreeing, contrary, opposite, repugnant, conflictory, discrepant, different, dissimilar, divergent, adverse, dissentient, unreconciled, unpacified.
[*in music*] **dissonant**, out of tune, tuneless, unmusical, unmelodious, inharmonious, harsh, rough, jarring, grating, cacophonous, jangling, untuneful, untunable.
quarrelsome, heated, unpacific, controversial, polemic, disputatious, factious, contentious, dissentious, inimical, hostile.
at strife, at odds, at loggerheads, at variance, at issue, at cross-purposes, at sixes and sevens, embroiled, torn, disunited, up in arms, at daggers drawn.

See also CONTENTION, DISAGREEMENT, ENMITY.—*Antonyms.* See CONCORD, HARMONY.

DISCOUNT.—I. *Nouns.* **discount**, abatement, deduction, concession, reduction, allowance, qualification, set-off, drawback; poundage, commission, rake-off (*slang*), percentage, rebate, depreciation, agio.
II. *Verbs.* **discount**, bate, rebate, abate, deduct, strike off, take off, reduce, mark down, allow, give, make allowance; depreciate, lessen, diminish, detract from; disregard.
III. *Adverbs.* **at a discount**, below par; out of favor (*colloq.*).

Antonyms. See PRICE.

---

discourage, *v.* dishearten, depress; advise against, divert; daunt, deter. See DEJECTION, DISSUASION, FEAR.

discourse, *v.* talk, discuss; declaim, lecture, expatiate. See CONVERSATION, SPEECH.

DISCOURTESY.—I. *Nouns.* **discourtesy**, impoliteness, incivility, rudeness, *brusquerie* (*F.*), ill-breeding, bad manners; tactlessness, discourteousness, rusticity, unmannerliness, lack (*or* want) of courtesy, disrespect, impudence, misbehavior; barbarism, barbarity, brutality, vulgarity, blackguardism, ungentlemanliness, conduct unbecoming a gentleman.
bad temper, spleen, ill humor, ill temper, temper, peevishness, surliness, churlishness, gruffness, bluntness, ill nature, crabbedness, groutiness (*U. S. colloq.*), grouchiness (*colloq.*), perversity, moroseness, black dog, sullenness, sternness, austerity, moodishness, captiousness, cynicism, acerbity, tartness, sourness, virulence, acrimony, asperity.
scowl, black looks, frown; sulks, short answer, rebuff; hard words, contumely, unparliamentary language, personality.
bear, brute, blackguard, beast; unlicked cub; crosspatch (*colloq.*), grouch (*slang*), sorehead (*U. S. slang*).
II. *Verbs.* **be discourteous**, be rude, treat with discourtesy, insult, affront, cheek (*slang*), make bold with, make free with; take a liberty; stare out of countenance, ogle, point at.
sulk, frown, scowl, glower, pout; snap, snarl, growl.
cut, slight, ignore, cold-shoulder (*colloq.*), snub, turn one's back upon, turn on one's heel, give the cold shoulder, keep at a distance keep at arm's length.

III. *Adjectives.* **discourteous,** uncourteous, uncourtly, undignified, indecorous, ill-bred, ill-mannered, ill-behaved, unmannerly, uncivil, impolite, unceremonious, disrespectful, unaccommodating, unneighborly, ungallant, ungracious, unpolished, unrefined; ungentlemanly; unladylike; pert, fresh (*slang*), forward, obtrusive, saucy, flippant, impudent, rude, vulgar.
bad-tempered, ill-tempered, ill-humored, crusty, tart, sour, crabbed, sharp, trenchant, sarcastic, caustic, virulent, bitter, acrimonious, venomous, contumelious, snarling, surly, perverse, grim, sullen, morose, splenetic, grouchy (*colloq.*) grouty (*U. S. colloq.*), cross, sulky, peevish, bristling, thorny; rough, rugged bluff, blunt, short, gruff, churlish, boorish, bearish; brutal, brusque, stern, harsh austere; cavalier.

See also DISRESPECT, IRASCIBILITY, SULLENNESS, VULGARITY.—*Antonyms.* See COURTESY.

DISCOVERY.—I. *Nouns.* **discovery,** detection, exposure, unfolding, showing, finding, sighting, espial, ascertainment, learning, disclosure, find, revelation, unearthing; invention, device, design, contrivance.
[*detective devices*] **detector,** detectagraph, detectaphone (*trade name*), burglar alarm seismograph, anemometer, etc.
II. *Verbs.* **discover,** find, ascertain, learn, hear, find out, elicit, trace out, make out, root out, dig up, uncover, unearth, disinter, bring to light, expose, manifest, display, reveal, unveil; determine, evolve, fix upon, espy, spot (*colloq.*), fathom, bring out, draw out, educe; invent, devise, contrive, design.
come upon, meet with, come across, light upon, fall in with, stumble upon; recognize, identify.
solve, resolve, unriddle, unravel, find a clew to, interpret, disclose, see through, detect, catch, scent, smell out, trace.
verify, confirm, prove, substantiate, clinch (*colloq.*), establish, make certain of identify, recognize, realize.

See also DISCLOSURE, INTERPRETATION, LOCATION, VISION.—*Antonyms.* See CONCEALMENT.

---

discredit, *v.* disgrace, shame, debase; doubt, disbelieve. See DISREPUTE, UNBELIEF.
discreditable, *adj.* disreputable, disgraceful, blameworthy. See VICE.
discreet, *adj.* cautious, prudent, politic, judicious, wary. See CARE.
discretion, *n.* prudence, wariness; choice, freedom, volition, option. See CAUTION, WILL.

DISCRIMINATION.—I. *Nouns.* **discrimination,** distinction, differentiation, diagnosis, nice perception; estimation; nicety, refinement, taste, judgment; tact, discernment, acuteness, clearness, acumen, insight, penetration.
II. *Verbs.* **discriminate,** distinguish, separate, differentiate, difference, draw the line, sift; estimate, sum up, criticize, take into account (*or* consideration), weigh carefully.
III. *Adjectives.* **discriminating,** discerning, critical, diagnostic, perspicacious, keen, fine, exquisite, perceptive, discriminative, distinctive, diacritical; nice, acute, deep, astute.

See also FASTIDIOUSNESS, JUDGE, TASTE.—*Antonyms.* See INDISCRIMINATION.

---

discursive, *adj.* deviating, digressive, rambling. See DEVIATION.
discuss, *v.* ventilate, agitate; investigate, examine, analyze; reason, argue, debate. See AGITATION, INQUIRY, REASONING.
discussion, *n.* public excitement; consideration, examination, study; argument, debate, controversy. See AGITATION, INQUIRY, REASONING.
disdain, *n.* scorn, derision; haughtiness, arrogance, airs. See CONTEMPT, INSOLENCE.

DISEASE.—I. *Nouns.* **disease,** illness, sickness, ailment, affection, malady, infirmity, invalidism, delicate health, loss of health, "the thousand natural shocks that flesh is heir to" (*Hamlet*); indisposition, complaint, disorder, distemper (*now chiefly used of dogs and horses*); qualm, seasickness, *mal de mer* (*F.*).

nausea; indigestion, dyspepsia, acidosis, antointoxication; malnutrition, want of nourishment; decline, prostration, collapse, break-down, decay; consumption, phthisis, tuberculosis, T. B. (*colloq.*), white plague.

seizure, attack, visitation, fit, ictus (*med.*), paroxysm, convulsion; epilepsy, falling sickness, apoplexy.

paralysis, stroke, shock (*colloq.*), palsy, hemiplegia (*one side only*), paraplegia *or* paraplegy (*lower half of body on both sides*), paresis; general paresis, general paralysis; diplegia (*as of the legs*); shaking palsy, *paralysis agitans* (*L.*), Parkinson's disease; infantile paralysis, acute anterior poliomyelitis (*med.*).

fever, feverishness, pyrexia (*med.*), febricity (*med.*), calenture (*med.*), inflammation; ague, malaria, malarial fever, black-water fever; dengue, breakbone fever; typhoid, enteric fever; typhus, jail fever, famine fever, spotted fever; scarlet fever, scarlatina, eruptive fever; yellow fever, yellow jack.

sore, ulcer, abscess, fester, boil, pimple, gathering, carbuncle, felon, canker, gangrene.

eruption, rash, brash, breaking out; scabies, itch, psora (*med.*); eczema, psoriasis (*med.*); prickly heat, lichen tropicus (*med.*), hives, nettlerash; herpes, shingles, herpes zoster (*med.*).

taint, virus, poison, pollution, infection, contagion; epidemic, endemic, plague, pestilence.

science of disease: pathology, therapeutics, ætiology *or* etiology, nosology, symptomatology, semeiology, diagnostics, diagnosis.

II. *Verbs.* **disease,** disorder, derange, afflict, cause disease in.

ail, suffer, be affected with, droop, flag, languish, sicken, pine, dwindle, waste away, fail, lose strength, lie helpless.

III. *Adjectives.* **diseased,** morbid, tainted, contaminated, poisoned, septic; mangy, leprous, cankered; rotten, withered; palsied, paralytic, hemiplegic, paraplegic, paretic; consumptive, tubercular, tuberculous, phthisic *or* phthisical.

sick, ill, not well, unwell, indisposed, ailing, poorly, seedy (*colloq.*), squeamish, qualmish; laid up, confined, bedridden, in hospital, on the sick list; disordered, out of health, out of sorts (*colloq.*), under the weather (*U. S.*).

sickly, infirm, unsound, unhealthy, sickish, weakly, drooping, flagging, lame, halt, crippled, halting.

See also INSANITY, UNHEALTHINESS, WEAKNESS.—*Antonyms.* See HEALTH.

---

disengage, *v.* disconnect, sever; disentangle, free, clear, extricate. See DISJUNCTION, LIBERATION.

disentangle, *v.* systematize, organize; separate, unfasten; unravel, extricate, free. See ARRANGEMENT, DISJUNCTION, LIBERATION.

disentitle, *v.* dispossess, disqualify, disfranchise. See RIGHTLESSNESS.

disfigure, *v.* impair, deface, mar, mutilate, mangle. See BLEMISH.

disgrace, *v.* degrade, dishonor, shame, discredit, humiliate. See DISREPUTE.

disgraced, *adj.* dishonored, shamed, in bad repute. See DISREPUTE.

disguise, *n.* blind, camouflage; mask, concealment, cloak, pretense. See AMBUSH, DECEPTION.

disgust, *v.* offend, nauseate, repel, revolt. See PAIN, WEARINESS.

disgust, *n.* aversion, loathing, repugnance; repletion, sickness. See DISLIKE, WEARINESS.

dish, *n. plat* (*F.*), dish of food; vessel, plate, platter, bowl, etc. See FOOD, RECEPTACLE.

dishabille, *n.* undress, negligee; kimono, wrapper. See CLOTHING.

dishonest, *adj.* untrue, fraudulent, false; crooked, dishonorable. See FALSEHOOD, IMPROBITY.

disincline, *v.* repel, disgust; indispose, deter. See DISLIKE, DISSUASION.

disinfect, *v.* fumigate, purify, cleanse, sanitate. See CLEANNESS.

disinherit, *v.* deprive, cut off, oust, disown. See TAKING, TRANSFER.

disintegrate, *v.* crumble, break up; disband, disperse. See DECOMPOSITION, DISJUNCTION.

disinter, *v.* exhume, dig up; unearth, bring to light. See DISCOVERY, INTERMENT.

disinterested, *adj.* impartial, fair, unbiased. See UNSELFISHNESS.

DISJUNCTION.—I. *Nouns.* **disjunction,** disconnection, disunion, separation, parting, partition, disengagement, dissociation, separateness; divorce; cæsura, division, subdivision, break, fracture, discontinuity, severance, cleavage, rupture, hernia (*med.*); dismemberment, dissection, disintegration, dispersion, disruption; detachment, segregation, isolation, insulation, insularity.
fissure, breach, rent, rift, crack, slit, split, cleft, cut, incision.
II. *Verbs.* **disjoin,** disconnect, disengage, disunite, dissociate, divorce, part, detach, separate, divide, sunder, subdivide, sever, dissever, cut off, segregate, set apart, keep apart, insulate, isolate; cut adrift, loose, unfasten, disentangle, unravel, undo, set free, liberate.
cut, chop, saw, snip, nip, cleave, rive, rend, slit, rip, split, splinter, chip, crack, snap, break, tear, lacerate, burst; wrench, rupture, hack, hew, gash, slash, slice, carve, quarter, dissect, anatomize; partition, parcel, portion, apportion, allocate, share.
disintegrate, dismember, dislocate, disrupt, disband, disperse, break up, crumble.
part, part company, separate, leave, take leave, quit, go away; alienate, estrange.
III. *Adjectives.* **disjoined,** discontinuous, disjunctive, discretive, discrete; detached, unconnected, disjoint, disjunct, isolated, insular; separate, apart, asunder, loose, free, adrift; unattached, unassociated, unannexed, distinct; reft, cleft, divided, split.
IV. *Adverbs.* **disjointly,** separately, one by one, severally, apart, asunder, in the abstract.
See also DECOMPOSITION, DISCONTINUITY, DISPERSION.—*Antonyms.* See JUNCTION.

DISLIKE.—I. *Nouns.* **dislike,** distaste, disrelish, disinclination, disfavor, dissatisfaction, displeasure, disapprobation, unwillingness, reluctance, backwardness.
repugnance, disgust, nausea, loathing, aversion, abomination, antipathy, abhorrence, horror, hatred, detestation; hate, animosity.
II. *Verbs.* **dislike,** disrelish; mind, object to, disapprove, disfavor, disesteem, have no taste for, turn up the nose at, look askance at; shun, avoid, eschew, shrink from, recoil from, shudder at.
loathe, abominate, detest, abhor, hate, contemn, despise.
repel, disincline, sicken, nauseate, pall, disgust, revolt, shock, make one's blood run cold.
III. *Adjectives.* **averse,** opposed, adverse, contrary, shy of, loath, sick of, heartsick, disinclined, unwilling, indisposed, reluctant.
repugnant, repulsive, repellent, abhorrent, insufferable, fulsome, nauseous, loathsome, offensive, disgusting, disagreeable.
uneatable, inedible, unappetizing, unpalatable, distasteful, unsavory.
unpopular, undesirable, unacceptable, uncared for, disliked, obnoxious, objectionable, unwished, unsought, out of favor.
See also AVOIDANCE, HATE, RESENTMENT, UNWILLINGNESS.—*Antonyms.* See DESIRE, PLEASURE.

---

dislocate, *v.* derange, disarrange, displace; disjoin, disunite. See DERANGEMENT, DISJUNCTION.
dislodge, *v.* disturb, misplace; oust, evict. See DISPLACEMENT, EJECTION.
disloyal, *adj.* false, traitorous, faithless, inconstant. See IMPROBITY.
dismal, *adj.* somber, gloomy, depressing; sorrowful, funereal, mournful. See DARKNESS, DEJECTION.
dismantle, *v.* demolish, destroy; undress, disrobe, strip. See DESTRUCTION, DIVESTMENT.
dismay, *n.* horror, terror, consternation, fright. See FEAR.
dismiss, *v.* discharge, send away; banish, dislodge; disband, let go. See ANNULMENT, EJECTION, LIBERATION.
dismissal, *n.* discharge, removal, sack (*slang*), deposition. See ANNULMENT.

DISOBEDIENCE.—I. *Nouns.* **disobedience,** insubordination, intractableness, unruliness, noncompliance, nonobservance, recalcitrance. waywardness, contumacy, stubbornness, obstinacy, perverseness; infraction, infringement, violation.
revolt, insurgence, rebellion, mutiny, outbreak, rising, uprising, outbreak, in-

surrection, riot, tumult, strike, defiance, sabotage; sedition, treason, high treason, lese majesty (*law*), *lèse-majesté* (*F.*); defection, secession, revolution; Bolshevism, Bolshevikism, revolutionary socialism.
insurgent, mutineer, rebel, traitor, *frondeur* (*F.*), malcontent; communist, Red (*or* red), Bolshevist, Bolshevik (*pl.* Bolsheviki) *or* bolshevik (*pl.* bolsheviks), radical socialist; Fenian, Sinn Feiner, seceder, Secessionist *or* Secesh (*U. S. colloq. or slang*); apostate, renegade, anarchist, nihilist.
II. *Verbs.* **disobey,** violate, infringe; shirk, slack; defy, set at defiance, set at naught, ignore, disregard, transgress, run riot, take the law into one's own hands; kick over the traces; refuse to support, bolt (*U. S. politics*); resist, strike, rise, rise in arms; secede, mutiny, rebel.
III. *Adjectives.* **disobedient,** unruly, ungovernable, unmanageable, refractory, naughty (*applied esp. to children or in playful censure*), mischievous, insubordinate, restive, defiant, undutiful, unduteous, contumacious, headstrong, perverse, obstinate, stubborn, unyielding, recusant, dissentient, recalcitrant.
lawless, riotous, mutinous, seditious, insurgent, revolutionary, nihilistic, anarchical, anarchistic, Red, Bolshevik.
See also DEFIANCE, NONOBSERVANCE, RESISTANCE.—*Antonyms.* See OBEDIENCE.

DISORDER.—I. *Nouns.* **disorder,** derangement, disarrangement, confusion, untidiness, disarray, jumble, botch, litter, farrago, mess, muss (*U. S.*), muddle, hodgepodge, imbroglio, clutter, medley; irregularity, anomaly; disunion, discord, anarchy, anarchism, chaos, disorganization.
complexity, complication, entanglement, intricacy, perplexity, network, maze, labyrinth; wilderness, jungle, coil, tangled skein, knot, Gordian knot.
turmoil, ferment, commotion, bustle, trouble, disturbance, row, convulsion, tumult, uproar, riot, rumpus (*colloq.*), fracas, *mêlée* (*F.*), bear garden, pandemonium, hell; Babel, Saturnalia, Donnybrook Fair, Bedlam.
malady, disease, ailment, sickness, illness, distemper, indisposition, complaint.
[*untidy man*] sloven, slouch (*slang*), slubberdegullion (*dial.*), slob (*slang*), guy, sight, *sagouin* (*F.*), ragamuffin: *opposite of* fop.
[*untidy woman*] slattern, slut, frump, drab, draggle-tail (*colloq.*), trollop, traipse *or* trapes (*dial.*), dowdy, slammock *or* slummock (*dial.*), *sagouine* (*F.*).
II. *Verbs.* **disorder,** disturb, derange, disarrange, confuse, discompose, jumble, litter, muddle, botch; entangle, ravel, ruffle, rumple, muss (*U. S. colloq.*).
III. *Adjectives.* **disorderly,** out of order, out of place, irregular, desultory, anomalous, disorganized, straggling, disheveled, unmethodical, unsystematic, untidy, slovenly, messy (*colloq.*), indiscriminate, chaotic, confused, hugger-mugger, turbid, disordered, deranged, topsy-turvy, disjointed, out of joint; perplexed, disconcerted, bewildered, embarrassed.
complex, intricate, complicated, perplexed, involved, raveled, entangled, knotted, tangled, inextricable, mazy, dædal.
riotous, turbulent, tumultuous, unquiet, troublous, agitated, boisterous, violent, noisy, rowdy, lawless.
slovenly, untidy, frowzy, unkempt, grubby (*colloq.*), slouchy (*colloq.*), frumpish, dowdy, sloppy (*colloq.*), slatternly; careless, slipshod.
See also DERANGEMENT, DISEASE, IRREGULARITY, MIXTURE, ROUGHNESS, VIOLENCE, WRONG.—*Antonyms.* See ORDER.

---

disorganize, *v.* derange, disarrange, disorder, disrupt. See DERANGEMENT.
disown, *v.* disclaim, repudiate, deny, renounce, reject, retract. See NEGATION, RESIGNATION.
disparage, *v.* underrate, belittle, decry, discredit; abuse, scoff at. See DISAPPROBATION, DISRESPECT.
disparaging, *adj.* condemnatory, derogatory, depreciatory, slanderous. See DISAPPROBATION.
dispatch, *v.* send off, dismiss; slay, murder. See EJECTION, KILLING.
dispatch, *n.* alacrity, promptness, expedition; speed, urgency, precipitation; message, letter, telegram. See ACTIVITY, HASTE, NEWS.
dispel, *v.* dissipate, dissolve; scatter, spread. See DESTRUCTION, DISPERSION.
dispense, *v.* distribute, allot, portion; bestow, administer. See APPORTIONMENT, GIVING.

DISPERSION.—I. *Nouns.* **dispersion,** scattering, dispersal, distribution, propagation, diffusion, dissipation, disjunction, dissemination, spread, broadcast, radiation, emission, divergence, apportionment, allotment, allocation.

II. *Verbs.* **disperse,** scatter, sow, disseminate, sow broadcast, propagate, diffuse, radiate, circulate, broadcast, spread, shed, bestrew, disband, dismember, dispel, cast forth, dislodge, eject, banish, rout, draft off; strew, cast, sprinkle, spatter, squatter (*dial.*); issue, deal out, retail, utter, dispense, apportion, allocate, distribute, administer.

III. *Adjectives.* **dispersed,** disseminated, strown, strewn, scattered, dispersive, dispensative, diffuse, diffusive, sparse, sporadic, broadcast, widespread, circulative, epidemic, adrift, stray; disheveled, unkempt.

See also APPORTIONMENT, DISJUNCTION, DIVERGENCE, WASTE.—*Antonyms.* See ASSEMBLAGE.

DISPLACEMENT.—I. *Nouns.* **displacement,** removal, transference, moving, shift, unshipment, transshipment, transposition, transfer, replacement, dislocation, derangement, disturbance, misplacement.

ejection, ejectment, expulsion, dispossession, ousting, ouster (*law*), eviction; exile, banishment, ostracism; discharge, dismissal, deposition, dethronement.

II. *Verbs.* **displace,** dislodge, disestablish, unseat, displant, uproot, discharge, dismiss, bounce (*U. S. slang*), sack (*slang*), fire (*slang*), depose, break (*colloq.*); set aside, remove, take away, cart away, draft off; empty, unload, unship, transfer, transpose, dispel; eject, expel, evict, banish, deport, exile.

disturb, derange, disorder, confuse, disarrange, misplace, dislocate, move.

vacate, abandon, give up, quit, depart, evacuate.

III. *Adjectives.* **displaced,** dislodged, disestablished, discharged, dismissed, fired (*slang*), out of a situation; unplaced, unsettled, unhoused, houseless, homeless, out of place.

See also DERANGEMENT, EJECTION, MOTION, TRANSFER.—*Antonyms.* See LOCATION, STABILITY.

---

display, *n.* exhibit, show; flaunt, parade, show off. See MANIFESTATION, OSTENTATION.

displease, *v.* annoy, vex, disturb, repel, offend. See PAIN.

displeasure, *n.* annoyance, discontent, vexation, distaste; indignation, anger. See PAINFULNESS, RESENTMENT.

DISPOSITION.—I. *Nouns.* **disposition,** temperament, prevailing spirit, emotion, passion, ruling passion; qualities, affections, temper, frame of mind, character, nature, spirit, idiosyncrasy, predilection, genius, turn of mind, bent, grain, tendency, disposedness, inclination, bias, predisposition, diathesis, proneness, proclivity, aptitude, propensity, vein, humor, mood, sympathy.

soul, heart, bosom, inner man; inmost recesses of the heart.

fervor, energy, ardor, fire, verve, force, zeal, *élan* (*F.*).

arrangement, disposal, distribution, plan, ordering, adjustment, regulation, dispensation, administration, management; assortment, array, grouping.

II. *Verbs.* **dispose,** arrange, regulate, order, distribute, adapt, adjust, set, fit; settle, finish, dismiss; give, bestow, deal out, employ, dispose of; incline, determine.

III. *Adjectives.* **disposed** (*to*), inclined, liable, prone, apt, subject, predisposed, having a bias; molded *or* moulded, cast, formed, framed.

inborn, innate, inbred, ingrained; deep-rooted, congenital, inherent, intrinsic, instinctive, natural; dyed-in-the-wool; blown-in-the-bottle.

IV. *Adverbs.* at heart; in the vein, in the mood.

See also SUBJECTION (*disposed*).

---

dispossess, *v.* eject, oust, deprive. See TAKING.

dispossession, *n.* deprivation, bereavement, disinheritance. See TAKING.

disprove, *v.* confute, refute, negative, rebut, defeat. See CONFUTATION.

dispute, *v.* differ, clash; wrangle, bicker; rebut, deny, confute; argue, debate; challenge, question. See DISAGREEMENT, DISCORD, NEGATION, REASONING, UNBELIEF.

dispute, *n.* wrangle, contention, argument, quarrel. See DISAGREEMENT, DISCORD, WORD.

disqualify, *v.* disable, incapacitate, unfit; disfranchise. See IMPOTENCE, RIGHTLESSNESS.

disquiet, *n.* commotion, turbulence; uneasiness, anxiety, restlessness, unrest. See AGITATION, CHANGEABLENESS.

disregard, *v.* slight, insult, affront; overlook, pass by, ignore; underrate, belittle. See DISRESPECT, NEGLECT, UNDERESTIMATION.

DISREPUTE.—I. *Nouns.* **disrepute,** discredit, dishonor, disfavor, disesteem, ill-repute, ill-favor, ingloriousness, derogation, abasement, debasement, degradation, "a long farewell to all my greatness" (*Henry VIII*); odium,—obloquy opprobrium, ignominy, disgrace, shame, humiliation, scandal, infamy, baseness, vileness, turpitude.

stigma, brand, reproach, criticism, reflection, imputation, slur, stain, spot, blot, blur, tarnish, taint, defilement, pollution, badge of infamy; bend sinister (*in heraldry, a mark of illegitimacy*), baton (*same significance*), bar sinister (*erroneously used for* bend sinister, *as a mark of illegitimacy*); object of scorn, byword.

II. *Verbs.* **be disreputable,** be inglorious, have a bad name, disgrace oneself, lose caste, fall from one's high estate, cut a sorry figure.

shame, disgrace, put to shame, dishonor, humiliate, mortify, discredit, degrade, debase, expel.

stigmatize, brand, vilify, defame, slur, tarnish, stain, blot, smirch, taint, sully; drag through the mire, heap dirt upon; post, send to Coventry, snub, show up (*colloq.*), reprehend.

disconcert, put out (*colloq.*), upset, discompose, disturb, faze (*colloq.*), embarrass, abash, discomfit, squelch, demoralize, confound, throw off one's center, put to the blush.

outshine, excel, outdo, eclipse, obscure, throw into the shade, overshadow, take the shine out of (*colloq.*), put in the background, outsparkle, outdazzle.

III. *Adjectives.* **disreputable,** dishonorable, discreditable, shameful, disgraceful, despicable; unbecoming, questionable, unworthy, derogatory, degrading, humiliating, scandalous, infamous, opprobrious, arrant, shocking, outrageous, notorious, ignominious, base, abject, vile, mean; beggarly, pitiful, petty, shabby.

disgraced, "shorn of its beams" (Milton), overcome, down-trodden, in bad repute, under a cloud, in the shade (*or* background); down in the world, down and out (*colloq.*), out at elbows, dishonored, shamed, discredited, degraded.

inglorious, nameless, obscure, unknown to fame, unnoticed, unnoted, unhonored, unglorified.

See also DISAPPROBATION, HARDNESS, IMPROBITY.—*Antonyms.* See REPUTE.

DISRESPECT.—I. *Nouns.* **disrespect,** disfavor, disesteem, disestimation, disrepute, disparagement, detraction; irreverence, slight, indignity, affront, dishonor, insult, discourtesy, scoffing; hiss, hissing, hoot, derision, taunt, sneer, flout, scoff, fling, gibe, jeer, sarcasm, mockery; insult, outrage, contumely, rudeness, disdain.

II. *Verbs.* **disrespect,** slight, disregard, undervalue, humiliate, cheapen, lower, depreciate, trifle with, pass by, push aside, overlook, be discourteous, treat with disrespect; insult, affront, outrage, browbeat.

disparage, dishonor, detract from, degrade, debase, desecrate, abuse, call names; throw mud at, vilify, run down, decry, belittle, derogate from, traduce, point at, indulge in personalities.

deride, scoff, sneer, laugh at, ridicule, gibe *or* jibe, mock, jeer, taunt, twit, flout, roast (*colloq.*), guy (*colloq.*), rag (*dial. Eng. and college slang*); burlesque; scout, hiss, hoot.

III. *Adjectives.* **disrespectful,** impolite, discourteous, uncivil, rude, disdainful, irreverent, derisive, disparaging, insulting, supercilious, sarcastic, scurrilous, foul, contemptuous, insolent, opprobrious.

unrespected, unregarded, disregarded, unenvied, unsaluted, ignored.

See also CONTEMPT, DETRACTION, DISCOURTESY.—*Antonyms.* See RESPECT.

dissatisfy, *v.* displease, offend, vex, annoy, provoke, anger, chafe, disaffect. See DISCONTENT.
dissect, *v.* cut up, anatomize; analyze, probe, examine. See DISJUNCTION, INQUIRY.
dissemble, *v.* disguise, hide, mask; feign, simulate, pretend; play the hypocrite. See CONCEALMENT, FALSEHOOD, IMPIETY.

DISSENT.—I. *Nouns.* **dissent,** disagreement, nonagreement, nonconcurrence, nonconsent, difference, variance, discordance, dissentience.
nonconformity, heterodoxy, protestantism, schism; disaffection, secession, recantation, recusancy.
dissension, discord, caviling, wrangling, quarrel, strife, bickering; discontent.
protest, objection, remonstrance, expostulation, contradiction, denial; noncompliance, rejection, demur.
dissentient, dissenter, nonconformist; sectary, separatist, protestant, heretic, schismatic, recusant, seceder, come-outer (*U. S. colloq.*).
II. *Verbs.* **dissent,** differ, disagree, demur, call in question, refuse to admit; cavil, quibble, wrangle, protest, repudiate; contradict, deny.
secede, retract, withdraw, retire, recant, revoke, forswear, crawl (*U. S. slang*).
III. *Adjectives.* **dissenting,** dissentient, negative; contradictory; unconvinced, unconverted.
sectarian, sectarial, denominational, schismatic, heterodox.
IV. *Adverbs.* at variance with, at odds with, at issue with; under protest.
See also APOSTASY, DIFFERENCE, DISAGREEMENT, FRICTION, HETERODOXY, NEGATION, REFUSAL.—*Antonyms.* See ASSENT.

DISSERTATION.—I. *Nouns.* **dissertation,** treatise, essay, thesis, theme; tract, tractate, discourse, memoir, disquisition, descant, lecture, sermon, homily, investigation, study, discussion, exposition.
commentary, review, critique, criticism, appreciation; diatribe, animadversion; article, leader (*chiefly Eng.*), editorial.
commentator, reviewer, critic, essayist, publicist, leader writer, editor.
II. *Verbs.* **dissertate** (*rare*), discourse, comment, explain, interpret, illuminate; treat of (ventilate, discuss, deal with, *or* go into) a subject; criticize, review, dissect.
See also INQUIRY, INTERPRETATION, REASONING.

DISSIMILARITY.—I. *Nouns.* **dissimilarity,** unlikeness, dissimilitude, diversity, disparity, divergence, variation, difference, heterogeneity, novelty, originality.
II. *Verbs.* **be dissimilar,** vary, differ, disaccord, change, alter, diverge, deviate, fluctuate, differ from, diversify.
III. *Adjectives.* **dissimilar,** unlike, different, distinct, various, diverse, diversified, heterogeneous, disparate, divergent, unique, new, novel, unprecedented, original.
See also DIFFERENCE.—*Antonyms.* See SIMILARITY.

---

dissipate, *v.* dispel, disperse; squander, fritter away. See DISPERSION, WASTE.
dissipated, *adj.* wild, fast, profligate. See INTEMPERANCE.
dissolute, *adj.* profligate, vicious, debauched. See LAXITY.
dissolution, *n.* death, destruction; decomposition, disintegration. See END, RESOLUTION.
dissolve, *v.* abolish, end, destroy; disintegrate, break up; vanish, fade; liquefy, evaporate. See ANNULMENT, DECOMPOSITION, DISAPPEARANCE, LIQUEFACTION.
dissonance, *n.* dissension, controversy, incongruity; discordance, harshness, jar, cacophony. See DISAGREEMENT, DISCORD.
dissonant, *adj.* harsh, inharmonious, discordant. See DISCORD.

DISSUASION.—I. *Nouns.* **dissuasion,** expostulation, dehortation (*rare*), diversion, remonstrance, deprecation, discouragement, damper, wet blanket.
curb, restraint, constraint, check, control, rein, repression.

II. *Verbs.* **dissuade,** cry out against, remonstrate, expostulate, warn; advise against, deprecate, dehort (*rare*).
disincline, indispose, shake, stagger; discourage, dishearten, disenchant; deter, hold back, restrain, repel, turn aside, divert from, damp, cool, chill, blunt, calm, quiet, quench.
III. *Adjectives.* **dissuasive,** dehortatory (*rare*), expostulatory, remonstrative; warning, admonitory, monitorial, monitory.
See also DEPRECATION, RESTRAINT.—*Antonyms.* See MOTIVE (*inducement*).

DISTANCE.—I. *Nouns.* **distance,** remoteness, farness; space, interval, span, reach, stride; far cry to; elongation; drift, offing, background; remote region; outpost, outskirt; horizon, sky line; foreign parts, *ultima Thule* (*L.*), *ne plus ultra* (*L.*), antipodes.
reserve, restraint, aloofness, coldness, frigidity, reservation, offishness, unresponsiveness.
[*control at a distance*] telautomatics (*elec.*).
II. *Verbs.* **be distant,** be far, etc. (see *adjectives*); extend to, stretch to, reach to, lead to, go to, spread to, stretch away to; range, outreach.
III. *Adjectives.* **distant,** far, far-away, remote, far-off, inaccessible, unapproachable, out-of-the-way; yon, yonder; ulterior; transatlantic, transalpine; ultramundane, antipodean.
reserved, aloof, cold, frigid, offish, unneighborly, uncommunicative, unresponsive, reticent, repellent, condescending, high-hat (*slang*).
IV. *Adverbs.* **far off,** far away, afar, afar off, away, beyond range, out of range, out of hearing, aloof; wide of, clear of; abroad, yonder, farther, further, beyond; far and wide, "over the hills and far away," from pole to pole, to the ends of the earth; farthest, ultimate, extreme, remotest.
apart, asunder, separately, wide apart, at arm's length; aside, away, aloof.
See also OVERRUNNING, PROGRESSION, SPACE, WAY.—*Antonyms.* See NEARNESS.

---

distasteful, *adj.* unpalatable, unsavory, bitter, disagreeable, displeasing, uninviting, unsatisfactory. See PAINFULNESS, SOURNESS.
distend, *v.* swell, expand, enlarge, extend, dilate. See EXPANSION.
distil, *v.* draw out, extract, rectify; evaporate. See EXTRACTION, VAPORIZATION.
distinct, *adj.* separate, apart; explicit, definite, clean-cut; clear, distinguishable. See DISJUNCTION, MANIFESTATION, VISIBILITY.
distinction, *n.* unlikeness, variance; differentiation; gracefulness, ease, refinement; dignity, importance, eminence, rank, greatness. See DIFFERENCE, DISCRIMINATION, ELEGANCE, REPUTE.
distinctive, *adj.* distinguishing, characteristic, peculiar. See DIFFERENCE.
distinguish, *v.* separate, differentiate, characterize; decide, determine; discern, perceive, descry. See DISCRIMINATION, JUDGE, VISION.
distinguished, *adj.* celebrated, famous, eminent, illustrious, renowned, noted. See REPUTE.

DISTORTION.—I. *Nouns.* **distortion,** twisting, deformation, contortion; knot, warp, buckle, screw, twist; crookedness, obliquity; deformity, malformation, kyphosis (*med.*), monstrosity, misproportion, asymmetry, anamorphosis, ugliness, disfigurement, grimace.
perversion, misdirection, misinterpretation, garble, misrendering, misreading, misconstruing, misconstruction, misrepresentation, misusage, misuse, misapplication.
II. *Verbs.* **distort,** contort, twist, gnarl, knot, warp, buckle, screw, wrench, wring, wrest, writhe, deform, misshape.
pervert, garble, misinterpret, misrender, misconstrue, misrepresent, misuse, misapply, misdirect, torture.
III. *Adjectives.* **distorted,** out of shape, irregular, one-sided, unsymmetric *or* unsymmetrical, asymmetric *or* asymmetrical (*chiefly tech.*), awry, wry, askew, crooked, gnarled; not true, not straight; deformed; misshapen, misproportioned,

ill-proportioned, ill-made, grotesque, humpbacked, hunch-backed, kyphotic (*med.*); bandylegged, bowlegged, knockkneed; clubfooted, taliped *or* talipedic, splayfooted.

See also FALSEHOOD, FORMLESSNESS, MISINTERPRETATION, OBLIQUITY, UGLINESS. —*Antonyms.* See SYMMETRY.

---

distract, *v.* divert, turn aside; confuse, bewilder. See INATTENTION.

distracted, *adj.* frantic, frenzied; puzzled, perplexed, distraught. See EXCITEMENT, UNCERTAINTY.

distress, *n.* affliction, sorrow, agony, anguish, grief, misery, misfortune, privation, want. See PAIN, POVERTY.

distress, *v.* grieve, sadden, hurt. See PAIN.

distressing, *adj.* painful, piercing, harrowing, heartrending, trying. See SEVERITY.

distribute, *v.* classify, separate, systematize; spread, scatter; allot, apportion, deal, dispense. See ARRANGEMENT, DISPERSION, MEASUREMENT.

district, *n.* division, tract, neighborhood, section, county, commune. See REGION.

distrust, *n.* suspicion, qualm, apprehension; doubt, disbelief, mistrust. See FEAR, UNBELIEF.

disturb, *v.* stir, shake; upset, muddle, confuse; move, misplace; disquiet, worry, trouble. See AGITATION, DERANGEMENT, DISPLACEMENT, PAIN.

disturbance, *n.* disorder, tumult; restlessness, perturbation, derangement. See AGITATION.

DISUSE.—I. *Nouns.* **disuse,** nonuse, desuetude, disusage, abandonment, relinquishment, nonemployment, neglect, discontinuance, want of practice; forbearance, abstinence.

II. *Verbs.* **disuse,** lay by, lay up, shelve, set aside, lay aside, leave off, have done with; supersede, discard, throw aside, relinquish, abandon; destroy, make away with, cast (*or* throw) overboard; dismantle.

not use, do without, dispense with, let alone, forbear, abstain, leave off, break off, be weaned from; spare, waive, neglect; keep back, reserve.

III. *Adjectives.* **disused,** done with, run down, worn out; unemployed, unapplied, unexercised, untouched, uncalled for, not required.

unaccustomed, unwonted, unused, unusual, strange, new, fresh, original; uninitiated, untrained, unskilled, unseasoned.

unconventional, informal, unofficial, unfashionable, unacademic, unorthodox, unstandardized; unrestrained, free and easy.

See also RIDDANCE.—*Antonyms.* See USE.

---

ditch, *n.* trench, drain, watercourse, fosse, moat. See CHANNEL.

dive, *v.* nose-dive; glide; plunge, pitch, dip, swoop, rush in. See AËRONAUTICS, PLUNGE.

DIVERGENCE.—I. *Nouns.* **divergence** *or* divergency, ramification, forking, furcation, branching, divarication, separation, detachment, dispersion, radiation, deviation; disagreement, difference.

II. *Verbs.* **diverge,** ramify, branch off, fork, part, sever, sunder, separate, fly off; spread, scatter, radiate, disperse; vary, dissent, disagree, differ.

III. *Adjectives.* **divergent,** radial, radiant (*as,* radiant *energy*), centrifugal; forking, furcate.

See also DEVIATION, DISPERSION.—*Antonyms.* See CONVERGENCE.

---

diversified, *adj.* varied, mixed, motley. See DIVERSITY.

diversion, *n.* pastime, recreation, sport; variation, break. See AMUSEMENT, CHANGE.

DIVERSITY.—I. *Nouns.* **diversity,** irregularity, inequality, unevenness, multiformity, unconformity, dissimilarity, dissimilitude, variation, unlikeness, variety difference, diversification, nonuniformity, divergence, heterogeneity, multifariousness.
II. *Verbs.* **diversify,** vary, variegate, make diverse, modify, diverge from.
III. *Adjectives.* **diversified,** varied, diverse, mixed, diversiform, multifarious, of various kinds; irregular, uneven, checkered, party- (*or* parti-) colored, variegated, motley.
See also CHANGE, DIFFERENCE, DISSIMILARITY, MULTIFORMITY.—*Antonyms.* See UNIFORMITY.

---

divert, *v.* entertain, regale, delight; deflect, switch, turn. See AMUSEMENT, DEVIATION.

DIVESTMENT.—I. *Nouns.* **divestment,** uncovering, unclothing, divestiture, unstripping, decortication, excoriation, exfoliation, desquamation; exuviation (*zoöl.*), molting, sloughing, ecdysis (*zoöl.*); nudity, bareness, nakedness, buff (*colloq.; as, to strip to the* buff); dishabille, undress.
baldness, hairlessness, alopecia, bald-headedness, bald-patedness; beardlessness, smooth-facedness; depilation.
II. *Verbs.* **divest,** uncover, expose, lay open, lay bare, denude, bare, strip; undress, disrobe, dismantle; put off, take off, doff.
molt *or* moult, shed (*feathers*), cast, slough, exuviate (*zoöl.*), mew (*archaic*).
peel, pare, decorticate, excoriate, skin, scalp, flay, bark, husk, hull, pod, shell (*as peas*); scale, desquamate (*tech.*), exfoliate (*tech.*).
III. *Adjectives.* **naked,** nude, bare, stark-naked, exposed, in a state of nature, *in puris naturalibus* (*L.*), undressed, undraped, unclad, ungarmented, unappareled, unclothed.
barefoot, barefooted, unshod, discalceate *or* discalced (*said esp. of friars, nuns, etc.*), sandaled.
bald, hairless, beardless; shaven, clean-shaven, smooth-faced, smooth, glabrous (*tech.*).
Antonyms. See CLOTHING.

---

divide, *v.* distribute, assign, allot; sever, sunder, separate, cleave, part, detach. See APPORTIONMENT, DISJUNCTION.
divination, *n.* prophecy, forecast; augury; guess. See PREDICTION, SORCERY, SUPPOSITION.
divine, *adj.* godlike, superhuman, celestial, holy; religious, theological. See DEITY, THEOLOGY.
divine service, exercises, devotions, prayer. See WORSHIP.
divisible, *adj.* separable. See PART.
division, *n.* split, rupture, breach, faction, schism; disconnection, parting; share, portion, apportionment; section, group, class, system, realm, sphere. See DISCORD, DISJUNCTION, PART, WORLD.

DIVORCE.—I. *Nouns.* **divorce,** divorcement, legal dissolution of marriage, dissolution of the marriage bond (*or* relation), *separatio a vinculo matrimonii* (*L.*), decree of nullity; *separatio a mensa et thoro* (*L.*), legal separation, judicial separation; separation, repudiation, separate maintenance; diffarreation (*Roman*), talak (*Moham.*); Reno ("*the Great Divide*" *of cross-word puzzles*).
[*of things*] severance, separation, disunion.
[*divorced person*] divorcee (*Anglicized form used for either*), *divorcé* (*F.; masc.*), *divorcée* (*F.; fem.*).
II. *Verbs.* **divorce,** dissolve union, put away, repudiate, separate.
sunder, sever, disunite, dissever (*as, to* divorce *a word from its true meaning*).
See also RIDDANCE, WIDOWHOOD.—*Antonyms.* See MARRIAGE.

---

divulge, *v.* impart, let slip, reveal See DISCLOSURE.
dizziness, *n.* giddiness, vertigo (*med.*). See INSANITY.
dizzy, *adj.* giddy, light-headed, confused, vertiginous. See INSANITY.

do, *v.* perform, achieve, execute, accomplish; dispatch, finish; make, construct, work out; avail, answer, serve. See ACTION, COMPLETION, PRODUCTION, SUCCESS.
docile, *adj.* tractable, obedient, submissive, gentle. See WILLINGNESS.
doctor, *n.* physician, surgeon, specialist. See REMEDY.
doctrine, *n.* creed, maxim, theory, dogma, principle. See BELIEF.
document, *n.* paper, writing, record. See INSTRUMENT.
dodge, *v.* elude, evade, escape; swerve, turn aside, duck. See AVOIDANCE, DEVIATION.
doer, *n.* performer, worker, operator, perpetrator, executor, deputy. See ACTION, AGENT.
dog, *n.* canine, pup, cur; sledge dog, husky. See ANIMAL, CARRIER.
dogma, *n.* doctrine, teaching, tenet. See BELIEF.
dogmatic, *adj.* bigoted, arrogant, dictatorial, opinionated. See CERTAINTY, MISJUDGMENT.
dogmatist, *n.* doctrinaire, bigot, zealot. See BLUSTERER.
dole, *n.* pittance, alms, mite. See INSUFFICIENCY.
dollar, *n.* cartwheel (*slang*), bone (*slang*); Mexican dollar, peso. See MONEY.
dolphin, *n.* delphinoid (*zoöl.*), porpoise. See ANIMAL (*cetaceans*).
domain, *n.* territory, sphere, realm, dominions, estate, lands. See REGION.
dome, *n.* cupola, vault, canopy. See CONVEXITY, HEIGHT.
domestic, *adj.* tame, broken; inland, home, family; stay-at-home; native, native-grown. See DOMESTICATION, INTERIORITY, SECLUSION, VEGETABLE.

DOMESTICATION.—I. *Nouns.* **domestication,** domesticity, taming, reclamation; breeding, raising, rearing.
veterinary art, farriery (*obsolescent in this sense*); manège, horsemanship.
menagerie, *Tiergarten* (*Ger.*), vivarium, zoölogical garden, zoo (*colloq.*); bear pit; aviary; apiary, beehive, hive; aquarium, fishery, fish hatchery, fish pond; hennery, incubator.
keeper, warden, herder, cowherd, neatherd, ranchero (*U. S.*), herdsman, *vaquero* (*Sp. Amer.*), cowboy, cow puncher (*U. S.*), cowkeeper, drover; grazier, shepherd, shepherdess; goatherd; trainer, breeder, horse trainer, broncho-buster (*slang*); bee keeper, apiarist, apiculturist.
veterinarian, veterinary surgeon, vet (*colloq.*), horse doctor; horseshoer, farrier.
[*place for domestic animals*] stable, livery, mews, barn, byre; fold, sheepfold; pen, sty; cage, hencoop.
II. *Verbs.* **domesticate,** tame, acclimatize, reclaim, domesticize (*rare*), train; corral, round up, herd; raise, breed, bring up.
[*relating to horses*] break in, gentle, break, bust (*U. S. slang*), break to harness, yoke, harness, harness up (*colloq.*), hitch, hitch up (*colloq.*), cinch (*U. S.*), drive, ride.
groom, tend, rub down, brush, curry, currycomb; water, feed, fodder; bed down, litter.
[*relating to fowls*] **hatch,** incubate, produce young, bring forth; sit, brood, cover,
III. *Adjectives.* **domesticated,** tame, habituated, domestic, broken, gentle. docile.
Antonyms. See ANIMAL (*wild*).

---

dominate, *v.* control, domineer, rule, govern, predominate. See AUTHORITY, POSSESSION.
domineer, *v.* tyrannize, command, bluster, dictate. See INSOLENCE.
don, *v.* put on, assume, wear. See CLOTHING.
donation, *n.* gift, present, grant, gratuity. See LIBERALITY.
donkey, *n.* ass, jackass; dolt, blockhead. See CARRIER, FOOL.
doom, *n.* sentence; judgment; fate, lot, fortune; ruin, death. See CONDEMNATION, DESTINY, DESTRUCTION.
door, *n.* entrance, gate, portal; barrier, obstacle; outlet, inlet. See BEGINNING, INCLOSURE, OPENING.

doorkeeper, *n.* *concierge* (*F.*), janitor, guard, gatekeeper. See STOPPER.
[1]**dot,** *n.* point, speck, particle, mite (*colloq.*), mote, jot. See LITTLENESS, SMALLNESS.
[2]**dot,** *n.* dowry, dower. See GIVING, PROPERTY.
double, *adj.* twofold, duplex, twin. See DUPLICITY.
double, *n.* bend, plait; counterpart, twin, duplicate; substitute, understudy. See [1]FOLD, SIMILARITY, SUBSTITUTION.
double, *v.* duplicate, repeat; grow, enlarge. See DUPLICATION, INCREASE.
doubt, *v.* disbelieve, question; mistrust, distrust, challenge, deny; waver, falter, hestitate. See IRRELIGION, UNBELIEF, UNCERTAINTY.
doubt, *n.* skepticism, agnosticism; suspicion, distrust; incredulity, disbelief; indecision, irresolution, misgiving. See IRRELIGION, JEALOUSY, UNBELIEF, UNCERTAINTY.
dower, *n.* legacy, inheritance. See PROPERTY.
down, *adv.* under, below, underneath, beneath. See LOWNESS.
downfall, *n.* misfortune, overthrow; crash, wreck; collapse, fall. See ADVERSITY, DESTRUCTION, FAILURE.
downhearted, *adj.* downcast, sad, depressed, discouraged, melancholy. See DEJECTION.
downright, *adv.* bluntly, plainly; completely, absolutely, utterly. See ARTLESSNESS, GREATNESS.
downy, *adj.* woolly, lanate, flocculent; soft, fluffy. See ROUGHNESS, SOFTNESS.

DOZEN.—I. *Nouns.* **dozen,** twelve; long dozen, baker's dozen, thirteen.
II. *Adjectives.* **dozenth,** twelfth, duodenary.

---

drab, *adj.* monotonous, dull; grayish, dun, leaden, dingy. See DULLNESS, GRAY.
draft, *n.* levy, contingent; submergence; drink, potion; conscription, muster; check, bill of exchange; sketch, forecast; drawing, picture; breeze, air. See COMBATANT, DEPTH, FOOD, LIST, MONEY, OUTLINE, REPRESENTATION, WIND.
draft, *v.* select, enlist; impress, conscript, commandeer; sketch, plan, model; compose, formulate. See CHOICE, COMPULSION, OUTLINE, WRITING.
draftsman, *n.* sketcher, delineator, designer. See REPRESENTATION.
drag, *v.* crawl, elapse; lag, trial, creep; haul, pull, tug. See LAPSE, SLOWNESS, TRACTION.
drain, *v.* leak, flow out, discharge; empty, draw off; impoverish, reduce; tax, wear, exhaust. See EGRESS, EJECTION, INSUFFICIENCY, WASTE.
drain, *n.* pipe, trench, sewer, outlet, ditch. See CHANNEL.
dram, *n.* drink, draft, potion. See PUNGENCY.

DRAMA.—I. *Nouns.* **the drama,** the stage, the theater *or* theatre, the play; theatricals, dramaturgy, histrionic art; buskin, sock, cothurnus; Melpomene (*Muse of tragedy*) and Thalia (*Muse of comedy*), Thespis ("*the first professor of our art.*"—Dryden).
play, drama, piece, composition, tragedy, comedy, opera, vaudeville, comedietta, curtain raiser, interlude, *entr'acte* (*F.*), *divertissement* (*F.*), afterpiece, farce, extravaganza, harlequinade, pantomime, burlesque, ballet, spectacle, masque, melodrama; comedy of manners; charade; mystery, miracle play, morality play.
act, scene, tableau, curtain; introduction, prologue, exposition, epilogue; libretto, book, text.
performance, representation, acting, rendition (*U. S.*), show (*colloq.*), stage setting, *mise en scène* (*F.*), stagecraft; acting, impersonation, stage business; slap-stick (*slang*), buffoonery, gag, patter.
theater *or* theatre, playhouse, amphitheater, moving-picture theater, moving pictures, movies (*colloq.*), cinematograph, cinema (*Brit. colloq.*), the silent drama, the silver screen, vitascope; vitaphone, talking pictures, movietone, talkies (*colloq.*), gabbies (*slang*), squawkies (*slang*), sound picture, kinetophone; puppet show, marionettes, Punch and Judy.
auditorium, auditory (*rare*), front of the house, front (*colloq. and professional*),

stalls (*chiefly Brit.*), parquet, orchestra, pit (*chiefly Brit.*), boxes, parterre boxes, stage (*or* proscenium) boxes, *baignoire* (*F.*), orchestra circle, dress circle, balcony, gallery.
scenery, scene; flat, drop, wing, screen, coulisse, side scene, transformation scene, curtain, act drop.
stage, the boards, footlights (*cant*), floats, limelight, spotlight; proscenium (*in the ancient theater, the stage*), movable stage, scene, flies.
theatrical costume, theatrical properties, props (*cant*).
cast, persons in the play, *dramatis personæ* (*L.*); rôle, part, character; repertoire, repertory.
actor, player, Thespian, performer; masker, mime, mimic; star, headliner; comedian, tragedian, photoplayer.
buffoon, mummer, pantomimist, *farceur* (*F.*), clown; pantaloon, harlequin, columbine; punch, punchinello.
company, first tragedian, prima donna, *diva* (*It.; pl. dive*), leading lady; lead; leading man; comedian, comedienne, juvenile lead, juvenile; villain, heavy lead, heavy, heavy father; *ingénue* (*F.*), soubrette; character man, character woman extra, mute, supernumerary, super *or* supe (*cant*).
dancer, ballet dancer, *danseuse* (*F.; fem.*), *coryphée* (*F.*), ballet girl, *ballerina* (*It.; pl. ballerine*), terpsichorean (*colloq.*), figurant (*masc.*), figurante (*fem.*), Terpsichore (*Muse*); ballet (*collective*), leg show (*slang*).
audience, house; orchestra, gallery, the gods (*colloq.*) gallery gods (*colloq.*), peanut heaven (*slang*).
dramatist, playwright, playwriter, dramatic author (*or* writer), photoplaywright.
II. *Verbs.* **dramatize**, make into a drama, represent dramatically, convert (*as a novel*) into a play, put on the stage, stage, produce, set.
act, play, perform, enact, personate, mimic; tread the stage (*or* boards); make one's début, take (act, *or* sustain) a part, star; rehearse, spout, rant.
III. *Adjectives.* **dramatic**, theatric *or* theatrical, histrionic, scenic; tragic, buskined; comic, farcical, tragi-comic, melodramatic, operatic; stagy, spectacular; impressive, striking, sudden, vivid.
IV. *Adverbs.* **on the stage**, on the boards; before the footlights, before an audience; in the limelight, in the spotlight; behind the scenes.

---

draw, *v.* attract, lure; describe, fabricate; sketch, portray, delineate; drag, pull, haul. See ATTRACTION, COMPOSITION, FINE ARTS, TRACTION.
drawback, *n.* obstacle, discouragement, difficulty, check. See HINDRANCE.
drawing, *n.* sketch, draft, design, picture, delineation. See FINE ARTS, REPRESENTATION.
dreadful, *adj.* frightful, horrible, tremendous, shocking, formidable. See FEAR.
dream, *n.* phantasy, vision, reverie, fancy; shadow, nothingness. See IMAGINATION, PSYCHICAL, RESEARCH, UNSUBSTANTIALITY.
dreamer, *n.* visionary, idealist. See MADMAN.
dreary, *adj.* depressing, somber, gloomy; monotonous, humdrum, dull. See DEJECTION, UNIFORMITY.
dregs, *n. pl.* sediment, settlings, lees, residue; trash, refuse, riffraff, scum. See DENSITY, REMAINDER, UNCLEANNESS.
drench, *v.* wet, soak, saturate. See WATER.
dress, *v.* clothe, attire, deck, drape; berate, scold; smooth, even, align; decorate, adorn, embellish; make ready, prepare, treat (*as a wound*). See CLOTHING, DISAPPROBATION, HORIZONTALITY, ORNAMENT, PREPARATION, REMEDY.
dress, *n.* garments, raiment, apparel, vesture, garb, clothes, covering, attire, costume. See CLOTHING, HABIT.
dressmaker, *n.* *modiste* (*F.*), seamstress. See CLOTHING.
dress suit, swallowtail (*colloq.*), tuxedo, tux (*colloq.*), dinner coat. See CLOTHING.
drift, *n.* heap, pile, mass; bearing, course; tenor, significance, import; trend, vein, bent, tone. See ASSEMBLAGE, DIRECTION, MEANING, TENDENCY.

drift, *v.* advance, move; float, be carried; heap up. See APPROACH, MOTION.
drill, *v.* bore, pierce; train, instruct. See OPENING, TEACHING.
drink, *v.* quaff, sip; tipple, carouse; imbibe, absorb; toast, pledge. See FOOD, RECEPTION, REPUTE.
drink, *n.* liquor, highball, cocktail; beverage, potion. See DRUNKENNESS, FOOD.
drinkable, *adj.* potable, potatory (*rare*). See FOOD.
drinking, *n.* potation, draft, libation; carousal. See FOOD, INTEMPERANCE.
drip, *v.* leak, ooze, drop, trickle, dribble. See RIVER.
drive, *v.* force, impel, oblige, urge; steer, manage, control; ride, travel; thrust, aim. See COMPULSION, DIRECTION, JOURNEY, PROPULSION.
drivel, *v.* babble, twaddle, dote. See IMBECILITY.
drivel, *n.* slobber, slaver; twaddle, nonsense. See EXCRETION, UNMEANINGNESS.
driver, *n.* whip, charioteer, coachman, teamster, chauffeur. See DIRECTOR, TRAVELER.
droop, *v.* sink, despond, decline; wither, fade; hang, lean, drop. See DEJECTION, DETERIORATION, PENDENCY.
drop, *n.* dash, particle, globule, bit. See SMALLNESS.
drop, *v.* fall, slide; sink; cease, discontinue; collapse, faint; discard, give up; drip, trickle. See DESCENT, END, IMPOTENCE, RELINQUISHMENT, RIVER.
dross, *n.* trash, rubbish, waste, garbage; leavings, sediment, dregs, grounds. See INUTILITY, UNCLEANNESS.
drought, *n.* aridness, parchedness, thirst; lack, dearth, scarcity. See DRYNESS, INSUFFICIENCY.
drown, *v.* submerge, suffocate; overpower, overwhelm, deaden (*sound*); drench. See KILLING, NONRESISTANCE, WATER.
drudge, *v.* plod, toil, grub, slave, grind. See EXERTION.
druggist, *n.* pharmacist, apothecary. See REMEDY.

DRUNKENNESS.—I. *Nouns.* **drunkenness,** intemperance, drinking, inebriety, inebriation, insobriety, intoxication, winebibbing; bacchanalia, libations; alcoholism, dipsomania; delirium tremens, D. T.'s (*colloq.*).
drink, intoxicant, stimulant, alcohol, spirit, liquor, Demon Rum, blue ruin (*slang*), booze (*colloq.*), wet goods (*slang*), grog, punch; punchbowl, cup, rosy wine, flowing bowl; dram, beverage; cocktail, highball (*U. S.*), peg (*Anglo-Indian origin: the word, not the habit*); champagne, brandy, whisky, rye, ale, beer, etc.; stirrup cup, parting cup, doch-an-dorrach (*Scot.*).
illicit distilling, bootlegging (*slang*), moonshining, moonshine *or* moonshine whisky (*colloq.*), hooch (*slang*), chain lightning (*slang*), home-brew; moonshiner (*colloq.*); bootlegger (*slang*), hijacker (*U. S. slang*); blind tiger, blind pig, speak-easy (*all U. S. slang*), oasis (*so regarded by some*).
drunkard, inebriate, dipsomaniac, drinker, lushington (*Eng. slang*), sot, toper, tippler, winebibber, hard drinker, soaker (*slang*), sponge (*slang*), boozer (*colloq.*); reveler, carouser; antiprohibitionist, wet (*slang: opposite of* dry).
II. *Verbs.* **get** (*or* be) **drunk,** see double; take a drop (*or* glass) too much; drink, tipple, booze (*colloq.*), soak (*slang*), carouse; drink hard (deep, *or* like a fish); liquor, liquor up (*both slang*), wet one's whistle (*colloq. or jocose*), raise the elbow, hit the booze (*slang*), crack a bottle.
intoxicate, inebriate, fuddle (*colloq.*), befuddle, stew (*slang*), mellow, stupefy, poison.
III. *Adjectives.* **drunk,** tipsy, intoxicated, inebriate, inebriated, in a state of intoxication, overcome, fuddled (*colloq.*), boozy (*colloq.*), full (*vulgar*), lit up (*slang*), elevated (*colloq.*), groggy (*colloq.*); screwed, tight, primed (*all slang*), muddled, stupefied, obfuscated, maudlin; blind drunk, dead drunk, drunk as a lord.
alcoholic, spirituous, distilled, ardent, strong, hard.
opposed to prohibition, antiprohibition; wet (*opposite of* dry; *as, a* wet *county: U. S. slang*).
See also INTEMPERANCE.—*Antonyms.* See SOBRIETY.

DRYNESS.—I. *Nouns.* **dryness,** aridness, aridity, parchedness, drought; desiccation, dehydration, evaporation.
shrewdness, keenness, sharpness, severity, cynicism; quaintness, gravity, impassiveness.
tediousness, dullness, lifelessness, dreariness, wearisomeness.
dry, prohibitionist (*U. S. slang*): *opposite of* wet.
II. *Verbs.* **dry,** dry up, soak up; sponge, swab, wipe, drain; parch, sear, bake kiln; desiccate, dehydrate, evaporate; preserve.
III. *Adjectives.* **dry,** rainless, fair, pleasant, fine; arid, sear *or* sere, parched, dried up, corky, shriveled up; droughty, thirsty, waterless, dried, desiccated, anhydrous; juiceless, sapless, waterproof, watertight; dry-footed, dry-shod.
[*of the voice*] **husky,** raucous rough, harsh, hoarse.
[*of wines, etc.*] **unsweet,** without sweetness, not fruity.
[*in fine arts*] **formal,** stiff, precise, hard.
[*relating to the legal sale of intoxicants*] **prohibited,** unpurchasable (*lawfully, of course*), unprocurable, bone-dry (*as, a* dry *town; a* dry *country*).
shrewd, keen, sharp, cynical; quaint, grave (*as,* dry *humour*).
tedious, dull, lifeless, wearisome, unprofitable, unfruitful, fruitless, uninteresting, jejune, pointless, sterile, barren, vapid, insipid.
meager, plain, bare, unadorned, unembellished (*as,* dry *facts*).
See also DULLNESS, WEARINESS.—*Antonyms.* See MOISTURE.

DUALITY.—I. *Nouns.* **duality,** dualism, twofoldness, doubleness, biformity, duplexity, duplicity; polarity.
two, couple, couplet, both, twain, brace, pair, deuce (*as in cards*), twins, binary, Castor and Pollux, gemini, fellow; yoke, span; distich, binomial (*algebra*).
II. *Verbs.* **pair,** couple, bracket, yoke, match, mate.
III. *Adjectives.* **dual,** twofold, double, duplicate, duplex, dualistic, biform, binary, binate (*bot.*), geminate, binomial; two, twin, twain (*archaic*), both.
coupled, paired, matched, conjugate, yoked, united, mated, bijugate (*bot.*).
See also DUPLICATION.

---

dubious, *adj.* doubtful, questionable, suspicious, uncertain. See SHADE (*equivocal*), UNCERTAINTY.
duck, *v.* bow, bob, dip; plunge, souse. See DEPRESSION, WATER.
duct, *n.* conduit, canal, pipe, tube. See CHANNEL.
ductile, *adj.* pliant, pliable, flexible, malleable, tractile; manageable, compliant, tractable, docile. See SOFTNESS, TRACTION, WILLINGNESS.
duel, *n.* affair of honor, single combat. See CONTENTION.
dues, *n. pl.* assessment, fee, tax. See PRICE.

DULLNESS.—I. *Nouns.* **dullness,** heaviness, flatness, stupidity, slowness, stagnation, sluggishness, apathy; dimness, obscurity; jejuneness, dryness, etc. (see *adjectives*); want of originality, dearth of ideas; matter of fact, commonplace. platitude, bromide (*colloq.*).
II. *Verbs.* **dull,** blunt (*as an edge*); deaden, stupefy, benumb; mitigate, moderate; blur, bedim, obscure, darken, cloud, tarnish.
be dull, fall flat, platitudinize, prose.
depress, deject, dampen, damp, throw cold water on, lay a wet blanket on, weaken, discourage, restrain, check.
III. *Adjectives.* **dull,** dry, uninteresting, heavy-footed, elephantine, ponderous, heavy; jejune, insipid, tasteless, unimaginative, flat-minded; tedious, cheerless, dreary, dismal, doleful; phlegmatic, stolid; inactive, stagnant, sluggish, lifeless, inert, listless, insensible, inanimate, dead.
[*of the understanding*] **slow,** stupid, crass, obtuse, dense, doltish, thick-headed, slow-witted, inapt.
[*of a surface*] **dim,** clouded, obscure, lusterless, blurred, lackluster, tarnished; matt, unglazed, unpolished, opaque.
[*of color*] **somber,** sober, gray, muddy, sad, subdued.
[*of style, etc.*] **bald,** meager, humdrum, monotonous, drab, commonplace, ordinary, matter-of-fact, prosy, prosaic, dry as dust, pointless, platitudinous; "weary, stale, flat, and unprofitable" (*Hamlet*)

[*of the weather*] overcast, gloomy, cloudy, leaden, murky, thick, lowering.
[*of sounds*] muffled, deadened, flat, subdued, softened, not clear.
See also BLUNTNESS, COLOR, DRYNESS, DUMBNESS, HEAVINESS, SLOWNESS, WEAKNESS.—*Antonyms*. See INTELLIGENCE, LIGHT, SHARPNESS, WIT.

DUMBNESS.—I. *Nouns*. **dumbness,** aphonia (*med.*), voicelessness, tonguelessness; silence, taciturnity, noiselessness; deaf-muteness, deaf-mutism, deaf-dumbness; mute, deaf-mute, dummy.
II. *Verbs*. **silence,** muzzle, muffle, suppress, smother, deaden, throttle, gag, strike dumb, dumbfound; hush, still, quiet.
III. *Adjectives*. **dumb,** voiceless, aphonic, nonvocal, speechless, tongueless, mute, mum, wordless, silent, taciturn, noiseless; inarticulate, tongue-tied.
dull, slow-witted, stupid: *in this sense,* dumb *is colloq., as used of "dumb Dora" and other "dumb-bells."*
See also TACITURNITY.—*Antonyms*. See VOICE.

DUPE.—I. *Nouns*. **dupe,** gull, cully, victim, easy mark (*slang*), soft mark (*slang*), sucker (*slang*), pigeon (*slang*), flat (*colloq.*), greenhorn, fool, puppet, cat's-paw; laughingstock, butt, April fool.
II. *Verbs*. **dupe,** deceive, delude, gull, trick, cheat, swindle, victimize.
be deceived, be the dupe of, fall into a trap, swallow (*or* nibble at) the bait, swallow whole, bite.
See also CREDULITY, DECEPTION, ERROR, FOOL.—*Antonyms*. See DECEIVER.

DUPLICATION.—I. *Nouns*. **duplication,** doubling, reduplication; iteration, repetition, renewal.
duplicate, facsimile, copy, transcript, replica, counterpart.
II. *Verbs*. **duplicate,** double, geminate (*tech.*), fold; facsimile, copy; redouble, reduplicate; repeat, renew, renovate.
III. *Adjectives*. **duplicate,** double, twofold, duplex, bifold; twin, second.
IV. *Adverbs*. **twice,** doubly, once more, over again, bis.
See also DUALITY, IMITATION, REPETITION.—*Antonyms*. See BISECTION.

---

duplicity, *n.* fraud, deceit, guile, double dealing. See FALSEHOOD.

DURABILITY.—I. *Nouns*. **durability,** durableness, permanence, continuance, persistence, diuturnity (*rare*), lastingness, standing; immutability, stability; survival; longevity; slowness, delay.
an age, æon *or* eon, century, an eternity, kalpa (*Hindu*); years, lifetime, a long time, a blue moon (*colloq.*); perpetuity.
II. *Verbs*. **dure** (*archaic*), last, endure, stand, remain, abide, continue, persist.
tarry, delay, dally, lag, drag on, protract, prolong; spin out, eke out, draw out; temporize, gain time.
outlast, outlive, outwear, survive, outgrow.
III. *Adjectives*. **durable,** lasting, permanent, fixed, immovable, stable, firm, enduring, persistent, continuing, chronic, long-standing, lifelong, livelong, long-lived, perennial, perpetual, endless.
prolonged, extended, protracted, spun out, lingering, long-winded, slow.
IV. *Adverbs*. **long,** for a long time, for an age, for ages, long ago; all the day long, the livelong day; all the year round; permanently, for good; to a great extent, all along.
See also PERMANENCE, PERPETUITY, SLOWNESS, STABILITY.—*Antonyms*. See TRANSIENCE.

---

duration, *n.* continuance, period, time, extent. See LENGTH.
during, *prep.* until, pending, throughout. See TIME.
dusk, *n.* twilight, gloaming, obscurit . See DIMNESS.
dust, *n.* powder; dirt, soil. See POWDERINESS, UNCLEANNESS.

DUTY.—I. *Nouns*. **duty,** deference, respect, reverence, homage, act of respect, devoir (*archaic*); obligation, bounden duty, moral obligation; "stern daughter of the voice of God" (Wordsworth); accountability, liability, onus, responsibility.
allegiance, fealty, tie; engagement, service, function, part, task, commission, **trust,** charge. business, office, calling

morality, morals, ethics, moral philosophy, ethical philosophy; the Ten Commandments, decalogue; conscientiousness, conscience, inward monitor, "still small voice" (*Bible*), sense of duty, virtue, rectitude, uprightness.
propriety, fitness, seemliness, decorum, decorousness, becomingness, correctness, *bienséance* (*F.*), the thing, the proper thing.
observance, attention, fulfillment, discharge, performance, acquittal, satisfaction, redemption; good behavior.
tax, impost, toll, levy, assessment, due, rate, custom, excise.
II. *Verbs.* **be the duty of,** behoove *or* behove (*used with* it *as subject*), belong, suit, become, befit, beseem; belong to, pertain to; rest with, fall to one's lot, devolve on, be incumbent on.
take upon oneself, be (*or* become) sponsor for, incur a responsibility; perform a duty, discharge an obligation, act one's part, redeem one's pledge, be at one's post, do one's duty.
impose a duty, enjoin, require, exact; bind, bind over; saddle with, prescribe, assign, call upon, look to, oblige.
III. *Adjectives.* **dutiable,** taxable, assessable, liable to duty.
dutiful, obedient, duteous, submissive, docile, tractable, compliant, respectful, reverent, reverential.
obligatory, binding, imperative, peremptory, mandatory, compulsive, necessitative, imperious, stringent, incumbent on.
amenable, liable, accountable, responsible, answerable.
right, meet, proper, becoming, fit, correct (*colloq.*), seemly, decent, just, appropriate, due, suitable, befitting, decorous, consistent; moral, ethical, conscientious.
IV. *Adverbs.* **dutifully,** obediently, etc. (see *adjectives*); with a safe conscience, as in duty bound, on one's own responsibility, at one's own risk.
See also BUSINESS, PROBITY, VIRTUE.—*Antonyms.* See DERELICTION.

---

dwarf, *n.* pygmy, Lilliputian, midget. See LITTLENESS.
dwell, *v.* reside, stay, lodge. See LIFE.
dwelling, *n.* abode, domicile, residence, house. See HABITATION.
dwindle, *v.* shrink, contract, lessen. diminish, decline. See DECREASE.
dye, *v.* tint, stain, tinge. See COLOR.
dying, *adj.* expiring, waning, passing, moribund. See DEATH.
dynamic, *adj.* impelling, driving; energetic, magnetic. See IMPULSE, POWER.

E

each, *adv.* respectively, apiece, severally, seriatim. See SPECIALTY.
eager, *adj.* ardent, zealous, fervent, earnest, intent. See ACTIVITY, FEELING.
eagerness, *n.* zeal, ardor, enthusiasm, keenness. See ACTIVITY.
eagle, *n.* bird of prey, *aquila* (*L.*), eaglet; bald eagle (*emblem of U. S.*), golden eagle, ringtail, harpy eagle, sea eagle, ern *or* erne. See ANIMAL.
[1]**ear,** *n.* heed, observance; organ of hearing, auricle, concha (*tech.*); lug, handle, knob. See ATTENTION, HEARING, INSTRUMENT.
[2]**ear,** *n.* spike (*of corn*), head. See EFFECT.

EARLINESS.—I. *Nouns.* **earliness,** punctuality, promptitude, readiness, expedition, quickness, haste, speed, swiftness, alacrity, instantaneity, suddenness, prematurity, precocity, prematureness, untimeliness, immaturity, hastiness, precipitation, anticipation; a stitch in time.
II. *Verbs.* **be early,** anticipate, foresee, foretaste, forestall, forerun, obviate; be early, be beforehand. take time by the forelock, steal a march upon; bespeak, secure, engage, preengage.
accelerate, expedite, quicken, hasten, haste, hurry, rush, press, forward, hustle
III. *Adjectives.* **early,** timely, seasonable, punctual. forward, prompt, speedy swift, alacritous.

premature, precipitate, anticipatory, untimely, inopportune, ill-timed; forward, precocious, advanced.
sudden, instantaneous, immediate, instant, prompt, unexpected.
imminent, threatening, overhanging, impending, coming, at hand; near.
IV. *Adverbs.* early, soon, anon, betimes, ere long, before long; punctually, in time; on time, on the dot (*slang*).
beforehand, previously, hitherto, heretofore, erenow (*archaic*); prematurely, too soon, precipitately, hastily; in anticipation, unexpectedly, unawares.
suddenly, forthwith, plump, immediately, instantaneously, at once, speedily, quickly, apace; at short notice, extempore, on the spur of the moment, on the spot, on the instant, at sight, offhand, straight, straightway, presently, by and by, directly.
See also INSTANTANEITY, VELOCITY.—*Antonyms.* See LATENESS.

---

earnest, *adj.* zealous, fervent, ardent, eager; grave, solemn, weighty; serious, purposeful, determined. See FEELING, IMPORTANCE, RESOLUTION.
earshot, *n.* range, carrying distance. See HEARING, [1]SOUND.
earth, *n.* soil, dirt, ground; globe, sphere, planet. See LAND, WORLD.
earthenware, *n.* pottery, crockery, stoneware. See CALEFACTION.
earthly, *adj.* mundane, material, temporal, secular. See IRRELIGION.
ease, *n.* contentment, enjoyment, complacency; readiness, expertness; unconstraint, naturalness; comfort, luxury. See [1]CONTENT, FACILITY, FREEDOM, PLEASURE.
easily, *adv.* smoothly, readily. See FACILITY.
eastern, *adj.* east, eastward, oriental: *opposite of* western. See SIDE.
easy, *adj.* untroubled, unconcerned, comfortable; unconstrained, smooth (*as style*); facile, simple; light, unexacting; mild, gentle, moderate, indulgent; compliant, tractable, manageable. See [1]CONTENT, ELEGANCE, FACILITY, LIGHTNESS, MILDNESS, WILLINGNESS.
easy-going, *adj.* satisfied, cheerful; careless, unconcerned; placid, tranquil. See [2]CONTENT, INDIFFERENCE, INEXCITABILITY.
eat, *v.* corrode, erode, rust; fare, feed, devour, consume. See DETERIORATION, FOOD.
eatable, *adj.* edible, esculent, comestible, nutritive. See FOOD.
eatables, *n. pl.* victuals, edibles. See FOOD.
eating, *n.* consumption, devouring, mastication. See FOOD.
ebb, *v.* decline, waste, decay; recede, withdraw. See DECREASE, RECESSION.
eccentric, *adj.* odd, peculiar; irregular, deviating, erratic. See INSANITY, UNCONFORMITY.
ecclesiastical, *adj.* priestly, religious, clerical, sacerdotal. See CHURCHDOM.
echo, *n*, reverberation, repercussion. See REPETITION.
echo, *v.* repeat, reproduce; resound, reverberate. See IMITATION, REPETITION.
eclipse, *v.* obscure, cloud, conceal; surpass, outshine, overshadow. See DARKNESS, REPUTE.

ECONOMY.—I. *Nouns.* **economy,** economization, Hooverism (*colloq.*), management, order, careful administration, organization, conduct; frugality, prudence, thrift, thriftiness, providence, sparingness, care, husbandry, retrenchment.
savings, hoard, store, thrift (*rare in this sense*) preservation, prevention of waste, save-all; parsimony.
II. *Verbs.* **economize,** be frugal, husband, Hooverize (*colloq.*), save; retrench, cut down expenses, skimp (*colloq.*), scrimp, scrape, stint, spare; make both ends meet, meet one's expenses, pay one's way; save (*or* invest) money, provide against a rainy day.
III. *Adjectives.* **economical,** frugal, careful, thrifty, saving, economizing, provident, chary, spare, sparing, parsimonious.
See also CONDUCT, ORDER, PARSIMONY, STORE.—*Antonyms.* See LIBERALITY, PRODIGALITY.

ecstasy, *n.* trance, frenzy, inspiration; bliss, rapture, exaltation. See IMAGINATION, PLEASURE.
eddy, *n.* countercurrent, swirl, whirlpool. See ROTATION.

EDGE.—I. *Nouns.* **edge,** verge, brink, brow, brim, curb, margin, border, frame, confine, skirt, rim, side, ledge, flange, mouth, lip, labium (*pl.* labia: *tech.*), labellum (*pl.* labella: *bot.*), labrum (*pl.* labra: *zoöl.*); featheredge (*as on a razor*).
threshold, sill, doorsill, groundsel, entrance, gate, door, portal, porch; beginning, outstart, inception; limen (*psychol.*).
shore, coast, strand, seashore, beach, waterside, foreshore, bank.
wharf, quay, landing, landing place, bunder (*Anglo-Indian*), bund (*Oriental*), dock, mole, pier.
fringe, border, edge, fimbriation, fimbria (*tech.*); edging, trimming, skirting, hem, selvage, welt; flounce, frill, furbelow, valance.
sharpness, keenness, intensity, zest, eagerness, penetration, penetrativeness; acrimony, bitterness, acridity.
II. *Verbs.* **edge,** coast, border, verge (on), skirt, fringe, hem; margin, marginate.
move edgewise, advance slowly, inch, inch along, hitch.
III. *Adjectives.* **marginal,** border, margined, marginate, limbiferous, limbic (*anat.*), littoral, coastal.
See also OPENING, SIDE.—*Antonyms.* See CENTRALITY, INTERIORITY.

---

edible, *adj.* eatable, esculent. See FOOD.
edict, *n.* order, proclamation, decree. See COMMAND.
edification, *n.* enlightenment, instruction, education. See TEACHING.
edifice, *n.* building, structure. See PRODUCTION.
edit, *v.* compile, compose, select, adapt; revise, correct, prepare; issue, publish. See COMPENDIUM, IMPROVEMENT, PUBLICATION.
edition, *n.* issue, impression, printing. See PUBLICATION.
educate, *v.* instruct, enlighten, edify, train, school, develop. See TEACHING.
educated, *adj.* well-informed, learned, scholarly, erudite. See KNOWLEDGE.
educational, *adj.* instructive, scholastic, didactic. See TEACHING.
educe, *v.* evolve, elicit, deduce, infer, develop, evoke. See EXTRACTION.
efface, *v.* cancel, erase, wipe out, blot. See OBLITERATION.

EFFECT.—I. *Nouns.* **effect,** consequence, result, resultant (*tech.*), end, conclusion, outcome, *dénouement* (*F.*), issue, event, upshot, catastrophe, aftergrowth, afterclap, aftermath, development, outgrowth; derivative, derivation; purport, meaning, intent, tenor, drift; general impression, impress, *ensemble* (*F.*).
product, production, yield, fruit, crop, harvest, produce; ear, spike (*of corn*), head; turnout, output; work, handiwork, fabric, performance; creature, creation; offspring, offshoot; first fruits, *primeur* (*F.*).
efficacy, effectiveness, weight, force, power, validity, efficiency, potency, virtue (*as, of no* effect).
execution, operation, performance, accomplishment, working, actuality, reality, realization (*as, to go into* effect).
[*in plural*] **effects,** movables, goods, personal estate, personalty.
II. *Verbs.* **effect,** produce, cause, make, do, perform, execute, carry out, complete, consummate, bring about, compass, fulfill, realize, effectuate.
be the effect of, be due to, be owing to; follow, proceed, originate in (*or* from), rise from, spring from, emanate from, come from, issue from, flow from, result from, result, accrue, fall (from *or* to); depend upon, hang upon, hinge upon, turn upon.
III. *Adjectives.* **owing to,** resulting from, derivable from, attributable to, ascribable to, due to, caused by; derived from, evolved from, derivative; hereditary.
consequential, resultant, sequential, consequent; eventual, secondary, indirect, contingent.

IV. *Adverbs.* **consequently,** therefore, ergo, argal (*both archaic*), hence, wherefore, it follows that, as a consequence, in consequence, as a natural result, inevitably, necessarily, eventually.

See also COMPLETION, JUDGMENT, PROPERTY.—*Antonyms.* See CAUSE.

---

effective, *adj.* adequate, telling, effectual, potent, operative, efficacious; efficient, capable. See POWER, USE.

effectual, *adj.* effective, operative, adequate, availing. See USE.

effeminate, *adj.* unmanly, delicate, soft, weak, womanish. See SOFTNESS, WEAKNESS.

effervesce, *v.* bubble, bead, hiss, fizz, ferment. See FOAM.

effervescence, *n.* bubbling, fermentation. See FOAM.

efficacious, *adj.* effective, adequate. See USE.

efficacy, *n.* potency, weight, strength, power, effectiveness. See EFFECT, VIRTUE.

efficient, *adj.* effective, operative; capable, competent. See POWER, SKILL.

effort, *n.* production, work, achievement; attempt, venture, struggle, endeavor, trial, labor. See COMPOSITION, EXERTION.

egg-shaped, *adj.* ovoid, ovate, oval, elliptical. See ROTUNDITY.

ego, *n.* self, personality, the I. See IMMATERIALITY, INTELLECT.

egoism, *n.* self-absorption, conceit, self-opinionatedness: *opposite of* altruism. See OVERESTIMATION, VANITY.

egoist, *n.* individualist, self-seeker: *opposite of* altruist. See OVERESTIMATION.

egotism, *n.* self-conceit, self-exaltation, vanity. See OVERESTIMATION, SELFISHNESS.

egotist, *n.* boaster, prig. See OVERESTIMATION.

EGRESS.—I. *Nouns.* **egress,** exit, departure, escape, discharge, issue, emanation, emergence, emersion, outbreak, outburst, eruption; evacuation, withdrawal; leakage, percolation, oozing, drain, drainage; gush, outpour, effluence, outflow, effusion, efflux.

export (*used esp. in pl.*), exportation; shipment: *opposite of* import.

emigration, exodus, departure, migration: *opposite of* immigration.

emigrant, migrant, colonist: *opposite of* immigrant.

outlet, vent, spout, faucet, tap, cock, beak, nozzle, snout; sluice, floodgate, conduit; mouth, opening, door, doorway, gate, debouch (*mil.*), debouchment; trail, path, pathway; port, porthole, loophole, skylight, window.

II. *Verbs.* **egress,** emanate, issue, go (come, pass, pour, *or* flow) out of, emerge, depart, exit; arise, appear, come forth.

exude, discharge, leak; run through, percolate; strain, distill; perspire, sweat; drain, seep (*dial. Eng. and U. S.*), ooze, filter, infiltrate, gush, spout, flow out, well, well out, pour, pour forth, effuse; trickle, find vent, escape, break forth, come forth, debouch, disembogue.

III. *Adjectives.* **emergent,** emerging, issuing, emanant, emanating; efflorescent, eruptive, porous, pervious, leaky; outgoing, outbound, outward-bound.

See also CHANNEL, ESCAPE, OPENING, RIVER, WAY.—*Antonyms.* See INGRESS.

EIGHT.—I. *Nouns.* **eight,** octave, octad (*esp. chem.*), octavo, octet (*as in music; also the first eight lines of a sonnet*), ogdoad, octonary, octagon (*geom.*), octahedron (*geom.*), octameter (*pros.*), octastyle (*arch.*), utas (*eccl.*), Octateuch (*Bible*), octosyllable.

II. *Verbs.* multiply by eight, make eightfold, octuple.

III. *Adjectives.* **eightfold,** octuple, octonary; octangular, octagonal, octohedral, octamerous (*bot. and zoöl.*), octadic, octavalent (*chem.*), octosyllabic.

EJECTION.—I. *Nouns.* **ejection,** emission, effusion, ejaculation (*archaic or tech.*), rejection, expulsion, eviction, dislodgment, dispossession, removal, ouster, ejectment, banishment, exile, deportation, expedition; discharge, evacuation, eruption, eruptiveness; tapping, drainage; emetic; vomiting, eructation. [*ejected matter*] ejecta (*as of a volcano*), *ejectamenta* (*L.; pl.*); vomit, spew (*dial.*); egesta (*physiol.*), excrements.

II. *Verbs.* **eject,** expel, extrude, reject, discard; ostracize, boycott; banish, exile, deport, expatriate; throw away (*or* aside), push out (*or* off), send off (*or* away); discharge, dismiss, fire (*slang*), turn (*or* cast) adrift; turn out, throw overboard.
evict, oust, dislodge, remove, dispossess, turn out of doors.
emit, send out, send forth, issue, pour out, dispatch, shed, express, exhale, breathe, vent, blow, gush, outpour, pour forth; squirt, spurt, spill.
empty, deplete, draw, exhaust, drain, sweep off, clear off; purge, void, cvacuate, draw off, tap, broach; eviscerate, gut.
eradicate, extirpate, exterminate, root out, uproot, root up, unearth, weed out, get out, eliminate, get rid of, do away with, shake off, abolish, destroy.
salivate, ptyalize (*med.*), slaver, slabber, slobber, drivel, drool, dribble; expectorate, spit, hawk, splutter, sputter.
vomit, spew; cast up, throw up, bring up; disgorge.
unpack, disburden; unchain, unmoor, unlash, unbind, loose, unstring, uncord, unlace, unloose, release; unlade, unload, dump (*chiefly U. S.*), unship.
III. *Adjectives.* **ejective,** expulsive, explosive, emissive, eliminant, eliminative (*physiol.*), extrusive (*chiefly geol.*), extruding, egestive (*physiol.*), emitting; vomitive, vomitory, emetic.
IV. *Interjections.* **begone!** get you gone! go away! depart! *allez-vous-en!* (*F.*), *va-t'en!* (*F.*), go! off with you! fade! (*slang*), chase yourself! (*slang*), away! scat! (*used chiefly in driving off a cat*), scoot! (*colloq.*), shoo! (*as in frightening away fowls*), aroint *or* aroynt! (*archaic*), avaunt! (*expressing contempt or aversion*).
See also DISPLACEMENT, PROPULSION, PUNISHMENT.—*Antonyms.* See INSERTION, RECEPTION.

---

elaborate, *adj.* complicated, studied, finished, detailed, perfected. See CURIOSITY, PREPARATION.
elaborate, *v.* execute, perfect; refine, develop. See COMPLETION, IMPROVEMENT.
elapse, *v.* slip, pass, glide, expire, intervene. See LAPSE, PASSAGE.
elasmobranch, *n.* placoid, selachian: *zoöl.* See ANIMAL.

ELASTICITY.—I. *Nouns.* **elasticity,** springiness, spring, resilience *or* resiliency, buoyancy; extensibility, ductility, tensibility, tensility, tensibleness; rebound, recoil, reflex; flexibility, adaptability, responsiveness.
[*comparisons*] India rubber, caoutchouc, gum elastic; whalebone.
II. *Verbs.* **be elastic,** spring back, recoil, rebound.
III. *Adjectives.* **elastic,** springy, resilient, buoyant; extensible, tensile, tensible, ductile; flexible, adaptable, responsive.
See also ENERGY, RECOIL, STRENGTH.—*Antonyms.* See INELASTICITY.

---

elate, *v.* flush, excite, gladden, delight, elevate. See CHEERFULNESS, ELEVATION.
elate, *adj.* joyful, exultant, flushed. See BOASTING, CHEERFULNESS, HEIGHT.
elder, *adj.* older, senior. See AGE.
eldest, *adj.* oldest, first-born. See AGE.
elect, *v.* choose, decide, fix upon; call, ordain. See CHOICE, CHURCHDOM.
election, *n.* poll, selection, vote, balloting. See CHOICE.
elector, *n.* voter, constituent. See CHOICE.
electric, *adj.* thrilling, stimulating; voltaic, galvanic, magnetic. See FEELING, POWER.
electrify, *v.* stimulate, animate; magnetize, charge; stun, bewilder, startle. See EXCITEMENT, POWER, WONDER.

ELEGANCE.—I. *Nouns.* **elegance,** refinement, grace, beauty, polish, finish, distinction, clarity, purity, purism, discrimination, felicity, ease; gracefulness, daintiness, euphony; taste, good taste, restraint, propriety, correctness, courtliness; symmetry, proportion, balance, rhythm; well-rounded (*or* well-turned) periods, flowing periods, Atticism.
[*affected elegance*] euphuism, Gongorism, cultism, Marinism.
euphuist, Gongorist, cultist, Marinist.
purist, stylist, classicist, Atticist.

II. *Adjectives.* **elegant,** refined, æsthetic, tasteful, graceful, comely, shapely, trim, pleasing, luxurious, ornate; symmetrical, rhythmic *or* rhythmical, balanced, well-proportioned; polished, discriminative, restrained, correct, artistic, finished, classic *or* classical, Attic, Ciceronian, Chesterfieldian, chaste, pure; unaffected, natural, unconstrained; easy, fluent, smooth, mellifluous, euphonious.
felicitous, happy, neat, appropriate, well-expressed, well-chosen, inspired.
Antonyms. See INELEGANCE.

---

element, *n.* origin, principle; constituent, ingredient, part. See CAUSE, COMPONENT.
elementary, *adj.* introductory, simple, rudimentary. See SIMPLENESS.

ELEVATION.—I. *Nouns.* **elevation,** raising, lifting, erection, lift, upheaval, upthrow, upcast, upthrust (*esp. geol.*); sublimation, exaltation, aggrandizement, promotion, advancement, eminence, dignity; prominence, relief, height, altitude.
[*elevated place*] hill, height, eminence, mount, rising ground, mountain.
[*elevating devices*] lever, crowbar, crow, jimmy *or* jemmy (*the burglar's "persuader"*); pulley, crane, derrick, windlass, capstan, winch, tiller; pedal, crank, jack, jackscrew; dredge, dredger.
elevator, lift (*chiefly Brit.*), hoist, chute, dumb waiter, spout (*esp. in a pawnshop*) moving stairway, escalator.
II. *Verbs.* **elevate,** raise, heighten, lift, erect, set up, tilt up, rear, hoist, boost (*U. S. colloq.*), lever, pry, prize, heave, scend (*said of a ship: opposite of* pitch) uplift, upraise, uprear; buoy, mount.
take up, drag up, fish up; dredge.
[*to raise in rank or station*] **exalt,** dignify, ennoble, promote, advance, heighten, aggrandize, honor.
[*to raise intellectually or morally*] **uplift,** refine, sublimate, glorify, inspire, animate.
[*to raise the spirits of*] **elate,** exhilarate, gladden, flush, excite, cheer; intoxicate (*jocose use of* elevate).
III. *Adjectives.* **elevated,** raised, etc. (see *verbs*); high, eminent, lofty, stilted, grandiose; upturned, rampant.
See also HEIGHT, REPUTE.—*Antonyms.* See DEPRESSION.

---

elf, *n.* sprite, fairy, pixie, gnome, goblin. See MYTHICAL BEINGS.
elicit, *v.* cause, call forth, educe, evoke, extort. See EXTRACTION.
eligible, *adj.* suitable, fit, qualified, desirable. See EXPEDIENCE.
eliminate, *v.* drop, neglect, pass over, omit, ignore; remove, cast out, eradicate, expel, weed out; simplify, clarify, refine. See EXCLUSION, EXTRACTION, SIMPLENESS.
elimination, *n.* removal, sifting, exclusion. See SIMPLENESS.
ellipse, *n.* oval. See CIRCULARITY.
eloquence, *n.* fluency, volubility; oratory, rhetoric; power, command of words. See LOQUACITY, SPEECH, VIGOR.
eloquent, *adj.* oratorical, rhetorical, declamatory; lofty, forceful. See SPEECH, VIGOR.
elucidate, *v.* clear, explain, expound, illustrate. See INTERPRETATION.
elude, *v.* evade, baffle, dodge, avoid, foil. See ESCAPE.
elusive, *adj.* slippery, tricky; intangible, fugitive. See AVOIDANCE, TRANSIENCE.
emanate, *v.* issue, spring, arise, proceed. See EGRESS.
emancipate, *v.* free, release, deliver, manumit, enfranchise. See LIBERATION.
embankment, *n.* bank, wall, levee, dike, barrier, rampart. See DEFENSE.
embark, *v.* board, set sail, sail; engage in, begin. See DEPARTURE, UNDERTAKING.
embarrass, *v.* hamper, encumber, complicate, perplex. See DIFFICULTY.
embarrassing, *adj.* awkward, delicate, perplexing. See DIFFICULTY.
embellish, *v.* decorate, adorn, beautify, enrich. See ORNAMENT.

embezzle, *v.* steal, peculate, defalcate, take by fraud. See STEALING.
embitter, *v.* sour, make bitter; exasperate, anger, irritate. See AGGRAVATION, DETERIORATION, SOURNESS.
emblem, *n.* symbol, token, sign, mark, badge, device. See INDICATION.
embody, *v.* incorporate, join, unite, organize; comprise, include, contain; express, voice; incarnate, actualize. See COMBINATION, INCLUSION, MANIFESTATION, MATERIALITY.
embrace, *v.* adopt, take up; comprise, embody; hug, caress; encircle, surround; clasp, infold; contain, include. See CHOICE, COMPOSITION, ENDEARMENT, ENVIRONMENT, [1]FOLD, INCLUSION.
emerge, *v.* issue, appear, rise, come forth. See EGRESS.
emergency, *n.* crisis, necessity, exigency, pinch, extremity. See CIRCUMSTANCE.
emergent, *adj.* emerging, issuing, emanant; efflorescent. See EGRESS.
emigrant, *n.* migrant, colonist: *correlative of* immigrant. See EGRESS.
emigration, *n.* migration, departure: *correlative of* immigration. See EGRESS.
eminence, *n.* distinction, importance; elevation, altitude. See GREATNESS REPUTE; HEIGHT.
eminent, *adj.* illustrious, distinguished, celebrated, noted. See GREATNESS, REPUTE.
eminently, *adv.* preëminently, supremely, notably, surpassingly. See GREATNESS, SUPERIORITY.
emit, *v.* send forth, outpour, discharge, issue. See EJECTION.
emotion, *n.* sensation, impression, sentiment, passion, sensibility. See FEELING.
emphasize, *v.* stress, accentuate; underline, mark. See AFFIRMATION, IMPORTANCE.
emphatic, *adj.* positive, decided, absolute; impressive, significant. See AFFIRMATION, IMPORTANCE.
employ, *v.* engage, hire; apply, devote, occupy, utilize. See BORROWING, USE.
employee, *n.* employé, helper, assistant, clerk. See SERVANT.
employer, *n.* proprietor, manager, director, boss. See MASTER.
employment, *n.* occupation, pursuit, work. See BUSINESS, SITUATION.
empower, *v.* commission, authorize; invest, enable, endow. See PERMISSION, POWER.
emptiness, *n.* void, vacuum, hollowness, vacuity, vacancy. See ABSENCE.
empty, *adj.* vacant, untenanted; unreal, inane, void, hollow; verbose, prolix, long-winded, garrulous. See ABSENCE, UNSUBSTANTIALITY, WIND (*wordy*).
empty, *v.* exhaust, deflate, drain, discharge, evacuate, unload. See CONTRACTION, EJECTION.
empty talk, babble, twaddle, fustian. See WIND.
empyrean, *adj.* empyreal, celestial, heavenly. See WORLD.
emulate, *v.* compete with, contend with, vie with, rival. See OPPOSITION, REPUTE.
enable, *v.* empower, authorize. See POWER.
enact, *v.* execute, perform, do; decree, order, ordain, pass. See ACTION, COMMAND, PASSAGE.
enchant, *v.* fascinate, captivate, delight; bewitch, charm, conjure. See PLEASURABLENESS, SORCERY.
encircle, *v.* ring, loop, girdle, circle, surround, compass, inclose. See ENVIRONMENT.
encounter, *v.* meet, come across; undergo, endure; contend, struggle. See ARRIVAL, EVENT, OPPOSITION.
encounter, *n.* skirmish, combat; collision, meeting. See CONTENTION, IMPULSE.
encourage, *v.* cheer, rally, hearten, reassure; advocate, promote. See HOPE, MOTIVE.

encroach, *v.* overstep, intrude, trespass; infringe, violate. See OVERRUNNING, RIGHTLESSNESS.

encumber, *v.* handicap, hamper, burden, obstruct, load down. See HINDRANCE.

END.—I. *Nouns.* **end,** limit, boundary (*as, the* ends *of the earth*).
[*final result*] **consequence,** result, issue, upshot; determination, decision; settlement, arrangement.
[*extreme part of anything*] **extremity,** tip, point, nib; tail, stub, tag; fag-end, remnant, fragment, foot, heel; head, top, horn; terminus, terminal, limit, goal, destination.
[*end of any event, series, state, or condition*] **close,** conclusion, termination, completion, finish, finis (*as of a book*), finale (*used esp. in music*), stoppage; expiration, expiry; period, term, last, extreme, *dénouement* (*F.*), wind-up (*colloq.*), consummation, final event, catastrophe (*as in a drama*), epilogue (*as in a play or discourse*), peroration; appendix (*pl.* appendixes *or* appendices), adjunct, supplement, addendum (*pl.* addenda); ending, last stage, fall of the curtain; knockout, K. O., sleep punch (*prize-ring slang*); deathblow, *coup de grâce* (*F.*), death, dissolution, destruction, doomsday.
[*decline of life*] close, closing period, declining period, evening, eventide (*poetic*), sunset.
object, purpose, aim, mark, intention, motive, final cause; goal, objective, butt; design.
II. *Verbs.* **end,** close, finish, terminate, conclude, cease, stop, drop, discontinue, come to a close, perorate, wind up (*colloq.*), put an end to, make an end of, abolish, destroy, bring to an end; achieve, accomplish, consummate; run out, pass away, expire, die.
III. *Adjectives.* **final,** terminal, conclusive, concluding, terminating, ending, finishing, crowning, last, farthest, extreme, ultimate; hindermost, rear.
ended, settled, decided, over.
IV. *Adverbs.* **finally,** conclusively, decisively, in fine; at the last; once for all.
over, at an end, by past, settled, done with.
See also CESSATION, COMPLETION, DEATH, EFFECT, INTENTION, REAR.—*Antonyms.* See BEGINNING.

---

endanger, *v.* jeopardize, expose, imperil. See COMPROMISE, DANGER.

ENDEARMENT.—I. *Nouns.* **endearment,** caress, blandishment, fondling, billing and cooing, dalliance, caressing, embrace; salute, kiss, smack, buss (*archaic*), osculation.
courtship, wooing, suit, court, attention, addresses, love-making, serenading; calf love (*colloq.*), amorous glances, ogle, side-glance, sheep's eyes, goo-goo eyes (*slang*).
flirting, flirtation, coquetry, gallantry, spooning (*slang*), petting (*colloq.*), necking (*slang*); love affair; amour, intrigue.
engagement, betrothal, affiance, handfast (*hist.*); marriage, honeymoon; love letter, *billet-doux* (*F.*); valentine.
flirt, coquette, gold digger (*slang*), vampire (*colloq.*), vamp (*slang*), Sheba (*slang: correlative of "sheik"*); male flirt, philanderer, cake eater (*slang*), tea hound (*slang*), sheik (*slang*), lounge lizard (*slang*); petter (*colloq.*), necker (*slang*), spoon (*slang*).
II. *Verbs.* **endear,** hold dear, prize, treasure, esteem, lose one's heart to, be enamored of, idolize.
caress, fondle, pet, smile upon, coax, wheedle, coddle, pamper, make much of, cherish, foster; clasp, hug, cuddle, fold to the heart, press to the bosom, fold in one's arms; snuggle, nestle, nuzzle; embrace, kiss, buss (*archaic*), salute.
court, make love, bill and coo, spoon (*slang*), toy, trifle, dally, flirt, pet, neck (*slang*), spark (*colloq.*), coquet, philander, pay one's court (*or* addresses) to; serenade, address, woo, set one's cap at (*colloq.*), sue.
propose, make (*or* have) an offer, pop the question (*colloq.*); become engaged, become betrothed; plight one's troth (*or* faith).
render dear, charm, attract; captivate, bewitch, enamor (*used chiefly in p. p.*) enrapture, win the affections of, take the fancy of.

III. *Adjectives.* **endearing,** winsome, attractive, charming, pleasing, enchanting, winning, sweet, delightful, irresistible, lovable; caressing, affectionate.
lovesick, lovelorn, languishing, pining; "sighing like furnace" (*As You Like It*); spoony (*slang*).
IV. *Adverbs.* **endearingly,** winsomely, etc. (see *adjectives*); in an endearing manner.
See also LOVE.—*Antonyms.* See HATE, REJECTION.

---

endeavor, *v.* attempt, try, strive, aim. See ESSAY, OFFER.
endeavor, *n.* attempt, trial, effort, striving. See OFFER.
endless, *adj.* continuous, unbroken; unlimited, interminable; boundless; eternal, never-ending, incessant, imperishable, undying. See CONTINUITY, INFINITY, PERPETUITY.
endow, *v.* settle upon, bestow, enrich; bequeath, dower. See GIVING.
endowment, *n.* bestowal, gift; faculty, power, capacity, aptitude, talent, bent. See GIVING, SKILL.
endue, *v.* invest, clothe, furnish. See POWER.
endure, *v.* encounter, experience; bear, suffer; last, stand, remain; permit, tolerate. See EVENT, FEELING, PERMANENCE, SUPPORT.

ENEMY.—*Nouns.* **enemy,** adversary, foe, foeman (*archaic or poetic*), antagonist, opponent, open (*or* bitter) enemy; snake in the grass; mortal aversion (*or* antipathy).
public enemy, enemy to society; anarchist, Red *or* red, terrorist, revolutionary revolutionist; seditionist, traitor, traitress (*fem.*).
See also OPPONENT.—*Antonyms.* See FRIEND.

ENERGY.—I. *Nouns.* **energy,** force, power, potency, efficacy, strength, puissance, might, vigor, intensity, life, fervor, spirit, verve, dash, animation, go (*colloq.*), pep (*slang*), fire, punch (*slang*), backbone (*colloq.*), vim (*colloq.*), mettle; high pressure.
kinetic energy, living force, *vis viva* (*L.*); potential energy, ergal (*physics*); dynamic force, motive power, driving force (*or* power); human dynamo.
[*unit of energy*] erg, dinamode.
activity, briskness, hustle (*colloq.*), alacrity, alertness, quickness; agitation, effervescence, ferment, fermentation, ebullition, perturbation, exertion, excitation, stir, bustle; voluntary energy, mental energy, resolution, stimulation.
II. *Verbs.* **energize,** stimulate, strengthen, invigorate, activate (*rare*), potentialize, kindle, excite, inflame, exert; sharpen, intensify, animate, enliven, pep up (*slang*), magnetize, electrify.
III. *Adjectives.* **energetic,** strong, forcible, active, strenuous, brisk, mettlesome, enterprising, go-ahead (*colloq.*), potent, powerful, forcible, forceful, emphatic; intense, keen, sharp, acute, incisive, trenchant.
poignant, virulent, caustic, escharotic (*med.*), corrosive, mordant; harsh, stringent, drastic.
See also ACTIVITY, EXCITEMENT, EXERTION, HARDNESS, POWER, STRENGTH, UNDERTAKING.—*Antonyms.* See INERTNESS, WEAKNESS.

---

enervate, *v.* unman, unnerve, devitalize; enfeeble, weaken, effeminate. See IMPOTENCE, SOFTNESS.
enforce, *v.* compel, oblige, force; urge, lash, goad. See COMPULSION, MOTIVE.
enfranchise, *v.* free, release; empower, license, qualify. See LIBERATION, PERMISSION.
engage, *v.* hire, employ; reserve, secure; bind, pledge; set about, take up; occupy, engross; fight, contend. See COMMISSION, EARLINESS, PROMISE, UNDERTAKING, USE, WARFARE.
engagement, *n.* occupation, employment; battle, encounter; betrothal; appointment, interview; agreement, pledge. See BUSINESS, CONTENTION, PROMISE, SOCIALITY, WORD.

ENGRAVING.—I. *Nouns.* **engraving,** chiseling, chalcography; line (mezzotint, *or* stipple) engraving; wood engraving, xylography; etching, aquatint *or* aquatinta; dry point, cerography, anaglyptography, anastatic process, glyptography (*gem engraving*); plate (copperplate, steel, process, *or* half-tone) engraving; zincography, gypsography, glyphography; chalk engraving, graphotype; photo-engraving, heliotypography, heliotypy, heliogravure, photogravure, rotogravure, lithography, photolithography, chromolithography.
printing; color printing, lithographic printing; type printing, three-color process.
impression, print, pull, proof, reprint, engraving, plate; steel-plate, copperplate; etching; aquatint, mezzotint; cut, woodcut; xylograph; anaglyptograph, cerograph, intaglio, glyphograph, photogravure, rotogravure, rotograph, photogravure, photo-engraving, half tone, heliotype, heliograph; lithograph, photolithograph, chromolithograph; illustration, picture, illumination; positive, negative, vignette, initial letter, tailpiece, *cul-de-lampe* (*F.*).
II. *Verbs.* **engrave,** grave, stipple, etch; bite, bite in; lithograph; print, imprint; prove, pull.
III. *Adjectives.* **engraved,** graven, cut, incised, sculptured, insculptured (*rare*), chalcographic.
See also PRINTING.

---

engross, *v.* occupy, engage, fill, absorb, control, monopolize; copy, write, transcribe. See TAKING, WRITING.
engrossed, *adj.* absorbed, intent, engaged, interested. See DEPTH, INATTENTION.
enhance, *v.* heighten, intensify, augment. See INCREASE.
enigma, *n.* riddle, question, puzzle, problem, conundrum. See SECRET.
enigmatical, *adj.* obscure, abstruse, incomprehensible, occult, secret, hidden; puzzling, intricate. See DARKNESS, UNINTELLIGIBILITY.
enjoin, *v.* counsel, admonish; charge, direct, order; exact, require; prohibit, restrain. See ADVICE, COMMAND, DUTY, PROHIBITION.
enjoy, *v.* like, relish, delight in, love, gloat over; hold, possess. See PLEASURE, POSSESSION.
enlarge, *v.* expand, extend, augment, broaden, magnify, swell, increase. See EXPANSION, GREATNESS.
enlighten, *v.* instruct, teach, illuminate, edify. See INFORMATION.
enlightenment, *n.* insight, understanding, elucidation. See LIGHT.
enliven, *v.* encourage, animate, inspire, exhilarate, rouse. See CHEERFULNESS.

ENMITY.—I. *Nouns.* **enmity,** hostility, antagonism, unfriendliness, animosity, hatred, hate, dislike, malevolence, ill will, malice, spite, malignity, repugnance, aversion, antipathy; heartburning, bitterness, rancor, venom, grudge; discord, alienation, estrangement.
II. *Verbs.* **be unfriendly,** keep (*or* hold) at arm's length; bear malice, fall out; take umbrage; alienate, estrange.
III. *Adjectives.* **unfriendly,** inimical, hostile, unfavorable, adverse, antagonistic, incompatible, indisposed; at enmity, at variance, at loggerheads, at daggers drawn, up in arms against.
on bad terms, not on speaking terms; cool, cold, estranged, alienated, disaffected, irreconcilable.
See also DISCORD, DISLIKE, HATE, MALEVOLENCE.—*Antonyms.* See FRIENDSHIP.

---

ennoble, *v.* exalt, dignify, glorify, elevate. See ELEVATION, REPUTE.
enormity, *n,* immensity, enormousness; atrocity, outrage. See GREATNESS, GUILT.
enormous, *adj.* huge, vast, immense, colossal, gigantic, prodigious, monstrous. See SIZE.
enough, *adj.* adequate, ample, abundant, plenteous, equal. See SUFFICIENCY.
enrage, *v.* anger, infuriate, incense, irritate. See RESENTMENT.
enrapture, *v.* delight, enchant, transport, charm, bewitch, entrance. See PLEASURABLENESS.

enrich, *v.* cultivate, develop; adorn, beautify; make wealthy, aggrandize. See IMPROVEMENT, ORNAMENT, WEALTH.
enroll, *v.* enter, register; enlist, serve. See LIST, WARFARE.
ensue, *v.* follow, happen, result, succeed. See EVENT, SUCCESS.
entangle, *v.* insnare, inveigle; embroil, perplex, embarrass; twist, snarl. See DECEPTION, DIFFICULTY, DISORDER.
enter, *v.* interpenetrate, share; go in, invade, penetrate; register, insert, file, record. See COMPONENT, INGRESS, LIST.
enterprise, *v.* energy, go (*colloq.*), venture, business, project. See ACTIVITY, UNDERTAKING.
enterprising, *adj.* eager, energetic, ambitious; venturesome, adventurous. See ACTIVITY, COURAGE.
entertain, *v.* divert, amuse, regale; heed, consider; welcome, receive; harbor, cherish. See AMUSEMENT, ATTENTION, SOCIALITY, THOUGHT.
enthrall, *v.* fascinate, charm; enslave, subjugate. See PLEASURABLENESS, SUBJECTION.
enthusiasm, *n.* ardor, fervor, vehemence, eagerness; optimism, assurance; fire, spirit, force. See ACTIVITY, FEELING, HOPE, VIGOR.
enthusiast, *n.* zealot, fanatic, devotee; live wire (*colloq.*). See ACTIVITY.
entire, *adj.* undivided, unbroken, perfect; total, gross, all. See COMPLETENESS, WHOLE.
entitle, *v.* designate, call, name; qualify, authorize. See NOMENCLATURE, RIGHTFULNESS.
entrails, *n. pl.* bowels, intestines. See INTERIORITY.
entrance, *n.* start, commencement, introduction; invasion, penetration, admittance, access, approach; door, gate, portal, entryway. See BEGINNING, INGRESS, RECEPTION, WAY.
entreat, *v.* beg, beseech, plead, implore, supplicate. See PLEA, REQUEST.
entreaty, *n.* petition, supplication, appeal, solicitation. See CRY, PLEA.
entwine, *v.* twist, twine, wreathe, weave, interlace. See CROSSING.
enumerate, *v.* count, number, reckon; recount, rehearse. See NUMERATION.
enunciate, *v.* declare, state, announce; articulate, pronounce. See AFFIRMATION, VOICE.
envelop, *v.* surround, wrap, inclose, infold, hide. See COVERING.
envelope, *n.* wrapping, cover, case, sheath; receptacle. See COVERING, INCLOSURE.
envious, *adj.* covetous, jealous, judging. See ENVY.

ENVIRONMENT.—I. *Nouns.* **environment, surroundings,** *milieu* (*F.*), external conditions (*in this sense,* environment *is biol.*), *entourage* (*F.*), encompassment; circumjacencies, outskirts, suburbs, purlieus, precincts, environs, neighborhood, vicinage, vicinity; background, setting, scene (*as, change of* scene).
II. *Verbs.* **environ, surround,** compass, encompass, inclose *or* enclose, encircle, loop, ensphere, circle, girdle, hedge, pen, confine, embrace, gird, belt, engird; skirt, hem in; circumscribe, beleaguer, besiege, invest, beset, blockade.
III. *Adjectives.* **surrounding,** encompassing, inclosing, circumjacent, circumambient, begirt; suburban, neighboring.
IV. *Adverbs.* **around, about,** nigh, near (*in this sense,* around *is colloq.*), without; on every side, on all sides.
See also CIRCUMSCRIPTION, NEARNESS.—*Antonyms.* See INTERJACENCE.

ENVY.—I. *Nouns.* **envy,** enviousness; emulation, rivalry, malice, ill will, spite, malignity, cupidity, covetousness, jealousy, grudgingness, mortification.
II. *Verbs.* **envy,** covet, grudge, begrudge; hanker after, long for, desire, crave.
III. *Adjectives* **envious,** invidious, covetous, desirous, jealous, suspicious, grudging, begrudged.
See also JEALOUSY.—*Antonyms.* See BENEVOLENCE, [2]CONTENT.

ephemeral, *adj.* transient, transitory, evanescent, short-lived, fleeting, diurnal. See TRANSIENCE.
epicure, *n.* *gourmet* (*F.*), epicurean. See FASTIDIOUSNESS.
episode, *n.* incident, occurrence, happening, action. See EVENT.
epistle, *n.* note, missive, communication. See LETTER.
epitome, *n.* brief, abstract, synopsis, abridgment, summary. See COMPENDIUM.
epoch, *n.* era, age, period, date. See TIME.

EQUALITY.—I. *Nouns.* **equality,** parity, equalization, symmetry, balance, poise; evenness, monotony, level; equivalence, equipollence *or* equipollency, equipoise, equilibrium; par, quits; distinction without a difference, identity, similarity; equal division, two-way split (*colloq.*), fifty-fifty (*colloq.*).
impartiality, fairness, justice, justness, equity, fair play; dispassionateness, disinterestedness, neutrality.
tie, dead heat; drawn game, drawn battle; neck-and-neck race.
match, peer, compeer, equal, mate, fellow, brother; equivalent, counterpart.
II. *Verbs.* **equal,** match, keep pace with, run abreast; come up to; balance, tie, parallel.
equalize, make equal, equate, level, dress (*mil.*), balance, handicap, trim, adjust, coördinate, poise; strike a balance; restore equilibrium, readjust.
III. *Adjectives.* **equal,** alike, like, identical; equable, uniform, even, level, monotonous; symmetrical, proportional, proportionate, commensurate, coördinate; on a par with, on a level with, up to the mark; just, equitable, impartial, fair.
equivalent, tantamount, comparable with; quits; synonymous, analogous, similar, correspondent, correlative, cognate; convertible; all one, all the same; drawn (*as a game*).
IV. *Adverbs.* **equally,** alike, evenly, without difference, justly; *pari passu* (*L.*), *ceteris paribus* (*L.*); to all intents and purposes.

See also COMPENSATION, IDENTITY, RIGHT, SIMILARITY, SUBSTITUTION.—*Antonyms.* See INEQUALITY.

---

equanimity, *n.* poise, self-control, calmness, composure, serenity, tranquillity. See INEXCITABILITY.
equidistance, *n.* equal distance; bisection. See MIDDLE.
equip, *v.* attire, dress, array; provide, furnish, fit out. See CLOTHING, PREPARATION.
equipment, *n.* outfit, apparel, accouterments; apparatus, gear, supplies. See CLOTHING, INSTRUMENT.
equivalent, *adj.* correspondent, interchangeable; tantamount, equal, convertible, identical, synonymous. See CORRELATION, EQUALITY, INTERPRETATION.
equivalent, *n.* *quid pro quo* (*L.*), equal; price, worth. See COMPENSATION, SUBSTITUTION.

EQUIVOCALNESS.—I. *Nouns.* **equivocalness,** equivocation, prevarication, quibbling, shuffling, evasion, equivoque *or* equivoke, double meaning; ambiguity, amphibology, amphiboly; sophistry, casuistry, duplicity, mental reservation, white lie, quibble, subterfuge.
conundrum, riddle, enigma, problem, puzzle; pun, word play; Sphinx, Delphic oracle.
II. *Verbs.* **equivocate,** shuffle, dodge, shift, quibble, palter, trifle, evade, tergiversate; prevaricate; have a double meaning.
III. *Adjectives.* **equivocal,** ambiguous, dubious, doubtful, uncertain, undetermined, perplexing, indeterminate, enigmatical, puzzling, mysterious, obscure, questionable, unintelligible, misleading, sophistical, casuistic *or* casuistical, amphibolous (*logic*), amphibolic, double-tongued.

See also CONCEALMENT, FALSEHOOD, SECRET, SHADE (*shady*).—*Antonyms.* See CERTAINTY, INTELLIGIBILITY, TRUTH.

era, *n.* epoch, period, age, cycle, eon or æon, kalpa (*Hindu*). See TIME.
eradicate, *v.* blot out, erase, exterminate; weed out, eliminate, uproot. See DESTRUCTION, EJECTION.
erase, *v.* efface, rub out, cancel, obliterate, expunge. See DESTRUCTION.
eraser, *n.* rubber, eradicator. See FRICTION.
erect, *adj.* vertical, perpendicular, upright. See RIGHT, STRAIGHTNESS.
erect, *v.* raise, rear, set up; build, construct, create, institute. See ELEVATION, PRODUCTION.
erosion, *n.* eating away, wearing away, disintegration. See DETERIORATION.
err, *v.* blunder, be mistaken, misjudge; transgress, sin. See ERROR, VICE.
errand, *n.* mission, business, charge, task. See COMMISSION.
erratic, *n.* eccentric, odd, peculiar, queer; changeable, uncertain, wandering. See CAPRICE, IRREGULARITY.

ERROR.—I. *Nouns.* **error,** fallacy, misconception, misapprehension, misunderstanding; aberration, obliquity, erroneousness, inexactness, fallaciousness, *non sequitur* (*L.*), *fallacia consequentis* (*L.: logic*), deception; iniquity, fault, transgression; laxity, misconstruction, misinterpretation; misjudgment, miscalculation, misstatement; fable.
[*chronological error*] **anachronism,** metachronism, parachronism, parepochism (*rare*).
mistake, fault, blunder, oversight, misprint, erratum (*pl.* errata), corrigendum (*pl.* corrigenda), slip, blot, flaw, trip, stumble, break (*colloq.*), bungle; slip of the tongue, *lapsus linguæ* (*L.*); slip of the pen, *lapsus calami* (*L.*), clerical error; bull, solecism, Malapropism, Spoonerism (*accidental transposition made famous by the Rev. W. A. Spooner of Oxford: "I am sorry to learn that you have been tasting your worms of late," said he to an undergraduate; "we all have a half-warmed fish in our bosoms"; "I have just received a blushing crow"; "for real enjoyment give me a well-boiled icycle." Asked if he sang, Mr. Spooner said: "I know only two tunes—'God Save the Weasel' and 'Pop Goes the Queen'." Spooner certainly added to the joy of nations.*)
delusion, false impression, illusion; self-deceit, self-deception; hallucination, mirage, dream, bubble, fancy; misconception, misbelief, heresy, false belief.
II. *Verbs.* **err,** be in error, be mistaken, be deceived; mistake, deceive oneself, blunder, nod, slip, slip up, stray, wander; misapprehend, misconceive, misunderstand, misreckon, miscount, miscalculate, misjudge; misbelieve, sin.
trip, stumble, lose oneself, go astray, fail, take the shadow for the substance.
mislead, misguide, lead astray, pervert, beguile, misinform, delude; falsify, misstate; deceive, lie,
III. *Adjectives.* **erroneous,** untrue, false, faulty, erring, fallacious, illogical, unreal, unfounded, ungrounded, groundless, unsubstantial, unsound, inexact, inaccurate, incorrect, mistaken; in error, deceived, out in one's reckoning; wide of the mark, at fault, at cross-purposes, at sea, bewildered.
illusive, illusory, delusive; unreal, deceptive, mock, imaginary, spurious, deceitful, untrustworthy.
exploded, refuted, discarded, rejected, discredited, obsolete, outworn, *passé* (*F.*).
See also DECEPTION, FALSEHOOD, IMAGINATION, MISINTERPRETATION, MISJUDGMENT, OBLIQUITY, SOPHISTRY, UNCERTAINTY, UNTRUTH, WRONG.—*Antonyms.* See TRUTH.

---

eruption, *n.* rash, breaking out; expulsion, discharge, outpour; outburst, outbreak, upheaval. See DISEASE, EJECTION, VIOLENCE.

ESCAPE.—I. *Nouns.* **escape,** flight, fleeing, hegira, evasion, retreat, withdrawal, departure, French leave.
[*means of escape*] fire escape, ladder, rope ladder, hook and ladder, fire net, life net; lifeboat, life raft, life buoy, life belt, cork jacket, life preserver, breeches buoy, life-saving gun (*or* mortar), life car, life line; parachute; secret passage, tunnel; secret chamber.

deliverance, release, liberation, emancipation, **freedom**, rescue, ransom; narrow escape, hairbreadth escape, close call (*colloq.*), near (*or* close) shave (*slang*), near squeak (*slang*); impunity, exemption, immunity.
outlet, egress, loophole, port, porthole; sluice, sluice gate, floodgate, hatch; escape pipe, waste pipe, waste weir; outflow, efflux, effluence, outpour, outgush, outburst, outrush; drain, culvert, sewer, cesspool; leak, leakage, seepage.
II. *Verbs.* **escape,** scape (*archaic*), fly, flee, run, run away; evade, avoid, elude, shun, wriggle out of; make one's escape, get off, get clear off, make off, give one the slip; skedaddle (*colloq.*), break loose, break away, make a get-away (*slang*), flee (*or* fly) the coop (*slang*), decamp, break jail.
issue, flow, flow out, emanate, stream, gush, spurt, debouch, exit; sally, sally forth, sortie, emerge.
III. *Adjectives.* **escaped,** fled, decamped, stolen away, scot-free, at large.

See also AVOIDANCE, DELIVERANCE, DERELICTION, LIBERATION.—*Antonyms.* See RETENTION.

---

escort, *n.* bodyguard, attendant, conductor, convoy. See KEEPER.
escort, *v.* attend, accompany, convoy, guard, usher, conduct. See SAFETY.
especial, *adj.* particular, special, exceptional. See SPECIALTY.

ESSAY.—I. *Nouns.* **essay,** trial, endeavor, attempt, try (*colloq.*), crack (*slang*), whack (*slang*), slap (*slang*), shy (*slang*), go (*colloq.*); aim, effort, struggle, venture, adventure, speculation, probation, experiment, undertaking.
[*literary composition*] tract, treatise, thesis, dissertation, disquisition.
II. *Verbs.* **essay,** try, aim, endeavor, attempt, undertake, strive; **venture,** adventure, speculate, tempt fortune; test, tempt (*archaic*), experiment.
III. *Adjectives.* **tentative,** experimental, empirical; problematic, **probationary;** makeshift, temporary.
IV. *Adverbs.* **tentatively,** experimentally, etc. (see *adjectives*); on examination, on trial, at a venture; by rule of thumb.

See also DISSERTATION, EXPERIMENT.—*Antonyms.* See INERTNESS, RESIGNATION.

---

essence, *n.* being, reality, quintessence, nature, life; purport, sense, pith. See EXISTENCE, MEANING, SUBJECTIVENESS.
essential, *adj.* constitutional, vital; indispensable, requisite, needful, necessary; inherent, basic, intrinsic; substantial, material. See FORM, REQUIREMENT, SUBJECTIVE, SUBSTANTIALITY.
essential, *n.* quality, attribute, characteristic; requisite. See PROPERTY, SECRET.
establish, *v.* verify, substantiate, prove; found, organize, institute; decide, determine; settle, stabilize, make firm, fix. See EVIDENCE, PRODUCTION, RULE, STABILITY.
established, *adj.* permanent, fixed, stable, settled, lasting. See PERMANENCE, REGULARITY.
estate, *n.* condition, station, rank; possessions, effects, interest, holdings, land. See DEGREE, PROPERTY.
esteem, *n.* estimation, admiration, regard, honor. See APPROBATION, RESPECT.
estimate, *v.* appraise, measure, consider, value; reckon, compute, calculate. See JUDGE, NUMERATION.
estimate, *n.* appraisal, estimation; criticism, report. See JUDGMENT.
estimation, *n.* valuation, calculation, appraisal; honor, esteem, regard. See JUDGMENT, RESPECT.
estrange, *v.* separate, withdraw, withhold; be unfriendly, fall out, alienate. See DISJUNCTION, ENMITY.
eternal, *adj.* endless, infinite, timeless, everlasting, deathless, immortal. See PERPETUITY, TIMELESSNESS.
eternalize, *v.* immortalize, perpetuate, preserve. See PERPETUITY.
ethereal, *adj.* heavenly, celestial; light, airy, gaseous. See HEAVEN, UNSUBSTANTIALITY.

ethics, *n.* science of morals, moral philosophy, moral principles, rules of conduct. See DUTY.
etiquette, *n.* manners, custom, decorum, good form, formality. See FASHION.
Eucharist, *n.* Communion, Lord's Supper, Sacrament. See RITE.
eulogize, *v.* extol, praise, laud. See OVERESTIMATION.
euphuism, *n.* cultism, Gongorism, affectation, mannerism. See ELEGANCE.
evacuate, *v.* vacate, quit, abandon; emit, discharge, empty. See DEPARTURE, EJECTION.
evade, *v.* shun, escape, parry, elude, baffle, foil; neglect, ignore, violate; quibble, equivocate, prevaricate. See AVOIDANCE, NONOBSERVANCE, SOPHISTRY.
evaporate, *v.* dehydrate, desiccate; vanish, disappear; gasify, vaporize. See DRYNESS, UNSUBSTANTIALLY, VAPORIZATION.
evasion, *n.* escape, elusion; subterfuge, excuse, shift, quibble, equivocation. See AVOIDANCE, SOPHISTRY.
even, *adj.* equal, like, equitable, impartial, just, fair; level, flat, smooth; abreast, alongside; true, straight, plumb; regular, unvaried, equable, unruffled, placid. See EQUALITY, HORIZONTALITY, PARALLELISM, STRAIGHTNESS, UNIFORMITY.

EVENING.—I. *Nouns.* **evening,** eve (*poetic*), even (*poetic*), decline of day, close of day, eventide, vespers (*eccl.*), evensong (*eccl.*), nightfall, curfew, dusk, candlelight, gloaming, twilight, cockshut (*dial.*), sunset, sundown, bedtime.
afternoon, *post meridiem* (*L.*), *p.m.;* middle age, decline of life, closing period.
[*close of the year*] **autumn,** fall, fall of the leaf, harvest time; autumnal equinox; Indian summer, St. Luke's summer (*so called in England when Indian summer occurs in October*), St. Martin's summer (*so called when occurring in November*).
winter, *hiems* (*L.*), cold season (*as in India*); old age, "sear and yellow leaf" (*Macbeth*), vale of years, decay, decrepitude, adversity; years (*as, a man of sixty* winters).
II. *Adjectives.* **vesper,** vespertine (*chiefly tech.*), nightly, nocturnal; autumnal.
wintry, winterly, hiemal, winterlike, brumal.
Antonyms. See MORNING.

EVENT.—I. *Nouns.* **event,** happening, occurrence, scene, incident, affair, transaction, proceeding, fact, circumstance, phenomenon, episode, particular, adventure, experience; crisis, pass, emergency, contingency, eventuality; hap (*archaic*), fortuity, lot; concern, business.
consequence, issue, result, termination, conclusion, sequel, end, outcome.
affairs, matters, things, doings; the world, life, the times; memorabilia (*pl.*).
II. *Verbs.* **happen,** occur, take place, transpire (*erroneous in this sense*), eventuate, chance, come, come to pass, take effect; present itself, fall out, turn out, befall, betide (*used only in 3d person; as, whate'er* betide; *woe* betide *him*); intervene, supervene, turn up, crop up, arrive; ensue, result; arise, start; take its course; pass off.
experience, encounter, undergo, bear, endure, go through; pass through, suffer, find, meet, taste, receive, have, meet with, fall to the lot of, be one's lot.
III. *Adjectives.* **eventful,** stirring, full of incident, memorable, momentous, weighty, consequential, important, striking, salient, signal.
happening, occurring, etc. (see *verbs*); current, doing, on foot, prevalent, prevailing, continuous; in question, at issue; incidental.
Antonyms. See DESTINY.

---

eventual, *adj.* coming, final, ultimate. See FUTURE.
ever, *adv.* perpetually, incessantly, always, constantly, continually, forever See PERPETUITY.
every, *adj.* each, all. See GENERALITY.
everyday, *adj.* customary, usual, habitual, conventional. See HABIT.
everyone, *n.* everybody, *tout le monde* (*F.*). See GENERALITY.
evict, *v.* oust, expel, remove, dispossess, put out. See EJECTION.

EVIDENCE.—I. *Nouns.* **evidence,** proof, exemplification, demonstration, illustration, indication, certainty; facts, premises, data, grounds; confirmation, corroboration, ratification, authentication.
testimony, testification, attestation, affirmation, admission, averment, declaration, deposition.
authority, warrant, credential, diploma, testamur (*Eng. universities*), voucher, certificate, muniments, document, deed, warranty; autograph, handwriting, signature, moniker (*slang*), seal, countersign; exhibit; citation, reference, quotation.
witness, eyewitness, observer, bystander, earwitness; testifier, deponent (*law*); conjuror, compurgator; sponsor.
II. *Verbs.* **evidence,** prove, document, make evident, evince, show, manifest, display, betoken, indicate, denote, imply, involve, argue, bespeak, tell, speak volumes, speak for itself, have weight, carry weight.
testify, bear witness, give evidence, depose, witness, swear, avouch, vouch for; certify, attest, acknowledge.
confirm, ratify, corroborate, indorse, support, bear out, vindicate, validate, establish, sustain, fortify, uphold, warrant, authenticate, substantiate, verify, prove, make good, make out a case, circumstantiate.
adduce, evidence, cite, quote, instance; refer to, call, call to witness, bring forward, bring into court; allege, plead.
III. *Adjectives.* **evidential,** evidentiary, documentary, corroborative, confirmatory, ratificatory, supportive, first-hand, cumulative, conclusive, final, decisive, determinative, indicative, deducible, inferential; significant, weighty, overwhelming, veracious, veridical.
oral, nuncupative (*said esp. of wills*), unwritten, verbal, hearsay, circumstantial, presumptive.
See also ASSENT, DEMONSTRATION, INDICATION, MANIFESTATION.—*Antonyms.* See COUNTEREVIDENCE.

---

evident, *adj.* clear, obvious, manifest, apparent, indubitable; visible, distinct. See CERTAINTY, MANIFESTATION, VISIBILITY.

EVIL.—I. *Nouns.* evil, ill, harm, hurt, injury, mischief, nuisance, drawback, disadvantage; "shocks that flesh is heir to" (*Hamlet*), adversity, misfortune, calamity, woe, bale (*chiefly poetic*), bane, disease, mental suffering, pain; disaster, accident, casualty, mishap, fatal mischief, catastrophe, tragedy, ruin.
blow, buffet, stroke, swipe (*colloq.*), *coup* (*F.*), scratch, bruise, wound, gash, stab, laceration, mutilation; mortal blow (*or* wound); damage, loss.
outrage, wrong, injury, damage, enormity, atrocity, foul play, bad turn, disservice.
[*moral badness*] **wickedness,** depravity, sin, iniquity, unrighteousness, turpitude, perverseness, perversity, obduracy, corruption, immorality, impiety, unregeneracy, villainy.
II. *Verbs.* **harm,** injure, hurt, damage, wrong, dishonor, outrage, disserve, impair.
III. *Adjectives.* **evil,** wicked, sinful, wrong, corrupt, vicious, depraved, bad, iniquitous, nefarious, unregenerate, unprincipled, villainous.
injurious, harmful, detrimental, deleterious, pernicious, damaging, disadvantageous, hurtful, prejudicial, mischievous, baleful, malefic, dire, fell, maleficent; unpropitious, calamitous, perverse, disastrous, destructive.
IV. *Adverbs.* **amiss,** wrongly, ill, improperly, faultily, astray; to one's cost.
See also ADVERSITY, BADNESS, BLACKNESS, DARKNESS, PAIN, PAINFULNESS, VICE. —*Antonyms.* See GOOD, GOODNESS.

EVILDOER.—I. *Nouns.* **evildoer,** evil worker, wrongdoer, mischief-maker, marplot; oppressor, tyrant; incendiary, firebrand, anarchist, nihilist, destroyer; barbarian, savage, vandal, Hun, Goth; iconoclast, terrorist.
villain, rascal, miscreant, knave, scoundrel, brute, ruffian, desperado, Apache, gunman, gangster, racketeer, hijacker (*slang*), rum-runner, bootlegger, bootie (*slang*); hoodlum (*colloq.*), tough (*U. S. colloq.*), bully, rough, hooligan (*slang*), thief, cutthroat; criminal classes.

monster, fiend, demon, devil incarnate, Frankenstein's monster; bloodsucker, vampire (*the bloodsucking variety*); harpy, siren; Fury, the Furies, the Erinyes, the Eumenides.
hag, hellhag, hell-cat, harridan, witch, beldam, strumpet, Jezebel.
cannibal, man-eater, anthropophagite, anthropophagist (*rare*), anthropophagi (*pl.*); ogre, ogress (*fem.*), ghoul, Aghori (*India*).
[*comparisons*] **wild beast,** ferine (*rare*); tiger, leopard, panther, hyena, catamount, catamountain, lynx, cougar, jaguar, puma; bloodhound, hellhound, sleuth-hound; gorilla; vulture.
cockatrice, adder; snake, serpent, cobra, asp, viper, rattlesnake, rattler, boa; alligator, crocodile; octopus.

See also BAD MAN, BANE, KILLING (*killer*).—*Antonyms.* See BENEFACTOR.

---

evil spirits, powers of darkness, host of hell, demons. See HELL, MYTHICAL BEINGS.
evince, *v.* show, indicate, manifest, exhibit, demonstrate, prove. See EVIDENCE.
evolution, *n.* Darwinism; unfolding, growth, development, evolvement. See ORGANIZATION, UNFOLDMENT.
evolutional, *adj.* evolutionary, ontogenic (*biol.*). See UNFOLDMENT.
evolve, *v.* construct, produce; develop, expand, work out. See PRODUCTION, UNFOLDMENT.
exact, *adj.* literal, verbatim; faithful, lifelike, close; correct, precise, rigorous, nice. See MEANING, SIMILARITY, TRUTH.
exact, *v.* demand, force, impose, extort; claim, required. See COMMAND. RIGHTFULNESS.
exactly, *adv.* precisely, absolutely; flat; literally, verbatim. See FLATNESS, TRUTH.

EXAGGERATION.—I. *Nouns.* **exaggeration,** overstatement, hyperbole (*rhet.*), expansion, amplification, enhancement, excess; fringe, embroidery; extravagance, stretch, high coloring, caricature; yarn (*colloq.*), traveler's tale, fish story (*colloq.*), tall story (*colloq.*); tempest in a teacup; much ado about nothing; puffery, boasting, rant.
II. *Verbs.* **exaggerate,** magnify, pile up, aggravate; amplify, overdo, strain, stretch (*colloq.*), enlarge, expand, overestimate, overstate, hyperbolize (*rhet.*) overdraw, overshoot the mark, overpraise, misrepresent, stretch a point, draw a long bow (*colloq.*), out-Herod Herod; overcolor, romance, heighten, embroider, color; puff, brag, boast.
III. *Adjectives.* **exaggerated,** magnified, etc. (see *verbs*); tall (*colloq.*), steep (*slang*), overdone, overwrought, hyperbolical (*rhet.*), extravagant, excessive, preposterous, egregious; bombastic magniloquent.

See also ABSURDITY, BOASTING, FALSEHOOD, INCREASE, MISREPRESENTATION, OVERESTIMATION.—*Antonyms.* See DECREASE, UNDERESTIMATION.

---

exalt, *v.* glorify, extol, praise; honor, promote, advance; elate, uplift; intensify, heighten. See APPROBATION, ELEVATION, INCREASE.
examination, *n.* investigation, trial, test; questioning, quiz (*U. S.*). See INQUIRY.
examine, *v.* test, try, inspect, investigate, question, scrutinize, scan, probe, audit, review. See ATTENTION, INQUIRY, [1]SOUND.
example, *n.* instance, illustration, case; specimen, sample; model, copy, pattern; problem, exercise. See CONFORMITY, PROTOTYPE, TEACHING.
exasperate, *v.* annoy, irritate, enrage, provoke, infuriate. See RESENTMENT.
excavation, *n.* pit, hole, cavity, opening, shaft. See CONCAVITY.
excavator, *n.* sapper, miner; dredger, steam shovel. See CONCAVITY.
exceed, *v.* pass, overstep, overdo, go beyond; excel, outdo, surpass, beat. See OVERRUNNING, SUPERIORITY.

excel, *v.* exceed, outstrip, outdo, outrival, surpass, eclipse. See SUPERIORITY.
excellence, *n.* merit, superiority, greatness, worth, distinction. See GOODNESS.
except, *prep.* save, but, excepting, barring. See EXCLUSION, UNCONFORMITY.
exception, *n.* offense, objection; omission, rejection; irregularity, peculiarity. See DISAPPROBATION, EXCLUSION, UNCONFORMITY.
exceptional, *adj.* extraordinary, uncommon, rare, unusual, superior. See NONIMITATION.
excerpt, *n.* extract, citation, quotation, selection: section, verse, sentence. See PASSAGE.
excess, *n.* dissipation, indulgence; superfluity, surplus, remainder. See INTEMPERANCE, REDUNDANCE.
excessive, *adj.* immoderate, extreme, unreasonable, vast. See DEPTH, GREATNESS.
exchange, *n.* trade, commerce; reciprocity, transportation, substitution; market. See BARTER, INTERCHANGE, MART.

EXCITABILITY.—I. *Nouns.* **excitability,** impetuosity, vehemence, boisterousness, turbulence; impatience, intolerance, irritability, irascibility, nervousness, disquiet, disquietude, restlessness, fidgets; agitation, trepidation, perturbation, ruffle, hurry, fuss, flurry, fluster, flutter; ferment; whirl; stage fright, thrill.
passion, excitement, flush, heat, fever, fire, flame, fume, tumult, effervescence, ebullition; gust, storm, tempest; burst, fit, paroxysm, explosion, outbreak, outburst, scene, agony.
violence, fury, fierceness, rage, furor, desperation, madness, distraction, raving, delirium; frenzy, hysterics; intoxication; towering rage, anger, towering (raging, *or* tearing) passion.
fixed idea (*psychol.*), *idée fixe* (*F.*), delusion, crankiness, monomania, fanaticism; Quixotism, Quixotry; fascination, infatuation.
II. *Verbs.* **be excitable,** etc. (see *adjectives*); fidget, fret, fuss, toss, worry.
fume, rage, foam; bear ill, wince, chafe, champ the bit, lose one's temper, break out, burst out, fly out, fly off the handle (*slang*), explode, flare up, flame up, fire up, boil, rave, rant, tear, go into hysterics; run riot, run amuck; raise Cain (*slang*), raise the devil (*slang*).
III. *Adjectives.* **excitable,** easily excited, mettlesome, high-mettled, skittish, high-strung, nervous, neurotic, peevish, irritable, impatient, intolerant, moody; restless, uneasy, unquiet, mercurial, galvanic, fidgety, fussy; feverish, hysterical, delirious.
vehement, demonstrative, violent, wild, furious, fierce, inflammable, fiery, hot-headed, overzealous, enthusiastic, impassioned, fanatical, rabid, mad, rampant, clamorous, uproarious, turbulent, tempestuous, boisterous.
impulsive, impetuous, rash, hasty, quick, passionate, uncontrolled, uncontrollable, heedless, reckless, madcap, rash, mad-brained, ungovernable, irrepressible, volcanic.
See also FEELING, FUEL, HEAT, IRASCIBILITY, RESENTMENT, SENSITIVENESS, VIOLENCE.—*Antonyms.* See INEXCITABILITY.

EXCITEMENT.—I. *Nouns.* **excitement,** excitation, stimulation, piquancy, provocation, inspiration, animation, agitation, perturbation; fascination, intoxication, delirium, heat, warmth, enravishment, entrancement, ebullition, ebullience, electrification, elation, impressiveness; irritation, passion, thrill, emotional appeal; melodrama, sensationalism, yellow journalism.
commotion, disturbance, bustle, to-do (*colloq.*), stir, ado, flurry, fluster, flutter, fuss, turmoil, ferment.
II. *Verbs.* **excite,** affect, touch, reach, impress, strike, interest, animate, inspire, smite, hit (*colloq.*), penetrate, pierce, move, imbue, infect, awake, wake; awaken, waken; call forth; evoke, provoke; raise up, summon up, call up, wake up, raise; rouse, arouse, stir, fire, kindle, enkindle, illumine, illuminate, inflame, irritate, sting, cut, pique, madden, infuriate.
go to one's heart, touch to the quick, rivet the attention; possess the soul, prey on the mind.

stimulate, inspirit, stir up, goad, brew, quicken, sharpen, whet, fillip, urge, spur, instigate, incite; infuse life into, give new life to, introduce new blood, fan, foster, heat, warm, foment, revive, rekindle, electrify, magnetize.
agitate, perturb, ruffle, fluster, flutter, flurry, shake, disturb, distract.
shock, stun, stagger, jar (*slang, when used of a person*), jolt (*slang*), strike dumb, astound, horrify, scandalize, petrify.
rage, storm, rave, flame, fume, foam, boil, seethe, simmer, flare up, flash up.
III. *Adjectives.* **excited,** wrought up, nervous, overwrought, hot, red-hot, flushed, feverish; raging, flaming, ebullient, seething, foaming, fuming, stung to the quick; wild, raving, frantic, mad, distracted, frenzied, beside oneself, *bouleversé* (*F.*).
exciting, impressive, stirring, telling, interesting, warm, glowing, fervid, spirit-stirring, thrilling; soul-stirring, heart-stirring, agonizing, sensational, melodramatic, hysterical; overpowering, overwhelming.
stimulating, exciting, stimulative, incentive, provocative, tantalizing, piquant, bracing, biting, spicy, stinging, keen, racy, poignant, pungent, appetizing, inspiring, electric.

See also ENERGY, EXCITABILITY, FEELING, HEAT, PLEASURABLENESS, RESENTMENT, VIOLENCE.—*Antonyms.* See INEXCITABILITY, INSENSITIVENESS, [1]REST.

---

exclaim, *v.* ejaculate, clamor, shout, vociferate. See CRY.

EXCLUSION.—I. *Nouns.* **exclusion,** debarring, debarment (*rare*), elimination, separation, seclusion, isolation, segregation, repudiation, ostracism, cut; omission, exception, rejection; prohibition, prevention, preclusion; boycott, embargo, blockade, economic pressure.
expulsion, ejection, exile, banishment, deportation, transportation (*as to a penal colony*), expatriation, excommunication, rustication (*as from a college*), suspension (*as of a student*); eviction, ejectment, dislodgment, dismissal, discharge.
outcast, exile, vagabond, outcaste (*one ejected from his caste, as in India*), outlaw, pariah, Ishmael, leper; outsider, rank outsider; foundling, castaway; expellee.
II. *Verbs.* **exclude,** bar, leave out, shut out; lay aside, put aside, set apart; neglect, omit, pass over; separate, weed out, segregate, eliminate, remove, strike off, strike out; repel, cut, send to Coventry, turn one's back upon, keep at arm's length, shut the door upon; reject, repudiate, blackball, ostracize; isolate, boycott, embargo, blockade.
expel, banish, drive out, eject, thrust out, relegate, exile, expatriate, outlaw, maroon; unchurch, excommunicate, disown (*as in the Society of Friends*), dismiss, fire (*slang*), oust, evict, rusticate (*as from a college*), suspend (*as a student*), drum out (*esp. of a regiment*), cashier.
III. *Adjectives.* **excluded,** unfrequented, unvisited; unwelcome, unbidden, unasked, uninvited, under a cloud.
homeless, houseless, desolate, friendless, lorn, forlorn, lonely, lonesome, solitary, single, estranged, isolated, deserted, abandoned, banished, outcast, derelict.
exclusive, inadmissible, exclusory, excluding, preclusive, prohibitive, preventive; select, restrictive, restricting, cliquish, clannish.
IV. *Prepositions.* **except,** save, saving, but, excepting, exclusive of, bating (*now rare*).

See also NEGLECT, PROHIBITION, SECLUSION, UNCONFORMITY.—*Antonyms.* See INCLUSION.

---

excommunicate, *v.* expel, unchurch. See EXCLUSION.
excrescence, *n.* outgrowth, swelling, appendage, protuberance; excess, superfluity. See CONVEXITY.

EXCRETION.—I. *Nouns.* **excretion,** discharge, elimination, exudation, extrusion, smegma (*physiol.*), secernment (*physiol.*), secretion, effusion, perspiration, sweat; evacuation, excrement, ordure, excreta (*pl.*), egesta (*pl.*), feces *or* fæces, stool, defecation; diarrhea *or* diarrhœa; hemorrhage, bleeding, flux; emanation, exhalation.
saliva, spittle, sputum (*pl.* sputa), spit, slaver, drivel.

II. *Verbs.* excrete, (*of animals and plants*), eliminate, discharge, eject, emit, expel, evacuate, pass, defecate; separate, secern (*physiol.*), secrete (*physiol.*), produce, elaborate; perspire, sweat, exude; exhale, emanate.
III. *Adjectives.* excretive, eliminative, ejective, eliminant, expellant *or* expellent; secretory, secretive (*physiol.*).

See also EJECTION.—*Antonyms.* See CONCEALMENT, FOOD, RECEPTION.

---

excruciating, *adj.* acute, agonizing, unbearable, racking. See PAINFULNESS.
excursion, *n.* trip, expedition, jaunt, tour, outing. See JOURNEY.
excusable, *adj.* forgivable, justifiable, pardonable. See VINDICATION.
excuse, *v.* exempt, free; pardon, forgive, overlook; apologize, justify. See EXEMPTION, FORGIVENESS, VINDICATION.
excuse, *n.* acquittal, release; plea, defense, justification, reason, apology. See FORGIVENESS, PLEA, VINDICATION.
execrable, *adj.* poor, wretched, inferior; abominable, detestable. See BADNESS.
execute, *v.* finish, complete, fulfill; perform; behead, hang, electrocute, lynch; seal, sign. See COMPLETION, MUSICIAN, PUNISHMENT, SECURITY.
execution, *n.* administration, achievement; operation, working; capital punishment; stamp, seal, signing; rendition, interpretation, performance. See ACTION, EFFECT, KILLING, PUNISHMENT, SECURITY, TOUCH.
executioner, *n.* hangman, electrocutioner, headsman. See SCOURGE.
executive, *n.* official, manager, administrator. See DIRECTOR.
exemplify, *v.* illustrate, quote, explain. See CONFORMITY.

EXEMPTION.—I. *Nouns.* **exemption,** freedom, immunity, privilege, irresponsibility, liberty, license, release, quittance, disengagement, discharge, excuse, exception, dispensation, absolution, exculpation, exoneration.
II. *Verbs.* **exempt,** release, acquit, absolve, exonerate, exculpate, discharge, remit; free, set at liberty, let off (*colloq.*), pass over, spare, excuse, overlook, dispense with; license, privilege; immunize.
III. *Adjectives.* **exempt,** free, immune, privileged, clear, at liberty, scot-free, released, unbound, unrestrained, unrestricted, unimpeded, untrammeled, unconfined; excusable, defensible, allowable, pardonable, forgivable, venial; irresponsible, not accountable.
devoid of, without, destitute of, void of, free of, unpossessed of, unblest with; exempt from, immune from.

See also ACQUITTAL, FORGIVENESS, FREEDOM, PERMISSION.—*Antonyms.* See DUTY, POSSESSION, RESTRAINT.

---

exercise, *n.* performance, operation; training, drill, sport, gymnastics; task, problem; application, employment. See AGENCY, EXERTION, TEACHING, USE.

EXERTION.—I. *Nouns.* **exertion,** effort, energy, push, attempt, essay, endeavor, trial; trouble, pains, duty; strain, stress, tug, pull, throw, stretch, struggle, spell, spurt; dead lift, heft (*dial.*).
exercise, exercitation, operation, working, use, practice, drill, training, discipline, play, gymnastics, field sports; violent exercise, breather (*colloq.*).
work, labor, toil, travail (*rare*), manual labor, sweat of one's brow, elbow grease (*jocose*), drudgery, grind, moil (*archaic*), slavery.
worker, toiler, man of action; plodder, laborer, drudge, slave, hack, grind (*college slang*), dig (*U. S.*); practitioner, performer, artist; handworker, handicraftsman, operative, journeyman, proletarian; working (*or* laboring) classes, proletariat, labor (*collective*).
II. *Verbs.* **exert oneself,** strive, strain, struggle, endeavor, bestir oneself, bring to bear, do, perform, exercise, vie, contend.
work, labor, toil, sweat, fag, toil and moil, drudge, grind, grub, plod, slave, pull, tug, ply; ply the oar.
work hard; rough it; put forth one's strength, buckle to, set one's shoulder to the wheel, do double duty; burn the candle at both ends, work (*or* fight) one's

way; do one's best, do one's utmost; take pains; strain every nerve; spare no efforts (*or* pains), leave no stone unturned.
III. *Adjectives.* **exertive,** laborious, toilsome, wearisome, burdensome, arduous, elaborate (*archaic in this sense*), uphill, Herculean; strenuous, energetic, painstaking, diligent, industrious, hard-working.
IV. *Adverbs.* **exertively,** laboriously, lustily, strenuously, with might and main, *manibus pedibusque* (*L.*), with all one's might, to the best of one's abilities, tooth and nail, *unguibus et rostro* (*L.*), hammer and tongs, heart and soul, by the sweat of one's brow, *suo Marte* (*L.*).
See also ACTIVITY, ENERGY, PERSEVERANCE, RESOLUTION.—*Antonyms.* See INACTIVITY, REPOSE.

---

exhale, *v.* breathe, expel, emit, send out, expire: *opposite of* inhale. See EXCRETION, WIND.
exhaust, *v.* finish, end; deflate, empty, drain, deplete; fag, tire, prostrate. See COMPLETION, EJECTION, FATIGUE.
exhaustive, *adj.* comprehensive, all-inclusive, thorough. See COMPLETENESS.
exhibit, *v.* produce, show; flaunt; display, present. See MANIFESTATION, OSTENTATION, PRODUCTION.
exhilarate, *v.* elate, inspirit, animate, invigorate, gladden. See CHEERFULNESS.
exigency, *n.* emergency, juncture; necessity, urgency, need. See CIRCUMSTANCE, DESIRE.
exile, *n.* banish, expel, expatriate. See EXCLUSION.

EXISTENCE.—I. *Nouns.* **existence,** being, entity, subsistence, life, vital principle, nature, quiddity, quid.
[*in philosophy*] *ens* (*L.;* being *in the abstract*), *esse* (*L.*), essence, true being, *actus* (*L.*), actuality, reality, actual existence.
[*in space*] presence, omnipresence, ubiquity, coexistence.
reality, actuality, fact, matter of fact, truth, verity, certainty.
science of existence: ontology.
II. *Verbs.* **exist,** be, subsist, live, breathe; vegetate, stand, lie; happen, take place; occur, prevail, obtain; continue, endure, abide, last, remain, stay, drag on (*or* along).
consist in, inhere in, lie in, be comprised in, be composed of.
III. *Adjectives.* **existent,** existing, being, subsistent, extant; afloat, on foot, current, prevalent.
real, actual, positive, absolute; veritable, true; substantial, essential, substantive (*now rare in this sense*), enduring, firm, solid; genuine, authentic, well-founded, well-grounded.
IV. *Adverbs.* **actually,** truly, verily (*archaic*), really, in fact, in reality, indeed.
See also LIFE.—*Antonyms.* See NONEXISTENCE.

---

exit, *n.* withdrawal, departure, emergence. See EGRESS.
exorbitant, *adj.* expensive, dear, extravagant; excessive, immoderate, unreasonable. See DEARNESS, GREATNESS.
expand, *v.* increase, unfold, dilate, rarefy, extend, enlarge. See EXPANSION.
expanse, *n.* stretch, reach, extent, breadth, vast (*poetic*). See SPACE.

EXPANSION.—I. *Nouns.* **expansion,** dilation, enlargement, extension, growth, increase, amplification, augmentation, aggrandizement; spread, increment, development, swell, dilatation; mydriasis (*of the pupil of the eye*); obesity, corpulence; dropsy, swelling, tumefaction, intumescence, diastole, distension, puffiness, inflation.
II. *Verbs.* [*to become larger*] **expand,** enlarge, dilate, distend, spread, stretch, widen, extend, diffuse; grow, wax, increase, swell, fill out; bud, shoot, sprout, germinate, put forth, open, burst forth; outgrow; overrun.
[*to render larger*] **enlarge,** augment, aggrandize; develop, amplify, spread out, magnify; inflate, blow up, puff; pack. stuff, pad, cram. bloat, fatten; exaggerate.

III. *Adjectives.* **expanded,** swollen, larger, expansive, widespread, overgrown, exaggerated, bloated, fat, turgid, tumid, dropsical; corpulent, obese, big, pudgy, plump; puffy, pursy, distended, mydriatic (*tech.*), bulbous; full-blown, full-grown.

See also SIZE.—*Antonyms.* See CONTRACTION.

---

expatiate, *v.* rant, dilate, enlarge, expand. See DIFFUSENESS.

expect, *v.* anticipate, await, trust, contemplate. See EXPECTATION.

EXPECTANCY.—I. *Nouns.* **expectancy** *or* expectance, hopefulness, trust, confidence, anticipation, prospect (*as, a legacy in* expectancy), expectation.

serenity, calmness, coolness, imperturbability, *sang-froid* (*F.*), evenness, equanimity, steadiness, placidity, poise, composure.

II. *Adjectives.* **expecting,** unamazed, astonished at nothing, *blasé* (*F.*), expected, foreseen, expectant.

serene, calm, undisturbed, imperturbable, nerveless, cool, cool-headed, unruffled, steady, unimaginative, tranquil, quiet, placid, composed, sedate, philosophical, impassive.

Antonyms. See HOPELESSNESS, NONEXPECTATION, WONDER.

EXPECTATION.—I. *Nouns.* **expectation,** anticipation, presumption, expectancy, hope, trust, confidence, assurance, reliance; prospect, foresight, contingency, reckoning, calculation; prediction, prognostication, suspense, torment of Tantalus, apprehension.

II. *Verbs.* **expect,** look for, look out for, look forward to; hope for, anticipate; have in prospect, keep in view; contemplate, promise oneself, wait for, watch for, await; foresee, prepare for, forestall; apprehend.

predict, foretell, prognosticate, forecast, forebode, presage, augur, prophesy.

III. *Adjectives.* **expectant,** expecting, waiting, in prospect, in expectation, vigilant, open-eyed, open-mouthed, agape, gaping; on tiptoe, ready, eager, prepared, provided for, provident; in suspense, on tenterhooks.

expected, foreseen, anticipated, in prospect, prospective, future, coming; in view, on the horizon, impending.

IV. *Adverbs.* **expectantly,** on the watch, on the alert, on the *qui vive* (*F.*), with muscles tense, on edge (*colloq.*), with bated breath; with ears pricked up, *arrectis auribus* (*L.*).

soon, quickly, presently, shortly, forthwith, anon (*archaic*).

See also FORESIGHT, FUTURE, HOPE.—*Antonyms.* See DISAPPOINTMENT, NONEXPECTATION.

EXPEDIENCE.—I. *Nouns.* **expedience** *or* expediency, desirability, desirableness, fitness, propriety, efficiency, utility, advantage, opportunity; opportunism, policy.

II. *Verbs.* **be expedient,** suit, befit; suit (*or* befit) the occasion.

III. *Adjectives.* **expedient,** desirable, advisable, wise, acceptable; convenient, worth while, meet, fit, fitting, due, proper, eligible, seemly, becoming, befitting; opportune, advantageous, suitable.

practicable, feasible, doable, performable, achievable, attainable, possible; usable: *opposite of* impracticable.

See also TIMELINESS, UTILITY.—*Antonyms.* See INEXPEDIENCE.

---

expedition, *n.* speed, promptness, dispatch, alacrity; tour, trip, jaunt, excursion; campaign, crusade. See ACTIVITY, JOURNEY, WARFARE.

expel, *v.* dislodge, dispossess, dispel, oust; banish, exile. See EJECTION, EXCLUSION.

EXPENDITURE.—I. *Nouns.* **expenditure,** outgo, outgoing, outlay, overhead (*business*), general costs, expense, cost; consumption (*of money, time, etc.*), laying out, disbursement, circulation.

[*money paid*] **payment,** settlement, discharge, acquittance; expenses (*esp. outlay that is to be reimbursed*), pay, remuneration; fee, footing, garnish (*hist. or slang*), subsidy, tribute, ransom, bribe, **donation, gift;** earnest, deposit, installment; **investment; purchase.**

II. *Verbs.* **expend,** spend, use, use up, consume, distribute; pay, disburse, run (*or* get) through, lay out, shell out (*slang*), ante up, fork out (*slang*); give, donate, subscribe; reward, fee, remunerate; subsidize.

III. *Adjectives.* **expensive,** costly, dear, high-priced, precious, high; lavish, prodigal, extravagant, liberal, free, profuse, beyond one's means (*or* income).

See also PAYMENT, PRICE, REWARD, USE, WASTE.—*Antonyms.* See RECEIPT.

---

expense, *n.* cost, outlay, charge. See EXPENDITURE, PRICE.

expensive, *adj.* costly, high, dear, exorbitant. See EXPENDITURE.

experience, *v.* encounter, undergo; brave, sustain, suffer; apprehend, realize, understand. See EVENT, FEELING, KNOWLEDGE, TASTE.

experienced, *adj.* capable, efficient, trained, qualified, skilled, See SKILL.

EXPERIMENT.—I. *Nouns.* **experiment,** essay, trial, tryout, attempt; analysis, assay (*esp. of precious metals*), investigation, examination, verification, probation, proof, criterion, test, crucial test, ordeal.

speculation, flyer (*colloq.*), venture, random shot, leap in the dark; feeler, *ballon d'essai* (*F.*), pilot balloon.

experimenter, experimentist (*rare*), assayer, analyst; prospecter, adventurer; speculator, gambler, plunger (*slang*), punter.

II. *Verbs.* **experiment,** essay, try, venture, make an experiment, make trial of; rehearse; put to the test (*or* proof), prove, verify, test.

grope, grope for, feel one's way, fumble, throw out a feeler; send up a pilot balloon; see how the land lies (*or* wind blows); feel the pulse; fish for, angle, trawl, cast one's net, try one's fortune.

III. *Adjectives.* **experimental,** probative, probatory, probational, probationary; analytic, speculative, tentative, empirical, experiential.

on trial, on examination, on (*or* under) probation, "on suspicion" (Elbert Hubbard), on approval (*commerce*); on one's trial, under suspicion.

See also ESSAY, INQUIRY, UNDERTAKING.

EXPERT.—I. *Nouns.* **expert,** adept, specialist, authority, proficient, virtuoso, connoisseur, master, master hand; top sawyer, crackajack (*slang*), dab (*colloq.*), dabster (*colloq.*), sharp (*slang*), past master; first fiddle, *première* (*F.*), prima donna (*Eng. pl.* prima donnas; *It. pl.* prime donne); prizeman, medalist, picked man; crack shot, dead shot (*both colloq.*), marksman.

veteran, old hand, old stager, old campaigner, man of business, man of the world.

genius, brilliant intellect (*or* mind), master mind, master spirit; Admirable Crichton, prodigy of learning, walking encyclopedia, mine of information.

[*one skilled in securing advantages*] diplomatist, diplomat, Machiavellian; politician, tactician, strategist.

II. *Adjectives.* **expert,** skilled, adroit, skillful, apt, deft, clever, proficient, crack (*colloq.*), dexterous, finished.

See also AUTHORITY, FACILITY, SKILL.—*Antonyms.* See BUNGLER.

---

expire, *v.* die, perish; cease, stop, terminate; breathe, exhale. See DEATH, END, WIND.

explain, *v.* solve, fathom, account for; elucidate, expound, criticize, comment. See ANSWER, INTERPRETATION.

explanation, *n.* key, secret, elucidation, explication. See ATTRIBUTION, INTERPRETATION.

explanatory, *adj.* illustrative, expository. See INTERPRETATION.

explicit, *adj.* definite, clear, plain, positive; open, unreserved, outspoken. See INFORMATION, INTELLIGIBILITY, MANIFESTATION.

explode, *v.* refute, disprove, expose; burst, detonate, discharge. See CONFUTATION, VIOLENCE.

exploded, *adj.* disproved, discredited, obsolete. See ERROR.

exploit, *n.* feat, achievement, deed, act, performance. See COURAGE.

exploit, *v.* abuse, misapply; utilize, profit by. See MISUSE, USE.

explore, *v.* seek, search, examine, investigate, inquire, into. See INQUIRY.
explosion, *n.* report, clap, detonation; outburst, blast, outbreak, paroxysm. See SNAP, VIOLENCE.
explosive, *adj.* hard (*phonetics*), sharp, abrupt. See HARDNESS, LETTER.
export, *n.* exportation, commodity. See EGRESS.
expose, *v.* endanger, imperil; denounce, brand; divulge, reveal, publish; uncover, bare, denude; offer, submit, exhibit, display. See DANGER, DISAPPROBATION, DISCLOSURE, DIVESTMENT, MANIFESTATION.
exposition, *n.* exposure, divulgence; explanation, commentary; exhibition, show (*colloq.*); fair. See DISCLOSURE, INTERPRETATION, MANIFESTATION, MART.
expostulate, *v.* remonstrate, dissuade; protest, object, rebuke. See ADVICE, DEPRECATION.
exposure, *n.* outlook, location; risk, peril; divulgement, exposition. See APPEARANCE, DANGER, DISCLOSURE.
expound, *v.* interpret, explain, set forth. See TEACHING.
express, *v.* press, squeeze out; represent, demonstrate, show, reveal; signify, denote; utter, word, describe. See EXTRACTION, MANIFESTATION, MEANING, PHRASE.
expression, *n.* statement, utterance, assertion; aspect, look; indication, representation; modulation, shading, interpretation; locution, wording, term. See AFFIRMATION, APPEARANCE, MANIFESTATION, MUSICIAN, PHRASE.
expressive, *adj.* indicative, suggestive; forceful, pithy, graphic. See INFORMATION, MEANING.
expulsion, *n.* ejection, banishment, dislodgment, dismissal. See EXCLUSION.
expurgate, *v.* purge, purify, cleanse. See CLEANNESS.
exquisite, *adj.* delicate, dainty; fastidious, discriminative, appreciative; choice, rare, high-wrought; charming, delightful; keen, sharp, intense. See BEAUTY, DISCRIMINATION, GOOD, PLEASURABLENESS, SHARPNESS.
extant, *adj.* existent, surviving. See EXISTENCE.
extemporaneous, *adj.* offhand, unprepared, improvised, spontaneous, impromptu. See IMPULSE, NONPREPARATION.
extemporize, *v.* improvise, make up. See NONPREPARATION.
extend, *v.* widen, stretch, increase, spread, enlarge; protract, prolong; stretch out, float, wave. See EXPANSION, LENGTH, STREAM.
extension, *n.* addition, enlargement, expansion, amplification, distension; lengthening, prolongation, continuation; extent, expanse, stretch, sweep. See INCREASE, PRODUCTION, SPACE.
extensive, *adj.* widespread, far-reaching, comprehensive; spacious, vast. See GREATNESS, SPACE.
extent, *n.* limit, measure, range; span, longitude; compass, proportions, size, bulk. See DEGREE, LENGTH, SPACE.
extenuate, *v.* forgive, pardon, palliate, excuse. See FORGIVENESS, VINDICATION.

EXTERIORITY.—I. *Nouns.* **exteriority,** outwardness, externality, externity (*rare*), externalization, exteriorization.
exterior, outside, surface, superficies; skin, covering, rind, finish, polish; face, facet; carapace (*as of a turtle*).
II. *Verbs.* **be exterior,** lie around, environ, envelop, encompass, invest, encircle, cover, shroud, wrap, veil, clothe.
exteriorize, externalize, objectify, visualize, actualize, envisage.
III. *Adjectives.* **exterior,** external, outward, extraneous, superficial; outer, outermost, outlying, outside, outdoor; outstanding; extrinsic, incidental.
IV. *Adverbs.* **exteriorly,** externally, outwardly, etc. (see *adjectives*); out, without, outwards, outdoors, out-of-doors, *extra muros* (*L.*), in the open air.
See also ENVIRONMENT.—*Antonyms.* See INTERIORITY.

exterminate, *v.* eradicate, root out, annihilate, blot out. See DESTRUCTION.
external, *adj.* outward, outside, extraneous, objective, superficial. See EXTERIORITY.
extinct, *adj.* exterminated, nonexistent, dead, gone, obsolete. See NONEXISTENCE.
extinction, *n.* annihilation, extermination, extirpation. See DESTRUCTION.
extinguish, *v.* blow out, smother; eradicate, suppress, end; quench, damp. See DARKNESS, DESTRUCTION, REFRIGERATION.
extol, *v.* praise, glorify, applaud, celebrate, exalt. See APPROBATION.
extort, *v.* wring, elicit, exact. See TAKING.
extortionate, *adj.* exorbitant, unreasonable; avaricious, grasping. See DEARNESS, DESIRE.
extra, *adj.* supplementary, additional, spare, redundant. See ADDITION.

EXTRACTION.—I. *Nouns.* **extraction,** drawing out, dislodgment, removal, elimination, extrication, evulsion, eradication, extirpation, extermination ejection, wrench; distillation, expression (*as of fruit juice*), squeezing; elicitation education.
descent, lineage, derivation, ancestry, origin, birth, stock, family, parentage.
[*something extracted*] **extract,** essence, decoction, abstract, distillation, juice.
quotation, selection, citation, excerpt, abstract, clipping, cutting, note, minute
II. *Verbs.* **extract,** draw; take out, draw out, draw forth, remove, extricate. eliminate, pull out, tear out, pluck out, pick out, get out; wring from, wrench; extort; root up, eradicate, stub, uproot, pull up, extirpate, weed out.
educe, elicit, evolve, bring forth, evoke, derive, deduce.
squeeze out, express, expel, extort, press out, distill.
See also EJECTION, PATERNITY, RECORD.—*Antonyms.* See INSERTION.

---

extracts, *n. pl.* clippings, citations, excerpts, selections, quotations. See COMPENDIUM.

EXTRANEOUSNESS.—I. *Nouns.* **extraneousness,** extrinsicality, exteriority, externality; exclusion; alienism.
foreign body (substance, *or* element).
alien, stranger, foreigner, newcomer, *novus homo* (*L.*), tenderfoot (*slang*). griffin (*Anglo-Indian*); immigrant, emigrant; outsider, barbarian, Guinea (*slang*), Wop (*slang*), Dago (*slang*), Chink (*slang*), Dutchman (*in careless or slang use, any Hollander or German*).
II. *Adjectives.* **extraneous,** foreign, alien, exterior, external; outlandish, barbaric, barbarian; exotic, extrinsic, extrinsical, unessential; excluded, inadmissible, exceptional.
III. *Adverbs.* **abroad,** in foreign parts, in foreign lands; oversea, overseas; absent, traveling, out of the country.
See also EXCLUSION, IRRELATION, OBJECTIVENESS.—*Antonyms.* See COMPONENT, INHABITANT.

---

extraordinary, *adj.* remarkable, eminent, rare, notable; uncommon, unusual, singular. See GREATNESS, UNCONFORMITY.
extravagant, *adj.* unreasonable, exorbitant; excessive, extreme; unreal, flighty, visionary; wasteful, lavish; absurd, fanciful, grotesque. See DEARNESS, GREATNESS, IMAGINATION, PRODIGALITY, RIDICULOUSNESS.
extreme, *adj.* last, final, utmost, farthest; excessive, inordinate, immoderate; ultra, advanced, radical. See END, GREATNESS, REVOLUTION.—**extreme unction,** last rites, viaticum. See RITE.
extremity, *n.* need, distress, destitution; edge, boundary, tip, limit. See ADVERSITY, END.
extricate, *v.* free, disentangle, liberate, relieve, disengage. See LIBERATION.
extrinsic, *adj.* external, outward, objective, unessential, extraneous. See OBJECTIVENESS.
exude, *v.* discharge, leak, ooze, trickle, drain. See EGRESS.

exult, *v.* triumph, crow, jubilate, rejoice, glory. See BOASTING, REJOICING.
exultant, *adj.* jubilant, elated, triumphant, pleased, satisfied, delighted. See PRIDE, REJOICING.
eye, *n.* visual organ, orb (*poetic*), optic (*jocose*); eyesight, perception. See VISION.
eye, *v.* watch, view, scrutinize, scan, inspect. See VISION.
eyeglasses, *n. pl. pince-nez* (*F.*), nippers. See OPTICAL INSTRUMENTS.
eyesore, *n.* offense, blemish, fright. See UGLINESS.

F

fable, *n.* allegory, parable, apologue, tale; fiction, myth. See DESCRIPTION, UNTRUTH.
fabric, *n.* construction, framework; tissue, material. See STRUCTURE, TEXTURE.
fabricate, *v.* misrepresent, falsify; invent, imagine, devise; construct, make, compose, frame. See FALSEHOOD, IMAGINATION, PRODUCTION.
fabrication, *n.* lie, invention, falsehood, fiction. See UNTRUTH.
fabulous, *adj.* extravagant, incredible, mythical, fictitious, legendary. See IMAGINATION, NONEXISTENCE.
face, *n.* features, physiognomy, countenance, aspect, visage, expression; outside, surface, right side; fore part, façade. See APPEARANCE, EXTERIORITY, FRONT.
face, *v.* cover, overlay, line; confront, encounter, brave, oppose. See COVERING, RESISTANCE.

FACILITY.—I. *Nouns.* **facility,** ease, easiness, capability, feasibility, practicability; flexibility, pliancy, ductility, smoothness, plain (smooth, *or* straight) sailing; mere child's play, cinch, snap (*both U. S. slang*).
skill, dexterity, adroitness, expertness, address, knack, quickness, readiness, ability, aptness.
[*in plural*] **facilities,** means, resources, conveniences, advantages, aids, appliances (*as,* facilities *for research*).
II. *Verbs.* **be easy,** run smoothly; have full play, obey the helm, work well, work smoothly.
facilitate, smooth, ease, lighten, free, clear, disencumber, disburden, unload, free from, disembarrass, unclog, disentangle, extricate, unravel, unknot, untie, unbind; humor, leave a loophole, leave the matter open; give full play, make way for, pave the way, bridge over, permit.
III. *Adjectives.* **facile,** easy, easily done, not difficult, feasible, practicable; within reach, accessible.
[*easy of access or converse*] **affable,** approachable, courteous, complaisant, cordial, mild, gentle, easy-going.
[*easily persuaded*] **pliant,** ductile, yielding, flexible, compliant, credulous.
[*working easily*] **expert,** dexterous, skillful, ready, quick, fluent (*as, to wield a* facile *pen*).
manageable, wieldy, tractable, submissive, yielding, ductile, pliant.
unburdened, unencumbered, unloaded, unobstructed, untrammeled; unrestrained, free, at ease, light.
IV. *Adverbs.* **easily,** readily, smoothly, swimmingly, with no effort.
See also POSSIBILITY, SKILL, SMOOTHNESS, WILLINGNESS.—*Antonyms.* See DIFFICULTY.

---

facsimile, *n.* copy, duplicate, replica, reproduction, counterpart. See IDENTITY.
fact, *n.* circumstance, incident; reality, actuality. See EVENT, EXISTENCE.
faction, *n.* dissension, rupture; clique, gang. See DISCORD, PARTY.

factor, *n.* instrument, constituent, cause, element; agent, solicitor. See MEANS, REPRESENTATIVE.
factory, *n.* manufactory, works, mill, foundry. See WORKSHOP.
faculty, *n.* quality, attribute, ability; aptitude, cleverness; professorate, teaching staff. See POWER, SKILL, TEACHER.
fad, *n.* hobby, craze, vogue, rage (*colloq.*). See FASHION.
fade, *v.* bleach, whiten; wither, droop, decay; pale, cloud; vanish, dissolve; languish, decline. See COLORLESSNESS, DETERIORATION, DIMNESS, DISAPPEARANCE, WEAKNESS.
failing, *n.* nonsuccess; indiscretion, slip; frailty, shortcoming, fault, foible. See FAILURE, LAPSE, WEAKNESS.

FAILURE.—I. *Nouns.* **failure,** unsuccess, nonsuccess, failing, nonfulfillment; labor in vain, no go (*colloq.*), inefficacy, vain attempt, "lame and impotent conclusion" (*Othello*); fiasco, fizzle (*colloq.*), washout (*slang*); frustration, disappointment.
blunder, error, default, deficiency, fault, omission, miss, oversight, delinquency, negligence, nonperformance, slip, trip, stumble; false step, *faux pas* (*F.*); scrape, mess, muddle, botch.
mishap, misfortune, mischance; decay, decline, deterioration; split, collapse, blow, deathblow, tragedy, explosion.
repulse, rebuff, defeat, rout, overthrow, discomfiture; beating, drubbing; subjugation, checkmate, fool's mate.
bankruptcy, insolvency, smash (*colloq.*), break, crash, wreck, ruin, fall, downfall; suspension (*temporary failure*).
II. *Verbs.* **fail,** be unsuccessful, make vain efforts, labor in vain, flunk (*colloq.*), bring to naught, make nothing of, fall short of, miss, miss one's aim (*or* the mark), slip, trip, stumble, blunder, miscarry; go to the wall (*colloq.*), lick the dust, be defeated, have the worst of it, lose the day, lose, go into the wilderness (*Eng. political cant*).
come to grief, flounder, falter, limp, halt, hobble, fall, tumble, run aground, split upon a rock, break down, sink, drown, founder, meet with disaster, turn out badly, succumb, collapse, come to nothing; become bankrupt (*or* insolvent), go up (*colloq.*); end in smoke, flat out (*U. S. colloq.*), fall through, hang fire, flash in the pan, go to wrack and ruin.
III. *Adjectives.* **failed,** unsuccessful, successless, failing, stickit (*Scot.*), at fault; unfortunate, luckless, unprosperous, abortive, sterile, fruitless, bootless; ineffectual, ineffective, inefficient, lame, insufficient, unavailing.
stranded, aground, grounded, swamped, struck, wrecked, shipwrecked, foundered, capsized.
undone, lost, ruined, broken, bankrupt, insolvent; played out, done up, done for (*both colloq.*); broken down, overborne, overwhelmed; all up with (*colloq.*); plowed (*Eng. Univ. cant*), plucked (*college cant*).
frustrated, thwarted, crossed, disconcerted; discomfited, checkmated, euchred, repulsed, vanquished, trimmed (*colloq.*), defeated; unhorsed, hard hit, stultified, befooled, dished (*colloq.*), foiled, victimized, sacrificed, hoist with one's own petard.
See also ADVERSITY, ERROR, INCOMPLETENESS, INUTILITY, NONPAYMENT, SHORTCOMING, UNSKILLFULNESS, WEAKNESS.—*Antonyms.* See SUCCESS.

FAINTNESS.—I. *Nouns.* **faintness,** feebleness, softness, lowness, gentleness, indistinctness, inaudibility; dimness, paleness, indefiniteness, faint sound, whisper, breath, undertone, murmur, hum, humming, souffle (*med.*), drone, buzz, purr, lap (*as of waves*), plash, babble, purl; sough, moan, rustle; tinkle; "still small voice" (*Bible*).
[*loss of strength*] **languor,** lassitude, weakness, exhaustion, giddiness, swoon, fainting, lipothymy (*med.*), syncope (*med.*).
silencer, muffler (*as in an automobile*); soft pedal, damper, mute, *sordino* (*It.*), sordine (*all five music*).
II. *Verbs.* **faint,** lose courage, give way (faint *in this sense is archaic*); swoon.
be faint, (*in sound*), whisper, breathe, mutter, murmur, hum, rustle, tinkle; purl, gurgle, ripple, babble, flow.

muffle, deaden, mute, hush, quiet, throttle, muzzle, subdue, repress, damp.
III. *Adjectives.* **faint,** low, dull, stifled, muffled, inaudible; indistinct, muttered, whispered, gentle, soft; purling, floating, flowing, liquid, soothing, dulcet; dim, feeble, pale.
[*lacking courage*] **timid,** timorous, pusillanimous, diffident, faint-hearted, half-hearted, funky (*slang*), cowardly, dejected, depressed.
[*lacking strength*] **weak,** feeble, languid, listless, torpid, sluggish, dull, sickly; lipothymial *or* lipothymic, giddy, inclined to swoon.
IV. *Adverbs.* **faintly,** feebly, softly, indistinctly, in a whisper, with bated breath, *sotto voce* (*It.*), aside; piano, pianissimo (*both music*), out of earshot; inaudibly. See also COLORLESSNESS, FATIGUE, IMPOTENCE, STAMMERING (*mumble, inarticulate*), WEAKNESS.—*Antonyms.* See LOUDNESS, STRENGTH.

---

fair, *adj.* beautiful, comely; spotless, unblemished; blond, light; clear, bright; medium, average, passable; equitable, just, impartial, reasonable, honest; sweet, winsome. See BEAUTY, CLEANNESS, COLORLESSNESS, GOOD, IMPERFECTION (*indifferent*), PROBITY, SWEETNESS.
fairness, *n.* justice, equity, impartiality. See PROBITY.
fairy, *n.* sprite, fay, pixy, elf. See MYTHICAL BEINGS.
fairylike, *adj.* sylphlike, elfish, dainty, exquisite. See MYTHICAL BEINGS.
faith, *n.* conviction, creed; trust, reliance, assurance. See BELIEF, HOPE.
faithful, *adj.* lifelike; constant, true, loyal, stanch; trustworthy, reliable, accurate. See COPY, PROBITY, TRUTH.
faithless, *adj.* treacherous, false, disloyal, unfaithful. See IMPROBITY.
fake, *n.* swindle, fraud, dodge: *slang.* See DECEPTION.
fall, *v.* decline, abate, diminish; drop, slip, slide, slope; crumble, collapse, perish, die; fail, come to grief; sin, err. See DECREASE, DESCENT, DESTRUCTION, FAILURE, VICE.—**fall short,** fail, want, lack, be deficient; *often with* of. See NONCOMPLETION, SHORTCOMING.
fall, *n.* failure, ruin; drop, tumble; downfall, crash, smash; autumn; declivity, slope. See ADVERSITY, DESCENT, DESTRUCTION, EVENING, OBLIQUITY.
fallacy, *n.* misconception, mistake, sophistry, inconsistency. See ERROR.
fallen, *adj.* overthrown, prostrate, powerless. See FLATNESS.
fallen angels, rulers of darkness, unclean spirits. See SATAN.
fallibility, *n.* unreliability, untrustworthiness. See UNCERTAINTY.
fallible, *adj.* questionable, unreliable. See UNCERTAINTY.
fallow, *adj.* uncultivated, untilled, unused. See NONPREPARATION.
false alarm, bugbear, bugaboo, bogy, hoax. See ALARM.

FALSEHOOD.—I. *Nouns.* **falsehood,** falseness, falsity, inaccuracy, misstatement, falsification, misrepresentation, deception, deceptiveness, dishonesty, untruthfulness, mendacity, lying, untruth, fib, lie; guile, perjury, false swearing, forgery, invention, fabrication; perversion, suppression, distortion, exaggeration, false coloring, prevarication, equivocation, mental reservation, evasion, fraud, mystification, concealment, simulation, dissimulation, dissembling, deceit; sham, pretense, pretending, profession, malingering.
duplicity, double dealing, insincerity, hypocrisy, cant, pharisaism; casuistry, Machiavellism; lip service, hollowness, mere show; quackery, charlatanism, charlatanry, humbug; cajolery, flattery, mealy-mouthedness, buncombe *or* bunkum, flimflam, gammon (*colloq.*), Judas kiss, perfidy, bad faith, cunning.
II. *Verbs.* **falsify,** misstate, misquote, misrepresent, belie; garble, gloss over, disguise, color, varnish, doctor (*colloq.*), fake, deacon (*colloq.*), adulterate, interpolate, cook (*slang*), dress up, embroider, exaggerate; fabricate, invent; trump up; forge; coin; hatch, spin, concoct.
prevaricate, equivocate, quibble, trim, shuffle, fence, beat about the bush.
dissemble, dissimulate, feign, assume; play false, play a double game; coquet; act (*or* play) a part; affect, pose; simulate, pass off for; counterfeit, sham, pretend, profess, make believe, deceive, malinger.
lie, tell a lie (*or* an untruth), fib, romance; swear falsely, forswear, perjure oneself, bear false witness.

III. *Adjectives.* **false,** untrue, deceitful, mendacious, unveracious, falsified, lying, untruthful, fraudulent, dishonest; evasive, disingenuous, hollow, insincere; artful, cunning, tricky, wily, sly; perfidious, treacherous, perjured, forsworn, faithless.

[*not genuine*] **counterfeit,** sham, make-believe, flash, artificial, spurious, feigned, theatrical (*as,* false *jewelry*); apparent, pseudo (*as,* false *indigo*).

[*not well founded*] **incorrect,** erroneous, inaccurate, unreliable, untrustworthy, wrong (*as, a* false *conclusion*).

hypocritical, canting, pharisaical, tartuffish *or* tartufish (*from the leading character in Molière's "Tartuffe"*), Machiavellian, double-tongued, double-dealing; two-faced, double-faced; smooth-spoken, smooth-tongued, plausible, mealy-mouthed; affected, canting, insincere, sanctimonious.

See also DECEPTION, ERROR, IMITATION, IMPROBITY, SOPHISTRY, UNTRUTH.—*Antonyms.* See VERACITY.

---

falter, *v.* waver, vacillate; stagger, stumble; stutter. See IRRESOLUTION, SLOWNESS, STAMMERING.

fame, *n.* glory, distinction, reputation, note, celebrity. See MEMORY, REPUTE.

familiarity, *n.* unconstraint, informality; disrespect, impudence; intimacy; experience, acquaintance. See FREEDOM, FRIENDSHIP, KNOWLEDGE.

familiar spirit, familiar, genius, guide, demon. See MYTHICAL BEINGS.

family, *n.* group, household, tribe, race; descent, ancestry, pedigree; parentage, forefathers; offspring, descendants. See CONSANGUINITY, CONTINUITY, PATERNITY, POSTERITY.

famine, *n.* dearth, destitution, starvation. See INSUFFICIENCY.

famous, *adj.* distinguished, renowned, celebrated, noted. See REPUTE.

[1]**fan,** *n.* devotee, enthusiast, follower: *slang.* See AMUSEMENT.

[2]**fan,** *n.* palm leaf, flabellum; blower, winnower. See WIND.

fan, *v.* blow, ventilate, cool, refresh, stimulate (*fig.*). See REFRIGERATION, WIND.

fanatic, *n.* zealot, enthusiast. See IMAGINATION.

fanciful, *adj.* whimsical, fantastic, unreal; odd, queer, grotesque; imaginary, ideal. See IMAGINATION, RIDICULOUSNESS, SUBJECTIVENESS.

fancy, *n.* humor, vagary, whim; inclination, wish; impression, thought; phantasy, daydream, illusion. See CAPRICE, DESIRE, IDEA, IMAGINATION.

fancy, *v.* surmise, suppose; like, affect; dream, conceive. See BELIEF, DESIRE, IMAGINATION.

fantastic, *adj.* extravagant, unreal, illusory, fanciful; grotesque, odd, queer, strange. See IMAGINATION, RIDICULOUSNESS.

fantasy, *n.* dream, illusion, fancy. See IMAGINATION.

far, *adv.* widely, remotely, afar: *often with* away *or* off. See DISTANCE.

far, *adj.* remote, distant, far-away. See DISTANCE.

farce, *n.* buffoonery, ridiculousness, burlesque; comedy, extravaganza. See ABSURDITY, DRAMA.

farewell! *interj.* good-by *or* good-bye! adieu! See DEPARTURE.

farewell, *n.* leave-taking, good-by, parting, adieu. See DEPARTURE.

farm, *n.* farmstead, ranch, plantation. See HABITATION.

farm, *v.* till, cultivate, sow. See HUSBANDRY.

farsighted, *adj.* farseeing, prudent; clear-sighted. See FORESIGHT, VISION.

farther, *adj.* beyond, more remote. See DISTANCE.

fascinate, *v.* delight, charm, captivate, enchant. See PLEASURABLENESS [1]SPELL.

fascination, *n.* attraction, charm, allurement, seduction, enchantment witchery. See PLEASURABLENESS, [1]SPELL.

FASHION.—I. *Nouns.* **fashion,** style, mode, vogue, *dernier cri* (*F.*), *ton* (*F.*), the latest thing, the go (*colloq.*), the rage, craze, fad, prevailing taste; custom, way usage, manner, appearance, shape, guise, trim, cut, dress, habit, taste, *hau ton* (*F.*).

society, *bon ton* (*F.*), *monde* (*F.*), good (*or* polite) society, civilized life, civilization; court, high life, world, fashionable world, "the glass of fashion and the mould of form" (*Hamlet*); upper ten thousand, upper ten (*colloq.*), *élite* (*F.*), smart set (*colloq.*), *beau monde* (*F.*), four hundred (*U. S. colloq. or jocose*), F. F. V.'s (*First Families of Virginia: U. S. colloq. or jocose*); Vanity Fair, Mayfair.

manners, breeding, politeness; air, demeanor, *savoir-faire* (*F.*), gentility, decorum, propriety, *bienséance* (*F.*), Mrs. Grundy; convention, conventionality, the proprieties; punctiliousness, punctilio, form, formality, etiquette.

II. *Verbs.* **fashion,** form, mold, design, pattern, shape; construct, contrive, compose, make, forge, execute, create, devise, originate, produce.

be fashionable, be the rage, have a run, pass current, follow the fashion, *savoir faire* (*F.*), *savoir vivre* (*F.*), keep up appearance, cut a dash (*colloq.*), go with the stream, be in the swim (*colloq.*).

III. *Adjectives.* **fashionable,** in fashion, *à la mode* (*F.*), stylish, modish, all the go (*colloq.*), all the rage (*colloq.*), *chic* (*F.*), swell (*slang*), smart, *recherché* (*F.*), presentable; punctilious, genteel, decorous, conventional.

polished, refined, polite, self-possessed, poised, easy, frank, unconstrained, unembarrassed, *dégagé* (*F.*); well-bred, gently bred, thoroughbred, high-bred, courtly, distinguished, *distingué* (*F.*); aristocratic, gentlemanly, ladylike.

See also COURTESY, FORM, HABIT, NOBILITY, TASTE.—*Antonyms.* See UNCONFORMITY, VULGARITY.

---

fast, *v.* abstain, starve. See FASTING.

fast, *adj.* dissolute, dissipated; firm, secure; steadfast, reliable; swift, rapid, quick. See INTEMPERANCE, JUNCTION, STABILITY, VELOCITY.

fasten, *v.* join, unite, attach; restrain, shackle, tie, secure. See JUNCTION, RESTRAINT, SECURITY.

fastening, *n.* catch, clasp; tie, lock, bond, chain. See SNAP, VINCULUM.

FASTIDIOUSNESS.—I. *Nouns.* **fastidiousness,** finicality, finicalness, meticulosity, etc. (see *adjectives*); nicety, hypercriticism, epicurism.

discernment, acuteness, discrimination, astuteness, keenness, sharpness, shrewdness, insight, perspicacity.

epicure, *gourmet* (*F.*), *bon vivant* (*F.; fem. bonne vivante*), epicurean, gourmand (*less fastidious than gourmet; obs. as* glutton); deipnosophist, gastronome *or* gastronomer (*lover of good living*), gastronomist, aristologist; Apicius.

[*excess of delicacy*] **prudery,** prudishness, primness, stiffness, coyness, preciousness.

II. *Verbs.* **be fastidious,** etc. (see *adjectives*); split hairs; mince matters; turn up one's nose at, disdain.

discriminate, distinguish, differentiate, have nice discrimination; have exquisite taste; be discriminative.

III. *Adjectives.* **fastidious,** finical, squeamish, fussy, pernickety (*colloq.*), particular, precise, scrupulous, overnice, meticulous, finicking *or* finicky, exacting, hard to please, difficult, dainty, nice, delicate, precious, overrefined, *précieuse* (*F.*), niminy-piminy, effeminate, dandified, prim, prudish, strait-laced; thin-skinned, querulous, critical, punctilious, hypercritical, overcritical.

discerning, discriminative, discriminating, judicious, astute, keen, sharp, subtle, perspicacious, sagacious.

Antonyms. See INDIFFERENCE, NEGLECT, UNWILLINGNESS.

FASTING.—I. *Nouns.* **fasting,** abstinence from food, voluntary abstinence, fast, famishment, starvation.

fast, fast day, fasting day, *jour maigre* (*F.*), Lent, spare (*or* meager) diet, lenten diet, short commons, Barmecide feast; banian (*or* banyan) day (*naut.: a day in which no meal is served out, or when the fare is particularly poor*).

II. *Verbs.* **fast,** starve, famish, perish with hunger; dine with Duke Humphrey, go hungry; abstain from food, go without food (*either entirely or partially, as a religious duty or in token of grief or penitence*).

III. *Adjectives.* **fasting,** lenten, quadragesimal; unfed, starved, half-starved, hungry.

Antonyms. See GLUTTONY.

fat, *adj.* corpulent, obese, fleshy, well-fed, portly, stout, chubby. See SIZE.
fatal, *adj.* deadly, mortal, destructive. See KILLING.
fate, *n.* future, hereafter; doom, predestination, lot. See DESTINY, NECESSITY.
fated, *adj.* destined, elect, appointed. See NECESSITY.
Fates, *n.* Mœræ. See MYTHICAL BEINGS (*minor deities*), NECESSITY.
father, *n.* pastor, priest, padre; parent, sire, pater (*colloq.*). See CLERGY, PATERNITY.
fatherland, *n.* country, home, native land. See LAND.
fatherly, *adj.* fatherlike, paternal, protecting, kind. See BENEVOLENCE, PATERNITY.

FATIGUE.—I. *Nouns.* **fatigue,** weariness, lassitude, tiredness, exhaustion; yawning, drowsiness.
[*in metals, due to repeated blows or strain*] deterioration, weakness.
[*cause of fatigue*] toil, labor, exertion, drudgery, fatiguing duties, tax.
faintness, fainting, swoon, syncope (*med.*), lipothymy (*med.*), exhaustion, collapse, prostration.
II. *Verbs.* **be fatigued,** yawn, gape, oscitate (*rare*); droop, sink, flag; gasp, pant, puff, blow, drop, swoon, faint, succumb.
fatigue, tire, bore, weary, irk (*archaic*), fag, flag, jade, harass, exhaust, wear out, prostrate.
tax, task, strain; overtask, overwork, overdo, overburden, overtax, overstrain.
III. *Adjectives.* **fatigued,** weary, tired, drowsy, haggard, toilworn, wayworn, footsore, faint, done up (*colloq.*), prostrate, spent, overtired, all in (*slang*), ready to drop, dog-tired, played out.
worn, worn-out, enfeebled, exhausted, battered, shattered, seedy (*colloq.*).
breathless, short of (*or* out of) breath, blown, puffing and blowing, panting, anhelous (*rare*), short-winded, short-breathed, dyspnœic *or* dyspneic (*med.*), asthmatic, broken-winded (*said of a horse*).
See also WEARINESS.—*Antonyms.* See CONTINUANCE, REFRESHMENT, RESTORATION.

---

fault, *n.* negligence, lapse, offense; flaw, blemish, defect; frailty, failing. See DERELICTION, IMPERFECTION, VICE.
fault-finding, *adj.* censorious, critical, captious, caviling. See DISAPPROBATION.
faulty, *adj.* imperfect, defective, deficient, unsound; unreliable, unretentive. See IMPERFECTION, SHORTNESS.
favor, *n.* patronage, sanction, support; approval, regard, commendation; boon, kindness, gift; partiality, favoritism. See AID, APPROBATION, GIVING, WRONG.
favorable, *adj.* auspicious, advantageous, propitious; helpful, beneficial. See FRIEND.
favorer, *n.* supporter, sympathizer, promoter, patron. See FRIEND.

FAVORITE.—*Nouns.* **favorite,** pet, idol, jewel, spoiled child, *enfant gâté* (*F.*), apple of one's eye, man after one's own heart; general (*or* universal) favorite; idol of the people; matinée idol.
[*one preferred above others*] **choice,** pick, selection, preference, option, best.
darling, beloved, love, dear, duck, honey, sweetheart.
See also LOVE.—*Antonyms.* See HATE (*object of hatred*).

---

fawn, *v.* cringe, crouch, toady, truckle. See SERVILITY.

FEAR.—I. *Nouns.* **fear,** timidity, diffidence, apprehensiveness, fearfulness, solicitude, anxiety, care, misgiving, mistrust, suspicion, qualm, hesitation; apprehension, dread, reverence (*as, the* fear *of God*), awe.
fright, affright (*archaic*), alarm, dread, terror, horror, dismay, consternation, panic, scare, funk (*colloq.*), cold feet (*slang*), mortal funk (*colloq.*), stampede (*as of horses*); trepidation, flutter, fear and trembling, perturbation, tremor.

quivering, shaking, trembling, quaking, palpitation, nervousness, restlessness, disquietude.

intimidation, daunting, etc. (see *verbs*); bullying; terrorism, reign of terror; terrorist, bully.

[*object of fear*] **bugbear,** bugaboo, scarecrow, bogy, hobgoblin, nightmare, specter, *bête noire* (*F.*).

II. *Verbs.* **fear,** be afraid, apprehend, dread, distrust; hesitate, falter, funk (*colloq.*), cower, crouch, skulk, take fright, take alarm; start, wince, flinch, shy, shrink, fly.

tremble, shake, shiver, shudder, flutter, quake, quaver, quiver, quail.

frighten, fright, affright, terrify, inspire (*or* excite) fear, bulldoze (*colloq.*), dismay, astound; awe, strike terror, appall, unman, petrify, horrify; startle, scare, alarm, stampede.

intimidate, daunt, cow, overawe, abash, deter, discourage; browbeat, bully, threaten, terrorize, bullyrag, badger.

haunt, obsess, beset, besiege; prey (*or* weight) on the mind.

III. *Adjectives.* **afraid,** frightened, alarmed, apprehensive, solicitous, anxious, fearful, timid, timorous, nervous, diffident, tremulous, shaky, faint-hearted, cowardly; aghast, awe-struck, awe-stricken, horror-stricken, panic-stricken.

[*inspiring fear*] **fearful,** dreadful, appalling, lurid, alarming, perilous, dread, fell, dire, direful, shocking, frightful, terrible, terrific, tremendous, formidable, redoubtable, horrid, horrible, ghastly, awful, awe-inspiring, distressing, revolting.

See also ALARM, COWARDICE, IRRESOLUTION, PAINFULNESS.—*Antonyms.* See COURAGE.

---

fearless, *adj.* dauntless, courageous, bold, daring. See COURAGE, HOPE.

feasible, *adj.* practicable, workable, suitable. See EXPEDIENCE, POSSIBILITY.

feast, *n.* banquet, repast, festival. See FOOD, GLUTTONY.

feat, *n.* achievement, exploit, deed. See COURAGE.

feather, *n.* plume, ornament, honor; plumage, quill, tuft, crest. See ORNAMENT, ROUGHNESS.

feature, *n.* lineament, outline; cast, make; characteristic, trait, quality, property. See APPEARANCE, FORM, INDICATION.

federation, *n.* association, league, union, coalition. See COMBINATION, PARTY.

fee, *n.* payment, pay, charge; tip, gratuity; compensation. See EXPENDITURE, GIVING, REWARD.

FEEBLENESS.—I. *Nouns.* **feebleness,** weakness, debility, enervation, infirmity; vapidity, etc. (see *adjectives*).

II. *Adjectives.* **feeble,** weak, infirm, enervated, impotent, powerless, debilitated, sickly, drooping, frail (*as, a* feeble *old man*).

[*lacking force, vigor, character, or intelligence*] **vapid,** insipid, flat, nerveless, spiritless, meager, trashy, flimsy, poor, dull, dry, bald, colorless, watery, tame, languid, prosy, prosaic, weak, slight, puny, careless, slovenly, loose, lax, slipshod, inexact; puerile, childish, rambling.

indistinct, hazy, dim, nebulous, misty, indefinite, uncertain, blurred, faint, vague.

See also POVERTY, SOPHISTRY (*weak*), WATER (*vapid*), WEAKNESS.—*Antonyms.* See VIGOR.

---

feed, *v.* fodder, graze, eat, devour; supply, furnish. See FOOD, PROVISION.

FEELING.—I. *Nouns.* **feeling,** emotion, sentiment, sensibility, sympathy, tenderness, concern, affection, pathos; sensation, impression, response, inspiration; suffering, endurance, sufferance.

[*in plural*] **feelings,** susceptibilities, sympathies (*as, to hurt one's* feelings).

fervor, fervency, unction, gusto, vehemence, heartiness, cordiality, earnestness, eagerness, gush (*colloq.*), *empressement* (*F.*), ardor, warmth, zeal, passion, *verve* (*F.*), enthusiasm, ecstasy.

thrill, tingle, tingling, excitement, kick (*slang*), shock, agitation, quiver, flutter, flurry, fluster, flush, blush, twitter, tremor, throb, throbbing, pulsation, palpitation, panting.

II. *Verbs.* feel, touch, handle, thumb, finger; test, examine, probe, find, discover perceive, understand, comprehend, know, see, discern, note, respond, remark receive an impression, be impressed with, enter into the spirit of.
bear, suffer, support, sustain, endure, brook, abide, experience, labor under brave, stand, taste, prove.
be perturbed (agitated, *or* excited), glow, flush, blush, crimson, change color mantle; darken, whiten, pale, tingle, thrill, heave, pant, throb, palpitate, tremble, quiver, flutter, twitter, shake, stagger, reel; wince.
III. *Adjectives.* feeling, sentient, sensitive, easily affected, emotional, demonstrative, susceptible, sensuous.
trenchant, keen, biting, caustic, pungent, sharp, lively, quick, acute, cutting, piercing, penetrative, incisive, racy, piquant, poignant.
impressive, effective, telling, striking, absorbing, penetrating, pervading; solemn, deep, profound, indelible, deep-felt, heartfelt, soul-stirring, electric, thrilling, rapturous, ecstatic, rapt.
earnest, eager, fervent, fervid, gushing (*colloq.*), warm, passionate, hearty, cordial, sincere, zealous, enthusiastic, glowing, ardent; longing, wistful.
rabid, raving, raging, feverish, fanatical, hysterical, impetuous, zealous.
IV. *Adverbs.* feelingly, sympathetically, compassionately, emotionally, understandingly.
heartily, cordially, willingly, sincerely, earnestly, gladly, *con amore* (*It.*), devoutly, eagerly, zealously, vigorously; with all the heart, with heart and soul, from the bottom of one's heart.
See also EXCITABILITY, PITY, SENSIBILITY, TAKING, TOUCH.—*Antonyms.* See INSENSITIVENESS.

---

feign, *v.* simulate, pretend; counterfeit, sham. See ACTION, UNTRUTH.
felicitous, *adj.* happy, neat, appropriate; well-chosen. See AGREEMENT, ELEGANCE.
fell, *v.* cut, hew, knock down. See HORIZONTALITY.
fellow, *n.* equal, peer; associate, companion; man, boy; student; mate, counterpart. See EQUALITY, FRIEND, MAN, SCHOLAR, SIMILARITY.
fellowship, *n.* companionship, association, intercourse. See FRIENDSHIP.
female, *n.* female person (*or* animal), she. See WOMAN.
feminist, *n.* suffragist, suffragette (*colloq. or cant*). See WOMAN.
fence, *n.* wall, barrier, stockade. See INCLOSURE.
ferment, *n.* disorder, tumult; yeast, leaven. See AGITATION, LEVITY.
ferment, *v.* effervesce, work, raise. See AGITATION, LEVITY.
fermentative, *adj.* yeasty, frothy, fermenting. See LEVITY.
fern-shaped, *adj.* fernlike, filiciform. See SYMMETRY.
ferocity, *n.* cruelty, brutality, savagery. See MALEVOLENCE.
fertile, *adj.* fruitful, teeming, prolific, productive, rich. See PRODUCTIVENESS, SWEETNESS, (*of land*).
fertilization, *n.* fecundation, impregnation, reproduction. See ORGANIZATION.
fertilizer, *n.* dressing, manure, compost, guano. See HUSBANDRY.
fervent, *adj.* ardent, vehement, impassioned, intense, fiery. See FEELING, HEAT.
fervor, *n.* ardor, fire, force, heartiness, vehemence. See DISPOSITION, FEELING.
festival, *n.* fête, feast; anniversary. See CELEBRATION, REGULARITY.
festivity, *n.* gayety, jollity, merrymaking, revelry. See AMUSEMENT.
fetch, *v.* yield, sell for; bring, carry, get. See PRICE, TRANSFER.

FETOR.—I. *Nouns.* fetor, malodor, offensive odor, bad smell, mephitis, stench stink, fume, fumet *or* fumette (*as of game*); foulness, graveolence (*rare*), fetidness, fustiness, mustiness; rancidity.
II. *Verbs.* be fetid, have a bad smell, smell, stink, smell strong, smell offensively
III. *Adjectives.* fetid, stinking, malodorous, smelling, offensive, mephitic noisome, graveolent (*rare*), foul, rank, rotten, putrid, suffocating; strong-smelling high, bad, strong, gamy, rancid, moldy *or* mouldy, tainted, musty.
Antonyms. See FRAGRANCE.

feudalism, *n.* feudal system (*hist.*), vassalage, serfdom. See AUTHORITY.
fever, *n.* feverishness, pyrexia (*med.*). See DISEASE.
feverish, *adj.* restless, excited; hot, flushed, fiery. See EXCITEMENT, HEAT.

FEWNESS.—I. *Nouns.* **fewness,** paucity, scarcity, scantiness, exiguity, sparseness, sparsity, rarity, infrequency; handful, small quantity; minority (*opposite of* majority), the smaller number, the less.
[*diminution of number*] **reduction,** diminution, lessening, thinning, weeding, elimination, decimation; eradication.
II. *Verbs.* **render few,** reduce, diminish, lessen, weed out, eliminate, exclude, thin, decimate.
III. *Adjectives.* **few,** scant, scanty; thin, **rare,** scarce, sparse, few and far between, exiguous, diminutive, infrequent.
See also INFREQUENCY, SMALLNESS.—*Antonyms.* See MULTITUDE.

---

fiber, *n.* thread, strand, tendril, fibril; grain, character. See FILAMENT, TEXTURE.
fickleness, *n.* changeableness, inconstancy. See IRRESOLUTION.
fiction, *n.* story, novel; invention, falsehood. See DESCRIPTION, UNTRUTH.
fidelity, *n.* exactness, accuracy; faithfulness, honesty, loyalty. See IDENTITY, PROBITY, TRUTH.
fidget, *v.* fuss, worry, fret. See EXCITABILITY.
field, *n.* course, ground; sphere, scope, realm; clearing, patch; pasture, meadow; expanse, extent. See ARENA, BUSINESS, HUSBANDRY, PLAIN, SPACE.
fiendish, *adj.* diabolical, devilish, monstrous, demoniacal. See HELL.
fierce, *adj.* grim, bellicose; fiery, fervid, impetuous, vehement; furious, violent, savage, ferocious. See COURAGE, SHARPNESS, VIOLENCE.
fiery, *adj.* vehement, passionate, ardent, impetuous; blazing, flaming; feverish, inflamed. See EXCITABILITY, HEAT, VIOLENCE.
fight, *n.* contest, struggle, strife, battle, combat. See CONTENTION.
fighter, *n.* contender, contestant, warrior, pugilist. See COMBATANT.

FIGURE.—I. *Nouns.* **figure,** numeral, number, digit, cipher, character; price, amount, sum, value: *in this sense,* figure *is colloq.*
form, shape, conformation, configuration, contour, outline, cut, cast, build; person, body, presence; impression, appearance; splendor, magnificence, show.
representation, image, likeness, effigy, symbol, emblem, pattern, design, drawing, diagram; type, representative.
[*in rhetoric*], **figure of speech,** trope, phrase, expression; image, imagery; personification, metaphor, simile, metonymy, synecdoche, catachresis, antonomasia, enallage; satire, irony; allegory, apologue, parable, fable.
II. *Verbs.* **figure,** depict, represent, sketch, delineate, picture, limn, blazon; shape, outline, form, fashion, image; embellish, adorn.
compute, reckon, calculate, numerate, cipher, cast: *in this sense,* figure *is colloq.*
symbolize, typify, emblemize, signify, mean, express; personify, metaphorize (*rare*), allegorize, fable, adumbrate, shadow forth, allude to.
III. *Adjectives.* **figurative,** typical, emblematical, symbolic, descriptive, topical, allusive, pictorial, plastic; **metaphorical,** allegoric *or* allegorical; ironic, ironical, satiric *or* satirical; euphemistic.
[*abounding in figures of speech*] **florid,** flowery, ornate, figured, embellished, showy, ostentatious, rhetorical, high-flown, euphuistic.
See also FORM, NUMBER, PHRASE, PRICE, REPRESENTATION.

FILAMENT.—I. *Nouns.* **filament,** fiber, fibril (*tech.*), hair, cilia (*pl.: biol. and bot.*), capillary, vein, strand, tendril, wire, harl, gossamer, cobweb.
thread, yarn, packthread, twist, linen, cotton.
string, twine, cord, rope, lanyard, braid, gut, wire (*esp. in music*), tape, ribbon; metal thread, wire.
strip, shred, slip, band, fillet, lath, splinter, shaving.
II. *Adjectives.* **filamentous,** threadlike, filamentar *or* filamentary, filar (*as a microscope*), fibrous, fibrillose (*bot.*), filiform, thready, stringy, ropy, wiry, hairy, hairlike, capilliform, capillary.
Antonyms. See LAYER.

file, *n.* catalogue, index, record, orderly collection (*of papers*). See LIST.
file, *v.* record, classify, arrange; march, line. See CONTINUITY, JOURNEY.
filial, *adj.* dutiful, sonlike, daughterly. See POSTERITY.
fill, *v.* hold, occupy; stuff, pack, cram, plug; satisfy, content, sate, satiate; distend, bloat, dilate, inflate; pervade, penetrate; replenish, renew. See BUSINESS, CLOSURE, COMPLETENESS, EXPANSION, PRESENCE, PROVISION.
film, *n.* skin, sheet, covering, membrane. See LAYER.
filth, *n.* vileness, obscenity; filthiness, dirt. See UNCLEANNESS.
final, *adj.* crowning, conclusive, ultimate; last, farthest. See COMPLETION, END.
finally, *adv.* conclusively, ultimately; lastly. See COMPLETION, END, REASONING.
financier, *n.* banker, capitalist. See SUFFICIENCY.
find, *v.* procure, gain; ascertain, discover; meet with, come upon; decide, determine; experience, perceive. See ACQUISITION, DISCOVERY, EVENT, JUDGE, KNOWLEDGE.—**find out,** ascertain, determine, learn, discover, decide, settle. See TAKING.
fine, *n.* mulct, forfeiture, damages, confiscation. See PENALTY.
fine, *v.* penalize, mulct, amerce, sequester. See PENALTY.
fine, *adj.* exquisite, elegant, polished, finished; acute, nice, fastidious; excellent, superior, splendid, admirable, choice, rare; skilled, competent; bright, pleasant; small, slender; tenuous, subtle, thin; sharp, keen; pure, refined; delicate, fine-grained: precise, exact. See BEAUTY, DISCRIMINATION, GOOD, LITTLENESS, RARITY, SHARPNESS, TEXTURE, TRUTH.

FINE ARTS.—I. *Nouns.* [*arts of design*] (1) **painting,** depiction, depicting, drawing, design, composition, treatment, arrangement, values, atmosphere, *chiaroscuro* (*It.*), black and white, notan (*Jap.*); tone, technique; perspective.
style, school; the grand style, high art; *genre* (*F.*), portraiture, landscape (marine, *or* historical) painting, still life; mosaic, fresco, encaustic painting; cubist, futurist, vorticist.
picture, painting, piece, tableau, canvas; fresco, cartoon; drawing, draft *or* draught, sketch, outline, study, daub; oil (*colloq.*), water color.
portrait, likeness, "counterfeit presentment" (*Hamlet*); head; silhouette; profile; miniature.
view, scene, prospect; landscape, *paysage* (*F.*), treescape (*rare*); seascape, sea view, seapiece; interior; panorama, diorama, bird's-eye view.
picture gallery, art gallery, art museum; studio, *atelier* (*F.*).
(2) **sculpture,** carving, modeling, sculpturing, molding, toreutics (*metal work*); statuary, marble, bronze.
statue, figure, piece, cast, bust, torso, statuette, figurina.
relief, relievo, low relief, bas-relief, basso-relievo; high relief, alto-relievo; intaglio, anaglyph, cameo, medallion, medal, celature.
(3) **architecture,** structure, construction, building, architectonics, civil architecture; ecclesiology (*church building and decoration*).
"Fine arts" also include poetry, music, dancing, and dramatic art.
II. *Verbs.* **paint,** design, limn, draw, sketch, pencil (*archaic*), color; daub, wash, stencil, depict; miniate (*as a manuscript*), illuminate, rubricate.
sculpture, carve, chisel, cut, cast, mold, model, sculp (*jocose or colloq.*).
III. *Adjectives.* **pictorial,** graphic, picturesque, delineatory; futurist, cubist, vorticist.
sculptured, carved, etc. (see *verbs*); engraved, glyphic, sculptural; Parian, marmoreal *or* marmorean, marble, marbled.
architectural, structural, constructive, architectonic *or* architectonical.
See also COLOR, ORNAMENT, PRODUCTION, REPRESENTATION.

---

finery, *n.* frippery, gewgaws. See ORNAMENT.
finger, *n.* organ of touch, digit. See TOUCH.
fingerprint, *n.* dactylogram. See INDICATION.
finish, *v.* conclude, end, accomplish, perfect. See COMPLETION.

finish, *n.* goal, conclusion; refinement, shapeliness. See END, SYMMETRY.
finished, *adj.* consummate, faultless; skilled, experienced; shapely, beautiful. See PERFECTION, SKILL, SYMMETRY.
fire, *n.* intensity, animation; flame, blaze, spark. See ENERGY, HEAT.
fire, *v.* shoot, discharge; kindle, light, ignite; animate, arouse, stir; illuminate. See ATTACK, CALEFACTION, EXCITEMENT, LIGHT.—**fire upon,** fire at, shoot at, bombard, shell. See ATTACK.
firearm, *n.* gun, piece, cannon, rifle, musket, etc. See ARMS.
fire eater, hotspur, tartar, pepperpot (*colloq.*), duelist. See IRASCIBILITY.
fire extinguisher, *extincteur* (*F.*); fireman. See REFRIGERATION.
fireplace, *n.* hearth, grate. See FURNACE.
firewood, *n.* kindling, fagots. See FUEL.
firing, *n.* discharge, volley. See ATTACK.
firm, *adj.* rigid, solid; fast, secure; determined, resolved; steadfast, stanch. See HARDNESS, JUNCTION, RESOLUTION, SECURITY, STABILITY.
firm, *n.* concern, house, corporation, partnership, company. See MERCHANT.
first, *adj.* original, foremost, leading, chief, principal. See BEGINNING, IMPORTANCE.
first, *adv.* in the first place, firstly, *imprimis* (*L.*); in preference, sooner, rather. See BEGINNING, CHOICE.
fishes, *n. pl.* Pisces (*L.*). See AMIMAL (*game and food fishes*).
fissure, *n.* rift, crack, split, cleft. See DISJUNCTION.
fit, *adj.* adapted, expedient, suitable, proper, adequate; qualified, capable. See AGREEMENT, RIGHT, SKILL.
fit, *v.* suit, befit; capacitate, enable, prepare, equip. See AGREEMENT, PREPARATION, QUALIFICATION.
fit, *n.* whim, notion; paroxysm, spasm. See CAPRICE, VIOLENCE.
fitness, *n.* aptness, aptitude, relevancy; propriety; capacity, ability, eligibility, competency. See AGREEMENT, DUTY, QUALIFICATION, SUFFICIENCY.

FIVE.—I. *Nouns.* **cinque,** quint (*card playing and music*), quincunx, quintuplet, pentad, fivesome (*Scot.*), quintet *or* quintette (*esp. music*), pentagon (*geom.*), pentameter (*pros.*), pentathlon (*athletics*); star, pentacle, pentalpha, pentagram, mullet (*heraldry*); estoile (*heraldry*); Pentateuch (*Bible*).
II. *Verbs.* multiply by five, make fivefold, quintuple, quintuplicate (*rare*).
III. *Adjectives.* **fivefold,** quintuple, quincuncial (*esp. bot.*), pentad (*chem.*), pentavalent (*chem.*), pentangular, pentagonal (*geom.*).

---

fix, *v.* arrange, dispose, adjust; fasten, attach; establish, place; conclude, decide, determine; settle, stabilize. See ARRANGEMENT, JUNCTION, LOCATION, RESOLUTION, STABILITY.—**fix the time,** record, chronicle, mark, register. See CHRONOMETRY.
fixed idea, delusion, monomania, *idée fixe* (*F.*). See EXCITABILITY.
flabby, *adj.* limp, flaccid. See SOFTNESS.
flaccid, *adj.* inelastic, flabby, limp; lax, unstrung. See INELASTICITY, SOFTNESS.
flag, *n.* banner, pennant, streamer. See INDICATION.
flag, *v.* fail, decline, languish, droop, lag. See WEAKNESS.
flagrant, *adj.* glaring, obvious; villainous, atrocious. See MANIFESTATION, VICE.
flame, *n.* fever, excitement, passion; blaze, fire; brightness, glow. See EXCITABILITY, HEAT, LIGHT.
flank, *v.* skirt, wing, border. See SIDE.
flap, *n.* lug, leaf, hanging piece; stroke, dab. See ADJUNCT, IMPULSE.
flap, *v.* flutter, oscillate, beat the wings; strike, slap. See AGITATION, IMPULSE.
flash, *v.* gleam, glitter, glisten. scintillate; snap (*as the eyes*); flare, discharge, burst. See LIGHT, SNAP, VIOLENCE.
flashy, *adj.* showy, garish, gaudy, tawdry. See COLOR.

[1]**flat**, *n.* stretch, lowland, level, expanse; shoal, shallow, morass. See PLAIN, SHALLOWNESS.
[2]**flat**, *n.* apartment, suite, floor. See HABITATION.

FLATNESS.—I. *Nouns.* **flatness,** levelness, smoothness, etc. (see *adjectives*).
plane, level (*or* flat) surface, even superficies, grade, level, stratum; plate, table, tablet, slab.
II. *Verbs.* **flatten,** level, smooth, plane, even, flat (*used chiefly in manufacturing processes*); throw down, fell, prostrate, squelch, squash; depress, deject.
III. *Adjectives.* **flat,** level, smooth, unbroken, plane, homaloid *or* homaloidal (*math.*), even, flush, horizontal; recumbent, supine, prostrate, flattened, complanate, oblate (*geom.*).
[*in music*] below pitch, minor, lower (*as, to sing* flat): *opposite of* sharp.
[*in phonetics*] **voiced,** sonant, intonated, vocal, tonic: *distinguished from* sharp *or* voiceless.
[*of pneumatic tires*] deflated.
[*laid low*] **fallen,** overthrown, destroyed, defeated, ruined, prostrate, powerless.
[*lacking interest*] **uninteresting,** monotonous, dull, insipid, tasteless, unsavory, unpalatable, lifeless, spiritless, vapid, tame, characterless, pointless; inactive, sluggish (*as, a* flat *market*); unglazed, unglossed (*as a painting*).
[*without qualification*] **positive,** unqualified, downright, absolute, peremptory, clear, plain, thorough, direct (*as, a* flat *refusal*); unvarying (*as, a* flat *rate*).
IV. *Adverbs.* **flat,** flatly, flatways *or* flatwise, lengthwise, horizontally.
[*without excess*] **exactly,** absolutely, literally, precisely (*as, ten seconds* flat).
See also DULLNESS, HORIZONTALITY, INSIPIDITY, LETTER (*voiced*), LOWNESS MUSIC, SMOOTHNESS, WATER (*weak*).—*Antonyms.* See CONCAVITY, CONVEXITY

---

flatter, *v.* compliment, cajole, soft-soap (*colloq.*), blarney. See FLATTERY, OIL

FLATTERER.—*Nouns.* **flatterer,** adulator, eulogist, laudator, encomiast, *prôneur* (*F.*), puffer, booster (*colloq.*), whitewasher; optimist.
toady, cringer, truckler, bootlicker (*slang or colloq.*), fawner, toadeater, lick-spit *or* lick-spittle, sycophant, parasite, hanger-on, tufthunter, pickthank (*archaic*).
Antonyms. See DETRACTOR.

FLATTERY.—I. *Nouns.* **flattery,** adulation, cajolery, blandishment, fawning, wheedling, obsequiousness, sycophancy, flunkeyism, toadyism, tufthunting. honeyed words, flummery, buncombe (*cant or slang*); blarney (*colloq.*), palaver, soft sawder (*slang*), soft soap (*colloq.*), butter (*colloq.*), jollying (*colloq.*), apple sauce (*slang*).
II. *Verbs.* **flatter,** overpraise, puff, wheedle, cajole, fawn upon, humor, pet, coquet, honey, soft-soap (*colloq.*), butter (*colloq.*), jolly (*colloq.*); truckle to, pander to, court; curry favor with, ingratiate oneself with, insinuate, fool to the top of one's bent.
III. *Adjectives.* **flattering,** adulatory, mealy-mouthed, honeyed, candied, smooth, smooth-tongued, oily, buttery (*colloq.*), unctuous, specious, plausible, servile, sycophantic, fulsome.
See also DECEPTION, PLEASURABLENESS.—*Antonyms.* See DETRACTION.

---

flatulence, *n.* windiness, gas; eructation. See WIND.
flaunt, *v.* brandish, display, blazon forth. See OSTENTATION.
flavor, *n.* relish, savor. See TASTE.
flaw, *n.* defect, fault, imperfection, spot; fissure, crack, break. See BLEMISH, INTERVAL.
flee, *v.* run, fly, avoid. See ESCAPE.
fleece, *v.* strip, despoil, rob, defraud. See TAKING.
fleet, *n.* navy, flotilla, squadron. See COMBATANT, SHIP.
fleet, *adj.* fleeting, brief, evanescent; swift, fast. See TRANSIENCE, VELOCITY.
flesh, *n.* muscular tissue, meat, pulp; man, humanity. See ANIMAL LIFE, FOOD, MANKIND.
flexible, *adj.* pliant, plastic, pliable, limber. See SOFTNESS.

flicker, *v.* gutter, glimmer; waver, flutter, quiver. See LIGHT, OSCILLATION.
flight, *n.* volley (*as of arrows*); departure, leaving, hegira, exodus. See ASSEMBLAGE, ESCAPE.
flighty, *adj.* extravagant, giddy, volatile, fickle. See CAPRICE.
flimsy, *adj.* slight, thin, unsubstantial; superficial, trivial, shallow. See UNIMPORTANCE, WEAKNESS.
flinch, *v.* wince, shrink, draw back. See FEAR.
fling, *v.* hurl, cast, pitch, heave. See PROPULSION.
flippant, *adj.* pert, trifling, impudent, impertinent. See INSOLENCE.
flirt, *n.* coquette; philanderer. See ENDEARMENT.
flit, *v.* leave, move; fly, speed, dart. See DEPARTURE, TRANSCIENCE.
float, *v.* drift, sail. See NAVIGATION.
flock, *n.* herd, pack, drove, multitude, company. See ASSEMBLAGE.
flog, *v.* beat, whip, strike, lash. See PUNISHMENT.
flood, *n.* downpour, deluge, inundation. See RIVER.
floor, *n.* pavement, flooring; stage, platform. See BASE, SUPPORT.
florid, *adj.* flowery, ornate, embellished, brilliant; flushed, high-colored. See FIGURE, MUSIC, RED.
flounder, *v.* welter, wallow; bungle, blunder, come to grief; hesitate, falter. See AGITATION, FAILURE, UNCERTAINTY.
flourish, *v.* brandish, wield; vaunt, strut; thrive, bloom, rise, prosper. See AGITATION, BOASTING, PROSPERITY.
flow, *v.* issue, emanate; run, glide. See EGRESS, MOTION, RIVER.
flower, *n.* pick, best; rosette, floral design; blossom, bloom. See CHOICE, ORNAMENT, VEGETABLE.—**flower of life,** flower of youth, springtide of life. See YOUTH.
flowery, *adj.* florid, embellished, ornate; blossomy, floral. See FIGURE, VEGETABLE.
flowing, *adj.* fluent, meandering, fluvial, streaming. See RIVER.
fluctuate, *v.* vacillate, waver, oscillate. See CHANGEABLENESS.
fluency, *n.* eloquence, volubility, loquaciousness. See LOQUACITY, ROTUNDITY.
fluent, *adj.* flowing, glib, ready, easy, voluble, eloquent, smooth. See FLUIDITY, LOQUACITY, SMOOTHNESS.

FLUIDITY.—I. *Nouns.* **fluidity,** liquidity, liquidness, fluidification, liquefaction, solubility: *opposite of* solidity.
[*lack of fixedness*] **instability,** changeableness, changeability, inconstancy, unstableness, fickleness, insecurity.
fluid, liquid; juice, sap, latex, lymph, chyle, rheum; gas (*compressible fluid*); solution, decoction.
blood, ichor (*Gr. myth.*), gore, claret (*slang*), cruor (*physiol.*), grume.
science of liquids at rest: hydrostatics, hydrodynamics, hydrokinetics; serology (*serums*).
II. *Verbs.* **fluidify,** fluidize, liquefy, render fluid; gasify.
III. *Adjectives.* **fluid,** liquid, flowing, fluent (*rare in literal sense*); soluble, liquefied, uncongealed; serous, sanious (*med.*), watery, ichorous, rheumy; sappy, juicy, succulent.
[*of speech, etc.*] **fluent,** flowing, easy, glib, facile, voluble.
See also GASEITY, LIQUEFACTION, RIVER (*fluids in motion*).—*Antonyms.* See DENSITY, STABILITY.

---

flurry, *n.* agitation, confusion, commotion, fluster; squall, gust. See EXCITABILITY, WIND.
flurry, *v.* excite, confuse, fluster, disconcert. See AGITATION.
flush, *v.* wash, drain, cleanse; glow, color, crimson, blush. See CLEANNESS, RED.
flush, *n.* glow, tinge; excitement, thrill; fever, redness, blush. See COLOR, FEELING, HEAT.

flute, *n.* groove, channel; fife, pipe. See FURROW, MUSICAL INSTRUMENTS.
flutter, *v.* waver, vacillate, vibrate; shake, quiver, tremble, palpitate. See CHANGEABLENESS, FEELING.
fly, *v.* soar, aviate; flutter, wave, float; shoot, scatter; flee, run, shun; flit, vanish; rush, dart; burst, explode. See AËRONAUTICS, AGITATION, DIVERGENCE, ESCAPE, TRANSIENCE, VELOCITY, VIOLENCE.
flyer, *n.* aviator, airman; venture; leaflet, handbill. See AËRONAUT, EXPERIMENT, PUBLICATION.

FOAM.—I. *Nouns.* **foam,** froth, spume, scum, head, cream, lather, suds (*colloq.*), yeast; surf, spray.
bubble, globule, bleb, vesicle, bulla (*med.*), blister, bladder.
effervescence, bubbling, ebullience *or* ebulliency, ebullition, fermentation; evaporation; aëration.
II. *Verbs.* **foam,** spume, froth, scum, head, cream, mantle.
effervesce, bubble, bead, hiss, boil, ferment, fizz, gurgle, sparkle; aërate.
III. *Adjectives.* **foamy,** frothy, spumous, spumescent, foaming, spumy, scummy, creamy, yeasty, lathery.
effervescent, bubbling, sparkling, *mousseux* (*F.*), fizzy, heady, up (*colloq.*); ebullient, boiling, intumescent.
See also AGITATION.—*Antonyms.* See SEMILIQUIDITY.

FOCUS.—I. *Nouns.* **focus,** center *or* centre, central point, core, nucleus; gathering place, rendezvous, rallying point, headquarters, resort, haunt, retreat, club; tryst, trysting place, place of meeting, *point de réunion* (*F.*).
II. *Verbs.* **focus,** center *or* centre, focalize, bring to a focus (*or* point), concentrate, converge, concenter *or* concentre, nucleate, corradiate (*rare*); rally, meet.
III. *Adjectives.* **focal,** central, pivotal, nuclear, concentrative.
See also CENTRALITY, CONVERGENCE.—*Antonyms.* See DISPERSION.

---

foe, *n.* adversary, opponent. See ENEMY.
fog, *n.* vapor, mist; obscurity, vagueness. See CLOUD, UNCERTAINTY.
foil, *v.* frustrate, balk, defeat, baffle, thwart. See HINDRANCE.
foil, *n.* contrast, set-off. See CONTRARIETY.

FOLD.—I. *Nouns.* **fold,** doubling, folding, double, plication, plicature, plica, bend, coil, lap, ply; syncline (*geol.*), isocline (*geol.*); crease, flexure, pleat, plait. tuck, gather; joint, elbow; crinkle, crumple, cockle, corrugation, furrow, dog's-ear; ruffle, flounce; wrinkle, pucker, crow's-feet.
II. *Verbs.* **fold,** double, plicate, lap, gather, pleat, plait, crease, wrinkle, knit (*as the brow*), contract, cocker, crinkle, curl, shrivel, rumple, corrugate, ruffle crumple, pucker; tuck, ruck, hem, gather; turn, wrap, infold, dog's-ear.
embrace, infold, envelop, clasp, entwine, interlace, wind round (*or* about), clutch, seize, inclasp, hug, embosom, inwrap, swathe.
III. *Adjectives.* **folded,** double, lapped, plaited, creased, etc. (see *verbs*); plicate (*tech.*), pliciferous (*tech.*).
Antonyms. See SMOOTHNESS, UNFOLDMENT.

---

fold, *n.* inclosure, pen; flock, congregation, church. See INCLOSURE, LAITY.
foliage, *n.* leafage, leaves. See VEGETABLE.
folk, *n.* people, nationality, tribe. See MANKIND.

FOLLOWING.—I. *Nouns.* **following,** followers, clientage, clientele, adherents, sequela (*rare*), dependents, retinue, train, attendance.
sequence, succession, run (*as in card playing*), series, order.
follower, attendant, adherent, disciple, proselyte, partisan, sectary, client; sycophant, parasite, satellite, dangler; pursuer, shadow, tail (*slang*), heeler; beau (*esp. of a maidservant*); successor, heir.
II. *Verbs.* **follow,** go after, attend, accompany, serve, dance attendance on; dog, shadow, hang on the skirts of, camp on the trail, trail, trace, hunt, chase, pursue; strive after, aim at, seek, court, woo.

succeed, come after, take the place of; ensue, result, be subsequent to.
copy, imitate, echo, ape, mimic, emulate, duplicate, borrow, adopt, accept.
heed, attend, notice, mind, observe, note, regard, watch; grasp, comprehend, understand, catch.
lag, loiter, linger, fall behind, saunter, tarry.
III. *Adjectives.* **following,** succeeding, next after, ensuing, consecutive, successive; consequent, consequential, sequential, sequent.
IV. *Adverbs.* **behind,** in the rear, after, subsequently, afterward, later than; in arrears, behindhand.

See also DEMONSTRATION, POSTERIORITY, PURSUIT, SEQUENCE, SERVANT, SUCCESS (*succeed*).—*Antonyms.* See PRECESSION.

FOLLY.—I. *Nouns.* **folly,** foolishness, fatuousness, fatuity, inanity, senselessness, unwisdom, irrationality, frivolity, levity, foolery, absurdity, trifling, ineptitude, giddiness, rashness, infatuation, extravagance, madness, eccentricity, inconsistency.
II. *Adjectives.* **foolish,** silly, fond (*archaic*), senseless, insensate, witless, brainless, shallow-brained, shallow; impolitic, unwise, nonsensical, imprudent, misguided, ill-advised, injudicious, inexpedient, indiscreet, unwary, incautious, inconsistent, improper, unreasonable, irrational, extravagant; fatuous, weak, idiotic, imbecile, stupid, inane, absurd, ridiculous, laughable, asinine; trivial, frivolous, useless, vain.

See also IMBECILITY.—*Antonyms.* See WISDOM.

---

fond, *adj.* affectionate, loving, tender; doting, indulgent. See LOVE, PART (*partial.*).
fondness, *n.* relish, liking, predilection. See DESIRE.

FOOD.—I. *Nouns.* **food,** nourishment, nutriment, sustenance, pabulum (*esp. food for the mind*), support, keep, nurture, subsistence; provender, corn, feed, feedstuff, fodder; provision, ration, board, commissariat; prey, forage, pasture, pasturage; fare, cheer; diet, dietary; regimen; staff of life, bread.
eatables, victuals (*esp. prepared food*), viands, comestibles, foodstuffs, edibles, grub (*slang*), eats (*colloq.*), flesh, roast, meat, dainties, delicacies; creature comforts, ambrosia, manna; good cheer, good living, high living, the fleshpots.
biscuit, cracker, pretzel, rusk, cracknel; hard-tack, sea biscuit, ship bread, ship biscuit.
eating, consumption, deglutition, devouring, devourment, mastication, rumination; epicurism, gastronomy; carnivorousness, gluttony; vegetarianism.
mouth, jaws, mandible (*esp. of birds*), maxilla (*zoöl.*), chops, gab (*Scot.*), gob (*dial. or vulgar*).
drinking, potation, draft *or* draught, libation; carousal, compotation, drunkenness.
table, cuisine, bill of fare, menu, *table d'hôte* (*F.*), *à la carte* (*F.*).
meal, repast, feed (*colloq.*), spread (*colloq.*); mess; course, dish, *plat* (*F.*), plate; refreshment, entertainment; refection, collation, picnic, feast, banquet, junket; potluck; chota hazri (*Anglo-Indian*), breakfast, *déjeuner* (*F.*), lunch, luncheon, tiffin (*Anglo-Indian*); tea, afternoon tea; dinner, supper.
mouthful, morsel, bite, sop, snack; titbit *or* tidbit, kickshaw.
drink, beverage, liquor, potion, dram, draft *or* draught.
restaurant, café, coffee house, chophouse, eating house, lunch room, cafeteria, automat, one-arm joint (*slang*).
II. *Verbs.* **feed,** nourish, sustain, foster, nurture, strengthen, satisfy, gratify; supply (*as with food*), deal out; graze (*cattle*).
eat, feed, fare, devour, swallow, consume, take; fall to, tuck in (*slang*), dine, refresh the inner man (*jocose*), banquet, feast; gormandize, gluttonize, bolt, dispatch, gulp; crunch, chew, masticate; peck (*colloq.*), nibble, gnaw, mumble.
live on, batten (*or* feast) upon; browse, graze, crop; bite, champ, munch, ruminate.
drink, quaff, sip, sup; lap; tipple, swig (*colloq.*), toss off, wet one's whistle (*colloq.*), guzzle, carouse.

III. *Adjectives.* **eatable,** edible, esculent, comestible, dietetic; culinary; nutritive, nutritious, alimentary; succulent.
underdone, rare, *saignant* (*F.*); well-done, *bien cuit* (*F.*); overdone; high (*of game*); ripe (*of cheese*).
drinkable, potable, potatory (*rare*); bibulous.
omnivorous, pantophagous (*rare*); carnivorous, flesh-eating, omophagous, omophagic, zoöphagous (*rare*), cannibal, predaceous; herbivorous, graminivorous, granivorous, phytivorous, phytophagous.

See also AMUSEMENT, DRUNKENNESS, GLUTTONY, PROVISION, VEGETABLE (*food plants*).—*Antonyms.* See EXCRETION, FASTING.

FOOL.—I. *Nouns.* **fool,** idiot, tomfool, wiseacre, witling, stupid, dunce, half-wit, simpleton, Simple Simon; donkey, ass, dolt, booby, noodle, imbecile, nincompoop (*colloq.*), oaf, blockhead, bonehead (*slang*), calf (*colloq.*), colt, mooncalf, gawk, numskull (*colloq.*), clod, clodhopper, rube (*U. S. slang*); lubber, lout, soft *or* softy (*colloq. or slang*), sap *or* saphead (*slang*), simp (*slang*), juggins (*slang*), owl, goose, gander, jay (*slang*), chump (*slang*), blockhead, lunkhead (*slang*); dotard, driveler; men of Bœotia, wise men of Gotham.
dupe, butt, victim, gull (*as, to make a* fool *of*).
buffoon, jester, clown, antic, merry-andrew, harlequin, punchinello, punch, pierrot, Scaramouch.
II. *Verbs.* **fool,** trifle, play the fool, idle, play, toy, jest, act like a fool.
dupe, deceive, befool, delude, gull, kid (*slang*), bamboozle, humbug, hoax, bluff; cheat, do (*slang*), bilk, diddle (*slang*), trick, best, flimflam (*both colloq.*).

See also BUNGLER, DECEPTION, DUPE, FOLLY, IGNORAMUS.—*Antonyms.* See SAGE.

---

foolhardy, *adj.* reckless, dare-devil, venturesome. See RASHNESS.
foolish, *adj.* nonsensical, laughable, absurd; unwise, indiscreet; silly, senseless, simple, imbecile. See ABSURDITY, FOLLY, SIMPLENESS.
foot, *n.* bottom, sole, hoof, paw; infantry. See BASE, COMBATANT.
footing, *n.* condition, situation, status, standing; foothold, purchase, support. See CIRCUMSTANCE, INFLUENCE.
footpath, *n.* path, walk, pathway, towpath, trial. See WAY.
footprint, *n.* track, trial, step. See INDICATION.
foot soldier, infantryman, rifleman, infantry. (*pl.*). See COMBATANT.

FOP.—I. *Nouns.* **fop,** dandy, swell (*colloq.*), toff (*Brit. slang*), exquisite, coxcomb, dude (*colloq.*), beau, buck (*archaic*), blade, dasher (*colloq.*), man about town, spark, popinjay, puppy (*contemptuous*), prig, jackanapes, jack-a-dandy, *petit maître* (*F.*), man milliner, carpet knight.
foppery, dandyism, coxcombry, foppishness, dudishness, dudism, exquisitism (*rare*).
II. *Adjectives.* **foppish,** foplike, dandyish, dapper, spruce, smart, dandified, coxcombical, vain.

See also AFFECTATION, OSTENTATION.—*Antonyms.* See DISORDER (*sloven*).

---

forbid, *v.* prohibit, restrain, ban, veto. See PROHIBITION.
force, *n.* army, host, array, troops, soldiery; emphasis, cogency; energy, strength, might; compulsion, constraint. See COMBATANT, MEANING, POWER, VIOLENCE.
forceful, *adj.* effective, telling, graphic, vivid. See VIGOR.
forcible, *adj.* weighty, forceful, convincing, powerful; vehement, violent, unrestrained; effective, telling, irresistible. See POWER, STRENGTH, VIGOR.
forcibly, *adv.* necessarily, perforce, by force. See COMPULSION.
fore, *adj.* foremost, headmost, anterior. See FRONT.
foreboding, *n.* apprehension, dread, presentiment, premonition. See FORESIGHT.
forecast, *v.* foretell, prophesy; project, design; augur, portend, signify. See FORESIGHT, PLAN, PREDICTION.
forefathers, *n. pl.* ancestors, forbears. See PATERNITY, VETERAN.

foregoing, *adj.* preceding, antecedent, former: *in time or place.* See PAST.
foreign, *adj.* alien, outlandish, exotic; irrelevant, inapplicable, remote. See EXTRANEOUSNESS, IRRELATION.
foreigner, *n.* alien, stranger, immigrant; outsider. See EXTRANEOUSNESS.
foremost, *adj.* initial, first; forward, fore; principal, chief, high (*as,* high *priest*), leading. See BEGINNING, HEIGHT, IMPORTANCE.
forerunner, *n.* announcer, harbinger, predecessor. See PRECURSOR.

FORESIGHT.—I. *Nouns.* **foresight,** prevision, foreknowledge, prescience, prenotion, preconception, precognition, prospect, anticipation, premeditation; prudence, sagacity, forethought, providence, longsightedness, farsightedness; shrewdness.
foreboding (*esp. of coming evil*), presentiment, premonition, presage, portent, prediction, forecast, omen, prognostic, boding, apprehension; second sight, clairvoyance.
II. *Verbs.* **foresee,** foreknow, anticipate, expect, contemplate, surmise; look forward to, look ahead (*or* beyond), see one's way; see how the land lies.
forecast, predict, prognosticate, augur, divine, forebode, foretell, prophesy, presage, portend, look into the future; warn, forewarn.
III. *Adjectives.* **foresighted,** prudent, discreet, judicious, circumspect, careful, sensible, wise, sagacious, watchful, provident.
foreseeing, prescient, anticipatory; farseeing, farsighted, longsighted; weatherwise; prospective; expectant.
See also EXPECTATION, FUTURE.—*Antonyms.* See NONEXPECTATION.

---

forest, *n.* wood, timberland, woodland. See VEGETABLE.
foretell, *v.* prophesy, predict, augur, portend, presage. See PREDICTION.
forethought, *n.* prudence, anticipation, premeditation, providence. See FORESIGHT.
forever, *adv.* always, eternally, constantly, incessantly, everlastingly, endlessly. See PERPETUITY.
forfeit, *n.* fine, forfeiture. See PENALTY.
forge, *v.* make, fabricate, devise; falsify, counterfeit. See FORM, STEALING.
forger, *n.* falsifier, counterfeiter, coiner. See THIEF.
forget, *v.* overlook, omit, disregard; be forgetful, obliterate. See NEGLECT, OBLIVION.
forgetful, *adj.* heedless, oblivious, neglectful. See OBLIVION.

FORGIVENESS.—I. *Nouns.* **forgiveness,** pardon, condonation, grace, remission, amnesty, oblivion; reprieve.
conciliation, reconciliation, pacification, appeasement, satisfaction, mollification, forbearance, propitiation.
excuse, acquittal, dispensation, absolution, release, quittance, indemnity; exoneration, exculpation, extenuation, justification, apology, essoin (*law*).
II. *Verbs.* **forgive,** pardon, remit, absolve, release, excuse, overlook, condone, wink at, pass over; acquit; reprieve, exonerate, clear, exculpate, justify, extenuate; think no more of, let bygones be bygones, bear with, allow for, make allowances for; pocket the affront, bury the hatchet, start afresh; give absolution; blot out one's sins (offenses, *or* transgressions), wipe the slate clean.
conciliate. propitiate, appease, reconcile, pacify, placate, mollify, satisfy; beg (*or* ask) pardon, make up a quarrel.
III. *Adjectives.* **forgiving,** placable, merciful, compassionate, clement, magnanimous, generous, conciliatory.
See also ACQUITTAL, PACIFICATION, VINDICATION.—*Antonyms.* See REVENGE.

---

forgotten, *adj.* unremembered, buried, lost. See OBLIVION, PAST.
fork, *v.* branch, ramify, diverge, divide. See ANGULARITY.
forlorn, *adj.* wretched, dismal; desolate, deserted, abandoned; desperate, hopeless. See DEJECTION, EXCLUSION, HOPELESSNESS.

FORM.—I. *Nouns.* **form,** figure, shape, make, formation, conformation, galbe (*F.: art*), format, get-up (*colloq.*), configuration, contour, outline, cut, build, cut of one's jib, set, frame, construction, stamp, type, cast, turn, mold, impression, pattern, fashion; structure, constitution, sculpture, architecture.
feature, outward appearance, lineament, phase, aspect, characteristic; posture, attitude, pose: *in this sense,* form *is archaic.*
body, person, figure, individual, fellow, being, creature, presence.
variety, kind, sort, species, genus, class, *genre* (*F.*), type, character, description, denomination, brand, race, color; manifestation.
mode, manner, way, method, style, fashion, procedure.
order, orderliness, arrangement, disposition, system, systematization, regularity, symmetry, harmony.
formality, ceremony, ceremonial, rite, ritual, punctilio, stiffness, precision, conventionality, etiquette; behavior, conduct, deportment.
condition (*esp. of health and training*), fitness, trim (*colloq.*), fettle, state, kilter (*colloq.*), shape (*as, in* form).
bench, long seat, settle, settee.
[*in English secondary schools*] class, grade, rank (*as, the sixth* form).
II. *Verbs.* **form,** shape, figure, fashion, carve, sculpture, cut, chisel, hew roughhew, sketch, block out; trim, model, knead, mold, pattern, cast, stamp, mint; build, construct, erect.
make, perform, do, achieve, devise, contrive, produce, effect, manufacture, constitute, establish, create, invent, forge, compose, conceive, prepare; organize, embody; arrange, adjust
contract (*as a habit*), acquire, develop, engender, beget, produce, incur.
[*to mold by discipline*] **train,** instruct, teach, drill, exercise, discipline, advance, expand, unfold.
III. *Adjectives.* **formal,** conventional, ceremonious, punctilious, ceremonial, ritualistic, liturgical; modal, perfunctory, outward, external, set.
precise, stiff, buckram, starched, prim, exact, rigid, unbending, inflexible, uncompromising, Procrustean; methodical, regular, orderly.
essential, constitutional, vital, inward, constituent, indispensable; apparent, manifest.
formative, plastic, formable, fictile, moldable, procreative, creative; impressible, sensitive, susceptible, impressionable, pliant, supple.
[*in biology*] plasmatic *or* plasmic, protoplasmic, plastic, metabolic.

See also ARRANGEMENT, COMPONENT, DRYNESS (*fine arts*), FASHION, FIGURE, ORDER, ORGANIZATION, OSTENTATION, PRODUCTION, WAY.—*Antonyms.* See FORMLESSNESS.

---

formation, *n.* structure, make-up; shape, conformation; creation, establishment. See COMPOSITION, FORM, PRODUCTION.
former, *adj.* earlier, foregoing, previous, antecedent. See PAST, PRIORITY.
formerly, *adv.* heretofore, previously, of old. See PAST.
formidable, *adj.* fearful, appalling, threatening. See FEAR.

FORMLESSNESS.—I. *Nouns.* **formlessness,** amorphism, amorphousness, shapelessness, misproportion, irregularity, deformity; disfigurement, defacement; mutilation.
II. *Verbs.* [*destroy form*] **deface,** disfigure, deform, mutilate, truncate, hack, foul, maim, derange, blemish, mar, scar.
III. *Adjectives.* **formless,** shapeless, amorphous, inform, unshapely, misshapen, unsymmetrical, asymmetric *or* asymmetrical, malformed, unformed, unhewn, unfashioned, unshapen; anomalous.
rough, rude, barbarous, craggy, coarse, uneven, rugged, scraggy.

See also DISTORTION.—*Antonyms.* See FORM, SYMMETRY.

---

formulate, *v.* express, state, embody. See SPECIALTY.
forsake, *v.* desert, abandon; renounce, drop. See RELINQUISHMENT.
fort, *n.* fortification, fortress. See DEFENSE.

fortify, *v.* corroborate, confirm, strengthen, brace, reënforce. See EVIDENCE, STRENGTH.
fortitude, *n.* endurance, firmness, hardihood. See COURAGE.
fortunate, *adj.* lucky, successful; auspicious, favorable. See PROSPERITY, TIMELINESS.
fortune, *n.* luck, accident; lot, fate; riches, means. See CHANCE, DESTINY, WEALTH.
forward, *adj.* ready, prompt; anterior, fore; bold, impudent, presumptuous; onward, advancing; extreme, radical, advanced. See EARLINESS, FRONT, INSOLENCE, PROGRESSION, REVOLUTION.
forward, *v.* advance, promote; transmit, send. See AID, TRANSFER.
fossil, *n.* remains, organic remains. See ORGANIZATION.
foster, *v.* nourish, rear; support, promote. See AID.
foul, *adj.* tainted, putrid; dishonorable, low, unfair; obscene, scurrilous; filthy, loathsome, odious, vile, hateful; stormy, dirty. See BADNESS, IMPROBITY, IMPURITY, UNCLEANNESS, WIND.
found, *v.* originate, institute; establish, settle, fix. See CAUSE, LOCATION.
foundation, *n.* groundwork, support; basis, reason. See BASE, CAUSE.
founder, *n.* originator, establisher, institutor. See PRODUCER.
founder, *v.* fall, stumble; flounder, collapse, fail; welter, swamp, sink. See DESCENT, FAILURE, PLUNGE.
fountain, *n.* origin, source; spring, fount. See CAUSE, RIVER.

FOUR.—I. *Nouns.* **four,** tetrad, quaternion, quadruplet, quaternary, quaternity (*rare*); square, foursquare, quadrate, quadrilateral; quadrangle, tetragon; quartet *or* quartette (*esp. music*), foursome (*golf*); quatrain (*prosody*), quarto.
II. *Verbs.* **square,** quadrate, reduce to a square.
III. *Adjectives.* **four,** quartile (*tech.*), quadric (*tech.*); square, foursquare, quadrangular, quadrilateral, tetragonal; quadratic, tetradic (*tech.*), quaternal (*rare*), quaternary.
See also QUADRISECTION, QUADRUPLICATION.

---

fourfold, *adj.* quadruple. See QUADRUPLICATION.
four-sided, *adj.* quadrilateral, tetrahedral (*tech.*). See SIDE.
fowl, *n.* bird, hen, rooster. See ANIMAL.
fox, *n.* reynard, tod, vixen (*fem.*). See ANIMAL.

FRACTION.—I. *Nouns.* **fraction,** fractional part; part, portion, fragment, scrap; breaking, division (*as of the bread in the Eucharist*).
II. *Verbs.* **fraction,** separate (*as by distillation*), fractionate, fractionize.
III. *Adjectives.* **fractional,** partial, portional (*rare*), fragmentary.
insignificant, small, inconsiderable, trivial, trifling, unimportant, petty, paltry, picayune *or* picayunish (*U. S. colloq.*).
See also PART.—*Antonyms.* See PLURALITY, UNITY, WHOLE.

---

fracture, *n.* rupture, breach, break, crack, fissure. See DISJUNCTION.
fragile, *adj.* frail, brittle; delicate, feeble. See BRITTLENESS, WEAKNESS.
fragment, *n.* portion, piece, particle, fraction. See PART.

FRAGRANCE.—I. *Nouns.* **fragrance,** aroma, redolence, perfume, bouquet; sweet smell (*or* odor), scent, nosegay (*rare in this sense*).
perfumery, perfumes, scents; incense, frankincense; musk, myrrh, attar, bergamot, balm, civet, potpourri, tuberose, hyacinth, heliotrope, rose, jasmine, lily, lily of the valley, violet, sweet pea, carnation; toilet water, cologne, *eau de cologne* (*F.*), cologne water; smelling salts; joss stick.
nosegay, bouquet, posy (*archaic or colloq.*), *boutonnière* (*F.*), buttonhole (*colloq.*); boughpot; spray, wreath, garland, chaplet, festoon.
[*containers*] smelling bottle, scent bottle, vinaigrette; atomizer, spray; scent bag, sachet; thurible (*eccl.*), censer, incense burner.

II. *Verbs.* **be fragrant,** etc. (see *adjectives*); have a perfume (*or* aroma); smell sweet, scent, perfume, embalm (*rare in this sense*).
III. *Adjectives.* **fragrant,** aromatic, redolent, spicy, balmy, scented, olent (*rare*), sweet-smelling, sweet-scented, perfumed, perfumy, odorous; incense-breathing, ambrosial.
See also SWEETNESS.—*Antonyms.* See FETOR.

---

frail, *adj.* brittle, fragile; lax, loose, dissolute; infirm, feeble. See BRITTLENESS, VICE, WEAKNESS.
frame, *v.* devise, invent; fashion, make, construct. See PLAN, PRODUCTION.
frame, *n.* border; shape, build; mood, condition; framework, skeleton. See EDGE, FORM, STATE, SUPPORT.
franchise, *n.* right, privilege, prerogative. See FREEDOM.
frank, *adj.* ingenuous, artless, free, open, outspoken, unreserved, honest, straightforward, direct, sincere, candid, transparent. See ARTLESSNESS, FREEDOM, OPENING, TRANSPARENCY.
frankness, *n.* candor, directness, openness. See ARTLESSNESS, FREEDOM, TRANSPARENCY.
frantic, *adj.* distracted, raving, frenzied, mad. See EXCITEMENT.
fraternity, *n.* brotherhood; club, society. See CONSANGUINITY, FRIENDSHIP, ORDER.
fraternize, *v.* associate, club, federate; mix with, consort with. See COMBINATION, SOCIALITY.
fraud, *n.* deceit, trickery; stratagem, trick. See DECEPTION.
freak, *n.* whim, vagary; monstrosity. See CAPRICE, UNCONFORMITY.

FREEDOM.—I. *Nouns.* **freedom,** liberty, independence; emancipation, liberation, release, manumission, enlargement; immunity, enfranchisement, exemption, franchise, privilege, prerogative, right.
scope, range, latitude, play, free play (*or* scope), swing, full swing, elbowroom, margin, rope, wide berth; liberty of action, unrestricted use; Liberty Hall.
frankness, candor, openness, ingenuousness, outspokenness, downrightness, unreservedness, directness.
ease (*in action*), facility, unembarrassment, unconstraint, naturalness.
boldness (*as of conception*), vigorousness, daring, powerfulness, strikingness.
familiarity, undue liberty, unceremoniousness, overfamiliarity, disrespect, impropriety, indecorum, unseemliness, impudence.
license, laxity, looseness, unrestraint, indulgence, self-indulgence, self-gratification, profligacy.
autonomy, self-government; political independence, self-determination, noninterference.
freeman, citizen, denizen, burgher, burgess, liveryman (*London*), nonunionist (*Australia*); freedman.
[*in early English history*] ceorl *or* churl, villein, free peasant.
independent, free lance, freethinker, free trader, nonpartisan.
II. *Verbs.* **free,** liberate, set free, release, emancipate, manumit, loose, rescue, ransom, redeem; unfetter, unbind, unchain, slip, clear, disentangle, extricate; disprison (*rare*), discharge, parole; give the reins to; make free of, enfranchise.
be free, have scope (*or* one's own way), do what one likes, have one's fling; paddle one's own canoe (*colloq.*); go at large, feel at home, stand on one's rights; take a liberty, presume, venture.
III. *Adjectives.* **free,** independent, at large, loose, scot-free; unconstrained, unconfined, unchecked, unhindered, unobstructed, unrestrained, unhampered, uncontrolled, ungoverned, unchained, unshackled, untrammeled, foot-loose, unfettered, unbridled, uncurbed, unmuzzled, unvanquished.
self-governing, autonomous, sovereign, self-directing, self-reliant, uncoerced.
unrestricted, unlimited, limitless, unbounded, illimitable; unqualified, plenary, full, absolute, arbitrary, unconditioned, unconditional; with unlimited power (*or* opportunity); discretionary.
unbiased, unprejudiced, impartial, dispassionate, disinterested, judicial, uninfluenced.

exempt, immune, freed, released, exempted, not liable; privileged, favored.
gratuitous, gratis, costless, chargeless; for nothing, for love.
ready, prompt, eager, alacritous, desirous, spontaneous, voluntary, unforced, freewill.
lavish, generous, open-handed, bounteous, liberal, free-handed, prodigal, munificent, handsome, bountiful; copious, profuse, unstinted; immoderate, extravagant.
frank, ingenuous, unreserved, free-spoken, communicative, candid, downright, outspoken, blunt, direct, unequivocal.
bold, daring, audacious, assured, confident, fearless; reckless; overfree, forward, familiar, overfamiliar, improper, impudent.
lax, loose, wanton, immoral, incontinent, dissipated, licentious, indecent.
[*in botany*] **separate,** distinct, unattached, discrete, disjunct, disjoint, disjoined.
free and easy, unconventional, unceremonious, careless, slack, unmindful, regardless, informal, Bohemian; at ease, *dégagé* (*F.*), at one's ease, quite at home.
IV. *Adverbs.* **freely,** at will, *ad libitum* (*L.*), with no restraint.
See also DELIVERANCE, DISJUNCTION, EXEMPTION, FACILITY, LIBERALITY, PRODIGALITY, RELIEF, TIME.—*Antonyms.* See DIFFICULTY, PARSIMONY, SUBJECTION.

---

freeze, *v.* congeal, harden, glaciate. See REFRIGERATION.
freight, *n.* cargo, shipment, lading. See TRANSFER.
frenzy, *n.* mania, furor; delirium, madness. See DESIRE, INSANITY.

FREQUENCY.—I. *Nouns.* **frequency,** repetition, iteration, frequence, oftenness, commonness; habitualness, habituality (*rare*), persistence; reiteration, recurrence; thickness, density, compactness, crowdedness, numerosity, numerousness, abundance.
frequenter, attender, habitué (*as of a theater*), resorter, fan (*sporting slang*), customer.
II. *Verbs.* **frequent,** resort to, visit, revisit, associate with, attend, haunt; infest, overrun, swarm over.
[*to do frequently*] **repeat,** reiterate, recur, keep on, hammer (at *or* away); renew, redouble, persist, continue; do nothing but.
III. *Adjectives.* **frequent,** repeated, ofttime (*rare*), often (*archaic*), not rare, thick-coming, incessant, perpetual, continual, constant; habitual, persistent, common, customary, general; numerous, abundant, thick.
IV. *Adverbs.* **frequently,** repeatedly, recurrently, in quick succession, at short intervals; often, oft (*archaic or poetic*), oftentimes, ofttimes (*archaic*); daily, every day, many a time and oft; habitually, commonly.
perpetually, continually, constantly, incessantly, at all times, ever and anon.
sometimes, occasionally, at times, once in a while, now and then, again and again.
See also HABIT, PRESENCE, REPETITION.—*Antonyms.* See INFREQUENCY.

---

fresh, *adj.* further, extra; keen, cool; gay, bright, unfaded; unskilled, untrained; new, undried, unmellowed; robust, vigorous, strong; novel, recent; untired, refreshed; wholesome, sweet; blooming, buoyant. See ADDITION, COLD, COLOR, DISUSE, GREEN, HEALTH, NEWNESS, REFRESHMENT, SWEETNESS, YOUTH.
freshen, *v.* refresh, brighten, strengthen, quicken, revive, renew, stimulate. See REFRESHMENT, SWEETNESS.
fret, *v.* irritate, chafe, annoy, harass, worry. See PAIN.
friar, *n.* brother, monk. See CLERGY.

FRICTION.—I. *Nouns.* **friction,** rubbing, attrition, abrasion, rub, resistance (*chiefly tech.*); massage, anatripsis (*med.*), frication, elbow grease (*colloq.*); erasure.
dissension, clashing, discord, disagreement, resistance, strife, wrangling, contention, quarrel.
eraser, rubber, India rubber.
II. *Verbs.* **rub,** friction (*rare*); abrade, scratch, scrape, scrub, fray, rasp, graze, curry, scour, polish, rub out, erase, file, grind; chafe, massage.

III. *Adjectives.* **frictional,** fricative (*phonetics*); attrite *or* attrited (*rare*), abrasive, abradant, anatriptic (*med.*).

See also COUNTERACTION.—*Antonyms.* See CONCURRENCE, LUBRICATION.

FRIEND.—I. *Nouns.* **friend,** well-wisher, intimate, confidant (*masc.*), confidante (*fem.*); *alter ego* (*L.*), other self; best (bosom, trusty, *or* fast) friend, *fidus Achates* (*L.*); brother, *frater* (*L.*); sister, *soror* (*L.*); neighbor, acquaintance.
favorer, supporter, sympathizer, promoter, ally, backer, patron, Mæcenas, advocate, partisan; good genius, tutelary saint; friend in need.
associate, comrade, mate, companion, *confrère* (*F.*), colleague, fellow, partner, copartner, consort, chum (*colloq.*), pal (*slang*), buddy (*colloq.*), side kick (*slang*), playfellow, playmate, schoolmate, schoolfellow, classmate; bedfellow, bunkie (*U. S. colloq.*), roommate, tentmate, shopmate, shipmate, messmate, commensal, fellow (*or* boon) companion.
[*famous friendships*] Pylades and Orestes, Castor and Pollux, Achilles and Patroclus, Theseus and Pirithoüs, Epaminondas and Pelopidas, Nisus and Euryalus, Damon and Pythias, David and Jonathan.
compatriot, countryman, countrywoman (*fem.*), fellow countryman; fellow townsman.
host, hostess (*fem.*), entertainer, Amphitryon ("*Le véritable Amphitryon est l'Amphitryon où l'on dine.*"—Molière); landlord, innkeeper, mine host, Boniface.
guest, visitor, frequenter, habitué, diner; *protégé* (*F.*); company (*collective*).
[*uninvited guest*] shadow, *umbra* (*L.*), parasite, sponge, sponger, crasher (*slang*), gate crasher (*slang*).
[*in plural*] **friends,** relatives, kinsmen, kinsfolk, folks (*colloq.*).
II. *Adjectives.* **friendly,** kind, amicable, friendlike, sociable, social, neighborly, hearty, cordial, warm-hearted, kindly, well-disposed, sympathetic, harmonious, affectionate, ardent, devoted; brotherly, fraternal, sisterly, companionable; friends with, at home with; on good (friendly, amicable, familiar, cordial, *or* intimate) terms; on visiting terms; intimate, confiding, familiar, affable; hail fellow well met; *sans façon* (*F.*); acquainted, on speaking terms, accessible, welcome.
favorable, propitious, promising, benign, conciliatory, favoring, fair, auspicious, advantageous, helpful, serviceable.

See also AID, AUXILIARY, FRIENDSHIP, THICKNESS.—*Antonyms.* See ENEMY.

FRIENDSHIP.—I. *Nouns.* **friendship,** amity, friendliness, kindliness, neighborliness, brotherliness, good will, sympathy, fellow feeling, response, benevolence, affection; harmony, concord, peace, cordiality, *entente cordiale* (*F.*), good understanding; partiality, favoritism.
sociability, sociality, companionship, intercourse, fraternization, companionability, companionableness, agreeableness; acquaintance, familiarity, intimacy.
brotherhood, fraternity, sodality; sisterhood, sorority, sorosis; fellowship, club, society, association (*as, the legal* brotherhood).
II. *Verbs.* **be friendly,** be friends, be acquainted with, know; have dealings with, sympathize with, have a leaning to, bear good will, love, make much of, befriend.
become friendly, make friends with, break the ice, be introduced to, make (*or* scrape) acquaintance with, get into favor, gain the friendship of; shake hands with, fraternize; receive with open arms, embrace.

See also AID, BENEVOLENCE, CONCORD, LOVE, PEACE.—*Antonyms.* See ENMITY.

---

fright, *n.* apprehension, alarm, dread, terror, consternation. See FEAR.
frighten, *v.* startle, excite, affright, terrify. See ALARM, FEAR.
frightful, *adj.* shocking, terrible, dreadful, horrible. See PAINFULNESS.
frigid, *adj.* freezing, icy; stiff, formal. See COLD, INDIFFERENCE.
fringe, *n.* edging, border. See EDGE.
fringed, *adj.* edged, bordered, fimbriate (*tech.*). See ROUGHNESS.
frivolity, *n.* lightness, flightiness, volatility. See LEVITY.
frivolous, *adj.* silly, useless; light-minded, fickle; trivial, trifling. See FOLLY, LIGHTNESS, UNIMPORTANCE.
frolic, *v.* gambol, caper, frisk, dance. See AMUSEMENT.

FRONT.—I. *Nouns.* **front,** foreground, forepart, beginning, forefront; face, frontage, frontispiece (*arch.*), frontal, façade, proscenium, auditorium (*in this sense,* front *is theatrical cant*); obverse (*of a medal*).
van, head, vanguard, advanced guard; line of battle; front rank, first line; outpost, Cossack post; vedette, sentinel, scout, picket.
brow, forehead; visage, physiognomy, phiz (*colloq.*), pan (*slang*), features, countenance; bow, stem, prow; jib, bowsprit.
bearing, carriage, port, mien, demeanor, air, presence.
II. *Verbs.* **front,** face, confront, meet, brave, dare, defy, oppose, buck (*U. S. slang*), buffet, breast; come to the front (*or* fore), lead.
[*to put a facing upon*] face, revet (*tech.*), veneer, overlay, cover (*as, to* front *a house with marble*).
III. *Adjectives.* **front,** frontal, foremost, fore, headmost; forward, anterior, first, chief.
IV. *Adverbs.* **frontwards,** forward, before, ahead, onwards; in front, in the van, in advance; in the foreground.
See also BEGINNING, EXTERIORITY, PRECESSION, RESISTANCE.—*Antonyms.* See REAR.

---

frontier, *n.* boundary, border. See LIMIT.
frontwards, *adv.* forward, onward, before. See FRONT.
frown, *v.* lower, scowl; disapprove, object. See DEJECTION, DISAPPROBATION.
fructify, *v.* fertilize, impregnate. See PRODUCTIVENESS.
frugal, *adj.* thrifty, saving, economical, careful, sparing. See HUSBANDRY.
frugality, *n.* thrift, economy, savingness. See HUSBANDRY.
fruit, *n.* reward, profit; consequence, result, outgrowth, harvest, crop. See ACQUISITION, EFFECT.
fruitful, *adj.* fertile, productive, prolific. See PRODUCTIVENESS.
fruitless, *adj.* vain, ineffectual, useless; unfruitful, barren. See INUTILITY, UNPRODUCTIVENESS.
frustrate, *v.* thwart, defeat, baffle, outwit, balk. See HINDRANCE.
frustrated, *adj.* defeated, foiled, thwarted. See FAILURE.

FUEL.—I. *Nouns.* **fuel,** firing, combustible, coal, hard coal, anthracite; soft coal, bituminous coal; cannel coal *or* cannel; brown coal, lignite; carbon, slack, coke, charcoal; turf, peat; oil, fuel oil, furnace oil, petroleum, kerosene; paraffin oil; gasoline, petrol; gas, coal gas, natural gas; electricity; ember, cinder.
[*sizes of coal*] steamboat (*largest*), broken *or* grate, egg, stove, chestnut *or* nut, pea, buckwheat.
firewood, fagot, kindling wood, kindlings, brushwood; log, stump, block, backlog, yule log.
tinder, punk, amadou, German tinder, spunk, touchwood.
torch, brand (*poetic*), firebrand, flambeau, light, link (*formerly used for lighting persons through dark or foggy streets, esp. in London; whence* linkboy, linkman), mussal *or* mushal (*Anglo-Indian*).
match, light, lucifer, tandstickor (*Swedish*), safety match, Congreve, fusee *or* fuzee, vesuvian; lighter, spill; flint and steel; pocket lighter.
II. *Verbs.* **fuel,** supply with fuel, coal, stoke; feed, fire, get (*or* procure) fuel.
III. *Adjectives.* **combustible,** inflammable, burnable, ignitible *or* ignitable, fiery, tindery: *opposite of* incombustible.
[*easily kindled*] **excitable,** irascible, fiery, quick, peppery, passionate, hot-tempered, choleric, hot-headed, hot-brained, irritable.
See also CALEFACTION, HEAT, OIL.

---

fugitive, *adj.* fleeting, transitory, passing. See TRANSIENCE.
fugitive, *n.* refugee, runaway, deserter. See AVOIDANCE, TRAVELER.
fulfill, *v.* accomplish, perform, effect; meet, satisfy, fill. See COMPLETION, OBSERVANCE.
full, *adj.* complete, entire; sonorous, orotund, rounded; sated, replete; ample, plenteous, copious, abundant. See COMPLETENESS, ROTUNDITY, SATIETY, SUFFICIENCY.

fullness, *n.* abundance, entirety; sonority, fluency (*of speech*). See COMPLETENESS, ROTUNDITY.
full-toned, *adj.* sonorous, full, deep. See DEPTH.
fumble, *v.* grope, feel; muff, bungle. See EXPERIMENT, UNSKILLFULNESS.
fume, *v.* rage, rave; smoke, reek. See EXCITABILITY, VAPORIZATION.
fun, *n.* merriment, jollity, play, sport. See AMUSEMENT.
function, *n.* role, capacity; task, service. See BUSINESS, DUTY.
function, *v.* act, operate, work, perform, go, take effect. See AGENCY.
fundamental, *adj.* essential, basic, elementary. See SUBJECTIVENESS.
funeral, *n.* burial, obsequies (*pl.*), funeral rites. See INTERMENT.
funereal, *adj.* dismal, gloomy, mournful, lugubrious. See DEJECTION.
funny, *adj.* droll, comic, comical, amusing, facetious, witty, ludicrous. See RIDICULOUSNESS, WIT.
Furies, *n. pl.* Erinyes, Eumenides. See MYTHICAL BEINGS, RESENTMENT.
furious, *adj.* angry, fuming, raging; turbulent, rushing, wild. See RESENTMENT, VIOLENCE.

FURNACE.—I. *Nouns.* **furnace,** stove, heater; retort, cupola, blast furnace, reverberatory *or* reverberatory furnace, calcar (*for glass and metal*); kiln, brick-kiln, limekiln; forge, fiery furnace, volcano; crucible, alembic, still; hot-air furnace, oil heater (*or* burner), gas heater, electric heater; range, kitchener (*Eng.*), cookstove, cooker, oven, brick oven, tin oven, fireless cooker.
crematory, crematorium; incinerator; pyre, funeral pile (*or* pyre).
[*heating appliances*] brazier, salamander, warming pan, foot-warmer, footstove; radiator, register, coil; boiler, caldron, pot, urn, kettle, double-boiler, *bain-marie* (*F.*); chafing-dish, electric iron, flatiron, sadiron; toaster, toasting fork.
hotbed, hothouse, conservatory; bakehouse, bakery; galley, caboose; washhouse, laundry.
fireplace, hearth, fireside, grate, firebox; andiron, firedog, fire-irons; poker, tongs, shovel, hob, trivet; damper, crane, pothooks, chains, turnspit, spit, gridiron.
hot bath, thermæ (*pl.*); Turkish (Russian, vapor, sitz, hip, shower, needle, or electric) bath; bathhouse, bathroom, lavatory.
[*severe test*] **ordeal,** trial, test, judgment, probation, trying experience, affliction, tribulation, misfortune, cross, visitation (*as, tried in the* furnace).
Antonyms. See REFRIGERATOR.

---

furnish, *v.* equip, fit out; provide, supply, purvey, cater, contribute. See GIVING, PREPARATION, PROVISION.

FURROW.—I. *Nouns.* **furrow,** groove, channel, flute, stria (*pl.* striæ), hollow, seam, cut, drill, line, wrinkle (*as on the forehead*), canaliculus (*anat. and zoöl.*), sulcation, rut, scratch, streak, crack, score, incision, slit.
trench, ditch, dike *or* dyke, moat, fosse, trough, gutter, cutting, depression; sap (*mil.*), boyau (*mil.*), zigzag (*mil.*), parallel (*mil.*).
II. *Verbs.* **furrow,** plow, channel, trench, ditch, sap, rut; groove, wrinkle, knit (*as the brow*), seam, chamfer, flute, corrugate, cut, chisel, carve, incise, engrave, grave, etch.
III. *Adjectives.* **furrowed,** grooved, channeled, sulcate, canaliculate *or* canaliculated, canalicular (*anat. and zoöl.*), canaliferous, striated, fluted, ribbed, corduroy.
See also INTERVAL, NOTCH.—*Antonyms.* See CONVEXITY, SMOOTHNESS.

---

further, *adj.* extra, supplementary; beyond, farther. See ADDITION, DISTANCE.
further, *v.* promote, assist, advance, forward. See AID.
furtive, *adj.* stealthy, skulking, sly, clandestine. See CONCEALMENT.
fury, *n.* rage, wrath; fierceness, turbulence. See RESENTMENT, VIOLENCE.
fuse, *v.* merge, consolidate; melt, liquefy. See COMBINATION, HEAT.
fuss, *n.* bustle, ado, excitement, stir. See AGITATION.
futile, *adj.* useless, unavailing, vain. See INUTILITY.

FUTURE.—I. *Nouns.* **future,** futurity, hereafter, time to come; morrow, to-morrow, by and by; millenium, doomsday, day of judgment, crack of doom; future state, life to come; destiny.
posterity, descendants, heirs, offspring, progeny, issue: *contrasted with* ancestry.
prospect, outlook, lookout (*chiefly Brit.*), forecast, foresight, prescience; hope, anticipation, expectation.
II. *Verbs.* **anticipate,** expect, await, foresee, preconceive, forebode, foretaste; get ahead of, forestall.
approach, near, draw near, come, come on; impend, hang over, threaten.
III. *Adjectives.* **future,** coming, prospective; impending, overhanging, imminent; next, near, close at hand; eventual, ulterior.
IV. *Adverbs.* **in future,** hereafter, prospectively, in course of time, eventually, ultimately, sooner or later, one of these days; on the knees of the gods.
soon, presently, shortly, anon (*archaic*), quickly, forthwith, early, betimes; on the eve (*or* point) of, about to.

See also DESTINY, EARLINESS, EXPECTATION, FORESIGHT, HEAVEN, POSTERIORITY. —*Antonyms.* See PAST.

G

gabble, *v.* jabber, chatter, prattle, clack, babble, prate. See LOQUACITY.
gag, *v.* throttle, choke, muffle, muzzle. See DUMBNESS.
gain, *n.* winnings, earnings; profit, advantage, benefit. See ACQUISITION, INCREASE.
gain, *v.* secure, get; attain, reach; thrive, flourish; win, persuade; allure. See ACQUISITION, ARRIVAL, GOOD, MOTIVE, STEALING.
gait, *n.* stride, step, pace. See MOTION.
gaiter, *n.* legging, spatterdash, spat. See CLOTHING.
Galaxy, *n.* the Milky Way, *Via Lactea* (*L.*): *astron.* See WORLD.
galaxy, *n.* cluster, assemblage, bevy, array. See MULTITUDE.
gale, *n.* storm, blow. See WIND.
gall, *v.* chafe, irritate; provoke, vex, annoy. See PAIN.
gallant, *adj.* brave, valiant; chivalrous, courtly. See COURAGE, COURTESY.
gallery, *n.* upper balcony, gallery gods (*colloq.*); art gallery, *salon* (*F.*); tunnel, passage, adit; portico, colonnade, balcony; bleachers (*U. S.*). See DRAMA, FINE ARTS, OPENING, RECEPTACLE, SPECTATOR.
gamble, *v.* bet, wager, punt. See CHANCE, PLUNGE.
gamble, *n.* risk, bet, wager, plunge, speculation. See CHANCE.
gambler, *n.* gamester, plunger, hazarder, speculator. See CHANCE, PLUNGE.
gambol, *v.* frolic, skip, frisk, romp. See LEAP.
game, *n.* play, diversion, entertainment; quarry, prey; contest, match; scheme, project. See AMUSEMENT, ANIMAL, CONTENTION, PLAN.
game fishes, sporting fishes, salmon, shad, etc. See ANIMAL.
gamester, *n.* gambler, sport. See AMUSEMENT.
gang, *n.* crew, horde, group, band, crowd; clique, set; troop, company. See PARTY.
gap, *n.* break, breach, opening; interruption, hiatus; notch, pass. See DISCONTINUITY, INTERVAL.
gape, *v.* stare, gaze; part, spread; yawn. See CURIOSITY, INTERVAL, OPENING.
garble, *v.* distort, pervert, falsify. See FALSEHOOD.
garden, *n.* *jardin* (*F.*), nursery, flower garden, ornamental grounds. See HUSBANDRY.
gardener, *n.* horticulturist, florist. See HUSBANDRY.
garish, *adj.* gaudy, showy, flashy, dazzling, glaring. See VULGARITY.
garland, *n.* wreath, festoon, chaplet. See ORNAMENT.
garment, *n.* dress, raiment, attire, habiliment, garb, apparel. See CLOTHING.

garnish, *v.* embellish, adorn, decorate, trim, beautify. See ORNAMENT
garret, *n.* attic, loft. See SUMMIT.
garrulity, *n.* talkativeness, loquaciousness. See LOQUACITY.

GASEITY.—I. *Nouns.* **gaseity,** gaseousness, vaporousness; aëration, aërification, gasification; flatulence *or* flatulency; volatility.
gas, elastic fluid, aëriform fluid, gaseous mixture; fluid, vapor, steam, air, ether, fume, effluvium, flatus; damp (*mining*), choke (*or* black) damp, mephitic air, fire damp, afterdamp (*occurring after an explosion of fire damp*); laughing gas, nitrous oxide; gasoline (*in this sense,* gas *is colloq.*).
[*combustible gases*] natural gas, coal gas, coke-oven gas, illuminating gas, water gas, acetylene, carbureted water gas, oil gas, etc.; hydrogen, parahydrogen, methane (*or* marsh gas), carbon monoxide, carbon dioxide (*or* carbonic-acid gas), nitrogen, oxygen.
bombast, empty talk, highfaluting (*colloq.*), fustian, grandiloquence, windbag, eloquence: *in this sense,* gas *is slang.*
science of elastic fluids: pneumatics, pneumatology; aërostatics (*including aëronautics*), aërodynamics.
II. *Verbs.* **gasify,** render gaseous; aërate, aërify; volatilize, vaporize.
III. *Adjectives.* **gaseous,** gasiform, aëriform, etheric (*physics*), ethereal, aëry, aërial, airy, vaporous, superheated; evaporable, volatilized, volatile; flatulent, gassy.
tenuous, thin (*as a fluid*), rare, subtile (*archaic*), subtle, unsubstantial, rarefied.
See also RARITY, UNSUBSTANTIALITY.—*Antonyms.* See DENSITY.

---

gash, *v.* cut, slit, slash. See DISJUNCTION.
gasoline, *n.* gas, (*colloq.*), petrol (*Brit.*). See OIL.
gasp. *v.* pant, puff, blow, wheeze. See FATIGUE, WIND.
gate, *n.* gateway, door, barrier; portal, postern, entrance. See INCLOSURE, OPENING.
gather, *v.* pick, pluck, cull, glean; collect, muster, convene, congregate, assemble; pucker, plait; infer, deduce, conclude; amass, accumulate, hoard; fester, suppurate. See ACQUISITION, ASSEMBLAGE, [1]FOLD, JUDGE, STORE, UNCLEANNESS.
gathering, *n.* assembly, meeting, crowd; abscess. See ASSEMBLAGE, DISEASE.
gaudy, *adj.* tawdry, flashy, showy, garish. See COLOR, UGLINESS.
gauge, *v.* estimate, judge, compute, evaluate. See MEASUREMENT.
gaunt, *adj.* lean, emaciated, haggard. See THINNESS.
gawky, *adj.* clumsy, awkward, clownish. See UNSKILLFULNESS.
gay, *adj.* blithe, lively, merry, jolly; bright, gaudy. See CHEERFULNESS, COLOR.
gaze, *v.* look, stare, watch. See VISION.
gear, *n.* equipment, garb; apparatus, machinery. See CLOTHING, INSTRUMENT.
gelatinous, *adj.* jellied, gelatinoid. See SEMILIQUIDITY.
gem, *n.* prize, flower; jewel, precious stone. See GOODNESS, ORNAMENT.

GENERALITY.—I. *Nouns.* **generality,** universality, catholicity, ecumenicity *or* œcumenicity, miscellany, miscellaneousness, collectiveness, indiscriminateness, promiscuity, promiscuousness; main body, the mass, the bulk, greatest part, majority; ruck, average, ordinary run, common run.
everyone, everybody, *tout le monde* (*F.*); all hands (*colloq.*), anybody.
vagueness, indefiniteness, uncertainty, inexplicitness, inexactness, inexactitude, looseness, indeterminateness, indetermination; vague (loose, *or* general) statement.
II. *Verbs.* **be general,** prevail, obtain, rage, reign, rule, subsist, predominate; stalk abroad.
generalize, make general, universalize, broaden, spread; form generalizations.
III. *Adjectives.* **general,** generic, collective; current, wide, broad, extensive, sweeping, comprehensive, widespread, popular; vague, unspecific, ill-defined, indefinite, impersonal, unspecified; every, all; encyclopedic, miscellaneous, panoramic, bird's-eye.
universal, catholic, pandemic, ecumenical *or* œcumenical (*esp. eccl.*), worldwide.

usual, ordinary, common, customary, prevailing, regular, habitual, wonted, accustomed; prevalent, rife.
IV. *Adverbs.* **generally,** commonly, extensively, as a rule, habitually, ordinarily, usually, always, in general, generally speaking, for the most part.
See also DISPERSION, HABIT.—*Antonyms.* See SPECIALITY, UNCONFORMITY.

---

generate, *v.* beget, engender, produce, reproduce, impregnate, procreate. See PRODUCTION.
generation, *n.* race, stock; age, lifetime; creation, formation. See CONSANGUINITY, PERIOD, PRODUCTION.
generosity, *n.* bounty; open-handedness, munificence, philanthropy; altruism, magnanimity. See BENEVOLENCE, LIBERALITY, UNSELFISHNESS.
generous, *adj.* magnanimous, unselfish; lavish, munificent; ample, abundant. See BENEVOLENCE, LIBERALITY, OPENING.
genesis, *n.* origin, birth, creation, formation. See PRODUCTION.
genial, *adj.* kindly, cordial, pleasant, hearty. See CHEERFULNESS.
geniality, *n.* good will, heartiness, cordiality. See WILLINGNESS.
genius, *n.* bent, propensity; master mind, brilliant intellect; inspiration, creative power. See DISPOSITION, EXPERT, INTELLECT.
gentle, *adj.* well-bred, courteous; docile, tame; lenient, tolerant; easy, gradual; well-born, highborn; tender, soothing; kindly, benign, sympathetic, compassionate. See COURTESY, DOMESTICATION, MILDNESS, MODERATION, NOBILITY, RELIEF, SOFTNESS.
gentleman, *n.* esquire, sahib (*India*), aristocrat, *gentilhomme* (*F.*). See MAN, PROBITY.
gentry, *n.* squirarchy, gentlefolk. See NOBILITY.
genuine, *adj.* sincere, frank, unaffected; real, honest, sterling, authentic, pure. See ARTLESSNESS, GOOD.
germ, *n.* rudiment, origin; seed, egg, embryo. See BEGINNING, CAUSE.
gesture, *n.* gesticulation, motion. See INDICATION.
get, *v.* obtain, procure, gain, attain, achieve, secure, receive; become; grasp, comprehend; persuade, induce; capture, take. See ACQUISITION, CONVERSION, INTELLIGIBILITY, MOTIVE, TAKING.—**get down,** alight, descend. See DESCENT.—**get on,** don, put on; advance, progress; succeed, prosper. See CLOTHING, PROGRESSION, PROSPERITY.—**get up,** ascend, climb, mount, arise; study, learn; prepare, arrange. See ASCENT, LEARNING, PREPARATION.
ghastly, *adj.* ashen, pallid, wan, grisly; hideous, horrible, fearful, terrible. See COLORLESSNESS, UGLINESS.
ghost, *n.* spirit, specter, apparition, phantom. See CORPSE, SHADE.
ghostlike, *adj.* ghostly, spectral, shadowy, phantom. See CORPSE.
giant, *n.* monster, colossus. See SIZE.
gibe, *n.* jeer, taunt, sneer, derision, ridicule. See DISRESPECT.
giddy, *adj.* fickle, flighty, volatile; dizzy, light-headed. See CAPRICE, INSANITY.
gift, *n.* donation, gratuity, present, offering, bequest, contribution, benefaction, bounty, boon, alms; talent, faculty, endowment, bent, aptitude. See GIVING, POWER.
gigantic, *adj.* enormous, immense, huge, colossal. See SIZE.
giggle, *v.* titter, snicker. See REJOICING.
gingersnap, *n.* ginger cookie. See SNAP.
gird, *v.* encircle, surround; secure, bind; brace, fortify, sustain. See ENVIRONMENT, JUNCTION, STRENGTH.
girdle, *n.* belt, baldric, girth, sash; band, ring. See CIRCULARITY, OUTLINE, VINCULUM.
girl, *n.* maiden, maid, damsel, lass; maidservant. See INFANT, SERVANT.
girth, *n.* circumference, girdle, belt, band, surcingle. See OUTLINE, VINCULUM.
gist, *n.* pith, essence, point, substance. See MEANING.

GIVING.—I. *Nouns.* **giving,** bestowal, bestowment, presentation, conferment, conferral, concession, cession; delivery, consignment, disposition, dispensation, endowment; investment, investiture; award, compensation.
charity, almsgiving, liberality, generosity, benevolence, philanthropy.
gift, donation, present, sportula (*pl.* sportulæ), shower (*as of gifts by a surprise party*), boon, favor, benefaction, grant, offering, bonus, honorarium, fee; consideration, oblation, sacrifice.
allowance, contribution, subscription, subsidy, subvention, tribute; pension, aid; pin money, pittance.
bequest, legacy, devise, will, dot, dowry, dower.
gratuity, alms, largess, bounty, dole, help, offertory, Christmas box, *douceur* (*F.*), tip, *pourboire* (*F.*), *Trinkgeld* (*Ger.*), baksheesh *or* bakshish, cumshaw (*China*), hand out (*slang*), lagniappe *or* lagnappe (*Louisiana*), pilon (*Southwestern U. S.*), pilonce (*Texas*), piloncillo (*Texas*).
bribe, bait, peace offering, graft (*colloq.*), sop, palm grease (*slang*).
giver, donor, presenter, conferrer, bestower, grantor; devisor (*law*), bequeather, testator; investor, subscriber, contributor; fairy godmother.
II. *Verbs.* **give,** bestow, grant, accord, award, donate (*chiefly U. S.*), confer; apportion, allot, assign, offer; present, give away, dispense, dispose of, give (*or* deal) out, fork out (*slang*), hand out, shell out (*slang*), distribute; allow, contribute, subscribe; pay, remunerate, compensate; spend, sacrifice.
[*to yield to pressure*] **relax,** slacken, loosen, unbend, ease, abate, relent.
[*to give in words*] **utter,** emit, articulate, voice, pronounce; announce, notify; describe, portray.
deliver, transfer, hand, hand over, pass, pass over, assign, turn over, make over, consign, surrender, give up, cede, relinquish, part with, shed; render, impart, communicate; commit, intrust.
concede, vouchsafe, yield, admit, allow, grant, permit; award, adjudge.
endow, settle upon, invest, vest in, enrich, bequeath, dower, leave, devise.
furnish, supply, provide, find, equip, help, administer to, afford, spare, accommodate with, indulge with, favor with; lavish, pour on, thrust upon.
bribe, tip, recompense, fee; grease the palm (*slang*), oil (*slang*), square (*colloq.*); buy, hire, suborn, corrupt.
give up, 1, cease from, stop, discontinue; succumb; **2, relinquish,** abandon, part with, resign, sacrifice, surrender, yield; **3, devote,** addict, apply, attach: *used esp. reflexively; as, to* give *oneself* up *to business.*
III. *Adjectives.* **given,** addicted, inclined, disposed, prone, attached, devoted, habituated (*as,* given *to drink*).
stated, specified, fixed, definite, named, specific, regular, settled, prearranged (*as, a* given *time*).
[*in mathematics and logic*] **assumed,** granted, taken as known, postulated, presupposed, suppositional, hypothetical.
charitable, liberal, beneficent, generous, kind, free-handed, open-handed, benevolent, philanthropic; eleemosynary, tributary.
See also LIBERALITY, PAYMENT, RELINQUISHMENT, REWARD.—*Antonyms.* See RECEIVING.

---

glad, *adj.* pleased, gratified, happy, joyful, content, cheerful. See PLEASURE.
gladden, *v.* delight, please, elate. See CHEERFULNESS, REJOICING.
glamour, *n.* fascination, allurement, charm, witchery; bewitchment, enchantment, magic. See MOTIVE, SORCERY.
glance, *n.* brush, graze; look, glimpse. See TOUCH, VISION.
gland, *n.* secreting organ, secretory. See CONCEALMENT.
glare, *v.* flare, glitter; lower, scowl. See LIGHT, VISION.
glaring, *adj.* brilliant, intense, dazzling; conspicuous, flagrant, notorious. See COLOR, MANIFESTATION.
glass, *n.* lens, microscope, telescope, spyglass; mirror, looking-glass; tumbler, goblet. See OPTICAL INSTRUMENTS, RECEPTACLE.
gleam, *n.* glow, beam, flash, ray, streak. See LIGHT.
glee, *n.* mirth, gayety, joyousness, merriment. See CHEERFULNESS.
glib, *adj.* fluent, ready, facile, voluble. See LOQUACITY.

glide, *v.* volplane, plane (*colloq.*); elapse, pass; slip, slide, coast, flow. See AËRONAUTICS, LAPSE, MOTION.
glider, *n.* motorless plane, sailplane. See AËRONAUTICS.
glimmer, *v.* gleam, flicker, twinkle, flash. See DIMNESS.
glimpse, *n.* glance, peep, view, squint (*colloq.*). See VISION.
glitter, *v.* glow, beam, glisten, shine, sparkle. See LIGHT.
gloat, *v.* rejoice, exult, revel, delight, glory. See BOASTING, PLEASURE.
globe, *n.* sphere, orb, ball. See ROTUNDITY.
gloom, *n.* duskiness, obscurity, dimness; depression, sadness, melancholy. See DARKNESS, DEJECTION.
glorify, *v.* transform, exalt; honor, distinguish; adore, magnify, praise. See ELEVATION, REPUTE, WORSHIP.
glory, *n.* grandeur, magnificence; brilliancy, effulgence, splendor, radiance; nimbus, halo; honor, renown, exaltation. See BEAUTY, LIGHT, REPUTE.
[1]**gloss,** *n.* deceptive appearance, speciousness; brightness, sheen, luster; glaze, polish, veneer. See DECEPTION, LIGHT, SMOOTHNESS.
[2]**gloss,** *n.* annotation, note, interlinear, translation; glossary. See INTERPRETATION, WORD.
glossy, *adj.* specious, deceptive; shiny, lustrous; smooth, polished. See DECEPTION, LIGHT, SMOOTHNESS.
glove, *n.* gauntlet, mitten. See CLOTHING.
glow, *v.* flush, be animated; burn, flame, blaze; gleam, shine. See FEELING, HEAT, LIGHT.
glower, *v.* glare, scowl, lower. See SULLENNESS.
glowing, *adj.* stirring, thrilling; burning, smoldering; flushed, ruddy. See EXCITEMENT, HEAT, RED.
glue, *v.* stick, fasten, fix, cement. See COHERENCE.
glum, *adj.* moody, surly, morose, sulky, gloomy. See DEJECTION.

GLUTTONY.—I. *Nouns.* **gluttony,** gormandizing, voracity, edacity, hoggishness, piggishness; abnormal hunger, polyphagia (*med.*), bulimia (*med.*); greed, greediness, gulosity (*rare*), rapacity; gastronomy, aristology, high living.
feast, banquet, good cheer, blow out (*slang*), junket, barbecue.
glutton, gormandizer, cormorant, belly-god (*archaic*), hog, pig (*colloq.; often used jocularly*), gorger, stuffer (*colloq.*), crammer (*colloq.*), trencherman.
II. *Verbs.* **gluttonize,** gormandize, gorge, stuff, cram, overeat, glut, satiate, indulge, eat one's fill, bolt, devour, gobble up, gulp, raven, eat out of house and home, play a good knife and fork.
III. *Adjectives.* **gluttonous,** greedy, gormandizing, edacious, ravenous, voracious, hoggish, piggish (*often used jocularly*), swinish, gross, omnivorous; overfed, gorged, overgorged.
See also DESIRE, FOOD, INSENSIBILITY.—*Antonyms.* See ASCETICISM, FASTIDIOUSNESS, FASTING.

---

gnaw, *v.* crunch, chew; rankle, distress. See FOOD, PAIN.
go, *v.* operate, work, run; leave, depart; fade, vanish, disappear, fall, die; lead, extend, reach; resort (to), visit; pass, elapse; move, wend, proceed, stir, advance; withdraw, retire. See AGENCY, DEPARTURE, DISAPPEARANCE, DISTANCE, JOURNEY, LAPSE, PROGRESSION, RECESSION.—**go about,** tack, wear (*naut.*); undertake, set about. See DEVIATION, UNDERTAKING.—**go off,** die, pass away; depart, go away; deteriorate, wither, fade; explode, be discharged. See DEATH, DEPARTURE, DETERIORATION, VIOLENCE.—**go through,** endure, experience, undergo; have passage, cut across, penetrate. See EVENT, INEXCITABILITY, PASSAGE.
go-between, *n.* interagent, medium; middleman, broker. See INSTRUMENTALITY, INTERJACENCE, REPRESENTATIVE.
god, *n.* divinity, deity. See MYTHICAL BEINGS.

God, *n.* Supreme Being, the Creator, Jehovah, the Lord. See DEITY.
godly, *adj.* devout, reverent, righteous. See PIETY.
gold, *n.* bullion, aurum (*tech.*); riches. See MONEY, WEALTH.
golden, *adj.* precious, excellent; gold, gilt, gilded, gold-colored, aureate. See GOOD, YELLOW.

GOOD.—I. *Nouns.* **good,** benefit, advantage, gain, profit, harvest, boon, good turn, favor, blessing, prize, windfall, godsend, good fortune, happiness, benison (*archaic*), benediction; improvement, interest, service, behoof, behalf; weal (*archaic*); commonweal *or* common weal; "consummation devoutly to be wished" (*Hamlet*).

[*in plural*] **goods,** wares, commodities, stock, stock in trade, merchandise, chattels, effects, movables (*law*), personal property, appurtenances, paraphernalia, traps (*colloq.*), things, gear.

II. *Verbs.* **be good,** be beneficial, etc. (see *adjectives*); be good as gold, be pure gold, look good to (*colloq.*), be the real thing; excel, transcend, stand the test, pass muster, pass an examination.

[*to strive for superiority*] **vie,** challenge comparison, contend, strive, emulate, rival.

benefit, profit, advantage, advance, avail, improve, serve, help, do good to, be beneficial.

gain, make progress, prosper, flourish, thrive, succeed; flower, blossom, bloom, fructify.

III. *Adjectives.* **good,** beneficial, favorable, fortunate, propitious, commendable, fit, appropriate, becoming, advantageous, profitable, useful, valuable; suitable, adequate, agreeable, pleasant, pleasing, edifying, congenial; excellent, admirable, thorough, superior, above par, buckra (*negro term, used in southern U. S. and West Indies; as a noun, it means "white man"*), nice, fine; sound, right, valid, effectual, genuine; salutary, wholesome, healthful; satisfactory, sufficient, up to the mark, desirable, unexceptionable, unobjectionable.

choice, best, select, picked, elect, *recherché* (*F.*), rare, *impayable* (*F.*), priceless, golden, unparalleled, peerless, matchless, unequaled, inimitable, bully (*slang*), tip-top (*colloq.*), top-hole (*slang*), first-rate, first-class, crackajack (*slang*), crack (*slang*), superfine, superexcellent of the first water; high-wrought, exquisite, fine, estimable, admirable, capital, priceless, precious, invaluable, gilt-edged (*colloq.*).

harmless, innocuous, innoxious, innocent, unoffending, inoffensive.

capable, efficient, competent, skillful, able, qualified, clever (*as, a* good *workman*).

[*morally good*] **virtuous,** moral, upright, exemplary, pious, devout, pure, innocent, unsullied, untainted, chaste; honorable, honest, fair, sincere.

kind, friendly, gracious, benign, kindly, kind-hearted, beneficent; benevolent, sympathetic, considerate, humane.

well-behaved, well-mannered, orderly, decorous, well-conducted, seemly, proper (*as,* good *manners*).

courageous, brave, stout-hearted, valorous, mettlesome, resolute, lion-hearted, manful, manly (*as, fight the* good *fight*).

goodly, 1, pleasing, comely, beautiful, graceful, bonny, well-favored, good-looking, handsome, personable, seemly, fair, excellent; **2, considerable,** large, substantial, sizable, tidy (*colloq.*), immense, colossal, ample, (*as, a* goodly *number*).

IV. *Adverbs.* **well,** aright, satisfactorily, favorably, in one's interest; worthily, justly, rightly, excellently; suitably, aptly, befittingly; abundantly, adequately, fully, quite.

See also APPROBATION, BEAUTY, PIETY, SAVORINESS, UTILITY, VIRTUE.—*Antonyms.* See DETERIORATION, EVIL.

---

good fellow, boon companion, good scout (*colloq.*). See SOCIALITY.
good-looking, *adj.* handsome, attractive. See BEAUTY.

GOOD MAN.—*Nouns.* **good man,** worthy, model, paragon, pattern, good example; hero, demigod, angel, saint; benefactor, "one who loves his fellow-men" (Hunt), good Samaritan, "little friend of all the world" (Kipling), philanthropist; a man among men, prince soul of honor, white man (*colloq.*).

See also BENEFACTOR.—*Antonyms.* See BAD MAN, EVILDOER.

good-natured, *adj.* amiable, pleasant, kindly, cordial. See BENEVOLENCE.

GOODNESS.—*Nouns.* **goodness,** excellence, merit, value, worth; generosity, kindness, virtue, benevolence, beneficence, favorableness, etc. (see *adjectives under* GOOD).

[*outstanding goodness*] **superexcellence,** supereminence, superiority, quintessence, perfection, *coup de maître* (*F.*), masterpiece, *chef d'œuvre* (*F.*), prime, flower, cream, *élite* (*F.*), pick, *crême de la crême* (*F.*), A1 *or* A number 1 (*colloq.*). nonpareil, flower of the flock, salt of the earth; gem of the first water, treasure, jewel, pearl, one in a thousand, *rara avis* (*L.*), prodigy, wonder, marvel.

See also GOOD, PERFECTION, SUPERIORITY, VIRTUE.—*Antonyms.* See BADNESS.

---

goods, *n. pl.* commodities, effects, wares, stock. See GOOD, PROPERTY.

GOOD WOMAN.—*Nouns.* **good woman,** ministering angel, heaven's noblest gift; "Earth's noblest thing,—a woman perfected" (Lowell); goddess, deity, queen, Madonna, virgin, maiden, Una (*Faërie Queene*).

Antonyms. See BAD WOMAN.

---

gorge, *n.* ravine, cañon, pass, defile. See INTERVAL.
gorge, *v.* gulp, bolt; gormandize, stuff, cram. See GLUTTONY.
gorgeous, *adj.* grand, superb, elegant, splendid, magnificent. See BEAUTY.
gossip, *n.* tattler, busybody; talk, rumor, report. See CURIOSITY, NEWS.
gossip, *v.* tell, repeat; tattle; chat, talk. See CONVERSATION.
government, *n.* administration, polity; state, body politic; control, regulation. See AUTHORITY, DIRECTION.—**government by women,** gynecocracy; metrocracy, matriarchy; petticoat rule. See AUTHORITY.
governor, *n.* ruler, chief, head; administrator, executive, master. See AUTHORITY, DIRECTOR.
gown, *n.* dress, robe, frock, garment. See CLOTHING.
grab, *v.* seize, take, snatch, grasp, clutch. See TAKING.
grace, *n.* charm, attractiveness, elegance; holiness, saintliness; favor, mercy, compassion; graciousness, tact, culture. See BEAUTY, PIETY, PITY, TASTE.
graceful, *adj.* easy, felicitous, fluent; willowy, supple; attractive, charming. See ELEGANCE, SOFTNESS, TASTE.
graceless, *adj.* awkward, inelegant; corrupt, depraved. See UGLINESS, VICE.
gracious, *adj.* kind, benign, merciful; obliging, courteous, affable. See BENEVOLENCE, COURTESY.
gradation, *n.* sequence, progression, series; grade, step; intensity, shading. See CONTINUITY, DEGREE, SHADE.
grade, *n.* gradation, amount; slope, incline; rank, standing. See DEGREE, OBLIQUITY, REPUTE.
gradual, *adj.* progressive, continuous, regular; moderate, deliberate, lingering, leisurely. See DEGREE, SLOWNESS.
gradually, *adv.* by degrees, little by little. See SLOWNESS.
graduate, *v.* modify, adjust; classify, place; measure, grade. See AGREEMENT, ARRANGEMENT, DEGREE.
graduation, *n.* commencement, promotion. See LEARNER.
graft, *v.* implant, join, ingraft. See INSERTION.
grain, *n.* temper, tendency; particle, bit; seed; contexture, surface. See DISPOSITION, LITTLENESS, POWDERINESS, TEXTURE.

GRAMMAR.—I. *Nouns.* **grammar,** rules of language, *jus et norma loquendi* (Horace); accidence, rudiments, elements, principles.

[*divisions of classical grammar*] orthography, orthoëpy, etymology (*or* inflection), syntax, prosody.

[*divisions of English grammar*] phonology, accidence, syntax.

[*parts of speech*] noun, adjective, pronoun, verb, adverb, preposition, conjunc-

tion, interjection; enclitic, affix, particle; case, declension, conjugation; parsing, analysis.
[*book*] grammatical textbook, treatise (*or* book) on grammar, manual (*or* handbook) of grammar.
propriety of speech, right use of language, correct diction, grammatical correctness.
grammarian, adept in grammar, grammatist (*rare*), grammaticaster (*grammatical pedant*); writer on grammar, grammatical author, philologist.
II. *Verbs.* **grammaticize,** parse, analyze, conjugate, decline, inflect; etymologize, philologize.
III. *Adjectives.* **grammatical,** correct (*grammatically*); syntactic *or* syntactical, prosodic *or* prosodical, inflectional; literal.
See also LANGUAGE, LETTER, WORD.—*Antonyms.* See SOLECISM.

---

grand, *adj.* stately, majestic, splendid, magnificent, sublime, glorious, impressive; pretentious. See GREATNESS, NOBILITY, PRIDE, REPUTE; OSTENTATION.
grandeur, *n.* eminence, loftiness, stateliness; magnificence, splendor, majesty. See GREATNESS, REPUTE.
grandfather, *n.* grandparent, grandpa, grandsire, forefather. See PATERNITY, VETERAN.
grandiloquence, *n.* bombast, highfaluting. See ORNAMENT.
grandmother, *n.* grandparent, grandma, granny. See VETERAN.
grant, *v.* give, allot, bestow; furnish, contribute; consent, admit, concede, permit; consign, convey. See GIVING, LENDING, PERMISSION, TRANSFER.
granular, *adj.* granulated, mealy, sandy, gritty, arenaceous. See POWDERINESS.
graphic, *adj.* descriptive, delineatory, pictorial; vivid, picturesque, telling, forcible. See FINE ARTS, INTELLIGIBILITY, VIGOR.
grapple, *v.* contend, struggle; seize, grasp. See OPPOSITION, TAKING.
grasp, *v.* understand, comprehend; clasp, seize. See INTELLIGIBILITY, TAKING.
grassland, *n.* meadowland, pasture. See PLAIN.
grassplot, *n.* lawn, plot, turf. See GREEN.
grate, *v.* grind, creak, scratch, rasp. See STRIDENCY.
grateful, *adj.* thankful; agreeable, refreshing, acceptable. See GRATITUDE, PLEASURABLENESS.
gratification, *n.* diversion, entertainment, feast; ease, comfort; dissipation, indulgence. See PLEASURE.
gratify, *v.* satisfy, please; indulge, humor. See PLEASURABLENESS.
grating, *n.* lattice, grille. See CROSSING.

GRATITUDE.—I. *Nouns.* **gratitude,** thankfulness, gratefulness, sense of obligation; acknowledgment, recognition; "a lively sense of favors to come" (*Talleyrand*); thanksgiving, giving thanks.
thanks, praise, benediction; pæan; *Te Deum* (*L.*), grace, requital, thank offering.
II. *Verbs.* **be grateful,** thank; give (render, return, offer, *or* tender) thanks, acknowledge, requite; lie under an obligation; never forget, overflow with gratitude.
III. *Adjectives.* **grateful,** thankful, obliged, appreciative, beholden, indebted to, under obligation, impressed; pleasing, pleasant, agreeable, gratifying.
IV. *Interjections.* **thanks!** many thanks! *merci!* (*F.*), *danke!* (*Ger.*), *danke schön!* (*Ger.*), *grazie!* (*It.*), gramercy! (*archaic*), much obliged! thank you! thank Heaven! Heaven be praised!
Antonyms. See INGRATITUDE.

---

gratuitous, *adj.* free, gratis; groundless, unwarranted. See CHEAPNESS, FREEDOM, SOPHISTRY.
gratuity, *n.* gift, present; tip, fee. See CHEAPNESS, GIVING.
grave, *adj.* dull, somber; sedate, solemn, sober; weighty, serious, momentous. See COLOR, DEJECTION, IMPORTANCE.

grave, *n.* tomb, vault, sepulcher, place of burial. See INTERMENT.
graveclothes, *n. pl.* cerements, shroud. See INTERMENT.
gravestone, *n.* tombstone, headstone, marker. See INTERMENT.
graveyard, *n.* cemetery, burial ground, churchyard. See INTERMENT.

GRAVITY.—I. *Nouns.* **gravity,** gravitation (*physics*), centripetal force, weight, heft (*U. S. and dial. Eng.*), heaviness, ponderousness, ponderosity; relative density (*or* weight), specific gravity; pressure, tonnage, load, burden, ballast, counterpoise; mass.
[*comparisons*] lead, millstone, ton, mountain. Ossa upon Pelion (*esp. in the phrase "to pile Ossa upon Pelion"*).
[*weighing instruments*] balance, scales, weighing scales, steelyard, weighbeam, scalebeam, beam, weighbridge, weighing machine.
science of gravity: statics.
sedateness, sobriety, seriousness, staidness, calmness, tranquillity, serenity, composure, solemnity.
importance, largeness, weight, significance, seriousness, greatness, magnitude, enormity, import, moment (*as, of great* moment), consideration, concern (*as, the* gravity *of an offense*).
II. *Verbs.* **gravitate,** sink (*as by gravity*), settle down, subside, precipitate; be attracted, tend, incline, point, head, lean.
weigh, load, press; cumber, bear heavily, balance, poise, counterbalance, equiponderate, counterweigh.
III. *Adjectives.* **gravitative,** centripetal, tending towards the center, gravitational.
weighty, heavy, hefty (*colloq.*), ponderous, ponderable; cumbersome, burdensome, cumbrous, unwieldy, massive.

See also DEJECTION, DESCENT, IMPORTANCE, TENDENCY, VIGOR.—*Antonyms.* See LEVITY.

GRAY.—I. *Nouns.* **gray** *or* grey; grayness *or* greyness; neutral tint, silver, silveriness, dove color, pepper and salt, *chiaroscuro* (*It.*), grisaille (*tech.*); dun, drab, etc. (see *adjectives*).
II. *Verbs.* **gray** *or* grey, make (*or* become) gray, grizzle, silver, dapple.
III. *Adjectives.* **gray** *or* grey, grizzled, grizzly, griseous, ashen, ashy, ash-colored, cinereous; dingy, leaden, livid, pearly, clouded, cloudy, misty, foggy, hoary, hoar, canescent, grayish, silver, silvery, silvered, silver-gray; iron-gray, dun, drab, dove-colored, dappled, dapple-gray, mouse-colored, stone-colored, slate-colored; sad, dull, somber; cool.
gray-haired, silver-haired, gray-headed, hoar-headed, hoary-headed, hoary, grizzly.

---

[1]**graze,** *v.* browse, crop, feed, pasture. See FOOD.
[2]**graze,** *v.* rub, scratch; brush, glance. See FRICTION, TOUCH.
grease, *v.* anoint, smear, oil, lubricate. See UNCTUOUSNESS.

GREATNESS.—I. *Nouns.* **greatness,** largeness, etc. (see *adjectives*); vastness, magnitude, size, bulk, mass, heap, multitude, quantity, volume, amplitude, content, measurement, measure; abundance, sufficiency, great quantity, deal (*colloq.*), power (*colloq.*), sight (*colloq.*); stock, store, load, shipload, immensity, infinity, enormity, might, strength, intensity, fullness.
eminence, distinction, grandeur, dignity; nobility, fame, importance.
II. *Verbs.* **be great,** etc. (see *adjectives*); soar, tower, loom, rise above, transcend; bulk, bulk large, know no bounds.
enlarge, expand, increase, grow, wax, magnify, swell, dilate, distend, broaden.
III. *Adjectives.* **great,** large, considerable, big, bulky, huge; titanic; voluminous, ample, abundant; many, numerous, manifold, multitudinous; goodly, precious.
world-wide, widespread, universal, cosmopolitan, far-reaching, far-famed, extensive.
vast, immense, enormous, extreme; inordinate, excessive, undue, extravagant, immoderate, unreasonable, exorbitant, outrageous, preposterous, unconscio-

able, monstrous, crass, gross; towering, stupendous, prodigious; terrible (*colloq.*), terrific (*colloq.*), dreadful (*colloq.*), fearful (*colloq.*).
unlimited, infinite, immeasurable, illimitable, boundless, limitless, interminate interminable, endless, inexhaustible; indefinite, absolute.
inexpressible, unutterable, indescribable, ineffable, unspeakable, nameless unnamable; fabulous.
absolute, positive, stark, decided, unconditional, unequivocal; perfect, complete, full, plenary, consummate, essential, thoroughgoing, thoroughpaced, thorough, sheer, unqualified, unalloyed; arrant, downright, flagrant, rank, unmitigated, glaring; profound, uttermost, intense, exquisite.
eminent, distinguished, remarkable, extraordinary, important, elevated, lofty, noble, mighty, supreme; notable, noteworthy, noticeable, esteemed, noted, signal, conspicuous, prominent, renowned, illustrious, famous, glorious, grand, majestic, august, dignified, sublime.
IV. *Adverbs.* [*in a great or high degree*] **greatly,** largely, etc. (see *adjectives*); much, indeed, very, very much, most; pretty (*rare*), in a great measure, passing, richly; on a large scale, by wholesale; mightily, powerfully; extremely, exceedingly, intensely, indefinitely, immeasurably, incalculably, infinitely.
[*in a positive degree*] **absolutely,** positively, truly, unconditionally, decidedly, unequivocally, essentially, fundamentally, radically, wholly, downright, in all conscience.
[*in a complete degree*] **wholly,** entirely, completely, utterly, altogether, quite, abundantly, amply, fully, widely.
[*in a supreme degree*] **preëminently,** superlatively, eminently, supremely, inimitably, incomparably.
[*in a too great degree*] **immoderately,** monstrously, preposterously, inordinately, superabundantly, unreasonably, exorbitantly, excessively, enormously, out of all proportion.
[*in a marked degree*] **remarkably,** particularly, singularly, curiously, uncommonly, unusually, peculiarly, notably, signally, strikingly, pointedly, mainly, chiefly; famously, egregiously, prominently, conspicuously, glaringly, emphatically, incredibly, amazingly, surprisingly, incredibly, stupendously.
[*in a violent degree*] **violently,** furiously, severely, desperately, boisterously, tremendously, extravagantly, *à outrance* (*F.*), with a vengeance.
[*in a painful degree*] **painfully,** sadly, sorely, bitterly, piteously, grievously, miserably, cruelly, woefully, balefully, lamentably, shockingly, frightfully, dreadfully, fearfully, terribly, horribly, distressingly.

See also HEIGHT, IMPORTANCE, INFINITY, QUANTITY, REPUTE, SIZE, SUPERIORITY, WHOLE.—*Antonyms.* See SMALLNESS.

---

greed, *n.* longing, craving, avarice, covetousness. See DESIRE.
greedy, *adj.* grasping, avaricious, rapacious; voracious, ravenous, gluttonous. See DESIRE, GLUTTONY.

GREEN.—I. *Nouns.* **green,** blue and yellow, olive, etc. (see *adjectives*); vert (*heraldry*), reseda *or* *réséda* (*F.*), mignonette, celadon, *corbeau* (*F.*), bice; greenness, verdancy, viridity.
[*comparisons*] emerald, chrysoprase; chrysolite, olivine, peridot; jasper, green chalcedony; malachite, beryl; verdigris, verd antique, aquamarine; absinth *or* absinthe, *crême de menthe* (*F.*), grass, sea water.
[*pigments*] terre-verte, green ocher *or* ochre, verditer, veridian, malachite green, sap green, cobalt green; Paris green, emerald green.
grassplot *or* grassplat, lawn; turf, sward, greensward; *maidan* (*Anglo-Indian*), common, campus (*U. S.*), heath (*as, village* green; *putting* green).
verdure, vegetation, greenery, green plants, vert (*Eng. forest law*).
vigor, virility, strength, lustiness, youth, freshness, health, vitality, stamina: *usually in the phrase "in the* green."
II. *Verbs.* **green,** make green, become green (*as with verdure*); verdigris (*rare*).
III. *Adjectives.* **green,** verdant, verdurous; emerald (pea, apple, sea, leaf, bottle, *or* Irish) green; grass-green, chlorine, chlorochrous; citrine *or* citrinous; olive, olive-green, olivaceous; blue-green, glaucous, berylline, aquamarine; greenish, virescent.

[*expressing immaturity*] **immature,** unripe, undeveloped, unfinished, crude, tender young, unfledged; raw, unseasoned.

inexperienced, young, callow, fresh, raw, untrained, unskilled, inexpert, undisciplined, unsophisticated, unversed, unacquainted, uninformed, ignorant, gullible.

[*expressing freshness*] **fresh,** recent, new; unmellowed (*as liquor*), undried (*as wood*), unfired (*as bricks*); uncured, unsmoked (*as meat*); unhealed (*as a wound*); untanned (*as hides*).

[*of the complexion*] **pale,** sickly-hued, sickly, sickly-looking, peaked (*colloq.*), peakish (*colloq.*), unhealthy.

See also CREDULITY, NEWNESS, NONPREPARATION, UNSKILLFULNESS.

---

greensward, *n.* turf, grass, sod, sward. See PLAIN.

greet, *v.* hail, accost, welcome; receive, admit, entertain. See COURTESY, RECEIVING.

greeting, *n.* salutation, welcome, salute. See COURTESY.

grief, *n.* sorrow, affliction, anguish, tribulation, woe; trial, distress, bereavement. See PAIN.

grievance, *n.* wrong, injustice, injury; annoyance, vexation. See EVIL, PAINFULNESS.

grieve, *v.* mourn, deplore; sadden, distress. See LAMENTATION, PAIN.

grievous, *adj.* intense, severe; atrocious, appalling. See PAINFULNESS.

grim, *adj.* fierce, ruthless; stern, inflexible, unyielding; forbidding, grisly, horrible. See MALEVOLENCE, RESOLUTION, UGLINESS.

grimy, *adj.* dirty, smutty, filthy, soiled. See UNCLEANNESS.

grind, *v.* file, sharpen, polish; harass, persecute; crush, pulverize; grate, rasp. See FRICTION, MALEVOLENCE, POWDERINESS, STRIDENCY.

grip, *v.* seize, clutch, grasp, hold. See TAKING.

grit, *n.* stamina, pluck; gravel, sand. See PERSEVERANCE, POWDERINESS.

groan, *v.* moan, whine, grumble. See CRY, LAMENTATION.

groom, *v.* tend, curry, rub down. See DOMESTICATION.

groove, *n.* channel, trench, opening; rut, routine. See FURROW, HABIT.

grope, *v.* search, hunt; fumble, feel. See EXPERIMENT, TOUCH.

gross, *adj.* bulky, huge; coarse, low. See GREATNESS, VULGARITY.

grotesque, *adj.* misshapen, deformed; bizarre, fantastic; odd, strange. See DEFORMITY, RIDICULOUSNESS, UNCONFORMITY.

ground, *n.* basis, foundation; earth, soil; reason, cause. See BASE, LAND, MOTIVE.

ground, *v.* fix, settle; instruct, inform. See STABILITY, TEACHING.

grounded, *adj.* stranded, aground. See FAILURE.

ground floor, street floor, *rez de chaussée* (*F.*). See LOWNESS.

groundless, *adj.* baseless, unauthorized, unfounded. See UNSUBSTANTIALITY.

grounds, *n. pl.* estate; dregs, lees. See PLAIN, UNCLEANNESS.

groundwork, *n.* basis, foundation; substructure, framework. See BASE, SUPPORT.

group, *n.* bunch, cluster, company, collection. See ASSEMBLAGE.

group, *v.* classify, sort, combine, cluster. See ARRANGEMENT.

grove, *n.* wood, tope (*Anglo-Indian*). See VEGETABLE.

grovel, *v.* cringe, crouch, creep, wallow, fawn. See SERVILITY.

grow, *v.* extend, enlarge, augment; cultivate, raise; wax, become; sprout, germinate; develop, thrive, flourish. See EXPANSION, HUSBANDRY, INCREASE, VEGETATION.

growl, *v.* grumble, complain; howl, snarl. See LAMENTATION, ULULATION.

grudge, *v.* covet, begrudge; withhold, stint. See ENVY, PARSIMONY.

gruesome, *adj.* hideous, ghastly, horrible, grisly. See UGLINESS.

gruff, *adj.* surly, blunt; coarse, harsh. See DISCOURTESY, STRIDENCY.

grumble, *v.* complain, murmur, mutter, growl. See DISCOUNT, LAMENTATION.

guarantee, *v.* pledge, undertake, assure, warrant, insure, secure (against, from, *or* in). See SECURITY.
guarantor, *n.* guarantee, surety, sponsor, bail. See SECURITY.
guaranty, *n.* guarantee, warranty, agreement, contract. See SECURITY.
guard, *v.* protect, shield, watch, safeguard, keep. See DEFENSE.
guard, *n.* protection, security, safeguard; convoy, escort; sentinel, watchman. See DEFENSE, SAFETY, STOPPER.
guardian, *n.* protector, custodian, preserver. See KEEPER, SAFETY.
guardianship, *n.* protection, custody, safe-keeping. See SAFETY.
guess, *v.* divine, conjecture, suspect, surmise. See SUPPOSITION.
guest, *n.* visitor, caller. See FRIEND.
guide, *v.* lead, escort; steer, regulate; train, instruct. See CONDUCT, DIRECTION, TEACHING.
guide, *n.* cicerone, courier, pilot; handbook, guidebook; dragoman; counselor, adviser. See DIRECTOR, INFORMATION, INTERPRETER, TEACHER.
guidebook, *n.* handbook, guide. See JOURNEY.
guild, *n.* association, society, union. See COMBINATION.
guile, *n.* deceit, treachery, cunning, craftiness. See DECEPTION.
guileless, *adj.* innocent, ingenuous, honest, unsuspicious. See ARTLESSNESS.
guilelessness, *n.* innocence, frankness, *naïveté* (*F.*), simple-mindedness, trust, unsophistication. See ARTLESSNESS, SIMPLICITY.

GUILT.—I. *Nouns.* **guilt,** guiltiness, culpability, criminality, blameworthiness, reprehensibility, censurability, censurableness; misconduct, misbehavior, malpractice, misdoing, wrongdoing, sinfulness, vice, depravity, turpitude.
misdeed, misdemeanor (*law*), transgression, fault, offense *or* offence, trespass injury, violation, infringement, sin, crime, felony, outrage, enormity, atrocity, capital crime; delinquency, misfeasance (*wrongful exercise of lawful authority*), malfeasance (*official misconduct*), nonfeasance (*neglect of some duty which one is legally bound to perform*), dereliction, negligence; extortion, corruption, malversation, malefaction, professional misconduct (*or* malpractice); deadly sin (*theol.*), mortal sin (*theol.*); "deed without a name" (*Macbeth*).
indiscretion, lapse, slip, misstep, trip, flaw, blot, omission, failing, failure; error, blunder, break (*U. S. colloq.*), *faux pas* (*F.*), peccadillo.
II. *Adjectives.* **guilty,** blamable, culpable, censurable, condemnable, reprehensible, blameworthy, delinquent; "weighed in the balances and . . . found wanting" (*Bible*); redhanded.
III. *Adverbs.* **guiltily,** culpably, etc. (see *adjectives*); *flagrante delicto* (*L.*), in the very act.
See also VICE.—*Antonyms.* See INNOCENCE.

---

guiltless, *adj.* blameless, faultless. See INNOCENCE.
guise, *n.* aspect, mien; semblance, form. See APPEARANCE.

GULF.—I. *Nouns.* **gulf,** bay, inlet, arm, bight, estuary, bayou (*U. S.*), fiord, frith *or* firth, mouth; lagoon, cove, creek, natural harbor, roadstead, roads; sound, strait, narrows.
chasm, abyss, cañon, rift, cleft, pit, deep (*poetic*), bottomless pit, crevasse, abysm.
whirlpool, eddy, swirl, vortex, maelstrom, Charybdis: *in this sense,* **gulf** *is poetic.*
II. *Verbs.* **gulf,** engulf, swallow up, suck down.
See also INTERVAL.

---

gullible, *adj.* unsuspicious, trustful, confiding. See CREDULITY.
gully, *n.* gulch, ravine, gorge. See INTERVAL.
gun, *n.* firearm, piece; cannon. See ARMS.
gunman, *n.* gangster, thug. See BAD MAN.
gunner, *n.* cannoneer, artilleryman; game shooter. See COMBATANT, PROPULSION (*marksman.*)

gush, *v.* spout, pour forth, flow, issue, emit, eject, rush. See EGRESS.
gushing, *adj.* enthusiastic, cordial; spouting, spurting; suave, smooth-tongued. See FEELING, STREAM, UNCTUOUSNESS.
gust, *n.* outburst (*as of passion*); blast, breeze, squall. See EXCITABILITY, WIND.
gusto, *n.* relish, delight, enjoyment, zest, enthusiasm. See PLEASURE.
gymnastic, *adj.* calisthenic, athletic. See CONTENTION.

H

HABIT.—I. *Nouns.* **habit,** wont, habitude, rule, practice, addiction, run, way, custom, usage, use, consuetude; mode, fashion, vogue, etiquette, procedure, prescription, prevalence, observance, conventionalism, conventionality; trick, knack, skill; beaten path, second nature, matter of course; tendency, aptitude, facilitation (*psychol.*).
rule, standing order, precedent, convention, routine, red tape, rut, groove.
dress (*esp. of religious order*), garb, attire, vestment, habiliment (*chiefly in pl.*), raiment, vesture, suit, gown, costume, frock (*as, a riding* habit).
constitution (*bodily and mental*), state, condition, temperament, character, appearance, make-up.
II. *Verbs.* **habit,** clothe, dress, garb, attire, array, accouter *or* accoutre.
habituate, inure, accustom, familiarize, addict, wont; harden, season, case-harden; train, naturalize, acclimate (*esp. without man's agency*), acclimatize; cling to, adhere to; acquire a habit; follow the beaten track (*or* path), move in a rut.
prevail, obtain, predominate, rule, reign, preponderate, rage; come into use, become a habit, take root; grow upon one.
III. *Adjectives.* **habitual,** customary, wonted, usual, routine, general, ordinary, common, frequent, everyday, household, familiar, well-trodden, well-known, trite, hackneyed, commonplace, conventional, regular, set, stock, established, prescriptive, stereotyped; fixed, rooted, permanent, inveterate, confirmed; besetting, ingrained, current, prevailing, prevalent.
wont, accustomed, habituated; in the habit of; used to, given to, addicted to; seasoned, imbued with, devoted to, wedded to.
IV. *Adverbs.* **habitually,** customarily, usually, etc. (see *adjectives*); *ex more* (*L.*), as usual, as things go, as the world goes; as a rule, for the most part, generally, most frequently.

See also CLOTHING, CONFORMITY, FREQUENCY.—*Antonyms.* See DISUSE.

HABITATION.—I. *Nouns.* **habitation,** abode, dwelling, lodging, domicile, residence, seat (*as, a* seat *of learning; country* seat), place, inhabitance (*rare*), address, berth, housing, sojourn (*temporary residence*), quarters, headquarters. [*in biology*] habitat, natural abode, natural home, native environment.
home, fatherland, motherland, country; homestead, hearth, hearthstone, fireside, chimney corner, ingleside; roof, household, housing; paternal domicile, *dulce domum* (*L.*), native soil, native land, "God's own country," down home (*colloq.*).
retreat, refuge, asylum, haunt, resort; lair, dugout, den, cave, cavern, grotto, hole, hiding place, cell, sanctum sanctorum, aerie *or* eyrie, rookery, hive; covert, perch, roost, nest, nidus (*pl.* nidi: *tech.*), arbor, bower.
anchorage, roadstead, roads; dock, basin, wharf, quay, port, harbor.
camp, bivouac, encampment, laager (*South Africa*), cantonment (*mil., as in India*), barracks, quarters.
tent, canvas, marquee, marquise, pavilion, wigwam, tepee, booth, kibitka (*Kirghiz*), tambu (*Hind.*); "A" tent, canoe tent, bell tent, fly tent, lean-to tent, pup tent, dog tent, shelter tent, wall tent.
hut, hovel, shanty, cabin, crib, shack (*colloq.*), miamia (*Australian aborigines*), igloo (*Eskimo*), chalet, log cabin, log house; barn, stable; byre, cowhouse, cowshed; booth, shed, stall, pen, fold; kennel, sty, cote, dovecote, coop, hutch.
house, mansion, place, villa, cottage, lodge, hermitage, *rus in urbe* (*L.*), country

seat, rotunda, tower, *château* (*F.*), castle, pavilion, hotel, court, manor house, hall, palace, kiosk, bungalow; apartment house, flat house; tenement, tenement house; flat, apartment, suite; three-decker, monitor building (*U. S.*); building, buildings.

farm, farmstead, grange, hacienda (*Sp. Amer.*), ranch, *estancia* (*Sp. Amer.*), plantation, pen (*West Indies*), mains (*Scot.*), barton (*Eng.*), croft (*Scot. Highlands*), location (*Australia*); dairy farm, dairy.

village, hamlet, thorp *or* thorpe (*now used chiefly in place names*), dorp (*Dutch*), wick (*rare except in place names*), rancho (*Sp. Amer.*), settlement, kraal (*South Africa*), clachan (*Scot.*), bustee *or* basti (*Anglo-Indian*), pueblo (*Indian village*).

town, borough, burgh (*Scot.*), burg (*U. S. colloq.*), city, capital, metropolis; county town, county seat.

street, place, terrace, parade, esplanade, board walk, embankment, road, row, lane, alley, wynd (*dial.*), court, quadrangle, quad (*colloq.*), close, yard, passage.

square, piazza (*as in Italy*), polygon, circus, crescent, block, arcade, colonnade, cloister; market place.

assembly room, auditorium, concert hall, armory, gymnasium; club, clubhouse, clubroom; lodge, lodge room, asylum (*Knights Templars*), hall, banquet hall, council chamber; cathedral, church, chapel, meetinghouse.

inn, hostelry (*archaic*), hotel, tavern, road house, saloon (*U. S. hist.*), barroom, speak-easy (*U. S. slang*), blind tiger (*U. S. slang*), blind pig (*U. S. slang*), pub (*Brit. colloq.*), public house, alehouse, *auberge* (*F.*), *posada* (*Sp.*), *Gasthof* (*Ger.*), *Wirtshaus* (*Ger.*), *albergo* (*It.*); grill room, chophouse, coffeehouse, eating-house; canteen, restaurant, buffet, café, *estaminet* (*F.*), cabaret, night club.

resthouse, serai (*Oriental*), dak bungalow (*India*), caravansary *or* caravanserai (*Oriental*), khan (*Oriental*), choultry (*Anglo-Indian*), hospice.

sanatorium, health resort, sanitarium; spa, watering-place; pump room.

II. *Adjectives.* **habitable,** inhabitable, livable *or* liveable, lodgeable, residential, tenantable, occupiable.

rural, rustic, Arcadian (*poetic*), agrarian, bucolic, country, pastoral, silvan *or* sylvan; agricultural, georgic, agrestic; countrified, provincial.

urban, town (*used attributively*), burghal, civic, metropolitan; suburban.

See also LOCATION, PRESENCE (*inhabit*), RECEPTACLE (*chamber*), REGION.

---

habitual, *adj.* customary, usual, regular, ordinary. See HABIT.

habituate, *v.* accustom, inure, familiarize. See HABIT, USE.

hack, *v.* cut, hew, haggle. See DISJUNCTION.

hackneyed, *adj.* trite, stale, banal, commonplace. See HABIT.

hag, *n.* witch, hellhag, harridan; crone, beldam. See BAD WOMAN, EVIL-DOER, VETERAN.

haggard, *adj.* worn, emaciated, gaunt. See FATIGUE, UGLINESS.

haggle, *v.* bargain, chaffer, higgle. See BARTER.

hail, *v.* salute, greet; call, accost. See COURTESY, SPEECH.

hail! *interj. ave*! (*L.*), hurrah! hello! welcome! all hail! See CELEBRATION, COURTESY, REPUTE.

hair, *n.* mop, thatch, locks. See ROUGHNESS.

hairless, *adj.* bald, clean-shaven, beardless, smooth-faced. See DIVESTMENT, SMOOTHNESS.

hairy, *adj.* hirsute, bristly, shaggy. See ROUGHNESS.

halcyon, *adj.* peaceful, calm, quiet, tranquil. See MODERATION.

hale, *adj.* sound, robust, vigorous, hardy. See HEALTHINESS.

half, *n.* moiety. See BISECTION.

half-breed, *n.* half-blood, half-caste. See MIXTURE.

half-hearted, *adj.* lukewarm, apathetic, listless. See INDIFFERENCE.

half truth, equivocation, white lie, suppression. See UNTRUTH.

half-witted, *adj.* foolish, mentally defective. See IMBECILITY.

hall, *n.* auditorium, assembly room; corridor, passage. See HABITATION, WAY.

hallelujah! *interj.* alleluia! hosanna! glory be to God! See WORSHIP.

hallow, *v.* consecrate, sanctify, enshrine. See PIETY.

hallucination, *n.* illusion, delusion, perception, phantasm. See ERROR.
halo, *n.* nimbus, aureole, aura. See LIGHT.
halt, *v.* stop, pause, stand still. See CESSATION.
halve, *v.* bisect, cut in two. See BISECTION.
hammer, *v.* pound, beat, strike; reiterate, drum. See IMPULSE, REPETITION.
hamper, *v.* obstruct, encumber, fetter, impede, restrict. See HINDRANCE.
hand, *n.* workman, laborer; pointer, guide; seaman, sailor; direction; handwriting, penmanship. See AGENT, INDICATION, MARINER, SIDE, WRITING.—**at hand,** handy, ready. See UTILITY.
hand, *v.* pass, give, convey, transmit. See TRANSFER.—**hand over,** give, transfer, deliver, surrender. See PASSAGE.
handbag, *n.* valise, grip (*colloq.*), portmanteau. See RECEPTACLE.
handbook, *n.* guidebook, manual. See INFORMATION.
handcuff, *v.* manacle, fetter, shackle. See RESTRAINT.
handicap, *v.* encumber, burden, hamper. See HINDRANCE.
handle, *v.* deal with, manage, control; work, operate; hold, feel; wield, manipulate. See DIRECTION, SERVANT, TOUCH, USE.
handle, *n.* hilt, shaft, haft. See INSTRUMENT.
handsome, *adj.* personable, comely; ample, generous, considerable. See BEAUTY, LIBERALITY.
handwriting, *n.* penmanship, hand, chirography. See WRITING.
handy, *adj.* dexterous, apt, quick, expert; available, convenient, ready. See SKILL, UTILITY.
hang, *v.* stick, cling; loiter, linger; fasten, suspend; dangle; kill, execute; float, wave. See COHERENCE, LATENESS, PENDENCY, PUNISHMENT, STREAM (*extend*).
hanker, *v.* long for, crave, covet. See DESIRE.
haphazard *adj.* random, accidental, aimless. See CHANCE.
happen, *v.* occur, take place, befall. See EVENT.
happiness, *n.* felicity, bliss, rapture; well-being, public welfare. See PLEASURE, UTILITY.
happy, *adj.* felicitous, apt; gay, sunny, contented; joyful, ecstatic; lucky, fortunate. See AGREEMENT, CHEERFULNESS, PLEASURE, TIMELINESS.
harangue, *n.* discourse, address, tirade. See SPEECH.
harass, *v.* torment, plague, pester, vex, annoy. See PAIN.
harbinger, *n.* sign, token; forerunner. See OMEN, PRECURSOR.
harbor, *n.* shelter, retreat; haven, port. See REFUGE.
harbor, *v.* cherish, foster, hold, entertain. See THOUGHT.
hard, *adj.* firm, rigid; strong, robust; unfeeling, unsympathetic; harsh, repellent; vigorous, violent; strenuous, laborious; oppressive, severe; puzzling, difficult; sharp, voiceless. See HARDNESS, STRENGTH (*phonetics*).
harden, *v.* accustom, inure, habituate; anneal, steel, make callous; blunt, caseharden; thicken, congeal. See HABIT, HARDNESS, INSENSITIVENESS, THICKNESS.
hardened, *adj.* obdurate, callous, irredeemable: *of persons.* See LOSS.
hardening, *n.* induration, scirrhosity (*as of a gland*). See HARDNESS.
hard-headed, *adj.* shrewd, keen, sharp. See INTELLIGENCE.
hard-hearted, *adj.* ruthless, cruel, unfeeling. See MALEVOLENCE.
hardihood, *n.* fortitude, intrepidity; audacity, impudence. See COURAGE, INSOLENCE.
hardly, *adv.* scarcely, rarely, barely. See INFREQUENCY.

HARDNESS.—I. *Nouns.* **hardness,** firmness, solidity, toughness, rigidity, etc. (see *adjectives*); inflexibility, temper, callosity; induration, petrifaction, ossification, fossilization; crystallization, glaciation, vitrification, vitrescence, vulcanization.

[*comparisons*] adamant, diamond, flint, stone, brick, pebble, cobble, cobblestone, rock, crag, marble, granite, quartz, crystal, fossil; cement, concrete; bone,

cartilage; block, board, deal board, oak; iron, steel, cast iron, wrought iron, rail; bakelite, durium, duralumin (*used in building airplanes: trade name*), osmium, iridosmium.
[*in medicine*] **hardening,** induration, scirrhosity (*as of a gland*), scleriasis (*as of the eyelid*), scleroma (*of tissues*), sclerosis (*also bot.*), scleroderma (*of the skin*); arteriosclerosis, hardening of the arteries.
II. *Verbs.* **harden,** render hard, temper, anneal, steel, braze, chill, case-harden, Harveyize, vulcanize; callous, crust, solidify, congeal, firm, indurate, starch, stiffen; bake, dry; cement, petrify, fossilize, ossify.
inure, habituate, discipline, train, toughen, strengthen, accustom, familiarize, acclimatize.
III. *Adjectives.* **hard,** firm, solid, rigid, stiff, implastic, unbending, unyielding, inflexible, stark, tense, taut; adamantine, stony, rocky, flinty, steely, brassy, brazen; horny, callous, bony, cartilaginous; indurate, indurated, scirrhous (*med.*), sclerosed, sclerotic, sclerous, scleroid (*bot. and zoöl.*).
robust, strong, hardy, inured, acclimatized, enduring, seasoned, tough (*as, the team was in* hard *condition*).
difficult, perplexing, intricate, involved; laborious, rigorous, severe, arduous, strenuous, trying, exacting, fatiguing, exhausting, uphill, painful, ticklish, oppressive.
[*difficult to impress*] **obdurate,** unfeeling, unsympathetic, hardened, callous, insensible, unsusceptible, stubborn, dour (*Scot.*), dure (*archaic*); close, grasping (*as, a* hard *heart*).
energetic, persevering, active, hearty, emphatic, vigorous, intense, earnest, profound, violent (*as, a* hard *worker or rider*).
disreputable, incorrigible, abandoned, reprobate, irreformable, shameless, depraved (*as, a* hard *gang: colloq. in this sense*).
[*of style, etc.*] **repellent,** repelling, repugnant, forbidding, harsh, grim, rigid, stiff, ungraceful, unattractive.
[*in phonetics*] **explosive** (*as* d, k, g), strong, sharp: *opposite of* soft.
voiceless (*as* p, t), surd, nonsonant: *opposite of* voiced.
[*of liquors*] **rough,** austere, acid, sour (*as,* hard *cider*).
strong, spirituous, ardent, alcoholic, distilled (*as,* hard *beverages*).
See also DIFFICULTY, HABIT, IMPENITENCE, INSENSITIVENESS, LETTER (*voiceless*), PAINFULNESS, ROUGHNESS, SEVERITY, STRENGTH.—*Antonyms.* See FACILITY, SOFTNESS.

---

hardship, *n.* affliction, trouble, calamity, reverse. See ADVERSITY.
hardy, *adj.* daring, resolute; tough, enduring. See COURAGE, STRENGTH.
harem, *n.* seraglio. See WOMAN.
hark, *v.* hearken, listen. See HEARING.
harlot, *n.* prostitute, strumpet, courtesan. See BAD WOMAN, LIBERTINE.
harm, *v.* damage, injure; wrong, dishonor. See DETERIORATION, EVIL, TOUCH (*impair*).
harmful, *adj.* injurious, detrimental, damaging, hurtful, mischievous. See EVIL.
harmless, *adj.* innocuous, inoffensive, innocent. See GOOD, INNOCENCE, SAFETY.

HARMONY.—I. *Nouns.* **harmony,** agreement, adaptation, conformity accord, accordance, concord, concurrence, consent, unity, unanimity, union; congruity, consistency, correspondence, unison; order, symmetry, proportion.
peace, tranquillity, pacification; friendliness, friendship, amity, understanding, *entente* (*F.*).
reconciliation, reconcilement, adjustment, settlement, coördination, collation, orientation.
[*in music*] **consonance,** accordance, accord, concord, tunefulness, euphony, tuneful sound; chordal structure, chord, consonant chord, triad; concentus, concent (*archaic*), diapason, music, symphony: *distinguished from* melody *and* rhythm.
science of harmony: harmony, harmonics; thorough bass, fundamental bass, counterpoint; faburden (*medieval music*)

harmonist, composer, musician, contrapuntist; harmonizer, collator (*esp. of parallel narratives*): *in music, distinguished from* melodist.
II. *Verbs.* [*to be harmonious*] **harmonize,** agree, accord, combine, cooperate, blend, unite, correspond, tally, suit.
[*to make harmonious*] arrange, adjust, reconcile, accord, attune, string, tune, modulate, put in harmony with, tune in (*radio: opposite of* tune out); adapt, set, orchestrate, symphonize, transpose.
III. *Adjectives.* **harmonious,** symmetrical, congruous, congruent, harmonistic, accordant, undiscordant, correspondent, conformable, proportionate.
peaceable, peaceful, amicable, friendly, neighborly, brotherly, cordial, congenial, sympathetic; unanimous, consentient.
[*in music*] **harmonic,** concordant, consonant, harmonizing, accordant, symphonious; in concord, in tune, in concert, in unison; agreeable, pleasing, sweet-sounding, pleasant-sounding, musical.

See also AGREEMENT, CONCORD, CONCURRENCE, CONFORMITY, MELODY, PURITY (*of sound*), TOUCH, UNITY.—*Antonyms.* See DISCORD.

---

harness, *v.* yoke, hitch up (*colloq.*); control, curb. See DOMESTICATION, RESTRAINT.

harrowing, *adj.* tragic, heart-rending, frightful. See PAINFULNESS.

harry, *v.* pillage, ravage; harass, hound. See DETERIORATION, MALEVOLENCE.

harsh, *adj.* stern, austere; stringent, drastic; sour, sharp; hard, rigorous; discordant, grating, raucous, rough. See DISCOURTESY, ENERGY, ROUGHNESS, SEVERITY, STRIDENCY.

harvest, *n.* outcome, issue; yield, crop. See EFFECT, STORE.

HASTE.—I. *Nouns.* **haste,** celerity, speed, quickness, dispatch, nimbleness, swiftness, rapidity, velocity, expeditiousness, alertness, promptitude.
[*undue haste*] **precipitation,** rush, impetuosity, precipitance *or* precipitancy, rashness; drive, bustle, hustle, scramble, flurry, fidget, scurry, scamper, scuttle, dash, spurt, forced march; urgency, hurry, acceleration.
II. *Verbs.* **hasten,** haste (*now chiefly literary*), make haste, dash on, push on, press on (*or* forward), hurry, speed, bustle, flutter, scramble, plunge, dash off, rush, express; bestir oneself, hustle (*colloq.*), race, fly, wing, spur, drive, lose no time, make short work of; work against time, work under pressure.
quicken, accelerate, dispatch, hurry, speed, expedite, precipitate, urge, whip, spur, press, flog, goad.
III. *Adjectives.* **hasty,** quick, speedy, expeditious, swift, rapid, hurried, cursory, passing, superficial.
precipitate, headlong, furious, boisterous, impetuous, rash, fiery, excitable, hot-headed, feverish, pushing, pressing, urgent.
IV. *Adverbs.* **hastily,** hurriedly, quickly, expeditiously, post-haste, hotfoot, precipitately, helter-skelter, hurry-skurry, slap-dash, slap-bang; full-tilt, full-drive; heels over head, headlong, pell-mell.
with haste, with speed, in haste, apace, amain; at short notice, immediately, posthaste; by cable, by telegraph, by wireless (*colloq.*), by aëroplane, by air mail, by return mail, by forced marches.

See also EXCITABILITY, INSTANTANEITY, IRASCIBILITY, VELOCITY.—*Antonyms.* See LEISURE.

---

hat, *n.* headdress, *chapeau* (*F.*), panama, derby (*U. S.*), sombrero, turban. See CLOTHING.

hatch, *v.* incubate; concoct, trump up; invent, originate. See DOMESTICATION, FALSEHOOD, IMAGINATION.

HATE.—I. *Nouns.* **hate,** hatred, aversion, detestation, abhorrence, loathing, repugnance, antipathy, execration, abomination, odium, ill will, malevolence, malignity, animosity, rancor, enmity, malice, implacability; disfavor, unpopularity, disaffection; alienation, estrangement, coolness; umbrage, pique, **grudge, spleen, bitterness, acrimony, bitterness of feeling;** ill blood, bad blood.

[*an object of hatred*] an abomination, an aversion, *bête noire* (*F.*), enemy, bitter pill, source of annoyance.
II. *Verbs.* **hate**, detest, abominate, abhor, loathe; recoil at, shudder at; shrink from, revolt against, execrate; dislike.
[*to provoke hatred*] **alienate**, estrange, repel, horrify, set against, sow dissension, disunite, set by the ears, envenom; incense, irritate, ruffle, vex, roil.
III. *Adjectives.* **hateful**, obnoxious, odious, abominable, nameless (*as vices*), repulsive, offensive, repellent, repugnant, loathsome, abhorrent, revolting, disgusting, shocking; unpleasant, unpalatable, disagreeable, forbidding; censurable, reprehensible, illaudable; invidious, malicious, spiteful, envious.
unloved, unbeloved, unlamented, undeplored, unmourned, uncared for, unvalued; disliked.
lovelorn, forsaken, rejected, jilted, crossed in love.
[*mutually hating*] at daggers drawn, at loggerheads, on bad terms, not on speaking terms, at odds, at outs.
See also BADNESS, DISLIKE, ENMITY, MALEVOLENCE, PAINFULNESS, RESENTMENT.—*Antonyms.* See LOVE.

---

haughty, *adj.* proud, supercilious, arrogant, overbearing. See HEIGHT, INSOLENCE.
haul, *v.* draw, pull, drag, lug. See TRACTION.
haunt, *v.* obsess, prey upon; visit, frequent. See FEAR, FREQUENCY.
haunt, *n.* resort, den, retreat. See FOCUS.
have, *v.* hold, possess, own. See POSSESSION.
haven, *n.* port, harbor; shelter, asylum. See REFUGE.
hazard, *n.* contingency, accident; peril, risk. See CHANCE, DANGER.
haze, *n.* mist, fog; vagueness, obscurity. See CLOUD, UNCERTAINTY.
head, *n.* caption, heading, title; grouping, category; chief, leader; fore, van; brains, judgment; top, tip, pate. See BEGINNING, CLASS, DIRECTOR, FRONT, INTELLECT, SUMMIT.
head, *v.* guide, manage, rule, control; precede, lead, take precedence. See DIRECTION, PRECEDENCE.
headdress, *n.* coiffure, headgear. See CLOTHING.
heading, *n.* title, caption, head. See BEGINNING.
headland, *n.* cliff, bluff, spur, cape, promontory. See CONVEXITY.
headlong, *adj.* rash, precipitate, furious, madcap. See HASTE.
headstrong, *adj.* willful, stubborn, perverse, wayward, ungovernable. See OBSTINACY, VIOLENCE.
headway, *n.* advance, progress. See PROGRESSION.
heal, *v.* repair, mend, cure. See REMEDY, RESTORATION.
healing art, practice of medicine, therapeutics; pathology. See REMEDY.

HEALTH.—I. *Nouns.* **health**, soundness, vigor, haleness, hardiness, good (perfect, excellent, *or* robust) health, euphoria *or* euphory (*rare*), *mens sana in corpore sano* (*L.*), sanity (*health of mind*); bloom, convalescence, strength, poise.
II. *Verbs.* **be in health**, enjoy good health, bloom, flourish.
return to health, recover, get better, take a new lease of life, convalesce, be convalescent, recruit; restore to health, cure.
III. *Adjectives.* [*conducive to health*] **healthful**, salubrious, health-giving, wholesome, salutary, beneficial (*as*, healthful *food*).
[*full of health, as a person or plant*] **healthy**, well, sound, strong, robust, hearty, euphoric (*rare*); fresh, green: healthful *and* healthy *are in the main interchangeable; but the tendency is to restrict* healthful *to that which conduces to health and to apply* healthy *to that which is in a state of health; as, a* healthy (*not* healthful) *child,* healthful (*not* healthy) *diet;* a healthful (*or* healthy) *climate.*
uninjured, unscathed, unmarred, unhurt, unharmed, without a scratch, safe and sound.
See also RESTORATION.—*Antonyms.* See DISEASE.

HEALTHINESS.—I. *Nouns.* **healthiness,** wholesomeness; soundness, healthfulness, salubrity, salubriousness; Hygeia.

II. *Adjectives.* [*conducive to health*] **healthy,** salubrious, salutary, wholesome, sanitary, prophylactic; benign, bracing, tonic, invigorating, hygienic (*as, a* healthy *climate;* healthy *exercise*): *in this sense, equivalent to* healthful.

nutritious, nourishing, nutrient, nutritive, alimental, eutrophic (*opposite of* dystrophic: *med.*), sustentative, substantial, digestible, eupeptic, digestive, peptic: *opposite of* innutritious.

[*enjoying health*] **hale,** sound, whole, robust, vigorous, hardy; rosy-cheeked, florid, blooming, chipper (*U. S. colloq.*), in fine fettle (*as, a* healthy *man*).

innocuous, harmless, innocent, innoxious, inoffensive, uninjurious; immune.

See also HEALTH, WHOLE.—*Antonyms.* See UNHEALTHINESS.

---

heap, *n.* mass, pile, stack, lump. See ASSEMBLAGE, SIZE.

HEARING.—I. *Nouns.* **hearing,** audition (*tech.*), auscultation (*esp. med.*); ear (*as for music*); audibleness, audibility; acoustics.

[*opportunity of being heard*] **audience,** interview, conference, admittance (*to a* hearing), attention (*as, to obtain a* hearing).

[*formal hearing*] **trial,** judicial examination.

[*hearing distance*] **earshot,** range, reach, carrying distance, sound.

[*organ of hearing*] **ear,** auricle (*external ear*), pinna (*anat. and zoöl.*), lug (*dial.*), concha; acoustic organ, auditory apparatus; eardrum, tympanum.

[*mechanical devices*] ear trumpet, speaking trumpet, ear phone; audiphone, dentiphone; stethoscope (*med.*); phonograph, graphophone (*trade-mark name*), gramophone, victrola (*trade-mark name*); dictophone (*mechanical eavesdropper*), dictograph (*both trade-mark names*); megaphone, amplifier, microphone, mike (*radio cant*), loud speaker *or* speaker (*radio*); telephone.

hearer, auditor, listener, eavesdropper (*secret listener*); disciple, follower.

[*in plural*] audience, auditory (*rare*), congregation; orchestra, pit (*chiefly Brit.*), pittites (*Eng. theatrical cant*); gallery, gods.

II. *Verbs.* **hear, hearken** *or* **harken, catch, listen, heed, hark** (*now rare, except as an imperative or interjection*), list (*archaic*), attend; strain one's ears, give attention, prick up one's ears, overhear; perceive, apprehend; give ear, give a hearing to, give audience to.

III. *Adjectives.* **hearing,** auditory, aural, otic (*tech.*), auricular, acoustic, auditive.

See also ATTENTION, LAWSUIT, TRIAL.—*Antonyms.* See DEAFNESS.

---

hearsay, *n.* rumor, report, talk. See NEWS.

heart, *n.* spirit, fortitude; soul, nature; midst, center; substance, essence, pith, core. See COURAGE, DISPOSITION, MIDDLE, SUBJECTIVENESS.—**by heart,** by rote. See MEMORY.

heartbroken, *adj.* disconsolate, miserable, forlorn, wretched. See PAIN.

hearten, *v.* nerve, reassure, rally, cheer, encourage. See COURAGE.

heartfelt, *adj.* profound, sincere, deep. See DEPTH, DEARNESS, FEELING.

heartily, *adv.* cordially, sincerely, earnestly, gladly, zealously. See FEELING.

heartless, *adj.* unfeeling, cruel, unsympathetic. See INSENSITIVENESS.

heart-shaped, *adj.* cordiform, cordate. See CURVATURE.

hearty, *adj.* cordial, warm, earnest; well, sound, vigorous. See FEELING HEALTH.

HEAT.—I. *Nouns.* **heat,** caloric, caloricity (*physiol.*), hotness, torridity, torridness, fervidity, fervency, fervidness, fervor, warmth; cauma (*med.*), temperature (*colloq. in the sense of supernormal heat, as of the human body*); glow, flush, fever, febricity (*med.*), pyrexia (*med.*), redness, blush.

[*intense heat*] **summer,** midsummer; dog days, canicular days, canicule (*rare*); baking heat, tropical heat, Bengal summer, broiling sun, vertical rays, sun at noon.

hot wind, hot wave, heat wave; khamsin (*Egypt*) harmattan (*West Africa*),

leste (*Madeira*), ***leveche*** (*Spain*), ***solano*** (*Spain*), sirocco (*Sahara, Italy, and coast of Mediterranean; applied also to the hot winds of Texas and Kansas*), simoom *or* simoon (*Arabia, Syria, etc.*).
fire, flame, blaze, ingle, spark, coal, scintillation, flash; bonfire, balefire, signal fire, beacon, alarm fire, needfire (*archaic*), wildfire, conflagration; sheet of fire, lambent flame.
science of heat: thermology, thermotics, thermodynamics, pyrology.
thermal unit (*physics*), calorie, British thermal unit, Board of Trade unit, B. T. U.
[*intensity of feeling*] **excitement,** agitation, fervor, ardor, warmth, animation, fervency; vehemence, rage, exasperation, frenzy.
II. *Verbs.* **heat,** make hot, hot (*colloq. or illiterate*), fire, bake, stove, mull (*as ale or wine*); calcine, incandesce; warm, chafe; calefy, tepefy.
excite, arouse, inflame, incense, enrage, exasperate, provoke, irritate; kindle, impassion, agitate, incite, stimulate.
be hot, glow, flush, bask, sweat, perspire, swelter, smoke, reek, stew, simmer, seethe, boil, decoct, burn, singe, scorch, scald, broil, blaze, flame, smolder, parch, pant.
thaw, liquefy, condense, melt, run, fuse, dissolve, liquate.
III. *Adjectives.* **heated,** hot, torrid, tropical, thermal (*as,* thermal *waters*), thermic, calorific; fiery, igneous, baking, roasting, parching, fervid, fervent, burning, flaming, glowing, reeking, smoking, smoldering, blazing, ablaze, afire, alight, live (*as coal*), incandescent; ebullient, boiling.
vehement, violent, passionate, fiery, ardent, agitated, fervid, fervent; raging, furious, precipitate, impetuous, frenzied, frantic.
excitable, irritable, irascible, nervous, high-strung, inflammable, hasty, wrathful, wrathy (*colloq.*), impatient; animated, brisk.
warm, mild, genial, sunny, sunshiny, calid (*archaic*); tepid, lukewarm.
close, sultry, stifling, stuffy, suffocating, oppressive, sweltering.
feverish, febrile, fevered, feverous, pyretic (*med.*), inflamed, burning, fiery.

See also CALEFACTION, EXCITABILITY, EXCITEMENT, FEELING.—*Antonyms.* See COLD.

---

heater, *n.* stove, radiator. See FURNACE.
heathen, *adj.* pagan, irreligious, idolatrous. See HETERODOXY.
heave, *v.* hoist, lift, raise. See ELEVATION.

HEAVEN.—I. *Nouns.* **heaven,** kingdom of heaven (*or* God), heavenly kingdom; heaven of heavens, highest heaven, empyrean (*as used by Dante and Milton*), abode of God, God's throne, throne of God; Paradise, Eden, Zion, Holy City, New Jerusalem, Heavenly City, City Celestial, abode of the blessed, abode of bliss.
[*mythological heaven or paradise*] Olympus; Elysium (*Greek*), Elysian fields, Islands (*or* Isles) of the Blessed, Happy Isles, Fortunate Isles, garden of the Hesperides; third heaven, seventh heaven; Valhalla (*Scandinavian*), Asgard (*Scandinavian*), Nirvana (*Buddhist*); happy hunting grounds (*N. Amer. Indian*).
future state, life after death, eternal home; resurrection, translation; apotheosis, deification; perfect felicity, heavenly bliss.
[*in plural*] **the heavens,** sky, welkin (*archaic*), firmament, canopy, sphere (*poetic*), empyrean, azure, blue vault above, hyaline (*poetic*), ether *or* æther, starry cope (*or* host); crystalline heavens, crystalline spheres (*Ptolemaic astronomy, alluded to in Paradise Lost*).
II. *Adjectives.* **heavenly,** celestial, supernal, unearthly, paradisaic *or* paradisaical, paradisiac *or* paradisiacal, angelic, divine, blessed, sacred, beatific; Elysian, Arcadian, Olympian.
[*relating to the heavens*] celestial; empyrean, empyreal (*these two words relate both to the firmament and to the highest heaven*); ethereal, uranic, astronomical; starry, stellar, stellary, sidereal, astral.

See also DEITY, PLEASURE, WORLD.—*Antonyms.* See HELL.

---

heavenly bodies, luminaries, stars, planets, etc. See WORLD.

HEAVINESS.—I. *Nouns.* **heaviness,** weight, gravity, ponderousness, ponderosity, massiveness.
[*of fabrics, etc.*] thickness, coarseness.
[*of style, etc.*] dullness, monotony, tediousness, uninterestingness, tiresomeness; tumidity, turgidity.
oppressiveness, severity, grievousness, onerousness, burdensomeness, cumbrousness, cumbersomeness, unwieldiness, irksomeness.
inertness, sluggishness, dullness, torpor, stupor, lethargy, languor, apathy, stolidity, inertia, languidness, lifelessness.
depression, dejection, oppression, sorrow, grief, gloom, melancholy, despondency, sadness (see *adjectives*).
II. *Verbs.* **be heavy,** be weighty, etc. (see *adjectives*); have weight, weigh; press, bear down; oppress, burden, crush.
weigh upon, prey upon, worry, distress, grieve, afflict.
make heavy, load, pack, burden, cargo, charge, lade, freight.
III. *Adjectives.* **heavy,** weighty, hefty (*colloq.*), ponderous, massive, unwieldy.
oppressive, hard, difficult, onerous, burdensome, severe, rigorous, grievous, troublesome (*as,* heavy *expenses; a* heavy *hand*).
languid, drowsy, sleepy, stolid, phlegmatic, inert, torpid, sluggish, apathetic, slow, listless, heavy-headed.
depressed, despondent, sad, low-spirited, doleful, dejected, weary, oppressed, heavy-laden, heavy-hearted.
dense, thick, close, abundant, copious (*as, a* heavy *growth of timber*).
thick, coarse, firm (*as,* heavy *linen*); wide, broad (*as, a* heavy *mark*).
stormy, violent; gloomy, overcast, cloudy, murky, leaden.
unusual, important, consequential, momentous; extraordinary, profound, intense, extreme; steep (*as a grade*).
[*of roads*] muddy, clinging, rough, washed-out, cloggy (*as,* heavy *going*).
[*of food*] soggy, indigestible; unleavened, unraised; strong (*as wines*).
[*of style, etc.*] dull, uninteresting, clumsy, stupid, tedious, monotonous, labored, laborious, turgid, tumid.
[*of theatrical roles*] serious, somber, grave (*as, a* heavy *part*).
[*of sounds*] loud, deep, bass, low-toned, full, powerful.
IV. *Adverbs.* **heavily,** weightily, etc. (see *adjectives*); with force; slowly, with difficulty, laboriously, tediously; wearily, dejectedly; grievously.
thickly, closely, densely; copiously, abundantly.
See also DEJECTION, DULLNESS, GRAVITY, INACTIVITY, PAINFULNESS, SLOWNESS.—*Antonyms.* See LEVITY, LIGHTNESS.

---

hector, *v.* domineer, bully, bluster. See INSOLENCE.
heed, *v.* attend, notice, regard, observe, note. See FOLLOWING.
heedful, *adj.* cautious, careful, thoughtful, mindful, attentive. See THOUGHT.
heedless, *adj.* negligent, remiss, careless, thoughtless; unobserving, undiscerning. See INATTENTION.

HEIGHT.—I. *Nouns.* **height,** altitude, elevation, perpendicular distance, highness, loftiness, pitch, stature, tallness, prominence, celsitude (*rare*), sublimity. apex, zenith, culmination.
[*that which is elevated*] **eminence,** hill, butte (*Western U. S.*); kop, kopje (*both South African*), mount, mountain, alp; bluff, cliff, peak, headland, foreland, promontory; ridge, range, chain, watershed, *arête* (*F.*), dune, rise, rising ground, down, brae (*Scot. and dial. Eng.*), uplands, highlands; knoll, knob (*chiefly in place names*), hummock, hillock, mound.
tower, pillar, column, obelisk, monument, belfry, steeple, spire, *flèche* (*F.*), minaret, campanile, turret, tourelle (*arch.*), dome, cupola; pagoda, pyramid; sikhra, vimana, gopura (*three types of pyramidal towers, as in Hindu and Buddhist temples*); skyscraper.
pole, spile, pile, stave, caber (*Scot.*), spar, stick, pikestaff, Maypole, flagstaff; mast, mainmast, topmast, topgallant mast.
high water, high tide, flood tide, spring tide.
[*highest point*] **summit,** apex, top, zenith, vertex, acme, pinnacle, culmination, extreme limit, *ne plus ultra* (*L.*), climax, meridian, turning point (*as, the* height *of a fever, storm, etc.*).

ceiling (*meteorol. and aëro.*), maximum altitude, absolute ceiling (*maximum height to which an aircraft can climb*), service ceiling (*maximum height at which an aircraft ceases to climb at a rate greater than* 100 *feet a minute, owing to diminishing atmospheric density; as, a* ceiling *of* 5,000 *feet*), ceiling height (*vertical distance to the lowest layer of clouds: meteorol.*).
measurement of altitudes: hypsometry, hypsography, altimetry; altimeter.
II. *Verbs.* **heighten,** elevate, exalt, upraise, uphoist, uplift, uprear, raise, rear, hoist, erect, set up, make higher.
intensify, strengthen, enhance, augment, increase, aggravate, advance, sharpen.
tower, soar, rear, uprise, rise, ascend, mount, spire, hover; overhang, impend (*rare in this sense*), beetle, jut, overtop, overlook, command; surmount, rise above, cap, culminate.
III. *Adjectives.* **high,** elevated, eminent, exalted, lofty, sublime; tall, gigantic, big, colossal; towering, soaring, elevated, aërial.
hilly, mountainous, rangy, Alpine; heaven-kissing, cloud-capt.
overhanging, impending, beetling, incumbent, overlying; superimposed.
foremost (*as in rank or importance*), first, chief, principal, head, top, main, leading, grand, supreme (*as,* high *priest;* high *society*).
intense, great, extreme, keen, marked; strong, mighty, powerful, potent (*as,* high *pressure;* high *passions*); deep, vivid (*as,* high *color*).
[*highly intellectual*] **recondite,** profound, abstruse, searching, deep, difficult, subtle, abstract (*as,* high *thinking*).
[*showing elation*] **elated,** pleased, gleeful, glad, delighted, exultant, joyous, gladful (*archaic*), joyful, mirthful (*as,* high *spirits*).
[*of manner or character*] **haughty,** arrogant, ostentatious, overbearing, domineering, uppish (*colloq.*), self-important, pompous, boastful, consequential, lordly, disdainful, contemptuous, contumelious, proud, magisterial (*as, a* high *look;* high *and mighty*); wrathful, angry, infuriated (*as,* high *words*).
[*of sounds*] **high-pitched,** shrill, sharp, high-toned, acute, loud, piercing.
[*of meat*] **tainted,** strongly scented, gamy, high-flavored.
[*of price*] **costly,** dear, expensive, high-priced.
higher, upper, superior, supernal, celestial, heavenly.
highest, topmost, uppermost; head, principal, supreme, crowning; apical, apicular.
IV. *Adverbs.* **on high,** high up, aloft, up, above, overhead; in the clouds.

See also CONVEXITY, ELEVATION, EXAGGERATION, SUMMIT.—*Antonyms.* See DEPTH, LOWNESS.

---

heinous, *adj.* atrocious, monstrous, hateful, abominable. See VICE.
heir, *n.* heiress (*fem.*), inheritor, inheritress (*fem.*). See POSSESSOR.

HELL.—I. *Nouns.* **hell,** underworld, abode of the dead, place of departed spirits, Sheol (*Hebrew*), the grave, purgatory.
bottomless pit, the pit, the abyss, infernal regions, inferno, abode of the damned, place of torment; Pandemonium, Abaddon, Tophet, Gehenna, Naraka (*Hinduism and Buddhism*), Avichi *or* Avici (*theos.*), Malebolge (*the eighth circle of hell, in Dante's "Inferno"*); hell fire, everlasting fire (*or* torment); worm that shall not die; evil resort (*as, a gambling* hell).
[*mythological hell*] Tartarus, Hades, Avernus; nether world, shades below, limbo, realms of Pluto; Nastrond (*Norse*), Niflhel (*Norse*); Amenti (*Egyptian*), Aralu (*Babylonian*).
Pluto, Rhadamanthus, Erebus, Charon, Cerberus; Persephone, Proserpina *or* Proserpine; Minos, Osiris.
[*river of Hades*] Styx, Stygian creek, Acheron (*river of woe*), Cocytus (*of wailing*), Phlegethon (*of fire*), Lethe (*of forgetfulness*).
evil spirits, infernal spirits, powers of darkness, hosts of hell (*or* evil); infernal concourse.
II. *Adjectives.* **hellish,** infernal, Stygian, Tartarean, Plutonian, Plutonic, Hadean (*rare*), chthonian; Satanic, Satanical, devilish.
fiendish, inhuman, diabolic *or* diabolical, demoniacal, satanic; wicked, malignant, destructive, detestable.

See also MYTHICAL BEINGS, SATAN.—*Antonyms.* See HEAVEN.

helmet, *n.* headpiece, casque, sallet, trench helmet. See CLOTHING.
helmet-shaped, *adj.* galeiform, galeate, cassideous (*bot.*). See CURVATURE.
help, *v.* assist, succor; support, befriend; relieve, ameliorate, remedy. See AID, IMPROVEMENT.
helper, *n.* assistant, coworker, partner, ally, colleague. See AUXILIARY.
helpful, *adj.* assisting, contributive, conducive, salutary, useful, beneficial, serviceable. See USE.
helpless, *adj.* powerless, incapable, crippled, dependent. See IMPOTENCE.
hen, *n.* fowl, Partlet, pullet. See ANIMAL.
hence, *adv.* therefore, so; thence, away. See ATTRIBUTION, DEPARTURE.
herald, *n.* forerunner, messenger, harbinger. See PRECURSOR.
herald, *v.* announce, introduce, usher in, proclaim. See PRECEDENCE, PREDICTION.
heraldry, *n.* heraldic science; heraldic devices, armorial bearings, blazonry, emblazonry, emblazonment. See ARMS, INDICATION.(*heraldry*).
herd, *n.* drove, flock. See MULTITUDE.
herder, *n.* herdsman, shepherd, cowherd, cowboy (*U. S.*). See DOMESTICATION.
here, *adv.* hither; hereabouts, in this place. See ARRIVAL, SITUATION.
hereafter, *adv.* ultimately, eventually, subsequently. See FUTURE.
hereditary, *adj.* ancestral; transmissible, inheritable. See POSTERITY, SUBJECTIVENESS.
heretic, *n.* infidel, unbeliever, skeptic. See HETERODOXY.
heritage, *n.* inheritance, patrimony, legacy. See POSSESSION, PROPERTY.
hermit, *n.* recluse, anchorite, solitary. See ASCETICISM.
heroic, *adj.* brave, valiant, fearless, gallant. See COURAGE.
hesitate, *v.* falter, pause; flounder, doubt. See IRRESOLUTION, UNCERTAINTY.

HETERODOXY.—I. *Nouns.* **heterodoxy,** unorthodoxy, error, false doctrine, heresy, schism, recusancy, backsliding, apostasy; materialism, unbelief, atheism.
bigotry, fanaticism, zealotry, iconoclasm; precisianism; sabbatarianism, puritanism, bibliolatry, hagiolatry.
sectarianism, nonconformity, dissent, disagreement, dissidence, secularism, denominationalism, separation, division; the isms, religious sects, the clash of creeds.
paganism, heathenism, heathendom, heathenry (*rare*), pagandom (*rare*), barbarism, animism, polytheism, pantheism, idolatry, idolism, superstition.
Mohammedanism, Islam, Islamism, Moslemism.
pagan, heathen, paynim (*archaic*); *giaour* (*Turk.*), kafir, non-Mohammedan; gentile; pantheist, polytheist, animist, idolater.
Mohammedan, Mussulman (*pl.* Mussulmans), Moslem *or* Muslim, Islamite, Islamist; Shiah, Shiite; Sunni, Sunnite; Osmanli, Motazilite, Wahabi, Ismaelian *or* Ismailian; Moor.
heretic, infidel, misbeliever, unbeliever, miscreant (*archaic in this sense*), apostate; backslider; antichrist, irreligionist, freethinker, atheist, agnostic, positivist, skeptic, materialist.
bigot, dogmatist, fanatic, zealot, dervish; iconoclast.
sectarian, sectary; seceder, separatist, recusant, dissenter, dissentient, dissident, nonconformist.
II. *Adjectives* **heterodox,** heretical, unorthodox, unscriptural, uncanonical, unchristian, apocryphal; antichristian; antiscriptural, schismatic, recusant, iconoclastic; sectarian, dissenting, secular; agnostic, atheistic, unbelieving, incredulous, freethinking, skeptical.
bigoted, narrow, prejudiced, illiberal, hidebound, dogmatical, fanatical; superstitious, credulous.
pagan, heathen, heathenish, unenlightened, paganish, gentile, paynim (*archaic*); polytheistic, pantheistic, animistic, idolatrous.
Mohammedan, Mussulman, Moslem *or* Muslim, Islamic *or* Islamitic; Moorish.
See also CREDULITY, DISSENT, IDOLATRY, IMPIETY, IRRELIGION, MISJUDGMENT.—*Antonyms.* See ORTHODOXY.

heterogeneous, *adj.* dissimilar, unlike, distinct, diverse. See DIFFERENCE.
hew, *v.* cut, chop, hack. See DISJUNCTION.
hidden, *adj.* latent, covered, secret, mysterious. See CONCEALMENT.
hide, *n.* coat, pelt, skin. See COVERING.
hide, *v.* secrete, veil, screen, cover; suppress, dissemble; skulk, sneak. See AMBUSH, CONCEALMENT.
hidebound, *adj.* narrow, bigoted, prejudiced. See IMPIETY.
hideous, *adj.* horrible, repulsive, revolting, frightful, detestable, odious. See UGLINESS.
hiding place, cache, recess, closet; asylum, shelter, retreat. See AMBUSH, REFUGE.
high, *adj.* tall, lofty; shrill, high-pitched; chief, foremost; profound, abstruse, costly, expensive; gamy. See HEIGHT.
highborn, *adj.* patrician, aristocratic, well-born. See NOBILITY.
highest, *adj.* topmost, uppermost, head, supreme. See SUMMIT.
high-flown, *adj.* pompous, extravagant, bombastic. See ORNAMENT.
high-minded, *adj.* great, magnanimous, noble. See UNSELFISHNESS.
high-pitched, *adj.* shrill, sharp, loud, piercing. See HEIGHT.
high rank, nobility, high descent; exalted station, power. See PURPLE.
high-spirited, *adj.* mettlesome, fiery, bold. See COURAGE.
high water, high tide, flood tide, spring tide. See HEIGHT.
highway, *n.* thoroughfare, road, turnpike. See WAY.
highwayman, *n.* bandit, footpad, thug. See THIEF.
hilarity, *n.* mirth, jollity, glee, gayety. See CHEERFULNESS.
hill, *n.* slope, ascent, mound, elevation. See CONVEXITY, HEIGHT.
hilly, *adj.* mountainous, rangy, steep. See HEIGHT.
hinder, *adj.* hind, last, hindmost. See POSTERIORITY.

HINDRANCE.—I. *Nouns.* **hindrance,** embarrassment, hampering, let (*archaic*), interruption, counteraction, interception, detention, retardation, delay, obstruction, stoppage, prevention, inhibition, restraint, preclusion, estoppel (*law*), restriction, determent; constriction, contraction, striction, coarctation (*med.*), stricture (*med.*); preventive, preventative, prophylactic (*med.*).

interference, interposition, obtrusion, meddlesomeness; discouragement, disapproval, disapprobation, censure, opposition.

impediment, obstacle, obstruction, barrier, difficulty, drawback, objection, disadvantage; knot, snag, hitch, *contretemps* (*F.*), setback, stumblingblock, lion in the path; ill wind, head wind.

check, clog, brake, anchor; trammel, tether; bit, snaffle, curb; drag, load, encumbrance *or* incumbrance, burden, onus, impedimenta; dead weight; umber, pack, kyack (*Western U. S.*); nightmare, incubus, old man of the sea; stay, stop. damper, wet blanket, kill-joy, crape-hanger (*slang*); dog in the manger, usurper, interloper, Buttinsky (*U. S. jocose*), hinderer, interferer, marplot, meddler; obstructionist, opponent.

II. *Verbs.* **hinder,** impede, delay, retard, detain, check, slacken, prevent, restrain, restrict, inhibit, debar, preclude; arrest, clog, obstruct, choke, barricade, block, dam up, bar, stop, stay, bolt, lock, put on the brake, put a stop to, interrupt, intercept, oppose, interfere, interpose.

avert, keep off, stave off, ward off; obviate; turn aside, draw off, prevent, forestall, nip in the bud; counteract, countercheck, remove.

encumber, hamper, cramp, clog, cumber, handicap; burden, saddle with, load with, act as a drag, overburden, overload, overwhelm, lumber, entrammel, trammel, incommode, discommode, discompose, perplex, embarrass, corner, tree (*colloq.*), nonplus.

thwart, frustrate, disconcert, balk, foil, contravene, counter, circumvent, baffle, override, defeat, spoil, mar, clip the wings of, cripple, damp, dishearten, discountenance, undermine; steal one's thunder, cut the ground from under one, take the wind out of one's sails.

III. *Adjectives.* **hindering,** obstructive, impedimental, impeditive, onerous, burdensome; cumbrous, cumbersome, hindersome (*dial.*); meddlesome. officious, intrusive, obstrusive.

preventive, preclusive, preventative, warding off, prophylactic (*med.*), deterrent, inhibitive, inhibitory, prohibitive, prohibitory, prohibitionary.

See also DIFFICULTY, OPPOSITION, PROHIBITION, RESTRAINT.—*Antonyms.* See AID.

---

hinge, *n.* pivot, axis, basis; joint, hook. See CAUSE, JUNCTION.

hint, *n.* suggestion, intimation, insinuation; reminder, allusion. See INFORMATION, MEMORY.

hint, *v.* whisper, intimate, suggest, insinuate, indicate. See INFORMATION.

hire, *v.* employ, engage; rent, lease. See BORROWING.

hiss, *v.* condemn; buzz, whiz. See DISAPPROBATION, SIBILATION.

historian, *n.* annalist, chronicler, historiographer, biographer. See RECORDER.

history, *n.* story, tale, narrative; biography, autobiography; chronicle, annals. See DESCRIPTION, RECORD.

hit, *v.* reach, touch; come upon, find; knock, strike, smite. See ARRIVAL, CHANCE, IMPULSE.

hitch, *v.* fasten, knot, yoke; hobble, limp. See JUNCTION, SLOWNESS.

hitch, *n.* jerk, pull, tug; stop, interruption; obstacle, impediment; limp, hobble; check, mischance, accident. See AGITATION, CESSATION, HINDRANCE, SLOWNESS, UNTIMELINESS.

hoard, *v.* treasure, collect, accumulate, save, amass. See STORE.

hoarse, *adj.* raucous, harsh, discordant, grating. See STRIDENCY.

hoary, *adj.* gray, grayheaded, white; venerable, ancient. See AGE.

hoax, *n.* trick, practical joke. See DECEPTION.

hoax, *v.* dupe, humbug, deceive, sell (*slang*). See DECEPTION, SALE.

hobble, *v.* shackle, hopple, fetter; limp, halt. See RESTRAINT, SLOWNESS.

hobby, *n.* avocation, fad, whim. See BUSINESS, MISJUDGMENT, SPECIALTY.

hodgepodge, *n.* jumble, medley. See MIXTURE.

hog, *n.* swine, sow, pig. See ANIMAL.

hoist, *v.* raise, lift, rear. See ELEVATION.

hold, *v.* accept, think, believe, entertain; cleave, stick, cohere, adhere; guard, defend, keep; include, admit, take; continue, persist, endure, last; have, possess, occupy, own; accommodate, contain, receive; force, repress, restrain, curb; clutch, grasp, grip, retain; carry, have capacity for; bear, sustain, maintain. See BELIEF, COHERENCE, DEFENSE, INCLUSION, PERMANENCE, POSSESSION, RECEIVING, RESTRAINT, RETENTION, STORE, SUPPORT.—**hold apart,** stand between, intervene, separate. See PART.—**hold out,** endure, last, continue, persist, carry on, persevere. See PERSEVERANCE.

hold, *n.* domination, control; ownership, claim; grasp, grip, seizure. See INFLUENCE, POSSESSION, RETENTION.

holding, *n.* tenure, possession; interest, claim. See PROPERTY.

hole, *n.* pit, cavity, excavation, hollow; cave, burrow; perforation, slot, puncture, gap. See CONCAVITY, OPENING.

holiday, *n.* gala day, celebration; recreation, vacation. See AMUSEMENT, REPOSE.

holiness, *n.* godliness, righteousness, sanctity. See PIETY.

hollow, *adj.* gaunt, sunken, depressed; deep-toned, sepulchral; false, specious, unsound, deceptive; void, empty, vacant. See CONCAVITY, RESONANCE, SOPHISTRY, UNSUBSTANTIALITY.

hollow, *n.* hole, cavity, depression; valley, basin, bowl; groove, channel. See CONCAVITY, FURROW.

holy, *adj.* consecrated, sacred; saintly, godly. See DEITY, PIETY.

Holy Ghost, Holy Spirit, Comforter, Intercessor. See DEITY.

holy orders, priesthood, ministry; ordination. See CHURCHDOM, RITE.

homage, *n.* submission, allegiance, devotion; deference, reverence, veneration, obeisance. See OBEDIENCE, RESPECT.

home, *n.* abode, house, residence, quarters, dwelling; seat, habitat, location; refuge, shelter, asylum; country, fatherland. See HABITATION.
homeless, *adj.* houseless, desolate, outcast. See EXCLUSION.
homely, *adj.* homelike, rustic, native; rude, common, unpretending; plain, unlovely. See PLAINNESS, SIMPLENESS, UGLINESS.
homesickness, *n.* nostalgia, *mal du pays* (*F.*). See REGRET.
homicide, *n.* slaying, manslaughter, murder. See KILLING.
homogeneity, *n.* correspondence, likeness, agreement. See UNIFORMITY.
honest, *adj.* open, sincere, frank; upright, honorable, trustworthy. See ARTLESSNESS, PROBITY.
honesty, *n.* uprightness, integrity, honor; sincerity, openness, frankness, candor, truthfulness. See PROBITY, TRANSPARENCY, VERACITY.
honeycombed, *adj.* favose, foveate, pitted. See CONCAVITY.
honor, *n.* decoration, title, distinction; uprightness, integrity; glory, fame, distinction; deference, esteem; reverence. See ORNAMENT, PROBITY, REPUTE, RESPECT, WORSHIP.
honor, *v.* accept (*as a draft*), pay; dignify, glorify, toast; reverence, revere. See PAYMENT, REPUTE, RESPECT.
honorable, *adj.* upright, respectable; noble, eminent; just, fair, trustworthy. See PROBITY, REPUTE, WHITENESS.
honorary, *adj.* gratuitous; nominal, titular. See CHEAPNESS, NOMENCLATURE.
hood, *n.* cowl, coif, capuche; capote (*as for a cabriolet*), calash, top; chimney-pot. See CLOTHING (*headdress*), COVERING.
hoodoo, *n.* voodoo, black magic, witchery, jinx (*slang*). See SORCERY, [1]SPELL.
hoodwink, *v.* blindfold; fool, delude, hoax. See BLINDNESS, CONCEALMENT, DECEPTION.
hook, *v.* crook, bend; link, fasten, catch. See CURVATURE, JUNCTION.
hook-shaped, *adj.* hooklike, hooked, unciform. See CURVATURE.
hoot, *v.* shout, condemn, deride, boo. See DISAPPROBATION.
hop, *v.* jump, spring, bound. See LEAP.

HOPE.—I. *Nouns.* **hope,** desire, sanguine expectation, trust, confidence, sanguineness, reliance, faith, belief, assurance, security; reassurance.
hopefulness, buoyancy, optimism, enthusiasm, aspiration; assumption, presumption; anticipation, expectation, expectance *or* expectancy.
daydream, pipe dream (*colloq.*), fancy, conceit, reverie, golden dream, mirage, castles in the air, *châteaux en Espagne* (*F.*), Utopia, millennium; airy hopes, fool's paradise, fond hope, dream of Alnaschar.
mainstay (*fig.*), chief (*or* main) support, staff, support, prop, pillar, strength; anchor, sheet anchor.
II. *Verbs.* **hope,** trust, confide, rely, lean upon; live in hope, rest assured.
hope for, desire, wish, wish for; expect, anticipate, promise oneself; presume, aspire.
be hopeful, look on the bright side of, make the best of it, hope for the best, hope against hope, take heart, be of good cheer; flatter oneself, lay the flattering unction to one's soul.
encourage, cheer, hearten, inspirit, hold out hope, comfort, fortify, animate, assure, reassure, buoy up, embolden; promise, bid fair, augur well.
III. *Adjectives.* **hopeful,** confident, in hopes, secure, sanguine, expectant, anticipative, anticipatory, optimistic, buoyant, elated, flushed, exultant, enthusiastic.
fearless, dauntless, courageous, stout-hearted, undaunted; unsuspecting, unsuspicious, undespairing, self-reliant.
auspicious, promising, favorable, propitious, prosperous, fortunate, reassuring, probable, encouraging, cheering, inspiriting, bright, roseate, rosy, *couleur de rose* (*F.*).

See also BELIEF, DESIRE, EXPECTATION, SUPPORT.—*Antonyms.* See HOPELESSNESS.

HOPELESSNESS.—I. *Nouns.* **hopelessness,** despair, desperation; despondency, disconsolateness, disconsolation, melancholy, depression, dejection, broken-heartedness; pessimism, miserabilism, malism; hope deferred, dashed hopes.
pessimist, miserabilist, cynic, malist, Job's comforter, hypochondriac; bird of ill omen: *opposite of* optimist.
II. *Verbs.* **be hopeless,** despair, lose (give up, *or* abandon) all hope, give up, give over, yield to despair; falter; despond.
III. *Adjectives.* **hopeless,** despondent, downcast, despairing, past (*or* beyond) recall, desperate, gone, in despair, forlorn, inconsolable, broken-hearted.
incurable, cureless, irremediable, remediless, immedicable (*rare*), irreparable, irrecoverable, irretrievable, irreclaimable, irredeemable, irrevocable, ruined, undone.
unpropitious, unpromising, unfavorable, inauspicious, ill-omened, threatening, lowering, ominous, sinister, minatory, menacing, ill-boding.
See also DEJECTION.—*Antonyms.* See HOPE.

---

horde, *n.* crowd, tribe, pack, throng. See ASSEMBLAGE.

HORIZONTALITY.—I. *Nouns.* **horizontality,** horizontalness, horizontalism, levelness, smoothness, flatness; level, dead level, plane, stratum.
recumbency, lying down, decumbence *or* decumbency, reclination, proneness, supination, prostration.
II. *Verbs.* **be horizontal,** lie, couch, repose, recline, lie flat; sprawl, loll.
render horizontal, lay, level, flatten, even, dress (*as stone*), smooth, raze; align, horizontalize (*rare*); prostrate, knock down, floor, fell, ground, cut (*or* hew) down, mow down; squelch (*colloq.*), squash (*colloq.*).
III. *Adjectives.* **horizontal,** level, even, plane, flush; flat, smooth.
recumbent, reclining, lying, prone, supine, prostrate; couchant (*esp. heraldry*), squatting.
[*in botany*] decumbent (*as stems or shoots*), procumbent, trailing, accumbent (*this also describes the position of the Romans at meals*), incumbent (*also zoöl.: as,* incumbent *hairs*).
IV. *Adverbs.* **horizontally,** level, etc. (see *adjectives*); on one's back; on all fours; on its beam ends.
See also DEPRESSION, FLATNESS, LAYER.—*Antonyms.* See VERTICALITY.

---

horn-shaped, *adj.* cornute, lance-shaped. See SHARPNESS.
horrible, *adj.* dreadful, appalling, frightful, hideous, execrable, dire, revolting. See FEAR, PAINFULNESS.
horror, *n.* abhorrence, loathing; terror, dread. See DISLIKE, FEAR.
horse, *n.* steed, mount; hack, nag, roadster; cavalry; trot (*school cant*); sawhorse, sawbuck (*U. S.*). See ANIMAL, CARRIER, COMBATANT, INTERPRETATION, SUPPORT.
horseman, *n.* rider, equestrian. See TRAVELER.
hospital, *n.* infirmary, clinic, sanitarium. See REMEDY.
hospitality, *n.* welcome, entertainment. See SOCIALITY.
[1]**host,** *n.* army, legion, array, throng. See COMBATANT, MULTITUDE.
[2]**host,** *n.* entertainer, hostess (*fem.*); landlord, innkeeper. See FRIEND, PROVISION.
hostage, *n.* pledge, guarantee. See SECURITY.
hostile, *adj.* unfriendly, antagonistic, warlike. See ENMITY.
hot, *adj.* burning, warm, torrid, sultry; fiery, ardent, violent; peppery, biting. See HEAT, PUNGENCY.
hot bath, thermæ (*pl.*); Turkish bath, vapor bath. See FURNACE.
hotel, *n.* tavern, inn, hostelry. See HABITATION.
hot-headed, *adj.* hasty, fiery, quick. See EXCITABILITY.
hot wind, heat wave, sirocco, simoom. See HEAT.
hound, *n.* dog, foxhound, bloodhound, etc.; miscreant, cur. See ANIMAL, BAD MAN.

hound, *v.* harass, harry, worry, bait, pursue, persecute. See MALEVOLENCE.
house, *n.* ancestry, family, line; lineage; legislature; home, abode, residence; firm, company. See CONTINUITY, COUNCIL, HABITATION, PARTY.
house, *v.* shelter, harbor, protect. See SAFETY.
household, *n.* family, establishment, ménage. See CONSANGUINITY.
housekeeping, *n.* housewifery, ménage. See CONDUCT.
hovel, *n.* hut, shack, shanty, cabin. See HABITATION.
hover, *v.* poise, hang; vacillate, waver; linger, hang about. See AIR, IRRESOLUTION, NEARNESS.
how, *adv.* in what manner, by what method. See WAY.
however, *adv.* yet, but, nevertheless, still. See COMPENSATION.
howl, *v.* yowl, ululate; wail, complain; roar, whistle, moan. See CRY, LAMENTATION, WIND.
hoyden, *n.* tomboy, romp. See INFANT.
hubbub, *n.* din, tumult, uproar, racket. See LOUDNESS.
huddle, *v.* lump, crowd, bundle, bunch. See ASSEMBLAGE.
hue, *n.* shade, tint, tinge, tone. See COLOR.
hug, *v.* clasp, embrace; cherish, prize; keep close to. See LOVE, NEARNESS.
huge, *adj.* vast, enormous, immense, gigantic. See SIZE.
hum, *n.* murmur, buzz, drone. See FAINTNESS.
human, *adj.* mortal, rational, civilized. See MANKIND.
human affairs, secular affairs, mundane interests, social life. See WORLD.
humane, *adj.* sympathetic, kind, tender-hearted. See BENEVOLENCE.
humanity, *n.* man, human race; benevolence, humanitarianism. See MANKIND, PHILANTHROPY.
humble, *adj.* meek, submissive, modest; poor, mean, paltry; lowly, obscure. See HUMILITY, INFERIORITY, LOWNESS, OBSCURITY, SIMPLENESS.
humbleness, *n.* lowliness; meekness. See OBSCURITY.
humbug, *n.* impostor, pretender; fraud, charlatanry. See DECEIVER, FALSEHOOD.
humbug, *v.* impose upon, hoax, trick, dupe. See DECEPTION.
humdrum, *adj.* prosaic, monotonous, tiresome. See DULLNESS.
humid, *adj.* damp, wet, dark. See MOISTURE.

HUMILITY.—I. *Nouns.* **humility,** humbleness, meekness, modesty, timidity, lowliness, abasement, self-abasement, submission, submissiveness, resignation, confusion, humiliation, mortification, humbled pride.

II. *Verbs.* **be humble,** deign, vouchsafe, condescend, humble oneself, stoop, submit, yield the palm, sing small (*colloq.*), hide one's face, hide one's diminished head, be humiliated, be put out of countenance, be shamed, be put to the blush; eat humble pie, eat crow.

humble, humiliate, snub, abash, abase, strike dumb, lower, cast into the shade, put to the blush, confuse, shame, put out of countenance, mortify, disgrace, degrade, crush.

III. *Adjectives.* **humble,** lowly, meek, modest, unassuming, unpretending, unpretentious, unambitious, humble-minded, sober-minded; poor, low-born, base-born, plain, simple, mean, inglorious, undistinguished, obscure; submissive, servile.

humbled, bowed down, abashed, ashamed, dashed, crestfallen, chopfallen, dejected, down in the mouth (*colloq.*), dumfoundered, flabbergasted (*colloq.*). shorn of one's glory.

IV. *Adverbs.* **humbly,** lowly, etc. (see *adjectives*); with downcast eyes, with bated breath, on bended knee.

See also INFERIORITY, MODESTY, SERVILITY, SUBMISSION.—*Antonyms.* See PRIDE.

---

humor, *n.* mood, temper; drollery, facetiousness. See DISPOSITION, WIT.
humor, *v.* indulge gratify, favor, oblige. See PERMISSION.

HUMORIST.—*Nouns.* **humorist,** wag, wit, reparteeist, banterer, *persifleur* (*F.*), wise-cracker (*slang*), epigrammatist, punster, *bel esprit* (*F.*), life of the party; joker, jester, droll, buffoon, comedian, merry-andrew, mime; tumbler, acrobat, mountebank, harlequin, pantaloon, punch, punchinello, clown; motley fool; caricaturist, grimacer.

Antonyms. See FOOL.

---

humorous, *adj.* funny, droll, amusing, comical. See WIT.

HUNDRED.—I. *Nouns.* **hundred,** century; centennium, centennial, centenary; centipede; centumvir (*Roman hist.*), centumvirate, centurion.

[*metric weights and measures*] cental (100 *lbs.*), centigram *or* centigramme, centiliter *or* centilitre, centimeter *or* centimetre, centiare, centistere.

II. *Verbs.* multiply by a hundred, make a hundredfold, centuple, centuplicate.

III. *Adjectives.* **hundredth,** centuple, centesimal, cental, centurial; centennial, centenary; centigrade; secular (*as, a* secular *festival*).

---

hunger, *n.* appetite; craving, voracity, bulimia (*med.*). See DESIRE, GLUTTONY.
hungry, *adj.* ravenous, starved, eager, craving. See DESIRE.
hunt, *v.* search, trace, ferret out; follow, chase. See INQUIRY, PURSUIT.
hunter, *n.* huntsman, sportsman. See KILLING.
hunting, *n.* the chase, the hunt, venery. See KILLING.
hurl, *v.* fling, cast, pitch, throw. See PROPULSION.
hurrah! *interj.* huzza! three cheers! See REJOICING.
hurrah, *n.* cheer, shout, huzza. See REJOICING.
hurricane, *n.* tempest, storm, whirlwind. See WIND.
hurry, *v.* hasten, speed, scurry; quicken, facilitate. See HASTE.
hurt *v.* injure, harm, damage; wound, bruise; distress, grieve. See BADNESS, DETERIORATION, PAIN.
hurt, *n.* bruise, wound; injury, harm; suffering, ache. See EVIL, PAIN.
hurtful, *adj.* harmful, injurious, detrimental. See BADNESS.
husband, *n.* spouse, Benedict; man, lord and master (*jocose*). See MARRIAGE.

HUSBANDRY.—I. *Nouns.* **husbandry,** agriculture, farming, geoponics, agronomy (*tech.*), agronomics, cultivation, tillage; gardening, vintage, viniculture; horticulture, arboriculture, forestry; floriculture; landscape gardening.

garden, *jardin* (*F.*), nursery, kitchen garden, market (*or* truck) garden, flower garden, botanic garden; greenhouse, hothouse, conservatory; grassplot, lawn; shrubbery, arboretum, orchard; vineyard, vinery, grapery, grape house; orangery.

field, meadow, mead (*poetic*), grassland, clearing, patch, glebe (*archaic or eccl.*), green, common.

fertilizer, dressing, manure, dung, compost, guano, lime, marl, chemicals, phosphate, bone dust.

frugality, thrift, economy, thriftiness, care, savingness, sparingness, economizing, management.

husbandman, agriculturist, farmer, yeoman, agronomist (*scientific farmer*), granger (*U. S.*), cultivator, tiller of the soil; gardener, mali (*India*), horticulturist, florist; pioneer, backwoodsman, woodcutter, logger, lumberman, lumberjack (*Northwestern U. S.*); forester.

II. *Verbs.* **husband,** economize, manage, make both ends meet; save, retrench.

cultivate, till, till the soil, farm, garden, grow, sow, plant; reap, mow, cut; manure, dress the ground; dig, spade, delve, hoe, plow *or* plough, harrow, rake, weed; seed, turf; transplant, thin out, bed, prune, graft: *in this sense,* husband *is archaic.*

III. *Adjectives.* **husbandly,** thrifty, frugal, economical, sparing, saving, provident, careful, unwasteful.

agricultural, rural, rustic, agrarian, country, georgic *or* georgical, geoponic *or* geoponical, agronomic *or* agronomical; agrestic, bucolic, pastoral, Arcadian.

arable, cultivable, cultivatable, tillable, plowable *or* ploughable.

See also CONDUCT, ECONOMY.—*Antonyms.* See NEGLECT, NONPREPARATION, PRODIGALITY.

hush, *v.* stifle, check, hide; soothe, calm, allay; quiet, still. See CONCEALMENT, MODERATION, SILENCE.
husky, *adj.* hoarse, rough, harsh, throaty. See DRYNESS, STAMMERING.
hut, *n.* hovel, shanty, shack, cabin. See HABITATION.
hybrid, *n.* cross, crossbreed. See MIXTURE.
hybrid, *adj.* crossbred, mixed, crossed, mongrel. See UNCONFORMITY.
hygienic, *adj.* sanitary, salutary, wholesome, clean. See HEALTHINESS.
hymn, *n.* song, psalm, chant; pæan, song of praise. See MUSIC, WORSHIP.
hyperphysical, *adj.* supernatural, psychical, spiritual. See PSYCHICAL RESEARCH.
hypnotic, *adj.* soporific, narcotic, lethargic; mesmeric, odylic. See INACTIVITY, PSYCHICAL RESEARCH.
hypochondriac, *n.* pessimist, self-tormentor. See DEJECTION.
hypocrisy, *n.* insincerity, pretense; pietism, cant, pharisaism. See FALSEHOOD, IMPIETY.
hypocrite, *n.* deceiver, cheat, dissembler. See IMPIETY.
hypocritical, *adj.* canting, sanctimonious, insincere. See FALSEHOOD, IMPIETY.
hypothesis, *n.* theory, assumption, postulate. See SUPPOSITION.
hysterical, *adj.* convulsive; emotional, uncontrolled. See FEELING.

I

icy, *adj.* frosty, frozen, freezing, glacial; chilling, frigid. See COLD.

IDEA.—*Nouns.* idea, mental impression, notion, conception, thought, apprehension, perception; sentiment, reflection, observation, consideration abstract idea.
[*way of thinking*] **opinion,** belief, theory, doctrine, impression, view, supposition judgment.
viewpoint, standpoint, point of view, angle, aspect.
[*mental image*] **image,** eidolon, form, representation, phantom; fantasy, fiction, fancy, conceit (*archaic in this sense*), imagination, creation, concept (*distinguished from* percept), recept (*psychol.*), generic image (*psychol.*).
[*plan of action*] **plan,** outline, sketch, draft, design, intention (*logic*).
[*in Platonic philosophy*] **archetype,** pattern, ideal, model, exemplar, prototype
[*in Hegelianism*] the realized ideal, the Absolute Idea, the Absolute, the Self-existent, the Self-determined.
See also IMAGINATION, THOUGHT.

---

ideal, *adj.* idealistic; abstract; impracticable, visionary. See IMAGINATION.
ideal, *n.* paragon, *beau idéal* (*F.*); archetype, exemplar. See PERFECTION, PROTOTYPE.

IDENTITY.—I. *Nouns.* **identity,** sameness, identicalness, likeness, selfsameness, oneness, unity, similarity, resemblance, correspondence, exactness, exactitude, fidelity; equality, coincidence, coalescence, convertibility; connature, connaturalness, connaturality, homogeneity; self, oneself; individuality, personality.
facsimile, copy, duplicate, ditto (*colloq.*), reprint, replica, reflex, reflection, reproduction, counterpart; same, selfsame.
monotony, uniformity, sameness, repetition, iteration, duplication, reduplication, reiteration, recurrence.
II. *Verbs.* **identify,** make (*or* treat as) identical, associate oneself with; unite, combine, coalesce, coincide.
[*to prove the identity of*] recognize, establish, determine, place, know, perceive.
III. *Adjectives.* **identical,** same, selfsame, like, one, ditto (*commercial*); similar, identic (*diplomacy: as, an* identic *note*), indistinguishable, equal, equivalent, coinciding, coincident, coalescent, convertible.

IV. *Adverbs.* **identically,** similarly, etc. (see *adjectives*); on all fours; *ibidem* (*L.*), *ibid.*

See also COPY, EQUALITY, PLACE, REPETITION, SIMILARITY.—*Antonyms.* See CONTRARIETY, DISSIMILARITY.

---

idiocy, *n.* foolishness, senselessness. See IMBECILITY.
idiot, *n.* fool, blockhead; cretin. See IMBECILITY.
idle, *adj.* inactive, unemployed, lazy; useless, worthless, futile; vacant, empty, unoccupied; vain, void, foolish, unprofitable. See INACTIVITY, INUTILITY, VACUITY, VANITY.
idle, *v.* loaf, dally, dillydally. See INACTIVITY.
idler, *n.* dawdler, lounger, loafer, laggard, dreamer. See INACTIVITY.

IDOLATRY.—I. *Nouns.* **idolatry,** idolatrousness, idolism, idolization, deification, idol worship, fetishism; apotheosis, canonization, excessive fondness, hero worship; fornication (*in Scriptural use*), demonism, demonology, devil worship.
sacrifice, offering, host (*archaic*), victim, burnt offering, hecatomb, holocaust, taurobolium (*Mithraism*), chiliomb, corban (*Jewish antiquities*); mactation, human sacrifice, immolation, self-immolation, suttee.
idol, image, golden calf, graven image, fetish, joss (*Chinese*), *lares et penates* (*L.*); false god, heathen deity, Baal, Moloch, Dagon, Juggernaut *or* Jagannath.
pet, darling, favorite, beloved, dautie (*Scot.*), fondling.
idolater, idolatress (*fem.*), idolizer, fetishist, idolist; worshiper, adorer.
II. *Verbs.* **idolize,** idolatrize, worship idols, worship, put on a pedestal, prostrate oneself before; make sacrifice to, deify, canonize; worship, adore.
III. *Adjectives.* **idolatrous,** idolistic, chthonian, fetishistic, prostrate before, prone before, worshiping, in the dust before, at the feet of.

See also FAVORITE, LOVE, SORCERY, WORSHIP.

---

if, *conj.* provided, in case that; whether. See SUPPOSITION.
ignition, *n.* kindling, conflagration. See CALEFACTION.
ignoble, *adj.* common, low, base, mean, vile. See PEOPLE, VULGARITY.

IGNORAMUS.—I. *Nouns.* **ignoramus,** illiterate, dunce, duffer, bonehead (*slang*), dolt, blockhead, dumb-bell (*slang*), thickhead (*colloq.*), numskull (*colloq.*); no scholar, lowbrow (*slang*), moron, cretin.
smatterer, dabbler, sciolist, half scholar; charlatan; four-flusher (*slang*), bluffer, wiseacre.
novice, greenhorn, plebe (*West Point cant*), beginner, tyro, newcomer, bungler.
II. *Adjectives.* **unlearned,** illiterate, dense, crass, thick, thickheaded, numskulled (*colloq.*), stupid, doltish, blockish, shallow, simple, dull, dumb (*colloq.*)

See also BUNGLER, DUPE, FOOL, LEARNER.—*Antonyms.* See EXPERT, SCHOLAR.

IGNORANCE.—I. *Nouns.* **ignorance,** illiteracy, nescience, illiterateness, ineducation (*rare*), unlearnedness, unacquaintance, darkness, unenlightenment, benightedness, benightment, blindness, incomprehension, moronism, cretinism; inexperience, simplicity, unawareness, unconsciousness.
sealed book; virgin soil, unexplored ground, *terra incognita* (*L.*); Dark Ages.
[*imperfect knowledge*] **smattering,** superficiality, sciolism, incapacity, half-learning, shallowness, glimmering, bewilderment.
[*affectation of knowledge*] **charlatanry,** charlatanism, quackery, bluff, four-flushing (*slang*), empiricism; pedantry, pedantism.
II. *Verbs.* **be ignorant** (*or* uninformed); be uneducated; know nothing of; ignore, be blind to, disregard.
III. *Adjectives.* **ignorant,** unknowing, unaware, unacquainted, uninformed, uninitiated, unwitting, unconscious; witless, unconversant, nescient.
illiterate, unread, uncultivated, uninstructed, untaught, untutored, unschooled, uneducated, inerudite, unlearned, unlettered, empty-headed, unintelligent.
shallow, superficial, sciolistic, green, rude, empty, half-learned, half-baked (*colloq.*), unscholarly, *au bout de son latin* (*F.*); unbookish, cretinous, moronic, lowbrow (*slang*).

in the dark, benighted, blinded, blindfold, hoodwinked; misinformed, at fault.
unknown, unapprehended, unexplained, unascertained, unperceived, unfamiliar, **un**investigated, unexplored, unheard of; concealed, hidden; untried, novel.
IV. *Adverbs.* **ignorantly,** unknowingly, etc. (see *adjectives*); unawares; for aught one knows; not that one knows.

See also CONCEALMENT, DARKNESS, UNCERTAINTY.—*Antonyms.* See KNOWLEDGE.

---

ignore, *v.* disregard; slight, omit, overlook. See IGNORANCE, NEGLECT.
ill, *adj.* harmful, evil; indisposed, sick. See BADNESS, DISEASE.
ill-advised, *adj.* injudicious, unwise, misadvised, infelicitous. See INEXPEDIENCE, UNSKILLFULNESS.
ill-bred, *adj.* ill-mannered, rude, uncivil, discourteous. See VULGARITY.

ILLEGALITY.—I. *Nouns.* **illegality,** illicitness, unlawfulness, illegitimateness, breach (*or* violation) of law, illegitimacy, invalidity, invalidness, unconstitutionality; contrabandism, smuggling, bootlegging (*colloq.*), contraband.
lawlessness, unruliness, disorderliness, disobedience; violence, brute force, despotism, tyranny, outlawry, mob (*or* lynch) law, anarchy.
II. *Verbs.* **illegalize,** make (*or* declare) illegal, illegitimatize, illegitimate; abrogate, invalidate, annul, vacate, void, nullify, quash.
violate the law, offend against the law, set the law at defiance, make the law a dead letter, take the law into one's own hands.
smuggle, bootleg (*colloq.*), run, poach.
III. *Adjectives.* **illegal,** unlawful, illegitimate, illicit, prohibited, contraband, actionable, unchartered, unconstitutional, lawless, unwarranted, unauthorized, unofficial, extrajudicial.
arbitrary, summary, irresponsible, discretionary; despotic, tyrannical, autocratic, tyrannous.
IV. *Adverbs.* **illegally,** unlawfully, etc. (see *adjectives*); with a high hand, in violation of law.

See also DISOBEDIENCE, PROHIBITION, RIGHTLESSNESS.—*Antonyms.* See LEGALITY.

---

illegitimate, *adj.* unlawful, illicit; bastard. See ILLEGALITY, RIGHTLESSNESS.
illiberal, *adj.* narrow-minded, bigoted; stingy, close. See NARROWNESS, PARSIMONY, SELFISHNESS.
illicit, *adj.* unlawful, prohibited; contraband. See ILLEGALITY.
illiterate, *adj.* unlearned, uneducated. See IGNORANCE.
ill-mannered, *adj.* ill-bred, rude, impolite. See VULGARITY.
ill-natured, *adj.* cross-grained, ill-tempered, quarrelsome. See UGLINESS.
illness, *n.* sickness, indisposition, malady, ailment. See DISEASE.
illogical, *adj.* unsound, fallacious, specious. See SOPHISTRY.
ill-timed, *adj.* inopportune, unseasonable. See UNTIMELINESS.
ill-treatment, *n.* persecution, cruelty, abuse. See BADNESS.
illuminant, *n.* light giver; gas, electricity, candle. See LUMINARY.
illuminate, *v.* explain, make clear; illumine, light up. See DISSERTATION. LIGHT.
illusion, *n.* fancy, phantasm, phantom, ghost, apparition. See DECEPTION, ERROR, VISION.
illusive, *adj.* illusory, unreal, deceptive, false. See ERROR.
illustrate, *v.* exemplify, elucidate, explain; adorn (*as with pictures*). See INTERPRETATION, ORNAMENT.
illustrious, *adj.* famous, distinguished, eminent, renowned. See REPUTE.
image, *n.* aspect, form; conception; statue, likeness; counterpart. See APPEARANCE, IDEA, REPRESENTATION, SIMILARITY.

MAGINATION.—I. *Nouns.* **imagination,** conception, fancy, flight of fancy, "thick-coming fancies" (*Macbeth*), creation, inspiration, imaginativeness, creative thought, originality, creation, invention; fiction, poetry, creative writing, fine art; "mind's eye" (*Hamlet*); "the mind's internal heaven" (Wordsworth); "such stuff as dreams are made on" (*Tempest*); poetic creation, idealized creation, imagery, word painting; ideality, idealism, romanticism, utopianism, castle-building, dreaming; frenzy, rhapsody, ecstasy, reverie, daydream, golden dream.

fantasy, conceit, fancy, notion, whim, vagary, figment, myth; romance, extravaganza; dream, vision; shadow, chimera, phantasm, illusion, phantom, "air-drawn dagger" (*Macbeth*), bugbear, nightmare; flying Dutchman, great sea serpent, man in the moon, castle in the air, castle in Spain, *château en Espagne* (*F.*), Utopia, Atlantis, Happy Valley (Johnson), fairyland; land of Prester John

visionary, idealist, seer, enthusiast, *exalté* (*F.*), romancer, dreamer, daydreamer, castle-builder, fanatic, rhapsodist, Don Quixote; romanticist; creative artist.

II. *Verbs.* **imagine,** fancy, conceive; idealize, realize; dream, dream of, give "to airy nothing a local habitation and a name" (*Midsummer Night's Dream*), indulge in reverie; create, picture, rhapsodize, "see visions and dream dreams" (*Bible*).

create, originate, devise, invent, hatch, make up, coin, fabricate, plan, scheme, improvise.

suppose, think, conjecture, guess, opine, believe, deem, apprehend, assume.

III. *Adjectives.* **imaginative,** original, inventive, creative, fictive, fertile, productive.

ideal, idealistic, poetic, romantic, intellectual, abstract, impracticable, imaginary, visionary, Utopian, quixotic, extravagant, high-flown, preposterous, flighty, unreal, unsubstantial, imaginational.

fanciful, fantastic *or* fantastical, fabulous, legendary, mythic *or* mythical, mythological, chimerical; whimsical, notional, fictitious, figmental, dreamy, shadowy, unreal; elfish, elfin, fairy, fairylike.

See also DESCRIPTION, DRAMA, IDEA, POETRY, SUPPOSITION, THOUGHT, UNSUBSTANTIALITY, VISION.

IMBECILITY.—I. *Nouns.* **imbecility,** feeble-mindedness, idiocy, cretinism (*tech.*), unintelligence, want of intelligence (*or* intellect), poverty of intellect, shallowness, silliness, foolishness, stupidity, hebetude, inanity, stolidity, fatuity, simplicity, puerility; senility, dotage, second childhood; old-womanishness, anility.

incompetence, incapacity, inability, unfitness, impotence, incapability, disability, inadequacy.

II. *Verbs.* **drivel,** twaddle, gabble, babble, trifle, dote, ramble; play the fool, fool; stultify oneself, talk nonsense.

III. *Adjectives.* **imbecile,** weak, feeble, fatuous, idiotic, silly, inane, feeble-minded, weak-minded, cretinous (*tech.*), half-witted, driveling, vacant, bewildered, weak in the upper story, crack-brained, nutty (*slang*), soft.

stupid, dull, heavy, clodpated, Bœotian, thick (*colloq.*), blockish, thick-skulled, bovine, muddle-headed, addle-headed, purblind, obtuse, blunt, stolid, doltish, sluggish, sottish, asinine, inapt; unintelligent, unintellectual, unreasoning; mindless, brainless; half-baked (*colloq.*), mentally deficient, unenlightened, unteachable, unwise.

childish, childlike, infantine, infantile, babyish, puerile, kiddish (*slang*); senile, anile; simple, credulous.

See also FOLLY, IGNORANCE.—*Antonyms.* See INTELLIGENCE.

---

imbue, *v.* instill, ingrain; tinge, suffuse. See INSERTION, MIXTURE.

IMITATION.—I. *Nouns.* **imitation,** copying, mimicking, apery, aping, mockery, parrotism, parrotry, echo, simulation, impersonation, disguise, masquerade, representation, semblance, pretense; copy; paraphrase, parody, adaptation; reproduction, quotation, repetition, duplication, reduplication.

counterfeit, sham, pretense, fake, Brummagem (*Eng.*), tinsel; forgery, make-believe, plagiarism, fraud.

imitator, copier, copyist, mimic, echo; cuckoo, parrot, mocking bird, catbird, ape, monkey; feigner, pretender; forger, counterfeiter.

II. *Verbs.* **imitate,** copy, mirror, reflect, reproduce, repeat; do like, follow, emulate, follow suit (*colloq.*), follow the example of, take after, model after, borrow, echo, reëcho, catch; match, parallel; forge, counterfeit.

mimic, ape, simulate, mock, take off, personate, impersonate, act, represent, parody, travesty, caricature, burlesque.

III. *Adjectives.* **imitative,** mock, mimic, apish, mimetic, echoic, sequacious (*archaic in this sense*), following, copying, reflecting, reflective; imitated, second-hand, pretended, feigned, modeled after, molded on, borrowed, counterfeit, forged, imitation, Brummagem (*Eng.*), flashy, sham, spurious, false, pseudo, near- (*as,* near-*silk*), imitational.

IV. *Adverbs.* **literally,** verbatim, *literatim* (*L.*), *sic* (*L.*), *verbatim et literatim* (*L.*), *mot à mot* (*F.*), word for word, precisely, exactly, textually.

See also COPY, DECEPTION, DRAMA, FALSEHOOD, REPRESENTATION.—*Antonyms.* See NONIMITATION, PROTOTYPE, TRUTH.

---

immaculate, *adj.* spotless, unsoiled; pure, virgin. See CLEANNESS, INNOCENCE.

immanent, *adj.* indwelling, inherent, intrinsic. See SUBJECTIVENESS.

IMMATERIALITY.—I. *Nouns.* **immateriality,** incorporeity, incorporeality, incorporality (*rare*), insubstantiality, unsubstantiality, spirituality, ethereality, etherealism, bodilessness; immaterialism (*philos.*), idealism, Platonism, Berkeleianism (*philos.*); spiritualism, spiritism, animism.

immaterialness, unimportance, insignificance, inconsequence (*rare in this sense*), triviality.

ego, self, personality, individuality; I, myself, me.

inner man, spirit, soul, psyche, pneuma, God within, higher self; subliminal self, subconscious self.

[*in theosophy*] etheric double (*or* self), *linga sharira* (*Sanskrit*); astral body, subtle body, desire (*or* kamic) body, *kama rupa* (*Sanskrit*); mental (*or* mind) body; causal body, spiritual body, bliss (*or* buddhic) body; spiritual (*or* higher) ego: *distinguished from* physical, dense, *or* gross body (*sthula sharira*).

immaterialist (*philos.*), Platonist; spiritualist, spiritist, rappist (*rare*); animist.

II. *Verbs.* **immaterialize,** incorporealize; spiritualize, dematerialize, dissolve disembody.

III. *Adjectives.* **immaterial,** incorporeal, incorporate, intangible, impalpable, unsubstantial, spiritual, metaphysical, Platonistic, hyperphysical, superphysical, extramundane, unearthly; spiritistic, animistic; discarnate, bodiless, asomatous, disembodied.

unimportant, insignificant, trivial, trifling, inconsequential, inconsiderable, inessential, nonessential, minor, slight, inappreciable, petty, small, little, diminutive, inferior.

subjective, personal, nonobjective, psychical; essential, real, substantial; inner, interior, internal, inherent, retrospective; illusory, imaginary, fanciful.

See also INTELLECT, UNIMPORTANCE, UNSUBSTANTIALITY.—*Antonyms.* See MATERIALITY.

---

immature, *adj.* undeveloped, unripe, raw, crude. See GREEN, NONPREPARATION.

immaturity, *n.* crudity, unripeness, undevelopedness, youthfulness. See NONPREPARATION, YOUTH.

immediate, *adj.* instant, prompt, present. See EARLINESS.

immediately, *adv.* speedily, forthwith, straightway, at once, now. See EARLINESS, STRAIGHTNESS.

immemorial, *adj.* ancient, remote, primitive. See OLDNESS.

immense, *adj.* vast, enormous, huge, gigantic. See SIZE.

immerse, *v.* dip, submerge, plunge, sink, duck. See INSERTION.

immigrant, *n.* incomer, newcomer, settler: *correlative of* emigrant. See INGRESS.

immigration, *n.* foreign influx; immigrants collectively: *correlative* of emigration. See INGRESS.

imminent, *adj.* coming, impending, threatening, near. See EARLINESS.

immoderately, *adv.* excessively, inordinately, extremely. See GREATNESS.

immoral, *adj.* licentious, dissolute, profligate, corrupt. See VICE.

immortal, *adj.* undying, imperishable, deathless. See PERPETUITY, REPUTE.
immovable, *adj.* stubborn, obdurate; fixed, stationary; steadfast, firm. See OBSTINACY, STABILITY.
immunity, *n.* privilege, freedom, dispensation. See EXEMPTION.
impact, *n.* collision, contact, impinging. See IMPULSE.
impair, *v.* injure, damage, lessen, weaken. See DETERIORATION, TOUCH.
impart, *v.* bestow, share, grant; tell, communicate. See GIVING, INFORMATION.
impartial, *adj.* equitable, average; fair, just, unbiased. See MID-COURSE, PROBITY.
impartiality, *n.* equity, fairness. See EQUALITY.
impassioned, *adj.* vehement, passionate; spirited, ardent. See EXCITABILITY, SENSITIVENESS.
impassive, *adj.* passionless, calm, serene; insensitive, insusceptible. See INEXCITABILITY, INSENSITIVENESS.
impatient, *adj.* hasty, restless, uneasy; irritable, peevish. See EXCITABILITY.
impediment, *n.* obstruction, difficulty, obstacle. See HINDRANCE.
impel, *v.* induce, force, incite; move, propel, drive. See IMPULSE, MOTION.
impend, *v.* hangover, beimminent, threaten, menace. See DESTINY.
impending, *adj.* threatening, menacing, looming, imminent. See DESTINY.
impenetrable, *adj.* impassable, impervious, impermeable; unfathomable, inscrutable, incomprehensible. See CLOSURE, UNINTELLIGIBILITY.

IMPENITENCE.—I. *Nouns.* **impenitence,** irrepentance, obduracy, incorrigibility, incorrigibleness, irreclaimability, irreclaimableness, callousness, relentlessness, gracelessness, recusancy, hardness of heart, heart of stone, seared conscience.

II. *Verbs.* **be impenitent,** steel the heart, harden the heart; die game, die and make no sign.

III. *Adjectives.* **impenitent,** obdurate, hard, hardened, callous, insensible, unfeeling, seared, recusant, unrepenting, unrepentant; relentless, remorseless, graceless, reprobate; lost, incorrigible, irreclaimable; unreclaimed, unreformed, wayward, refractory, unconverted.

Antonyms. See PENITENCE.

---

imperative, *adj.* authoritative, peremptory; essential, necessary, urgent. See COMMAND, REQUIREMENT.
imperceptible, *adj.* undiscernible, unnoticeable; inappreciable, slight. See INVISIBILITY, SMALLNESS.

IMPERFECTION.—I. *Nouns.* **imperfection,** imperfectness, incompleteness, faultiness, defectiveness, weakness, frailty, failure, omission, error, deficiency, inadequacy, defection, badness, unsoundness, immaturity.

fault, defect, flaw, "little rift within the lute" (Tennyson), foible, failing, weak point; screw loose; taint, blemish, spot, stain; weakness, shortcoming, drawback; transgression, offense, misdeed, vice.

II. *Verbs.* **be imperfect,** have a defect, lie under a disadvantage; not pass muster, fall short, miss the mark.

III. *Adjectives.* **imperfect,** deficient, defective, faulty, vicious (*as pronunciation*), corrupt, bad, unsound, tainted, out of order; warped, injured, impaired, disfigured; crude, incomplete, unfinished, abortive, undeveloped, garbled, mutilated; insufficient, short, partial, scanty, limited, inadequate, unsuitable; below par.

indifferent, middling, ordinary, mediocre, average, tolerable, fair, passable, soso *or* so-so, milk-and-water, moderate, decent, not bad, not amiss; admissible, bearable.

inferior, secondary, second-rate, one-horse (*colloq.*), small, petty, mean, two-by-four (*colloq.*).

IV. *Adverbs.* **imperfectly,** incompletely, inadequately; almost, to a limited extent, pretty, moderately, *couci-couci* (*F.*), *comme ci comme ça* (*F.*), tolerably; all things considered, considering.

See also BADNESS, INCOMPLETENESS, INFERIORITY, NONPREPARATION, SHORTCOMING. TOUCH. WEAKNESS.—*Antonyms.* See PERFECTION.

imperil, *v.* endanger, hazard, expose, risk, jeopardize. See DANGER.
imperishable, *adj.* indestructible; undying, enduring. See PERPETUITY, REPUTE.
impersonate, *v.* personate, act, play; personify, typify. See REPRESENTATION.
impertinent, *adj.* rude, impudent, saucy; irrelevant. See INSOLENCE, IRRELATION.
impetuous, *adj.* rash, hasty, headlong; furious, raging. See IMPULSE, VIOLENCE.

IMPIETY.—I. *Nouns.* **impiety,** irreverence, undutifulness, ungodliness, sin, irreligion, profaneness, profanity, blasphemy, profanation; desecration, sacrilege; scoffing, ribaldry.

[*assumed piety*] **hypocrisy,** pietism, cant, pious fraud; lip-devotion, lip-service; formalism, austerity; sanctimony, sanctimoniousness, pharisaism, precisianism, sabbatarianism; sacerdotalism; bigotry, *odium theologicum* (*L.*), blue laws.

apostasy, recusancy, nonconformity, backsliding, tergiversation, recreancy, secession, lapse, perversion, reprobation.

hypocrite, dissembler, tartufe *or* tartuffe, deceiver, pretender, Mucker (*Ger.*) Pecksniff (*Martin Chuzzlewit*), Tartufe (*hypocritical priest in Molière's "Tartufe"*), Mawworm (*Bickerstaff's comedy, "The Hypocrite"*), Holy Willie (Burns); Scribes and Pharisees (*New Testament*).

bigot, Pharisee, sabbatarian, formalist, precisian, pietist, devotee, ranter, religionist, fanatic.

sinner, wrongdoer, transgressor, scoffer, blasphemer, sabbath breaker; worldling.

[*in plural*] the wicked, the evil, the unjust, the reprobate, children of darkness.

II. *Verbs.* **be impious,** etc. (see *adjectives*); profane, desecrate, violate, contaminate, defile, pollute, blaspheme, revile, scoff, swear; commit sacrilege.

dissemble, simulate, pretend, play the hypocrite, hypocritize (*rare*), cant snuffle.

III. *Adjectives.* **impious,** irreligious, ungodly, profane, ribald, irreverent, sacrilegious, blasphemous; unhallowed, unsanctified, unregenerate; hardened, perverted, reprobate; undutiful, disobedient.

hypocritical, canting, pietistical, sanctimonious, unctuous, pharisaical, overrighteous, deceitful, double-faced, two-faced, tartufish *or* tartuffish.

bigoted, fanatical, hidebound, narrow, narrow-minded, intolerant, prejudiced, illiberal, small, little; provincial, parochial, insular, untraveled.

See also DECEIVER, FALSEHOOD, IRRELIGION, MALEDICTION, MISJUDGMENT, OBSTINACY.—*Antonyms.* See PIETY.

---

implant, *v.* infix, plant; instill, inculcate. See INSERTION, TEACHING.
implanted, *adj.* ingrafted, inset, infused, instilled. See OBJECTIVENESS.
implement, *n.* tool, utensil. See INSTRUMENT.
implicate, *v.* associate, incriminate, connect, involve. See ACCUSATION.
implication, *n.* allusion, inference, hint, intimation, innuendo. See LATENCY, MEANING.
implied, *adj.* tacit, inferential, understood. See MEANING.
implore, *v.* beseech, entreat, pray, beg. See REQUEST.
imply, *v.* involve, entail, include; insinuate, hint. See EVIDENCE, INFORMATION.
impolite, *adj.* rude, uncivil, boorish. See DISCOURTESY.
import, *v.* matter, concern; indicate, imply; bring in, introduce. See IMPORTANCE, MEANING, RECEPTION.
import, *n.* significance, force; importation; purport, drift. See IMPORTANCE, INGRESS, MEANING.

IMPORTANCE.—I. *Nouns.* **importance,** consequence, moment, prominence, consideration, mark; weight, ponderosity, materialness, import, significance, concern, emphasis, interest, standing, distinction, caliber, influence; value, usefulness; greatness; superiority, notability, figure, self-importance, pomposity, self-sufficiency.

salient point, outstanding feature; distinctive feature, essential matter, precise thing, *sine qua non* (*L.*), "the be-all and the end-all" (*Macbeth*); cardinal point;

substance, gist, sum and substance, gravamen, cream, salt, core, kernel, heart, nucleus; key, keynote; keystone, corner stone; trump card.
gravity, seriousness, solemnity; pressure, urgency, press, stress; matter of life and death.
[*person of importance*] **personage,** figure, somebody, big wig (*jocose*), great gun, big gun (*colloq.*), big boy (*colloq.*), magnate, grandee, bashaw, pasha (*Turkish*), nabob, Mogul, panjandrum, "The Grand Panjandrum himself" (*a mock title occurring in some nonsense lines by Samuel Foote*), his nibs (*jocose*); top sawyer (*colloq.*), first-fiddle, prima donna, chief, leader, boss, burra sahib *or* bara sahib (*India*), cock of the walk.
II. *Verbs.* **be important,** be somebody, be something; import, signify, matter, carry weight; come to the front, lead the way, take the lead, play first fiddle.
value, care for, set store upon (*or* by), treasure, prize, appreciate.
emphasize, stress, accentuate, feature, punctuate, lay stress on; mark, underline, underscore.
III. *Adjectives.* **important,** of importance, substantial, big (*colloq.*), consequential, material, considerable; weighty, ponderous, influential, notable, prominent, marked, outstanding, salient, signal, memorable, remarkable, particular, rare, unusual, special, noteworthy; stirring, eventful.
grave, serious, earnest, grand, solemn, impressive, momentous, critical, commanding, imposing.
urgent, pressing, critical, crucial, instant, imperative, exigent.
principal, leading, first, foremost, staple (*as a commodity*), chief, main, prime, primary; capital, superior, paramount, preëminent, supreme; essential, vital, radical, cardinal.
significant, telling, impressive, trenchant, emphatic, decided, positive, forceful, pregnant.
IV. *Adverbs.* **importantly,** substantially, materially, etc. (see *adjectives*); in the main, *par excellence* (*F.*), above all, in the first place, to crown all.

See also GRAVITY, GREATNESS, INFLUENCE, MATERIALITY, NOBILITY, REPUTE.—*Antonyms.* See UNIMPORTANCE.

---

impose, *v.* inflict, enjoin, levy, tax. See PRICE.—**impose upon,** palm off, delude, victimize. See DECEPTION.
imposing, *adj.* stately, impressive, majestic, commanding. See REPUTE.

IMPOSSIBILITY.—I. *Nouns.* **impossibility,** impracticability, infeasibleness, infeasibility, insuperableness, insuperability, hopelessness, incredibility.
II. *Verbs.* **be impossible,** etc. (see *adjectives*); have no chance whatever, be a waste of time.
attempt impossibilities; square the circle, find the elixir of life, discover the philosopher's stone, discover the grand panacea, find the fountain of youth, discover the secret of perpetual motion; wash a blackamoor white; make bricks without straw, weave a rope of sand, be in two places at once, gather grapes from thorns, *prendre la lune avec les dents* (*F.*).
III. *Adjectives.* **impossible,** not possible, absurd, contrary to reason, unlikely, unreasonable, incredible, visionary, impractical, improbable, hopeless, unimaginable, unthinkable, inconceivable.
impracticable, unachievable, infeasible *or* unfeasible, insurmountable, insuperable, inaccessible, unattainable, unobtainable; out of the question; impassable, impervious, innavigable; self-contradictory, incompatible.

See also HOPELESSNESS.—*Antonyms.* See POSSIBILITY.

---

impostor, *n.* humbug, pretender, quack. See DECEIVER.
imposture, *n.* deception, trick, fraud, imposition. See CUNNING.

IMPOTENCE.—I. *Nouns.* **impotence,** feebleness, weakness, inability, disability, incapacity, incapability, disablement, ineptitude, inefficiency, incompetence, disqualification; inefficacy, failure, washout (*slang*).
helplessness, powerlessness, prostration, paralysis, collapse, exhaustion, atony (*med.*), senility, superannuation, decrepitude, infirmity, imbecility, inanition.

weakling, tenderling, cripple; old woman, muff (*colloq.*), milksop, betty, molly-coddle, sissy (*colloq.*), mother's darling.
II. *Verbs.* **be impotent,** etc. (see *adjectives*), collapse, fail, flunk (*school slang*), fizzle out (*colloq.*), cave in, break down, end in smoke, go by the board; faint, swoon, drop.
render impotent (*or* powerless), disable, disarm, incapacitate, sterilize (*biol.*), disqualify, unfit, invalidate, demoralize, weaken, enfeeble, shatter, exhaust, undermine, deaden, cramp, tie the hands; prostrate, paralyze, muzzle, cripple, maim, lame, hamstring, strangle, throttle, silence, put *hors de combat* (*F.*), spike the guns, unhinge, put out of gear.
unman, unnerve, devitalize, attenuate, enervate; emasculate, effeminize (*rare*), castrate. geld, alter (*colloq.*), spay (*referring to a female animal*).
III. *Adjectives.* **impotent,** powerless, weak, helpless; incapable, unable, incompetent, inefficient, ineffective, unfit, unfitted, unqualified, disqualified; crippled, disabled; senile, decrepit, infirm, superannuated; paralytic, paralyzed, nerveless, out of joint, out of gear; unnerved, unhinged; done up (*colloq.*), done for (*colloq.*)- dead-beat (*colloq.*), spent, all in (*slang*), exhausted, shattered, prostrate, demoralized; harmless, unarmed, weaponless, defenseless, *hors de combat* (*F.*).
nugatory, null and void, inoperative, good for nothing, invalid, unsound, ineffectual, inadequate, inefficacious, fruitless, futile, useless.

See also FAILURE, INSUFFICIENCY, INUTILITY.—*Antonyms.* See POWER.

---

impoverish, *v.* deplete, exhaust, drain; pauperize, reduce. See INSUFFICIENCY, POVERTY.
impracticable, *adj.* infeasible. See IMPOSSIBILITY.
impress, *v.* interest, strike, inspire; mark, imprint; affect, act upon. See EXCITEMENT, INDICATION, TOUCH.
impressible, *adj.* impressionable, sensitive, susceptible, emotional, facile. See SENSITIVENESS, SOFTNESS.
impression, *n.* opinion, notion; stamp, imprint; sensation, perception, feeling. See BELIEF, ENGRAVING, SENSIBILITY.
impressive, *adj.* effective, stirring, stately, imposing; solemn, grave; moving, affecting. See FEELING, PRIDE, SAGE, TOUCH.
imprison, *v.* confine, incarcerate. See RESTRAINT.
imprisoned, *adj.* in custody, incarcerated, jailed, immured. See PRISONER.

IMPROBABILITY.—I. *Nouns.* **improbability,** unlikelihood, inconceivableness, bare possibility; long odds; incredibility, incredibleness, doubtfulness.
II. *Verbs.* **be improbable,** etc. (see *adjectives*); go beyond reason, strain one's credulity; have small chance.
III. *Adjectives.* **improbable,** unlikely, rare, unheard of, inconceivable, unimaginable, incredible, implausible, doubtful, unbelievable, questionable.

Antonyms. See PROBABILITY.

IMPROBITY.—I. *Nouns.* **improbity,** dishonesty, dishonor, disrepute, disgrace; fraud, lying; bad faith, falsity, infidelity, faithlessness, unrighteousness; Judas kiss, Iscariotism, betrayal, perfidy, perfidiousness, treachery, double dealing; malpractice, wrongdoing, professional misconduct; degradation, turpitude, moral turpitude, laxity; shuffling, trimming.
breach of trust (*or* faith), disloyalty, divided allegiance, hyphenated allegiance (*cant*), treason, high treason; apostasy.
rascality, knavery, villainy; roguery, scoundrelism, reprobacy (*rare*), baseness, foul play; jobbing, jobbery, job, corruption, graft (*colloq.*), venality, corruption, sharp practice.
II. *Verbs.* **play false;** break one's word (*or* promise), jilt, betray, forswear, swear falsely, perjure (*used reflexively*); grovel, sneak, sell oneself, squeal (*slang*), peach (*slang*), sell, knife (*U. S. slang*), go back on (*colloq.*), go over to the enemy.
III. *Adjectives.* **dishonest,** dishonorable, unconscientious unscrupulous, unprincipled, fraudulent, false-hearted; unfair, one-sided; double, double-tongued, double-faced, time-serving, crooked, tortuous, Machiavellian, slippery, fishy (*colloq.*), questionable.

infamous, ignominious, arrant, foul, base, vile, low, villainous, rascally, knavish recreant, contumelious, odious, sordid, ignoble, despicable, contemptible, abject, mean, shabby, little, paltry, dirty, scurvy, sneaking, groveling, corrupt venal, purchasable.
derogatory, discreditable, disreputable, unworthy, ignoble, scandalous, degrading, undignified, unbefitting, *infra dignitatem* (*L.*), *infra dig.*, ungentlemanly, unchivalric, unmanly, inglorious.
faithless, false, unfaithful, disloyal, perfidious, treacherous; perjured, traitorous, untrue, Iscariotic *or* Iscariotical, untrustworthy, trustless; lost to shame, dead to honor.
IV. *Adverbs.* **dishonestly,** dishonorably, etc. (see *adjectives*); *mala fide* (*L.*); like a thief in the night, by crooked paths, by foul means.

See also APOSTASY, DECEPTION, DISREPUTE, FALSEHOOD, VICE.—*Antonyms.* See PROBITY.

---

improper, *adj.* unsuitable, inappropriate, unbecoming; indelicate, indecent; incorrect, unjustified. See RIGHTLESSNESS, VICE, WRONG.
impropriety, *n.* unfitness, imprudence, indecorum. See RIGHTLESSNESS.

IMPROVEMENT.—I. *Nouns.* **improvement,** amelioration, betterment, melioration, amendment, emendation; enrichment, advancement, advance, promotion, preferment, elevation, increase; recovery.
cultivation, refinement, culture, civilization, *Kultur* (*Ger.*), polish, menticulture (*rare*) mind culture, march of intellect; acculturation (*ethnol.*), race culture, euthenics (*through environment*), eugenics (*through heredity*).
reform, reformation, progress; revision, radical reform; correction, development, elaboration; purification, repair, reconstruction, reclamation.
reformer, reformist, progressive, radical.
II. *Verbs.* **improve,** mend, amend, better, ameliorate, help, relieve. rectify, correct, repair, restore; improve upon; enrich, mellow, elaborate, refine, develop.
revive, renew, refresh, revivify, recreate, invigorate, strengthen, freshen, recruit.
promote, cultivate, advance, forward, further, speed, push, enhance, bring forward, foster, aid, profit, benefit.
revise, edit, review, make corrections, doctor, emend, correct, rectify, touch up, polish, make improvements, amend.
reform, remodel, reëstablish, reconstruct, refashion, new-model, reorganize, reclaim, civilize, lift, uplift, ennoble, raise, regenerate, inspire.
III. *Adjectives.* **improved,** mended, etc. (see *verbs*); better, preferable, all the better for; progressive, superior.
improvable, amendable, curable, corrigible, correctable.

See also PROGRESSION, RESTORATION.—*Antonyms.* See DETERIORATION.

---

improvise, *v.* extemporize, compose. See IMPULSE.
impudence, *n.* self-assertion, audacity, nerve (*slang*), effrontery. See INSOLENCE.
impudent, *adj.* saucy, impertinent, rude, bold. See INSOLENCE.

IMPULSE.—I. *Nouns.* **impulse,** impulsion, impelling force, impetus, momentum, moment (*tech.*), pressure, push, thrust, shove, boom, boost (*U. S. colloq.*), drive, kick, scend (*naut.*), start, send-off, propulsion.
crash, clash, collision, smash (*colloq.*), smash-up (*colloq.*); encounter, shock, brunt, bump; impact, *élan* (*F.*), charge, onset; percussion, concussion.
blow, stroke, knock, tap, rap, slap, smack, pat, dab, flap, fillip; bang, hit, clip (*slang*), jab, bat, poke, swat (*slang*), whack, thwack, cuff, buffet, punch, thump, kick, cut, thrust, lunge; carom, cannon (*Brit.: billiards*).
science of mechanical forces: mechanics, dynamics, kinetics.
[*mental impetus*] **incitement,** incentive, actuation, motive, encouragement, abetment, instigation, influence, call; sudden thought, flash, inspiration, improvisation, impromptu.
proclivity, tendency, inclination, propensity, itch, cacoëthes (*as for writing*), desire, proneness, bias, set, leaning, passion, liking, taste, turn, twist, bent, predisposition.

II. *Verbs.* **impel,** drive, urge, urge forward, propel, push, boost (*U. S. colloq.*) boom; pelt, throw, start, set going, elbow, shoulder, shove, thrust, prod, poke, stick, butt, jog, jolt.
strike, hit, slap, knock, thump, beat, hammer, bang, slam, bat, dash, punch, plug (*slang*), clip (*slang*), thwack, whack, smash, wham (*slang*), ram, batter, tamp, stamp, buffet, cudgel, belabor; lunge, jab, kick; tap, rap, pat, flap, dab, peck, peckle, pick.
collide, foul, bump, butt, meet, clash, crash, telescope, hurtle, jostle.
incite, induce, influence, instigate, abet, actuate, encourage, force, constrain.
improvise, extemporize, act on the spur of the moment, rise to the occasion; compose.
III. *Adjectives.* **impulsive,** impellent, impelling, moving, driving, propulsive, dynamic.
impetuous, hasty, quick, rash, precipitate, passionate, hot, ungovernable, heedless, capricious, incautious.
extemporaneous, improvised, unpremeditated, spontaneous, inspirational, unprompted, snap (*colloq.*); natural, unguarded, offhand.
IV. *Adverbs.* **impulsively,** rashly, quickly, unpremeditatedly; extempore, extemporaneously, impromptu, offhand.

See also EXCITABILITY, MOTIVE, PROPULSION, PUNISHMENT, RASHNESS.—*Antonyms.* See PREDETERMINATION, RECOIL.

---

impunity, *n.* exemption (*from punishment*), immunity. See ACQUITTAL.

IMPURITY.—I. *Nouns.* **impurity,** uncleanness, foulness, filth, corruption, unwholesomeness, pollution, defilement, feculence.
debasement, deterioration, taint, corruption, adulteration, vitiation.
unchastity, lewdness, grossness, immodesty, indelicacy, ribaldry, indecency, obscenity; lust, carnality, incontinence, concupiscence, immorality, salacity; dissipation, libertinism, sensuality.
II. *Verbs.* **be impure,** etc. (see *adjectives*); seduce, ravish, violate, rape, debauch, defile, force, deflower, ruin.
III. *Adjectives.* **impure,** unclean, foul, dirty, filthy, feculent, defiled, fetid, polluted, nasty, unwholesome.
debased, adulterated, mixed, deteriorated, vitiated, doctored (*colloq.*), drugged; spurious, snide (*slang*), inferior, base (*as, an* impure *diamond*).
[*ceremonially impure*] **unpurified,** uncleansed, defiled, unholy, unhallowed, unsanctified, unblessed *or* unblest.
unchaste, lewd, indelicate, immodest, improper, risky, *risqué* (*F.*), off-color, suggestive, shameless, indecent, coarse, smutty, obscene, Fescennine, ribald, filthy, gross, vile, licentious, dissolute, incontinent, immoral, unclean, libidinous, lustful, lascivious, lecherous, sensual, concupiscent, salacious, Paphian.

See also INELEGANCE, LIBERTINE, UNCLEANNESS.—*Antonyms.* See PURITY.

---

inability, *n.* incapacity, weakness; incompetence, inefficiency. See IMPOTENCE, UNSKILLFULNESS.
inaccurate, *adj.* wrong, incorrect, inexact. See ERROR.

INACTION.—I. *Nouns.* **inaction,** passiveness, passivity, watchful waiting, nonresistance, *laissez faire* (*F.*), noninterference, Fabian policy; neglect, inactivity, idleness, inertness; stagnation, vegetation, rest, loafing, *dolce far niente* (*It.*), want of occupation, unemployment.
sinecure, easy post (position, billet, *or* job), soft snap *or* soft thing (*slang*), cinch (*U. S. slang*), snap (*slang*).
II. *Verbs.* **be inactive,** not do, not act, not attempt; abstain from doing, do nothing, hold, spare; leave (*or* let) alone; let be, let pass, let things take their course, live and let live; rest upon one's oars; stand aloof; refrain, relax one's efforts; desist, stop, pause, wait, cool one's heels (*colloq.*), pass (*or* beguile) the time, waste time.
undo, unmake, do away with; take down, take to pieces; annul, make null and void, abolish, expunge, destroy, ruin.

III. *Adjectives.* **passive,** inactive, inert, sluggish, torpid; unresisting, nonresistant, noninterfering, patient; quiescent, resigned, indifferent, apathetic, impassive, impassible.
unoccupied, unemployed, unbusied (*rare*), vacant, idle, loafing, resting, disengaged, out of employ (work, *or* a job).

See also CESSATION, INACTIVITY, INERTNESS, RELINQUISHMENT, REPOSE, [1]REST.—*Antonyms.* See ACTION.

INACTIVITY.—I. *Nouns.* **inactivity,** inaction, inactiveness, inertness, do-nothingness, do-nothingism, faineance *or* faineancy, sluggishness, idleness, sloth, indolence, ergophobia, laziness, inexertion; remissness, relaxation, dawdling, pottering; idling, otiosity, deedlessness; passiveness, lull, quiescence, rest, peace.
languor, dullness, stagnation, torpor, stupor, somnolence, drowsiness, kef (*as produced by bhang*), dreaminess, heaviness, hypnotism, lethargy.
sleep, slumber, rest, repose; forty winks (*colloq.*), nap, doze, siesta, catnap, snooze (*colloq.*); Morpheus, Somnus, the Dustman (*folklore*), the Sandman; dreamland, Land of Nod; dream, reverie, sopor (*med.*), coma, trance, catalepsy, hypnosis; hibernation, dormancy, torpidity, æstivation (*zoöl.: opposite of* hibernation).
idler, drone, do-little, *fainéant* (*F.*), dawdler, truant; dead one (*slang*), dummy, *flâneur* (*F.*), lounger, loafer, slow coach, laggard, sluggard; tramp, beggar, bum (*slang*), hobo (*U. S.*), Weary Willie (*colloq.*), sundowner (*Australia*), afternoon farmer, lazzarone (*It. pl.* lazzaroni: *Naples*), bummer (*U. S. slang*), lazybones (*colloq.*); opium eater, lotus eater, dreamer; cocaine addict, coke fiend (*slang*), snowbird (*slang*), dope fiend (*slang*), hophead (*slang*).
II. *Verbs.* **be inactive,** do nothing; dawdle, drawl, lag, hang back, slouch, loll, lounge, loaf, loiter; sleep at one's post; take it easy, vegetate.
idle, loaf, laze, idle (fritter, *or* fool) away time, dillydally, potter, putter (*U. S.*), dabble.
sleep, slumber, be asleep, oversleep, hibernate, æstivate (*zoöl.*); doze, snooze (*colloq.*), drowse, nap, take a nap; fall asleep, drop asleep; nod, go to bed, turn in.
languish, expend itself, flag, decline, droop, sink, pine, hang fire; relax.
III. *Adjectives.* **inactive,** unoccupied, unemployed, disengaged; motionless, passive, inert, stagnant, lifeless, inanimate, dull, heavy, leaden, torpid, sluggish, logy (*U. S.*); peaceful, quiet, quiescent.
indolent, lazy, slothful, idle, remiss, slack, *fainéant* (*F.*), do-nothing, shiftless, languid, listless, maudlin; dilatory, laggard, slow, pottering, flagging.
sleeping, asleep, slumbering, dozing, dormant, dead, comatose; in the arms (*or* lap) of Morpheus.
sleepy, slumberous, slumbery, drowsy, dozy, dreamy, Morphean, somnolent, lethargic *or* lethargical, heavy, heavy with sleep; soporific, hypnotic.

See also INACTION, INSENSIBILITY, LATENESS, SLOWNESS, VEGETATION.—*Antonyms.* See ACTIVITY.

---

inadequate, *adj.* incomplete, scanty, defective, lacking. See INSUFFICIENCY.
inadvertence, *n.* heedlessness, carelessness, thoughtlessness. See INATTENTION.
inadvisable, *adj.* unwise, imprudent. See INEXPEDIENCE.
inane, *adj.* empty, senseless, silly, idiotic; dull, unintelligent, unreasoning. See FOLLY, VACUITY.
inappreciabl , *adj.* imperceptible, infinitesimal. See SMALLNESS.
inappreciative, *adj.* unappreciative, unresponsive. See UNDERESTIMATION.
inappropriate, *adj.* unsuitable, improper. See DISAGREEMENT.
inapt, *adj.* inapplicable, unsuitable, unskillful. See DISAGREEMENT.
inarticulate, *adj.* mute; confused, indistinct, thick. See DUMBNESS, STAMMERING, THICKNESS.

INATTENTION.—I. *Nouns.* **inattention,** heedlessness, disregard, unconcern, want of thought, inadvertence, carelessness, absent-mindedness, thoughtlessness, negligence, inconsideration, want of consideration, inconsiderateness; oversight, neglect.

abstraction, absence of mind, absorption, engrossment, detachment, preoccupation, distraction, reverie, brown study (*colloq.*), woolgathering, daydream.

II. *Verbs.* **be inattentive** (*or* unobservant); overlook, disregard; pass by, neglect; think little of; pay no attention to; dismiss from one's mind, drop the subject, think no more of; turn a deaf ear to, turn one's back upon.

bewilder, perplex, confuse, disconcert, discompose, fluster, flurry, befuddle, fuss (*colloq.*), rattle (*colloq.*), muddle; distract the attention (thoughts, *or* mind); put out of one's head.

III. *Adjectives.* **inattentive,** unobservant, undiscerning, unmindful, unheeding, regardless; listless, apathetic, indifferent, blind, deaf; volatile, scatter-brained, harebrained, flighty, giddy; unreflecting; inconsiderate, thoughtless, heedless, wild, harum-scarum (*colloq.*), careless, neglectful.

absent, absent-minded, musing, lost, rapt, engrossed, preoccupied, abstracted, *distrait* (*F.*), woolgathering, dreamy, far-away, dazed; lost in thought, in the clouds, in a reverie, off one's guard, caught napping.

See also INDIFFERENCE, NEGLECT.—*Antonyms.* See ATTENTION.

---

inaudible, *adj.* unhearable, low, indistinct, muffied. See DEAFNESS, FAINTNESS.

inaugurate, *v.* institute, launch, initiate; install, invest. See BEGINNING, CELEBRATION.

inauspicious, *adj.* unfavorable. ill-starred, unlucky, ominous. See ADVERSITY, OMEN.

inborn, *adj.* innate, natural, inherent, inbred. See DISPOSITION.

incapable, *adj.* incompetent, unable, unfitted, inefficient. See INSUFFICIENCY.

incapacity, *n.* incapability, incompetence. See IMPOTENCE.

incarnate, *v.* embody, incorporate; animate, materialize. See ANIMAL LIFE, MATERIALITY.

incautious, *adj.* rash, indiscreet, imprudent; overconfident, careless, heedless. See RASHNESS, SECURITY.

incendiary, *n.* fire bug (*U. S.*), pyromaniac. See CALEFACTION.

incentive, *n.* spur, stimulus, encouragement, goad. See MOTIVE.

incessant, *adj.* continual, uninterrupted, unceasing. See FREQUENCY.

incident, *n.* occurrence, affair, episode, circumstance. See EVENT.

incidental, *adj.* occasional, casual, secondary, subordinate. See IRRELATION, OBJECTIVENESS.

incite, *v.* induce, actuate, constrain, arouse, stir, urge, instigate, impel. See IMPULSE, MOTIVE.

incitement, *n.* incentive, motive, encouragement, instigation. See IMPULSE.

incivility, *n.* impoliteness, rudeness, bad manners. See DISCOURTESY.

inclement, *adj.* pitiless, cruel, merciless; severe, cold, bitter, violent. See PITILESSNESS, SEVERITY.

inclination, *n.* fondness, liking; slant, slope; leaning, propensity, bent. See DESIRE, OBLIQUITY, TENDENCY.

inclined plane, sloping plane, slope. See INSTRUMENT (*mechanical powers*), OBLIQUITY.

INCLOSURE.—I. *Nouns.* **inclosure** *or* enclosure, inclosing, encompassment, encincture; receptacle, case, wrapper, envelope; cincture, girdle.

[*inclosed place*] pen, fold, corral, pound, pinfold; sty, shed, stall; paddock, pasture, croft; *enceinte* (*F.*), circumvallation.

yard, court, curtilage, close, garth, compound (*Oriental*), quadrangle; barnyard. farmyard, stockyard, barton (*Eng.*), cattlefold, bawn (*Irish*).

fence, paling, rail, railing, pale (*archaic*), weir, wall; hedge, hedgerow.

barrier, barricade, bar, obstruction, cordon, stockade; gate, gateway, door, hatch; boom (*mil.*), entanglement; barrage (*mil.*).

dike, ditch, fosse, trench, drain, moat; levee, bank, estacade (*mil.*).

II. *Verbs.* **inclose** *or* enclose, surround, encircle, encompass, circumscribe, hedge, rope, corral, pen, box, case, incase, envelop, shut in, insert.

See also CIRCUMSCRIPTION, DEFENSE, ENVIRONMENT, PRISON, RECEPTACLE.—*Antonyms.* See FREEDOM, SPACE.

INCLUSION.—I. *Nouns.* **inclusion,** admission, comprehension, subsumption, comprisal, reception; embodiment, incorporation, composition, formation, constitution; congenerousness, kindred, relationship.

II. *Verbs.* **include,** comprise, subsume, comprehend, contain, hold, admit, embrace, receive, inclose, encircle, involve, incorporate, cover, embody, reckon among, number among, number, count; refer to; place under, arrange under, take into account.

III. *Adjectives.* **inclusive,** inclosing, surrounding, encircling, inclusory (*rare*), included, including; compendious, extensive, wide, comprehensive, full, large, sweeping, all-embracing; congeneric (*esp. biol.*), congenerous, kindred.

See also CIRCUMSCRIPTION, CLASS, COMPONENT, COMPOSITION.—*Antonyms.* See EXCLUSION.

INCOHERENCE.—I. *Nouns.* **incoherence** *or* incoherency, immiscibility, nonadhesion; looseness, laxity, relaxation; loosening, disjunction.

incongruity, inconsistency, incompatibility, unsuitableness, impropriety, disagreement, inharmony, irreconcilableness, irreconcilability, incompatibility, dissonance, discordance *or* discordancy; illogicality, inconsequence, absurdity.

II. *Verbs.* **loosen,** make loose, slacken, detach, disjoin, disengage, loose, undo; free, release, unfasten; relax.

III. *Adjectives.* **incoherent** (*physically disconnected*), nonadhesive, immiscible, noncohesive, detached, loose, slack, lax, relaxed, segregated, unconsolidated, uncombined.

incongruous, inconsistent, inconsequent, incompatible, unsuitable, unfit, improper, inharmonious, discordant, dissonant, disagreeing, variant, contradictory, illogical, absurd, irreconcilable, discrepant, incongruent, contrary, antagonistic, incoördinate.

See also CONTRARIETY, DIFFERENCE, DISJUNCTION.—*Antonyms.* See COHERENCE.

---

incombustible, *adj.* uninflammable, fireproof. See REFRIGERATION.

income, *n.* receipts, earnings, revenue, emoluments. See ACQUISITION.

in common, commonly, equally, shared, in joint use. See PARTICIPATION.

incompatible, *adj.* uncongenial, unsympathetic, inharmonious, inconsistent. See DISAGREEMENT.

incompetence, *n.* inability, incapability, inefficiency, disqualification. See IMBECILITY, IMPOTENCE.

incompetent, *adj.* incapable, inefficient, unfit, unqualified, disqualified; unskilled, inexpert. See IMPOTENCE, POVERTY (*inefficient*), UNSKILLFULNESS.

INCOMPLETENESS.—I. *Nouns.* **incompleteness,** imperfectness, imperfection, immaturity; defect, deficiency, shortcoming, lack, want, insufficiency, shortness, inadequacy.

[*part wanting*] deficit, omission, shortage; break, interval: missing link.

II. *Verbs.* **be incomplete,** fall short of, lack, want, need, require.

III. *Adjectives.* **incomplete,** uncompleted, imperfect, unfinished; defective, deficient, wanting, failing, in arrear, short, short of; hollow, meager, scarce, perfunctory, sketchy, crude, immature, undeveloped.

mutilated, garbled, distorted, defaced, hashed, mangled, maimed, butchered, docked, truncated.

See also IMPERFECTION, INSUFFICIENCY, NONCOMPLETION, NONPREPARATION, PART, SHORTCOMING.—*Antonyms.* See COMPLETENESS.

---

incomprehensible, *adj.* unfathomable, inscrutable, impenetrable. See UNINTELLIGIBILITY.

inconceivable, *adj.* unthinkable, unimaginable, incredible. See IMPOSSIBILITY.

incongruity, *n.* inconsistency, incompatibility, disagreement; absurdity. See INCOHERENCE.

incongruous, *adj.* inconsistent, inharmonious, absurd, unsuitable. See DISAGREEMENT, INCOHERENCE.

inconsiderate, *adj.* neglectful, thoughtless, careless. See INATTENTION.

inconsistency, *n.* incompatibility, incoherence, contradiction. See DISCORD.
inconsistent, *adj.* fickle, changeable; incompatible, inharmonious; fallacious, illogical. See CAPRICE, DISCORD, SOPHISTRY.
inconspicuous, *adj.* unobtrusive, unnoticeable. See INVISIBILITY.
inconstant, *adj.* fickle, faithless, unsteady. See CHANGEABLENESS.
inconvenient, *adj.* unsuitable, inopportune, unseasonable, troublesome. See INEXPERIENCE.
incorporate, *v.* unite, blend, fuse, merge; federate, consolidate; embody. See COMBINATION, MATERIALITY.
incorrect, *adj.* wrong, fallacious, mistaken, inaccurate, untrue. See ERROR, FALSEHOOD, UNTRUTH.
incorrigible, *adj.* depraved, intractable, irreclaimable. See VICE.

INCREASE.—I. *Nouns.* **increase,** augmentation, addition, enlargement, accession, reinforcement, extension, expansion, dilation, dilatation, spread, growth, increment, accretion, development, accumulation, inflation, enhancement, aggrandizement, intensification, aggravation, exaggeration; rise (*as, in price*), advance.
multiplication, procreation, begetting, production, propagation, generation, breeding, prolification, proliferation (*biol.*), reproduction, histogenesis *or* histogeny (*biol.*); progeny, offspring, issue.
profit, benefit, interest, advantage, gain, clean-up (*slang*), gettings (*pl.*), produce, product, bonus, bunce (*slang*), velvet (*slang*), graft, plunder, booty, rake-off (*U. S. slang*).
II. *Verbs.* [*make greater*] **increase,** augment, add to, enlarge, magnify, aggrandize, greaten (*archaic*), multiply, spread, enhance, raise, boost (*colloq.*), inflate, extend, double, deepen, lengthen, heighten, exalt, strengthen, thicken, redouble reinforce; intensify, aggravate, exacerbate, exaggerate.
[*become greater*] grow, augment, wax, become, mount, rise, ascend, swell; multiply, be fruitful (*or* fertile), be prolific, proliferate (*biol.*).
III. *Adjectives.* **increasing,** growing, crescent, crescive, augmenting, waxing, increscent, enlarging, swelling, augmentative, multiplying, intensifying, intensive, intensitive (*rare*).
See also ADDITION, ASCENT, DISPERSION, EXPANSION, PRODUCTION.—*Antonyms.* See DECREASE.

---

incredibility, *n.* unbelievability, inconceivability. See UNBELIEF.
incredible, *adj.* doubtful, unbelievable, inconceivable. See UNBELIEF.

INCREDULITY.—I. *Nouns.* **incredulity,** incredulousness, skepticism, Pyrrhonism, doubt, disbelief, unbelief, miscreance (*archaic*).
unbeliever, misbeliever, skeptic *or* sceptic, doubting Thomas, disbeliever, agnostic, infidel, Pyrrhonist, freetbinker, heretic, nullifidian.
II. *Verbs.* **be incredulous,** distrust, doubt, skepticize *or* scepticize, suspect, refuse to believe; turn a deaf ear to, hold aloof.
III. *Adjectives.* **incredulous,** skeptical *or* sceptical, distrustful, doubtful, dubious, mistrustful, suspicious; dissenting, disbelieving, unbelieving, nullifidian, Pyrrhonean *or* Pyrrhonic; heretical, heterodox; agnostic *or* agnostical.
See also IRRELIGION, UNBELIEF.—*Antonyms.* See CREDULITY.

---

incur, *v.* bring on, fall into, acquire. See CONTRACTION.
incurable, *adj.* irreparable, irremediable, remediless. See HOPELESSNESS.

INCURIOSITY.—I. *Nouns.* **incuriosity,** incuriousness, apathy, unconcern, indifference, insouciance, Laodiceanism, nonchalance, carelessness, heedlessness, disregard, inattentiveness.
II. *Verbs.* **be incurious** (*or* indifferent), have no curiosity, be bored by, take no interest in, mind one's own business.
III. *Adjectives.* **incurious,** uninquisitive, uninquiring, indifferent, insouciant, nonchalant, heedless, careless, inattentive, bored, uninterested, apathetic, adiaphorous, impassive.
See also INDIFFERENCE. INSENSIBILITY.—*Antonyms.* See CURIOSITY, DESIRE.

incursion, *n.* attack, inroad, raid, foray, hostile invasion. See DESCENT.
indebted, *adj.* owing, liable; beholden, obliged. See DEBT, GRATITUDE.
indecent, *adj.* immodest, improper, indelicate, obscene, immoral. See IMPURITY, UNCLEANNESS.
indecision, *n.* uncertainty, hesitation. See IRRESOLUTION.
indefinite, *adj.* vague, indeterminate; undecided; equivocal. See UNCERTAINTY.
indent, *v.* dent, dint, score, jag; requisition. See CONCAVITY, NOTCH, REQUEST.
indentation, *n.* dent, dint, depression, cut, serration. See CONCAVITY, NOTCH.
independence, *n.* liberty, self-government; sufficiency, affluence. See FREEDOM, WEALTH.
independent, *adj.* free, unfettered, self-directing, self-reliant, autonomous, self-governing; irrespective (*of*), exclusive (*of*), separate (*from*); well-to-do, affluent. See FREEDOM, IRRELATION, WEALTH.
independent, *n.* free lance, freethinker, nonpartisan. See FREEDOM.
indescribable, *adj.* inexpressible, ineffable. See WONDER.

INDICATION.—I. *Nouns.* **indication,** denotation, implication, connotation, suggestion, inference, symptom, evidence, particularization, description, specification; proof, demonstration; dactylography, Bertillon system.
sign, token, symbol, mark, note, signum (*L. pl.* signa), device, emblem, cipher, type, figure, indicium (*usually in pl.* indicia); asterisk, star; reference, reference mark, index, indicant, indicator, pointer, cue, hint, clew *or* clue, key; omen, presage, prognostication, portent, boding, foretoken, warning, foreboding, prognostic, foreshowing, augury.
characteristic, trait, diagnostic (*esp. med.*), feature, peculiarity, lineament, quality, property, cast, trick, earmark.
footprint, track, trail, scent, spoor, step, footstep, footmark, vestige, trace, pug *or* pag (*Anglo-Indian*), pad, ichnite *or* ichnolite (*fossil footprint*).
gesture, gesticulation, motion; wink, glance, leer; nod, shrug, beck; touch, nudge; byplay, dumb show, pantomime, chironomy; deaf-and-dumb alphabet, dactylology; freemasonry.
signal, beacon, flare, flare-up, fiery cross (*Scot. hist.*), rocket, watch fire, beacon fire, watchtower; telegraph, radio beacon, wigwag, semaphore, heliograph, target (*U. S. railroads*); searchlight, flashlight; calumet, peace pipe.
call, command, summons, reveille, taps (*U. S.*), last post (*Brit.*), trumpet call, bugle call; tattoo, beat of drum, drumbeat; whistle, hooter, siren, horn, bell, alarm, alarum, tocsin; battle cry, rallying cry.
mark, impression, imprint, line, stroke, dash, score, streak, scratch, tick, dot, notch, nick, blaze; hachure (*map drawing*), contour line.
[*for identification*] badge, countermark, hall mark, trade mark, emblem, insignia (*pl.*), decoration; voucher, docket, countercheck, counterfoil; stub, duplicate, tally, tag, slip, label, ticket, counter, check, chip, stamp; credentials; monogram, seal, signet; fingerprint, dactylogram; brand; caste mark, tilka (*Hindu*); shibboleth; watchword, catchword, password, *mot d'ordre* (*F.*), *mot de passe* (*F*)., cue; sign, countersign, pass, grip; open-sesame.
signature, autograph, sign manual, moniker (*slang*), John Hancock (*U. S. slang*), subscription, indorsement, frank, mark, cross, signum (*L. pl.* signa).
banner, flag, colors, streamer, pennant, pennon, ensign, standard; eagle, oriflamme, blue peter, jack, union jack; "Old Glory" (*colloq.*), Stars and Stripes; tricolor.
[*heraldry*] crest; arms, coat of arms, armorial bearings; hatchment, escutcheon *or* scutcheon; shield, supporters; livery, uniform; cockade, epaulet, brassard, chevron; garland, chaplet; love knot, favor.
[*of locality*] guidepost, waypost, signpost, fingerpost, sign, signboard; milestone, milepost, landmark, beacon, cresset, cairn, flagstaff, hand, pointer; vane, cock, weathercock, weathervane; North Star, polestar, Polaris; seamark, lighthouse, pharos; address, direction, name.
[*of diagrace*] brand, fool's cap, stigma, stripes, broad arrow, mark of Cain.
II. *Verbs.* **indicate,** betoken, connote, signify, denote, imply, manifest, evidence, discover, reveal, display, disclose, evince, present, exhibit, register,

measure, read (*said of a recording instrument*), show, designate, specify, note, underscore, underline; typify, symbolize, prefigure, represent, stand for, mark, stamp, imprint, impress, earmark, sign, seal, nick, blaze; label, ticket.
signal, notify, inform, signalize (*rare*); wave, beckon, nod, wink, glance, leer; nudge, shrug, gesticulate, saw the air, "suit the action to the word" (*Hamlet*).
III. *Adjectives.* indicative, indicatory, significative, significant, significatory, expressive, characteristic, individual, emblematic, symbolic *or* symbolical, typical, representative, suggestive, indicant, connotative, denotative, symptomatic, diagnostic.

See also ARMS, ATTENTION, EVIDENCE, INFORMATION, MANIFESTATION, MEANING, OMEN, PREDICTION, RECORD, [1]SPELL, WARNING.—*Antonyms.* See CONCEALMENT, OBLITERATION.

---

indict, *v.* accuse, arraign, charge. See ACCUSATION.

INDIFFERENCE.—I. *Nouns.* indifference, unconcern, nonchalance, insouciance, supineness, disdain, inattention, phlegmaticness, phlegmatism, indifferency (*rare*), apathy, lukewarmness, insensibility, stoicism, Laodiceanism, adiaphorism, unconcernedness; neutrality, impartiality, disinterestedness, inertia, indetermination; coolness, coldness, frigidity.
mediocrity, passableness, ordinariness, tolerableness, commonplaceness; moderation, average.
unimportance, insignificance, inconsiderableness, inferiority, triviality, paltriness, immaterialness (*as, a matter of* indifference).
II. *Verbs.* be indifferent, stand neuter, take no interest in, have no desire for, have no taste for, not care for, care nothing for (*or* about); not mind, make light of; spurn, disdain.
III. *Adjectives.* indifferent, cold, frigid, lukewarm, cool; neutral, impartial, disinterested; apathetic, uninterested, nonchalant, insouciant, heedless, listless, careless, easy-going, unconcerned, phlegmatic; stoical, impassive, stolid, Laodicean, unimpressible, insensible, impassible; half-hearted, unambitious, undesirous, unsolicitous.
mediocre, passable, neutral, moderate, reasonable, temperate, modest, ordinary average, tolerable, commonplace, fair, medium, middling.
unimportant, insignificant, inconsiderable, immaterial, inconsequential, trifling, paltry, small, slight, petty, inappreciable, inferior.
unattractive, unalluring, unprepossessing, undesired, uncoveted, undesirable, unwished, unvalued.

See also COLD, IMPERFECTION, INATTENTION, INCURIOSITY, INSENSITIVENESS, UNIMPORTANCE.—*Antonyms.* See DESIRE.

---

indigenous, *adj.* native; innate, inherent. See INHABITANT, SUBJECTIVENESS.
indigestible, *adj.* innutritious, undigestible (*rare*). See UNHEALTHINESS.
indignation, *n.* displeasure, anger, vexation, wrath. See RESENTMENT.
indirect, *adj.* circuitous, roundabout, rambling; crooked, covert, underhand. See DEVIATION, LATENCY.
indiscretion, *n.* slip, lapse, blunder, imprudence. See GUILT.

INDISCRIMINATION.—I. *Nouns.* indiscrimination, indistinction, indistinguishability, indistinguishableness, confusion, jumble, promiscuity, promiscuousness, want of discernment; uncertainty, doubt.
II. *Verbs.* confound, confuse, jumble, mix, intermingle, blend; baffle, bewilder.
III. *Adjectives.* indiscriminate, indistinguishable, undistinguished, undistinguishable; mixed, promiscuous, jumbled, higgledy-piggledy, chaotic, heterogeneous, diverse, omnigenous, miscellaneous; undistinguishing, undiscriminating, indiscriminative.

See also DISORDER, MIXTURE, MULTIFORMITY, UNCERTAINTY.—*Antonyms.* See DISCRIMINATION.

indispensable, *adj.* requisite, necessary, vital, essential. See NECESSITY, REQUIREMENT.
indistinct, *adj.* dim, faint, obscure, vague, shadowy, blurred. See DIMNESS, FEEBLENESS, INVISIBILITY.
individual, *adj.* special, particular, specific, proper, personal. See SPECIALTY.
individual, *n.* person, somebody; one, unit, entity. See MANKIND, UNITY.
individuality, *n.* personality, character; peculiarity, originality; oneness. See SPECIALTY, UNCONFORMITY, UNITY.
indivisible, *adj.* inseparable, indissoluble, infrangible. See DENSITY, WHOLE.
indolence, *n.* idleness, sloth, laziness, ease. See INACTIVITY.
indolent, *adj.* lazy, idle, sluggish, slothful. See INACTIVITY.
indomitable, *adj.* unconquerable, invincible, unyielding. See STRENGTH.
indorse, *v.* support, recommend; sign, inscribe. See APPROBATION, COMPACT.
induce, *v.* bring about, effect; influence, impel, urge. See CAUSE, MOTIVE.
inducement, *n.* incentive, enticement, consideration. See MOTIVE.
induction, *n.* installation (*as of a priest*); generalization, conclusion, inference: *in this sense, contrasted with* deduction. See CHURCHDOM, REASONING.
indulge, *v.* revel; humor, favor, gratify, pamper. See INTEMPERANCE, MILDNESS, PLEASURABLENESS.
industrious, *adj.* assiduous, dilligent, busy, hard-working. See ACTIVITY.
industry, *n.* diligence, assiduity, assiduousness; occupation, labor. See ACTIVITY, BUSINESS.
ineffective, *adj.* inefficient, inefficacious, impotent, useless, unavailing. See WEAKNESS.
ineffectual, *adj.* useless, futile, unavailing. See INUTILITY.
inefficient, *adj.* incompetent, incapable; ineffective. See IMPOTENCE, POVERTY.

INELASTICITY.—I. *Nouns.* **inelasticity,** flaccidity, flaccidness, laxity, flabbiness; inductility, irresilience (*rare*), inextensibility.
II. *Adjectives.* **inelastic,** flaccid, flabby, irresilient, inductile, unyielding, inflexible, inextensible.
Antonyms. See ELASTICITY.

INELEGANCE.—I. *Nouns.* **inelegance,** ungracefulness, awkwardness, stiffness, impurity, coarseness, vulgarity; poor (*or* bad) diction, cacology, loose construction, ill-balanced sentences; fustian, bombast; barbarism, slang, solecism; mannerism, affectation; "unlettered Muse" (Gray).
II. *Adjectives.* **inelegant,** graceless, ungraceful, unrefined, unpolished, uncultivated, uncultured, uncourtly, coarse, rough, homespun, uncouth, crude, rude, barbarous, vulgar, common, harsh, abrupt; dry, cramped, awkward, still, constrained, formal, forced, labored, halting; artificial, mannered, affected, ponderous, turgid, tumid, bombastic, inflated, swollen, fustian, euphuistic.
See also NEOLOGY, ORNAMENT, SOLECISM, UGLINESS.—*Antonyms.* See ELEGANCE.

INEQUALITY,—I. *Nouns.* **inequality,** disparity, dissimilarity, dissimilitude, odds, difference, unevenness, disproportion, irregularity, diversity; variableness, inconstancy, changeableness; insufficiency, inferiority, shortcoming, deficiency, inadequacy.
II. *Adjectives.* **unequal,** uneven, disparate, partial, inadequate, deficient, insufficient; overbalanced, unbalanced, top-heavy, lopsided, irregular.
unequaled, unmatched, peerless, inimitable, unique, unsurpassed, incomparable, unapproached, unparalleled, unrivaled, matchless.
See also DIFFERENCE, DISSIMILARITY.

INERTNESS,—I. *Nouns.* **inertness,** inertia, *vis inertiæ* (*L.; physics*), inertion (*rare*), inactivity, torpor, sluggishness, laziness, sloth, indolence, inaction, languor, quiescence, passivity, passiveness, stagnation.
[*mental inertness*] dullness, lifelessness, lethargy, supineness, negligence, apathy, inexcitability, irresolution, indecision, vacillation, obstinacy.
II. *Verbs.* **be inert,** be inactive, etc. (see *adjectives*); **hang fire, smolder.**

III. *Adjectives.* **inert,** inactive, passive, torpid, sluggish, leaden, logy (*U. S.*), dull, heavy, slack, tame, slow, supine, slothful, indolent, lazy, idle, lethargic, comatose, apathetic, languid, listless, sleepy, stagnant, lifeless, dead.
latent, concealed, hidden, dormant, slumbering, smoldering, unexerted.

See also HEAVINESS, INACTIVITY, INEXCITABILITY, INSENSITIVENESS, IRRESOLUTION, [1]REST, VEGETATION.—*Antonyms.* See ENERGY.

---

inevitable, *adj.* sure, unavoidable, assured. See CERTAINTY.
inexact, *adj.* inaccurate, incorrect, erroneous; loose, indefinite. See ERROR, UNINTELLIGIBILITY.

INEXCITABILITY,—I. *Nouns.* **inexcitability,** imperturbability, even temper, tranquil mind, dispassion, inirritability, toleration, tolerance, patience; passiveness, inertia, impassibility, stupefaction.
equanimity, evenness, equability, poise, staidness, gravity, sobriety, composure, placidity, *sang-froid* (*F.*), coolness, calmness, tranquillity, serenity, content; quiet, quietude, peace of mind; philosophy, stoicism, self-possession, self-control, self-command, self-restraint; presence of mind.
resignation, acquiescence, submission, sufferance, endurance, resignedness, compliance, patience of Job, "patience on a monument" (*Twelfth Night*), long-suffering, forbearance, longanimity, fortitude, moderation, restraint.
II. *Verbs.* **bear,** endure, undergo, suffer, bear with, put up with, tolerate, brook, abide, bide (*archaic*), stand, submit to, resign oneself to, acquiesce in, go through, support, brave, disregard; digest, eat, swallow, pocket, stomach; carry on, carry through; make light of, make the best of, make "a virtue of necessity" (Chaucer).
compose, appease, tranquilize, calm, quiet, assuage, propitiate, repress, restrain, master one's feelings, set one's mind at ease (*or* rest), calm down, cool down.
III. *Adjectives.* **inexcitable,** imperturbable, passionless; unsusceptible, dispassionate, cold-blooded, enduring, stoical, Platonic, philosophical, staid, sober, grave; sedate, demure, cool-headed, level, well-balanced, steady, level-headed, composed, collected, temperate, unstirred, unruffled, unperturbed; easy-going, peaceful, placid, calm; quiet, tranquil, serene, cool, undemonstrative.
meek, mild, submissive, humble, unassuming, forbearing, patient, gentle, tolerant, long-suffering, clement; tame, subdued, unoffended, unresisting, spiritless.

See also CONTENT, MODERATION, [1]REST, RESTRAINT, SUBMISSION.—*Antonyms.* See EXCITABILITY.

---

inexcusable, *adj.* unpardonable, unjustifiable. See ACCUSATION.
inexhaustible, *adj.* unfailing, unlimited. See SUFFICIENCY.

INEXPEDIENCE,—I. *Nouns.* **inexpedience,** undesirableness, undesirability, inadvisability, impropriety, unfitness, inutility, disadvantage, inconvenience, discommodity, disadvantageousness.
II. *Verbs.* **be inexpedient,** come amiss, embarrass, put to inconvenience.
III. *Adjectives.* **inexpedient,** undesirable, inadvisable, ill-advised, impolitic, unwise, imprudent, inopportune, disadvantageous, unprofitable, unfit, inappropriate, unsuitable, objectionable, ineligible, inadmissible, inconvenient, discommodious, unsatisfactory, inept, improper, unseemly.
clumsy, awkward, cumbrous, cumbersome, lumbering, lumbersome, ungainly, unwieldy, hulky, unmanageable, unskillful, unhandy, ungraceful.

See also DISAGREEMENT, INUTILITY, UNSKILLFULNESS, UNTIMELINESS.—*Antonyms.* See EXPEDIENCE.

---

inexperienced, *adj.* fresh, raw, unskilled, unversed, untrained. See GREEN, UNSKILLFULNESS.
inexpressible, *adj.* unutterable, unspeakable, indescribable, ineffable. See GREATNESS. UNINTELLIGIBILITY.

INEXTENSION.—*Nouns.* **inextension,** nonextension; point, dot, speck, spot.
See also SMALLNESS.—*Antonyms.* See EXPANSION, SPACE.

infallible, *adj* unfailing, reliable, indubitable, certain, sure. See CERTAINTY.
infamous, *adj* contemptible, shameful, abominable. See IMPROBITY.
infancy, *n.* babyhood, childhood; cradle. See YOUTH.

INFANT.—I. *Nouns.* **infant,** babe, baby, *bambino* (*It.*), nursling, suckling, papoose (*N. Amer. Indian*), weanling.
[*in law*] minor (*male or female*); pupil, ward.
child, little one, *enfant* (*F.*), bairn (*Scot.*), tot, chick, mite, kid (*slang*), butcha *or* bacha (*Hind.*), whelp (*usually contemptuous*), cub (*jocose or contemptuous*), brat (*usually contemptuous*), chit (*colloq.*), pickaninny (*in U. S., colored child; also jocose*), lambkin (*endearing term*), imp (*mischievous child*), urchin; elf, cherub.
youth, boy, lad, laddie (*chiefly Scot.*), stripling, youngster, slip, sprig (*usually contemptuous*), callant (*Scot.*), gossoon (*Anglo-Irish*), whippersnapper (*colloq.*), schoolboy, hobbledehoy (*colloq.*), young hopeful, cadet.
scion, descendant, offspring, sapling, seedling, olive-branch; nestling, chicken, duckling; larva, grub, chrysalis, cocoon, caterpillar; fry, tadpole; calf, maverick (*Western U. S.*); colt (*masc.*), filly (*fem.*), foal; pup, puppy; kitten; lamb, kid, eanling, yeanling, cosset, pet lamb.
girl, lass, lassie (*chiefly Scot.*), wench (*dial.*), damsel, damosel (*archaic*), demoiselle, colleen (*Anglo-Irish*), girleen (*Anglo-Irish*), girlie (*colloq.*), schoolgirl, maid, maiden, virgin, nymph; flapper (*slang*), minx (*chiefly playful*), tomboy, hoyden, romp, baggage (*playful*).
II. *Adjectives.* **infantile,** infantine, childish, childlike, kiddish (*colloq.*), babyish, kittenish, dollish, doll-like; boylike, puerile, boyish; girlish, girl-like; newborn; callow, unfledged, newfledged.

See also YOUTH.—*Antonyms.* See VETERAN.

---

infantry, *n.* foot, rifles, foot soldiers. See COMBATANT.
infantryman, *n.* infantry soldier, foot soldier, rifleman, doughboy (*U. S. slang*). See COMBATANT.
infatuation, *n.* gullibility; folly, passion. See CREDULITY, LOVE.
infection, *n.* contamination, infecting, influence, epidemic. See TRANSFER.
infectious, *adj.* catching, communicable, epidemic, pestilential: *an* infectious *disease is a germ disease which may or may not be contagious.* Cf. CONTAGIOUS. See TAKING, TRANSFER, UNHEALTHINESS.
infer, *v.* deduce, gather, conclude. See JUDGE.
inference, *n.* conclusion, implication. See DEDUCTION.

INFERIORITY.—I. *Nouns.* **inferiority,** deficiency, shortcoming, inadequacy, imperfection; poorness, meanness, baseness, smallness, littleness, shabbiness, indifference.
[*personal inferiority*] subordination, subjection, juniority, subordinacy (*rare*), subservience, submission; commonalty, the people, rank and file, the masses.
II. *Verbs.* **be inferior,** fall short of, come short of, not come up to; become smaller, decrease, hide its diminished head, retire into the shade, take a back seat (*colloq.*), yield the palm, play second fiddle.
III. *Adjectives.* **inferior,** smaller; less, lesser, reduced, deficient, lower, subordinate, minor, junior, secondary, humble; second-rate, one-horse (*U. S. colloq.*), small, petty, two-by-four (*U. S. colloq.*), unimportant, insignificant, paltry, poor, shabby.
IV. *Adverbs.* **inferiorly,** subordinately, under, below; under par, below par; at the bottom of the scale, at a low ebb, at a disadvantage.

See also IMPERFECTION, INEQUALITY, LOWNESS, SMALLNESS, UNIMPORTANCE.—*Antonyms.* See SUPERIORITY.

---

infernal, *adj.* diabolical, hellish, fiendish. See VICE.
infidelity, *n.* faithlessness, treachery; skepticism, unbelief. See IMPROBITY, IRRELIGION.

INFINITY.—I. *Nouns.* **infinity,** infinitude, infiniteness, endlessness, interminateness, immensity, boundlessness, immeasurableness, immeasurability, illimitableness, illimitability, inexhaustibleness, inexhaustibility; perpetuity, immortality.
II. *Verbs.* **be infinite,** have no limits (*or* bounds), go on forever.
III. *Adjectives.* **infinite,** immense, numberless, countless, untold, unnumbered, innumerable, incalculable, illimitable, without limit, limitless, boundless, interminable, interminate, all-embracing, unbounded, unlimited; measureless, immeasurable, unmeasured, unfathomable, perpetual, endless, without end.
See also PERPETUITY, SPACE.—*Antonyms.* See CIRCUMSCRIPTION, LIMIT.

---

infirm, *adj.* feeble, decrepit; unsound, failing. See WEAKNESS.
inflame, *v.* animate, kindle, intensify; irritate, arouse, excite. See ENERGY, VIOLENCE.
inflammable, *adj.* combustible, ignitible. See CALEFACTION.
inflate, *v.* blow up, pump up, distend; raise; puff up. See EXPANSION, INCREASE, VANITY, WIND.
inflated, *adj.* pompous, bombastic, turgid. See OVERESTIMATION.
inflect, *v.* vary, modulate; bend, curve, deflect; decline, conjugate. See CHANGE, CURVATURE, GRAMMAR.
inflexible, *adj.* firm, stiff, rigid; unyielding, grim, stern. See HARDNESS, RESOLUTION.
inflict, *v.* impose, wreak, put upon. See SEVERITY.
infliction, *n.* calamity, affliction, adversity, curse, disgrace. See SCOURGE.

INFLUENCE.—I. *Nouns.* **influence,** power, influentiality, ascendancy, capability, potency, pull (*colloq.*), drag (*slang*), favor, weight, bias, importance, pressure, interest, credit, hold, domination, sway, control, authority, dominance, mastery, supremacy, predominance, prevalence, upper hand, reign, rule; spell, magic, magnetism.
footing, foothold, standing, foundation, stable position; support, purchase, vantage ground, advantage, play, leverage; *locus standi* (*L.*), *pou sto* (*Gr.* ποῦ στῶ), bases for operations.
protection, patronage, championship, favor, aid, support, encouragement, guidance, auspices; tower of strength, patron, benefactor.
II. *Verbs.* **influence,** affect, persuade, move, induce, incline, bias, actuate, work upon, magnetize; guide, direct, regulate, lead; determine, impel, modify.
be influential, be potent, etc. (see *adjectives*); carry weight, make one's influence felt; weigh, tell, count; take root, take hold.
pervade, impregnate, permeate, penetrate, infiltrate, fill, run through, be rife, rage, prevail, spread like wildfire.
control, rule, govern, sway, wield, dominate, subject, manage, master, predominate, override, overpower, overbear, have (*or* gain) the upper hand, get control of, take the lead, pull the strings; turn the scale; set the fashion, lead the dance.
III. *Adjectives.* **influential,** potent, effective, important, weighty, powerful, strong, authoritative, substantial, recognized, predominant, dominant, controlling; prevalent, rife, rampant.
See also AUTHORITY, IMPORTANCE, INSTRUMENTALITY, MOTIVE, POWER.—*Antonyms.* See IMPOTENCE, INERTNESS.

---

infold, *v.* inclose, incase, envelop, surround. See CIRCUMSCRIPTION.
informal, *adj.* unconventional, unceremonious. See UNCONFORMITY.

INFORMATION.—I. *Nouns.* **information,** enlightenment, acquaintance, intelligence, knowledge; mention, telling, narration, recital, account, description, specification, particularization, itemization, estimate, instruction; communicativeness, intercommunication; publicity, spotlight (*colloq.*), limelight (*colloq.*), notoriety.
hint, suggestion, insinuation, innuendo, inkling, whisper, cue; byplay, gesture; word to the wise, *verbum sapienti* (*L.*), tip (*colloq.*), pointer (*U. S. colloq.*); **subaudition, subauditur, reading between the lines.**

communication, notice, message, intimation, monition, representation, proclamation, annunciation, announcement, *communiqué* (*F.*), letter, telegram, cable, wire (*colloq.*), wireless (*colloq.*); news, tidings, report, advice, statement, return, record.
informant, authority, teller, harbinger, messenger, herald, reporter, newsmonger, exponent, mouthpiece, spokesman, interpreter; tipper, tipster (*colloq.*).
informer (*usually one who informs against another*), complainant, accuser, spy, eavesdropper, *mouchard* (*F.*), spotter (*slang*), detective, dick (*slang*), tec (*slang*), shadow, sleuth (*colloq.*), busy (*Eng. thieves' slang*), under-cover man (*police cant*); nark (*cant*), stool pigeon, stoolie (*slang*), squealer, squeaker (*slang*), peacher (*slang*); whistle guy (*U. S. slang*).
guide, cicerone, pilot, conductor, steerer; guidebook, handbook, manual, vade mecum, map, plan, chart, gazetteer; itinerary.
II. *Verbs.* **inform,** tell, acquaint, impart, apprise, tip (*slang*), advise, notify instruct, enlighten, teach; state, declare, assert, affirm, mention, express, intimate, represent, communicate; signify, specify, retail, describe, explain confide to, give inside information, give the low-down (*slang*).
announce, report, bring (send, *or* leave) word, annunciate, enunciate, proclaim, make known, promulgate, publish, disseminate; broadcast, put (*or* go) on the air (*radio cant*); telegraph, cable, wireless, wire (*colloq.*), telephone, phone (*colloq.*).
hint, insinuate, allude to, glance at, indicate, suggest, intimate, breathe, whisper, imply, let fall, tip *or* tip off (*colloq.*), give a pointer to (*colloq.*), tip the wink (*slang*), prompt, give the cue.
undeceive, set right, correct, disabuse, open the eyes of.
III. *Adjectives.* **informative,** instructive, informing, teaching, informatory, informational, educational, instructional, didactic *or* didactical, preceptive, pedagogic *or* pedagogical, intelligential; advisory, monitory, admonitory, monitorial.
explicit, express, plain-spoken, plain, unequivocal, unambiguous, open, aboveboard, clear, definite, emphatic, specific.
declaratory, expository, exegetical, declarative, predicative, expressive, affirmative, enunciative, communicative, communicatory.

See also ACCUSATION, ADVICE, AFFIRMATION, INDICATION, KNOWLEDGE, NEWS, PUBLICATION, TEACHING.—*Antonyms.* See CONCEALMENT.

INFREQUENCY.—I. *Nouns.* **infrequency,** infrequence, rareness, uncommonness, seldomness, rarity, sparseness, fewness.
II. *Adjectives.* **infrequent,** uncommon, rare, unique, unusual, few, scant, scarce, sporadic, occasional; unprecedented, unheard of.
III. *Adverbs.* **infrequently,** seldom, rarely, scarcely, hardly; not often, unoften, uncommonly, scarcely ever, hardly ever; sparsely, occasionally, sporadically; once in a blue moon (*colloq.*).

Antonyms. See FREQUENCY.

---

infringe, *v.* violate, transgress; intrude, trespass. See NONOBSERVANCE, RIGHTLESSNESS.
infringement, *n.* infraction; transgression, encroachment; literary theft. See NONOBSERVANCE.
infuse, *v.* instill, implant, infix, introduce; tinge, imbue; pour into, mingle. See INSERTION, MIXTURE.
ingenious, *adj.* resourceful, inventive, clever, adroit. See SKILL.
ingenuous, *adj.* frank, open, naïve, candid. See ARTLESSNESS.
inglorious, *adj.* humble, obscure; disgraceful, shameful. See DISREPUTE.
ingratiating, *adj.* winning, tactful, charming, attractive. See COURTESY.

INGRATITUDE.—I. *Nouns.* **ingratitude,** ungratefulness, thanklessness, unthankfulness; "benefits forgot" (*As You Like It*); thankless task, thankless office.
II. *Verbs.* **be ungrateful,** be unthankful, etc. (see *adjectives*); forget benefits, feel no obligation; bite the hand that fed one.

III. *Adjectives.* **ingrate,** ungrateful, unthankful, thankless, ingrateful (*rare*), inappreciative, unmindful.
unacknowledged, unavowed, unthanked, unrequited, unreturned, unrewarded; ill-requited, ill-rewarded, forgotten, unremembered.
Antonyms. See GRATITUDE.

---

ingredient, *n.* constituent, element, part. See COMPONENT.

INGRESS.—I. *Nouns.* **ingress,** entrance, introgression, entrée, incoming, *début* (*F.*), entry, influx, intrusion, inroad, incursion, invasion, irruption; penetration, interpenetration, infiltration; insinuation, insertion.
import (*used esp. in pl.*), importation, imported commodity: *opposite of* export.
immigration, incoming population, foreign influx: *opposite of* emigration.
immigrant, incomer, newcomer, colonist: *opposite of* emigrant.
inlet, entrance, orifice; bay, recess, nook; bight, gulf, arm, fiord, firth, bayou (*Southern U. S.*); opening, mouth, door, path, way.
II. *Verbs.* **enter,** come in, go in (*or* into), pass into, pour in, flow in; set foot on; burst (*or* break) in upon, intrude, butt (*or* horn) in (*slang*), trespass, invade; penetrate, interpenetrate, filter into, infiltrate.
III. *Adjectives.* **ingressive,** entering, inceptive (*gram*); incoming, entrant (*rare*), ingoing, inbound, inward.
See also INSERTION, OPENING, RECEPTION, WAY.—*Antonyms.* See EGRESS.

INHABITANT.—I. *Nouns.* **inhabitant,** resident, dweller, residentiary; inmate, inhabiter, occupier, occupant, householder, indweller, addressee, tenant, incumbent; settler, squatter, backwoodsman, planter, habitant (*Canada and Louisiana*), colonist; islander; denizen, citizen; burgher, townsman, burgess; villager, cottager, cotter; boarder, lodger, roomer (*U. S.*).
native, aborigine (*pl.* aborigines), aboriginal, autochthon (*pl.* autochthones); indigene.
population, inhabitants, people, folk, nation, state, race, community; colony, settlement.
II. *Verbs.* **inhabit,** live in, dwell in, occupy; sojourn, abide, stay, reside, domicile, live, take up one's abode, lodge, room (*U. S.*), tenant, roost (*colloq.*), bunk (*colloq.*); populate, people.
III. *Adjectives.* **inhabitable,** habitable, tenantable, occupiable, residential; livable *or* liveable, endurable.
inhabited, occupied, tenanted, peopled; populous.
indigenous, native, original, aboriginal, autochthonous, autochthonal, endemic, domestic, home-bred, domiciled; naturalized; vernacular.
See also HABITATION, MANKIND, PEOPLE.

---

inhale, *v.* breathe (in), inbreathe, inspire (*lit.*): *opposite of* exhale. See WIND.
inherent, *adj.* intrinsic, innate, inseparable, essential. See COMPONENT.
inherit, *v.* acquire, receive, obtain, possess, succeed. See TRANSFER.
inheritance, *n.* legacy, heritage, patrimony. See PROPERTY.
inhibit, *v.* suppress, repress, prohibit, check. See RESTRAINT.
inhuman, *adj.* savage, barbarous, cruel, brutal. See MALEVOLENCE.
iniquity, *n.* wrongdoing, sin, crime, wickedness, unrighteousness. See VICE.
initial, *adj.* first, introductory, commencing, primary. See BEGINNING.
initiate, *v.* start, institute, inaugurate; admit, introduce, take in; instruct, ground. See BEGINNING, RECEPTION, TEACHING.
inject, *v.* introduce, insert, interject, throw in, force in, lug in. See INSERTION, INTERJACENCE.
injunction, *n.* order, direction, admonition, requirement. See COMMAND.
injure, *v.* damage, mar, impair; wound; wrong, dishonor; maltreat, hurt, harm. See DETERIORATION, EVIL, MALEVOLENCE.
injurious, *adj.* harmful, detrimental, disadvantageous, destructive. See EVIL.
injury, *n.* outrage, abuse; damage, impairment; wound, hurt. See BADNESS, DETERIORATION, EVIL.

injustice, *n.* unfairness, inequity, partiality, injury, foul play. See WRONG.
inkling, *n.* hint, suggestion, suspicion. See INFORMATION.
inland, *adj.* internal, upcountry; domestic, home. See INTERIORITY.
inlet, *n.* entrance; bay, arm, waterway, channel. See INGRESS.
inn, *n.* hotel, tavern. See HABITATION.
innate, *adj.* inherent, inborn, inbred, natural. See COMPONENT.
inner, *adj.* inside, internal, inward. See INTERIORITY.
inner man, stomach (*as in "refresh the inner man": jocose*); soul, spirit. See FOOD, IMMATERIALITY.
innkeeper, *n.* innholder, landlord, mine host. See PROVISION.

INNOCENCE.—I. *Nouns.* **innocence,** blamelessness, harmlessness, innocuousness, artlessness, guilelessness, ingenuousness, *naïveté* (*F.*), simplicity; purity, chastity, sinlessness, guiltlessness, incorruption, impeccability; clean hands, clear conscience.
innocent, new-born babe, young child, lamb, dove; simple person, simpleton, idiot.
II. *Adjectives.* **innocent,** not guilty, unguilty, guiltless, faultless, stainless, spotless, clear, immaculate, unsullied, upright, untainted, sinless, pure, blameless, inculpable, unoffending, unerring, undefiled, above suspicion, irreproachable, unimpeachable, virtuous, chaste; guileless, *naïve* (*F.*), ingenuous, artless, simple, "more sinned against than sinning" (*Lear*).
harmless, inoffensive, innoxious, innocuous, hurtless, safe (*as, an* innocent *remedy*).
lawful, legitimate, legal, rightful permitted, unprohibited, right, warrantable, not contraband (*as,* innocent *trade*).
devoid, destitute, wanting, lacking, void, unprovided (*as,* innocent *of clothes: colloq. or jocose in this sense*).
III. *Adverbs.* **innocently,** unguiltily, etc. (see *adjectives*); with clean hands, with a clear (*or* safe) conscience.
See also ARTLESSNESS, PROBITY, PURITY, VIRTUE.—*Antonyms.* See GUILT.

---

innocuous, *adj.* harmless, innocent, inoffensive. See HEALTHINESS.
innovation, *n.* alteration, variation, diversion, novelty, novation (*rare*). See CHANGE, NEWNESS.
innumerable, *adj.* numberless, countless, myriad. See INFINITY.
innutritious, *adj.* unnourishing, innutritive, indigestible. See LOWNESS, UNHEALTHINESS.

INODOROUSNESS.—I. *Nouns.* **inodorousness,** absence (*or* want) of smell. deodorization, disinfection, purification, fumigation; deodorizer, deodorant, disinfectant.
II. *Adjectives.* **inodorous,** scentless, odorless, without smell (*or* odor); deodorized.
Antonyms. See ODOR.

---

inoffensive, *adj.* blameless, unoffending; harmless, innocuous. See INNOCENCE.
inopportune, *adj.* inconvenient, unseasonable. See UNTIMELINESS.

INORGANIZATION.—I. *Nouns.* **inorganization,** inanimation (*rare*); lapidification, fossilization, lithification; mineral kingdom, mineral world; unorganized (*or* inorganic) matter, inanimate matter.
science of the mineral kingdom: mineralogy, geology, geognosy, geoscopy, lithology, petrology, metallurgy.
II. *Verbs.* **petrify,** calcify, lapidify, lithify; mineralize.
pulverize, turn to dust, comminute, triturate, levigate, powder, pound, grind, crumble.
III. *Adjectives.* **inorganic,** unorganized, disorganic (*rare*), lithoid *or* lithoidal, mineral, azoic (*geol.*), inanimate.
[*in philology*] extraneous, unessential, abnormal, irregular (*as, the* s *in* demesne).
Antonyms. See ORGANIZATION.

INQUIRY.—I. *Nouns.* **inquiry,** investigation, research, scrutiny, search, quest, pursuit, prosecution, inquest, inquisition, percontation (*rare*), exploration; trial, test, assay, examination, review, inspection, analysis, titration (*chem.*), titrimetry (*chem.*), docimasy, dissection, anatomy, induction, study, sifting; ventilation, calculation, consideration; exploitation, survey, reconnaissance, reconnoissance (*tech.*), reconnoitering, espionage; lantern of Diogenes.
interrogation, questioning, examination, quiz (*U. S.*), third degree (*colloq.*), catechism, Socratic method, cross-examination, cross-interrogation (*law*), challenge, interpellation (*parliamentary*); discussion, debate.
question, query, interrogatory (*law*), problem, poser, desideratum, point (*or* matter) in dispute, moot point, issue, question at issue, subject, topic; bone of contention, enigma, mystery, knotty point, debatable point, *quodlibet* (*L.*); puzzle, riddle, conundrum, cross-word puzzle; demand, request.
inquirer, investigator, inquisitor, inspector, querist, questioner, questionist. examiner, catechist; scrutator, scrutinizer; analyst.
II. *Verbs.* **inquire,** seek, search, make inquiry, look for, scan, reconnoiter, explore, sound, rummage, rake, scour, ransack, pry, peer, spy, look round; overhaul, survey, look behind the scenes; nose, nose out, hunt out, fish out, ferret out, unearth, track, seek a clew (*or* clue), hunt, trail, shadow, mouse, dodge, trace, pursue, experiment; leave no stone unturned.
examine, study, consider, calculate; dip (*or* dive) into, probe, sound, fathom, analyze, separate, discriminate, reduce, resolve, titrate (*chem.*), test, make an analysis; anatomize, dissect, parse, sift, winnow, thresh out; investigate, look into, scrutinize, look over, overlook, inspect, discuss, canvass, subject to examination, quiz; audit, tax, pass in review, put to the proof.
question, ask, demand; interrogate, interpellate (*as a cabinet minister*), catechize, pump; cross-question, cross-interrogate (*law*), cross-examine; put through the third degree (*colloq.*), grill (*colloq.*), roast (*colloq.*), badger, heckle (*as a parliamentary candidate*); challenge, doubt, controvert, dispute, charge, accuse.
III. *Adjectives.* **inquiring,** inquisitive, inquisitorial, analytic, investigative, zetetic, interrogative, questioning, curious, prying, percontatorial (*rare*).
questionable, doubtful, uncertain, undecided, problematical, dubious, moot, debatable, disputable, controversial, arguable, controvertible, suspicious, tentative, undetermined; proposed, under consideration, in question, in dispute, in issue.
See also CURIOSITY, EXPERIMENT, PURSUIT, REQUEST, UNBELIEF, UNCERTAINTY.—*Antonyms.* See ANSWER.

---

inquistive, *adj.* inquiring; meddlesome, prying. See CURIOSITY.

INSANITY.—I. *Nouns.* **insanity,** lunacy, madness, mania, dementia, idiocy; derangement, fugue (*psychol.*), dissociated mental activity, mental alienation, unsoundness of mind, mental derangement, frenzy, raving, delirium, lightheadedness, aberration, wandering, delusion, hallucination, obsession; monomania, craze, fanaticism, infatuation, eccentricity, strangeness, oddity, twist.
dizziness, giddiness, vertigo (*med.*), swimming, sunstroke, siriasis (*med.*).
delirium tremens, D. T.'s œnomania (*med.*), the horrors (*colloq.*), *mania a potu* (*L.*), blue devils (*colloq.*), blue-devilism, jimjams (*slang*), blue Johnnies (*Australian*), pink spiders (*slang*), snakes in the boots (*slang*), gallon distemper (*slang*).
II. *Verbs.* **be** (*or* **become**) **insane,** lose one's senses (*or* reason), go mad, rave, dote, ramble, wander, drivel, go off one's head (*colloq.*).
[*to drive insane*] **insanify** (*rare*), derange, madden, dement, craze, unhinge, unbalance, shatter, loco (*U. S. colloq.*), infatuate, obsess, befool; turn the brain, send one out of one's head (*colloq.*).
III. *Adjectives.* **insane,** mad, lunatic, crazy, crazed, disordered, crack-brained, cracked (*colloq.*), touched; bereft of reason, unhinged, insensate, beside oneself, demented, maniacal, daft, frenzied, maddened, deranged, moonstruck, stark mad, *non compos mentis* (*L.*); fanatical, infatuated, rabid, mad as a hatter, mad as a March hare.
giddy, dizzy, vertiginous, wild, flighty, distracted, distraught, bewildered.

delirious, light-headed, incoherent, rambling, wandering, frantic, frenzied, raving, off one's head.
eccentric, odd, peculiar, idiosyncratic, funny (*colloq.*), bizarre, strange, unusual, singular, cranky, queer, nutty (*slang*).
See also DERANGEMENT, IMBECILITY.—*Antonyms.* See SANITY.

---

insatiable, *adj.* voracious, unappeasable, unquenchable. See DESIRE.
inscribe, *v.* enroll, register; mark, engrave. See LIST, WRITING.
insect, *n.* bug, fly. See ANIMAL, LITTLENESS.
insecurity, *n.* risk, peril, jeopardy. See DANGER.

INSENSIBILITY.—I. *Nouns.* **insensibility,** unfeelingness, insentience, insensibleness, induration, insensitiveness, numbness, obtuseness, dullness, torpor, sluggishness, inactivity, torpidity, stolidity, stupidity, apathy, indifference, incuriosity, lethargy, lifelessness, unconsciousness, stupor, coma, sleep, hypnosis, anæsthesia, paralysis; anæsthetization, anociassociation (*med.*).
[*anæsthetic agent*] **anæsthetic,** opium, ether, chloroform, chloral, morphine, morphia; nitrous oxide, laughing gas; cocaine, novocaine; knock-out drops (*U. S. slang*).
II. *Verbs.* **render insensible,** blunt, dull, deaden, obtund, numb, benumb, stupefy, stun; anæsthetize, put to sleep, hypnotize, paralyze.
glut, clog, surfeit, sate, satiate, overcloy, overgorge.
III. *Adjectives.* **insensible,** unfeeling, senseless, callous, thick-skinned, pachydermatous, hard, hardened, casehardened, proof, obtuse, dull, apathetic, lethargic, indifferent, insentient, unconscious; paralytic, palsied, numb, inanimate, dead.
See also INACTIVITY, INSENSITIVENESS.—*Antonyms.* See SENSIBILITY, SENSITIVENESS.

INSENSITIVENESS.—I. *Nouns.* **insensitiveness,** insensibility, insensibleness, inertness, inertia, imperturbation, impassibility, impassivity, unimpressionableness, apathy, dullness, insusceptibility; lukewarmness, indifference, insouciance, nonchalance, unconcern, stoicism, coldness, frigidity, callousness, callosity, hardness; obtundity, hebetude, dullness.
torpor, torpidity, lethargy, coma, catalepsy, trance, suspended animation; sleep, stupor, stupefaction, daze; paralysis, numbness.
II. *Verbs.* **be insensitive,** not mind, not care, not be affected by; take no interest in; disregard, set at naught, make light of.
render insensitive, numb, benumb, obtund, blunt, hebetate, paralyze, deaden, stun, stupefy.
harden, steel, caseharden, sear, toughen, inure, indurate; brutalize.
III. *Adjectives.* **insensitive,** insensible, unconscious, impassive, insusceptible, unimpressionable, unimpressible; passionless, spiritless, heartless, soulless, unfeeling, stony, obdurate.
apathetic, phlegmatic, dull, frigid, cold, cold-blooded, cold-hearted; inert, supine, sluggish, torpid, sleepy, languid, languorous, unemotional, inexcitable, lackadaisical, listless, half-hearted; numb, numbed; comatose, stupefied.
indifferent, lukewarm, careless, mindless, inattentive, unconcerned, incurious, insouciant, heedless, nonchalant.
unaffected, unruffled, unimpressed, unexcited, unmoved, unstirred, untouched, unshocked, unanimated, unblushing.
callous, thick-skinned, pachydermatous, impervious, hard, hardened, indurated, inured, casehardened; imperturbable, unfelt.
IV. *Adverbs.* **insensitively,** insensibly, etc. (see *adjectives*); *æquo animo* (*L.*); in cold blood; with dry eyes; with withers unwrung.
See also INACTIVITY, INDIFFERENCE, INEXCITABILITY, INSENSIBILITY.—*Antonyms.* See SENSITIVENESS.

INSERTION.—I. *Nouns.* **insertion,** implantation, introduction, ingress; interpolation, intercalation, embolism, epenthesis (*phonetics*), interlineation, insinuation, injection, inoculation, infusion; immersion, submersion, submergence, dip, plunge.
[*thing inserted*] **insert,** inset, inlay, panel, addition.

II. *Verbs.* **insert,** introduce, put in (*or* into), inject, imbed, inlay, inweave, parenthesize, interject, interpolate, inset, intercalate, interline, interlineate, interpage, infuse, instill, infix, inoculate, impregnate, imbue.
graft, ingraft, bud, plant, implant, inarch (*tech.*).
obtrude, thrust in, stick in, ram in, stuff in, tuck in, press in, drive in, pierce; intrude, intervene.
immerse, merge, immerge, plunge, dip, duck, baptize; bathe, imbathe, steep, soak; sink, bury, inter.
See also ADDITION, INGRESS, INTERJACENCE, INTERMENT, OPENING (*perforate*), RECORD.—*Antonyms.* See EXTRACTION.

---

in short, in brief, briefly. See COMPENDIUM.
insight, *n.* preception, penetration, discernment. See INTUITION, KNOWLEDGE.
insignia, *n.* badges, emblems, signs, marks. See INDICATION, ORDER, SCEPTER.
insignificance, *n.* unimportance, worthlessness, triviality. See CHEAPNESS.
insignificant, *adj.* petty, unimportant, trivial, small; pitiable, sorry. See FRACTION, POVERTY.
insincere, *adj.* hypocritical, deceitful, two-faced. See FALSEHOOD.
insinuate, *v.* ingratiate, curry favor with; hint, intimate; insert, introduce. See FLATTERY, INFORMATION, INTERJACENCE.

INSIPIDITY.—I. *Nouns.* **insipidity,** tastelessness, unsavoriness, etc. (see *adjectives*).
II. *Adjectives.* **insipid,** tasteless, unsavory, unflavored, savorless, weak, stale, *fade* (*F.*), flat, wishy-washy (*colloq.*), milk-and-water, watery.
vapid, dull, uninteresting, jejune, barren, sterile, meager, lean, thin; pointless, monotonous, lifeless, dead, spiritless, unanimated, heavy, prosy, prosaic.
Antonyms. See SAVORINESS, TASTE.

---

insist, *v.* maintain, hold; require, demand. See AFFIRMATION, COMPULSION.
insnare, *v.* entrap, decoy, allure, catch. See DECEPTION.

INSOLENCE.—I. *Nouns.* **insolence,** haughtiness, arrogance, airs, overbearance, toploftiness (*colloq.*), domineering, bluster, swagger, contempt, intrusiveness, bumptiousness, assumption, presumption; disdain, insult, abuse, oppression.
impertinence, sauciness, malapertness, cheek (*colloq. or slang*), rudeness, pertness, unmannerliness, incivility, sauce (*colloq.*), lip (*slang*), flippancy.
impudence, self-assertion, assurance, audacity, nerve (*slang*), freshness, brazenness, front, face, effrontery, boldness, hardihood, gall (*slang*), shamelessness.
II. *Verbs.* **be insolent,** give oneself airs, arrogate, assume, presume; make bold make free, take a liberty; lay down the law, look big, stare out of countenance, outface, outlook, outstare, outbrazen, brazen out.
domineer, bully, dictate, hector; lord it over, snub, browbeat, intimidate, bluster, swagger, bulldoze (*colloq.*), terrorize, dragoon.
III. *Adjectives.* **insolent,** haughty, arrogant, imperious, magisterial, high and mighty, toplofty (*colloq.*), overbearing, dictatorial, arbitrary, high-handed, supercilious, intolerant, overweening, bumptious, domineering, blustering, swaggering, hectoring, rollicking, roistering, devil-may-care; oppressive, abusive, insulting; "full of sound and fury" (*Macbeth*).
impertinent, rude, saucy, pert, flippant, fresh (*U. S. slang*), unmannerly, intrusive, meddlesome.
impudent, rude, disrespectful, self-assertive, cheeky (*colloq.*), audacious, presumptuous, assuming; shameless, brazen, brazen-faced, bold, forward, immodest, unblushing, unabashed, barefaced, brazen-faced, lost to shame.
IV. *Adverbs.* **insolently,** haughtily, etc. (see *adjectives*); *de haut en bas* (*F.*), with a high hand, *ex cathedra* (*L.*).
See also DEFIANCE, DISRESPECT, VANITY.—*Antonyms.* See COURTESY, SERVILITY.

---

insolvency, *n.* bankruptcy, failure. See NONPAYMENT.
insolvent, *n.* defaulter, bankrupt. See NONPAYMENT.
insomnia, *n.* sleeplessness, wakefulness. See ACTIVITY.

inspect, *v.* review, oversee; examine, investigate. See ATTENTION, VISION.
inspiration, *n.* creative impulse; stimulation; revelation, truth; inhalation. See IMAGINATION, MOTIVE, SCRIPTURES, WIND.
inspire, *v.* animate, infuse, enliven, stimulate. See EXCITEMENT.
instability, *n.* changeability, fickleness, unsteadiness, unstableness. See CHANGEABLENESS, FLUIDITY.
install, *v.* invest, induct; set, place. See CELEBRATION, LOCATION.
installment, *n.* part payment, portion. See PART.
instance, *n.* illustration, example. See CONFORMITY.
instant, *adj.* immediate, instantaneous, direct, sudden. See INSTANTANEITY.
instant, *n.* moment, minute, jiffy (*colloq.*). See INSTANTANEITY.

INSTANTANEITY.—I. *Nouns.* **instantaneity,** instantaneousness; suddenness, abruptness, promptness, immediateness.
moment, instant, second, split second, twinkling, flash, trice, jiffy (*colloq.*), breath.
II. *Adjectives.* **instantaneous,** momentary, sudden, abrupt, prompt, immediate, instant, hasty, quick as thought (*or* lightning).
III. *Adverbs.* **instantaneously,** instanter, instantly, presto, in no time, forthright (*archaic*), at once, eftsoon *or* eftsoons (*archaic*), in a trice, in a jiffy (*colloq.*), suddenly, in the twinkling of an eye, promptly, immediately, now, in the same breath; extempore, on the spur of the moment, without hesitation, plump.
See also EARLINESS, HASTE.—*Antonyms.* See LATENESS, NEGLECT, PERPETUITY.

---

instead, *adv.* in lieu (*of*), in place (*of*). See COMMISSION, SUBSTITUTE.
instigate, *v.* stimulate, urge, provoke, incite. See MOTIVE.
instill, *v.* infuse, impart, implant. See INSERTION.
instinct, *n.* prompting, impulse. See NECESSITY.
instinctive, *adj.* intuitive, innate, natural. See INTUITION, SUBJECTIVENESS.
institute, *v.* start, originate, found, inaugurate, organize. See BEGINNING.
instruct, *v.* direct, order; notify, tell; educate, teach. See COMMAND, INFORMATION, TEACHING.
instruction, *n.* charge, injunction, precept; tuition, education. See ADVICE, TEACHING.
instructor, *n.* tutor, master. See TEACHER.
instructorship, *n.* mastership, preceptorship, tutorship, professorship. See TEACHER.

INSTRUMENT.—I. *Nouns.* **instrument,** means, agent, medium, channel, machinery, wherewithal *or* (*less commonly*) wherewith, material supplies, *matériel* (*F.: distinguished from* personnel).
device, contrivance, apparatus, appliance, convenience, mechanism; tool, implement, utensil, machine, motor, engine; lathe, gin; automaton, mechanical man, robot.
gear, equipment, plant, *matériel* (*F.*), outfit, appliances, contrivances, tools, tackle, rigging, harness, trappings, fittings, accouterments, appointments, furniture, upholstery; chattels, paraphernalia, belongings.
[*mechanical powers*] (1) **lever,** crow, crowbar, jimmy *or* jemmy (*usually in sections for the burglar's convenience*), pry, prize (*dial.*), jack, pawl, tumbler, trigger; treadle, pedal; arm, limb, wing, oar, sweep, paddle, helm, tiller, swingle, cant hook, handspike, marlinespike *or* marlinspike (*naut.*).
(2) **wheel and axle** (*continuous lever*), wheelwork, clockwork, wheels within wheels, pinion, crank, winch, cam, capstan, wheel, drum, flywheel, cogwheel, gear; sprocket wheel, chain wheel.
(3) **pulley,** tackle, purchase, Weston's pulley block, crane, derrick; belt, crossed belt, endless belt.
(4) **inclined plane,** sloping plane, slope.
(5) **wedge** (*double inclined plane*), chock, shim, quoin, **keystone, voussoir** (*arch.*), cleat, block, glut, cotter, key (*esp. in U. S.*), embolus.

(6) **screw** (*inclined plane around a cylinder*), external (*or* male) screw, internal (*or* female) screw, Archimedean screw, differential (*or* Hunter's) screw, endless (*or* perpetual) screw, worm, screw propeller; jackscrew, screw jack.
handle, hilt, haft, shaft, shank, helve (*as of an ax*), bail (*as of a kettle*), grasp (*esp. of an oar*), grip, tiller, snath *or* snead (*of a scythe*), rounce (*printing*), crank, stale (*as of a rake dial. Eng.*), ear, lug, crop, knob, knocker.
[*legal document*] **document,** writing, record, paper; deed, contract, bond, note, bill, mortgage, grant.
II. *Adjectives.* **instrumental,** helpful, contributory, contributive, conducive, serviceable, subservient, ministrant; intermediate, intermediary, mediatorial.
labor-saving, useful, mechanical, machinelike, machinal (*rare*), ingenious, efficient, automatic; power-driven, motor-driven, electric.

See also MEANS, MUSICAL INSTRUMENTS, SECURITY.

---

instrumentalist, *n.* instrumental performer; organist, pianist, violinist, etc.: *distinguished from* vocalist. See MUSICIAN.

INSTRUMENTALITY.—I. *Nouns.* **instrumentality,** means, agency, working, operation, action, mediation, intervention, help, aid, assistance, contribution, subservience, procurement, influence, pull (*slang*).
medium, vehicle, tool, instrument; interagent, intermediary, friend at court, go-between, minister, handmaid, servant.
II. *Verbs.* **be instrumental,** subserve, aid, assist, promote, further, minister to, serve; mediate, intervene, come (*or* go) between, interpose, use one's influence.
III. *Adverbs.* **somehow,** someway, by some means, somehow or other; by hook or by crook.
IV. *Prepositions.* **through,** by, for, *per* (*L.*), by means of, by (*or* through) the agency of, by dint of, by (*or* in) virtue of; by reason of, in consequence of, by way of.

See also AGENCY, MEANS, UTILITY, VEHICLE.

---

insufferable, *adj.* unbearable, intolerable. See PAINFULNESS.

INSUFFICIENCY.—I. *Nouns.* **insufficiency,** inadequacy, inadequateness, incompetence, deficiency, shortage, scarcity, imperfection, shortcoming; paucity, stint, scantiness, meagerness, bare subsistence.
want, need, lack, poverty, exigency, necessity, starvation, famine, drought, dearth.
dole, mite, pittance; trifle, modicum; short allowance (*or* commons); half rations.
depletion, exhaustion, reduction, emptiness, evacuation, vacancy; ebb tide; low water.
II. *Verbs.* **be insufficient,** want, lack, need, require; be in want, live from hand to mouth.
render insufficient, impoverish, beggar, stint, drain, ruin, pauperize, exhaust, drain of resources.
III. *Adjectives.* **insufficient,** inadequate, scanty, unequal, incommensurate, scant, scarce, infrequent, rare, deficient, wanting, lacking, incomplete, imperfect; ill-furnished, ill-provided, ill-stored; short of, out of, destitute of, devoid of, bereft of, denuded of, slack, at a low ebb; empty, vacant, bare; dry, drained.
incapable, incompetent, unfit, inefficient, unable, disqualified; perfunctory, careless, superficial.
unprovided, unsupplied, unreplenished, unprepared, unfurnished; unfed; empty-handed.
meager, thin, spare, thin, slim, poor, slight, slender, bare, barren, scurvy, stingy, stinted; starved, emaciated, under-nourished, underfed, half-starved, famine-stricken, famished; at the end of one's tether; without resources, in want.
IV. *Adverbs.* **insufficiently,** inadequately, etc. (see *adjectives*); in default of, for want of; failing.

See also INCOMPLETENESS, IMPERFECTION, POVERTY, SHORTCOMING.—*Antonyms.* See SUFFICIENCY.

insular, *adj.* insulated, isolated; narrow, illiberal. See ISLAND, NARROWNESS.
insulate, *v.* isolate, detach. See DISJUNCTION.
insult, *v.* affront, offend. See DISCOURTESY.
insurance, *n.* assurance, guarantee. See PROMISE.
insure, *v.* guarantee, warrant, secure; underwrite. See CERTAINTY, SECURITY.
insurgent, *n.* rebel, traitor. See DISOBEDIENCE.
insurrection, *n.* rebellion, revolt, uprising. See RESISTANCE.
intact, *adj.* uninjured, entire, untouched. See COMPLETENESS.
intangible, *adj.* impalpable, vague, dim. See IMMATERIALITY.
integrity, *n.* uprightness, honesty; entirety, wholeness, completeness. See PROBITY, WHOLE.
integument, *n.* skin, coat, hide. See COVERING.

INTELLECT.—I. *Nouns.* **intellect,** mind, brains, understanding, comprehension, insight, intuition, perception, cognition, reason; rationality, intellectual faculties (*or* powers), intellectuality, intellectualism; senses, consciousness, observation, percipience, mentality, intelligence; association of ideas, conception, wisdom, judgment, parts, capacity, genius; wit; nous (*colloq., except in philosophical sense*), talent, ability; ideality, idealism, imagination.

ego, the I, soul, spirit; heart, breast, bosom; inner man, heart's core, *penetralia mentis* (*L.*); subconscious self, subliminal consciousness.

[*seat of thought*] **brain,** headpiece, head, skull, cranium (*L. pl.*, crania), sensorium (*tech.*), noddle (*colloq.*), brain box, brain pan, gray matter (*colloq.*); cerebrum (*anat.*), cerebellum (*anat.*), the little brain; hind-brain, epencephalon (*anat.*).

science of mind: psychology, psychoanalysis, psychiatry; mental philosophy; metaphysics, ontology, epistemology, speculative philosophy, philosophy.

II. *Verbs.* **intelligize** (*rare*), think, understand, reason, intellectualize, ratiocinate, reflect, cogitate, mediate, ruminate, contemplate, judge, conceive; philosophize, syllogize.

note, notice, perceive, realize, observe, regard, heed, see, mind, mark; take notice of; be aware of.

III. *Adjectives.* **intellectual,** mental, gifted, brainy (*colloq.*), talented, clever, scholarly, learned, well-informed, bright, quick, smart, quick-witted, keen, intelligent, imaginative, inventive, rational, spiritual; percipient, conscious.

See also IMAGINATION, INTELLIGENCE, SKILL, THOUGHT, WISDOM.—*Antonyms.* See IMBECILITY, VACUITY.

INTELLIGENCE.—I. *Nouns.* **intelligence,** capacity, comprehension, apperception (*psychol.*), understanding, intellect, brains, parts, sagacity, mother wit, wit, *esprit* (*F.*), nous (*colloq.*), mentality, hard-headedness, gumption (*colloq.*), acuteness, acumen, keenness, smartness, longheadedness, subtlety, cunning, penetration, perspicacity, discernment, good judgment, discrimination, refinement.

notification, notice, advice, instruction, report, information, news, tip (*colloq.*), low-down (*slang*), dope (*sporting slang*).

II. *Verbs.* **be intelligent,** understand, comprehend, see at a glance, discern, discriminate, penetrate, see through, seize, apprehend, twig (*slang*), follow; have one's wits about one, scintillate, be brilliant, coruscate.

III. *Adjectives.* **intelligent,** sensible, understanding, intellectual; clever, able, quick of apprehension, keen, acute, alive, awake, bright, quick, sharp, quick-witted, knowing, wide-awake, shrewd, hard-headed, smart, long-headed, astute; clear-headed, long-sighted, calculating, thoughtful, farsighted, discerning, perspicacious, penetrating, penetrative, piercing, sharp as a needle, brainy (*colloq.*): *opposite of* unintelligent.

See also DISCRIMINATION, INTELLECT, NEWS, SENSIBILITY, TASTE, WISDOM.—*Antonyms.* See IMBECILITY.

INTELLIGIBILITY.—I. *Nouns.* **intelligibility,** clearness, clarity, explicitness, lucidity, perspicuity, precision, plain speaking, plainness, simplicity, comprehensibility.

II. *Verbs.* **render intelligible,** simplify, elucidate, clarify, explain, interpret; popularize.

understand, comprehend, perceive, sense (*colloq.*), get, take in, catch, grasp, seize, fathom, follow; master.
III. *Adjectives.* **intelligible,** clear, lucid, perspicuous, transparent, comprehensible.
plain, distinct, explicit, palpable, obvious, manifest, legible, evident, positive, clear-cut, to the point, definite, precise; unequivocal, unmistakable.
graphic, vivid, telling, expressive, descriptive, delineatory, picturesque, pictorial.
See also INTERPRETATION, MANIFESTATION, PERSPICUITY, SIMPLENESS, SIMPLICITY.—*Antonyms.* See OBSCURITY, UNINTELLIGIBILITY.

INTEMPERANCE,—I. *Nouns.* **intemperance,** excess, immoderation, excessiveness, extravagance, unrestraint, overabundance.
self-indulgence, self-gratification, free-living, dissipation, high living, indulgence, prodigalism, pleasure, luxury, luxuriousness, dissoluteness, fastness, drunkenness, inebriety; license, tragalism, sensuality, animalism, voluptuousness, debauchery, crapulence; epicurism, epicureanism, sybaritism.
revel, revels, revelry, orgy, spree, debauch, jollification (*colloq.*), hot time (*slang*), racket, carousal, drinking bout, saturnalia.
II. *Verbs.* **be intemperate,** indulge, exceed; live high (*or* on the fat of the land), dine not wisely but too well; revel, carouse, run riot, live hard, sow one's wild oats, plunge into dissipation, paint the town red (*colloq.*), hit the booze (*slang*).
III. *Adjectives.* **intemperate,** excessive, immoderate, unbridled, unrestrained, uncurbed, inordinate, extravagant, ungovernable; extreme, severe, inclement.
self-indulgent, self-gratifying, wild, fast, dissolute, dissipated, crapulous, lax, profligate; indulged, pampered, luxurious, Sybaritic *or* Sybaritical, Epicurean; nursed in the lap of luxury.
sensual, voluptuous, carnal, fleshly, gross, gluttonous; bestial, brutish, hoggish, piggish, porcine, swinish, animal; lewd, lascivious, lecherous, licentious, lustful, concupiscent, libidinous, goatish, salacious, wanton, Cyprian, Paphian.
drunken, inebrious, sottish, bibacious, crapulent; boozy *or* bousy (*colloq.*), dipsomaniacal, winebibbing.
See also DRUNKENNESS.—*Antonyms.* See TEMPERANCE.

---

intend, *v.* purpose, design, plan, mean. See INTENTION.
intense, *adj.* intensified, rich (*in color*), dark; extreme, profound; violent, acute, keen, concentrated, ardent. See DEPTH, HEIGHT, STRENGTH.
intensify, *v.* heighten, strengthen, sharpen, aggravate. See HEIGHT, INCREASE.
intensity, *n.* strength, power, force, vigor. See DEGREE, ENERGY.

INTENTION,—I. *Nouns.* **intention,** intent, purpose, design, plan, intentionality, determination, decision, resolve, resolution, fixed purpose, proposal, view, contemplation, ambition, project, undertaking; final cause, *raison d'être* (*F.*).
object, aim, end; drift, tendency, inclination, set, bent; destination, objective, "the be-all and the end-all" (*Macbeth*), mark, point, goal, target, butt, bull's-eye; prey, quarry, game.
significance, meaning, import, upshot, purport, implication, connotation, force, signification, denotation.
II. *Verbs.* **intend,** purpose, design, mean, have in view, desire, bid for, labor for, aspire to, aim at, pursue; contemplate, meditate, think of, dream of, talk of; premeditate, destine, propose, project, plan, calculate (*U. S. colloq.*).
III. *Adjectives.* **intentional,** designed, intended, purposed, purposive, deliberate, voluntary, willing, contemplated, free, spontaneous, disposed, inclined advised, express, determinate.
IV. *Adverbs.* **intentionally,** designedly, etc. (see *adjectives*); advisedly, wittingly, knowingly, purposely, on purpose, by design, studiously, pointedly; deliberately, in cold blood.
See also MEANING, PREDETERMINATION, TENDENCY, UNDERTAKING.—*Antonyms.* See CHANCE.

---

inter, *v.* bury, entomb. See INTERMENT.
intercede, *v.* intervene, arbitrate, interpose. See MEDIATION.
intercept, *v.* interrupt, cut off, stop; catch, seize. See HINDRANCE, TAKING.

INTERCHANGE,—I. *Nouns.* **interchange,** exchange; *quid pro quo* (*L.*), commutation, permutation, transmutation, intermutation, transposition, transposal, shuffling, shuffle; swap (*colloq.*), barter, intercourse, commerce; tit for tat, substitution, interchangeableness, interchangeability, commutability; retaliation, reprisal; retort, requital, cross fire.

reciprocation, alternation, reciprocalness, correlation, correspondence, equivalence, mutuality, reciprocity, give-and-take.

II. *Verbs.* **interchange,** exchange, bandy, transpose, counterchange, change, substitute, convert; barter, trade, dicker (*U. S. colloq.*), swap (*colloq.*), give and take, commute, retaliate, retort; requite, return.

reciprocate, alternate, vary, shuttle, gig, seesaw, give in return; correspond, correlate.

III. *Adjectives.* **interchangeable,** exchangeable, fungible (*tech.*), commutable, changeable, transmutable, returnable, substitutive, synonymous.

[*mutually interchangeable*] **reciprocal,** mutual, give-and-take, correlative, correspondent, equivalent, complementary, interchanging.

IV. *Adverbs.* **interchangeably,** by turns, turn about *or* turn and turn about, alternately, in succession; in exchange, *vice versa* (*L.*), conversely.

See also BARTER, CORRELATION, PASSAGE, RETALIATION, SUBSTITUTION.

---

intercourse, *n.* communion, converse; association, fellowship, dealings. See CONVERSATION, SOCIALITY.

interest, *n.* sum, payment; benefit, advantage, profit; concern, regard; weight, power; possession, holding, share; claim, title, due. See DEBT, GOOD, IMPORTANCE, INFLUENCE, PROPERTY, RIGHT.

interest, *v.* affect, touch; animate, arouse. See EXCITEMENT.

interested, *adj.* attentive, engrossed; partial, prejudiced; self-interested. See ATTENTION, MISJUDGMENT, SELFISHNESS.

interesting, *adj.* exciting, alluring, fascinating, pleasurable. See EXCITEMENT, LOVE, PLEASURABLENESS.

interfere, *v.* clash, oppose; interpose, meddle. See HINDRANCE, INTERJACENCE.

interference, *n.* interposition; disapproval, meddlesomeness, opposition. See HINDRANCE.

INTERIORITY,—I. *Nouns.* **interiority,** inwardness, interiorness, innerness, internality, internalness, internalization.

interior, inside, center *or* centre, interspace; womb, belly, heart, bosom, breast; bowels, entrails, intestines, guts (*esp. of animals vulgar as applied to man*), viscera (*tech.*), inner parts; recess (*esp. in pl.*), innermost recesses, penetralia; substance, marrow, pith, spirit, soul, innermost, interne (*poetic*).

inland (*often* inlands), hinterland, midland (*usually in pl.*), in-country (*Scot.*), upcountry (*colloq.*), backwoods, the sticks (*slang*).

II. *Verbs.* **intern,** confine, keep (*or* place) within, internalize; circumscribe, inclose *or* enclose, shut in, envelop, encompass; embed, insert.

III. *Adjectives.* **interior,** internal, intern (*archaic*), inner, inside, inward, inmost, innermost, intimate; innate, inborn, inbred, intrinsic, inherent, deep-seated, ingrained, implanted, inwrought, inwoven, infixed, indwelling, immanent.

inland, upcountry, midland, internal; domestic (*not foreign*), home, native, home-bred, intraterritorial.

visceral, splanchnic (*tech.*), intestinal, duodenal, rectal, abdominal, ventral, cœliac *or* celiac, stomachic.

IV. *Adverbs.* **interiorly,** internally, inwardly, inly, *ab intra* (*L.*), inwards; indoors, within; ben (*Scot.*), in, inside, at home, in the bosom of one's family.

V. *Prepositions.* **within,** inside of, in, inclosed by; not beyond, not exceeding; in the reach of, in the limits of.

See also CIRCUMSCRIPTION, INSERTION, INTERJACENCE, SUBJECTIVENESS.—*Antonyms.* See EXTERIORITY.

INTERJACENCE,—I. *Nouns.* **interjacence** *or* interjacency, interposition, interlocation, intervention, interference, intrusion, obtrusion, intercurrence, intermediation, interpenetration; interjection, interpolation, parenthesis, interlineation, interspersion, intercalation, insertion, insinuation.

partition, septum (*tech.*), dissepiment, diaphragm, midriff, mediastinum (*anat.*); panel, bulkhead, wall, party wall.
intermediary, go-between, interagent, intermedium, intervener, middleman, medium.
interloper, intruder, obtruder, interferer, intermeddler, interrupter, trespasser, buttinsky (*slang*), meddler.
II. *Verbs.* [*lie between*] **intervene,** interpose; permeate, interpenetrate, pervade, interfuse.
[*put between*] **interject,** interpose, introduce, import, insert, intercalate, implant, insinuate, inject, interpolate, interjaculate, throw in, force in, [illegible] in, parenthesize, interlard, intersperse, infiltrate, ingrain, infuse; dovetail, mortise, splice.
interfere, intrude, obtrude, intermeddle, intervene; butt in (*slang*), horn in (*slang*), thrust in; clash, conflict, collide, encounter.
III. *Adjectives.* **interjacent,** intervening, intervenient, interplane (*as, the* interplane *struts of an airplane*), interjectional, parenthetical, episodic; medial, mesial (*zoöl.*), intermediate, mean, mesne (*law*), middle, intermediary, intercalary, intrusive; embosomed, merged.
IV. *Adverbs.* **between,** at intervals, in the midst, betwixt and between (*colloq.*), in the thick of, betwixt, midway, halfway, atween (*archaic*).
See also COUNTERACTION, HINDRANCE, INSERTION.—*Antonyms.* See ENVIRONMENT.

---

interlace, *v.* intertwine, interweave. See JUNCTION.
interloper, *n.* meddler, intruder, interferer. See INTERJACENCE.
interlude, *n.* interval, pause, intermission. See TIME.
intermediary, *n.* go-between, mediator. See INTERJACENCE.
intermediate, *adj.* middle, intervening. See MEAN.

INTERMENT,—I. *Nouns.* **interment,** burial, sepulture, inhumation, entombment: *opposite of* disinterment.
obsequies, funeral rites, funeral, obit, exequies; knell, passing bell, death bell, tolling; wake, dirge, coronach (*Scot. and Irish*), requiem, elegy, epicedium, dead march, muffled drum.
bier, litter, hearse, catafalque.
cremation, burning, incineration, incremation (*rare*); pyre, funeral pile.
undertaker, funeral director, mortician.
mourner, weeper, lamenter, keener (*Ireland*); mute; pallbearer, bearer.
graveclothes, shroud, winding sheet, cerecloth, cerements.
coffin, casket (*U. S.*), box, kist (*Scot.*); shell, sarcophagus; urn, cinerary urn, mortuary urn.
grave, burial place, pit, sepulcher *or* sepulchre, tomb, "the lone couch of his everlasting sleep" (Shelley), last home, long home, vault, mausoleum, crypt, catacomb (*usually in pl.*); cairn, cromlech, barrow, tumulus, mastaba (*Egypt*), tope *or* stupa (*Buddhist*); dokhma, Tower of Silence (*Parsi*); crematorium, crematory, burning ghat *or* ghaut (*Hindu*).
graveyard, burial ground, burying ground, bone yard (*U. S. slang*), cemetery necropolis, polyandrion (*classical*); churchyard, God's acre; potter's field, golgotha; ossuary, charnel house; deadhouse, morgue, mortuary.
gravestone, headstone, tombstone, monument, stone, shaft, cross, footstone, marker; epitaph, inscription.
autopsy, necropsy (*med.*), necroscopy (*med.*), post-mortem examination, postmortem.
disinterment, exhumation, disentombment.
II. *Verbs.* **inter,** bury, entomb, inhume, inhumate (*rare*), sepulcher *or* sepulchre, ensepulcher (*rare*), inearth, grave (*archaic*), tomb, sepulture (*rare*); inurn, urn (*rare*); consign to the grave (*or* tomb), lay in the grave.
cremate, incinerate, incremate, burn.
disinter, exhume, disinhume (*rare*), disentomb, unbury, unearth; disclose, uncover.
III. *Adjectives.* **mortuary,** funeral, funebrial (*rare*), sepulchral, funereal, burial, funerary, exequial, cinerary, feral; elegiac, epicedial.
IV. *Adverbs.* **in memoriam** (*L.*), *hic jacet* (*L.*), *ci-gît* (*F.*), *post obitum* (*L.*) *post mortem* (*L.*), beneath the sod, at rest; R. I. P. (*L.; requiescat in pace*).
See also CORPSE, DEATH.

intermittent, *adj.* recurring, recurrent (*as a fewer*), periodic. See REGULARITY.
intern, *v.* confine, shut in. See INTERIORITY.
internal, *adj.* inland, inside, inner; innate, inherent. See INTERIORITY.
interpolate, *v.* insert, introduce; falsify, mix. See ADDITION, INTERJACENCE, MIXTURE.
interpose, *v.* interrupt, interfere, intervene; mediate. See HINDRANCE, INTERJACENCE, MEDIATION.

INTERPRETATION,—I. *Nouns.* **interpretation,** explanation, elucidation, explication, exposition, *éclaircissement* (*F.*), definition, meaning, diagnosis; solution, answer, key, clew *or* clue, *mot de l'énigme* (*F.*).
translation, rendering, rendition, reddition, construction, version, reading; rewording, paraphrase, sense, free translation; metaphrase, interlineary translation, gloss, verbal (literal, *or* word-for-word) translation, Bohn, key, *clavis* (*L.*).
crib, pony, horse, cab (*Eng.*), trot: *all school cant.*
commentary, note, gloss, comment, annotation, scholium (*L. pl.* scholia), exegesis, explanation (*esp. critical*), exposition, exemplification, illustration, reflection, deduction, inference, animadversion.
equivalent, equivalent meaning, analogue, synonym (*opposite of* antonym), pœcilonym (*rare*), polyonym (*rare*); apposition, convertible terms.
II. *Verbs.* **interpret,** explain, define, construe, literalize, translate, render; spell out, decode, read, decipher, make out, unravel, disentangle, solve; read between the lines, clear up, account for, elucidate, throw (*or* shed) light upon; unfold, expound, comment upon, commentate (*rare*), annotate, gloss, margin, exemplify; illustrate; simplify, popularize.
paraphrase, reword, rephrase, restate, repeat, state differently, rehash, express broadly; synonymize, express by a synonym.
III. *Adjectives.* **interpretative,** explanatory, expository, exegetical, explicative, explicatory, definitional, definitive, elucidative, illustrative, exemplificative, annotative, inferential, scholiastic, hermeneutic *or* hermeneutical; interpretational, constructive.
equivalent, consignificant, convertible, synonymous, synonymic *or* synonymical, pœcilonymic (*rare*), polyonymic (*rare*); paraphrastic, illiteral (*rare*); metaphrastic, literal, word-for-word.
IV. *Adverbs.* **in explanation,** that is to say, *id est* (*L.*), to wit, namely, *videlicet* (*L.*), in other words.
literally, precisely, actually, strictly speaking; in plain terms (words, *or* English); *literatim* (*L.*), verbatim, *verbatim et literatim* (*L.*).
See also ANSWER, DISSERTATION, MEANING, WORD.—*Antonyms.* See MISINTERPRETATION.

INTERPRETER.—*Nouns.* **interpreter,** expositor, expounder, explainer, exponent, demonstrator; translator, annotator, commentator, scholiast; oneirocritic (*dreams*), oracle.
spokesman, speaker, mouthpiece, spokeswoman (*fem.*), prolocutor (*esp. chairman of the lower house of convocation in Church of England*), chairman, foreman (*of a jury*), orator, oratress (*fem.*); representative, delegate, ambassador, plenipotentiary; advocate, pleader, mediator, intercessor.
guide, conductor, leader, director, pilot, mercury, dragoman, *valet de place* (*F.*), courier, cicerone, showman, barker (*colloq.*), steerer, runner (*U. S. cant*).
See also ORACLE.

---

interrogation, *n.* question, examination. See INQUIRY.
interrupt, *v.* suspend, stop, cut short; obstruct, check. See CESSATION, HINDRANCE.
intersect, *v.* cross, cut, pierce, decussate (*tech.*). See CROSSING.
interspace, *n.* space, gap, interstice, crevice. See INTERVAL.

INTERVAL.—I. *Nouns.* [*intervening time*] **interval,** space, period, spell, term, season, pause, interlude, interim, meantime, interregnum, recess, interruption, intermedium (*obsolescent in this sense*), parenthesis.

[*intervening space*] **interspace,** space, interstice, gap, break, hiatus, lacuna (*L. pl.* lacunæ), cæsura, separation, division; void, vacancy, vacuum, incompleteness, deficiency; *hiatus valde deflendus* (*L.*).
cleft, crevice, crack, fissure, chimney (*mountaineering*), slit, chink, cranny, opening, hole, puncture, rift, flaw, fault, fracture, rent, gash, cut, breach.
gorge, defile, pass, ravine, canon, crevasse, abyss, abysm, chasm, *couloir* (*F.*), gulf, notch (*U. S.*), gap, gully, gulch (*U. S.*), nullah (*India*), *barranco* (*Sp.*), clough, cleuch *or* cleugh (*Scot.*).
[*in music*] difference of pitch, step, tone; whole step, major second; half step, minor second, semitone; complement, diastem (*ancient music*), schisma, diaschisma; comma, comma syntonum, comma ditonicum, Pythagorean comma; ditone, diesis, enharmonic diesis, quarter tone; discord, dissonance; prime (*or* unison), second, third, fourth, fifth (*or* quint), sixth, seventh, octave.
II. *Verbs.* **interval,** space, dispart, separate, set at intervals.
gape, yawn, open, crack, dehisce, hiate (*rare*), spread, cleave.
III. *Adjectives.* **intervallic** (*rare*), with an interval, spaced, gaping, chinky, breachy, dehiscent, rimose *or* rimous, rimulose (*bot. and zoöl.*); fissury, fissural, cloven.

See also ABSENCE, DEGREE, DISCONTINUITY, DISJUNCTION, INTERJACENCE, MUSIC, OPENING, SPACE, TIME.—*Antonyms.* See CONTACT.

---

intervene, *v.* interrupt, break in; occur, happen; come between, interfere; elapse (*as time*); interpose, arbitrate, intercede. See DISCONTINUITY, EVENT, INTERJACENCE, LAPSE, MEDIATION.
interview, *n.* conference, meeting, consultation. See CONVERSATION.
intestinal, *adj.* visceral, rectal, duodenal. See INTERIORITY.
intimate, *adj.* familiar, thick (*colloq.*), close, near; singular, exceptional. See FRIEND, NEARNESS, THICKNESS, SPECIALTY.
intimidate, *v.* bully, terrify, frighten, overawe, cow. See FEAR.
intolerable, *adj.* unbearable, insufferable. See PAINFULNESS.
intolerance, *n.* bigotry, dogmatism. See OBSTINACY.
intoxicate, *v.* inebriate. See DRUNKENNESS.
intoxicated, *adj.* inebriated, drunk, tipsy. See DRUNKENNESS.
intractable, *adj.* perverse, obstinate, refractory, unmanageable. See UNCONFORMITY.
intricate, *adj.* involved, complicated, complex. See DISORDER.
intrigue, *n.* amour, love affair, liaison; scheme, plot, conspiracy. See ENDEARMENT, PLAN.
intriguer, *n.* busybody, meddler; schemer, plotter. See ACTIVITY, CUNNING.
intrinsic, *adj.* inherent, innate, inborn, essential. See SUBJECTIVENESS.
introduce, *v.* start, institute; insert, place in; usher in, present. See BEGINNING, INTERJACENCE, PRECEDENCE.
introduction, *n.* presentation; preface, foreword; insertion, admittance. See COURTESY, PRECURSOR, RECEPTION.
introductory, *adj.* prefatory, preliminary, opening. See BEGINNING.
intrude, *v.* infringe, trespass, obtrude. See OVERRUNNING.
intrust, *v.* confide, consign; charge, invest. See COMMISSION.

INTUITION.—I. *Nouns.* **intuition,** immediate apprehension, immediate knowledge (*or* cognition), spiritual insight, perception, direct (*or* sense) perception. *Anschauung* (*philos.*); innate knowledge, insight, instinctive knowledge, intuitiveness, penetration, perceptivity, perceptiveness, discernment, sagacity, perspicacity, divination, presentiment, clairvoyance, inspiration.
II. *Verbs.* **judge intuitively,** judge by intuition; hazard a proposition; talk at random.
III. *Adjectives.* **intuitive,** instinctive, impulsive, intuitional, inspirational, perceptive, involuntary, automatic, natural, inherent, innate.
IV. *Adverbs.* **intuitively,** instinctively, etc. (see *adjectives*); by intuition.

See also KNOWLEDGE.—*Antonyms.* See REASONING.

inure, *v.* accustom, familiarize, habituate, harden. See HABIT, HARDNESS.

INUTILITY.—I. *Nouns.* **inutility,** uselessness, unprofitableness, worthlessness, inefficacy, futility; ineptitude, inadequacy, unfitness; inefficiency, incompetence, unskillfulness, labor in vain; triviality, frivolity, nugacity.

refuse, rubbish, junk, lumber, litter, odds and ends, shoddy; rags, leavings, orts (*archaic*), scum, dregs, garbage, dross, trash, sweepings, offscourings, waste, rubble, *débris* (*F.*); chaff, stubble, weeds, tares.

II. *Verbs.* **be useless,** labor in vain, go a-begging, fail, seek (*or* strive) after impossibilities; use vain efforts, beat the air, pour water into a sieve, bay the moon, cast pearls before swine, carry coals to Newcastle, kick against the pricks.

render useless, dismantle, dismast, disqualify; disable, cripple, lame, hamstring, hock *or* hough, spike guns, clip the wings; put out of gear, put out of kilter (*colloq.*).

III. *Adjectives.* **inutile,** useless, futile, unavailing, bootless, inoperative, inefficacious, inadequate, inept, inefficient, ineffectual, incompetent, "weary, stale, flat, and unprofitable" (*Hamlet*), unserviceable, unprofitable, unproductive, ill-spent, profitless, gainless, fruitless; superfluous, unneeded, unnecessary, uncalled for.

worthless, meritless, valueless, unsalable, not worth a straw, good-for-nothing (*or* naught), losel (*archaic*), trashy, dear at any price; vain, idle, empty, inane, effete, barren, sterile, impotent, worn out, obsolete; not worth powder and shot.

See also DISUSE, IMPOTENCE, INSUFFICIENCY, REDUNDANCE, UNIMPORTANCE, UNPRODUCTIVENESS.—*Antonyms.* See UTILITY.

---

invade, *v.* harry, assail; encroach, trespass. See ATTACK, INGRESS.

invalid, *adj.* unsound, null, void, inoperative, nugatory. See IMPOTENCE.

invalidate, *v.* nullify, cancel. See ANNULMENT.

invaluable, *adj.* priceless, precious. See GOOD, USE.

invariable, *adj.* regular, constant, unchangeable. See UNIFORMITY.

inveigle, *v.* allure, insnare, decoy, entangle. See DECEPTION.

invent, *v.* create, originate, contrive, devise. See IMAGINATION.

INVERSION.—I. *Nouns.* **inversion,** subversion, reversion, contraposition, eversion, ectropion (*as of the eyelids*), reversal, transposition, transposal; intussusception (*med.*), invagination (*tech.*); opposition, polarity; contrariety, contradiction; upset, capsizal, capsize, somersault, somerset, *culbute* (*F.*), overturn, revulsion, revolution; turn of the tide.

[*in rhetoric*] anastrophe, hyperbaton, hysteron proteron, hypallage, palindrome, metathesis (*gram.*).

II. *Verbs.* **invert,** reverse, inverse (*rare*), subvert, turn, upset, overturn, capsize, upturn, topple, overbalance, evert (*archaic*); turn upside down, turn topsy-turvy, *culbuter* (*F.*), turn the tables, overthrow, *bouleverser* (*F.*); put the cart before the horse; introvert, invaginate, intussuscept, transpose.

be inverted, turn (go, *or* wheel) about; turn (tilt, *or* topple) over, turn turtle, capsize, overturn.

III. *Adjectives.* **inverted,** reversed, etc. (see *verbs*); wrong side out (*or* up); inside out; upside down, bottom upward, on one's head, topsy-turvy, *sens dessus dessous* (*F.*).

inverse, reverse, opposite, converse, antipodal; inverted, reversed, transposed, hyperbatic, palindromic *or* palindromical (*rhet.*).

IV. *Adverbs.* **inversely,** conversely, by inversion; heels over head, head over heels.

See also CHANGE, CONTRARIETY, OPPOSITE, REVERSION.—*Antonyms.* See PERMANENCE.

---

invest, *v.* install, induct; array, dress; besiege, surround; put at interest; endow, confer. See CELEBRATION, CLOTHING, ENVIRONMENT, LENDING, PLACE, POWER.

investigate, *v.* look into, examine, probe. See INQUIRY.

invigorate, *v.* stimulate, refresh, enliven, animate, energize. See STRENGTH.
invincible, *adj.* unyielding, uncompromising; unconquerable, irresistible, indomitable. See RESISTANCE, STRENGTH.

INVISIBILITY.—I. *Nouns.* **invisibility,** imperceptibility, indistinctness, indefiniteness, obscurity; concealment, latency, seclusion, retirement, delitescence, delitescency; mystery, mystification; smoke screen.
II. *Verbs.* **be invisible** (*or* imperceptible); be hidden, hide, lurk, couch, escape notice (*or* observation).
render invisible, veil, shroud, screen, cloud, blind, enshroud, mask, ensconce, conceal; put out of sight.
III. *Adjectives.* **invisible,** imperceptible, undiscernible, indistinguishable, unnoticeable; unseen, viewless (*rare*), unapparent, inconspicuous, covert, latent, hidden, concealed, masked, enshrouded, cloaked, screened, shrouded, veiled, suppressed; out of sight, not in sight.
indistinct, dim; dark, obscure, darksome, shadowy, indefinite, undefined, ill-defined, blurred, out of focus, misty, hazy, feeble, faint, nebulous, confused, uncertain, vague, mysterious.
See also BLINDNESS, CONCEALMENT, DIMNESS, LATENCY.—*Antonyms.* See VISIBILITY.

---

invite, *v.* tempt, lure, attract; ask, bid, summon. See MOTIVE, REQUEST.
invoice, *n.* itemized list; manifest, bill of lading. See LIST.
invoke, *v.* entreat, beseech, implore; conjure, evoke; pray, supplicate. See REQUEST, WORSHIP.
involuntary, *adj.* instinctive, reflex, automatic. See NECESSITY.
involve, *v.* implicate, entangle; imply, mean. See COMPOSITION, LATENCY.
involved, *adj.* intricate, mazy, complicated. See CONVOLUTION.
inward, *adj.* internal, inner, inside. See INTERIORITY.
iota, *n.* jot, bit, particle, white, speck, mite. See SMALLNESS.

IRASCIBILITY.—I. *Nouns.* **irascibility,** irritability, bad temper, temper, anger, irritation, crossness, irascibleness, grouchiness (*slang*), huffishness, petulance, tartness, acerbity, acrimony, asperity, churlishness, pugnacity, excitability; a word and a blow.
shrew, vixen, virago, dragon, scold, spitfire, termagant, fury; Xanthippe *or* Xantippe.
fire eater (*colloq.*), hotspur, Squire Western (*Tom Jones*), tartar, brabbler (*archaic*), pepperpot (*colloq.*), duelist.
II. *Verbs.* **be irascible,** have a temper, be possessed of the devil, have the temper of a fiend, fire up, flare up, storm, rage, scold, go on (*colloq.*), fume, fly off the handle (*slang*).
III. *Adjectives.* **irascible,** bad-tempered, irritable, excitable, thin-skinned, peppery, waspish, fiery, passionate, choleric, "sudden and quick in quarrel" (*As You Like It*), splenetic, nettlesome (*rare*), quick-tempered, hot-tempered, spleeny, hasty, quick, warm, hot, petulant, fretful, querulous, captious, moody, cross, fractious, peevish, snappish, impatient, captious, moodish, sensitive, touchy, testy, pettish, huffy, huffish, cross-grained, cross, shrewish, ill-natured, ill-humored, churlish, grouchy (*slang*).
quarrelsome, contentious, cantankerous (*colloq.*), wrangling, dissentious, disputatious, ugly (*U. S. colloq.*), pugnacious, hostile, belligerent, factious.
See also CONTENTION, DISCORD, EXCITABILITY, RESENTMENT, SNAP, SULLENNESS.—*Antonyms.* See CHEERFULNESS, CONCORD, INEXCITABILITY.

---

iridescent, *adj.* prismatic, opalescent. See CHANGEABLENESS, VARIEGATION.
irksome, *adj.* fatiguing, tiresome, tedious, wearisome. See DIFFICULTY.
irony, *n.* sarcasm, satire. See RIDICULE.
irrational, *adj.* illogical, unreasonable, untenable, absurd. See ABSURDITY, SOPHISTRY.

IRREGULARITY.—I. *Nouns.* **irregularity,** uncertainty, unpunctuality, capriciousness, etc. (see *adjectives*); aberration, abnormality, abnormity, singularity, anomaly.
laxity, intemperance, immorality, looseness, disorderliness, lawlessness.
II. *Adjectives.* **irregular,** uncertain, unpunctual, capricious, fitful, flickering, rambling, spasmodic, variable, unsettled, mutable, changeable, erratic, uneven, unequal, immethodical, unmethodical, unsystematic, confused, disordered, disarranged, unsymmetrical, asymmetric *or* asymmetrical, unnatural, abnormal, anomalous, aberrant (*esp. biol.*), unconformable, exceptional, uncanonical, illegitimate, heteromorphic (*tech.*), unusual, singular, odd; crooked, devious.
disorderly, unruly, wild, lawless, turbulent, intemperate, vicious, immoral, dissolute, inordinate, excessive.
[*of surfaces*] **uneven,** rough, unequal, unlevel, humpy, jagged, hummocky, bunchy, hilly, rugged, lumpy, broken; holey, pitted.
III. *Adverbs.* **irregularly,** uncertainly, etc. (see *adjectives*); by fits and starts, by fits, intermittently.

See also DISCONTINUITY, DISORDER, DISTORTION, DIVERSITY, MULTIFORMITY, ROUGHNESS, UNCONFORMITY.—*Antonyms.* See REGULARITY.

IRRELATION.—I. *Nouns.* **irrelation,** unrelatedness, dissociation, disconnection, disjunction; inconsequence, disagreement, heterogeneity, unconformity, inapplicability, impropriety, impertinency, irrelevancy.
II. *Verbs.* **be irrelative,** have no relation to, have no bearing upon, have nothing to do with; drag in by the head and shoulders, travel out of the record, wander from the subject.
III. *Adjectives.* **irrelative,** unrelated, unallied, independent, exclusive, separate, disconnected, unconnected, irrespective; incommeasurable, unconformable, divergent, heterogeneous; strange, alien, foreign, outlandish, exotic, extraneous, isolated, insular; remote, far-fetched, detached, apart, forced, out-of-the-way, segregate, secluded, separate, abstracted, neither here nor there; *à propos de bottes* (*F.*).
irrelevant, inapplicable, impertinent (*in the sense of* not pertinent), inconsequent, unrelated, inappropriate, unessential, inapposite, beside the mark (*or* point).
incidental, casual, chance, contingent, accidental, fortuitous, subordinate, parenthetical, episodic, collateral, secondary, accessory; *obiter dictum* (*L.*).
IV. *Adverbs.* **irrelatively,** disconnectedly, inappositely, incidentally, parenthetically, by the way, by the by, *en passant* (*F.*).

See also DISAGREEMENT, DISJUNCTION, UNCONFORMITY, UNIMPORTANCE.—*Antonyms.* See RELATION.

---

irrelevant, *adj.* inapplicable, inappropriate, unrelated, inconsistent. See IRRELATION, SOPHISTRY.

IRRELIGION.—I. *Nouns.* **irreligion,** impiety, irreligionism, ungodliness, irreverence, godlessness, wickedness; laxity, apathy, indifference.
skepticism *or* scepticism, doubt, unbelief, disbelief, incredulity, agnosticism, freethinking; materialism, hylotheism, rationalism, positivism, Comtism, Pyrrhonism, Humism; atheism, infidelity, antichristianity, antichristianism.
irreligionist, skeptic, unbeliever, heretic, *giaour* (*Turkish*), zendik (*Arabic*), infidel, atheist, miscreant (*archaic*), heathen, alien, gentile, Nazarene; freethinker, rationalist, materialist, positivist, Comtist, agnostic, Pyrrhonist, nullifidian, *esprit fort* (*F.*), nihilist.
II. *Verbs.* **be irreligious,** doubt, disbelieve, skepticize, *or* scepticize, question, lack faith, deny the truth.
III. *Adjectives.* **irreligious,** undevout, godless, graceless, ungodly, irreverent, profane, impious, blasphemous; unholy, unsanctified, unhallowed.
skeptical *or* sceptical, freethinking, agnostic *or* agnostical, incredulous, Pyrrhonean, Pyrrhonic, positivistic, materialistic *or* materialistical, unbelieving, unconverted, faithless, atheistic, nullifidian, unchristian, antichristian.
worldly, mundane, earthly, carnal, worldly-minded, unspiritual, unregenerate.

See also IMPIETY, INCREDULITY, UNBELIEF.—*Antonyms.* See ORTHODOXY, PIETY, THEOLOGY, WORSHIP.

irresistible, *adj.* overwhelming, overpowering, puissant. See STRENGTH.

IRRESOLUTION.—I. *Nouns.* **irresolution,** indecision, indetermination, shilly-shally, instability, uncertainty, irresoluteness, fickleness, caprice, vacillation, timidity, cowardice, demur, suspense, hesitation, hesitancy, changeableness, fluctuation; levity, pliancy, weakness, lukewarmness.
waverer, trimmer, timeserver, opportunist, Vicar of Bray, turncoat, shilly-shallier; shuttlecock, butterfly.
II. *Verbs.* **be irresolute,** dilly-dally, hesitate, hover, shilly-shally, hum and haw, demur, debate, balance; dally with, coquet with; go halfway, compromise, be afraid, "let 'I dare not' wait upon 'I would' " (*Macbeth*), remain neuter.
waver, vacillate, fluctuate, falter, change, alternate, shuffle, straddle, palter, shirk, trim; play fast and loose; blow hot and cold.
III. *Adjectives.* **irresolute,** wavering, undecided, undetermined, uncertain, fickle, unreliable, irresponsible, half-hearted, capricious, inconstant, vacillating, vacillant (*rare*), variable, changeful, changeable, mutable, unstable, unsteady; light, giddy, volatile, light-minded, lightsome, frivolous, featherbrained, feather-headed, hen-headed (*colloq.*).
weak, spineless, invertebrate, feeble-minded, frail, timid, cowardly, pliant.
IV. *Adverbs.* **irresolutely,** undecidedly, etc. (see *adjectives*); in faltering accents; off and on.
See also CAPRICE, CHANGEABLENESS, COWARDICE, FEAR, INERTNESS, OSCILLATION, UNCERTAINTY, WEAKNESS.—*Antonyms.* See RESOLUTION.

---

irritable, *adj.* ill-humored, peevish, petulant, fretful. See IRASCIBILITY.
irritate, *v.* annoy, provoke, ruffle, exasperate. See PAIN, TOUCH.
irritating, *adj.* exasperating, galling, annoying, irksome. See PAINFULNESS.
irritation, *n.* exasperation, annoyance. See RESENTMENT.

ISLAND.—I. *Nouns.* **island,** isle (*chiefly poetic, except in proper names*), islet, ait, eyot, holm (*common in English place names*), calf (*small island near a larger*), reef, ridge, bar, atoll, key (*as in Florida*); archipelago: *opposite of* mainland.
islander, islandman (*rare or local*), islandress (*fem.: rare*), islesman, isleman (*rare*), insular (*rare as a noun*), *insulaire* (*F.*).
II. *Verbs.* **island,** insulate, isolate; isle, enisle.
III. *Adjectives.* **insular,** island, seagirt (*chiefly poetic*), isolated; archipelagic.
narrow-minded, prejudiced, petty, narrow, illiberal, bigoted, circumscribed, parochial.

---

isolate, *v.* insulate, set apart, segregate. See DISJUNCTION.
isolation, *n.* solitude, loneliness, separation, aloofness. See SECLUSION.
issue, *n.* outcome, result; outflow, discharge; outlet, exit; question, point in question; children, progeny. See EFFECT, EGRESS, INQUIRY, POSTERITY.
issue, *v.* leave, go out; follow, proceed; flow out, emerge; distribute, circulate; publish. See DEPARTURE, EFFECT, ESCAPE, MONEY, PUBLICATION.

ITCHING.—I. *Nouns.* **itching,** formication (*med.*), paræsthesia (*med.*), tingling, prickling; tickling, titillation.
itch, scabies, psora (*med.*), pruritus (*med.*), prurigo (*med.*); mange, scab (*of sheep*).
desire, hankering, longing, yearning, craving, orexis (*med.*), cacoëthes (*as, cacoëthes scribendi, itch for writing*), mania, propensity, inclination, prurience *or* pruriency.
II. *Verbs.* **itch,** tingle, creep, thrill, sting; prick, prickle.
desire, crave, hanker after, yearn for, long for, covet, wish for
tickle, titillate, kittle (*Scot. and dial.*); please, divert, enliven.
III. *Adjectives.* **itchy,** itching, crawly, creepy, tingling, etc. (see *verbs*); scabious, mangy, psoric, psoroid (*med.*), formicative, pruriginous, pruritic (*med.*); prurient, lustful, longing.
ticklish, tickly, sensitive (*to tickling*); kittle (*dial.*), kittlish (*Scot. and dial.*), critical, unstable, insecure, risky, dangerous.
See also DESIRE.—*Antonyms.* See INDIFFERENCE, NUMBNESS.

item, *n.* detail, particular, entry; article, piece (*as of news*). See PART.
itinerant, *adj.* traveling, peripatetic, wayfaring, nomadic. See JOURNEY.
itinerary, *n.* route, course; record of travel; guidebook. See JOURNEY.

J

jabber, *v.* babble, chatter, twaddle, gabble, gibber. See UNMEANINGNESS.
jack, *n.* lever, lifting device; bower (*cards*). See INSTRUMENT, KNAVE.
jacket, *n.* coat, sack, doublet; casing, wrapper. See CLOTHING.
jagged, *adj.* uneven, notched, sharp, craggy. See ROUGHNESS.
jail, *n.* lockup. See PRISON.
jangle, *n.* clang, dissonance; wrangle, bickering. See DISCORD.
jar, *n.* jolt, shock, vibration. See AGITATION.
jargon, *n.* gibberish; lingo, cant, slang. See ABSURDITY, NEOLOGY.

JEALOUSY.—I. *Nouns.* **jealousy,** distrust, mistrust, apprehension, heartburn, envy, grudging, resentment, doubt, suspicion; "green-eyed monster" (*Othello*); yellows (*archaic*), jaundiced eye; "the injured lover's hell" (*Paradise Lost*).
solicitude, watchfulness, care, concern, anxiety.
II. *Verbs.* **be jealous,** view with jealousy, grudge, begrudge, envy; doubt, distrust, mistrust, suspect, misdoubt.
III. *Adjectives.* **jealous,** jaundiced, yellow-eyed, envious, distrustful, suspiciously vigilant, apprehensive, suspicious, resentful.
solicitous, anxious, concerned, careful, watchful (*as*, jealous *of one's good name*); zealous (*archaic*).
See also ENVY, YELLOW.—*Antonyms.* See BENEVOLENCE, ²CONTENT, TRUST.

---

jeer, *v.* scoff, taunt, ridicule, gibe. See DISRESPECT.
jelly, *v.* jellify, gellatinize, jell (*U. S. colloq.*). See SEMILIQUIDITY.
jeopardy, *n.* peril, risk, hazard. See DANGER.
jerk, *v.* jolt, thrust, twitch; throw, flick, toss. See AGITATION, SNAP.
jest, *n.* witticism, joke; fun, sport. See WIT.
jester, *n.* joker, wit, comedian; clown, buffoon. See HUMORIST.
jet, *v.* spout, gush, spurt, shoot. See RIVER.
jewelry, *n.* gems, jewels. See ORNAMENT.
jingle, *v.* clink, tinkle. See RESONANCE.
job, *n.* piece of work, task. See BUSINESS.
jocularity, *n.* merriment, facetiousness, jesting. See WIT.
jog, *v.* jolt, push, nudge, shake. See IMPULSE.
join, *v.* connect, hitch, bind; combine, unite, associate. See JUNCTION, PARTY.
joining, *adj.* uniting, connecting; connective, copulative (*gram.*). See JUNCTION.
joint, *n.* connection, juncture; articulation; *Slang*: den, dive (*U. S.*). See JUNCTION, VICE.
joint, *adj.* joined, united, corporate, combined. See JUNCTION, PARTY.
jointly, *adv.* together, in common. See JUNCTION.
joke, *n.* butt; jest, witticism. See LAUGHINGSTOCK, WIT.
jolly, *adj.* joyful, gay, merry, vivacious. See CHEERFULNESS.
jolt, *v.* jar, jerk, shake, jounce. See IMPULSE.
jostle, *v.* push, elbow, shove, crowd. See AGITATION.
journal, *n.* diary, record; periodical, newspaper, magazine. See CHRONOMETRY, PUBLICATION.
journalist, *n.* reporter, newspaperman; editor. See BOOK, RECORDER.

JOURNEY.—I. *Nouns.* **journey,** excursion, expedition, tour, trip, circuit, pilgrimage, hadj *or* hajj (*to Mecca*), peregrination, jaunt, outing, airing, drive, ride, trek (*South Africa*); march, walk, promenade, constitutional (*colloq.*),

stroll, saunter, ramble, hike (*colloq.*), tramp, turn, run, stalk, perambulation; voyage, cruise, sail, passage; travel, traveling, wayfaring, campaigning; motoring, automobiling; globe-trotting (*colloq.*), sight-seeing.
riding, equitation, horsemanship, manège, ride and tie.
roving, vagrancy, nomadism, *Wanderlust* (*Ger.*); vagabondism, vagabondage, hoboism (*U. S.*); migration, emigration, gadding, flitting, flit.
route, course, itinerary, plan, circuit, path, road, airway, air route.
guidebook, guide, roadbook, handbook; Baedeker, Bradshaw.
procession, parade, cavalcade, caravan, file, *cortège* (*F.*), column, train.
stopping place, stop, station, depot (*U. S.*), terminal (*U. S.*), terminus, railway station; camp, encampment, post.
journeyer, traveler, wanderer, tourist, tripper, excursionist, rambler, migrant, rover, hiker (*colloq.*), walker, pilgrim, wayfarer, hadji *or* hajji (*pilgrim to Mecca*); voyager, trekker (*South Africa*); rider, driver, motorist, flyer, aviator.
II. *Verbs.* **journey**, travel, go, tour, peregrinate, trek (*South Africa*), pilgrim; voyage, cruise, sail; take (*or* go) a journey; take wing, flit, migrate, emigrate; spin, speed, cycle (*colloq.*), bicycle, wheel (*colloq.*); trolley (*colloq.*); motor, drive, auto (*colloq.*); fly.
roam, wander, rove, range, prowl, jaunt, ramble, stray, stroll, saunter, perambulate, nomadize, meander, straggle; gad, gad about.
walk, march, step, tread, pace; plod, trudge, pad, stump, traipse *or* trapes (*colloq. or dial*), wend (*archaic*); hike (*colloq.*), tramp; stalk, stride; strut, bowl along, toddle, paddle, peg on, jog on, shuffle on, bend one's steps, promenade, track, patrol, pace up and down; march in procession, defile, file off.
slide, coast, skim, skate, glide, skid, toboggan, ski.
take horse, ride, drive, trot, amble, canter, gallop, prance, frisk, caracole.
go to, repair to, resort to, hie to, betake oneself to, visit.
III. *Adjectives.* **journeying**, traveling, etc. (see *verbs*); itinerant, ambulatory, peripatetic, roving, rambling, gadding, vagrant, wandering, migratory, nomadic wayfaring; wayworn, travel-stained.
self-propelling, self-acting, self-moving, locomotive, locomotory (*rare*), locomobile, automotive, automobile, automatic, motile.

See also MOTION, NAVIGATION, TRAVELER, VEHICLE.—*Antonyms.* See [1]REST.

---

jovial, *adj.* jolly, gay, merry, convivial. See CHEERFULNESS.
joy, *n.* delight, elation, gladness, happiness, mirth, gayety. See PLEASURE.
jubilant, *adj.* exultant, elated, joyful. See REJOICING.

JUDGE.—I. *Nouns.* **judge**, justice, justiciar *or* justiciary (*Eng. and Scot. hist.*), judicator, deemster (*Isle of Man and archaic*); hakim, mollah, ulema, mufti, cadi *or* kadi (*all Moham.*); bencher (*archaic*), alcalde (*Sp.*), podesta (*It.*), justice (*or* judge) of assize; magistrate, police magistrate, beak (*slang*); his worship (*Eng.*), his honor, his lordship (*Brit.*); the court; Lord Chancellor, Master of the Rolls, Vice Chancellor, Lord Chief Justice (*all Brit.*), Chief Justice; Rhadamanthus, Solomon, Minos.
arbitrator, arbiter, umpire, referee, referendary (*rare*), censor, inspector, assessor, moderator, master, receiver.
connoisseur, critic, expert, adept, virtuoso (*It. pl.* virtuosi), epicure, *cognoscente* (*It.; pl. cognoscenti*); reviewer, annotator, commentator; literalist, verbalist.
jury, panel, inquest (*esp. a coroner's*), country (*Eng. law*); grand jury; petit jury *or* petty jury, trial jury.
juror, juryman, talesman; grand juror, grand juryman; petit juror, petit juryman.
II. *Verbs.* **judge**, adjudicate, decide, settle, adjudge, try, arbitrate, umpire; decree, pronounce, rule, confirm, sentence, doom, award, find; try a case; act as judge; sit in judgment; pronounce judgment; criticize, censure, condemn.
appraise, estimate, rate, assess, rank, value, count, account, appreciate, prize, price; size up (*colloq.*).
[*to exercise the judgment*] **distinguish**, discern, discriminate, determine, ascertain, decide, resolve, form an opinion; come to (*or* arrive at) a conclusion.
review (*as a book*), comment upon, criticize, examine, survey, investigate, dissect, flay; write a review.

conclude, reckon, suppose, consider, opine, presume, think, esteem, believe, imagine, deem, regard; deduce, derive, infer, gather, collect, glean.
III. *Adjectives.* **judicial,** judicatory, judicatorial, judicative; legal, juridical, juristic; determinate, positive, conclusive.
discriminating, discerning, discriminative, critical, perspicacious, judgmatic *or* judgmatical (*colloq.*), impartial.
censorious, condemnatory, critical, severe, hypercritical, reprobative, reprehensive, captious, faultfinding.
judicious, prudent, wise, sagacious, sensible, rational, discreet, cautious, well-advised, well-considered, politic.

See also DISCRIMINATION, INQUIRY, JURISDICTION, SAGE, TASTE, TRIBUNAL, WISDOM.

JUDGMENT.—*Nouns.* **judgment,** result, conclusion, upshot, deduction, inference, corollary, decision, resolution, opinion, determination; finding, award, verdict, sentence, decree; arbitration, adjudication, arbitrament.
estimate, appraisal, appraisement, valuation, estimation, assessment, appreciation, consideration, award; criticism, review, critique, notice, report.
discernment, discrimination, perspicacity, keenness, sharpness, shrewdness, longheadedness, astuteness, tact, discretion, taste, acumen; sense, common sense, sagacity, circumspection, good sense, horse sense (*colloq.*).
[*decree of the people*] **plebiscite,** voice, vote, suffrage, franchise, ballot, poll, election, referendum; *vox populi* (*L.*).

See also BELIEF, CHOICE, CONDEMNATION, DISCRIMINATION, INTELLECT, WISDOM.—*Antonyms.* See MISJUDGMENT.

---

juicy, *adj.* sappy, succulent. See FLUIDITY.
jumble, *v.* confuse, mix up, disarrange. See DISORDER.
jump, *v.* hop, bound, spring. See LEAP.

JUNCTION.—I. *Nouns.* **junction,** joining, union, connection, hook-up (*radio; as, a coast-to-coast* hook-up), combination, conjugation, concatenation, confluence, meeting, communication, conjunction, coherence, attachment, annexation, assemblage, reunion; concourse, consolidation, alliance, coalition, combine (*U. S. colloq.*); marriage, wedlock.
joint, joining, juncture, connection, articulation, pivot, hinge, mortise, miter, dovetail, splice, weld, knee, elbow, knot, node (*bot.*), commissure (*tech.*), suture (*anat.*), raphe (*tech.*), closure, seam, gore, gusset; link, bond.
juncture, emergency, pass, contingency, predicament, crisis, concurrence, conjuncture, quandary, strait, extremity, pinch.
II. *Verbs.* **join,** unite, connect; associate; put together, piece together, coalesce, blend, merge, mix, mingle, combine, embody, incorporate, compound, conjoin, consolidate, league, band.
attach, fix, fasten, bind, secure, tighten, clinch, tie, pinion, strap, sew, lace, stitch, knit, button, buckle, hitch, lash, truss, splice, gird, tether, moor, picket, chain; fetter, hook, link, yoke, couple, bracket; marry; bridge over, span; pin, nail, screw, bolt, hasp, lock, clasp, clamp, rivet; solder, cement, weld, fuse; rabbet, mortise, miter, dovetail; graft, ingraft; append, add, annex, adjoin.
interlace, entwine, interweave, interknit, weave, plait, intertwine, interlock; entangle.
III. *Adjectives.* **joining,** uniting, etc. (see *verbs*); conjunctive, connective, conjunctival, combinative, copulative (*gram.*).
joint, joined, united, etc. (see *verbs*); corporate, conjunct, compact, concurrent, coincident, correal (*civil law*); hand in hand.
firm, fast, close, tight, taut, secure, inseparable, indissoluble.
IV. *Adverbs.* **jointly,** unitedly, together, in conjunction with, intimately, firmly.

See also ARRIVAL, ASSEMBLAGE, COHERENCE, COMBINATION, CONTACT, MARRIAGE, PARTY, VINCULUM.—*Antonyms.* See DISJUNCTION.

---

juncture, *n.* emergency, contingency, extremity. See JUNCTION.
junior, *adj.* younger, minor, subordinate, inferior, later. See INFERIORITY, YOUTH.

JURISDICTION.—I. *Nouns.* **jurisdiction,** sphere of authority, sovereign power, authority, magistracy, soc *or* soke (*hist.*), circuit, range, province, dominion, control, administration of justice; judicature, judiciary.
department, office, division, bureau; secretariat, cutcherry *or* cutchery (*India*).
II. *Adjectives.* **jurisdictional,** justiciable, judicable, juridical, jurisdictive (*rare*), administrative, executive.
See also AUTHORITY, JUDGE, SAFETY, TRIBUNAL.

---

juror, *n.* juryman. See JUDGE.
jury, *n.* panel; trial jury, grand jury, petit jury. See JUDGE.
just, *adj.* impartial, fair, equitable. See PROBITY, RIGHT.
justice, *n.* fairness, impartiality; uprightness, integrity. See RIGHT.
justification, *n.* excuse, vindication. See DEFENSE.
justify, *v.* warrant, excuse, vindicate, exonerate. See VINDICATION.
jut, *v.* protrude, project, overhang. See CONVEXITY.
juvenile, *adj.* youthful, immature, undeveloped, young, puerile. See YOUTH.

K

keen, *adj.* eager, ardent; acute, discerning; bitter, cutting, stinging; shrewd, quick; keen-edged. See DESIRE, DISCRIMINATION, FEELING, INTELLIGENCE, SHARPNESS.
keen-edged, *adj.* keen, fine, acute. See SHARPNESS.
keep, *v.* observe, fulfill; carry on, manage; continue, persist; maintain, sustain; confine, repress, withold; hold, have, retain. See CELEBRATION, CONDUCT, PERMANENCE, PRESERVATION, RESTRAINT, RETENTION.
keep, *n.* donjon, stronghold; support, maintenance, living; charge, care. See DEFENSE, FOOD, RESTRAINT.

KEEPER.—I. *Nouns.* **keeper,** custodian, conservator, curator, warden, wardsman (*rare*), ranger, gamekeeper, warder, jailer *or* gaoler, turnkey, castellan, guard, watch, watchdog, watchman, doorkeeper, chokidar (*India*), durwan (*India*), janitor, *concierge* (*F.*); sentry, sentinel, picket, patrol; vanguard, outpost, Cossack post, rearguard; coastguard.
escort, bodyguard, attendant, conductor, safe-conduct, safeguard, burkundaz (*India*), convoy.
guardian, protector, tutor, governor; duenna, chaperon, governess, nurse, *bonne* (*F.*), ayah (*India*), amah (*Oriental*).
See also DOMESTICATION, SAFETY.—*Antonyms.* See PRISONER.

---

keepsake, *n.* souvenir, memento, token. See MEMORY.
kernel, *n.* seed, grain, nucleus; essence, pith, gist, core. See CENTRALITY, IMPORTANCE.
key, *n.* explanation, solution; trot (*cant*); tonality, pitch; opener. See INTERPRETATION, MUSIC, OPENING.
keynote, *n.* tonic; fundamental principle. See MUSIC, SUBJECTIVENESS.
kick, *v.* strike (*with foot*), spurn; find fault, object; recoil, rebound. See IMPULSE, OPPOSITION, RECOIL.
kidnap, *v.* abduct, steal, carry away. See TAKING.

KILLING.—I. *Nouns.* **killing,** slaying; homicide, manslaughter; murder, assassination; gore, blood, dispatch, death, bloodshed, effusion of blood; slaughter, carnage, butchery, massacre, *pogrom* (*Russia*); *noyade* (*F.; Reign of Terror*).
war, warfare, battle, jihad *or* jehad (*Moham.*), crusade, war to the death, hostilities; Armageddon.

deathblow, finishing stroke, *coup de grâce* (*F.*), quietus; execution, judicial murder, electrocution, guillotinade (*F.*), martyrdom.

suffocation, strangulation, strangling, thuggee (*India*), garrote *or* garrotte; hanging, etc. (see *verbs*).

fatal accident, violent death, casualty, calamity, disaster, catastrophe, tragedy.

killer, slayer, slaughterer, butcher, murderer, lyncher, Cain, assassin, cutthroat, garroter *or* garrotter, thug, strangler, gunman, manslayer, Apache, bandit, bravo (*professional assassin*), hatchet man (*menace of Chinatown*); executioner, hangman, decapitator, guillotineer *or* guillotiner, poisoner, head-hunter, cannibal. regicide, parricide, matricide, fratricide, sororicide, vaticide (*prophet*), infanticide: *this cheerful list of* -cides *denotes both doer and deed.*

suicide, self-murder, self-destruction, hara-kiri (*Jap.*), seppuku (*Jap.*), suttee (*former practice of Hindu widows*); car of Jagannath *or* Juggernaut (*erroneously supposed that devotees cast themselves before it*).

sacrifice, sacrificial offering, immolation, burnt offering, holocaust, hecatomb.

[*destruction of animals*] **slaughter,** slaughtering, butchering, killing.

hunting, venery, the chase, the hunt, fox-hunting, deerstalking, big-game hunting, shikar (*India*), sport; coursing, shooting, pig-sticking, boar-hunting; falconry, hawking; angling, fishing.

hunter, huntress (*fem.*), huntswoman (*rare*), Diana; Nimrod, big-game hunter, lion hunter, tiger hunter, sportsman, shikari (*India*), gunner, stalker, deerstalker, jäger (*Ger.*), huntsman; fisherman, angler; gunner, gun (*cant*); poacher, trapper, ferreter; falconer, hawker (*rare*).

slaughterhouse, shambles, *abattoir* (*F.*), butchery.

II. *Verbs.* **kill,** put to death, slay, shed blood; murder, assassinate, poison, butcher, slaughter, put an end to; lynch, finish, destroy, dispatch *or* despatch, do to death, do for (*colloq.*), take for a ride (*euphemism of gunmen and racketeers*), bump off (*slang*), brain, burke, knock on the head, shoot, hunt; run through, saber *or* sabre, stab, bayonet, put to the sword; decimate, massacre; immolate, sacrifice.

strangle, garrote *or* garrotte, hang, throttle, choke, stifle, suffocate; smother, asphyxiate, drown.

execute, behead, decapitate, guillotine; hang, gibbet, crucify; electrocute.

die a violent death, commit suicide; kill (make away with, *or* put an end to) oneself.

III. *Adjectives.* **mortal,** fatal, tragic, deadly, lethal, lethiferous; mutually destructive, internecine; suicidal.

murderous, slaughterous, sanguinary, bloody, blood-stained, gory, red-handed; bloodthirsty, bloody-minded, homicidal.

See also ARMS, DEATH, PUNISHMENT, WARFARE.—*Antonyms.* See AID, DELIVERANCE.

---

kind, *n.* type, sort, stamp, species, character, nature. See CLASS.

kind, *adj.* benign, indulgent, lenient, gracious, obliging, tender, mild. See GOOD, MILDNESS.

kindle, *v.* set on fire, light, ignite; arouse, stir, fire. See CALEFACTION, EXCITEMENT.

kindness, *n.* benignity, graciousness, gentleness, goodness, compassion; service, favor. See BENEVOLENCE, MILDNESS; GOOD.

kindred, *n.* kinship, relationship; ancestry, ancestors, relatives, folks (*colloq.*). See CONSANGUINITY, PEOPLE.

kindred, *adj.* sympathetic, congenial; akin, related, cognate; similar. See CONCORD, CONSANGUINITY, SIMILARITY.

king, *n.* monarch, sovereign. See MASTER.

kingdom, *n.* realm, dominion, empire. See REGION.

kingly, *adj.* regal, imperial, royal, majestic. See AUTHORITY.

kinsman, *n.* relative, relation. See CONSANGUINITY.

kiss, *v.* caress, smack, osculate; brush, graze. See ENDEARMENT, TOUCH.

knack, *n.* trick, expertness, dexterity, cleverness. See SKILL.

KNAVE.—*Nouns.* **knave,** rogue, villain, rascal, scoundrel, miscreant, budmash (*India*), caitiff, cheat, shyster (*U. S.*), sharper, trickster.
traitor, betrayer, archtraitor, Judas; plotter, complotter, colluder, accomplice, conspirator; reptile, serpent, snake in the grass, wolf in sheep's clothing, sneak, squealer (*slang*), squeaker (*slang*), telltale, mischief-maker; renegade, recreant.
[*playing card*] **jack,** *valet* (*F.*), varlet (*obsolete*), pam (*knave of clubs in five-card loo*), bower (*euchre*).
[*archaic and original sense*] **boy, lad, servant, manservant, male servant, menial,** retainer.

See also APOSTASY, BAD MAN.

---

kneel, *v.* genuflect, bend the knee. See DEPRESSION.
knickknack, *n.* gewgaw, trinket, bauble, gimcrack. See UNIMPORTANCE.
knight, *n.* Templar; paladin, champion; gallant, cavalier; chevalier. See CLERGY, DEFENSE, LOVE, NOBILITY.
knit, *v.* contract, wrinkle; unite, weave, interlace. See [1]FOLD, JUNCTION.
knob, *n.* lump, protuberance, bunch. See CONVEXITY.
knock, *v.* rap, tap; bump, collide, hit, strike. See IMPULSE.
knoll, *n.* hummock, rise, mound, hillock. See HEIGHT.
knot, *n.* group, cluster; lump, bunch; tangle, snarl, problem; fastening, tie. See ASSEMBLAGE, CONVEXITY, DIFFICULTY, VINCULUM.

KNOWLEDGE.—I. *Nouns.* **knowledge,** cognition, cognizance, apperception (*psychol.*), comprehension, apprehension, recognition, appreciation, judgment, understanding, intuition, cryptæsthesia *or* cryptesthesia (*psychol.*), subconscious perception, consciousness, perception; enlightenment, light; impression, perception, discovery, revelation; insight, privity, ken, familiarity, acquaintance, information, experience.
learning, erudition, lore, scholarship, science; letters, literature; book learning, bookishness, general information; education, culture, cultivation, attainments, acquirements, accomplishments, proficiency, higher education, liberal education.
II. *Verbs.* **know,** perceive, apprehend, cognize, discern, ken, recognize, see, comprehend, understand, realize, conceive, appreciate, fathom, make out, experience; wot (*archaic*), wot of (*archaic*), be aware of, ween (*archaic*), trow (*archaic*), savvy (*slang*).
learn, study, con, peruse, master, acquire, get, evolve; find, discover, hear of, read, ascertain.
III. *Adjectives.* **knowable,** ascertainable, discoverable, discernible, distinguishable, understandable, cognizable, cognoscible, perceptible, comprehensible.
knowing, conscious, cognitive, percipient, perceptive, apperceptive (*psychol.*), appercipient (*psychol.*), understanding, intelligent, informed, knowledgeable.
wide-awake, alert, keen, shrewd, cunning, artful, fly (*slang*), astute, canny (*as, a* knowing *look*).
stylish, smart, *chic* (*F.*), snappy (*colloq.*), fashionable, modish, tony (*slang*), dressy (*colloq.*), elegant: *in this sense,* knowing *is colloq.*
aware of, cognizant of, conscious of, *au fait* (*F.*), acquainted with, privy to, in the secret; alive to; apprized of, informed of, let into; undeceived.
educated, instructed, erudite, learned, lettered, well-informed, well-versed, well-read, well-grounded, well-educated; *savant* (*F.*), bluestocking (*applied only to women*), blue (*used here of literary women and not of jazz*), literary, cultured, cultivated, enlightened, high-brow (*slang*), bookish, scholastic, solid, profound, deep-read, book-learned, accomplished; self-taught, self-instructed, self-educated, autodidactic (*rare*).
known, ascertained, well-known, understood, recognized, received, noted, notorious, proverbial; familiar, hackneyed, trite, commonplace.

See also BELIEF, CUNNING, DISCOVERY, JUDGMENT, LANGUAGE, LEARNING, SKILL, TEACHING, WISDOM.—*Antonyms.* See IGNORANCE.

L

labor, *n.* work, toil, drudgery, task. See EXERTION.—**labor of love,** unrewarded effort, unpaid service. See WILLINGNESS.
laborer, *n.* workman, hand, workingman. See AGENT.
laborious, *adj.* uphill, toilsome; hard-working, energetic. See EXERTION.
labor-saving, *adj.* useful; motor-driven, mechanical. See INSTRUMENT.
labyrinth, *n.* maze, perplexity, intricacy. See SECRET.
lace, *n.* net, mesh, netting; fancywork, openwork; cord, thong, lacing. See CROSSING, ORNAMENT, VINCULUM.
lace, *v.* interlace, embroider, weave; fasten, tighten, unite; flavor, dash; beat, lash. See CROSSING, JUNCTION, MIXTURE, PUNISHMENT.
lacerate, *v.* tear, mangle; hurt, distress. See PAIN.
lack, *n.* deficiency, shortage, want, insufficiency; fault, demerit, failing. See INCOMPLETENESS, VICE (*defect*).
lack, *v.* need, want, call for. See REQUIREMENT.
lad, *n.* youth, boy, stripling. See INFANT.
ladle, *n.* dipper, bail, scoop, spoon. See RECEPTACLE.
ladylove, *n.* sweetheart, mistress. See LOVE.
lag, *v.* loiter, tarry, delay, linger. See FOLLOWING.
laicize, *v.* secularize, popularize. See LAITY.
lair, *n.* den, cave, hole, burrow. See HABITATION.

LAITY.—I. *Nouns.* **laity,** laymen; flock, fold, congregation, assembly, brethren, people; society *or* parish (*U. S. Congregational churches*).
layman, laic, secular (*eccl.*), parishioner, catechumen; nonprofessional.
II. *Verbs.* **laicize,** secularize, democratize, popularize.
III. *Adjectives.* **lay,** laic *or* laical, secular, civil, temporal, profane, congregational, popular, nonclerical; nonprofessional, nonexpert, unprofessional (*as, lay opinion*). *opposite of* clerical, ecclesiastical, professional.
Antonyms. See CLERGY, EXPERT.

LAKE.—I. *Nouns.* **lake,** lagoon, loch (*Scot.*), lough (*Irish*), tarn, broad (*as, the Norfolk* broads, *England*); pond, mere, pool, lakelet, tank (*Anglo-Indian*), reservoir; salina, salt pond; well, artesian well; ditch, dike *or* dyke, dam, race.
lake dweller, lacustrian, lacustrine dweller (*or* inhabitant), pile dweller.
lake dwelling, lacustrine dwelling, pile dwelling, crannog (*prehistoric Celtic*), *palafitte* (*F.*), *Pfahlbauten* (*Ger.; pl.*).
II. *Adjectives.* **lake,** lacustrine (*as, the* lacustrine, *or lake-dwelling, period*), lacustral (*rare*), lacustrian (*rare*).

---

lame, *adj.* limping, crippled; ineffectual, ineffective, weak. See IMPOTENCE, WEAKNESS.
lamellar, *adj.* scaly, lamellate. See LAYER.

LAMENTATION.—I. *Nouns.* **lamentation,** lament, wail, complaint, plaint, mourning, jeremiad, murmur, mutter, grumble, groan, moan, whine, whimper, sob, sigh, suspiration (*rare*); wailing, howl, outcry, cry, scream; frown, scowl.
weeping, sobbing, crying, tears, cry (*colloq.*), lachrymation (*rare*), flood of tears, fit of crying, lachrymals (*pl.*).
mourning, weeds (*colloq.*), widow's weeds, crape, armozeen, deep mourning; sackcloth and ashes.
dirge, funeral song, death song, coronach (*Scot. and Irish*), keen (*Irish*), ullalulla (*Irish*), requiem, elegy, threnody, epicedium, nenia (*rare*).
mourner, lamenter, keener (*Irish*), mute, weeper, howler, wailer; Niobe, Heraclitus (*the "Weeping Philosopher"*).
II. *Verbs.* **lament,** mourn, deplore, grieve, keen (*Irish*), weep over; bewail, bemoan, condole with, wail, sorrow, fret, moan, groan, howl, roar, scream, yell, yelp, rend the air.

sigh, give (*or* heave) a sigh; "waft a sigh from Indus to the pole" (Pope); suspire (*rare*).
cry, weep, sob, greet (*archaic or Scot.*), blubber, snivel, whimper, shed tears, burst into tears, cry one's eyes out.
complain, murmur, mutter, grumble, growl, grouse (*colloq.*), whine, clamor, croak, grunt.
III. *Adjectives.* **lamentable,** mournful, doleful, sorrowful, sad, pitiful, regrettable, woeful, piteous, pitiable, deplorable, pathetic, miserable, wretched, grievous.
lamenting, clamorous, sorrowing, sorrowful, mournful, lamentable, tearful, lachrymose, plaintive, querulous; in tears, "like Niobe, all tears" (*Hamlet*); bathed in tears; in mourning; in sackcloth and ashes.
IV. *Interjections.* **alas!** alack! ah me! woe is me! ochone *or* ohone! (*Irish and Scot.*), heigh-ho! alackaday *or* lackaday! (*archaic*), alas the day! *O tempora, O mores!* (*L.*).
See also BADNESS (*lamentable*), CONDOLENCE, CRY, DEJECTION, INTERMENT, PAIN.
—*Antonyms.* See REJOICING.

---

lamina, *n.* plate, scale, flake. See LAYER.
laminate, *v.* foliate, flake; plate, overlay. See LAYER.

LAND.—I. *Nouns.* **land,** earth, ground, carpet (*aviation slang*), soil, dry land, *terra firma* (*L.*); continent; mainland, main; peninsula, chersonese; delta; neck (*or* tongue) of land, isthmus, cape, promontory, highland; plain, desert, oasis; campus, yard, farm, grounds, frontage; real estate, realty, property, acres, premises (*law*), estate.
coast, shore, strand, playa (*Sp.*), beach; bank; seaboard, seaside, seacoast, seashore; reclamation, made land.
soil, glebe, clay, loam, marl, gravel, mold *or* mould, subsoil, clod, clot (*dial.*), divot (*golf*).
clay, argil, potter's clay, slip; kaolin (*porcelain manufacture*), bole; till, bowlder clay; cloam (*dial. Eng.*), cledge (*dial. Eng.*), metal, clunch, shale, wacke.
rock, crag, cliff, bowlder *or* boulder, stone.
native land, mother country, motherland, fatherland, home, homeland; realm, region.
landsman (*opposite of* seaman), landlubber (*sailor's slang*), non-sailor, landman; tiller of the soil, farmer, husbandman, agriculturist, backwoodsman.
II. *Verbs.* **land,** disembark, debark, come to land, come (*or* go) ashore, cast anchor, arrive; alight, descend, settle, stop.
catch, capture, get, take, secure, gain, seize, bag, net (*as, to* land *a fish*).
III. *Adjectives.* **terrestrial,** earthly, terrene, earthy, telluric, tellurian, mundane, worldly; littoral, riparian, riparious, riparial (*zoöl.*), alluvial; landed, prædial *or* predial, territorial, continental, midland.
IV. *Adverbs.* **ashore,** on shore, on land, on dry land, on *terra firma* (*L.*); aground, stranded.
See also ARRIVAL, HABITATION, PLAIN, PROPERTY, REGION.—*Antonyms.* See OCEAN, WATER.

---

landholder, *n.* landowner, proprietor, tenant. See POSSESSOR.
landlubber, *n.* landsman, lubber. See BUNGLER.
landsman, *n.* non-sailor; farmer. See LAND.
lane, *n.* ocean lane, sea route; alley, bypath. See OCEAN, OPENING.

LANGUAGE.—I. *Nouns.* **language,** speech, tongue, mother (vulgar, *or* native) tongue; King's (*or* Queen's) English; vernacular, bât (*Anglo-Indian*), dialect, brogue, patois, lingo (*chiefly jocose or contemptuous*), argot, slang; idiom, accent, phraseology, diction, vocabulary, use of words, verbal expression, style.
universal language, pasigraphy (*a loose use*), international language; Volapük, Esperanto (*or* La Lingvo internacia), Ido, Mondolingue, Novilatiin, Kosmos, Myrana, Spelin, Universala, Idiom Neutral, Ro: *the first three are the best known.*
literature, letters, polite literature, *belles-lettres* (*F.*), Muses, humanities, *litteræ humaniores* (*L.*), dead languages, classics; republic of letters.

[*science of language*] **linguistics,** glossology, glottology, philology, comparative philology, lexicology, linguistic science.
II. *Verbs.* **language,** (*archaic*), express, say, speak, utter, voice, put into words, phrase, couch, signify, present, state, tell, give expression to; sling the bât (*Anglo-Indian slang for "speak the vernacular"*).
III. *Adjectives.* **linguistic,** linguistical, glossological, glottological, philological, lexicological, glottic; dialectal, dialectic, vernacular, current, colloquial, slangy; literary, belletristic; polyglot, polyglottous (*rare*).

See also GRAMMAR, KNOWLEDGE, PHRASE, SCHOLAR, SPEECH, STYLE, WORD.

---

languid, *adj.* listless, sluggish, heavy, dull, inert; drooping, faint. See HEAVINESS, WEAKNESS.
languish, *v.* decline, droop; pine, yearn, grieve; fail, grow feeble. See INACTIVITY, PAIN, WEAKNESS.
languor, *n.* exhaustion, lassitude, weakness, listlessness, dullness, stagnation. See FAINTNESS, HEAVINESS, INACTIVITY.
lank, *adj.* angular, lean, gaunt, awkward, ungainly. See ANGULARITY.

LAPSE.—I. *Nouns.* [*of time*] **lapse,** passing, progress, passage, flow, tide, march, flight, sweep, elapse (*rare*), course, duration; expiration, expiry, termination, end.
age, æon *or* eon; lifetime, month of Sundays (*colloq.*).
[*slip of the tongue or pen*] **slip,** fault, error, flaw, peccadillo, slight mistake, omission, negligence, inadvertence; *lapsus calami* (*L.*), *lapsus linguæ* (*L.*).
[*moral slip*] **failing,** delinquency, indiscretion, shortcoming, offense, failure, dereliction, collapse, miscarriage, secession, recreancy, backsliding, apostasy, relapse.
II. *Verbs.* **lapse,** fail, slip, err; backslide, secede, fall.
[*of time*] **pass,** slip, by, slip away, glide, go; expire, end.
elapse, intervene, lapse, flow, run, proceed, advance, pass; fly, slip, slide, glide; crawl, drag; expire, go by, pass by, be past.
III. *Adverbs.* **in time,** in due time (season, *or* course), in course of time, in the fullness of time, eventually, sooner or later.

See also CESSATION, DESCENT, PASSAGE, PAST, RELAPSE, TIME.

---

large, *adj.* big, great, spacious, comprehensive. See SIZE.
lascivious, *adj.* lewd, lustful, lecherous, sensual, wanton. See IMPURITY.
lash, *v.* scold, rate; beat, flog, whip. See DISAPPROBATION, PUNISHMENT.
last, *v.* wear, endure; continue, remain. See DURABILITY, PERMANENCE.
lasting, *adj.* enduring, permanent, continuing. See LENGTH.
late, *adj.* tardy, slow; recent, new. See LATENESS.

LATENCY.—I. *Nouns.* **latency,** dormancy, quiescence, abeyance, inactivity, passiveness, passivity, inertness, inertia; concealment, suppression, evasion, obscurity, secrecy, reticence, reserve, mystery, mystification, cabalism, occultism, mysticism, anagoge, symbolism; ambiguity, hidden meaning, occult meaning, Delphic oracle; undercurrent.
allusion, insinuation, implication, inference, hint, suggestion, reference, intimation, innuendo.
II. *Verbs.* **be latent,** lurk, smolder *or* smoulder, underlie, make no sign; escape observation (detection, *or* recognition); lie hid, lie in ambush, couch, sneak.
involve, imply, connote, import, implicate, contain, mean, signify, allude to, typify, represent, symbolize, emblematize.
III. *Adjectives.* **latent,** lurking, dormant, potential, concealed, hidden, invisible, undisclosed, unseen, unapparent, unknown, unsuspected, quiescent, inactive, in abeyance, abeyant; cryptic, steganographic (*rare*), cryptographic *or* cryptographical; secret, occult, esoteric, anagogic *or* anagogical, mystic, mystical, veiled, recondite; symbolic, emblematic *or* emblematical, figurative.
indirect, inferential, implicative, implicational; implied, implicit, understood, unexpressed, tacit; allusive, covert, under cover, concealed, underground, underhand, crooked, tortuous, clandestine.

IV. *Adverbs.* **latently,** covertly, secretly, privily, stealthily, clandestinely, in secret, in private, hugger-mugger, *sub rosa* (*L.*), *sub silentio* (*L.*), with closed doors, *à huis clos* (*F.*), *in camera* (*L.*); behind the scenes, in the background; below the surface, between the lines.

See also CONCEALMENT, INERTNESS, INVISIBILITY, PITFALL.—*Antonyms.* See MANIFESTATION.

LATENESS.—I. *Nouns.* **lateness,** tardiness, lingering, loitering, lagging, delay, tarriance (*archaic*), retardation, protraction, prolongation, procrastination; postponement, adjournment, prorogation, deferment, respite, reprieve, truce, stop, stay, suspension, moratorium, remand, mora (*Roman and civil law*), default, remand, continuance (*law*).

II. *Verbs.* **be late,** tarry, wait, stay, bide, take time; dawdle, linger, loiter, gain time; hang fire; stand over, lie over; hang.

put off, defer, delay, lay over, suspend; stave off; retard, postpone, remand, continue (*law*), adjourn, prorogue, procrastinate; dally, prolong, protract, spin out, draw out; table, lay on the table, shelve; reserve, temporize, stall (*colloq.*), filibuster (*U. S.*).

be kept waiting, dance attendance; cool one's heels (*colloq.*), wait impatiently; await, expect, wait for, sit up for.

III. *Adjectives.* **late,** tardy, dilatory; slow, behindhand, backward, unpunctual; overdue, belated, delayed, long-delayed, far advanced; posthumous.

recent, not long past, fresh; quondam, former, *ci-devant* (*F.*), sometime, foregoing, outgoing, retiring; deceased, dead, defunct, late.

IV. *Adverbs.* **late,** backward, behindhand, ago; behind time, too late; ultimately, late in the day, at the eleventh hour, at length, at last.

slowly, leisurely, deliberately, tardily, at one's leisure.

See also DEATH, INACTIVITY, NEWNESS, PAST, SLOWNESS.—*Antonyms.* See EARLINESS.

---

latent, *adj.* hidden, concealed, invisible. See LATENCY.
lateral, *adj.* oblique, sidelong. See SIDE.
latitude, *n.* range, scope, independence, liberality. See FREEDOM.
latter, *adj.* second-mentioned; later. See POSTERIORITY.
laud, *v.* praise, compliment, applaud. See APPROBATION.
laugh, *v.* giggle, chuckle, roar, guffaw. See REJOICING.
laughable, *adj.* risible, amusing, comic, droll, funny. See RIDICULOUSNESS.

LAUGHINGSTOCK.—*Nouns.* **laughingstock,** butt, gazingstock, game, fair game, target, sport, jest, mockery, buffoon, monkey, figure of fun (*colloq.*), joke, byword, April fool, queer fish (*colloq.*); oddity, original.

See also DUPE, RIDICULE.

---

laughter, *n.* laugh, guffaw, snicker, titter; mirth. See REJOICING.
launch, *v.* start, set going; hurl, throw. See BEGINNING, PROPULSION.
lavish, *adj.* profuse, unstinted; excessive, extravagant. See FREEDOM.
lavish, *v.* squander, waste, dissipate. See PRODIGALITY.
law, *n.* jurisprudence; statute, ordinance, regulation; custom, usage, convention, principle. See LEGALITY, RULE.
law-abiding, *adj.* peaceable, quiet, submissive. See ORDER.
lawful, *adj.* legal, legitimate, allowable, licit. See INNOCENCE, PERMISSION, RIGHTFULNESS.
lawless, *adj.* mutinous, insurgent; unrestrained, unruly. See DISOBEDIENCE, DISORDER.
lawlessness, *n.* unruliness, disorderliness; anarchy, terrorism, license. See ILLEGALITY, LAXITY.
lawn, *n.* green, terrace, grassplot, grass land, glade (*archaic*). See PLAIN.

LAWSUIT.—I. *Nouns.* **lawsuit,** suit, action, case, cause, suit in law, judicial contest, litigation; assumpsit, replevin; legal proceedings (*or* action), prosecution, arraignment, accusation, impeachment; presentment, true bill, indictment.
summons, subpœna, citation; writ, brieve (*Scots law*); *habeas corpus* (*L.*).
arrest, apprehension, seizure; attachment, legal seizure; committal, commitment; imprisonment.
pleadings, allegations, *procès-verbal* (*F.*), declaration, bill, claim; affidavit, libel; answer, counter allegations, counterclaim, plea, demurrer, rebutter, rejoinder; surrebutter, surrejoinder; interpleader.
hearing, trial; judgment, sentence, finding, verdict; appeal, writ of error; decision, decided case, precedent.
litigant, suitor, libelant; plaintiff, defendant.
II. *Verbs.* **litigate,** go to law, appeal to the law, contest; bring to justice (trial, *or* the bar), put on trial, accuse, prefer (*or* file) a claim; cite, summon, summons, subpœna, serve with a writ, arraign; sue, prosecute, indict, impeach; attach, distrain; commit, apprehend, arrest, give in charge.
try, hear a cause, hear, sit in judgment; adjudicate, judge, adjudge, decide.
III. *Adjectives.* **litigious,** fond of litigation, contentious, litigant, disputatious, controversial, belligerent, pugnacious, quarrelsome; litigatory.

See also ACCUSATION, ACQUITTAL, ACTION, CONDEMNATION, RESTRAINT, TRIBUNAL.

LAWYER.—I. *Nouns.* **lawyer,** attorney, public attorney, attorney-at-law, mouthpiece (*slang*), legal adviser, advocate, solicitor (*chiefly Brit.*), writer (*Scot.*) conveyancer, barrister *or* barrister-at-law (*chiefly Brit.*), counselor-at-law, counsel, counselor, King's counsel *or* K. C. (*Eng.*), vakil (*India*), moolvee (*Moham.*), pleader, special pleader; procurator, proctor; bencher (*Eng.*), sergeant-at-law (*Eng.*), jurist, legist, jurisconsult, jurisprudent.
[*inferior or tricky lawyer*] pettifogger, shyster (*U. S.*), sharking lawyer, rascally attorney.
bar, legal profession, barristers (*Eng.*), Inns of Court (*Eng.*); court, tribunal.
II. *Verbs.* **practice law,** practice at (*or* within) the bar, plead; be called to (*or* within) the bar; admitted to the bar; take silk (*become a K. C.*).

See also JUDGE, LEGALITY, PLEA (*pleader*).

LAXITY.—I. *Nouns.* **laxity,** laxness, looseness, slackness; negligence, remissness; toleration, lenity, latitude, freedom, relaxation; dissoluteness, profligacy.
anarchy, lawlessness, disorder, misrule, license, insubordination, disorganization, mob rule, mob law, lynch law, nihilism, terrorism, reign of violence.
[*deprivation of power*] **dethronement,** discrownment, deposal, deposition, degradation, abdication; usurpation.
II. *Verbs.* **be lax,** hold a loose rein, *laisser faire* (*F.*), *laisser aller* (*F.*), give the reins to, give rope enough, give free rein to; tolerate; relax; misrule.
have one's fling, act without authority, act on one's own responsibility, usurp authority.
dethrone, depose, discrown, degrade; abdicate.
III. *Adjectives.* **lax,** loose, slack, relaxed; careless, remiss, negligent, weak, incoherent, vague, unexacting; unbridled, reinless, licensed, unrestrained, unconfined.
dissolute, profligate, licentious, wanton, reckless, wild, free, debauched, lewd, immoral.
anarchical, anarchic, lawless, unauthorized, ungoverned, insubordinate, ungovernable, disorganized, chaotic; nihilistic, terroristic, red, revolutionary.
[*of the bowels*] **loose,** open, relaxed, diarrheal, diarrheic, purged.

See also DISORDER, FREEDOM, INCOHERENCE, IRREGULARITY, MILDNESS, NEGLECT, SOFTNESS, VICE.—*Antonyms.* See AUTHORITY, SEVERITY.

---

lay, *adj.* secular, nonclerical. See LAITY.
lay, *v.* charge, ascribe; impose, inflict; place, put, deposit; put forward, present, submit. See ATTRIBUTION, COMMAND, LOCATION, OFFER.

LAYER.—I. *Nouns.* **layer,** stratum, course, couch, bed, seam, coping, substratum, floor, stage, story, tier; fold, lap, ply; slab, tablet, flag.
lamina (*chiefly tech.*), plate, scale, flake, lamella, leaf, sheet, film, membrane, skin, caul, tympan (*tech.*), dura mater *or* dura (*anat.*), arachnoid (*anat.*), pia

mater (*anat.*), meninges (*anat.; sing.* meninx); chorion (*embryol.*), endocardium (*anat.*), endocarp (*bot.*), endocyst (*zoöl.*), endoderm (*zoöl.*), epithelium (*biol.*), endodermis (*bot.*), blastoderm (*embryol.*), hypoblast (*embryol. and zoöl.*), hypodermis (*zoöl.*), ectoderm (*zoöl.*), epiblast (*biol.*), epiblema (*bot.*), mesoblast (*embryol. and zoöl.*), mesoderm (*embryol. and zoöl.*), germ layer (*embryol.*); coat, peel, slice, shaving, paring, wafer; stratification, lamination, foliation, scaliness; scurf, furfur, dandruff *or* dandriff.
paper, newsprint, newspaper, writing paper, note paper, papyrus, onionskin, tissue, *pelure* (*F.*), foolscap.
II. *Verbs.* **laminate,** plate, coat, foliate (*as a mirror*), foil, veneer, overlay, cover, stratify.
scale, flake, delaminate, desquamate (*med.*), exfoliate; peel, pare, shave, slice, skive.
III. *Adjectives.* **lamellar,** lamellate *or* lamellated, scaly, scalelike, lamelliform, laminate, laminose (*rare*), platelike, laminated, flaky, scurfy, furfuraceous, foliaceous, foliated, squamous, stratified, stratiform (*anat.*), straticulate (*geol.*), leafy, micaceous, schistose *or* schistous, spathic, spathose; filmy, membranous, membranaceous, arachnoid (*anat.*), membranoid (*rare*).
See also COVERING.—*Antonyms.* See FILAMENT.

---

layman, *n.* secular; nonprofessional. See LAITY.
lazy, *adj.* indolent, idle, slothful; sluggish. See INACTIVITY.
lead, *v.* guide, conduct, pilot, counsel; induce, persuade; stand first, head; contribute, conduce. See DIRECTION, MOTIVE, PRECEDENCE, TENDENCY.
leaden, *adj.* lurid, overcast, lowering, gloomy; ashen, lead-colored; heavy sluggish. See DIMNESS, GRAY, INERTNESS.
leader, *n.* conductor, coryphæus; commentary, editorial; chief, head, commander; guide, bellwether, front horse; tendon. See DIRECTOR, DISSERTATION, MASTER, PRECURSOR, VINCULUM.
leadership, *n.* direction, guidance, supremacy. See AUTHORITY.
leaf, *n.* scale, flake, sheet; frond, blade, petal, lamina (*bot.*), leaflet. See LAYER, VEGETABLE.
leafage, *n.* foliage, leaves (*collectively*), foliation. See VEGETABLE.
league, *v.* join, federate, unite, band together. See COMBINATION.
leak, *v.* become known, transpire; issue, escape, ooze. See DISCLOSURE, EGRESS.
lean, *v.* depend, rely; slant, incline, bend. See HOPE, OBLIQUITY.
lean, *adj.* skinny, lanky, gaunt. See POVERTY, THINNESS.

LEAP.—I. *Nouns.* **leap,** jump, hop, spring, bound, vault, saltation (*rare*).
caper, skip, prance, hop, dance, spring, buck, frisk, romp, gambol, curvet caracole, demivolt, gambado, dido (*U. S. colloq.*).
[*comparisons*] kangaroo, wallaby, chamois, goat, jerboa, frog, grasshopper locust, cricket, flea.
II. *Verbs.* **leap,** jump, hop, spring, bound, vault, clear, ramp, skip; cut capers (*colloq.*), cavort (*U. S.*), caper, prance, dance, frisk, gambado, gambol, frolic, romp, curvet, caracole, cut a dido (*U. S. colloq.*), bob, bounce, flounce; buck, buck-jump.
III. *Adjectives.* **leaping,** jumping, etc. (see *verbs*); saltatory, saltatorial; frisky, frolicsome, lively, skittish, capersome, rompish.
See also AGITATION, ASCENT.—*Antonyms.* See PLUNGE.

---

learn, *v.* hear of, discover; master, gain knowledge. See KNOWLEDGE, LEARNING.
learned, *adj.* scholarly, erudite. See LEARNING.

LEARNER.—*Nouns.* **learner,** scholar, student, pupil, *élève* (*F.*), schoolboy, schoolgirl, subfreshman, freshman, plebe (*West Point*), sophomore, junior, senior, undergraduate; monitor, prefect; classman, alumnus (*pl.* alumni), alumna (*fem.; pl.* alumnæ), graduate (*in the U. S., applied to one who has com-*

pleted a prescribed course in any school or college; in England, used only of the holder of an academic degree), graduate student, postgraduate student; disciple, follower, chela (*India*), proselyte, apostle, evangelist.
beginner, novice, tyro, abecedarian, alphabetarian; tenderfoot (*slang or colloq.*), *débutant* (*F.; fem. débutante*), greenhorn, recruit, rooky (*slang*); initiate, apprentice, probationer, neophyte, catechumen.
classmate, fellow student (*or* pupil), condisciple (*rare*), schoolfellow, schoolmate.
class, form, grade, room, division, remove (*in some English schools, an intermediate or special class*); seminar, seminary; promotion, graduation.

See also SCHOLAR.—*Antonyms.* See TEACHER.

LEARNING.—I. *Nouns.* **learning,** acquisition of knowledge (*or* of skill), acquirement, attainment, knowledge, lore, mental cultivation, scholarship, erudition, schoolcraft (*archaic*), opsimathy (*education late in life*), wisdom, wide reading; study, inquiry, enlightenment.
apprenticeship, tutelage, novitiate, pupilage.
II. *Verbs.* **learn,** acquire (gain, imbibe, pick up, *or* obtain) knowledge *or* learning; master, grind (*college slang*), cram (*colloq.*), get up, learn by heart, prepare, study, read, peruse, con, pore over, wade through, plunge into; burn the midnight oil; be taught, serve an apprenticeship.
III. *Adjectives.* **learned,** well-informed, erudite, scholarly, scholastic, studious, well-read, widely read, accomplished, able, well-grounded, well-educated, lettered, wise.

See also KNOWLEDGE, WISDOM.—*Antonyms.* See TEACHING.

---

lease, *v.* let, rent, demise (*law*). See LENDING.
lease, *n.* holding, tenure. See PROPERTY.
leash, *n.* brace and a half (*as of hares*); thong, couple. See THREE, VINCULUM.
least, *adj.* smallest, slightest, minimum. See SMALLNESS.
leathery, *adj.* tough, leatherlike, coriaceous. See TENACITY.
leave, *v.* start, go away, vacate; bequeath, devise; resign, renounce; abandon, desert. See DEPARTURE, GIVING, RELINQUISHMENT.
leaven, *n.* yeast, barm. See LEVITY.
leave-taking, *n.* farewell, parting, adieu. See DEPARTURE.
lecture, *v.* scold, rebuke; hold forth, discourse, instruct. See DISAPPROBATION, SPEECH.
ledge, *n.* ridge, projection; strip, rim; shelf, bench; berm (*fortification*). See CONVEXITY, EDGE, SUPPORT, WAY.

LEFT.—I. *Nouns.* **left,** sinistrality, sinistration; left-hand division (*as of an army*).
left-hand (*or* side), near side (*of a horse or vehicle: opposite of* off side), port *or* larboard (*naut.*), Gospel side (*eccl.*), cantorial side (*north side of choir: eccl.*), verso (*of a book: opposite of* recto); south paw (*U. S. slang*).
[*European politics*] **Left,** radicals, liberals, democrats: *those seated on the left of the presiding officer, distinguished from* Center (*moderates*) *and* Right (*monarchists and conservatives*).
II. *Adjectives.* **left,** leftward, left-hand, near (*as of animals or vehicles*), larboard *or* port (*naut.*); sinister, sinistral, sinistrous, sinistrorse (*bot.*), sinistrorsal (*rare*).
left-handed, sinistral; ambiguous, doubtful, questionable, uncertain, clumsy, awkward, unlucky, sinister, double-edged, equivocal (*as, a* left-handed *compliment*); morganatic (*as, a* left-handed *marriage*).

Antonyms. See RIGHT.

---

leg, *n.* limb, member; shank. See PART, SUPPORT.

LEGALITY.—I. *Nouns.* **legality,** conformity to law, lawfulness, legitimacy, legitimateness; legitimation, legitimization, legalization, authorization.
law, rule (*or* rules), code, constitution, charter, act, enactment, statute, canon, ordinance, ordonnance (*as in France*), institution, regulation, by-law, decree, proclamation, ukase, precept, decision, command, order, standing order; equity,

common law; unwritten law, *lex non scripta* (*L.*); law of nations, international law; constitutionality, justice, right, equity; divine commandment, divine revelation, will of God; jurisprudence; nomology (*tech.*), codification, legislation, litigation (*as, to go to* law); legal knowledge (*or* learning); legal profession (*with* the).
II. *Verbs.* **legalize,** legitimize, legitimate, make legal (*or* legitimate), legitimatize, authorize, sanction; regulate, legislate; enact, ordain, decree; codify, formulate.
III. *Adjectives.* **legal,** legitimate, licit, lawful, legalized, authorized, valid, sound, according to law; vested, constitutional, chartered, statutory; legislative; judicial, juridical.
IV. *Adverbs.* **legally,** legitimately, etc. (see *adjectives*); in the eye of the law; by right, by law, *de jure* (*L.*).
See also COMMAND, PERMISSION, PRECEPT, RIGHT, RIGHTFULNESS, RULE.—*Antonyms.* See ILLEGALITY.

---

legend, *n.* myth, story, tradition; inscription, motto. See DESCRIPTION, RECORD.
leggings, *n. pl.* gaiters, chaps, puttees. See CLOTHING.
legible, *adj.* plain, distinct, decipherable. See INTELLIGIBILITY.
legislator, *n.* lawmaker, lawgiver, statesman, Congressman. See DIRECTOR.
legislature, *n.* lawmaking body, parliament, congress. See COUNCIL.
legitimate, *adj.* lawful, legal, regular. See RIGHTFULNESS.

LEISURE.—I. *Nouns.* **leisure,** spare time, spare moments, vacant hour; freedom, otiosity, idleness, holiday, ease, convenience, opportunity; time to spare, time; *otium cum dignitate* (*L.*).
II. *Verbs.* **have leisure,** take one's time (leisure, *or* ease); repose, rest, loaf, lounge, loiter, move slowly, while away the time, be master of one's time, be an idle man.
III. *Adjectives.* **leisured,** unoccupied, unemployed, disengaged, inactive, idle, spare, vacant, otiose, otiant (*rare*).
leisurely, unhurried, slow, easy, languid, hasteless, deliberate.
See also INACTION, REPOSE, SLOWNESS, TIME.—*Antonyms.* See HASTE.

LENDING.—I. *Nouns.* **lending,** advancing, accommodating, etc. (see *verbs*); loan, advance, accommodation, mortgage, investment.
lender, bestower, granter; pawnbroker, money lender, my uncle (*slang*), *tante* (*F.: colloq.*), usurer, Shylock.
pawnshop, loan company, popshop (*slang*), *mont-de-piété* (*F.*), spout (*slang*), uncle's (*slang*), three balls, golden balls.
II. *Verbs.* **lend,** advance, accommodate with; lend on security, loan (*chiefly U. S.*), let out, place (*or* put) out to interest, place, put, intrust, invest; embark, risk, venture, sink.
grant, furnish, give, impart, contribute, bestow, afford, confer (*as, to* lend *aid*).
let, lease, hire, rent, demise (*law*); sublet, sublease, underlet.
III. *Adverbs.* **in advance,** on loan, on security.
See also SECURITY.—*Antonyms.* See BORROWING.

LENGTH.—I. *Nouns.* **length,** longitude (*chiefly jocose or tech.*), longness (*rare*), extent, span, fly (*as of a flag*), measure, distance, mileage; range, reach, compass, magnitude, size, limit; lengthiness, prolixity, amplification; quantity (*prosody and phonetics*).
line, row, series, sequence, succession, chain, concatenation, train, string, queue, stream, course; bar, rule, stripe, streak, stroke; chord, radius.
[*of time*] **duration,** extent, stretch, continuance; term, space, period.
[*single piece*] **piece,** portion, part, fragment, coil, roll, run (*as, a* length *of rope*).
lengthening, prolongation, production, protraction; elongation, stretching, stretch, tension, extension.
linear measure, measurement of length, lineal measure; line, nail, inch, hand, palm, foot, cubit, yard, ell, fathom, rood, pole, furlong, mile, knot (*naut.*), league; chain; meter, kilometer, centimeter, etc.
II. *Verbs.* **be long,** stretch out, sprawl; extend to, reach to, stretch to; "drag its slow length along" (Pope).

lengthen, let out, extend, elongate, stretch, prolong, produce (*geom.*), protract; draw out, finedraw, wiredraw, spin out.
[*in military usage*] rake (*as with gunfire*), enfilade, sweep.
III. *Adjectives.* lengthy (*used of speech, writing, etc.*), long, longish, protracted, drawn out, interminable, diffuse, prolix, sesquipedalian, long-winded, tedious, wearisome, tiresome.
long, extended, elongated, elongate (*rare*), lengthened, outstretched; protracted, prolonged, great; far-reaching, far-seeing, distant, far-away.
[*extended in time*] **lasting,** continuing, enduring; tedious, long-drawn, long-spun, long-winded, prolix; slow, tardy, dilatory, delayed, lingering.
[*in phonetics and prosody*] prolonged, relatively more prolonged, sustained; accented, stressed: *opposite of* short.
tall, lengthy (*colloq. in this sense*), high, lofty; lank, lanky, long-limbed, rangy, gangling (*colloq.*).
linear, lineal, longitudinal, direct; serial, running, consecutive.
[*in criminology*] **long-headed,** dolichocephalic (*opposite of* brachycephalic), dolichocephalous.
IV. *Adverbs.* **lengthwise,** longitudinally, along, endlong; in a line, tandem, from end to end, from stem to stern, over all, fore and aft; from head to foot, from top to toe.
See also DIFFUSENESS, DURABILITY, HEIGHT, SLOWNESS.—*Antonyms.* See BREADTH, CONTRACTION, SHORTNESS.

---

lenient, *adj.* easy, tolerant, gentle. See MILDNESS.
lens, *n.* eyepiece, ocular. See OPTICAL, INSTRUMENTS.
less, *adj.* lower, inferior; smaller, lesser. See INFERIORITY, SMALLNESS.
less, *adv.* to a smaller extent, not so much. See DEDUCTION.
lessen, *v.* reduce, diminish, moderate, lower, shorten. See DECREASE, TAKING (*take in*).
lesson, *n.* recitation, instruction; exercise, task. See TEACHING.
let, *v.* lease, rent; allow, admit. See LENDING, PERMISSION.
lethargy, *n.* drowsiness, apathy, stupor. See INSENSIBILITY.

LETTER.—I. *Nouns.* **letter,** character, symbol, type, hieroglyphic; capital, majuscule (*paleography*), uncial, upper case (*printing*); small letter, lower case (*printing*), minuscule (*paleography*); alphabet, ABC; consonant, vowel, diphthong, mute, surd, sonant, liquid, nasal, labial, palatal, cerebral, dental, guttural.
syllable, unit of pronunciation, single utterance, phone (*phonetics*); monosyllable, dissyllable, polysyllable; prefix, suffix, affix, particle.
spelling, orthography; phonetic spelling, phonetics; transliteration.
cipher, device, monogram, anagram; acrostic, double acrostic; code, cryptograph, cryptogram.
epistle, missive, communication, line (*colloq.*), note, billet, message; decretal (*eccl.*), decretal epistle, rescript; bull (*papal*).
[*in plural*] **letters,** literature, *belles-lettres* (*F.*), polite literature; learning, erudition (*as, a man of* letters).
II. *Verbs.* **letter,** inscribe, stamp, mark, sign, initial.
cipher, write in cipher, code; decipher, decode, transliterate, reveal.
spell, orthographize, form words, trace out.
III. *Adjectives.* **lettered,** inscribed, stamped, marked (*as with letters*).
literate, educated, cultivated, cultured; learned, erudite, literary (*as, a* lettered *person*).
literal, verbal, written, alphabetical; syllabic, sonorous; strict, true, close.
[*in phonetics*] **voiced,** (*as,* b, d, g, m, v), tonic, sonant, vocalized, vocal, sonantized (*rare*), phonetic, intonated, subvocal, subtonic, phthongal; soft, weak, flat: *opposite of* voiceless.
voiceless (*as* p, f, s, t, k), toneless, surd, nonvocal, nonsonant, nonintoned, breathed; hard, strong, sharp: *opposite of* voiced.
mute, silent, unpronounced, unuttered, unarticulated; stopped (*as the consonants* p, b, t, d, k, g), shut, checked.
See also CORRESPONDENCE, PRINTING, WRITING.

letter carrier, postman, mailman, mail carrier. See CARRIER, MESSENGER.
level, *adj.* even, equal; flat, plane, smooth; horizontal; well-balanced, steady; uniform. See EQUALITY, FLATNESS, HORIZONTALITY, INEXCITABILITY, UNIFORMITY.
level, *v.* raze, lay in ruins; roll, flatten. See DESTRUCTION, SMOOTHNESS.
lever, *n.* crowbar, pry, handspike, arm. See ELEVATION, INSTRUMENT.
leverage, *n.* advantage; hold, power, force. See PURCHASE.

LEVITY.—I. *Nouns.* **levity,** lightness, buoyancy, imponderability, volatility, airiness, levitation; fermentation, effervescence, ebullience *or* ebulliency.
[*comparisons*] feather, fluff, down, thistledown, cobweb, gossamer, straw, cork, bubble, mote, dust, air, ether.
leaven, ferment, yeast, barm; zyme, enzyme, diastase, pepsin (*all chem.*).
frivolity, jocularity, flightiness, unsteadiness, fickleness, wantonness, inconstancy, changeableness, inconsideration, thoughtlessness.
II. *Verbs.* **levitate,** become (*or* make) buoyant, float, swim, rise, soar, hang, waft; uplift, upraise, buoy up: *opposite of* gravitate.
ferment, work, raise; leaven, pepsinate (*tech.*), effervesce.
III. *Adjectives.* **levitative,** buoyant, floating, floaty, light, gossamery, volatile, subtle, ethereal, airy, imponderable, imponderous.
fermentative, fermenting, yeasty, barmy, frothy, foamy.
[*in chemistry*] zymotic, zymic, enzymic, enzymatic (*rare*), zymogenic, zymolytic, diastatic, peptic.

See also CHANGEABLENESS, IRRESOLUTION, UNIMPORTANCE.—*Antonyms.* See GRAVITY.

---

levy, *n.* muster, draft; tax, assessment. See COMBATANT, PRICE.
lewd, *adj.* licentious, lustful, gross, obscene. See IMPURITY.
lexicographer, *n.* dictionary maker, lexicologist. See WORD.

LIABILITY.—I. *Nouns.* **liability,** liableness, accountability, accountableness, responsibility, answerableness; possibility, chance, accident, casualty, contingency, exposedness.
[*in plural*] **liabilities,** obligations, debts: *opposite of* assets.
II. *Verbs.* **be liable,** incur, lay oneself open to, be subjected to, run the chance, stand a chance; lie under, expose oneself to, open a door to.
III. *Adjectives.* **liable,** subject, in danger, open to, exposed to, apt to, obnoxious to (*now rare*), answerable, accountable, amenable, responsible, dependent on.
contingent, incidental, possible, casual, accidental, chance, fortuitous; on the cards, within range of, at the mercy of; provisional, conditional, provisory, dependent.

See also DEBT, DUTY.—*Antonyms.* See DERELICTION, EXEMPTION.

---

liar, *n.* prevaricator, fibber, story-teller (*colloq.*). See DECEIVER.
libel, *n.* slander, calumny, lampoon. See DETRACTION.

LIBERALITY.—I. *Nouns.* **liberality,** generosity, open-handedness, large-heartedness, free giving, munificence; bounteousness, hospitality, charity, philanthropy.
donation, gift, grant, present, gratuity, benefaction, largess, bounty.
broad-mindedness, open-mindedness, toleration, tolerance, catholicity, magnanimity, large-mindedness, candor, impartiality.
II. *Verbs.* **be liberal,** spend freely, shower down upon, spare no expense, open one's purse strings, give *carte blanche* (*F.*), give with both hands; keep open house.
liberalize, make liberal, broaden, widen, expand, catholicize, democratize.
III. *Adjectives.* **liberal,** generous, charitable, hospitable; bountiful, beneficent, free-handed, bounteous, ample, large, abundant, handsome; unsparing, ungrudging; unselfish; open-handed, large-hearted; munificent, princely; free, unrestricted.

broad-minded, unprejudiced, open-minded, tolerant, magnanimous, unbigoted, broad, independent, eclectic, catholic, liberalistic, democratic; candid, impartial.
IV. *Adverbs.* **liberally,** generously, etc. (see *adjectives*); ungrudgingly, unstintedly, with open hands.

See also BENEFACTOR, BENEVOLENCE, BREADTH, EXPENDITURE, GIVING.—*Antonyms.* See ECONOMY, NARROWNESS, PARSIMONY.

LIBERATION.—I. *Nouns.* **liberation,** freeing, liberating, deliverance, loosing, enlargement (*setting at large*), release, emancipation, enfranchisement, disenthrallment *or* disenthralment, disimprisonment, manumission; redemption, extrication; acquittance, absolution, acquittal, discharge, dismissal; rescue, escape, liberty, freedom.
[*in chemistry*] separation, disengagement, analysis, release from combination (*as gases*).
liberator, deliverer, emancipator, rescuer, redeemer, preserver.
II. *Verbs.* **liberate,** free, set free, emancipate, release, disenthrall, disimprison, enfranchise, manumit; demobilize, disband, discharge, dismiss; let go, let loose, let out, deliver, rescue; absolve, acquit, reprieve.
unfetter, untie, loose, loosen, relax; unbolt, unbar, unhand, unfasten, unbind, unchain, disengage, disentangle; clear, extricate.
[*in chemistry*] separate, disengage, analyse, free from combination.
III. *Adjectives.* **liberated,** freed, released, etc. (see *verbs*); out of harness; one's own master; at large, at liberty, free.

See also ACQUITTAL, DELIVERANCE, DISJUNCTION, ESCAPE, FREEDOM.—*Antonyms.* See RESTRAINT.

LIBERTINE.—*Nouns.* **libertine,** voluptuary, rake, *roué* (*F.*), debauchee, deceiver, Lothario, Don Juan.
harlot, courtesan, strumpet, prostitute, unfortunate, frail (*slang*), broad (*slang*), wanton, demimondaine, *lorette* (*F.*), *cocotte* (*F.*), pick-up, wren (*slang*), chippy (*U. S. slang*), streetwalker, woman of the town, woman of easy virtue, *fille de joie* (*F.*), Cyprian, demirep, white slave; Jezebel, Messalina, Delilah, Thais, Phryne, Aspasia, Lais.
mistress, paramour, kept woman, hetæra *or* hetaira (*ancient Greece*), concubine, doxy (*archaic or dial.*), leman (*archaic*), sultana, *bona roba* (*It.*).
procurer, pimp, pander, mackerel (*archaic*), *maquereau* (*F.: slang*); procuress (*fem.*), bawd, *conciliatrix* (*L.*), *entremetteuse* (*F.*).

See also DRUNKENNESS, IMPURITY.—*Antonyms.* See GOOD MAN, GOOD WOMAN, PURITY.

---

liberty, *n.* independence, emancipation, privilege, franchise, exemption, right. See FREEDOM.
librarian, *n.* bibliothec (*rare*), curator. See BOOK.
library, *n.* public library, bibliotheca. See BOOK.
license, *n.* lawlessness, laxity, unrestraint, licentiousness; permit, authority. See FREEDOM, PERMISSION.
[1]**lie,** *v.* fib, deceive, tell a lie. See FALSEHOOD.
[2]**lie,** *v.* repose, recline; be, remain; be located. See HORIZONTALITY, PRESENCE, SITUATION.

LIFE.—I. *Nouns.* **life,** vitality, being, existence, animate existence, essence, soul, animation; life force, vital principle, vital spark, vital flame, lifeblood; respiration, breath, breath of life; vivification, vitalization; growth force (*or* energy), bathmism (*biol.*); revival, revivification.
living being, living creature, person; living beings (*collectively*), living organisms (*as, marine* life).
human existence, period (*or* duration) of life, lifetime; biography, memoir (*as, a short* life; *the* life *of Shelley*).
manner of living, mode of life, course of living, course, career; human affairs, social manners.

vivacity, animation, energy, liveliness, sprightliness, alertness, spirit, vigor, activity (*as, full of* life); vivifying influence, moving spirit (*as, the* life *of the party*).
science of life, physiology, biology, biochemistry, embryology.
II. *Verbs.* **live,** be alive, breathe, subsist, exist, be, walk the earth; continue in life (*or* existence), continue, remain, endure; fare.
be born, see the light, come into the world; quicken, revive; come to life.
give birth to, bring to life, bring forth, produce, bear; put life into, vitalize; vivify, reanimate, restore, resuscitate, revivify.
dwell, reside, abide, stay, lodge, domicile, sojourn, hang out (*slang*).
III. *Adjectives.* **living,** alive, live, existing, viable (*said of a newborn infant*); breathing, quick (*archaic*), animate, alive and kicking (*colloq.*), tenacious of life; vital, vivifying.
[*in biology*] organic, organized; biotic, zoëtic.
[*not dead or outworn*] **vigorous,** active, energetic, ardent, brisk, humming (*slang*), operative, working; unquenched, unexhausted, burning; quickening, enlivening, refreshing.
vivacious, lively, animated, sprightly, spirited, alert, sportive, light-hearted.
[*true to life*] **lifelike,** vivid, clear, strong, striking, resembling, resemblant (*rare*), speaking (*as, a* living *portrait*).
See also ACTIVITY, EXISTENCE, PERMANENCE, PRESENCE, RESTORATION, WORLD.—*Antonyms.* See DEATH.

---

lifeless, *adj.* dead, defunct; inactive, torpid. See DEATH, INERTNESS.
lifelike, *adj.* faithful, exact, true, accurate. See COPY, LIFE, SIMILARITY.
lift, *v.* rise; raise, hoist, elevate. See ASCENT, ELEVATION.
ligature, *n.* slur (*music*); cord, tie, link, band, bracket, brace. See MUSIC, VINCULUM.

LIGHT.—I. *Nouns.* **light,** ray, beam, stream (*of light*), streak, pencil, sunbeam, moonbeam; aurora, dawn, daybreak, daylight, day, sunshine, sunlight, sun, starlight, moonlight; illumination, radiation, phosphorescence, lucency, lightness; glare, glow, afterglow.
[*phenomena*] reflection, reflex, refraction, dispersion, interference, polarization.
halo, glory, nimbus, aureole, *vesica piscis* (*L.: eccl. art*), aura, corona.
lustre *or* lustre, sheen, shimmer, gloss, brightness, shining, glowing, resplendence, brilliancy, splendor, effulgence, radiance, iridescence, refulgence *or* refulgency, luminosity, luminousness.
flash, gleam, sparkle, glint, glitter, coruscation, scintillation, flame, blaze, glare, shimmer, spark, scintilla, glance, glisten.
lightning, levin (*poetic*), fulguration (*rare*), fulminating, fulmination, thunderbolt, bolt.
science of light: optics, photology, photics, photometry, catoptrics; radiology, photography; phototelegraphy, radiotelegraphy; radioscopy, radiotherapy, ray-therapy; X-rays, Röntgen rays; ultra-violet ray, infra-red rays.
pane, windowpane; quarrel (*arch.*), quirk (*diamond-shaped pane*); square of glass, compartment, panel (*as of a stained-glass window*), skylight, fanlight; sash, window.
enlightenment, illumination, *Aufklärung* (*Ger.: philos.*); insight, knowledge, education, learning, comprehension, elucidation, *éclaircissement* (*F.*), explanation, explication.
appearance, aspect, view, phase, look, complexion; angle, viewpoint, point of view.
II. *Verbs.* **light,** ignite, kindle, enkindle, set fire to, set burning; rekindle, relume, relight.
illuminate, brighten, illumine, illume (*poetic*), light up, lighten, enlighten, irradiate.
shine, glow, glitter, glisten, gleam; flare, blaze, glare, shimmer, glimmer, flicker, sparkle, scintillate, coruscate, flash, beam.
dazzle, bedazzle, daze, blind, bewilder, confuse.
III. *Adjectives.* [1]**light** (*not dark*), bright, clear, shiny, sunny, lucent, ablaze, aglow, cloudless, unobscured, unclouded, sunshiny.
pale, whitish, white, blond, colorless, bleached, wan, pallid, wannish, faint, dim, ashen (*as,* light *complexion;* **light** *gray*).

luminous, shining, bright, radiant, brilliant, illuminated, illuminate (*archaic*), nitid, lustrous, vivid, splendid, lucid, resplendent, refulgent, lambent; fulgurant, flashing, scintillant, phosphorescent.
glossy, burnished, glassy, sheeny, shiny, polished.
[*scientific*] optic, optical, catoptric *or* catoptrical; actinic, radioactive, radiological, photological, photic, photogenic (*biol.*), photometric *or* photometrical, photographic.

See also APPEARANCE, CALEFACTION, HEAT, KNOWLEDGE, LUMINARY.—*Antonyms.* See DARKNESS.

LIGHTNESS.—I. *Nouns.* **lightness,** buoyancy, airiness, levity; frivolity, etc. (see *adjectives*).
II. *Verbs.* **lighten** (*make less heavy*), disburden, ease, make easier, make lighter; relieve, alleviate, allay, assuage, soothe, mitigate, calm; cheer, gladden.
III. *Adjectives.* **[2]light** (*not heavy*), feathery, airy, ethereal, buoyant, floating, volatile, imponderable; portable, transportable.
[*of food*] digestible, eupeptic, peptic, easy to digest; moderate, frugal; well leavened, not soggy (*as pastry*), not strong (*as wine*).
[*of soil*] porous, loose, sandy, open, friable, pulverable.
[*of a syllable or vowel*] unaccented, unemphatic, unstressed, unemphasized, weak, obscure.
frivolous, light-minded, thoughtless, unsteady, unsettled, volatile, fickle, flighty, inconstant; undignified, flippant, trifling; light-headed, dizzy, delirious.
wanton, wayward, forward, perverse; loose, lax, unchaste, immoral.
cheerful, gay, light-hearted, sanguine, airy, buoyant, gladsome, happy, sunny, cheery, genial, smiling, jolly, jocund, bright, blithe (*as, a* light *heart*).
nimble, active, brisk, swift, quick, agile, tripping, fleet-footed, light-footed, light-heeled, light-limbed, graceful, quick-moving.
unimportant, slight, small, trifling, trivial, inconsiderable, inappreciable, minor, insignificant, immaterial (*as, make* light *of*).
easy, unoppressive, unburdensome, unexacting; facile, gentle, effortless, soft, moderate, convenient (*as,* light *taxes;* light *task*).
IV. *Adverbs.* lightly, gently, moderately, delicately; nimbly, briskly, swiftly; frivolously, thoughtlessly; flippantly, slightingly, indifferently; cheerfully, gayly; wantonly, etc. (see *adjectives*).

See also CHEERFULNESS, FACILITY, LEVITY, UNIMPORTANCE, WEAKNESS.—*Antonyms.* See HEAVINESS.

---

lightning, *n.* electrical discharge. See LIGHT.
light year, unit of stellar distance. See SPACE.
like, *adj.* resembling, analagous, twin. See SIMILARITY.
like, *v.* enjoy, relish, fancy. See PLEASURE.
likeness, *n.* shape, form, guise; portrait, copy; resemblance. See APPEARANCE, REPRESENTATION, SIMILARITY.
liking, *n.* fondness, predilection, inclination, appetite. See TASTE.
limb, *n.* scamp, imp; member, arm, wing, leg, branch, bough. See BAD MAN, PART.

LIMIT.—I. *Nouns.* **limit,** boundary, bound, border, edge, utmost extent, *ne plus ultra* (*L.*), bourn, verge, end, extreme, pale, confine, term, period, termination, terminus, terminal; boundary line, frontier, march, mark (*hist.*); landmark, pillars of Hercules; Rubicon, turning point.
limitation, restriction, qualification, condition, reservation, circumscription, finiteness, restraint; stint, allotment, allowance, quota.
II. *Verbs.* **limit,** bound, compass, confine, define, determine, delimit, demarcate, circumscribe, restrain, restrict, stint, condition, qualify.
III. *Adjectives.* **limited,** circumscribed, circumscript, restrained, restricted, narrow, narrowed, confined, bounded, finite, limitate (*rare*), conditioned, qualified; bordering, border, boundary, frontier, terminal, limitary, restrictive.
definite, determinate, fixed, clear-cut, defined, specific, exact, precise, unequivocal.

See also CIRCUMSCRIPTION, CONTRACTION, EDGE, END, PERIOD, QUALIFICATION, RESTRAINT, SMALLNESS.—*Antonyms.* See FREEDOM, INFINITY.

limp, *adj.* flabby, flexible, flaccid, flimsy, drooping, soft. See SOFTNESS.
limp, *v.* hobble, hitch, halt, walk lamely. See SLOWNESS.
line, *v.* cover, interline. See LINING.
line, *n.* occupation, branch, department; route, course, way; streak, stroke, mark; row, file, rank, series; lineage, descent; string, cord, rope, cable. See BUSINESS, DIRECTION, INDICATION, LENGTH, POSTERITY, VINCULUM.
lineage, *n.* family, ancestry, line. See DESCENT, SIDE.
lineal, *adj.* linear, longitudinal; direct, hereditary. See LENGTH, POSTERITY.
lineament, *n.* feature, outline. See APPEARANCE.
linear, *adj.* lineal; narrow, threadlike. See LENGTH, NARROWNESS.
linear measure, measurement of length. See LENGTH.
linger, *v.* loiter, delay, remain, tarry, dawdle. See LATENESS.
lingua franca, pidgin English, Hindustani, Volapük, Esperanto, etc. See NEOLOGY.
linguist, *n.* glossolalist, glottologist, polyglot. See SCHOLAR.
linguistic, *adj.* glossological, philological, linguistical. See LANGUAGE.
linguistics, *n.* comparative philology, linguistic science. See LANGUAGE.

LINING.—I. *Nouns.* **lining,** coating, inner coating, inner surface; filling, stuffing, wadding, padding; facing, bushing; sheathing, wainscoting, wainscot, panelwork, brattice (*mining*).
II. *Verbs.* **line,** stuff, incrust, wad, pad, quilt, fur, fill, face, ceil, overlay, bush, sheathe, wainscot.
Antonyms. See COVERING.

---

link, *n.* bond, tie; loop. See RELATION, VINCULUM.
link, *v.* unite, couple, connect. See JUNCTION.
lion, *n.* king of beasts; celebrity. See ANIMAL, REPUTE.
lip, *n.* margin, rim, labium (*tech.*); *Slang*: impudence. See EDGE, INSOLENCE

LIQUEFACTION.—I. *Nouns.* **liquefaction,** liquescence *or* liquescency, deliquescence; liquation, eliquation, melting, fusion; thaw; solubleness; dissolution.
solvent, dissolvent, resolvent, resolutive, menstruum, diluent; dissolving agent.
solution, decoction, infusion. mixture, apozem (*rare*), cremor (*rare*), lixivium, lye; flux.
II. *Verbs.* **liquefy,** liquidize, fluidize, fluidify; melt, fuse, dissolve, resolve, deliquesce, liquate, run; hold in solution.
[*in phonetics*] palatalize make palatal, front, soften (*as*, gn *in* "*mignonette*"; gl *in* "*seraglio*").
III. *Adjectives.* **liquescent,** liquefiable, soluble, dissolvable, dissoluble, deliquescent, melting, liquefying, colliquative (*med.*); diluting, diluent, solvent, dissolvent, resolvent, resolutive (*rare*), liquefactive.
See also FLUIDITY.—*Antonyms.* See DENSITY, VAPORIZATION.

---

liquid, *adj.* flowing, fluid; vowel-like. See FLUIDITY, PURITY (*of sounds*), SMOOTHNESS.
liquidate, *v.* discharge, settle, clear, pay up. See PAYMENT.
liquor, *n.* drink, alcoholic drink; liquid, fluid; dram, beverage. See DRUNKENNESS, FLUIDITY, FOOD.

LIST.—I. *Nouns.* **list,** catalogue *or* catalog, inventory, schedule, scroll, register, roll, rota, panel (*jury*), class roll, muster roll, muster, beadroll (*esp. R. C. Ch.*), roll of honor, roster, poll, ballot, ticket (*U. S. politics*), slate (*polit. cant*), docket (*U. S.*); prospectus, programme *or* program, syllabus, synopsis, scheme. canon, contents, index, table, bulletin, calendar; census, statistics, returns, cadastre *or* cadaster, *cadre* (*F.*), directory, gazetteer, atlas; book, ledger; account, invoice, bill, manifest, bill of lading; menu, bill of fare; score, tally, file, row.
dictionary, wordbook, lexicon, glossary, vocabulary, gradus (*prosody*), thesaurus (*pl.* thesauri).

II. *Verbs.* **list,** register, enter, record, inscribe, tally, enroll, inventory, schedule, catalogue, file, index, docket (*U. S.*), calendar, tabulate, post (*bookkeeping*), slate (*U. S.*), book, invoice, bill, manifest, tabulate, census, impanel (*as jurors*), enroll, draft, poll.

See also CONTINUITY, RECORD.

---

listen, *v.* give ear, hearken, attend. See HEARING.
listless, *adj.* inattentive, spiritless, uninterested. See INDIFFERENCE.
lists, *n. pl.* field, ring. See ARENA.
literal, *adj.* verbal, written; exact, word-for-word, precise. See LETTER, MEANING.
literally, *adv.* verbatim, *literatim* (*L.*). See IMITATION.
literary, *adj.* bookish, learned, belletristic. See BLUE, KNOWLEDGE, LANGUAGE.
literate, *adj.* educated; learned, literary. See LETTER.
literature, *n.* literary work, *belles-lettres* (*F.*), letters. See LANGUAGE.
litigant, *n.* suitor; plaintiff, defendant. See LAWSUIT.
litigate, *v.* go to law, contest. See LAWSUIT.
litigious, *adj.* contentious, litigant; litigatory. See LAWSUIT.
litter, *n.* jumble, disarray, mess; stretcher, palanquin. See DISORDER, VEHICLE.
litter, *v.* jumble, disorder, confuse, scatter. See DERANGEMENT.

LITTLENESS.—I. *Nouns.* **littleness,** smallness, etc. (see *adjectives*); exiguity, inextension, parvitude (*rare*); abridgment, compendium, abstract, summary, epitome, brief, digest, synopsis, syllabus; rudiment, embryo; vanishing point; microcosm (*opposite of* macrocosm).
dwarf, pygmy, Negrillo (*African*), Negrito (*Asiatic*), midget, Lilliputian, Pigwiggen, elf; doll, puppet, manikin; Tom Thumb, hop-o'-my-thumb, homunculus.
[*in bacteriology*] **microbe,** germ, microörganism, bacterium (*pl.* bacteria), bacillus (*pl.* bacilli), microzyme (*biol.*), microphyte (*bot.*), micrococcus, zoöglœa, schizomycete (*bot.*); spore, zygote (*bot.*), zygospore (*opposite of* oöspore), arthrospore (*opposite of* endospore), zoöspore, gamete (*biol.*), gonidium (*bot.*).
[*in zoölogy*] **animalcule,** animalculum (*pl.* animalcula), protozoan, rhizopod, foraminifer, mastigopod, mastigophore, amœba, infusorian, rotifer, paramecium, radiolarian, gregarine, gregarinid, protamœban; moner, moneron; proton, anlage (*Ger. pl.* anlagen), primordium (*pl.* primordia).
insect, arthropod, hexapod, ephemerid, ephemera, bug (*popular, U. S.*), emmet, ant, fly, gnat, arachnid, mite, grub, larva.
particle, speck, dot, iota, mote, scrap, morsel, fraction, fragment, jot, mite (*colloq.*), crumb, grain; stiver, sou; spark, scintilla, powder, dust; atom, molecule, monad, ion, magneton (1/100 *of the diameter of an atom*), electron, corpuscle.
little, small amount (*or* quantity), trifle, modicum, whit, dab, bit (*colloq.*), pinch, dash, touch, tinge; small scale, small degree, miniature.
a little (*used adverbially*), rather, somewhat, to some extent.
[*measurement of minute distances*] micrometer, vernier, interferometer.
[*study of microscopic objects*] **microscopy,** micrography, microphysics; microphotography, photomicography, photomicroscopy; micromotion, microscopic movement.
II. *Verbs.* **be little,** lie in a nutshell; became small, decrease; contract.
III. *Adjectives.* **little** (*opposite of* big, great), small (*opposite of* large), minute, fine, diminutive, exiguous; limited, cramped; puny, tiny, wee (*colloq.*), young, elfin, miniature, pocket, undersized, stunted, minikin, runty (*U. S.*), dwarf, dwarfed, dwarfish, nanoid, pygmy, Lilliputian; infinitesimal, homeopathic, microscopic, micromotion, invisible, imperceptible, evanescent, atomic, molecular, microbic, microbial, animalcular, embryonic; insignificant, inconsiderable, slight, unimportant; brief, short (*in duration*).
contemptible, mean, sorry, beggarly, paltry, trivial, petty, small, narrow, illiberal, ungenerous, shallow, scurvy, low.

IV. *Adverbs.* little, slightly, not much, somewhat, rather; in a small compass, in a nutshell; on a small scale.

See also CONTRACTION. DECREASE, IMPIETY (*bigoted*), SHORTNESS, SMALLNESS, THOUGHT, UNIMPORTANCE.—*Antonyms.* See SIZE.

---

live, *v.* exist, be; dwell, reside. See LIFE.
liveliness, *n.* life, alacrity, vivacity, animation. See CHEERFULNESS.
lively, *adj.* alert, brisk, numble, quick; gay, jolly, animated. See ACTIVITY, CHEERFULNESS.
living, *adj.* alive, existing, breathing; vital. See LIFE.
lizard, *n.* lacertian (*zoöl.*), newt, gecko, etc. See ANIMAL (*reptiles*).
load, *n.* cargo, freight; burden, weight. See [2]CONTENT, HEAVINESS.
loadstone, *n.* lodestar, polestar, magnet. See ATTRACTION.
loafer, *n.* slacker, idler, time-killer, lounger. See DERELICTION, INACTIVITY.
loathe, *v.* despise, abhor, detest, hate, abominate. See DISLIKE.
local, *adj.* regional, sectional, topographic, limited. See REGION, SITUATION.

LOCATION.—I. *Nouns.* **location,** locating, establishing, localization, delimitation, establishment, lodgement, settlement, installation, stationing, fixation, emplacement, orientation; placing, disposition, allocation, arrangement; stowage packing, lading.

place, situation, position, spot, locality, locale (*properly* local), region, tract, part, neighborhood, district; site, station, post, locus (*L. pl.* loci), whereabouts *or* whereabout.

anchorage, mooring, roadstead, road, harborage, harbor, shelter.

park (*as for wagons or military supplies*), *parc* (*F.*), parking space (*as for automobiles*), artillery encampment, artillery park.

habitation, abode, domicile, residence; encampment, camp, settlement, plantation, colony; barracks, cantonment, quarters; "a local habitation and a name" (*Midsummer Night's Dream*).

naturalization, acclimatization, acclimation (*esp. without man's agency*), habituation, inurement, domestication, colonization.

II. *Verbs.* **locate,** place, situate, establish, settle, repose, set, seat, put, lay, deposit, plant, store, station, park (*as an automobile*), pitch, camp, post, quarter lodge, localize, stow, house, cradle, install; fix, root, graft; load, lade, pack; moor, tether, picket, tie, stake; embed, imbed, insert.

billet on, quarter upon, saddle with.

settle, take up one's abode (*or* residence), settle down, take root, strike root, anchor, cast anchor, establish (*or* locate) oneself; keep house, bach (*slang*); squat. burrow, get a footing; bivouac, encamp, pitch one's tent: *in this sense,* locate *is U. S. colloq.*

naturalize, acclimatize, acclimate (*esp. without man's agency*), habituate, inure, domesticate; found, colonize, people.

determine (*the location of*), mark off, mark out, delimit, limit, delimitate, localize, position, bound, define (*as, to* locate *a mining claim*).

discover, detect, find, spot (*colloq.*), catch, discern, see espy, descry (*as, to* locate *a leak*).

III. *Adjectives.* **located,** placed, etc. (see *verbs*); situate, ensconced, imbedded, rooted; moored, at anchor.

See also HABITATION, INSERTION, PLACE, PRESENCE, REGION, SITUATION.—*Antonyms.* See DISPLACEMENT.

---

lock, *v.* fasten, secure. See JUNCTION.
lodge, *v.* stop, remain; reside, dwell. See LOCATION, PRESENCE.
lofty, *adj.* elevated, high; proud, lordly; exalted, sublime. See HEIGHT, PRIDE, VIGOR.
logical, *adj.* deducible, consistent. See REASONING.
loincloth, *n.* dhoti (*Hindu*), lungi (*Burmese*). See CLOTHING.
loiter, *v.* lag, linger, dawdle, saunter. See SLOWNESS.
lone, *adj.* sole, only, single, solitary. See UNITY.

lonely, *adj.* unfrequented; lonesome, solitary. See SECLUSION, UNITY (*alone*).
long, *adj.* extended, great; tiresome, tedious; extensive. See LENGTH.
long, *adv.* for a long time, to a great extent, all along. See DURABILITY.
long-headed, *adj.* discerning, shrewd; dolichocephalic. See INTELLIGENCE, LENGTH.
longing, *n.* yearning, craving, eagerness. See DESIRE.
look, *v.* seem, appear; heed, notice; see, eye, glance. See APPEARANCE, ATTENTION, VISION.
look, *n.* aspect, phase, expression; glance, glimpse, view, gaze, contemplation. See APPEARANCE, VISION.
lookout, *n.* outlook, view, prospect; beacon, watchtower, crow's-nest (*naut.*); scout, spy, watch, sentinel. See APPEARANCE, VISION, WARNING.
loop, *n.* eyelet, eye, circlet, ring, hoop, grommet, coil, noose, fold, frog; circuit. See CIRCULARITY, CURVATURE.
loose, *adj.* unfastened, detached; uncompact, open, uncombined; relaxed, slack; dissipated, immoral; vague, rambling. See FREEDOM, INCOHERENCE, LAXITY, SOPHISTRY.
loose, *v.* unfasten, detach, free, release. See LIBERATION.
loosen, *v.* detach, unfasten; slacken, relax. See INCOHERENCE.
loot, *n.* plunder, spoils, prize. See BOOTY.

LOQUACITY.—I. *Nouns.* **loquacity,** loquaciousness, talkativeness, garrulity, multiloquence, polylogy (*rare*); verbosity, volubility, eloquence, fluency, flow of words, *copia verborum* (*L.*), *flux de paroles* (*F.*), gift of the gab (*colloq.*); effusion, effusiveness, gush, slush.
chatter, jabber, prattle, twaddle, gabble, small talk, idle talk, gossip, prate, *bavardage* (*F.*), cackle, *caqueterie* (*F.*), rattle, clack, gibble-gabble, blather *or* blether, talkee-talkee (*colloq.*), gab (*colloq.*), jaw (*low*), hot air (*slang*), boloney (*slang*).
talker, chatterer, chatterbox, rattle, windbag (*slang*), blatherskite (*U. S. colloq.*), babbler, ranter, proser, driveler, gossip, magpie, jay, parrot; *moulin à paroles* (*F.*).
II. *Verbs.* **be loquacious,** talk glibly, pour forth, prate, palaver, patter, prose, maunder, chatter, blab, gush, prattle, jabber, jaw (*low*), babble, gabble, cackle, clack, blather *or* blether, expatiate, gossip, talk at random, talk nonsense.
III. *Adjectives.* **loquacious,** talkative, garrulous, multiloquent, polyloquent (*rare*), long-winded, long-tongued, chattering, chatty, declamatory, fluent, eloquent, voluble, effusive, glib.
See also CONVERSATION, DIFFUSENESS, SPEECH.—*Antonyms.* See TACITURNITY.

---

lordly, *adj.* haughty, proud; noble, dignified. See HEIGHT, REPUTE.
lore, *n.* learning, information. See KNOWLEDGE.

LOSS.—I. *Nouns.* **loss,** destruction, ruin, perdition, wreck, shipwreck, demolition, crash, downfall, fall, undoing, overthrow, defeat, failure.
privation, bereavement, dispossession, deprivation, riddance, forfeiture, lapse; damage, harm, misfortune, injury, cost, penalty; waste, leakage, death, casualties (*mil.*).
II. *Verbs.* **lose,** incur a loss, be deprived of, fail to keep, fail to win, suffer loss (disadvantage, *or* defeat), drop (*slang*), be without, forfeit; miss, mislay, wander from, go astray.
waste, squander, dissipate, lavish, get rid of, let, slip, throw away, misspend fritter away, play ducks and drakes with.
destroy, ruin, wreck, fall, crash, shatter, break, crush out, raze, dissolve, consume, shipwreck, demolish, kill: *usually in the passive; as, the crew was* lost.
lose itself, hide (*or* obscure) itself; become obscured, become merged, become engrossed in.
III. *Adjectives.* **lost,** destroyed, ruined, wrecked, etc. (see *verbs*).
missing, absent, gone, invisible, wanting, abstracted, minus (*colloq., except in math.*), parted with; stray, strayed, wandering, astray, perplexed, bewildered.

bereft, bereaved, deprived of, shorn of, denuded, cut off; rid of, quit of, out of pocket, forfeit, unredeemed.
[*of persons*] **hardened,** insensible, obdurate, callous, unfeeling; incorrigible, irredeemable, abandoned, irreclaimable, outcast.

See also ABSENCE, DEATH, FAILURE, HOPELESSNESS, IMPENITENCE, OBLIVION, RELINQUISHMENT, UNCERTAINTY, WASTE.—*Antonyms.* See ACQUISITION, INCREASE.

---

lot, *n.* fate, fortune; portion, allotment, number. See DESTINY, QUANTITY.

LOUDNESS.—I. *Nouns.* **loudness,** noisiness, vociferance, vociferousness, clamorousness, uproariousness; sonority, sonorousness, resonance, intensity, power, vehemence.
ostentation, flashiness, showiness, garishness, gaudiness, vividness, vulgarity.
noise, din, clang, clangor, clatter, roar, uproar, charivari, hubbub, racket, ballyhoo (*colloq.*), hullabaloo, pandemonium, fracas, outcry, vociferation, clamor, shouting; blare, blast, trumpet blast, flourish of trumpets, fanfare; peal, swell, alarum, boom, detonation, explosion, crash, thunder; stentor, bomb, cannon, artillery, guns, barrage, drum fire, bombardment, *rafale* (*F.*).
II. *Verbs.* **be loud,** etc. (see *adjectives*); peal, swell, clang, clash, boom, thunder, roar; deafen, stun, rend the air, awake the echoes, resound; speak up, shout, bellow, vociferate, din, clamor.
III. *Adjectives.* **loud,** sonorous, deep, full, powerful, emphatic, vehement, noisy, blatant, clangorous, thundering, deafening, ear-splitting, piercing, shrill, obstreperous, blustering, turbulent, uproarious, clamorous, clamant, vociferant, vociferous, full-mouthed, loud-mouthed, loud-voiced, stentorian.
ostentatious, showy, flashy, garish, glaring, vivid, gaudy, pretentious, spectacular, theatrical, pompous, conspicuous, obtrusive, vulgar, offensive, unrefined.
IV. *Adverbs.* **loudly,** noisily, etc. (see *adjectives*); lustily, aloud; at the top of one's lungs, in full cry.

See also CRY, RESONANCE, ROLL, SOUND, VULGARITY.—*Antonyms.* See FAINTNESS, SILENCE.

LOVE.—I. *Nouns.* **love,** affection, fondness, liking, friendship, attachment, regard, fancy, admiration, inclination, infatuation, enthusiasm, passion, fervor, flame, rapture, devotion, yearning, tender passion, enchantment, gallantry, adoration, idolization, idolism, idolatry.
[*Christian love*] **charity,** good will, benevolence, brotherly love, fellow-feeling, heart, sympathy, tenderness, charitableness, beneficence, liberality, almsgiving.
mother love, maternal love, parental affection, natural affection, storge (*Gr.*).
charm, attractiveness, fascination, attraction, winsomeness, grace, appeal, pleasingness, affinity; popularity, popular regard.
[*god of love*] Cupid *or* Amor (*Roman*), Eros (*Gr.*), Kama (*Hindu*), Freya *or* Freyja (*Norse*); Astarte (*Phœnician*), Aphrodite (*Gr.*), Venus (*Roman*); myrtle (*sacred to Venus*).
love affair, love suit, romance, amour, intrigue, *affaire de cœur* (*F.*), *affaire d'amour* (*F.*).
lover, suitor, *fiancé* (*F.*), follower (*colloq.*), admirer, adorer, wooer, beau, boy friend (*colloq.*), inamorato (*now rare*), sweetheart, swain, young man (*colloq.*), flame (*colloq.*), love, beloved, truelove; Lothario, amorist, gallant, knight, cavalier, *cavalier servente* (*It.*), *cicisbeo* (*It.; pl. cicisbei*), *amoroso* (*It.*).
ladylove, sweetheart, sweetie (*colloq.*), Dulcinea, mistress, inamorata, darling, favorite, beloved, queen, belle, idol, angel, goddess; betrothed, *fiancée* (*F.*).
[*in tennis*] nothing, no score.
II. *Verbs.* **love,** like, fancy, care for, take an interest in, sympathize with; be in love with, regard, revere, take to, set one's affections on, adore, idolize, idolatrize, dote on (*or* upon), make much of, hold dear, prize; hug, cling to, cherish, caress, fondle, pet, feast one's eyes upon.
charm, attract, attach, fascinate, delight, captivate, bewitch, enamor, allure, transport, enchant, enrapture, turn the head.

III. *Adjectives.* **lovable,** adorable, lovely, sweet, winning, winsome, charming, engaging, interesting, lovesome (*archaic*), alluring, seductive, attractive, enchanting, captivating, fascinating, bewitching, amiable, angelic.
loved, beloved, well beloved, dearly beloved; dear, precious, darling, pet; favorite, popular.
loving, affectionate, tender, sympathetic, amorous, amatory, erotic, uxorious, lovesick, fond, ardent, impassioned, passionate, rapturous, devoted, motherly, sisterly.

See also BENEVOLENCE, DEARNESS, DESIRE, ENDEARMENT, FAVORITE, FRIENDSHIP.

---

love affair, amour, intrigue. See ENDEARMENT.
lovelorn, *adj.* jilted, forsaken. See HATE.
lovely, *adj.* exquisite, charming, delightful. See BEAUTY, PLEASURABLENESS.
lover, *n.* suitor, wooer; paramour. See LOVE.
lovesick, *adj.* languishing, pining. See ENDEARMENT.
lowborn, *adj.* baseborn, common, humble, ignoble, plebeian. See PEOPLE.
lower house, second chamber, House of Representatives, House of Commons. See COUNCIL.

LOWNESS.—I. *Nouns.* **lowness,** flatness, levelness, flattishness, depression, hollowness, hollow, deepness, depth; prostration, debasement, recumbency.
coarseness, indelicacy, baseness, offensiveness, broadness, grossness, impropriety, etc. (see *adjectives*).
vault, crypt, dungeon, cavern, cellar, cell, serdab (*archæol.*); underground room, basement; sub-basement, hold.
ground floor, street floor, *rez de chaussée* (*F.*).
low tide, low water, ebb tide, neap tide, neap: *opposite of* high tide, spring tide, flood tide.
II. *Verbs.* **be low,** lie low, underlie; crouch, cower, squat, grovel, wallow, welter.
lower, let down, pull down, haul down, take down, depress, sink, drop, dip, duck, strike (*as sail*), douse (*naut.*).
reduce, diminish, decrease, curtail, shorten, lessen, flatten, slacken, abate.
degrade, humble, debase, humiliate, abase, dishonor, disgrace.
III. *Adjectives.* **low,** not high, unelevated; flat, level, low-lying, depressed, basal, profound, deep; decumbent, prostrate; crouched, squat.
[*of sounds*] subdued, gentle, soft, moderate, grave, deep, low-pitched, low-toned.
humble (*as in rank*), unpretentious, modest, lowly, obscure, low-born, inferior, submissive, unimportant, commonplace, common, undignified, ordinary, mean, plebeian, menial.
weak (*as in strength*), feeble, exhausted, weakly, inferior, decrepit, enervated, prostrated, sickly, debilitated, asthenic (*med.*); depressed, dejected, dispirited, downcast.
unfavorable, sinister, ill, contrary, adverse, disparaging, unfriendly, depreciative (*as, a* low *opinion*).
coarse, indelicate, base, offensive, broad, low-minded, gross, improper, unbecoming, vulgar, unrefined, ill-bred, unpolished, crude; depraved, abandoned, degraded, abject, disreputable, dishonorable, mean, scurvy, rascally, low-down (*colloq.*).
[*of quantity, intensity, etc.*] **moderate,** mediocre, indifferent, subnormal; inconsiderable, trifling, petty, light, small, scant, slight, limited (*as, a* low *temperature; a* low *number*).
cheap, inexpensive, moderate, low-priced, reasonable (*as, a* low *price*).
[*of diet*] **innutritious,** ill-nourishing, innutritive, unnutritious, innutrient (*rare*), inalimental (*rare*); simple, plain, frugal, spare.
[*of a dress*] low-necked, *décolleté* (*F.*), low-cut.
lower, inferior, subordinate, subject, under, nether; less advanced (*biol.*), earlier (*geol.*), subjacent.
lowest, nethermost, lowermost, undermost.
IV. *Adverbs.* **under,** beneath, underneath, below, down, downward; underfoot, underground; downstairs, belowstairs; at a low ebb; below par.

See also BASE, CONCAVITY, DEPRESSION, FAINTNESS, FLATNESS, HORIZONTALITY, PEOPLE, SMALLNESS, SOFTNESS, VULGARITY.—*Antonyms.* See HEIGHT.

loyal, *adj.* faithful, true, leal (*poetic*), stanch, trustworthy. See PROBITY.

LUBRICATION.—I. *Nouns.* **lubrication,** lubrifaction (*rare*), lubrification (*rare*), oiling, greasing; anointing, anointment.
oiliness, unctuousness, unctuosity, oleaginousness, greasiness; smoothness, lubricity, polish, gloss, slipperiness.
lubricant, lubricator; oil, grease, dope (*slang*), plumbago, graphite, alemite (*trade name*); ointment, unguent, unguentum (*pharm.*), nard, spikenard; pomade, pomatum; salve, balm, oleamen, unction, lenitive (*med.*), emollient (*med.*); synovia (*anat.*), synovial fluid.
II. *Verbs.* **lubricate,** lubrify (*rare*), oil, grease; lather, soap; wax; anoint; pomade.
III. *Adjectives.* **lubricant,** lubricating, lubricous, oily, oleaginous, unctuous, oleous *or* oleose (*rare*), oleic (*chem.*), unguinous; unguentary, unguentous; greasy, smooth, slippery.
See also OIL, SMOOTHNESS.—*Antonyms.* See FRICTION.

---

lucid, *adj.* plain, clear, understandable; limpid, pellucid. See PERSPICUITY TRANSPARENCY.
lucidity, *n.* clarity, clearness, unambiguity. See CERTAINTY.
luck, *n.* fortune, hap; good fortune. See CHANCE, PROSPERITY.
lucky, *adj.* fortunate, favorable, providential. See TIMELINESS.
lull, *n.* pause, calm, respite. See CESSATION.

LUMINARY.—I. *Nouns.* **luminary,** light, ray, gleam, flash, beam, flame, spark, scintilla.
[*heavenly bodies*] sun, sol, orb of day, day-star (*poetic*); star, starlet, planet, nova (*astron.*); evening star, Vesper, Hesper, Hesperus; morning star, Phosphor (*poetic*), Lucifer; Cynosure, polestar, North Star, Polaris; Dog Star, Sirius, Canicula; moon, Luna, Phœbe, Cynthia; constellation; galaxy, Milky Way, *Via Lactea* (*L.*).
sun god, Helios, Phœbus Apollo, Hyperion, Sol, Ra *or* Re (*Egypt*), Shamash (*Babylon and Assyria*).
illuminant, light giver; gas, gaslight, electric light, headlight, searchlight, ceiling light (*for determining the height of clouds trigonometrically at night: aëro.*), flashlight, spotlight, limelight, calcium light; lamplight, lamp, lantern, dark lantern, bull's-eye; candle, taper, rushlight; night-light, night lamp, *veilleuse* (*F.*); torch, flambeau, link (*suggestive of the pea-soup fogs of an earlier London*), brand; gaselier, chandelier, electrolier; candelabrum, sconce, luster *or* lustre, candlestick; fireworks, pyrotechnics.
signal light, flare, flare-up, rocket, balefire, beacon fire; lighthouse.
polar lights, northern lights, merry dancers, aurora borealis (*L.*), **aurora australis** (*L.*); aurora, zodiacal light.
will-o'-the-wisp, *ignis fatuus* (*L.*), jack-o'-lantern, friar's lantern; St. Elmo's fire (*or* light), corposant; double corposant, Castor and Pollux (*naut.*).
luminescence, phosphorescence, self-luminousness, fluorescence, noctilucence (*rare*); triboluminescence, tribophosphorescence (*by friction*), chemiluminescence *or* chemicoluminescence (*by chemical action*), electroluminescence (*by electric action*), crystalloluminescence (*by crystallizing*), photoluminescence (*by exposure to light*), autoluminescence (*of radioactive bodies*); firefly, fire beetle, glowworm.
II. *Adjectives.* **self-luminous,** autoluminescent (*tech.*), phosphorescent, phosphoric, luminescent, fluorescent, noctilucent (*rare*), radiant.
See also HEAT, LIGHT, WORLD.—*Antonyms.* See SHADE.

---

luminous, *adj.* shining, bright, brilliant, radiant. See LIGHT.
lump, *n.* protuberance, bunch; mass, block; main part, bulk; total, lot. See CONVEXITY, SIZE, WHOLE.
lunatic, *n.* maniac, insane person. See MADMAN.
lung, *n.* respiratory organ, gill, branchia (*zoöl.*). See WIND.
lurch, *v.* stagger, lean, roll, sway. See OBLIQUITY.

lure, *v.* fascinate, draw, attract, allure, entice, decoy. See ATTRACTION.
lurid, *adj.* wan, dismal, stormy, gloomy, murky; ghastly, terrible; sensational, melodramatic. See DIMNESS, FEAR, YELLOW.
lurk, *v.* hide, sneak, skulk, slink. See CONCEALMENT, LATENCY.
luscious, *adj.* delicious, rich, delectable. See SAVORINESS.
luster, *n.* sheen, gloss, splendor, brightness. See LIGHT.
lusty, *adj.* stalwart, vigorous, hearty, robust. See STRENGTH.
luxuriant, *adj.* fertile, fruitful; rank, dense, abundant. See PRODUCTIVENESS, VEGETATION.
luxurious, *adj.* voluptuous, self-indulgent; gratifying, comfortable, costly. See INTEMPERANCE, PLEASURE.
luxury, *n.* indulgence, prodigalism; luxuriousness, ease, comfort. See INTEMPERANCE, PLEASURE.
lyric, *n.* poem, song, ode, canzonet. See POETRY.

M

machine, *n.* mechanism, engine; organization, ring, gang; conveyance, car. See INSTRUMENT, PARTY, VEHICLE.
mad, *adj.* crazy, demented; frenzied, wild, reckless. See INSANITY, VIOLENCE.
madam, *n.* mistress, lady, *madame* (*F.*), ma'am (*colloq.*). See TITLE, WOMAN.

MADMAN.—*Nouns.* **madman,** lunatic, maniac, bedlamite (*archaic*), raver, dement, loony *or* luny (*slang*), nut (*slang*), phrenetic; automaniac, monomaniac, paranoiac, crank (*colloq.*).

See also FOOL, INSANITY.—*Antonyms.* See SAGE.

Madonna, *n.* the Virgin Mary, Our Lady. See ANGEL.
magazine, *n.* periodical; storehouse, warehouse. See BOOK, STORE.
magic, *n.* witchcraft, necromancy, enchantment. See SORCERY.
magic, *adj.* magical, witching, weird; enchanting. See SORCERY.
magician, *n.* sorcerer, conjurer, wizard. See DECEIVER.
magisterial, *adj.* overbearing, pompous, dictatorial. See ORACLE.
magnanimous, *adj.* noble, generous, high-minded. See UNSELFISHNESS.
magnetism, *n.* attraction, magnetic power. See INFLUENCE.
magnificent, *adj.* majestic, grand, sublime, glorious. See REPUTE.
magnifier, *n.* magnifying glass, microscope. See OPTICAL INSTRUMENTS.
magnify, *v.* enlarge, augment, amplify. See INCREASE.
magnitude, *n.* size, bulk; quantity; importance. See GREATNESS.
maid, *n.* unmarried woman, virgin; girl, maidservant, help (*U. S.*). See CELIBACY, SERVANT.
maidenly, *adj.* maidenlike, girlish, gentle, modest; chaste, virgin. See WOMAN.
maidservant, *n.* maid, lady's maid, nurse, girl. See SERVANT.
mail, *n.* postal service; post, letters. See MESSENGER.
mail, *v.* post, dispatch, send (*by mail*), ship, forward, express (*U. S.*). See TRANSFER.
maim, *v.* cripple, disable, mutilate, injure. See DETERIORATION.
main, *n.* pipe, conduit; mainland; sea. See CHANNEL, LAND, OCEAN.
main, *adj.* primary, chief, principal, leading. See IMPORTANCE.
mainstay, *n.* strength, support, prop. See HOPE.
maintain, *v.* claim, assert; provide for; sustain, keep, uphold, continue. See AFFIRMATION, PRESERVATION, SUPPORT.
maintenance, *n.* defense, conservation; sustenance, livelihood, living, upkeep. See PRESERVATION, SUPPORT.

majestic, *adj.* imposing, stately, noble, magnificent, regal. See GREATNESS.
major, *adj.* higher, greater. See SUPERIORITY.
majority, *n.* manhood, adulthood, full age; greater number, bulk, preponderance; *opposite of* minority *and distinguished from* plurality. See ADOLESCENCE, PLURALITY, SUPERIORITY.
make, *v.* constitute, compose; cause, occasion, impel, force; construct, fashion, manufacture, prepare, created; devise, invent. See COMPONENT, COMPULSION, FORM.
makeshift, *n.* apology, stop-gap, shift. See SUBSTITUTION.
make-up, *n.* formation, structure, constitution. See COMPOSITION.
malady, *n.* illness, sickness, complaint, ailment. See DISEASE, DISORDER.
malcontent, *n.* faultfinder; radical, anarchist. See DISCONTENT, OPPONENT.
male, *adj.* masculine. See MAN.

MALEDICTION.—I. *Nouns.* **malediction,** curse, malison (*archaic*), imprecation, denunciation, execration; anathema, ban (*archaic or eccl.*), proscription, excommunication, commination, thunders of the Vatican, fulmination: *opposite of* benediction.
abuse, revilement, vilification, vituperation, obloquy, contumely, invective, diatribe, tongue-lashing; disparagement, calumniation, aspersion, scandalization, slander, libel, defamation, dispraise, backbiting, traduction; evil speaking, foul (bad, strong, *or* unparliamentary) language, billingsgate, blackguardism, cursing, profane swearing, expletive, oath, foul invective, ribaldry, scurrility
II. *Verbs.* **curse,** imprecate, damn, swear at; execrate, blaspheme, vituperate, scold, beshrew (*archaic*), maledict (*rare*), anathematize, denounce, proscribe, excommunicate, fulminate, thunder against; curse by bell, book, and candle; devote to destruction.
III. *Adjectives.* **maledictory,** imprecatory, cursing, anathematic *or* anathematical, execratory, blasphemous.
IV. *Interjections.* **curse!** woe! betide! confusion seize! beshrew! (*archaic*), *ruat cœlum!* (*L.*), damn! blast! devil take! hang! a plague upon! out upon! aroint *or* aroynt! (*archaic*).
See also BANE, DISAPPROBATION.—*Antonyms.* See APPROBATION.

---

malefactor, *n.* criminal, culprit, evildoer, felon. See SCOURGE.

MALEVOLENCE.—I. *Nouns.* **malevolence,** bad intent, bad intention, unkindness, uncharitableness, ill-nature, ill-will, bad blood, animosity, enmity, hate, malice, malignancy, malignity, maliciousness; malice prepense (*law*) malice aforethought (*law*); grudge, spite, resentment, pique, bitterness, gall. venom, rancor, virulence, hardness of heart, heart of stone, obduracy; evil eye, cloven foot (*or* hoof).
ill turn, bad turn; affront, indignity; tender mercies (*ironical*); "unkindest cut of all" (*Julius Cæsar*).
cruelty, brutality, savagery, ferocity, savageness, ferity, blood-thirstiness, outrage, atrocity, fiendishness, "sharp-tooth'd unkindness" (*Lear*), ill-usage, persecution, barbarity, inhumanity, hard-heartedness, ruthlessness, pitilessness, mercilessness, truculence, ruffianism; Inquisition, torture.
II. *Verbs.* **bear malice,** harbor a grudge; hurt, annoy, injure, harm, wrong, outrage, malign; molest, worry, harry, bait, hound, dragoon, harass, persecute, oppress, grind, maltreat, illtreat; give no quarter, have no mercy.
III. *Adjectives.* **malevolent,** ill-disposed, ill-intentioned, ill-natured, ill-conditioned, evil-minded, evil-disposed, venomous, malicious, malign, malignant, maleficent; rancorous, vicious, spiteful, treacherous, faithless, perfidious; caustic, bitter, envenomed, acrimonious, virulent; grinding, galling, harsh, disobliging, unkind, unfriendly; stepmotherly, novercal; neglectful, ungracious, churlish, surly, sullen.
cold-blooded, cold-hearted, hard-hearted, stony-hearted, bloodless, cold, unnatural; ruthless, grim, pitiless, relentless, unfeeling, merciless, heartless.
cruel, brutal, brutish, savage, ferocious, ferine, feral, blood-thirsty, inhuman; barbarous, fell, truculent, atrocious, fiendish, diabolic *or* diabolical, demoniac *or* demoniacal, devilish, infernal, hellish.

IV. *Adverbs.* **malevolently,** maliciously, etc. (see *adjectives*); with bad intent; with the ferocity of a tiger; with hellish delight.

See also ENMITY, HATE, PITILESSNESS, RESENTMENT, REVENGE.—*Antonyms.* See BENEVOLENCE.

---

malformation, *n.* deformity, disfigurement. See DISTORTION.
malice, *n.* hate, ill-will, malignity, spite. See MALEVOLENCE.
malpractice, *n.* wrongdoing, improper (*or* illegal) treatment, professional negligence (*of a patient*), illegal conduct. See IMPROBITY, WRONG.
maltreat, *v.* abuse, injure, mistreat, ill-use. See BADNESS.

MAN.—I. *Nouns.* **man,** homo (*L.*), *Homo sapiens* (*L.*), male, he, masculine; chap (*colloq.*), wight (*now chiefly jocose*), swain, fellow, blade, beau, goodman (*archaic*), yeoman, gaffer (*dial. Eng.; correlative of* gammer); gentleman, sir, sahib (*India*), esquire, hidalgo (*Sp.*), caballero (*Sp.*), don (*Sp.*), duniwassal (*Scot. Highlands*); husband (*in phrase* man and wife); vassal, servant, workman, employee.

mister, Mr., *monsieur* (*F.; abbr.* M., *pl.* MM. *or* Messrs.), *Herr* (*Ger.*), *signor* (*It.; used before name*), *signore* (*It.*), *singorino* (*It.; dim. of signore*), *señor* (*Sp.*), *senhor* (*Pg.*), sahib (*India; used after name*).

[*male animal*] cock, drake, gander, dog, boar, stag, hart, buck, horse, stallion, entire *or* entire horse, gelding; bull, bullock, ox, steer, stot (*provincial Eng.*), ram, tup; he-goat, billy-goat (*colloq.*); tom, tomcat; rooster, capon; milter (*fish*).

mankind, human race, humanity, human beings (*collectively*).

II. *Verbs.* **man,** furnish with men, people, garrison, station (*naut.*); strengthen, fortify, brace.

III. *Adjectives.* **manly,** manlike, brave, resolute, determined, undaunted, virile, hardy, manful, daring, courageous, stout, stout-hearted, intrepid, fearless, bold, noble, upright, heroic; unwomanly, unfeminine.

male (*opposite of* female), masculine (*opposite of* feminine), manlike (*opposite of* womanlike, *suggests masculine traits, esp. foibles*), manly (*opposite of* boyish, childish, *suggests the finer qualities*), mannish (*characteristic of* man *as opposed to* woman: *used chiefly of men-aping women*).

See also AGENT, COURAGE, DEFENSE, MANKIND, PREPARATION, PROBITY, SERVANT. —*Antonyms.* See WOMAN.

---

manage, *v.* handle, conduct, manipulate, engineer; superintend. See DIRECTION.
manageable, *adj.* docile, governable, tractable. See FACILITY.
management, *n.* administration, guidance, direction, control. See CONDUCT.
manager, *n.* superintendent, supervisor, overseer. See DIRECTOR.
mandate, *n.* degree, charge, injunction. See COMMAND, ORDER, REQUIREMENT.
maneuver, *n.* stratagem, scheme, ruse, artifice. See CUNNING.
[1]**mangle,** *v.* mutilate, hack, tear, lacerate. See DETERIORATION.
[2]**mangle,** *v.* press, smooth, iron. See SMOOTHNESS.
manhood, *n.* maturity, majority. See ADOLESCENCE.
mania, *n.* enthusiasm, craze; lunacy, madness. See DESIRE, INSANITY.

MANIFESTATION.—I. *Nouns.* **manifestation,** showing, demonstration, presentation, exhibition, show, display, parade, production, revelation, unfoldment, expression, evincement, indication, disclosure, show-down, exposition, revealment, unveiling, baring, uncovering, *exposé* (*F.*), publication, divulgence, divulgation (*rare*), divulgement, declaration, publicity; plain speaking, plainness, openness, candor, *épanchement* (*F.*); prominence, saliency, conspicuousness.

[*public display*] display, exhibition, exposition, show (*colloq.*), performance, representation, production, staging; exhibit; séance, materialization (*Spiritualism*); epiphany, theophany.

II. *Verbs.* **manifest,** bring forth, bring forward, make visible, materialize, express, embody (*as an idea in words*), represent, set forth, indicate, point out, prove; exhibit, evidence, produce, show, show up, expose; hold up, show forth,

unveil, bare, uncover, undrape, display, demonstrate, lay open, unroll, evince, develop, disclose, discover, betray, bring to light, elicit, disinter, draw out, bring out; manifest oneself; speak out, declare, proclaim, publish; translate, transcribe, decipher, decode; make out.
be manifest (*or* plain), appear, transpire, leak out, come to light, be disclosed; speak for itself, go without saying, be self-evident, loom large.
III. *Adjectives.* **manifest,** apparent; evident, open, patent, palpable, tangible, naked, bare, overt, conspicuous, visible, salient, striking, prominent, in the foreground, notable, pronounced, ostensible, avowed.
plain, intelligible, clear, self-evident, perceptible, lucid, explicit, express, defined, definite, distinct, obvious, unmistakable; conclusive, indubitable, indisputable, plain as a pikestaff (*colloq.*), clear as day, obvious, bald, undisguised, literal, downright, unreserved, frank, plain-spoken.
flagrant, glaring, notorious, bold, shameless, brazen, daring, loud (*colloq.*), *risqué* (*F.*), arrant, flaunting, barefaced, audacious, immodest, outrageous.
IV. *Adverbs.* **manifestly,** openly, plainly, aboveboard, *cartes sur table* (*F.*), in plain sight, in the open, in broad daylight; without reserve; at first blush, *prima facie* (*L.*), on the face of.

See also DEMONSTRATION, DISCLOSURE, INTELLIGIBILITY, PLAINNESS, PUBLICATION, VISIBILITY.—*Antonyms.* See CONCEALMENT, LATENCY.

---

manipulate, *v.* engineer, maneuver, manage; wield, handle, operate. See DIRECTION, USE.

MANKIND.—I. *Nouns.* **mankind,** man; human race (species, kind, *or* nature); mortality, flesh, humanity, the earth, generation.
mankind (*accent on man-*), male sex, men (*collectively*): *opposite of* womankind.
science of man, anthropology, anthropography, anthropometry, somatology, ethnology, ethnography.
human being, person, personality, personage; individual, creature, fellow creature, mortal, body, somebody, one, some one; soul, living soul; party (*slang or vulgar*), head, hand, human (*chiefly jocose*).
people, persons, folk, public, society, world; community, general public; nation, state, realm, republic; commonweal, commonwealth; body politic; the masses, commonalty, proletariat, the general (*archaic*), multitude, million, crowd, demos (*pl.* demi), democracy, populace, commons, population, "the peepul"; lords of creation; ourselves.
II. *Adjectives.* **human,** humanistic, hominine (*rare*), anthropoid, mortal; personal, individual.
public, general, common, national, state, provincial, political, civil (*not naval or military*), civic, municipal, social; cosmopolitan, world-wide, universal.

See also INHABITANT, MAN, PEOPLE, WORLD.

---

manly, *adj.* brave, strong, noble, masculine. See MAN, STRENGTH.
manner, *n.* sort, kind; behavior, address; fashion, mode, method. See CLASS, CONDUCT, WAY.
mannerism, *n.* peculiarity, idiosyncrasy. See AFFECTION.
manners, *n.* politeness, breeding. See FASHION.
man of means, millionaire, capitalist, financier, plutocrat. See PROSPERITY, SUFFICIENCY.
man of substance, man of means, independent gentleman. See PROSPERITY, SUFFICIENCY.
man-of-war, *n.* warship, battleship, dreadnaught, cruiser. See COMBATANT.
manservant, *n.* valet, *valet de chambre* (*F.*), footman, butler, man. See SERVANT.
mantle, *n.* cloak, robe, shawl, cape, covering. See CLOTHING.
manufacture, *v.* make, construct, fabricate. See PRODUCTION.
manure, *n.* fertilizer, dressing, dung, compost. See HUSBANDRY.
manuscript, *n.* original, copy, document, deed, instrument. See WRITING.
many, *adj.* numerous, various, myriad. See MULTITUDE.

many-sided, *adj.* multi ateral, polyhedral (*geom.*). See MULTIFORMITY, SIDE.
map, *n.* chart, plan, diagram. See REPRESENTATION.
mar, *v.* damage, injure; mutilate, deface, disfigure. See DETERIORATION, FORMLESSNESS.
marauder, *n.* raider, plunderer, pillager, brigand. See THIEF.
march, *v.* walk, parade, file, defile. See JOURNEY.
margin, *n.* limit, border, brink, rim. See EDGE.
marginal, *adj.* margined, marginate, limbic (*anat.*), littoral, coastal. See EDGE.
marine, *adj.* nautical, naval, maritime. See SHIP.

MARINER.—*Nouns.* **mariner,** sailor, seaman, seafarer, seafaring man, sea dog (*colloq.*), water dog (*colloq.*), tarpaulin (*archaic*), *matelot* (*F.*), old salt (*colloq.*), shellback (*slang*), lithsman (*hist.*), Jack, Jack Tar *or* jack-tar, tar, bluejacket, jacky (*landsman's term*), gob (*U. S. slang*), limy *or* lime-juicer (*U. S. sailors' slang for a British tar, because of the compulsory use of lime juice to prevent scurvy*); marine, jolly (*slang*), leatherneck (*slang; used esp. of U. S. marines*), devil dog (*slang for U. S. marine*); midshipman, middy (*colloq.*); able seaman, A.B., hand, lascar (*India*), khalasi (*India*), galiongee *or* galionji (*Turkish*); crew; captain, commander, master mariner, skipper, old man (*colloq.*), navigator; afterguard (*as on a racing yacht*); mate; boatswain; boatman, ferryman, waterman, lighterman, longshoreman; gondolier; oar, oarsman, rower.

steersman, helmsman, pilot, coxswain, cox (*colloq.*).

Antonyms. See LAND (*landsman*).

---

mark, *n.* standard, measure; line, impression, stroke, streak, scratch; badge, symbol, sign; target, goal, object; distinction, importance, note. See DEGREE, INDICATION, INTENTION, REPUTE.
mark, *v.* stamp, impress; denote, designate; observe, notice, regard. See INDICATION, INTELLECT.
marked, *adj.* conspicuous, prominent, noticeable. See SPECIALTY.
market, *n.* marketplace. See MART.
marksman, *n.* sharpshooter, crack shot, rifleman. See PROPULSION.

MARRIAGE.—I. *Nouns.* **marriage,** matrimony, wedlock, union, intermarriage, miscegenation (*whites with negroes*); nuptial tie, nuptial knot, *vinculum matrimonii* (*L.*), match.

wedding, nuptials, espousals, spousals, hymeneals (*rare*), hymeneal rites, hymen, bridal, leading to the altar, nuptial benediction, confarreation (*Roman*); honeymoon.

bride, bridegroom, groom; bridesmaid, maid of honor, matron of honor; best man, groomsman, bridesman, attendant, usher.

marriage song, nuptial ode, wedding song, hymeneal, epithalamium.

married man, benedict, Benedick, partner, spouse, mate, yokefellow, yokemate, husband, hubbie (*colloq.*), lord *or* lord and master (*poetic or jocose*), baron (*old law*), man (*dial.*), consort, goodman (*archaic or dial.*).

married woman, wife, wedded wife, spouse, helpmeet, helpmate, better half, rib (*jocose*), goodwife (*archaic or dial.*), squaw, matron, queen, empress, lady (*archaic or uncultivated*), feme (*law*).

married couple, man and wife, baron and feme (*old law*), newly-weds (*colloq.*), wedded pair, wedded couple, Darby and Joan, Philemon and Baucis.

[*kinds of marriage*] monogamy, monogyny (*tech.*), monandry (*opposite of* polyandry); bigamy (*two at a time*), deuterogamy (*one after another*), second marriage, digamy; trigamy; polygamy, polygyny (*plurality of wives*), polyandry (*plurality of husbands*), Mormonism (*as was*); levirate (*ancient Jewish*), niyoga (*Hindu*), lobola (*South Africa; by purchase*), endogamy (*within the clan*), exogamy (*outside the clan*), hetærism *or* hetairism (*communal marriage*); morganatic marriage, left-handed marriage; *mésalliance* (*F.*), misalliance; *mariage de convenance* (*F.*), marriage of convenience; companionate marriage, trial marriage, common-law marriage.

matchmaker (*amateur or professional*), match promoter, marriage schemer; matrimonial agent, marriage broker, schatchen (*Yiddish*).
II. *Verbs.* **marry,** take to oneself a wife; be married, be spliced (*colloq.*); wed, espouse, wive (*archaic*), lead to the altar, join, couple, be made one, unite in holy wedlock.
III. *Adjectives.* **matrimonial,** marital, conjugal, connubial, wedded; nuptial, hymeneal, spousal, bridal.
betrothed, affianced, plighted, engaged.
See also JUNCTION, PROMISE, RITE.—*Antonyms.* See CELIBACY.

MARSH.—I. *Nouns.* **marsh,** swamp, morass, marish (*poetic or dial.*), marshland, mash (*dial.*), flow (*Scot. and dial. Eng.*), moss (*as on the Scottish border*), peat bog, fen, bog, quagmire, slough, pocosin *or* dismal (*Southern U. S.*), corcass (*Ireland*), maremma (*It.*), carr *or* car (*local Eng.*), jhil (*India*), vlei (*South Africa*), ciénaga (*Sp.*), baygall (*Southern U. S.*); mud, slush.
II. *Adjectives.* **marsh,** marshy, swampy, boggy, morassy (*rare*), fenny, fennish, paludal, paludine, paludous, palustral (*rare*), poachy, quaggy, squashy, spongy, muddy, miry, soft.
Antonyms. See ISLAND.

MART.—*Nouns.* **mart,** market, marketplace, cheap (*as in* Cheap*side: archaic*), rialto (*rare*), gunge *or* gunj (*India*), bazaar *or* bazar (*primarily Oriental*), staple, fair, exposition, exchange, stock exchange, 'change, bourse, curb, curb market, the street (*brokers' cant*).
shop, store, emporium, department store, chain store, *magasin* (*F.*), *boutique* (*F.*), establishment; stall, booth; office, chambers, countinghouse, bureau.
warehouse, storehouse, *entrepôt* (*F.*), depot, magazine, depository, repository, loft, pantechnicon (*Eng.*).
See also STORE.

---

martial, *adj.* military, warlike. See WARFARE.
martial law, military government. See AUTHORITY.
marvel, *n.* prodigy, miracle, phenomenon, rarity, curiosity. See WONDER.
marvelous, *adj.* wonderful, incredible, miraculous. See WONDER.
masculine, *adj.* strong, virile, manly. See MAN.
mask, *n.* visor, disguise, masquerade, domino. See AMBUSH.
mask, *v.* cover, hide, veil, disguise. See CONCEALMENT.
masquerader, *n.* domino, masker, mummer, mime. See CONCEALMENT.
Mass, *n.* Eucharist, Lord's Supper, Holy Communion. See RITE, WORSHIP.
mass, *n.* lump, heap, pile; amount, portion; bulk, bigness; main body, majority. See ASSEMBLAGE, QUANTITY, SIZE, WHOLE.
massacre, *n.* butchery, slaughter, carnage. See KILLING.
massage, *n.* rubbing, kneading, stroking, shampoo. See FRICTION, TOUCH.
massive, *adj.* bulky, weighty, huge, immense. See SIZE.
mast, *n.* pole, spar, mainmast, topmast, flagstaff. See HEIGHT.

MASTER.—I. *Nouns.* **master,** controller, director, proprietor, owner, employer, old man (*familiar*), leader, boss (*slang*), big shot (*gangsters' slang*), king-pin (*colloq.*), master mind; lord, commander, commandant, captain, chief, chieftain; paterfamilias, patriarch, head, senior, governor, margrave (*hist.*), dictator; sirdar, sachem, sagamore, burra (*or* bara) sahib (*India*), sheikh, emir, aga *or* agha (*Turkish*).
potentate, ruler, sovereign, monarch, liege, liege lord, suzerain, overlord, crowned head, emperor, imperator, king, majesty, protector, president; autocrat, despot, tyrant, oligarch.
cæsar, kaiser, czar *or* tsar, sultan, caliph, imam *or* imaum (*Moham.*), shah, padishah, khan, shereef *or* sherif, mikado, doge, mogul, great mogul, inca; prince, duke, archduke; maharajah, rajah, rao, gaekwar, thakur, nizam, amir *or* ameer, mirza, nawab (*Indian ruling chiefs*).
empress, queen, sultana, czarina *or* tsarina, princess, infanta, duchess; maharani (*Hindu*), rani (*Hindu*), begum (*Moham.*).

regent, viceroy, khedive, mandarin, tetrarch, satrap, bey, beg, pasha, three-tailed pasha (*Turkish*).
the authorities, the powers that be, the government, staff; official, functionary, man in office, person in authority.
[*military authorities*] marshal, field marshal, generalissimo; commander-in-chief, general, brigadier general, brigadier, lieutenant general, major general, colonel, lieutenant colonel, major, captain, subahdar (*India*), ressaldar *or* risaldar (*India*), lieutenant, lieut (*U. S. slang*), jemadar (*India*), subaltern, sublieutenant, second lieutenant, shavetail (*U. S. slang*); officer, staff officer, aide-de-camp (*pl.* aides-de-camp), adjutant, ensign, cornet, cadet; noncommissioned officer; sergeant, top-sergeant (*U. S.*), corporal.
[*civil authorities*] mayor, prefect, chancellor, provost, magistrate, syndic, archon (*Gr.*), corregidor (*Sp.*), alcalde (*Sp.*); burgomaster, seneschal, alderman, warden, constable.
[*naval authorities*] admiral, admiralty; commodore, captain, commander, lieutenant, naval officer; midshipman, midshipmite (*sailor's perversion*), naval cadet; skipper, master, mate.
conqueror, victor, subduer, subjugator, vanquisher, defeater, winner.
schoolmaster, teacher, preceptor, tutor, instructor, principal, guru (*India*), pedagogue, dominie (*chiefly Scot.*), *maestro* (*It.; pl. maestri: esp. of music*).
proficient, expert, adept, crack (*colloq.*), sharp (*slang*), dabster (*colloq.*), dab (*colloq.*), specialist, virtuoso; technicist, technician, master hand.
[*courtesy title*] **master** (*now restricted to boys, as when addressed by servants*), dan (*archaic*), sir, chota (*or* chhota) sahib (*India*).
II. *Verbs.* **master,** overpower, overcome, subdue, vanquish, subjugate, conquer, defeat; control, rule, regulate, govern, direct, superintend, manage, boss (*colloq.*).
learn, acquire, get, learn thoroughly, grasp, become an adept in, become proficient.
III. *Adjectives.* **master,** chief, principal, main, leading, prime, cardinal, commanding, controlling (*as,* a master *clock*).
masterful, self-willed, arbitrary, domineering, imperious, haughty, arrogant, dictatorial, overbearing, bossy (*colloq.*), high-handed, autocratic, lordly, magisterial, authoritative, commanding.
masterly, skillful, expert, finished, adroit, able, accomplished, gifted, talented, dexterous, deft, proficient.
See also DIRECTOR, EXPERT, LEARNING, NOBILITY, POSSESSOR, SUCCESS, TEACHER.
—*Antonyms.* See SERVANT.

---

masterpiece, *n. chef-d'œuvre* (*F.*), masterwork. See PERFECTION, SKILL.
master stroke, feat, hit, stroke, *coup de maître* (*F.*). See SUCCESS.
mastery, *n.* upper hand, sway, dominion, acquisition. See SUCCESS.
[1]**match,** *n.* lucifer, safety match, fusee *or* fuzee. See FUEL.
[2]**match,** *n.* competition, contest; equal, mate; union, matrimony; parallel, counterpart. See CONTENTION, EQUALITY, MARRIAGE, SIMILARITY.
matchless, *adj.* unequaled, supreme, peerless. See SUPERIORITY.
matchmaker, *n.* marriage broker. See MARRIAGE.
mate, *n.* match, counterpart; comrade, companion. See EQUALITY, FRIEND.

MATERIALITY.—I. *Nouns.* **materiality,** corporeity, physical nature, materialness, bodiliness, corporality, material existence; incarnation, flesh and blood; substantiality (*chiefly legal*).
matter, body, substance, brute matter, protoplasm, stuff, element, principle, parenchyma (*tech.*), material, substratum; *corpus* (*L.*), hyle (*philos.*).
[*material thing*] object, article, thing, something; still life.
science of matter: physics, natural philosophy, physical science; somatology, somatics; materialism, hylotheism, hylism, hylozoism.
materialist, physicist, somatist, somatologist, substantialist, hylicist, hylotheist, hylozoist.
II. *Verbs.* **materialize,** incorporate, embody, incarnate, personify, materiate (*rare*), substantialize, exteriorize, externalize, substantiate.
III. *Adjectives.* **material,** bodily, corporeal, corporal, physical, incarnate, materialized, embodied; sensible, sensuous, tangible, palpable, ponderable,

substantial; unspiritual, temporal, materialistic, somatic (*biol.*), somatologic *or* somatological, hylic, hylotheistic, hylozoistic.
objective, impersonal, external, nonsubjective.
important, significant, consequential, momentous, serious, grave, weighty, substantial, essential, indispensable.

See also HETERODOXY, IMPORTANCE, SUBSTANTIALITY.—*Antonyms.* See IMMATERIALITY.

MATERIALS.—*Nouns.* **materials,** substances, elements; raw (*or* unmanufactured) materials; supplies, essentials, stores, *matériel* (*F.*), munitions, provisions, means; baggage, property, fuel, fabrics; contingents, reënforcements, relays.
timber (*used also fig.; as, presidential* timber), wood, lumber, stumpage (*U. S.*), raff (*dial.*); beam, joist, rafter, tiebeam, balk *or* baulk, tie, truss, scantling, rib (*as of a vessel*).
material, matter, substance, constituent, component, element; stuff, goods, fabric, grist, staple, ore, metal.
data (*sing.* datum), facts, conditions, premises (*logic and law*); memoranda, notabilia, notes, documents, information, abstracts; perceptions, ideas (*as,* material *for thought*).

See also ARMS, FOOD, MEANS, PROPERTY, PROVISION, STORE.

---

materia medica, pharmacy; medicines. See REMEDY.
maternal, *adj.* motherly, sympathetic, kind, parental. See PATERNITY.
mathematician, *n.* mathematical scholar; computer. See NUMERATION.
matrimonial, *adj.* nuptial, connubial, marital. See MARRIAGE.
matrimony, *n.* wedlock, marriage. See RITE.
matron, *n.* housekeeper, supervisor; married woman. See DIRECTOR, MARRIAGE.
matter, *n.* subject matter, topics, subjects; trouble, embarrassment; affair, thing; body, substance; subject, theme. See [1]CONTENT, DIFFICULTY, EVENT, MATERIALITY, TOPIC.
matter, *v.* import, signify, have weight. See IMPORTANCE.
matter-of-fact, *adj.* prosaic, unimaginative. See PLAINNESS.
mature, *adj.* developed, ripe; perfected, completed. See ADOLESCENCE, PREPARATION.
mature, *v.* complete, consummate; mellow, ripen. See PERFECTION, PREPARATION.
maturity, *n.* ripeness, development, completion. See OLDNESS.

MAXIM.—I. *Nouns.* **maxim,** rule, principle, precept, law, conclusion, truth, apothegm, aphorism, dictum, saying, adage, saw, proverb, byword, motto, epigram, sentence, mot (*Gallicism*), reflection, commonplace, *cliché* (*F.*), moral, golden rule.
axiom, self-evident truth, theorem, formula, truism, postulate.
II. *Verbs.* **utter maxims,** apothegmatize, aphorize, make aphorisms, epigrammatize.
III. *Adjectives.* **aphoristic,** apothegmatic (*rare*), sententious, pithy, piquant, epigrammatic *or* epigrammatical, proverbial, axiomatic.
IV. *Adverbs.* **aphoristically,** sententiously, etc. (see *adjectives*); as the saying is, as they say.

See also BELIEF, IDEA, PRECEPT, RULE.—*Antonyms.* See ABSURDITY.

---

maximum, *adj.* greatest, highest, utmost, supreme. See SUPERIORITY.
maze, *n.* labyrinth, network; perplexity, confusion. See CONVOLUTION, DIFFICULTY.
meadow, *n.* field, grassland, pasture. See PLAIN.
meager, *adj.* plain, bare, unembellished; thin, emaciated; scanty, poor. See DRYNESS, INSUFFICIENCY.
meal, *n.* repast, refreshment. See FOOD, SOCIALITY.

mean, *v.* intend, aim; signify, express, convey. See INTENTION, MEANING.
[1]**mean,** *adj.* shameful, contemptible; stingy, parsimonious, close; low, common, ordinary; small, ungenerous, petty; poor, paltry, worthless, unimportant. See DISREPUTE, PARSIMONY, PEOPLE, SMALLNESS, UNIMPORTANCE.

MEAN.—I. *Nouns.* **mean,** medium, average, normal, medial estimate, mean proportion, balance, run, rule, golden mean, middle; mediocrity, moderation, measure, compromise, neutrality.
II. *Verbs.* **average,** reduce to a mean, equate, split the difference, strike a balance, pair off; go, run.
III. *Adjectives.* [2]**mean,** intermediate, intervening, medium, middle, moderate; medial, median, average, normal, standard; neutral.
mediocre, middling, ordinary; middle-class, *bourgeois* (*F.*), commonplace.
IV. *Adverbs.* **on an average,** in the long run; in round numbers; taking one with another; *communibus annis* (*L.*), in average years.
See also COMPROMISE, MID-COURSE, MIDDLE.

MEANING.—I. *Nouns.* [*that which is meant*] **meaning,** intent, purpose, intention, aim, object, design, scheme.
[*that which is signified*] **sense,** significance, signification, import, purport, drift, bearing, tenor, force, pith, essence, spirit; implication, denotation, suggestion, allusion, acceptation, interpretation, connotation, upshot, substance, value, effect, burden, gist, sum and substance; argument, content, matter, text, subject matter, subject.
II. *Verbs.* **mean,** have in mind, intend, purpose, resolve, destine, aim, direct.
signify, denote, import, imply, argue, connote, suggest, intimate, allude to, point to, indicate, convey, symbolize, express, purport, drive at, involve, declare, state, affirm, utter, betoken, manifest, touch on, tell of, speak on.
III. *Adjectives.* **meaning,** expressive, significant, significative, significatory, meaningful, suggestive, allusive, indicative, eloquent, explicit, clear, intelligible, pithy, pregnant with (*or* full of) meaning; ominous, portentous, bodeful, boding, prognostic, pithy.
implied, implicit, understood, tacit, assumed, connoted, involved, inferred; potential, virtual.
synonymous, pœcilonymic (*rare*), polyonymic (*rare*), tantamount, equivalent, equal, equipollent.
literal, verbal, verbatim, exact, real, word for word, textual.
See also AFFIRMATION, INFORMATION, INTENTION, INTERPRETATION, LATENCY, MANIFESTATION, [1]SPELL (*indicate*), TRUTH.—*Antonyms.* See UNMEANINGNESS.

---

meaningless, *adj.* unmeaning, senseless, vague, inexpressive. See UNMEANINGNESS.

MEANS.—I. *Nouns.* **means,** instrumentality, agency, medium, measure, instrument, factor, aid, engine (*archaic*), constituent, element, contributing force (*as, a* means *to an end*): *used as sing. in this sense.*
resources, wherewithal, ways and means; capital, wealth, money, revenue, income; property, estate, stock in trade, provision, appliances, conveniences, expedients, wheels within wheels; sheet anchor, reserve, remnant, last resource.
II. *Verbs.* **have the means,** have something to draw upon, possess the wherewithal, have powerful friends, have friends at court.
III. *Adverbs.* **by means of,** by the agency of, by the aid of, by dint of; with, wherewith, wherewithal.
See also AID, INSTRUMENT, INSTRUMENTALITY, MATERIALS, MONEY, PROVISION, STORE, WEALTH.

---

mean-spirited, *adj.* base, groveling, despicable. See POVERTY.
meantime, *adv.* meanwhile, in the interim, *ad interim* (*L.*). See TIME.
measure, *n.* dimensions, extent, size; gauge, rule, criterion; step, action; rhythm, meter; capacity, amount. See DEGREE, MEASUREMENT, PLAN, POETRY, QUANTITY.

MEASUREMENT.—I. *Nouns.* **measurement,** measure, admeasurement, mensuration (*tech.*), metage, survey, valuation, appraisement, assessment, estimate, estimation; dead reckoning (*naut.*); reckoning, gauging; amount, quantity, degree, extent, size, dimensions, capacity, limit; horse power, candle power, foot candle, magnifying power, foot pound, foot ton, erg, dinamode.
measure, gauge, rule, standard, assize, norm, norma (*tech.*), pattern, model, type, scale, canon, criterion; yard measure, two-foot rule, foot rule, rule; level, spirit level; plumb line, plumb rule, plummet, plumb bob; log, log line, patent-log (*naut.*); calipers, dividers, compass; square, set square, steel square, try-square, T square; meter, line, tape, chain, rod, check.
water line, light water line, load water line, load-line mark, Plimsoll mark *or* Plimsoll line (*all naut.*); floodmark, tide mark, high-water mark.
[*in printing*] width (*of a column or page*).
[*in poetry*] rhythm, meter; metrical unit; melody, tune.
[*course of action*] **step,** plan, course, procedure, proceeding, means, provision, act, bill, enactment (*as, a precautionary* measure; *a legislative* measure).
[*due amount or degree*] **share,** portion, lot, allotment, apportionment proportion, division, allowance, ratio, quota.
[*in plural*] **measures** (*geol.*), beds, strata (*as, coal* measures).
scale, graduation, graduated scale; vernier, quadrant, Gunter's scale, Gunter's quadrant, transit *or* transit theodolite, theodolite; beam, steelyard, balance, weighing machine, weighbridge, platform scale.
latitude and longitude, declination and right ascension, altitude and azimuth.
[*scientific measurement*] geometry, stereometry, hypsometry, altimetry; geodesy, cartography, hypsography, topography, cadastration, triangulation, surveying, land surveying.
surveyor, land surveyor, geodesist, topographer, cartographer.
II. *Verbs.* **measure,** meter, mete (*archaic*); value, compute, determine, assess, rate, appraise, estimate, form an estimate; standardize; span, pace, step, inch, divide, space, graduate, calibrate, caliper, dial, gauge, scale, balance, weigh, poise, plumb, probe, sound, fathom; survey, plot, graph, trace, block in, block out, lay out, delimit, rule, draw to scale.
distribute, deal out, apportion, allot, allocate, mete out, share, dole, assign, admeasure, divide, portion out, set apart.
traverse, pass through (*or* over), cross, overpass, track, range, itinerate (*rare*), travel through: *in this sense,* measure *is poetic.*
III. *Adjectives.* **measurable,** mensurable, gaugeable, fathomable, determinable, computable.
measured, uniform, regular, equal, moderated, steady, rhythmical, metrical; deliberate, calculated, premeditated, studied, weighed (*as,* measured *tread;* measured *language*).

See also DEGREE, PLAN, QUANTITY, SIZE.

---

meddle, *v.* interfere, obtrude. See ACTIVITY.
meddlesome, *adj.* pushing, officious, intrusive, forward. See ACTIVITY.
meddlesomeness, *n.* prying, obtrusiveness, interference, officiousness. See ACTIVITY, CURIOSITY.

MEDIATION.—I. *Nouns.* **mediation,** mediatorship, instrumentality, intermediation, intervention, interposition, interference, intercession; parley, negotiation, arbitration, good offices; compromise.
mediator, intercessor, reconciler, propitiator, peacemaker, pacificator, negotiator, interagent, intermediary, intermedium, diplomatist, arbitrator, umpire, moderator.
II. *Verbs.* **mediate,** intercede, interpose, interfere, intervene, step in, negotiate; meet halfway, mediatize (*rare*), arbitrate, propitiate, reconcile.
III. *Adjectives.* **mediatory,** mediating, mediatorial, intercessory, intermedial, intermediary, interventional, propitiatory, reconciliatory; diplomatic.

See also AGENCY, COMPROMISE, CONCORD, DEITY, INSTRUMENTALITY, PACIFICATION.
—*Antonyms.* See EVILDOER.

---

medicine, *n.* physic, medicament, nostrum; leechcraft (*archaic*). See REMEDY.

MEDIOCRITY.—I. *Nouns.* **mediocrity,** ordinariness, middle state, golden mean, average capacity, normality, moderation, moderate (*or* average) circumstances; respectability, commonplaceness.
middle classes, *bourgeoisie* (*F.*).
II. *Verbs.* preserve a middle course; strike the golden mean, jog on, get along (*colloq.*), get on tolerably (*or* respectably).
III. *Adjectives.* **mediocre,** ordinary, average, normal, moderate, commonplace, medium, middling, indifferent, fair, soso (*colloq.*), passable, presentable, respectable, everyday, tolerable, admissible, second-rate, undistinguished, middle-class, *bourgeois* (*F.; fem. bourgeoise*).
See also INDIFFERENCE, MEAN, MID-COURSE, MODERATION, SMALLNESS.

---

meditate, *v.* plan, consider; muse, reflect. See INTENTION, THOUGHT.
medium, *n.* interagent, intermediary; middle; clairvoyant, seer; agency, interagency. See INSTRUMENTALITY, MEAN, PSYCHICAL RESEARCH, VEHICLE.
medley, *n.* jumble, potpourri, hodgepodge. See MIXTURE.
meek, *adj.* mild, submissive, humble, patient. See INEXCITABILITY.
meet, *v.* harmonize, concur; come upon, encounter; gather, collect, congregate; join, unite, intercept; match, equal; satisfy, fulfill. See AGREEMENT, ARRIVAL, ASSEMBLAGE, CONVERGENCE, EQUALITY, OBSERVANCE.
meeting, *n.* encounter; gathering, convention, assemblage; union, connection. See ARRIVAL, COUNCIL, JUNCTION.
melancholy, *adj.* depressed, sad; depressing, gloomy. See BLUE, DEJECTION.
mellow, *adj.* softened, sweet, delicate; mature, seasoned, ripe. See COLOR, PREPARATION.

MELODY.—I. *Nouns.* **melody,** tunefulness, melodiousness, euphony, sweetness, mellifluence, musicalness, musical quality.
air, tune, chime, carillon, measure, lay, song, aria, run, *ranz des vaches* (*Swiss*), chant; plain song, plain chant, Gregorian chant, *cantus firmus* (*New L.*), *cantus planus* (*New L.*): theme, melodic theme; descant, treble, soprano, chief voice part: *distinguished from* harmony *and* rhythm. Melody *is the rhythmical succession of single notes;* harmony, *the combination of simultaneous notes so as to form chords.*
timbre, clang, tone color, quality, clang tint, *Klangfarbe* (*Ger.*).
melodist, composer of melodies; singer, lyrist, bard, vocalist: *distinguished from* harmonist.
II. *Verbs.* **melodize,** make melody; compose melodies, set to melody.
III. *Adjectives.* **melodious,** melodic, musical, tuneful, tunable, euphonious; sweet, mellow, mellifluous, mellifluent, sweet-sounding, dulcet, mellisonant (*archaic*), soft; enchanting, siren, alluring; lyric, melic, songful; clear, silvery, silver-toned, fine-toned, full-toned, deep-toned, rich, Orphean, canorous, resonant, ringing.
See also HARMONY, MUSIC, POETRY, SWEETNESS.—*Antonyms.* See DISCORD.

---

melt, *v.* liquefy, fuse, dissolve, soften; blend, merge; fade, disappear. See CALEFACTION, CONVERSION, TRANSIENCE.
melting pot, crucible, caldron. See WORKSHOP.
member, *n.* element, constituent; limb, organ. See COMPONENT, PART.
memoir, *n.* biography. See DESCRIPTION.
memorable, *adj.* notable, remarkable, signal. See IMPORTANCE.
memorial, *adj.* commemorative. See CELEBRATION.
memorial, *n.* memento, monument, commemoration. See RECORD.

MEMORY.—I. *Nouns.* **memory,** remembrance, memoria (*L.*), retention, retentiveness; retentive (tenacious, trustworthy, *or* ready) memory, readiness, recollection, mental reproduction, retrospect, retrospection, reminiscence; recognition; afterthought, idea.
reminder, hint, suggestion, memorandum (*pl.* memoranda), token, memento, souvenir, keepsake, relic, token of remembrance, remembrancer; monumental

record, memorial, testimonial, monument; commemorative record, commemoration, jubilee.
[*posthumous repute*] fame, celebrity, renown, reputation; repute, notoriety.
art of memory, mnemonics, *memoria technica* (*L.*), mnemotechny, mnemotechnics (*rare*), artificial memory, mnemonization; Mnemosyne (*goddess of memory*).
II. *Verbs.* **remember,** retain the memory of, keep in mind, retain, bear in mind, haunt one's mind (*or* thoughts); brood over, dwell upon; keep the wound open; retain, keep, treasure, hold in remembrance; reward.
recall, recollect, recognize, bethink oneself, call up, summon up, retrace, conjure up, call (*or* bring) to mind, review, look back upon; rake up the past, revive, renew, redeem from oblivion, call to remembrance.
[*to cause to remember*] **remind,** suggest, hint, prompt; put (*or* keep) in mind; refresh the memory, jog the memory; commemorate; memorialize, memorial (*rare*).
memorize, commit to memory; con, con over, fix in the mind, engrave (stamp, grave, *or* impress) upon the memory; learn by heart, learn, master, get, know by rote, have at one's fingers' ends.
note, make a note of, put down, record, chronicle.
III. *Adjectives.* **memorial** (*as a tablet, festival, etc.*), commemorative, commemoratory (*rare*), commemorational; "lest we forget—" (Kipling).
reminiscent, remindful, suggestive, reminiscential (*rare*), recollective; remembered, recollected, mindful, unforgotten, unforgetable, fresh, green, vivid, enduring, never to be forgotten, indelible; within one's memory; memorable.
IV. *Adverbs.* **by heart,** by rote, by (*or* from) memory, *memoriter* (*L.*), without book, word for word.
in memory of, *in memoriam* (*L.*), to the memory of; *beatæ memoriæ* (*L.*), of blessed memory.

See also CELEBRATION, IMPORTANCE, RECORD, REPUTE, RETENTION.—*Antonyms.* See OBLIVION.

---

mend, *v.* correct, better; repair, patch. See IMPROVEMENT, RESTORATION.
mendicancy, *n.* begging, beggary. See POVERTY.
menial, *n.* domestic, servitor. See SERVANT.
mental, *adj.* intellectual, psychological. See INTELLECT.
mentality, *n.* intellectuality, keenness, penetration, acumen. See INTELLECT, VIGOR.
mention, *v.* specify, refer to, remark. See INFORMATION.
mercenary, *adj.* hireling, venal; grasping, sordid, selfish. See SELFISHNESS.

MERCHANDISE.—I. *Nouns.* **merchandise,** wares, commodities, goods, effects, articles, stock, produce, goods for sale, vendibles, stock in trade, cargo.
II. *Verbs.* **merchandise,** trade, traffic, barter, buy and sell, deal, merchant (*rare*).

See also BARTER, BUSINESS.

MERCHANT.—I. *Nouns.* **merchant,** trader, dealer, commission merchant, consignee, mercantile agent, factor; monger (*now chiefly in combination; as, fish*monger), chandler (*as, ship* chandler), merchantman (*archaic*), regrater; tradesman, shopkeeper, shopman, retailer, salesman: merchant *is now used only of a wholesale trader.*
[*in plural*] **merchantry,** merchants, tradesfolk, tradespeople, tradesmen.
peddler *or* pedlar, hawker, huckster, sutler, *vivandier* (*F.*; *fem. vivandière*), chapman, packman, costermonger, colporteur, tallyman (*rare*), cheap jack (*slang*), faker (*slang*), duffer (*Eng. slang*); canvasser, solicitor (*U. S.*).
[*dealer in money*] banker, cambist, moneyer (*rare*), financier; money changer, changer (*archaic*), money broker, exchange broker, discount broker, bill broker; stockbroker, broker, stockjobber, jobber (*Eng.*), buyer, seller; bull, bear (*stock exchange*); money lender, money broker, usurer, Marwari (*India*).
firm, company, partnership, corporation, association, trust, concern, house, *maison* (*F.*).
II. *Adjectives.* **merchant,** commercial, mercantile, mercatorial (*rare*), trading.
merchantable, marketable, salable, vendible, staple (*rare in this sense*).

See also PARTY, PURCHASE, REPRESENTATIVE, SALE.

merciful, *adj.* lenient, clement, compassionate, benignant, kind. See PITY.
merciless, *adj.* ruthless, unfeeling, relentless, pitiless. See PITILESSNESS.
mercy, *n.* mildness, leniency, compassion. See PITY.
mere, *adj.* simple, sheer, stark, bare, plain. See SIMPLENESS, SMALLNESS.
merely, *adv.* simply, barely, solely, along. See SIMPLENESS.
merge, *v.* blend, mingle, fuse, consolidate. See COMBINATION.
merit, *n.* due, credit, desert; excellence, worth. See RIGHTFULNESS, VIRTUE.
merited, *adj.* due, deserved, condign; just, right, fit. See RIGHTFULNESS.
merry, *adj.* joyous, gay, jolly, mirthful. See CHEERFULNESS.
mesmerism, *n.* hypnotism, hypnosis. See PSYCHICAL RESEARCH.
mesmerize, *v.* magnetize, hypnotize. See PSYCHICAL RESEARCH.
mess, *n.* botch, muddle; hodgepodge, jumble. See DIFFICULTY, MIXTURE.
message, *n.* communication, word, dispatch. See NEWS.

MESSENGER.—*Nouns.* **messenger,** envoy, emissary, angel (*Biblical*), legate, nuncio (*rare*), internuncio, delegate, intermediary, go-between, apparitor (*eccl.*), king's messenger, state messenger, pursuivant, *parlementaire* (*F.*), marshal, herald, bode (*archaic*), harbinger, forerunner, precursor; trumpeter, crier, bellman; Gabriel, Hermes, Mercury, Iris, Ariel.
courier, runner, express, hircarra (*India*), peon (*India*), chuprassy (*India*), estafette, chiaus (*Turkey*), intelligencer, dispatch rider (*or* bearer), commissionaire; postboy, errand boy, bell boy, bell hop (*slang*).
mail, post, post office; air mail, aërial mail; dak *or* dawk (*India*); mail boat, post boat, mailer, mail train; postman, mailman, letter carrier, *facteur* (*F.*); carrier pigeon.
telegraph, cable, wire (*colloq.*), radiotelegraph, radio, wireless telegraph, wireless (*colloq.*).
telephone, phone (*colloq.*), radiophone, radiotelephone, wireless telephone.
reporter, newspaperman, pressman (*cant*), journalist, gentleman (*or* representative) of the Press; staff correspondent, own correspondent, special correspondent, war correspondent.
scout, spy, informer, secret agent, observer, secret observer, sleuth (*colloq.*), detective, tec (*slang*); police spy, stool pigeon, stoolie (*slang*), nark (*slang*), undercover man (*police cant*).
See also INFORMATION, TRAVELER.

---

messmate, *n.* buddy (*colloq.*), companion, commensal. See FRIEND.
metaphorical, *adj.* figurative, allegorical. See FIGURE.
metaphysical, *adj.* incorporeal, immaterial; transcendental, ontological; oversubtle; abstract, speculative, visionary. See IMMATERIALITY, INTELLECT, SOPHISTRY, THOUGHT.
metaphysics, *n.* ontology, epistemology, speculative philosophy. See INTELLECT.
meteorological, *adj.* climatic, atmospherical, barometric. See AIR.
meter *or* **metre,** *n.* rhythm, measure. See POETRY.
method, *n.* system, design, plan, order; manner, mode, fashion. See ARRANGEMENT, WAY.
methodical, *adj.* regular, businesslike, systematic. See ARRANGEMENT, ORDER.
methodize, *v.* classify, organize, systematize. See ARRANGEMENT.
mettle, *n.* spirit, pluck, stamina. See COURAGE.
mettlesome, *adj.* courageous, valiant, fiery, high-spirited. See PRIDE.
microbe, *n.* germ, bacterium, bacillus. See LITTLENESS.
microscopic, *adj.* minute, animalcular, atomic. See LITTLENESS.
microscopy, *n.* micrography, microphotography. See LITTLENESS.

MID-COURSE.—I. *Nouns.* **mid-course,** middle way, middle course, midway (*rare*), mean, golden mean, *aurea mediocritas* (*L.*), *juste-milieu* (*F.*), *mezzo termine* (*It.*), middle term; *ariston metron* (*Gr.* ἄριστον μέτρον), moderation.
straight course (path, *or* passage), cut, short cut, crosscut; great-circle sailing.

half measure, half-and-half measure, fifty-fifty (*colloq.*), give-and-take, compromise, mutual concession, adjustment, equalization; neutrality, impartiality.
II. *Verbs.* **steer a middle course,** keep the golden mean, go straight, avoid extremes; sit on the fence.
compromise, compound, settle, make a compromise, go halfway, concede half, go fifty-fifty (*colloq.*), equalize, even.
III. *Adjectives.* **midmost,** middlemost, midway, halfway, median, medial, middle, equidistant, intermediate, interjacent; direct, straight.
impartial, just, even, equitable, average, moderate, unbiased, unwarped; neutral.
See also DIRECTION, MEAN, *n.*, MIDDLE.—*Antonyms.* See CIRCUIT.

MIDDLE.—I. *Nouns.* **middle,** midst, midmost (*rare*), mid (*archaic*), thick, mean, medium, middle term; center, core, kernel, nucleus, hub, nave, navel, omphalos (*anat.*), umbilicus (*anat.*), nombril (*heraldry*), heart, bull's-eye, cazimi (*astrol.*); midship (*naut.*).
equidistance, equal distance, half distance, interjacence; equidivision (*rare*), bisection; equator, diaphragm, midriff; halfway house; medial line (*geom.*), mesial line.
II. *Adjectives.* **middle,** medial, mesial (*zoöl.*), mean, mid, midmost, middlemost, central, axial, pivotal; equidistant, intermediate, mediate (*rare*), intermediary, equatorial; midland, inland.
III. *Adverbs.* **midway,** halfway, in the middle (*or* mean); amidships (*naut.*); *in medias res* (*L.*).
See also CENTRALITY, INTERJACENCE, MEAN, *n.*—*Antonyms.* See BEGINNING, END, OUTLINE.

---

middle age, maturity, full age, prime of life. See ADOLESCENCE.
middle-aged, *adj.* mature; matronly (*fem.*). See ADOLESCENCE.
middleman, *n.* go-between, intermediary, medium, broker. See INTERJACENCE.
midmost, *adj.* halfway, middle, middlemost. See MID-COURSE.
midnight, *n.* dead of night, 12 p.m. See DARKNESS.
midway, *adj.* halfway, equidistant. See MIDDLE.
mien, *n.* bearing, action, deportment, attitude, appearance. See AIR.
might, *n.* force, vigor, energy, ability, efficacy. See POWER.
migrate, *v.* emigrate, trek (*South Africa*), wander; move periodically. See JOURNEY.

MILDNESS.—I. *Nouns.* **mildness,** gentleness, moderation, temperateness, considerateness, lenity, clemency, tenderness, humanity, compassion, mercy, quarter, indulgence, tolerance, toleration, favor, forbearance, etc. (see *adjectives*).
II. *Verbs.* **be mild,** be gentle, etc. (see *adjectives*); bear with, tolerate, suffer, endure; have (*or* show) mercy, *parcere subjectis* (*L.*), spare the vanquished, give quarter.
indulge, favor, gratify, humor, spoil, coddle, pamper, pet, cosset.
milden, make (*or* become) mild, soften, mollify, calm, mellow, sweeten; mitigate, alleviate, allay, ease, relieve, ameliorate.
III. *Adjectives.* **mild,** gentle, easy, moderate, temperate, tranquil, calm, placid, bland, soft, suave; kind, considerate, conciliatory, gracious, amiable, benign, complaisant, easy-going, indulgent, tolerant; lenient, merciful, clement, compassionate, tender, humane; forbearing, forbearant, meek, submissive, pacific, unassuming, mild-spoken.
soothing, mollifying, assuasive, lenitive, tranquilizing, demulcent, emollient; operating gently (*as a cathartic*).
tame, feeble, insipid, vapid, dull, flat, jejune, spiritless, half-hearted, unanimated (*as,* a mild *joke;* a mild *attempt*).
[*of weather*] **temperate,** genial, balmy, soft, warm, pleasant, calm, summery, moderate.
[*of tobacco*] not strong (*as,* a mild *cigar*).
See also INEXCITABILITY, MODERATION, SOFTNESS, TEMPERANCE.—*Antonyms.* See SEVERITY.

military, *adj.* martial, soldierly, warlike: *opposite of* civil. See WARFARE.
milky, *adj.* lacteal, lactescent; pearly, whitish, cloudy; effeminate, timorous, weak; milk-white. See SEMILIQUIDITY, SEMITRANSPARENCY, WEAKNESS, WHITENESS.
mimic, *v.* ape, mock, take off, impersonate. See IMITATION.
mind, *n.* consciousness, understanding, reason, judgment; intent, inclination, purpose. See INTELLECT, WILL.
mind, *v.* perceive, heed, note; object to, disrelish. See ATTENTION, DISLIKE.
mingle, *v.* combine, blend, merge, join. See COMBINATION, MIXTURE.
minimum, *n.* modicum, least. See SMALLNESS.
minister, *n.* rector, pastor, divine; envoy, ambassador. See CLERGY, DEPUTY.
ministry, *n.* service, ministration; priesthood, clergymen; agency, administration, government. See AID, CLERGY, DIRECTION.
minor, *adj.* secondary, lesser, subordinate. See INFERIORITY.
minority, *n.* the smaller, the less; nonage, childhood, pupilage: *opposite of* majority. See FEWNESS, YOUTH.
minstrel, *n.* bard, singer. See MUSICIAN.
minus, *adj.* less, negative (*math.*), diminished; *Colloq.:* deprived of, lacking. See DEDUCTION.
minute, *adj.* precise, accurate; fine, small. See CARE, LITTLENESS.
minuteness, *n.* exactness, precision, attention to detail. See ATTENTION.
minutiæ, *n. pl.* minor details, particulars. See SMALLNESS, SPECIALTY.
miraculous, *adj.* marvelous, supernatural, incredible. See WONDER.
mire, *n.* mud, filth, slime, ooze, slough. See UNCLEANNESS.
mirror, *n.* reflector, looking-glass. See OPTICAL INSTRUMENTS.
mirth, *n.* jollity, gayety, hilarity, glee. See CHEERFULNESS.

MISANTHROPY.—I. *Nouns.* **misanthropy,** hatred of mankind, misanthropism; selfishness, egoism, egotism; sullenness, moroseness, cynicism, cynicalness; want of patriotism, incivism, unpatriotism.
hatred of women, misogyny, misogynism.
misanthrope, man-hater, misanthropist, egoist, egotist, cynic, Timonist; Timon, Diogenes.
woman hater, misogynist, misogyne (*rare*).
II. *Adjectives.* **misanthropic** *or* misanthropical, antisocial, unpatriotic; egoistical, egotistical, selfish; sullen, morose, cynical, Diogenic.
woman-hating, misogynic, misogynous, misogynistic.
See also SELFISHNESS, SULLENNESS.—*Antonyms.* See PHILANTHROPY.

---

misapprehend, *v.* misunderstand, mistake. See ERROR.
miscalculate, *v.* err, blunder. See MISJUDGMENT.
miscarry, *v.* be unsuccessful, come to naught. See FAILURE.
miscellaneous, *adj.* mixed, promiscuous, indiscriminate; many-sided (*as, a* miscellaneous *writer*). See MIXTURE, MULTIFORMITY.
miscellany, *n.* anthology, collectanea; jumble, medley. See ASSEMBLAGE, MIXTURE.
mischief, *n.* hurt, harm, trouble. See EVIL.
misconception, *n.* mistake, misapprehension, misunderstanding. See MISJUDGMENT.
misconduct, *n.* misdeed, misbehavior, wrongdoing. See GUILT.
misdate, *v.* date wrongly, predate, postdate. See ANACHRONISM.
misdeed, *n.* misdemeanor, crime, offense. See GUILT.
miser, *n.* skinflint, niggard, hoarder. See PARSIMONY.
miserable, *adj.* wretched, forlorn; worthless, poor, pitiable. See PAIN, UNIMPORTANCE.
misery, *n.* wretchedness, woe, distress, unhappiness. See PAIN.
misfortune, *n.* disaster, calamity, trouble, accident. See ADVERSITY.

misgiving, *n.* doubt, mistrust, distrust, qualm, apprehension. See UNBELIEF.
mishap, *n.* misfortune, disaster, mischance. See FAILURE.

MISINTERPRETATION.—I. *Nouns.* **misinterpretation,** misapprehension, misexplanation, misexplication, misconstruction, misrendering, misunderstanding, misconception, misapplication; cross-purposes; mistake.
misrepresentation, perversion, distortion, misstatement, exaggeration, abuse of terms, misuse of words, catachresis (*rhet. and philol.*), travesty, falsification.
II. *Verbs.* **misinterpret,** mistranslate, misconstrue, misapprehend, misunderstand, misconceive, misjudge, misspell, misrender, misexplain, mistake, misapply.
misrepresent, pervert, misstate, garble, falsify, distort; stretch (strain, twist, *or* wrest) the sense *or* meaning; travesty, caricature.
III. *Adjectives.* **misinterpreted,** mistranslated, etc. (see *verbs*); catachrestic *or* catachrestical.
bewildered, dazed, confused, rattled (*slang*), perplexed, snarled, mixed, bemazed, benighted, befogged, puzzle-headed.
See also ERROR, FALSEHOOD, MISREPRESENTATION.—*Antonyms.* See INTERPRETATION.

MISJUDGMENT.—I. *Nouns.* **misjudgment,** misconstruction, warped judgment, miscalculation, miscomputation, misconception, misinterpretation, hasty conclusion.
preconception, foregone conclusion, preconceived idea; prejudgment, presumption, predilection, prepossession; presentiment, foreboding; fixed idea, *idée fixe* (*F.*), obsession.
prevarication, equivocation, evasion, subterfuge, quirk, quibble, shift, dodge, artifice, shuffle.
bias, partiality, one-sidedness, prejudice, favor; warp, twist; hobby, whim, fad, crotchet, craze, cult.
partisanship, clannishness, partisanism, party spirit, *esprit de corps* (*F.*), prestige, class prejudice, class consciousness, provincialism, race prejudice.
II. *Verbs.* **misjudge,** misconstrue, miscalculate, misdeem (*archaic*), misconjecture, misconceive, misunderstand; overestimate, underestimate.
prejudge, forejudge, presuppose, presume; dogmatize; have a bias, run away with the notion; jump to a conclusion; blunder.
bias, warp, twist; prejudice, prepossess, influence.
III. *Adjectives.* **misjudging,** ill-judging, wrong-headed, prejudiced, prepossessed; shortsighted, purblind; partial, interested, one-sided, warped, biased, superficial.
narrow, narrow-minded, hidebound, provincial, parochial, insular; mean-spirited, confined, illiberal, intolerant, infatuated, fanatical, positive, dogmatic, dictatorial, pragmatic; egotistical, conceited, bigoted, unreasonable, *opiniâtre* (*F.*), obstinate, stubborn, *entêté* (*F.*), opinionated; stupid, credulous, gullible.
See also ERROR, OVERESTIMATION, UNDERESTIMATION.—*Antonyms.* See JUDGMENT.

---

mislay, *v.* misplace, lose. See DERANGEMENT.
mislead, *v.* lead astray, delude, misinform, deceive. See ERROR.
mismanage, *v.* misdirect, misconduct. See UNSKILLFULNESS.
mismanagement, *n.* misconduct, misguidance, misdirection, maladministration. See UNSKILLFULNESS.

MISNOMER.—I. *Nouns.* **misnomer,** misnaming; *lucus a non lucendo* (*L.*); malapropism, Mrs. Malaprop.
nickname, *sobriquet* (*F.*), *or* soubriquet, by-name, pet name, assumed name, pseudonym, alias, *nom de guerre* (*F.*), *nom de plume* (*English formation*), pen name, stage name, *nom de théatre* (*F.*).
II. *Verbs.* **misname,** miscall, misterm, nickname; take an assumed name.
III. *Adjectives.* **misnamed,** miscalled, nicknamed; *soi-disant* (*F.*), self-styled, pseudonymous, so-called, quasi.
nameless, anonymous (*abbr.* anon.), innominate. unnamed, unknown, unacknowledged; pseudo.
Antonyms. See NOMENCLATURE.

misplace, *v.* disturb, disarrange, place (*or* set) wrongly. See DISPLACEMENT.
mispronounce, *v.* misspeak, missay (*rare*). See STAMMERING.

MISREPRESENTATION.—I. *Nouns.* **misrepresentation,** misstatement, falsification, exaggeration, distortion, anamorphosis, bad likeness, daub, scratch.
burlesque, travesty, take-off, parody, caricature, extravaganza, burletta, mock-heroic, mock tragedy, paratragœdia *or* paratragedia, mimicry, mockery, ridicule.
II. *Verbs.* **misrepresent,** distort, overdraw, exaggerate, falsify, understate, overstate, stretch, wrest the sense (*or* meaning), give a false coloring, put a bad (*or* false) construction on.
burlesque, travesty, buffoon, mimic, mock, satirize, ridicule, parody, caricature.
See also FALSEHOOD, MISINTERPRETATION, MISTEACHING.—*Antonyms.* See REPRESENTATION.

---

misrule, *n.* misgovernment, maladministration, mismanagement. See UNSKILLFULNESS.
miss, *v.* want, lack; miscarry, fail, lose; omit, let slip, skip, overlook. See DESIRE, FAILURE, NEGLECT.
misshapen, *adj.* deformed, crooked, disfigured, unshapely. See UGLINESS.
missile, *n.* projectile. See ARMS, PROPULSION.
missing, *adj.* gone, wanting, absent. See LOSS.
mission, *n.* calling, work; errand, charge; embassy. See BUSINESS, COMMISSION.
misstatement, *n.* misrepresentation, error, falsification. See UNTRUTH.
mist, *n.* haze, haziness, fog, dimness. See CLOUD.
mistake, *v.* err, stray, slip, sin, blunder, misapprehend, miscalculate. See ERROR, UNSKILLFULNESS.
mistake, *n.* blunder, slip, oversight; misunderstanding. See ERROR.

MISTEACHING.—I. *Nouns.* **misteaching,** misinstruction, miseducation (*rare*), misinformation, misguidance, misdirection, misleading, perversion, sophistry, the blind leading the blind.
II. *Verbs.* **misteach,** misinstruct, misinform, miseducate, misdirect, misguide, pervert; deceive, mislead, misrepresent, lie.
render unintelligible, bewilder, mystify, befog, confuse, conceal.
See also DECEPTION, FALSEHOOD, SOPHISTRY.—*Antonyms.* See TEACHING.

---

mister, *n.* Mr., *monsieur* (*F.*). See MAN.
mistress, *n.* head, matron; paramour, kept woman; ladylove, sweetheart; madam, lady, Mrs. See DIRECTOR, LIBERTINE, LOVE, WOMAN.
misunderstanding, *n.* dispute, quarrel; mistake, miscomprehension. See DISAGREEMENT, ERROR.

MISUSE.—I. *Nouns.* **misuse,** misusage, misemployment, misapplication, perversion, misappropriation; abuse, ill usage, maltreatment, profanation, prostitution (*as of abilities*), desecration; waste.
II. *Verbs.* **misuse,** misemploy, misapply, misappropriate, exploit; desecrate, abuse, ill-use, ill-treat, maltreat, prostitute, profane, squander, waste; debase, profane.
overwork, overtax, overtask, overlabor, overburden, overstrain; tire, jade, fatigue, harass, exhaust.
See also WASTE.—*Antonyms.* See USE.

---

mitigate, *v.* lessen, alleviate, soften, abate. See MODERATION.

MIXTURE.—I. *Nouns.* **mixture,** admixture, minglement, blend, compound, combination, union, association, amalgamation, mix (*colloq.*), intermixture, immixture, commingling, composite, alloyage, junction; alloy, amalgam; compositeness, complexity, complexus, complication; instillation, infusion, transfusion; impregnation, infiltration; interlarding, interpolation, adulteration.
[*thing mixed*] **tinge,** tincture, touch, dash, vein, shade, strain, *soupçon* (*F.*), smack, spice, seasoning, infusion.

medley, jumble, hodgepodge, *mélange* (*F.*), hash, mess, mingle-mangle, olla-podrida, salmagundi, olio, miscellany, omnium-gatherum (*colloq.*), Noah's ark, farrago, *pasticcio* (*It.; pl. pasticci*), potpourri, patchwork, *pastiche* (*F.*), chowchow, gallimaufry; mosaic, motley.
half-breed, half-caste, half-blood, mestizo (*fem.* mestiza), mestee (*West Indies*), Eurasian, crossbreed; mulatto, quadroon, octoroon; mule, cross, hybrid, mongrel.
II. *Verbs.* **mix**, blend, combine, mingle, pour into, commingle, intermingle, scramble (*as eggs*), interlard, interpolate, intertwine, interweave, join, compound, amalgamate, alloy, cross; adulterate.
imbue, infuse, diffuse, suffuse, transfuse, instill, infiltrate, saturate, impregnate, lace (*a beverage*), fortify (*as wine*), flavor, dash, tinge, tincture, entincture, season.
[*to unite with in company*] **unite**, associate, join, have intercourse, conjoin, betroth, fraternize.
III. *Adjectives.* **mixed**, blended, etc. (see *verbs*); composite, half-and-half, heterogeneous; motley, variegated, miscellaneous, promiscuous, indiscriminate; hybrid, mongrel.
IV. *Prepositions.* **among**, amongst, amid, amidst, in the midst of, with.

See also COMBINATION, JUNCTION, LIQUEFACTION.—*Antonyms.* See DISJUNCTION, SIMPLENESS.

---

moan, *v.* wail, groan, lament, bemoan. See CRY.
mob, *n.* rabble, populace; crowd, throng. See MULTITUDE.
mob law, mob rule, anarchy. See AUTHORITY.
mock, *v.* scorn, deride, defy; mimic, ape. See DISRESPECT, IMITATION.
mock, *adj.* counterfeit, sham, false, pretended. See DECEPTION.
mode, *n.* vogue, style; manner, method, procedure. See FASHION, FORM, STATE.
model, *n.* pattern, prototype, design; standard, criterion; manikin. See COPY, PERFECTION, REPRESENTATION.

MODERATION.—I. *Nouns.* **moderation**, temperateness, moderateness, temperance, gentleness, mildness, lenity, quiet, sobriety; mental calmness, composure, tranquilization, pacification; abatement, diminution, assuagement, mitigation, relaxation.
moderator, temperer, mitigator; sedative, lenitive, demulcent, palliative; balm, opiate.
umpire, arbitrator, mediator; presiding officer (*as of a town meeting*), president, chairman.
II. *Verbs.* **moderate**, temper, mollify, soften, mitigate, palliate, alleviate, allay, assuage, appease, lull, soothe, compose, still, calm, quiet, tranquilize, hush, quell, sober, pacify, smooth, cool; slacken, slack, lessen, abate, decrease; deaden, smother, weaken, check, tame, curb, restrain, blunt, subdue, chasten.
III. *Adjectives.* **moderate**, temperate, reasonable, lenient, measured; gentle, mild, calm, unruffled, cool, sober, quiet, tranquil, still, untroubled, peaceful, halcyon, peaceable, pacific.
IV. *Adverbs.* **moderately**, temperately, etc. (see *adjectives*); in moderation, in reason, within bounds.

See also CHEAPNESS, [2]CONTENT, DECREASE, INEXCITABILITY, LOWNESS, MILDNESS, SLOWNESS, SMALLNESS, SOBRIETY, TEMPERANCE.—*Antonyms.* See GREATNESS, REDUNDANCE, VIOLENCE.

---

modern, *n.* modernist; neologist. See NEWNESS.
modernism, *n.* modernness; the latest thing, *dernier cri* (*F.*). See NEWNESS.

MODESTY.—I. *Nouns.* **modesty**, diffidence, demureness, timidity, bashfulness, shyness, humility, retiring disposition, unobtrusiveness; blush, blushing; reserve, constraint.
II. *Verbs.* **be modest**, retire, give way to, keep one's distance, keep in the background; hide one's light under a bushel.
III. *Adjectives.* **modest**, diffident, demure, retiring, humble, timid, timorous, bashful, shy, coy, sheepish, blushing; unpretending, unpretentious, unobtrusive,

unassuming, unpresumptuous, quiet, unostentatious, reserved, constrained; seemly, becoming, virtuous.

IV. *Adverbs.* modestly, diffidently, demurely, etc. (see *adjectives*); quietly, privately; without ceremony, *sans façon* (*F.*).

See also HUMILITY, POVERTY (*insignificant*), SMALLNESS.—*Antonyms.* See BOASTING, OSTENTATION, VANITY.

---

modicum, *n.* minimum, little. See SMALLNESS.

modification, *n.* alteration, variation; limitation, condition. See CHANGE, QUALIFICATION.

modify, *v.* transform, alter, vary, moderate; qualify, limit, restrict. See CHANGE, QUALIFICATION.

modulation, *n.* modification, inflection, variation. See CHANGE.

Mohammedan, *adj.* Mussulman, Moslem, Islamic. See HETERODOXY.

Mohammedan, *n.* Moslem, Mussulman. See HETERODOXY.

Mohammedanism, *n.* Islam, Moslemism. See HETERODOXY.

MOISTURE.—I. *Nouns.* **moisture,** moistness, humidity, dampness, damp, wet, mugginess; dew, fog drip (*as from trees*), false dew (*exuded from vegetation*); exhalation, exudation, humidification.

II. *Verbs.* **moisten,** wet, damp, sponge, humidify, bedew; drench, soak, sodden, seethe, sop; saturate, infiltrate.

III. *Adjectives.* **moist,** damp, watery, humid, wet, wettish, vaporous, dank, muggy, dewy, rainy; tearful, lachrymose; juicy.

soaked, sodden, saturated, dabby, soggy, pappy, soft, soppy, sloppy; swampy, marshy, poachy; reeking, dripping, soaking, wringing wet, wet through.

See also EGRESS (*exude*), MARSH, WATER.—*Antonyms.* See DRYNESS.

---

mold, *n.* kind, stamp, cast; shape, formation; matrix, die. See CLASS, FORM, PROTOTYPE.

mold, *v.* turn, influence; fashion, create, cast, shape. See CONVERSION, FORM.

moldy, *adj.* musty, tainted, rancid, stale. See FETOR.

molecule, *n.* atom, monad, particle. See LITTLENESS, SMALLNESS.

molest, *v.* harm, bother, disturb, annoy. See MALEVOLENCE.

mollify, *v.* calm, appease, soothe, allay. See MODERATION.

molly, *n.* milksop, sissy, mollycoddle. See WOMAN.

molt, *v.* shed (*feathers*), cast, exuviate, slough. See DIVESTMENT.

molten, *adj.* fused, smelted, melted. See CALEFACTION.

moment, *n.* consequence, weight; instant, second, twinkling. See IMPORTANCE, INSTANTANEITY.

momentum, *n.* impetus, moment (*tech.*), energy. See IMPULSE.

monarch, *n.* sovereign, ruler, emperor. See MASTER.

monarchy, *n.* kingdom, empire, autocracy, realm. See AUTHORITY.

monastery, *n.* abbey, convent, cloister, priory. See TEMPLE.

monasticism, *n.* monachism, monkhood, monastic life. See CHURCHDOM.

MONEY.—I. *Nouns.* **money,** finance, funds, treasure, wealth, capital, principal (*distinguished from* interest *or* income), corpus (*pl.* corpora: *law*), stock, assets, supplies, ways and means, wherewithal *or* wherewith, sinews of war, almighty dollar, cash; great wealth, riches, money to burn (*colloq.*); power *or* mint of money (*colloq.*), good sum, millions, thousands.

[*slang terms*] dough, jack, spondulics *or* spondulix, rhino, simoleons, mazuma, gingerbread, kale, moss, long green, salt, dust, insect powder, tin, chink, blunt, brass, dibs, chips, beans, rocks, clinkers, plunks, horse nails, iron men, mopuses, bucks, bones, wad, oof, ooftish, yellow boys, thick 'uns (*sovereigns*), shekels, barrel (*chiefly political*), velvet (*money gained without effort*), palm oil (*bribe or tip*), the needful, the ready, the actual, corn in Egypt; plum (£100,000), grand ($1000), monkey (£500), century (£100 *or* $100), pony (£25); tenner (£10 *or* $10), ten spot; fiver (£5 *or* $5), five spot; cart wheel (*silver dollar*), bob (*shilling*), tanner (*sixpence*), two bits (*quarter*).

sum, amount, aggregate, sum total; balance, balance sheet; proceeds, receipts.
currency, circulating medium, specie, coin, piece, hard cash; dollar sterling; pounds, shillings, and pence, £ s. d.; sovereign, quid (*Brit. slang*), guinea; purse, ready money, wallet, roll, wad (*slang*).
precious metal, noble metals (*opposite of* base metals), gold, silver, bullion, ingot, bar, nugget; platinum (*not used for coins*).
petty cash, pocket money, pin money, spending money, change, small coin, chicken feed (*slang*).
wampum, wampumpeag, seawan *or* seawant, roanoke, cowrie.
science of coins: numismatics.
paper money, note, bill, money order, bank note, bond, bill of exchange, check (*esp. U. S.*) *or* cheque (*esp. Brit.*), promissory note, note of hand, IOU, draft, order, warrant, coupon, debenture, greenback (*U. S.*), long green (*U. S. slang*).
solvency, soundness, stability, solidity, reliability, responsibility.
II. *Verbs.* **total**, amount to, come to, mount up to, tot up to (*colloq.*).
monetize, put into circulation, utter, issue, circulate, fiscalize: *opposite of* demonetize.
III. *Adjectives.* **monetary**, pecuniary, fiscal, financial; sterling; **numismatic**, nummular, nummary, nummulary.
moneyed, wealthy, rich, affluent, opulent, well-to-do.
solvent, sound, solid, stable, substantial, reliable, good, responsible, having a good rating.
See also PROPERTY, WEALTH.

---

monk, *n.* friar, religious, cenabite, monastic. See CLERGY.
monkey, *n.* simian, ape, gorilla, baboon; imitator; *Slang:* £500. See ANIMAL, IMITATION, MONEY.
monopolize, *v.* corner, engross, forestall (*hist.*), hog (*slang*). See POSSESSION.
monopoly, *n.* monopolism, exclusive possession; exclusive control, limitation, restriction. See POSSESSION, RESTRAINT.
monotonous, *adj.* humdrum, tedious, tiresome, unvaried. See REPETITION.
monotony, *n.* sameness, repetition, tedium. See IDENTITY.
monster, *n.* fiend, devil; freak, monstrosity; giant; legendary animal, gorgon, minotaur. See EVILDOER, PRODIGY, SIZE, UNCONFORMITY.
monstrous, *adj.* enormous, huge, titanic; ugly, unsightly; abnormal, unnatural; flagrant, atrocious, outrageous. See GREATNESS, SIZE, UGLINESS, UNCONFORMITY, VICE.
month, *n.* moon, lunation. See PERIOD.
monument, *n.* gravestone, tombstone; memorial, testimonial. See INTERMENT, RECORD.
mood, *n.* humor, temper, vein. See DISPOSITION.
moon, *n.* month, lunation; satellite; Luna, Diana. See PERIOD, WORLD.
moon-shaped, *adj.* lunar, luniform, crescent-shaped. See CURVATURE.
moor, *n.* heath, wold, moorland, waste. See PLAIN, SPACE.
mope, *v.* brood, pine, languish. See DEJECTION.
moral, *adj.* ethical; probable, reasonable; just, righteous, honorable, honest. See DUTY, PROBABILITY, VIRTUE.
morality, *n.* virtue, uprightness; ethics, morals. See DUTY.
morbid, *adj.* sickly, unhealthy, unwholesome. See DISEASE.

MORNING.—I. *Nouns.* **morning**, morn, morningtide (*poetic*), matins (*eccl.*), forenoon, *ante meridiem* (*L.*), a.m., prime, dawn, daybreak, dayspring (*poetic*), peep of day, break of day, aurora, sunrise, sunup (*U. S. colloq.*), daylight, cockcrow.
noon, midday, noonday, noontime, noontide, meridian.
spring, springtime, springtide, seedtime, vernal season, blossom time; vernal equinox.
summer, summertime, summertide, midsummer.

II. *Adjectives.* **morning,** matutinal, matin, matinal (*as, morning exercises*).
noon, noonday, midday.
spring, vernal.
summer, æstival *or* estival.
Antonyms. See EVENING.

---

morose, *adj.* moody, gloomy, crabbed, glum, sour. See SULLENNESS, SOURNESS.
morphology, *n.* morphography, comparative anatomy. See ZOÖLOGY.
morsel, *n.* bit, scrap, crumb, piece. See SMALLNESS, TASTE.
mortal, *adj.* deadly, fatal; human; perishable, short-lived. See KILLING, MANKIND, TRANSIENCE.
mortification, *n.* vexation, humiliation, confusion. See PAINFULNESS.
mortuary, *adj.* funeral, burial, mourning. See INTERMENT.
mortuary, *n.* deadhouse, morgue. See INTERMENT.
mother, *n.* female parent, progenitress, mamma, mater (*colloq.*). See PATERNITY.
motherhood, *n.* maternity; motherliness. See PATERNITY.
motif, *n.* theme, subject. See MOTIVE.

MOTION.—I. *Nouns.* **motion,** movement, move, agitation, action, gesture; motive power, mobility, movableness; direction, inclination, tendency, drift, driftage, set, course, stream, flow, flux, stir.
proposal, proposition, recommendation, suggestion, submission (*as, a motion to adjourn*).
gait, step, tread, footfall, stride, stalk; walk, rack, amble, single foot, canter, pace, trot, jog, gallop, run.
rate, clip (*colloq.*), velocity, speed, pace; port, carriage.
journey, progress, travel, locomotion; excursion, expedition, passage, pilgrimage; voyage, sail, cruise.
II. *Verbs.* **motion,** gesture, sign, gesticulate, beckon, nod, wave, direct, guide, invite.
move, go, hie, gang (*Scot. and dial.*), budge, stir, pass, flit; hover around (*or* about), shift, slide, glide, roll, flow, stream, run, drift, sweep along; wander, walk, rush; progress, advance; act; take action.
displace, shift, remove, unseat, dislodge, disturb; transfer, translate, transport.
propose, suggest; offer, recommend, make a motion, submit (*as a resolution*).
[*set in motion*] impel, stir, actuate, prompt, influence; propel, drive, urge, rouse, arouse, stimulate, incite, instigate, constrain, compel; render movable, mobilize.
touch, affect, agitate, excite, melt, soften, impress, perturb (*as, to* move *to tears*).
III. *Adjectives.* **moving,** impelling, motive, motor (*tech.*), motile, mobile, movable; shifting, restless, changeable, mercurial, erratic, nomadic, traveling, transitional.
touching, affecting, pathetic, appealing, impressive.
IV. *Adverbs.* **under way,** on the move (wing, fly, tramp, *or* march).
See also BEGINNING, EXCITEMENT, IMPULSE, JOURNEY, OFFER, PROPULSION, TRANSFER.—*Antonyms.* See [1]REST.

---

motionless, *adj.* immovable, inert, still, quiet, stationary, stagnant. See DEATH, [1]REST.

MOTIVE.—I. *Nouns.* **motive,** reason, cause, ground, call, principle, mainspring, pro and con, reason why, wherefore (*colloq.*), the why and the wherefore (*colloq.*), root, basis, occasion, rationale, object, purpose, excuse, intention, secret motive, ulterior motive.
inducement, consideration, attraction, loadstone, magnet, magnetism, temptation, enticement, allurement, glamour, witchery, charm, spell, fascination, blandishment, cajolery, seduction, voice of the Sirens.
influence, prompting, dictate, instance; urge, impulse, incitement, press, insistence, instigation; inspiration, persuasion, encouragement, exhortation, advice,

solicitation; pull (*slang*), drag (*slang*), power, potency, control, authority, supremacy, ascendancy.
incentive, stimulus, spur, fillip, whip, goad, provocative, whet.
bribe, lure, decoy, bait, sop, bribery and corruption, grease (*slang*), graft (*colloq.*), sop to Cerberus, palm oil (*jocose*).
[*in artistic composition*] **motif,** dominant feature (*or* idea), theme, subject, salient element.
instigator, inciter, prompter, abettor, firebrand.
tempter, temptress (*fem.*), seducer, enchantress (*fem.*), vampire (*colloq.*), vamp (*slang*); Siren, Circe, Lorelei.
II. *Verbs.* **induce,** move, motive, draw, inspire, prompt, stimulate, rouse, arouse, animate, lead, sway, win over, gain, prevail on, urge, lobby (*chiefly U. S.*), influence, bias, dispose, incline, predispose, persuade, get, bring round, carry, overcome, talk over, conciliate, enlist, engage, invite, court; whet, incite, provoke, instigate, actuate, motivate, advocate, encourage.
tempt, entice, allure, captivate, fascinate, bewitch, hypnotize, charm, magnetize, wheedle, coax, lure, inveigle, overpersuade.
bribe, corrupt, square (*slang*), oil, grease, grease the palm, tamper with, suborn
enforce, force, impel, constrain, compel, make, gar (*Scot.*), drive, propel, whip, lash, goad, spur, prick, egg on, hound on, hurry on.
III. *Adjectives.* **motive,** impelling, impulsive, operating, energic, energizing (*as,* motive *power*).
persuasive, hortative, hortatory, inviting, suasive, tempting, seductive, attractive, fascinating; provocative.
IV. *Adverbs.* **because,** therefore, by reason of, for the sake of, on account of, on that account, consequently.
V. *Conjunctions.* **because,** since, for, as, inasmuch as, forasmuch as.
See also CAUSE, EXCITEMENT, IMPULSE, INTENTION.—*Antonyms.* See CAPRICE.

---

motor boat, power boat, motor launch. See SHIP.
mottled, *adj.* spotted, dappled, party-colored. See VARIEGATION.
motto, *n.* proverb, adage, saw, aphorism. See MAXIM.
mound, *n.* hillock, rise, knoll. See HEIGHT.
mount, *v.* climb, scale; rise, grow, augment. See ASCENT, INCREASE.
mountain, *n.* mount, peak, hill, alp, range. See HEIGHT.
mourn, *v.* grieve, bewail, lament, sorrow, deplore. See PAIN.
mourner, *n.* lamenter, weeper, wailer. See INTERMENT, LAMENTATION.
mourning, *n.* grief, sorrow; weeds, black. See LAMENTATION.
mouth, *n.* jaws, chops, gab (*Scot.*); estuary, outfall; entrance, aperture, hole. See FOOD, GULF, OPENING.
mouthful, bite, morsel, bit. See FOOD.
movable, *adj.* transportable, portable. See TRANSFER.
move, *v.* recommend, suggest; go, budge, stir; affect, arouse; induce, impel persuade; transport, carry; change residence. See ADVICE, MOTION, MOTIVE, TAKING, TRANSFER.
movement, *n.* performance, exercise, operation, labor; move, agitation, gesture; transfer, moving. See ACTION, MOTION, TRANSFER.
moving, *adj.* motive, motile, traveling; pathetic, touching. See MOTION, PAINFULNESS.
mud, *n.* mire, slime, silt, ooze, muck. See SEMILIQUIDITY, UNCLEANNESS.
muddle, *n.* mess, jumble; confusion, perplexity. See DIFFICULTY, DISORDER.
muffle, *v.* wrap, cover, conceal; damp, mute; stifle, hush, gag. See CLOTHING, FAINTNESS, NONRESONANCE, SILENCE.
muffled, *adj.* subdued, softened, deadened. See DULLNESS, FAINTNESS.
muffler, *n.* scarf, tippet; silencer, silencing device. See CLOTHING, FAINTNESS, NONRESONANCE, VEHICLE (*allied terms*).
muggy, *adj.* damp, humid, close. See MOISTURE.
mule, *n.* hinny, hybrid; obstinate person See CARRIER, OBSTINACY.

MULTIFORMITY.—I. *Nouns.* **multiformity,** variety, diversity, omniformity, omnifariousness, multifariousness, polymorphism (*esp. biol.*), diversification.
II. *Adjectives.* **multiform,** multifold, multifarious, multiplex, variform (*rare*), omniform, omnifarious, diversiform, polymorphic, polymorphous, proteiform, protean, multiphase, many-sided, miscellaneous (*as a writer*).
diversified, diverse, irregular, manifold, varied, indiscriminate, **various, of every** description, mixed, heterogeneous, motley, variegated, mosaic.
Antonyms. See CONFORMITY, RULE.

---

multiplication, *n.* production, procreation, breeding. See INCREASE.

MULTITUDE.—I. *Nouns.* **multitude,** crowd, throng, press, great number, mob, assembly, numbers, scores, legion, host, array, army, assemblage, aggregation, galaxy, cloud; heap (*colloq.*), power (*colloq.*), sight (*colloq.*), lot (*colloq.*), lots (*colloq.*); swarm, bevy, flock, herd, drove, shoal, school, flight, covey, hive, brood, litter, farrow; multiplicity, multitudinousness, profusion.
II. *Verbs.* **be numerous,** swarm with, teem with, be alive with, **crowd, swarm,** outnumber, multiply; people.
III. *Adjectives.* **multitudinous,** numerous, teeming, outnumbering, alive with, thick, rife, abundant, widespread, prevalent; populous, crowded, studded, profuse, manifold, sundry, divers, several, many, various, endless, galore (*colloq.*); numerous as the sands on the seashore; numerous as the hairs on the head.
See also ASSEMBLAGE, GREATNESS.—*Antonyms.* See FEWNESS.

---

mumble, *v.* mutter, murmur. See STAMMERING.
mundane, *adj.* earthly, worldly, terrestrial. See WORLD.
murder, *n.* slaying, manslaughter, homicide. See KILLING.
murderer, *n.* killer, slayer, cutthroat, assassin. See KILLING.
murderous, *adj.* bloodthirsty, bloody, sanguinary. See KILLING.
murmur, *v.* rustle, hum; grumble, mutter. See FAINTNESS, LAMENTATION.
muscular, *adj.* brawny, stalwart, sinewy. See STRENGTH.
muse, *v.* meditate, ponder, mull, ruminate. See THOUGHT.
Muses, *n. pl.* the Nine, sacred Nine. See MUSICIAN.

MUSIC.—I. *Nouns.* **music,** melody, harmony; polyphony (*opposite of* homophony), contrapuntal composition; strain, tune, air, measure; minstrelsy; piece of music, *morceau* (*F.*); rondo, rondeau, caprice, *capriccio* (*It.*), nocturne, serenade, serenata, *pastorale* (*It.*), pastoral; cavatina, fantasia, *toccata* (*It.*); fugue, canon; incidental music, medley, potpourri.
[*instrumental music*] orchestral score, full score; composition, *opus* (*L.; pl. opera*); concert piece; *concerto* (*It.*); symphony, sonata, symphonic poem, tone poem; program music, chamber music; movement; overture, prelude, *Vorspiel* (*Ger.*); voluntary, accompaniment.
lively music, polka, reel, jig, hornpipe, mazurka, bolero, galop, gavot *or* gavotte, cotillion *or cotillon* (*F.*); fox trot, two-step, blues (*cant*); ragtime, jazz, syncopation; martial music, pibroch, march; *allegro* (*It.*).
slow music, Lydian measures; *largo* (*It.*), adagio, *andante* (*It.*), lullaby, cradle song, *berceuse* (*F.*); dirge, coronach (*Scot. and Irish*), dead march; minuet, waltz.
[*vocal music*] chant; psalm, psalmody, hymnology, hymnody; hymn; canticle; oratorio; opera, grand opera, music drama, operetta; cantata; song, *Lied* (*Ger.; pl. Lieder*), *chanson* (*F.*), strain, canzonet, lay, ballad, ditty, carol; recitative *or* recitativo, aria, arietta.
solo, duet, *duo* (*It.*), trio, quartet, quintet, sestet, septet, double quartet, chorus; part song, descant, glee, madrigal, catch, round, chorale; antiphon; inside part, second, alto, tenor, bass; score, vocal score.
concert, musicale, musical (*colloq.*), entertainment, recital, chamber concert, popular concert *or* pop (*colloq.*), singsong (*colloq.*), sing (*colloq.*), open-air concert; morning concert, *aubade* (*F.*).
[*musical terms*] pitch, timbre, intonation, tone, tonality, overtone; harmonization, orchestration, modulation, figuration, phrasing, syncopation, resolution, suspension; colorature, *coloratura* (*It.*), variations, roulade, run, cadenza, ca-

dence, bravura, *fioritura* (*It.; pl. fioriture*), trill *or* shake, turn, *arpeggio* (*It.*); staff *or* stave, line, space, brace, bar, rest; slur, vinculum; scale, gamut, key, clef, chord; keynote, tonic; passage, phrase, theme.

note, symbol, character, musical note; sharp, flat, natural; grace, grace note, *appoggiatura* (*It.*), *acciaccatura* (*It.*).

breve, semibreve *or* whole note, minim *or* half note, crotchet *or* quarter note, quaver *or* eighth note, semiquaver *or* sixteenth note, demisemiquaver *or* thirty-second note; sustained note, undertone, drone, burden (*of a bagpipe*), bourdon.

interval, step; first, second, third, fourth, etc., diatessaron (*ancient music*); half step, half tone, semitone; harmonic interval, melodic interval.

solmization, solfeggio, sol-fa, tonic sol-fa

II. *Adjectives.* **musical**, melodious, melodic, tuneful, canorous, euphonious, harmonious, symphonic, symphonious, contrapuntal; orchestral, instrumental; classic *or* classical (*distinguished from* popular), modern; vocal, choral, lyric, operatic, dramatic; philharmonic, music-loving: *opposite of* unmusical.

florid, embellished, brilliant, flowery, elaborate, ornate, figurate, figural, figured.

See also HARMONY, MELODY.

MUSICAL INSTRUMENTS.—*Nouns.* **musical instruments**; orchestra (*including* strings, wood winds, brass winds, *and* percussives), concert orchestra, *Kapelle* (*Ger.*); band, string band, military band, brass band, jazz band.

[*stringed instruments*] violin, Cremona, Stradivarius *or* Strad (*colloq.*), fiddle (*colloq. or depreciatory*), kit (*of the old dancing master*); crowd (*Celtic*), rebec *or* rebeck, viol, viola, viola d'amore (*It.*), viola da braccio (*It.*), tenor viol, viola da gamba (*It.*), bass viol, violoncello *or* cello, double bass, contrabass, contrabasso (*It.*), violone (*It.*).

harp, lyre, lute, archlute, theorbo, cithara, cither, cittern, gittern, zither, psaltery, vina *or* bina (*India*), samisen (*Jap.*), balalaika (*Russia*), guitar, banjo, banjo-zither, mandolin, ukelele (*Hawaii*) *or* uke (*colloq.*), mandola.

piano *or* pianoforte, harpsichord, clavichord, clavier, clarichord *or* manichord (*medieval*), spinet, virginal.

[*wind instruments*] organ, pipe organ, reed organ; harmonium, melodion, seraphine, accordion, concertina; bagpipes, doodlesack (*Scot.*); Panpipe, Pandean pipes, syrinx (*pl.* syringes); mouth organ, harmonicon *or* harmonica; whistle.

wood winds, flute, fife, piccolo, pipe, flageolet, clarinet *or* clarionet, oboe, bassoon, contrafagotto (*It.*), double bassoon, serpent, saxophone, reed instrument.

brass winds, trumpet, trump (*archaic*), cornet, clarion (*poetic*), horn, bugle, French horn, bugle horn, post horn, saxhorn, sackbut (*medieval*), trombone, tuba, sax-tuba, bombardon, bass tuba, ophicleide, euphonium; lituus (*pl.* litui: *Roman antiquities*), conch, lure (*for calling cattle*).

[*percussion instruments*] drum, bass drum, kettledrum, timbal, timpano (*pl.* timpani), side drum, snare drum, tambour, taboret, tom-tom *or* tam-tam (*Oriental*), tambourine, timbrel; cymbals, bells, glockenspiel, carillon, xylophone, marimba, vibraphone, triangle, etc.

[*mechanical*] automatic piano, piano player, player piano, player; hurdy-gurdy, street piano; hand organ, barrel organ; phonograph, victrola (*trade-mark name*), graphophone, gramophone, music box *or* musical box; calliope.

MUSICIAN.—I. *Nouns.* **musician**, *artiste* (*F.*), performer, virtuoso, player, minstrel, bard; composer, *maestro* (*It.*), harmonist, contrapuntist; instrumentalist, organist, pianist, accompanist; violinist, fiddler, (*colloq. or derogatory*), flutist, flautist, harpist *or* harper, lutist *or* lutanist, fifer, trumpeter, cornetist, bugler, piper, drummer.

orchestra, band; strings, woodwind, brass; brass band, military band, German band, jazz band; *Kapelle* (*Ger.*); street musicians, waits.

vocalist (*opposite of* instrumentalist), singer, melodist, warbler, song bird; songster, songstress, *cantatrice* (*It. or F.*), chantress (*poetic*), soprano, mezzo-soprano, contralto; tenor, barytone, bass; chanter, caroler, chorister; chorus singer; choir, chorus, voices.

Orpheus, Apollo; the Muses, the Nine, sacred Nine, tuneful Nine, **tuneful quire** (*archaic*); Polyhymnia *or* Polymnia, Erato, Euterpe, Terpsichore.

[*song birds*] nightingale, philomel (*poetic*), bulbul, lark, thrush, **mavis**, **oriole**.

conductor, director, leader, *Kapellmeister* (*Ger.*), bandmaster, choirmaster concert master, drum major; cantor, precentor, song leader.
performance, execution, touch, expression.
II. *Verbs.* **play,** perform, execute, render, read, tune, tune up, pipe, flute whistle, pipe up, strike up, sweep the chords, strike the lyre; fiddle, bow, scrape (*derogatory*); blow (*or* wind) the horn; twang, pluck, pick; pound, thump, tickle the ivories (*slang*), strum, thrum, drum; accompany.
conduct, direct, lead, wield the baton, beat time.
compose, set to music, arrange, harmonize, orchestrate.
sing, chant *or* chaunt (*archaic*), cantillate (*rare*), intone, troll, warble, carol (*poetic*), yodel, hum, twitter, chirp, chirrup, lilt, quaver, trill, shake; sol-fa, solmizate.

---

muster, *v.* collect, gather, convene, convoke, assemble. See ASSEMBLAGE.
mute, *adj.* silent, inarticulate, speechless; unpronounced. See DUMBNESS, LETTER, SILENCE.
mutilate, *v.* amputate, excise, detruncate; mangle, maim, disfigure. See DEDUCTION, FORMLESSNESS.
mutilated, *adj.* maimed, mangled; garbled, distorted. See INCOMPLETENESS.
mutiny, *n.* uprising, rebellion, revolt, insurrection; insubordination. See REVOLUTION.
mutter, *v.* grumble, complain; mumble. See LAMENTATION, STAMMERING.
mutual, *adj.* reciprocal, correlative. See INTERCHANGE.
muzzle, *v.* hush, silence, quiet; gag, bind. See FAINTNESS, RESTRAINT.
mysterious, *adj.* obscure, abstruse, occult, incomprehensible, hidden. See DARKNESS.
mystery, *n.* riddle, enigma. See SECRET.
mystic, *adj.* occult, esoteric; mysterious, inscrutable, unknowable. See CONCEALMENT, LATENCY.
mystify, *v.* perplex, puzzle, befog, bewilder. See UNINTELLIGIBILITY.
myth, *n.* tradition, fable; fancy, fantasy. See DESCRIPTION, IMAGINATION.

MYTHICAL BEINGS.—I. *Nouns.* **god,** goddess (*fem.*), divinity, spirit, power, numen (*L.; pl.* numina), godling, godkin, tutelary deity, tutelary, *lar* (*L.; pl. lares*), *lar familiaris* (*L.*); *di majores* (*L.*), the greater gods; *di minores* (*L.*), the lesser gods; heathen gods and goddesses; pantheon.
the Fates *or* Mœræ: Clotho (*Spinner*), Lachesis (*Disposer of Lots*), Atropos (*Inflexible One*).
gods of the sea: Poseidon (Neptune) *and* Amphitrite, Triton, Oceanus, Oceanides (*offspring of Oceanus*), Nereus *and the* Nereids, Thetis, Galatea, Proteus.
gods of the earth: Gæa *or* Gaia, Rhea *or* Cybele; Dionysus, Bacchus (*wine*); Priapus (*fruitfulness*); Pan (*literally,* "the pasturer"), Faunus (*flocks, herds, forests, and wild life*); Demeter, Ceres (*agriculture and fertility*).
gods of the nether world: Hades, Pluto (*King*); Persephone, Proserpine (*Queen*): Hecate; Furies, Erinyes (*sing.* Erinys), Eumenides.
[*classical*] Uranus (*Heaven*), Gæa (*Earth*); Titans (*children of Uranus and Gæa*): Cronus *and* Rhea (*parents of the Olympians*), Oceanus *and* Tethys, Hyperion *and* Theia (*parents of Helios, Selene, and Eos*), Cœus *and* Phœbe, Iapetus *and* Themis, Creus *and* Mnemosyne (*goddess of memory, and mother of the Muses*); Titaness (*fem.*).
Olympian deities, Olympians: Zeus, Jupiter *or* Jove (*King*); Hera, Juno (*Queen*); Athena *or* Athene, Minerva (*wisdom*); Apollo *or* Phœbus Apollo (*the sun*); Artemis, Diana (*the moon and hunting*); Aphrodite, Venus (*love and beauty*); Hephæstus, Vulcan (*smith*); Ares, Mars (*war*); Hermes, Mercury (*messenger*); Hestia, Vesta (*the hearth*).
minor deities: Themis, the Graces, the Muses; Eros, Cupid (*love*); Nike (*victory*), Iris (*rainbow*), Hebe (*youth*), Ganymede (*cupbearer of the gods*), Helios (*the sun*), Selene (*the moon*), Eos (*the dawn*), Eileithyia (*childbirth*), Asclepius (*healing*), Nemesis (*retributive justice*), Tyche (*fortune*).
[*Norse*] Ymir (*primeval giant*), Odin *or* Woden (*the All-father,* =*Zeus*), Frigg *or* Frigga (*wife of Odin*); the Æsir: Thor (*the Thunderer*). Balder (=*Apollo*), Freyr

(*fruitfulness*), Tyr (*war*), Bragi (*poetry and eloquence*), Idun (*goddess of Spring, wife of Bragi*), Höder (*blind god of the winter*), Heimdall (*warder of Asgard*), Loki (*evil*), Sigyn (*wife of Loki*), Hel (*goddess of death,* = *Persephone*).
the Vanir: Njorth (*the winds and the sea*), Frey (*prosperity and love*), Freya (*goddess of love and beauty,* = *Venus*).
[*Egyptian*] Ra *or* Amun-Ra (*the sun god*), Osiris (*judge of the dead*), Isis (*wife of Osiris*), Horus (*the morning sun; son of Osiris and Isis*), Anubis (*jackal-god, brother of Horus, a conductor of the dead*), Nephthys (*sister of Isis*), Set (*evil deity, brother of Osiris*), Thoth (*clerk of the under world*), Bast *or* Bubastis (*a goddess with the head of a cat*), the Sphinx (*wisdom*).
[*Hindu*] **Vedic gods:** Dyaus (*Heaven*), Indra (*cloud-compeller*), Varuna (*the sky, also the waters*), Surya (*the sun*), Soma ("*the Sustainer*"), Savitar ("*the Inciter,*" *a sun god*), Agni (*fire*), Vayu (*winds*), the Marutas (*storm gods*), Ushas ("*the Dawn,*" *goddess of wisdom*).
[*Various*] Baal (*Semitic*); Astarte *or* Ashtoreth (*Phœnician goddess of fertility and love*); Bel (*Babylonian*); The Great Spirit (*N. American Indian*).
nymph, dryad, hamadryad, wood nymph; oread, mountain nymph; naiad, fresh-water nymph; nereid, sea nymph; Oceanid, ocean nymph; Pleiades *or* Atlantides, Hyades (*daughters of Atlas*); siren, Lorelei.
fairy, fay, sprite; nix (*fem.* nixie), water sprite; brownie *or* browny, pixy, elf (*pl.* elves); banshee; kobold, troll, hobgoblin, gnome, salamander, sylph, kelpie; faun; peri, undine, sea maid, mermaid (*masc.* merman); Mab, Oberon, Titania, Ariel; Puck, Robin Goodfellow; Leprechaun; the good folk, the little men, the little people, elfenfolk.
[*maleficent spirits*] fiend, devil, demon, evil spirit, incubus (*pl.* incubi), succubus (*pl.* succubi), cacodæmon *or* cacodemon; ogre, ogress (*fem.*), Scylla, ghoul, vampire, lamia, harpy, afreet, evil jinni (*pl.* jinn), genie, evil genius (*pl.* genii) barghest; Flibbertigibbet (*King Lear*), bad fairy, imp; dwarf (*sometimes helpful, sometimes malignant*), Alberich (*Ger.; king of the dwarfs*), Andvari, Reginn (*both Volsunga Saga*), Mimer (*demonic smith who reared Siegfried*); satyr.
changeling, elf-child; werewolf, *loup-garou* (*F.*) lycanthrope, berserk *or* berserker (*Norse*).
bugbear, bugaboo, bogy *or* bogey *or* bogie, goblin, hobgoblin, boggart, spook, poker (*rare*).
familiar spirit, familiar, genius, guide, good genius, demon, daimon.
mythology, mythical lore, folklore, fairyism, fairy mythology.
II. *Adjectives.* **mythical,** mythic, mythological, fabulous, legendary.
fairylike, sylphlike, elfin, elflike, elfish, nymphlike; dainty, exquisite.
demoniac, demoniacal, fiendish, fiendlike, devilish, evil, ghoulish; pokerish (*U. S. colloq.*), bewitched, hoodooed (*U. S. colloq.*); demonic.
See also UNCONFORMITY (*legendary beings*).

N

nag, *v.* find fault, scold, pester, fret, irritate, annoy. See DISCORD.
nail, *n.* finger nail, unguis (*pl.* ungues), claw, talon; pin, peg, spike, treenail, brad. See RETENTION, VINCULUM.
naked, *adj.* nude, bare, stripped, uncovered. See DIVESTMENT.
name, *n.* designation, epithet; fame, reputation. See NOMENCLATURE, TITLE, REPUTE.
name, *v.* designate, mention, appoint; call, term, style. See COMMISSION. NOMENCLATURE.
nameless, *adj.* obscure, inglorious; unnamable, indescribable; abominable, repulsive; anonymous, unnamed. See DISREPUTE, GREATNESS, HATE, MISNOMER.
namely, *adv.* to wit, *videlicet* (*L.*), *viz.* See SPECIALTY.
nap, *n.* pile, surface. See ROUGHNESS, TEXTURE.
narcotic, *n.* opiate, sedative, drug. See REMEDY.
narrate, *v.* relate, tell, recite, recount, describe. See DESCRIPTION.
narrative, *n.* story, history, account. recital. See DESCRIPTION.

narrator, *n.* teller, describer, recorder, relator, chronicler, novelist, *raconteur* (*F.*). See DESCRIPTION.

narrow-minded, *adj.* narrow, illiberal, prejudiced, insular. See ISLAND, NARROWNESS.

NARROWNESS.—I. *Nouns.* **narrowness,** slenderness, etc. (see *adjectives*); closeness, exiguity; hair's (*or* finger's breadth, line, strip, streak.

neck, cervix (*pl.* cervixes *or* cervices: *tech.*), jugulum (*pl.* jugula: *zoöl.*), hals *or* halse (*Scot. and dial. Eng.*), clod (*of beef*), scrag (*of mutton or beef; slang of a person's neck*), nape, scruff, nucha (*pl.* nuchæ); gula (*pl.* gulæ: *zoöl.*), auchenium (*pl.* auchenia: *zoöl.*).

constriction, compression, contraction, angustation (*rare*), narrowing, stricture, coarctation (*med.*); isthmus, hourglass, sandglass; pass, ravine, ghat *or* ghaut (*India*); channel, strait, narrows (*pl.*), canal.

II. *Verbs.* **narrow,** taper, reduce, constrict, contract, limit, restrict, reduce, lessen, diminish.

III. *Adjectives.* **narrow,** slender, thin, fine, threadlike, linear, delicate, finespun, taper, slim; scant, scanty, spare, contracted, circumscribed, limited, close, confined, confining, strait (*archaic and Biblical*), pent, cramped, exiguous, incapacious, straitened, meager, small, restricted.

[*with little margin*] **near,** close, hairbreadth, bare (*as, a* narrow *escape*).

niggardly, mean, parsimonious, selfish, illiberal, ungenerous, covetous, avaricious, stingy, close.

illiberal, bigoted, prejudiced, self-centered, hidebound, narrow-minded, uncharitable, narrow-hearted, insular, parochial.

scrutinous, critical, scrutinizing, careful, close, searching, attentive, near, exact, accurate, precise.

See also IMPIETY, MISJUDGMENT, SELFISHNESS, THINNESS.—*Antonyms.* See BREADTH, LIBERALITY.

---

nasty, *adj.* foul, filthy; obscene, smutty; nauseating, loathsome. See IMPURITY, PAINFULNESS.

native, *adj.* inborn, inherent; indigenous, natural. See COMPONENT, VEGETABLE.

native, *n.* aborigine, countryman, countrywoman. See INHABITANT.

native land, fatherland, home, country. See LAND.

natural, *adj.* regular, normal; unaffected, spontaneous; innate, inborn, intrinsic; ingenuous, unsophisticated. See RULE, SIMPLENESS, SUBJECTIVENESS, TRUTH.

naturalist, *n.* botanist, zoölogist. See ORGANIZATION.

naturalization, *n.* acclimatization, habituation; denization. See LOCATION.

naturalize, *v.* acclimatize, habituate, inure; colonize. See HABIT, LOCATION.

nature, *n.* kind, sort; temperament, character, bent; constitution, essence; universe, creation. See CLASS, DISPOSITION, SUBJECTIVENESS, WORLD.

naughty, *adj.* wayward, disobedient, mischievous. See DISOBEDIENCE.

nausea, *n.* seasickness, qualm; loathing, disgust, aversion. See DISEASE, DISLIKE.

nauseate, *v.* revolt, sicken, disgust. See PAIN.

nauseous, *adj.* repulsive, sickening, loathsome. See UNSAVORINESS.

NAVIGATION.—I. *Nouns.* **navigation,** navigating, seamanship; piloting, pilotage, pilotship; voyaging, seafaring.

voyage, cruise, sail, passage, circumnavigation; boating, yachting, cruising; aquatics.

steerageway, headway, way, sternway, leeway.

[*means of propulsion*] oar, scull, sweep, pole; paddle, screw, propeller, turbine; sail, canvas.

II. *Verbs.* **navigate,** sail, cruise, steam, circumnavigate; steer, direct, manage, pilot, con *or* conn (*naut.*); sail over (*or* on), plough the deep (*or* waves), put to sea, set sail; coast, hug the shore; scud, boom (*as a ship under full sail*), ride, ride the waves, gather way, make sail, spread sail, carry sail.

row, paddle, pull, scull, punt, oar (*poetic*), propel, ply the oar.
float, swim, skim, drift, ride (*as at anchor*), waft, tide, drive; buoy, buoy up.
III. *Adjectives.* **nautical**, maritime, marine, naval; seafaring, seagoing, ocean-going; coasting; navigable.
aquatic, natatory, natatorial; natant (*esp. bot.*), natational, floating, swimming.
IV. *Adverbs.* **under way**, in motion, under sail (canvas, *or* steam), afloat; on the wing.
See also AËRONAUTICS, MARINER, SHIP.

---

navy, *n.* naval forces, fleet. See COMBATANT.

NEARNESS.—I. *Nouns.* **nearness**, closeness, etc. (see *adjectives*), proximity, propinquity, vicinity, vicinage, neighborhood, contiguity, adjacency.
short distance, short cut; earshot, close quarters, range, stone's throw; gunshot, bowshot; hair's breadth, span.
purlieus, neighborhood, vicinage, environs, *alentours* (*F.*), *faubourg* (*F.*), suburbs, confines, outskirts, *banlieue* (*F.*).
bystander, spectator, onlooker, witness; neighbor.
nearing, approach, advance, approximation, access; convergence, meeting, coming.
II. *Verbs.* **be near**, adjoin, abut, neighbor, border upon, verge upon; approximate; stand by, hang about, hover over, cling to, clasp, hug, huddle.
near, approach, draw near, approximate, come (*or* bring) near, converge, press, cram, throng, crowd, huddle, mob, herd.
III. *Adjectives.* **near**, nigh, close (*or* near) at hand, close, warm (*colloq.*), vicinal (*rare*), neighboring, bordering upon, contiguous, adjacent, adjoining; proximate, approximate; at hand, handy, impending, imminent, forthcoming.
[*of animals and vehicles*] left: *opposite of* off.
intimate, dear, familiar, close (*as, a* near *friend*), closely related (*as, a* near *relative*).
direct, short, quick, straight, immediate (*as, a* near *way*).
close, narrow, bare, hairbreadth (*as, a* near *escape*).
stingy, niggardly, closefisted, parsimonious, close, mean, narrow, penurious.
substitutive, makeshift, tentative, experimental, provisional; imitative, imitational, imitation, pseudo, counterfeit, resembling (*as,* near *beer*).
IV. *Adverbs.* **near**, nigh, hard by, close to, close upon, hard upon; next door to; within reach (call, hearing, earshot, *or* range), in sight of; at close quarters; beside, alongside, cheek by jowl, side by side, in juxtaposition; at the heels of, on the verge of, at the point of; closely (*as,* near *akin*).
nearly, closely; approximately, almost, about, all but, thereabouts, roughly, in round numbers, roundly, generally, well-nigh, barely.
See also APPROACH, CONTACT, CONVERGENCE, EARLINESS, ENVIRONMENT, FUTURE, NARROWNESS, PARSIMONY, PRESENCE, SIMILARITY.—*Antonyms.* See DISTANCE.

---

nearsighted, *adj.* myopic, shortsighted. See DIM-SIGHTEDNESS.
neat, *adj.* felicitous, pat; tidy, trim, spruce, orderly; unmixed, pure; adroit, deft, skillful, clever. See AGREEMENT, CLEANNESS, SIMPLENESS, SKILL.

NECESSITY.—I. *Nouns.* **necessity**, inevitableness, unavoidableness, certainty.
necessitation, compulsion, force, obligation, coercion, constraint, subjection; Hobson's choice, no choice; stern (*or* dire) necessity, last resort; instinct, blind impulse, natural tendency (*or* impulse).
destiny, fatality, fate, kismet, destinism (*rare*), fatalism, doom, election, predestination, predetermination, determinism, necessitarianism; lot, cup (*Biblical*), dispensation, portion, God's will, will of Heaven, Heaven; fortune, wheel of fortune, stars, planets, astral influence, book of fate.
fates, Parcæ (*L.*), Sisters three, Norns, Weird Sisters (*Macbeth*), Mœræ (*Gr.*): Clotho ("*Spinner*" *of the thread of life*), Lachesis ("*Disposer of Lots,*" *who decides its length*), Atropos ("*Inflexible One,*" *who cuts it off*).
need, want, indigence, urgency, exigency, needfulness, requirement, requisiteness, indispensableness.
necessary, requisite, essential, *sine qua non* (*L.*): *often in plural.*
necessitarian, necessarian, fatalist, determinist; automaton, pawn.

II. *Verbs.* **necessitate,** make necessary, cause, compel, force, drive, oblige, impel, constrain, coerce, make, gar (*Scot.*).
destine, doom, foredoom, devote; predestine, foreordain, preordain, predetermine, appoint.
III. *Adjectives.* **necessary,** inevitable, inevasible, unavoidable, irrevocable, inexorable, unpreventable, ineluctable, irresistible; binding, compulsory.
fated, destined, fateful, set apart, devoted, elect, appointed.
involuntary (*opposite of* free), instinctive, automatic, blind, mechanical; unconscious, unwitting, unthinking; unintentional.
indispensable, needful, essential, requisite, vital.
necessitous, needy, poor, indigent, penniless, destitute, poverty-stricken, pinched, pinching, narrow.
IV. *Adverbs.* **necessarily,** etc. (see *adjectives*); of necessity, of course; willy-nilly, *nolens volens* (*L.*), *coûte que coûte* (*F.*); compulsorily, by force, *bon gré, mal gré* (*F.*).

See also COMPULSION, POVERTY, PREDETERMINATION, SUBJECTION.—*Antonyms.* See CHANCE, WILL.

---

neck, *n.* cervix (*tech.*), gula (*pl.* gulæ: *zoöl.*), nape, scruff; constriction, narrowing; isthmus, strait, pass. See NARROWNESS.
neckcloth, *n.* neckerchief, necktie, scarf, cravat, tie. See CLOTHING.
necrology, *n.* obituary, register of deaths. See DEATH.
necromancy, *n.* black art, magic, enchantment. See SORCERY.
need, *n.* want, lack, requirement; destitution, privation; occasion, indispensableness. See NECESSITY, POVERTY, USE.
needless, *adj.* superfluous, unnecessary. See REDUNDANCE.
nefarious, *adj.* base, detestable, wicked, shameful. See VICE.

NEGATION.—I. *Nouns.* **negation,** denial, disavowal, disclaimer (*chiefly law*), disclamation, disaffirmation, refutation, contradiction, *démenti* (*F.*), protest, dissent, repudiation, rejection, recantation, revocation; retractation, rebuttal, confutation; refusal.
nullity, blankness, negativity, negativeness, annihilation, obliteration.
II. *Verbs.* **negative,** veto, refuse, reject, disallow, set aside, ignore; offset, neutralize, cancel.
deny, contradict, contravene, controvert, gainsay, disaffirm, negate, nullify, disprove, refute; dispute, impugn, traverse, confute, rebut, join issue upon, bring (*or* call) in question, give the lie to, belie.
disclaim, disown, repudiate, disavow, abjure, forswear, renounce; recant, revoke.
III. *Adjectives.* **negative,** denying, negatory, nullifying; dissentient, contradictory, contrary, repugnant, recusant.
IV. *Adverbs.* **no,** nay, not, nowise, not at all, not in the least, quite the contrary, *tout au contraire* (*F.*), on no account, by no means.

See also APOSTASY, CONFUTATION, DISSENT, NONEXISTENCE, REFUSAL, REJECTION.—*Antonyms.* See AFFIRMATION.

NEGLECT.—I. *Nouns.* **neglect,** disregard, inattention, slight, negligence, culpa (*law*), heedlessness, thoughtlessness, carelessness, unwariness, remissness, laches (*law*), default, paraleipsis (*rhet.*), omission, procrastination; supineness, apathy; imprudence, improvidence, recklessness; slovenliness, untidiness; inexactness, inaccuracy, incorrectness.
neglector, trifler, waiter on Providence, Micawber, drifter (*colloq.*), procrastinator, dillydallier, waster (*colloq.*), slacker (*slang*).
II. *Verbs.* **neglect,** disregard, slight, omit, cut (*colloq.*), overlook, forget, pass over, miss, skip, pass by, let pass, gloss over, let slip; wink at, connive at, ignore; *laisser aller* (*F.*), let go, not trouble oneself with (*or* about); let the grass grow under one's feet.
scamp, trifle, fribble, slur, skimp (*colloq.*), skim, skip, take a cursory view of, run over, dip into; slur (*or* slip) over; push aside, throw into the background, sink.
delay, defer, procrastinate, put off, postpone, adjourn, shelve, pigeonhole, table, lay on the table.

III. *Adjectives.* **neglectful,** negligent, heedless, careless, forgetful, thoughtless, culpose (*law*), unwary, unguarded, remiss, inattentive, indifferent, regardless, unwatchful, supine, apathetic, nonchalant, offhand, perfunctory, inconsiderate, improvident, unthrifty, thriftless, imprudent, reckless; disorderly, slovenly, dirty, untidy, lax, loose, slack; inaccurate, inexact, untrustworthy.
neglected, uncared for, unheeded; disregarded, unimproved, unattended to, unregarded; abandoned, shelved, shunted.
IV. *Adverbs.* **neglectfully,** negligently, etc. (see *adjectives*); anyhow, in any old way (*colloq.*); *per incuriam* (*L.*).
See also DERELICTION, INATTENTION, NONCOMPLETION, NONOBSERVANCE, NONPREPARATION.—*Antonyms.* See CARE.

---

negotiable, *adj.* transferable, assignable, conveyable. See TRANSFER.
negotiate, *v.* bargain, contract, arrange. See COMPACT.
negro, *n.* African, Ethiopian, darky (*colloq.*). See BLACKNESS.
neighborhood, *n.* vicinity, district, community. See NEARNESS.

NEOLOGY.—I. *Nouns.* **neology,** neologism, innovation, neoterism, newfangled expression; coined word, manufactured term, vogue word, nonce word, genteelism, poeticism; caconym, barbarism, corruption; antiphrasis (*rhet.*).
[*in theology*] rationalism, neologism.
dialect, brogue, patois, provincialism, broken English, Anglicism, Briticism, Gallicism, Scotticism, Hibernicism; Americanism; Gypsy lingo, Romany.
lingua franca, pidgin (*or* pigeon) English (*the "business English" of the Chinese*), Hindustani (*India*), kitchen Kafir (*South Africa*), Chinook (*used by Indians and traders in the Northwest*); Volapük, Esperanto, Ido.
jargon, dog Latin, gibberish; confusion of tongues, Babel; cant, shop, lingo, slang, back slang, argot, thieves' Latin, Billingsgate.
pseudonym, pen name, *nom de guerre* (*F.*), *nom de plume* (*an English formation*); assumed name, alias, nickname, by-name, byword, soubriquet, *sobriquet* (*F.*).
neologist, word-coiner, coiner of words, jargonist; innovator, neoterist.
II. *Verbs.* **neologize,** neoterize, coin words; Americanize, Anglicize, Gallicize; jargonize, jargon.
III. *Adjectives.* **neologic,** neological, neologistic *or* neologistical, neoteristic; barbarous, jargonic (*rare*).
See also FIGURE, MISNOMER.—*Antonyms.* See ELEGANCE, WORD.

---

nerve, *n.* resolution, grit; vigor, vitality. See COURAGE, STRENGTH.
nerve, *v.* invigorate, embolden, brace, strengthen. See COURAGE, STRENGTH.
nervous, *adj.* sensitive, high-strung; neurotic. See EXCITABILITY.
nest, *n.* set (*as of boxes*), series; cradle, nursery, hotbed; aerie, nidus (*pl.* nidi: *tech.*); retreat, haunt, den, resort. See ASSEMBLAGE, CAUSE, HABITATION.
nestle, *v.* snuggle, cuddle. See ENDEARMENT.
net, *n.* web, mesh; snare, trap. See CROSSING, DECEPTION.
nettle, *v.* provoke, irritate, annoy, ruffle. See PAIN.
network, *n.* openwork; interlacing, reticulation, interconnection (*as of radio stations*). See CROSSING.

NEUTRALITY.—I. *Nouns.* **neutrality,** aloofness, nonpartisanship, noninterference; indifference, inertness, unconcern; indecision, indetermination, impartiality.
neutral, neuter, nonparticipant, nonparticipator, noncontestant, common friend, bystander, onlooker.
II. *Adjectives.* **neutral,** neuter, nonpartisan, noninterfering, unconcerned, inert; impartial, indifferent, middling, nonchalant, irresolute, undecided; indeterminate, vague, colorless; betwixt and between (*colloq.*), neither one thing nor the other.
[*in biology*] **asexual,** sexless, neuter; sterile, barren.
See also INDIFFERENCE, MEAN, *n.*, MID-COURSE.—*Antonyms.* See COÖPERATION.

---

neutralize, *v.* offset, counterbalance. See COUNTERACTION.
never, *adv.* at no time, nevermore. See TIMELESSNESS.

NEWNESS.—I. *Nouns.* **newness,** freshness, etc. (see *adjectives*); novelty, innovation, neoterism, renovation, restoration; youth, juvenility, immaturity.
modernism, modernness, modernity, modernization, *dernier cri* (*F.*), latest thing, latest fashion.
modern, modernist, neoteric; neologist, neoterist.
upstart, parvenu, *nouveau riche* (*F.*), profiteer, snob, mushroom.
II. *Verbs.* **renew,** refresh, revive, rejuvenate, resurrect; renovate, regenerate, revamp, refurbish, repair, restore; modernize, render modern, bring up-to-date.
III. *Adjectives.* **new,** fresh, recent, modern, neoteric, late, later, novel, new-fashioned, newfangled, just out (*colloq.*), up-to-date (*colloq.*), brand-new, fire-new, span-new, *fin-de-siècle* (*F.*), advanced, twentieth-century, spick-and-span, unhandled, newfledged, young, new-born, green, raw, immature, virgin.
renewed, renovated, reinvigorated, recreated, modernized; fresh, additional, further.
unaccustomed, unfamiliar, strange, unused, unusual, untried, bizarre, different.
IV. *Adverbs.* **newly,** freshly, etc. (see *adjectives*); afresh, anew, lately, recently, latterly, of late.

See also DISSIMILARITY, RESTORATION, YOUTH.—*Antonyms.* See OLDNESS.

NEWS.—I. *Nouns.* **news** (*construed as sing.*), information, intelligence, tidings; rumor, hearsay, *oui-dire* (*F.*), story, copy (*cant*), beat *or* scoop (*newspaper cant*), report, bruit, cry; talk, gossip, scandal, newsmongery, tittle-tattle; canard, misreport, fabricated report, hoax.
message, word, advice, communication, letter, bulletin, broadcast, dispatch *or* despatch; telegram, wire (*colloq.*), flash (*colloq.*), cable (*colloq.*), wireless telegram, wireless (*colloq.*), marconigram, radiotelegram, radiogram, radio (*colloq.*); telephone message (*or* call), radiophone (*or* wireless telephone) message.
newsmonger, gossip, quidnunc, gossiper, tattler, busybody, talebearer, scandalmonger, telltale, informer, chatterer; narrator, recounter, reciter.
II. *Adjectives.* **current,** circulating, rife, prevailing, persisting, prevalent, general, noised abroad, rumored, circulated, in circulation, in every one's mouth.

See also DISCLOSURE, INFORMATION, WORD.—*Antonyms.* See SECRET.

---

newspaper, *n.* journal, gazette, daily, paper. See PUBLICATION, RECORD.
New Testament, Gospels, Acts, Epistles, Apocalypse. See SCRIPTURES.
nice, *adj.* discerning, critical; overrefined, squeamish; pleasing, attractive; exact, accurate; delicate, fine. See DISCRIMINATION, FASTIDIOUSNESS, PLEASURABLENESS, TRUTH.
niche, *n.* recess, corner, hollow, nook. See ANGULARITY.
nick, *v.* cut, jag, indent. See NOTCH.
nickname, *n.* diminutive, pet name, *sobriquet* (*F.*). See MISNOMER.
niggardly, *adj.* mean, stingy, near, close, parsimonious. See NARROWNESS, NEARNESS.
night, *n.* nightfall, nighttime, midnight. See DARKNESS.
nimble, *adj.* spry, agile, alert, brisk, lively. See LIGHTNESS.

NINE.—I. *Nouns.* **nine,** ennead, nonary (*rare*), novenary, nonagon (*geom.*), ennastyle (*arch.*), novena (*R. C. Ch.*), nonuplet (*music*).
II. *Adjectives.* **ninefold,** nonuple, novenary; enneastyle (*arch.*).

---

nip, *v.* cut off, clip; check growth of. See DISJUNCTION, SHORTNESS.
no, *adv.* not at all, not so, by no means. See NEGATION.

NOBILITY.—I. *Nouns.* **nobility,** nobleness, greatness, dignity, loftiness, generosity, magnanimity; impressiveness, grandeur, stateliness, magnificence.
rank, condition, distinction, eminence, preëminence, *pur sang* (*F.*), blood, birth, high descent, order, quality.
[*the nobility*] aristocracy, patriciate, *noblesse* (*F.*), *haut monde* (*F.*), peerage, upper classes, the classes, upper ten thousand, upper ten (*colloq.*), *élite* (*F.*), four hundred (*U. S. colloq. or jocose*), F. F. V.'s (First Families of Virginia: *U. S. colloq. or jocose*); lords, house of lords (*or* peers), optimates (*ancient Rome*), samurai (*Jap.*); baronage; fashionable world, high life; Shriners (*collectively*).

gentry (*next below the nobility*), squirarchy *or* squirearchy, gentlefolk, **landed** proprietors, *petite noblesse* (*F.*), magnates.
noble, nobleman, peer, lord, aristocrat, patrician, don (*Sp.*), hidalgo (*Sp.*), grandee, magnate, magnifico (*as of Venice*), daimio (*Jap.*); Shriner (*A. A. O. N. M. S.*).
[*male titles*] king, prince, duke, marquis, earl, viscount, baron, baronet, **knight**, chevalier, count, esquire, laird (*Scot.*); shahzada (*"king's son"*), kumar *or* kunwar (*"prince"*), maharaja, raja, rana, jám, thakur (*all Hindu*); nawab, sultan, mir, ameer *or* amir, khan, mirza, nizam (*all Moham.*); signior, seignior; *signor* (*It.*), *señor* (*Sp.*), *senhor* (*Pg.*), effendi (*Turkey*), sheik *or* sheikh (*Moham.*), pasha (*Turkey*), mirza (*when prefixed, = "Mr."; when appended, = "Prince"*), sahib (*India*), huzur (*India*).
[*female titles*] empress, queen, princess, duchess, marchioness, viscountess, countess; shahzadi, kumari *or* kunwari, maharani, rani (*all Hindu*); sultana, begum *or* begam (*both Moham.*); lady, *doña* (*Sp.*), *dona* (*Pg.*); *signora* (*It.*), *señora* (*Sp.*), *senhora* (*Pg.*).
[*dignity or domain*] kingship, dukedom, duchy, marquisate, earldom; **viscount**ship, viscounty, lordship, baronetcy, knighthood.
[*person of note*] **notability**, celebrity, lion, notable, great gun (*colloq.*), bigwig (*jocose*), great man, star (*esp. theatrical*), magnate (*as, a steel* magnate), dignitary (*esp. of the Church*), swell (*colloq.*); squire, gentleman (*esp. in the historic sense*); a man among men; "every inch a king" (*Lear*).
II. *Adjectives.* **noble**, illustrious, famous, renowned, great, lofty, sublime, high, elevated, exalted, eminent, superior, worthy, dignified, togaed, togated, honorable; magnanimous, liberal, generous, large-hearted, great-hearted, chivalrous, bounteous, munificent.
highborn, aristocratic, patrician, princely, courtly, titled, well-born, gentle, **blue**-blooded, of gentle birth (*or* blood): *opposite of* lowborn, plebeian.
grand, stately, impressive, magnificent, fine, splendid, imposing, **brilliant**, majestic, regal, imperial, royal.
See also FASHION, GREATNESS, IMPORTANCE, MASTER, PROBITY, REPUTE, VIRTUE.—*Antonyms.* See PEOPLE.

---

nobody, *n.* upstart; nonentity, jackstraw. See PEOPLE, UNIMPORTANCE.
nod, *v.* bow, greet, salute; doze, nap; sign, signal. See COURTESY, INACTIVITY, INDICATION.
noise, *n.* din, clamor, uproar, racket. See LOUDNESS.
noiseless, *adj.* quiet, still, hushed, soundless. See SILENCE.
noisy, *adj.* boisterous, uproarious, clamorous, blatant. See LOUDNESS.
nomad, *n.* wanderer, rover. See TRAVELER.

NOMENCLATURE.—I. *Nouns.* **nomenclature**, terminology, glossology, toponomy (*of places*), technology, orismology (*tech.*); baptism, naming.
name, appellation, compellation, appellative, designation, denomination, title, head, heading; style, proper name; prænomen (*as among the ancient Romans*), Christian name, given name (*colloq.*), first name; cognomen, patronymic, surname, eponym, moniker (*slang*), epithet, agnomen, nickname, soubriquet, alias; handle to one's name.
term, expression, locution, word, noun, substantive, phrase, idiom, technical term; cant.
II. *Verbs.* **name**, call, term, denominate, designate, style, entitle, clepe (*archaic*), dub (*colloq. or jocose*), christen, baptize, nickname, characterize, specify, label.
III. *Adjectives.* **named**, called, etc. (see *verbs*); hight (*archaic*), yclept (*archaic or jocose*); known as; titular, nominal, honorary.
See also INDICATION.

---

nonalcoholic, *adj.* nonintoxicating. See TEMPERANCE.
nonchalance, *n.* unconcern, carelessness, insouciance. See INDIFFERENCE.

NONCOMPLETION.—I. *Nouns.* **noncompletion**, nonfulfillment, nonperformance, inexecution, neglect, shortcoming, deficiency, incompletion, incompleteness; drawn battle, drawn game; work of Penelope; Sisyphean labor.

II. *Verbs.* leave unfinished, leave undone, neglect, disregard, let alone, let slip; lose sight of; fall short of, fail to obtain (attain, *or* reach), do things by halves, hang fire; collapse.

III. *Adjectives.* **uncompleted,** incomplete, unfinished, unaccomplished, unperformed, unexecuted; sketchy, defective, imperfect, inchoate, uncomplete (*rare*).

in progress, in hand, going on, proceeding, on the stocks, on the anvil, in preparation, under construction.

See also INCOMPLETENESS.—*Antonyms.* See COMPLETION.

---

nonconformist, *n.* heretic, separatist. See DISSENT.

nonconformity, *n.* heresy, heterodoxy; originality, individuality. See DISSENT, UNCONFORMITY.

nondescript, *adj.* odd, indescribable, unclassifiable. See UNCONFORMITY.

nonentity, *n.* nonsubsistence, nullity; nobody, cipher. See NONEXISTENCE, UNIMPORTANCE.

nonessential, *adj.* unnecessary, irrelevant, incidental. See UNIMPORTANCE.

NONEXISTENCE.—I. *Nouns.* **nonexistence,** inexistence (*rare*), nonbeing, nonsubsistence, *non esse* (*L.*), not-being, nonentity; nullity, nihility, nihilism; blank, *tabula rasa* (*L.*), void, vacuum; nothingness, emptiness, absence.

annihilation, extinction, destruction, abolition, extirpation, obliteration, extinguishment, nullification.

II. *Verbs.* **not exist,** be null and void; cease to exist; pass away, perish, be (*or* become) extinct, die out, disappear, vanish, fade, dissolve, melt away, be no more, die.

annihilate, render null, nullify, abrogate, extinguish, blot out, destroy, remove, displace, vacate; obliterate, extirpate, uncreate.

III. *Adjectives.* **nonexistent,** inexistent (*rare*), negative, blank; null, missing, absent.

unreal, unsubstantial, shadowy, spectral, ideal, visionary, baseless.

unborn, uncreated, unconceived, unproduced, unmade, unbegotten.

extinct, gone, lost, departed, defunct, dead, passed away, passed on, perished, annihilated; extinguished, quenched.

fabulous, fictitious, imaginary, chimerical, legendary, mythical, feigned, apocryphal, supposititious.

See also ABSENCE, DEATH, DISAPPEARANCE, IMAGINATION, UNSUBSTANTIALITY.—*Antonyms.* See EXISTENCE.

NONEXPECTATION.—I. *Nouns.* **nonexpectation,** unforeseen contingency, the unforeseen; surprise, blow, shock; bolt out of the blue; astonishment, amazement; wonder, bewilderment; disappointment, disillusion, miscalculation.

II. *Verbs.* **be unexpected,** come unawares, turn up, burst (*or* flash) upon one; take by surprise, catch unawares, catch napping.

surprise, startle, stun, stagger, throw off one's guard; spring upon, take by surprise, catch (*or* take) unawares, astonish, amaze, astound, electrify.

III. *Adjectives.* **nonexpectant,** surprised, startled, thunderstruck, astonished, unwarned, unaware, off one's guard.

unexpected, unanticipated, unlooked for, unforeseen, unheard of; startling, sudden.

IV. *Adverbs.* **unexpectedly,** suddenly, abruptly, unawares, without notice (*or* warning), like a bolt from the blue.

See also INSTANTANEITY, MISJUDGMENT, NONPREPARATION, WONDER.—*Antonyms.* See PREPARATION.

NONIMITATION.—I. *Nouns.* **nonimitation,** originality, inventiveness, origination, creativeness.

II. *Adjectives.* **unimitated,** uncopied, original, archetypal, prototypal, prototypic, primordial, creative, inventive; unmatched, unparalleled, unexampled, inimitable, unique, unwonted, out-of-the-way, exceptional, rare, uncommon, real, Simon-pure.

See also UNCONFORMITY.—*Antonyms.* See IMITATION.

NONOBSERVANCE.—I. *Nouns.* **nonobservance,** nonobservation, nonacquiescence, nonperformance, noncompliance, evasion, failure, omission, neglect, laches (*law*), slackness, laxness, laxity, informality; lawlessness, disobedience.
infringement, infraction; violation, contravention, encroachment, inroad, invasion, transgression; piracy, literary (*or* artistic) theft, unauthorized appropriation (*or* reproduction). plagiarism.
II. *Verbs.* **omit, leave** undone, evade, neglect, skip, slip, elude, cut (*colloq.*), set aside, ignore; **shut** (*or* close) one's eyes to.
infringe, transgress, violate, contravene; encroach, intrude, invade; purloin, steal, pirate (*a book, etc.*), appropriate, plagiarize.
discard, lay aside, cast off, reject, abandon, repudiate, protest, nullify, declare null and void, cancel, rescind, revoke, recall, retract, abolish.
III. *Adjectives.* **nonobservant,** inattentive, neglectful, elusive, evasive, slippery, casual, lax; transgressive, lawless.
See also DISOBEDIENCE, RIGHTLESSNESS.—*Antonyms.* See OBSERVANCE.

NONPAYMENT.—I. *Nouns.* **nonpayment,** failure (*or* neglect) to pay, **default;** protest, repudiation; misappropriation, defalcation, embezzlement.
insolvency, bankruptcy, failure; run upon a bank.
insolvent, defaulter, bankrupt, lame duck (*stock exchange cant*), debtor; levanter, absconder, welsher (*racing slang*); defalcator, embezzler.
II. *Verbs.* **default,** not pay, fail, break, stop payment; run up bills, get into debt, outstrip (*or* outrun) the constable (*colloq.*); become insolvent (*or* bankrupt), be gazetted (*Brit.*); embezzle, defalcate, swindle.
protest, dishonor, repudiate, nullify.
IV. *Adjectives.* **defaulting,** in arrear, behindhand, in debt; beggared, insolvent, bankrupt, ruined, broken.
See also DEBT, INSUFFICIENCY, POVERTY, STEALING.—*Antonyms.* See PAYMENT.

NONPREPARATION.—I. *Nouns.* **nonpreparation,** unpreparation, want of preparation, unpreparedness, negligence, inadvertence, improvidence.
immaturity, crudity, rawness, unripeness, incipience *or* incipiency, incompleteness, rudimentariness, undevelopedness; abortion, abortiveness, prematurity.
[*absence of art*] nature, state of nature; virgin soil, unweeded garden; rough diamond; raw material.
II. *Verbs.* **be unprepared,** lack preparation; lie fallow; live from hand to mouth.
extemporize, improvise, provide (*or* do) offhand, cook up, fix up.
III. *Adjectives.* **unprepared,** unequipped, unprovided, unfurnished, unorganized, unready, unfit, unadapted, unsuitable, unfitted, unqualified, unsuited, disqualified; unripe, kutcha *or kachcha* (*Anglo-Indian*), raw, uncooked, unbaked, green, callow; crude, coarse, incomplete, rough, roughhewn.
rudimentary, rudimental, vestigial, incomplete, imperfect, embryonic, premature, inchoate, undeveloped, immature, unfledged, unhatched.
untaught, uneducated, uncultivated, uncultured, untrained, untutored, unlicked.
fallow, unsown, untilled, uncultivated, unplowed *or* unploughed, idle, lea (*Eng.*).
shiftless, improvident, thriftless, unthrifty, happy-go-lucky, careless, heedless, negligent, slack, remiss, lax, inefficient, thoughtless, inconsiderate, wasteful, prodigal.
extemporaneous, unpremeditated, improvised, extempore, extemporized, improvisatory, impromptu, offhand, spontaneous, extemporary, extemporal.
IV. *Adverbs.* **unpreparedly,** extemporaneously, unpremeditatedly, etc. (see *adjectives*); on the spur of the moment, without premeditation, without preparation, by surprise.
See also IMPULSE, NONEXPECTATION.—*Antonyms.* See PREPARATION.

NONRESONANCE.—I. *Nouns.* **nonresonance,** nonvibration, nonvibrancy, deadness, dullness, hollowness, heaviness; dead sound, pounding, pound, thud, thump; damper, sordine, mute (*as on a violin*); muffler, silencer (*as on an automobile*); muffled drums.
II. *Verbs.* **muffle,** deaden, dampen, drown, overwhelm, overpower, mute; stop (*or* deaden) the sound.
III. *Adjectives.* **nonresonant,** nonvibrant, deadened, dead, hollow, heavy muffled, silenced, mute.
Antonyms. See RESONANCE.

nonsense, *n.* silliness, absurdity, bosh (*colloq.*) trash. See UNMEANINGNESS.
nook, *n.* corner, recess, niche. See ANGULARITY.
noon, *n.* midday, noonday. See MORNING.
noose, *n.* loop, lariat, lasso, halter. See VINCULUM.
normal, *adj.* usual, typical, regular. See CONFORMITY.
northern, *adj.* north, northerly, northward: *opposite of southern.* See OPPOSITE.
nosegay, *n.* bouquet, posy. See FRAGRANCE.
notability, *n.* celebrity, notable, dignitary, lion. See NOBILITY.
notable, *adj.* remarkable, renowned, distinguished. See REPUTE.

NOTCH.—I. *Nouns.* **notch,** dent, nick, score, nock (*as of an arrow*), cut, indent, indentation, serration, denticulation, serrulation, indention (*printing*).
saw, tooth, crenel *or* crenelle, scallop, vandyke, jag; battlement, embrasure, machicolation, crenelation, castellation.
pass, defile, cut, gap, gut, neck, *col* (*F.*), gully, passage, gorge: *common in New England place names; as,* *Crawford* Notch.
II. *Verbs.* **notch,** nick, mill, score, cut, dent, indent, jag, scarify, scallop, gash, crimp, vandyke; crenelate *or* crenellate.
III. *Adjectives.* **notched,** crenate, scalloped, emarginate *or* emarginated (*tech.*), dentate, toothed, palmate *or* palmated, serrate *or* serrated, serriform, sawlike, serrulate *or* serrulated; machicolated, castellated.
See also INDICATION, INTERVAL.—*Antonyms.* See SMOOTHNESS.

---

note, *n.* notice, regard, observation; letter, epistle, missive; mark, sign, token, feature; comment, annotation, explanation, remark; musical note, tone; minute, memorandum; distinction, fame. See ATTENTION, CORRESPONDENCE, INDICATION, INTERPRETATION, MUSIC, RECORD, REPUTE.
note, *v.* heed, notice, remark, observe; jot down. See INTELLECT, MEMORY, RECORD, WRITING.
noted, *adj.* celebrated, famous, renowned, eminent. See REPUTE.
noteworthy, *adj.* remarkable, exceptional, extraordinary. See GREATNESS.
nothing, *n.* trifle, bagatelle; naught, *nihil* (*L.*), zero, cipher; nothingness, blank. See UNIMPORTANCE, UNSUBSTANTIALITY.
notice, *n.* regard, note, observation; announcement, notification; placard, circular, poster; consideration, recognition, civility. See ATTENTION, INFORMATION, PUBLICATION, RESPECT.
notice, *v.* heed, remark, observe, regard; see, detect, note. See ATTENTION, OBSERVANCE.
noticeable, *adj.* conspicuous, prominent. See GREATNESS.
notification, *n.* notice, news, information. See INTELLIGENCE.
notify, *v.* tell, acquaint, apprise. See ADVICE, INFORMATION.
notion, *n.* inclination, fancy; conception, belief, opinion, theory. See DESIRE, IDEA.
notoriety, *n.* publicity, notoriousness. See PUBLICATION.
notwithstanding, *adv.* nevertheless, yet, although, however. See COMPENSATION.
notwithstanding, *prep.* despite, in spite of. See COMPENSATION.
nourish, *v.* foster, support; feed, sustain. See AID, FOOD.
nourishment, *n.* nutriment, sustenance. See FOOD.
novel, *adj.* new, different, unusual, unique. See NEWNESS.
novice, *n.* greenhorn, tyro, amateur, beginner. See IGNORAMUS, LEARNER.
now, *adv.* at present, immediately, at this moment. See PRESENT, STRAIGHTNESS.
nowise, *adv.* noway, in no manner, not at all. See SMALLNESS.
noxious, *adj.* injurious, harmful, pernicious. See BADNESS.
nucleus, *n.* core, kernel, heart. See CENTRALITY.
nude, *adj.* bare, naked, unclothed, exposed. See DIVESTMENT.

nudge, *v.* jog, push, touch (*with the elbow*), poke. See INDICATION
nugatory, *adj.* futile, useless, ineffectual. See IMPOTENCE, UNIMPORTANCE.
nuisance, *n.* annoyance, bother, pest, bore. See PAINFULNESS.
nullity, *n.* blankness, negativeness, annihilation, obliteration, nothingness. See NEGATION.
numb, *adj.* benumbed, deadened, insensible. See NUMBNESS.

NUMBER.—I. *Nouns.* **number,** symbol, character, numeral, figure, numero (*abbr.* No., *pl.* Nos.), cipher, digit, integer, folio, round number; series.
sum, difference, product, total, summation, aggregate, tally, tale, quantity, amount; collection, assemblage, company; multitude, many; problem, example (*arith.*).
ratio, proportion, quota, percentage; progression; arithmetical progression.
power, root, exponent, index, logarithm, modulus.
[*in plural*] **numbers,** poetry, verses, verse, rime *or* rhyme, metrical composition.
II. *Verbs.* **number,** count, reckon, enumerate, tell (*as money*), compute, calculate, numerate; call over, run over, take an account of, tell off, cipher, score, reckon up, total, cast up, tot up (*Eng. colloq.*), sum up, sum; call the roll, muster, poll; estimate, make an estimate; add, subtract, multiply, divide, algebraize extract roots.
page, foliate, paginate, mark, affix numbers to.
check, tick, mark, prick, tally, audit, balance, take stock, overhaul, prove, demonstrate.
comprise, contain, consist of, amount to, equal, embrace, take in.
III. *Adjectives.* **numberable,** countable, reckonable, computable, numerable, calculable.
proportional, commeasurable, commensurate, proportionate.
See also MULTITUDE, NUMERATION, POETRY.

NUMBNESS.—I. *Nouns.* **numbness,** benumbedness, torpor, torpidity, dullness, insensibility, anæsthesia, narcosis (*med.*), narcotization, narcotism (*med.*); pins and needles (*colloq.*).
II. *Verbs.* **numb,** deaden, benumb, paralyze, narcotize (*tech.*), drug, stupefy, torpify, dull.
III. *Adjectives.* **numb,** benumbed, deadened, dulled, torpid, stupefied, paralyzed, asleep, numbed, comatose, insensible, dazed, unfeeling; impalpable, intangible; dull, lifeless, inert.
See also INSENSIBILITY.—*Antonyms.* See SENSIBILITY, TOUCH.

NUMERATION.—I. *Nouns.* **numeration,** numbering, counting, calculation, computation, reckoning, enumeration, tale, tally; roll call, muster, poll, census, lustrum (*Roman hist.*); statistics.
arithmetic, algebra, differential calculus, calculus of differences, mathematics.
[*operations*] addition, subtraction, multiplication, division; proportion, rule of three; practice, equations, extraction of roots, reduction, involution, evolution, approximation, interpolation, differentiation, integration.
[*instruments*] abacus, suan pan (*Chinese*); logometer, slide rule, Napier's bones (*or* rods); calculating machine, adding machine, cash register, arithmometer, arithmograph, comptometer (*trade-mark name*).
mathematician, algebraist, geometrician, trigonometrician, arithmetician, calculator, actuary, statistician.
numeral, digit, number, figure; cardinal number.
II. *Verbs.* **numerate,** count, reckon, calculate, enumerate, number, compute, estimate, call over, tell off, divide off.
III. *Adjectives* **numeral,** numerary, numerative, numerical; arithmetical, analytic, algebraic, statistical.
See also LIST, NUMBER.

---

numerous, *adj.* many, various, plentiful, myriad, thick. See MULTITUDE, THICKNESS.
nun, *n.* sister, *religieuse* (*F.*). See CLERGY.
nuptial, *adj.* bridal, connubial. See MARRIAGE.

nurse, *v.* cherish, foster; take care of, tend; bring up. See AID, REMEDY.
nurture, *v.* nourish, foster, rear; train, educate. See AID, PREPARATION.
nutritious, *adj.* nourishing, wholesome, nutritive, digestible. See FOOD. HEALTHINESS.
nymph, *n.* dryad, undine. See MYTHICAL BEINGS.

O

oaf, *n.* blockhead, idiot, dunce, numskull (*colloq.*); lout. See FOOL, PEOPLE.
oar, *n.* oarsman, rower, stroke; paddle, scull, sweep. See MARINER, NAVIGATION.
oath, *n.* pledge, sworn statement; curse, profanity. See AFFIRMATION, MALEDICTION.
obdurate, *adj.* unfeeling, hardened; stubborn, firm, unyielding, inflexible. See HARDNESS, OBSTINACY.

OBEDIENCE.—I. *Nouns.* **obedience,** observance, compliance, subservience, duteousness, obeisance (*archaic in this sense*), submission, subjection; nonresistance, passivity, passiveness, resignation, submissiveness, ductility, obsequiousness, servility.
allegiance, faithfulness, fidelity, constancy, loyalty, fealty, homage, deference, devotion.
II. *Verbs.* **obey,** give ear to, mind, heed, comply, do one's bidding, attend to orders, conform, submit, yield, serve faithfully (loyally, devotedly, *or* without question); be resigned to, be submissive to, serve; play second fiddle.
III. *Adjectives.* **obedient,** complying, compliant, submissive, pliant, supple, unresisting, attentive, yielding, dutiful, duteous, complaisant; loyal, faithful, devoted; under beck and call, under control; acquiescent, resigned, passive, nonresistant, nonresisting, law-abiding.
servile, cringing, fawning, truckling, subservient, obsequious, sycophantic.
IV. *Adverbs.* **obediently,** compliantly, etc. (see *adjectives*); in obedience to, in compliance with; as you please.
See also OBSERVANCE, SERVILITY, SUBJECTION, SUBMISSION.—*Antonyms.* See DISOBEDIENCE.

---

obeisance, *n.* bow, curtsy, salaam (*Oriental*); homage, genuflection, prostration. See COURTESY, SUBMISSION.
object, *v.* kick, protest, resist, disapprove. See OPPOSITION.
object, *n.* aim, goal, objective; thing. See END, INTENTION, MATERIALITY.
objection, *n.* criticism, exception; barrier, drawback. See DISAPPROBATION, HINDRANCE.
objectionable, *adj.* obnoxious, offensive, undesirable. See DISLIKE.

OBJECTIVENESS.—I. *Nouns.* **objectiveness,** objectivity, objectivation, objectization, externalism, externality, externalization, exteriorization, extrinsicality, extraneousness; *non ego* (*L.*).
II. *Verbs.* **objectivate,** objectify, externalize, visualize, exteriorize, actualize, envisage.
III. *Adjectives.* **objective,** external, extraneous, extrinsic, outward, nonsubjective; actual, positive, real.
incidental, accidental, nonessential, unessential, fortuitous, casual, chance, subsidiary, contingent, ascititious, adscititious, secondary, supplementary, collateral, accessory.
implanted, ingrafted, infixed, inset, insinuated, infused, instilled, introduced.
IV. *Adverbs.* **objectively,** externally, etc. (see *adjectives*).
See also EXTRANEOUSNESS, MATERIALITY.—*Antonyms.* See SUBJECTIVENESS.

---

obligation, *n.* indebtedness, responsibility; contract, agreement, bond. See DUTY, PROMISE.

obligatory, *adj.* binding, imperative, compulsory, incumbent on. See DUTY.
oblige, *v.* favor, accommodate; force, make, impel. See AID, COMPULSION.
obliging, *adj.* kind, helpful, accommodating, gracious. See COURTESY.

OBLIQUITY.—I. *Nouns.* **obliquity,** inclination, incline, slope, retreat (*backward slope: aëro.*), slant, rake, leaning, tilt, bias, diagonal, bevel, zigzag, list, twist, sag, cant, lurch, bend, curve; distortion, deviation, divergence.
acclivity (*upward slope*), steepness; rise, ascent, pitch, gradient (*chiefly Brit.*), grade (*U. S.*), inclined plane, ramp; rising ground, hill, bank, khudd (*India*), glacis; cliff, precipice.
declivity (*downward slope*), dip, fall, descent, downhill.
[*measure of inclination*] clinometer, Abney level, inclinometer (*as used on aircraft*); sine, cosine, angle, hypotenuse *or* hypothenuse.
[*moral and intellectual obliquity*] **error,** mistake, errancy, slip, twist, fallacy, fallaciousness, erroneousness, flaw, fault, delinquency, transgression, misdeed, offense, sin.
II. *Verbs.* **oblique,** deviate, swerve, diverge, deflect, veer, sheer, incline, slue *or* slew; march obliquely (*mil.*).
be oblique, slope, slant, lean, cant, incline, retreat (*slope backward, as a wing tip: aëro.*), shelve, decline, descend, bend; heel over, careen, reel, lurch, roll, slouch, sag, sidle, skid.
render oblique, sway, bias; slope, slant, cant, tilt; incline, bend, crook; zigzag, stagger (*tech.*); distort.
III. *Adjectives.* **oblique,** sloping, tilted, slanting, aslope, slant, bevel, plagihedral (*as quartz crystals*), supine, inclined, askew, asquint, bias, aslant, diagonal, transverse, athwart; indirect, wry, awry, crooked; sinuous, zigzag.
acclivous, rising, ascending; steep, abrupt, precipitous, uphill.
declivous, descending, falling, declining, shelving, declivitous, downhill.
underhand, shifty, tricky, shuffling, indirect, devious, deceitful, evasive, disingenuous, unfair, unscrupulous, dishonest, crooked.
IV. *Adverbs.* **obliquely,** on one side, askew, askance *or* askant, aslope, slant, awry, edgewise, at an angle; sidelong, sidewise, slantwise.
See also CUNNING, CURVATURE, DEVIATION, DISTORTION.—*Antonyms.* See PARALLELISM, STRAIGHTNESS.

OBLITERATION.—I. *Nouns.* **obliteration,** erasure, expunction, cancellation, deletion; blot; effacement, extinction, annihilation; *tabula rasa* (*L.*).
II. *Verbs.* **obliterate,** efface, erase, expunge, cancel, dele (*printing*), delete, rub out, strike out, scratch out, rule out, wash out, blot out, expurgate, deface, render illegible, annihilate, destroy, exterminate.
be effaced, leave no trace; "leave not a rack behind" (*Tempest*).
III. *Adjectives.* **obliterated,** erased, expunged, unrecorded, unregistered, wiped out (*colloq.*).
See also DESTRUCTION, NONEXISTENCE.—*Antonyms.* See RECORD.

OBLIVION.—I. *Nouns.* **oblivion,** forgetfulness, obliviousness, obliviscence (*rare*), obliteration of the past; short (treacherous, untrustworthy, slippery, *or* failing) memory; amnesia, decay (failure, lapse, *or* loss) of memory; waters of oblivion, Lethe.
amnesty, general pardon, pardon (*as, an act of* oblivion).
II. *Verbs.* **forget,** be forgetful; fall (*or* sink) into oblivion; have a short memory; lose, lose the memory of, escape (*or* slip) one's memory, disremember (*archaic or dial.*), efface from the memory, obliterate, lose sight of, unlearn; consign to oblivion, think no more of; let bygones be bygones.
III. *Adjectives.* **oblivious,** forgetful, unmindful, heedless, disregardful, neglectful; forgetting, amnesic *or* amnestic, insensible to the past, Lethean.
forgotten, unremembered, past recollection, gone, lost, gone out of one's head, out of mind, buried (*or* sunk) in oblivion.
See also PAST, SILENCE.—*Antonyms.* See MEMORY.

---

obnoxious, *adj.* offensive, repulsive, odious. See HATE.
obscene, *adj.* indecent, smutty, coarse, lewd. See IMPURITY.

OBSCURITY.—I. *Nouns.* **obscurity,** dimness, nebulosity, nebulousness, darkness, duskiness, gloom, cloudiness, indistinctness, obfuscation, obscuration, occultation.
vagueness, indefiniteness, unclearness, ambiguity, inexactness, inaccuracy, unintelligibility, unintelligibleness, intricacy, confusion, abstruseness, involution, mystery, mysteriousness.
humbleness, lowliness, humility; namelessness, inconspicuousness, unassumingness; seclusion, privacy, retirement.
II. *Verbs.* **obscure,** dim, bedim, bemist, becloud, befog, cloud, shroud, conceal, hide, darken; obfuscate, confuse, bewilder, mystify, perplex.
III. *Adjectives.* **obscure,** dusky, dim, shadowy, dark, darksome, shaded, indistinct, misty, blurred, hazy, nebulous, eclipsed, inconspicuous, hidden.
unintelligible, incomprehensible, involved, intricate, difficult, abstruse, enigmatical, mysterious, blind, doubtful, vague, indefinite, ill-defined, loose, confused, unclear, ambiguous.
humble, lowly, mean, plebeian, baseborn, lowborn, ignoble, unknown, unnoticed, nameless, unhonored, inglorious, undistinguished, unsung (*poetic*), uncelebrated; secluded, retired, remote.

See also DARKNESS, DEPTH, INVISIBILITY, OPACITY, SHADE, SMALLNESS, UNINTELLIGIBILITY.—*Antonyms.* See PERSPICUITY.

---

obsequies, *n. pl.* funeral, burial service. See INTERMENT.
obsequious, *adj.* fawning, cringing, truckling. See SERVILITY.

OBSERVANCE.—I. *Nouns.* **observance,** attention, keeping, holding, acknowledgment, adhesion, compliance, acquiescence, obedience, concurrence, fulfillment, satisfaction, discharge; acquittance, acquittal; fidelity.
rite, ceremony, custom, performance, practice, form, customary act, ordinance (*eccl.*), rule.
II. *Verbs.* **observe,** comply with, respect, acknowledge, abide by, hold, heed, obey, follow, cling to, adhere to, be faithful to, act up to; meet, carry out, execute, perform, discharge, keep one's word (*or* pledge), redeem, fulfill (*as a promise*), keep faith with; celebrate, solemnize, regard.
notice, perceive, see, discover, detect, behold, note, mark, eye, watch, take notice of, examine.
remark, utter, say, state, mention, comment, descant, express, animadvert.
III. *Adjectives.* **observant,** attentive, mindful, heedful, watchful, regardful.
obedient, submissive, faithful, true, loyal, honorable; punctual, punctilious, scrupulous, as good as one's word.

See also CONFORMITY, DUTY, HABIT, OBEDIENCE, PROBITY.—*Antonyms.* See NONOBSERVANCE.

---

observation, *n.* remark, comment; notice, regard, consideration. See AFFIRMATION, ATTENTION.
observe, *v.* respect, obey, follow; notice, see; remark, say. See OBSERVANCE.
obsess, *v.* haunt, prey upon, beset, besiege. See FEAR.
obsolete, *adj.* out-of-date, outworn, disused, antiquated. See OLDNESS.
obstacle, *n.* hindrance, stumblingblock, obstruction, barricade. See DIFFICULTY, OPPOSITION, PRISON (*barrier*).

OBSTINACY.—I. *Nouns.* **obstinacy,** stubbornness, pertinacity, doggedness, mulishness, unyieldingness, recalcitrance *or* recalcitrancy, noncompliance, tenacity, cussedness (*U. S. colloq.*), perverseness, persistency, firmness, resoluteness, resolution, perseverance, immovability, inflexibility, obduracy, self-will, contumacy, perversity.
bigotry, intolerance, narrow-mindedness, opinionativeness, dogmatism; fixed idea, *idée fixe* (*F.*), prejudice, fanaticism, zealotry, infatuation, monomania.
bigot, dogmatist, zealot, enthusiast, fanatic, bitter-ender (*U. S. politics*), irreconcilable, incompatible, mule, recalcitrant, stickler.
II. *Verbs.* **be obstinate,** stickle, take no denial, be wedded to an opinion, hug a belief, persist, die hard, not yield an inch, stand out.

III. *Adjectives.* **obstinate,** tenacious, stubborn, obdurate, inflexible, unbending, immovable, unchangeable, inexorable, determined, mulish, balky, pig-headed, pertinacious, persistent, unyielding, firm, unmoved, hard-set, hardbitted *or* hardbitten (*as a horse*), untoward, perverse, forward, wayward, refractory, dogged; sullen, sulky.

opinionated, self-willed, opinionative, opinioned, stiff-necked, hidebound, headstrong, heady, ungovernable, willful, intractable, refractory, cross-grained, perverse, unruly, incorrigible, wayward, contumacious; bigoted, prejudiced, dogmatic, arbitrary, positive.

IV. *Adverbs.* **obstinately,** tenaciously, etc. (see *adjectives*); with dogged resolution; with set jaw; no surrender; to the bitter end.

See also CERTAINTY, HARDNESS, MISJUDGMENT, PERMANENCE, PERSEVERANCE, RESOLUTION, TENACITY, WILL.—*Antonyms.* See APOSTASY, IRRESOLUTION.

---

obstreperous, *adj.* riotous, noisy, clamorous, vociferous. See VIOLENCE.

obstruct, *v.* choke, stop, block; retard, check, impede. See HINDRANCE.

obtain, *v.* procure, get, attain, gain, acquire, secure. See ACQUISITION, SECURITY.

obtainable, *adj.* accessible, procurable. See POSSIBILITY.

obtrude, *v.* thrust in, intrude. See INSERTION.

obtuse, *adj.* blunt (*of angles*); dull, stupid, stolid, dense, thick. See BLUNTNESS, DULLNESS, OPACITY.

obvious, *adj.* plain, patent, evident, clear. See MANIFESTATION.

occasion, *n.* reason, ground; event, happening; opening, opportunity. See CAUSE, CIRCUMSTANCE, TIMELINESS.

occasional, *adj.* incidental, irregular, casual. See TIMELINESS.

occult, *adj.* mystic, hidden, secret, mysterious. See LATENCY.

occupant, *n.* tenant, occupier, holder, inhabitant. See POSSESSOR.

occupation, *n.* calling, profession, pursuit; tenure, occupancy. See BUSINESS, POSSESSION.

occupy, *v.* inhabit, dwell, live in, tenant; take up, fill, have, hold; busy, engross; employ, make use of. See INHABITANT, POSSESSION, USE.—**occupy oneself with,** have in hand, undertake. See BUSINESS.

occur, *v.* happen, take place, come. See EVENT, PASSAGE.

occurrence, *n.* incident, transaction, affair, proceeding. See CIRCUMSTANCE, PASSAGE.

OCEAN.—I. *Nouns.* **ocean,** sea, great sea, main (*poetic*), high seas, deep, salt water, *kala pani* (*Hind.*), briny deep, brine, "the whelming brine" (Cowper), vasty deep, the wave (*poetic*), mere (*archaic*), watery waste, the hyaline (*poetic*), pond *or* herring pond (*esp. the Atlantic: jocose or colloq.*), the Seven Seas; waters, waves, billows, tide, offing.

[*mythological*] Neptune, Poseidon, Oceanus, Thetis, Triton, Naiad, Nereid; sea nymph, Siren, mermaid, merman; trident.

[*Anglo-Saxon kennings*] swan bath, swan road, sea fowl's bath, whale path, home of the whale, realm of monsters.

ocean lane, lane, sea route, lane route, steamer lane, steamer track.

oceanography (*static and dynamic*); hydrography, bathymetry; oceanographer, hydrographer.

II. *Adjectives.* **oceanic,** pelagic, marine, maritime; seaworthy, seagoing; oceanographic *or* oceanographical, hydrographic *or* hydrographical; bathygraphic, bathymetric *or* bathymetrical, bathybic (*biol.*), benthonic (*biol.*).

Antonyms. See LAND.

---

ocular, *adj.* visual, optic; visible, perceptible. See VISION.

odd, *adj.* over, left, extra; curious, strange, unusual, quaint, droll, queer; lone, single. See REMAINDER, RIDICULOUSNESS, UNITY.

oddity, *n.* singularity, strangeness, eccentricity; curiosity, freak, queer person, crank (*colloq.*). See INSANITY, UNCONFORMITY.

odds, *n.* advantage, probability; difference, disparity. See CHANCE, INEQUALITY.
odious, *adj.* repulsive, offensive, hateful, detestable. See PAINFULNESS.

ODOR.—I. *Nouns.* **odor** *or* odour, smell, scent, perfume, essence, aroma, bouquet (*of wine*), redolence, odoriferousness, odoriferosity, emanation, effluvium (*pl.* effluvia: *esp. a noxious emanation*), exhalation; fume, trail, trace, savor *or* savour.
repute, estimation, character, name, reputation, fame, regard (*as, in good* odor).
[*sense of smell*] olfaction, olfactory; olfactory organs, olfactories.
II. *Verbs.* **have an odor** (*or* scent); smell, exhale; give out a smell (*or* odor); scent.
smell, scent, snuff, sniff, nose (*now rare*), inhale.
III. *Adjectives.* **odorous,** odoriferous, strong-scented, redolent, pungent, savory, aromatic, sweet-smelling, perfumed, sweet-scented, olent (*rare*).
[*relating to the sense of smell*] olfactory, olfactive (*rare*); quick-scented, keen-scented.
See also FRAGRANCE.—*Antonyms.* See INODOROUSNESS.

---

of course, consequently, naturally. See DEMONSTRATION.
offend, *v.* disgust, displeasure, anger, wound. See PAINFULNESS.
offense, *n.* assault, onset, crime, sin, outrage; displeasure, pique; affront, slight, indignity. See ATTACK, GUILT, RESENTMENT.
offensive, *adj.* aggressive, combative; repulsive, disgusting; foul, tainted; unsavory, uninviting, revolting. See ATTACK, HATE, UNCLEANNESS, UNSAVORINESS.

OFFER.—I. *Nouns.* **offer,** proffer, tender, bid, advance, submission, presentation, overture, proposal, proposition; motion, ultimatum, invitation, offering; nomination, candidature.
endeavor, attempt, try, essay, trial, effort, exertion, striving.
II. *Verbs.* **offer,** proffer, present, tender, bid, propose, suggest, propound (*as an opinion*), lay, lay before, submit, put forward, bring forward, advance, extend, press, urge upon, hold out; move, make a motion, start, invite, place at one's disposal, make possible; offer up, sacrifice.
[*offer oneself*] **volunteer,** bestow, proffer, tender, offer voluntarily, make an offer, express readiness, come forward, be a candidate, present oneself, stand for, bid for; seek; be at one's service.
endeavor, attempt, try, undertake, strive, essay, venture, dare; make, give, do (*as, to* offer *resistance*).
III. *Adjectives.* **offered,** proffered, etc. (see *verbs*); disengaged, on hire, to let, for sale, in the market.
See also GIVING, SALE, SUBMISSION, WILLINGNESS.—*Antonyms.* See REFUSAL, REQUEST, REQUIREMENT.

---

offering, *n.* gift, sacrifice; proposition; collection, offertory. See GIVING, OFFER, WORSHIP.
offhand, *adv.* impromptu, extempore. See IMPULSE.
office, *n.* function, service; position, post. See AGENCY, BUSINESS.
officer, *n.* office holder, official, functionary. See DIRECTOR.
official, *adj.* authentic, authoritative. See AUTHORITY.
official, *n.* dignitary, functionary, officer. See MASTER.
officialism, *n.* bureaucracy, red-tapism. See AUTHORITY.
officiate, *v.* serve, function, preside. See BUSINESS, RITE.
officious, *adj.* meddlesome, pushing, obtrusive. See ACTIVITY.
officiousness, *n.* meddlesomeness, interference, inquisitiveness, meddling. See ACTIVITY.
offset, *v.* balance, cancel, counterbalance. See COUNTERACTION.
offshoot, *n.* shoot, branch, scion, ramification. See ADJUNCT.
offspring, *n.* children, progeny, descendants. See POSTERITY.
often, *adv.* repeatedly, frequently, oftentimes. See FREQUENCY.

OIL.—I. *Nouns.* *oleum* (*L.*), lubricant, fat, grease, olein; glycerin *or* glycerine; petrolatum (*pharm.*), cosmoline, vaseline, petroleum jelly; ointment, pomade, pomatum, unguent, liniment; soap, Castile soap, marine soap, soft soap; wax, cerate (*pharm.*), vegetable wax; mineral wax, ozocerite, ceresin *or* ceresine, fossil wax.
[*vegetable oils*] bay (*or* bayberry), cacao (*or* cocoa) butter, castor, coconut, cottonseed, croton, kekune (artist's candlenut, *or* Spanish-walnut), kundah (*or* talicoona), linseed, maize (*or* corn), makassar, olive (*or* sweet), palm, peanut (arachis, *or* groundnut), rape (*or* colza), turpentine, etc.
[*animal oils and fats*] cod-liver (*or* shore), crocodile, dœgling (arctic-sperm, *or* bottlenose), dugong, melon (*of cetaceans*), menhaden (*or* pogy), neat's-foot, oleo, porpoise, seal, shark, sperm, train, tunny, walrus, whale; cream, butter, lard, dripping, tallow, suet, blubber; stearin, tristearin; palmitin, tripalmitin.
[*mineral oils*] petroleum (mineral, rock, *or* natural), benzine, naphtha; gasoline *or* gasolene, gas (*colloq.*), petrol (*chiefly Brit.*); paraffin *or* paraffine; mineral colza (mineral seal, *or* mineral sperm); kerosene (*or* coal oil), fuel oil, furnace oil; fatty (*or* fixed) oils, volatile (*or* essential) oils.
[*in art*] oils (*colloq.*), oil colors, oil paintings.
II. *Verbs.* **oil,** lubricate, grease, lard, smear, begrease, pinguefy; anoint, salve, chrism (*rare*).
bribe, square (*colloq.*), tip (*colloq.*), corrupt, suborn, square (*slang*), grease the palm (*slang*).
flatter, soft-soap (*colloq.*), butter (*colloq.*), adulate, suavify (*rare*), blarney, blandish (*as, to* oil *the tongue*).
III. *Adjectives.* **oily,** unctuous, oleaginous, greasy, oleic, unguinous, sebaceous, fatty, fat, pinguid, oleous *or* oleose (*rare*), slippery, lubricous; soapy, saponaceous; lardy, lardaceous; buttery, butyraceous.
smooth, glib, unctuous, plausible, suave, bland, fawning, insinuating, ingratiating, subservient, compliant, supple.
IV. *Adverbs.* **oilily,** unctuously, etc. (see *adjectives*); blandly, smoothly.
See also LUBRICATION, SMOOTHNESS, UNCTUOUSNESS.

---

oiliness, *n.* greasiness, unctuousness. See LUBRICATION.
oily, *adj.* greasy, oleaginous, unctuous; smooth, plausible. See OIL.
ointment, *n.* salve, unguent, balm. See LUBRICATION.
old man, boss (*slang*), employer; father, governor (*slang*), pater (*colloq.*); grandfather, patriarch, graybeard. See MASTER, PATERNITY, VETERAN.

OLDNESS.—I. *Nouns.* **oldness,** age, antiquity, eld (*poetic*), venerableness, hoariness, ancientness, agedness.
maturity, matureness, ripeness, maturation, maturement (*rare*), full development.
decline, decay, impairment, deterioration, decadence, ebb, wane.
senility, old age, superannuation, dotage, debility, weakness, infirmity, senile decay, anility, second childhood, decrepitude.
antiquities, ancient relics, remains, reliquiæ, fossils, *disjecta membra* (*L.*), monuments; eoliths, paleoliths, neoliths; antiquarianism, archæology *or* archeology, paleontology.
tradition, custom, usage, immemorial usage, common law, unwritten law; Sunna *or* Sunnah (*Moham.*), prescription; folklore.
II. *Verbs.* **be old,** have had its day, have seen its day.
become old, age, ripen, mature; fade, deteriorate, decay.
III. *Adjectives.* **old,** ancient, antique; time-honored, venerable, hoary; elder; eldest, firstborn.
primitive, prime, primeval, primiginous, primigenial, primigenious, primary, primal, primordial, aboriginal; antediluvian, prehistoric, dateless, patriarchal, Noachian, ancestral, archaic, classic, Vedic, Pre-Raphaelite, medieval.
immemorial, traditional, prescriptive, unwritten, inveterate, rooted.
antiquated, of other times, of the old school, old world; obsolete out-of-date, out-of-fashion, unfashionable, outworn, gone by, *passé* (*F.*), stale, old-fashioned, exploded, extinct, time-worn, crumbling; old as the hills; old as Methuselah (*or* Adam).
See also AGE.—*Antonyms.* See NEWNESS.

Old Testament, Septuagint, the Law, the Prophets. See SCRIPTURES.
old woman, crone, hag; granny, dowager (*colloq.*). See VETERAN.

OMEN.—I. *Nouns.* **omen,** portent, presage, prognostic, auspice, augury, sign, token, indication, foretoken, foreboding, prognostication, warning, bodement, boding, prophecy; harbinger; halcyon birds; bird of ill omen; signs of the times.
II. *Verbs.* **omen,** augur, forebode, presage, divine, foreshow, soothsay, predict, foretell.
III. *Adjectives.* **ominous,** portentous, significant, boding, presageful, prophetic, oracular; suggestive, indicative: *now used chiefly in an unfavorable sense.*
auspicious, favorable, propitious, fortunate, prosperous, promising, lucky, halcyon, of good omen.
inauspicious, unfavorable, unpromising, unfortunate, unlucky, ill-omened, ill-starred, ill-boding, threatening, lowering.
See also INDICATION, PREDICTION.

---

ominous, *adj.* inauspicious, unpromising; portentous, premonitory. See HOPELESSNESS, PREDICTION.
omission, *n.* elimination, exception, rejection, cut; deficit, shortage; evasion, failure, neglect. See EXCLUSION, INCOMPLETENESS, NONOBSERVANCE.
omit, *v.* overlook, skip; leave undone, evade. See NEGLECT, NONOBSERVANCE.
omnipotence, *n.* infinite power, almightiness. See POWER.
omnivorous, *adj.* eating, everything, all-devouring. See FOOD.
on, *adv.* ahead, forward, onward. See PROGRESSION.
once, *adv.* formerly; ever. See TIME.
one, *adj.* single, sole, solitary, individual. See UNITY.
onerous, *adj.* oppressive, burdensome, difficult. See HEAVINESS.
one-sided, *adj.* asymmetric, unsymmetrical, awry; biased, partial, unfair; unilateral (*tech.*). See DISTORTION, MISJUDGMENT, SIDE.
onlooker, *n.* observer, witness, bystander, looker-on. See SPECTATOR.
ooze, *v.* leak, filter, percolate. See EGRESS.

OPACITY.—I. *Nouns.* **opacity,** opaqueness, nontranslucency, nontransparency, intransparency, obscurity, obfuscation, nubilation, cloudiness, darkness, filminess, mistiness; film, nebula, cloud; imperviousness (*physics*).
[*obscurity of sense*] **unintelligibility,** unintelligibleness, incomprehensibleness, inexplicableness, unfathomableness, enigma, mystification.
[*mental dimness*] **obtuseness,** dullness, stupidity, obtusity (*rare*), stolidity, thickheadedness, dull-wittedness.
II. *Verbs.* **opaque,** obfuscate, becloud, darken, obscure, make opaque, etc. (see *adjectives*).
III. *Adjectives.* **opaque,** nontranslucent, nontransparent, intransparent, impervious to light; filmy, cloudy, misty, foggy, vaporous, dim, dark, smoky, fuliginous, fumy, reeky, murky, smeared, turbid, thick, muddy, dirty.
obscure, unintelligible, incomprehensible, inexplicable, unfathomable, enigmatical, mysterious.
obtuse, dull-witted, stupid, dull, stolid, Bœotian.
See also CLOUD, DULLNESS.—*Antonyms.* See TRANSPARENCY.

OPENING.—I. *Nouns.* **opening,** aperture, hole, cleft, fissure, gap, chasm, yawning, dehiscence, oscitance *or* oscitancy; perforation, puncture; eye, eyelet, slot, loophole, peephole, keyhole, penhole; vent, venthole, blowhole, airhole; interstice, foramen, pore, orifice; crater, moutn, sucker, muzzle, nozzle, throat, gorge, hals *or* halse (*Scot. and dial. Eng.*), weasand (*archaic*), windpipe, fauces (*pl.: tech.*), gullet; outlet, inlet; width, span, spread.
window, casement, lattice, light, skylight, fanlight, bay window, bow window, oriel, dormer, bull's-eye, *œil-de-bœuf* (*F.*); port, porthole, embrasure, splay; fenestration (*arch.*).
portal, doorway, entrance, entranceway, gate, porch, postern, wicket, trapdoor, hatch. door, cellarway, hatchway. lich-gate. *porte-cochère* (*F.*); portico, veranda piazza (*U. S.*).

way, path, clearing, avenue, vista, aisle, glade, mall, lane, alley, thoroughfare; channel, fairway, gully, passage, passageway, gateway; driveway, drive.
tube, pipe, main, canal, gut, fistula, duct, tubule, tubulus (*rare*), tubulure (*chem.*), tubulation, catheter (*med.*), hose, pipette, bronchiole (*anat.*), bronchus (*anat.*): smokestack, chimney, flue; bore, caliber, diameter.
tunnel, mine, pit, adit, shaft, gallery, drift, crosscut, airway.
sieve, strainer, colander, riddle, screen, griddle (*mining*); honeycomb.
beginning, start, commencement, inchoation, inception, inauguration, initiation, first step, first appearance, initial stage (*or* part).
opportunity, chance, scope, show (*U. S. colloq.*), space, place, suitable occasion, favorable conjuncture.
opener, opening device, key, pass-key, master key, *passe-partout* (*F.*), open-sesame.
II. *Verbs.* **open,** ope (*poetic*), gape, dehisce, yawn, fly open, expand, crack, split, part, divaricate, spread out; lead, give.
perforate, pierce, tap, bore, drill, mine; transpierce, transfix; enfilade, impale, spike, spear, gore, spit, stab, pink, puncture, lance; stick, prick, riddle, punch, stave in.
uncover, unclose, unseal, uncork, unwrap, undo, unfold, unlock, unstop, deobstruct (*rare*), unclutch, unclench, discover; unveil, unsheathe, undrape, uncurtain; reveal, bare, expose.
begin, commence, start, inaugurate, initiate, institute, originate, introduce, broach; have a first performance (*theatrical*).
III. *Adjectives.* **open,** agape, gaping, yawning, dehiscent, patulous, distended, expanded, extended; unclosed, ajar, unobstructed, unclogged; uncovered, unprotected, exposed, unconcealed, patent, bare.
tubular, cannular, fistulous, tubate, tubiform, tubulose *or* tubulous, tubulate; foraminous, pervious, permeable; vascular, follicular, porous, honeycombed.
accessible, approachable, get-at-able (*colloq.*), come-at-able (*colloq.*), reachable, available; responsive, amenable.
frank, candid, sincere, unreserved, undissembling, unfeigned honest, artless, guileless, ingenuous, genuine, open-hearted, free-hearted.
generous, liberal, open-handed, free-handed, free, lavish, bountiful, bounteous, benevolent.
plain, obvious, apparent, evident, unmistakable, manifest, patent, overt, public clear, palpable, conspicuous (*as,* open *admiration;* open *guilt*).
unsettled, undecided, undetermined, unadjusted, pending, pendent, tabled (*as a motion*), uncertain, irresolute (*as, an* open *account or question*).

See also ARTLESSNESS, BEGINNING, DISCLOSURE, INTERVAL, TIMELINESS, VERACITY.—*Antonyms.* See CLOSURE.

---

operate, *v.* work, function, act; manage, direct; take effect. See AGENCY, CONDUCT, TAKING (*perform*).
operative, *adj.* acting, working, effective, effectual. See AGENCY.
opiate, *n.* sedative, drug, narcotic. See MODERATION.
opinion, *n.* belief, theory, judgment, view. See IDEA.
opinionated, *adj.* hidebound, bigoted, prejudiced, positive. See OBSTINACY.

OPPONENT.—I. *Nouns.* **opponent,** antagonist, adversary, enemy, foe, assailant; opposite party, the opposition.
oppositionist wrangler, disputant, obstructer, obstructionist, filibuster *or* filibusterer (*U. S. politics*), extremist, bitter-ender (*U. S. politics*).
malcontent, irreconcilable, agitator, demagogue, reactionist, reactionary, anarchist, Red, *frondeur* (*F. hist.*), revolutionary, revolutionist, rebel, seditionist, seditionary.
rival, competitor, contestant, contender, entrant, emulator; the field (*collective*).
II. *Adjectives.* **opponent,** opposite, confronting, adverse, antagonistic, competitive.

See also ENEMY.—*Antonyms.* See AUXILIARY.

---

opportune, *adj.* seasonable, apropos, suitable, felicitous. See TIMELINESS.
opportunity, *n.* chance, occasion. See OPENING.
oppose, *v.* cross, thwart; withstand, confront; resist, combat, repel. See CROSSING, OPPOSITION, RESISTANCE.

OPPOSITE.—I. *Nouns.* **opposite,** contrary, antipodes, reverse, inverse, counterpart, obverse (*opposite of* reverse), antithesis; pole (*as of an electric cell*), terminal point, extremity; opposite side, *vis-à-vis* (*F.*); contraposition, opposition, polarity, inversion.
antipodes, underworld (*not that of the crook and the racketeer*), opposite poles; North and South.
II. *Adjectives.* **opposite,** reverse, converse; antipodal, antipodean, diametrical, antithetic, counter, fronting, facing, opposing, oppositive, polar (*as in character*), diametrically opposite (*or* different); contrary, contradictory, antagonistic, adverse, repugnant, hostile.
northern, north, northerly, northward, hyperborean, boreal, septentrional, polar, arctic.
southern, south, southerly, meridional, southward, austral, antarctic.
III. *Adverbs.* **over,** over the way, over against; against, face to face, *vis-à-vis* (*F.*); across, beyond, "down under" (*referring esp. to Australia and New Zealand*).
See also CONTRARIETY, INVERSION.—*Antonyms.* See SIDE, SIMILARITY.

OPPOSITION.—I. *Nouns.* **opposition,** antagonism, oppugnancy, impugnation, contravention, defiance, resistance, counteraction, hindrance, counterplot, restraint, counterinfluence, crossing, withstanding, obstruction, filibuster (*U. S. politics*); contrariness, contrariety, contrast, diversity, repugnance.
conflict, discord, hostility, want of harmony, clashing, collision, clash, strife, encounter, struggle, contention, fight, combat, battle.
competition, rivalry, emulation, race, handicap, contest; tug of war.
obstacle, impediment, hindrance, snag, difficulty, stumblingblock, bar, clog, check, baffle (*tech.*), obstruction; opposite party, minority party, the left (*European legislatures*).
II. *Verbs.* **oppose,** counteract, withstand, resist, defy, gainsay, oppugn, contravene, obstruct, hinder, restrain, countervail, check, counteract, cross, thwart, pit against, face, confront, cope with; object, kick, protest (*or* vote) against; disfavor; contradict, belie, antagonize.
encounter, meet, stem, breast, buffet the waves, resist, grapple with, kick against the pricks, contend with (*or* against), do battle with (*or* against).
compete, emulate, rival, vie with, strive, contend, race; outvie, outrival, force out, drive out of business.
set opposite (*without antagonism*), face, confront, contrast; present, exhibit.
III. *Adjectives.* **oppositional,** opposing, adverse, opposed, oppugnant, antagonistic, oppositive, contrary, filibusterous, hostile, warring, unfriendly, inimical, cross, unfavorable, sinister, unpropitious; at cross-purposes, at variance, at issue, at daggers drawn, in hostile array.
competitive, emulous, rival, competitory, cut-throat; in rivalry with, in friendly rivalry.
IV. *Prepositions.* **against,** facing, opposite to, *versus* (*L.*), adverse to, in opposition to, counter to.
despite, in spite of, mauger *or* maugre (*archaic*), in despite of, in defiance of, notwithstanding, against, in the teeth of, in the face of.
See also CONTENTION, CONTRARIETY, COUNTERACTION, COUNTEREVIDENCE, CROSSING, DISAGREEMENT, FRONT, HINDRANCE, RESISTANCE, RESTRAINT.—*Antonyms.* See COÖPERATION.

---

oppositionist, *n.* obstructionist, filibusterer, reactionary. See OPPONENT.
oppress, *v.* burden, weigh down; persecute, tyrannize. See HEAVINESS, MALEVOLENCE.
oppressive, *adj.* burdensome, hard, grievous; cruel, tyrannical. See HEAVINESS, SEVERITY.

OPTICAL INSTRUMENTS.—*Nouns.* **optical instruments,** optical devices; optometrical devices: ophthalmoscope, skiascope, retinoscope, amblyoscope, corneal microscope.
telescope (refracting, reflecting), glass (*colloq.*), tube (*Milton's "glazed optic tube"*), spyglass, equatorial, reflector, refractor, lorgnette binocular, Galilean telescope, polemoscope, opera glass, field glass, prism binocular, achromatic

telescope, helioscope; teinoscope, prism telescope; telespectroscope; finder, view finder; altiscope, hyposcope, periscope, omniscope.
magnifier, magnifying glass, reading glass; microscope (simple *or* single, compound, projecting, dissecting, petrological, portable); ultramicroscope, photomicroscope.
lens (plano-concave, double concave *or* biconcave, plano-convex, double convex *or* biconvex, convexo-concave *or* meniscus, concavo-convex), eyepiece, ocular, objective, bull's-eye *or* bull's-eye condenser, glass, crystalline lens (*of the eye*); achromatic lens, converging (*or* convex) lens, diverging (*or* concave) lens, telephoto (*or* telephotographic) lens; Huygenian (*or* Huyghenian) eyepiece, Huygenian, negative eyepiece, Campani's eyepiece; eyeglass, quizzing glass, monocle; burning glass, sunglass, convex lens; prism.
camera, camera obscura, camera lucida, photographing apparatus, hand camera, kodak (*trade-mark name*), pinhole camera, magazine camera, panoramic (view, enlarging, stereoscopic, binocular, etc.) camera; magic lantern, megascope, stereopticon; stereoscope, telestereoscope, kaleidoscope, pseudoscope.
cinematograph *or* kinematograph, moving-picture machine, animatograph, biograph, bioscope, kinetoscope, vitagraph, vitascope, zoetrope (*optical toy*).
mirror, glass, looking-glass, reflector, speculum, pier glass, cheval glass; hand glass, hand mirror.
spectacles, glasses, barnacles (*colloq.*), gig lamps (*slang*), eyeglasses, *lorgnon* (*F.*), bifocals, *pince-nez* (*F.*), nippers (*slang*), horn-rimmed spectacles (*or* glasses), specs (*colloq.*); colored spectacles, preserves (*colloq.*), goggles.
[*various optical devices*] spectroscope, spectrometer, telespectroscope, reflecting goniometer, polariscope, polarimeter, abdominoscope (*med.*), gastroscope (*med.*), telelectroscope *or* telectroscope, spectroheliograph *or* photospectroheliograph; photometer, lucimeter; optometer, eriometer, actinometer, radiometer, spectrophotometer, spectropolarimeter.
optical sciences: optics, optometry, skiascopy, microscopy, spectrology, spectrometry, spectroscopy, abdomenoscopy (*med.*), gastroscopy (*med.*).
optician, oculist, optometrist, microscopist, spectroscopist.
See also LIGHT.

---

optional, *adj.* elective, discretionary, nonobligatory. See CHOICE.

ORACLE.—I. *Nouns.* **oracle,** prophet, prophetess (*fem.*), seer, seeress (*fem.*), sibyl, soothsayer, augur, diviner, haruspex (*ancient Rome*); sorcerer, sorceress (*fem.*), evocator, evocatrix (*fem.*), wizard, python, pythoness (*fem.*), witch, medium, clairvoyant, palmist; fortune teller.
Delphian (*or* Delphic) oracle, Pythia; oak of Dodona; Tiresias (*blind Theban soothsayer*), Cumæan sibyl (*consulted by Æneas*), Witch of Endor (*consulted by Saul*), Cassandra (*whose prophecies no one believed*), Sphinx; Sibylline Leaves, Sibylline Books; Mother Shipton.
weather prophet, clerk of the weather (*jocose*), weather man (*colloq.*), weather spy (*rare*), weather forecaster, meteorologist (*dare we include him among the prophets?*); weather bureau, Old Probabilities *or* Old Prob. (*jocose nickname for U. S. weather bureau*).
[*prophetic almanacs*] Zadkiel, Old Moore, Old Farmer's Almanac.
wise man, sage, wiseacre (*archaic or ironical*), authority, mentor; Solomon, "second Daniel," Solon, Nestor.
[*in plural*] **oracles,** inspired utterances (*or* revelations), divine oracles; the Scriptures.
II. *Adjectives.* **oracular,** Delphian *or* Delphic, sibylline, orphic, cryptic, occult, cabalistic, esoteric, mystic, Dodonæan *or* Dodonean, pythonic, enigmatical, ambiguous, veiled, obscure, prophetic.
magisterial, authoritative, sententious, dogmatic, dictatorial, arrogant, pompous, august, grave, solemn, commanding, stately, imperious.
See also INTERPRETER, PREDICTION, SAGE, SORCERER.

---

oral, *adj.* spoken, vocal, verbal. See SPEECH.
orally, *adv.* vocally, phonetically. See SPEECH.

ORANGE.—I. *Nouns.* **orange,** reddish yellow, old gold, gold color, henna. [*pigments*] ocher *or* ochre, Mars orange, cadmium.
II. *Adjectives.* **orange,** reddish yellow, ocherous *or* ochreous, ochery *or* ochry, orange-colored, apricot, gold-colored, flame-colored, warm, hot, glowing.
See also YELLOW.

---

oration, *n.* address, discourse. See SPEECH.
oratory, *n.* declamation, expression, elocution, eloquence. See SPEECH.
orchestra, *n.* instrumental performers, band. See MUSICIAN.
ordain, *v.* appoint, elect, frock, install, invest. See CHURCHDOM, COMMISSION.
ordained, *adj.* called, appointed, invested. See CLERGY.
ordeal, *n.* trial, test, cross. See FURNACE (*severe test*).

ORDER.—I. *Nouns.* **order,** arrangement, disposition, disposal, systematization, system, method, course, routine, economy, array; regularity, uniformity, symmetry, harmony; established usage, customary procedure, prescribed practice.
rank, class, group, division, grade (*of Christian ministry*), status, kind, sort, station, position, estate, degree, caste (*as, the lower* orders; *the military* order).
fraternity, brotherhood, society, company, association, community (*as, the Franciscan* order; *Masonic* order).
insignia (*pl.; sing.* insigne), badges, emblems, decorations.
sequence, succession, consecution, series, gradation, rotation, procession, progression (*as, alphabetical* order).
mandate, injunction, direction, instruction, commission, authorization, authority, precept, command, charge, warrant, rule, regulation.
[*conformity to law*] **orderliness,** law-abidingness, public tranquillity, obedience, quiet, peace, discipline, subordination.
[*in banking, etc.*] **written direction,** draft, bill of exchange, promissory note, check *or* cheque; commercial paper, negotiable instrument.
[*in biology*] **category** (*between "class" and "family"*), group, division, classification, taxonomy.
[*in architecture*] type (*esp. of column and entablature*), mode, style.
classical orders: (1) *Greek.* Doric, Ionic, Corinthian; (2) *Roman.* Tuscan, Composite.
II. *Verbs.* **order,** regulate, rule, manage, control, dispose, arrange, adjust, time, systematize, classify, methodize, organize, standardize; array (*archaic in this sense*).
[*to give an order to*] **command,** bid, direct, tell, enjoin, charge, instruct, adjure; prescribe, authorize, appoint, ordain (*eccl.*), decree.
[*to give an order for*] **bespeak,** engage, secure, stipulate for, book, reserve, retain, arrange for.
III. *Adjectives.* **orderly,** regular, in order, in trim, neat, tidy, *en règle* (*F.*), methodical, uniform, symmetrical, shipshape, businesslike, well-regulated, systematic.
law-abiding, obedient, compliant, controllable, submissive, peaceable, quiet, tranquil, disciplined, dutiful, loyal.
IV. *Adverbs.* **in order,** methodically, systematically, in turn, in its turn; step by step, by regular stages, *seriatim* (*L.*); by clockwork.
See also COMMAND, FORM, OBEDIENCE, REQUIREMENT.—*Antonyms.* See DISORDER.

---

ordinance, *n.* decree, order, rule, law, enactment. See COMMAND.
ordinary, *adj.* usual, regular, common; commonplace, average, inferior. See CONFORMITY, MEDIOCRITY.
ordnance, *n.* artillery, cannon, guns. See ARMS.

ORGANIZATION.—I. *Nouns.* **organization,** systematization, arrangement, classification, regimentation, methodization, coördination, synthetization, formation, creation, structure, construction, organizing, constitution.
organism, organic structure; bion (*physiological individual*), morphon (*morphological individual*).
organized nature, animated nature; living beings; biota (*biol.*), animal and plant life, fauna and flora.

fossil, petrified organism, organic remains, *disjecta membra* (*L.*), prehistoric remains; petrifaction, fossilization.

[*organized social body or system*] **organic whole,** assemblage, aggregation, combination, machine (*as of government or a political party*), system, association, society, club, establishment, enterprise, business, trust.

[*science of life*] **biology** (*including* zoölogy, botany, physiology, anatomy, embryology, cytology, histology, *and allied sciences*), natural history (*now commonly restricted to a study of animal life, treated in a popular manner*); organic chemistry; cell theory, metabolism, mutation, evolution, Darwinism, Lamarckism, Weismannism *or* Neo-Darwinism; biogenesis *or* biogeny, ontogeny, phylogeny.

protoplasm, plasma *or* plasm, bioplasm, cytoplasm, metaplasm, idioplasm, karyoplasm *or* nucleoplasm (*opposite of* cytoplasm), trophoplasm; biophore (*Weismann's hypothetical vital unit*), bioblast (*Altmann*), plasome (*Weisner*), pangen (*De Vries*), biogen (*Verworn*); cell, plastid, blastomere, nucleolus, centrosome, chromosome, vacuole; protoplast, energid, protozoan, amœba, spore, zooid, zoöspore.

ovum (*female*), egg cell, egg, germ cell (*distinguished from* somatic cell), germinal matter, germ plasm; oöspore, zygote, oösperm, oösphere (*unfertilized*), ovule; oöcyte, oœcium, ovicell, gamete; spawn (*as of fish*).

sperm (*male*), sperm cell, sexual cell, spermatozoön (*pl.* spermatozoa), spermatozoid, spermatocyte; seed, semen, milt (*roe of male fish*).

fertilization, fecundation, impregnation; spermatogenesis, blastogenesis oögenesis, reproduction.

biologist, zoölogist, naturalist, botanist, bacteriologist, embryologist.

II. *Verbs.* **organize,** systematize, systemize, methodize, coördinate, correlate, shape, frame, make, establish, assemble, form, arrange, construct, build.

III. *Adjectives.* **organic,** having organs, organized, coördinated, structural, systematic, fundamental, inherent, constitutional; vital, biotic.

protoplasmic, primordial, primitive; plasmic, plasmatic; cellular, cellulous, vacuolated, vacuolar, nuclear, nucleate, nucleolar, amœboid, amœbic, protozoan.

See also ARRANGEMENT, PLAN, PRODUCTION, ZOÖLOGY.—*Antonyms.* See INORGANIZATION.

---

orgy, *n.* debauch, carousal, revelry. See INTEMPERANCE.

origin, *n.* source, commencement, derivation, rise. See BEGINNING, CAUSE.

original, *adj.* primary, initial; inventive, creative; novel, unique. See BEGINNING, IMAGINATION, UNCONFORMITY.

originate, *v.* start, inaugurate, initiate; spring, arise, issue; create, invent, devise. See BEGINNING, DESCENT, IMAGINATION.

ORNAMENT.—I. *Nouns.* **ornament,** ornamentation, adornment, decoration, embellishment, enrichment; illustration, illumination, ornature (*rare*), ornateness, flamboyance *or* flamboyancy.

decorative design, decorative art; fretwork, tracery, filigree, arabesque, Moresque, Morisco, vermiculated work, vermiculation, foliation, imbrication, cuspidation, reeding; scroll, spiral, wave, flourish, running scroll, guilloche, zigzag, diaper, diapering, interlacing, strapwork, checkering *or* checquering, striping, lining, banding, paneling, panelwork, spotting, powdering; frostwork (*as on silver*), tooling, inlaid work, parquetry, figurework, *repoussé* (*F.*), *repoussage* (*F.*), wrought-iron work, bent-iron work, metal work; *appliqué* (*F.*), enamel, niello, *cloisonné* (*F.*), *champlevé* (*F.*); stenciling, graffito *or* *sgraffito* (*It.*), batik; *L'Art-Nouveau* (*F.*), New Art.

[*architectural*] molding *or* moulding, listel, fillet, fascia, torus, billet, ovolo, bead, astragal, reed, cavetto, scotia, *congé* (*F.*), apophyge, cyma (*L. pl.* cymæ), *cyma recta* (*L.*), *cyma reversa* (*L.*), ogee, beak, splay; egg and dart, egg and tongue, egg and anchor; volute, scrollhead (*of a vessel*), cartouche, finial, terminal, boss, cusp, acanthus, fret; foil, trefoil, quatrefoil, cinquefoil; patera, relief, relievo; pilaster, column, caryatid (*L. pl.* caryatides), atlantes (*pl.; sing.* atlas), telamones (*pl.; sing.* telamon); frieze, cornice.

[*floral*] wreath, garland, chaplet, crown, coronet, bays, laurel, festoon; bouquet, posy (*archaic or colloq.*), nosegay, flower; "daisies pied and violets blue" (*Love's Labor's Lost*).

[*fancywork*] embroidery, broidery (*archaic*), needlework; lace, guipure, point *or* point lace, tatting, insertion, crochet, edging, Valenciennes, Mechlin, duchesse lace, pillow lace, bobbinet; brocade, brocatel; tapestry, arras.
[*trimmings*] fringe, tassel, knot, frog; shoulder knot, aglet *or* aiglet, aiguillette, epaulet; rosette, bow; feather, plume, panache, aigrette; fillet, snood; sash, scarf, baldric, girdle, belt.
jewelry *or* jewellery, *bijouterie* (*F.*); tiara, crown, coronet, diadem; jewel, *bijou* (*F.; pl. bijoux*), gem, stone, precious stone, ice (*slang for* diamonds); trinket, pendant, lavaliere, locket, necklace, torque, bracelet, bangle, armlet, anklet; brooch, pin; chain, chatelaine; ring, earring, star, badge (*as of an order*).
finery, frippery, tinsel, clinquant, spangle, excess of ornament; pride, show, ostentation.
bric-a-brac (*collective*), knickknacks, curiosities, curios, scrimshaw (*U. S. sailors' cant*).
grandiloquence, magniloquence, purple patches, flowers of rhetoric, declamation, floridness, flourish, trope, euphuism, affectation, high-flown diction, lexiphanicism, bombast, rodomontade, rant, highfaluting *or* highfalutin, spreadeagleism (*U. S. colloq.*), inflation, pretension, buncombe (*cant or slang*), balderdash, extravagance, fustian, fine writing, sesquipedality, sesquipedalism, sesquipedalianism, Johnsonese, macrology.
[*mark of distinction*] **honor,** dignity, decoration, title, degree, distinction, rank, compliment, "blushing honors" (*Henry* VIII).
II. *Verbs.* **ornament,** embellish, enrich, decorate, adorn, beautify, ornamentalize, deck, bedeck; trick up (*or* out), prink, bedizen, trim, dress out, dress up, dress, array, smarten, spruce up (*colloq.*), doll up (*slang*); garnish, furbish, polish, gild, varnish, enamel, paint; spangle, bespangle, bead, embroider; chase, tool, scrimshaw (*U. S. sailors' cant*); emblazon, blazon, illuminate, miniate (*as a manuscript*), rubricate.
III. *Adjectives.* **ornamental,** decorative, fancy, beautifying, embellishing, adorning; inwrought, inlaid, filigreed, fretted, festooned.
smart, gay, trim, dapper, well-groomed, new-spangled, spruce, trig, fine, stylish, modish, fashionable, *chic* (*F.*).
ornate, ornamented, decorated, adorned, beautified, flowery, florid, rich; gilt, begilt, gilded, glittering, refulgent, resplendent; showy, flashy, gorgeous, garish, gaudy, tawdry, meretricious.
[*of literary style*], **grandiloquent,** magniloquent, rhetorical, pedantic, declamatory, grandiose, sesquipedalian, Johnsonian, orotund, sonorous, pompous, stilted, high-sounding, euphuistic, flamboyant, bombastic, high-flown, lexiphanic, inflated, swollen, turgid, turgescent, tumid, flashy, frothy, plethoric, overloaded.

See also REPUTE, TITLE, VULGARITY.—*Antonyms.* See BLEMISH, PLAINNESS, SIMPLICITY.

ORTHODOXY.—I. *Nouns.* **orthodoxy,** soundness, strictness, religious truth, true faith, truth, soundness of doctrine, canonicity, canonicalness, convention; Christianity, Catholicism, "the faith once delivered to the saints."
the church, Church Militant, Church Triumphant, Holy Church, Church of Christ, Catholic (Universal, *or* Apostolic) Church; Established (*or* State) Church; the Bride of the Lamb; temple of the Holy Ghost; Christians, Christendom.
canon (*eccl.*), rule, law, regulation, decision, decree; thirty-nine articles; creed, confession of faith, Apostles' Creed *or* the Creed, Nicene Creed, Athanasian Creed.
II. *Adjectives.* **orthodox,** sound, strict, faithful, catholic, Christian, evangelical, scriptural, textual, literal, monotheistic, canonical, conventional, approved.

See also BELIEF, CONFORMITY, TRUTH.—*Antonyms.* See HETERODOXY.

OSCILLATION.—I. *Nouns.* **oscillation,** vibration, fluctuation, variation, libration, nutation, vibratility, undulation, pulsation; pulse, beat, throb.
alternation, reciprocation, seesaw, teeter (*U. S.*), to-and-fro; coming and going; ebb and flow, flux and reflux, systole and diastole; ups and downs.
vacillation, wavering, irresolution, indecision, faltering, hesitation.
swing, sway, wave, beat, shake, wag; lilt, rhythm.
[*scientific instruments*] oscillograph, oscilloscope; oscillator, oscillometer, vi-

brator, vibroscope, vibrograph; seismoscope (*for detecting earthquakes*), seismograph.
II. *Verbs.* **oscillate,** vibrate, undulate, wave, librate, nutate; wabble *or* wobble, rock, sway, pendulate, swing, dangle; pulsate, throb, beat; wag, waggle; nod, bob, curtsy; vacillate, waver, falter, fluctuate, reel, quake; quiver, quaver, shake, wriggle, flicker, flutter, tremble; roll, toss, pitch, flounder, stagger, totter.
alternate, vary, reciprocate, teeter (*U. S.*), seesaw; crossruff (*card playing*); pass and repass, ride and tie, hitch and hike, hitch-hike (*colloq.*); ebb and flow, come and go.
III. *Adjectives.* **oscillatory,** oscillating, vibratory, vibrative, oscillative (*rare*), libratory, undulatory, pulsatory (*as an electric current*), vibratile, pendulous, vacillatory, to-and-fro, reciprocative; seismic *or* seismical.
IV. *Adverbs.* **to and fro,** back and forth, shuttlewise, in and out, up and down, seesaw, zigzag, wibble-wobble (*colloq.*), from side to side.
See also AGITATION, CHANGEABLENESS, REGULARITY.—*Antonyms.* See [1]REST.

---

ostensible, *adj.* outward, professed, pretended, apparent. See PLEA.
ostensibly, *adv.* apparently, seemingly, professedly. See PLEA.

OSTENTATION.—I. *Nouns.* **ostentation,** display, show, *étalage* (*F.*), parade, pretension, pretense, ostentatiousness, pomposity, flourish, pomp, magnificence, splendor, pageantry, array, state, solemnity; dash (*colloq.*), splurge (*colloq.*), splash (*colloq.*), front (*slang*), veneer, gloss, glitter, clinquant, tinsel, frippery, foppery.
pageant, parade, demonstration, spectacle, exhibition, exposition, procession, turnout (*colloq.*); fête, field day, gala, gala day; review, march past, promenade, "insubstantial pageant" (*Tempest*).
ceremony, ceremonial, ritual, form, formality, etiquette, punctilio.
II. *Verbs.* **be ostentatious,** show off, display, exhibit, brandish, flaunt, air, parade, wave, dangle, sport, emblazon; cut a dash (*colloq.*), put up a front (*slang*), swagger, make a splurge (*colloq.*), exult, blazon forth.
III. *Adjectives.* **ostentatious,** pretentious, ambitious, showy, dashing, conspicuous, garish, gaudy, flaunting, glittering, gay, splendid, magnificent, sumptuous, gorgeous, palatial.
theatrical, theatric, dramatic, spectacular, scenic, stagy (*derogatory*), dramaturgic.
formal, stiff, starched, punctilious, ceremonial, ceremonious, ritualistic; solemn, stately, majestic; *en grande tenue* (*F.*), in full dress (*or* regalia), in best bib and tucker (*colloq.*), in one's Sunday best, *endimanché* (*F.*).
pompous, vainglorious, grand, bombastic, boastful, arrogant, self-important, consequential, presumptuous; conceited, egotistic, priggish, cocky (*colloq.*); swaggering, grandiloquent, turgid.
IV. *Adverbs.* **ostentatiously,** pretentiously, etc. (see *adjectives*); with flourish of trumpet, with beat of drum, with flying colors.
See also BOASTING, LOUDNESS, ORNAMENT, PRIDE, VANITY.—*Antonyms.* See MODESTY.

---

ostracize, *v.* banish; exclude, bar, blackball. See EXCLUSION.
other, *adj.* extra, remaining; separate, distinct, another. See ADDITION, DIFFERENCE.
oust, *v.* evict, remove, depose, dismiss, dislodge. See EJECTION.
out, *adv.* outside, without. See EXTERIORITY.
outbreak, *n.* uprising, insurrection, revolt; eruption, outburst. See DISOBEDIENCE, VIOLENCE.
outcast, *n.* castaway, pariah, outsider, exile, outlaw. See EXCLUSION, UNCONFORMITY.
outcome, *n.* consequence, outgrowth, issue, result. See EFFECT.
outcry, *n.* clamor, tumult, uproar. See CRY.
outdo, *v.* surpass, exceed, excel, outstrip. See SUPERIORITY.
outer, *adj.* external, outside, outward. See EXTERIORITY.
outfit, *n.* equipment, gear. See CLOTHING.

outflow, *n.* outpour, effluence, outgush, issue, escape. See EGRESS, STREAM.
outgrowth, *n.* offshoot; development, outcome. See EFFECT.
outlandish, *adj.* barbarous, strange, grotesque, odd. See RIDICULOUSNESS.
outlast, *v.* survive, outlive, outwear. See DURABILITY.
outlaw, *n.* bandit, fugitive. See BAD MAN, EXCLUSION.
outlet, *n.* spout, faucet, conduit; opening, vent, exit. See EGRESS, ESCAPE.

OUTLINE.—I. *Nouns.* **outline, contour, boundary, pale, lines, features, lineaments,** *tournure* (*F.*), **bounds, circuit, circumference, perimeter, periphery; profile, silhouette, configuration, relief; coast line, horizon.**
girdle, belt, band, baldric, girth, cingle (*rare*), **cincture, cingulum** (*tech.*), **cummerbund** (*Anglo-Indian*), **zonar, zone, circlet, cordon, zodiac; tire** *or* **tyre, felloe** *or* **felly.**
draft *or* **draught, drawing, design, sketch, skeleton, program, synopsis, conspectus, delineation, map, chart, diagram, rough, draft, epitome, summary,** *ébauche* (*F.*); **main features** (*pl.*), **general principles** (*as,* outlines *of philosophy*).
II. *Verbs.* **outline, delineate, contour, trace, sketch, block, profile, silhouette, circumscribe, delimit.**
draft, draw up, sketch, plan, describe, model, diagram, depict, portray, paint, design (*as, to* outline *a speech or a campaign*).
III. *Adjectives.* **outlinear, delineatory, outlined, contoured, circumferential; synoptic** *or* **synoptical.**
See also APPEARANCE, CIRCULARITY, CIRCUMSCRIPTION, FORM, INCLOSURE, PLAN.

---

outlive, *v.* survive, outlast. See PERMANENCE.
outlook, *n.* view, scene, vista; prospect, forecast. See APPEARANCE, FUTURE.
outlying, *adj.* distant, remote, frontier. See EXTERIORITY.
output, *n.* yield, product, outturn. See ACQUISITION.
outrage, *n.* injury, wrong, affront, abuse; transgression, infraction, violation, ravishment. See EVIL, VIOLENCE.
outrun, *v.* outstrip, pass, outdistance. See OVERRUNNING.
outset, *n.* commencement, start, departure. See BEGINNING.
outshine, *v.* excel, outdo, overshadow, eclipse. See DISREPUTE.
outside, *adj.* outer, outward, external. See EXTERIORITY.
outskirts, *n. pl.* purlieus, environs, suburbs. See ENVIRONMENT, NEARNESS.
outspoken, *adj.* bluff, blunt, plain-spoken, frank, unreserved. See ARTLESSNESS, PLAINNESS.
outstanding, *adj.* unsettled, unpaid; eminent, prominent, signal. See DEBT, IMPORTANCE.
outstretched, *adj.* extended, expanded, outspread. See BREADTH.
outstrip, *v.* outrun, outpace, outdistance, pass; eclipse. See OVERRUNNING, SUPERIORITY.
outward, *adj.* out, outside, outer. See EXTERIORITY.
outweigh, *v.* overbalance, exceed, overweigh. See SUPERIORITY.
outwit, *v.* get the better of, circumvent, frustrate. See DECEPTION.
oval, *adj.* ovate, ovoid, elliptical. See CIRCULARITY.
over, *adv.* by, past; across; extra, remaining; again, once more; beyond. See END, OPPOSITE, REDUNDANCE, REPETITION, SUPERIORITY.—**over and above**, besides, overmuch, too, extra. See REDUNDANCE.
overawe, *v.* intimidate, cow, daunt. See FEAR.
overbalance, *v.* outweigh, surpass, preponderate. See SUPERIORITY.
overbearing, *adj.* lordly, domineering, dictatorial. See INSOLENCE.
overcast, *adj.* leaden, cloudy, dark, gloomy. See DULLNESS.
overcautious, *adj.* timorous, unenterprising. See CAUTION.
overcharge, *v.* extort, fleece. See DEARNESS.
overcoat, *n.* topcoat, greatcoat, ulster, raglan. See CLOTHING.
overcome, *v.* surmount, subdue, conquer, overthrow. See SUCCESS.
overcóme, *adj.* crushed, defeated, downcast. See DEJECTION, DISREPUTE.

overdo, *v.* stretch, strain; overwork, overtask. See EXAGGERATION, FATIGUE
overdue, *adj.* delayed, belated, tardy. See LATENESS.

OVERESTIMATION.—I. *Nouns.* **overestimation,** overvaluation, overrating, rodomontade, hot air (*slang*), apple sauce (*slang*), gush (*colloq.*); blind optimism, megalomania, eulogy, overpraise; exaggeration, hyperbole; much ado about nothing; tempest in a teacup.

egoism, individualism, solipsism (*philos.*), self-seeking, self-absorption, self-centration, self-opinionatedness, selfishness: *opposite of* altruism.

egotism, self-conceit, self-exaltation, self-glorification, self-concentration, selfishness, self-applause, self-praise, conceit, vanity, conceitedness, self-importance, self-conceitedness, self-complacency, self-satisfaction, self-admiration, bumptiousness, self-assertiveness; self-love, self-interestedness, egoism; wegotism (*excessive use of the editorial "we": jocose*).

egoist, individualist, solipsist (*philos.*), self-seeker: *opposite of* altruist.

egotist, self-applauder, self-exalter. self-glorifier; braggart, boaster, swaggerer, braggadocio, rodomont; prig, coxcomb, peacock, *poseur* (*F.; fem. poseuse*), puppy (*derogatory*).

II. *Verbs.* **overestimate,** overvalue, overrate, overprize; overpraise, overesteem, rate (*or* estimate) too highly, magnify, glorify, extol, panegyrize, eulogize, puff (*colloq.*), boost (*U. S. colloq.*), crack up (*colloq.*).

III. *Adjectives.* **overestimated,** overrated, overprized, overextolled, inflated, puffed up, bloated. turgid.

See also EXAGGERATION, VANITY.—*Antonyms.* See UNDERESTIMATION.

---

overflow, *v.* run over, overrun, abound; flood, inundate. See OVERRUNNING, REDUNDANCE; RIVER.
overhang, *v.* jut, beetle, command, overtop. See HEIGHT.
overhanging, *adj.* beetling, projecting, imminent. See HEIGHT PENDENCY.
overhaul, *v.* examine, look over. See INQUIRY.
overhead, *adv.* above, aloft, up. See HEIGHT.
overhead, *n.* general costs (*business*). See EXPENDITURE.
overjoyed, *adj.* delighted, enraptured, transported. See PLEASURE.
overlapping, *adj.* imbricate, shingled, lapstreak (*said of boats*). See COVERING.
overlay, *v.* cover, superimpose, overspread. See COVERING.
overload, *v.* overburden, overcharge, overwhelm. See HINDRANCE, REDUNDANCE.
overlook, *v.* oversee, supervise, superintend; excuse, condone; overtop, command; inspect, examine; skip, miss, disregard. See DIRECTION, FORGIVENESS, HEIGHT, INQUIRY, NEGLECT.
overpower, *v.* subdue, overcome, defeat, overwhelm, conquer. See SUCCESS.
overpowering, *adj.* overwhelming, irresistible. See STRENGTH.
overrate, *v.* overvalue, overprize. See OVERESTIMATION.
override, *v.* overrule, cancel, repeal. See ANNULMENT.
overrule, *v.* set aside, revoke; override, overcome. See ANNULMENT, AUTHORITY.

OVERRUNNING.—I. *Nouns.* **overrunning,** overflowing, overspreading, overstepping, transgression, transilience *or* transiliency (*rare*), encroachment, infraction, inroad, infringement, transcendence, advance, overrun.

II. *Verbs.* **overrun,** run over, spread over, overspread, overgrow (*as with weeds*), infest, grow over; overflow, overwhelm, deluge, inundate.

outrun, outstrip, outpace, outstride, outdistance, outrace, pass, go beyond, go by, shoot ahead of, override, outride, outrival, outdo, beat, distance, throw into the shade, eclipse; surmount, tower above, surpass, outgo; overshoot the mark.

overstep, transgress, trespass, encroach, infringe, intrude, invade.

ravage, pillage, harry, harass, despoil, devastate, trample down, lay waste.

III. *Adverbs.* **ahead,** in advance, to the front, beyond the mark.

See also DETERIORATION, REDUNDANCE.—*Antonyms.* See SHORTCOMING.

oversee, *v.* supervise, superintend, manage, boss (*colloq.*). See DIRECTION.
overshoe, *n.* arctic, rubber, galosh. See CLOTHING.
oversight, *n.* supervision, management; blunder, slip. See DIRECTION, ERROR.
overstate, *v.* overdo, overdraw, exaggerate. See EXAGGERATION.
overstep, *v.* infringe, intrude, trespass, transgress. See OVERRUNNING.
overtake, *v.* come up to, reach, catch. See ARRIVAL.
overthrow, *v.* upset, overturn; demolish, ruin; overcome, defeat. See DEPRESSION, DESTRUCTION, SUCCESS.
overtop, *v.* command, overlook; surpass, excel. See HEIGHT, SUPERIORITY.
overturn, *n.* upset, overthrow, reversal, reconstruction. See REVOLUTION.
overwhelm, *v.* submerge, crush, overpower, overcome. See DESTRUCTION.
overwork, *v.* overdo; overtax, overtask, overburden; tire, exhaust. See FATIGUE, MISUSE.
ovum, *n.* egg, egg cell. See ORGANIZATION.
owe, *v.* be indebted, be in debt. See DEBT.
owing to, resulting from, attributable to, caused by. See EFFECT.
own, *v.* confess, admit, acknowledge; have, hold. See DISCLOSURE, POSSESSION.
owner, *n.* proprietor, holder, master. See POSSESSOR.
ownership, *n.* proprietorship, possessorship, holding. See POSSESSION.

P

pace, *n.* step, stride; gait, rack, amble; rate, speed. See MOTION, VELOCITY.
pace, *v.* step, tread, walk, amble. See JOURNEY.
pacific, *adj.* conciliatory; calm, peaceful, peaceable. See PACIFICATION, PEACE.

PACIFICATION.—I. *Nouns.* **pacification,** conciliation, reconciliation, reconcilement; accommodation, arrangement, adjustment; terms, compromise; amnesty.
peace offering, propitiatory gift; olive branch; calumet, peace pipe.
truce, armistice, suspension of arms (*or* hostilities); Truce of God (*hist.*); flag of truce, white flag, treaty of peace; cartel; *parlementaire* (*F.*).
II. *Verbs.* **pacify,** tranquilize, compose, calm, still, quiet, appease, assuage, soothe, soften, alleviate, allay, mitigate; reconcile, propitiate, placate, conciliate, meet halfway, hold out the olive branch, heal the breach, make peace, restore harmony, bring to terms, win over.
raise a siege, sheathe the sword, bury the hatchet, lay down one's arms, turn swords into plowshares; outlaw war.
III. *Adjectives.* **pacifiable,** placable, propitiatory, appeasable, forgiving.
pacificatory, conciliatory, mollifying, propitiating, reconciliatory, pacific.
See also MODERATION, PEACE.—*Antonyms.* See CONTENTION, WARFARE.

---

pack, *n.* gang, drove, multitude; load, bundle, burden. See ASSEMBLAGE, HINDRANCE.
pack, *v.* cram, stuff, crowd; load, fill, stow. See EXPANSION, LOCATION.
package, *n.* bundle, parcel, packet. See ASSEMBLAGE.
pact, *n.* agreement, bargain. See COMPACT.
pad, *v.* stuff, fill, augment, enlarge. See EXPANSION.
pagan, *n.* heathen, idolater. See HETERODOXY.
page, *n.* call boy, bell boy, footboy, lackey. See SERVANT.
page, *v.* give numbers to, mark. See NUMBER.
pageant, *n.* spectacle, parade, exhibition. See OSTENTATION.

PAIN.—I. *Nouns.* **pain,** suffering, ache, hurt, smart, twinge, pang, gripe, pinch, nip, squeeze, shooting, cut, laceration, lancination, sore, soreness, discomfort.
spasm, seizure, paroxysm, gripes, colic, throe, convulsion, eclampsia (*med.*);

crick, stitch, cramp; throb, palpitation, throbbing; laryngismus (*med.*), holotony, tetanus, tonic spasm, entasia (*med.*); clonic spasm.
torture (*physical or mental*), torment, agony, anguish, rack, crucifixion, martyrdom; hell upon earth, reign of terror.
care, anxiety, solicitude, concern, worry, cark (*archaic*), trouble, trial, ordeal, shock, blow, fret, burden, load.
grief, sorrow, distress, dolor (*poetic*), affliction, woe, bitterness, heartache, heavy (aching, bleeding, *or* broken) heart, broken-heartedness.
misery, unhappiness, infelicity, tribulation, wretchedness, despondency, despair, desolation, extremity, prostration, depth of misery, slough of despond; nightmare, incubus, ephialtes.
[*in plural*] **pains,** labor, toil, effort, trouble, diligence, painstaking, assiduity, laboriousness, toilsomeness, toilsome effort (*as, to take* pains).
childbirth, parturition, travail (*archaic*), childbed, labor; delivery, eutocia (*easy*), dystocia (*difficult*), *accouchement* (*F.*), confinement.
sufferer, victim, prey, martyr, wretch, shorn lamb.
II. *Verbs.* [*to give or inflict pain*] **pain,** hurt, wound, lacerate, pierce, prick, sting, stab, cut; gall, fret, gnaw, corrode, grate, chafe, bite; torture, rack, torment, crucify, agonize, wring, convulse, harrow; flog, maltreat, abuse, punish, smite, assail.
annoy, vex, displease, irritate, provoke, anger, fash (*Scot.*), incommode, disturb, discompose, cross, thwart, perplex; molest, tease, tire, irk, bore, fret, bother, pester, trouble, plague, worry; harass, harry, badger, heckle (*Brit.*), bait, beset, infest, persecute, mortify; nettle, pique, roil, rile (*colloq. and dial.*), ruffle, aggrieve, affront, enrage.
distress, grieve, afflict, cut up (*colloq.*), deject, sadden, depress, make unhappy, cut to the heart (*or* quick); break the heart; make the heart bleed.
disgust, offend, nauseate, sicken, repel, revolt, shock, disenchant, horrify, appal.
[*to undergo pain*] suffer, feel, endure, undergo, bear, sustain, experience (*pain or grief*); ail, ache, smart, tingle, shoot, twinge, agonize, bleed; writhe, wince; bear the cross; quaff the bitter cup, fall on evil days, come to grief, "sup full of horrors" (*Macbeth*).
fret, chafe, gall, sit on thorns, wince, worry oneself, fret and fume; take to heart; rankle, fester, inflame.
grieve, mourn, lament, sorrow, yearn, repine, pine, droop, languish, sink, despair, give way, break down, break one's heart.
III. *Adjectives.* **pained,** afflicted, suffering, worried, anxious, hurt, aching, griped, sore, raw, excoriated, chafed, galled; on the rack, ill at ease, uneasy, uncomfortable, disquieted, disturbed, discontented, weary.
unhappy, infelicitous, poor, wretched, miserable, woebegone, comfortless, cheerless, heart-sick, dejected, careworn, heavy-laden, stricken, doomed, devoted, accursed, unfortunate, undone, crushed, lost, stranded, victimized, ill-used.
sad, grieved, sorrowful, mournful, dismal, melancholy, sorry, gloomy; concerned, cut up (*colloq.*), chagrined, horrified, mortified, horror-stricken; heartbroken, heartstricken, broken-hearted.

See also DEJECTION.—*Antonyms.* See PLEASURE.

PAINFULNESS.—I. *Nouns.* **painfulness,** trouble, care, trial, affliction, visitation, infliction, misfortune, mishap; injury, wound, cross, blow, stroke, burden, load, curse.
annoyance, grievance, nuisance, vexation, irritation, chagrin, pique, mortification, worry, bore, bother, "sea of troubles" (*Hamlet*), hornet's nest, plague, pest, sore subject, skeleton in the closet; thorn in the flesh.
displeasure, distaste, dissatisfaction, disapprobation, discomfort, disquiet, discomposure, uneasiness, inquietude; discontent, dislike, disfavor, aversion.
II. *Adjectives.* **painful,** hurtful, afflictive, aching; grave, hard, harsh, acute, poignant, sharp, severe, raw, sore, cruel, biting, caustic, consuming, corroding, cutting, excruciating, agonizing, torturous.
grievous, piteous, dolorous, distressing, cheerless, dismal, disheartening, depressing, dreary, melancholy, woeful, mournful, deplorable, pitiable, rueful, lamentable, sad; affecting, moving, touching, pathetic.
unpleasant, unpleasing, displeasing, disagreeable, unpalatable, bitter, distasteful, uninviting, unwelcome, undesirable, unsatisfactory, unacceptable.

irritating, provoking, annoying, disquieting aggravating (*colloq.*), exasperating, galling, vexatious; troublesome, worrisome, tiresome, irksome, cumbersome, burdensome, cumbrous, onerous, heavy, oppressive; pestering, bothering, harassing, worrying, tormenting.
insufferable, intolerable, insupportable, unbearable, unendurable.
shocking, terrific, grim, appalling, crushing; dreadful, fearful, frightful, tremendous, dire, heartbreaking, heart-rending, harrowing, rending.
odious, hateful, execrable, repulsive, repellent, horrid, horrible; offensive, obnoxious, objectionable; nauseous, disgusting, revolting, nasty, loathsome, vile, hideous.
disastrous, calamitous, ruinous, destructive, tragic *or* tragical, desolating, withering, baleful; unfortunate, hapless, unlucky, ill-starred, inauspicious, untoward.
toilsome, laborious, arduous, wearisome, hard, severe, difficult (*as, a* painful *journey*).
painstaking, assiduous, diligent, persevering, industrious, sedulous, hard-working, careful, conscientious: *in this sense,* painful *is archaic.*
III. *Adverbs.* **painfully,** laboriously, etc. (see *adjectives*); with pain; in agony, in torment; *de profundis* (*L.*), out of the depths.

See also ADVERSITY, GREATNESS, PAIN, PUNGENCY.—*Antonyms.* See PLEASURABLENESS.

---

painstaking, *adj.* diligent, careful, particular. See EXERTION, PAINFULNESS.
paint, *v.* depict, describe; color, daub; draw sketch. See DESCRIPTION, FINE ARTS.
¹painter, *n.* rope (*of a boat*). See VINCULUM.
²painter, *n.* colorist, landscapist, portraitist, depictor. See ARTIST.
painting, *n.* depiction, portraiture; picture, canvas. See FINE ARTS.
pair, *n.* couple, brace; fellows, mates; team, span. See DUALITY, SIMILARITY, VEHICLE.
pair, *v.* couple, bracket, yoke, match, mate. See DUALITY.
palatable, *adj.* appetizing, toothsome, tasty; agreeable, pleasing. See SAVORINESS, PLEASURABLENESS.
pale, *adj.* ashen, wan, blanched; dim, faint; whitish, blond; sickly hued, sickly, unhealthy. See COLORLESSNESS, DIMNESS, LIGHT; GREEN, (*of complexion*).
pale, *n.* boundary, border, confines. See LIMIT.
pale, *v.* blanch, fade, grow dim. See COLORLESSNESS, DIMNESS.
pall, *v.* satiate, weary, cloy, sicken. See SATIETY.
palliate, *v.* relieve, mitigate, smooth, soften, lessen; extenuate, excuse. See MODERATION, SMOOTHNESS, SOFTNESS, VINDICATION.
pallor, *n.* paleness, sallowness, bloodlessness, etiolation. See COLORLESSNESS.
palpitate, *v.* throb, pulsate, beat. See AGITATION.
paltry, *adj.* insignificant, contemptible, pitiful; sorry, pitiable; trifling, mean, trivial. See PITY, POVERTY, UNIMPORTANCE.
pamper, *v.* indulge, humor, coddle, spoil, overindulge. See PLEASURABLENESS.
panacea, *n.* cure-all, relief, cure. See REMEDY.
pane, *n.* windowpane, glass. See LIGHT.
panegyric, *n.* eulogy, laudation, encomium. See APPROBATION.
pang, *n.* twinge, throe, paroxysm. See PAIN.
panic, *n.* terror, consternation, fright. See FEAR.
pant, *v.* yearn, long for; gasp, puff, blow. See DESIRE, FATIGUE.
papacy, *n.* the Vatican, papal system, pontificate. See CHURCHDOM.
papal, *adj.* pontifical, apostolic, popish. See CHURCHDOM.
paper, *n.* newsprint, writing paper, foolscap, etc.; bill, note, paper money; newspaper, journal; document, deed, certificate; composition, article. See LAYER, MONEY, PUBLICATION, RECORD, WRITING.
paper money, bill, note, bank note. See MONEY.

par, *n.* balance, level, equal footing; face value, par value. See EQUALITY, PRICE
parable, *n.* allegory, apologue. See FIGURE, TEACHING.
parade, *n.* procession, march; pretension, display. See CONTINUITY, OSTENTATION.
parade, *v.* display, exhibit, flaunt; vent, publish. See AIR.
paradise, *n.* Elysium; bliss. See HEAVEN.
paradox, *n.* inconsistency, self-contradictory statement. See ABSURDITY.
paragon, *n.* pattern, model, pink, nonpareil. See PERFECTION.

PARALLELISM.—I. *Nouns.* **parallelism,** equidistance, coextension, concentricity, collaterality, collateralism, collimation (*tech.*); similarity, resemblance correspondence, analogy.
parallel, parallel position; resemblance, similarity, conformity, comparison counterpart, duplicate, match, analogue, correlative, equivalent.
II. *Verbs.* **parallel,** be (*or* set) parallel, equal, collimate (*tech.*); correspond to, match, equal, follow, parallelize, equate, collate, compare.
III. *Adjectives.* **parallel,** coextensive, equidistant; collateral, concentric, concurrent; abreast, aligned, even.
analogous, correspondent, corresponding, similar, like, equal, equivalent, cognate, correlative.
IV. *Adverbs.* **alongside,** abreast, side by side, neck and neck, broadside on, stem to stem, bow to bow, on a level, cheek by jowl.
See also AGREEMENT, IMITATION, SIDE, SIMILARITY, SYMMETRY.

---

paralysis, *n.* palsy, stroke. See DISEASE.
paralyze, *v.* disable, incapacitate, demoralize, cripple, unnerve; deaden, obtund. See IMPOTENCE, INSENSIBILITY, INSENSITIVENESS.
paramount, *adj.* supreme, chief, dominant. See SUPERIORITY.
parapet, *n.* embankment, breastwork, rampart, wall. See DEFENSE.
paraphernalia, *n. pl.* belongings, equipment, accessories. See PROPERTY.
paraphrase, *n.* rewording, free translation. See INTERPRETATION.
paraphrase, *v.* reword, rehash, rephrase. See INTERPRETATION.
parasite, *n.* commensal (*biol.*), inquiline (*biol.*); hanger-on, sycophant. See SERVILITY.
parcel, *n.* package, bundle; group, bunch, collection; portion, division. See ASSEMBLAGE, PART.
parched, *adj.* arid, scorched, roasted. See DRYNESS.
pardon, *v.* excuse, overlook, make allowance. See FORGIVENESS.
pardonable, *adj.* excusable, forgivable, justifiable. See VINDICATION.
pare, *v.* reduce, diminish, remove; shave, slice, cut, skive (*as leather*). See CONTRACTION, DEDUCTION, LAYER.
parent, *n.* father, mother; source, author. See PATERNITY.
parental, *adj.* fatherly, paternal; motherly, maternal; tender, protecting. See PATERNITY.
paring, *n.* shaving, slice, peeling, peel. See LAYER, SMALLNESS.
parity, *n.* equalization, equivalence, fifty-fifty (*colloq.*). See EQUALITY.
park, *n.* common, public gardens, pleasure grounds; parking space (*as for automobiles*), artillery encampment; chase (*Eng.*). See AMUSEMENT, LOCATION, PLAIN, VEGETABLE (*woodland*).
park, *v.* inclose; station, stand, leave (*as an automobile*). See CIRCUMSCRIPTION, LOCATION.
parley, *v.* palaver, confer, debate, discuss. See CONVERSATION.
parlor, *n.* best room (*colloq.*), drawing room. See RECEPTACLE.
parochial, *adj.* narrow, provincial, hidebound; parish (*used attributively*), local. See MISJUDGMENT, REGION.
parody, *n.* burlesque, travesty. See COPY, IMITATION.
paroxysm, *n.* fit, outburst; seizure, spasm. See EXCITABILITY, PAIN, VIOLENCE.
parry, *v.* dodge, avert, ward off; evade, fence. See AVOIDANCE, CONFUTATION.

PARSIMONY.—I. *Nouns.* **parsimony,** parsimoniousness, niggardliness, closefistedness, closeness, stinginess, stint, illiberality, avarice, avidity, rapacity, extortion, venality, cupidity, selfishness; frugality, economy, cheeseparing.
miser, niggard, churl, screw, skinflint, curmudgeon, moneygrubber, pinchfist; harpy, extortioner, extortionist, usurer.
Harpagon (Molière's *L'Avare*), Silas Marner (George Eliot), Euclio (Plautus).
II. *Verbs.* **be parsimonious,** pinch, screw, gripe, stint, grudge, begrudge, withhold, hold back, starve, famish; grasp, grab, have an itching palm; cheapen, beat down, drive a hard bargain.
III. *Adjectives.* **parsimonious,** penurious, stingy, miserly, mean, shabby, near, niggardly, close, tight-fisted, close-fisted, close-handed, tight (*colloq.*), cheeseparing (*colloq.*), scrimping, meager, sparing, grudging, illiberal, ungenerous, churlish, sordid, mercenary, venal, covetous, avaricious, greedy, grasping, rapacious, extortionate.
IV. *Adverbs.* **parsimoniously,** stingily, etc. (see *adjectives*); with a sparing hand.
See also DESIRE, ECONOMY, SELFISHNESS.—*Antonyms.* See PRODIGALITY.

---

parson, *n.* rector, preacher, clergyman. See CLERGY.
parsonage, *n.* manse, parish house, rectory. See TEMPLE.

PART.—I. *Nouns.* **part,** portion, fragment, fraction, division, parcel (*as of land: law*), subdivision, sector, segment, detachment; item, detail, particular; aught, any.
[*of printed matter*] book, number, fascicle, fasciculus, *livraison* (*F.*), section, chapter, article, passage, paragraph, clause, verse.
piece, lump, bit, cut, cutting; chip, chunk, slice, scrap, swatch (*cant*), sample, crumb, morsel, moiety, particle; installment.
member, organ, element, component, constituent, ingredient; limb, leg, arm; wing, ala (*pl.* alæ: *tech.*), alula (*pl.* alulæ: *zoöl.*), elytrum (*pl.* elytra: *zoöl.*), pinion, sail (*of a windmill*); scion, branch, bough, joint, link, offshoot, ramification, spur, twig, spray, sprig, switch, withe, runner, tendril, sarmentum (*pl.* sarmenta: *bot.*); leaf, leaflet; stump.
[*portion allotted*] **share,** allotment, portion, partition, section, division, apportionment, quota, proportion, quantum, lot, dividend, divvy (*slang*), dole, allowance; duty, concern, function, office.
rôle, character, personification, impersonation (*as, to play a* part).
side (*as in a controversy*), party, faction, interest, cause, behalf.
[*in plural*] **parts,** regions, districts, quarters, localities, latitudes, scenes, spots, places.
talents, powers, abilities, qualities, faculties, capabilities, accomplishments, gifts, endowments (*as, a man of* parts).
II. *Verbs.* **part,** divide, disjoin, separate, sever, dissever, disconnect, sunder, disunite, dispart, rend, cleave, cut, bisect, carve, saw, break, snap, dislimb, disjoint, dismember, disbranch, disband, dissociate, detach; analyze, discriminate.
hold apart (*as combatants*), intervene between, interpose between, separate, stand between.
share, apportion, portion, allot, divide, distribute, parcel out ("*they* parted *my garments among them*": *archaic in this sense*).
depart, go away, leave, quit, take leave, bid farewell; die, pass away.
part with (*or* from), relinquish, give up, yield, renounce, abandon, release.
III. *Adjectives.* **partial,** fragmentary, fractional, component, aliquot (*math.*), sectional, incomplete, imperfect, not entire.
biased, one-sided, prejudiced, interested, unfair, unjust, inequitable, warped, prepossessed.
fond (*esp. in a foolish or excessive way*), doting, indulgent, overfond, desirous (*as,* partial *to sweets*).
partible, separable, divisible, severable, dissolvable, dissoluble, dividual, distinct.
IV. *Adverbs.* **partly,** in part, partially, incompletely, in some measure (*or* degree).
piecemeal, by degrees, little by little piece by piece, bit by bit, by installments.
See also APPORTIONMENT, BUSINESS, COMPONENT, DISJUNCTION, DRAMA, FRACTION, SMALLNESS, SNAP, TITLE.—*Antonyms.* See WHOLE.

partake, *v.* share (in), participate, take: *with* of *or* in. See PARTICIPATION.
partiality, *n.* predilection, preference; bias, favor, one-sidedness. See DESIRE, MISJUDGMENT.
partially, *adv.* partly; incompletely, somewhat, comparatively, rather. See PART, SMALLNESS.

PARTICIPATION.—I. *Nouns.* **participation,** partaking, sharing, joint possession, communion, partnership, joint tenancy; joint (*or* common) stock; community, community of possessions, communism, communalism, communization, sovietism (*Russia*), collectivism, national ownership, socialism; coöperation.
participator, participant, partaker, sharer, partner; shareholder; joint tenant; tenants in common; coheir.
communist, communalist, Communard (*F. hist.*), collectivist; socialist; radical socialist, Bolshevist, Bolshevik (*pl.* Bolsheviki).
II. *Verbs.* **participate,** partake, share, share in, join in, chip in (*colloq.*), go shares, go cahoots (*slang*), go halves; share and share alike.
communize, communalize, sovietize; have (*or* possess) in common.
III. *Adjectives.* **participative,** participating, participatory, sharing; coöperative, coöperating, profit-sharing; socialistic, communistic, communalistic.
IV. *Adverbs.* **in common,** commonly, equally, shared, in joint use; share and share alike.
See also COÖPERATION, PARTY.

---

particle, *n.* affix, preposition, conjunction, interjection; speck, atom, molecule, iota, scrap, bit, jot. See GRAMMAR, LITTLENESS.
particular, *adj.* fussy, overnice; special, noteworthy; individual, separate, specific, personal, private; critical, careful, exact. See FASTIDIOUSNESS, IMPORTANCE, SPECIALTY, TRUTH.
particular, *n.* item, fact, detail, datum. See PART, RESPECT, SPECIALTY.
particularize, *v.* itemize, detail, specify, formulate. See DESCRIPTION, SPECIALTY.
parting, *n.* leave-taking, farewell; separation, division. See DEPARTURE, DISJUNCTION.
partisan, *n.* adherent, supporter, follower, champion. See AUXILIARY.
partisanship, *n.* cliquishness, clannishness, party spirit, provincialism. See MISJUDGMENT, PARTY.
partition, *n.* separation, division; diaphragm, wall; section, portion. See DISJUNCTION, INTERJACENCE, PART.
partly, *adv.* partially, incompletely, somewhat. See PART.
partner, *n.* associate, participant, sharer, companion, mate. See ACCOMPANIMENT.
partnership, *n.* company, association, alliance. See ACCOMPANIMENT, COOPERATION.

PARTY.—I. *Nouns.* **party,** faction, cause, denomination, sect, class, communion; side, crew, team; band, detachment, horde, posse, phalanx; caste, family, gens (*Roman hist.*), clan.
community, body, group, fellowship, solidarity, freemasonry; fraternity, sodality, brotherhood, fraternal order; sisterhood, sorority.
clique, knot, circle, set, coterie, club; gang, ring, push (*slang; in Australia, a gang of larrikins*), machine, junto, cabal, camarilla.
corporation, corporate body, guild, company, partnership, firm, house; combination, combine (*U. S. colloq.*), trust; merger, holding company.
society, association, institute, institution; union, trade-union, league, syndicate, alliance, coalition, federation, confederation, confederacy; *Verein* (*Ger.*), *Bund* (*Ger.*), *Zollverein* (*Ger.*); tong (*Chinese*).
[*political parties*] Democrats, Republicans, Tories, Whigs, Conservatives, Liberals, Radicals, Socialists, Fascisti (*It.; sing.* Fascista); Constitutional

Democrats *or* Cadets, Social Democrats, Menshiviki (*sing.* Menshivik), Minimalists, Bolsheviki (*sing.* Bolshevik), Maximalists (*the last four are Russian*).
partisanship, cliquishness, cliquism, partyism, party system, party spirit.
social gathering, company, assemblage, reception, gathering, tamasha (*Anglo-Indian*), tea party, dinner party, etc.
[*one concerned, as in a contract or lawsuit*] **participator,** participant, sharer, signer, accessory, litigant, suitor (*law*), plaintiff, defendant.
person, individual, somebody, someone, one, fellow (*chiefly colloq.*), chap (*colloq.*), bloke (*slang*), duck (*slang*), bird (*slang*), guy (*slang*), cove (*slang*), bozo (*slang*), man: *in this sense,* party *is slang or vulgar.*
II. *Verbs.* **unite,** join, combine, league, associate, amalgamate, band together, club together, coöperate, consolidate, incorporate, confederate, ally, federate, federalize.
III. *Adjectives.* **united,** joined, combined, etc. (see *verbs*); joint, conjoint; corporate, confederated, allied, federal; organized, syndicated, unionized; fraternal, brotherly, Masonic; cliquish, cliquy, thick as thieves (*colloq.*).
IV. *Adverbs.* **unitedly,** jointly, etc. (see *adjectives*); side by side, hand in hand, shoulder to shoulder, in the same boat, *en masse* (*F.*), unanimously.
See also ASSEMBLAGE, COMBINATION, COÖPERATION, SIDE, SOCIALITY.

---

party-colored, *adj.* many-colored, variegated, mottled. See COLOR, VARIEGATION.
[1]pass, *n.* cut, defile, gorge. See NOTCH.
[2]pass, *n.* lunge, thrust; condition, state, situation, predicament; permit, license, passport. See ATTACK, CIRCUMSTANCE, PERMISSION.
passable, *adj.* mediocre, tolerable, fair, ordinary. See BEAUTY, IMPERFECTION.

PASSAGE.—I. *Nouns.* **passage,** passing, going, movement, motion; ingress, access, entrance; egress, exit, issue, evacuation, departure, migration, wing, flight; enactment (*of a measure or law*), sanction.
[*of time*] **lapse,** progress, transition, course, run, efflux, effluxion, expiry, revolution.
[*motion through*] **transit,** passage through, passage over, transition, intercurrence, transmission; permeation, infiltration, percolation, penetration, interpenetration; osmosis *or* osmose (*physics*), diosmosis *or* diosmose, endosmosis *or* endosmose (*osmosis inward*), exosmosis *or* exosmose (*osmosis outward*).
voyage, journey, crossing, cruise, sail, route.
[*means of passing*] **way,** path, road, thoroughfare, avenue; pass, defile, notch (*U. S.*), gap, neck, gut; canal, channel, passage, meatus (*anat.*), iter (*anat.*), aqueduct, conduit; ford, ferry, bridge; passageway, vestibule, lobby, entry, hall, corridor, cloister, gallery, tunnel, sap, drift, communication, overpass, underpass, chute; flue, chimney.
[*mutual act*] **interchange,** change, exchange, negotiation; altercation, collision, brush, encounter, contest, skirmish, just *or* joust, fight (*as, a* passage *of or at arms*).
[*portion of literary composition*] **excerpt,** extract, portion, quotation, citation, pericope (*esp. from the Bible*), text, selection; paragraph, section, clause, sentence, verse.
[*portion of music*] phrase, measure, bar; roulade, run, flourish.
occurrence, incident, event, deed, act, transaction, exploit, feat: *in this sense,* passage *is archaic.*
II. *Verbs.* pass (*used with* along, down, on, over, *etc.*), go, move, proceed, extend, flow, stream, run, continue, move past, flow past.
circulate, be current, be received, gain currency.
depart, leave, go away, quit, withdraw; pass away, perish, die (*as, to* pass *hence*).
elapse (*as time*), lapse, go by, glide by, be spent, be lost, vanish, flit, disappear, slip by (*or* away), steal away.
occur, happen, befall, betide, arise, take place, come, be present.
go through, have passage, force (make, thread, *or* worm) one's way, find a way (*or* vent), cross, traverse, overpass, go over, proceed across, cut across, ford, thread, penetrate, perforate, permeate.
enact (*as a bill*), ratify, sanction, approve, establish, decree. ordain.

pledge (*one's word or oath*), promise, plight, undertake, agree, vow, swear, contract, engage, subscribe.
utter, deliver, express, voice, pronounce (*as, to* pass *judgment*).
hand over, deliver, give, transfer, make over, surrender, yield control of, consign, relinquish, commit.
[*to go beyond*] **surpass,** exceed, overstep, excel, transcend, surmount, outrun, outstrip, outdo.
[*to pass the time*] **spend,** pass away, expend, employ, use, consume, while away live through, beguile, moon, idle, languish away.
III. *Adjectives.* **passing,** going by, transient, transmigratory, departing; fleeting ephemeral, evanescent, fugacious, transitory, cursory, incidental.
IV. *Adverbs.* **passing,** exceedingly, surpassingly, extraordinarily, unusually, excessively, very, preëminently (*as,* passing *strange*).

See also CESSATION, CONVERSION, CROSSING, DISAPPEARANCE, EVENT, JOURNEY, LAPSE, MOTION, NAVIGATION, NONEXISTENCE, NOTCH, OPENING, SUPERIORITY, TIME, TRANSFER.

---

passion, *n.* feeling, excitement, emotion; ardor, desire, infatuation; anger, wrath, fury. See EXCITABILITY, LOVE, RESENTMENT.
passive, *adj.* inert, quiet; resigned, apathetic, indifferent. See INACTION.
passiveness, *n.* passivity, nonresistance, inactivity, quiescence; inertia. See INACTION, INERTNESS.
passport, *n.* safe-conduct, pass. See PERMISSION.
password, *n.* countersign, watchword. See INDICATION, WORD.

PAST.—I. *Nouns.* **past,** time gone by, past time, days of yore, former days (*or* times), eld (*poetic*), days of old, times past, langsyne, long ago, bygone days, yesterday, the olden time, heretofore (*rare*), foretime (*rare*).
antiquity, antiqueness, ancientness, time immemorial, history, remote time; remote past; paleontology, archæology, paleology, antiquarianism.
antiquary, antiquarian, virtuoso; archæologist, paleologist; *laudator temporis acti* (*L.*), dryasdust; the Rev. Dr. Dryasdust (*an imaginary person made use of by Scott to introduce some of his novels*), Jonathan Oldbuck (Scott's *The Antiquary*), Herr Teufelsdröckh (*Sartor Resartus*).
ancestry, lineage, ancestors, forefathers, forbears *or* forebears.
past life, past career, history, record: *esp. one that will not bear inquiry; as, a woman with a* past.
II. *Verbs.* **be past,** have expired, have run its course, have had its day; cease, vanish, pass, pass by (*or* away), lapse, blow over.
III. *Adjectives.* **past,** gone, gone by, over, passed away, bygone, elapsed, lapsed, agone (*archaic*), expired, extinct, exploded, forgotten, irrecoverable; obsolete, antiquated, outworn.
former, earlier, prior, previous, antecedent, *ci-devant* (*F.*), whilom (*archaic*), sometime, pristine, quondam, late; ancestral, ancient.
foregoing, preceding, last, latter; recent.
retrospective, retroactive, looking back (*or* backward); archæological.
IV. *Adverbs.* **formerly,** of old, of yore, erst (*archaic or poetic*), erstwhile (*archaic*), whilom (*archaic*), time was, ago, anciently, aforetime, once, one day, long ago; lately, latterly, of late; ere now, before now, hitherto, heretofore; already, yet, up to this time, from time immemorial.
past, by, beyond (*as, to sweep* past).
V. *Prepositions.* **past,** beyond (*in time*), after; beyond (*in place*), farther than

See also OLDNESS.—*Antonyms.* See FUTURE, [1]PRESENT.

---

pastime, *n.* diversion, recreation, play, entertainment. See AMUSEMENT.
pastor, *n.* minister, clergyman, rector, preacher. See CLERGY.
pastry, *n.* pie crust; cakes. See SWEETNESS.
pasture, *n.* pasturage; paddock, croft; meadow, field, lea. See FOOD, INCLOSURE, PLAIN.
pasty, *adj.* pale, pallid; sticky, glutinous, viscid. See COLORLESSNESS, SEMILIQUIDITY.

pat, *v.* rap, tap, strike (*gently or caressingly*), smack, beat. See IMPULSE.
pat, *adj.* appropriate, apt, felicitous, timely. See AGREEMENT.
patch, *v.* piece together, reconstruct, adjust; repair, mend, revamp. See COMPROMISE, RESTORATION.
patent, *adj.* evident, obvious, apparent, clear, plain. See MANIFESTATION.

PATERNITY.—*Nouns.* **paternity,** fathership, fatherhood, progenitorship (*rare*); parentage, male parentage; paternal headship, paternal rule.
parent, father, sire, *père* (*F.*), old man (*colloq.*), papa (*a child's word*), pop (*slang*), dad (*colloq.*), governor (*slang*), paterfamilias, pater (*colloq.*), daddy (*colloq.*), ancestor, genitor (*rare*), forefather, progenitor, author, begetter, originator procreator; grandfather, grandsire.
motherhood, maternity, motherhead (*archaic*).
mother, mamma *or* mama, ma (*colloq. or childish*), mammy (*a child's word*), mam (*colloq.*), mater (*colloq.*), materfamilias, matriarch; dam (*used esp. of quadrupeds*); venter (*law*); progenitress, progenitrix.
stem, trunk, tree, stock, stirps, pedigree, house, lineage, line, family, race, tribe, sept, clan; genealogy, family tree, descent, extraction, birth, ancestry; forefathers, forbears *or* forebears.
II. *Adjectives.* **paternal,** fatherly, fatherlike; protecting, shielding, protective, sheltering, tender, affectionate, parental; ancestral, lineal, racial, patriarchal; phyletic (*biol.*), phylogenetic (*biol.*).
maternal, motherly, motherlike, affectionate, sympathetic, kind, parental.
See also BENEVOLENCE, CONSANGUINITY, PRODUCER.—*Antonyms.* See POSTERITY.

---

path, *n.* course, route; footway; footpath, trail. See DIRECTION, WAY.
pathetic, *adj.* touching, sad, pitiful, distressing, heartrending. See PAINFULNESS, PITY, TOUCH.
patience, *n.* endurance, submission; tolerance, leniency; persistence, constancy. See [2]CONTENT, INEXCITABILITY, PERSEVERANCE.
patient, *adj.* gentle, forbearing, long-suffering, tolerant. See INEXCITABILITY.
patrician, *adj.* aristocratic, blue-blooded, noble. See NOBILITY.
patriotism, *n.* love of country. See PHILANTHROPY.
patron, *n.* supporter, backer, benefactor, champion, defender. See AUXILIARY.
patronage, *n.* favor, support, interest; auspices. See AID.
[1]**patter,** *v.* chatter, jabber; mumble, mutter. See LOQUACITY, STAMMERING.
[2]**patter,** *v.* pitapat, pitterpatter, tap. See ROLL.
pattern, *n.* model, example, mold; paragon, ideal. See COPY, PERFECTION.
pauper, *n.* beggar, mendicant. See POVERTY.
pause, *n.* stop, wait, inaction, hesitation; lull, suspension, discontinuance. See CESSATION, [1]REST.
pause, *v.* cease, stop, halt, desist. See CESSATION, [1]REST.
pavement, *n.* floor, flooring, paving; sidewalk, causeway. See BASE, WAY.
pawn, *v.* pledge, hock (*slang*), pop (*slang*). See BORROWING, SECURITY.
pawnbroker, *n.* loan broker, uncle (*slang*). See LENDING.
pawnshop, *n.* loan company, popshop (*slang*), uncle's (*slang*). See LENDING.

PAYMENT.—I. *Nouns.* **payment,** defrayal, defrayment, discharge, settlement, acquittance, quittance, clearance, liquidation, satisfaction, reckoning, arrangement, compounding.
acknowledgment, release; receipt, voucher.
repayment, repaying, reimbursement, recoupment, remuneration, satisfaction, requital, retribution.
pay (*that which is paid*), reward, recompense, compensation, return; hire, wages, stipend, salary; percentage, brokerage, commission, royalty, salvage, demurrage; tribute, subsidy, fee, blood money; deposit, earnest, installment *or* instalment.
II. *Verbs.* **pay,** defray, make payment; pay one's way, expend, put down, lay down; discharge, settle, foot the bill (*colloq.*), meet, honor (*as a draft*), accept, acknowledge, remit, satisfy, pay in full, clear, liquidate, pay up; cash (*as a check*); be profitable, be remunerative.

repay, refund, reimburse, reward, indemnify, recompense, remunerate; requite, redeem; disgorge, make repayment.

III. *Adjectives.* **payable**, due, owing, matured, maturing; profitable.

paying, remunerative, gainful, profitable, remuneratory (*rare*), compensative, compensatory; out of debt, all clear, all straight, solvent.

IV. *Adverbs.* **at sight**, at first sight, on presentation (*as of a draft*); money down, cash down, on the nail (*slang*), cash on delivery, C.O.D.

See also COMPENSATION, EXPENDITURE, MONEY, REWARD, TAKING.—*Antonyms.* NONPAYMENT, RECEIPT.

PEACE.—I. *Nouns.* **peace**, tranquillity, calm, equanimity, quietude, composure, rest, repose, concord, harmony; public quiet (*or* order); friendliness, amity peacefulness; pacifism, neutrality; piping time of peace, cessation of war (*or* hostilities), truce; pipe of peace, calumet.

II. *Verbs.* **be at peace**, keep the peace, make peace, pacify, placate, conciliate.

III. *Adjectives.* **peaceable** (*inclined to peace*), pacific, calm, tranquil, still, undisturbed, untroubled, peaceful, halcyon; bloodless; neutral, pacifistic, unbelligerent, "too proud to fight" (Woodrow Wilson).

peaceful (*at peace*), quiet, tranquil, restful, placid; harmonious, concordant, amicable.

See also CONCORD, FRIENDSHIP, HARMONY, MODERATION, PACIFICATION, [1]REST, SILENCE.—*Antonyms.* See CONTENTION, DISCORD, WARFARE.

---

peacemaker, *n.* mediator, intercessor. See CONCORD.

peace offering, satisfaction, reparation, olive branch. See PACIFICATION.

peak, *n.* crag, pinnacle; top, crest, apex, height. See SHARPNESS, SUMMIT.

peal, *n.* blast, resounding, boom, reverberation. See LOUDNESS.

pearly, *adj.* grayish, silvery; nacreous; whitish. See GRAY, SEMITRANSPARENCY, WHITENESS.

pear-shaped, *adj.* pyriform, obconic. See ROTUNDITY.

peasant, *n.* farmer, rustic, countryman. See PEOPLE.

peck, *v.* nibble, eat; pick, strike, jab. See FOOD, IMPULSE.

peculiar, *adj.* particular, especial; odd, strange, queer. See SPECIALTY, UNCONFORMITY.

peculiarity, *n.* idiosyncrasy, individuality; oddity, eccentricity. See SUBJECTIVENESS, UNCONFORMITY.

pedagogic, *adj.* educational, scholastic, academic. See TEACHING.

pedant, *n.* prig, doctrinaire, theorist. See AFFECTATION, SCHOLAR.

pedantic, *adj.* affected, stilted; formal, precise, narrow. See AFFECTATION, SCHOOL.

peddle, *v.* hawk, retail. See SALE.

peddler, *n.* hawker, vender, huckster. See MERCHANT.

pedestrian, *n.* foot traveler, walker. See TRAVELER.

pedigree, *n.* ancestry, descent, lineage, genealogy. See CONTINUITY.

peel, *v.* pare, skin, strip. See DIVESTMENT.

peel, *n.* rind, skin. See COVERING.

[1]**peep,** *v.* cheep, chirp, chirrup. See ULULATION.

[2]**peep,** *v.* peek, peer, look. See VISION.

peer, *v.* peep, peek, pry. See VISION.

peer, *n.* match, equal; nobleman, lord. See EQUALITY, NOBILITY.

peerless, *adj.* unrivaled, matchless, supreme, unequaled. See SUPERIORITY.

peevish, *adj.* cross, touchy, irritable, fretful. See IRASCIBILITY.

peg, *n.* highball (*U. S.*); pin, bolt, dowel, thole, spike. See DRUNKENNESS, VINCULUM.

pelf, *n.* filthy lucre, ill-gotten gain, mammon. See ACQUISITION, WEALTH.

pelt, *n.* skin (*of an animal*), hide, fur. See COVERING.

pelt, *v.* strike, beat, drive; hurl, throw, pitch, fling. See IMPULSE, PROPULSION.

pen, *n.* corral, pound, fold, paddock. See INCLOSURE.

[1]pen, *v.* shut in, confine; impound, cage, coop, restrain. See INCLOSURE, RESTRAINT.

[2]pen, *v.* write (*as a letter*), indite, inscribe. See WRITING.

PENALTY.—I. *Nouns.* **penalty,** penal retribution, punishment, chastisement, suffering, penalization, pain, penance, *peine forte et dure* (*F.*).

fine, mulct, amercement, assessment, forfeit, forfeiture, damages, sequestration, confiscation, deodand (*hist.*), præmunire (*hist.*); handicap (*sporting cant*).

II. *Verbs.* **penalize,** make penal, punish, chastise, castigate, imprison.

fine, mulct, amerce, confiscate, sequestrate, sequester; forfeit, escheat (*law*); handicap (*sporting cant*).

See also PUNISHMENT.—*Antonyms.* See REWARD.

---

penance, *n.* suffering, discipline, fasting, flagellation. See ATONEMENT, RITE.

PENDENCY.—I. *Nouns.* **pendency,** dependence, suspension, pendulousness, pendulosity (*rare*), pensileness, pensility, hanging, droop, inclination; overhang (*as of the upper wing of a biplane*).

pendant, hanging appendage; drop, eardrop, lavaliere, *pendeloque* (*F.*); tippet, tassel, lobe; tail, train, queue, pigtail; pendulum.

chandelier, gaselier, electrolier; corona (*as in churches*), *corona lucis* (*L.*), crown, circlet.

suspense (*as of a suit or petition*), indetermination, suspension, continuance.

II. *Verbs.* **be pendent,** hang, depend, swing, dangle, droop; flap, daggle, draggle, trail; beetle, jut, overhang.

suspend (*cause to depend*), hang, sling, hook up, hitch, fasten to, append.

III. *Adjectives.* **pendent,** pendulous, hanging, drooping, decumbent (*bot.*), dangling, pensile, suspended, weeping (*as a willow*), nodding, cernuous (*as a flower*), dependent.

caudate *or* caudated, tailed, caudal, tail-like.

overhanging, beetling, jutting over, imminent, projecting, impending; overlapping, overlying, imbricate, imbricated (*as shingles*).

pending, undecided, unsettled, in suspense, unresolved, undetermined, in continuance; impending, imminent.

Antonyms. See SUPPORT.

---

penetrate, *v.* pierce, affect, excite; filter into, enter, invade; discern, see through; perforate, permeate, pass through. See EXCITEMENT, INGRESS, INTELLIGENCE, PASSAGE.

penetrative, *adj.* piercing, acute, penetrating; discerning, astute. See FEELING, INTELLIGENCE.

PENITENCE.—I. *Nouns.* **penitence,** contrition, compunction, repentance, remorse, regret, self-reproach, self-reproof, self-accusation, self-condemnation, qualms of conscience, "compunctious visitings of nature" (*Macbeth*).

acknowledgment, confession, apology, recantation; penance, sackcloth and ashes.

penitent, repentant (*rare*); Magdalen; prodigal son, returned prodigal, "a sadder and a wiser man" (Coleridge).

II. *Verbs.* **repent,** be sorry for, rue, regret, think better of, recant; plead guilty, acknowledge, confess, cry *peccavi* (*L.*), humble oneself, beg pardon, apologize; turn over a new leaf, put on the new man.

reform, reclaim, regenerate, redeem, convert, amend, improve, correct, restore, make a new man of.

III. *Adjectives.* **penitent,** repentant, contrite, conscience-smitten, conscience stricken, remorseful, regretful, sorry, compunctious, self-accusing; touched, affected, melted, softened.

See also ATONEMENT, REGRET.—*Antonyms.* See IMPENITENCE.

---

penitentiary, *n.* prison house, state prison, house of correction. See PRISON.

penmanship, *n.* handwriting, chirography. See WRITING.

pen name, pseudonym, *nom de guerre* (*F.*). See MISNOMER.

pennant, *n.* pennon, flag, banner, streamer. See INDICATION.

penniless, *adj.* impecunious, moneyless, indigent, needy, poor. See POVERTY.
pension, *n.* annuity, allowance, settlement. See RECEIPT.
pensive, *adj.* melancholy; meditative, reflective, thoughtful, amusing. See DEJECTION, THOUGHT.
penurious, *adj.* miserly, stingy, parsimonious. See PARSIMONY.
penury, *n.* indigence, pauperism, destitution. See POVERTY.

PEOPLE.—I. *Nouns.* [*body of persons forming a characteristic group*] **people,** folk, race, tribe, clan, nation, state, country, city, etc.
[*persons indefinitely*] inhabitants, population, public; individuals, persons, folks, men.
[*members of one's family*] kindred, relatives, folks (*colloq.*); ancestry, ancestors.
[*the masses as contrasted with the higher classes*] **populace,** commonalty, the people, democracy, *hoi polloi* (*Gr.* οἱ πολλοί), *bourgeoisie* (*F.*), lower classes (*or* orders), common herd, rank and file, the many, the general (*archaic*), the crowd, the ruck, the multitude, the million, the masses, the mobility (*jocose*), the peasantry, proletariat, great unwashed (*term of contempt first applied by Edmund Burke*).
rabble, mob, scum, rout, horde, canaille, dregs of society, trash, riffraff, ragtag and bobtail.
commoner, one of the people, democrat, plebeian, *roturier* (*F.*), yeoman, republican, *bourgeois* (*F.*).
peasant, countryman, boor, churl, serf, swain, clown, hind (*Eng.*), clod, clodhopper, yokel (*Eng.*), oaf, lout, hawbuck (*dial.*), bumpkin, plowman, hayseed (*slang*), rustic, rube (*U. S. slang*), Tony Lumpkin (Goldsmith); tiller of the soil, ryot (*India*), fellah (*Arabic; pl.* fellahin *or* fellaheen), gossoon (*Anglo-Irish*), *contadino* (*It.; pl. contadini*); hewers of wood and drawers of water; sons of Martha; gamin, street Arab, mudlark.
upstart, parvenu, nobody, snob, mushroom, adventurer, *nouveau riche* (*F.; pl. nouveaux riches*), *bourgeois gentilhomme* (*F.*).
vagrant, vagabond, wanderer, tramp, gaberlunzie (*Scot.*), bum (*U. S. slang*), hobo *or* bo (*U. S.*), sundowner (*Australia*), floater, caird (*Scot.*), panhandler (*slang*), beggar, ragamuffin; outcast, pariah.
II. *Verbs.* **people,** populate, fill (*or* stock) with people, settle: *opposite of* depopulate.
III. *Adjectives.* **peopled,** inhabited, populous, settled, full of people, occupied.
plebeian, proletarian, lowborn, baseborn, risen from the ranks, humble, unknown to fame, obscure, untitled: *opposite of* aristocratic.
ignoble, common, mean, low, menial, servile, base, vile, sorry, scrubby, beggarly; vulgar, low-minded; snobbish, parvenu, low-bred: *opposite of* noble.
rustic, countrified, country, backwood *or* backwoods, hobnailed, clownish, geoponic (*pedantic or jocose*), agricultural, clodhopping, loutish, boorish, churlish, rude, carlish, unpolished: *opposite of* urban.
barbarous, barbarian, barbaric, heathenish, paganish, uncivilized, savage: *opposite of* civilized.
See also CONSANGUINITY, MANKIND.—*Antonyms.* See NOBILITY.

---

perceive, *v.* see, know, comprehend, understand. See FEELING.
percentage, *n.* fee, compensation; allowance, agio. See COMMISSION, DISCOUNT.
perceptible, *adj.* perceivable, cognizable; discernible, visible. See KNOWLEDGE, VISIBILITY.
perception, *n.* discernment, apprehension, penetration; understanding, cognizance. See IDEA, KNOWLEDGE.
perceptive, *adj.* knowing, percipient, cognitive. See KNOWLEDGE.
perch, *v.* alight, settle, roost. See [1]REST.
percolate, *v.* filter, ooze, permeate; trickle, drip. See EGRESS, RIVER (*flow*).
perdition, *n.* fall, downfall; loss, ruin. See DESTRUCTION, FAILURE.
peremptory, *adj.* absolute, conclusive; binding, compulsory; arbitrary, tyrannical. See AUTHORITY, COMPULSION, SEVERITY.
perennial, *adj.* consecutive, successive: endless, long-lived. See CONTINUITY, DURABILITY.

PERFECTION.—I. *Nouns.* **perfection,** perfectness, indefectibility, faultlessness, excellence, finish, superexcellence, transcendence, perfectiveness, perfectivity; impeccability, impeccancy; maturity, development, perfectionment (*rare*), consummation, accomplishing, completion, idealization.
[*a perfect thing or person*] **paragon,** model, pattern, *beau idéal* (*F.*), ideal, *ne plus ultra* (*L.*), standard; pink, pink (*or* acme) of perfection, nonesuch *or* nonsuch, nonpareil, phœnix *or* phenix, flower, queen (*fig.*), mirror, "the observed of all observers" (*Hamlet*); Admirable Crichton, Roland, Bayard; *chevalier sans peur et sans reproche* (*F.*).
masterpiece, masterwork, *chef-d'œuvre* (*F.*), masterstroke, prize-winner, prize.
II. *Verbs.* **perfect,** bring to perfection, ripen, mature; improve, put the finishing touch to (*or* upon), complete, finish, consummate, accomplish, crown, perfectionate (*rare*); idealize.
III. *Adjectives.* **perfect,** faultless, immaculate, spotless, impeccable, unblemished, sound, entire, whole, complete, ripe, perfected, indefectible, blameless, flawless, scatheless, intact; consummate, finished, ideal.
best, model, standard; inimitable, unparalleled, unparagoned, unequaled, choice, prime, beyond all praise.
utter, absolute, downright, entire, total, complete (*as, a* perfect *stranger*) perfect *nonsense: colloq. in this sense*).
IV. *Adverbs.* **perfectly,** faultlessly, etc. (see *adjectives*); to perfection, with a finish, *ad unguem* (*L.*), to a nicety, exactly; clean, clean as a whistle.
See also BEAUTY, COMPLETENESS, COMPLETION, GOODNESS, SUMMIT, SUPERIORITY. —*Antonyms.* See IMPERFECTION.

---

perforate, *v.* prick, pierce, puncture, penetrate, drill, bore. See OPENING.

PERFORATOR.—*Nouns.* **perforator,** piercer, borer; auger, gimlet, drill, awl, bradawl, scoop, corkscrew, dibble, trepan, lancet, probe, stylet, stiletto, bodkin, needle, punch, punching machine, puncher (*telegraphy*); gouge, chisel.
Antonyms. See STOPPER.

---

perform, *v.* do, act; work, operate; achieve, discharge, fulfill; enact, personate, play, execute; sustain, assume (*a rôle*). See ACTION, AGENCY, COMPLETION, DRAMA, MUSICIAN, SUPPORT, TAKING.
performance, *n.* action, acting, representation; creation, achievement; execution, touch, playing. See DRAMA, EFFECT, MUSICIAN.
performer, *n.* doer, executor, actor, player; instrumentalist, virtuoso. See AGENT, DRAMA, MUSICIAN.
perfume, *n.* aroma, scent, perfumery. See FRAGRANCE.
perfumery, *n.* perfumes, scent; incense, attar, cologne, etc. See FRAGRANCE.
perfunctory, *adj.* careless, mechanical, crude. See INCOMPLETENESS.
perhaps, *adv.* haply, by chance, peradventure. See POSSIBILITY.
peril, *n.* risk, hazard, exposure. See DANGER.

PERIOD.—*Nouns.* **period** (*of time*), interval, span, cycle, season, spell, term, semester, quarter, month, lunation, moon, year, twelvemonth, octave, *novena* (*L.*); quinquennium, quinquennial, luster *or* lustre, lustrum (*L. pl.* lustra); decade, decennial, decennium; generation, pilgrimage, lifetime, century; time, date, epoch, era, eon, age, kalpa (*Hindu*), millenium; duration, continuance.
limit, bound, end, termination, conclusion, completion, close, stop.
[*in punctuation*] full stop, full point.
[*in rhetoric*] complete sentence (*esp. one of several clauses, in which completion of the sense is suspended till the close*).
See also AGE, REGULARITY, TIME.—*Antonyms.* See IRREGULARITY, LAPSE.

---

periodic, *adj.* epochal, cyclic, seasonal; recurring, intermittent. See REGULARITY.
periodical, *adj.* periodic, regular, recurring, intermittent. See REGULARITY.
periodical, *n.* magazine, periodic publication. See BOOK.
periodicity, *n.* regular recurrence, reoccurrence. See REGULARITY.

perish, *v.* die, expire; be destroyed, crumble, break up; pass away, cease to exist. See DEATH, DESTRUCTION, NONEXISTENCE.
perishable, *adj.* mortal, temporal, impermanent, short-lived. See TRANSIENCE.
perjure, *v.* forswear: *used reflexively.* See IMPROBITY.
perjury, *n.* forswearing, false swearing, fraud, perversion. See FALSEHOOD.

PERMANENCE.—I. *Nouns.* **permanence,** fixedness, duration, permanency, continuance, fixity, persistence, endurance, durableness, durability; standing, *status quo* (*L.*); maintenance, preservation, conservation, conservatism; law of the Medes and Persians; immovableness, stability, constancy, changelessness, immutability, immutableness, inflexibility, obstinacy.
II. *Verbs.* **endure,** persist, remain, stay, tarry, rest, hold, last, continue, bide, abide, dwell, maintain, keep; stand fast, subsist, live, outlive, survive; hold one's ground (*or* footing).
III. *Adjectives.* **permanent,** durable, fixed, abiding, lasting, pucka *or pakka* (*Anglo-Indian*), stable, settled, established, irremovable; unaltered, unchanged, intact, inviolate, persistent, constant, enduring, conservative; unfailing, unfading, amaranthine.
IV. *Adverbs.* **permanently,** durably, etc. (see *adjectives*); *in statu quo* (*L.*), *uti possidetis* (*L.: Roman and civil law*); at a stand, at a standstill; finally, for good.
See also DURABILITY, OBSTINACY, REGULARITY, [1]REST, STABILITY, UNIFORMITY.—*Antonyms.* See CHANGE.

---

permeate, *v.* penetrate, pass through; pervade, overspread. See PASSAGE, PRESENCE.

PERMISSION.—I. *Nouns.* **permission,** leave, *congé* (*F.*), allowance, sufferance, tolerance, toleration, connivance; permissibleness, liberty, law, license, concession, grace; indulgence, favor, dispensation, exemption, release; authorization, warranty, accordance, admission.
permit, warrant, sanction, authority, imprimatur, firman (*Turkey; pl.* firmans), purwannah (*Anglo-Indian*), pass, safe-conduct, safeguard, passport; license, *carte blanche* (*F.*), grant, charter, patent.
II. *Verbs.* **permit,** let, allow, admit; suffer, tolerate, recognize, concede, accord, vouchsafe, favor, oblige, humor, gratify, indulge. stretch a point, wink at, connive at.
grant, empower, charter, enfranchise, privilege, license, authorize, warrant, sanction; intrust, commission.
III. *Adjectives.* **permissible,** allowable, admissible, unprohibited, unforbidden, licit, lawful, legitimate, legal, legalized, chartered.
permissive, permitting, allowing, facultative, optional; tolerated, suffered, sanctioned.
IV. *Adverbs.* by (*or* with) leave, under favor of, by all means.
See also CONSENT, FREEDOM.—*Antonyms.* See PROHIBITION.

---

pernicious, *adj.* harmful, detrimental, ruinous, wicked, malign. See BADNESS.
perpendicular, *adj.* upright, vertical, plumb. See RIGHT (*erect*).
perpetrate, *v.* commit, do, inflict, practice, perform. See ACTION.
perpetration, *n.* committal, performing, performance. See COMMISSION.

PERPETUITY.—I. *Nouns.* **perpetuity,** unceasingness, endlessness, continuity, everlastingness, perdurability, perpetuation, eternity, sempiternity, age; immortality.
II. *Verbs.* **perpetuate,** preserve (*from oblivion*), perennialize (*rare*), continue, eternize, eternalize, immortalize.
III. *Adjectives.* **perpetual,** eternal, everlasting, continual, endless, sempiternal, interminable, illimitable, infinite, boundless, unending, ceaseless, incessant, uninterrupted, unceasing; eterne (*poetic*); unfading, amaranthine, perennial. perdurable, never-ending, deathless, immortal, undying, imperishable.

IV. *Adverbs.* **perpetually,** eternally, etc. (see *adjectives*); constantly, always, ever, evermore (*archaic*), aye; forever, for aye, in all ages, without end, to the end of time, to the "last syllable of recorded time" (*Macbeth*), till doomsday, to the crack of doom; *in sæcula sæculorum* (*L.*).

See also CONTINUANCE, DURABILITY, FREQUENCY, STABILITY.—*Antonyms.* See INSTANTANEITY, TRANSIENCE.

---

perplex, *v.* bewilder, disconcert, distract; puzzle, confuse, confound, nonplus. See INATTENTION, UNCERTAINTY.

perplexity, *n.* predicament, quandary; hesitation, uncertainty, puzzle, bewilderment. See DIFFICULTY, UNCERTAINTY.

perquisite, *n.* gratuity, tip, bonus, bribe, *douceur* (*F.*). See REWARD.

persecute, *v.* oppress, annoy, trouble; molest, maltreat, injure. See MALEVOLENCE, PAINFULNESS.

PERSEVERANCE.—I. *Nouns.* **perseverance,** continuance, persistence, push, determination, aggressiveness, industry, effort, application, pertinacity, resolution, tenacity (*or* singleness) of purpose, firmness, constancy, steadiness, patience, indefatigability.

grit, stamina, backbone, sand (*slang*), pluck, bottom, courage, endurance, tenacity, staying power, bulldog courage.

II. *Verbs.* **persevere,** persist, hold on, hold out, continue, endure, stick to, cling to, adhere to, keep on, plod, carry on; keep to one's course, hold (*or* maintain) one's ground; bear up, keep up, hold up; go all lengths, go through fire and water; die in harness, die at one's post.

III. *Adjectives.* **persevering,** steady, constant, determined, steadfast, unwavering, unfaltering, undeviating, unswerving; plodding, industrious, persistent, persisting, pertinacious, strenuous, indefatigable, indomitable, unflagging, untiring, unwearied, unwearying, unflinching, game to the last.

IV. *Adverbs.* **perseveringly,** steadily, etc. (see *adjectives*); without fail, through thick and thin, through fire and water, through evil report and good report, *per fas et nefas* (*L.*); sink or swim, at any price, rain or shine, fair or foul, *vogue la galère* (*F.*).

See also ACTIVITY, CONTINUANCE, EXERTION, PERMANENCE, STABILITY.—*Antonyms.* See INACTIVITY, IRRESOLUTION.

---

persist, *v.* continue, carry on; endure, abide, rest, stand; persevere, plod; remain, endure. See CONTINUANCE, PERMANENCE, PERSEVERANCE, TIME.

persistent, *adj.* enduring, durable; permanent, constant, unchanged, steadfast; persevering, unfailing. See DURABILITY, PERMANENCE, PERSEVERANCE.

person, *n.* man, human being, humanity; individual, somebody; body, substance. See MANKIND, PARTY, SUBSTANTIALITY.

personage, *n.* somebody, figure, celebrity. See IMPORTANCE.

personal, *adj.* individual, private, own, particular, special. See SPECIALTY.

personality, *n.* censure, blame, invective, offensive remark; self, ego; person, individual; notable, celebrity; individuality. See DISAPPROBATION, IMMATERIALITY, MANKIND, REPUTE, SPECIALTY.

personalty, *n.* personal property, chattels, goods, movables. See PROPERTY.

personate, *v.* impersonate, pose as, act the part of. See REPRESENTATION.

personation, *n.* simulation, impersonation, dramatic performance. See REPRESENTATION.

personify, *v.* exemplify, symbolize; embody; personate, represent. See FIGURE, MATERIALITY, REPRESENTATION.

perspicacity, *n.* keenness, discrimination; acuteness, penetration, shrewdness. See FASTIDIOUSNESS, INTELLIGENCE.

PERSPICUITY.—I. *Nouns.* **perspicuity,** explicitness, lucidity, lucidness, clearness, limpidity, intelligibility, palpableness, definiteness, exactness, plainness, perspicuousness.

II. *Adjectives.* perspicuous, clear, lucid, pellucid, limpid, explicit, luminous, exact, unambiguous, plain, sharp-cut, distinct, intelligible, palpable, evident, manifest.

See also INTELLIGIBILITY, MANIFESTATION, TRANSPARENCY, TRUTH.—*Antonyms.* See OBSCURITY.

---

perspire, *v.* excrete, exude, sweat, swelter. See EXCRETION, HEAT.

persuade, *v.* convince, assure, satisfy; induce, prevail upon, win over. See BELIEF, MOTIVE.

persuasible, *adj.* persuadable, amenable, docile, tractable. See WILLINGNESS.

persuasion, *n.* conviction; influence, insistence, exhortation. See BELIEF, MOTIVE.

persuasive, *adj.* convincing, suasive, tempting, seductive. See MOTIVE.

pert, *adj.* rude, forward, bold, obtrusive; saucy, impudent, flippant. See DISCOURTESY, INSOLENCE.

pertain, *v.* belong, appertain; affect, concern, relate, refer: *followed by* to. See POSSESSION, RELATION.

pertinacious, *adj.* persistent, firm, constant, resolute, unyielding. See TENACITY.

pertinacity, *n.* persistence, resoluteness, perseverance, obstinacy. See TENACITY.

pertinent, *adj.* apt, belonging to; applicable, relevant, apposite. See AGREEMENT, RELATION.

perturbation, *n.* turmoil, disturbance, tumult; disquiet, restlessness; ado, flutter; trembling, trepidation. See AGITATION, EXCITABILITY, EXCITEMENT, FEAR.

peruse, *v.* read, study, con. See LEARNING.

pervade, *v.* permeate, fill, penetrate, overspread. See INFLUENCE, PRESENCE.

pervasion, *n.* permeation, penetration, saturation. See PRESENCE.

perverse, *adj.* stubborn, obstinate, obdurate; wayward, reactionary; petulant, cross, ill-tempered. See OBSTINACY, REPRESSION, SULLENNESS.

perversion, *n.* misconstruction, misrepresentation, misusage, garble. See DISTORTION.

perversity, *n.* perverseness, obduracy, contumacy; wickedness. See OBSTINACY, VICE.

pervert, *v.* distort, garble, misrepresent, falsify; mislead, lead astray; misstate, misinterpret; equivocate, quibble. See DISTORTION, ERROR, MISINTERPRETATION, SOPHISTRY.

pessimism, *n.* depression, gloom, blues (*colloq.*); despair, despondency; morbidity. See DEJECTION, HOPELESSNESS.

pessimist, *n.* Job's comforter, cynic; alarmist, knocker (*slang*), depreciator See HOPELESSNESS, UNDERESTIMATION.

pest, *n.* pestilence, nuisance; ugly customer, seditionary, traitor. See BANE, PITFALL.

pester, *v.* vex, annoy, displease, plague, worry. See PAINFULNESS.

pestilence, *n.* epidemic, plague. See DISEASE.

pet, *n.* favorite, darling, beloved. See IDOLATRY.

pet, *v.* caress, fondle, coddle; cherish. See ENDEARMENT, LOVE.

petition, *v.* ask, plead, entreat, implore. See REQUEST.

petition, *n.* request, entreaty; prayer, supplication. See REQUEST, WORSHIP.

PETITIONER.—*Nouns.* **petitioner,** solicitor, applicant, suppliant, supplicant, orator (*law*), oratrix (*fem.: law*), suitor, candidate, postulant (*esp. for holy orders*), claimant, aspirant, competitor, bidder; place hunter, pothunter; salesman, drummer (*U. S.*), canvasser.

runner (*U. S.*), hotel runner, steerer (*U. S.*), touter (*colloq.*), tout (*colloq.*); barker (*colloq.*).

beggar, mendicant, panhandler (*slang*), cadger, schnorrer (*Yiddish*), clapperdudgeon (*archaic*); fakir, dervish (*both Moham.*); almsman, beadsman *or* bedesman, bluegown (*Brit.*).

See also REPRESENTATIVE (*salesman*), SERVILITY (*sycophant*).—*Antonyms.* See GIVING (*giver*).

---

petrify, *v.* thicken, stiffen; stupefy, paralyze, shock; harden, ossify; calcify, mineralize; astonish, stun. See DENSITY, EXCITEMENT, HARDNESS, INORGANIZATION, WONDER.

petroleum, *n.* rock oil, benzine, naphtha, kerosene, etc. See OIL.

petty, *adj.* mean, beggarly, contemptible; unimportant, trifling. See DISREPUTE, UNIMPORTANCE.

petty cash, change, spending money, pocket money, pin money. See MONEY.

petulant, *adj.* peevish, fretful, irritable, cross. See CROSSING, IRASCIBILITY.

phantom, *n.* ghost, spirit, apparition; unreality, shadow, vision. See APPEARANCE, SPECTER, UNSUBSTANTIALITY.

phase, *n.* angle, form, shape; guise, aspect, situation, position, status. See APPEARANCE, CIRCUMSTANCE, SIDE.

phenomenon, *n.* fact, occurrence; marvel, wonder. See EVENT, PRODIGY.

PHILANTHROPY.—I. *Nouns.* **philanthropy,** universal good will, altruism, humanity, humanitarianism, large-heartedness, benevolence, public welfare, commonweal *or* common weal.

public spirit, patriotism, nationality, love of country, *amor patriæ* (*L.*).

philanthropist, altruist, humanitarian, patriot, lover of mankind, *amicus humani generis* (*L.*), good Samaritan, salt of the earth; "little friend of all the world" (Kipling): *opposite of* misanthrope.

II. *Adjectives.* **philanthropic** *or* philanthropical, humanitarian, public-spirited, patriotic; humane, large-hearted, benevolent, generous, liberal, charitable, altruistic.

See also BENEVOLENCE, UNSELFISHNESS.—*Antonyms.* See MISANTHROPY.

---

philosophical, *adj.* calm, rational, imperturbable; contemplative, deliberative, speculative. See INEXCITABILITY, THOUGHT.

phlegmatic, *adj.* cold, apathetic, unemotional, languid, inert. See INSENSITIVENESS.

phonetic, *adj.* voiced, tonic; phonic, phonetical, sonant; vocal, lingual, oral, spoken. See LETTER, [1]SOUND, SPEECH.

phonograph. *n.* gramophone, victrola (*trade-mark name*). See HEARING.

photograph, *n.* print, film, snapshot. See REPRESENTATION.

photographer, *n.* photographist, daguerreotypist. See REPRESENTATION.

PHRASE.—I. *Nouns.* **phrase,** expression, locution; idiom, turn of expression, peculiar expression, set phrase, idiomatic turn of speech; pithy saying, motto, proverb, metaphor, euphemism, figure, trope, figure of speech.

phraseology, diction, language, wording, phrasing, style, choice of words, mode of expression, literary power.

II. *Verbs.* **phrase,** express, word, put, describe, style, designate, call, dub, denominate; put into words, express by words, voice, couch in terms, clothe in words; speak by the card (*i.e., with precision*), speak by the book.

III. *Adverbs.* in round (*or* set) terms; in set phrases.

See also STYLE.

---

physic, *n.* medicine, dose, pill, drug, laxative. See REMEDY.

physician, *n.* consultant, adviser; doctor, surgeon, specialist. See ADVICE, REMEDY.

phytologist, *n.* botanist, horticulturist. See BOTANY.

piazza, *n.* veranda, porch, portico. See OPENING, RECEPTACLE.

pick, *v.* get, gain; choose, select; gather, pluck, cull. See ACQUISITION, CHOICE, TAKING.

pick, *n.* preference; best, choicest, *élite* (*F.*), cream, flower. See CHOICE, GOODNESS.
picket, *n.* stake, post, pale; sentry, sentinel, guard, patrol. See SHARPNESS, WARNING.
picket, *v.* inclose, fence, palisade; tether, restrain; guard, patrol. See CIRCUMSCRIPTION, RESTRAINT, WARNING.
pickle, *v.* preserve, salt, brine, corn, marinade. See PRESERVATION.
pickpocket, *n.* cutpurse, pickpurse (*rare*), dip (*slang*). See THIEF.
picnic, *n.* excursion, outing, festivity, junket. See AMUSEMENT.
pictorial, *adj.* graphic, depicting, delineatory. See FINE ARTS.
picture, *n.* representation, view, display, tableau; canvas, painting, drawing, sketch, study. See APPEARANCE, FINE ARTS.—**picture gallery,** art gallery, art museum, *salon* (*F.*). See FINE ARTS.
picturesque, *adj.* pictorial, artistic, attractive; graphic, vivid. See BEAUTY, VIGOR.
picturesqueness, *n.* pictorial quality, vividness, force. See COLOR (*in literature*).
piece, *n.* fragment, portion; bit, morsel, moiety. See LENGTH, PART.
piece, *v.* patch, repair, transform; put together, unite, combine. See CHANGE, JUNCTION.
piecemeal, *adv.* little by little, piece by piece, by degrees. See PART.
pier, *n.* breakwater, mole; landing place, wharf, quay; pillar, shaft, buttress. See REFUGE, SUPPORT.
pierce, *v.* wound, stab; affect, penetrate; perforate, bore; chill, nip. See DETERIORATION, EXCITEMENT, OPENING, REFRIGERATION.
piercing, *adj.* biting, cutting; sharp, acute, keen; shrill, high. See COLD, FEELING, STRIDENCY.

PIETY.—I. *Nouns.* **piety,** religiousness, devoutness, veneration, reverence, godliness, dutifulness, devotion, religion, theism, faith; religiosity, holiness, saintship, sanctity, spirituality, spiritual-mindedness, charism (*theol.*), grace, humility, worship, consecration.
beatification, regeneration, conversion, sanctification, salvation, inspiration, bread of life; Body and Blood of Christ.
pietist (*often used disparagingly*), devotionalist, devotionist (*rare*), devotee, Christian, Saint, believer, convert, theist; the faithful (*collective*).
II. *Verbs.* **be pious,** have faith, believe, receive Christ; venerate, revere, adore, worship, be converted, be on God's side, stand up for Jesus, fight the good fight, keep the faith.
regenerate, convert, edify, inspire, sanctify, hallow, keep holy, beatify, consecrate, enshrine.
III. *Adjectives.* **pious,** religious, devout, devoted, reverent, reverential, godly, humble, dutiful, pure, pure in heart, holy, spiritual, saintly, saintlike; believing, faithful, Christian.
regenerate, born again (*relig.*), regenerated, redeemed, reformed, converted, Christianized; charismatic, inspired, consecrated; elected, adopted, justified, sanctified; unearthly, not of the earth.
Antonyms. See IMPIETY.

---

pig, *n.* swine, hog, boar, sow (*fem.*). See ANIMAL.
pigment, *n.* coloring matter, paint, stain, dye. See COLOR.
pile, *n.* mass, heap; edifice, structure. See ASSEMBLAGE, PRODUCTION.
pilfer, *v.* rob, thieve, plunder, filch. See STEALING.
pilgrimage, *n.* expedition, crusade; life, lifetime. See JOURNEY, PERIOD.
pillage, *n.* theft, plunder, depredation, spoliation. See STEALING.
pillar, *n.* column, obelisk, pedestal; prop. See HEIGHT, SUPPORT.
pilot, *n.* airman, aviator; adviser, counselor; guide; steersman, helmsman. See AËRONAUT, DIRECTOR, INFORMATION, MARINER.
pimple, *n.* excrescence, pustule, papule. See CONVEXITY.

pin, *n.* scarfpin, brooch, badge; fastener, coupler, dowel, thole, peg, spike. See ORNAMENT, VINCULUM.

pin, *v.* fasten, secure, attach, hold. See JUNCTION.

pincers, *n.* nippers, pliers, forceps. See RETENTION.

pinch, *v.* tighten, squeeze, compress; nip, hurt; chill, bite. See CONTRACTION, PAIN, REFRIGERATION.

pinch, *n.* plight, crisis, exigency; predicament, strait, emergency; nip, pinching; stress, pressure. See CIRCUMSTANCE, DIFFICULTY, PAIN, REQUIREMENT.

pine, *v.* mope, languish, droop, wither; crave, long for. See DEJECTION, DESIRE.

pinnacle, *n.* top, crown, peak, acme. See SUMMIT.

pioneer, *n.* forerunner, leader. See PRECURSOR.

pious, *adj.* religious, devout, holy, reverential. See PIETY.

pipe, *n.* fife, flute, flageolet, hornpipe, pipes (*pl.*); tube, passage, main; tobacco pipe, brier, meerschaum, clay. See MUSICAL INSTRUMENTS, OPENING, RECEPTACLE.

piquant, *adj.* stimulating, pungent, piercing; keen, sharp, tart, strong. See FEELING, PUNGENCY.

pique, *v.* offend, irritate, infuriate; cut, sting, nettle. See EXCITEMENT, PAINFULNESS.

pirate, *n.* sea-robber, freebooter, buccaneer, corsair. See THIEF.

pirate, *v.* plunder, steal, plagiarize, appropriate. See STEALING.

pistol, *n.* revolver, automatic, derringer, gat (*slang*). See ARMS.

pit, *n.* hollow, crater, excavation; mine, abyss, chasm, Hades; parquet (*theater*); snare, trap. See CONCAVITY, DEPTH, DRAMA, PITFALL.

pitch, *v.* reel, toss, lurch; dip, slope; cast, throw, heave; erect, set up. See OSCILLATION, PLUNGE, PROPULSION, VERTICALITY.

pitch, *n.* height, range, peak, acme; dip, decline, drop; tone, timbre; rise, ascent. See DEGREE, DESCENT, MELODY, OBLIQUITY.

piteous, *adj.* pathetic, deplorable, pitiable. See PAINFULNESS, PITY.

PITFALL.—*Nouns.* **pitfall,** trap, snare, gin, trapfall, springe, traphole, *trou-de-loup* (*F.; pl. trous-de-loup: mil.*), deadfall, ambush; pit, mine, void, chasm, crevasse, abyss, abysm.

[*hidden dangers for mariners*] rocks, reefs, sunken rocks, snags; sands, quicksands; shoals, shallows, shelf, bank (*as, the* banks *of Newfoundland*), flat; lee shore, rockbound coast.

whirlpool, vortex, eddy, maelstrom, Charybdis, gulf (*poetic*); eagre, bore, tidal wave; undertow, rapids, tide race, current.

[*human*] pest, nuisance, curse, ugly customer; incendiary, firebug (*slang*); firebrand, seditionary, seditionist, traitor, assassin; hornets' nest.

sword of Damocles; wolf at the door; snake in the grass, *anguis in herba* (*L.*), snake in one's bosom.

See also AMBUSH, DECEPTION, LATENCY.—*Antonyms.* See REFUGE.

---

pith, *n.* essence, substance; gist, core, kernel, soul. See MEANING, SUBJECTIVENESS.

pithy, *adj.* brief, terse, laconic, sententious; forceful, powerful. See CONCISENESS, VIGOR.

pitiable, *adj.* wretched, woeful, deplorable; miserable, pathetic; insignificant, despicable. See BADNESS, PAINFULNESS, PITY.

pitiful, *adj.* piteous, lamentable; deplorable, pitiable; mean, disreputable compassionate, tender, merciful, sympathetic. See BADNESS, CONTEMPT DISREPUTE, PITY.

PITILESSNESS.—I. *Nouns.* **pitilessness,** mercilessness, etc. (see *adjectives*); inclemency, severity, inexorability, inflexibility, hard-heartedness, callousness barbarity, savagery, malevolence.

II. *Verbs.* **be pitiless,** turn a deaf ear to; shut the gates of mercy, have no mercy, give no quarter.
III. *Adjectives.* **pitiless,** merciless, ruthless, unpitying, unmerciful, inclement, grim-visaged, harsh, cruel, remorseless, unfeeling, unkind, hard-hearted, stony, obdurate, barbarous, savage, ferocious, Draconian; unrelenting, inflexible, relentless, inexorable.
See also MALEVOLENCE, REVENGE, SEVERITY.—*Antonyms.* See PITY.

---

pittance, *n.* mite, dole; driblet, small portion. See INSUFFICIENCY, QUANTITY.
pitted, *adj.* pock-marked; alveolate, honeycombed, favose. See BLEMISH, CONCAVITY.

PITY.—I. *Nouns.* **pity,** compassion, commiseration, sympathy, fellow-feeling, tenderness, tender-heartedness, soft-heartedness, yearning, forbearance, humanity, mercy, clemency; leniency, lenity, charity, ruth (*poetic*), long-suffering; quarter, grace.
pitier, sympathizer, condoler, commiserator; friend, well-wisher, advocate, patron, partisan, champion, defender.
II. *Verbs.* **pity,** commiserate, compassionate, have (*or* feel) pity, condole, sympathize, feel for, be sorry for.
forbear, relent, relax, give quarter, *parcere subjectis* (*L.*).
excite pity, touch, affect, soften, melt, melt the heart, move.
III. *Adjectives.* **piteous** (*calling for pity*), compassionate, tender; mournful, distressing, lamentable, deplorable, sorrowful, sad, rueful, doleful, miserable, wretched (*as a* piteous *look or cry*).
pitiable (*calling for pity or contempt*), lamentable, sorrowful, woeful, piteous, sad, miserable (*as, a* pitiable *plight*); insignificant, contemptible, sorry (*as, a* pitiable *appearance*).
pitiful (*full of pity*), compassionate, sympathetic, pitying, tender-hearted, soft-hearted, touched; humane, humanitarian, clement, merciful, forbearing, lenient: *said of persons.*
[*eliciting compassion*] pathetic, touching, moving, affecting, distressing, heart-rending, lamentable, piteous: *said of things; as, a* pitiful *cry.*
[*to be pitied for its littleness or meanness*] paltry, contemptible, miserable, despicable, insignificant, abject, base, mean (*as, a* pitiful *ambition*).
See also CONDOLENCE.—*Antonyms.* See PITILESSNESS.

---

pivot, *n.* focus, turning point; joint, hinge; axle, axis. See CAUSE, JUNCTION, ROTATION.
placard, *n.* bill, poster, advertisement, notice. See PUBLICATION.

PLACE.—I. *Nouns.* **place,** spot, locality, situation, site, location, locus (*esp. tech.*), situs, position, region, neighborhood, locale (*properly* local'), scene, tract, latitude, longitude, whereabouts, point, part; premises: *patio* (*Sp.*), courtyard, square, *place* (*F.*), quadrangle, *cortile* (*It.; pl. cortili*), peristyle, *piazza* (*It.*), *plaza* (*Sp.*), forum (*L.*); hamlet, village, town, city, stronghold; space, room, stead; compartment, niche, nook, hole, corner; building, residence, seat, mansion, abode.
rank, position, grade, precedence, status, standing, condition, station; occupation, calling, appointment, employment, office, post, charge, trust, function, order, sphere.
II. *Verbs.* **place,** put, fix, set, stick, lay, deposit, rest, repose, settle, locate, dispose, stand, station, lodge, establish, plant, install; order, arrange, array, marshal, organize.
appoint, assign, name, nominate, commission, delegate, charge, intrust, induct, ordain; secure for.
invest (*as funds*), lay out, put; venture, risk, embark; make an investment, put out to interest, lend, intrust.
identify (*as by connecting with some place*), recognize, know, perceive; establish, settle, fix, assign.
III. *Adverbs.* **somewhere,** in some place, here and there, *passim* (*L.*), somewhither (*archaic*): *opposite of* nowhere.
See also ARRANGEMENT, BUSINESS, HABITATION, LOCATION, SIDE, SITUATION.

placid, *adj.* calm, peaceful, gentle, serene, unruffled, undisturbed. See INEXCITABILITY.

PLAIN.—I. *Nouns.* **plain,** level land, open country, lowland, flat, basin, champaign, reach, stretch, expanse, prairie (*or* plains), grassland, downs, heath, wold, moor, moorland, llano (*S. Amer.*), *vega* (*Sp. Amer. and Philippine Islands*), pampas (*esp. in Argentina*), savanna (*as in Brazil; also, a treeless plain, as in Florida*), campo (*S. Amer.*), tundra (*Arctic*), steppe (*Russia*), sebka *or* sebkha (*N. Africa*), playa (*as in Texas, Arizona, and New Mexico*), alkali flat; mesa (*as in Southwestern U. S.*), mesilla (*small mesa*), plateau, table-land; uplands, fell (*Brit.*), veldt *or* veld (*S. Africa*), bush, waste, wild, desert.
meadow, mead, pasture, lea, haugh (*Scot. and dial. Eng.*), pasturage, field.
lawn, green, plot, grassplat.
sward, greensward, turf, sod, grass; heather.
grounds, estate, land, park, common, campus (*U. S.*), maidan (*India*).
II. *Adjectives.* **campestral,** campestrine, campestrian; champaign, flat, open.

See also FLATNESS.—*Antonyms.* See HEIGHT, LAKE.

PLAINNESS.—I. *Nouns.* **plainness,** clearness, obviousness, etc. (see *adjectives*); homeliness, simplicity, severity; household words, plain English.
candor, openness, frankness, unreserve, sincerity, candidness, plain-spokenness.
II. *Verbs.* **speak plainly,** come to the point, plunge *in medias res* (*L.*), waste no words, call a spade a spade.
III. *Adjectives.* **plain,** flat, level, even, smooth, plane.
manifest, clear, obvious, evident, distinct, unmistakable, apparent, patent, palpable, open, intelligible, explicit, uninvolved.
candid, guileless, artless, ingenuous, unaffected, unsophisticated, sincere, frank, honest, straightforward, downright, unreserved, outspoken, blunt, plain-spoken.
simple (*without beauty, ornament, or luxury*), unornamented, unadorned, unembellished, unpolished, unvarnished; severe, neat, chaste, pure, Saxon; commonplace, matter-of-fact, plain-spoken; workaday, prosaic, sober.
homely, homespun, homelike, rustic, natural, native; ill-looking, ill-favored, hard-favored, ugly.
IV. *Adverbs.* **plainly,** clearly, etc. (see *adjectives*); honestly, candidly, bluntly; point-blank; in plain words (*or* English), in common parlance.

See also INTELLIGIBILITY, MANIFESTATION, OPENING, SIMPLENESS, UGLINESS, VISIBILITY.

---

plaintive, *adj.* sorrowful, melancholy, sad, mournful. See LAMENTATION.

PLAN.—I. *Nouns.* **plan,** design, scheme, project, undertaking, racket (*as, a bootlegging* racket: *slang*), game, method, line, proposal, proposition, suggestion, idea, conception, projection, planning, resolution, motion; organization, arrangement, system, systematism.
outline, method, *modus operandi* (*L.*), sketch, skeleton, draft, plot (*of a story*), rough draft, layout (*colloq.*), representation, drawing, *ébauche* (*F.*), diagram, map, chart, copy; forecast, program *or* programme, agenda (*pl.*), memoranda (*pl.*), prospectus; order of the day, protocol, platform, plank, slate (*U. S.*), ticket (*U. S.*); rôle; policy.
contrivance, invention, expedient, receipt, nostrum, artifice, gadget (*slang*), device; stratagem, trick, shift, makeshift.
measure, step, action, course, procedure; stroke, *coup* (*F.*), *coup de maître* (*F.*), masterstroke; trump, trump card; bright idea, clever move (*or* stroke); *cheval de bataille* (*F.*).
intrigue, cabal, plot, conspiracy, wire pulling, machination; mine.
planner, projector, prompter, designer, organizer, founder, author, artist.
II. *Verbs.* **plan,** scheme, design, frame, contrive, project, forecast, draft, sketch, devise, invent, hatch concoct; hit upon; shift, manage, wangle (*slang*); prepare, block out, cast, recast, arrange, shape out a course, map out, organize, systematize, systemize, form, build, construct; digest, mature.
plot, intrigue, maneuver *or* manœuvre, machinate, scheme, conspire; cabal, complot, counterplot, mine, countermine, lay a train.

III. *Adjectives.* **planned,** arranged, devised; under consideration, *sur le tapis* (*F.*), on the carpet, on the tapis; in course of preparation.

See also ARRANGEMENT, CONDUCT, CUNNING, IDEA, NECESSITY, ORDER, PREPARATION.

---

plane, *n.* level surface, grade, level, stratum. See FLATNESS.
plane, *v.* level, smooth, even, shave. See SMOOTHNESS.
plant, *n.* equipment, machinery; organism, growth, shoot, herb, flower, etc.; *Slang*: hoax, trap, snare. See INSTRUMENT, VEGETABLE, DECEPTION.
plant, *v.* bed, sow, transplant; implant, set; place, put, deposit. See HUSBANDRY, INSERTION, LOCATION.
plastic, *adj.* formative, moldable, impressible, pliant. See FORM.
plate, *n.* coat, coating, veneer; utensil, dish, platter. See LAYER, RECEPTACLE.
plateau, *n.* table-land, mesa. See PLAIN.
platform, *n.* policy, scheme, plank; rostrum, stage, dais; foundation, scaffold See PLAN, SCHOOL, SUPPORT.
platitude, *n.* truism, commonplace, banality, triteness. See DULLNESS.
plaudit, *n.* applause, clapping, acclaim, acclamation, encomium. See APPROBATION.
plausible, *adj.* probable, credible, reasonable, specious, fair-spoken; vindicatory, defensible, justifiable. See PROBABILITY, VINDICATION.
play, *v.* act, impersonate, represent; work operate, move; sport, frolic, toy, dally, idle; perform, execute. See ACTION, AGENCY, AMUSEMENT, MUSICIAN.
play, *n.* game, gambol, romp, prank; piece, tragedy, comedy, opera; scope, range, room, latitude, sweep. See AMUSEMENT, DRAMA, FREEDOM.
player, *n.* actor, comedian, tragedian; player piano; performer, instrumentalist. See DRAMA, MUSICAL INSTRUMENTS, MUSICIAN.
playful, *adj.* sportive, rollicking, frolicsome, frisky; mirthful, roguish, jolly, jocose. See AMUSEMENT, CHEERFULNESS.
plaything, *n.* toy, doll; trifle, bauble, trinket, bagatelle. See AMUSEMENT, UNIMPORTANCE.

PLEA.—I. *Nouns.* **plea,** pretext, excuse, vindication, justification, apology, argument, allegation, claim, pleading, defense; ostensible reason (*or* motive); color, gloss, guise.

pretense, subterfuge, mask, simulation, artifice, fabrication, show, assumption, pretext, feint, bluff, feigning, sham, dust thrown in the eye; blind, lame excuse, makeshift, shift.

entreaty, prayer, appeal, cry, request, call, supplication, intercession, suit, petition, importunity.

pleader, advocate, intercessor, entreater, supporter, vindicator, defender; attorney, lawyer, counsel, barrister.

II. *Verbs.* **plead,** allege, excuse, vindicate, defend, argue, reason, answer, rejoin, reply, rebut, surrebut (*law*), surrejoin (*law*); use as a plea, take one's stand upon; state, affirm, protest, asseverate, avouch, avow, aver; color, gloss over, make a pretext of, pretend.

entreat, supplicate, beg, implore, pray, ask, appeal, request, beseech, importune, petition, sue (*as,* to plead *with a judge*).

III. *Adjectives.* **pleadable,** defensible, maintainable, tenable, supportable, justifiable, excusable, vindicable.

ostensible, apparent, seeming, pretended, alleged, professed.

IV. *Adverbs.* **pleadingly,** entreatingly, beseechingly, earnestly, importunately, by supplication.

ostensibly, apparently, etc. (see *adjectives*); under color of, under the pretense of, under the plea of.

See also ANSWER, LAWSUIT, REASONING, REQUEST, VINDICATION.

---

pleasantry, *n.* banter, chaff, jocularity, persiflage, jest. See WIT.
please, *interj.* do, pray, will you, if you please. See REQUEST.

PLEASURABLENESS.—I. *Nouns.* **pleasurableness,** pleasantness, agreeableness, jocundity, gayety, delectability, pleasingness, amusement, treat; dainty, *bonne bouche* (*F.*), titbit, sweets, sweetmeats; salt, savor.
attraction, attractiveness, fascination, captivation, invitingness, enchantment, witchery, seduction, winning ways, winsomeness, loveliness, beauty, charm, sex appeal (*or* S. A.: *cant*), "it" (*slang*); biological urge (*or* B. U.: *cant*).
II. *Verbs.* **please,** charm, delight, pleasure (*poetic*), gratify, captivate, fascinate, enchant, enrapture, enthrall; enravish, ravish, bewitch, transport, entrance, gladden, tickle, cheer, lætificate (*rare*), enliven, attract, allure, take one's fancy, interest, excite, thrill; stimulate, amuse, relieve, divert, refresh, treat, tickle the palate, titillate, hit, suit; satisfy (*as the appetite*), appease, satiate, quench; indulge, coddle, pamper, spoil, overindulge, humor, flatter.
III. *Adjectives.* **pleasurable,** pleasure-giving, pleasing, pleasant, amiable, agreeable, palatable, interesting, grateful, gratifying, acceptable, delightful, delectable (*archaic or ironical*), charming, exquisite, lovely, ravishing, voluptuous, sensuous, luxurious, rapturous, thrilling, heartfelt, felicitous, ecstatic, heavenly; joyful, jolly (*colloq.*), gladsome, delightsome, glad, genial, cordial, welcome, refreshing, invigorating, restful, comfortable; nice, delicate, dainty, delicious, sweet, dear, beloved.
attractive, inviting, prepossessing, engaging, winning, winsome, magnetic, fascinating, seductive, alluring, taking, captivating, killing (*colloq.*), enticing, bewitching, enchanting, entrancing, enravishing; appetizing; cheering, exciting.
IV. *Adverbs.* **pleasurably,** pleasingly, etc. (see *adjectives*); in clover (*colloq.*); in paradise, in elysium; at one's ease, on a bed of roses, on flowery beds of ease.
See also AMUSEMENT, SAVORINESS, SWEETNESS.—*Antonyms.* See PAINFULNESS.

PLEASURE.—I. *Nouns.* **pleasure,** gratification, enjoyment, joy, gladness, delight, glee, elation, jubilation, cheer, sunshine, cheerfulness, delectation, relish, zest, gusto, thrill, kick (*slang*), stimulus, exhilaration, satisfaction, complacency, solace, well-being, good.
happiness, felicity, bliss, beatitude, exaltation, enchantment, transport, rapture, ecstasy; paradise, heaven, elysium, seventh heaven.
[*sensuous enjoyment*] **gratification,** diversion, entertainment, treat, refreshment, feast, banquet; sport, amusement, indulgence, self-gratification, gayety, jollity, merriment, hilarity, mirth; ease, comfort, luxury, luxuriousness, lap of luxury; bed of roses, purple and fine linen, creature comforts; round of pleasure, dissipation, sensuality (*as, carnal* pleasure).
will, desire, wish, choice, volition, discretion, purpose (*as, to consult his* pleasure).
II. *Verbs.* **enjoy,** like, relish, be pleased with, derive pleasure from, take pleasure in, delight in, rejoice in, indulge in, revel in, bask in, luxuriate in, wallow in; feast on, smack the lips, gloat over, love; take a fancy to (*colloq.*), take to (*colloq.*).
enjoy oneself, joy (*archaic*), be happy, be in clover (*colloq.*); tread on enchanted ground; go into raptures; feel at home, breathe freely, bask in the sunshine.
III. *Adjectives.* **pleased,** gratified, contented, content, glad, gladsome, gleeful, elate, blithe, joyful, joyous, happy, blest, blessed, blissful, beatified; in raptures, in ecstasies.
overjoyed, entranced, enchanted; **raptured,** enraptured, ravished, transported; fascinated, captivated.
pleasing, delightful, pleasant, agreeable, pleasurable, gratifying, lovely, sweet, delicious, fragrant, refreshing, grateful, comforting, cordial, genial; sensuous, palatable, melodious, harmonious, ecstatic, beatific, painless, cloudless, unalloyed.
comfortable, cheering, satisfying, satisfactory, easeful, restful, at east, cosy, snug, luxurious, in comfort; consolatory, encouraging.
IV. *Adverbs.* **pleasingly,** delightfully, etc. (see *adjectives*); in a pleasing manner.
See also AMUSEMENT, CHEERFULNESS, SWEETNESS.—*Antonyms.* See PAIN.

---

plebeian, *adj.* lowborn, obscure, common, vulgar. See PEOPLE.
plebiscite, *n.* vote, ballot, referendum. See JUDGMENT.
pledge, *n.* word, troth, betrothal, vow, oath, contract, guarantee; **bond,** surety, guaranty, deposit, pawn, earnest. See PROMISE, SECURITY.

pledge, *v.* pawn; plight, vow, undertake, contract; engage, bind oneself; honor, toast. See BORROWING, PASSAGE, PROMISE, REPUTE.
pledged, *adj.* promised, bound, affianced; pawned. See PROMISE, SECURITY.
plentiful, *adj.* ample, enough, plenteous, abundant, copious. See SUFFICIENCY.
plenty, *n.* abundance, amplitude, profusion, copiousness. See SUFFICIENCY.
pleonastic, *adj.* tautological, verbose, wordy, circumlocutory. See REDUNDANCE.
pliant, *adj.* yielding flexible, compliant. See FACILITY.
plight, *n.* predicament, dilemma, scrape, crisis; word, pledge, betrothal; case, condition, situation. See CIRCUMSTANCE, PROMISE, STATE.
plod, *v.* toil, drudge; persist, persevere; walk, trudge, lumber. See ACTIVITY, PERSEVERANCE, SLOWNESS.
plodding, *adj.* diligent, persevering, hardworking. See ACTIVITY.
plot, *n.* scheme, intrigue, conspiracy; skeleton (*of a story*), outline; patch, field, paddock, inclosure. See PLAN, REGION.
plot, *v.* intrigue, scheme, contrive, conspire, machinate. See PLAN.
plow, *v.* channel, turn up; cultivate, till. See FURROW, HUSBANDRY.
pluck, *v.* pick, pull, gather. See TAKING.
pluck, *n.* bravery, valor, daring, heroism; grit, stamina, backbone; will, determination. See COURAGE, PERSEVERANCE, RESOLUTION.
plug, *n.* cork, wadding, padding, stopple, spigot. See STOPPER.
plumage, *n.* feathers, feathering, down. See ROUGHNESS.
plumb, *adj.* straight, true; erect, perpendicular, vertical. See STRAIGHTNESS, VERTICALITY.
plume, *n.* feather, panache, aigrette, quill. See ORNAMENT, ROUGHNESS.
plummet, *n.* plumb, lead, bob, plumb line. See DEPTH.
plumb, *adj.* direct, blunt, unqualified; fat, corpulent, chubby, fleshy, stout. See ARTLESSNESS, ROTUNDITY, SIZE.
plumbness, *n.* chubbiness, obesity, stoutness, corpulence. See ROTUNDITY, SIZE.
plunder, *v.* pillage, rifle, loot, despoil, forage, smuggle. See STEALING.
plunder, *n.* loot,, spoil, pillage, stolen goods; gain, advantage. See BOOTY, INCREASE, STEALING.

PLUNGE.—I. *Nouns.* **plunge,** dip, header (*colloq.*), ducking, dive, nose dive (*aviation*), submergence, submersion, immersion; reckless speculation (*slang in this sense*); critical step.
plunger, diver; piston.
gambler (*esp. a reckless one*), punter, hazarder, speculator, gamester: *in this sense,* plunger *is slang.*
II. *Verbs.* **plunge,** dip, souse, duck; dive, plump, swoop, drop; take a header (*colloq.*); make a plunge; bathe; pitch (*as a ship*).
submerge, submerse, immerse; douse, engulf, thrust into, send to the bottom; go to the bottom, founder, sink, collapse.
welter, wallow, roll, toss, tumble about.
[*to throw oneself into*] **dive in,** rush in, enter violently, penetrate, pierce.
gamble (*recklessly*), bet, punt, play, game, wager: *in this sense,* plunge *is slang.*
III. *Adjectives.* **plunging,** dipping, diving, dropping; submergible, submersible.
See also DEPTH.—*Antonyms.* See LEAP.

PLURALITY.—I. *Nouns.* **plurality,** large number, several, multitude, majority (*opposite of* minority), excess of votes (*esp. over those for the next opponent when there are more than two candidates: distinguished from* majority, *or a number greater than half of the total votes cast*).
II. *Verbs.* **pluralize,** make plural, express in the plural.
III. *Adjectives.* **plural,** more than one, upwards of. some, certain.
[*in grammar*] not singular (*or* dual).
See also MULTITUDE.—*Antonyms.* See FEWNESS.

ply, *v.* exert, apply; work (at), wield, use, manipulate. See EXERTION, SUE.
pocket, *n.* cavity, hollow, air pocket (*aëro*); pouch, purse, wallet. See CONCAVITY, RECEPTACLE.
pocketbook, *n.* purse, wallet, *portemonnaie* (*F.*). See TREASURY.

POETRY.—I. *Nouns.* **poetry,** poetics, poesy (*archaic*), rime *or* rhyme, minstrelsy (*archaic*), verse, song; assonance, alliteration, numbers, meter, measure, rhythm; blank verse, heroic verse; free verse, *vers libre* (*F.*); imagism, symbolism.

Muse, Apollo, Pierian spring, Helicon, Parnassus; inspiration, fire of genius.
versification, riming *or* rhyming, orthometry (*rare*), prosody; scansion, scanning.
poem, metrical composition; epic, ballad, *canzone* (*It.; pl. canzoni*), lyric, ode, idyl *or* idyll, eclogue, pastoral, sonnet, roundelay, rondeau, rondel, madrigal; pastoral poem, pastoral, bucolic; epode, elegy; dramatic (didactic, satirical, narrative, *or* lyric) poetry; satire; anthology, posy (*archaic*); *disjecti membra poetæ* (*L.*).

canto, stanza, verse, stave, line, verselet, couplet, distich; tristich, tercet, triplet; quatrain, tetrastich, pentastich, hexastich, heptastich, octastich; refrain, chorus, burden; octave, sestet.

[*bad poetry*] doggerel *or* doggrel, Hudibrastic verse; macaronics, macaronic verse; "not poetry, but prose run mad" (Pope).

poet, writer of poems, poetess (*fem.*), maker (*archaic*), Parnassian; poet laureate, laureate; bard, lyrist, scop (*hist.*), idylist *or* idyllist, scald *or* skald, sonneteer, rhapsodist, satirist, troubadour, trouvère; minstrel, jongleur; Minnesinger, Meistersinger; minor poet, versifier; rimer *or* rhymer, rimester, poetaster, poetling, poeticule, poetizer (*all six derog.*); vers-librist, imagist, symbolist; *genus irritabile vatum* (*L.*).

II. *Verbs.* **poetize,** poeticize, sing, write poetry; string verses together, versify, make verses, rime *or* rhyme, "lisp in numbers" (Pope).

III. *Adjectives.* **poetic** *or* poetical; lyric *or* lyrical, tuneful, metrical, idyllic, Heliconian, Parnassian, Pierian; epic, epodic, elegiac, iambic, dactylic, spondaic, trochaic, anapestic; Ionic, Sapphic, Alcaic, Pindaric, Dicæan.

Antonyms. See PROSE.

---

poignant, *adj.* keen, sharp, biting, piercing; pungent. See PAIN, PUNGENCY.
point, *n.* punctuation mark; period, limit; salient feature, precise thing; aim, object, intent; spot, site; spike, pin, needle; speck, jot; case, point at issue. See CESSATION, END, IMPORTANCE, INTENTION, PLACE, SHARPNESS, SMALLNESS, TOPIC.
point-blank, *adv.* straight, direct; plainly, clearly, honestly, bluntly. See DIRECTION, PLAINNESS.
pointed, *adj.* brief, concise, direct, terse, pithy; sharp, spiked, barbed. See CONCISENESS, SHARPNESS.
poise, *n.* equipoise, equilibrium; balance, self-possession, composure, equanimity. See EQUALITY, INEXCITABILITY.
poison, *n.* virus, toxin. See BANE.—**science of poisons,** toxicology. See BANE.
poison, *v.* envenom, corrupt, infect, defile; kill, murder. See DETERIORATION, KILLING.
poisonous, *adj.* virulent, deadly, noxious, toxic, venomous. See BADNESS, BANE.
poke, *v.* nudge, thrust, jab. See IMPULSE.
polar, *adj.* opposite; arctic, antarctic. See POLAR, SUMMIT.
polar lights, northern lights, aurora; *aurora borealis* (*L.*), *aurora australis* (*L.*). See LUMINARY.
[1]**pole,** *n.* axis, hub, pivot; terminal point, extremity. See CENTRALITY, OPPOSITE.
[2]**pole,** *n.* rod, mast, flagstaff; shaft, post. See HEIGHT, SUPPORT.
polestar, *n.* magnet, cynosure; lodestar, guiding star, guide; Polaris, North Star. See ATTRACTION, DIRECTION, LUMINARY.

policeman, *n.* patrolman, officer, cop (*slang*), policewoman (*fem.*). See SAFETY.
policy, *n.* strategy, tactics, administration, management; rôle, platform, plank. See CONDUCT, PLAN.
polish, *v.* rub, scour, burnish, brighten. See FRICTION, SMOOTHNESS.
polish, *n.* politeness, breeding, culture, refinement; gloss, glaze; brightness, luster; discrimination, tact. See COURTESY, LUBRICATION, SMOOTHNESS, TASTE.
polished, *adj.* polite, refined, well-bred, cultivated; courtly, fashionable, *à la mode* (*F.*). See COURTESY, FASHION.
polite, *adj.* civil, courteous, gallant, well-bred, refined, polished. See COURTESY.
politic, *adj.* discreet, noncommittal, artful, wary, strategic; wise, prudent, sagacious, judicious. See CAUTION, WISDOM.
poll, *n.* ballot, election; register, voting list; poll tax; head, skull. See CHOICE, LIST, PRICE, SUMMIT.
pollute, *v.* corrupt, demoralize, contaminate, defile; soil, foul, taint. See DETERIORATION, UNCLEANNESS.
poltroon, *n.* coward, craven, dastard. See COWARDICE.
pommel, *v.* beat, drub, trounce, maul, pound, sandbag. See PUNISHMENT.
pomp, *n.* style, magnificence, splendor, display, ostentation. See PRIDE, STATE.
pompous, *adj.* vainglorious, self-important, boastful, arrogant. See OSTENTATION.
ponder, *v.* think, reflect, weigh, meditate, muse, deliberate. See THOUGHT.
ponderous, *adj.* massive, bulky, heavy, weighty. See GRAVITY.
pony, *n.* Shetland, broncho; crib, horse (*student slang*). See CARRIER, INTERPRETATION.
pool, *n.* tarn, pond, reservoir; puddle. See LAKE.
pool, *v.* combine, conduce, contribute, coöperate. See COÖPERATION.
poor, *adj.* inferior, below par, defective, faulty; thin, spare, emaciated, underfed; moneyless, beggarly, indigent, insolvent; weak, flimsy, loose. See BADNESS, INSUFFICIENCY, POVERTY, SOPHISTRY.
poorness, *n.* dearth, scarcity, meagerness, want. See POVERTY.
populace, *n.* masses, rabble, common people, proletariat. See PEOPLE.
popular, *adj.* approved, praised; chosen, elect; desirable, pleasing, in demand; celebrated, noted, distinguished, famous, admired. See APPROBATION, CHOICE, DESIRE, REPUTE.
population, *n.* people, inhabitants, nation, race. See INHABITANT.
porch, *n.* entrance, portal, portico; veranda, piazza. See OPENING, RECEPTACLE.
porous, *adj.* perforated, honeycombed; open, loose, sandy; permeable, pervious. See CONCAVITY, LIGHTNESS, OPENING.
[1]port, *n.* harbor, haven, shelter. See REFUGE.
[2]port, *n.* porthole, embrasure. See OPENING.
[3]port, *n.* air, carriage, bearing, demeanor. See APPEARANCE.
[4]port, *n.* left side (*of a vessel*), larboard: *opposite of* starboard. See LEFT.
portable, *adj.* movable, transmissible, transportable. See TRANSFER.
portage, *n.* passage, route; carrying, transportation. See TRANSFER.
portal, *n.* doorway, gateway, entry, entrance. See OPENING.
portend, *v.* presage, bode, forebode, augur, foretoken, signify. See PREDICTION.
portent, *n.* sign, token, foreboding; marvel, phenomenon. See OMEN, WONDER.
porter, *n.* gatekeeper, guard, warder, sentinel; bearer, red cap (*U. S.*). See STOPPER, CARRIER.
portico, *n.* porch, veranda, colonnade. See RECEPTACLE.
portion, *n.* share, ration, measure, dividend, allotment; piece, fragment, section, morsel. See APPORTIONMENT, PART.

portly, *adj.* corpulent, fleshy, stout, bulky; imposing, stately. See SIZE.
portmanteau, *n.* traveling bag, Gladstone bag. See RECEPTACLE.
portrait, *n.* painting, miniature, picture, likeness, photograph. See FINE ARTS, REPRESENTATION.
portray, *v.* draw, picture, depict, delineate, describe, act, represent. See REPRESENTATION.
[1]**pose,** *v.* question, quiz; puzzle, nonplus. See INQUIRY, UNCERTAINTY.
[2]**pose,** *v.* attitudinize; affect; lay down, propound. See AFFECTATION, AFFIRMATION.
pose, *n.* attitude, posture, position; aspect, condition, figure. See FORM, SITUATION.
position, *n.* post, station, office, job; phase, condition; status, rank, caste; place, site, locality. See BUSINESS, CIRCUMSTANCE, REPUTE, SITUATION.
positive, *adj.* decided, emphatic; inescapable, certain; unqualified, peremptory, absolute. See AFFIRMATION, DEATH, FLATNESS.

POSSESSION.—I. *Nouns.* **possession,** possessing, ownership, seizin *or* seisin (*law*), possessorship, proprietorship, occupancy, occupation, hold, holding, tenure, tenancy, *métayage* (*F.*), métayer system, dependency.
[*exclusive possession*] **monopoly,** corner, retention, impropriation (*Eng. eccl. law*), exclusive possession, preoccupancy; monopolism.
[*future possession*] **heritage,** inheritance, birthright, patrimony, heirship, reversion.
[*in plural*] **possessions,** belongings, property, holdings, assets, estate, wealth, stocks, shares, bonds; realty, real estate, real property; personalty (*law*), personal property, goods, chattels; subject territory, dominions.
II. *Verbs.* **possess,** have, hold, maintain, take up, fill, occupy, enjoy, be possessed of, own, control, command, inherit.
belong to, appertain to, pertain to; be in one's possession, vest in.
seize, take, gain, win, acquire, appropriate, commandeer (*mil.: originally used of the Boers*), grab, bag, kent (*archaic*).
monopolize, corner, forestall (*hist.*), hog (*slang*); engross, occupy, busy.
dominate, control, influence, actuate, obsess, bedevil (*as, to* possess *with rage;* possessed *by a devil*).
III. *Adjectives.* **possessing,** worth, possessed of, master of, in possession of, possessory; endowed (blest, fraught, laden, *or* charged) with.
on hand, in hand, in store, in stock; at one's command, at one's disposal.
See also PROPERTY, SORCERY, TRANSFER, WEALTH.—*Antonyms.* See LOSS, POVERTY, RELINQUISHMENT, TRANSFER.

POSSESSOR.— *Nouns.* **possessor,** holder, occupant, occupier, tenant, métayer, freeholder, tenant at will, lessee, leaseholder, renter, lodger.
owner, proprietor, proprietress (*fem.*), master, mistress, lord.
landholder, landowner, landlord, landlady, patroon (*U. S. hist.*); lord of the manor, lord paramount, laird (*Scot.*), duniwassal (*Scot.*), yeoman; landed gentry.
[*future possessor*] **heir,** heiress (*fem.*), inheritor, inheritress *or* inheritrix (*fem.*); joint heir, coheir, coheiress (*fem.*), coparcener (*law*), parcener (*law*); heir apparent, heir presumptive.

POSSIBILITY.—I. *Nouns.* **possibility,** potentiality, potency, practicability, feasibility, workableness, workability.
contingency, chance, hazard, toss-up (*colloq.*), probability.
II. *Verbs.* **be possible,** stand a chance; admit of, bear.
render possible, put in the way of, bring to bear, bring together
III. *Adjectives.* **possible,** conceivable, imaginable, thinkable, cogitable, credible, compatible, likely.
practicable, feasible, potential, performable, doable, actable, workable, achievable; within reach, accessible, surmountable; attainable, obtainable.
IV. *Adverbs.* **possibly,** perhaps, perchance, peradventure, haply, mayhap (*archaic*), maybe; if possible, God willing, *Deo volente* (*L.*), D. V.
See also CHANGE, LIABILITY, UNCERTAINTY.—*Antonyms.* See IMPOSSIBILITY.

[1]post, *n.* office, place, incumbency; station, position. See BUSINESS, SITUATION.
[1]post, *v.* place, station, billet on, quarter. See LOCATION.
[2]post, *n.* post office, mail, air mail. See MESSENGER.
[2]post, *v.* enter, book, post up, slate, register; send by mail, mail, dispatch; hasten, speed. See RECORD, TRANSFER, VELOCITY.
[3]post, *n.* prop, pillar, pedestal, column. See SUPPORT.
[3]post, *v.* publish, announce, placard. See PUBLICATION.
postdate, *v.* date after, misdate; *opposite of* antedate. See ANACHRONISM.
poster, *n.* advertisement, bill, placard. See PUBLICATION.

POSTERIORITY.—I. *Nouns.* **posteriority,** subsequence *or* subsequency, sequel, following, sequence, succession, remainder, continuance, prolongation; futurity, future; successor; lineage, race, descent.
posterior *or* posteriors, buttocks (*of an animal*), hinder parts.
II. *Verbs.* **follow after,** ensue, result, come after, go after; succeed, supervene.
III. *Adjectives.* **posterior,** later, subsequent, following, after, succeeding, successive, ensuing; latter, more recent, second-mentioned; posthumous, future, after-dinner, postprandial: *opposite of* prior.
hinder, hind, rear, after, hindmost, posticous (*bot.*), postjacent: *opposite of* anterior.
IV. *Adverbs.* **posteriorly,** subsequently, posterior (*rare*), after, afterward, since, later; next, close upon, thereafter, thereupon, eftsoon (*archaic*), after a while (*or* time).
See also FOLLOWING, FUTURE, SEQUENCE.—*Antonyms.* See PRIORITY.

POSTERITY.—I. *Nouns.* **posterity,** progeny, offspring, descendants, seed (*Biblical*), breed, issue, spawn (*contemptuous*), brood, family, children, heirs; rising generation; future time.
descendant, offshoot, scion, olive branch, chip of the old block, heir, heiress (*fem.*); heir-apparent, heir-presumptive.
child, son, *fils* (*F.*), daughter, *fille* (*F.*), bairn (*Scot.*), bantling (*often depreciatory*), brat (*usually contemptuous*), papoose (*Amer. Indian*), infant, baby, kid (*colloq.*), imp, cherub, tot, innocent, urchin, chit (*colloq.*), pickaninny.
descent, lineage, filiation, sonship, line, succession, heredity, pedigree, family, origin, birth, extraction; primogeniture.
II. *Adjectives.* **filial,** sonlike, daughterly, dutiful.
lineal, in a direct line (*opposite of* collateral), direct, progenial (*rare*); hereditary; phyletic (*biol.*), phylogenic *or* phylogenetic (*biol.*), diphyletic (*biol.*).
See also FUTURE.—*Antonyms.* See PATERNITY.

---

posthaste, *adv.* rashly, headforemost; apace, hastily, swiftly, speedily. See RASHNESS, VELOCITY.
post-mortem, *n.* examination (*after death*), autopsy. See INTERMENT.
postpone, *v.* defer, delay, retard, procrastinate; shelve, table, prorogue, adjourn. See LATENESS, NEGLECT.
posture, *n.* position, pose; condition, attitude, aspect. See FORM, SITUATION.
pot, *n.* mug, tankard, jug, kettle, vessel. See RECEPTACLE.
potent, *adj.* able, capable, forceful; strong, mighty, puissant, powerful. See POWER, STRENGTH.
potentate, *n.* ruler, monarch, sovereign, emperor, king. See MASTER.
potential, *adj.* latent, dormant; magnetic, dynamic. See LATENCY, POWER.
pottery, *n.* crockery, china, earthenware, porcelain. See CALEFACTION.
poultry, *n.* fowls, hens, chickens, ducks, geese. See ANIMAL.
pound, *v.* thump, drum; beat, bruise, pulverize. See MUSICIAN, POWDERINESS.
pour, *v.* issue, emerge, flow out of; shower, rain, flood. See EGRESS, RIVER.

POVERTY.—I. *Nouns.* **poverty,** indigence, penury, pennilessness, necessity, want, neediness, need, lack, privation, destitution, distress, difficulties, wolf at the door, straits, low water (*slang*), *res angusta domi* (*L.*), broken (*or* loss of)

fortune, "a beggarly account of empty boxes" (*Romeo and Juliet*), **impecuniosity** pauperism, insolvency.
beggary, mendicancy, mendicity, mendication (*rare*), begging.
poorness, scarcity, dearth, deficiency, meagerness, inferiority (*as,* poverty *of soil;* poverty *of ideas*).
poor man, pauper, mendicant, beggar, starveling, *pauvre diable* (*F.*); bankrupt, insolvent.
II. *Verbs.* **be poor,** want, lack, *n'avoir pas le sou* (*F.*), starve, live from hand to mouth, have seen better days, go to rack and ruin; beg one's bread, run into debt.
impoverish, reduce, reduce to poverty, pauperize, beggar, fleece, ruin, ruinate; exhaust.
III. *Adjectives.* **poor,** needy, necessitous, indigent, poverty-stricken, badly off, moneyless, penniless; impecunious, short of money, *sans le sou* (*F.*), hard up, barefooted, beggarly, beggared, destitute; reduced, distressed, pinched, straitened, embarrassed, involved, insolvent.
scanty, inadequate, scant, deficient, insufficient, imperfect, short, scarce (*as, a* poor *crop*).
lean, emaciated, thin, spare, scraggy, bony, scrawny (*U. S.*), rawboned (*as, a* poor *horse*).
feeble, weak, debilitated, impotent, powerless, dejected, spiritless (*as,* poor *health;* poor *spirits*).
mean-spirited, base, groveling, despicable (*as, a* poor *specimen of a man*).
paltry, sorry, pitiable, wretched, small (*as,* poor *consolation*).
unfavorable, disadvantageous, unfortunate, luckless, unsuccessful, contrary, hapless, unlucky (*as,* poor *business;* poor *fellow*).
uncomfortable, restless, disturbed, unrestful (*as, a* poor *night*).
inefficient, ineffective, incapable, incompetent, disqualified, unfit (*as, a* poor *workman*).
insignificant, humble, unimportant, unpretentious, modest (*as, in my* poor *opinion*): *often ironical or jocose.*
shabby, mean, inelegant, inferior, worn, faded, seedy (*colloq.*), indifferent (*as,* poor *clothes*).
[*of land*] **sterile,** barren, unproductive, unfruitful, infertile, exhausted (*as,* poor *soil*).
See also DEBT, INSUFFICIENCY, NONPAYMENT.—*Antonyms.* See WEALTH.

POWDERINESS.—I. *Nouns.* **powderiness,** friableness, friability, pulverulence, dustiness, grittiness, sandiness, arenosity, granulation.
powder, dust, sand, shingle, grit; sawdust; meal, bran, flour, farina, rice, spore, sporule, efflorescence (*chem.*); pounce, crumb, seed, grain; particle; cosmetic; explosive, gunpowder.
[*reduction to powder*] pulverization, comminution, granulation, disintegration, abrasion, detrition, attenuation, trituration, levigation, multure; limation, filing.
[*pulverizing instruments*] mill, grater, rasp, file, pestle and mortar, grindstone, quern, millstone.
II. *Verbs.* **powder,** pulverize, comminute, granulate, triturate, levigate, reduce to powder; scrape, file, abrade, grind, grate, rasp, pound, bray, bruise, beat, crush, craunch *or* cranch, crunch, crumble, disintegrate.
sprinkle, besprinkle, scatter, strew, bepowder, flour, dust, pounce.
III. *Adjectives.* **powderable,** pulverable, pulverizable, friable, crumbly, shivery.
powdery, pulverulent, granular, mealy, floury, farinaceous, branny, dusty, sandy, arenaceous, arenose, gritty, scurfy, furfuraceous (*esp. bot.*), lepidote (*bot.*), lentiginous.

POWER.—I. *Nouns.* **power,** potency, potentiality, powerfulness, efficacy, puissance, arm, might, strength, pressure, energy, dynamic energy, vigor, force; validity, cogency; vantage ground; mechanical energy, applied force, motive power.
authority, warrant, *carte blanche* (*F.*), weight, control, influence, predominance, command, government, ascendancy, sway, omnipotence, almightiness.
ability, competence, efficiency, capability, efficacy, capacity, capableness, talent,

aptitude, skill; enablement, faculty, quality, affection, attribute, endowment, virtue, gift, property, qualification.
II. *Verbs.* **empower,** give (*or* confer) power, enable, commission, authorize, license, delegate, sanction, permit, legalize; invest, endue; endow, arm, strengthen.
energize, activate, potentialize, dynamize (*med.*), strengthen, animate, quicken, electrify, galvanize, magnetize.
III. *Adjectives.* **powerful,** puissant, potent, capable, able, competent; strong, forceful, forcible, vigorous, weighty, valid, cogent; effective, effectual, efficient, efficacious, adequate; influential, predominant, mighty, potential (*rare in this sense*), omnipotent, almighty.
dynamic *or* dynamical, active, energetic, potent, capacitive (*elec.*), high-powered, functional (*med.*); electric, galvanic, magnetic.
IV. *Adverbs.* **powerfully,** potently, etc. (see *adjectives*); by virtue of, by dint of.
See also AUTHORITY, ENERGY, INFLUENCE, NUMBER, PRODUCTIVENESS, STRENGTH. —*Antonyms.* See IMPOTENCE, POWERLESSNESS.

POWERLESSNESS.—I. *Nouns.* **powerlessness,** forcelessness, strengthlessness, etc. (see *adjectives*); disablement, incapacity, paralysis, impotence.
II. *Adjectives.* **powerless,** forceless, strengthless, mightless, weak, helpless, crippled, prostrate, disabled, incapacitated, impotent, paralyzed, paralytic, paraplegic (*med.*); unarmed, defenseless, weaponless: *opposite of* powerful.
See also IMPOTENCE, WEAKNESS.—*Antonyms.* See POWER.

---

practicable, *adj.* practical, useful; possible, feasible, workable, achievable. See EXPEDIENCE, POSSIBILITY.
practical, *adj.* useful, matter-of-fact, pragmatical, operative; virtual, effective. See AGENCY, SUBSTANTIALITY.
practice, *v.* act, do, perform, prosecute; drill, train; apply, exercise. See ACTION, TEACHING, USE.
practice, *n.* habit, method, manner, procedure; application, exercise, play; drill, training. See CONDUCT, EXERTION, TEACHING.
prairie, *n.* grassland, savanna, steppe, llano (*Sp. Amer.*). See PLAIN, SPACE.
praise, *v.* commend, extol, applaud, eulogize; laud, glorify. See APPROBATION, WORSHIP.
praise, *n.* laud, acclaim, applause, commendation, exaltation; grace, benediction, thanksgiving. See APPROBATION, WORSHIP.
praiseworthy, *adj.* commendable, laudable, good, meritorious. See APPROBATION.
prance, *v.* dance, caper, cavort (*colloq.*), frisk, gambol; rear, jump, spring. See AGITATION, LEAP.
prance, *n.* caper, skip, dance. See LEAP.
prank, *n.* trick, frolic, escapade. See CAPRICE.
prattle, *n.* chatter, jabber, babble. See LOQUACITY, SPEECH.
pray, *v.* ask, beg, solicit, petition; offer prayer. See REQUEST, WORSHIP.
prayer, *n.* petition, entreaty, supplication; thanksgiving, praise. See REQUEST, WORSHIP.
preach, *v.* lecture, sermonize, moralize. See RITE, TEACHING.
preacher, *n.* pastor, minister, clergyman. See CLERGY.
preamble, *n.* preface, prelude, prologue, introduction. See PRECURSOR.
precarious, *adj.* uncertain, critical; insecure, unstable, dubious. See DANGER, TRANSIENCE.
precaution, *n.* anticipation, forethought; caution, warning, safeguard, provision. See CARE, PREPARATION.

PRECEDENCE.—I. *Nouns.* **precedence** *or* precedency, antecedence, precession, anteposition, the lead, *le pas* (*F.*), superiority, anteriority, priority, preference, advantage, importance, consequence; premise.
II. *Verbs.* **precede,** forerun, come before, antecede, come first; head, lead, lead

the way; introduce, herald, usher in: rank, take precedence, outrank, outstrip. **preface,** premise, prelude, preamble, introduce.
III. *Adjectives.* **preceding,** antecedent, precursory, preliminary, precursive, prodromal (*med.*), introductory, prefatory, precedent (*now rare*); anterior, prior, before; former, foregoing, aforesaid, aforementioned, aforestated, said.
IV. *Adverbs.* **before,** in front, ahead, forward, foremost, headmost, in the van (*or* lead), onward.
[*in time*] earlier, sooner, previously, heretofore, above, already, ere now, hitherto, beforehand: *opposite of* after.
See also FRONT, IMPORTANCE, PRECURSOR, PRIORITY, REPUTE, SUPERIORITY.—*Antonyms.* See SEQUENCE.

---

precedent, *n.* usage, custom, practice; case, decision; original, model, standard. See HABIT, LAWSUIT, PROTOTYPE

PRECEPT.—*Nouns.* **precept,** direction, instruction, charge, command, order, commandment, injunction, behest, mandate fiat, decree, ordinance, prescript, prescription; recipe, receipt; golden rule.
rule, regulation, canon, law, *corpus juris* (*L.*), *lex scripta* (*L.*), code, convention; unwritten law, *lex non scripta* (*L.*), common law; canon law; act, statute, rubric; maxim, principle; model, form, formula, formulary.
See also COMMAND, MAXIM, PRECEPT, REQUIREMENT.

PRECESSION.—*Nouns.* **precession,** precedence, antecedence, priority; lead, van, front.
See also PRECEDENCE, PRECURSOR, PRIORITY.—*Antonyms.* See FOLLOWING, SEQUENCE.

---

precinct, *n.* boundary, limit, environs (*pl.*); district, area. See ENVIRONMENT, REGION.
precious, *adj.* valuable, costly, dear; overrefined, overnice; beloved, darling. See DEARNESS, FASTIDIOUSNESS, LOVE.
precious metal, gold, silver, platinum. See MONEY.
precious stone, gem, jewel. See ORNAMENT.
precipice, *n.* bluff, cliff, declivity. See VERTICALITY.
precipitate, *adj.* hasty, impetuous, headlong, rash, hot-headed. See HASTE, RASHNESS.
precipitation, *n.* rush, impetuosity, rashness; condensation, rainfall. See HASTE, RIVER.
precipitous, *adj.* steep, sheer, uphill. See OBLIQUITY.
precise, *adj.* prim, rigid, unbending; exact, definite, punctilious. See FORM, TRUTH.
preclude, *v.* check, hinder, debar, stop, prevent, prohibit. See HINDRANCE.
precocious, *adj.* forward, premature, advanced. See EARLINESS.
preconception, *n.* preconceived idea (*or* opinion), prejudgment. See MISJUDGMENT.

PRECURSOR.—I. *Nouns.* **precursor,** forerunner, harbinger, herald, avant-courier, pioneer; antecedent, precedent, predecessor; outrider; leader, bellwether, forelooper *or* foreloper (*South Africa*); prognostic, omen, sign, presage, token.
prelude, preamble, preface, prologue, foreword, proem, exordium, introduction, prelusion, prolegomena (*pl.; sing.* prolegomenon), prolepsis (*tech.*), protasis; heading, frontispiece, groundwork, preparation; overture, voluntary; premises (*logic and law*).
II. *Adjectives.* **precursory,** preliminary, introductory, prefatory, prelusive *or* prelusory, preludial, proemial (*rare*), prodromal (*esp. med.*), inaugural, inauguratory (*rare*), preceding.
See also OMEN, PRECEDENT, PREDICTION, PREPARATION, PRIORITY.—*Antonyms.* See SEQUEL.

predacious, *adj.* predatory, plundering, pillaging, raptorial (*zoöl.*). See TAKING.
predatory, *adj.* plundering, robbing, predacious. See TAKING.
predecessor, *n.* antecedent, forerunner, ancestor, progenitor. See PRECURSOR.
predestinate, *v.* preordain, predestine, foreordain. See DEITY, PREDETERMINATION.

PREDETERMINATION.—I. *Nouns.* **predetermination,** predeliberation, premeditation, preordination, predestination, *parti pris* (*F.*), foregone conclusion, resolve; project, intention; necessity, fate, destiny, kismet.
II. *Verbs.* **predetermine,** premeditate, preordain, predestine, preresolve, resolve, resolve beforehand, ordain.
III. *Adjectives.* **predeterminate,** premeditated, predesigned, prepense (*as, malice* prepense), studied, designed, calculated, aforethought; foregone.
well-laid, well-devised, well-weighed, maturely considered, prearranged, deliberate, well-considered, cut and dried.
IV. *Adverbs.* **predeterminately,** premeditatedly, deliberately, advisedly, intentionally, with eyes open, in cold blood.
See also INTENTION, PLAN.—*Antonyms.* See IMPULSE.

---

predicament, *n.* dilemma, quandary, fix, emergency, crisis. See CIRCUMSTANCE, DIFFICULTY.

PREDICTION.—I. *Nouns.* **prediction,** prophecy, prognostication, vaticination, augury, forecast, premonition, foreboding, presage; soothsaying, divination, fortune-telling, sorcery, magic, spell, charm, omen, oracle, horoscope; astrology, necromancy.
declaration, announcement, notification, enunciation, intimation, proclamation: bulletin, program *or* programme, advice, notice, platform.
II. *Verbs.* **predict,** forecast, prognosticate, prophesy, auspicate (*rare*), divine, foretell, foresee, read, forewarn, presage, augur, bode, forebode, foretoken, betoken, portend, shadow forth, signify, point to.
herald, usher in, announce, proclaim, advise, intimate, annunciate, cry; lower, threaten.
III. *Adjectives.* **predictive,** prophetic, fatidic *or* fatidical, vaticinal, haruspical; oracular, fatiloquent (*rare*), Sibylline; weatherwise.
ominous, portentous, premonitory, augural, significant, monitory, prescient; auspicious, propitious; pregnant with, big with the fate of.
See also EXPECTATION, OMEN, ORACLE, SORCERY, WARNING.

---

predilection, *n.* preference, partiality; bias, prejudice. See DISPOSITION, MISJUDGMENT.
predominant, *adj.* ruling, controlling, supreme. See POWER.
preëminent, *adj.* conspicuous, distinguished, renowned; foremost, paramount, superior, supreme. See REPUTE, SUPERIORITY.
preëminently, *adv.* supremely, superlatively, inimitably. See GREATNESS.
preface, *n.* premise, preliminary, foreword, introduction, preamble, prelude. See PRECURSOR.
preface, *v.* introduce, precede, premise. See PRECEDENCE.
prefatory, *adj.* precursory, preliminary, introductory. See PRECURSOR.
prefer, *v.* choose, select, fancy, adopt. See CHOICE.
prefix, *n.* affix, adjunct: *opposite of* suffix. See ADDITION.
pregnant, *adj.* weighty, significant, potential; big (*as with young*), teeming, parturient. See IMPORTANCE, PRODUCTIVENESS.
prejudge, *v.* presume, presuppose, judge beforehand. See MISJUDGMENT.
prejudice, *n.* bias, predilection, prepossession, preconscious opinion, intolerance. See MISJUDGMENT.
preliminary, *adj.* introductory, prefatory, preparatory. See PREPARATION.
prelude, *n.* introductory movement; introduction, preface. See MUSIC PRECURSOR.

premature, *adj.* too early, forward, untimely; unprepared, incomplete, immature, unripe. See EARLINESS, NONPREPARATION.
prematurity, *n.* prematureness, precocity, untimeliness, immaturity, precipitation. See EARLINESS.
premeditate, *v.* plan, resolve, predesign, predeliberate, predetermine. See PREDETERMINATION.
premises, *n. pl.* facts, data, testimony; land, real estate, building; terms. See EVIDENCE, PLACE, REASONING.
premium, *n.* prize, recompense, bounty, bonus. See RECEIPT, REWARD.
premonition, *n.* presentiment, forewarning, admonition. See PSYCHICAL RESEARCH, WARNING.
premonitory, *adj.* portentous, ominous, threatening, minatory, cautionary. See WARNING.
preoccupation, *n.* prepossession, engrossment, distraction, absence of mind, inattentiveness. See ABSENCE, INATTENTION.

PREPARATION.—I. *Nouns.* **preparation,** provision, arrangement, anticipation, precaution, forecast, rehearsal; adaptation, elaboration, formation, manufacture, evolution, development, ripening, maturation (*tech.*); concoction, digestion, hatching, incubation; dissemination, propaganda; groundwork, substructure, base, basis, foundation; scaffold, scaffolding, *échafaudage* (*F.*).
[*of men*] training, education, equipment, inurement; novitiate.
[*of food*] cooking, cookery, culinary art.
[*of the soil*] tilling, plowing, sowing, semination, cultivation.
preparedness, readiness, fitness; ripeness, mellowness, maturity.
preparer, preparator (*tech.*), trainer, coach, teacher, pioneer; forerunner, avant-courier, *avant-coureur* (*F.*), *avant-courrier* (*F.*), precursor; sappers and miners (*mil.*), engineers.
II. *Verbs.* **prepare,** prime, get (*or* make) ready, arrange, make preparations, settle preliminaries, get up; concoct, cook, dress, brew; fix, devise, fabricate; prepare the ground, lay the foundations, erect the scaffolding; roughhew, block out.
mature, ripen, mellow, season, bring to maturity, **nurture;** elaborate, perfect, complete, develop, hatch.
equip, arm, man; fit out, fit up, rig, dress, accouter *or* accoutre, array, outfit, appoint, gird, furnish, provide.
prepare for, guard against, forearm; make provision for; provide against; set one's house in order, make all snug; clear decks, clear for action.
be prepared, be ready, hold oneself in readiness, watch and pray, keep one's powder dry, lie in wait for, anticipate, foresee.
III. *Adjectives.* **preparatory,** preparative, introductory, preliminary, provisional, inchoate; provident, forehanded (*U. S.*), precautionary; in embryo, in hand, in train; afoot, afloat; on foot, brewing, hatching, forthcoming.
prepared, ready, cut and dried; available, at one's elbow, ready for use, usable, all ready; handy.
ripe, mature, pucka *or* *pakka* (*Anglo-Indian*), mellow; seasoned, practiced, experienced.
elaborate, labored, high-wrought, worked up, finished, perfected.
IV. *Adverbs.* **in preparation,** in anticipation of; afoot, astir, abroad.
See also ARRANGEMENT, FORESIGHT, PLAN, PROVISION, TEACHING.—*Antonyms.* See NONPREPARATION.

---

preponderance, *n.* predominance, ascendancy, supremacy, outweighing. See INFLUENCE, SUPERIORITY.
prepossessing, *adj.* attractive, engaging, inviting. See PLEASURABLENESS.
preposterous, *adj.* absurd, nonsensical; imaginative, unreal; ridiculous, extravagant; unfit, improper. See ABSURDITY, IMAGINATION, RIDICULOUSNESS, RIGHTLESSNESS.
prerogative, *n.* right, privilege, claim, birthright. See RIGHTFULNESS.

prescribe, *v.* advise, suggest, advocate, urge; order, appoint, decree; allot, ordain, legalize. See ADVICE, COMMAND, RIGHTFULNESS.

prescription, *n.* direction, decree, edict, mandate; recipe, receipt, medicine. See COMMAND, REMEDY.

PRESENCE.—I. *Nouns.* **presence,** attendance; occupancy, occupation, residence, inhabitance, inhabitancy, habitancy; whereness, ubiety, ubiquity, omnipresence.
pervasion, penetration, saturation, permeation, diffusion.
proximity, nearness, propinquity, neighborhood, vicinity.
bearing, carriage, port, mien, air, demeanor, appearance.
II. *Verbs.* **be present,** make one of, look on, attend, *assister* (*F.*), **remain, find** (*or* present) oneself; lie, stand.
frequent, resort to, haunt, visit; infest, overrun; revisit.
pervade, permeate, penetrate, diffuse; overspread; fill, run through, saturate.
III. *Adjectives.* [*being in a certain place*] **present,** situate, resident, domiciled; moored, anchored, at anchor; ubiquitous, omnipresent.
[*not past or future*] **current,** existing, actual, latest, existent, occurring; instant, immediate.
IV. *Adverbs.* here, there, everywhere; aboard, on board, at home, afield: on the spot; *in propria persona* (*L.*), in person.
See also EXISTENCE, LOCATION, SPECTATOR.—*Antonyms.* See ABSENCE.

[1]**PRESENT.**—I. *Nouns.* **the present,** now, nonce, the present juncture (*or* occasion); the times, time being; twentieth century; epoch, day, hour, crisis.
[*in plural*] **presents** (*law*), documents, instruments, deeds, writings (*as,* "*know all men by these* presents").
II. *Adverbs.* **at this time, at this moment,** now, at present; today, nowadays; already; even now, but now, just now; for the time being, for the nonce; *pro hac vice* (*L.*), for this occasion; contemporary (*of persons*), contemporaneous (*of events*).
See also INSTANTANEITY.—*Antonyms.* See FUTURE, PAST, TIME.

---

[2]**present,** *n.* gift, offering, donation, favor, bonus. See GIVING.

present, *v.* give, bestow, assign, pass, deliver, hand over; proffer, tender. See GIVING, OFFER.

presentiment, *n.* apprehension, foreboding; forecast, prophecy, augury. See PREDICTION, PSYCHICAL, RESEARCH.

presently, *adv.* immediately, at once; soon, shortly, by and by. See EARLINESS, EXPECTATION.

PRESERVATION.—I. *Nouns.* **preservation,** conservation, keeping, saving, safe-keeping, economy, maintenance, support, salvation, deliverance, protection.
[*means of preservation*] **preservative,** preserver; prophylaxis; hygiene, hygienics; dehydration, evaporation, drying, canning, pickling; ensilage.
II. *Verbs.* **preserve,** maintain, keep, uphold, sustain, support, keep up, keep alive, conserve, save, rescue, make safe, take care of, guard, secure, protect, shield; husband, economize.
embalm, dry, season, smoke, kipper, cure, salt, brine, corn, marinade, marinate, pickle, bottle, pot, tin (*chiefly Brit.*), can; dehydrate, evaporate; kyanize.
III. *Adjectives.* **preserved,** maintained, etc. (see *verbs*); unimpaired, uninjured, unhurt, unmarred; safe, safe and sound, intact, unbroken, with a whole skin.
See also CARE, CONTINUANCE, DEITY, DELIVERANCE, PERMANENCE, PROVISION, SAFETY, STORE.—*Antonyms.* See DESTRUCTION, WASTE.

---

preside, *v.* control, direct, manage, superintend. See AUTHORITY, DIRECTION.

president, *n.* head, chief, principal, chairman, presider; ruler, chief executive. See AUTHORITY, DIRECTOR, MASTER.

press, *v.* throng, crowd; force, compel; hug, embrace; squeeze out; weigh, bear upon; urge upon, emphasize, stress; solicit, entreat, importune; smooth, iron. See ASSEMBLAGE, COMPULSION, ENDEARMENT, EXTRACTION, GRAVITY, OFFER, REQUEST, SMOOTHNESS.

press, *n.* crowd, throng, crush; pressure, urgency; printing press; newspapers (*collectively*); repository, wardrobe. See ASSEMBLAGE, IMPORTANCE, PRINTING, PUBLICATION, RECEPTACLE.
pressing, *adj.* urgent, persistent, critical, exacting. See IMPORTANCE.
pressure, *n.* distress, affliction; compression, impression, heaviness; stress, compulsion, urgency; persuasion, persuasiveness. See ADVERSITY, GRAVITY, IMPORTANCE, INFLUENCE.
presume, *v.* venture, take the liberty; assume, infer, deduce; expect, presuppose. See FREEDOM, PROBABILITY, SUPPOSITION.
presumption, *n.* haughtiness, arrogance; inference, deduction, conclusion; audacity, impetuosity. See INSOLENCE, PROBABILITY, RASHNESS.
presuppose, *v.* presume, assume, take for granted. See SUPPOSITION.
pretend, *v.* dissemble, make believe, feign, sham, simulate; lie, counterfeit. See FALSEHOOD, UNTRUTH.
pretender, *n.* impostor, claimant (*as to a throne*), feigner, hypocrite, humbug. See DECEIVER, RIGHTLESSNESS.
pretense, *n* semblance, simulation; pomposity, sham, show; excuse, subterfuge, makeshift; evasion, pretext. See IMITATION, OSTENTATION, PLEA, UNTRUTH.
pretension, *n.* pretense, airs, ostentation, profession, claim (*true or false*). See AFFECTATION, VANITY.
pretentious, *adj.* affected, unnatural; ostentatious, conspicuous; showy, tawdry, garish; vain, conceited. See AFFECTATION, OSTENTATION, UGLINESS (*gaudy*), VANITY.
pretext, *n.* excuse, justification, vindication; sham, evasion, pretense. See PLEA, UNTRUTH.
pretty, *adj.* fair, comely, fine, beautiful. See BEAUTY.
prevail, *v.* be, exist; be general, be prevalent; obtain, predominate, rule; triumph, overcome See EXISTENCE, GENERALITY, HABIT, SUCCESS.—**prevail upon,** induce, persuade, urge. See MOTIVE.
prevalence, *n.* sway, power; dominance, preponderance. See INFLUENCE, SUPERIORITY.
prevalent, *adj.* rife, general, prevailing, current. See GENERALITY, HABIT.
prevaricate, *v.* deviate, equivocate, quibble. See FALSEHOOD.
prevarication, *n.* evasion, subterfuge, quibble. See FALSEHOOD, MISJUDGMENT.
prevent, *v.* hinder, impede, check, restrain, prohibit, stop. See HINDRANCE.
prevention, *n.* interception, restriction, obstruction, stoppage, preventive. See HINDRANCE.
preventive, *adj.* preclusive, deterrent, warding off. See HINDRANCE.
previous, *adj.* foregoing, preceding, prior, former. See PRIORITY.
prey, *n.* prize, spoil, pillage; game, quarry; victim. See BOOTY, INTENTION, PAIN.
prey, *v.* wear (upon), deject; plunder, pillage, ravage. See DEJECTION, TAKING.

PRICE.—I. *Nouns.* price, worth, value; estimation, valuation, appraisement, amount, cost, expense, charge, rate, quotation, outlay, figure, demand, fare, hire, wages; par, face value, par value, money's worth; market price, price current, price list.
dues, duty, toll, tax, avania (*Turkey*), impost, tariff, levy; capitation, poll tax, poll, pollage (*rare*); custom, excise, *octroi* (*F.*), assessment, taxation, benevolence (*hist.*), exactment, exaction, tithe, ransom; salvage, towage; brokerage, wharfage, freightage.
reward, recompense, compensation, renumeration, pay, prize, return, guerdon, requital (*as, the* price *of toil*).
II. *Verbs.* price, set (*or* fix) a price, appraise, assess, tax, levy, impose, rate, charge, demand, ask, require, exact; ask the price of (*colloq.*).
fetch, sell for, cost, bring in, yield, afford.
III. *Adjectives.* taxable, assessable, dutiable, tithable, ratable.
See also REWARD, SUBSTITUTION.—*Antonyms.* See DISCOUNT, INUTILITY.

priceless, *adj.* costly, expensive; precious, invaluable. See DEARNESS, GOODNESS.

prick, *v.* urge, incite, spur, goad; pierce, stick, puncture; wound, sting. See MOTIVE, OPENING, PAIN.

prickly, *adj.* bristly, barbed, bearded, thorny, stinging. See ROUGHNESS, SHARPNESS.

PRIDE.—I. *Nouns.* **pride,** haughtiness, proudness, high notions, hauteur, vainglory, arrogance, superciliousness, disdain, haughtiness, *morgue* (*F.*), self-importance, self-complacency, lordliness, loftiness, self-conceit, self-exaltation, egotism, pomposity, swank (*slang*), side (*slang*), swagger, toploftiness (*colloq.*), self-sufficiency; exultation, elation.

self-esteem, self-respect, self-approbation, dignity, decorum, stateliness, augustness; gravity, seemliness, befittingness, becomingness.

ostentation, show, display, parade, ostentatiousness, pomp, glory, dazzle, splendor (*as, the* pride *of war*).

II. *Verbs.* **be proud,** presume, swagger, peacock (*fig.*), prance, swell, strut, hold one's head high, look big, carry with a high hand; ride the high horse, give oneself airs; plume, pride oneself.

III. *Adjectives.* **proud,** haughty, arrogant, prideful, lordly, supercilious, disdainful, bumptious, magisterial, imperious, pompous, toplofty (*colloq.*), consequential, overweening, presumptuous, uppish (*colloq.*), egotistical, lofty, high, mighty, swollen, puffed up, flushed, vainglorious; purse-proud, fine.

dignified, stately, lordly, lofty-minded, high-souled, high-minded, high-mettled, high-flown, high-toned.

stiff, starched up (*colloq.*), straitlaced, prim, affected, constrained, formal, stiff-necked.

exultant, elated, pleased, satisfied, elate, joyous, delighted.

grand, splendid, imposing, noble, impressive, stately, majestic, magnificent, ostentatious (*as,* proud *titles*).

mettlesome, spirited, courageous, vigorous, valiant, brave, game (*colloq.*), high-spirited, fiery (*as, a* proud *steed*).

IV. *Adverbs.* **proudly,** haughtily, etc. (see *adjectives*); with head erect; with nose in air, with nose turned up; with a sneer, with curling lip; *en grand seigneur* (*F.*).

See also BOASTING, INSOLENCE, OSTENTATION, REPUTE, VANITY.—*Antonyms.* See HUMILITY.

---

priest, *n.* clergyman, minister, *abbé* (*F.*), father. See CLERGY.

priggish, *adj.* affected, conceited, egotistic, pedantic. See AFFECTATION.

prim, *adj.* stiff, formal, precise, demure. See AFFECTATION, FASTIDIOUSNESS, PRIDE.

primary, *adj.* prime, initial, first; primitive, original; chief, principal. See BEGINNING, CAUSE, IMPORTANCE.

prime, *adj.* first, initial; main, chief, leading; primitive, primeval. See BEGINNING, IMPORTANCE, OLDNESS.

primitive, *adj.* prime, primal, primary, primeval, aboriginal, prehistoric, antiquated, old-fashioned. See OLDNESS.

primness, *n.* stiffness, formality; prudery, prudishness. See AFFECTATION, FASTIDIOUSNESS.

prince, *n.* sovereign, ruler, heir apparent, prince of the blood, princess (*fem.*); greatest, chief. See MASTER, NOBILITY, SUPERIORITY.

princely, *adj.* liberal, munificent; noble, royal, titled; generous, magnanimous. See LIBERALITY, NOBILITY, UNSELFISHNESS.

principal, *adj.* prime, main, chief, foremost, leading. See IMPORTANCE.

principal, *n.* head, chief, leader; capital, corpus (*pl.* corpora: *law*), original sum. See DIRECTOR, MONEY.

principle, *n.* theory, conviction, tenet, doctrine; rule, precept, law; justice, equity, integrity; source, origin, nature, cause. See BELIEF, MAXIM, PROBITY, SUBJECTIVENESS.

PRINTING.—I. *Nouns.* **printing,** typography, *ars artium omnium conservatrix* (*L.*), composition, typesetting, presswork; type, linotype, monotype.
print, impression, impress, imprint, letterpress, text, matter, context.
proof, pull, slip, trial impression, galley, galley proof, page proof, foundry proof, plate proof; revise.
printer, compositor, typesetter, pressman.
proof-reader, proof-corrector, reader, corrector of the press; copyholder.
printing press, press, printing machine, cylinder press, rotary press, web press.
II. *Verbs.* **print,** impress, imprint, stamp, strike off; compose, go to press, see through the press; publish, issue, bring out; reprint, reissue.
III. *Adjectives.* **typographic** *or* typographical, printed, in type.
See also BOOK, ENGRAVING, PUBLICATION.—*Antonyms.* See WRITING.

PRIORITY.—I. *Nouns.* **priority,** antecedence, anteriority, preëxistence, precedence, seniority; superiority, preëminence.
II. *Verbs.* **antecede,** go before (*in time or place*), precede, preëxist, forecome (*rare*); forerun, have precedence, outrank, lead, head; presage, herald, usher in, announce, introduce, present.
be beforehand, anticipate, forestall, steal a march upon, have (*or* gain) the start; surpass, outstrip.
III. *Adjectives.* **prior,** previous, preceding, anterior, antecedent, preëxistent; former, aforementioned, foregoing, before-mentioned, aforesaid, said, introductory, prefatory; first, superior.
IV. *Adverbs.* **before,** prior to, earlier, previously, beforetime (*archaic*), aforetime (*archaic*), hitherto, heretofore, erenow, formerly, erewhile *or* erewhiles (*archaic*), already, yet, beforehand; on the eve of.
See also PAST, PRECEDENCE, PRECURSOR.—*Antonyms.* See POSTERIORITY.

PRISON.—*Nouns.* **prison,** prison house; jail *or* gaol, jug (*slang*); cage, coop; den, cell; stronghold, fortress, keep, donjon, dungeon, Bastille, oubliette, penitentiary, quod (*slang*), stir (*slang*), choky (*Anglo-Indian*), State prison, lockup, **clink** (*colloq.*), station house, station (*colloq.*), pen (*also slang for penitentiary*); penal settlement; workhouse (*U. S.; in England, a workhouse is a poorhouse*), house of correction, reformatory, reform school.
[*restraining devices*] shackle, bond, gyve, fetter, irons, pinion; manacle, handcuff, bracelet (*jocose*); wristlet (*slang*), snitcher (*slang*), twister; strait-waistcoat, stocks, pillory; vise *or* vice, bandage, splint, strap; muzzle, gag, bit, curb, snaffle, bridle; rein, reins, lines (*U. S. and dial. Eng.*), ribbons (*colloq.*), halter, tether, picket, band, cord; bar, bolt, lock, padlock, chain; brake, drag, check.
barrier, obstruction, obstacle; hedge, fence, rail, paling, palisade, stockade, wall, barricade, boom, barbed-wire entanglement (*mil.*).
[*for stray animals*] pound, pinfold *or* penfold, greenyard (*Eng.*).
See also HINDRANCE, RESTRAINT.

PRISONER.—I. *Nouns.* **prisoner,** captive (*as in war*), *détenu* (*F.; fem. détenue*), culprit, convict, jailbird *or* gaolbird, *forçat* (*F.*); ticket-of-leave man (*Eng.*).
II. *Verbs.* stand committed; be imprisoned, serve time.
III. *Adjectives.* **imprisoned,** incarcerated, confined, committed, jailed, in prison, in custody, in charge, behind bars, in durance vile, under lock and key, under hatches.
Antonyms. See KEEPER.

---

privacy, *n.* retirement; solitude, retreat, secrecy. See SECLUSION.
private, *adj.* retired, sequestered; special, individual, personal. See SECLUSION, SPECIALTY.
privation, *n.* deprivation, dispossession, bereavement, forfeiture; indigence, want. See LOSS, POVERTY.
privilege, *n.* liberty, favor, exemption, immunity; prerogative, personal right. See FREEDOM, RIGHT.
privileged, *adj.* exempt, immune, allowed, authorized, licensed. See RIGHTFULNESS.

prize, *n.* reward, privilege, advantage; laurel, decoration, medal. See ACQUISITION, TROPHY.

---

prize, *v.* value, esteem, cherish, hold dear. See LOVE.

PROBABILITY.—I. *Nouns.* **probability,** likelihood, likeliness, chance, prospect, presumption, credibility, *vraisemblance* (*F.*), appearance, verisimilitude, plausibility; color, semblance, show of.

II. *Verbs.* **be probable,** lend color to; point to; imply, bid fair, promise, stand (*or* run) a good chance.

presume, infer, gather, conclude, deduce, suppose, take for granted, expect, count upon, flatter oneself; venture, advance.

III. *Adjectives.* **probable,** likely, hopeful, presumable, moral, presumptive, apparent, verisimilar, in a fair way.

credible, believable, trustworthy; reasonable, *ben trovato* (*It.*), well-founded, specious, plausible, colorable, ostensible.

IV. *Adverbs.* **probably,** presumably, etc. (see *adjectives*); seemingly, in all probability, belike (*archaic*), most likely, to all appearance; *prima facie* (*L.*).

See also BELIEF, CHANCE, EXPECTATION, PREDICTION, TOPIC.—*Antonyms.* See IMPROBABILITY.

---

probation, *n.* test, trial, examination. See EXPERIMENT.

probe, *v.* investigate, sift, search, explore, verify; sound, measure, fathom. See INQUIRY, MEASUREMENT.

PROBITY.—I. *Nouns.* **probity,** integrity, rectitude, uprightness, honesty, faith, honor, good faith, *bona fides* (*L.*), clean hands, morality, virtue, respectability, constancy, faithfulness, fidelity, loyalty, trustworthiness, truth, veracity, candor, singleness of heart.

fairness, fair play, justice, equity, impartiality, principle.

punctiliousness, punctilio, delicacy, scrupulosity, scrupulousness, scruple; point of honor.

man of honor, man of his word, gentleman, *gentilhomme* (*F.*), *preux chevalier* (*F.*), Chevalier Bayard, *galantuomo* (*It.*), "a verray parfit gentil knight" (Chaucer); white man (*U. S. slang*), square shooter (*colloq.*), trump (*slang*), brick (*slang or colloq.*).

II. *Verbs.* **be honorable,** speak the truth, make a point of; do one's duty, play the game (*colloq.*); redeem one's pledge, keep one's promise (*or* word) keep faith with, not fail.

III. *Adjectives.* **honorable,** upright, honest, veracious, truthful, virtuous, noble, reputable, respectable; fair, right, just, equitable, impartial, square, aboveboard; manly, straightforward, frank, candid, open-hearted.

loyal, constant, faithful, stanch *or* staunch, true, leal (*Scot. and literary*), devoted, tried, trusty, trustworthy, incorruptible.

conscientious, right-minded, high-principled, high-minded, scrupulous, religious, strict; nice, punctilious, correct.

stainless, unstained, unsullied, inviolate, untainted, uncorrupt, innocent, pure, undefiled, undepraved.

chivalrous, jealous of honor, *sans peur et sans reproche* (*F.*), knightly, chivalric, valorous, generous, high-spirited.

IV. *Adverbs.* **honorably,** uprightly, etc. (see *adjectives*); on the square (*colloq.*), in good faith, on the up-and-up (*slang*), in all honor, by fair means, with clean hands.

See also DUTY, REPUTE, VERACITY.—*Antonyms.* See IMPROBITY.

---

problem, *n.* query, question, issue, enigma; theorem, proposition, exercise. See INQUIRY, TOPIC.

problematical, *adj.* doubtful, uncertain, perplexing, enigmatic. See UNCERTAINTY.

proboscis, *n.* nose, snout, trunk (*of an elephant*). See CONVEXITY.

procedure, *n.* act, proceeding; course, process, method. See AGENCY, WAY.

proceed, *v.* glide, elapse; issue, emanate, move, pass, go on, continue, advance, progress. See LAPSE, PROGRESSION.

proceeding, *n.* step, procedure, measure, process, move, transaction. See ACTION.

proceeds, *n. pl.* earnings, receipts, yield; balance, gain, profit. See ACQUISITION, MONEY.

process, *n.* practice, way, course, method, procedure. See CONDUCT.

procession, *n.* succession, sequence, progression; parade, caravan, column, cavalcade, file. See CONTINUITY, JOURNEY.

proclaim, *v.* announce, circulate, publish, broadcast. See PUBLICATION, [1]SOUND.

proclivity, *n.* propensity, proneness, tendency, inclination. See IMPULSE.

procrastination, *n.* delay, postponement, protraction, dilatoriness; omission, negligence. See LATENESS, NEGLECT.

procure, *v.* get, obtain, acquire; effect, bring about; buy, gain, hire. See ACQUISITION, CAUSE, PURCHASE.

procurer, *n.* pimp, pander, bawd, procuress (*fem.*). See LIBERTINE.

PRODIGALITY.—I. *Nouns.* **prodigality,** extravagance, unthriftiness, **waste,** wastefulness, profusion, profuseness, lavishness; profuse liberality.

prodigal, spendthrift, waster, wastrel (*an erroneous use*), high roller (*U. S. slang*), squanderer, spender, Prodigal Son.

II. *Verbs.* **prodigalize,** squander, lavish, sow broadcast, pour forth like water, shower, spill, waste, dissipate, exhaust, drain, overdraw.

III. *Adjectives.* **prodigal,** profuse, thriftless, unthrifty, improvident, **wasteful,** squandering, extravagant, lavish, dissipated; penny-wise and pound-foolish.

IV. *Adverbs.* **prodigally,** profusely, etc. (see *adjectives*); with an unsparing hand.

See also BAD MAN (*prodigal*), LIBERALITY, REDUNDANCE, WASTE.—*Antonyms.* See PARSIMONY.

---

prodigious, *adj.* huge, vast, immense, enormous, portentous, monstrous; astonishing, wonderful. See GREATNESS, WONDER.

PRODIGY.—*Nouns.* **prodigy,** phenomenon, wonder, wonderwork, wonderment, marvel, miracle; sign, portent; freak, freak of nature, monstrosity, monster; curiosity, infant prodigy, lion, sight, spectacle, *coup de théâtre* (*F.*).

See also UNCONFORMITY.

---

produce, *n.* product, fruit, yield; stock, goods, commodity. See ACQUISITION, MERCHANDISE.

PRODUCER.—*Nouns.* **producer,** originator, inventor, author, founder, generator, mover, architect, builder, artist, creator, maker, prime mover, introducer; grower, agriculturist, horticulturist, raiser, manufacturer.

Antonyms. See DESTROYER.

---

product, *n.* produce, outcome; yield, output, result. See ACQUISITION, EFFECT.

PRODUCTION.—I. *Nouns.* **production,** producing, creation, origination, causation, constitution, establishment, organization, construction, formation, fabrication, manufacture; building, architecture, erection; workmanship, performance, achievement; flowering, efflorescence, fruition, completion; genesis, birth, parturition, gestation; evolution, development, growth; breeding; propagation, procreation, fecundation, impregnation, proliferation (*biol.*).

[*in geometry*] extension, lengthening, prolongation, continuation.

[*that which is produced*] product, result, effect, fruit, work, yield, offspring, performance; composition, publication, *opus* (*L.; pl. opera: music*), opuscule; authorship: *in this sense,* production *is used esp. of literary or artistic work.*

structure, building, edifice, erection, pile, compages, fabric, framework.

II. *Verbs.* **produce,** perform, operate, do, make, form, construct, fabricate, frame, contrive, manufacture; fashion, invent, cause, originate, bring about, occasion, induce, superinduce; build, raise, rear, erect; establish, constitute, compose, evolve, coin, organize, institute; achieve, accomplish.

bear, yield, furnish, blossom, flower, bear fruit, fructify; bring forth, give birth

to, usher into the world; yean, lamb, farrow (*said of swine*), drop (*said esp. of sheep*), throw (*said of animals*), foal, calve, fawn, whelp, cub, kitten.
generate, beget, engender, reproduce, propagate, proliferate (*biol.*), fecundate, impregnate, conceive, form (*in the womb*), create, procreate, progenerate (*rare*); breed, hatch, develop, bring up, rear, foster, nurture, cultivate.
exhibit, show, lead forth, display, present, bring forward (*as, to* produce *a witness*).
[*in geometry*] extend, prolong, lengthen, continue.
III. *Adjectives.* **producible,** productible, causable, generative, generant; performable, achievable.

See also ACQUISITION, CAUSE, COMPLETION, COMPOSITION, EFFECT, INCREASE, PREPARATION.—*Antonyms.* See DESTRUCTION.

PRODUCTIVENESS.—I. *Nouns.* **productiveness,** productivity, fecundity, fertility, fruitfulness, fructuousness, fructification, proliferation (*biol.*), creativeness, inventiveness, propagation, multiplication, luxuriance.
II. *Verbs.* **render productive,** fructify, fecundate, impregnate, fertilize, pollinate (*bot.*), spermatize; generate, produce, conceive; spawn, multiply, teem.
III. *Adjectives.* **productive,** prolific, fertile, fructiferous, fruitbearing, fruitful, uberous, proliferous, copious, teeming, fructuous, plenteous, luxuriant; creative, generative, life-giving, formative, constructive, inventive, originative, causative, producing.
pregnant, *enceinte* (*F.*), parturient, gravid, heavy, big (*as with young*), great, gestant (*rare*).

See also CAUSE, PRODUCTION.—*Antonyms.* See UNPRODUCTIVENESS.

---

profane, *v.* defile, desecrate, pollute; abuse, debase. See IMPIETY, MISUSE.
profess, *v.* admit, own, affirm, avow; pretend, feign; teach (*as in a university*). See AFFIRMATION, FALSEHOOD, TEACHING.
profession, *n.* acknowledgment, avowal, declaration; calling, vocation; pretense, sham, evasion. See AFFIRMATION, BUSINESS, UNTRUTH.
professorship, *n.* chair, instructorship, mastership. See TEACHER.
proficient, *adj.* expert, adept, masterly; dexterous, adroit, skillful. See MASTER, SKILL.
profit, *n.* earnings, gain, return; advantage, interest, benefit, product. See ACQUISITION, INCREASE.
profit, *v.* benefit, advantage, aid, gain; advance, improve; avail, serve. See ACQUISITION, IMPROVEMENT, UTILITY.
profitable, *adj.* gainful, productive, advantageous; paying, remunerative, lucrative; useful, helpful, serviceable. See ACQUISITION, RECEIPT, USE.
profitably, *adv.* beneficially, productively, advantageously. See ACQUISITION.
profound, *adj.* heavy, undisturbed, deep; heartfelt, deep-felt; great, intense; erudite, learned. See DEPTH, FEELING, GREATNESS, KNOWLEDGE.
profuse, *adj.* lavish, wasteful, extravagant, prodigal; redundant, excessive, overmuch. See PRODIGALITY, REDUNDANCE.
profusion, *n.* multiplicity; excess, extravagance, waste, superfluity; plenty, abundance. See MULTITUDE, PRODIGALITY, SUFFICIENCY.
progeny, *n.* offspring, children, family, descendants. See POSTERITY.
prognosticate, *v.* foretell, predict, prophesy, augur. See PREDICTION.
program, *n.* outline, draft, forecast, prospectus, syllabus. See LIST, PLAN.

PROGRESSION.—I. *Nouns.* **progression,** progress, progressiveness, advance, advancement, ongoing, march, onward motion, speed, headway; rise, improvement, development, growth.
course, passage, procession, movement, process, lapse (*of time*).
series, gradation, rate (*as, arithmetical* progression); succession, motion, sequence (*music*).
II. *Verbs.* **progress,** advance, proceed, go, go on, get on, gain ground, forge ahead, press onward, step forward, speed, make progress (head, *or* headway); **go ahead,** shoot ahead, distance, make up leeway; improve, reform, amend.

III. *Adjectives.* **progressive,** advancing, increasing; advanced, enterprising forward, onward, forward-looking, go-ahead (*colloq.*), up-to-date.

IV. *Adverbs.* **progressively,** enterprisingly; forward, onward; forth, on, ahead, under way, in progress, *in transitu* (*L.*)

See also CONTINUITY, IMPROVEMENT, JOURNEY, MOTION, NONCOMPLETION, ORDER, VELOCITY.—*Antonyms.* See REGRESSION.

---

progressive, *adj.* continuous, successive; improving, advancing; advanced, enterprising, up-to-date. See CONTINUITY, IMPROVEMENT, PROGRESSION.

PROHIBITION.—I. *Nouns.* **prohibition,** forbiddance, disallowance, inhibition, veto, interdict, interdiction, injunction, embargo, ban, taboo *or* tabu, proscription, restriction, prevention; contraband; forbidden fruit; Volstead Act, 18th amendment (*U. S.*).

II. *Verbs.* **prohibit,** forbid, inhibit, enjoin, disallow, bar, debar, hinder, prevent, restrain, restrict, withhold, limit, circumscribe, interdict, taboo *or* tabu, proscribe; exclude, shut out.

III. *Adjectives.* **prohibited,** forbidden, vetoed, contraband, taboo *or* tabu; illegal, unlicensed, unauthorized.

prohibitionary, interdictive, interdictory, inhibitive, inhibitory; dry (*colloq.*).

prohibitive, prohibitory, exclusive, restrictive, proscriptive.

See also DRYNESS, HINDRANCE, ORDER, RESTRAINT.—*Antonyms.* See PERMISSION.

---

project, *v.* jut, protrude, bulge; intend, purpose; devise, design, scheme; cast, fling, hurl. See CONVEXITY, INTENTION, PLAN, PROPULSION.

projectile, *n.* missile, bullet, shell. See ARMS.

projection, *n.* prominence, protuberance, protrusion, extension. See CONVEXITY.

prolific, *adj.* fertile, productive, fruitful. See PRODUCTIVENESS.

prolix, *adj.* diffuse, wordy, verbose, lengthy; tedious. See DIFFUSENESS, WEARINESS.

prologue, *n.* introduction, prelude, preface, preamble. See BEGINNING, PRECURSOR.

prolong, *v.* continue, sustain, perpetuate; protract, extend; draw out, lengthen. See CONTINUANCE, DURABILITY, LENGTH.

prolonged, *adj.* extended, protracted; long, drawn-out. See DURABILITY, LENGTH.

prominence, *n.* bulge, swelling, excrescence, protuberance; projection, embossment; eminence, importance. See CONVEXITY, RELIEF, REPUTE.

prominent, *adj.* protuberant, convex, raised, projecting; marked, salient, important; eminent, distinguished, influential, conspicuous. See CONVEXITY, IMPORTANCE, REPUTE.

promiscuous, *adj.* indiscriminate, confused; mixed, miscellaneous. See INDISCRIMINATION, MIXTURE.

PROMISE.—I. *Nouns.* **promise,** engagement, undertaking, word, troth, plight (*archaic*), pledge, parole, word of honor, vow, oath, profession, assurance, earnest, foretaste, warranty, guarantee, insurance, obligation, stipulation, contract, covenant.

betrothal, affiance, espousal, engagement, subarrhation (*rare*), marriage contract (*or* vow); plighted faith.

II. *Verbs.* **promise,** engage, undertake, make (form, *or* enter into) an engagement, covenant, contract, agree, bargain, stipulate, bind (*or* pledge) oneself; resolve, determine, vow, swear, give (*or* pledge) one's word; betroth, plight faith.

assure, warrant, guarantee, foretoken, vouch for, attest, answer for, be answerable for; secure, give security, underwrite, subscribe.

III. *Adjectives.* **promised,** affianced, betrothed, engaged; pledged, bound, committed, compromised.

promising, assuring, hopeful, likely, flattering, encouraging, auspicious, propitious.

promissory, stipulating, contractual, covenantal, votive; under hand and seal, upon oath (*or* affirmation).

IV. *Adverbs.* **promisingly**, assuringly, etc. (see *adjectives*); confidently; in all soberness.

See also AFFIRMATION, COMPACT, EVIDENCE, SECURITY, UNDERTAKING, WORD.

---

promontory, *n.* cape, headland. See HEIGHT.

promote, *v.* improve, cultivate, advance, further, dignify. See IMPROVEMENT.

promoter, *n.* encourager, planner, organizer, founder. See PLAN.

promotion, *n.* advancement, preferment; graduation. See IMPROVEMENT, LEARNER.

prompt, *adj.* alert, active, ready, quick; early, seasonable, punctual, immediate, instant. See ACTIVITY, EARLINESS.

prompt, *v.* mention, suggest, tell; remind; induce, actuate, incite. See INFORMATION, MEMORY, MOTIVE.

prone, *adj.* disposed, predisposed, propense, inclined; flat, horizontal, prostrate, recumbent. See DISPOSITION, HORIZONTALITY.

pronounce, *v.* assert, affirm, declare; conclude, judge; speak, say, deliver; utter. See AFFIRMATION, JUDGMENT, SPEECH, VOICE.

pronunciation, *n.* articulation, enunciation, utterance, orthoëpy. See VOICE.

proof, *n.* verification, confirmation, conclusiveness; ratification, corroboration; test, trial; impression. See DEMONSTRATION, EVIDENCE, EXPERIMENT, PRINTING.

proof-reader, *n.* proof-corrector, reader. See PRINTING.

prop, *v.* uphold, brace, truss, stay. See SUPPORT.

prop, *n.* stay, staff, brace, fulcrum. See SUPPORT.

propagate, *v.* multiply, increase, produce, breed, generate; disseminate, publish, spread. See PRODUCTION, PUBLICATION.

propel, *v.* impel, drive, push, thrust, force. See PROPULSION.

propensity, *n.* inclination, bent, proclivity, aptitude. See DISPOSITION, TENDENCY, WILLINGNESS.

proper, *adj.* right, just, equitable; meet, appropriate, pertinent, seemly, befitting; own, individual, personal, special. See RIGHT, RIGHTFULNESS, SPECIALTY.

PROPERTY.—I. *Nouns.* **property**, possession, tenure, ownership, proprietorship, lordship, dominion.

right, interest, title, claim, demand, holding, estate, patent, copyright, vested interest; use, trust, benefit; term, lease, settlement, demise (*law*), conveyance; remainder, reversion.

dower, dowry, dot, jointure, inheritance, heritage, patrimony, legacy, gift, bequest, endowment.

assets, belongings, means, resources, circumstances, wealth, money; estate and effects.

realty, real estate, land, ground, lands, landed (*or* real) property; tenements; freehold, copyhold, leasehold; manor, domain, demesne; farm, plantation, ranch.

territory, state, kingdom, principality, realm, empire, dependency, protectorate, sphere of influence, mandate.

personalty, personal property (estate, *or* effects), chattels, goods, effects, movables; stock, stock in trade, paraphernalia, equipage, appurtenances: *opposite of* realty.

baggage, luggage (*esp. Brit.*), impedimenta (*pl.; esp. mil.*), encumbrances, traps (*colloq.*), things (*colloq.*), kit, *saman* (*Hind.*); bag and baggage.

quality, attribute, essential, characteristic, singularity, peculiarity, trait, feature, mark, qualification, virtue.

II. *Adjectives.* **propertied**, landed, well-to-do, prosperous, well off, thriving, flourishing, rich.

See also AUTHORITY, CREDIT, LAND, POSSESSION, PURCHASE, RECEIPT.

prophecy, *n.* forecast, augury, prognostication, presage. See PREDICTION.
prophet, *n.* seer, soothsayer, diviner, prognosticator. See ORACLE.
prophetic, *adj.* presageful, predictive, oracular. See PREDICTION.
prophylactic, *adj.* protective, preservative; preventive. See HEALTHINESS, HINDRANCE.
propinquity, *n.* proximity, adjacence, vicinity. See NEARNESS.
propitiate, *v.* atone; mediate, intercede; pacify, conciliate, reconcile. See ATONEMENT, MEDIATION, PACIFICATION.
propitiatory, *adj.* atoning, sacrificial, expiatory. See ATONEMENT.
propitious, *adj,* auspicious, favorably disposed, gracious, encouraging; prosperous, thriving, fortunate; timely, well-timed, opportune. See HOPE, PROSPERITY, TIMELINESS.
proportion, *n.* share, quota; ratio, distribution; dimensions, magnitude; adjustment, uniformity. See APPORTIONMENT, RELATION, SIZE, SYMMETRY.
proportional, *adj.* proportionate, commensurable. See NUMBER.
proportionate, *adj.* proportional, commensurate; proportionable. See AGREEMENT, EQUALITY, RELATION.
proposal, *n.* proposition, recommendation, suggestion; overture, proffer, tender. See MOTION, OFFER, REQUEST.
propose, *v.* offer marriage; intend, purpose; suggest, recommend; proffer, tender; propound, See ENDEARMENT, INTENTION, MOTION, OFFER, SUPPOSITION.
proposition, *n.* proposal, overture; project, undertaking; thesis, predication, statement; theorem, problem. See OFFER, PLAN, REASONING, TOPIC.
propound, *v.* set forth, suggest, propose. See SUPPOSITION.
proprietor, *n.* master, owner, lord. See POSSESSOR.
propriety, *n.* aptness, fitness, appropriateness; correctness, conventionality, decorum, *savoir-faire* (*F.*). See AGREEMENT, DUTY.

PROPULSION.—I. *Nouns.* **propulsion,** projection, propelment, *vis a tergo* (*L.*); push, shove, thrust, impulse, jaculation, ejection; throw, fling, toss, shot, discharge, shy; festination (*med.*); impelling influence.
science of propulsion, gunnery, ballistics.
missile, projectile; arrow, fléchette, steel dart (*as dropped from an airplane*), spear, dart, boomerang; shot, shell, ball, grenade, bomb.
marksman, sharpshooter, good shot, dead shot, crack shot; rifleman, gunner.
archer, bowman, toxophilite, sagittary (*rare*).
II. *Verbs.* **propel,** impel, drive onward (*or* forward), push, thrust, force, dash, drive; project, throw, fling, cast, put (*as a shot*), pitch, toss, jerk, heave, shy, jaculate (*rare*), hurl, dart, lance, tilt; sling, pelt, pitchfork; send, let off, fire off, discharge, shoot; launch, send forth, let fly; expel, eject.
start, put (*or* set) in motion, set going, give an impulse to.
III. *Adjectives.* **propulsive,** driving, urging, impellent; projectile, ballistic.
See also ARMS, EJECTION, IMPULSE, ROTATION.—*Antonyms.* See TRACTION.

---

prosaic, *adj.* dull, uninteresting, unimaginative, prosy, commonplace; sober, matter-of-fact. See DULLNESS, PLAINNESS.
proscribe, *v.* condemn; curse, excommunicate; interdict, prohibit, outlaw. See CONDEMNATION, MALEDICTION, PROHIBITION.

PROSE.—I. *Nouns.* **prose,** nonmetrical composition; prosaicness, prosaicism (*rare*); tedious discourse, unimaginativeness.
prose writer, essayist, monographer, monographist, biographer, historian, novelist; prosaist.
II. *Verbs.* **prose,** write prose (*or* in prose), prosify, talk prosily.
III. *Adjectives.* **prosaic** *or* **prosaical,** prosy, matter-of-fact, unimaginative, unromantic, dull, tedious, uninteresting, commonplace, sober, practical; long-winded, prolix, loquacious.
prose, unpoetical, unmetrical, nonmetrical, unrimed *or* unrhymed, in prose; plain, prosaic, matter-of-fact.
See also DESCRIPTION, DULLNESS, PLAINNESS.—*Antonyms.* See POETRY.

prosecute, *v.* sue, indict, arraign; continue, follow, carry on, pursue. See LAWSUIT, PURSUIT.
proselyte, *n.* convert, neophyte. See CONVERSION.
prospect, *n.* sight, scene, vista, view, landscape; anticipation, expectancy; promise, outlook, hope. See APPEARANCE, EXPECTATION, FUTURE.
prospective, *adj.* expected, coming, foreseen. See EXPECTATION, FUTURE.
prospectus, *n.* syllabus, description; sketch, scheme, design. See LIST, PLAN

PROSPERITY.—I. *Nouns.* **prosperity,** prosperousness, success, weal (*archaic*), welfare, well-being, thrift, affluence, luck, good fortune, good luck, happiness, blessings, godsend; bed of roses; fat of the land.
man of substance, man of means (*or* wealth), moneyed man, independent gentleman, *rentier* (*F.*), made man; spoiled child of fortune.
upstart, parvenu, *nouveau riche* (*F.*), profiteer, mushroom.
II. *Verbs.* **prosper,** thrive, flourish, succeed, be successful, turn out well, light on one's feet, swim with the tide, rise in the world, get on; bask in the sunshine, have a run of luck, make one's fortune, feather one's nest, make one's pile (*slang*); flower, blossom, bloom, fructify, bear fruit; fatten, batten, increase.
III. *Adjectives.* **prosperous,** thriving, flourishing, successful, booming, well off, well-to-do, at one's ease, rich, fortunate, lucky; palmy, halcyon.
auspicious, propitious, providential, favorable, promising, rosy, fair, bright.
IV. *Adverbs.* **prosperously,** thrivingly, etc. (see *adjectives*); swimmingly; as good luck would have it.
See also GOOD, SUCCESS, WEALTH.—*Antonyms.* See ADVERSITY.

---

prostrate, *adj.* stretched out, prone, recumbent; powerless, helpless; resigned. See FLATNESS, IMPOTENCE, SUBMISSION.
prosy, *adj.* dull, stupid, jejune; prosaic, tedious. See DULLNESS, WEARINESS
protect, *v.* guard, watch over, shelter, preserve, defend. See SAFETY.
protection, *n.* preservation, defense, safeguard; care, custody, safe-keeping; aid, support, championship. See DEFENSE, INFLUENCE, RESTRAINT, SECURITY
protective, *adj.* defensive, shielding. See DEFENSE.
protector, *n.* defender, guardian, patron, champion; chaperon, custodian, warden. See DEFENSE, SAFETY.
protest, *v.* default, repudiate, not pay. See NONPAYMENT.
protest, *n.* disapproval, disapprobation; expostulation, remonstrance, contradiction; objection, protestation. See DEPRECATION, DISSENT, REPRESENTATION.
protoplasm, *m.* plasma, bioplasm, metaplasm. See ORGANIZATION.

PROTOTYPE.—I. *Nouns.* **prototype,** original, model, pattern, precedent, standard, criterion, norm, rule, test, type, archetype, exemplar, example, paradigm; ideal, copy, text, design.
die, mold *or* mould, matrix, last, mint, seal, punch, stamp, intaglio, negative.
II. *Verbs.* be an example, set an example.
III. *Adjectives.* **prototypal,** prototypic, original, archetypal, archetypical, exemplary.
Antonyms. See COPY.

---

protract, *v.* continue, prolong; defer, postpone, dally, put off; extend, lengthen. See CONTINUANCE, LATENESS, LENGTH.
protrude, *v.* bulge, project, jut, thrust out. See CONVEXITY.
protuberance, *n.* prominence, projection, excrescence, bulge. See CONVEXITY.
protuberant, *adj.* bulging, swelling, prominent, projecting. See CONVEXITY.
proud, *adj.* lofty, haughty, arrogant, vainglorious, puffed up; dignified, stately, lordly, majestic. See PRIDE, REPUTE.
prove, *v.* demonstrate, show, substantiate, confirm, verify; try, test, check. See DEMONSTRATION, EXPERIMENT.
proverb, *n.* adage, saying, axiom, precept. See MAXIM.

provide, *v.* lay in, supply, replenish, furnish, contribute. See PROVISION.
provided, *adv.* if so, in case of, in the event of, on condition; if, though, supposing. See CIRCUMSTANCE, QUALIFICATION.
providential, *adj.* auspicious, fortunate; seasonable, timely, opportune. See PROSPERITY, TIMELINESS.
provider, *n.* caterer, commissary, steward, victualer. See PROVISION.
province, *n.* sphere, function, field; section, department; district, division. See BUSINISS, CLASS, REGION.
provincial, *adj.* rustic, rural, countrified; intolerant, illiberal, narrow-minded, insular. See HABITATION, MISJUDGMENT.

PROVISION.—I. *Nouns.* **provision** (*chiefly in plural in this sense*), supply, stock, store, hoard, reserve, accumulation, grist, resources, equipment, furnishing, *matériel* (*F.: distinguished from* personnel); food, eatables, rations, fare, provender, viands, victuals, groceries, purveyance, commissariat.
preparation, readiness, preparedness, arrangement, providing, provident care, anticipation.
proviso, condition, stipulation, agreement, prerequisite, precondition, postulate, terms, clause, covenant, reservation, reddendum (*pl.* reddenda).
provider, caterer, purveyor, commissary, quartermaster, steward, purser, compradore (*China*), *restaurateur* (*F.*), khansamah (*India*), victualer *or* victualler, sutler; housekeeper; landlord, innkeeper, innholder, mine host; grocer, fishmonger, provision merchant.
provision shop, provision store, market, public market; grocery (*U. S.*), grocery store, groceteria (*cant*); fish market, fish shop, delicatessen.
II. *Verbs.* **provide,** make provision, lay in, lay in a stock (*or* store), procure beforehand; arrange, prepare, plan; lay by, gather into barns, store, conserve, keep, preserve.
supply, furnish, equip, outfit; cater, victual, provision, purvey, forage; stock, make good, replenish, fill; recruit, feed.
stipulate, contract, covenant, agree, engage, bargain, condition.
III. *Adjectives.* **provisional,** temporary, provisionary, provisory, makeshift, contingent, incidental, impermanent: *opposite of* permanent.
IV. *Adverbs.* **provisionally,** temporarily, etc. (see *adjectives*).
See also AID, ECONOMY, FOOD, PREPARATION, STORE, TRANSIENCE.—*Antonyms.* See WASTE.

---

proviso, *n.* stipulation, condition, agreement, covenant, reservation. See PROVISION.
provisory, *adj.* conditional, conditionate, conditioned, dependent, subject; provisional. See CONDITIONS, PROVISION.
provocation, *n.* annoyance, vexation; affront, indignity. See AGGRAVATION, RESENTMENT.
provoke, *v.* irritate, exasperate; evoke, elicit; excite, call forth; annoy, nettle, vex, anger. See AGGRAVATION, CAUSE, EXCITEMENT, RESENTMENT.
prowess, *n.* valor, bravery, heroism. See COURAGE.
prowl, *v.* slink, sneak, lurk; ramble, rove. See CONCEALMENT, JOURNEY.
proximity, *n.* propinquity, neighborhood, vicinity. See NEARNESS, PRESENCE.
proxy, *n.* agency, delegacy; substitute, procurator, agent, representative. See COMMISSION, DEPUTY.
prude, *n.* formalist, puritan: *usually a woman.* See AFFECTATION.
prudence, *n.* circumspection, discretion, policy, foresight, tact. See WISDOM.
prudent, *adj.* careful, wary, heedful, cautious; wise, discreet, circumspect, politic. See CAUTION, WISDOM.
prudery, *n.* primness, stiffness; prudishness, coyness. See AFFECTATION, FASTIDIOUSNESS.
prudish, *adj.* demure, prim, precise, strait-laced. See AFFECTATION, FASTIDIOUSNESS.
prune, *v.* thin, trim, thin out, lop. See DEDUCTION, HUSBANDRY.

[1]**pry,** *v.* prize, lever, raise, force, pull apart: *with* up *or* open. See ELEVATE.
[2]**pry,** *v.* search, ferret out; seek, ransack, reconnoiter; peep, peek, peer. See CURIOSITY, INQUIRY, VISION
pseudo, *adj.* false, counterfeit, spurious; mock, simulated. See IMITATION, SIMILARITY.
pseudonym, *n.* pen name, *nom de plume* (*F.*). See MISNOMER, NEOLOGY.

PSYCHICAL RESEARCH.—I. *Nouns.* **psychical research,** psychical (*or* psychic) investigation; supernormal (spiritistic, *or* mediumistic) phenomena; psychophysics, mysticism, occultism.
the subconscious, the subconscious (*or* subliminal) self, ego, astral body; aura; subconsciousness, subliminal consciousness; dual personality, secondary personality, multiple personality, obsession, possession; self-projection.
psychotherapy, psychotherapeutics, psychiatry, psychoanalysis, **Freudianism; hysteria, neurasthenia; dreams, visions, apparitions, hallucinations; psychopathology, mind cure.**
[*phenomena*] **telepathy, thought transference** (*or* **transmission**), **telepathic transmission; cryptæsthesia** *or* **cryptesthesia, subconscious perception, second sight,** clairvoyance, clairaudience, psychometry.
premonition, forewarning, presentiment, prevision; premonitory apparition, wraith, fetch, double.
automatism, automatic writing, ouija **board, planchette, trance writing; trance speaking, inspirational speaking.**
spiritualism, spiritism, spirit communication, spirit manifestations; **trance,** ecstasy, spirit control (*or* possession); spirit rapping, table tipping (*or* turning), mediumistic communications; séance; materialization.
mesmerism, animal magnetism; mesmeric trance; hypnotism, hypnotic suggestion, hypnotic sleep, hypnosis; self-hypnotism, autohypnotism, autosuggestion psychic, medium, seer, clairvoyant, clairaudient; guide, control.
II. *Verbs.* **psychologize, investigate the abnormal** (supernormal, **subconscious,** *or* subliminal), pursue psychological (*or* psychical) investigations.
mesmerize, magnetize, **hypnotize, place under control, induce hypnosis, place in a trance.**
III. *Adjectives.* **psychical,** psychic, psychological; spiritistic, spiritualistic, spiritual; subconscious; subliminal, supernormal, hyperphysical, metaphysical, transcendental; telepathic, mediumistic, clairvoyant, clairaudient, psychometric; hypnotic, mesmeric, magnetic, odylic; mystic *or* mystical, occult.
See also IMMATERIALITY, INTELLECT.

---

psychotherapy, *n.* psychotherapeutics, mind cure. See PSYCHICAL RESEARCH.
public, *adj.* common, general, state, national, civil; published, known, notorious. See MANKIND, PUBLICATION.

PUBLICATION.—I. *Nouns.* **publication,** announcement, promulgation, propagation, proclamation, pronouncement, ventilation, divulgation.
publicity, notoriety, limelight (*colloq.*), spotlight (*colloq.*), publicness, *réclame* (*F.*), currency, flagrancy, cry, hue and cry, bruit, report; *vox populi* (*L.*).
the Press, the Fourth Estate, public press; newspaper, paper, daily, **journal,** gazette.
[*that which is published*] **book,** work, tome, volume; booklet, brochure, **pamphlet,** magazine.
edition, issue, printing, impression; redaction, revision, new edition.
advertisement, placard, bill, flyer (*cant*), leaflet, *affiche* (*F.*), broadside, **handbill,** poster; circular, notice, program *or* programme, manifesto, edict.
II. *Verbs.* **publish,** make public, broach, announce, utter, divulge, air, **vent,** ventilate, circulate, propagate, promulgate, spread, spread abroad, divulgate, rumor, diffuse, disseminate; emit, edit, get out, issue; bring before the public, give to the world, drag into the limelight (*colloq.*); report, voice, bruit, trumpet, proclaim, herald, blazon, noise abroad, advertise, placard, press-agent.
telegraph, cable, wire (*colloq.*), wireless (*colloq.*), broadcast, radiocast, put (*or* go) on the air (*colloq.*).

III. *Adjectives.* **published, current, in circulation, issued; general, common, public, notorious, flagrant, arrant.**
IV. *Adverbs.* **publicly, in public, in open court, with open doors.**

See also AIR, DISCLOSURE, INFORMATION, MANIFESTATION, NEWS, PRODUCTION.—*Antonyms.* See CONCEALMENT.

---

publicity, *n.* outlet, utterance, vent; limelight (*colloq.*), notoriety. See AIR, PUBLICATION.
public spirit, patriotism, love of country, civic interest. See PHILANTHROPY.
pucker, *v.* wrinkle, ruffle, gather, cockle. See [1]FOLD.
puerile, *adj.* boyish, childish, juvenile; trifling, trivial, foolish, weak, nonsensical. See INFANT, UNIMPORTANCE.
puff, *v.* commend, praise; brag, boast; blow, inflate; pant, gasp; swell (*as with pride*): *usually with* up. See APPROBATION, BOASTING, EXPANSION, FATIGUE, VANITY.
pugilism, *n.* boxing, prize fighting. See CONTENTION.
pugilist, *n.* prize fighter, boxer. See COMBATANT.
pugnacious, *adj.* quarrelsome, contentious, belligerent. See CONTENTION, IRASCIBILITY.
pull, *v.* extract, draw out; row, paddle; drag, draw, haul, tow. See EXTRACTION, NAVIGATION, TRACTION.
pull, *n.* gravity, magnetism; power, sway; tug, wrench. See ATTRACTION, INFLUENCE, TRACTION.
pulley, *n.* purchase, tackle. See INSTRUMENT.

PULPINESS.—I. *Nouns.* **pulpiness, pulpousness, grumousness, fleshiness, coagulation.**
pulp, flesh [*as of fruit*], sarcocarp (*bot.*), pap, sponge, paste, pomace, mash, dough, batter, curd, grume, jam, poultice.
II. *Verbs.* **pulp, mash, squash** (*colloq.*), **macerate; inspissate, incrassate, gelatinate, coagulate.**
III. *Adjectives.* **pulpy, pultaceous** (*rare*), **grumous, fleshy** (*as fruit*), **pulpous, spongy, pappy, crass, thick, gelatinous; baccate** (*bot.*), **berrylike.**
Antonyms. See HARDNESS, UNCTUOUSNESS.

---

pulpit, *n.* ministry, priesthood; platform, rostrum, desk, ambo. See CLERGY, TEMPLE.
pulsate, *v.* beat, throb, palpitate. See OSCILLATION, REGULARITY.
pulse, *v.* beat, throb, pulsate. See AGITATION.
pulverable, *adj.* powderable, pulverizable, crumbly, friable. See POWDERINESS.
pulverize, *v.* powder, crumble, crunch, grind, granulate. See INORGANIZATION POWDERINESS.
pump, *v.* catechize, draw out, interrogate; inflate, blow up. See INQUIRY, WIND.
pun, *n.* play upon words, word-play. See ABSURDITY, WIT.
punch, *v.* beat, knock, strike; pierce, puncture, perforate. See IMPULSE, PERFORATOR.
punctilious, *adj.* ceremonious, formal, strict, severe; precise, exact, scrupulous, conscientious. See OSTENTATION, TRUTH.
punctiliousness, *n.* punctilio, scrupulousness, scrupulosity. See PROBITY.
punctual, *adj.* prompt, early; precise, punctilious; regular, periodical. See EARLINESS, OBSERVANCE, REGULARITY.
punctuate, *v.* point, interpunctuate, interrupt; accentuate. See CESSATION, IMPORTANCE.
punctuation, *n.* period, comma, semicolon, etc. See CESSATION.
puncture, *v.* prick, pierce, perforate. See OPENING.

PUNGENCY.—I. *Nouns.* **pungency,** acridity, sharpness, keenness, tartness, etc. (see *adjectives*); tang, nip, *haut goût* (*F.*); piquancy, poignancy, causticity, acrimony.
dram, stimulant, cordial, nip, potion, drop, sip, bracer (*colloq.*), eye-opener (*slang*), hair of the dog (that bit you), thimbleful, pick-me-up (*colloq.*) liqueur.
tobacco, Lady Nicotine, nicotine, weed (*colloq.*), bacca, bacco, *or* baccy (*all three colloq.*); smoke (*slang*), cigar, Havana, cheroot, stogy; cigarette, fag (*slang*); pipe, chew, snuff.
II. *Verbs.* **render pungent,** season, flavor, spice, bespice, salt, pepper, pickle, brine, devil, curry.
III. *Adjectives.* **pungent,** biting, acrid, stinging, pricking, piercing, sharp, tart, piquant, poignant, racy, acid, sour, bitter; hot, peppery, spicy, spiced, seasoned, gamy, high, strong, high-flavored, full-flavored, high-seasoned.
salt, saline, salty, saltish, briny, brackish.
[*of reproof, satire, etc.*] **caustic,** stinging, cutting, mordant, biting, trenchant, severe, sharp, satirical, acrimonious, acrid, bitter-tempered, tart, keen, irritating, pointed.
painful, penetrating, sharp, severe, agonizing, excruciating, racking, torturous, tormenting, poignant.
[*mentally stimulating*] **piquant,** stimulating, racy, smart, spirited, lively, vigorous, inspiring, stimulative.
[*in botany*] sharp-pointed, prickly-pointed.
See also CONDIMENT, SHARPNESS, SOURNESS, TASTE.—*Antonyms.* See INSIPIDITY.

PUNISHMENT.—I. *Nouns.* **punishment,** punition (*rare*), chastisement, chastening, correction, castigation; discipline, infliction, trial; judgment, penalty, rod, penance, retribution, Nemesis, retributive justice; rough treatment.
[*forms of punishment*] imprisonment, transportation, banishment, expulsion, exile, involuntary exile, ostracism, penal servitude, hard labor, galleys; lash, beating, flagellation, bastinado, blow, stripe, cuff, kick, buffet, pummel; torture, rack, pillory, cyphonism, cangue (*China*).
capital punishment, execution; hanging, scaffold; electrocution, electric chair; shooting, decapitation, beheading; garrote *or* garrotte, thuggee (*India*), strangling, strangulation; crucifixion, impalement, martyrdom; *auto-da fé* (*Pg.; pl. autos-da-fé*), *auto-de-fe* (*Sp.*), the stake; harakiri (*Jap.*), happy dispatch (*jocular*), lethal chamber, hemlock (*the poison drunk by Socrates*).
II. *Verbs.* **punish,** chastise, chasten, castigate, strafe (*used originally by British soldiers in the World War*), correct, inflict punishment; tar and feather; masthead, keelhaul.
visit upon, pay, reward (*ironical*), settle, settle with, do for (*colloq.*), get even with, make an example of; give it one (*colloq.*)
strike, smite, spank, cuff, bethwack, wham (*slang*), thwack, thump, beat, buffet, thrash, pommel, lace, drub, trounce, belabor; trim (*colloq.*), cowhide, lambaste (*slang*), lash, flog, scourge, whip, horsewhip, birch, cane, switch, lay about one, beat black and blue; sandbag, blackjack; pelt, stone.
execute, kill; bring to the block (*or* gallows), behead, decapitate, decollate, guillotine; hang (*p. p.* hanged, *not* hung, *for the death penalty*), electrocute, shoot, burn (*also used as slang for* electrocute); strangle, garrote *or* garrotte (*Spanish method*), bowstring, drown; gibbet, crucify, impale, lynch, break on the wheel.
torture, agonize, torment, excruciate, rack, put on (*or* to) the rack, martyr, martyrize.
banish, exile, transport, deport, expel, ostracize; rusticate; drum out (*esp. mil.*), dismiss, disbar, disbench (*Eng. law*); unfrock (*as a priest*).
III. *Adjectives.* **punitive,** penal, punitory, corrective, disciplinary, inflictive, castigatory.
See also IMPULSE, PENALTY, RESTRAINT, SCOURGE.—*Antonyms.* See ACQUITTAL, REWARD.

---

puny, *adj.* tiny, undersized, undeveloped. See LITTLENESS.
pupil, *n.* disciple, student, schoolboy, schoolgirl, tyro. See LEARNER, SCHOLAR.
puppet, *n.* cat's-paw, tool; figure, manikin, doll. See AUXILIARY, REPRESENTATION.

purblind, *adj.* dim-sighted, half-blind; obtuse, dull, stupid. See DIM-SIGHTEDNESS, IMBECILITY.

PURCHASE.—I. *Nouns.* **purchase,** buying, emption (*rare*), acquisition, purchasing, shopping; preëmption (*esp. law*), coemption (*Roman law*), ransom.
[*thing purchased*] **property,** acquisition, acquirement, possession, buy (*colloq.*), bargain, gain, acquist, booty; value (*in yield*).
[*mechanical advantage*] **leverage,** advantage, hold, power, force; tackle.
purchaser, buyer, vendee (*correlative of* vendor: *chiefly legal*), emptor (*law*), customer, client, patron; clientele (*collective*).
II. *Verbs.* **purchase,** buy, acquire, procure, gain, obtain; invest in, shop, market, go a-shopping, bargain; rent, hire, repurchase, buy in, redeem, ransom.
III. *Adjectives.* **purchasable,** buyable, procurable, obtainable; venal, mercenary, hireling, corrupt.
See also EXPENDITURE, PAYMENT, SUPPORT, TAKING.—*Antonyms.* See SALE.

---

pure-blooded, *adj.* thoroughbred, full-blooded. See PURITY.
purge, *v.* pardon, absolve, atone; cleanse, purify, clarify. See ATONEMENT, CLEANNESS.
purify, *v.* clean, cleanse, chasten, purge. See CLEANNESS.
purist, *n.* stylist, classicist, formalist, stickler. See ELEGANCE.
puritanical, *adj.* prudish; rigid, strict, severe. See AFFECTATION, BLUE, SEVERITY.

PURITY.—I. *Nouns.* **purity,** pureness, cleanness, clearness, fineness; simpleness, homogeneity; faultlessness, correctness, propriety.
[*moral pureness*] **innocence,** continence, chastity, decorum, decency, delicacy, modesty, virtue, pudicity, immaculateness, immaculacy, virginity.
virgin, vestal, maiden; Lucretia, Diana, Athena Parthenos.
II. *Adjectives.* **pure,** unmixed, unadulterated, unalloyed, homogeneous, simple, clear, mere, absolute, sheer; genuine, perfect, real, true, correct, classic.
[*morally undefiled*] **innocent,** guiltless, sincere, clean, decent, decorous, delicate, unpolluted, undefiled, stainless, unstained, spotless, unsullied, guileless, untainted, immaculate, white, untarnished, unblemished, chaste, continent, honest (*archaic in this sense*), modest, incorrupt, virtuous, virgin, holy: *applied to persons, actions, thoughts, etc.*
[*of sounds*] **undiscordant,** euphonious, smooth, liquid, soft, harmonious, mathematically perfect (*music*); single, unmixed, simple (*as a vowel sound*).
[*of science and mathematics*] **theoretic** *or* theoretical, speculative, unapplied, abstract: *distinguished from* applied.
[*of unmixed descent*] **pure-blooded,** full-blooded, thoroughbred.
III. *Adverbs.* **purely,** simply, merely, absolutely, solely; completely, entirely, wholly, perfectly; innocently, guiltlessly, etc. (see *adjectives*).
See also CLEANNESS, GOODNESS, INNOCENCE, PIETY, SIMPLENESS, TRUTH, VIRTUE, WHITENESS.—*Antonyms.* See IMPURITY.

---

purlieus, *n. pl.* neighborhood, environs, confines, bounds, outskirts. See ENVIRONMENT, NEARNESS.
purloin, *v.* filch, thieve, rob, steal. See STEALING.

PURPLE.—I. *Nouns.* purple, violet, lilac, heliotrope, etc. (see *adjectives*); gridelin, amethyst, damson, purpure (*heraldry*); punicin, archil, cudbear, bishop's purple, royal purple, Tyrian purple.
high rank, exalted station, lofty position, cardinalate; great wealth, power.
II. *Verbs.* **purple,** make purple, empurple.
III. *Adjectives.* purple, violet, lilac, heliotrope, mauve, violaceous, plum-colored, lavender, puce, purplish, purpurescent, amethystine, magenta, solferino; livid, cyanotic (*med.*).

---

purport, *n.* sense, significance, import. See MEANING.
purpose, *n.* intent, aim, view, end; resolve, resolution. See INTENTION, WILL.
purse, *n.* wallet, pocketbook, moneybag. See TREASURY.

PURSUIT.—I. *Nouns.* **pursuit,** pursuing, following, prosecution, pursuance, quest, search, adventure, enterprise, undertaking.
chase, hunt, *battue* (*F.*), race, steeplechase; hunting, fox hunting, chevy *or* chivy (*Eng.*), coursing, sport, shooting, shikar (*India*); angling, fishing.
vocation, business, calling, employment, occupation, profession; hobby, fad, avocation.
pursuer, chaser, stalker, hunter, huntsman, the field; sportsman, shikari (*India*), Nimrod; hound.
II. *Verbs.* **pursue,** prosecute, follow, shadow; carry on, undertake, engage in, set about, endeavor, woo, seek, fish, fish for, trace, aim at, aim after, take up, go in for, stick to, press on, push, follow up, be absorbed in, ride one's hobby.
chase, give chase, stalk, course, hunt, hound, chevy *or* chivy (*Eng.*).
III. *Adjectives.* **pursuing,** prosecuting, following, etc. (see *verbs*); in quest of, in pursuit, in full cry, in hot pursuit, on the scent.
See also ACTION, APPROACH, BUSINESS, CONTINUANCE, ESSAY, FOLLOWING, INQUIRY, UNDERTAKING.—*Antonyms.* See AVOIDANCE.

---

purvey, *v.* cater, provision, furnish, provide. See PROVISION.
pus, *n.* suppuration, matter, humor. See UNCLEANNESS.
push, *v.* impel, urge; propel, drive, shove; prosecute, follow up. See IMPULSE, PROPULSION, PURSUIT.
push, *n.* pinch, crisis, exigency; effort, endeavor; thrust, shove, pressure; persistence, determination, aggressiveness. See DIFFICULTY, EXERTION, IMPULSE, PERSEVERANCE.
pusher, *n.* enthusiast, hustler (*colloq.*), go-getter (*slang*). See ACTIVITY.
put, *v.* place, lay, set, deposit, plant, locate; cast, throw. See LOCATION, PROPULSION.—**put off,** delay, defer, suspend, postpone. See LATENESS NEGLECT.
putrefy, *v.* decay, decompose, rot. See DECOMPOSITION.
putrid, *adj.* corrupt, rotten, decayed, decomposed. See UNCLEANNESS.
puzzle, *n.* complication, mystification, enigma, riddle, conundrum; perplexity, dilemma. See SECRET, UNCERTAINTY.
puzzle, *v.* perplex, confuse, confound. See UNCERTAINTY.
puzzled, *adj.* bewildered, perplexed, nonplused, disconcerted. See UNCERTAINTY.
pygmy, *n.* dwarf, midget, Lilliputian. See LITTLENESS.

Q

quack, *n.* impostor, charlatan, empiric, mountebank. See DECEIVER.
quackery, *n.* charlatanry, charlatanism, humbug, empiricism. See AFFECTATION.

QUADRISECTION.—I. *Nouns.* **quadrisection,** quadripartition; quartering; fourth, quarter, quartern.
II. *Verbs.* **quadrisect** (*rare*), quarter, divide into four parts.
III. *Adjectives.* **quartered,** quadrifid (*as a petal*), quadripartite (*esp. arch.*), quadrifoliate (*bot.*), quadriphyllous (*bot.*), quadrifoliolate (*bot.*), four-way (*as a valve*).
See also FOUR.—*Antonyms.* See QUADRUPLICATION.

QUADRUPLICATION.—I. *Nouns.* **quadruplication,** quadruplicature (*rare*).
II. *Verbs.* **quadruplicate,** quadruple, increase fourfold, multiply by four, fourfold, biquadrate (*rare*), quadruplex (*telegraphy*).
III. *Adjectives.* **quadruplicate,** fourfold, quadruple, biquadratic (*math.*), quadruplex, quadrigeminal (*tech.*), four-cycle (*as a motor*); fourth.
IV. *Adverbs.* **quadruple,** fourfold; fourthly, in the fourth place.
Antonyms. See QUADRISECTION.

quaff, *v.* drink, drain, swig (*colloq.*), take a pull at (*colloq.*). See FOOD.
quail, *v.* cower, shrink, flinch, blench. See COWARDICE.
quaint, *adj.* curious, fanciful; strange, odd, queer. See RIDICULOUSNESS, UNCONFORMITY.
quake, *v.* shake, tremble, shiver, shudder, quiver; vibrate. See AGITATION, OSCILLATION.

QUALIFICATION.—I. *Nouns.* **qualification,** limitation, restriction, modification, coloring; allowance, consideration, extenuating circumstances; mitigation, abatement.
condition, proviso, stipulation, provision, arrangement; exception, exemption, saving clause.
fitness, competency, eligibility, suitableness, capacity, ability, endowment; enablement, capacitation: *opposite of* disqualification.
II. *Verbs.* **qualify,** limit, modify, restrict, narrow, restrain; temper, soften, moderate, assuage, mitigate, abate, reduce, diminish; affect, give a color to, allow for, take into account.
fit, capacitate, enable, adapt, prepare, equip, empower, make competent, entitle.
III. *Adjectives.* **qualified,** fit, competent, capable, fitted, able, accomplished, eligible.
limited, modified, restricted, narrowed, circumscribed (*as, a* qualified *statement*): *opposite of* unqualified.
qualifying, limiting, etc. (see *verbs*); restrictive, limitative, conditional, provisory, provisional, modificatory, qualificatory, contingent, exceptional, hypothetical; palliative, extenuating, extenuatory.
IV. *Adverbs.* **provided,** if, unless, but, yet; according as; conditionally, admitting, supposing; even, although, though, for all that.
See also CHANGE, POWER, SUPPOSITION, UNCERTAINTY, UNCONFORMITY.—*Antonyms.* See IMPOTENCE, RIGHTLESSNESS, UNSKILLFULNESS.

---

quality, *n.* high descent, rank; characteristic, qualification, nature, grade, kind. See NOBILITY, PROPERTY.
quandary, *n.* plight, predicament; doubt, dilemma. See STATE, UNCERTAINTY.

QUANTITY.—I. *Nouns.* **quantity,** amount, bulk, volume, mass, abundance, measure, measurement, substance, strength, extension, weight, content, magnitude, extent, size number, sum, aggregate, length, duration.
[*definite quantity*] portion, share, quantum, proportion, quota, dole, driblet, pittance; armful, handful, mouthful, spoonful; stock, batch, lot, dose.
science of quantity: mathematics, mathesis (*rare*).
II. *Adjectives.* **quantitative,** of quantity; some, any, more or less.
See also DEGREE, GREATNESS, SIZE.

---

quarrel, *n.* dispute, controversy, strife, squabble, altercation, wrangle. See DISCORD.
quarrel, *v.* cavil, wrangle, disagree, dispute, fall out, clash, altercate, litigate. See DIFFERENCE.
quarrelsome, *adj.* contentious, controversial, irascible, fiery, pugnacious. See DISCORD, IRASCIBILITY.
quarter, *n.* clemency, mercy; three months; one fourth, quartern; direction, point, place, district. See MILDNESS, PERIOD, QUADRISECTION, REGION.
quarter, *v.* locate, lodge, post, station; cut up, divide, carve. See LOCATION, QUADRISECTION.
quarters, *n. pl.* lodgings (*esp. mil.*), abode, shelter. See HABITATION.
[1]**quash,** *v.* nullify, invalidate, stop. See ANNULMENT.
[2]**quash,** *v.* crush, quell, suppress. See DESTRUCTION.
quaver, *v.* quiver, shake, tremble, shudder; vibrate, oscillate. See AGITATION, OSCILLATION.
quay, *n.* wharf, dock, pier, landing. See EDGE.

queen, *n.* inamorata, goddess, belle; femal monarch, queen consort, empress; paragon, nonesuch. See LOVE, MASTER, NOBILITY, TITLE, PERFECTION.
queer, *adj.* peculiar, singular, strange, unusual. See UNCONFORMITY.
quell, *v.* calm, quiet, still; conquer, subdue, put down. See [1]REST, SUCCESS.
quench, *v.* cool, damp; extinguish, slake, sate, satiate. See REFRIGERATION, SATIETY.
querulous, *adj.* squeamish, fastidious; touchy, irritable, quarrelsome; plaintive, complaining, whining, fretful. See FASTIDIOUSNESS, IRASCIBILITY, LAMENTATION.
query, *n.* question, issue, problem. See INQUIRY.
question, *n.* query, interrogation, problem, enigma, puzzle, issue. See INQUIRY.
question, *v.* ask, sound, examine, seek, inquire; doubt, challenge, dispute. See INQUIRY, UNBELIEF.
questionable, *adj.* undecided, problematical; inconceivable, suspicious, disputable, debatable. See INQUIRY, UNCERTAINTY.
quibble, *n.* equivocation, evasion, subterfuge; quirk, shift, shuffle, cavil. See EQUIVOCALNESS, MISJUDGMENT.
quick, *adj.* prompt, alert, ready; clever, sharp, keen, intelligent; alive, living; transient, brief, fleeting; rapid, brisk. See ACTIVITY, INTELLIGENCE, LIFE, TRANSIENCE, VELOCITY.
quicken, *v.* work, take effect; sharpen, whet, stimulate; hurry, expedite, accelerate; revive, revivify, resuscitate; animate, energize, strengthen. See AGENCY, EXCITEMENT, HASTE, LIFE, POWER.
quickly, *adv.* soon, forthwith, speedily, apace. See EARLINESS.
quickness, *n.* alertness, agility, dispatch, haste. See ACTIVITY.
quiet, *adj.* gentle, meek, undemonstrative; unruffled, peaceful; modest, unobtrusive; motionless, quiescent; still, hushed, calm. See INEXCITABILITY, MODERATION, MODESTY, [1]REST, SILENCE.
quiet, *n.* calm, gentleness, tranquillity; repose, relaxation; hush, stillness, peace. See MODERATION, [1]REST, SILENCE.
quirk, *n.* quibble, equivocation, subterfuge; quip, conceit. See MISJUDGMENT, WIT.
quit, *v.* depart, vacate, abandon; leave, relinquish, resign. See DEPARTURE, RELINQUISHMENT.
quite, *adv.* wholly, completely, totally; positively. See COMPLETENESS.
quitter, *n.* shirker, slacker (*colloq.*), deserter. See AVOIDANCE.
quiver, *v.* quaver, shake, shudder, quake, tremble; vibrate, oscillate. See AGITATION, OSCILLATION.
quiz, *v.* examine, question. See INQUIRY.
quota, *n.* allotment, apportionment, share, proportion. See QUANTITY.
quotation, *n.* reference, citation; rate, current price, market price. See EVIDENCE, PRICE.
quote, *v.* cite, instance, illustrate; repeat, adduce. See CONFORMITY, EVIDENCE, TAKING.

R

rabble, *n.* mob, horde, scum, trash, riffraff, canaille. See PEOPLE.
rabid, *adj.* fanatical, furious, raging, mad. See FEELING.
[1]**race,** *n.* career, walk, province; sluice, mill race, tide race; contest, run, sprint. See CONDUCT, RIVER, VELOCITY.
[2]**race,** *n.* lineage, stock, family, tribe, nation. See CONSANGUINITY.
racial, *adj.* ancestral, lineal, phyletic (*biol.*). See PATERNITY.
rack, *v.* stretch, strain. rend, torment, harass, torture. See PAIN.

racket, *n.* carousal, dissipation; uproar, clatter, noise, fracas; *Slang:* scheme, trick, game, undertaking. See INTEMPERANCE, LOUDNESS, PLAN.
racy, *adj.* sharp, piquant, stimulating; vigorous, spirited. See PUNGENCY, VIGOR.
radiance, *n.* brilliancy, luster, splendor; brightness, radiation, radiancy, illumination. See BEAUTY, LIGHT.
radiant, *adj.* beaming, shining, sparkling, brilliant. See BEAUTY, LIGHT.
radiate, *v.* shine, light, heat; shed, diffuse, spread. See DISPERSION, DIVERGENCE.
radiation, *n.* diffusion, emission, dissemination. See DISPERSION, DIVERGENCE.
radical, *adj.* extreme, complete; essential, vital; rebellious, insurgent; fundamental, original. See COMPLETENESS, IMPORTANCE, REVOLUTION, SUBJECTIVENESS.
radio, *n.* radiotelegraphy, radiotelephony, wireless (*colloq.*). See LIGHT, MESSENGER.
radiograph, *n.* skiagraph, X-ray photograph. See REPRESENTATION.
rage, *n.* craze, mania; mode, style, vogue; passion, fury, storm, violence, madness. See DESIRE, FASHION, RESENTMENT.
rage, *v.* storm, rave, fume, foam, boil. See EXCITEMENT, RESENTMENT.
raid, *n* invasion, foray; plunder, pillage. See ATTACK, STEALING.
raid, *v.* invade, assault, fall upon. See ATTACK, DESCENT.
railing, *n.* fence, paling, rail, barrier; banister. See INCLOSURE, SUPPORT.
raillery, *n.* chaff, banter, pleasantry. See RIDICULE.
railroad, *n.* railway (*esp. Brit. when used of steam roads*), line, track, tramway. See WAY.
raiment, *n.* clothing, attire, wearing apparel, garments. See CLOTHING.
rain, *n.* rainfall, drizzle, shower, downpour, cloudburst. See RIVER.
rain, *v.* pour, shower, sprinkle, drizzle. See RIVER.
rain gauge, pluviometer, pluviograph, udometer, hyetometer. See RIVER.
rainy, *adj.* wet, drizzly, showery. See RIVER.
raise, *v.* lift, heave, hoist; excite, arouse, heighten; advance, enhance, exalt; leaven, work, ferment, effervesce; produce, start, breed, grow. See ELEVATION, EXCITEMENT, INCREASE, LEVITY, PRODUCTION.
rake, *v.* gather, collect; comb, scratch, scrape; ransack, scour; enfilade (*mil.*), sweep. See ASSEMBLAGE, CLEANNESS, INQUIRY, LENGTH.
rally, *v.* encourage, rouse, revive; meet, assemble, collect, unite, reunite. See COURAGE, FOCUS.
ram, *v.* cram; dam, stop; tamp, beat, drive; strike, butt. See CLOSURE, IMPULSE.
ramble, *v.* stroll, saunter, wander, roam, stray; digress, maunder; rave. See DEVIATION, DIFFUSENESS, INSANITY.
ramification, *n.* branching, arborescence, radiation, bough, branch, offshoot. See PART, SYMMETRY.
ramiform, *adj.* branched, ramose, dendriform, tree-shaped. See SYMMETRY.
rancid, *adj.* rank, strong-smelling; bad, offensive, foul, tainted. See FETOR, UNCLEANNESS.
random, *adj.* casual, accidental, haphazard, unexpected, irregular. See CHANCE.
range, *n.* series, rank, line, row; stove, cooking stove; latitude, scope, extent, reach, compass. See CONTINUITY, FURNACE, SPACE.
rangy, *adj.* long-limbed, lanky, lank, slender. See LENGTH.
rank, *adj.* fetid, rancid, foul, strong-scented; extreme, utter, unmitigated, flagrant; acrid, strong; dense, luxuriant, wild, overgrown. See FETOR, GREATNESS, STRENGTH, VEGETATION.
rank, *n.* line, row, file, series; grade, order, class; blood, birth, quality; group, division; position, standing, status, caste. See CONTINUITY, DEGREE, NOBILITY, ORDER, PLACE, REPUTE.

rankle, *v.* inflame, irritate, gall; fester, ulcerate. See PAIN, UNCLEANNESS.
ransack, *v.* seek, search, explore; plunder, pillage, rifle, sack. See INQUIRY, STEALING.
rap, *n.* blow, knock, slap, tap, whack, cuff. See IMPULSE.
rapacity, *n.* extortion, rapaciousness, theft. See TAKING.
rape, *v.* ravish, violate, defile, force. See IMPURITY.
rapid, *adj.* swift, speedy, quick, fleet, fast. See VELOCITY.
rapid, *n.* chute, shoot, torrent, dalles (*U. S. and Canada*): *usually in plural.* See PITFALL, RIVER.
rapt, *adj.* enraptured, absorbed, engrossed. See THOUGHT.
rapture, *n.* bliss, ecstasy, enchantment, transport. See PLEASURE.
rarefy, *v.* thin, attenuate; refine, purify. See RARITY, SENSIBILITY.

RARITY.—I. *Nouns.* **rarity,** tenuity, subtlety, rareness, thinness, ethereality; rarefaction, attenuation, expansion, inflation.
uncommonness, infrequency, unwontedness, sporadicalness, singularity, sparseness, scarcity, fewness.
curio, article of virtu, work of art, bric-a-brac (*collective*), knickknack, a find, curiosity.
II. *Verbs.* **rarefy,** attenuate, thin, subtilize (*rare*), expand, dilate, enlarge: *opposite of* condense.
refine, purify, cleanse, defecate, depurate, clarify, clear, spiritualize.
III. *Adjectives.* **rare,** subtle, thin, fine, tenuous, subtile (*now rare*), compressible, flimsy, slight, light, porous; rarefied, unsubstantial.
uncommon, infrequent, unusual, scarce, few, sparse, sporadic, occasional, exceptional, singular, extraordinary.

See also CUNNING, CURIOSITY, FEWNESS, GASEITY, GOODNESS, INFREQUENCY, NONIMITATION, THINNESS, UNCONFORMITY.—*Antonyms.* See CURIOSITY, DENSITY, MULTITUDE.

---

rascal, *n.* scoundrel, reprobate, villain, knave, rogue. See BAD MAN.
rascality, *n.* knavery, villainy, roguery, baseness. See IMPROBITY.

RASHNESS.—I. *Nouns.* **rashness,** temerity, imprudence, incautiousness, indiscretion, overconfidence, presumption, audacity, precipitancy, hastiness, precipitation, impetuosity, foolhardiness, heedlessness, thoughtlessness, carelessness, desperation.
gaming, gambling; blind bargain, leap in the dark; fool's paradise.
desperado, madcap, dare-devil, *enfant perdu* (*F.*), Hotspur, Hector; scapegrace, Don Quixote, knight-errant, Icarus; adventurer, gambler, gamester; fire eater, bully, bravo.
II. *Verbs.* **be rash,** stick at nothing, play a desperate game, run into danger, play with fire (*or* edged tools); rush on destruction, tempt Providence, go on a forlorn hope.
III. *Adjectives.* **rash,** incautious, indiscreet, injudicious, imprudent, improvident, uncalculating, impulsive, hasty, overhasty, thoughtless, heedless, unwary, careless, venturesome, venturous, adventurous, quixotic; overconfident, overweening.
reckless, wild, madcap, desperate, devil-may-care, death-defying, bold, fearless, intrepid, hardy; hot-headed, headlong, headstrong, breakneck, foolhardy, harebrained, precipitate.
IV. *Adverbs.* **rashly,** incautiously, etc. (see *adjectives*); posthaste, headforemost, *tête baissée* (*F.*).

See also CHANCE, HASTE, INATTENTION, NEGLECT, NONEXPECTATION.—*Antonyms.* See CAUTION.

---

rate, *n.* ratio, proportion, quantity, amount; velocity, speed, pace; worth, value, market price. See DEGREE, MOTION, PRICE.
rather, *adv.* slightly, fairly, somewhat, tolerably. See UNIMPORTANCE.
ratification, *n.* approval, sanction, indorsement, confirmation. See ASSENT, COMPACT.

ratify, *v.* sanction, approve, indorse, corroborate, confirm. See ASSENT, COMPACT.
ratio, *n.* proportion, quota; rate, percentage, amount; comparison. See DEGREE, NUMBER, RELATION.
rational, *adj.* sane, sound, normal. See SANITY.
rattle, *v.* clatter, clack, prattle; daze, confuse, embarrass. See ROLL, UNCERTAINTY.
ravage, *v.* pillage, harry, devastate, despoil, overrun. See OVERRUNNING.
rave, *v.* fume, rant, rage; ramble, wander, be made. See EXCITABILITY, INSANITY.
ravenous, *adj.* greedy, rapacious, voracious, omnivorous. See DESIRE.
ravine, *n.* forge, gully, gulch (*U. S.*), defile, cañon. See CHANNEL, INTERVAL.
raw, *adj.* chilly, piercing, cutting; immature, crude, unripe, uncooked, unprepared; excoriated, galled, chafed; unskilled, untrained, green, inexperienced; wind-swept, exposed, bleak. See COLD, NONPREPARATION, PAIN, UNSKILLFULNESS, WIND.
[1]ray, *n.* batoid (*zoöl.*), sting ray, sawfish. See ANIMAL (*elasmobranchs*).
[2]ray, *n.* beam, sunbeam, moonbeam, radiance. See LIGHT.
raylike, *adj.* radiated, actinoid, actiniform. See SYMMETRY.
raze, *v.* destroy, demolish, fell, level, efface. See DESTRUCTION.
reach, *v.* attain, arrive at, overtake; affect, impress, influence; stretch out, extend. See ARRIVAL, TOUCH; EXCITEMENT, LENGTH.
reach, *n.* span, extent, expanse, range, scope, compass. See DEGREE, LENGTH.
reaction, *n.* response; rebound, reflex (*physiol.*), retroaction; return, reverting, backlash (*tech.*). See ANSWER, RECOIL, REVERSION.
reactionary, *n.* recalcitrant, reactionist. See RECOIL.
read, *v.* indicate, show; interpret, decipher; peruse, con, study, learn; reproduce, render; foresee, foretell; utter, deliver; perceive, discern. See INDICATION, INTERPRETATION, LEARNING, MUSICIAN, PREDICTION, SPEECH, VISION.
reader, *n.* peruser; literary adviser; proof-corrector; reading book; elocutionist, reciter; lecturer. See BOOK, PRINTING, SCHOOL, SPEECH, TEACHER.
ready, *adj.* expert, dexterous, skillful, fluent; prompt, eager, spontaneous; available, handy. See FACILITY, FREEDOM, PREPARATION, UTILITY.
real, *adj.* existing, substantial; positive, absolute, true, actual, veritable, genuine. See EXISTENCE, TRUTH.
realism, *n.* naturalism, truth to nature, realness. See TRUTH.
realistic, *adj.* vivid, graphic, true to life. See DESCRIPTION.
reality, *n.* entity, being; fact, truth, actuality. See EXISTENCE.
realize, *v.* produce, clear; accomplish, discharge, perfect; idealize, imagine; apprehend, recognize, understand; sell, obtain. See ACQUISITION, COMPLETION, IMAGINATION, KNOWLEDGE, SALE.
realty, *n.* real estate, landed property. See PROPERTY.
reap, *v.* crop, cut, gather, harvest. See TAKING.

REAR.—I. *Nouns.* **rear,** back, posterior, hind part, hindmost part, rearward, rear rank, rear guard; background, setting, hinterland, reverse (*as of a coin: opposite of* obverse); after-part, stern, poop; tailpiece, heel, heelpiece; back door, postern, postern door; rumble, rumble seat; occiput (*tech.*); nape, scruff.
rump, croup, buttock, fundament, seat, crupper (*of a horse*), podex (*zoöl.*), breech, dorsum (*esp. anat.*), tergum (*zoöl.*), loin; dorsal region, hind quarters.
tail, brush (*of a fox*), scut (*as of a hare*), flag (*as of a setter*), dock, caudal appendage, cauda (*tech.*), empennage (*of an airplane*); appendage, narrative (*both jocose*).
wake, train, trail, track, path, trace, pug (*India*), spoor.
II. *Verbs.* **be behind,** bring up the rear, fall astern; heel, tag, shadow, follow, pursue.

III. *Adjectives.* **rear,** back, hindermost *or* hindmost, hind, after, mizzen (*naut.*), rearmost, rearward, posterior, hinder; caudal (*anat.*), dorsal; backswept *or* swept-back (*as the wing of an airplane*).
IV. *Adverbs.* **behind,** in the rear (*or* background), at the heels of; aft, abaft, astern, rearward, backward.
See also END, FOLLOWING, PURSUIT, SEQUEL.—*Antonyms.* See FRONT.

---

rear, *v.* elevate, raise, lift, erect, hoist; build, establish, make, construct; foster, nourish, breed; instruct, train; uprear, upraise. See ELEVATION, PRODUCTION, TEACHING, VERTICALITY.
reason, *n.* motive, ground, occasion, explanation; sanity, common sense, rationality. See CAUSE, INTELLECT.
reasonable, *adj.* cheap, low-priced, moderate, fair; credible, well-founded, plausible. See MODERATION, PROBABILITY.

REASONING.—I. *Nouns.* **reasoning,** dialectics, dialecticism, relationalism (*philos.*), syllogization, logic, induction (*from particulars to generals*), generalization, inference; deduction (*from generals to particulars*), syllogism, ratiocination; synthesis, analysis; dialogism, enthymeme (*logic*), sorites (*logic*).
argumentation, debate, discussion, wrangling, logomachy, disputation, pilpulism (*esp. Talmudic*), controversy, contention; polemics; arguments, reasons, pros and cons.
argument, case, plea, proposition, terms, premises, data, principle; comment, inquiry, review, ventilation, agitation.
reasoner, logician, dialectician, casuist, polemic; disputant, controversialist, eristic, wrangler, arguer, debater, logomach *or* logomachist.
II. *Verbs.* **reason,** discourse, converse, think, ratiocinate, consider, examine, discuss, debate; explain, support, justify; argue, dispute, contend, wrangle; chop logic; controvert, deny; canvass.
III. *Adjectives.* **reasoning,** rational, ratiocinative; argumentative, controversial, dialectic, polemical, disputations.
logical, syllogistic, inductive, deductive, synthetic *or* synthetical, analytic *or* analytical; relevant, germane, legitimate, sound, valid.
IV. *Adverbs.* **therefore,** hence, as a deduction, consequently, accordingly, *ergo* (*L.*), thus, so, wherefore, then, thence, whence, argal (*archaic*).
finally, lastly, in conclusion, in fine, after all, on the whole.
See also CONTENTION, INQUIRY, JUDGMENT, NEGATION, THOUGHT.—*Antonyms.* See INTUITION, SOPHISTRY.

---

rebate, *n.* decrement, discount, decrease, reduction, allowance. See DEDUCTION.
rebel, *v.* revolt, mutiny, strike, resist. See DISOBEDIENCE.
rebellion, *n.* defiance, resistance, mutiny, revolt, insurrection. See REVOLUTION.
rebellious, *adj.* defiant, refractory, insubordinate, mutinous. See DEFIANCE.
rebound, *v.* spring back, fly back, kick, ricochet. See RECOIL.
rebuff, *n.* check, repulse, snub. See FAILURE.
rebuff, *v.* snub, refuse, deny, repudiate, repel. See REPULSION.
rebuild, *v.* reconstruct, reorganize, reëstablish, restore. See RESTORATION.
rebuke, *v.* reprehend, chide, admonish, reprove. See DISAPPROBATION.
rebuke, *n.* reprimand, reproof, correction, scolding. See DISAPPROBATION.
rebut, *v.* retort, refute, oppose, confute. See CONFUTATION.
recall, *v.* cancel, revoke, retract, nullify; remember, recollect, review, retrace. See ANNULMENT, MEMORY.
recant, *v.* repent, renounce, objure, repudiate, recall. See PENITENCE.
recapitulate, *v.* repeat, restate, review, summarize. See COMPENDIUM.
recast, *v.* remodel, refashion, reform, reconstruct. See REVOLUTION.
recede, *v.* withdraw, retreat, ebb, revert, return, regress. See RECESSION.

RECEIPT.—I. *Nouns.* **receipt,** reception, acceptation, acceptance, admission, getting, receiving, taking, recipience *or* recipiency; recipe.
[*in commerce*] **acknowledgment** (*in writing*), voucher, acquittance, quittance, discharge.
[*in plural*] **receipts,** income, *rente* (*F.*), revenue, earnings, returns, avails, proceeds; rent, rental, rent roll.
premium, bonus, bounty, prize, drawings, reward, gain, fee, commission, share, hand-out (*slang*).
pension, annuity, allowance, pittance, jointure, alimony.
II. *Verbs.* **receipt,** acknowledge, put a receipt on, give a receipt for.
be in receipt of, have coming in, receive, get, take, acquire; draw from, derive from.
yield, bring in, afford, return; accrue.
III. *Adjectives.* **remunerative,** profitable, gainful, paying, lucrative, remuneratory (*rare*), well-paying, interest-bearing, well-invested.
See also ACQUISITION, PAYMENT, RECEIVING, REWARD.—*Antonyms.* See EXPENDITURE.

RECEIVING.—I. *Nouns.* **receiving,** acquisition, obtainment, procuration; reception, acceptance, admission.
receiver, recipient; assignee, legatee, feoffee (*law*), trustee, grantee, lessee; beneficiary, donee, pensioner; treasurer, teller, collector; fence (*colloq.*), receiver of stolen goods; receptacle.
II. *Verbs.* **receive,** take, accept, get, obtain, come by, gain, acquire, pocket, take in, catch.
[*to accept as true*] **believe,** credit, accept, approve, assent to, agree to, admit, allow, adopt, embrace.
understand, comprehend, learn, apprehend, perceive, grasp, follow.
greet (*as a visitor*), welcome, admit, entertain, see, hold reception.
hold, contain, retain, accommodate, carry, inclose, include.
undergo, experience, be subjected to, meet, encounter, catch, bear, endure, sustain, support, suffer, submit to.
be received, come in, come to hand, go into one's pocket; fall to one's lot (*or* share), accrue.
III. *Adjectives.* **receiving,** taking, accepting, etc. (see *verbs*); receptive, recipient; pensionary, stipendiary.
See also ACQUISITION, INCLUSION, RECEIPT, RECEPTION, SOCIALITY, TAKING.—*Antonyms.* See GIVING.

---

recent, *adj.* fresh, modern; foregoing, outgoing, retiring, deceased; novel, new. See LATENESS, NEWNESS.
recently, *adv.* lately, newly. See NEWNESS.

RECEPTACLE.—*Nouns.* **receptacle,** container, receiver; vessel, utensil, vase, amphora, *tazza* (*It.*), epergne, canister, jar; compartment, cell, torus (*bot.*); crypt, hole, corner, niche, recess, nook, pigeonhole; mouth.
stomach, paunch, belly, bread basket (*slang*), ingluvies (*zool.*), crop, craw, maw, gizzard; psalterium (*of ruminants*), omasum, manyplies.
sac (*tech.*), cyst, pocket, vesicle, vesica, bladder, sound (*of a fish*), blister, bleb, theca (*L. pl.* thecæ), bursa, utricle, sacculus (*pl.* sacculi: *anat.*), saccule, cavity, ventricle, sinus (*L. pl.* sinus); capsule, follicle, pod, calyx (*pl.* calyxes *or* calyces).
bag, sack, wallet, scrip (*archaic*), purse, portemonnaie (*F.*), poke (*chiefly dial*), pocket, pouch; knapsack, rucksack, duffel bag, haversack, satchel, reticule, saddlebags; *portefeuile* (*F.*), portfolio, brief case, valise, grip (*colloq.*), suitcase, handbag, Boston bag, traveling-bag, Gladstone bag, portmanteau.
case, incasement, chest, box, bin, bunker (*Scot.*), manger, rack, crib; coffer, caddy, casket; pyx, monstrance (*R. C. Ch.*); reliquary, shrine; caisson; trunk, Saratoga trunk, bandbox, hatbox; sheath, scabbard, socket.
basket, pannier, hamper, skep, crate, corbeil (*arch.*), pottle, corf (*dial. Eng. and Scot.*), creel; bassinet, cradle.
tobacco pipe, pipe, brier *or* briar, meerschaum, clay (*colloq.*), TD (*U. S. colloq.*), dudeen, churchwarden; calabash, corn cob, underslung (*or* Dawes)

pipe; hookah, hubble-bubble, calean *or* qalyan (*Persian*), nargile *or* narghile (*Persian*), chibouk *or* chibouque (*Turkish*); peace pipe, calumet.
[*for liquids*] cistern, tank, vat, caldron *or* cauldron, barrel, cask, keg, tun, butt, firkin, tub; bottle, decanter, ewer, cruse, carafe, canteen, flagon; demijohn; flask, stoup *or* stoop, noggin, vial, phial; cruet, caster; urn, percolator, coffeepot, coffee urn, teapot, tea urn, samovar; bucket, pail; pot, tankard, jug, pitcher, mug, porringer; receiver, retort, alembic, crucible; can, kettle, saucepan, skillet, spider (*colloq.*); bowl, basin, jorum (*colloq.*), pan, patella, punch bowl, cup, goblet, beaker, chalice, cylix, tumbler, glass.
plate, platter, dish, porringer, trencher, tray, waiter, salver; saucer, patera (*L. pl.* pateræ).
ladle, dipper, bail, scoop, simpulum (*Roman*), cyathus (*pl.* cyathi) *or* kyathos (*pl.* kyathoi: *classical archæol.*); spoon, labis (*Eastern Ch.*), *éprouvette* (*F.; used in assaying*).
repository, depository, closet, cupboard, cabinet, ambry, locker, cuddy, wardrobe, clothespress, press, chiffonier, almirah (*Anglo-Indian*), buffet, bureau, chest of drawers, commode, sideboard; escritoire, secretary, writing desk, *secrétaire* (*F.*), desk, davenport; bookcase, bookrack, bookstand, bookshelf, canterbury; till, safe, drawer; shelf, *étagère* (*F.*), whatnot.
chamber, apartment, room, cabin; office, court, hall, suite of rooms, apartment (*U. S.*), flat, tenement; saloon, *salon* (*F.*), parlor, living (sitting, drawing, *or* reception) room, best room (*colloq.*), boudoir; anteroom, waiting room; bedroom, dormitory, cubicle, ward (*as in a hospital*); refectory, dining room, *salle à manger* (*F.*), breakfast room; nursery, schoolroom; library, study; studio; smoking room, den, sanctum, adytum.
attic, loft, garret; cellar, vault, hold, cockpit; cubbyhole; basement, kitchen, pantry, scullery; storeroom, lumber room; dairy, laundry, coach house, barn, garage, hangar; outhouse, penthouse, lean-to, shed, shelter.
porch, entrance, vestibule, lobby, hall, galilee (*eccl.*); stoop (*U. S.*), veranda piazza (= *veranda: U. S.*); colonnade, triforium, arcade, stoa, portico, loggia, gallery (*Southern U. S.*), sun parlor, sleeping porch.
bower, arbor, pergola, kiosk, pandal (*Southern India*).
See also CONCAVITY, HABITATION, INCLOSURE, STORE.

RECEPTION.—I. *Nouns.* **reception**, admission, admittance, entrance, entrée; importation; initiation, introduction, absorption, immission, injection, insertion, introception, imbibation, ingurgitation, swallowing, inhalation, suction, sucking; receipt, receiving, recipience.
welcome, greeting, *bienvenue* (*F.*), entertainment, demonstration, salutation.
[*formal meeting of guests*] levee, at-home, drawing-room, ruelle, matinée, soirée, party, assembly, durbar (*India*).
[*mental acceptance*] **credence**, belief, acceptance, acknowledgment, allowance, admission, recognition, concession, open-mindedness, receptivity.
II. *Verbs.* **give entrance to**, give the entrée, introduce, usher, usher in, show in, admit, initiate; receive, import, bring in; absorb, ingest, drink, drink in, assimilate, imbibe, instill, implant, induct, inhale; let in, take in.
swallow, gulp, ingurgitate, consume, take, eat, drink, engorge, englut, bolt.
III. *Adjectives.* **receptive**, recipient, receptual, susceptible, open-minded, retentive; absorbent, absorptive, sorbefacient (*med.*).
See also COURTESY, FOOD, INSERTION, SOCIALITY.—*Antonyms.* See EJECTION, REJECTION.

---

recess, *n.* interval, break, respite, intermission, vacation; corner, niche, alcove, nook. See CESSATION, RECEPTACLE.

RECESSION.—I. *Nouns.* **recession**, retirement, withdrawal, retreat, regression, retrogression, retrocession; departure, flight.
II. *Verbs.* **recede**, go, go back, move back, retire, withdraw, regress, retrocede, return, retrograde, ebb; shrink; drift away, depart, sheer off, retreat, retire, fall back, desist; run away, fly, flee.
III. *Adjectives.* **recessive**, receding, regressive, backward, retrogressive.
See also REGRESSION.—*Antonyms.* See APPROACH.

recipient, *n.* receiver, assignee, beneficiary, pensioner; fence. See RECEIVING.
reciprocal, *adj.* mutual, correlative, complementary. See CORRELATION, INTERCHANGE.
reciprocate, *v.* correspond, correlate; alternate, vary. See CORRELATION, INTERCHANGE.
reciprocation, *n.* reciprocity, mutuality, correspondence; alternation, give-and-take. See CORRELATION, INTERCHANGE.
reciprocity, *n.* exchange, correlation, alternation, reciprocation. See INTERCHANGE.
recital, *n.* mention, recounting, narration, account. See REPETITION.
recitation, *n.* recital, narration; discourse, declamation; lesson. See REPETITION, SPEECH, TEACHING.
recite, *v.* relate, narrate, recount, repeat, recapitulate; speak, deliver. See DESCRIPTION, REPETITION, SPEECH.
reckless, *adj.* defiant, daring; rash, madcap, breakneck. See RASHNESS.
reckon, *v.* compute, enumerate, calculate, number. See ADDITION.
reckoning, *n.* calculation, computation, estimation; settlement, arrangement, satisfaction. See NUMERATION, PAYMENT.
reclaim, *v.* amend, correct, reform, regenerate; redeem, recover. See PENITENCE, RESTORATION.
recline, *v.* lie, lean; rest, take one's ease. See HORIZONTALITY, REPOSE.
recluse, *n.* hermit, anchorite. See SECLUSION.
recognition, *n.* notice, identification; acknowledgment, appreciation; cognition, comprehension; concession, allowance, acceptance. See ATTENTION, GRATITUDE, KNOWLEDGE, RECEPTION.
recognize, *v.* acknowledge, accede, acquiesce; identify, verify, know, perceive, apprehend; see, behold, notice. See ASSENT, KNOWLEDGE, VISION.

RECOIL.—I. *Nouns.* **recoil,** rebound, repercussion, recalcitration, *contrecoup* (*F.*), kick, boomerang, blacklash, ricochet, elasticity; reflux, reverberation, resonance, repulse; retroaction, reflex (*physiol.*), reaction, revulsion, shrinking, flinch, shrink, funk (*colloq.*).
reactionary, recalcitrant, reactionist.
II. *Verbs.* **recoil,** react, rebound, kick, spring, fly back, repercuss (*rare*), resile, ricochet; reverberate, echo.
shrink, flinch, shy, jib, balk, blench, start back, draw back, start, quail, wince, funk (*colloq.*), cringe.
III. *Adjectives.* **recoiling,** reflu nt, ebbing; recalcitrant, reactionary, refractory.
See also ELASTICITY, REVERSION.—*Antonyms.* See IMPULSE.

---

recollection, *n.* remembrance, reminiscence, retrospect. See MEMORY.
recommence, *v.* commence, again, begin again, renew. See BEGINNING.
recommend, *v.* advise, counsel, suggest, prescribe; sanction, endorse. See ADVICE, APPROBATION.
recommendation, *n.* counsel, exhortation, advocacy; testimonial. See ADVICE, APPROBATION.
recompense, *v.* pay, remunerate, requite, compensate, indemnify. See COMPENSATION, REWARD.
recompense, *n.* repayment, requital, remuneration. See COMPENSATION, REWARD.
reconcile, *v.* regulate, adjust, harmonize, settle; pacify, placate, conciliate, propitiate. See AGREEMENT, ²CONTENT, PACIFICATION.
reconciliation, *n.* reconcilement, reunion, adjustment, settlement. See AGREEMENT, HARMONY.
recondite, *adj.* profound, abstruse, deep, occult. See CONCEALMENT, HEIGHT.
recondition, *v.* renovate, renew, restore, rebuild. See RESTORATION.
reconnoiter, *v.* inquire, search, scan, explore. See INQUIRY.

RECORD.—I. *Nouns.* **record,** memorial, momento, monument, testimonial, medal, cross, ribbon, garter, commemoration, hatchment, escutcheon *or* scutcheon; slab, tablet, trophy, obelisk, pillar, hoarstone (*Eng. hist.*), column, monolith.
trace, vestige, relic, remains; scar, cicatrix (*pl.* cicatrices); footstep, footmark, footprint; track, mark, wake, trail, scent, spoor, pug (*India*), *piste* (*F.*)
[*written record*] **register,** registry, minute, note, memorandum, memorabilia (*pl., sing.* memorabile), *procès-verbal* (*F.; procès-verbaux*), report; roll, list, entry, indorsement *or* endorsement; inscription, copy, duplicate, docket; deed, paper, document, deposition, affidavit; certificate.
notebook, memorandum book; bulletin, bulletin board, score board, score sheet; card index, file.
newspaper, daily, gazette, magazine.
calendar, diary, ephemeris (*archaic*), log, journal, daybook, ledger, cashbook.
archive, scroll, return; almanac, gazetteer, census report, statistics; Congressional Record, Hansard (*Brit. Parliament*); state paper, government publication, bluebook, green book (*esp. It.*), white book (*esp. Ger., Pg., and Jap.*); yellow book, *livre jaune* (*F.*); report, account, minutes, proceedings, transactions, chronicle, annals; legend; history, biography, factum (*pl.* facta), achievement.
registration, registry, enrollment, tabulation; entry, booking; signature, sign manual.
II. *Verbs.* **record,** put (*or* place) upon record, chronicle, calendar; report, commit to writing, write, transcribe, inscribe, attest, note, put (*or* set) down, mark, sign, enter, book, post, insert, print; mark off, tick off; register, list, enroll, inscroll, file, catalogue.
commemorate, celebrate, memorialize, historify, historicize, emblaze, emblazon, monumentalize, hand down to posterity.
[*to record photographically*] **register,** simulate, represent, depict, portray, delineate: *in photoplay cant,* register *is most commonly used; as, to* register *grief.*
III. *Adjectives.* **recording,** inscribing, registering; self-recording, autographic.
See also CELEBRATION, DESCRIPTION, EVIDENCE, INDICATION, LIST, SUPERIORITY.
—*Antonyms.* See OBLITERATION.

RECORDER.—*Nouns.* **recorder,** notary, clerk, registrar, register (*as of deeds*), prothonotary, amanuensis, secretary, recording secretary, scribe, stenographer, bookkeeper; *custos rotulorum* (*L.*), Keeper of the Rolls, Master of the Rolls (*Eng.*).
annalist, historian, historiographer, chronicler, biographer; antiquary, antiquarian, archæologist; memorialist.
journalist, newspaperman, reporter, gentleman (*or* representative) of the Press, interviewer; publicist, author, editor.
[*recording instrument*] recording apparatus, tracer, marker, scorer, timer, autographic recorder, telegraphone, siphon recorder (*elec.*), electrograph, telautograph, telephotograph, telespectroscope, telethermograph, seismograph, etc.; phonograph, gramophone, time clock; adding machine, arithmometer, comptometer, calculating machine, cash register; turnstile, ticker, stock ticker, tape; speedometer, pedometer, patent log (*naut.*).

---

recount, *v.* describe, portray, narrate, tell, report, recite, rehearse, enumerate. See DESCRIPTION.
recoup, *v.* redeem, reimburse, compensate. See COMPENSATION.
reckon, *v.* regain, retake, retrieve, repossess; repair, heal, cure, rally, revive. See ACQUISITION, RESTITUTION, RESTORATION.
recovery, *n.* salvage, redemption, return, revival. See ACQUISITION, RESTITUTION, RESTORATION.
recreant, *adj.* cowardly, craven; faithless, false. See COWARDICE, UNTRUTH (*unfaithful*).
recreation, *n.* refreshment, play, pastime, relaxation. See AMUSEMENT.
recruit, *v.* regale, repair, restore, revive, recuperate. See IMPROVEMENT.
recruit, *n.* helper, supporter; rookie (*U. S. slang*); tyro, new member. See AUXILIARY, COMBATANT, LEARNER.
rectangular, *adj.* normal (*geom.*), orthogonal, square. See ANGULARITY, VERTICALITY.

rectify, *v.* amend, correct, improve; straighten, adjust. See IMPROVEMENT, STRAIGHTNESS.
rectitude, *n.* uprightness, integrity, honesty, justice, equity. See PROBITY.
recumbent, *adj.* prone, prostrate, lying, reclining. See HORIZONTALITY.
recuperation, *n.* restoration (*to health*), recovery, convalescence. See REFRESHMENT.
recur, *v.* return, repeat, alternate, reappear. See REGULARITY, REPETITION.
recurrence, *n.* repetition, iteration, frequence; return. See FREQUENCY, REGULARITY.

RED.—I. *Nouns.* **red,** scarlet, cardinal, etc. (see *adjectives*); coquelicot, gules (*heraldry*), gridelin, pompadour, *chaudron* (*F.*); *couleur de rose* (*F.*), *rose du Barry* (*F.*), damask, flesh color, flesh tint, morbidezza (*painting*), *sang-de-bœuf* (*F.*).
[*comparisons*] ruby, garnet, *grenat* (*F.*), carbuncle; rose, peony; rust, iron mold (*or* mould).
[*dyes and pigments*] cinnabar, cochineal, ponceau, stammel, fuchsine, minium, vermilion, annatto *or* annotto, madder, ruddle, red lead; Indian red, light red, Venetian red, rouge, archil red, cudbear.
redness, ruddiness, rubescence, rubicundity, rubricity, rubification, erubescence, blush, flush, warmth, color.
Red (*or* red), extremist, revolutionary, revolutionist, nihilist, anarchist, Red Republican, bolshevik, communist, intransigent.
II. *Verbs.* **redden,** rouge, crimson, incarnadine, rubricate (*as a manuscript*), miniate, empurple, rouge; ruddle, rust.
blush, flush, color, color up, mantle, redden.
III. *Adjectives.* **red,** scarlet, cardinal, vermilion, *sang-de-bœuf* (*F.*), carmine, crimson, cramoisy *or* cramoisie (*archaic*), pink, rose, rose-colored, flesh-colored, salmon, salmon-colored, rosy, roseate, coral, coralline, peach-colored, cerise, cherry, maroon, carnation, magenta, solferino, damask, rubric; miniaceous, miniate (*rare*), rubricate, rubineous, ruby, ruby-red; blood-red, gory, sanguineous, sanguine, bloody, murrey; warm, hot.
reddish, rufous, vinaceous, wine-colored, wine red, claret, claret-colored, flame-colored; bricky, reddish brown, brick-colored, rust-colored.
red-complexioned, high-colored, red-faced, florid, rubicund, ruddy, red, ruddy-faced, burnt, blowzy, blowzed, flushed, hectic, inflamed, glowing, sanguine, blooming, erubescent.
[*of hair*] auburn, chestnut, sandy, carroty, Titian red, brick-red, reddish brown.
[*of animals*] bay, sorrel, chestnut.
Red (*or* red), anarchistic, revolutionary, terroristic, nihilistic, bolshevist *or* bolshevik, ultraradical, intransigent, *intransigeant* (*F.*), irreconcilable.
See also DISOBEDIENCE (*insurgent*).

---

reddish brown, bay, chestnut, russet, terra cotta. See BROWN.
redeem, *v.* atone for, reform; fulfill, perform; reclaim, recover, retrieve, ransom, reinstate. See ATONEMENT, OBSERVANCE, RESTORATION.
red-letter day, festival, holiday, fête, memorable occasion. See CELEBRATION.
redress, *v.* rectify, right, repair, correct, amend. See RELIEF, REMEDY.
redress, *n.* reparation, amends, reformation, correction. See RELIEF, RESTORATION.
reduce, *v.* shorten, abbreviate, subtract, minimize, decimate, thin; lower, abase, degrade; abate, diminish; subdue, conquer, subjugate. See DECREASE, DEPRESSION, LOWNESS, SUBJECTION.
reduced, *adj.* cheap, low-priced, marked down; decreased, diminished, shortened, curtailed; poor, needy, impoverished. See CHEAPNESS, INFERIORITY, POVERTY.
reduction, *n.* decrease, diminution, abridgment, abatement; deoxidization (*chem.*); lessening, thinning; conquest, subjugation. See CONTRACTION, CONVERSION, FEWNESS, SUBJECTION.

REDUNDANCE.—I. *Nouns.* **redundance** *or* redundancy, too much, too many, superabundance, superfluity, supersaturation, exuberance, profuseness, profusion, plenty, repletion, plethora, glut, engorgement, congestion, surfeit, overdose, oversupply, overflow, inundation, deluge, avalanche, *embarras de richesses* (*F.*); pleonasm (*rhet.*), tautology, verbosity, diffuseness; excess, surplus, overplus, surplusage, remainder.

II. *Verbs.* **superabound,** overabound, swarm; bristle with, overflow, run over; run riot, overrun, overstock, overdose, overfeed, overload, overburden, overshoot the mark; gorge, glut, cloy, surfeit, satiate, choke, suffocate, pile up, lavish, lay on thick, load, drench, inundate, deluge, flood, whelm, overwhelm, engulf; send (*or* carry) coals to Newcastle; "to gild refined gold, to paint the lily, to throw a perfume on the violet" (Shakespeare, *King John*).

III. *Adjectives.* **redundant,** exuberant, inordinate, superabundant, excessive, excess, overmuch, replete, profuse, lavish, prodigal, plentiful, copious, fulsome, immoderate, exorbitant, extravagant, overflowing; gorged, stuffed, turgid, swollen.

superfluous, unnecessary, needless, uncalled for, *de trop* (*F.*), supernumerary, spare, duplicate, supererogatory, useless.

pleonastic, tautological, verbose, diffuse, wordy, periphrastic, circumlocutory, ambagious.

IV. *Adverbs.* **over and above,** overmuch, too much, too far; over, too, in addition, besides; over head and ears, over one's head; up to one's eyes; extra, beyond the mark.

See also ADDITION, DIFFUSENESS, OVERRUNNING, PRODIGALITY, REMAINDER.—*Antonyms.* See INSUFFICIENCY.

---

reef, *n.* shoal, ridge, bar, islet. See ISLAND.

reel, *v.* whirl, sway, stagger, be giddy. See AGITATION.

reënforce, *v.* augment, strengthen, fortify. See ADDITION.

reënforcements, *n. pl.* supports, recruits, auxiliaries (*mil.*). See AID.

reëstablish, *v.* restore, replace, reinstate, rebuild, reconstruct. See RESTORATION.

refashion, *v.* recast, remodel, reshape, reconstruct, rearrange. See IMPROVEMENT, REVOLUTION.

refer, *v.* attribute, impute; call, cite, quote; relate, concern; commit, relegate, submit: *followed by* to. See ATTRIBUTION, EVIDENCE, RELATION, SUBMISSION, TOUCH.

reference, *n.* ascription; citation, allusion; reference mark; connection, respect, relationship; relegation, assignment. See ATTRIBUTJON, EVIDENCE, INDICATION, RELATION, TRANSFER.

reference book, encyclopedia, dictionary, thesaurus; concordance, gazetteer, yearbook. See BOOK.

refine, cleanse, clarify, purify, spiritualize, rarefy, improve. See RARITY, SENSIBILITY.

refined, *adj.* cultivated, cultured well-bred, polished. See TASTE.

refinement, *n.* nicety, subtlety; betterment, purification; cultivation, culture, elegance, finish. See DISCRIMINATION, IMPROVEMENT, TASTE.

reflect, *v.* imitate, copy, reproduce, mirror; think, contemplate, ponder, study, weigh. See IMITATION, THOUGHT.

reflection, *n.* image, echo; reproach, criticism; reflex; musing, deliberation, idea, remark. See COPY, DISREPUTE, LIGHT, THOUGHT.

reflux, *n.* flowing back, backwater, ebb, refluence. See REGRESSION.

reform, *v.* remodel, reconstruct, reëstablish; reclaim, redeem, regenerate, convert, correct, improve, restore. See IMPROVEMENT, PENITENCE.

reform, *n.* amendment, reformation, reconstruction, correction, progress. See IMPROVEMENT.

reformation, *n.* reform, correction, amendment, purification. See IMPROVEMENT.

reformer, *n.* reformist, progressive. See IMPROVEMENT.

refraction, *n.* fallacy of vision, nearsightedness, myopia; divergence, deflection, dispersion. See DIM-SIGHTEDNESS, LIGHT.
refractory, *adj.* obstinate, stubborn, sullen, self-willed, unruly, unmanageable, ungovernable, intractable, contumacious. See OBSTINACY.
refrain, *v.* abstain, forbear, withhold, desist. See AVOIDANCE.
refrain, *n.* burden (*of a song*), chorus, undersong. See REPETITION.

REFRESHMENT.—I. *Nouns.* **refreshment** (*of mind or body*), reinvigoration, restoration, renewal, revival, recovery, renovation, repair, recuperation, reanimation; relief, recreation, diversion, relaxation.
[*that which refreshes*] **regalement,** regale, bait (*as on a journey*), lunch, food or drink; *usually in pl.*
II. *Verbs.* **refresh,** brace, strengthen, exilarate, reinvigorate, reanimate, brisken, brisk, reënliven, revivify, restore, renew, renovate, repair, revive, recreate; recruit, recuperate, recover (*or* regain) one's strength, get better; cool, air, freshen; regale, cheer, give (*or* take) refreshment (*esp. drink*); refresh the inner man.
freshen (*the memory*), quicken, strengthen, brighten, revive, renew, freshen up, stimulate.
III. *Adjectives.* **refreshed,** strengthened, etc. (see *verbs*); freshened, invigorated, vigorous, fresh, fit, unwearied, untired.
refreshing, refreshful, invigorating, recuperative, restorative; restful, genial, delectable, delicious.
See also FOOD, PLEASURABLENESS, RELIEF, RESTORATION, STRENGTH.—*Antonyms.* See FATIGUE.

REFRIGERATION.—I. *Nouns.* **refrigeration,** cooling, infrigidation, gelation, regelation (*physics*), congelation, glaciation; solidification.
fire extinguisher, *extincteur* (*F.*), fire annihilator; asbestos, amianthus, earth flax, mountain flax; fireman, fire brigade, fire department, fire engine, pyroleter.
II. *Verbs.* **refrigerate,** cool, freeze in ice, chill, fan, infrigidate, precool (*as fruit for shipment*), regelate (*physics*), congeal, benumb, petrify; pinch, nip, cut, pierce, bite; chill to the marrow.
extinguish, put out, stamp out; quench, smother, stifle, douse (*slang*), damp, slack, annihilate.
III. *Adjectives.* **refrigerative,** cooling, refrigeratory, refrigerant, frigorific *or* frigorifical, chilling.
incombustible, unflammable, uninflammable; fireproof, asbestic: *opposite of* combustible.
See also COLD.—*Antonyms.* See CALEFACTION.

REFRIGERATOR.—*Nouns.* **refrigerator,** ice box, ice chest, refrigerating machine (*or* engine), ice machine, freezing machine, freezer; icehouse, cold storage; refrigerator car, refrigerating plant; frigidarium; ice bag, ice pack, cold pack; ice pail, cooler, refrigeratory.
refrigerant, refrigerative (*rare*), freezing mixture, ice, ammonia.
Antonyms. See FURNACE.

REFUGE.—*Nouns.* **refuge,** sanctuary, retreat, defense, rock, fastness, stronghold, fortress, castle, keep; asylum, *sanctum sanctorum* (*L.*), shelter, *abri* (*F.*), dugout, covert, ark, home, hiding place, last resort, *dernier ressort* (*F.*).
anchorage, roadstead; breakwater, mole, port, haven, harbor, pier, jetty, embankment, quay, wharf, bund (*Oriental*), bunder (*Oriental*), landing place.
anchor, kedge, killick, sheet (*or* waist) anchor, bower, patent anchor, screw anchor, mushroom anchor, grapnel, grappling iron; mainstay, support, safeguard.
See also AVOIDANCE, DEFENSE, ESCAPE, SECLUSION.—*Antonyms.* See PITFALL.

---

refund, *v.* repay, reimburse. See PAYMENT.

REFUSAL.—I. *Nouns.* **refusal,** noncompliance, rejection, declension, declination, nonacceptance, flat (*or* point-blank) refusal; repulse, rebuff; discountenance, disapprobation.
denial, disallowance, disclaimer (*esp. law*), repudiation, disavowal, dissent,

negation, disaffirmation, disbelief, abnegation, protest, renunciation, recusancy, nonconformity; revocation, annulment.
II. *Verbs.* refuse, decline, turn down (*slang*), dissent, disavow, deny, disallow, disclaim, protest, repudiate, reject, discard, veto, rescind, negative, withhold one's assent, grudge, begrudge; stand aloof, be deaf to, turn one's back upon, discountenance, forswear, set aside, renounce, abandon, give up, cast off.
resist, dispute, oppose, gainsay, contest, obstruct, withstand, thwart, frustrate, repel, repulse, rebuff, overthrow, defeat.
III. *Adjectives.* refusing, declining, etc. (see *verbs*); recusant, dissentient, uncomplying, unconsenting, noncompliant, deaf to.
IV. *Adverbs.* on no account, not for the world, not on your life (*colloq.*), nothing doing (*slang*).

See also ANNULMENT, DISSENT, PROHIBITION, REJECTION.—*Antonyms.* See OFFER, PERMISSION.

---

refuse, *n.* rubbish, junk, litter, leavings, garbage. See INUTILITY.
refute, *v.* confute, disprove, defeat, overthrow, silence; oppose, deny, weaken, rebut. See CONFUTATION, COUNTEREVIDENCE.
regain, *v.* recover, retrieve, recapture. See ACQUISITION.
regal, *adj.* royal, sovereign, kingly, imperial, autocratic. See AUTHORITY.
regalement, *n.* regale, entertainment, gratification. See REFRESHMENT.
regalia, *n. pl.* insignia, emblems, decorations; sovereignty. See SCEPTER.
regard, *v.* see, notice, look, view, mark, attend, gaze; esteem, consider, heed; hold, suppose, take (for). See ATTENTION, RESPECT, TAKING.
regard, *n.* esteem, value, affection. See DEARNESS.
regardful, *adj.* attentive, mindful, thoughtful, heedful, observant. See ATTENTION.
regardless, *adj.* heedless, thoughtless, careless, indifferent, negligent. See INATTENTION.
regenerate, *adj.* regenerated, reformed, converted. See PIETY.
regenerate, *v.* revive, generate anew (*as a storage battery*), reëstablish; convert, reform, inspire. See IMPROVEMENT, PIETY.
regeneration, *n.* transformation, revival, reformation, regenerateness. See CONVERSION, RESTORATION.
regent, *n.* vicegerent, ruler, governor. See DEPUTY, MASTER.

REGION.—I. *Nouns.* **region,** sphere, ground, soil, area, tract, space, place, arena, clearing, domain, territory, realm, hemisphere, quarter, scene, terrain (*mil.*), locality, locale (*properly* local'), spot, location, situation, part; orb, circuit, circle, pale.
county, shire, canton, province, department, *arrondissement* (*F.*), commune, district, parish, diocese, township, ward, *enciente* (*F.*), precinct, wapentake (*hist.*), soke (*hist.*) hundred, riding, bailiwick; walk, march, beat; enclave, exclave; principality, duchy, palatinate, archduchy, dukedom, dominion, colony, commonwealth, country; fatherland, motherland; kingdom, empire.
plot, piece, patch, lot, plot, square, block; field, garth, paddock, close, inclosure.
clime (*poetic*), realm, latitude, meridian, zone, climate.
II. *Adjectives.* regional, sectional local, parochial; regionalistic, regionary, topographical; insular, provincial, territorial.

See also HABITATION, INCLOSURE, LIMIT, PLACE, SPACE.

---

register, *n.* registry, minute, entry, list, roll, archives. See RECORD.
register, *v.* enroll, enter, book; depict, portray, delineate. See LIST, RECORD.
registrar, *n.* register, clerk, official recorder. See RECORDER.
registration, *n.* registry, enrollment. booking, entry. See RECORD.

REGRESSION.—I. *Nouns.* **regression,** retrogression, regressiveness, retreat, withdrawal, retirement, recession, retrogradation, recidivism, relapse, reversion countermotion, countermovement, countermarch, remigration; deterioration tergiversation backsliding, fall, declension.

reflux, refluence, backwater, ebb, return, *volte-face* (*F.*), rebound, recoil, reëntry, regress; contrary; flexure, inflexion (*math.*).

II. *Verbs.* **regress,** go back, recede, return, retreat, retire, retrograde, revert, back, back out (*colloq.*), crawfish (*U. S. slang*), balk, shy, jib, retrogress, back down (*colloq.*), withdraw, recoil, rebound; turn back, fall back, put back, lose ground; drop astern, backwater, put about (*naut.*), veer, double, wheel, countermarch; ebb, regurgitate.

III. *Adjectives.* **regressive,** backward, recessive, retrograde, retrogressive, returning, refluent, reflex, resilient, contraclockwise, counterclockwise; **balky,** perverse, recidivous, reactionary, declining.

retroactive, retrospective, *ex post facto* (*as law: L.*).

IV. *Adverbs.* **regressively,** recessively, etc. (see *adjectives*); back, backward *or* backwards, reflexively, to the right-about, *à reculons* (*F.*), *à rebours* (*F.*).

See also RECESSION, RECOIL.—*Antonyms.* See PROGRESSION.

REGRET.—I. *Nouns.* **regret,** repining; sorrow, grief, misgiving, concern, remorse, contrition, mourning, lamentation, repentance, penitence, compunction, self-condemnation, self-accusation, self-reproach; bitterness, heartburning, rue, disappointment, vexation, dissatisfaction.

homesickness, nostalgia, *mal du pays* (*F.*), *maladie du pays* (*F.*), nostalgy (*rare*), *Heimweh* (*Ger.*).

II. *Verbs.* **regret,** deplore, bewail, lament, grieve, mourn, wail, sorrow, *infandum renovare dolorem* (*L.*); repine, rue, rue the day, repent, leave an aching void.

III. *Adjectives.* **regretful,** repining, sorrowful, sorry, penitent, mournful, compunctious, remorseful, apologetic, rueful; homesick, nostalgic.

See also LAMENTATION, PENITENCE.—*Antonyms.* See CONTENT, INSENSITIVENESS.

REGULARITY.—I. *Nouns.* **regularity,** conformity, compliance, adaptation, conformation; harmony, symmetry, accordance, correspondence, congruity, etc. (see *adjectives*).

periodicity, regular recurrence, reoccurrence, return, intermittence *or* intermittency, alternation, rhythm; oscillation, vibration; beat, ictus, pulse, pulsation; systole and diastole; round, revolution, cycle, rota (*rare in this sense*), rotation, bout, turn; routine, punctuality, steadiness.

anniversary, yearly (*or* periodic) observance, celebration, commemoration; biennial, triennial, quadrennial, quinquennial, sextennial, septennial, octennial, decennial; jubilee, centennial, centenary, bicentennial, bicentenary, tercentenary; birthday, natal day, fête day, saint's day, feast, festival, fast, holiday.

Christmas, yule, *Noel* (*F.*), yuletide, Christmastide; New Year's Day, Ash Wednesday, Maundy Thursday, Good Friday, Easter; Halloween, All Saints' Day, Allhallows, Hallowmas, Allhallowmas; All Souls' Day; Candlemas; Memorial (*or* Decoration) Day, Independence Day, Labor Day, Thanksgiving, ground-hog day, woodchuck day; St. Swithin's Day, Midsummer Day, May Day; Dewali (*Hindu*), Holi (*Hindu*); Muhurram, Ramadan, Bairam (*all Moham.*); leap year, bissextile.

rhythm, cadence, cadency, *rhythmus* (*L.*), lilt, swing, measured movement, measure, harmonious correlation; regular recurrence, periodicity.

II. *Verbs.* **regularize,** normalize, systematize, methodize, symmetrize, standardize; regulate, dispose, adjust, arrange.

recur, reoccur, reappear, occur again, come round again, return, revolve, alternate, intermit; pulsate, beat.

III. *Adjectives.* **regular,** normal, customary, typical, natural, habitual, usual, conventional, uniform, constant, steady, unvarying, punctual; methodical, orderly, systematic *or* systematical; regular as clockwork.

symmetrical, symmetric, even, well-balanced, well-proportioned, harmonious, congruous, accordant, consistent.

permanent, fixed, lasting, standing (*as an army*), established, settled (*as, a regular profession*).

thorough, genuine, indubitable, unmitigated, complete, perfect (*as, he is a regular brick: colloq.*).

periodic, periodical, cyclic, cyclical, recurrent, recurring, epochal, termly (*rare*), seasonal, serial, intermittent, rhythmic; pulsatile, throbbing, pulsating, pulsative, pulsatory; alternate, every other; every.

IV. *Adverbs.* **regularly**, normally, etc. (see *adjectives*); at regular intervals, at stated times, at fixed (*or* established) periods; *de die in diem* (*L.*), from day to day, day by day.
by turns, in turn, in rotation, alternately, off and on, ride and tie, hitch and hike, round and round.

See also ARRANGEMENT, COMPLETENESS, ORDER, OSCILLATION, RULE, STRAIGHTNESS, SYMMETRY, UNIFORMITY.—*Antonyms.* See IRREGULARITY.

---

rehabilitate, *v.* reconstruct, repair, restore, reinstate, reëstablish. See RESTITUTION.
rehearse, *v.* drill, try, essay, test, verify; repeat, tell over, enumerate, recapitulate, describe. See EXPERIMENT, REPETITION.
reign, *v.* rule, sway, govern, administer; prevail. See AUTHORITY.
reins, *n. pl.* lines (*U. S. and dial. Eng.*), ribbons (*colloq.*). See PRISON (*restraining devices*).

REJECTION.—I. *Nouns.* **rejection,** repudiation, disallowance, disapproval; denial, disbelief, disproof, refutation, disproval; discard, dismissal, repellence, repulsion, repulse, exclusion; refusal, declination, declension, veto.
II. *Verbs.* **reject,** set (*or* lay) aside, give up, exclude, except; pluck up, spurn, cast out; repudiate, scout, disbelieve, deny, disprove, disclaim, discard, jilt, repel, cast off, relegate, remove, eject, cashier, dismiss, pluck (*as a candidate*), plow (*Eng. university cant*), send to the right about; fling overboard, cast (throw, *or* toss) to the winds.
decline, refuse, negative, disallow, disapprove, withhold consent, turn down (*slang*), veto; abnegate, abjure, renounce.
III. *Adjectives.* **rejected,** excluded, etc. (see *verbs*); out of the question, not to be thought of; forsaken, jilted.

See also EJECTION, EXCLUSION, NEGATION, REFUSAL.—*Antonyms.* See ASSENT, CHOICE, OFFER, RECEIVING, RECEPTION.

REJOICING.—I. *Nouns.* **rejoicing,** exultation, exultance *or* exultancy, delight, joy, elation, gladness, triumph, jubilation, flush, reveling, frolicsomeness, heyday, mirth, merrymaking, pæan; *Te Deum* (*L.*), thanksgiving; congratulation.
smile, simper, smirk, grin; broad grin, sardonic grin.
laughter, giggle, titter, snicker, snigger, crow, chuckle, shout; cachinnation, guffaw, burst (fit, shout, roar, *or* peal) of laughter.
cheer, shout, hurrah, huzza, cheering; yell (*U. S. and Canada*), college yell; tiger (*colloq.*).
II. *Verbs.* **rejoice,** congratulate oneself, hug oneself, clap one's hands, fling up one's cap, dance, skip, leap with joy; sing, carol, chirrup, chirp, hurrah, cry for joy, delight, joy, exult, triumph, make merry, jubilate; crow, vaunt, gloat.
[*to give joy to*] **gladden,** cheer, delight, please, blithen, transport, exhilarate.
smile, simper, smirk, grin, laugh in one's sleeve.
laugh, giggle, titter, snigger, snicker, chuckle, cackle; burst out, shout, roar, shake (*or* split) one's sides, cachinnate.
III. *Adjectives.* **rejoicing,** jubilant, exultant, triumphant, flushed, elated; laughing, convulsed (*or* shaking) with laughter.
IV. *Adverbs.* **rejoicingly,** jubilantly, etc. (see *adjectives*); laughingly; in fits of laughter.
V. *Interjections.* **hurrah!** huzza! hip, hip, hurrah! three cheers! banzai! (*Jap.*), *viva!* (*It.*), *vive!* (*F.*), *vivat!* (*F.*).

See also AMUSEMENT, CELEBRATION.—*Antonyms.* See LAMENTATION.

---

rejoin, *v.* reply, respond, retort, rebut; join, meet, unite. See ANSWER, ASSEMBLAGE.
rejoinder, *n.* response, reply, retort, rebuttal. See ANSWER.
rejuvenescence, *n.* rejuvenation, reinvigoration, renewal of youth. See YOUTH.

RELAPSE.—I. *Nouns.* **relapse,** lapse, reversion, falling back, retrogradation, retrogression; recidivism (*criminology*), recidivity, recrudescence, backsliding, apostasy, fall, deterioration.
II. *Verbs.* **relapse,** lapse, fall (*or* slip) back, have a relapse, be overcome, be overtaken, yield again to, fall again to, sink again, return, revert, regress, retrograde, recidivate (*rare*), backslide, fall.
III. *Adjectives.* **relapsing,** recidivous, recidivistic, recrudescent, retrograde, retrogressive; backsliding.
See also DETERIORATION, REGRESSION, REVERSION.—*Antonyms.* See RESTORATION.

RELATION.—I. *Nouns.* **relation,** narration, recital, rehearsal, account, report, narrative, tale, statement, description, detail, explanation.
connection, bearing, relevancy, relevance, application, pertinency, reference, concern, respect; alliance, nearness, correlation, propinquity, interconnection, rapport, interrelation, applicability, appositeness, apposition, relationship, relativity, reciprocal dependence, relative position; analogy, association, similarity, homogeneity.
ratio, proportion, commensurateness, comparison, commensurability, comparative relation.
link, tie, bond, couple, coupler, coupling; *liaison* (*F.: mil.*), intercommunication.
relationship, kinship, consanguinity, blood, affinity, kindred.
relative, kin, kinsman, kinswoman, connection, cognate (*mother's side*), agnate (*father's side*), affine (*by marriage*), sib (*rare*), in-law (*colloq. or jocose*).
II. *Verbs.* **relate,** recount, narrate, tell, recite, rehearse, report, state, describe, detail, explain, mention, repeat, record, chronicle.
connect, associate, unite with, link, bind, correlate; bring into relation with, bring to bear upon.
relate to, refer to, bear upon, regard, concern, touch, affect, pertain to, belong to, appertain to (*formal*).
III. *Adjectives.* **related,** connected, associated, affiliated, allied, collateral, cognate, akin, paronymous, (*said of words*), conjugate, affinitive, correlative, conjoint; *en rapport* (*F.*).
[*of persons*] **akin,** kindred, allied, consanguineous; affinal (*by marriage*), affined, affine; cognate (*esp. on mother's side*), agnate (*esp. on father's side*), german (*as, cousin*-german), sib (*archaic and Scot.*).
relative, pertaining, referring, referential, connective, relating to, belonging to, referable to, in respect to, with reference to; germane, relevant, pertinent, applicable, in the same category, equiparant (*rare*).
comparative, not absolute; approximative, approximating, approximate, near, comparable, contrastive; proportional, proportionate, proportionable; allusive.
IV. *Adverbs.* **relatively,** comparatively, etc. (see *adjectives*).
V. *Prepositions.* **concerning,** as regards, respecting, pertaining to, with regard to, as to, as for, with relation to, anent, about, in respect to, in (*or* with) reference to, in connection with, in the matter of.
See also AGREEMENT, CONSANGUINITY, CORRELATION DESCRIPTION, NEARNESS, RESPECT, SIMILARITY.—*Antonyms.* See IRRELATION.

---

relax, *v.* loosen, abate, weaken, mitigate, relent, soften, appease, lessen; slacken, unbend, rest. See GIVING, REPOSE.
relaxation, *n.* recreation, diversion; loosening; mitigation. See AMUSEMENT, INCOHERENCE, MODERATION.
relaxed, *adj.* lax, loose, slack, negligent, careless, remiss. See LAXITY.
release, *v.* free, let go, discharge, acquit, exempt, loose, liberate. See LIBERATION.
relegate, *v.* banish, remove, transpose; assign, consign. See EXCLUSION, TRANSFER.
relent, *v.* soften, submit, relax, forbear. See PIETY.
relentless, *adj.* impenitent, remorseless, unyielding; unfeeling, merciless, ruthless, unpitying, malevolent. See IMPENITENCE, MALEVOLENCE.
relevant, *adj.* relative, apposite, germane, applicable, pertinent, apropos. See RELATION

reliable, *adj.* trustworthy, dependable, unfailing. See See CERTAINTY, SAFETY.
reliance, *n.* assurance, confidence, credence, trust, dependence, hope. See BELIEF.
relic, *n.* token, memento, keepsake; trace, survival, remains. See MEMORY, RECORD.

RELIEF.—I. *Nouns.* **relief,** deliverance, alleviation, mitigation, palliation, assuagement, amelioration, allayment (*rare*), lightening, softening, easement; lenitive, palliative, restorative, assuasive.
solace, consolation, comfort, diversion, variety, relaxation, rest, ease, respite.
succor, aid, help, assistance, encouragement, support, reënforcement, service; release, rescue.
redress, reparation, amends, rectification, correction, righting, indemnification, repair, remedy.
prominence, projection, protrusion, excrescency, embossment.
[*in sculpture*] **relievo,** *relievo* (*It.*); high relief, *alto-relievo* (*It.*); half relief, *mezzo-rilievo* (*It.*); low relief, bas-relief, *basso-relievo* (*It.*); *stiacciato* (*It.; as on coins*); hollow relief, *cavo-rilievo* (*It.*), *intaglio rilevato* (*It.*), cœlanaglyphic sculpture (*as used by the Egyptians*); cameo (*opposite of* intaglio).
[*distinctness of outline*] **vividness,** sharpness, distinctness, definition, prominence (*as, in bold* relief).
II. *Verbs.* **relieve,** ease, alleviate, palliate, soothe, salve, soften, assuage, allay, charm; lessen, abate, mitigate, lighten, diminish, remove, free; remedy, cure, restore.
cheer, comfort, console, solace, hearten, give comfort, encourage, gladden, divert, vary, inspirit, enliven, strengthen, invigorate; pat on the back.
succor, aid, help, assist, support, sustain; deliver, rescue.
redress, repair, remedy, readjust, right, indemnify, make amends to (*or* for).
[*to take one's turn*] **free,** release, disengage, spell, take the place of, relay (*as, to* relieve *a sentry*).
III. *Adjectives.* **relieving,** soothing, assuaging, assuasive, palliative, lenitive, balmy, balsamic, soft, gentle, comforting; curative, remedial.

See also AID, CONVEXITY, FINE ARTS, PLEASURABLENESS.—*Antonyms.* See AGGRAVATION.

---

religion, *n.* godliness, faith, worship; theology. See PIETY.
religious, *adj.* pious, devout, godly, holy, spiritual; conscientious, strict, scrupulous; theological, canonical, divine. See PIETY, PROBITY, THEOLOGY.
religious, *n.* monk, friar, nun, cenobite. See CELIBACY, CLERGY.

RELINQUISHMENT.—I. *Nouns.* **relinquishment,** abandonment, desertion, dereliction, defection, secession, withdrawal; discontinuance, renunciation, abrogation, resignation, retirement, demission, abdication; surrender, yielding, cession.
derelict (*a thing abandoned, as a tract of land or a ship*), jetsam, jettison; dereliction (*new land gained by the retreat of a body of water*); waif, foundling; outcast, human wreck.
II. *Verbs.* **relinquish,** give up, abandon, desert, forsake, leave in the lurch; go back on (*colloq.*); leave, quit, vacate, resign, demit (*as an office or a Masonic lodge membership*), cease from, surrender, yield, cede, let go, forbear, lay down, abdicate; give away, dispose of, part with, dismiss; throw (*or* fling) away, jettison; maroon.
renounce, forego, waive, have done with, drop, nol-pros (*law*), withdraw, revoke, recall, reject, cast off, lay aside, set aside, spare, discard, disclaim, disavow, deny, disown, repudiate.
[*in debate*] give up the point (*or* argument), pass to the order of the day, move the previous question, table, table the motion.
III. *Adjectives.* **relinquished,** abandoned, etc. (see *verbs*); cast off, derelict. ownerless; disowned, disinherited, divorced.

See also GIVING, RIDDANCE.—*Antonyms.* See PURSUIT, RETENTION.

relish, *n.* appetizer, seasoning; gratification, satisfaction, zest. See CONDIMENT, PLEASURE.

reluctance, *n.* distaste, disinclination, unwillingness, aversion, repugnance. See DISLIKE.

rely, *v.* trust, depend, confide, hope. See REPOSE, [1]REST.

REMAINDER.—I. *Nouns.* **remainder,** residue, remains, remnant, rest, relic; leavings, odds and ends, residuum, *caput mortuum* (*L.*), educt, result; dregs, draff, lees, heeltap, refuse, stubble, ruins, wreck, skeleton, fossil, stump, butt (*as of a cigar*), rump.

surplus, excess, overplus, surplusage, balance (*commercial slang*); superfluity, redundance; survival.

[*in plural*] **remains,** relics (*now rare in this sense*), dead body, corpse, organic remains, reliquiæ; *disjecta membra* (*L.*), scattered parts; bones, ashes; posthumous works.

II. *Verbs.* **remain,** be left, survive, subsist, exist; exceed, be over.

stay, continue, last, endure; rest, tarry, wait, halt; sojourn, abide, dwell, stop, live, reside.

III. *Adjectives.* **remaining,** left, residual, residuary, surplus, remanent, supplementary, over, odd, surviving; net; superfluous, over and above, outlying, outstanding; remainder, refuse, left, left over.

See also EXISTENCE, REDUNDANCE, [1]REST.—*Antonyms.* See ADJUNCT, DECREMENT.

---

remark, *v.* utter, state, express, mention; observe, notice. See OBSERVANCE

remark, *n.* comment, observation, assertion, statement. See AFFIRMATION.

remarkable, *adj.* distinguished, noteworthy, memorable, important; rare, uncommon, unusual, extraordinary, wonderful. See GREATNESS, UNCONFORMITY.

remarkably, *adv.* singularly, uncommonly, unusually, notably, conspicuously. See GREATNESS.

REMEDY.—I. *Nouns.* **remedy,** help, aid, assistance, counteraction, relief, reparation, redress; corrective, counteractive, antifebrile, febrifuge; antipoison, antitoxin, antibody (*physiol. chem.*), antiserum (*med.*), antidote, emetic; prophylactic, antiseptic, germicide, disinfectant; restorative, specific, stimulant, tonic, pick-me-up (*colloq.*), bracer; cure, sovereign remedy panacea.

narcotic, opium, morphine; belladonna, atropine, stramonium, hyoscyamine; lactucarium,cocaine,hashish,Indian hemp, bhang (*India*), dope (*slang*); sedative.

medicine, physic, simples, drug, potion, draft, dose, bolus, pill, electuary, linoture *or* linctus, medicament, recipe, receipt, prescription; patent medicine, nostrum; elixir, balm, balsam, cordial, ptisan, tisane.

salve, ointment, oil, lenitive, lotion, embrocation, liniment.

healing art, leechcraft (*archaic*), practice of medicine, pathology, nosology, ætiology, symptomatology, therapeutics; pharmaceutics, pharmacy, pharmacology, materia medica; allopathy, homeopathy *or* homœopathy, eclecticism; surgery; osteopathy, chiropractic; faith cure, faith healing; psychiatry, psychotherapy, psychotherapeutics; vocational therapy; dentistry, dental surgery.

treatment, medical treatment, regimen, diet; dietary, dietetics; operation, the knife (*colloq.*), surgical operation; major operation.

hospital, infirmary, surgery, clinic, *maison de santé* (*F.*), *hôtel-Dieu* (*F.*), *hôpital* (*F.*), pesthouse, lazarhouse, lazaretto, lazaret; sanitarium, sanatarium, sanatorium; nursing home; springs, baths, spa; asylum, home; Red Cross.

dispensary, drug store, chemist's shop (*Brit.*).

doctor, physician, leech (*archaic*), medical man, general practitioner, medical attendant; specialist, consultant; surgeon, chirurgeon (*archaic*).

orthopedist, laparotomist; sawbones (*slang*); aurist, oculist, dentist, dental surgeon; osteopath, osteopathist; Æsculapius, Hippocrates, Galen; chiropractor, masseur (*fem.* masseuse), rubber; nurse, attendant, trained nurse, district nurse practical nurse; sister, nursing sister.

druggist, pharmacist, pharmaceutical chemist, apothecary, chemist (*Brit.*).

II. *Verbs.* remedy, cure, heal, restore, relieve, palliate; doctor (*colloq.*), minister to, treat, attend, nurse, dress (*as a wound or a wounded man*); dose, physic, drug, medicate.
redress, rectify, right, repair, renew, retrieve, correct, amend, satisfy.
III. *Adjectives.* remediable, curable, restorable, retrievable, recoverable, healable, medicable.
remedial, curative, healing, recuperative, recuperatory, restorative; sanatory, sanative, prophylactic; medical, medicinal, therapeutic, surgical; tonic, sedative, palliative, lenitive; allopathic, homeopathic, eclectic; aperient, laxative, cathartic, purgative; aseptic (*as a wound or dressing*), antiseptic, antitoxic; alexipharmic, antidotal.
dietetic, dietetical, dietary, alimentary; nutritious, nutritive; peptic, digestive, digestible.
reparative, amendatory, corrective, indemnificatory, compensatory.
See also IMPROVEMENT, RESTORATION.—*Antonyms.* See BANE, DISEASE.

---

remember, *v.* recollect, recall, retrace. See MEMORY, RETENTION.
remembrance, *n.* recollection, retrospect, reminiscence; reminder, token, souvenir, memento, keepsake. See MEMORY.
remind, *v.* suggest, hint, call up, prompt. See MEMORY.
reminder, *n.* hint, memorandum, memento, souvenir, keepsake. See MEMORY.
reminiscent, *adj.* suggestive, remindful, retrospective. See MEMORY.
remiss, *adj.* idle, indolent, shiftless, slow, tardy; lax, slack, negligent, careless. See INACTIVITY, LAXITY.
remission, *n.* cancellation, discharge; pardon, absolution. See CESSATION, FORGIVENESS.
remit, *v.* forgive, pardon, absolve, condone, release, excuse; send (*money*). See FORGIVENESS, PAYMENT.
remnant, *n.* residue, rest, trace; fragment, scrap. See REMAINDER.
remonstrance, *n.* protest, expostulation, dissuasion, reproof. See DISAPPROBATION.
remorse, *n.* compunction, qualm, repentance, regret, self-reproach. See PENITENCE.
remote, *adj.* distant, out-of-the-way, isolated; unrelated, foreign, far-fetched, inappropriate. See DISTANCE, IRRELATION.
removal, *n.* withdrawal, abandonment; elimination, dislodgment; transference, shift, change. See DEPARTURE, EXTRACTION, TRANSFER.
remove, *v.* depart, retire; displace, dismiss; reduce, smooth, raze. See DEPARTURE, DISPLACEMENT, SMOOTHNESS.
remunerate, *v.* pay, compensate, repay, requite, reimburse. See REWARD.
remunerative, *adj.* profitable, gainful, paying, lucrative; compensatory, reparative; useful, beneficial, valuable. See RECEIPT, REWARD, USE.
renaissance, *n.* awakening, rebirth, revival, regeneration. See RESTORATION.
rend, *v.* break, tear, burst, split, rupture. See DISJUNCTION.
render, *v.* give, deliver, impart, furnish, yield, surrender; explain, define, translate. See GIVING, INTERPRETATION.
renew, *v.* replace, restore, reëstablish, rebuild; refresh, revive, renovate, regenerate. See DUPLICATION, NEWNESS.
renewal, *n.* renovation, renewing; iteration, recurrence; revival, regeneration; resumption, replacement, repair. See NEWNESS, REPETITION, REPRODUCTION, RESTORATION.
renewed, *adj.* renovated, freshened; additional. See NEWNESS.
renounce, *v.* abjure, forswear, disavow, disclaim, reject, repudiate; desert, abandon, relinquish, surrender. See APOSTASY, RELINQUISHMENT, RESIGNATION.
renovate, *v.* renew, refresh, revive, repair. See NEWNESS.
renown, *n.* fame, celebrity, reputation, greatness, distinction, exaltation. See REPUTE.

renowned, *adj.* famous, eminent, distinguished, illustrious, notable. See GREATNESS.
[1]rent, *n.* tear, split, break, fissure, opening, rupture. See DISJUNCTION.
[2]rent, *n.* rental, rent roll. See RECEIPT.
reorganize, *v.* reform, remodel, reconstruct, rearrange, reëstablish. See CONVERSION, RESTORATION.
[1]repair, *v.* go, resort, betake oneself. See JOURNEY.
[2]repair, *v.* remedy, renew, restore, mend, amend, recruit. See RESTORATION.
repair, *n.* reconstruction, mending, reparation, renovation, renewal. See IMPROVEMENT, RESTORATION.
reparation, *n.* redress, amends, requital, recompense, restoration. See RESTITUTION.
reparative, *n.* corrective, amendatory, compensatory. See REMEDY.
repartee, *n.* reply, retort, rejoinder; banter. See ANSWER, WIT.
repay, *v.* pay back, refund, reimburse, requite, recompense. See PAYMENT.
repayment, *n.* repaying, reimbursement, remuneration, requital. See PAYMENT.
repeal, *v.* recall, revoke, rescind, cancel. See ANNULMENT.
repeat, *v.* iterate, recur, echo, recite, rehearse. See FREQUENCY, REPETITION.
repeated, *adj.* frequent, recurrent, redundant, tautological. See REPETITION.
repel, *v.* dispel, disperse, scatter; sicken, disgust, revolt; rebuff, repulse. See DEFENSE. DISLIKE, REPULSION.
repellent, *adj.* repugnant, grim, harsh, forbidding; hideous, unattractive. See HARDNESS, UGLINESS.
repent, *v.* regret, rue. See PENITENCE.
repentant, *adj.* penitent, contrite, remorseful, sorry. See PENITENCE.

REPETITION.—I. *Nouns.* **repetition,** iteration, recapitulation, reiteration, recurrence, return, renewal, rehearsal, duplication, reduplication, monotony harping, monotone, ding-dong (*colloq.*), jingle; recurrence, reappearance; succession, run; alliteration; vibration, resonance; battology, tautology, redundance, pleonasm; *rifacimento* (*It.*), *réchauffé* (*F.*).
echo, reverberation, repercussion, reflection *or* reflexion, return, reply, reëcho.
refrain, burden (*of a song*), ritornelle (*mus.*), *ritornello* (*It.*), chorus, undersong, bob; tag, catchword, stock phrase.
twice-told tale, old story, chestnut (*slang*), old song, old stuff (*slang*); second edition.
recital,mention,retailing, recounting, narration, account, enumeration; rehearsal.
copy, reproduction, replica, duplicate, double, facsimile.
II. *Verbs.* **repeat,** iterate, reiterate, reproduce, echo, reëcho, drum, harp upon, hammer; resume, return to, recapitulate, reword, retell, paraphrase; renew, redouble, reduplicate, duplicate, battologize.
recur, return, reappear; revert, turn back, go back, come back, be repeated.
recite, narrate, relate, tell over, tell, rehearse, recount, enumerate, state, record.
III. *Adjectives.* **repetitious,** repetitive, repetitional, repetitionary, repeated, recurrent, recurring, reduplicative, frequent, incessant; tautological, redundant, pleonastic.
monotonous, harping, iterative, unvaried, singsong, ding-dong (*colloq.*), dreary, wearisome.
aforesaid, aforenamed, above-mentioned, aforementioned, said, forenamed, forementioned, beforesaid (*archaic*), named.
IV. *Adverbs.* **repeatedly,** often, again, anew, afresh, once more, over; ditto, encore, *de novo* (*L.*), *da capo* (*It.*), bis; again and again, over and over, frequently.
See also AFFIRMATION, COPY, FREQUENCY, HABIT, IMITATION, REPRODUCTION, RESTORATION, SIMILARITY.—*Antonyms.* See FEWNESS, UNITY.

---

repine, *v.* mope, pine, fret, complain. See DEJECTION.
replace, *v.* restore, repay, return, reinstate; supplant, supersede. See RESTORATION, SUBSTITUTE.

repletion, *n.* profusion, satiation, saturation, glut, surfeit. See SATIETY.
reply, *n.* response, retort, rejoinder, acknowledgment, repartee. See ANSWER.
report, *v.* announce, narrate, proclaim, publish, broadcast, herald, advertise; note, write. See INFORMATION, PUBLICATION, RECORD.
report, *n.* account, statement, record; advice, tidings; rumor, hearsay; fame reputation; clap, explosion. See DESCRIPTION, INFORMATION, NEWS, REPUTE, SNAP.
reporter, *n.* journalist, newspaperman; registrar. See BOOK, MESSENGER, RECORDER.
[1]**repose,** *v.* lay, place, deposit, put, set, rest. See LOCATION.

REPOSE.—I. *Nouns.* **repose,** rest, quiet, calm, stillness, tranquillity, quietness, peacefulness, peace; inactivity, leisure, relaxation; breathing time, halt, stay, pause, respite; sleep, slumber, doze.
composure (*of manner*), self-possession, self-command, ease, dignity, unconstraint, freedom, facility.
day of rest, *dies non* (*L.*), Sabbath, Lord's day, Sunday, First day; holiday, red-letter day, gala day; vacation, recess.
II. *Verbs.* [2]**repose,** rest, take rest, take one's ease, lie, settle, couch, lie down, recline, go to rest (bed, *or* sleep), sleep, slumber.
relax, unbend, unbrace, slacken, breathe, take breath, rest upon one's oars, pause; take a holiday, shut up shop, take it easy; lie fallow.
rely, confide, trust, count upon, depend, bank, build, lean.
III. *Adjectives.* **reposed,** calm, tranquil, peaceful, composed, reposeful, quiet unstrained, relaxed.
holiday, festal; ferial (*rare*); sabbatic *or* sabbatical.
IV. *Adverbs.* **reposedly,** calmly, etc. (see *adjectives*); at rest.
See also CESSATION, INACTION, INACTIVITY, LEISURE, [1]REST.—*Antonyms.* See EXERTION.

---

repository, *n.* depository, storeroom, storehouse, vault. See RECEPTACLE.
reprehensible, *adj.* blamable, culpable, blameworthy. See GUILT.

REPRESENTATION.—I. *Nouns.* **representation,** depiction, imitation, illustration, delineation, imagery, portraiture; design, designing; art, fine arts; exhibition, delineation, show, sight; spectacle.
personation, simulation, impersonation, personification; dramatic performance.
description, sketch, statement, relation, account, narration, report.
[*argument against something*] **protest,** protestation, objection, expostulation, remonstrance, challenge, kick (*colloq.*), declaration, assertion, asseveration, expostulation.
[*mechanical representation*] **photography,** heliography (*still used in photo-engraving*), daguerreotypy; X-ray photography, radiography, skiagraphy, telephotography; television.
photograph, photo (*colloq.*), print; boudoir, cabinet, carte de visite (*pl.* cartes de visite), diamond, imperial, panel, snapshot, ping-pong (*cant*); daguerreotype, platinotype, cyanotype, telephoto.
radiograph, X-ray photograph, X-ray (*colloq.*), radiogram, skiagraph *or* sciagraph, skiagram *or* sciagram.
drawing, picture, sketch, draft *or* draught; tracing, copy.
image, effigy, icon, symbol, emblem; portrait, likeness, resemblance, reproduction, facsimile.
figure, figurehead, puppet, doll, manikin, lay figure, model, marionette, fantoccini, waxwork; statue, statuette, bust.
map, plan, chart; diagram; ground plan, projection, elevation; atlas, outline view, bird's-eye view.
draftsman *or* draughtsman, sketcher, delineator, drawer, designer, artist.
photographer, daguerreotypist; photographist, radiographer, X-ray photographer, skiagrapher.
II. *Verbs.* **represent,** delineate, depict, portray, picture limn, draw, sketch, figure, shape, paint, sculpture, mold *or* mould, engrave, trace, copy, reproduce

photograph, snapshot, film (*as for motion pictures*), illustrate; symbolize, typify, exemplify.

personate, impersonate, dress up (*colloq.*), pose as, act, play, assume a character, personify; mimic, imitate; stand for, act for, stand in the place of, be substitute (*or* deputy) for.

[*represent in words*] **describe**, define, outline, adumbrate, shadow forth, sketch, exhibit, show, present; relate, narrate, report, state, express, set forth, depict, portray.

See also COPY, DEPUTY, DESCRIPTION, DRAMA, FIGURE, FINE ARTS, IMITATION, INDICATION, MANIFESTATION.

REPRESENTATIVE.—I. *Nouns.* **representative**, agent, delegate, commissioner, emissary, envoy, messenger; trustee, consignee, nominee; deputation, committee.

factor, steward, bailiff, clerk, secretary, attorney, solicitor (*law*), proctor; broker, go-between, middleman, negotiator.

diplomatist, diplomat, ambassador, plenipotentiary, diplomatic agent, resident, consul, legate, attaché, congressman, congresswoman, senator, representative, member of parliament, M.P., assemblyman, councilor.

salesman, traveler, traveling salesman, commercial traveler, drummer (*U. S.*), traveling man; retail salesman (*or* saleswoman), clerk (*U. S.*).

II. *Adjectives.* **representative**, representing, acting for, delegated, deputed, delegatory, procuratory, agential (*rare*); consular, ambassadorial.

typical, typifying, portraying, similar, like, imitative, illustrative, descriptive, figurative.

See also AGENT, DEPUTY.

---

repress, *v.* check, restrain, constrain, restrict, curb, control, suppress, subdue. See RESTRAINT.

reprieve, *n.* pardon, remission; respite, suspension. See ACQUITTAL, FORGIVENESS, LATENESS.

reprimand, *n.* blame, censure, reproach, reproof, rebuke. See DISAPPROBATION.

reprisal, *n.* requital, retaliation. See INTERCHANGE.

reproach, *v.* blame, censure, rebuke, upbraid, condemn. See ACCUSATION.

reproach, *n.* blame, censure, disapproval, reprehension; stigma, slur, disgrace, dishonor. See DISAPPROBATION, DISREPUTE.

reprobate, *n.* sinner, rascal, scoundrel, scamp. See BAD MAN.

REPRODUCTION.—I. *Nouns.* **reproduction**, renovation, restoration, renewal, revival, regeneration, revivification, palingenesis, recreation, resuscitation, reanimation, resurrection, resurgence, reappearance, generation, propagation, multiplication.

copy, repetition, reconstruction, representation, imitation.

II. *Verbs.* **reproduce**, revive, renovate, renew, restore, repeat, regenerate, revivify, resuscitate, reanimate, refashion; multiply, propagate, generate.

copy, imitate, repeat, reconstruct, represent, portray.

III. *Adjectives.* **reproductive**, progenitive, generative, germinative, proliferous, conceptive, gametal (*biol.*); renascent, resurgent, reappearing; hydra-headed.

See also COPY, IMITATION, PRODUCTION, RESTORATION, SIMILARITY.—*Antonyms.* See DESTRUCTION.

---

reproof, *n.* censure, rebuke, admonition, correction, reprimand. See DISAPPROBATION.

reprove, *v.* scold, chide, rebuke, admonish, correct. See DISAPPROBATION.

reptile, *n.* reptilian, saurian, ophidian, snake, lizard, etc.; groveler, viper (*fig.*). See ANIMAL, KNAVE.

republic, *n.* democracy, state, commonwealth. See AUTHORITY, MANKIND.

repudiate, *v.* disclaim, protest, ignore, nullify; disown, renounce, reject, divorce. See NONOBSERVANCE, REJECTION.

repugnance, *n.* contradictoriness, antagonism, antipathy, aversion, detestation. See CONTRARIETY, DISLIKE, REPULSION.
repugnant, *adj.* incompatible, inconsistent, contradictory; opposed, hostile; distasteful, offensive, repulsive. See DISAGREEMENT, DISLIKE, REPULSION.

REPULSION.—I. *Nouns.* **repulsion,** repellence *or* repellency, driving back (*or* away), repulse, rejection, rebuff, spurning, discarding.
repugnance, aversion, antipathy, dislike, loathing, abhorrence, hatred, detestation, disgust; hostility, antagonism.
II. *Verbs.* **repulse,** repel, drive back, beat back, oppose, resist, chase; dispel, send off, send away, reject, discard.
rebuff, snub, refuse, deny, repudiate; keep at arm's length, turn one's back upon, give the cold shoulder.
III. *Adjectives.* **repulsive,** repellent, repelling; harsh, cold, frigid, reserved, stern, unsympathetic, forbidding (*as,* repulsive *manners: archaic in this sense*).
repugnant, offensive, loathsome, disgusting, abhorrent, hateful, odious, revolting, nauseating.
See also DISLIKE, FAILURE, HATE, REFUSAL, RESISTANCE, UGLINESS.—*Antonyms* See ATTRACTION.

REPUTE.—I. *Nouns.* **repute,** reputation, distinction, mark, name, figure, note, notability, éclat, "the bubble reputation" (*As You Like It*), vogue, celebrity, fame, report, renown, popularity, *aura popularis* (*L.*), public esteem, popular favor, glory, honor; credit, prestige, account, regard, respect.
dignity, stateliness, impressiveness, solemnity, grandeur, luster, splendor, nobility, nobleness, excellence, majesty, sublimity.
rank, standing, precedence, *pas* (*F.*), station, place, status, position, order, grade, degree, caste, condition.
eminence, greatness, height, prominence, conspicuousness, importance, celebrity, preëminence, supereminence, elevation, exaltation; dedication, consecration, ordination, enthronement.
[*person of repute*] **celebrity,** worthy, hero, man of mark (*or* rank), lion, notability, notable, personality, somebody, *rara avis* (*L.*), "the observed of all observers" (*Hamlet*), cynosure, center of attraction; "a mother in Israel" (*Bible*); scholar, *savant* (*F.*), paragon, star, pillar of the state (*or* church); "the choice and master spirits of this age" (*Julius Cæsar*), *élite* (*F.*), constellation galaxy.
ornament, honor, feather in one's cap, halo, aureole, nimbus; "blushing honors" (*Henry VIII*), laurels.
[*posthumous fame*] **commemoration,** remembrance, niche in the temple of fame, memory, celebration, canonization, enshrinement, glorification, immortality, immortal name, *magni nominis umbra* (*L.*).
II. *Verbs.* **repute,** account, reckon, think, consider, esteem, regard, call, judge, deem, believe, hold: *usually in passive.*
be distinguished, shine, shine forth, figure, cut a figure, cut a dash (*colloq.*), flourish, flaunt, acquire (*or* gain) honor, play first fiddle, bear the palm, take precedence; win laurels (*or* golden opinions).
surpass, outdo, outstrip, excel, outrival, outvie, eclipse, overshadow, outshine, throw into the shade.
emulate, rival, vie with, compete with.
honor, give (do, *or* pay) honor to, accredit, dignify, glorify, pledge, toast, drink; lionize, look up to, exalt, aggrandize, elevate, exalt to the skies, ennoble, enthrone, signalize, immortalize, deify; consecrate, dedicate to, devote to; enshrine, inscribe, blazon.
III. *Adjectives.* **reputable,** estimable, worthy, honorable, respectable, creditable; in good odor, in favor, in high favor.
distinguished, noted, of note, honored, popular, remarkable, notable, celebrated, renowned, famous, famed, *distingué* (*F.*), far-famed, illustrious, glorious, splendid, brilliant, radiant.
eminent, prominent, conspicuous, towering, foremost, great, peerless, preeminent, dignified, proud, noble, honorable, lordly, grand, magnificent, stately, august, princely, imposing, solemn, transcendent, majestic, sacred, sublime, heroic, *sans peur et sans reproche* (*F.*).

imperishable, deathless, immortal, undying, amaranthine, unfading, fadeless, *œre perennius* (*L.*).
reputed, supposed, imagined, conjectural, suppositive, putative (*esp. tech.*).
IV. *Interjections.* **hail!** all hail! *ave!* (*L.*), *viva!* (*It.*), *vive!* (*F.*), long life to! glory be to! honor be to!

See also APPROBATION, EXPERT, IMPORTANCE, MASTER, NOBILITY, ODOR, PROBITY, SAVORINESS, TROPHY.—*Antonyms.* See DISREPUTE.

REQUEST.—I. *Nouns.* **request,** solicitation, invitation, call, petition, suit, prayer, entreaty, beseechment, obsecration, impetration, obtestation, importunity, imploration, supplication, invocation; requisition, claim, demand, interpellation.
proposal, motion, overture, advancement, application, suggestion, offer, instance, submission, proposition, canvass, address, appeal.
II. *Verbs.* **request,** ask, beg, crave, sue, pray, petition, solicit, canvass; invite, bid, summon; beg leave, beg a boon, apply to, call to, call for, order, requisition, indent, make a request, make application, claim, demand.
entreat, beseech, plead, supplicate, implore, seek (*archaic*), conjure, adjure; apostrophize, cry to, kneel to, appeal to; invoke, evoke; press, urge, tease, besiege, importune, dun, clamor for, cry aloud, cry for help.
III. *Adjectives.* **requesting,** beseeching, etc. (see *verbs*); precatory, precative, supplicatory, suppliant, supplicant, postulant; solicitous, urgent, clamorous, importunate; cap in hand.
IV. *Interjections.* **please,** prithee (*archaic*), I pray thee (*archaic*), do, pray, be so good as, be good enough, have the goodness, vouchsafe (*archaic*), will you, if you please.

See also COMMAND, INQUIRY, WILL, WORSHIP.—*Antonyms.* See DEPRECATION, REFUSAL.

REQUIREMENT.—I. *Nouns.* **requirement,** need, want, requisite, essential, needfulness, essentiality, necessity, exigency, urgency, indispensability, compulsion, extremity, *sine que non* (*L.*), stress, pinch, case of need, case of life or death, desideratum.
demand, requisition, request, call, claim; run, sale, market, call for.
mandate, order, command, injunction, charge, precept, direction, bidding, behest, decree, ultimatum.
II. *Verbs.* **require,** need, want, stand in need of, call for, lack, desire.
demand, requisition, exact, claim; direct, bid, order, command, enjoin, decree.
III. *Adjectives.* **requisite,** needful, necessary, indispensable, imperative, essential, called for; in demand, in request, requisitory.
urgent, exigent, pressing, instant, crying, insistent.
IV. *Adverbs.* of necessity, *ex necessitate rei* (*L.*); at a pinch.

See also COMMAND, COMPULSION, DESIRE, DUTY, INSUFFICIENCY, REQUEST, TAKING.—*Antonyms.* See CONSENT, SUBMISSION.

---

requisite, *adj.* necessary, needful, essential, indispensable. See REQUIREMENT.
requisite, *n.* essential, necessity, vital part. See REQUIREMENT, SECRET.
requisition, *n.* claim, demand, request, order. See REQUIREMENT.
requital, *n.* return, compensation, recompense; desert, revenge, reprisal, retribution. See INTERCHANGE, RETALIATION.
requite, *v.* avenge, retaliate; repay, compensate, recompense. See REVENGE, REWARD.
rescue, *v.* release, extricate, deliver, liberate, ransom, free, save. See DELIVERANCE.
research, *n.* investigation, analysis, study. See INQUIRY.
resemblance, *n.* likeness, semblance, analogy, affinity, agreement. See SIMILARITY.
resemble, *v.* match, parallel, look like, be like, be similar, agree. See SIMILARITY.

RESENTMENT.—I. *Nouns.* **resentment,** displeasure, animosity, anger, choler, wrath, ire, indignation, exasperation, vexation, annoyance, irritation, irascibility, warmth, ferment, excitement, ebullition; asperity, acrimony, bitterness, virulence, spleen, bile, gall, acerbity, soreness; dudgeon, pique, umbrage, huff, pet, tiff, tantrum (*colloq.*), sulks; fit, angry mood, wrathful indignation; enmity, hatred, hate, ill will, malignity, revenge.
fury, rage, vehemence, *acharnement* (*F.*), towering rage, passion; outburst, explosion, paroxysm, storm, violence, vials of wrath; hot blood, high words.
Furies, Erinyes (*sing.* Erinys), Eumenides: Alecto, Megæra, Tisiphone.
[*cause of resentment*] **provocation,** affront, offense, indignity, insult, slight, grudge; last straw, sore subject; buffet, blow, box on the ear, rap on the knuckles; ill turn, outrage, *casus belli* (*L.*).
II. *Verbs.* **resent,** take amiss, take offense, take umbrage, take exception, take in ill part; pout, frown, scowl, lower, snarl, growl, gnash, snap; redden, color; look black, look daggers.
be angry, fly into a rage, bridle up, bristle up, fire up, flare up; chafe, mantle, fume, kindle, fly out, boil, boil with indignation (*or* rage); rage, storm, foam; hector, bully, bluster; lose one's temper; vent one's spleen (*or* rage), cut up rough (*slang*), stamp with rage, burst with anger, raise Cain (*slang*); breathe revenge.
[*to cause resentment*] **provoke,** affront, offend, give offense (*or* umbrage), hurt the feelings; insult, ruffle, heckle (*Brit.*), nettle, huff, pique, peeve (*slang*), chafe, wound, incense, inflame, enrage, anger, exasperate, irritate, excite, fret, sting, envenom, embitter, infuriate, madden, lash into fury, set by the ears; rankle.
III. *Adjectives.* **resentful,** resentive (*rare*), touchy, huffy, offended, indignant, bitter, sore, hurt, acrimonious, virulent; up in arms, on one's high ropes (*colloq.*), in high dudgeon; revengeful, malignant.
angry, wroth, irate, ireful, wrathful, irascible, fuming, raging, hot under the collar (*slang*), infuriated, *acharné* (*F.*), infuriate, rageful, convulsed with rage; fierce, wild, furious, fiery, rabid, savage, violent.
IV. *Adverbs.* **resentfully,** indignantly, etc. (see *adjectives*); in the heat (*or* height) of passion, in an ecstasy of rage.

See also DISCOURTESY, HATE, IRASCIBILITY, REVENGE, SULLENNESS, VIOLENCE.—*Antonyms.* See ENDEARMENT, INEXCITABILITY, PLEASURE.

---

reserve, *n.* restraint, aloofness, coldness, unresponsiveness, shyness, modesty; concealment, secrecy, suppression; supply, savings, provision. See DISTANCE, LATENCY, STORE.
reserved, *adj.* set apart, booked, bespoken; aloof, distant, uncommunicative, offish, cold. See DESTINY, DISTANCE.
reservoir, *n.* reserve supply, tank, cistern. See STORE.
reside, *v.* live, abide, dwell, stay, lodge, room (*U. S.*). See INHABITANT.
residence, *n.* stay, sojourn; abode, lodging, domicile, house. See HABITATION.
residue, *n.* rest, remains, remnant, leavings, surplus. See REMAINDER.

RESIGNATION.—I. *Nouns.* **resignation,** surrender, relinquishment, forsaking, retirement, abdication; renunciation, retractation, retraction, disclaimer, abandonment, abjuration, disclamation.
resignedness, acquiescence, submission, compliance, patience, endurance.
II. *Verbs.* **resign,** give up, throw up, lay down, surrender, relinquish, vacate, hand over (*as an office or a property*); retire, withdraw, quit, leave, abandon, desert; give up office, tender (*or* hand in) one's resignation, make vacant, abdicate.
renounce, forego, abjure, disclaim, disavow, disown, retract, deny, reject; wash one's hands of.
III. *Adjectives.* **resigned,** yielding, submissive, unresisting, acquiescent, compliant, submissive, passive, philosophical, reconciled.

See also [2]CONTENT, HUMILITY, INEXCITABILITY OBEDIENCE, SUBMISSION.—*Antonyms.* See ABROGATION, DISCONTENT, POSSESSION.

RESIN.—I. *Nouns.* **resin,** pine resin, rosin (*specific*), colophony *or* colophonium; gum, lac, shellac, varnish, mastic, elemi, animé, oleoresin, megilp *or* magilp, copal, japan, lacquer, sealing wax; amber, ambergris; bitumen, pitch, tar, asphalt *or* asphaltum.
II. *Adjectives.* **resinous,** resiny, rosiny, gummous, gummy, gummed, waxed, lacquered, tarry, pitched, pitchy, bituminous, asphaltic.

RESISTANCE.—I. *Nouns.* **resistance,** stand, front, withstanding, renitency, oppugnance *or* oppugnancy (*rare*), hindrance, impeding, blocking, opposition, recalcitrance, repugnance, repulsion; counter tendency, reaction, load (*mechanics*); opposing force (*as, the* resistance *of fluids*).
[*in electricity*] impedance, nonconductivity; reactance, inductive resistance.
repulse, repelling, repulsion, repercussion, rebuff, rejection, snub, refusal.
insurrection, revolt, uprising, insurgence, rebellion, revolution, *levée en masse* (*F.*), *Jacquerie* (*F. hist.*), riot, mutiny, disorder; strike, turnout (*colloq.*), lockout; boycott, interdiction, isolation; sabotage.
II. *Verbs.* **resist,** withstand, obstruct, stand against, stop, stand, stand firm, stand fast (*or* one's ground); check, hinder, frustrate, thwart, impede, counteract, neutralize, countervail; stem.
[*to strive against*] **oppose,** antagonize, oppugn (*rare*), confront, face, front, breast, encounter, grapple with, make a stand, defend, show a bold front, withstand an attack, repel, repulse; breast the wave (*or* current), stem the tide (*or* torrent); revolt, rebel, rise up in arms, strike, fly in the face of; turn out, boycott; attack, fight; *prendre le mors aux dents* (*F.*), take the bit between the teeth, sell one's life dearly, die hard, stand at bay.
III. *Adjectives.* **resistant,** resisting, resistive, opposing, recalcitrant, renitent, repulsive, repellent, repelling, refractory, repugnant; up in arms.
unyielding, indomitable, firm, stubborn, iron, tenacious, uncompromising, obdurate, hard, inflexible, immovable, inexorable, unconquerable, unsubduable, invincible.

See also ATTACK, COUNTERACTION, DEFENSE, DISOBEDIENCE, OBSTINACY, OPPOSITION, REFUSAL, WARFARE.—*Antonyms.* See OBEDIENCE, RETALIATION, SUBMISSION.

---

resistless, *adj.* irresistible, invincible, unconquerable, overpowering. See STRENGTH.

RESOLUTION.—I. *Nouns.* **resolution,** determination, resoluteness, firmness, steadfastness, constancy, tenacity, resolvedness, boldness, courage, perseverance, fortitude, obstinacy; stamina, pluck, manliness, sand (*slang*), grit (*colloq.*), backbone, clear grit, strength of mind (*or* will), iron will; energy, vigor; zeal, devotion, devotedness.
self-control, self-mastery, self-command, *aplomb* (*F.*), self-possession, self-assurance, *retenue* (*F.*), self-reliance, self-restraint, self-denial; moral strength (*or* courage).
separation, decomposition, disintegration, solution, dissolution, conversion, analysis; disentanglement, unraveling.
resolve, decision, will, purpose, finding, judgment, decree, official determination, conclusion, declaration (*as, a legislative* resolution).
[*in medicine*] **disappearance** (*as of inflammation without suppuration*), dispersion, removal, termination.
II. *Verbs.* **resolve,** determine, decide, will, purpose, make up one's mind, decide upon, form a resolution, conclude, fix, bring to a crisis, take a decisive step, take upon oneself, devote oneself to, take one's stand, stand firm, nail one's colors to the mast; insist upon, make a point of, set one's heart upon; stick at nothing, make short work of, not stick at trifles; persevere, persist, go the limit (*slang*), go the whole hog (*slang*), go all lengths, go through fire and water; "ride in the whirlwind and direct the storm" (Addison).
separate, split up, break up, disintegrate, reduce, transform, change, convert, analyze, decompose, dissolve.
solve (*as a problem*), unravel, disentangle, unfold, explain, answer, elucidate interpret, decipher; clear up, settle, dispel, banish, remove.

decide (*by a formal vote*), express, declare, determine on, conclude, decree, pass upon.

III. *Adjectives.* **resolute,** resolved, determined, strong-willed, strong-minded. self-possessed, earnest, serious; decided, peremptory, unflinching, firm, steadfast, fixed, constant, bold, sturdy, iron, game, gritty (*colloq.*), plucky, tenacious, indomitable, inexorable, relentless; obstinate, unyielding, *tenax propositi* (Horace), inflexible, unbending; set, deliberate, prepense (*chiefly in "malice prepense"*), intentional, premeditated, grim, stern, irrevocable, unalterable, unshaken.

IV. *Adverbs.* **resolutely,** in earnest, earnestly; on one's mettle, manfully, like a man; at all costs, *coûte que coûte* (*F.*).

See also CONVERSION, COURAGE, DISCOVERY, INTENTION, OBSTINACY, PERSEVERANCE, STABILITY.—*Antonyms.* See IRRESOLUTION.

RESONANCE.—I. *Nouns.* **resonance,** vibration, reverberation, reflection *or* reflexion; ringing, tintinnabulation, bell-note, ring, chime, boom, roar, clang, clangor, rumble, thunder, roll; nasality, twang; snoring, snore.

[*in music*] base, *basso* (*It.*), *basso profondo* (*It.*); barytone *or* baritone, contralto; pedal point, organ point.

II. *Verbs.* **resound,** reverberate, reëcho, sound, echo, ring in the ear, peel, vibrate, tintinnabulate, ring, chime, tinkle, jingle, chink, clink; gurgle, mutter, murmur, plash; boom, roar, thunder, roll, rumble.

III. *Adjectives.* **resonant,** resounding, reverberant, reverberating, sonorous, vibrant, ringing, plangent, roaring, booming, thunderous, thundering; deep-toned, deep-mouthed; hollow, sepulchral.

See also REPETITION, ROLL, [1]SOUND.—*Antonyms.* See NONRESONANCE.

---

resort, *v.* meet, convene, assemble, congregate; go, repair, frequent, haunt; have recourse (to). See ASSEMBLAGE, PRESENCE, USE.

resort, *n.* haunt, retreat, refuge; recourse. See HABITATION, USE.

resound, *v.* sound, ring, reverberate, echo, reëcho. See RESONANCE.

resources, *n. pl.* capital, property, income, reserve, wealth. See MEANS.

RESPECT.—I. *Nouns.* **respect,** regard, consideration, notice, recognition, civility, courtesy, attention, deference, reverence, honor, esteem, estimation, veneration, admiration; approbation.

homage, fealty, obeisance, genuflection, kneeling, prostration; salaam, kotow *or* kowtow (*Chinese*).

relation, reference, relationship, connection, bearing, aspect (*as, with respect to*)

particular, detail, point, circumstance, regard, point of view (*as, in this respect*).

[*in plural*] **respects** (*as, to pay one's* respects), regards, greetings, compliments, *devoirs* (*F.*), duty, *égards* (*F.*).

II. *Verbs.* **respect,** regard, esteem, value, admire, think much of, entertain respect for, look up to, defer to, pay attention to, pay respect to, do honor to; do the honors, hail, show courtesy, pay homage to, honor, venerate, revere, reverence, worship, hallow; observe due decorum, stand upon ceremony, keep one's distance, make room; treat with consideration, spare.

command respect, inspire respect; awe, impose, overawe, confound, dazzle.

relate to, be concerned with, pertain to, bear upon, appertain to, have regard to: *now rare except in participle.*

III. *Adjectives.* **respected,** esteemed, valued, estimable; time-honored, venerable; emeritus.

respectful, deferential, decorous, reverential, ceremonious, polite, attentive, courteous; bareheaded, cap in hand; prostrate.

IV. *Adverbs.* **respectfully,** deferentially, etc. (see *adjectives*); with all respect, with due respect, with the highest respect; in deference to; *pace tanti viri* (*L.*).

See also APPROBATION, COURTESY, OBSERVANCE, REPUTE, WAY.—*Antonyms.* See DISRESPECT.

---

respectable, *adj.* moderate, fair, mediocre, presentable; reputable, upright See MEDIOCRITY, PROBITY.

respective, *adj.* particular, several, individual. See APPORTIONMENT.

respectively, *adj.* severally, separately, each to each. See APPORTIONMENT.
respire, *v.* breathe, live. See WIND.
respite, *n.* reprieve; pause, break, recess, interval, intermission; delay, postponement. See ACQUITTAL, CESSATION, LATENESS.
resplendent, *adj.* splendid, brilliant, radiant, refulgent, beaming, lustruos, shining, luminous. See BEAUTY.
response, *n.* reply, retort, rejoinder, repartee, echo. See ANSWER.
responsible, *adj.* liable, amenable, accountable, answerable. See LIABILITY.
responsive, *adj.* respondent, replying, answering; impressionable, sympathetic. See ANSWER, SENSITIVENESS.

---

[1]REST.—I. *Nouns.* **rest,** repose, resting, sleep, slumber, siesta, relaxation; quiet, calm, quiescence, stillness, peace, hush, silence, dead calm, tranquillity, quietness, peacefulness; stagnation, stagnancy, fixity, immobility, motionlessness, catalepsy; quietism.
pause, lull, cessation, intermission, stop, cæsura (*prosody*), full stop, let-up (*colloq.*), breathing spell, stand, standstill, deadlock, dead stand; embargo.
resting place, lodging place, shelter, refuge, haven, retreat; camp, encampment, bivouac; bed, couch, hammock, pillow; home, abode; goal, destination, bourn.
support, prop, stay, seat, trestle, pillar, foundation.
II. *Verbs.* **rest,** repose, sleep, slumber; lie, lean, recline, lounge, couch, pillow; relax, unbend; be still, be quiet, be let alone; stand still, stand fast, stand firm; lie still, keep quiet; vegetate, stagnate; be dead, lie in the grave.
pause, stop, halt, stop short, hold, cease, abstain, let up (*colloq.*), desist, discontinue, remain, stay, wait, stand, tarry, mark time, pull up, draw up; bring to, heave to, lay to, anchor, cast anchor, come to anchor, ride at anchor, lie to; rest on one's oars, rest on one's laurels, take breath; alight dismount, arrive, settle, settle down, perch, roost.
quell, becalm, hush, calm, allay, pacify, appease, still, tranquilize, stay, lull to sleep; lay an embargo on.
rely, depend, trust, lean upon, repose in.
III. *Adjectives.* **restful,** peaceful, reposeful, comfortable, quiet, still, calm, tranquil, silent, hushed.
resting, sleeping, slumbering, dormant (*bot.*), quiescent, unagitated, undisturbed, unruffled, motionless, moveless, at rest, at a stand, at a standstill, at anchor; stock-still; sedentary, untraveled, stay-at-home; becalmed, stagnant, unmoved, immovable, stable, fixed, stationary.
IV. *Interjections.* **stop! stay! avast!** (*naut.*), **halt! hold! hold hard! whoa! quit!** (*U. S. colloq.*).
See also CESSATION, HABITATION, INACTIVITY, LOCATION, REPOSE, SOFTNESS, SUPPORT.—*Antonyms.* See CONTINUANCE, EXERTION, MOTION.

---

[2]rest, *n.* residue, surplus, remnant. See REMAINDER.
restaurant, *n.* eating place, café, cafeteria. See FOOD.
restful, *adj.* peaceful, reposeful, comfortable, tranquil, soothing. See [1]REST.
resthouse, *n.* dak bungalow (*India*), hospice, caravansary. See HABITATION.
resting place, goal, haven, bivouac; couch, bed. See [1]REST.

RESTITUTION.—I. *Nouns.* **restitution,** return, restoration, reinstatement, reinvestment, rehabilitation, reparation, atonement; amends, compensation, indemnification, remuneration, reimbursement.
recovery, retrieval, recapture, repossession, replevin (*law*), redemption, release, reversion.
II. *Verbs.* **restitute** (*now rare*), restore, return, give back, render, give up, let go, release, remit, disgorge; recoup, reimburse, compensate, indemnify, refund; reinvest, reinstate, rehabilitate, repair, make good.
recover, get back, retrieve, regain, reclaim, replevy *or* replevin (*law*), reobtain, repossess, reacquire, recapture, redeem; take back again.
III. *Adjectives.* **restitutory,** reparative, amendatory, restorative, remedial, restitutive; indemnificatory, compensatory; redemptive, reversionary.
See also ACQUISITION, RESTORATION.—*Antonyms.* See TAKING.

restless, *adj.* changeable, unsettled, roving, transient, sleepless, unquiet, uneasy, agitated, fidgety, fitful. See CHANGEABLENESS, EXCITABILITY.

restlessness, *n.* disquiet, unrest, agitation, perturbation; fidgetiness, fidgets. See CHANGEABLENESS.

RESTORATION.—I. *Nouns.* **restoration,** replacement, reinstatement, reëstablishment, rehabilitation, *rifacimento* (*It.*), remodeling, reconstruction, reproduction, renovation, redintegration, repair, reparation, renewal, revival, resuscitation, revivification, reanimation, reorganization; redemption, restitution, return, rectification, relief, redress, retrieval, resumption, reclamation, recovery, regainment.

renaissance, renascence, rebirth, new birth, rejuvenescence, palingenesis, regenesis, regeneration, regeneracy, resurrection, resurgence.

[*recovery of health*] **recovery,** cure, convalescence, recuperation, recruitment, recruiting, recruital.

restorer, reviver, renewer, replacer; mender, repairer, tinker, cobbler.

II. *Verbs.* **restore,** put back, replace, return, reseat, reinstate, reinstall, rehabilitate, reëstablish, reconstruct, rebuild, reorganize, rearrange, convert, recondition, redintegrate, make whole, renew renovate, place *in statu quo* (*L.*); regenerate, rejuvenate.

repair, mend, put in repair, retouch, tinker, cobble, patch up, darn; **stanch** *or* staunch, calk *or* caulk, splice.

redeem, reclaim, recover, retrieve, rescue; recoup, repay, refund.

cure, heal, remedy, doctor (*colloq.*), bring round, set on one's legs.

resuscitate, revive, reanimate, revivify, reinvigorate, refresh.

recover, rally, revive, come to, come round, come to oneself, pull through, weather the storm, be oneself again; get well, survive, reappear, come to life again.

III. *Adjectives.* **restorable,** replaceable, renewable, reproducible, recoverable, reclaimable, retrievable, remediable, curable, healable, medicable.

restorative, recuperative, curative, remedial, recuperatory, healing, sanatory, sanative; reparative, reparatory.

restored, redivivous (*rare*), convalescent, rejuvenated, renascent; none the worse.

See also REFRESHMENT, REMEDY, REPRODUCTION, RESTITUTION.—*Antonyms.* See DETERIORATION, RELAPSE.

RESTRAINT.—I. *Nouns.* **restraint,** hindrance, deterrence, determent, coercion, compulsion, discipline, control, check, curb, stop, limitation, restriction, protection, monopoly; prohibition, economic pressure, blockade.

constraint, constrained manner, repression, unnaturalness, embarrassment, reserve.

confinement, detention, imprisonment, incarceration, durance vile; durance, duress, bondage, thrall (*poetic*), thralldom, limbo, captivity, servitude.

safe-keeping, care, custody, keep, keeping, possession, charge, ward, guardianship, protection.

restrainer, restrictionist, protectionist, monopolist, repressionist.

II. *Verbs.* **restrain,** check, curb, rein in, restrict, debar, hinder, constrain, coerce, compel, harness, control, govern, bridle, muzzle, gag, hold in leash, hold back, pull in, stop short, snub, withhold, repress, strangle, inhibit, suppress, keep under; smother, hold, prohibit, limit.

fasten, enchain, fetter, shackle, trammel, pinion, manacle, handcuff, hobble, bind, swathe, swaddle; tether, picket, tie, secure.

confine, shut up (*or* in), lock up, detain, hold in custody; box up, bottle up, cork up, seal up, blockade, hem in, bolt in, wall in, rail in; impound pen, coop, inclose, cage, imprison, incarcerate, immure, entomb; put in irons, clap (*or* lay) under hatches, cast into prison.

arrest, apprehend, pinch (*slang*), nab (*colloq.*), take into custody, take (*or* make) prisoner, lead captive, send to prison, commit; give in charge (*or* custody).

III. *Adjectives.* **restrained,** imprisoned, pent up, wedged in, icebound, snowbound, windbound, weatherbound; "cabined, cribbed, confined" (*Macbeth*), laid by the heels.

stiff, narrow, prudish, strait-laced, hidebound; constrained, repressive, suppressive, reserved.

IV. *Adverbs.* **under restraint**, under lock and key, behind bars, under hatches; in confinement, in captivity, under arrest; in prison, in stir (*slang*), in jail, in custody, doing time (*colloq. or slang*); on parole, on probation, on ticket of leave (*Brit.*).

See also CIRCUMSCRIPTION, COMPULSION, DISSUASION, MODERATION, PRISON, PRISONER, PROHIBITION, SIMPLENESS, SUBJECTION.—*Antonyms.* See LAXITY, LIBERATION, PERMISSION.

---

restrict, *v.* limit, check, prohibit, inhibit, restrain, obstruct, confine. See RESTRAINT.

restriction, *n.* limitation, discipline, control. See RESTRAINT.

restriction, *adj.* prohibitive, prohibitory; qualificatory, limitative. See PROHIBITION, QUALIFICATION.

result, *n.* issue, eventuality, end, termination, consequence, outcome, effect; inference, deduction, opinion, finding, verdict, resolution. See EFFECT, JUDGMENT, SEQUENCE.

resume, *v.* continue, recommence, renew, recapitulate. See BEGINNING, REPETITION.

resuscitate, *v.* restore, reanimate, revive, revivify. See RESTORATION.

retail, *v.* relate (*in detail*), recount; sell, hawk, peddle, distribute. See INFORMATION, SALE.

retain, *v.* remember; keep, hold, reserve, secure. See MEMORY, RETENTION.

retake, *v.* regain, recover, retrieve, recapture. See ACQUISITION.

RETALIATION.—I. *Nouns.* **retaliation**, reprisal, requital, desert, retribution, punishment, *lex talionis* (*L.*), retortion (*international law*), counterstroke, counterproject, counterplot, counterblast; retort, recrimination, accusation, revenge, *revanche* (*F.*), compensation; a Roland for an Oliver, measure for measure, diamond cut diamond, tit for tat, give and take, blow for blow, and eye for an eye; bommerang, the biter bit.

II. *Verbs.* **retaliate**, require, return, repay, retort, turn upon; pay, pay off, pay back; cap, match; reciprocate, turn the tables upon, return the compliment, give as good as was sent, return like for like, exchange blows; give and take, be quits, be even with, pay off old scores.

III. *Adjectives.* **retaliatory**, retaliative, retributive, avenging, requiting, recriminatory, reciprocal.

See also ACCUSATION, INTERCHANGE, REVENGE.—*Antonyms.* See FORGIVENESS, RESISTANCE.

---

retard, *v.* postpone, put off, defer; impede, check, hamper, obstruct, detain. See DELAY, HINDRANCE.

retardation, *n.* delay, hindrance, deceleration (*mech.*). See SLOWNESS.

RETENTION.—I. *Nouns.* **retention**, retaining, keeping, hold, maintenance; grasp, gripe, grip, tenacity, retentiveness, retentivity.

memory, remembrance, recollection, recollecting, reminiscence.

[*prehensile organs*] claw, talon, pounce (*of a bird of prey*), nail, finger nail, unguis (*pl.* ungues: *tech.*), clutch (*chiefly in pl.*), hook (*slang*), ungula (*pl.* ungulæ: *tech.*), manus (*pl.* manus: *tech.*), chela (*zoöl.*), nipper (*as of a crab*), pincer; tentacle, tentaculum (*pl.* tentacula: *zoöl.*); finger, digit; hand, fist, paw.

tooth, fang, tusk, snag, tang, tush (*esp. a horse's canine*), incisor, canine (*zoöl.*), molar; grinders (*slang*).

[*instruments for gripping*] pincers *or* pinchers, nippers, pliers, tweezers, *pincette* (*F.*), forceps; Stillson wrench, monkey wrench, vise.

II. *Verbs.* **retain**, keep, hold, maintain, hold fast, clinch, clench, clutch, grip, grasp, gripe, hug, embrace; secure, withhold, detain, restrain, hold (*or* keep) back; husband, reserve, save, preserve, have (*or* keep) in stock, have in reserve, keep in pay (*as, to* retain *a lawyer*); entail, tie up, settle.

remember, recall, recollect, keep in mind (*or* memory), bear in mind.

III. *Adjectives.* **retentive, keeping, holding, maintaining, detentive; unforfeited, undeprived; inalienable.**

[*of the memory*] **tenacious, retaining, having a good memory, unforgetting reliable.**

See also MEMORY, POSSESSION, PRISONER, STABILITY, STORE. TENACITY.—*Antonyms.* See OBLIVION, RELINQUISHMENT.

---

reticence, *v.* reserve, secretiveness, uncommunicativeness. See CONCEALMENT.

retinue, *n.* followers, attentants, suite, train, escort. See ACCOMPANIMENT, SERVANT.

retire, *v.* depart, leave, withdraw, go to bed, retreat, resign, recede. See DEPARTURE.

retirement, *n.* withdrawal, retreat, regression, departure; abdication, abandonment; privacy, concealment, solitude, isolation. See RECESSION, RESIGNATION, SECLUSION.

[1]**retort,** *n.* rejoinder, replay, repartee. See ANSWER.

[2]**retort,** *n.* alembic, crucible. See RECEPTACLE.

retract, *v.* recant, rescind, revoke, withdraw, disavow, recall, forswear, abjure, disclaim, renounce. See ANNULMENT.

retreat, *n.* haunt, habitat, resort, refuge, asylum; retirement, departure, withdrawal, recession; cell, hermitage, cloister, convent. See HABITATION, REGRESSION, SECLUSION.

retreat, *v.* withdraw, recede, retire, depart. See AVOIDANCE.

retribution, *n.* requital, desert, compensation, recompense, penalty, judgment, nemesis. See RETALIATION .

retrieve, *v.* recover, regain, redeem, reclaim, restore, reëstablish, revive, repair. See RESTORATION.

retroactive, *adj.* retrospective, regressive. See REGRESSION.

retrograde, *adj.* inverse, regressive, retrogressive, backward. See REGRESSION.

retrospect, *n.* retrospection, recollection, reminiscence. See MEMORY.

retrospective, *adj.* retroactive, looking back (*or* backward). See PAST.

return, *v.* reply, respond; recur, reappear; restore, give back; reverse, revert, turn back, retreat. See ANSWER, REGULARITY, RESTITUTION, REVERSION.

return, *n.* reply, response; home-coming, reëntry; profit, proceeds, income, results (*pl.*); report, statement; recurrence; restoration, recovery. See ANSWER, ARRIVAL, RECEIPT, RECORD, REPETITION, RESTITUTION.

reunion, *n.* assembly, meeting, convention. See ASSEMBLAGE.

reveal, *v.* divulge, tell, announce, disclose, publish, unmask, unveil, unseal, open, expose. See DISCLOSURE.

revel, *v.* sport, disport, carouse; delight in. See AMUSEMENT, INTEMPERANCE, PLEASURE.

revel, *n.* orgy, carousal, spree, saturnalia. See AMUSEMENT, INTEMPERANCE.

revelation, *n.* divulgence, unveiling, *exposé* (*F.*). exposure, detection, find; inspiration, Bible, Apocalypse. See DISCLOSURE, SCRIPTURES.

revelry, *n.* merrymaking, jollification (*colloq.*), carousal, orgy. See INTEMPERANCE.

REVENGE.—I. *Nouns.* **revenge, vengeance, revengefulness, retaliation, vindictiveness, vengefulness, implacability, rancor, ruthlessness, malevolence; vendetta, death feud, eye for an eye, tooth for a tooth, blood for blood; day of reckoning.**

revenger (*rare*), **avenger, Nemesis, Erinys** (*pl.* **Erinyes**), **Eumenides** (*pl.*), **Furies.**

II. *Verbs.* **revenge, avenge, retaliate, vindicate, requite, take revenge, have one's revenge; breathe vengeance, wreak one's vengeance; give no quarter, take no prisoners.**

harbor revenge, keep the wound open, bear malice; rankle, rankle in the breast

III. *Adjectives.* **revengeful**, vengeful, vindictive, revenging, malicious, resentful, rancorous; pitiless, ruthless, rigorous, avenging, retaliative; unforgiving, unrelenting; inexorable, implacable, relentless, remorseless, stony-hearted.

See also MALEVOLENCE, PITILESSNESS, RETALIATION.—*Antonyms.* See FORGIVENESS.

---

reverberate, *v.* rebound, reflect; resound, echo. See RECOIL, RESONANCE, ROLL.
reverberation, *n.* echoing, reëchoing, reflection. See RESONANCE, ROLL.
revere, *v.* honor, venerate, reverence, worship, hallow. See RESPECT.
reverence, *n.* veneration, awe, homage. See RESPECT.
reverie, *n.* abstraction, absorption, musing, daydream, dream. See INATTENTION.
reverse, *n.* misfortune, calamity, infliction, check, defeat; back (*as of a coin, medal, shield: opposite of* obverse), converse, other side, verso (*left-hand page of a book: opposite of* recto). See ADVERSITY, OPPOSITE.
reverse, *v.* revoke, annul, rescind, retract; invert, transpose. See ANNULMENT, INVERSION.

REVERSION.—I. *Nouns.* **reversion**, return, returning, reverting, revulsion; turning point, turn of the tide, *status quo ante bellum* (*L.*); alternation, rotation, recurrence; inversion, recoil, blacklash (*tech.*), reaction; retrospection, restoration, reconversion; relapse, regression, retrogression, recidivism (*esp. of a criminal*), atavism (*biol.*), throwback; escheat (*law*), succession.

II. *Verbs.* **revert**, return, turn back, go back, recur, relapse, recidivate (*rare*), regress, recoil, retreat; restore; undo, unmake; turn the tide, turn the scale.

III. *Adjectives.* **reversionary**, reversional, regressive, retrogressive, reactionary, revulsionary, revulsive; atavistic (*biol.*).

See also ATTENTION, PROPERTY, RECOIL, REGRESSION, RELAPSE, REPETITION, RESTITUTION, RESTORATION, TRANSFER.—*Antonyms.* See CONTINUANCE.

---

review, *v.* analyze, consider, edit, revise, correct, comment upon. See JUDGE.
review, *n.* epitome, synopsis, analysis, digest; commentary, critique; pageant, parade; reconsideration, reflection. See COMPENDIUM, DISSERTATION, OSTENTATION, THOUGHT.
revile, *v.* upbraid, abuse, reproach, execrate, vilify. See DISAPPROBATION.
revise, *v.* review, reëxamine, edit, correct, overhaul, polish. See IMPROVEMENT.
revival, *n.* renewal, regeneration, revivification; revival meeting, camp meeting. See REPRODUCTION, RESTORATION, WORSHIP.
revive, *v.* renew, refresh, revivify, reanimate, resuscitate. See IMPROVEMENT, RESTORATION.
revocation, *n.* recall, repeal, repudiation, retraction; abrogation. See ANNULMENT.
revoke, *v.* annul, cancel, repeal, rescind, recall, retract. See ANNULMENT.
revolt, *n.* rebellion, mutiny, outbreak, strike, insurgence, desertion. See DISOBEDIENCE.
revolting, *adj.* objectionable, offensive, repulsive, nauseous. See PAINFULNESS.

REVOLUTION.—I. *Nouns.* **revolution**, revolving, circular motion, rotation, gyration, turn, course, circuit, round, circumvolution, wheel, whirl, gyre (*poetic*); cyclic recurrence, cycle.

[*complete change*] **overturn**, upset, overthrow, reversal, fundamental reconstruction (*as,* a revolution *in thought*).

[*violent change of government*] **rebellion**, *bouleversement* (*F.*), revolt, uprising, insurrection, rising, mutiny, debacle, subversion, breakup, destruction; political upheaval, *coup d'état* (*F.*); counter-revolution; bolshevism.

spasm, convulsion, throe, revulsion; upheaval, cataclysm, earthquake, eruption, explosion.

II. *Verbs.* **revolutionize**, change fundamentally, recast, remodel, new-model, refashion, reform, reconstruct, break with the past, change the face of.

III. *Adjectives.* **revolutionary,** radical, extreme, intransigent, ultra, advanced, forward; insurgent, Red (*or* red), bolshevistic, insurrectionary, rebellious, mutinous; convulsionary, cataclysmal, cataclysmic, catastrophic.

See also CHANGE, DESTRUCTION, DISOBEDIENCE, REGULARITY, ROTATION.—*Antonyms.* See CONTINUANCE, PERMANENCE, SUBJECTION, SUBMISSION.

---

revolve, *v.* turn, rotate, roll, spin, whirl. See ROTATION.

REWARD.—I. *Nouns.* **reward,** recompense, remuneration, meed, guerdon, bounty, bonus, prize, indemnity, indemnification; quittance, compensation, reparation, redress, acknowledgment, requital, amends, sop, consideration, return, *quid pro quo* (*L.*); atonement, retribution, punishment.

allowance, salary, stipend, wages, pay, payment, emolument; tribute; premium, fee, honorarium; hire; mileage, extra pay, batta (*India*); solatium, smart money (*Brit.*).

perquisite, perks (*slang*), gratuity, vail (*now rare*), tip, *douceur* (*F.*), baksheesh *or* bakshish, donation, consideration; dasturi *or* dustoori (*India*), rake-off (*slang*), graft, bribe, hush money, blackmail.

II. *Verbs.* **reward,** recompense, repay, requite, remunerate, compensate, pay, fee, tip, bribe; make amends, indemnify; redress, atone, satisfy, acknowledge, remember.

III. *Adjectives.* **remunerative,** compensative, profitable, lucrative, remuneratory (*rare*), compensatory; retributive, reparative.

See also COMPENSATION, GIVING, PRICE.—*Antonyms.* See PENALTY.

---

rhetoric, *n.* eloquence, elocution, expression, declamation; grandiloquence. See SPEECH.

rhythm, *n.* meter, measure; cadence, swing. See POETRY, REGULARITY.

rhythmic, *adj.* melodious; rhythmical, regular. See NELODY, REGULARITY.

rick, *adj.* intense, strong, dark, deep; sufficient, abundant, enough; wealthy, moneyed, affluent. See DEPTH, SUFFICIENCY, WEALTH.

riches, *n. pl.* money, fortune, means, affluence. See WEALTH.

rich man, moneyed man, capitalist, millionaire. See WEALTH.

rickety, *adj.* weak, frail, shaky, tumbledown. See WEAKNESS.

RIDDANCE.—I. *Nouns.* **riddance,** freeing, disencumberment, clearing, disencumbrance, disembarrassment, extrication; escape, release. freedom. deliverance (*as, a good* riddance).

II. *Verbs.* **rid** (*followed by* of), free, disencumber, disburden, clear, scour, sweep (*as, to* rid *the sea of pirates*).

get rid of, become free (*or* delivered) from; abolish, eject, drive away.

divorce, cut off, separate, disunite, sunder, sever; desert, disinherit, repudiate, put away, dissolve (union).

See also DELIVERANCE, EJECTION, LOSS, RELINQUISHMENT.—*Antonyms.* See RETENTION.

---

riddle, *n.* enigma, puzzle, problem, mystery. See SECRET, UNINTELLIGIBILITY.

rider, *n.* attachement, amendment, corollary, codicil, additional clause; horseman, equestrian. See ADJUNCT, TRAVELER.

ridge, *n.* rim, rib, seam; hogback, chine, range, watershed. See CONVEXITY, HEIGHT.

RIDICULE.—I. *Nouns.* **ridicule,** disparagement, derision, scoffing, mockery, banter, irony, satire, sarcasm, squib, skit, quip, persiflage, raillery, chaff, *badinage* (*F.*), asteism (*rhetoric*); grin, snicker *or* snigger, leer, sneer, jibe.

burlesque, parody, travesty, mimicry, farce, caricature.

buffoonery, foolery, buffoonism, practical joke, horseplay.

II. *Verbs.* **ridicule,** deride, disparage, laugh at, grin at, smile at; snicker *or* snigger; banter, chaff, joke, josh (*U. S. slang*), guy (*colloq.*), roast (*colloq.*), haze (*U. S.*), rag (*Eng. slang*), make merry with, make fun of.

burlesque, satirize, parody, skit, caricature, cartoon, travesty.

III. *Adjectives.* **derisive,** sarcastic, ironical, satirical, quizzical, burlesque, mock, mock-heroic, Hudibrastic.

See also AMUSEMENT, DISRESPECT, LAUGHINGSTOCK.—*Antonyms.* See APPROBATION.

RIDICULOUSNESS.—I. *Nouns.* **ridiculousness.** comicality, laughableness, strangeness, oddity, drollery, farce, comedy, burlesque, buffoonery; bull, Irish bull, Hibernianism, Spoonerism; bombast, anticlimax, bathos; extravagance, absurdity, laughingstock, scream (*slang*).

II. *Verbs.* **be rediculous,** play the fool, make a fool of oneself, commit an absurdity.

III. *Adjectives.* **ridiculous,** ludicrous, comic *or* comical, waggish, quizzical, droll, funny, amusing, risible, laughable, farcical, serio-comic.

odd, grotesque, whimsical, fanciful, fantastic, queer, rum (*slang*), quaint, bizarre, eccentric, strange, outlandish, out-of-the-way, baroque.

preposterous, absurd, unreasonable, irrational, nonsensical, monstrous, extravagant, *outré* (*F.*); bombastic, inflated, stilted, burlesque, mock-heroic.

See also ABSURDITY, FOLLY, RIDICULE, UGLINESS, UNMEANINGNESS.—*Antonyms.* See BEAUTY, LAMENTATION, TASTE, WISDOM.

---

[1]**riding,** *n.* district, subdivision (*of a country*). See REGION.

[2]**riding,** *n.* horsemanship, equitation, equestrianism. See JOURNEY.

rife, *adj.* prevalent, general, common, current; numerous, abundant, plentiful. See GENERALITY, MULTITUDE.

riffraff, *n.* mob, rabble. See BAD MAN.

rift, *n.* fissure, cleft, crack, slit, breach. See INTERVAL.

RIGHT.—I. *Nouns.* **right,** what ought to be, what should be, rectitude, integrity, probity, uprightness, propriety, fitness; morality, virtue, goodness, honor, straight course.

justice, equity, equitableness, propriety, fairness, fair treatment, fair play, square deal (*colloq.*), impartiality; lawfulness, legality, *summum jus* (*L.*), strict law, *strictum jus* (*L.*); scales of justice, even-handed justice, *suum cuique* (*L.*), fair field and no favor.

Astræa, Nemesis, Themis, Rhadamanthus.

privilege, prerogative, grant, power, liberty, advantage, license, immunity, exemption.

claim, title, interest, due, droit (*law*); justification.

right hand (*or* side), dexter, off side (*of a horse or vehicle: opposite of* near side), starboard (*naut.*), Epistle side (*eccl.*), decanal side (*south side of choir: eccl.*), recto (*of a book: opposite of* verso), right-hand division (*as of an army*).

[*European politics*] **Right,** conservatives, nonarchists, reactionaries: *those seated on the right of the presiding officer, distinguished from* Center (*moderates*) *and* Left (*radicals and democrats*).

II. *Verbs.* **right,** regulate, rule, make straight; correct, restore, adjust; do right, recompense, vindicate, do justice to, see justice done, see fair play, hold the scales even, give every one his due; *audi alteram partem* (*L.*).

III. *Adjectives.* [*not crooked*] **right,** straight, direct, rectilinear, right-lined; lineal, linear.

[*not oblique*] **erect,** upright, vertical, plumb, perpendicular (*as,* right *ascension*).

[*not wrong*] **correct,** accurate, regular, strict, unmistaken, unerring, inerrant, inerrable, perfect, infallible (*as, the* right *solution*).

just, upright, righteous, true, good, reasonable, equitable, honest, square, genuine, fair, equable, evenhanded, equal; rightful, justifiable, legitimate, lawful, legal.

fit, becoming, suitable, proper, correct, meet, fitting, seemly, appropriate, *comme il faut* (*F.*); right as a trivet, right as rain; orderly, well done.

desirable, favorable, fortunate, advantageous, preferable, convenient, well advised.

[*in good condition*] **sound,** satisfactory, sane, well, hale, healthy.

[*not left*] **dextral,** dexterous *or* dextrous (*rare in this sense*), right-handed, dexter, dextrorse (*bot.*).

IV. *Adverbs.* **rightly,** uprightly, in justice, *à bon droit* (*F.*), in equity, in reason, without distinction of (*or* regard to) persons, upon even terms; properly, appropriately, fitly; correctly, etc. (see *adjectives*).

See also DUTY, LEGALITY, PERMISSION, PROBITY, PROPERTY, RIGHTFULNESS, STRAIGHTNESS, TITLE, TRUTH, VIRTUE.—*Antonyms.* See LEFT, WRONG.

---

righteous, *adj.* virtuous, godly, pure, noble, upright, just. See VIRTUE.

RIGHTFULNESS.—I. *Nouns.* **rightfulness,** right, dueness, due, privilege, prerogative, prescription, title, claim, pretension, legality, lawfulness, justness, demand, birthright.

immunity, license, exemption, liberty, franchise; vested interest (*or* right).

authorization, sanction, permission, authority, charter, deed, warrant; constitution; bond.

desert, merit, due, meed, worth.

claimant, claimer, appellant, plantiff, libelant; heir, inheritor, heiress (*fem.*); heir apparent, heir presumptive; legal heir, heir at law; pretender.

II. *Verbs.* **have right to,** have claim (*or* title) to, be entitled to, belong to; deserve, merit, be worthy of.

demand, claim, lay claim to, requisition, reclaim, exact; insist on (*or* upon), make a point of, require, assert, assume, arrogate.

entitle, give (*or* confer) a right, authorize, sanction, legalize, ordain, prescribe, allot; qualify, capacitate, name.

III. *Adjectives.* **rightful,** fitting, correct, square, due, appropriate, just, true; equitable, right, creditable, fit, proper, meet, befitting, becoming, seemly, decorous.

lawful, legitimate, legal, licit, legalized, allowable.

privileged, allowed, sanctioned, warranted, authorized; ordained, prescribed, constitutional, chartered, enfranchised.

prescriptive, presumptive, absolute, inalienable, inviolable, sacrosanct.

merited, due to, deserved, condign (*archaic, except of punishment*).

IV. *Adverbs.* **rightfully,** fittingly, lawfully, etc. (see *adjectives*); by right, *de jure* (*L.*), by divine right; *ex officio* (*L.*); on the square (*colloq.*), on the level (*colloq.*).

See also AUTHORITY, LEGALITY, PERMISSION.—*Antonyms.* See ILLEGALITY, RIGHTLESSNESS.

RIGHTLESSNESS.—I. *Nouns.* **rightlessness,** undueness, *malum prohibitum* (*L.; pl. mala prohibita: law*); invalidity of title, unrightfulness, unlawfulness, illegality, illegitimacy, falseness; loss of right, disfranchisement, forfeiture.

impropriety, unfitness, unseemliness, unsuitability, indecorum, imprudence, incivility, indecency, indecorousness; solecism.

usurpation, assumption, seizure, dispossession, infringement, tort (*law*), violation, breach, encroachment, exaction, imposition.

usurper, pretender, impostor, arrogator.

II. *Verbs.* **infringe,** encroach, trench on, trespass, intrude; exact, arrogate, usurp, violate; get under false pretenses, sail under false colors.

disentitle, dispossess, disfranchise, disqualify, invalidate; illegitimate, illegitimatize, bastardize.

III. *Adjectives.* **rightless,** unlawful, illegal, illicit, unconstitutional, unauthorized, unwarranted, unsanctioned, undue, tortious (*law*), unfair, unjust, unequitable, unjustified; disqualified, unqualified; unprivileged, unchartered; undeserved, unmerited, unearned.

illegitimate, irregular, spurious, false, illogical, usurped, unlawful; bastard misbegotten, natural.

improper, unfit, unbefitting, unseemly, unsuitable, unmeet, *contra bonos mores* (*L.*), unbecoming, misbecoming, indecorous, inappropriate, incongruous, inaccurate, incorrect; out of the question, not to be thought of, preposterous; pretentious, would-be; indelicate, imprudent, indecent, immodest, immoral.

See also ILLEGALITY, WRONG.—*Antonyms.* See RIGHTFULNESS.

---

rigid, *adj.* conventional, regular; hard, firm, stiff, unpliant; exact, correct, precise. See CONFORMITY, HARDNESS, TRUTH.

rim, *n.* brim, brink, margin, border. See EDGE.

rind, *n.* peel, skin, integument, coat, coating, bark, crust, hull. See COVERING.
¹ring, *v.* resound, peal, chime, tinkle, jingle. See RESONANCE.
²ring, *v.* encircle, inclose, surround, environ, girdle. See CIRCULARITY.
¹ring, *n.* chime, ringing, clangor, bell-note. See RESONANCE.
²ring, *n.* lists, prize ring; circle, hoop, band, finger ring; clique, gang, set, faction, machine. See ARENA, CIRCULARITY, PARTY.
riot, *n.* revolt, insurgence, rebellion, strike; turmoil, disturbance, row, violence, pandemonium. See DISOBEDIENCE, DISORDER.
riotous, *adj.* turbulent, disorderly, boisterous, lawless, violent. See DISORDER.
ripe, *adj.* perfected, consummate, complete; mature, mellow; prepared, seasoned. See PERFECTION, PREPARATION.
ripen, *v.* perfect, complete, mature, mellow, season. See PERFECTION.
ripple, *n.* gurgle, babble, purl, lap (*of waves*), murmur; wavelet, undulation. See FAINTNESS, RIVER.
rise, *v.* mount, ascend, arise, take off, go up; begin, start, originate; revolt, rebel, strike; thrive, propser. See ASCENT, BEGINNING, DISOBEDIENCE, PROSPERITY.
rise, *n.* slope, grade, hill; origin, cause, source; addition, gain, expansion, advance, progress. See ASCENT, BEGINNING, INCREASE, PROGRESSION.
rising, *adj.* climbing, mounting, ascending; aspiring. See ASCENT.
risk, *v.* speculate, hazard, dare, stake, bet, venture. See CHANCE, DANGER.
risky, *adj.* hazardous, dangerous; *risqué* (*F.*), suggestive. See DANGER, IMPURITY.

RITE.—I. *Nouns.* **rite,** ceremony, observance, function, duty, form, solemnity, sacrament.
sermon, discourse, preaching, preachment, exhortation, khutbah (*Moham.*), religious harangue, homily, lecture, pastoral.
worship, service, ministration, ministry; adoration, devotion, prayer, invocation of saints, confession, the confessional; absolution, remission of sins; reciting the rosary, telling one's beads; thurification, incense; asperges (*R. C. Ch.*), aspersion, holy water.
Seven Sacraments! (1) baptism, immersion, christening, chrism; baptismal regeneration; font.
(2) **confirmation,** laying on (*or* imposition) of hands.
(3) **Eucharist,** Mass, Lord's Supper, Communion, Holy Communion, the sacrament, the holy sacrament, celebration; consecrated elements, bread and wine, intinction, impanation, subpanation, transubstantiation, real prsence.
(4) **penance,** penitential acts, fasting, maceration, sackcloth and ashes, flagellation, castigation.
(5) **extreme unction,** last rites, viaticum.
(6) **holy orders,** ordination, consecration.
(7) **matrimony,** marriage, wedlock.
[*sacred articles*] relics, rosary, beads, reliquary, host, pyx, Agnus Dei, pax; cross, rood, crucifix; censer, thurible; Sangraal, Holy Grail; *Pietà* (*It.*).
ritual, liturgy, *rituale* (*L.*), manual, rubric, canon, ordinal, missal, breviary, Mass book, beadroll, litany, prayer book Book of Common Prayer; psalter, psalm book, hymn book, hymnal.
ritualism, ceremonialism; liturgics, liturgiology.
ritualist, ceremonialist; liturgist, liturgiologist; High Churchman, Anglican.
II. *Verbs.* **officiate,** act, perform service; do duty, minister; celebrate, administer the sacrament (*or* Holy Eucharist).
preach, sermonize, address the congregation, hold forth, evangelize, homilize lecture.
III. *Adjectives.* **ritual,** ritualistic, ceremonial, liturgic *or* liturgical, High Church, Anglican.
See also OBSERVANCE, WORSHIP.

---

rival, *n.* competitor, contestant, antagonist, adversary, emulator. See OPPONENT.

rival, *v.* challenge, compete with, vie with, emulate; surpass, outrival, eclipse. See CONTENTION, REPUTE.

rivalry, *n.* competition, emulation, race, contest. See OPPOSITION.

RIVER [water in motion].—I. *Nouns.* **river,** stream, reach, affluent, tributary, feeder, anabranch (*anastomosing branch: Australia*).

rivulet, streamlet, brook, brooklet, gill *or* ghyll, runlet, runnel, branch (*U. S.*), creek, run, burn (*Scot. and dial*), rill, rillet, beck (*Eng.*); spring, fount, fountain, jet, *jet d'eau* (*F.*), squirt, spout, splash, rush, gush.

current, stream (*esp. the swiftest part of it*), course, flow, flux, tide, race, sluice, tide race, mill race, torrent, rapids, flood; undercurrent, undertow; spring tide, high tide, flood tide, full tide; neap, neap tide; ebb, ebb tide, reflux, refluence.

whirlpool, vortex, eddy, maelstrom, Charybdis, gurge (*rare*), gulf (*chiefly figurative*).

waterfall, fall, cascade, cataract, Niagara, force *or* foss (*Eng. dial.*), linn *or* lin (*Scot.*); chute, shoot, rapid, dalles (*U. S. and Canada*).

wave, undulation, billow, surge, swell; bore, eagre, tidal wave; comber, beach comber, roller; ripple, wavelet, riffle (*U. S.*); surf, sea, ground swell, heave; breakers, white horses, whitecaps.

rain, condensation, precipitation; shower, wet, fall, pour, drizzle, scud (*dial.*), mizzle (*dial.*), plash, *serein* (*F.*), downpour, drencher, cloudburst, deluge, flood, inundation, waterspout; rainy season, rains, monsoon, bursat *or* barsat (*Hind.*).

rain gauge, pulviometer, pluviograph, ombrometer, undomograph, udometer, hyetometrograph, hyetometer.

[*for measuring tides and the heights of rivers*] **marigraph,** fluviograph, fluviometer, nilometer, hydrometrograph.

science of fluids in motion: hydrodynamics; hydraulics, hydrostatics, hydrokinetics, hydromechanics.

II. *Verbs.* **flow,** run, stream, gush, pour, spout, roll, jet, well, issue, ooze, spurt, geyser; drop, drip, dribble, trickle, distil, percolate; purl, gurgle, babble, murmur, meander; surge, swirl, regurgitate, overflow, inundate, deluge, flow over, splash, plash, swash.

flow into, fall into, open into, drain into; discharge itself, disembogue.

[*to cause a flow*] **pour,** pour out, discharge, emit, spill, splash, shower down; irrigate, drench.

[*to stop a flow*] **stop,** close, seal, occlude, obstruct, stanch *or* staunch, check, dam, plug, stop up, cork, dam up, obstruct, choke, cut off.

rain, shower, sprinkle, drizzle, spit (*colloq.*); set in, pour.

III. *Adjectives.* **riverain,** riparian, riparial (*zoöl.*), riparious; riverine, riverside.

flowing, fluent, meandering, flexuous, fluvial, streamy, tidal; choppy, rolling.

rainy, showery, drizzly, drizzling, wet, pluvious.

See also EGRESS, EJECTION, FLUIDITY, WATER.

---

road, *n.* path, route, course, roadway, highway, railway. See WAY.

roadway, *n.* street, thoroughfare, road. See WAY.

roam, *v.* wander, rove, prowl, jaunt, ramble. See JOURNEY.

roar, *v.* boom, thunder; bellow, howl, cry, bay, bray, wail, laugh; storm, rage. See LOUDNESS, ULULATION, VIOLENCE.

roar, *n.* bawl, yell; din, uproar; guffaw; boom, thunder; howl, bellow; detonation. See CRY, LOUDNESS, REJOICING, RESONANCE, ULULATION, VIOLENCE.

roast, *v.* cook, grill, bake, broil, parch, dry; *Colloq.:* banter, chaff, guy (*colloq.*). See CALEFACTION, RIDICULE.

rob, *v.* steal, thieve, appropriate, plagiarize, embezzle, forge. See STEALING.

robber, *n.* pillager, burglar, highwayman, bandit, pirate. See THIEF.

robbery, *n.* depredation, plunder, theft, piracy, plagiarism. See STEALING.

robe, *n.* gown, habit, dress, costume, attire. See COSTUME.

robot, *n.* automaton, mechanical man. See INSTRUMENT.

robust, *adj.* strong, hardy, seasoned, tough, sound. See HARDNESS.

rock, *v.* vibrate, totter, sway, wabble, swing. See OSCILLATION.

rock, *n.* bowlder, stone (*U. S.*), crag, cliff; reef; defense, protection, safeguard. See LAND, PITFALL, REFUGE, SAFETY.

rocky, *adj.* hard, stony, flinty, craggy, rugged, rough; callous, unfeeling. See HARDNESS, ROUGHNESS.
rod, *n.* switch, birch; staff, wand; *Slang*: revolver, pistol, automatic. See SCOURAGE, SUPPORT,; ARMS.
rogue, *n.* villain, rascal, scoundrel. See KNAVE.
roguish, *adj.* playful, sportive, knavish, mischievous. See AMUSEMENT.
role, *n.* task, function; charater, impersonation. See CONDUCT, PART.

ROLL.—I. *Nouns.* **roll,** scroll, document; register, record, list, rota, catalogue, inventory, schedule.
[*of bread*] small loaf, loaflet, biscuit (*U. S.*), scone (*Scot.*), bap (*Scot.*), twist.
roller, cylinder, barrel, drum, treadle (*Scot. and dial.*), trundle, rundle, truck, trolley, wheel.
[*reverberatory and protracted sound*] **reverberation,** echoing, rumbling, rumble, drumming, *berloque* (*F.*), resonance, bombilation, bombination, booming, boom, thunder cannonade, drum fire, barrage; ratatat, rubadub, pitapat, quaver, pitter-patter, tattoo, devil's tattoo, racket, rattle, clutter, clatter, clangor, charivari, howl, dingdong, peal of bells, whir, drone.
II. *Verbs.* **roll,** revolve, rotate, wheel, trundle, turn, turn over, whirl, gyrate; bowl.
wrap, envelop, wind, muffle, swathe, fold, whip, lap, bind; infold, inwrap, involve, inclose.
smooth, level, press, flatten, spread, even (*as, to* roll *a lawn*).
sway, incline, lean, lurch, reel, swing, gybe, yaw (*as a ship*), wallow, welter.
[*relating to sounds*] **reverberate,** reëcho, resound; drum, boom, roar, thunder, bombinate, rumble; clack, clatter, rattle; patter, pitapat, pitpat, pitter-patter; whir, rustle, hum; trill (*as certain songsters*), shake, quaver; tootle, chime, peal; tick, beat.
undulate (*as a surface*), wave, swell, billow.
III. *Adjectives.* **rolling,** revolving, rotating, etc. (see *verbs*); undulatory, wavy, undulating (*as,* rolling *country*).

See also CIRCUIT, CONVOLUTION, LIST, MOTION, RESONANCE, RIVER (*flow*), ROTATION, SMOOTHNESS.—*Antonyms.* See SNAP, UNFOLDMENT.

---

romance, *n.* fiction, novel, story, tale; imaginativeness; love affair; falsehood, exaggeration. See DESCRIPTION, IMAGINATION, LOVE, UNTRUTH.
romantic, *adj.* idealistic, fanciful, poetic, fictitious, imaginary, extravagant; sentimental. See IMAGINATION, SENSITIVENESS.
romp, *v.* caper, frisk, gambol, dance, leap. See AMUSEMENT.
roof, *n.* cover, thatch, slates, shingles; shelter, house, dwelling, home. See COVERING, HABITATION.
room, *n.* chamber, apartment, lodging place; scope, compass, capacity, range. See RECEPTACLE, SPACE.
roommate, *n.* chum, comrade, bedfellow, bunkie (*U. S. colloq.*), tentmate. See FRIEND.
roomy, *adj.* spacious, extensive, expansive. See SPACE.
root, *n.* underground part, embedded part, basic part, basic element, radical, bottom; source, reason, motive, rationale; radix. See BASE, CAUSE, NUMBER.
[1]**root,** *v.* unearth, uproot, eradicate, extirpate; plant, embed, place, set; take root, settle. See EJECTION, LOCATION.
[2]**root,** *v.* shout for, applaud, encourage; *U. S. slang.* See APPROBATION.
rope, *n.* cord, line, halyard (*naut.*), painter, cable, hawser, halter, lariat, lasso. See FILAMENT, VINCULUM.
roseate, *adj.* rose-colored (*lit. and fig.*), rosy. See RED.
rosy, *adj.* hopeful, favorable; blooming, flushed, blushing. See HOPE, RED.
rot, *v.* decay, decompose, putrefy; defile, corrupt, taint, degenerate. See DECOMPOSITION, DETERIORATION, UNCLEANNESS.

ROTATION.—I. *Nouns.* **rotation,** revolution, turning, turn, wheel, gyration, circulation, roll, circumgyration, circumrotation, turbination, circumvolution (*rare*); whirligig, whirlabout; convolution.
whirl, reel, spin, twirl, turn, pirouette, gyre, swirl, whir; vortex, eddy, surge, whirlpool, maelstrom, Charybdis; cyclone, tornado, twister (*U. S.*); vertigo, vertiginousness.
succession, sequence, round, procession, series, run, cycle, order, course, alternation.
[*comparisons*] wheel, screw, turbine, propeller; whirligig, whirlabout, top, teetotum, windmill, treadmill; turnspit, jack, smokejack; flywheel, gearwheel, cogwheel, roller, caster, sheave, pulley; gyroscope, gyrostat; merry-go-round.
pivot, axle, axis, gudgeon, swivel, hinge, pin, gimbals; arbor, mandrel, reel, spool, bobbin, cop, quill, pirn (*dial.*) whorl, wharve.
science of rotary motions: trochilics, gyrostatics.
II. *Verbs.* **rotate,** revolve, spin, rev (*aviation cant*), turn, turn round, encircle, circulate, swirl, gyrate, gyre, wheel, trundle, roll, twist, twiddle (*as one's thumbs*), twirl, whirl; roll up, furl; box the compass; spin like a top (*or* teetotum).
III. *Adjectives.* **rotatory,** rotary, rotating, rotational, rotative, trochilic.
whirling, gyral, gyratory, revolving, gyrational, vertiginous, vortical, vorticose, circumvolutory, circumgyratory, circumrotatory; Ixionian.
See also REGULARITY.—*Antonyms.* See UNFOLDMENT.

---

rotten, *adj.* decayed, corrupt, putrid; foul, unclean, impure, fetid. See DETERIORATION, UNCLEANNESS.

ROTUNDITY.—I. *Nouns.* **rotundity,** rotundness, roundness, sphericity, globularity, cylindricity, spheroidicity *or* spheroidity, globosity; completeness, entirety.
cylinder, cylindroid, barrel, drum; roll, roller, rolling-pin, rundle, column.
sphere, globe, ball, spheroid, globoid, geoid, ellipsoid; drop, spherule, globule; bulb, bullet, pellet, pill, marble, pea, knob.
[*of speech*] **fullness,** sonority, sonorousness, fluency, grandiloquence, magniloquence.
[*of persons*] **plumpness,** chubbiness, obesity, stoutness, podginess, buxomness, *embonpoint* (*F.*).
II. *Verbs.* **round,** fill out, make rotund, render spherical, sphere, form into a sphere, roll into a ball.
III. *Adjectives.* **rotund,** round, rounded out, rotundate, circular, spherical, spheroidal, globular, globate (*rare*), globoid, globous, globose; bulbous, fungiform; conic, conical; cylindric *or* cylindrical, cylindroid *or* cylindroidal; beadlike, bead-shaped, monilated, moniliform; pea-shaped, pisiform; *teres atque rotundus* (*L.: said of a wise man*); round as an orange (an apple, a ball, a billiard ball, *or* a cannon ball).
bell-shaped, campaniform, campanulate, campanulous, campaniliform (*rare*), campanular.
egg-shaped, ovoid, ovate, oviform, oval, elliptical, ellipsoid *or* ellipsoidal, obovate (*bot.*), obovoid (*bot.*).
pear-shaped, pyriform, obconic *or* obconical.
[*of speech, literary style, etc.*] **full,** rounded, sonorous, orotund, magniloquent, grandiloquent, mouth-filling, flowing, fluent.
[*of persons*] **plump,** chubby, obese, stout, fat, podgy, buxom, full-fleshed, full-formed, crummy (*Eng. slang*).
See also CIRCULARITY, CURVATURE.—*Antonyms.* See ANGULARITY, STRAIGHTNESS.

ROUGHNESS.—I. *Nouns.* **roughness,** unevenness, irregularity; asperity, rugosity, corrugation, nodosity, nodulation, hispidity, villosity, pilosity, hairiness etc. (see *adjectives*); texture, grain, tooth.
hair, filament, down, pubescence (*bot. and zoöl.*), fimbria (*pl.* fimbriæ: *tech.*), fringe, villus (*pl.* villi: *tech.*); wool, fur, coat, mat, thatch (*jocose*), mop, shock, tangle, shag, mane, pompadour, topknot, elf locks, scolding locks (*colloq.*), scalp lock; tress, lock, curl, ringlet; eyelashes, lashes, cilia (*sing.* cilium); beard, whiskers, side whiskers, burnsides (*U. S. colloq.*), mutton chops (*slang*), imperial, Vandyke, goatee; moustache.

bristle, seta (*L. pl.* setæ: *tech.*), setula *or* setule (*tech.*), striga (*pl.* strigæ: *bot.*), pappus (*bot.*), feeler, vibrissa (*pl.* vibrissæ: *as cat's whiskers or the hairs in the nostrils of man*); awn (*bot.*), beard (*as of barley*), arista (*L. pl.* aristæ: *tech.*).
feather, plume, quill, plumule (*zoöl.*), filoplume (*zoöl.*), scapular (*chiefly in pl.: zoöl.*), covert (*zoöl.*), beam *or* beam feather (*esp. of a hawk*), pinion, remex (*pl.* remiges); tuft, crest, panache (*esp. on a helmet*).
plumage, feather (*chiefly in pl.*), feathering, down, mail (*breast feathers, esp. of a hawk*), mantle, hackle (*as of a hen*), mirror (*as of a duck's wing*), speculum (*L. pl.* specula).
nap, pile, shag; fleece, wool, fluff, down, fur; cotton, silk, velvet, plush, duvetyn.
II. *Verbs.* **roughen,** rough, rough up, crinkle, ruffle, crumple, rumple; corrugate; stroke the wrong way, rub the fur the wrong way.
III. *Adjectives.* **rough,** uneven, bumpy (*said esp. of a natural disturbance of air currents which causes uneven flight*), irregular, unlevel, rocky, broken, craggy, cragged, rugged, jagged; cross-grained, gnarled, gnarly, knotted, knotty, nodose (*tech.*), nodular, nodulated, nodulose, scraggly, scraggy; wrinkled, wrinkly, corrugated, crinkly, rugose, rugulose; scaly, scabrous, coarse (*in texture*).
hairy, hirsute, tufted, bushy, bearded, shaggy; ulotrichous (*anthropol.*), woolly-haired, woolly-headed; unshorn, unshaven, pilose, pileous, pilous (*rare*), pappose (*bot.*), ciliate *or* ciliated (*as a leaf*), filamentous, crinose (*rare*), crinite, villous, nappy, trichoid, hairlike.
bristly, prickly, setose, setaceous, setulose, hispid, hispidulous (*tech.*), strigose (*bot. and zoöl.*), strigate (*bot.*); setiferous, setigerous; "like quills upon the fretful porcupine" (*Hamlet*).
downy, fluffy, pubescent; velvety; woolly, flocculent, flaccose (*esp. bot.*), lanate, lanuginose *or* lanuginous, tomentose (*tech.*); silky, sericeous (*tech.*); feathery, plumate (*zoöl.*), plumose, plumous.
fringed, edged, bordered, fimbriate (*tech.*), befringed, fimbriated, laciniate *or* laciniated (*esp. bot.*), laciniose, cirrate (*zoöl.*).
crude, unwrought, roughhewn, unfashioned, uncut (*as a diamond*), formless, shapeless; incomplete, unfinished, imperfect, rudimentary, vague; preliminary, approximate, inexact, passable, general (*as a sketch or guess*).
[*of the sea or the weather*] **tempestuous,** boisterous, turbulent, violent, wild, stormy, inclement.
[*harsh to the ear*] **harsh,** discordant, grating, jarring, inharmonious, gruff, hoarse, raucous; aspirated (*as, the* rough *breathing in Greek*).
[*harsh to the taste*] **tart,** acrid, sharp, austere, sour, astringent (*as,* rough *wine*).
unrefined, coarse, rugged, unpolished, unkempt, uncultivated, uncultured, rude, blunt, gruff, brusque, churlish, uncivil, discourteous.
disorderly, riotous, noisy, unrestrained, vehement, rowdy, rowdyish, uproarious.
unfeeling, inconsiderate, hard, harsh, cruel, insensate; severe, drastic.
IV. *Adverbs.* **roughly,** unevenly, irregularly, etc. (see *adjectives*); harshly, cruelly, severely; incompletely, approximately, generally.

See also DISCOURTESY, FORMLESSNESS, HARDNESS, SEVERITY, STRIDENCY, TEXTURE, VIOLENCE.—*Antonyms.* See SMOOTHNESS.

---

round, *adj.* rounded, circular, oval; globular, spherical, orbed, bulbous rotund. See CIRCULATORY, ROTUNDITY.
round, *n.* revolution, course, turn, lap, ring, cycle, circle; routine. See CIRCUIT, REGULARITY.
rouse, *v.* excite, agitate, touch, move, inspire, stimulate, whet, incite. See EXCITEMENT, MOTIVE.
rout, *v.* overcome, conquer, beat, vanquish. See SUCCESS.
route, *n.* path, road, course, track, itinerary, circuit. See JOURNEY, WAY.
routine, *n.* beat, round, walk; red tape, convention; course, method, system, procedure. See BUSINESS, HABIT, ORDER.
rove, *v.* roam, wander, range, prowl, ramble. See JOURNEY.
roving, *n.* wandering, vagrancy, emigration, *Wanderlust* (*Ger.*), See JOURNEY.
row, *v.* pull, paddle, punt, scull. See NAVIGATION.
[1]**row,** *n.* quarrel, brawl, riot, uproar. See VIOLENCE.
[2]**row,** *n.* rank, file, series, line; street, court. See CONTINUITY, HABITATION.

rowdy, *n.* roisterer, ruffian, brawler, tough (*U. S.*). See BAD MAN, BLUSTERER.
rowdyism, *n.* ruffianism, blackguardism. See VULGARITY.
rower, *n.* oar, oarsman, sculler. See MARINER.
royal, *adj.* regal, kingly, imperial, majestic; princely, courtly. See AUTHORITY, NOBILITY.
royalty, *n.* kingship, sovereignty; percentage, share, compensation. See AUTHORITY, PAYMENT.
rub, *v.* smooth, scour, polish, burnish, curry; pet (*an animal*), stroke, knead, massage. See FRICTION, TOUCH.
rubbish, *n.* waste, refuse, trash, junk, litter, *débris* (*F.*). See INUTILITY.
rude, *adj.* impudent, insulting, churlish, unpolished, uncultured, vulgar; rough, barbarous, coarse, uneven. See DISCOURTESY, FORMLESSNESS.
rudiment, *n.* germ, seed, embryo, root. See CAUSE.
rudimentary, *adj.* elementary, primal, original, embryonic; simple, undeveloped, premature. See BEGINNING, NONPREPARATION.
rudiments, *n. pl.* elements, first principles, first steps, ABC. See BEGINNING.
rueful, *adj.* sorrowful, mournful; regretful, penitent. See DEJECTION, REGRET.
ruffian, *n.* rough, rowdy, bully, hoodlum. See BAD MAN.
ruffle, *v.* rumple, muss, dishevel; excite, perturb, agitate, irritate, vex; ruff, plait, flounce, pucker, crinkle. See DISORDER, EXCITEMENT, ROUGHNESS.
rug, *n.* floor covering, mat, carpet. See COVERING.
rugged, *adj.* cragged, jagged, uneven, rough; unkempt, seamed, wrinkled; harsh, stern. See ROUGHNESS.
ruin, *n.* downfall, overthrow, failure, wreck, destruction. See ADVERSITY.
ruin, *v.* smash, shatter, demolish, overthrow, crush, fell, destroy; violate, seduce; imporverish, beggar. See DESTRUCTION, IMPURITY, POVERTY.
ruinous, *adj.* disastrous, calamitous, destructive; decayed, dilapidated. See DESTRUCTION, DETERIORATION.

RULE.—I. *Nouns.* **rule,** regulation, law, measure, decision, ruling, prescription, precept, canon, guide, maxim, formula, convention, standard, test, criterion, model, precedent, rut, system, even tenor; habit, routine, custom, *règlement* (*F.*), order, method; nature, principle; order of things, normal condition (*or* state), normality, normalcy, ordinary (*or* natural) condition; standing order, hard and fast rule, Procrustean law, law of the Medes and Persians.

uniformity, regularity, constancy, consistency; punctuality, exactness, clockwork precision.

sway, government, dominion, empire, authority, control, direction, jurisdiction, sovereignty, regnancy, reign.

ruler, straightedge, strip; slide rule, folding rule, parallel ruler.

II. *Verbs.* **rule,** control, govern, reign, guide, conduct, direct, command, manage; prevail, predominate, obtain; curb, bridle, restrain.

decide, determine, settle, fix, establish, conclude, decree, adjudicate, judge, hold, pass upon.

III. *Adjectives.* **ruling,** controlling, governing, reigning, etc. (see *verbs*); predominant, regnant.

uniform, regular, symmetrical, constant, steady, according to rule; normal, natural, habitual, customary; methodical, systematic, orderly.

See also AUTHORITY, CONFORMITY, HABIT, INFLUENCE, JUDGMENT, LEGALITY, PRECEPT.—*Antonyms.* See DISOBEDIENCE, LAXITY, MULTIFORMITY.

---

ruler, *n.* chief, governor, head, president, director, sovereign, emperor, king, etc.; rule, straightedge. See AUTHORITY, MASTER, RULE.
ruling, *adj.* paramount, supreme, commanding, sovereign. See AUTHORITY.
rumble, *n.* rumble seat; rumbling, thunder, reverberation. See REAR, ROLL.
rumor, *n.* hearsay, report, talk, gossip, scandal. See NEWS.
rump, *n.* buttocks, croup (*of a horse*); remnant, fag-end. See REAR, REMINDER.
rumple, *v.* dishevel, wrinkle, crumple, ruffle, muss. See ROUGHNESS

run, *v.* proceed, elapse; drive, propel, operate, turn; flow, pour, stream, spread, sprint, gallop, flee. See LAPSE, MOTION, RIVER, VELOCITY.
run, *n.* way, wont; average, rule; stream, brook, flow; roulade; course, succession; trot, gallop, canter. See HABIT, MEAN, MOTION, MUSIC, REPETITION, VELOCITY.
rung, *n.* round, rundle, step, spoke. See SUPPORT.
runner, *n.* tendril, sarmentum (*bot.*); hotel runner, touter; courier, messenger. See PART, PETITIONER, TRAVELER.
rupture, *n.* quarrel, schism, feud, faction; break, burst, split, fracture, hernia (*med.*). See DISCORD, DISJUNCTION.
rural, *adj.* rustic, country, agricultural, agrarian, pastoral, bucolic. See HABITATION, HUSBANDRY.
ruse, *n.* trick, hoax, artifice, stratagem, subterfuge. See CUNNING.
rush, *v.* swarm, flock; storm, charge, assault; speed, dash, sweep, scurry, dart, tear. See ASSEMBLAGE, ATTACK, HASTE, VELOCITY.
rush, *n.* crowd, throng; precipitation, dash, charge, drive. See ASSEMBLAGE, HASTE.
rust, *v.* corrode, oxidize, deteriorate. See DETERIORATION.
rustic, *adj.* rural, countrified, agricultural, agrarian, pastoral; awkward, crude, rude, plain, simple. See HUSBANDRY, PEOPLE.
rustic, *n.* countryman, peasant, swain. See PEOPLE.
rustle, *v.* crackle, swish; *Slang:* hustle; steal (*cattle*). See FAINTNESS, ACTIVITY, STEALING.
rusty, *adj.* rusted, time-worn, decrepit, inactive, antiquated. See DETERIORATION.
rut, *n.* groove, track, channel; course, habit, practice. See FURROW, RULE.
ruthless, *adj.* cruel, pitiless, merciless, relentless. See MALEVOLENCE.

S

Sabbath, *n.* Sunday, Lord's day, First day, day of rest. See REPOSE.
sac, *n.* cyst, pocket, vesicle. See RECEPTACLE.
sacrament, *n.* ceremony, sacred rite. See RITE.
sacred, *adj.* holy, hallowed, inviolable; scriptural, biblical. See DEITY, SCRIPTURES.
sacrifice, *n.* victim, offering, hecatomb, suttee; immolation, holocaust. See IDOLATRY, KILLING.
sacrifice, *v.* immolate; destroy, demolish; surrender, give up, offer. See ATONEMENT, DESTRUCTION, GIVING.
sad, *adj.* dark, dull, sober; pensive, gloomy, woeful, melancholy; painful, mournful. See COLOR, DEJECTION, PAIN.
sadden, *v.* depress, discourage, deject, distress, grieve. See DEJECTION, PAIN.
safeguard, *n.* protection, guard; pass, passport, safe-conduct. See DEFENSE, PERMISSION, SAFETY.
safe-keeping, *n.* care, custody, charge, safety. See RESTRAINT.

SAFETY.—I. *Nouns.* safety, security, safeness, surety, impregnability, invulnerableness, invulnerability; escape, danger past (*or* over), coast clear.
safeguard, defense, safekeeping, protection, palladium, auspices, championship; safe-conduct, escort, convoy, guard, ward, custody, tutelage; guardianship, wardship, wardenship; rock, tower, shield, bulwark, sheet anchor; means of escape.
protector, defender, champion, paladin, guardian, preserver, life saver, warden, warder, custodian, duenna, chaperon, patron, guardian angel, tutelary deity (*or* saint).
watchman, patrolman, policeman, policewoman, police officer, officer (*colloq.*),

roundsman (*U. S.*), constable, *gendarme* (*F.*); cop, copper, bobby (*all slang*), blue coat (*colloq.*), detective, bull (*U. S. slang*), harness bull (*U. S. slang*), dick (*slang*), spotter (*slang*); sheriff, deputy; sentinel, sentry, scout.
watchdog, bandog, mastiff, bloodhound, police dog; Cerberus.
armed force, garrison, life guard, State guard, militia, regular army, marines, navy; man-of-war, battleship, cruiser, etc.; air force.
II. *Verbs.* **protect**, defend, fend (*archaic*), ward, guard, safeguard, watch over, take care of, preserve; cover, screen, shelter, house, harbor, shroud; flank, take precautions, "make assurance double sure" (*Macbeth*).
escort, support, convoy, accompany, conduct.
watch, mount guard, patrol, scout, spy, picket.
III. *Adjectives.* **safe**, secure, sound, whole, on *terra firma* (*L.*); on the safe side; under cover, under lock and key; out of danger, protected; at anchor, high and dry, above water; safe and sound, unscathed, uninjured, untouched, unharmed, unmolested, unhurt, unthreatened, unexposed.
snug, seaworthy, airworthy, weatherproof, watertight, waterproof, fireproof; bombproof, shellproof.
denfensible, tenable, proof against, invulnerable, unattackable, unassailable, "founded upon a rock" (*Bible*), impregnable.
guardian, tutelary, protective, defensive, preservative, protecting.
reliable, trustworthy, dependable, trusty, unfailing, certain, sure; cautious, circumspect, prudent.
harmless, innocuous, innoxious, innocent inoffensive, hurtless.
IV. *Adverbs.* **safely**, securely, etc. (see *adjectives*); with impunity; *ex abundanti cautela* (*L.*).

See also DEFENSE, ESCAPE, PRESERVATION, RESTRAINT, SECURITY.—*Antonyms* See DANGER.

---

sagacious, *adj.* discerning, penetrating, astute; shrewd, sage, wise. See DEPTH, WISDOM.

SAGE.—I. *Nouns.* **sage**, wise man; master mind, thinker, philosopher, *savant* (*F.*), pundit, man of learning; wiseacre (*archaic or ironical*).
authority, expert, specialist, luminary, shining light, oracle, mentor, Solon, Solomon, Buddha, Confucius, Mentor, Nestor, the Magi; Seven Wise Men of Greece, Seven Sages, "second Daniel," *magnus Apollo* (*L.*).
II. *Adjectives.* **sage**, wise, sagacious, sapient, erudite, authoritative, weighty; venerable, venerated, revered, reverenced, honored.
judicious, discreet, prudent, shrewd. well judged, discerning, acute, perspicacious, keen-sighted, clear-sighted.
solemn, grave, oracular, impressive, awe-inspiring; wise-looking, solemn-faced.

See also EXPERT, SCHOLAR, WISDOM.—*Antonyms.* See FOOL, IGNORAMUS.

---

sail, *v.* embark, take ship; cruise, navigate. See DEPARTURE, NAVIGATION.
sailing vessel, sailer, clipper, ship, brig, schooner, yacht. See SHIP.
sailor, *n.* seaman, tar, bluejacket. See MARINER.
salary, *n.* wages, remuneration; pay, compensation, stipend. See ACQUISITION, REWARD.

SALE.—I. *Nouns.* **sale**, disposal; vend (*Eng.*), vent (*rare*), vendition; auction, roup (*Scot.*), vendue, Dutch auction.
salableness, salability, marketability, vendibility, vendibleness.
salesmanship, selling ability, art of selling.
seller, vender, vendor (*law*); auctioneer, merchant, wholesaler, jobber, retailer, peddler; salesman, saleswoman.
II. *Verbs.* **sell**, vend, market, dispose of, make a sale, effect a sale; auction, sell at (*esp. U. S.*) auction, sell by (*esp. Brit.*) auction, put up to (*or* at) auction; dispense, offer, furnish, trade, barter, bargain, exchange, retail; deal in, sell off (*or* out), turn into money, realize; hawk, peddle; dump, unload, place; undersell.
win over, prevail on, persuade, convince: *an overworked slang sense of* sell.
betray (*by breach of trust*), deliver up, sell out (*slang*), play false, trick, knife (*slang*).

hoax, gull, cheat, deceive, trick, impose upon, string (*slang*), take in (*colloq.*): *in this sense*, sell *is slang.*
III. *Adjectives.* **salable,** marketable, vendible, merchantable; staple, in demand, popular.

See also BARTER, OFFER.—*Antonyms.* See PURCHASE.

---

salesman, *n.* commercial traveler, drummer (*U. S.*); clerk (*U. S.*). See REPRESENTATIVE.
salesmanship, *n.* selling ability, art of selling. See SALE.
salient, *adj.* notable, marked, signal; conspicuous, prominent. See IMPORTANCE, VISIBILITY.
saliva, *n.* spittle, sputum, spit. See EXCRETION.
salivate, *v.* ptyalize (*med.*), slaver. See EJECTION.
sallow, *adj.* pale, ashy; yellowish, jaundiced. See COLORLESSNESS, YELLOW.
saloon, *n.* bar, alehouse, pub (*Brit. slang*); hall, *salon* (*F.*), drawing-room. See HABITATION (*inn*), RECEPTACLE (*chamber*).
salt, *adj.* saline, salty, brackish. See PUNGENCY.
salubrity, *n.* healthfulness, salubriousness. See HEALTHINESS.
salute, *v.* bow, curtsy, uncover, kiss, salaam; hail, accost, greet. See COURTESY, SPEECH.
salvation, *n.* redemption, deliverance; regeneration. See DEITY, PIETY.
salve, *n.* ointment, lotion, liniment. See REMEDY.
same, *adj.* identical, selfsame, like, one; similar, equal. See IDENTITY.
sameness, *n.* duplication, exactness, counterpart, coincidence; likeness, resemblance. See IDENTITY, SIMILARITY.
sample *n.* example, specimen. See CONFORMITY, PART.
sanatorium, *n.* sanitarium, health resort. See HABITATION, REMEDY.
sanctify, *v.* sanction, justify; bless, hallow, consecrate, beatify. See DEITY, PIETY.
sanction, *n.* authorization, permission, authority, indorsement, license, approbation. See RIGHTFULNESS.
sanctuary, *n.* retreat, shelter, asylum, temple. See REFUGE.
sandy, *adj.* granular, gritty; carroty, brick-red. See POWDERINESS, RED.
sanguinary, *adj.* bloody, blood-stained, bloodthirsty, murderous. See KILLING.

SANITY.—I. *Nouns.* **sanity,** soundness, saneness, rationality, sobriety, poise, balance, reason, senses, common sense, horse sense (*colloq.*), sound mind, *mens sana* (*L.*); lucidity, lucid interval.
II. *Verbs.* **become sane,** come to one's senses, sober down, cool down, see things in proper perspective.
render sane, bring to one's senses, sober, bring to reason.
III. *Adjectives.* **sane,** rational, normal, wholesome, healthy, underanged, right-minded, sound, sound-minded, in possession of one's faculties, *compos mentis* (*L.*), mentally sound.
sensible, reasonable, sober, moderate, just, wise, intelligent, understanding (*as,* sane *views*).
IV. *Adverbs.* **sanely,** rationally, etc. (see *adjectives*); in reason, within reason, within bounds.

See also INTELLIGENCE, WISDOM.—*Antonyms.* See INSANITY.

---

sap, *n.* fluid, vital juice; vitality. See FLUIDITY, VIGOR.
sap, *v.* undermine, mine, tunnel; weaken, enervate. See CONCAVITY, WEAKNESS.
sarcasm, *n.* cynicism, acrimony; satire, sneer, taunt. See DETRACTION, DISAPPROBATION.
sarcastic, *adj.* satirical, sardonic, cynical, biting, ironical. See RIDICULE.

SATAN.—I. *Nouns.* **Satan,** the Devil, Lucifer, Belial, Beëlzebub, Mephistopheles, Mephisto, Samael, Asmodeus, Abaddon, Apollyon, Eblis (*Arabian*), Ahriman (*Zoroastrianism*), *Diabolus* (*L.*), Satanas (*archaic*), Shaitan (*Moham.*), *le Diable* (*F.*), Deil (*Scot.*); the Tempter, the Evil One, the Evil Spirit, the Old Serpent, the Author of Evil, the Archenemy, the Archfiend, the Father of Evil, the Father of Lies, the Prince of Darkness, the Prince of the Devils, his Satanic Majesty.

[*popular euphemisms*] Old Harry, Lord Harry, Old Nick, Auld Clottie (*Scot., in reference to the cloven foot*), Old Gentleman, Old One *or* Old 'un, Old Roger, Old Scratch, Auld Hornie (*Scot.*), Davy Jones (*sailors'* term).

fallen angels, unclean spirits, maleficent spirits, rulers of darkness, the powers of darkness.

Moloch, Mammon, Azazel, Beëlzebub (*in "Paradise Lost," the fallen angel next to Satan*); Belial (*in "Paradise Lost," one of the fallen angels*); Loki (*Norse myth.*).

Satanism, devilism, diabolism, diabolology *or* diabology, devil worship, demonism, demonology, demonoaltry, witchcraft; Manichæism *or* Manicheism; Black Mass, Black Magic.

Satanist, diabolist, demonist, demonolater, demonologist; Manichæan *or* Manichean.

II. *Verbs.* **Satanize,** demonize, diabolize (*rare*); bedevil, bewilder, possess, obsess.

III. *Adjectives.* **Satanic** *or* satanic, satanical, diabolic *or* diabolical, devilish, demoniac *or* demoniacal, infernal, hellborn.

See also HELL, MYTHICAL BEINGS (*maleficent spirits*).—*Antonyms.* See ANGELS.

SATIETY.—I. *Nouns.* **satiety,** fullness, repletion, satisfaction, saturation, plenitude, glut, surfeit, satiation.

II. *Verbs.* **sate,** satiate, satisfy, saturate, cloy, quench, slake, pall, glut, gorge, surfeit; bore, tire, spoil; have one's fill.

III. *Adjectives.* **satiated,** full, replete, satisfied, gorged, overgorged, overfed. *blasé* (*F.*), sick of, fed up (*slang*).

See also FATIGUE, SUFFICIENCY, WEARINESS.—*Antonyms.* See INSUFFICIENCY.

---

satire, *n.* irony, sarcasm, mockery. See FIGURE, RIDICULE.

satirical, *adj.* cynical, withering, sardonic; satiric, ironical; derisive, sarcastic. See DISAPPROBATION, FIGURE, RIDICULE.

satisfaction, *n.* amends, compensation, indemnification; contentment, contentedness; settlement, discharge; gratification, enjoyment; repletion, surfeit, sufficiency. See ATONEMENT, [2]CONTENT, PAYMENT, PLEASURE, SATIETY.

satisfactory, *adj.* dependable, reliable; sufficient, adequate, ample, enough. See BELIEF, [2]CONTENT.

satisfied, *adj.* convinced, confident, contented, gratified; full, satiated, replete, *blasé* (*F.*). See BELIEF, [2]CONTENT, SATIETY.

satisfy, *v.* convince, assure, persuade; quench, slake, gratify; surfeit, satiate; do, suffice. See BELIEF, PLEASURABLENESS, SATIETY, SUFFICIENCY.

saturate, *v.* fill; soak, seethe, sop. See COMPLETENESS, MOISTURE.

sauce, *n.* relish, appetizer; sauciness, impudence. See CONDIMENT, INSOLENCE.

saucy, *adj.* sprightly, debonair; impertinent, flippant, rude, disrespectful. See CHEERFULNESS, DISCOURTESY.

saunter, *v.* stroll, rove, ramble, wander. See JOURNEY, SLOWNESS.

savage, *adj.* brutal, brutish, ferocious, fiendish; raging, rabid, violent; unpolished, uncivilized, wild, barbarous. See MALEVOLENCE, RESENTMENT, VULGARITY.

savage, *n.* barbarian, brute, desperado, cutthroat, vandal. See EVILDOER.

save, *v.* rescue, deliver, liberate; economize, scrimp, hoard, husband; preserve, conserve, secure, keep. See DELIVERANCE, ECONOMY, PRESERVATION.

save, *prep.* except, excepting, barring, but. See UNCONFORMITY.

savings, *n. pl.* hoard, store. See ECONOMY.

Savior, *or* **Saviour.** *n.* Jesus Christ, The Messiah, The Redeemer. See DEITY.

SAVORINESS.—I. *Nouns.* **savoriness,** tastiness, palatability, pleasingness, daintiness, toothsomeness, delectability.
savor, taste, smack, *goût* (*F.*), flavor, relish, tang, tinge, piquancy, zest; odor, scent, aroma, bouquet; property, quality; reputation, name.
appetizer, *apéritif* (*F.*), *hors d'œuvres* (*F.*).
delicacy, tidbit, dainty, choice morsel, *bonne bouche* (*F.; pl. bonnes bouches*); ambrosia, nectar.
II. *Verbs.* **be savory,** tickle the palate (*or* appetite), tempt the appetite, taste good, flatter the palate; suggest the presence of.
savor, taste, smack of, smell; relish, like, enjoy, smack the lips, appreciate.
III. *Adjectives.* **savory,** tasty, palatable, good, pleasing, nice, dainty, exquisite, delicate, delectable (*archaic or ironical*), toothsome, appetizing, piquant, delicious, distinctive; rich, luscious, ambrosial, nectareous.
[*pleasing morally*] **reputable,** respectable, creditable, honorable, estimable.

See also TASTE.—*Antonyms.* See UNSAVORINESS.

---

say, *v.* assert, affirm, state, declare; express, voice; speak, talk, utter, pronounce, recite. See AFFIRMATION, LANGUAGE SPEECH.
saying, *n.* remark, assertion, dictum, observation; aphorism, adage, saw, proverb, byword. See AFFIRMATION, MAXIM.
scab, *n.* incrustation, scale, slough; *Trade-unionist cant:* strike breaker, black leg, rat. See COVERING; APOSTASY.
scaffold, *n.* block, guillotine, gallows; scaffolding, framework, platform. See SCOURGE, SUPPORT.
[1]scale, *n.* balance, steelyard, weighing machine. See GRAVITY.
[1]scale, *v.* weigh, measure. See MEASUREMENT.
[2]scale, *n.* coating, film, flake, scab, incrustation. See LAYER.
[2]scale, *v.* strip, peel, husk; flake, shave, skive, pare. See DIVESTMENT, LAYER.
[3]scale, *n.* series, graduation; rate, ratio; dimensions, measure, rule, pattern, model; gamut, run. See CONTINUITY, DEGREE, MEASUREMENT, MUSIC.
[3]scale, *v.* climb, clamber, ascent, mount. See ASCENT.
scaly, *adj.* squamate, squamous, scalelike. See COVERING.
scamp, *n.* rascal, scapegrace, rapscallion, wretch. See BAD MAN.
scamp, *v.* trifle, skimp (*colloq.*), slur. See NEGLECT.
scandal, *n.* slander, defamation, calumny, vilification; rumor, report, gossip, tattle. See DETRACTION, NEWS.
scandalize, *v.* horrify, shock, revolt. See DISAPPROBATION.
scant, *adj.* meager, stinted, scarce, insufficient, inadequate; few, narrow, poor, small, short. See INSUFFICIENCY, POVERTY, SHORTNESS.
scanty, *adj.* scarce, infrequent, inadequate, insufficient, few, exiguous; small, meager, limited; sparse, thin. See POVERTY, SMALLNESS, THINNESS.
scarce, *adj.* infrequent, few, rare, inadequate, scant. See INSUFFICIENCY.
scarcity, *n.* dearth, fewness, infrequency, deficiency, rareness. See INSUFFICIENCY.
scarlet, *adj.* bright red, cardinal, crimson. See RED.
scatter, *v.* dispel, disperse, sow, spread, radiate. See DIRPERSION.
scattered, *adj.* dispersed, disseminated, broadcast, strewn. See DISPERSION.
scene, *n.* view, prospect, landscape, spectacle, scenery; tableau, division of an act; flat (*theat.*), slide; surroundings, setting; occurrence, happening; outbreak, disturbance. See APPEARANCE, DRAMA, ENVIRONMENT, EVENT, EXCITABILITY.
scenery, *n.* view, landscape, seascape; scene, screen. See APPEARANCE, DRAMA.
scent, *v.* trace, track; perfume; sniff, snuff, smell; suspect, smell a rat (*colloq.*). See DISCOVERY, FRAGRANCE, ODOR, UNBELIEF.
scent, *n.* smell, fragrance, perfume; track, trail, spoor. See ODOR, RECORD.

SCEPTER.—I. *Nouns.* scepter *or* sceptre, rod, baton, verge, rod of empire, wand, staff, truncheon, mace, fasces (*Roman*), lituus (*Roman*), thyrsus (*Bacchus*); caduceus, Hermes' staff, Mercury's rod (staff, *or* wand); gavel; staff of office, emblem (*or* badge) of authority.
[*regal insignia*] crown, coronet, diadem; orb; pall; robes of state, ermine, purple; Prince of Wales' feathers, triple plume; signet, seal, privy seal *or* signet (*Eng.*); uræus (*Egyptian*); cap of maintenance (dignity, *or* estate).
[*ecclesiastical insignia*] tiara (*papal*), triple crown; ring, keys; miter *or* mitre, crozier, crook, staff; cardinal's hat; bishop's apron (sleeves, lawn, *or* gaiters), shovel hat, biretta, fillet.
[*military insignia*] star, bar, eagle, crown (*Brit.*), oak leaf, Sam Browne belt; shoulder strap, shoulder knot, aiguillette *or* aglet, *fourragère* (*F.*), epaulet; chevron, stripe.
regalia, insignia, paraphernalia, badges, emblems, ensigns, decorations.
throne, royal seat, chair, chair of state, seat, musnud *or* masnad (*Oriental*), divan, gaddi *or* guddee (*India*), Peacock Throne (*Oriental*), dais, woolsack (*seat of Eng. Lord Chancellor in the House of Lords*).
sovereignty, sway, dominion, power, sovereign authority, royal power, the throne, the crown, royalty, regality, regalia, sovranty (*poetic*).
II. *Verbs.* **scepter** *or* sceptre, enthrone, throne, enthronize (*archaic*), crown, seat, regalize (*rare*).
III. *Adjectives.* **sceptered** *or* sceptred, enthroned, crowned; royal, regal, sovereign, imperial.
See also AUTHORITY, INDICATION, TITLE.

---

scheme, *n.* design, project, idea, purpose, plot. See PLAN.
schemer, *n.* trickster, ingriguer, plotter. See CUNNING.
scheming, *adj.* designing, intriguing, crafty, artful. See CUNNING.

SCHOLAR.—I. *Nouns.* **scholar,** learned man, *savant* (*F.*); learned woman, *savante* (*F.*); pundit (*India*), moolvi (*Moham.*), guru (*Hindu*), schoolman, professor, academician, doctor, fellow, don (*Eng. Univ. cant*), graduate, postgraduate, gownsman, classicist, Latinist, Hellenist, Græcist, Hebraist, Sanskritist; sinologist, sinologue; linguist, glossolalist; philosopher, philomath, scientist; etymologist, philologist, lexicographer, glossographer, glossologist, lexicologist, scholiast, commentator, annotator; *littérateur* (*F.*), man of letters, man of learning *literati* (*L.; pl.*), *homo multarum literarum* (*L.*), giant (*or* colossus) of learning, walking encyclopedia; Admirable Crichton, prodigy.
bookworm, bibliophile, bibliomaniac, *helluo librorum* (*L.*), *bas bleu* (*F.; fem.*), bluestocking (*colloq.*), high-brow (*slang*), grind *or* dig (*U. S. college slang*).
pedant, doctrinaire, pedagogue, pantologist, Dr. Pangloss.
student, learner, pupil, schoolboy, freshman, junior, sophomore, senior, classman; studious person; close observer (*as, a* student *of life*).
II. *Adjectives.* **scholarly,** learned, well-read, well-grounded, well-educated, erudite, *savant* (*F.*), polyglot, high-brow (*slang*), blue (*colloq.*), academic, scholastic; brought up at the feet of Gamaliel.
See also KNOWLEDGE, LEARNER, SAGE, TEACHER.—*Antonyms.* See IGNORAMUS.

---

scholarship, *n.* erudition, knowledge; fellowship, studentship (*rare in U. S.*). See LEARNING, TROPHY.

SCHOOL.—I. *Nouns.* **school,** academy, lyceum, palæstra *or* palestra (*wrestling school*); seminary, college, phrontistery *or* phrontisterion (*rare or jocose*), educational institution, institute; university, 'varsity (*colloq.*), Alma Mater; day school, boarding school, private school, *pensionnat* (*F.*).
[*elementary*] **elementary school,** common school, dame school (*hist.*), grade (district, primary, nursery, kindergarten, *or* grammar) school; voluntary school (*Brit.*), board school (*Brit.*), mission school, National school (*Eng.*); junior high school (*intermediate: U. S.*).
[*secondary*] **secondary school,** preparatory school, high school, Latin school, grammar school (*in Great Britain, an endowed Latin school*), public school (*in Great Britain, an endowed school of high rank, such as Eton, Harrow, Winchester, etc.*); *lycee* (*F.*), *Gymnasium* (*Ger.*), *Realschule* (*Ger.*); normal school, training

college; military academy, naval academy; summer school, graduate school post-graduate school; correspondence school, university extension; fresh-water college (*U. S. slang*).

[*vocational*] **vocational school,** trade school, occupational school, school of art, commercial *or* business school, library school, polytechnic school, technological school, technical school, conservatory (*chiefly U. S.*), conservatoire.

Sunday school, Sabbath school, Bible school, Bible class.

class, division, form, grade, room; seminar.

schoolroom, classroom, recitation room, room, lecture room, lecture hall, theater *or* theatre, amphitheater *or* amphitheatre.

desk, reading desk, lectern, ambo, pulpit, forum, stage, rostrum, platform, dais.

schoolbook, textbook, manual, vade mecum; grammar, primer, New England Primer, abecedary, abecedarium, hornbook (*hist.*), reader, reading book.

[*in philosophy, art, etc.*] **sect,** denomination, disciples, followers, adherents, imitators, band, group (*as, the Hegelian* school; *the* school *of Raphael*).

II. *Verbs.* **school,** educate, instruct, teach, indoctrinate, train, drill, tutor; discipline, govern, control, bring under control.

III. *Adjectives.* **scholastic,** scholarlike, academic, clerkly (*archaic*), educational, instructional, cultural, collegiate, tuitionary.

pedantic, formal, modal, precisian, precise, hidebound, narrow.

See also LEARNER, LEARNING, TEACHER.

---

schoolmaster, *n.* teacher, pedagogue, preceptor, tutor, instructor. See MASTER.

science, *n.* formulated knowledge, scientific knowledge; efficiency. See SKILL.

scientific, *adj.* systematic, accurate, exact. See TRUTH.

scion, *n.* descendant, offspring, heir; bud, shoot, joint, slip. See INFANT, PART.

scoff, *v.* deride, sneer, ridicule, mock, jeer, taunt. See DISAPPROBATION, DISRESPECT.

scold, *v.* chide, rate, upbraid, rail. See DISAPPROBATION.

scope, *n.* range, compass, latitude, play, margin, liberty. See FREEDOM, SPACE.

scorch, *v.* singe, burn, sear. See HEAT.

score, *n.* scratch, streak; tally, account; composition; twice ten. See FURROW, LIST, MUSIC, TWENTY.

scorn, *n.* disdain, contemptuousness, derision, mockery. See CONTEMPT.

scorn, *v.* despise, disdain, abhor, detest. See CONTEMPT.

scoundrel, *n.* rascal, villian, knave, reprobate. See BAD MAN.

scour, *v.* rub, cleanse, scrub. See CLEANNESS, FRICTION.

SCOURGE.—I. *Nouns.* **scourge,** whip, lash, strap, thong, cowhide, knout, cat, cat-o'-nine-tails, black-snake, bullwhack (*U. S.*), rawhide, quirt, sjambok (*S. Africa*), kurbash (*Turkish*), chabuk (*Hind.*), azote (*Sp. Am.*), plet (*Russian*); rope's end.

rod, cane, stick, rattan, birch, birch rod; rod in pickle; switch, ferule, cudgel, truncheon.

[*other instruments of punishment*] **pillory,** stocks, whipping post, ducking stool, cucking stool, brank, trebuchet *or* trebucket, tumbrel (*wheeled cucking stool*); triangle, wooden horse, Iron Maiden of Nuremberg; thumbscrew, boot, rack, wheel; treadmill, crank, galleys; bed of Procrustes.

scaffold; block, ax, maiden (*Scot. hist.*), guillotine; stake; cross, gallows, gibbet, tree; noose, rope, halter, bowstring; death chair, electric chair, chair.

executioner, deathsman (*archaic*), headsman, hangman, Jack Ketch (*hist.*), carnifex (*Roman*), electrocutioner, garroter *or* garrotter, torturer, tormentor (*formerly an executioner*); firing party *or* firing squad (*mil.*); lynching party, necktie party (*slang*); lyncher.

[*condemned person*] **malefactor,** criminal, culprit, *condamné* (*F.*), victim, felon.

infliction, calamity, affliction, misfortune, suffering, punishment, vengeance, curse; pestilence, war, famine.

II. *Verbs.* **scourge,** whip, lash, flog; chastise, castigate, punish, harass, afflict.

See also PUNISHMENT.—*Antonyms.* See ACQUITTAL, REWARD.

scout, *n.* sentinel, watch, spy, observer, informer. See MESSENGER, SAFETY.
scowl, *v.* frown, glower, lower. See DISCOURTESY, SULLENNESS.
scramble, *v.* clamber, scrabble; contend, struggle; mix (*as eggs*). See ASCENT, CONTENTION, MIXTURE.
scrapbook, *n.* album, memory book. See CONPENDIUM.
scrape, *v.* shave, pare; save, economize; scratch, rub, smooth, rasp, clean; grate, file. See DEDUCTION, ECONOMY, FRICTION, POWDERINESS.
scrape, *n.* difficulty, predicament, emergency, fix. See DIFFICULTY.
scratch, *v.* scrape, rub, dig, rasp, abrade; scribble, scrawl. See FRICTION, WRITING.
scrawl, *v.* scribble, scratch, scrabble. See UNMEANINGNESS, WRITING.
scream, *v.* yell, screech, yelp; whistle, howl, roar. See CRY, WIND.
screen, *n.* curtain, blind, cover, cload; safeguard, bulwark, shield, breastwork; sieve, strainer; partition, shutter, blind. See AMBUSH, DEFENSE, OPENING, SHADE.
screen, *v.* sift, winnow, riddle; conceal, cover, cloak, camouflage, veil, mask, shelter, protect. See CLEANNESS, CONCEALMENT.
screw, *n.* twist, screwing; worm, jackscrew, screw propeller; miser, skinflint See DISTORTION, INSTRUMENT, PARSIMONY.
scribble, *v.* scrawl, scratch. See UNMEANINGNESS, WRITING.
scribble, *n.* scrawl, scrawling, scrabble, cacography. See UNMEANINGNESS, WRITING.
scribe, *n.* writer, amanuensis, penman, author. See WRITING.
scrimmage, *n.* tussle, scuffle, struggle, *mêlée* (*F.*), scrummage (*Rugby football*); row, brawl. See CONTENTION, DISCORD.

SCRIPTURES.—I. *Nouns.* **Scriptures,** sacred (*or* inspired) writings; revelation, divine inspiration, theopneusty (*rare*), afflatus.
[*Biblical*] **The Bible,** the Book, the Book of Books, the Good Book, the Word, the Word of God, Holy Writ, Holy Scriptures, Gospel.
Old Testament, Septuagint, Vulgate, Pentateuch, Octateuch; the Law, the Prophets; Hagiographa, Hierographa; Apocrypha.
Masora *or* Masorah; Talmud, Mishna, Gemara.
New Testament; Gospels, Evangelists, Acts, Epistles, Apocalypse, Revelation, Good Tidings, Glad Tidings.
inspired writers, prophet, evangelist, apostle, disciple, saint; the Fathers, the Apostolic Fathers; Holy Men of old.
[*Non-Biblical*] The Vedas, Upanishads, Puranas, Sutras, Sasta *or* Shastra, Tantra, Bhagavad Gita (*all Brahmanic*); The Koran *or* Alcoran (*Moham.*); Zendavesta, Avesta (*Zoroastrian*); Tripitaka, Dhammapada (*Buddhist*); Agamas (*Jain*); Granth, Adigranth (*Sikh*); the Kings (*Chinese*); the Eddas (*Scandinavian*).
II. *Adjectives.* **Scriptural,** Biblical, sacred, prophetic; evangelical, evangelistic, apostolic, apostolical, patristic *or* patristical; inspired, theopneustic (*rare*), apocalyptic, revealed; ecclesiastical, canonical, textual, textuary.
See also HETERODOXY, ORTHODOXY, THEOLOGY.

---

scroll, *n.* outline, synopsis; volute (*arch.*), cartouche, spiral; record, schedule. See LIST, ORNAMENT, ROLL.
scrub, *v.* clean, cleanse, wash, mop, scour, polish. See CLEANNESS, FRICTION.
scruple, *n.* scrupulousness, hesitation, qualm, doubt. See UNWILLINGNESS.
scrupulous, *adj.* strict, precise, careful, punctilious, conscientious. See CARE.
scrutinous, *adj.* critical, searching, attentive, exact. See NARROWNESS.
scrutiny, *n.* study, examination, search, inquiry. See ATTENTION.
sculptor, *n.* molder, modeler, carver, statuary. See ARTIST.
sculpture, *n.* carving, modeling, sculpturing, statuary. See FINE ARTS.
scum, *n.* froth, cream, spume; dross. See FOAM, INUTILITY.
scurfy, *adj.* scaly, flaky, furfuraceous. See LAYER.

scurrilous, *adj.* opprobrious, abusive, foul-mouthed, low, foul. See DISRESPECT.
sea, *n.* deep waters, tide, flood; wave, billow. See OCEAN.
seacoast, *n.* seaboard, seaside, seashore. See LAND.
seal, *n.* authority, confirmation; signet, stamp, impression. See EVIDENCE, INDICATION, PROTOTYPE.
seal, *v.* plug, lock secure, confine, occlude; close, conclude, clinch, ratify. See CLOSURE, COMPLETION.
seam, *n.* scar, cicatrix; line, wrinkle (*as on the forehead*); joint, juncture, suture (*anat.*); stratum, bed. See BLEMISH, FURROW, JUNCTION, LAYER.
seaman, *n.* sailor, seafarer. See MARINER.
seaplane, *n.* waterplane, hydro-airplane. See AËRONAUTICS.
search, *v.* seek, probe, examine, explore, sound, investigate. See INQUIRY.
search, *n.* investigation, research, scrutiny, quest. See INQUIRY.
searching, *adj.* penetrating, keen, sharp, scrutinizing. See SHARPNESS.
season, *n.* period, term, spell; seasonableness, proper time. See TIME, TIMELINESS.
season, *v.* harden, habituate, acclimatize; blend, tincture, flavor, salt, pepper, spice. See HABIT, MIXTURE, PUNGENCY.
seasonable, *adj.* early, prompt, punctual; timely, opportune. See EARLINESS, TIMELINESS.
seat, *n.* abode, residence, mansion; buttocks, breech; site, location, station; chair, bench, sofa, throne, saddle. See HABITATION, REAR, SITUATION, SUPPORT.
seaweed, *n.* algæ (*pl.*), dulse, kelp, rockweed. See VEGETABLE.
secede, *v.* rebel, mutiny; withdraw, retire. See DISOBEDIENCE, DISSENT.

SECLUSION.—I. *Nouns.* **seclusion,** privacy, retirement, delitescence, withdrawal, concealment, rustication, *villeggiatura* (*It.*), solitude, isolation, obscurity, background, separation, reclusion, recess, loneliness, voluntary exile, anchoretism, aloofness.
unsociability, unsociableness, insociableness. dissociability, disociality, inhospitality, domesticity, self-sufficiency.
retreat, cell, hermitage, cloister, convent; study, library, den (*colloq.*), sanctum sanctorum.
recluse, hermit, anchoret *or* anchorite, eremite, santon; pillarist, stylite: caveman, cave-dweller, troglodyte; cynic, Diogenes.
II. *Verbs.* **seclude oneself,** keep aloof, withdraw, keep apart, separate oneself, shut oneself up; sport one's oak (*Eng. Univ. slang*); deny oneself, rusticate, retire, embower *or* imbower, retire from the world; take the veil.
III *Adjectives.* **secluded,** retired, private, solitary; sequestered, hidden, secret, covert, outlying, remote, back, aloof, out of the world; "the world forgetting, by the world forgot" (*Pope*); lonely, unfrequented.
unsociable, unsocial, insociable, dissocial, reserved, stand-offish, inhospitable, *sauvage* (*F.*), unclubbable (*colloq.*), cynical, anchoretic *or* anchoretical, hermitical, eremitic *or* eremitical, troglodytic; snug, domestic, stay-at-home.
uninhabited, unoccupied, untenanted, tenantless, abandoned, deserted.
Antonyms. See SOCIALITY.

---

[1]second, *n.* supporter, attendant; interval; tone; alto. See AUXILIARY, MUSIC.
[2]second, *n.* moment, instant, twinkling. See INSTANTANEITY.
second, *v.* stand by, back; support, encourage. See AID.
secondary, *adj.* second, subordinate, inferior. See INFERIORITY.
secondhand, *adj.* used, worn, not new; not originla. See DETERIORATION, OLDNESS.
second thought, reconsideration, retrospection, afterthought. See THOUGHT.

SECRET.—I. *Nouns.* **secret,** mystery, arcanum (*chiefly in pl.*, arcana); maze, labyrinth, intricacy, tangle, problem, poser; *terra incognita* (*L.*), sealed book; privacy, privity, confidence, communication.

enigma, riddle, puzzle, conundrum, charade, rebus, logogriph, *crux criticorum* (*L.*); Sphinx.
essential, substantial, life, vital part, indispensable element, requisite.
solution, key, open-sesame, clew *or* clue, explanation, interpretation, exegesis, elucidation, *dénouement* (*F.*), outcome, issue.
II. *Adjectives.* **secret**, concealed, hidden, confidential, unrevealed, undisclosed, untold, privy, private, unknown, veiled, screened, masked, cloaked, ensconced, unseen, dark, obscure, disguised, secluded, retired; involved, tortuous, circuitous, labyrinthine, mazy, meandrous; enigmatic *or* enigmatical, cryptic *or* cryptical, occult, inscrutable.
secretive, close, uncommunicative, silent, taciturn, reticent; insidious, sly, stealthy, furtive, clandestine, underhand, covert, surreptitious.
III. *Adverbs.* **secretly**, privily, privately, in private, in secret, clandestinely, covertly.
See also CONCEALMENT, DIFFICULTY, INQUIRY, INTERPRETATION, LATENCY, UNINTELLIGIBILITY.—*Antonyms.* See ARTLESSNESS, DISCLOSURE, MANIFESTATION, NEWS.

---

secretary, *n.* writing desk, escritoire; clerk, stenographer, typist, amanuensis. See RECEPTACLE, RECORDER.
secrete, *v.* conceal, hide; cache; separate, omit. See CONCEALMENT, EXCRETION.
secreting organ, secretive gland, glandular organ. See CONCEALMENT.
secretory, *adj.* secretive, glandular. See CONCEALMENT.
sect, *n.* denomination, creed, party, faction. See CLASS, PARTY, SCHOOL.
sectarian, *adj.* denominational; schismatic, intolerant. See DISSENT, HETERODOXY.
sectarianism, *n.* dissent, nonconformity, denominationalism. See HETERODOXY.
secular, *adj.* worldly, temporal, nonclerical, lay. See LAITY.

SECURITY.—I. *Nouns.* **security**, secureness, stability, strength, firmness, solidity, fastness, tightness, reliableness, impregnability: *opposite of* insecurity.
confidence (*of power or safety*), assurance, assuredness, unconcern, certainty, certitude, ease, self-sufficiency; overconfidence, cocksureness.
protection, defense, guard, safeguard, safety, shelter, bulwark.
guaranty, guarantee, assurance, insurance, warranty, engagement, undertaking, agreement, contract, covenant; pledge, vadium (*law*), collateral, earnest, stake, deposit, pawn, bail, gage, tie; debenture, bond, stock, scrip, consol, mortgage; bill of sale, hypothecation, pignoration, surety, lien, promissory note, note, IOU, bill, bill of exchange, personal security.
acceptance (*of a bill*), indorsement *or* endorsement, signature, execution; stamp, seal.
authentication, verification, warrant, certificate, voucher, receipt, attested copy.
deed, instrument, title deed, indenture; charter, paper, parchment, settlement, will, testament, codicil.
[*one who becomes surety for another*] **guarantor**, guarantee, surety, warrantor (*law*), sponsor, insurer, bail, mainpernor (*hist.*), mainprise (*hist.*); hostage; godfather, godmother.
[*in plural*] **securities**, negotiable instruments, shares, stocks, bonds, government paper.
II. *Verbs.* **secure**, guard, protect, defend, preserve, make safe, fortify.
guarantee, vouch, contract, undertake, warrant, assure, insure, underwrite, indorse, accept.
execute (*as a deed*), complete, make; stamp, sign, seal, deliver.
give security, give bail, go bail; pawn, put in pawn, pledge, pop (*slang*), spout (*slang*), hock (*slang*), impignorate, mortgage, hypothecate.
obtain, acquire, get, procure, bag, gain, win, achieve, attain; bespeak, preëngage.
[*to make fast*] **fasten**, tie, bind, shackle, fetter; close, confine, seal, inclose *or* enclose, cage, imprison, restrain.
III. *Adjectives.* **secure**, untroubled, unmolested, undisturbed, easy (*in mind*), confident, careless, light-hearted, unconcerned, care-free.

incautious, careless, overconfident, heedless, negligent, unsuspecting, unwary. **confident** (*in opinion*), certain, sure, positive, cocksure, assured, self-sufficient, self-confident.

[*free from danger*] **safe**, unexposed, guarded, protected, preserved, insured.
[*in safe keeping*] **secured**, guarded, protected, preserved; in custody.
firm, steady, reliable, strong, fast, tight; impregnable, unassailable.
pledged, pawned, impignorate, in pawn, up the spout (*slang*); on deposit, at stake, as earnest.

IV. *Adverbs.* **securely**, safely, in security; firmly, etc. (see *adjectives*).

See also ACQUISITION, JUNCTION, RESTRAINT, SAFETY, TAKING (*take up*), TREASURY.—*Antonyms.* See DANGER.

---

sedate, *adj.* grave, staid, demure, serious; inexcitable, serene, composed. See DEJECTION (*serious*), INEXCITABILITY.

sedateness, *n.* sobriety, seriousness, calmneess, tranquillity. See GRAVITY.

sediment, *n.* dregs, lees, grounds, deposit. See DENSITY, UNCLEANNESS.

sedition, *n.* treason, agitation, lese majesty. See DISOBEDIENCE.

seduce, *v.* allure, mislead; ravish, violate, rape, deflower. See DECEPTION, IMPURITY.

sedulous, *adj.* diligent, persevering, untiring, assiduous. See ACTIVITY.

see, *v.* attend, mark, notice; perceive, apprehend, comprehend, realize; behold, discern, recognize. See ATTENTION, KNOWLEDGE, VISION.

seed, *n.* germ, egg, sperm, semen; stone (*of a fruit*), pip; progeny, offspring; grain. See CAUSE, DENSITY, POSTERITY, POWDERINESS.

seek, *v.* search, explore, inquire; try, attempt. trace. See INQUIRY, PURSUIT.

seem, *v.* appear, look. See APPEARANCE, [1]SOUND.

seemly, *adj.* meet, fitting, becoming, expedient; right, proper, suitable. See EXPEDIENCE, RIGHTFULNESS.

seer, *n.* prophet, diviner, soothsayer. See ORACLE.

seesaw, *v.* teeter (*U. S.*), alternate, crossruff (*card playing*). See OSCILLATION.

seethe, *v.* boil, decoct; soak, sop, saturate. See HEAT, MOISTURE.

seize, *v.* grasp, fathom, understand; take, appropriate; snatch, grab, clutch See INTELLIGIBILITY, POSSESSION, TAKING.

seizure, *n.* access, paroxysm, convulsion, fit, spell, stroke; assumption, infringement. See AGITATION, ATTACK, DISEASE, RIGHTLESSNESS.

seldom, *adv.* rarely, occasionally, infrequently. See INFREQUENCY.

select, *v.* pick, choose, glean; differentiate. See CHOICE, SPECIALTY.

selection, *n.* designation, specification, classification. See CLASS.

self-assertive, *adj.* self-asserting, bumptious, forward, presumptuous. See INSOLENCE.

self-control, *n.* poise, equanimity; self-denial, self-command, self-possession. See INEXCITABILITY, RESOLUTION.

self-defense, *n.* self-preservation, resistance. See DEFENSE.

self-denial, *n.* self-control, self-sacrifice, stoicism, devotion. See RESOLUTION, UNSELFISHNESS.

self-educated, *adj.* self-taught, self-instructed, autodidactic (*rare*). See KNOWLEDGE.

self-esteem, *n.* self-respect, self-approbation; conceit. See PRIDE.

self-governing, *adj.* autonomous, sovereign, self-directing. See FREEDOM.

self-importance, *n.* self-conceit, consequence, consequentialness, pompousness, pomposity, arrogance. See PRIDE.

self-indulgent, *adj.* self-gratifying, wild, fast, dissipated, profligate. See INTEMPERANCE.

SELFISHNESS.—I. *Nouns.* **selfishness**, self-love, self-regard, self-indulgence, self-worship, self-seeking, self-interest; egotism, egoism. selfism (*rare*), suicism (*rare*); illiberality, meanness, hoggishness, piggishness.

self-seeker, timeserver, monopolist, nepotist, dog in the manger, hog, road-hog (*colloq.*); toady, sycophant, tuft-hunter; fortune hunter, gold digger (*slang*).
II. *Verbs.* **be selfish,** indulge (*or* pamper) oneself; feather one's nest; have an eye to the main chance, live for oneself alone.
III. *Adjectives.* **selfish,** self-seeking, self-indulgent, self-interested; self-centered; egotistic *or* egotistical, egoistic *or* egoistical.
illiberal, mean, niggardly, stingy, ungenerous, narrow-minded; mercenary, hireling, venal, sordid, covetous, grasping, piggish, hoggish.
worldly, unspiritual, earthly, earthly-minded, mundane, worldly-minded, worldly-wise; timeserving, interested.
IV. *Adverbs.* **selfishly,** ungenerously; for private ends, from selfish motives.

See also DESIRE, MISANTHROPY, PARSIMONY, VANITY.—*Antonyms.* See UNSELFISHNESS.

---

self-luminous, *adj.* phosphorescent, luminescent, radiant. See LUMINARY.
self-propelling, *adj.* self-acting, self-moving, locomotive, automatic. See JOURNEY.
self-satisfied, *adj.* self-complacent, smug, conceited. See VANITY.
self-seeker, *n.* monopolist, timeserver. See SELFISHNESS.
self-sufficiency, *n.* self-confidence, self-complacency, self-admiration, conceit. See SUFFICIENT, VANITY.
self-willed, *adj.* obstinate, unyielding, headstrong. See WILL.
sell, *v.* vend, market, auction, peddle, retail, trade; betray; *Slang*: deceive, hoax. See SALE.
seller, *n.* vender, vendor (*law*), merchant, auctioneer. See SALE.
semblance, *n.* counterpart, facisimile, cast, model; representation, reproduction; likeness, resemblance. See COPY, IMITATION, SIMILARITY.
semicircle, *n.* half circle. See CIRCULARITY.

SEMILIQUIDITY.—I. *Nouns.* **semiliquidity,** semifluidity, colloidality (*tech.*); stickiness, viscidity, viscosity, gummosity (*rare*), gummosis (*bot.*), glutinosity, adhesiveness, mucosity, pastiness, thickening, spissitude, inspissation, jellification, incrassation, coagulation.
mud, slush (*esp. half-melted snow*), sludge, slosh, slime, ooze, mire, muck, dirt.
II. *Verbs.* **thicken,** inspissate, incrassate, coagulate, clot, curd, curdle, clabber (*as milk*), lopper (*dial.*); congeal, gelatinize, jellify, jelly, jell (*colloq.*); mash, squash (*colloq.*), crush, churn, beat up.
squelch (*as when walking in wet boots or through slush*), quelch (*dial.*), squish (*dial.*), squash (*colloq.*).
III. *Adjectives.* **semiliquid,** semifluid, semifluidic, half-melted, half-frozen; milky, lacteal, lacteous, lactescent, lactiferous, emulsive; clotted, curdled, thick, crass, uliginose *or* uliginous, succulent (*esp. bot.*).
gelatinous, gelatinoid, tremelloid (*bot.*), tremellose (*bot.*), colloidal, muculent (*bot.*), gelatiniform, jellied.
sticky, glutinous, viscid, viscous, adhesive, mucilaginous, ropy, pasty, tacky, gummy, gummous, albuminous, slimy, mucid, mucous, pituitous.

See also COHERENCE, DENSITY.—*Antonyms.* See FLUIDITY, FOAM, RARITY.

---

seminary, *n.* academy, lyceum, college. See SCHOOL.

SEMITRANSPARENCY.—I. *Nouns.* **semitransparency,** opalescence, milkiness, pearliness; mistiness, cloudiness, haziness, fogginess, filminess, frostiness.
[*comparisons*] muslin, gauze; mica, amber, mother-of-pearl, nacre, opaline, frosted glass, opal glass; mist, film.
II. *Verbs.* **cloud,** frost, cloud over, frost over, opalize.
III. *Adjectives.* **semitransparent,** semidiaphanous, semiopaque, semipellucid, opalescent, opaline, pearly, nacreous, milky, frosted; hazy, misty, cloudy, clouded, filmy, foggy.

See also CLOUD.—*Antonyms.* See OPACITY, TRANSPARENCY.

send, *v.* impel, hurl, fling, toss, push, thrust, drive; deliver, ship, dispatch, mail. See PROPULSION, TRANSFER.

senilty, *n.* decrepitude, superannuation, infirmity; old age, dotage. See IMPOTENCE, OLDNESS.

senior, *adj.* older, elder, oldest, firstborn. See AGE.

seniority, *n.* primogeniture; precedence. See AGE, PRIORITY.

sensate, *v.* feel, perceive, apprehend, sense. See SENSIBILITY.

sensation, *n.* feeling, emotion. See SENSIBILITY.

sensational, *adj.* lurid, exciting, stirring, melodramatic. See EXCITEMENT, YELLOW.

sense, *n.* import, significance, essence; feeling, emotion, sensation; sapience, rationality. See MEANING, SENSIBILITY, WISDOM.

senseless, *adj.* absurd, nonsensical, unreasonable; foolish, stupid, witless; insensible, unfeeling, unconscious; meaningless, unmeaning. See ABSURDITY, FOLLY, INSENSIBILITY, UNMEANINGNESS.

SENSIBILITY.—I. *Nouns.* **sensibility,** discernment, taste, receptivity; delicacy of feeling, sympathy, feeling, impressibility, susceptibility; cryptæsthesia *or* cryptesthesia (*psychol.*), subconscious perception; hyperæsthesia (*med.*), anaphylaxis (*med.*), æsthesia *or* esthesia, affectibility, sensitiveness; sensibleness, etc. (see *adjectives*).

sensation, impression, consciousness, feeling, sense, emotion.

II. *Verbs.* **sensate,** feel, perceive, apprehend, be sensitive to, sense.

render sensitive, sharpen, refine, rarefy, purify, spiritualize; excite, stimulate, sensitize (*tech.*), stir, cultivate.

cause sensation, impress, excite, produce an impression.

III. *Adjectives.* **sensible,** perceptible, apprehensible, discernible, observable, cognizable, perceivable, tangible; impressible, sensitive, susceptible; appreciable.

cognizant, aware, conscious, observant; convinced, satisfied, persuaded (*as, sensible of being tired*).

[*of good sense*] **intelligent,** understanding, reasonable, moderate, judicious, wise, discreet, sober, sound, practical.

IV. *Adverbs.* **sensibly,** perceptibly, intelligently, etc. (see *adjectives*).

See also SANITY, SENSITIVENESS, WISDOM.—*Antonyms.* See INSENSIBILITY.

SENSITIVENESS.—I. *Nouns.* **sensitiveness,** sensitivity (*chiefly tech.*), sensibility, perceptivity, perceptiveness; impressibility, susceptibility, susceptivity, susceptibleness, affectibility; vivacity, tenderness, feeling, emotion, sentimentality, sentimentalism.

II. *Verbs.* **be sensitive,** have a tender (*or* warm) heart; take to heart, shrink, wince, blench, quiver.

III. *Adjectives.* **sensitive,** impressible, impressionable, sensible, sentient, conscious, alive, alive to impressions, sensuous, perceptive, susceptive, susceptible, impressionable, responsive, sympathetic; warm-hearted, tender-hearted, soft-hearted, tender; sentimental, romantic; enthusiastic, impassioned, spirited, mettlesome, vivacious, lively, expressive, mobile.

excitable, oversensitive, supersensitive, hypersensitive, moody, impatient, inflammable, nervous, thin-skinned, fastidious.

acute, sharp, keen, intense, vivid, lively; discerning, discriminating, nice, subtle, delicate (*as a balance*).

uncertain, fluctuating, indeterminate, shaky, unsteady, inconstant, variable (*as, a sensitive market*).

IV. *Adverbs.* **sensitively,** impressibly, sensibly, acutely, uncertainly, etc. (see *adjectives*); to the quick, on the raw.

See also EXCITABILITY, FASTIDIOUSNESS, SENSIBILITY, SOFTNESS (*impressible*).—*Antonyms.* See INSENSITIVENESS.

---

sensual, *adj.* voluptuous, carnal, fleshly, gross, salacious. See INTEMPERANCE.

SENSUALIST.—*Nouns.* **sensualist,** Sybarite, voluptuary, man of pleasure, epicure, epicurean, *gourmet* (*F.*); gourmand, glutton, pig, hog, animal; votary of Epicurus; free liver, hard liver, libertine, Heliogabalus.

sensuous, *adj.* sentient, susceptible; emotional, pleasurable. See FEELING.
sentence, *n.* penalty, death warrant; decision, decree, verdict; expression, saying. See CONDEMNATION, JUDGMENT, MAXIM.
sententious, *adj.* concise, laconic, terse, pithy, crisp. See CONCISENESS.
sentient, *adj.* sensitive, susceptible, emotional. See FEELING.
sentiment, *n.* emotion, sympathy, tenderness; thought, preception, impression. See FEELING, IDEA.
sentimental, *adj.* simpering, languishing; romantic. See AFFECTATION, SENSITIVENESS.
sentinel, *n.* sentry, watch, guard, patrol, picket. See WARNING.
separate, *v.* bisect, divide, split; disjoin, disconnect, disunite, part, divorce; change, break up, split up, analyze. See BISECTION, DISJUNCTION, RESOLUTION.
separate, *adj.* separated, disconnected, parted, divorced, distinct, unattached, disjoined. See DISJUNCTION, FREEDOM.
separation, *n.* parting, divorce, disconnection, separateness; seclusion, isolation, segregation; disengagement, analysis; decomposition, disintegration, solution. See DISJUNCTION, EXCLUSION, LIBERATION, RESOLUTION.

SEQUEL.—*Nouns.* **sequel,** continuation, resumption; postscript, supplement, appendix, postlude, epilogue, peroration, codicil (*of a will*); suffix, tail, queue, train, wake, trail, rear; retinue, suite, appendage, tag, aftergrowth, afterpiece afterpart; afterthought, second thoughts, *arrière-pensée* (*F.*).
upshot, result, end, consummation, conclusion, solution, outgrowth, fruit, issue, final issue, *dénouement* (*F.*), consequence, effect, product, event, outcome, after effect, sequela (*pl.* sequelæ: *esp. med.*).
See also ADJUNCT, EFFECT, END, SEQUENCE.—*Antonyms.* See PRECURSOR.

SEQUENCE.—I. *Nouns.* **sequence,** succession, following, train, consecutiveness, coming after; consecution, series, progression, gradation, run (*as in card playing*), straight (*poker*); suite, set.
result, sequel, consequence, resultant, effect, issue, conclusion, event; aftermath, aftercrop, aftergrowth; afterclap, afterglow, aftertaste, aftersensation (*psychol.*).
continuation, prolongation, extension, continuity; mantle of Elijah; order of succession.
II. *Verbs.* **succeed,** come after, ensue, come next, follow, take the place of.
append, place after, subjoin, attach, suffix.
III. *Adjectives.* **sequent,** following, succeeding, subsequent, ensuing, sequential, consequent; proximate, next, consecutive.
IV. *Adverbs.* **after,** subsequently, behind, afterward, later.
See also FOLLOWING, ORDER, POSTERIORITY, REAR, SEQUEL.—*Antonyms.* See PRECEDENCE.

---

serene, *adj.* calm, cool, placid, unruffled, tranquil. See EXPECTANCY, INEXCITABILITY.
serenity, *n.* calmness, imperturbability, composure. See EXPECTANCY, INEXCITABILITY.
serf, *n.* bondman, slave, vassal, thrall. See SERVANT.
series, *n.* rank, file, line, row, chain, string; graduation, succession. See CONTINUITY, PROGRESSION.
serious, *adj.* sedate, staid, earnest, solemn; grand, impressive, important, weighty. See DEJECTION, IMPORTANCE.
sermon, *n.* discourse, preaching, exhortation, homily. See RITE, TEACHING.

SERVANT.—I. *Nouns.* **servant,** retainer, yeoman (*hist.*), follower, attendant, gillie (*Scot.*), henchman; squire, page, usher, cupbearer, trainbearer; equerry, groom, jockey, hostler *or* ostler, servitor (*archaic*), domestic, menial, help, helper, assistant, subordinate, secretary, clerk, stenographer, agent, underling, apprentice, understrapper, employee; bell boy, bell-hop (*slang*), chokra (*Hind.*), tiger, buttons (*colloq.*), caddie; valet, *valet de chambre* (*F.*), man, manservant (*pl.* menservants), bearer (*Anglo-Indian*), khitmutgar (*India*), orderly, messenger

boots (*Brit.*), butler, khansamah (*India*), steward (*on ship*), stewardess (*fem.*), **waiter,** lackey, footman, flunky (*colloq.*); boy (*any colored male servant, as in the Orient, South Africa, etc.*).
maidservant, maid, handmaid (*archaic*), lady's maid, abigail, ancilla (*rare*); nurse, *bonne* (*F.*), ayah (*India*), nursemaid, amah (*Oriental*); girl, help (*U. S. local*), cook, scullion, Cinderella; general servant (*Brit.*), general (*colloq.*), maid-of-all-work, domestic; washerwoman, laundress, charwoman.
dependent, hanger-on, satellite, parasite, *protégé* (*F.*), ward, hireling, mercenary, puppet, creature.
bondman, bondwoman (*fem.*), bondmaid (*fem.*), bondsman, bondswoman (*fem.*), serf, slave, bondslave, villein (*hist.*), vassal, thrall, churl *or* ceorl (*hist.*), helot (*ancient Sparta*), peon (*Latin America*).
subject, liege, liegeman, liege subject; native-born subject, naturalized subject.
retinue, train, suite, *cortège* (*F.*), following, bodyguard, staff, court.
[*body of assistants*] **staff,** force, office force (*or* staff); employees, workers, crew, the help (*esp. U. S.*).
II. *Verbs.* **serve,** minister to, help, aid, assist, succor, wait (attend, *or* dance attendance) upon; squire, valet, tend, do for (*colloq.*), attend; work for, be useful to, coöperate with, oblige; do service for, obey; officiate, act.
[*relating to the serving of food*] dish up, set on table, place, set ready, arrange; distribute, deal out, portion, help.
[*to meet the needs of*] **suffice,** satisfy, content; avail, answer, do, be suitable, suit, be sufficient for; benefit, subserve, promote, forward, further, advance, conduce to, contribute to.
treat, act toward, behave toward, require, use, deal by, pay out (*as, he* served *me shabbily*).
undergo, endure, sustain, pass through, pass, spend (*as, to* serve *a term in jail*).
handle (*as artillery*), work, operate, manipulate, manage.
supply, provide, furnish, accommodate, find, deliver, render (*as, to* serve *a town with gas*).
[*in various games*] put in play, deliver, pitch, throw, bowl.
III. *Adjectives.* **serviceable,** useful, helpful, coöperative, coöperating, advantageous, beneficial, convenient, valuable, handy; durable, lasting, practical.
See also AID, AUXILIARY, BUSINESS, INSTRUMENTALITY, OBEDIENCE, REPRESENTATIVE, UTILITY, WARFARE.—*Antonyms.* See MASTER.

---

service, *n.* good turn, kindness; servitude, employ, yoke, obedience; wear, use, utilization, aid, helpfulness; campaigning; office, duty; devotion. See GOOD, SUBJECTION, UTILITY, WARFARE, WORSHIP.
serviceable, *adj.* useful, helpful, advantageous, beneficial, convenient, durable, practical; subservient, utilitarian. See SERVANT, USE.

SERVILITY.—I. *Nouns.* **servility,** slavery, subjection, dependence; obsequiousness, slavishness, servileness, toadyism, subserviency; abasement, humility, prostration, toadeating, fawning, flunkyism, sycophancy.
sycophant, parasite, fawner, flatterer, cringer, snob, toady, toadeater, flunky, hanger-on, timeserver, Vicar of Bray; beat (*slang*), dead beat (*slang*); heeler, wardheeler (*both U. S. political cant*); carpet knight, *cavaliere servente* (*It.*); sponge, sponger, truckler, bootlicker (*colloq. or slang*).
[*in biology*] **parasite,** commensal, inquiline; ectozoön (*pl.* ectozoa: *external*), epizoön (*pl.* epizoa); entozoön (*pl.* entozoa: *internal*), intestinal worm; saprophyte; epiphyte (*med.*).
II. *Verbs.* **cringe,** bow, stoop, kneel; fawn, crouch, cower, sneak, crawl, sponge, toady, grovel; be servile, dance attendance on; go with the stream, follow the crowd, worship the rising sun; be a timeserver, *avaler des couleuvres* (*F.*).
III. *Adjectives.* **servile,** slavish, enslaved, dependent, subject, thrall, bond; subservient, obsequious, oily, pliant, cringing, fawning, truckling, groveling, sniveling, mealy-mouthed; sycophantic, parasitic *or* parasitical, abject, prostrate, base, mean, sneaking, timeserving.
IV. *Adverbs.* **servilely,** slavishly, obsequiously, etc. (see *adjectives*); "in a bondman's key" (*Merchant of Venice*); hat (*or* cap) in hand.
See also FLATTERY, HUMILITY, OBEDIENCE, SUBJECTION.—*Antonyms.* See CONTEMPT, INSOLENCE.

session, *n.* sitting (*as of a court*), meeting, conference, hearing. See COUNCIL.
set, *v.* coagulate, curdle; bar, exclude; put, lay, seat, locate, deposit, plant; whet, sharpen, strop; fix, settle, establish, stabilize. See DENSITY, EXCLUSION, LOCATION, SHARPNESS, STABILITY.
set, *n.* group, clique, coterie; party, faction, clan; trend, aim, drift, run, tendency. See ASSEMBLAGE, CLASS, DIRECTION.
set-off, *n.* offset, counterpoise. See COMPENSATION.
settle, *v.* adjust, reconcile, determine, stipulate; choose, elect, decide, determine; sink, subside, gravitate, drop; anchor, take root; pay, discharge, liquidate; alight, settle down; set, fix, stabilize. See ARRANGEMENT, CHOICE. DESCENT, LOCATION, PAYMENT, [1]REST, STABILITY.
settlement, *n.* adjustment, reconciliation; agreement, stipulation; colony, encampment; discharge, liquidation, defrayal; conveyance, disposition. See ARRANGEMENT, COMPACT, LOCATION, PAYMENT, SECURITY.
settler, *n.* colonist, squatter, immigrant; resident, dweller. See INHABITANT.

SEVEN.—I. *Nouns.* **seven,** heptad (*esp. chem.*), heptagon (*geom.*), heptahedron (*geom.*), heptameter (*pros.*), heptastich (*pros.*); septet (*esp. music*), septuor; heptarchy, Heptateuch (*Bible*), septennate (*period of seven years*).
II. *Verbs.* multiply by seven, make sevenfold, septuple.
III. *Adjectives.* **sevenfold,** septuple; heptad (*chem.*), heptavalent (*chem.*); heptangular, heptagonal, heptahedral, heptamerous (*bot.*), heptasyllabic; septennial, septenary.

SEVENTY.—I. *Nouns.* **seventy,** threescore and ten; septuagenarian, septuagenary; Septuagesima, Septuagint (*Greek version of the Old Testament, said to have been made by* 70 *translators*).
II. *Adjectives.* **seventieth,** septuagenary, septuagesimal.

---

sever, *v.* disjoin, divide, rend, dissever; fork, sunder, separate. See DISJUNCTION, DIVERGENCE.
several, *adj.* sundry, divers, various. See MULTITUDE.
severance, *n.* separation, disunion, disconnection, parting, dissociation, disjunction. See DIVORCE.

SEVERITY.—I. *Nouns.* **severity,** strictness, harshness, etc. (see *adjectives*); severeness, cruelty, sharpness, rigor, stringency, inclemency; austerity, gravity, seriousness; strictness, exactness, rigorousness, chasteness (*of style*).
[*arbitrary power*] tyranny, despotism, absolutism, autocracy, domination, oppression, assumption, usurpation, dictatorship, inquisition, reign of terror, iron rule, coercion, martial law.
bureaucracy, red-tapery, red-tapism, officialism, departmentalism.
tyrant, despot, autocrat, Draco, oppressor, inquisitor, extortioner; disciplinarian, martinet, stickler.
II. *Verbs.* **be severe,** etc. (see *adjectives*); assume, arrogate, usurp, take liberties, domineer, bully, tyrannize, put on the screw, be hard upon, illtreat, rule with a rod of iron, oppress, override, trample under foot, ride roughshod over, coerce; inflict, impose, wreak, hurl, drive.
III. *Adjectives.* **severe,** strict, hard, harsh, dour (*Scot.*), rigid, stern, rigorous, uncompromising, exigent, *exigeant* (*F.*), unyielding, hard-shell (*U. S. colloq.*), exacting, searching, inexorable, inflexible, obdurate, austere, relentless, stringent, peremptory, absolute, arbitrary, imperative, coercive, tyrannical, extortionate, oppressive, Draconian, barbarous, grinding, inquisitorial, iron-handed, cruel, arrogant; formal, punctilious, puritanical, precise, exact, prudish, strait-laced, forbidding.
[*of style, as in art and literature*] **unadorned,** unornamented, plain, restrained, suppressed, strict, terse, clear-cut, chaste, vigorous, nervous.
[*strict in judgment*] censorious, carping, faultfinding, caviling, hypercritical, sharp, biting, cutting, condemnatory, acrimonious, tart, sarcastic, bitter, keen, satirical.

[*of pain or anguish*] **distressing, painful, piercing, keen, sharp, afflictive, harrowing,** heartrending, grievous, worrying, carking (*archaic*), distressful, trying.
[*of weather*] **inclement, violent, extreme, rough, stormy, boisterous, vehement,** cold, bitter, rigorous.
IV. *Adverbs.* **severely, strictly, censoriously,** etc. (see *adjectives*); with a high (strong, tight, *or* heavy) hand; at the point of the sword (*or* bayonet).
See also COMPULSION, DISAPPROBATION, INSOLENCE, MALEVOLENCE, PAINFULNESS, PITILESSNESS, SHARPNESS, SIMPLENESS.—*Antonyms.* See MILDNESS.

---

sew, *v.* stitch, tack, bind, mend. See JUNCTION.
sex, *n.* gender, male or female. See CLASS.
shabby, *adj.* worn, threadbare; shameful, beggarly; stingy, miserly, penurious, mean; inelegant, inferior, faded, seedy. See DETERIORATION, DISREPUTE, PARSIMONY, POVERTY.
shack, *n.* shed, cabin, hut, hovel, shanty. See HABITATION.
shackle, *n.* bond, fetter, manacle, impediment, obstruction. See PRISON.

SHADE.—I. *Nouns.* **shade,** comparative darkness, dimness, obscurity, umbra (*tech.*), shadow, cloud, mist, dusk, duskiness, gloom, umbrage (*archaic or poetic in this sense*), somberness, seclusion; retreat, nook, *kala jagah* (*Hind.*).
screen (*against light or heat*), protection, shelter; awning, canopy, shutter, blind, window shade, venetian *or* Venetian blind, *jalousie* (*F.*), chick (*India*), *portière* (*F.*), purdah (*India*), curtain; globe (*as for a lamp*); veil, mantle, mask, yashmak (*Turkish*).
umbrella, gamp (*one large and loosely tied*), gingham (*colloq.*), chatta (*India*), chatri (*India*); sunshade, parasol, *en-tout-cas* (*F.*).
blinkers, blinders (*for horses*), eye shield, goggles, colored spectacles, smoked glasses.
[*departed spirit*] **ghost,** spirit, phantom, specter *or* spectre, shadow, apparition, manes (*pl.*), lemures (*pl.: Roman religion*).
trace, touch, tinge, suspicion (*colloq.*), *soupçon* (*F.*), suggestion, adumbration, hint, trifle, dash, flavor, smack, degree, slight difference.
[*in drawing and painting*] **gradation, intensity, depth, shading, variation;** hachure, crosshatching, stipple *or* stippling.
II. *Verbs.* **shade,** screen, cover, hide, ensconce, shelter, veil, cloak, shroud, canopy, curtain, mask, protect.
obscure, dim, cloud, eclipse, becloud, obfuscate, obumbrate (*rare*), beshade, beshadow, bedarken, overshadow.
[*in drawing and painting*] **darken,** blacken, deepen, intensify, gradate; hachure, crosshatch, stipple, shadow.
III. *Adjectives.* **shady,** umbrageous, shadowy, shadeful (*rare*), shaded, sheltered, dark, obscure.
equivocal, dubious, suspicious, questionable, doubtful, uncertain, mysterious, fishy (*slang*), disreputable (*as,* shady *conduct*).
See also AMBUSH, COLOR, CONCEALMENT, COVERING, DARKNESS, DEGREE, DIMNESS.—*Antonyms.* See LIGHT, LUMINARY.

---

shadow, *n.* shade, obscuration, adumbration, eclipse; ghost, phantom, apparition; reflection. See DARKNESS, SPECTOR, UNSUBSTANTIALITY.
shadow, *v.* becloud, overcast, darken; dim, shade; follow, trail, trace, pursue. See CLOUD, DIMNESS, FOLLOWING.
shaft, *n.* air shaft, chimney stack; pit, well; stem, shank, handle, helve; pole, thill; pillar, obelisk. See AIR PIPE, DEPTH, INSTRUMENT, SUPPORT.
shake, *v.* tremble, flutter, quiver, quaver, quake; shiver, chill; dissuade, discourage, dishearten; shudder, quail; oscilate, vibrate. See AGITATION, COLD, DISSUASION, FEAR, OSCILLATION.

SHALLOWNESS.—I. *Nouns.* **shallowness,** want of depth, superficiality; veneer.
shallow, shallow place, shoal, flat; bar, sandbank.
II. *Verbs.* **shallow,** become shallower, make shallow, decrease in depth, fill in (*or* up), silt up.

III. *Adjectives.* **shallow,** depthless, shoal, shoaly, fleet (*dial. in this sense*), superficial, slight; skin-deep, ankle-deep, knee-deep.
[*not deep intellectually*] superficial, trivial, empty, silly, inane, frivolous, shallow-brained, shallow-pated; meretricious, flashy, trashy, flimsy; half-learned, half-baked (*colloq.*), ignorant, lowbrow (*slang*), empty-headed.
See also IGNORANCE.—*Antonyms.* See DEPTH.

---

sham, *n.* imitation, counterfeit, make-believe, brummagem. See DECEPTION.
sham, *adj.* make-believe, counterfeit, feigned, pretended. See DECEPTION.
shame, *n.* disgrace, dishonor, humiliation, ignominy, mortification. See DISREPUTE.
shame, *v.* humiliate, disgrace, dishonor, degrade, debase. See DISREPUTE, HUMILITY.
shameful, *adj.* disgraceful, infamous, disreputable. See DISREPUTE.
shameless, *adj.* flagrant, brazen, audacious, immodest, outrageous. See MANIFESTATION.
shape, *n.* frame, figure, configuration, outline, contour, cut, aspect, guise. See APPEARANCE, FORM.
shapeless, *adj.* formless, unshapely, misshapen, amorphous; *opposite of* shapely. See FORMLESSNESS.
shapely, *adj.* well-formed, trim, symmetrical, neat. See CLEANNESS, SYMMETRY.
share, *n.* portion, allotment, apportionment, quota, dividend, lot, allowance. See MEASUREMENT, PART.
share, *v.* divide, portion, apportion, allot, distribute; partake, participate. See PART, PARTICIPATION.
shark, *n.* carchariid (*zoöl.*), man-eater. See ANIMAL (*elasmobranchs*).

SHARPNESS.—I. *Nouns.* **sharpness,** keenness, acuity, acumination, saliency, spinosity, mucronation (*tech.*); acuteness, etc. (see *adjectives*).
point, spike, spine, spiculum (*pl.* spicula: *zoöl.*), spit, needle, pin; prick, barb, apiculus; thorn, thistle; calcar (*L. pl.* calcaria: *tech.*), gaff (*of a gamecock*), spur, rowel; horn, antler; snag, tag, tooth, tusk, tine.
beard, cheval-de-frise (*pl.* chevaux-de-frise), porcupine, hedgehog, brier, bramble, thistle, bur *or* burr; currycomb, comb.
peak, crag, crest, *arête* (*F.*), cone, sugar loaf; spire, aiguille (*as in the Alps*), pyramid, steeple.
cutting-edge, knife-edge, blade, edge tool, cutlery, knife, penknife, razor; scalpel, lancet; plowshare, colter; hatchet, ax *or* axe, mattock, adz *or* adze, cleaver, scythe, sickle, bill, billhook; scissors, shears, sword.
sharpener, hone, strop, grindstone, whetstone, oilstone, rubstone, steel, emery, carborundum, sharper.
II. *Verbs.* **be sharp,** etc. (see *adjectives*); taper to a point; bristle with; cut.
sharpen, whet, point, barb, set, strop, grind, reset; acuminate, spiculate (*rare*), cuspidate.
III. *Adjectives.* **sharp,** keen; fine, acute, pointed, aciculate (*tech.*), acicular, needle-shaped, acuate, aculeate, acuminate, cuspidate *or* cuspidated, cuspate *or* cuspated, mucronate *or* mucronated, tapering; spiked, spiky, studded, peaked, ridged, salient; spiny, thorny, bristling, bristly, setaceous, bristled, echinate *or* echinated (*like a hedgehog*), prickly, muricate *or* muricated, pectinate (*esp. bot.*), comb-shaped, barbate, barbed, spurred, bearded, awned, aristate, thistly, briery; craggy, jagged, angular, snaggy.
keen-edged, cutting, edged, sharp-edged, knife-edged; cultrate (*natural hist.*); sharpened, set, sharp as a needle, keen as a razor.
cone-shaped, conical, conic, coniform (*rare*); pyramidal, pyramidic *or* pyramidical.
horn-shaped, cornute *or* cornuted, corniform, hornlike, corniculate, horned.
spear-shaped, hastate, hastiform (*rare*), lance-shaped, lanceolate (*tech.*), lanceolar (*rare*).
star-shaped, stellate *or* stellated, stelliform, stellular, starlike, radiated, starry.

sword-shaped, ensate (*bot.*), ensiform (*as a leaf*), gladiate (*bot.*), xiphoid (*anat.*).
tooth-shaped, dentiform, dentoid, odontoid, toothlike.
well-defined, sharp-cut, clear-cut, clear, distinct, clean-cut (*as*, a sharp *outline*)
[*of taste or smell*] **pungent,** acrid, poignant, acid, tart, sour, biting, piquant.
[*of sound*] **shrill,** piercing, penetrating, penetrative, acute.
[*trying to the feelings*] **severe,** intense, painful, distressing, excruciating, shooting, lancinating, keen (*as*, sharp *pain*).
[*of perception*] **discerning,** penetrating, acute, shrewd, quick, clever, sharp-sighted, sharp-witted, keen-witted, sagacious, discriminating, discriminate, critical, scrutinous, sensitive, astute (*as*, sharp *sight;* sharp *judgment*).
vigilant, alert, attentive, observant, wary, circumspect, searching (*as, a* sharp *lookout*).
fierce, fiery, violent, ardent, fervid, vigorous, brisk, speedy, impetuous, eager, precipitate, furious (*as, a* sharp *struggle*).
steep, abrupt, precipitous, sheer, vertical, sudden (*as, a* sharp *ascent*).
[*of language or import*] **cutting,** biting, sarcastic, caustic, acrimonious, bitter, tart, harsh, stern, trenchant, pointed (*as, a* sharp *reproof*).
[*quick to take advantage*] **unscrupulous,** close, exacting, artful, dishonest, unprincipled.
[*in music*] high (*in pitch*), acute; major (*interval*), augmented: *opposite of* flat.
[*in phonetics*] voiceless, surd, hard; *distinguished from* flat *or* voiced.
IV. *Adverbs.* **sharp,** precisely, promptly, exactly (*as, five o'clock* sharp).
sharply, keenly, acutely, poignantly, piercingly, etc. (see *adjectives*).
See also ARMS, DISAPPROBATION, EDGE, ENERGY, FASTIDIOUSNESS, INTELLIGENCE, LETTER (*voiceless*), PAINFULNESS, PERFORATOR, PUNGENCY, SEVERITY, SHARPNESS, STRIDENCY.—*Antonyms.* See BLUNTNESS, DULLNESS, FLATNESS.

---

sharpshooter, *n.* sniper, skirmisher, marksman, rifleman. See ATTACK, COMBATANT.
shatter, *v.* dash, burst, smash, crash, destroy; impair, enfeeble, exhaust, demoralize. See DESTRUCTION, IMPOTENCE.
shave, *v.* shear, slice; shorten, mow, crop, cut, slip. See CONTRACTION, SHORTNESS.
sheath, *n.* case, scabbard, sheathing, pod, casing, wrapping, envelope. See COVERING.
shed, *n.* shack, hut, cabin, lean-to. See HABITATION.
sheep, *n. ovis* (*L.*), lamb, ewe (*fem.*), ram (*masc.*). See AKIMAL.
sheer, *adj.* unqualified, unconditional; utter, downright; fine, transparent; vertical, steep. See COMPLETENESS, THINNESS, VERTICALITY.
shelf, *n.* ledge, bracket, mantelpiece, console. See SUPPORT.
shell, *v.* bombard, bomb, torpedo; pod, husk. See ATTACK, DIVESTMENT.
shelter, *n.* cover, screen, protection; retreat, sanctuary, asylum, covert. See COVERING, REFUGE.
shepherd, *n.* pastor; herder (*of sheep*), shepherdess (*fem.*). See CLERGY, DOMESTICATION.
shield, *n.* screen, protection, shelter, refuge; armor, buckler, ægis; escutcheon. See COVERING, DEFENSE, INDICATION.
shift, *v.* move, veer, gybe, swerve, turn; waver, vary, fluctuate, alter, lapse; deflect; divert, sidetrack; contrive, manage. See CHANGE, CONVERSION, DEVIATION, PLAN.
shift, *n.* change, alteration; chemise; dodge, expedient, artifice, quibble; sophism, subterfuge. See CHANGE, CLOTHING, MISJUDGEMNT, SOPHISTRY.
shiftless, *adj.* thriftless, lazy, indolent; careless, negligent, slack, remiss. See INACTIVITY, NONPREPARATION.
shifty, *adj.* tricky, crafty, wily, deceptive. See CUNNING.
shine, *v.* glow, glitter, glisten, gleam, beam. See LIGHT.
shingled, *adj.* overlapping, imbricate. See COVERING.
shiny, *adj.* glossy, burnished, glassy, polished; bright, sunny. See LIGHT, SMOOTHNESS.

SHIP.—I. *Nouns.* **ship,** vessel, boat, sail, craft, bottom; merchantman, argosy (*poetic*), galleon, merchant ship; freighter, freight steamer, coaster, whaler whaling vessel, slaver (*hist.*), collier; packet, mail boat; liner, leviathan (*rhetorical*), floating palace (*or* hotel), ocean greyhound; steamship, steamer, steamboat, tug, trawler, fishing boat, fisherman.
[*ships collectively*] **fleet,** flotilla, armada, navy (*esp. war vessels*), marine, squadron, division, convoy, escort; shipping, tonnage.
sailing vessel, sailer, clipper ship, windjammer (*colloq.*), full-rigged ship, bark *or* barque; shipentine, four-masted bark *or* barque; brig, brigantine, barkentine, schooner, fore-and-after (*colloq.*); sloop, yacht, cutter, revenue cutter (*U. S.*), yawl, ketch, smack, lugger, junk (*Chinese*), dhow (*Arab*), felucca, caravel *or* carvel, cat, catboat, sailboat.
boat, rowboat; shallop, skiff, pinnace; launch; lifeboat, pilot boat, longboat, jolly-boat, gig, pair-oar, cockboat, tender, cockleshell; dory, canoe, dugout, dinghy, punt, outrigger; scow, barge, lighter, flatboat, praam, pontoon, catamaran; ferryboat, ferry bridge, float, raft; ice-boat, ice-yacht.
coracle, currach *or* curragh (*Gaelic*), gondola, galley, trireme, sampan (*Oriental*), bunderboat (*India*), caïque (*Levant*), umiak *or* oomiak (*Eskimo*), kayak, dahabeah (*Nile*); hulk, derelict.
motor boat *or* motorboat, power boat; cabin cruiser, motor launch, hydroplane, speed boat, sea sled; auxiliary vessel (cruiser, *or* yacht), auxiliary; outboard motor.
II. *Verbs.* **ship,** put (*or* take) on board, send away, dispatch *or* despatch, express (*U. S.*), mail transmit, transport, freight, export; embark, go on board, take ship.
III. *Adjectives.* **marine,** maritime, naval, nautical, seafaring, ocean-going; A1, A1 at Lloyd's; seaworthy; oceanic, pelagic, thalassic.
IV. *Adverbs.* **afloat,** aboard; on board, on shipboard, at sea, in naval service.
unsettled, unfixed, adrift, floating, uncontrolled, unguided, unstable.

See also AËRONAUTICS (*aircraft*), COMBATANT (*man-of-war*), MARINER, NAVIGATION, TRANSFER.—*Antonyms.* See VEHICLE.

---

shirk, *v.* avoid, evade, blink, malinger. See AVOIDANCE.
shirker, *n.* shirk, quitter, evader, slacker (*colloq.*), truant. See AVOIDANCE, COWARDICE.
shiver, *v.* shake, tremble, quiver, quake; chill; shatter, smash, destroy. See AGITATION, COLD. DESTRUCTION.
shoal, *n.* crowd, throng, school (*of fish*). See MULTITUDE.
shock, *v.* offend, scandalize; stun, stagger; disgust, repel, revolt, horrify. See DISAPPROBATION. EXCITEMENT, PAIN.
[1]**shock,** *n.* heap, pile, stack. See ASSEMBLAGE.
[2]**shock,** *n.* stroke, attack, paroxysm, seizure, apoplexy, paralysis; thrill, excitement, agitation; concussion, crash, collision, impact; blow, ordeal. See DISEASE, FEELING, IMPULSE, PAIN.
[3]**shock,** *n.* mop (*of hair*), mass, tangle. See ROUGHNESS.
shocking, *adj.* shameful, disgraceful, scandalous, arrant; fearful, direful, appalling; grim, crushing. See DISREPUTE, FEAR, PAINFULNESS.
shoe, *n.* Oxford *or* oxford, boot; horseshoe; skid, clog, brake; tire. See CLOTHING, HINDRANCE, VEHICLE.
shoemaker, *n.* bootmaker, cordwainer (*archaic*), cobbler. See CLOTHING.
shoot, *v.* bud, sprout, expand, develop; kill, hunt; discharge, fire off, hurl, propel, let fly; dart, rush, dash. See EXPANSION, KILLING, PROPULSION, VELOCITY.
shop, *n.* store, emporium; stall, booth. See MART, STORE.
shore, *n.* coast, strand, beach, bank, seacoast, seashore. See EDGE, LAND.

SHORTCOMING.—I. *Nouns.* **shortcoming,** failing, weakness, fault, imperfection, flaw, defect, falling short; default, omission, failure, neglect, carelessness, remissness, defalcation, delinquency; labor in vain, no go (*colloq.*), washout (*slang*), flivver (*slang*), fizzle (*colloq.*), slump (*colloq.*); flash in the pan.

incompleteness, deficiency, inadequacy, deficit, shortage, insufficiency; noncompletion, nonfulfillment.
II. *Verbs.* **fall short,** come short of, not reach; be deficient, want; keep within bounds (the mark, *or* compass).
collapse, fail, break down, flat out (*U. S.*), come to nothing; fall down, slump, fizzle out (*all colloq.*); peter out (*slang*), fall through, fall to the ground; cave in (*colloq.*), end in smoke, miss the mark.
III. *Adjectives.* **deficient,** inadequate, defective, insufficient, lacking, imperfect, incomplete, minus, short, short of; perfunctory, remiss, at fault.
See also FAILURE, IMPERFECTION, INCOMPLETENESS, INEQUALITY, INFERIORITY, INSUFFICIENCY, NONCOMPLETION, NEGLECT.—*Antonyms.* See OVERRUNNING, PERFECTION.

---

shorthand, *n.* stenography, phonography; cipher. See WRITING.
short-headed, *adj.* brachycephalic (*opposite of* dolichocephalic), broad-headed. See SHORTNESS.

SHORTNESS.—I. *Nouns.* **shortness,** brevity, curtness, consciseness, littleness, etc. (see *adjectives*); a span.
abridgment, shortening, abbreviation, retrenchment, curtailment, epitomization, contraction, condensation, reduction, epitome; elision, ellipsis.
II. *Verbs.* **shorten,** curtail, retrench, abridge, abbreviate; take in, scrimp, reduce; compress, contract; epitomize, abstract, summarize, condense; truncate, cut, trim, pare down, clip, dock, lop, prune, shear, shave, mow, crop, stunt, nip, cramp, dwarf, check the growth of; foreshorten (*drawing*).
III. *Adjectives.* **short** (*not long*), brief, curt, little, curtate; pug, *retroussé* (*F.*), turned up; stubby, pudgy, squatty, stumpy.
[*not tall*] **undersized,** undergrown, stunted, stumpy (*colloq.*), thickset, chunky (*U. S.*), scrub, stocky, squat, dumpy, runty (*colloq.*), dwarfish, diminutive.
concise, laconic, condensed, terse, compact, succinct, compendious, pithy, laconic, summary.
curt (*in language*), abrupt, uncivil, snappish, harsh, sullen, petulant, cross (*as, a* short *answer*).
scant, scanty, inadequate, deficient, insufficient, niggardly, scrimpy, poor, small, limited (*as, a* short *supply of food*): *opposite of* ample.
[*easily broken*] crisp, friable, crumbly, crumbling (*as,* short *pastry*).
[*of stocks, crops, etc.*] unpossessed (*at time of sale*), unowned.
[*in phonetics and prosody*] unprolonged, brief, unsustained; unstressed (*as a syllable*), unaccented: *opposite of* long.
[*in craniology*] **short-headed,** brachycephalic (*opposite of* dolichocephalic), brachycephalous, broad-headed.
IV. *Adverbs.* **short,** abruptly, curtly, suddenly (*as, to stop* short).
[*of memory*] faulty, unreliable, retentive, narrow, at fault.
See also BRITTLENESS, COMPENDIUM, CONCISENESS, CONTRACTION, DEDUCTION, DISCOURTESY, INCOMPLETENESS, LITTLENESS.—*Antonyms.* See LENGTH.

---

shortsighted, *adj.* myopic, nearsighted, dim-sighted; misjudging, ill-judging. See DIM-SIGHTEDNESS, MISJUDGMENT.
short-winded, *adj.* short-breathed, dyspnœic (*med.*), broken-winded. See FATIGUE.
shout, *v.* yell, bawl, halloo, whoop; hurrah, cheer; yelp, bark. See CRY, REJOICING, SNAP.
show, *v.* appear, seem, look, loom; present, display, exhibit; prove, verify, demonstrate, establish; produce, expose; direct, guide, teach. See APPEARANCE, ATTENTION, DEMONSTRATION, MANIFESTATION, TEACHING.—**show off,** boast, brag, strut, exult, exaggerate. See OSTENTATION.—**show up,** expose, denounce, criticize. See DISAPPROBATION.
show, *n.* showing, exposition, exhibition; performance, representation; parade, pomp, flourish, array, glitter. See DEMONSTRATION, DRAMA, OSTENTATION.

shower, *n.* flight (*as of arrows*), volley; shower bath; copious bestowal (*as of gifts*); rain, flurry, fall. See ASSEMBLAGE, CLEANNESS, GIVING, RIVER (*rain*).
showy, *adj.* ornate, flashy, loud, gorgeous, garish, gawdy, tawdry, specious, meretricious. See ORNAMENT, UGLINESS, VULGARITY.
shrew, *n.* vixen, scold, spitfire, fury, termagant. See IRASCIBILITY.
shrewd, *adj.* sharp, acute; alert, keen, dry; astute, knowing, sagacious, sapient. See CUNNING, DRYNESS, KNOWLEDGE, WISDOM.
shrewdness, *n.* keenness, sharpness; farsightedness, sagacity. See DRYNESS, FORESIGHT.
shriek, *v.* scream, screech, squeal, yelp. See CRY.
shrill, *adj.* piercing, penetrating, acute, strident, thin. See SHARPNESS, STRIDENCY, THINNESS.
shrink, *v.* shrivel, dwindle, contract, decrease; flinch, shy, balk, blench, quail, wince, cringe. See AVOIDANCE, CONTRACTION, RECOIL.
shrivel, *v.* contact, shrink; wrinkle, rumple. See CONTRACTION, [1]FOLD.
shroud, *n.* screen, cloak, veil; winding sheet, cerecloth; stay (*naut.*), guy. See CONCEALMENT, INTERMENT, SUPPORT.
shudder, *v.* shiver, chill; shake, quake, tremble. See COLD, FEAR.
shuffle, *v.* shift, change, waver, fluctuate, vacillate; quibble, fence, equivocate; alternate, palter; slouch, shamble, trudge. See CHANGEABLENESS, FALSEHOOD, IRRESOLUTION, SLOWNESS.
shun, *v.* avoid, evade, elude, eschew. See AVOIDANCE, DISLIKE.
shut, *v.* close, bar, stop, seal, lock; slam, clap. See CLOSURE.
shy, *adj.* wary, cautious; timid, fearful; modest, bashful, coy, sheepish. See CAUTION, COWARDICE, MODESTY.

SIBILATION.—I. *Nouns.* **sibilation,** hissing; hiss, buzz; zip, siss (*U. S. colloq.*) fizz *or* fiz, fizzle, sizzle (*U. S. colloq.*), spit (*as of a cat*), swish, whiz *or* whizz, wheeze, siffle (*med.*), *râle* (*F.: med.*); sneeze, sneezing, sternutation.
II. *Verbs.* **sibilate,** hiss, sizz, siss (*U. S. colloq.*), goose (*theatrical slang*), spit, fizz *or* fiz, fizzle, sizzle (*U. S. colloq.*), whiz, buzz, rustle, swish, wheeze, whistle, squash, squelch (*as of wet boots*).
III. *Adjectives.* **sibilant,** hissing, sibilous (*rare*), sibilatory (*rare*), rustling, wheezy.
See also DISAPPROBATION, DISRESPECT, SOFTNESS (*phonetics*).

---

sick, *adj.* ill, unwell, ailing, indisposed, nauseated; satiated, gorged, surfeited. See DISEASE, SATIETY.
sicken, *v.* ail, droop, pine, fail; repel, nauseate, disgust, pall. See DISEASE, DISLIKE, UNSAVORINESS.
sickle-shaped, *adj.* falcate, falciform. See CURVATURE.
sickly, *adj.* sickish, weakly, infirm, unhealthy. See DISEASE.
sickness, *n.* illness, ailment, malady, infirmity, disorder. See DISEASE.

SIDE.—I. *Nouns.* side, flank, pleuron (*zoöl.*), paries (*pl.* parietes: *biol.*), flitch (*of bacon*), loin, wing, hand, haunch, hip, leg (*of a triangle*); check, jowl *or* jole; quarter, lee; profile; gable, gable-end; broadside, page, outer surface, face; slope, declivity; laterality (*rare, except as med.*).
edge, margin, verge, border, bound, limit, brim, brink, rim, curb, lip, hem, fringe.
place, locality, region, situation, position, location, quarter, section, division, part; latitude, longitude; point, direction, point of the compass; East, Orient, Levant; West, Occident.
phase, aspect, appearance, angle, point of view.
party, faction, sect; team, crew; interest, cause, part, behalf.
[*line of descent*] **lineage,** descent (*through one parent*), parentage, family, ancestry; spear side (*male line*); distaff side, spindle side (*female line*).
swagger, braggadocio, prententiousness, dog (*slang*), pretension, arrogance, airs (*as, to put on side: slang*).

II. *Verbs.* **flank,** skirt, wing, border; outflank, outmaneuver (*mil.*), enfilade.
side, put (*or* push) aside, jostle, elbow: *in this sense,* side *is colloq.*
side with, take the part of, befriend, aid, uphold, back up, second, advocate, countenance, unite with, coöperate with, rally round.
III. *Adjectives.* **side,** lateral, parietal (*tech.*), flanking, skirting; sideling, sloping, inclined; sidelong (*as a glance*), sidewise, sideward, sideway, oblique, collateral, indirect, incidental, minor (*as, a* side *issue*).
eastern, east, eastward, orient, oriental, Levantine, auroral.
western, west, westerly, westward, occidental, Hesperian.
one-sided, unilateral (*esp. law and bot.*); partial, biased, unfair, unjust, prejudiced, influenced.
two-sided, bilateral, dihedral (*tech.*); bifacial (*as the Roman Janus*).
three-sided, trilateral (*geom.*), triquetrous (*tech.*).
four-sided, quadrilateral (*esp. geom.*), tetrahedral (*tech.*).
many-sided, multilateral, polyhedral *or* polyhedrical (*geom.*), polyhedric (*rare*), polyhedrous (*rare*); versatile: *opposite of* one-sided.
IV. *Adverbs.* **sidelong,** laterally, obliquely, sideling, indirectly; askew, askance *or* askant.
sidewise, sideways, laterally, broadside on; abreast, alongside, neck and neck, side by side, beside, aside; by, by the side of, right and left; to windward, to leeward (*naut.*); on her beam ends (*as a vessel*).
See also AID, COÖPERATION, EDGE, LEFT, OBLIQUITY, PART, PARTY, RIGHT.—*Antonyms.* See FRONT, OPPOSITE, REAR.

---

siege, *n.* investment, blockade, bombardment, cannonade. See ATTACK.
siesta, *n.* nap, doze, midday nap. See INACTIVITY.
sieve, *v.* strainer, colander, riddle, screen. See CROSSING, OPENING.
sift, *v.* winnow, sieve, bolt, screen, riddle; examine, quiz, investigate. See CLEANNESS, INQUIRY.
sigh, *v.* long for, yearn for; lament, grieve; sough. See DESIRE, LAMENTATION, WIND.
sight, *n.* view, scene, prospect, show, spectacle; marvel, phenomenon, curiosity, monstrosity; eyesight, visibility. See APPEARANCE, PRODIGY, VISION.—**at sight,** at first sight, on presentation (*as of a draft*). See VISION.
sign, *n.* mark, notice, device, emblem, symbol; foreboding, augury, warning, prophecy; marvel, portent. See INDICATION, OMEN, PRODIGY.
signal, *n.* sign, gesture, call, cue, cry, alarm, beacon, telegraph, wigwag. See INDICATION.
signal, *adj.* eventful, momentous, remarkable, conspicuous, noteworthy. See GREATNESS, SUBSTANTIALITY.
signal, *v.* notify, inform, beckon, nod, glance, nudge. See INDICATION.
signal light, flare, rocket, balefire; lighthouse. See LUMINARY.
signature, *n.* autograph, sign manual, moniker (*slang*). See INDICATION.
significance, *n.* weight, influence; meaning, purport, implication, signification. See IMPORTANCE, INTENTION.
significant, *adj.* telling, forceful, pithy, pregnant. See IMPORTANCE, MEANING.
signify, *v.* mean, denote, import, suggest, indicate, symbolize. See MEANING.

SILENCE.—I. *Nouns.* **silence,** stillness, quiet, peace, hush, still (*poetic*), quietude, quietness, soundlessness, noiselessness, lull, rest (*music*), muteness, taciturnity; silence of the tomb (*or* grave).
[*absence of mention*] **oblivion,** forgetfulness, obscurity, namelessness; secrecy, hiddenness, concealment, uncommunicativeness, reserve, reticence.
II. *Verbs.* **silence,** still, hush, quiet, stifle, muffle, gag, muzzle, throttle, choke, strangle, put to silence; stop, quell, suppress.
III. *Adjectives* **silent,** still, noiseless, quiet, calm, soundless, stilly (*poetic*) hushful, hushed; soft, peaceful, undisturbed; solemn, reverential, impressive, awful, deathlike.
[*making no utterance*] **speechless,** mute, dumb, inarticulate, voiceless, tongueless: taciturn, reserved, uncommunicative, mum.

unspoken, unuttered, unexpressed, unsaid; tacit, implied, understood. [*in phonetics*] mute, unpronounced, aphonic (*as* p *in* cupboard).
IV. *Adverbs.* **silently,** noiselessly, etc. (see *adjectives*); *sub silentio* (*L.*), in dead silence.
V. *Interjections.* **silence!** hush! soft! whist! whisht! (*Irish and dial.*), mum! tut! sh! chut! *pax!* (*L.*), *chup!* (*Hind.*), *chup raho!* (*Hind.*), *tais-toi!* (*F.*).
See also CONFUTATION, DUMBNESS, [1]REST, SUCCESS (*quell*), TACITURNITY.—*Antonyms.* See [1]SOUND, VOICE.

---

silencer, *n.* muffler (*as in an automobile*); soft pedal, damper. See FAINTNESS.
silliness, *n.* weakness, foolishness, folly; imbecility. See SIMPLICITY.
silly, *adj.* stupid, absurd; simple, childish, feeble-minded, weak-minded, half-witted. See ABSURDITY, CREDULITY, IMBECILITY.
silver, *n.* small coin, pin money, small change. See CHANGE, MONEY.

SIMILARITY.—I. *Nouns.* **similarity,** resemblance, likeness, similitude, semblance, affinity, approximation, parallelism, agreement, analogy, correspondence; brotherhood, family likeness; identity, sameness, uniformity, repetition.
counterpart, duplicate, facsimile, copy, equal, like, analogue, homologue, parallel, congener, match, fellow, companion, pair, mate, twin, double, brother, sister; type, image, simile, comparison; one's second self, *alter ego* (*L.*); chip of the old block, birds of a feather, *par nobile fratrum* (*L.; often ironical*), *Arcades ambo* (*L.*), *et hoc genus omne* (*L.*).
II. *Verbs.* **resemble,** look like, favor (*colloq.*), follow, echo, reproduce, take after, bear resemblance; savor of, smack of; approximate; parallel, match, imitate, copy, rime (*or* rhyme) with.
III. *Adjectives.* **similar,** resembling, corresponding, like, alike, twin, duplicate, consimilar (*rare*), parallel, homologous, analogous, of a piece; akin to, allied to, correlative, cognate, congeneric (*esp. biol.*), congenerous, kindred, connatural, isogamous (*biol.*).
approximate, near, close, something like, closely resembling, fairly close (*or* correct); pseudo, mock, simulating, representing.
lifelike (*as a portrait*), faithful, exact, true, accurate, true to life, the very image of, cast in the same mold.
IV. *Adverbs.* **as if,** as though, so to speak; as it were, as if it were; *quasi* (*L.*), just as.
See also AGREEMENT, CONFORMITY, IDENTITY, RELATION, REPETITION, UNIFORMITY.—*Antonyms.* See DISSIMILARITY.

SIMPLENESS.—I. *Nouns.* **simpleness** (*freedom from mixture*), singleness, purity, etc. (see *adjectives*); homogeneity, uniformity.
elimination, sifting, purification, separation, removal, expulsion, abstraction; exclusion.
unaffectedness, artlessness, ingenuousness, *naïveté* (*F.*), simplicity, naturalness, modesty.
foolishness, silliness, *niaiserie* (*F.*), guilelessness, weakness (*of intellect*), fatuity credulity, ignorance.
II. *Verbs.* **simply,** render simple (*or* simpler), disinvolve, disintricate (*rare*), disentangle, abbreviate (*math.*), reduce to simplicity; chasten, restrain, strip of ornament, disornament (*rare*).
eliminate, expel, exclude, abstract, separate, excrete, get rid of; sift, winnow, bolt, clear, purify, clarify, refine.
III. *Adjectives.* **simple,** single, pure, neat, uncompounded, unmixed, unblended. incomplex, uncombined, unmingled, unadulterated, unalloyed, *pur et simple* (*F.*), uniform, homogeneous; ultimate, elemental, elementary: *opposite of* compound.
uninvolved, unelaborate, uncomplicated; easy, understandable, plain, clear, intelligible (*as, a* simple *machine;* simple *language*): *opposite of* complex.
unadorned, unembellished, unornamented, inornate, unvarnished, unpretentious, unluxurious, plain, homelike homely, homespun, ordinary (*as,* simple *dress;* simple *fare*).
[*free from affectation*] unaffected, natural, unstudied, inartificial, ingenuous, naïve, artless, straightforward, undesigning, unsophisticated, unsuspecting,

simple-minded, sincere, modest, simple-hearted; chaste, strict, severe, restrained; *simplex munditiis* (*L.*).
[*of low degree*] **humble,** lowly, lowborn, unpretending, poor, obscure, undistinguished, plebeian.
[*of moderate understanding*] **foolish,** silly, feeble-minded, weak-minded, ignorant, unlearned, inexperienced, credulous, childish, weak, fatuous.
[*of small value*] **unimportant,** trifling, trivial, insignificant, paltry, petty.
[*not other than*] **mere,** such, bare, naked, plain, sole, dry, unqualified (*as, the* simple *facts*).
IV. *Adverbs.* **simply,** singly, purely, etc. (see *adjectives*); merely, barely, solely, alone.
See also ARTLESSNESS, CLEANNESS, CREDULITY, DISJUNCTION, FOLLY, IGNORANCE, IMBECILITY, PLAINNESS, PURITY.—*Antonyms.* See MIXTURE, ORNAMENT.

---

simpleton, *n.* stupid, dunce, dolt, imbecile, half-wit. See FOOL.

SIMPLICITY.—*Nouns.* **simplicity,** clearness, clarity, lucidity, perspicuity, intelligibleness, intelligibility, definiteness, simpleness, easiness, straightforwardness.
plainness (*as of dress or style*), neatness, homeliness; chasteness, restraint, severity, naturalness, unaffectedness; beauty unadorned.
guilelessness, innocence, ingenuousness, simple-mindedness, unsuspiciousness, trust, trustfulness, trustingness, unsophistication, *naïveté* (*F.*), artlessness, sincerity, openness, frankness.
[*lack of common sense*] **silliness,** weakness, foolishness, folly, imbecility, inanity, fatuity, fatuousness; weakness of intellect.
See also IMBECILITY, INTELLIGIBILITY, PLAINNESS, SIMPLENESS.—*Antonyms.* See ORNAMENT, UNINTELLIGIBILITY.

---

simulate, *v.* feign, counterfeit, sham, assume; imitate, ape, mimic, impersonate. See FALSEHOOD, IMITATION.

SIMULTANEOUSNESS.—I. *Nouns.* **simultaneousness,** coinstantaneousness, coinstantaneity, simultaneity, synchronism, coexistence, coincidence, concurrence, contemporaneousness, contemporariness, coevality, coetaneousness; isochronism.
II. *Verbs.* **coexist,** concur, accompany, keep pace with; synchronize.
III. *Adjectives.* **simultaneous,** coinstantaneous, coexistent, coexisting, coincident, synchronous, synchronal, concomitant, concurrent; contemporary (*esp. of persons*), contemporaneous (*esp. of events*), coeval, coetaneous.
IV. *Adverbs.* **simultaneously,** coinstantaneously, etc. (see *adjectives*); at the same time, together, in concert; in the same breath.

---

sin, *n.* misdeed, transgression; wickedness, iniquity. See GUILT, VICE.
sin, *v.* err, transgress. See VICE.
since, *adv.* subsequently, after, afterward. See POSTERIORITY.
since, *conj.* because, for, whereas, inasmuch as, seeing that. See ATTRIBUTION.
sincere, *adj.* artless, frank, open, ingenuous; warm, hearty, cordial; true, honest, unfeigned, truthful, veracious. See ARTLESSNESS, FEELING, TRUTH. VERACITY.
sincerity, *n.* honesty, genuineness, frankness, unaffectedness, integrity, probity. See TRUTH.
sinecure, *n.* easy post, cinch (*U. S. slang*), sure thing, easy job. See INACTION, SNAP.
sinewy, *adj.* muscular, wiry, well-knit, strong. See STRENGTH.
sinful, *adj.* evil, wicked, vicious, unprincipled, unrighteous. See VICE.
sing, *v.* chant, hum, twitter, lilt, trill; carol, jubilate, crow, rejoice. See MUSICIAN, REJOICING.
single, *v.* scorch, burn, sear. See HEAT.
singer, *n.* vocalist, solosit, warbler, chanter, caroler. See MUSICIAN.

single, *adj.* unmarried, unwedded, celibate; pure, simple, elemental, uncompounded, unalloyed; one, sole, lone, solitary. See CELIBACY, SIMPLENESS, UNITY.

singly, *adv.* individually, severally, separately, independently. See UNITY.

singular, *adj.* unique, rare, odd, remarkable, strange, unusual; one, alone, unattended. See UNCONFORMITY, UNITY.

sinister, *adj.* evil, disastrous; unlucky, malign; left-handed, sinistral. See ADVERSITY, BADNESS, LEFT.

sink, *v.* humble, abse, debase, degrade; engulf, swamp, scuttle, submerge, destroy; drown, founder, succumb. See DEPRESSION, DESTRUCTION, FAILURE.

sinless, *adj.* pure, blameless, unerring, undefiled. See INNOCENCE.

sinner, *n.* evildoer, wrongdoer, transgressor, blasphemer. See BAD MAN, IMPIETY.

sinuous, *adj.* winding, circling, snaky, serpentine, tortuous. See CONVOLUTION.

siren, *n.* fog signal, alarm signal; temptress, vampire; Lorelei. See ALARM, MOTIVE, MYTHICAL BEINGS.

sister, *n.* nun, *sorer* (*L.*), kinswoman; chum (*colloq.*), companion, fellow-member; mate, twin, couterpart. See CLERGY, CONSANGUINITY, FRIEND, SIMILARITY.

sit, *v.* sit down, squat, recline, perch; brood, incubate. See DEPRESSION, DOMESTICATION.

SITUATION.—I. *Nouns.* **situation,** position, locality, location, place, site, station, seat, post, spot, whereabouts, ground, environment, bearings, direction, latitude and longitude; footing, status, standing, standpoint, stage; aspect, attitude, posture, pose, set (*colloq.*).

topography, chorography, geography; map, plan, chart.

state, condition, circumstance (*usually in pl.*), pass, predicament, case, plight; juncture, crisis, critical point (*as in drama*).

employment (*as of a domestic servant*), place, position, office, berth, billet.

II. *Verbs.* **be situated,** be located, lie; have its seat in.

III. *Adjectives.* **situated,** located, fixed, established, settled; conditioned, circumstanced.

local, sectional, topical (*esp. med. in this sense*), limited, topographic *or* topographical, chorographic *or* chorographical (*of a region or district*), regional, provincial, territorial.

IV. *Adverbs.* **in position,** *in situ* (*L.*), *in loco* (*L.*), in place; *passim* (*L.*), here and there; here, hereabouts; there, thereabouts.

See also BUSINESS, CIRCUMSTANCE, DIRECTION, LOCATION, PLACE, REGION.

SIX.—I. *Nouns.* **six,** half a dozen; hexad (*esp. chem.*), hexavalent (*chem.*); sextuplet, sextet (*esp. music*), sestet (*of a sonnet*), hexagram, hexagon (*geom.*), hexahedron (*geom.*), hexameter (*pros.*), hexarchy, hexapod (*six-footed animal*), hexastich (*pros.*), hexapody (*pros.*), hexastyle (*arch.*), Hexateuch (*Bible*).

II. *Verbs.* multiply by six, make sixfold, sextuple.

III. *Adjectives.* **sixfold,** sextuple, sexpartite; hexad (*chem.*), sextuplex (*telegraphy*), hexangular, hexagonal, hexahedral, hexastyle (*arch.*), hexatomic (*chem.*), hexamerous (*bot.*), sexennial.

SIXTY.—I. *Nouns.* **sixty,** threescore; sexagenarian, sexagenary; Sexagesima (*approximately the sixtieth day before Easter*).

II. *Adjectives.* **sixtieth,** sexagesimal, sexagenary.

SIZE.—I. *Nouns.* **size,** dimensions, proportions, measurement, measure; magnitude, bulk, volume, quantity, weight; expanse, extent, area, largeness, greatness, amplitude, mass; capacity, content, tonnage, cordage; caliber *or* calibre, internal diameter, bore.

corpulence, obesity, plumpness, *embonpoint* (*F.*), corporation (*colloq.*), fatness, obeseness, polysarcia (*med.*), stoutness, pinguitude (*rare*).

hugeness, enormousness, immensity, immenseness, monstrousness, giganticness, stupendousness; bigness, massiveness, bulkiness, sizableness.
giant, giantess (*fem.*), Brobdingnagian, Goliath, Antæus, Polyphemus, Colossus, Titan, Briareus, Hercules, Cyclops, Gog and Magog, Gargantua; colossus, polypheme (*rare*), "Triton among the minnows" (*Coriolanus*); monster, mammoth, whale, behemoth, leviathan, elephant, hippopotamus, jumbo (*colloq.*).
[*great quantity*] **heap**, pile, lump, lot, power (*colloq.*), sight (*colloq.*), swad (*U. S. slang*), clod, block, hunk (*colloq.*), stack; tumulus, mound, hillock, hill, mount, mountain.
II. *Verbs.* **size**, adjust, arrange, grade, gauge, classify, range, graduate, group, sort, match.
size up (*colloq.*), estimate, rate, appraise, form a judgment of, form an estimate of (*as, to* size up *a person*).
III. *Adjectives.* **sizable**, considerable, fairly large, big, great, large, massive, bulky, substantial, tidy (*colloq.*), ample, voluminous, capacious, spacious, comprehensive; mighty, towering, fine, magnificent.
corpulent, obese, stout, fat, plump, chubby; brawny, fleshy, burly; portly, imposing.
unwieldy, hulky, hulking, lubberly, cumbrous, cumbersome, ponderous, hippopotamic, lumpish, overgrown; puffy, swollen, bloated.
huge, immense, enormous, hugeous (*jocose*), gigantic gigantean, Titanic, mighty, vast, vasty (*archaic*); stupendous, monster, monstrous, elephantine, megatherian *or* megatherine, mammoth; giant, colossal, Cyclopean, Brobdingnagian, Gargantuan.

See also ASSEMBLAGE, EXPANSION, GREATNESS, INFINITY, SPACE.—*Antonyms.*—See LITTLENESS, SMALLNESS.

---

skeleton, *n.* outline, draft, sketch; remains; framework. See PLAN, REMAINDER, SUPPORT.
skeptic, *n.* unbeliever, heretic, atheist, infidel. See INCREDULITY, IRRELIGION.
skeptical, *adj.* freethinking, agnostic, atheistic, unbelieving. See IRRELIGION.
skepticism, *n.* doubt, unbelief, disbelief, agnosticism. See IRRELIGION.
sketch, *v.* depict, represent; paint, draw, design; outline, diagram, draft. See DESCRIPTION, FINE ARTS, PLAN.
sketchy, *adj.* crude, imperfect, imcomplete, undeveloped, perfunctory. See NONCOMPLETION.

SKILL.—I. *Nouns.* **skill**, skillfulness, address, dexterity, adroitness, expertness, proficiency, competence, *curiosa felicitas* (*L.*), felicity, capability, capacity, qualification, mastery, efficiency, excellence, deftness, featness (*archaic*), adeptness, facility, finish, technique, execution, technic, craft, cunning (*archaic in this sense*), knack, trick, sleight; technical (*or* practical) knowledge, art, science, scientific (*or* formulated) knowledge.
cleverness, talent, ability, ingenuity, parts, talents, faculty, endowment, acquirement, attainment, accomplishment, forte, turn, gift, genius, inspiration, intelligence, sharpness, readiness, aptness, aptitude, resourcefulness, inventiveness, ingenuity; *ars celare artem* (*L.*).
worldly wisdom, knowledge of the world, *l'usage du monde* (*F.*), *savoir-faire* (*F.*); tact, mother wit, discretion, finesse; management, strategy, statesmanship.
masterpiece, masterwork, *chef d'œuvre* (*F.*), *coup de maître* (*F.*), *tour de force* (*F.*).
II. *Verbs.* **be skillful**, excel in, be master of; have a turn for.
take advantage of, make the most of, profit by, make a killing (*slang, esp. financial*), make a hit, make a virtue of necessity, make hay while the sun shines
III. *Adjectives.* **skillful** *or* skilful, dexterous, adroit, expert, apt, handy, quick, deft, artful, subtle, feat (*archaic*), slick (*slang*), ready, smart, proficient, good at, at home in, master of, conversant with; masterly, crack (*colloq.*), crackajack (*slang*), accomplished, *au fait* (*F.*).
experienced, practiced, skilled, up in, in practice, competent, efficient, workmanlike, businesslike, qualified, capable, fitted, fit for, up to the mark, up and coming (*U. S. dial.*), trained, initiated, sophisticated, prepared, primed, finished.
clever, able, ingenious, felicitous, neat, gifted, talented, resourceful, inventive

scientific; shrewd, sharp, cunning; neat-handed, artistic, fine-fingered, nimble-fingered, ambidextrous, sure-footed.
IV. *Adverbs.* skillfully, dexterously, etc. (see *adjectives*); artistically, with skill, with fine technique, *secundum artem* (*L.*), with consummate skill; like a machine. See also CUNNING, EXPERT, FACILITY, IMAGINATION, INTELLIGENCE.—*Antonyms.* See UNSKILLFULNESS.

---

skin, *n.* integument, pellicle, peel, rind, shell (*of a ship*). See COVERING.
skin, *v.* peel, scalp, flay, excoriate, slough. See DIVESTMENT.
skip, *v.* caper, prance, hop, dance, frisk, gambol. See LEAP, REJOICING.
skirmish, *n.* conflict, combat, encounter, fight, fracas, mêleé. See CONTENTION.
skirt, *n.* petticoat, overskirt, kilt; border, rim, confine, margin. See CLOTHING.
skulk, *v.* slink, lurk, sneak, crouch, prowl. See CONCEALMENT, COWARDICE.
sky, *n.* heavens, firmament, welkin (*archaic*), empyrean. See WORLD.
slack, *adj.* insufficient, underdone; lax, loose, relaxed, incoherent, negligent, weak; remiss, lawless, inattentive; careless, heedless, inefficient; slow, sluggish, dull, torpid, lazy; indifferent, laggard, unwilling. See INSUFFICIENCY, LAXITY, NONOBSERVANCE, NONPREPARATION, SLOWNESS, UNWILLINGNESS.
slacken, *v.* loosen, relax; lessen, moderate, soften, mitigate; retard, slow. See INCOHERENCE, MODERATION, SLOWNESS.
slacker, *n.* shirker, quitter; loafer, idler, dawdler. See AVOIDANCE, DERELICTION.
slake, *v.* slacken, retard, abate, moderate; allay, quench, sate, satiate. See MODERATION, SATIETY.
slander, *n.* scandal, calumny, defamation, vilification. See DETRACTION.
slant, *n.* slope, inclination, incline, tilt, list. See OBLIQUITY.
slap, *v.* strike, hit, whack, tap, rap. See IMPULSE.
slate, *n.* plank, platform, ticket, rôle, policy. See PLAN.
slattern, *n.* frump, slut, drab, trollop. See DISORDER.
slaughter, *n.* murder, slaying; carnage, butchery, massacre; slaughtering, butchering (*of animals*). See KILLING.
slaughterhouse, *n.* shambles, *abattoir* (*F.*), butchery. See KILLING.
slave, *n.* toiler, drudge; bondman, serf, thrall. See EXERTION, SERVANT.
slavery, *n.* toil, drudgery; bondage, thralldom, serfdom. See EXERTION, SUBJECTION.
slay, *v.* kill, murder, assassinate, butcher; slaughter, dispatch. See KILLING.
sled, *n.* sleigh, sledge, bobsled, pung; toboggan. See VEHICLE.
sleep, *n.* slumber, nap, doze, snooze (*colloq.*), rest, repose; insensibleness, coma, stupor. See INACTIVITY, INSENSIBILITY.
sleep, *v.* slumber, nap, doze, drowse, nod. See INACTIVITY.
sleeping, *adj.* asleep, slumbering, dormant. See INACTIVITY.
sleepless, *adj.* unsleeping, untiring; wakeful, insomnious (*rare*); watchful, vigilant. See ACTIVITY, CARE.
sleepy, *adj.* drowsy, dozy, dreamy, somnolent, lethargic. See INACTIVITY.
slender, *adj.* slim, thin, fine, narrow, spare, small, lean, lank, skinny, gaunt. See NARROWNESS, THINNESS.
sleuth, *n.* detective, spy, shadow; bloodhound. See INFORMATION.
slice, *v.* shave, skive, pare, cut, delaminate. See DISJUNCTION, LAYER.
slide, *v.* slip, glide, skid, skate, coast, toboggan. See JOURNEY, MOTION.
slight, *adj.* frail, feeble, weak, infirm; light, flimsy, unsubstantial; shallow, depthless, superficial. See FEEBLENESS, RARITY, SHALLOWNESS.
slight, *v.* evade, disregard, ignore; snub, humiliate, insult; defer, delay, procrastinate, postpone, shelve. See DERELICTION, DISRESPECT, NEGLECT.
slight, *n.* indignity, affront, negligence, discourtesy, contempt. See DISRESPECT.

slightly, *adv.* somewhat, rather, fairly, inconsiderably. See UNIMPORTANCE.
slim, *adj.* slender, thin, frail, unsubstantial, spare, poor. See NARROWNESS.
slime, *n.* ooze, mire, sludge, mud. See SEMILIQUIDITY, UNCLEANNESS.
slimy, *adj.* viscous, glutinous, mucid; slippery. See SEMILIQUIDITY, UNCTUOUSNESS.
slip, *v.* slide, skid, glide; trip, blunder, err, miscarry, backslide, fall; elapse, pass, glide, fly. See DESCENT, FAILURE, LAPSE.
slip, *n.* loose dress lining, pinafore; pillowcase, pillowslip; strip, shred; trip, misstep, indiscretion; stripling; blunder, mistake, peccadillo; error, barbarism, impropriety. See CLOTHING. COVERING, FILAMENT, GUILT, INFANT, LAPSE, SOLECISM.
slippery, *adj.* changeful, irresolute; tricky, fickle, undependable; lax, nonobservant, neglectful, evasive; smooth, slick (*colloq.*), glassy, polished; unctuous, greasy, oily, waxy, soapy. See APOSTASY, IMPROBITY, NONOBSERVANCE, SMOOTHNESS, UNCTUOUSNESS.
slobber, *v.* slaver, drivel, drool. See EJECTION.
slope, *n.* incline, grade (*U. S.*), slant, tilt, acclivity, declivity. See OBLIQUITY.
sloping, *adj.* declivitous; slanting, oblique, bevel. See DESCENT, OBLIQUITY.
sloven, *n.* slouch (*slang*), untidy fellow. See DISORDER.
slovenly, *adj.* untidy, unkempt, dowdy, slatternly. See DISORDER.

SLOWNESS.—I. *Nouns.* **slowness,** tardiness, dilatoriness, etc. (see *adjectives*); sluggishness, lentor (*rare*), languor; drawl; jog-trot, dog-trot, amble, walk, limp, hitch, hobble, hop, slow-down (*colloq.*), mincing steps; dead march, slow march.
retardation, delaying, hindrance, delay, retard, deceleration (*mech.*), negative (*or* minus) acceleration (*mech.*), retardment, obstruction, obstacle: *opposite of* acceleration.
deliberation, caution, coolness, deliberateness, circumspection, wariness, watchfulness, prudence, measuredness.
dullness, tediousness, tedium, monotony, uninterestingness, cheerlessness, stupidity.
slow goer, slow coach (*colloq.*), loiterer, sluggard, drone, slugabed (*archaic*) poke (*U. S. slang*), slow poke (*slang or colloq.*), dawdler; tortoise, snail.
II. *Verbs.* **slow,** retard, delay, decelerate (*mech.*), slacken speed, slow down, slacken, relax, check, moderate, rein in, **curb**; reef, shorten (*or* take in) sail; brake, backwater, back pedal.
move slowly, creep, crawl, lag, walk, linger, loiter, saunter, plod, trudge, lumber, trail, drag, worm one's way, inch, inch along, jog on, toddle, waddle, slouch, shuffle, halt, hobble, hitch, limp, shamble; flag, falter, totter, stagger; mince; take one's time.
III. *Adjectives.* **slow,** tardy, dilatory, snail-like, crawling, lingering, late, behindhand, slow-gaited, slow-paced, leisurely; deliberate, gradual, gentle, moderate; languid, sluggish, inert, inactive, stagnant, slack, logy (*U. S. colloq.*), torpid, lazy, dopey (*slang*), heavy, apathetic, phlegmatic, lymphatic.
dull, tedious, irksome, wearisome, cheerless, dismal, stupid, boring, uninteresting, humdrum, prosaic (*as, a* slow *evening*).
IV. *Adverbs.* **slowly,** tardily, etc. (see *adjectives*); slow, at half speed in slow time; with clipped wings; under easy sail; adagio, *larghetto* (*It.*), *largo* (*It.*).
gradually, by degrees, step by step, bit by bit, inch by inch, little by little, *peu à peu* (*F.*), by slow degrees.
See also DULLNESS, INACTIVITY, INERTNESS, LATENESS.—*Antonyms.* See VELOCITY.

---

sluggish, *adj.* inactive, drowsy, sleepy, dull, torpid, logy (*U. S.*), lifeless; inert, slow, languid, lazy, slothful, apathetic, supine. See INACTIVITY, INERTNESS, INSENSITIVINESS.
slumber, *n.* sleep, rest, repose, nap, doze, siesta, snooze (*colloq.*). See INACTIVITY.
slur, *v.* accuse, blame; defame, vilify, stigmatize, asperse; slight, scamp, skip. See ACCUSATON. DISREPUTE, NEGLECT.

slush, *n.* gush, effusiveness; sludge, slosh, ooze. See LOQUACITY, SEMILIQUIDITY.
sly, *adj.* underhand, crafty, tricky, wily, stealthy. See CONCEALMENT, CUNNING.
small arms, portable firearms, rifle, carbine, pistol, etc. See ARMS.

SMALLNESS.—I. *Nouns.* **smallness,** littleness, etc. (see *adjectives*); paucity, fewness, sparseness, scarcity; insignificance, unimportance, inconsiderableness.
small quantity, modicum, minimum; atom, particle, molecule, electron, corpuscle, point, speck, fleabite, dot, mote, jot, iota; minutiæ (*pl.*), details; tittle, spark; grain, scruple, minim; drop, sprinkling, dab, dash, tinge, dole, mite, bit, nip, pinch, snick, snack (*dial.*), snatch, slip, morsel, crumb, fragment, trifle, fraction, scrap, shred, tag, rag; snip, silver, splinter, chip, peeling, paring, shaving, hair; thimbleful, handful, capful, mouthful; a drop in the bucket, a drop in the ocean.
II. *Verbs.* **be small,** lie in a nutshell.
diminish, lessen, decrease, contract, shrink, dwindle, wane.
III. *Adjectives,* **small** (*opposite of* large), little (*opposite of* big, great), diminutive, stunted, sawed-off (*as a shotgun*), tiny, puny, wee (*colloq.*), runty (*U. S.*) Lilliputian, dapper, *petite* (*F.; said of a girl or woman*), pygmy *or* pigmy, miniature, minikin, minute; fine, comminuted, triturated, pulverized; scanty, scant, limited, lesser, moderate, meager *or* meagre, few, sparse; narrow, slender, slight.
inappreciable, inconsiderable, homeopathic *or* homœopathic, infinitesimal, atomic, microscopic, molecular, evanescent.
mere, simple, sheer, stark, bare, naked, plain, nothing but.
unimportant, trivial, inconsequential (*rare in this sense*), slight, paltry, trifling, petty, insignificant (*as,* small *talk*).
[*of the voice*] **soft,** gentle, faint, low; clear, thin.
[*of diluted liquors*] **diluted,** weak, thin, watery, washy, light, mildly alcoholic (*as,* small *beer*).
[*socially undistinguished*] **obscure,** humble, retired, modest, lowly, unpretentious. poor (*as, to live in a* small *way*).
[*morally mean*] **small-minded,** petty, paltry, ungenerous, mean, scurvy, base, sordid, unworthy, selfish, narrow-minded.
less, lesser, smaller, inferior, minor, lower.
least, smallest, slightest, lowest, minimum, minimal.
IV. *Adverbs* [*in a small degree*] **smally** (*rare*), to a small extent, on a small scale; slightly, imperceptibly, faintly, feebly, passably, imperfectly, insufficiently; miserably, wretchedly.
[*in a certain or limited degree*] **partially,** in part, incompletely, restrictedly, somewhat, to a certain extent, *pro tanto* (*L.*), in a certain degree, comparatively, rather, in some degree *or* measure; simply, only, purely, merely; at least, at most, *tant soit peu* (*F.*), ever so little, thus far, after a fashion.
almost, nearly, well-nigh, nigh, not quite, all but, near upon, close upon, near the mark; within an ace (*or* inch) of, on the brink of; scarcely, hardly, barely, only just, no more than.
[*in an uncertain degree*] **about,** nearly, approximately, *circa* (*L.*), say (*imperative*), thereabouts, somewhere about, somewhere near.
[*in no degree*] **nowise,** noway *or* noways, in no manner, not at all, not in the least, not a bit, not a jot, in no wise, in no respect, by no means, on no account.

See also DECREASE, FEWNESS, INFERIORITY, LITTLENESS, PART, UNIMPORTANCE.—*Antonyms.* See GREATNESS, SIZE.

---

smart, *adj.* quick, vigorous, prompt; trim, spruce; stylish, *chic* (*F.*); adroit; skillful; keen, witty, brilliant, clever, sprightly. See ACTIVITY, CLEANNESS, ORNAMENT, SKILL, WIT.
smarten, *v.* array, deck, bedeck, prink, trim, dress. See ORNAMENT.
smash, *v.* shatter, crush, destroy. See DESTRUCTION.
smatterer, *n.* dabbler, sciolist. See IGNORAMUS.
smattering, *n.* superficiality, glimmering, sciolism. See IGNORANCE.
smear, *v.* daub, bedaub, besmear, cover; blur, smirch, spot, soil; salve, grease. See COVERING, UNCLEANNESS, UNCTUOUSNESS.

smell, *v.* scent, sniff, inhale; suspect, scent out, nose. See ODOR, UNBELIEF.
smile, *v.* simper, smirk, grin. See REJOICING.
smog, *n.* smoke fog: *portmanteau word.* See CLOUD.
smoke, *v.* reek, fume, burn; cure (*as hams*), kipper (*as herrings*); puff, inhale, vapor, vaporize. See HEAT, PRESERVATION, VAPORIZATION.
smoky, *adj.* fuliginous, sooty, fumy, reeky. See OPACITY.
smolder, *v.* burn, smoker, smother; hang fire, be inert. See HEAT, INERTNESS.

SMOOTHNESS.—I. *Nouns.* **smoothness,** evenness, etc. (see *adjectives*); polish, gloss, glaze, shine, levigation; lubrication, lubricity.
[*smooth surfaces*] billiard table, bowling green, lawn; glass, ice, asphalt, marble, alabaster; velvet, silk, *charmeuse* (*F.*), taffeta, satin.
smoother, sleeker, slicker (*founding*), roller, steam roller, mangle; iron, flatiron, sadiron, electric iron; chamois *or* shammy, burnisher; pumice, pumice stone; sandpaper, emery paper; plane.
II. *Verbs.* **smooth,** smoothen (*rare*), even, level, flatten, roll, grade, macadamize; press, mangle, iron; scour, sandpaper, pumice, buff, file; plane, shave, mow.
polish, burnish, furbish, sleek, slick, levigate, planish, glance (*metal working*), luster *or* lustre, varnish, glaze, gloss; lubricate, oil, grease, wax, anoint.
palliate, gloze, soften, extenuate, excuse, mitigate; ease, calm, quiet, mollify, alleviate, assuage, soothe.
remove (*as an obstruction*), displace, dislodge, reduce, raze, get rid of.
III. *Adjectives.* **smooth,** even, level, plane, flat, unwrinkled, regular, uniform; slick (*colloq.*), sleeky, sleek, glossy, lustrous, satiny, shiny, silken, sikly, velvety, velutinous, lubricous, slippery, glassy, greasy, glairy, oily, polished, *glacé* (*F.*), glabrous (*as a leaf*), glabrate (*tech.*), levigate, leiodermatous; smooth as glass (monumental alabaster, ice, ivory, satin, velvet, *or* oil); slippery as an eel.
[*without hair*] **hairless,** bald; clean-shaven, beardless, whiskerless, shaven, smooth-chinned, smooth-faced; pelon (*as a dog: Sp. Amer.*).
unruffled, calm, tranquil, serene, undisturbed, quiet, still; mild, pleasant, equable, agreeable (*as,* smooth *water; a* smooth *temper*).
suave, bland, smooth-spoken, smooth-tongued, glib, flattering, ingratiatory, ingratiating, silky, soft-spoken, unctuous, oily, smug, plausible, fair-spoken, insinuating, insinuative; soothing, conciliatory, complimentary, polite (*as,* smooth *words*).
[*of diction*] **fluent,** flowing, easy, voluble, rhythmic *or* rhythmical, polished (*as,* smooth *verse*).
[*of musical sound*] **smooth-sounding,** melodious, euphonious, harmonious, running, *legato* (*It.*), liquid.
[*in phonetics*] liquid, vowel-like (*as* l, m, n, r); unaspirated (*as, the* smooth *breathing in Greek*).
IV. *Adverbs.* **smoothly,** smooth, evenly, etc. (see *adjectives*).
See also CONCORD, FLATNESS, HORIZONTALITY, LUBRICATION, MODERATION, OIL, ROLL, SOFTNESS, SWEETNESS, UNIFORMITY.—*Antonyms.* See ROUGHNESS.

---

smother, *v.* choke, stifle, suffocate; deaden, weaken; govern, hold, suppress. See KILLING, MODERATION, RESTRAINT.
smuggler, *n.* contrabandist, runner (*colloq.*), rum runner. See THIEF.
snake, *n.* serpent, reptile, viper, ophidian. See ANIMAL.

SNAP.—I. *Nouns.* **snap,** bite, nip, catch, snatch, seizure (*as with the teeth*).
crack (*as of a whip*), click, smack, blow, fillip, flip, flick, rap, tap, etc. (see *verbs*); clack, fico (*archaic*), sound; thud, thump; break, breaking, rupture; crepitation (*esp. tech.*), crackling, decrepitation (*tech.*); yelp, bark, yap, yell, shout, toot.
report, pop, shot, clap, burst, crash, fulguration, fulmination, thunderclap thunderburst (*rare*), eruption, blowout (*tire*), explosion, discharge, detonation, firing, salvo, volley.
fastening (*as of a bracelet*), catch, clasp, fastener; spring hook, nsap hook, spring catch.
gingersnap, ginger cookie: *chiefly in plural.*
vigor, energy, vim (*colloq.*), go (*colloq.*), briskness, crispness, liveliness, life, dash,

verve, spirit, enthusiasm, *élan* (*F.*), pep (*slang*): *in this sense,* snap *is colloq*
[*brief, intense period*] **spell,** turn, interval, season, period (*as, a* snap *of cold weather*).
[*an easy time or thing*] **sinecure,** cinch (*U. S. slang*), mere child's play, straight sailing, sure thing, easy job (*as, a soft* snap: *slang*).

II. *Verbs.* **snap,** snatch (*esp. with the teeth*), catch, grab, grasp, seize; bite, nip.
break (*suddenly*), fracture, rend, splinter, shatter, burst, split, part asunder (*as, to* snap *a twig*).
crack, pop, crash, clap, slam, shut, bang, thump, knock, rap, tap, clash, twang, click; crackle, decrepitate (*tech.*), crepitate; yelp, yap, bark, fire, explode, rattle, toot, burst on the ear; miss fire (*as a gun*).
jerk (*as a baseball*), fling, throw, toss, flick, fillip, project, whisk, whip, dart.
[*of the eyes*] **flash,** sparkle, glance, glint, glitter, glisten, gleam.
[*to speak crossly*] **snarl,** growl, bark, gnar *or* gnarr, gnarl; chide, rebuke, censure, cavil, carp: *usually with* at.

III. *Adjectives.* **snappish,** snarly, snarling, threatening (*to bite*), currish, surly, peevish, testy, irritable, ill-natured, cross; curt, short, brusque, blunt, tart.

See also ACTIVITY, CLOSURE, DISCOURTESY, DISJUNCTION, IRASCIBILITY, RESENTMENT.—*Antonyms.* See COURTESY, JUNCTION, ROLL.

---

snare, *n.* trap, pitfall, spring, gin. See DECEPTION.
snarl, *v.* growl, carp, rebuke, chide; mutter, threaten, bark, yelp, ululate. See DISCOURTESY, SNAP, THREAT, ULULATION.
snatch, *v.* seize, grab, clutch, grip. See TAKING.
sneak, *v.* skulk, slink, creep; *Slang:* filch, steal. See CONCEALMENT, STEALING.
sneer, *v.* jeer, scoff, ridicule, taunt, gibe. See DISRESPECT.
snigger, *v.* snicker, titter, giggle. See REJOICING, RIDICULE.
snob, *n.* toady, truckler; upstart, parvenu. See SERVILITY, VULARITY.
snooze, *n.* sleep, slumber, nap, doze, drowse. See INACTIVITY.
snort, *v.* snore, grunt. See CRY, ULULATION.
snub, *v.* cut, slight, ignore; rebuke, humble, humiliate, crush; check. See DISCOURTESY, HUMILITY, RESTRAINT.
[1]**snuff,** *v.* extinguish, put out, stifle, smother. See DARKNESS.
[2]**snuff,** *v.* smell, sniff, inhale; snuffle, sniffle. See ODOR, WIND.
snug, *adv.* trim, firm, close, compact; cozy, comfortable. See CLOSURE, PLEASURE.
snuggle, *v.* nestle, nuzzle, cuddle. See ENDEARMENT.
soak, *v.* drench, saturate, steep. See WATER.
soaked, *adj.* sodden, saturated, soggy, reeking, dripping, drenched. See MOISTURE.
soar, *v.* fly aloft, aviate, glide; tower, loom, transcend; rise, mount, ascend. See AERONAUTICS, GREATNESS, HEIGHT.
sob, *v.* sigh, cry, weep; sough. See LAMENTATION, WIND.

SOBRIETY.—I. *Nouns.* **sobriety,** soberness, moderation, temperateness, temperance, abstention, abstemiousness, abstinence; blue-ribbonism, total abstinence, teetotalism, nephalism (*rare*).
sober-mindedness, calmness, sedateness, gravity, solemnity, seriousness, earnestness, etc. (see *adjectives*); soundness, rationality, reasonableness.
water drinker, hydropot (*rare*), teetotaler, total abstainer, nephalist (*rare*), Rechabite, blue-ribboner, blue-ribbonist, dry (*slang*), prohibitionist; abstainer, abstinent.

II. *Verbs.* **sober,** make sober, become sober, soberize (*rare*); take (*or* sign) the pledge.
moderate, calm, allay, temper, cool down, steady, brace, nerve.

III. *Adjectives.* **sober,** temperate, abstentious, abstemious, abstinent, teetotal, unintoxicated, ascetic, austere; moderate, regular, steady, sane, well-balanced, dispassionate, cool, calm, unimpassioned, collected, inexcitable, unruffled, self-possessed, self-controlled, rational, reasonable, sound.

sober-minded, sedate, staid, grave, solemn, somber *or* sombre, sombrous, serious, earnest, thoughtful, demure.
[*of color*] **subdued,** inconspicuous, quiet, plain, drag, gray, sad, dull, dull-looking.
IV. *Adverbs.* soberly, temperately, abstemiously, moderately, etc. (see *adjectives*); in a sober manner, calmly, coolly, gravely, sober-mindedly.

See also MODERATION, SANITY, TEMPERANCE, WISDOM.—*Antonyms.* See DRUNKENNESS, INTEMPERANCE.

---

socialism, *n.* communism, collectivism, nationalism; communalism. See AUTHORITY, PARTICIPATION.

SOCIALITY.—I. *Nouns.* **sociality,** sociability, sociableness, companionableness, companionability, social intercourse, intercourse, association, company, society, companionship, comradeship, fellowship, consociation, clubbism, urbanity, intimacy, familiarity, *esprit de corps* (*F.*); family (*or* social) circle, family hearth, circle of acquaintance.
conviviality, good fellowship, joviality, jollity, festivity, merry-making; hospitality, heartiness, cheer; loving cup, festive board; "the feast of reason and the flow of soul" (Pope).
welcome, greeting, salutation, *bienvenue* (*F.*); hearty (*or* warm) reception; hearty welcome (*or* greeting), the glad hand (*slang*).
good fellow, boon companion, bawcock (*archaic*), *bon enfant* (*F.*), good scout (*colloq.*), good mixer (*colloq.*), a j'iner (*U. S. colloq.*); *bon vivant* (*F.*).
social gathering, social reunion, assembly, social, sociable (*U. S.*), party, entertainment, reception, levee, at home, *conversazione* (*It.*), soirée, matinée; garden party, coming-out party (*colloq.*), surprise party, tea party, tea fight (*slang*), *thé dansant* (*F.*); hen party (*colloq.*), stag *or* stag party (*colloq.*), smoker (*colloq.*), stag dinner (*colloq.*), bachelor dinner, hunt dinner; Dutch treat (*colloq.*); *partie carrée* (*F.*), rout (*archaic*), drum (*hist.*), kettledrum, *ridotto* (*It.*), wedding breakfast; ball, hunt ball, dance, dinner dance, festival; bee, corn husking (*U. S.*), corn shucking (*U. S.*), husking, husking bee (*U. S.*); house raising, house-warming, hanging of the crane.
breakfast, luncheon, lunch; picnic lunch, basket lunch, picnic; tea, afternoon tea, five o'clock tea, cup of tea, dish of tea (*esp. Brit.*); dinner, potluck, high tea, banquet.
visit, call, morning call, interview, visiting, round of visits; official visit, visitation; tryst, appointment, engagement, date (*colloq.*).
II. *Verbs.* **be sociable,** know, be acquainted, associate with, consort with, club together, bear one company, join, make advances, neighbor *or* neighbour, mingle, hobnob, mix, fraternize, intercommunicate.
visit, pay a visit, call at, call upon, leave a card, drop in, look in.
entertain, receive, welcome; give a party, keep open house, have the latchstring out, do the honors, kill the fatted calf.
III. *Adjectives.* **sociable,** companionable, clubbable (*colloq.*), cozy *or* cosy, chatty, conversable, communicative, conversational; convivial, festive, festal, jovial, jolly, hospitable, neighborly, social, familiar, intimate, friendly, genial, affable; accessible, informal, democratic, free and easy, hail fellow well met.
social, sociable, consociative (*rare*), gregarious, coöperative, interdependent.
[*in biology*] communistic, commensal (*as ants*); colonial, compound (*as ascidians*); grouped, massed (*as certain plants*).
IV. *Adverbs.* **sociably,** companionably, etc. (see *adjectives*); socially, *en famille* (*F.*), in the family circle; on terms of intimacy; in the social whirl; *sans façon* (*F.*), *sans cérémonie* (*F.*), arm in arm.

See also AMUSEMENT, COURTESY, FOOD, FRIENDSHIP, PARTY.—*Antonyms.* See EXCLUSION, SECLUSION.

---

society, *n.* high life, *élite* (*F.*), four hundred (*colloq.*), smart set; man, human race; association, union, league, federation. See FASHION, MANKIND, PARTY.
sod, *n.* clod, clot (*dial.*); sward, greensward. See LAND, PLAIN.
sodden, *adj.* soaked, soaking, saturated, soggy, reeking, dripping. See MOISTURE.
sofa, *n.* couch, davenport, day-bed, ottoman, settee. See SUPPORT.

SOFTNESS.—I. *Nouns.* **softness,** pliableness, flexibility, pliancy, pliability, malleability, ductility, tractility, extensibility, extendibility, plasticity, flaccidity, laxity, flabbiness, flocculence, mollescence, mollities (*med.*), mollification, softening; smoothness, gentleness, etc. (see *adjectives*).
[*comparisons*] butter, down, silk, putty, dough, pudding; cushion, feather bed, pillow, padding, wadding; clay, wax.
II. *Verbs.* **soften,** render, soft, etc. (see *adjectives*); mollify, mellow, milden, dulcify; melt, thaw, dissolve, moisten, macerate; squash (*colloq.*), mash, knead, massage.
bend, give, yield, relax, relent; deflex, flex, deflect.
palliate, mitigate, assuage, extenuate, alleviate, allay, appease, lessen, abate.
subdue (*as tone or color*), temper, tone down, restrain, chasten, modify, moderate, qualify, lower.
enervate, enfeeble, weaken, debilitate; effeminate, effeminize (*rare*).
III. *Adjectives.* **soft,** supple, pliant, pliable, flexible, flexile; lissom, graceful, lithe, lithesome, limber; extensible, ductile, malleable, tractable, tractile, plastic, yielding; relaxed, softened, flexuous, limp, flimsy; mellow, pulpy, doughy, pasty, spongy, œdematous *or* edematous (*tech.*), medullary (*tech.*), pithy; argillaceous, clayey: *opposite of* hard.
downy, woolly, fleecy, lanate, lanuginose *or* lanuginous, sericeous (*tech.*), silky, villous (*esp. bot.*), flocculent, flocky, fluffy, feathery.
[*not rough or harsh*] **smooth,** satiny, velvety, silky; delicate, fine, agreeable, flowing, **gentle,** kind, kindly, genial, amiable, benign, gracious, mild, tender, soft-hearted, tender-hearted, sympathetic, compassionate; courteous, polite, complaisant.
soft-spoken, conciliatory, complimentary, affable, plausible.
[*of the weather*] damp, wet, rainy, moist, thawing.
mild, mellow, balmy, summery, clement, warm (*as, a* soft *winter;* soft *air*).
restful, reposeful, quiet, peaceful, comfortable, undisturbed (*as,* soft *slumbers*).
effeminate, unmanly, pusillanimous, timorous, weak, silly, foolish, amorous, spoony (*slang*).
impressible, impressionable, susceptible, sensitive, emotional, facile.
[*of muscles*] **flaccid,** flabby, lax, unstrung, untrained, undertrained, unhardened.
[*of sounds*] low, low-toned, low-pitched, subdued, faint, melodious, smooth (*as* soft *music; a* soft *voice*).
[*in phonetics*] sibilant, spirant (*as* g *in* gin, c *in* cede); sonant, voiced, tonic, flat: *opposite of* hard.
unaspirated, smooth (*as, a* soft *breathing in Greek*).
softening, emollient, mollescent, demulcent, mollient (*rare*), assuasive, lenitive, lenient.
IV. *Adverbs.* **softly,** in a soft manner; soft, gently, quietly, mildly, etc. (see *adjectives*); low, not loud.
V. *Interjections.* soft! (*archaic*), hush! be quiet! hold! stop! not so fast! gently!
See also FAINTNESS, LETTER (*voiced*), MARSH, MODERATION, MOISTURE, PITY, SILENCE, SMALLNESS, SWEETNESS, TOUCH, WEAKNESS.—*Antonyms.* See HARDNESS, LOUDNESS.

---

soggy, *adj.* soaked, sodden, saturated. See MOISTURE.
[1]soil, *n.* loam, dirt, earth, ground; country. See LAND.
[2]soil, *n.* smear, smudge, stain. See UNCLEANNESS.
soil, *v.* smear, spot, daub, blot, stain. See UNCLEANNESS.
sojourn, *v.* tarry, lodge, dwell. See INHABITANT.
solace, *n.* consolation, comfort, cheer. See RELIEF.
soldier, *n.* private, doughboy (*U. S.*), guardsman, warrior. See COMBATANT.
sole, *adj.* one, lone, single, solitary, only, individual. See UNITY.

SOLECISM.—I. *Nouns.* **solecism,** idiomatic blunder, grammatical error, slip, error, slip of the pen, slip of the tongue, bull, Hibernianism; barbarism (*illiterate or unacceptable expression*), impropriety.
II. *Verbs.* **solecize,** commit a solecism, murder the King's (*or* Queen's) English, use bad grammar, break Priscian's head.
III. *Adjectives.* **solecistic** *or* solecistical, ungrammatical, unidiomatic, improper, incorrect, inaccurate, faulty, illiterate.
Antonyms. See GRAMMAR.

solely, *adv.* barely, merely, purely, exclusively, singly, alone. See UNITY.
solemn, *adj.* sober, serious, sad, mournful; grave, awe-inspiring, wise-looking; impressive, reverential, devotional. Se DEJECTION, SAGE, SILENCE.
solicit, *v.* beg, beseech, plead, implore, entreat. See REQUEST.
solicitous, *adj.* anxious, concerned, careful. See JEALOUSY.
solicitude, *n.* care, watchfulness, concern, ansiety. See JEALOUSY, THOUGHT.
solid, *adj.* unanimous, united; dense, compact, impermeable, thick, massive; strong, nourishing, nutritive; substantial, stable, firm; genuine, trustworthy; sober, staid. See CONCORD, DENSITY, STRENGTH, SUBSTANTIALITY, WISDOM (*prudent*).—**solid body,** solid, mass, block, lump. See DENSITY.

SOLILOQUY.—I. *Nouns.* **soliloquy,** monologue, apostrophe (*rhet.*), monology (*the habit*).
soliloquist, soliloquizer, monologuist, monologian (*rare*); monologist, monopolizer of conversation.
II. *Verbs.* **soliloquize,** monologize, monologue, monologuize, talk to oneself, think aloud; say aside, address an imaginary audience, apostrophize.
III. *Adjectives.* **soliloquizing,** soliloquacious (*rare*), monologic *or* monological, apostrophic.
Antonyms. See CONVERSATION.

---

solitary, *adj.* lonely, lonesome, isolated, secluded; sole, lone, single, alone. See SECLUSION, UNITY.
solitude, *n.* isolation, reclusion, privacy, loneliness. See SECLUSION.
solmization, *n.* solfeggio, sol-fa. See MUSIC.
solution, *n.* key, clew *or* clue, explanation, interpretation; decoction, infusion, mixture. See ANSWER, SECRET, LIQUEFACTION.
solve, *v.* unriddle, unravel, interpret, resolve, discover. See DISCOVERY, RESOLUTION.
solvency, *n.* soundness, stability, solidity, reliability. See MONEY.
solvent, *adj.* dissolvent, diluent; sound, solid, stable. See LIQUEFACTION, MONEY.
solvent, *n.* dissolvent, resolvent, resolutive, diluent. See LIQUEFACTION.
somber, *adj.* dusky, dim, overcast; gloomy, dismal; grave, sober, dull, subdued. See DARKNESS, DEJECTION, DULLNESS.
somehow, *adv.* in some way, by some means. See INSTRUMENTALITY.
sometimes, *adv.* occasionally, at times. See FREQUENCY.
somewhere, *adv.* in some place, here and there. See PLACE.
son, *n.* male child, boy, junior, scion, heir, descendant. See POSTERITY.
song, *n.* lay, aria, air, chant, carol. See MUSIC.
sonorous, *adj.* resonant, full-toned; loud, deep, full; high-sounding, soniferous See DEPTH, LOUDNESS, [1]SOUND.
soon, *adv.* presently, shortly, early, forthwith, betimes. See FUTURE.
soothe, *v.* lull, compose, still, calm, quiet, relieve. See MODERATION, RELIEF.
soothing, *adj.* mollifying, assuasive, transquilizing. See MILDNESS.
sop, pacifier, bribe, lure, bait. See MOTIVE.

SOPHISTRY.—I. *Nouns.* **sophistry,** specious reasoning, casuistry, jesuitry, equivocation, fallaciousness, evasion, speciousness, deception, sophistication, mystification, mental reservation, perversion, chicane, chicanery, trickery, hair-splitting, quibbling, begging of the question, *petitio principii* (*L.*), *post hoc ergo propter hoc* (*L.*), *non sequitur* (*L.*), reasoning in a circle, *circulus in probando* (*L.*), nonsense, absurdity, error.
sophism, paralogism (*logic*), amphibology *or* amphiboly, ambiguity, fallacy, quibble, quick, subterfuge, shift, subtlety, quillet (*archaic*), *quodlibet* (*L.*), antilogy, inconsistency; "a delusion, a mockery, and a snare" (Denman); **claptrap,** mere words; "lame and impotent conclusion" (*Othello*).
sophist, casuist, quibbler, paralogist, prevaricator, shuffler.

II. *Verbs.* **sophisticate,** quibble, subilize, split hairs, refine, equivocate, prevaricate, shuffle, cavil, palter, shift, dodge, elude, evade, mystify, mislead, varnish, gloss over, falsify, misrepresent, pervert, misteach, beg the question, reason in a circle, beat about the bush, put oneself out of court

adulterate (*as wine, etc.*), vitiate, corrupt, debase, drug, alloy, load, thin, deteriorate, tamper with.

III. *Adjectives.* **sophistical** *or* sophistic, specious, captious, casuistic, pilpulistic (*esp. in Talmudic study*), hair-splitting, paralogistic, jesuitic *or* jesuitical, oversubtle, metaphysical, abstruse, fallacious, misleading, paralogical, unsound, invalid, illogical, deceptive, illusory, illusive, plausible, evasive, false, groundless, hollow, unscientific, untenable, inconclusive, incorrect, fallible, unproved; inconsequent, irrational, incongruous, unreasonable, inconsequential, self-contradictory, inconsistent, unconnected, irrelevant, inapplicable, unwarranted, gratuitous.

weak, feeble, poor, flimsy, loose, vague, preposterous, nonsensical, absurd, foolish, frivolous, pettifogging, quibbling.

sophisticated, worldly-wise, knowing, shrewd, astute, experienced, fly (*slang*), artful, wide-awake, knowing what's what (*colloq.*), knowing what o'clock it is (*colloq.*), knowing one's onions (*slang*).

IV. *Adverbs.* **sophistically,** speciously, fallaciously, illogically, etc. (see *adjectives*).

See also ABSURDITY, FALSEHOOD, MISTEACHING.—*Antonyms.* See REASONING, TRUTH.

SORCERER.—I. *Nouns.* **sorcerer,** magician, wizard, necromancer, conjuror, prestidigitator; charmer, exorcist, voodoo, theurgist, mage (*poetic*), thaumaturge, thaumaturgist, medicine man, witch doctor, shaman; astrologer, soothsayer.

sorceress (*fem.*), pythoness, enchantress, siren, harpy; witch, hag.

Cagliostro, Merlin, Comus; Circe, weird sisters, Grææ *or* Graiæ, witch of Endor

See also ORACLE, [1]SPELL.

SORCERY.—I. *Nouns.* **sorcery,** magic, black magic, the black art, necromancy, thaumaturgy, theurgy, demonology, witchcraft, witchery, wizardry, fetishism, hoodoo (*colloq.*), voodoo, voodooism; shamanism, obi *or* obiism; conjuration, invocation, incantation, divination, sortilege; hocus-pocus, spell, enchantment, bewitchment, glamour; obsession, possession.

II. *Verbs.* **practice sorcery,** cast a nativity (*or* horoscope), conjure, voodoo, hoodoo (*colloq.*); fascinate, entrance; charm, enchant, bewitch, bedevil, witch, hypnotize, cast a spell; call up spirits, raise ghosts, command jinn (*or* genii).

III. *Adjectives.* **magic,** magical, necromantic, incantatory, Circean, witching, weird, cabalistic, talismanic.

See also PREDICTION, [1]SPELL.

---

sordid, *adj.* base, ignoble; greedy, grasping, covetous, avaricious, niggardly. See IMPROBITY, PARSIMONY.

sore, *adj.* painful, hurtful, severe, raw; sullen, offended, vexed, hurt, resentful. See PAINFULNESS, RESENTMENT.

sore, *n.* ulcer, abscess, fester, boil, gall; soreness, discomfort. See DISEASE, PAIN.

sorrow, *n.* misfortune, trial, blow; grief, distress, affliction. See ADVERSITY, PAIN.

sorry, *adj.* sad, grieved, sorrowful, gloomy; regretful, remorseful, apologetic; beggarly, poor, mean, miserable. See PAIN, REGRET, UNIMPORTANCE.

sort, *n.* kind, manner, nature, type, character. See CLASS.

sort, *v.* assort, allot, classify, adjust, fit. See ARRANGEMENT.

soul, *n.* spirit, psyche, ego, heart, spiritual being; human being, person; life, essence, substance, cause. See DISPOSITION, IMMATERIALITY, INTELLECT, MANKIND, SUBJECTIVENESS.

sound, *adj.* legal, valid; solvent, secure, stable, firm; orthodox, authorized, approved, strict, canonical; whole, perfect, faultless, unblemished; satisfactory, sane, well, hale, healthy; pure, sterling, unadulterated. See LEGALITY, MONEY, ORTHODOXY, PERFECTION, RIGHT, TRUTH.

---

[1]**SOUND.**—I. *Nouns.* **sound,** noise, report, sonority, sonorousness, sonorescence (*physics*), sonification, stridulation (*as of insects*); audibility, resonance, vibration, reverberation, polyphony; strain, tone, intonation, key, modulation, tune, cadence, accent, twang; utterance, phonation, sonancy, articulation, voice.
earshot, hearing, range, hearing, distance.
science of sound: acoustics, diacoustics, catacoustics; phonetics, phonology phonography; telephony, radiophony.
II. *Verbs.* [1]**sound,** make a noise, give out sound, emit sound, give forth; ring, resound, reverberate; blow (*as a trumpet*), blare.
proclaim (*by or as by sound*), make known, announce, call, cry, sing, hymn, herald, spread abroad, broadcast, publish; indicate, order; celebrate, honor, commemorate.
examine (*as the chest*), try, test, auscultate (*med.*).
[*to convey an impression*] **seem,** appear, look (*as, the tale* sounds *false*).
III. *Adjectives.* **sounding,** sonorous, soniferous, resonant, high-sounding, sonoric, melodious, ringing; ear-splitting, stertorous; audible, distinct, clear; acoustic, auditory.
phonetic, phonic; vocal, sonant, voiced, tonic, intonated, vocalized, phthongal, sonantized (*rare*).

See also CRY, FAINTNESS, LETTER (*phonetics*), LOUDNESS, MELODY, MUSIC, RESONANCE, ROLL, SIBILATION, SNAP, STRIDENCY, ULULATION (*animal sounds*), VOICE. —*Antonyms.* See SILENCE.

---

[2]**sound,** *n.* passage (*of water*), strait, channel. See GULF.
[3]**sound,** *v.* fathom, take soundings, measure; probe, examine, sift. See DEPTH, INQUIRY.
sounding, *n.* depth of water: *naut.* See DEPTH.
source, *n.* origin, rise, cause, fountain, genesis. See BEGINNING.

SOURNESS.—I. *Nouns.* **sourness,** acerbity, acidity, acetosity, tartness, acid; sharpness, asperity, bitterness; moroseness, sullenness, etc. (see *adjectives*).
[*comparisons*] vinegar, verjuice, crab, lemon, alum.
II. *Verbs.* **sour,** acidify, acidulate, acetify, turn; ferment.
embitter, exacerbate, exasperate, irritate, envenom, make bitter (*or* more bitter).
III. *Adjectives.* **sour,** acid, acidulated, acerb, acetic, acetose, acetous, acidulous, acrid, tart, rancid, turned (*as milk*), curdled, musty, vinegary, foxy (*as wine, beer, etc.*), sourish, subacid, green, acescent; rough, sharp, hard, unripe, astringent, styptic.
distasteful, disagreeable, bitter, acrimonious, unpleasant, unpalatable, unsavory, offensive, displeasing.
[*of persons or temper*] **morose,** sullen, crabbed, soured, peevish, caustic, ill-humored, sour-tempered, vinegary, cross, cantankerous, snappish, testy, unamiable, glum, crusty, surly, harsh, austere, misanthropic.
[*of soil*] cold, wet, acid; unfertile, unproductive, unfavorable.

See also AGGRAVATION, DISCONTENT, DISCOURTESY, ROUGHNESS (*tart*).—*Antonyms.* See SWEETNESS.

---

southern, *adj.* south, southerly, meridional: *opposite of* northern. See OPPOSITE.
souvenir, *n.* token, reminder, memento, keepsake, relic. See MONEY.
sovereign, *n.* ruler, potentate, monarch, suzerain, king. See MASTER.
sovereignty, *n.* sway, dominion, power; royalty. See SCEPTER.
sow, *v.* disperse, scatter, disseminate, bestrew; plant. See DISPERSION, HUSBANDRY.

SPACE.—I. *Nouns.* **space,** extension, extent, proportions, spaciousness, expanse, stretch, spread, expansion; distance, interval, interspace, interstice, gap; abyss, chasm, void, vacuum; capacity, accommodation, room; field, margin, area, scope, compass, range, latitude, sweep, play, swing, elbowroom, leeway, seaway, headway; sphere, arena.

open space, free space, country, rural regions; waste, desert, wild, wilderness; moor, down, downs, upland, moorland; prairie, steppe, llano (*Sp. Amer.*), campagna.

[*unlimited space*] **infinity,** immensity, vast (*poetic*), boundlessness, endlessness; interplanetary (interstellar, intercosmic, *or* intergalactic) space; plenum (*opposite of* vacuum), ether, heavens; creation, universe, world, wide world.

[*measurement of interstellar space*] **light year** (*distance over which light can travel in a year*); parsec *or* secpar (*about* 3¼ *light years*).

[*of time*] **interval,** duration, time, period, while; interim, interlude, intermission, interregnum, interstices (*pl.; R. C. Ch.*).

II. *Verbs.* **space,** set at intervals, interspace, interval, put spaces between (*as in printing or typewriting*); arrange, set out, spread out, extend, open up (*or* out), separate, disaggregate, dissociate, disassociate, disunite.

III. *Adjectives.* **spacious,** roomy, commodious, extensive, expansive, capacious, ample, large, magnificent, comprehensive; widespread, vast, world-wide, wide, far-flung, boundless, vasty (*archaic*), limitless, endless, infinite; shorelesx, trackless, pathless; spatial, steric (*chem.*).

IV. *Adverbs.* **spaciously,** extensively, etc. (see *adjectives*); by and large; everywhere, far and near (*or* wide); here, there, and everywhere; from pole to pole, "from China to Peru" (Johnson), "from Indus to the pole" (Pope), "from Dan to Beersheba" (*Bible*), "from the four corners of the earth" (*Merchant of Venice*), from all points of the compass; to the four winds, to the uttermost parts of the earth.

See also DEGREE, INFINITY, INTERVAL, PLACE, REGION, WORLD.—*Antonyms.* See INEXTENSION.

---

span, *v.* stretch across, cover, join, connect; measure. See JUNCTION, MEASUREMENT.

spank, *v.* punish, strike, smite, slap, thwack, beat, thrash, whip. See PUNISHMENT.

spar, *v.* contend, contest, strive, box; fight, strke, brawl. See CONTENTION, DISCORD.

spare, *v.* excuse, pass over; afford, give; forbear, yield, cede; let be, let pass. See EXEMPTION, GIVING, INACTION, RELINQUISHMENT.

spare, *adj.* sparing, frugal, chary, provident; meager, scanty, thin, lean, gaunt, half-starved; additional, extra, supplementary, superfluous, needless. See ECONOMY, INSUFFICIENCY, REDUNDANCE.

sparing, *adj.* economical, frugal, thrifty, saving, provident, close, scrimping, stingy. See ECONOMY, PARSIMONY.

sparkle, *v.* glint, glitter, glimmer, glisten, gleam, twinkle. See LIGHT.

sparse, *adj.* scattered, sporadic; few, scant, scarce, infrequent. See DISPERSION, FEWNESS.

spasm, *n.* seizure, throe, paroxysm, convulsion; revulsion, upheaval, cataclysm, eruption, earthquake. See AGITATION, PAIN, REVOLUTION.

spasmodic, *adj.* intermittent, fitful, irregular; convulsive. See IRREGULARITY, VIOLENCE.

spatter, *v.* bespatter, defame; scatter, sprinkle; soil, spot; splash, swash, wet. See DETRACTION, DISPERSION, UNCLEANNESS, WATER.

speak, *v.* talk, say, utter, tell, declare, soliloquize; pronounce, vocalize, articulate, whisper. See SPEECH, VOICE.

speaker, *n.* chair, chairman; loud speaker (*radio*); spokesman, orator, speechmaker. See DIRECTOR, HEARING, SPEECH.

spear, *n.* lance, pike, javelin. See ARMS.

spear-shaped, *adj.* hastate, lance-shpaed. See SHARPNESS.

SPECIALTY.—I. *Nouns.* **specialty,** special pursuit, object of special attention, special product (manufacture, *or* feature); work of a specialist, pet study, hobby, speciality.
individuality, personality, character, selfness (*rare*), originality.
characteristic, distinctive feature, trait, particularity, diagnostic (*tech.*), peculiarity, trick, mannerism, idiosyncrasy, idiocrasy, *je ne sais quoi* (*F.*), differentia (*pl.* differentiæ: *logic*), singularity.
particulars, details, circumstances, items, counts; minutiæ, minute details.
[*in law*] sealed contract; instrument (*or* deed) under seal.
specialist, expert, sharp (*slang*), specializer, connoisseur, virtuoso (*masc.; It. pl.* virtuosi), virtuosa (*fem.; It. pl.* virtuose); technicist, technician.
II. *Verbs.* **specialize,** pursue specially, concentrate on, study intensively; limit, modify (*as a statement*).
[*in biology*] **differentiate,** exhibit differentiation, adapt, set apart, become individual.
specify, particularize, formulate, individualize, designate, mention, determine, denote, indicate, point out, select, itemize, enter into detail, descend to particulars.
III. *Adjectives.* **special,** especial, particular, individual, specific, proper, personal, original, private, respective, definite, minute, certain, peculiar, unique, marked, appropriate, exclusive, restricted, intimate; singular, exceptional, extraordinary, uncommon; typical, representative, characteristic.
IV. *Adverbs.* **specially,** especially, particularly, etc. (see *adjectives*); expressly, in particular; *in propria persona* (*L.*); *ad hominem* (*L.*); for my part; *pro hac vice* (*L.*), *pro re nata* (*L.*).
each, apiece, one by one, seriatim, severally, respectively, in detail.
namely, that is to say, *videlicet* (*L.; abbr.* viz.), scilicet (*abbr.* scil., sc.), to wit (*chiefly legal*).
See also EXPERT, TENDENCY, UNCONFORMITY.—*Antonyms.* See GENERALITY.

---

species, *n.* kind, sort, type, classification, variety. See CLASS.
specimen, *n.* sample, example, instance, representative. See CONFORMITY.
specious, *adj.* plausible, ostensible; misleading, fallacious, illusory, sophistical, casuistic. See PROBABILITY, SOPHISTRY.
speck, *n.* spot, speckle, stain; dot, mite (*colloq.*), mote, jot, bit, particle. See BLEMISH, LITTLENESS.
spectacle, *n.* exhibition, exposition; pageant, show; parade, review, procession, demonstration; sight, wonder. See APPEARANCE, DRAMA, OSTENTATION, PRODIGY.
spectacles, *n. pl.* glasses, eyeglasses. See OPTICAL INSTRUMENTS.

SPECTATOR.—*Nouns.* **spectator,** beholder, observer, *assistant* (*F.*), looker-on, onlooker, witness, eyewitness, bystander, passer-by; sightseer, rubberneck (*slang*), spy, scout, sentinel.
[*collectively*] attendance, crowd, house, grandstand, bleachers (*U. S.*), gallery, customers (*as at a prize fight: cant*).
See also DRAMA, PRESENCE, VISION, WARNING.

SPECTER.—I. *Nouns.* **specter** *or* spectre, ghost, apparition, vision, spirit, sprite, shade, shadow, wraith, banshee, White Lady, spook (*now jocose*), phantom, phantasm, materialization (*Spiritualism*), astral body, aura, etheric body (*or* self), double; lemures (*pl.: Roman relig.*); will-o'-the-wisp, friar's lantern, *ignis fatuus* (*L.; pl. ignes fatui*).
II. *Adjectives.* **spectral,** ghostly, ghostlike, spiritual, wraithlike, weird, uncanny, eerie, spooky (*colloq.*), haunted; unearthly, supernatural, visionary, illusory.
See also DIM-SIGHTEDNESS, LUMINARY (*will-o'-the-wisp*), PSYCHICAL RESEARCH.

---

speculate, *v.* risk, venture, hazard; think, reflect, ponder; conjecture, theorize, imagine, suppose. See CHANCE, THOUGHT, WONDER.
speculation, *n.* venture, hazard, wager, bet, flyer (*colloq.*). See CHANCE, EXPERIMENT.

SPEECH.—I. *Nouns.* **speech,** locution, talk, parlance, utterance, conversation, verbal intercourse, oral communication, word of mouth, prattle, palaver, whisper, soliloquy, apostrophe.
oration, recitation, delivery, speech, speaking, address, discourse, declamation, allocution, lecture, harangue, sermon, appeal, invocation, exhortation, tirade; stump speech, public speaking, political speaking, the stump; travelogue *or* travelog, salutation, greeting, salutatory (*U. S.*), valedictory (*U. S.*); peroration.
oratory, elocution, expression, eloquence, rhetoric, declamation; grandiloquence, multiloquence, burst of eloquence, command of words (*or* language), gift of the gab (*colloq.*), *copia verborum* (*L.*), *usus loquendi* (*L.*).
speaker, spokesman, mouthpiece, prolocutor, interlocutor, speechmaker, orator, oratress *or* oratrix (*fem.*), public speaker, lecturer, prelector *or* prælector (*as in a university*), preacher; platform orator, spellbinder, stump orator; *improvisatore* (*It.; pl. improvvisatori*), *improvvisatrice* (*It. fem.; pl. improvvisatrici*), improviser, improvisator; rhetorician, elocutionist, reciter, reader (*U. S.*); Hermes, Demosthenes, Cicero.
II. *Verbs.* **speak,** talk, say, utter, pronounce, deliver, breathe, let fall, rap out, blurt out; tell, proclaim, delcare, make known; soliloquize; converse, talk together, hold intercourse.
address, speak to, accost, salute, hail, call to, greet; apostrophize, appeal to, invoke, memorialize.
declaim, hold forth, harangue, stump (*colloq.*), spout, orate, spellbind, speechify (*derisive*); rant; recite, read, render, lecture, sermonize, discourse, expatiate.
III. *Adjectives.* **spoken,** oral, unwritten, nuncupative (*chiefly of wills*), not written, parol (*law*), acroamatic *or* acroamatical (*as the esoteric teachings of Aristotle*); phonetic, phonic; voiced, lingual.
eloquent, oratorical, rhetorical, elocutionary, declamatory, grandiloquent, facund (*archaic*), Demosthenian, Ciceronian, Tullian.
IV. *Adverbs.* **orally,** by word of mouth, *viva voce* (*L.*), vocally, from the lips of, nuncupatively (*of wills*); phonetically.
See also CONVERSATION, INFORMATION, LOQUACITY, SOLILOQUY, VOICE.—*Antonyms.* See DUMBNESS, SILENCE, TACITURNITY.

---

speechless, *adj.* dumb, mute, mum, silent, inarticulate. See SILENCE.
speed, *n.* swiftness, celerity, rapidity. See VELOCITY.
speed, *v.* hie, hasten, spurt, sprint, rush. See VELOCITY.

---

[1]**SPELL.**—I. *Nouns.* **spell,** charm, incantation, exorcism, abracadabra, cantrip (*chiefly Scot.*), open sesame; evil eye, jinx (*slang*), hoodoo (*colloq.*), malicious animal magnetism (*abbr.* M. A. P.).
talisman, amulet, phylactery, philter, fetish; wishbone, merrythought, furcula (*pl.* furculæ: *tech.*), furculum (*pl.* furcula: *anat. and zoöl.*); mascot, rabbit's foot, scarabæus *or* scarab; veronica; swastika, fylfot, triskelion *or* triskele, gammadion.
wand, caduceus, rod, divining rod, witch hazel, Aaron's rod.
[*magic wish-givers*] Aladdin's lamp, Aladdin's casket, magic casket, magic ring, magic belt, magic spectacles, wishing cap, Fortunatus's cap; seven-league boots; magic carpet; cap of darkness, Tarnkappe (*Siegfried*), Tarnhelm.
fascination, enchantment, bewitching, bewitchment, captivation, witchery, seduction, allurement, entrancement.
II. *Verbs.* **spell,** form letters, orthographize (*rare*), transliterate, decipher, make out, form.
indicate, signify, mean, denote, typify, involve (*as, war* spells *ruin*).
fascinate, enchant, bewitch, allure, captivate, entrance, enrapture, spellbind.
See also INFLUENCE, LETTER, SORCERY.

---

[2]**spell,** *n.* turn, interval, season, period. See SNAP.
spelling, *n.* orthography; phonetics, transliteration. See LETTER.
spend, *v.* expend, use, consume, pass (*as time*); squander. See PASSAGE, WASTE.
spendthrift, *n.* prodigal, waster, spender, squanderer. See PRODIGALITY.
spent, *adj.* fatigued, exhausted, overtired, worn out, played out, prostrate; weak, effete. See FATIGUE, WEAKNESS.
sperm, *n.* semen, seed, sperm cell. See ORGANIZATION.

sphere, *n.* realm, compass, department, scope, province; globe, ball, spheroid, globoid. See BUSINESS, ROTUNDITY.
spice, *v.* bespice, season, flavor. See PUNGENCY.
spill, *v.* run over, run out, pour out, shed (*as blood*), drain, deplete. See EJECTION, WASTE.
spin, *v.* prolong, protract; rotate, twirl, whirl. See LENGTH, ROTATION.
spine, *n.* spike, barb, thorn; backbone, spinal column, chine (*of an animal*), ridge. See SHARPNESS, SUPPORT.
spinster, *n.* celibate, bachelor-girl, old maid; new woman. See CELIBACY, WOMAN.
spiral, *adj.* coiled, helical, cochlear, screw-shaped. See CONVOLUTION.
spirit, *n.* energy, vim, liveliness, vigor, vivacity; daring, boldness; life, soul; sense, drift, bearing; ghost, shade, phantom, apparition, vision; character, nature, individuality, disposition, mood. See ACTIVITY, COURAGE, IMMATERIALITY, MEANING, SPECTER, SUBJECTIVENESS.
spirited, *adj.* brisk, lively, animated, vivacious, frishy; mettlesome, plucky; glowing, sparkling. See ACTIVITY, COURAGE, VIGOR.
spiritual, *adj.* supernatural, unearthly; immaterial, incorporeal, intangible; mental, intellectual; pure, saintly, holy. See DEITY, IMMATERIALITY, INTELLECT, PIETY.
spiritualism, *n.* apiritism, spirit communication. See PSYCHICAL RESEARCH.
spirituous, *adj.* alcoholic, ardent, hard. See DRNNKENNESS, STRENGTH.
[1]spit, *v.* pierce, transfix, impale. See OPENING.
[2]spit, *v.* splutter, eject, expectorate; shower, sprinkle. See EJECTION, RIVER.
spite, *n.* resentment, pique, bitterness, malice, grudge. See MALEVOLENCE.
spiteful, *adj.* malicious, venomous, churlish, bitter. See MALEVOLENCE, VICE.
splash, *v.* plash, spatter; bespatter, besmear, spot. See RIVER, UNCLEANNESS.
splendid, *adj.* glorious, illustrious, brilliant, radiant. See REPUTE.
splendor, *n.* brilliancy, radiance; luster, brightness, sheen; showiness, display, parade; glory, dignity, majesty, grandeur. See BEAUTY, LIGHT, OSTENTATION, REPUTE.
splice, *v.* join, unite, connect, knit, mortise; *Slang:* marry. See JUNCTION.
split, *v.* crack, snap, break; cleave, rive, rend, burst. See BRITTLENESS, DISJUNCTION.
spoil, *v.* decay, deompose; hamper, hinder, handicap; rob, plunder, pillage, despoil; mar, impair, ruin, destroy. See DECOMPOSITION, HINDRANCE, STEALING, UNSKILLFULNESS.
spoil, *n.* plunder, prize, prey, loot. See BOOTY.
spoken, *adj.* oral, unwritten; phonetic, voiced, lingual. See SPEECH.
spokesman, *n.* speaker, mouthpiece, chairman, orator. See INTERPRETER, SPEECH.
sponsor, *n.* witness, testifier; insurer, guarantor; godfather, godmother. See EVIDENCE, SECURITY.
spontaneous, *adj.* improvised unpremeditated, inspirational; voluntary, free, unasked. See IMPULSE, WILLINGNESS.
spool, *n.* bobbin, reel, quill, pirn (*dial.*). See ROTATION.
sport, *n.* gamester, gambler; game, play, recreation, merriment; hunting, fishing. See AMUSEMENT, KILLING.
sportsman, *n.* hunter, Nimrod, sportswoman (*fem.*). See AMUSEMENT, KILLING.
spot, *n.* stain, blot, blotch, freckle, patch; point, locality, situation, site, scene. See BLEMISH, PLACE.
spotless, *adj.* clean, stainless, perfect, guiltless, immaculate. See BEAUTY. INNOCENCE.
spotted, *adj.* spotty, speckled, freckled, flecked. See VARIEGATION.
spouse, *n.* mate, partner, husband, wife. See MARRIAGE.

spout, *n.* outlet, tube, beak, nozzle, gargoyle, waterspout; shoot (*esp. in a pawnshop*), lift; jet, squirt, gush, rush. See CONDUIT, EGRESS, ELEVATION, RIVER.
sprain, *v.* strain, wrench, rick (*Brit.*). See WEAKNESS.
[1]spray, *n.* wreath, garland; sprig, twig, bough, branch. See FRAGRANCE, PART.
spray, *n.* surf, spume. See FOAM.
spray, *v.* vaporize, atomize. See VAPORIZATION.
spread, *v.* sow, strew, scatter, diffuse, sprinkle; radiate, disperse; expand, extend, open, unfurl; broaden, universalize; publish, circulate, disseminate, broadcast, promulgate; level, flatten. See DISPERSION, DIVERGENCE, EXPANSION, GENERALITY, PUBLICATION, ROLL (*smooth*).
spread, *n.* expansion, stretch, range, compass, scope; *Colloq.*: meal, feast. See SPACE; FOOD.
sprightly, *adj.* gay, lively, airy, bright, spirited, animated; witty, sparkling. See CHEERFULNESS, WIT.
spring, *v.* jump, hop, bound, vault, bounce, arise; fly back, rebound. See LEAP, RECOIL.
spring, *n.* fountain, font, source, origin, motive; springiness, resilience; jump, hop, bound, vault, recoil, rebound; springtide, seedtime, vernal season. See CAUSE, ELASTICITY, LEAP, MORNING.
sprinkle, *v.* disperse, scatter, sow, diffuse, spread; besprinkle, bestrew, powder, flour, dust; moisten, dabble, irrigate. See DISPERSION, POWDERINESS, WATER.
sprinkler, *n.* nozzle, spray, atomizer. See WATER.
sprout, *v.* germinate, bud, shoot, grow. See EXPANSION.
spruce, *adj.* trim, tidy, neat, clean, smart. See BEAUTY.
spur, *n.* projection, bluff, headland; incitement, stimulus, goad; branch, arm, offshoot; rowel, prick, barb, calcar (*tech.*). See CONVEXITY, MOTIVE, PART, SHARPNESS.
spur, *v.* hasten, quicken, press; prick, goad, urge, incite. See HASTE, MOTIVE.
spurious, *adj.* sham, make-believe, assumed, counterfeit, illegitimate. See DECEPTION.
spurn, *v.* despise, contemn, scorn, disdain, reject. See CONTEMPT.
[1]spurt, *v.* gush, jet, well, spout, squirt. See RIVER.
[1]spurt, *n.* jet, spout, splash, gush. See RIVER.
[2]spurt, *v.* sprint, rush, dash. See VELOCITY.
[2]spurt, *n.* burst, sprint, rush, dash. See VELOCITY.
spy, *n.* watch, scout, patrol, sentinel. See SAFETY, SPECTATOR.
squalid, *adj.* uncleanly, slovenly, unkempt. See UNCLEANNESS.
squall, *n.* gust, blast, flurry. See WIND.
squall, *v* bawl, scream, shriek. See CRY.
squander, *v.* lavish, waste, dissipate, prodigalize. See PRODIGALITY.
square, *n.* quadrate, qaudrilateral, tetragon; measure, set-square; quadrangle, *place* (*F.*), *plaza* (*Sp.*), forum (*L.*). See FOUR, MEASUREMENT, PLACE.
square, *v.* compensate, equalize, balance, recoup; quadrate. See COMPENSATION, FOUR.
squash, *v.* crush, squeeze, quell; pulp, mash. See DESTRUCTION, PULPINESS.
squat, *adj.* crouched, crouching; squatty, dumpy, pudgy, stubby. See LOWNESS, SHORTNESS.
squeamish, *adj.* qualmish, nauseated; fastidious, nice, overnice, finical. See DISEASE, FASTIDIOUSNESS.
squeeze, *v.* contract, constrict; compress, condense, press. See CONTRACTION, DENSITY.
squelch, *v.* silence, disconcert; quell, quash, crush; squash, flatten; quelch (*dial.*), squish (*dial.*). See CONFUTATION, DESTRUCTION, FLATNESS, SEMILIQUIDITY.

squint, *n.* strabismus (*med.*), cross-eye, squinting. See DIM-SIGHTEDNESS.

stab, *v.* bayonet, saber; kill; pierce, transfix, stick; cut, hurt, wound. See KILLING, OPENING, PAIN.

STABILITY.—I. *Nouns.* **stability,** firmness, steadiness, fixity, establishment, fixedness, immovableness, immovability, immobility, solidity, stiffness, soundness, permanence, coherence, immutability, unchangeableness, stabilization: *opposite of* instability.

[*of character or purpose*] steadfastness, constancy, steadiness, stableness, firmness, devotedness, resolution, perseverance, faith, adherence; obduracy, obstinacy; vitality, virility, vigor.

[*comparisons*] rock, pillar, tower, foundation; leopard's spots, Ethiopian's skin; law of the Medes and Persians.

II. *Verbs.* **stabilize,** fix, ground, set, establish, stablish (*archaic*), settle, consolidate, found, institute, organize, install, confirm, secure, keep, retain; make sure, make good, set on its legs (*colloq.*), set on its feet, perpetuate.

be firm, stick fast, stand firm, remain firm, stand pat (*colloq.*), strike root, take root, settle down; build one's house on a rock, weather the storm.

III. *Adjectives.* **stable,** fixed, firm, strong, solid, fast, sound, valid, steady, steadfast, established, settled, staple, rooted, deep-rooted, deep-seated, ineradicable, immovable, anchored, moored; lasting, abiding, durable, permanent, persistent, stereotyped, constant, perennial; confirmed, inveterate; vested, incontrovertible: *opposite of* unstable.

unchangeable, immutable; unaltered, unalterable, invariable, undeviating; irretrievable, irrevocable, irreversible, indissoluble, indestructible, imperishable, perpetual, immortal, undying, irremovable, indelible.

stuck fast, transfixed, aground, stranded, high and dry.

[*steady in purpose*] steadfast, constant, steady, unwavering, answering, firm, resolute, stanch *or* staunch, loyal, faithful; obdurate, obstinate.

IV. *Adverbs.* **stably,** fixedly, firmly, etc. (see *adjectives*); in a stable manner.

V. *Interjections.* stet (*proof correcting*), let it stand!

See also DURABILITY, OBSTINACY, PERMANENCE, [1]REST, STRENGTH, UNIFORMITY.—*Antonyms.* See CHANGEABLENESS.

---

stable, *n.* livery, mews, barn, byre. See DOMESTICATION.

staff, *n.* force, assistants, personnel; crew, workers, employees; club, cudgel; stave (*music*); pole, shaft, crook, crutch, stick, cane, walking-stick. See AGENT, SERVANT, ARMS, MUSIC, SUPPORT.

stage, *n.* amount, measure, point, mark; the theater, the boards; fotting, standing, standpoint; scaffold, platform, dais, rostrum, stand; period, step, space, instar (*zoöl.*); stagecoach. See DEGREE, DRAMA, SITUATION, SUPPORT, TIME, VEHICLE.

stagger, *v.* sway, reel, totter; hesitate, falter; surprise, startle, astonish, bewilder, stun. See OSCILLATION, SLOWNESS, WONDER.

stagnant, *adj.* idle, inactive, dormant, sluggish, lifeless; listless, languid, inert. See DETERIORATION, INERTNESS.

stagnate, *v.* vegetate, be inactive. See [1]REST.

staid, *adj.* serious, sedate, grave, demure. See DEJECTION.

stain, *n.* blot, spot, smudge, discoloration; dye, pigment, tint; paint, enamel, varnish; taint, stigma, disgrace. See BLEMISH, COLOR, COVERING, DISREPUTE.

stainless, *adj.* spotless, cleanly, immaculate, unsoiled; pure, innocent, unstained, untainted. See CLEANNESS, PROBITY, PURITY.

stairway, *n.* staircase, stairs, companion (*naut.*), escalator. See ASCENT.

stake, *n.* wager, bet, hazard; martyrdom, *auto-da-fé* (*Pg.: pl. autos-da-fé*); earnest, deposit, pledge; post, pale. See CHANCE, PUNISHMENT, SECURITY, SUPPORT.

stale, *adj.* insipid, flat, vapid, tasteless; dull, commonplace. See INSIPIDITY.

stalk, *n.* stem, axis, pedicel (*tech.*), petiole (*bot. and zoöl.*)., See SUPPORT.

stalwart, *adj.* courageous, resolute; strong, sturdy, lusty. See COURAGE STRENGTH.

STAMMERING.—I. *Nouns.* **stammering** (*imperfect speech*), stuttering, hesitation, impediment in one's speech, inarticulateness; lisp, drawl, tardiloquence (*rare*), nasalism, nasality, nasal accent; twang; falsetto, brogue; cacoëpy, mispronunciation.

II. *Verbs.* **stammer,** stutter, hesitate, falter, halt, stumble, sputter, splutter, hem, haw, hem and haw.

mumble, mutter, patter, grumble, murmur, mump, maunder; jabber, gabble, gibber; drawl, mouth; croak; quaver, waver, snuffle, clip one's words, mince, lisp, speak thickly, talk incoherently.

mispronounce, misspeak, missay (*rare*), murder the language, murder the King's English.

III. *Adjectives.* **stammering,** stuttering, etc. (see *verbs*); throaty, guttural, husky; lisping, inarticulate, indistinct; mispronounced, cacoëpistic.

IV. *Adverbs.* **stammeringly,** falteringly, inarticulately; *sotto voce* (*L.*).

Antonyms. See SPEECH.

---

stamp, *n.* cast, form, make, grade, rate, brand; type, mold, design, pattern, impression; badge, label, ticket; seal, last, matrix. See CLASS, FORM, INDICATION, PROTOTYPE.

stanch, *adj.* steady, steadfast, unwavering, loyal, true; sound, water-tight. See PROBITY, SAFETY.

stand, *v.* bear, suffer, tolerate, brook, brave; last, endure, hold, abide; pause, stop, tarry, settle. See INEXCITABILITY, PERMANENCE, [1]REST.—**stand against,** withstand, obstruct, thwart. See RESISTANCE.—**stand by,** befriend, second, abet; clasp, huddle. See AID, NEARNESS.—**stand for,** indicate, betoken, represent. See INDICATION.

standard, *n.* emblem, banner, ensign; measure, rate, stage, point; model, pattern, criterion, rule, test. See INDICATION, MEASUREMENT, PROTOTYPE. **standard time,** sone time, civil time. See CHRONOMETRY.

standing, *n.* condition, status; *status quo* (*L.*); position, locality, station, standpoint, footing; reputation, rank, sphere, degree. See CIRCUMSTANCE, PERMANENCE, SITUATION, STATE.

stanza, *v.* verse, stave, strophe, tristich, quatrain, etc. See POETRY.

staple, *adj.* principal (*as a commodity*), chief; established, settled. See IMPORTANCE, STABILITY.

star, *n.* principal actor (*or* actress), headliner; pentacle, pentagram, estoile (*heraldry*); asterisk; self-luminous body, fixed star, starlet (*dim.*), planet (*esp. astrol.*); celebrity, cynosure; *in plural*: fate, destiny, fortune. See DRAMA, FIVE, INDICATION (*typography*). LUMINARY, REPUTE, WORLD (*heavenly* bodies); NECESSITY.

starboard, *n.* right side (*of a vessel*): *opposite of* port. See RIGHT.

stare, *v.* gaze, gape, rubberneck (*U. S. slang*); stand out, be conspicuous (*as,* staring *colors*). See CURIOSITY, VISION, VISIBILITY.

star-shaped, *adj.* stellate, stellular, starlike, radiated. See SHARPNESS.

start, *v.* begin, commence, undertake, initiate, inaugurate; depart, set out, dislocate, loosen; arise, occur; wince, flinch, shy; push, thrust, drive. See BEGINNING, DEPARTURE, DERANGEMENT, EVENT, FEAR, PROPULSION.

startle, *v.* frighten, scare, alarm, start; surprise, astonish, stagger, stun. See FEAR, NONEXPECTATION.

starve, *v.* fast, famish, perish, weaken; be in need (*or* want). See FASTING, POVERTY.

STATE.—I. *Nouns.* **state,** condition, mode, nature, category, situation, status, position, circumstance (*usually in pl.*), state of affairs, case; diathesis (*med.*), bodily condition; lot, mood, temper, appearance. aspect.

plight, pass, predicament, quandary, dilemma, pinch, pickle, *impasse* (*F.*), corner, fix (*colloq.*).

frame, fabric, stamp, mold *or* **mould; structure, framework, texture, constitution.**

mode, manner, style, character, complexion, fashion, guise, way, form, build, shape; tone, tenor, trim, fettle, kilter (*U. S. colloq.*).
standing (*as in society*), reputation, position, rank, quality, estate, station, sphere.
pomp, style, dignity, grandeur, magnificence, splendor, display, pageantry, ostentation (*as, to travel in state*).
body politic (*pl.* bodies politic), commonwealth, nation, polity, democracy, federation, government, civil power, civil government (*distinguished from ecclesiastical; as, Church and* State), territory; *often* State *in this sense.*)
II. *Adjectives.* state (*or* State), pertaining to the state (*or* to a state of the Union), governmental, public, national, state-owned.
ceremonial, formal, ceremonious, official; set apart, reserved (*for state occasions*).
See also APPEARANCE, AUTHORITY, CIRCUMSTANCE, SITUATION.

---

stated, *adj.* specified, fixed, definite, named, specific, settled. See GIVING.
stately, *adj.* formal, ceremonious, solemn, majestic, ostentatious; august, imposing. See OSTENTATION, REPUTE.
statement, *n.* allegation, assertion, declaration, averment; account, record, report. See AFFIRMATION, DESCRIPTION.
statesman, *n.* legislator, lawgiver, Solon. See DIRECTOR.
statesmanship, *n.* statecraft, state management. See DIRECTION.
station, *n.* stage, step; terminal, stop, depot (*U. S.*); standing, rank, status, degree, caste, condition; location, position, sphere, place, site, seat, post. See DEGREE, JOURNEY, REPUTE, SITUATION.
station, *v.* set, locate, place, situate, establish, settle. See LOCATION.
statue, *n.* figure, cast, bust, statuette. See FINE ARTS, REPRESENTATION.
status, *n.* rank, standing, footing, station, place, position, caste, condition, situation, state. See CIRCUMSTANCE, REPUTE.
statute, *n.* law, enactment, regulation, decree, rule. See LEGALITY, PRECEPT.
stay, *v.* cease, stop, discontinue, desist; hinder; detain, delay, prevent; continue, last, endure, rest, wait, halt, tarry, linger, sojourn, abide, dwell, live, reside; fasten, hold, brace, truss, prop. See CESSATION, HINDRANCE, REMAINDER, SUPPORT.
steadfast, *adj.* constant, steady, persevering, firm, loyal. See PERSEVERANCE, STABILITY.
steady, *adj.* calm, cool, undisturbed, unruffled, sedate; regular, uniform, unvarying; normal, habitual, customary, systematic; stable, firm, fixed, constant, unwavering, steadfast, faithful. See EXPECTANCY, REGULARITY, RULE, STABILITY, TRUTH.

STEALING.—I. *Nouns.* **stealing,** theft, thievery, robbery, direption (*rare*); swindling, cheating, defrauding; rapacity, thievishness; depredation, abstraction, appropriation, steal (*colloq.*), crib (*colloq.*), plagiarism, embezzlement, peculation, fraud, swindle, forgery, larceny, pilfering; kleptomania.
plunder, pillage, spoliation, sack, rapine, brigandage, highway robbery, holdup (*slang*); raid, foray, razzia; piracy, privateering, buccaneering, filibustering, hijacking (*slang*); burglary, housebreaking, shoplifting, cattle stealing, cattle lifting (*colloq.*), cattle rustling (*U. S. slang*), abaction (*rare*); extortion, *chantage* (*F.*), blackmail, kidnaping *or* kidnapping.
den of thieves, den of robbers, nest of thieves, den of Cacus (*Roman mythology*); Alsatia, Whitefriars.
II. *Verbs.* steal, thieve, rob, purloin, pilfer, take, filch, bag, sneak (*slang*), pinch (*slang*), prig (*cant*), crib (*colloq.*), palm, finger, abstract; misappropriate, appropriate, plagiarize, pirate.
abduct, convey away, carry off, impress, make (*or* run) off with, run away with, kidnap, hold for ransom, spirit away, seize, lift, rustle (*cattle: slang*).
plunder, pillage, filibuster, rifle, sack, loot, ransack, spoil, despoil, burgle (*colloq. and jocose*), strip, gut, forage, maraud, poach, hijack (*slang*), smuggle, hold up, stick up (*slang*); levy blackmail.
swindle, cheat, cozen, defraud, victimize, bunko *or* bunco, pluck, fleece, diddle

(*colloq.*), trick, chouse, rook, pigeon (*slang*), bilk; peculate, embezzle; obtain under false pretenses; live by one's wits.
counterfeit, forge, coin, circulate bad money, shove the queer (*slang*).
gain (*insidiously*), win, accomplish, draw over, allure (*as, to* steal *one's affections*).
[*to move secretly or silently*] **creep,** go stealthily, pass privily, sneak, slink, withdraw; introduce, insinuate.
III. *Adjectives.* **thievish,** light-fingered, pilfering, thieving, larcenous; predacious (*as animals*), predatory, raptorial, plundering, piratical.
See also AVOIDANCE, BOOTY, CONCEALMENT, DECEPTION, TAKING, THIEF.—*Antonyms.* See RESTORATION.

---

stealth, *n.* stealthiness, furtiveness, slyness, caution, cunning. See CONCEALMENT.
steamboat, *n.* steamship, steamer. See SHIP.
steed, *n.* horse, charger, mount. See ANIMAL, CARRIER.
steep, *v.* soak, drench, saturate. See WATER.
steep, *adj.* sloping, declivitous; abrupt, sheer, precipitous, vertical. See DESCENT, SHARPNESS.
steer, *v.* guide, pilot, direct, manage, drive. See DIRECTION.
steersman, *n.* helmsman, pilot. See MARINER.
stem, *n.* bow (*of a ship*), prow; trunk, stock, house, lineage, line, family, race; stalk, peduncle (*bot.*), pedicel (*bot.*). See FRONT, PATERNITY, SUPPORT.
stench, *n.* stink, smell, odor, fume, fetor. See BANE.
step, *n.* stair (*usually in pl.*), ladder; grade, rank; plan, course, measure, proceeding, act; gait, pace, tread, footfall; interval (*music*); footstep, footmark, footprint. See ASCENT, DEGREE, MEASUREMENT, MOTION, MUSIC, RECORD.
stepmotherly, *adj.* novercal, harsh, unkind, neglectful, unmotherly. See MALEVOLENCE.
sterile, *adj.* abortive, fruitless; barren, unproductive. See FAILURE, POVERTY.
sterilize, *v.* asepticize, antisepticize, disinfect; make sterile, incapacitate, Tyndallize (*tech.*), Pasteurize (*as milk*). See CLEANNESS, IMPOTENCE, UNPRODUCTIVENESS.
sterling, *adj.* standard, of standard purity; genuine, true; pure, noble. See MONEY, TRUTH, VIRTUE.
stern, *adj.* grim, unyielding, resolute; severe, strict, hard, exacting, cruel, pitiless. See RESOLUTION, SEVERITY.
stern, *n.* after-part, poop (*naut.*). See REAR.
stet, *interj.* let it stand: *used in proof correcting.* See STABILITY.
steward, *n.* factor, manager; provider, purveyor, purser; attendant, waiter (*on ship*), stewardess (*fem.*). See AGENT, DIRECTOR, PROVISION, SERVANT.
stick, *v.* cease, check, hold, discontinue; cohere, adhere, cling; continue, endure, persevere, persist; push, thrust; stab, prick, pierce, penetrate, perforate, impale; put, place. See CESSATION, COHERENCE, CONTINUANCE, IMPULSE, OPENING, PLACE.
sticky, *adj.* glutinous, viscid, adhesive, gummy, slimy. See SEMILIQUIDITY.
stiff, *adj.* constrained, affected, stilted, formal, prim, prudish, restrained, firm, solid, rigid, tense, unyielding. See AFFECTATION, HARDNESS, PRIDE; RESTRAINT.
stiffen, *v.* harden, starch, petrify, coagulate, thicken, jelly. See DENSITY, HARDNESS, THICKNESS.
stiffening, *n.* solidification, jellification, inspissation. See THICKNESS.
stifle, *v.* choke, suffocate, smother; muffle, suppress. See KILLING, SILENCE.
stigma, *n.* brand, reproach, blot, stain. See DISREPUTE.
stigmatize, *v.* brand, vilify, defame, slur. See DISREPUTE.
still, *adj.* calm, unruffled, quiet, tranquil. See MODERATION.
stimulant, *n.* intoxicant, bracer. (*colloq.*); restorative, tonic. See PUNGENCY, REMEDY.

stimulate, *v.* excite, energize, kindle, inspirit, sharpen, quicken, awaken, goad, whet, spur, instigate, incite. See EXCITEMENT, MOTIVE.
stimulating, *adj.* exciting, provocative, inspiring, bracing; pungent, keen, piquant, vigorous, spirited; suggestive, stimulative. See EXCITEMENT, PUNGENCY, SUPPOSITION.
sting, *v.* irritate, pique, cut; itch, tingle; prick, nettle, smart, burn. See EXCITEMENT, ITCHING, PAIN.
sting, *n.* fang, thorn, prick, nettle. See BANE.
stingy, *adj.* close, mean, parsimonious, miserly, niggardly. See NEARNESS, PARSIMONY.
stipend, *n.* recompense, remuneration, pay, salary. See REWARD.
stipulate, *v.* contract, covenant, agree, engage, bargain, condition. See PROVISION.
stir, *n.* agitate, bestir, move, disturb; fire, kindle, inflame, goad, quicken, stimulate. See AGITATION, EXCITEMENT.
stock, *n.* cattle, herds, live stock; race, strain, breed; stem, truck; load, cargo, goods, wares, produce, commodity; supply, hoard, funds, capital, resources. See ANIMAL, CONSANGUINITY, PATERNITY, MERCHANDISE, STORE.
stocking, *n.* hose, hosiery (*pl.*), sock. See CLOTHING.
stocky, *adj.* squat, dumpy, chunky (*U. S.*), thick-set. See SHORTNESS.
stolid, *adj.* dull, impassive, tedious, phlegmatic, stupid. See DULLNESS, IMBECILITY..
stomach, *n.* appetite, keenness, hunger, inclination; paunch, belly, craw. See DESIRE, RECEPTACLE.
stone, *n.* nutlet, pit (*U. S.*), pyrene (*of a fruit*); rock, pebble; gravestone, headstone, tombstone; gem. See DENSITY, HARDNESS, INTERMENT, ORNAMENT.
stony, *adj.* rocky, flinty, adamantine; unfeeling, obdurate, pitiless; cragged, rough. See HARDNESS, PITILESSNESS, ROUGHNESS.
stool, *n.* hassock, footstool, cricket. See SUPPORT.
stoop, *v.* couch, bend, cower; submit, yield, condescend, acquiesce, comply, accede. See DEPRESSION, SUBMISSION.
stop, *v.* cease, desist, stay, pause, halt, rest, arrive; close, block, lock, bar, barricade; seal, occlude, obstruct, stanch, check; call at, tarry, visit. See CESSATION, CLOSURE, RIVER, TOUCH.
stop, *n.* comma, semicolon, colon, period *or* full stop; stopping place, station, depot (*U. S.*), terminus; truce, stay, respite, reprieve, postponement, suspension, interruption. See CESSATION, JOURNEY, LATENESS.
stop! *interj.* hold! stay! halt! whoa! See CESSATION, [1]REST.

STOPPER.—I. *Nouns.* **stopper,** stopple, plug, cork, bung, tampion (*esp. for a cannon*), spike, spill, spile, stopcock, tap, faucet; valve, spigot; rammer, ram, ramrod; piston, stop-gap; wadding, stuffing, padding; dossil, pledget, sponge (*surg.*), tourniquet.
doorkeeper, gatekeeper, janitor, janitress *or* janitrix (*fem.*), *concierge* (*F.*), porter, warder, durwan (*Hind.*), beadle, usher, guard, sentinel, tiler *or* tyler (*Freemasonry*); beefeater, yeoman of the guard (*Tower of London*), Cerberus, watchdog.
II. *Verbs.* **stopper,** stopple, plug, cork, bung, seal, close, stop.
See also CLOSURE.—*Antonyms.* See PERFORATOR.

---

stopping place, stop, station, depot (*U. S.*), terminus. See JOURNEY.

STORE.—I. *Nouns.* store, accumulation, abundance, hoard; stock, supply, stock in trade, reserve supply, fund, mine, vein (*as of coal*), bed, lode, quarry; spring, fount, fountain, well; treasure, reserve, reserve fund, savings, nest egg.
crop, harvest, vintage, yield, product, gleaning.
storehouse, depository, repository, repertorium (*rare*), repertory, magazine, *étape* (*F.*), warehouse, godown (*Oriental*), golah (*Anglo-Indian*), *entrepôt* (*F.*),

depot, cache, clamp (*as of potatoes: Eng. dial.*), garner, granary, grain elevator, silo; safe-deposit vault; armory; arsenal, stable, barn: storeroom, store closet; larder, buttery, stillroom (*Eng.*), cellar.
shop (*place of sale*), department store, emporium, establishment, chain store, market, business, *magasin* (*F.*), *boutique* (*F.*): *in the United States,* store *is the more common term,* shop *denoting a place of manufacture and repair.*
reservoir, receptacle, receiver, cistern, tank, standpipe, basin, fore bay *or* forebay, water back (*as used in brewing*), lodge (*as for wine: rare*), *aljibar* (*Sp. Amer.*); gasometer; pond, mill pond.
[*in plural*] **stores** (*of food or of special articles, accessories, etc.*), supplies, provisions, furnishings, necessaries, equipment (*as, marine* stores; *military* stores).
II. *Verbs.* **store,** furnish, provide, supply, equip, stock (*as, to* store *a ship;* store *the mind*).
[*to collect a supply*] **accumulate,** amass, collect, gather, scrape up (*or* together) aggregate, pile up, heap up, stack, load; garner, harvest.
preserve, save, lay up, stow, stow away, put by, file, lay by, set by, store up, bottle, pack, can; conserve, hoard, hoard up, treasure up, save up, bank, deposit; cache, hide, bury; warehouse, reservoir; reserve, retain, husband, keep, keep back, hold back; husband one's resources, put by for a rainy day.
[*of a receptacle*] **hold,** contain, keep, accommodate, carry, have capacity for.
III. *Adjectives.* **stored,** accumulated, preserved, etc. (see *verbs*); in store, in reserve, spare, supernumerary.

See also ASSEMBLAGE, GREATNESS, MART, PRESERVATION, PROVISION, TREASURY.—*Antonyms.* See WASTE.

---

storehouse, *n.* depository, magazine, warehouse, granary, silo. See STORE.
storm, *n.* onset, assault; excitement, commotion, tumult, outburst; tempest, hurricane, whirlwind, tornado, cyclone. See ATTACK, EXCITABILITY, WIND
storm, *v.* assault, besiege, beset, beleaguer, invest; rage, foam, fume, boil; riot, rampage; blow, rain, hail, snow. See ATTACK, RESENTMENT, VIOLENCE, WIND.
stormy, *adj.* turbulent, raging, riotous, uproarious, violent; windy, blustering, tempestuous. See SEVERITY, VIOLENCE, WIND.
[1]**story,** *n.* stratum, floor, stage, tier, level. See LAYER.
[2]**story,** *n.* account, record, report, anecdote, tale, history, annals. See DESCRIPTION.
stout, *adj.* courageous, brave, resolute; corpulent, obese, fat, plump, chubby, fleshy; solid, firm, tough, sound. See COURAGE, SIZE, STRENGTH.
straddle, *v.* bestride, bestraddle; trim, vacillate. See BISECTION, IRRESOLUTION.

STRAIGHTNESS.—I. *Nouns.* **straightness,** directness, rectilinearity, rectilinearness; chord, secant (*geom.*); straight (bee, right, *or* direct) line; short cut; erectness, uprightness, etc. (see *adjectives*); inflexibility.
II. *Verbs.* **be straight,** have no turning, go straight, steer for.
straighten, set (*or* put) straight, plumb; unbend, unfold, uncurl, uncoil, unravel; rectify, put in order, straight (*rare*).
III. *Adjectives.* **straight,** rectilinear, rectilineal, right-lined, direct, even, right, true, in a line; undeviating, unswerving, undistorted, uninterrupted, unbroken, invariable, inflexible, straight as an arrow: *opposite of* angular, curved, crooked.
erect, upright, perpendicular, plumb, vertical.
[*of hair*] lank, limp, not curly, not wavy.
[*morally erect*] **upright,** honest, honorable, square, just, incorrupt, incorruptible, fair, sound, pure; straightforward, candid, frank, truthful.
[*in proper order or place*] **regular,** normal, accurate, correct, orderly; even, level, symmetrical.
[*slang senses*] undiluted, unmixed, unmodified, plain (*as, whiskey* straight); reliable, trustworthy (*as, a* straight *tip*); out-and-out, thorough-going, unreserved, unqualified (*as, a* straight *Democrat*); flat, unvarying, evenly priced (*as, cigars ten cents* straight).
IV. *Adverbs.* **straight,** directly, straightforwardly, lineally, straightly, exactly in a bee line, in a direct course, point-blank.

immediately, at once, forthwith, straight away (*slang*), now, straightway, forthright (*archaic*), presto, instantly: *in this sense,* straight *is archaic.*
See also DIRECTION, PROBITY, VERACITY.—*Antonyms.* See ANGULARITY, CONVOLUTION, CURVATURE.

---

straightway, *adv.* suddenly, forthwith, immediately, speedily. See EARLINESS.
strain, *v.* drain, filter, percolate, separate, ooze, distill, dilute; task, tax, overtax, overstrain, overexert, sprain. See CLEANNESS, EHRESS, FATIGUE.
stranded, *adj.* aground, wrecked, shipwrecked; doomed, lost. See FAILURE, PAIN.
strange, *adj.* unusual, uncommon, remarkable; remote, far-fetched, alien, foreign; odd, queer, outlandish, grotesque, quaint, droll, ececentri; inconceivable, incredible. See CURIOSITY, IRRELATION, RIDICULOUSNESS, WONDER.
stranger, *n.* alien, foreigner, newcomer, immigrant, outsider. See EXTRANEOUSNESS.
strangle, *v.* contract, tighten, squeeze; hang, choke, garrote, throttle, stifle, suffocate, smother; suppress, repress; still, quiet. See CONTRACTION, KILLING, RESTRAINT, SILENCE.
stratagem, *n.* artifice, trick, maneuver, deception, imposture. See CUNNING, PLAN.
strategy, *n.* maneuvering, craftiness; generalship, art of war. See CUNNING, WARFARE.
stratification, *n.* lamination, foliation, scaliness. See LAYER.
stray, *v.* wander, meander, rove; go astray, err, transgress. See DEVIATION, VICE.
streak, *n.* stripe, line, bar, stroke. See LENGTH, VARIEGATION.

STREAM.—I. *Nouns.* **stream,** flow, current, course, tide, flood, race, rush; river, rivulet, streamlet, brook; tributary, affluent, confluent: wave, torrent, flood: drift, tide, tendency.
outflow, efflux, effluence, effusion, outgush, outrush, outgo, issue, escape, outrun.
II. *Verbs.* **stream,** flow, run, glide, move, pour, trickle, spout, gush, discharge; emit, issue, pour out, shed, radiate, emanate.
[*relating to a banner, hair, etc.*] **extend,** stretch out, stretch, outstretch, outspread, float, wave; hang, droop, trail.
III. *Adjectives.* **streaming,** flowing, etc. (see *verbs*); streamline (*as an automobile body*); radiating, radiant, effulgent.
See also ASSEMBLAGE, LIGHT, MOTION, RIVER, WIND.

---

street, *n.* avenue, road, terrace, highway, thoroughfare, boulevard. See HABITATION, WAY.

STRENGTH.—I. *Nouns.* **strength,** power, potency, puissance, energy, vigor, force; main (physical, *or* brute) force; lustihood, stamina, nerve, muscle, brawn, sinews, thews, physique, grit, virility, vitality; spring, elasticity; solidity, firmness, etc. (see *adjectives*); intensity, degree, potency; validity, security.
athletics, athleticism, agonistics, gymnastics, calisthenics; feats of strength.
[*strong man*] athlete, gymnast, acrobat; Atlas, Hercules, Antæus, Samson, Goliath; giant refreshed.
[*comparisons*] adamant, steel; iron, oak, heart of oak; iron grip.
science of forces: dynamics, statics.
II. *Verbs.* **strengthen,** brace, fortify, buttress, sustain, harden, steel; gird, set up, gird up one's loins; recruit, set on one's legs (*colloq.*); vivify, invigorate, nerve, stimulate, energize, animate, reman, refresh, restore, confirm, reënforce *or* reinforce.
III. *Adjectives.* **strong,** vigorous, hard, robust, hale, healthy, robustious (*jocose*), sturdy, husky (*colloq.*), hardy, muscular, brawny, wiry, well-knit, sinewy, strapping, stalwart, lusty, able-bodied, athletic, doughty (*archaic or facetious*), buckra (*Southern U. S.*); Herculean, Atlantean, Cyclopean, Briarean, Titanic; well-equipped, powerful, potent, puissant, mighty; strong as a lion (horse, *or* an ox).

resistless, irresistible, invincible, impregnable, unconquerable, indomitable; incontestable, valid; overpowering, overwhelming, all-powerful, formidable, indefatigable.
manly, manful, virile, in the prime of manhood; masculine, male.
[*able to resist force*] **solid,** firm, stout, tough, sound, stanch *or* staunch, stable, settled, steady, stiff; compact, cohesive, tenacious, resistant.
unweakened, unworn, unexhausted, unspent, unwithered, fresh, blooming; in full force (*or* swing); in the plenitude of power; in fine (*or* high) feather (*colloq.*).
vigorous, energetic, forceful, cogent, potent, pithy, meaty, terse, effective, weighty, decided, convincing, striking, forcible, able, capable, masterful (*as arguments or literary style*).
vehement, violent, impetuous, forcible, brisk, smart, lively, fresh (*as, a* strong *wind;* strong *tide*).
intense, concentrated, keen, acute, deep, passionate, ardent, poignant, warm, vivid, extreme (*as, a* strong *liking*).
[*of odor or flavor*] **rank,** high, gamy, rancid, ill-smelling, malodorous, fetid, offensive; pungent (*as cheese or onion*), acrid, sharp, penetrating.
[*of the voice*] **powerful,** effective, telling, impressive, loud, far-reaching; rhetorical, oratorical.
[*of language*] **forcible,** violent, unrestrained, uncurbed, vehement, abusive, blasphemous.
[*in phonetics*] hard, sharp, voiceless: *opposite of* weak.
[*of food*] **solid,** substantial, nourishing, nutritive, nutrient, nutritious.
[*of drink*] **spirituous,** alcoholic, proof, ardent, bodied, heavy, nappy (*rare*), beady, hard, stiff, full of kick (*slang*); neat, undiluted, straight (*slang*).
IV. *Adverbs.* **strongly,** vigorously, etc. (see *adjectives*); by force, by main force.
See also DEGREE, ENERGY, FETOR, GREATNESS, HEALTH, LETTER (*voiceless*), POWER, PUNGENCY, QUANTITY, REFRESHMENT, RESTORATION, TENACITY.—*Antonyms.* See WEAKNESS.

---

strenuous, *adj.* active, energetic, ardent, zealous; resolute, persevering, sedulous, indefatigable. See ACTIVITY, PERSEVERANCE.
stress, *n.* effort, tug, pull, strain; urgency, pressure, weight, significance; accent, accentuation, emphasis. See EXERTION, IMPORTANCE, VOICE.
stretch, *v.* expand, distend, dilate, widen, spread; extend, lengthen, protract; misrepresent, distort, exaggerate. See EXPANSION, LENGTH, MISREPRESENTATION.
strict, *adj.* stiff, formal, rigid, uncompromising, orthodox; correct, scrupulous, conscientious, religious, punctilious; severe, hard, harsh, stern, exacting, obdurate; exact, accurate, literal, just. See CONFORMITY, PROBITY, SEVERITY, TRUTH.
stricture, *n.* denunciation, censure; contraction, compression, constriction. See DISAPPROBATION, NARROWNESS.

STRIDENCY.—I. *Nouns.* **stridency,** stridor, harshness, hoarseness, throatiness, gutturalness, thickness, roupiness, raucousness, cacophony, dissonance, discord; shrillness, sharpness; creak, jar, screak, squeak; creaking, crashing, static (*radio*), grating; twang, nasality.
high note, shrill note; soprano, treble, tenor, alto, falsetto; head voice, *voce di testa* (*It.*), head tone; shriek, cry, wail, pipe.
[*shrill instruments*] whistle, pipe, fife, piccolo; bagipies, doodlesack (*Scot.*), pipes; Panpipe, syrinx (*L. pl.* syringes).
II. *Verbs.* **stridulate,** grate, creak, saw, snore, buzz, grit, grind, rasp, jar, burr, pipe, twang, jangle, clank; set the teeth on edge, pierce (*or* split) the ears, scream, yelp, *écorcher les oreilles* (*F.*), screech, screak, squeak, shrill.
III. *Adjectives.* **strident,** grating, harsh-sounding, harsh, discordant, cacophonous, stridulous, stridulatory, creaking, jangling, jarring; hoarse, coarse, roupy, thick, gutteral, raucous, metallic, cracked, ragged, rude, rough, gruff, grum, hollow. sepulchral.
shrill, high, high-pitched, sharp, thin, acute, keen, penetrating, piercing, penetrative.
See also CRY, DISCORD.—*Antonyms.* See CONCORD, MELODY, SILENCE, SWEETNESS.

strife, *n.* contest, struggle, opposition, conflict, fight, battle, combat, warfare; friction, quarrel, dispute, litigation. See CONTENTION, DISCORD.
strike, *v.* disobey, resist, secede, mutiny, rebel, boycott; hit, slap, rap, thump, beat, hammer; punish, smite, spank, lash, thrash, flog, whip, switch, stone; astonish, electrify, stun. See DISOBEDIENCE, IMPULSE, PUNISHMENT, WONDER.
strike breaker, scab (*trade-unionist cant*). See APOSTASY.
string, *n.* cord, twine, twist. See FILAMENT.
strip, *v.* divest, uncover, expose, denude, bare, disrobe, shed, skin, peel, remove, take off; steal, plunder, loot, despoil. See DIVESTMENT, STEALING.
strip, *n.* shred, slip, band, fillet, lath, splinter, shaving. See FILAMENT.
strive, *v.* contend, contest, struggle, wrestle, tussle, fight; endeavor, attempt, try, aim, venture. See CONTENTION, ESSAY.
stroke, *n.* shock, attack, paralysis; injury, hurt, damage, loss; blow, knock, bang; mark, scar, dash, line; measure, move, step; masterstroke, feat, hit, go. See DISEASE, EVIL, IMPULSE, INDICATION, PLAN, SUCCESS.
stroll, *n.* saunter, ramble, tramp, walk. See JOURNEY.
strong, *adj.* energetic, enterprising, forceful, powerful; rank, strong-smelling, rancid, musty, fetid; spirituous, ardent, alcoholic, hard; pungent, biting, hot, high-flavored; vigorous, stout, robust, hardy, healthy, sturdy, mighty, tenacious, tough, solid, firm. See ENERGY, FETOR, HARDNESS, PUNGENCY, STRENGTH, TENACITY.
stronghold, *n.* fort, fortress, fortification, citadel. See DEFENSE.
strong-minded, *adj.* strong-willed, firm, resolute, indomitable. See COURAGE.

STRUCTURE.—I. *Nouns.* **structure,** make, form, construction, make-up, build, configuration, conformation, frame, framework, anatomy, fabric, composition, texture, fiber, mold *or* mould, architecture, stratification, arrangement, nature, compages, compaction (*rare*), organization, constitution, organism.
building, erection, pile edifice; superstructure, substructure; house, cottage, bungalow, etc.
science of structures, organology, organography, osteology, myology, splanchnology, neurology, angiology, angiography, adenology, adenography, morphology; histology, microscopic anatomy, tectonics, architecture.
II. *Adjectives.* **structural,** constructional, tectonic, architectural, geotectonic (*geol.*), formational, formative, organic, anatomic *or* anatomical.
See also FORM, HABITATION, ORGANIZATION, PRODUCTION, TEXTURE.—*Antonyms.* FORMLESSNESS, INORGANIZATION.

---

struggle, *v.* contend, contest, strive; flounder. See CONTENTION, DIFFICULTY.
struggle, *n.* trial, endeavor, attempt, venture; effort, stress, strain, tug. See ESSAY, EXERTION.
strut, *v.* swagger, prance, peacock (*fig.*). See BOASTING, PRIDE.
stubborn, *adj.* obstinate, obdurate, inflexible, refractory, mulish. See OBSTINACY.
stuck fast, aground, stranded, transfixed. See STABILITY.
student, *n.* learner, pupil, schoolboy, schoolgirl; keen observer. See SCHOLAR.
studious, *adj.* well-read, well-informed, scholarly, lettered; thoughtful, contemplative. See LEARNING, THOUGHT.
study, *n.* model, representation; reading, inquiry, enlightenment; library, studio, den. See COPY, LEARNING, RECEPTACLE.
study, *v.* examine, consider, question, probe, analyze, investigate; think, reflect, reason, weigh, consider, ponder. See INQUIRY, THOUGHT.
stuff, *v.* humbug, delude, fool, sell (*slang*); pack, puff, press; cram, gorge, gormandize; line, wad, pad. See DECEPTION, EXPANSION, GLUTTONY, LINING.
stumble, *v.* trip, lurch, topple, totter, pitch, stagger; err, blunder, slip, fail. See DESCENT, ERROR.
stumblingblock, *n.* obstacle, hindrance, impediment, snag. See DIFFICULTY.

stump, *n.* snag, protuberance; challenge, dare; log, block; remnant, stub; political speaking; rod, upright. See CONVEXITY, DEFIANCE, FUEL, REMAINDER, SPEECH, SUPPORT.
stun, *v.* astonish, surprise, astound, dumbfound, daze, electrify, stupefy, petrify, confound, stagger, overpower. See WONDER.
stunt, *v.* check (*growth*), nip, cramp, dwarf. See SHORTNESS.
stunted, *adj.* dwarfed, shrunken, runty (*U. S.*), undersized. See LITTLENESS, SHORTNESS.
stupefy, *v.* dull, deaden, obtund, numb, stun, hypnotize, paralyze; astound, electrify, petrify. See INSENSIBILITY, WONDER.
stupendous, *adj.* enormous, towering, prodigious, marvelous, monstrous, wonderful. See GREATNESS, WONDER.
stupid, *adj.* dense, slow, crass, obtuse, thick-headed, dull, stolid, doltish, witless, thick (*colloq.*), dumb (*colloq.*). See DENSITY, DULLNESS, IMBECILITY, THICKNESS.
stupidity, *n.* dullness, foolishness, crassness, ignorance, ineptitude. See DENSITY.
stupor, *n.* daze, stupefaction, lethargy, torpidity. See INACTIVITY, INSENSITIVENESS.
sturdy, *adj.* firm, resolute; strong, stout, robust. See RESOLUTION, STRENGTH.
stutter, *v.* stammer, falter, hesitate, halt, stumble, splutter. See STAMMERING.
sty, *n.* pen, shed, pigsty, lair, den. See INCLOSURE, UNCLEANNESS.

STYLE.—I. *Nouns.* **style,** diction, mode, phraseology, wording, composition, mode of expression, idiom, choice of words; mode of speech, command of language, literary power, authorship, artistry; distinctiveness, distinction, finish; manner, way, fashion, form, character; sort, kind, make, pattern, shape.
II. *Verbs.* **style,** term, name, call, designate, dub, denominate, title, entitle, characterize.
word, phrase, express by words, put into (*or* clothe in) words, couch, write; apply the file; put into style (*as a manuscript*).
See also FASHION, FINE ARTS, NOMENCLATURE, PHRASE, SPEECH, TASTE, TITLE.

---

stylish, *adj.* modish, fashionable, smart, *chic* (*F.*). See FASHION, KNOWLEDGE.
suave, *adj.* bland, fair-spoken, glib, smooth, oily, unctuous, flattering. See COURTESY, SMOOTHNESS, UNCTUOUSNESS.
suavity, *n.* politeness, gallantry, urbanity, blandness. See COURTESY, UNCTUOUSNESS.
subconscious, *adj.* subliminal, supernormal, psychic. See PSYCHICAL RESEARCH.
subconscious, the, the subliminal self, subconsciousness. See PSYCHICAL RESEARCH.
subdue, *v.* temper, restrain, moderate; suppress, crush. See SOFTNESS, SUCCESS.
subdued, *adj.* gentle, soft, moderate, grave, deep, low-toned; plain, quiet, inconspicuous, dull, drab. See LOWNESS, SOBRIETY.
subject, *n.* liege, liegeman; subordinate; matter, theme. See SERVANT, TOPIC.

SUBJECTION.—I. *Nouns.* **subjection,** dependence, subordination; thrall, thralldom, enthrallment *or* enthralment, bondage, serfdom, slavery, enslavement, servitude, yoke, feudalism, vassalage; conquest, reduction, subjugation.
service, employment, employ, occupation; tendence, aid, obligation, duty; tutelage, constraint, submission, obedience.
II. *Verbs.* **be subject,** be at the mercy of, depend upon; fall a prey to, fall under; serve, obey, submit to; drag a chain.
subject, control, expose, make liable; treat; tame, break in, master, subdue, vanquish, subjugate, reduce, defeat, overcome; tread down, weigh down, keep under, enthrall, enslave, lead captive, rule, hold in bondage (*or* leading strings).
III. *Adjectives.* **subject,** dependent, subordinate, inferior; feudal, feudatory; under control; in leading strings, in harness; servile, slavish, enslaved, down-

trodden, henpecked; under one's thumb, tied to one's apron strings, at one's beck and call, used as a doormat, a slave to, at the mercy of, on the hip.
disposed (*to*), liable, prone, inclined, apt, expressed (*as*, subject *to headache*).
conditional (*upon*), dependent, incidental, contingent, provisional, on the assumption of (*as*, subject *to your approval*).
IV. *Adverbs.* **under,** below, underneath, in a subordinate position, at the feet of, under orders (*or* command), at one's orders.

See also INFLUENCE, LIABILITY, OBEDIENCE, PRISON, RESTRAINT, SERVANT, SEVERITY, SUBMISSION, SUCCESS.—*Antonyms.* See FREEDOM.

SUBJECTIVENESS.—I. *Nouns.* **subjectiveness,** subjectivity, introspection, introspectiveness, self-examination, nonobjectiveness, inwardness, interiority, innateness, intrinsicality, inherence, immanence, indwelling; ego, egohood, solipsism (*philos.*).
essence, quiddity, quintessence, hypostasis (*pl.* hypostases: *tech.*), essential nature, hyparxis (*pl.* hyparxes: *rare*), elixir; gist, keynote (*as of a policy*), pith, core, kernel, marrow, backbone, heart, soul, life, lifeblood, flower, substance, essentialness.
nature, character, type, principle, constitution, quality, structure, inner nature, interior, disposition, diathesis (*med.*), spirit, humor, temper, tenor, temperament, mood, aspect, feature, grain, vein; endowment, capacity, capability; idiocrasy, idiosyncrasy, peculiarity; distinctiveness, individuality.
II. *Adjectives.* **subjective,** introspective, introversive, contemplative, nonobjective, idiocratic, idiosyncratic, individual: *opposite of* objective.
intrinsic, inner, internal, interior, inherent, implanted, essential, natural, native, ingenerate, innate, inborn, inbred, ingrained, indwelling, immanent, inwrought; fundamental, radical, incarnate, hereditary, inherited, congenital, connate, indigenous, native; in the grain, bred in the bone, inseparable, constitutional, running in the blood, instinctive; characteristic, ineradicable, fixed: *opposite of* extrinsic.
fanciful, imaginary, illusory, imaginative, fancied, visionary, chimerical, whimsical, imaginational, ideal.
III. *Adverbs.* **subjectively,** introspectively, intrinsically, etc. (see *adjectives*); in the main, in effect, at bottom, virtually, practically, substantially.

See also IMMATERIALITY, INTERIORITY, SUBSTANTIALITY, TENDENCY.—*Antonyms.* See OBJECTIVENESS.

---

subjoin, *v.* add, annex, affix; append, attach, suffix. See ADDITION, SEQUENCE.
subjugate, *v.* subject, subdue, quell, overcome, enthrall, enslave. See SUBJECTION.
sublet, *v.* sublease, underlet. See LENDING.
sublime, *adj.* grand, august, stately, noble, majestic, sacred; great, high, elevated, exalted, heroic. See REPUTE, UNSELFISHNESS.
subliminal self, spirit, soul, the subconscious. See IMMATERIALITY, INTELLECT, PSYCHICAL RESEARCH.
submerge, *v.* submerse, immerse, inundate, duck, engulf, sink. See PLUNGE, WATER.

SUBMISSION.—I. *Nouns.* **submission,** acquiescence, compliance, deference, obedience, submissiveness, resignation, humility, meekness, humbleness, passiveness, nonresistance.
surrender, yielding, cession, capitulation, relinquishment, abandonment, renunciation, recedence, backdown (*colloq.*), recession.
obeisance, homage, kneeling, genuflexion, curtsy, kotow (*Chinese*), salaam (*Oriental*), prostration.
II. *Verbs.* **submit,** succumb, yield, defer to, acquiesce, be submissive, comply, accede, resign oneself, bend, stoop, submit with a good grace.
surrender, cede, capitulate, come to terms, lay down one's arms, hand over one's sword, strike one's flag, give way, give ground, give in, give up, cave in (*colloq.*), bend before the storm, knuckle down to (*colloq.*), knuckle under (*colloq.*), grin and bear it, pocket the affront, make a virtue of necessity.

yield obeisance, obey, kneel to, bow to, pay homage to, cringe to, truckle to; kneel, bow submission, curtsy, kotow (*Chinese*).
refer, commit, make over, relegate, leave (*as, to* submit *a case to the court*).
offer (*as an opinion*), put forward, affirm, adduce, move, propose, urge, tender, present, advance, proffer, volunteer, set forth, propone (*rare or Scot.*), state, propound.
III. *Adjectives.* **submissive,** yielding, obedient, pliant, compliant, acquiescent; passive, unresisting, resigned; crouching, prostrate, humble, meek, docile, obsequious, subservient, deferential, obeisant (*rare*), unassertive.
untenable, indefensible, inexcusable, insupportable, unsupportable.

See also HUMILITY, OBEDIENCE, SUPPOSITION.—*Antonyms.* See DEFIANCE, RESISTANCE.

---

subordinate, *adj.* inferior, second-rate, dependent, secondary. See INFERIORITY.

subscribe, *v.* authorize, approve, agree, assent, underwrite, indorse, sign, attest; give, contribute. See COMPACT, GIVING.

subsequent, *adj.* posterior, later, following, succeeding, ensuing. See POSTERIORITY.

subservient, *adj.* aiding, auxiliary, accessory, subsidiary; servile, subordinate. See AID, SERVILITY.

subside, *v.* wane, ebb, abate; decline, sink, droop, settle. See DECREASE, DESCENT.

subsidence, *n.* wane, decline, ebb, reflux, refluence. See DECREASE.

subsist, *v.* exist, be, breathe; endure, persist, live. See EXISTENCE, PERMANENCE.

subsistence, *n.* being, entity, life; sustenance, nurture, nourishment. See EXISTENCE, FOOD.

substance, *n.* matter, body, stuff, material, element, substratum; sense, significancy, import, drift, burden, spirit; solidity, weight, content, extent; essence, pith, core, heart, soul, life; means, resources, income, property, estate. See MATERIALITY, MEANING, QUANTITY, SUBJECTIVENESS, WEALTH.

SUBSTANTIALITY.—I. *Nouns.* **substantiality,** substantialness, materiality, hypostatization, reification; corporeity, hypostasis (*tech.*), physical nature, flesh and blood, substance, matter; thing, object, article, something; person, creature, being, entity, body; element, substantial, vital part; substratum, groundwork, foundation; actuality, trueness, realness, verity, tangibility, factuality.
II. *Verbs.* **substantialize,** actualize, materialize, hypostatize, reify, realize, substantiate, embody.
III. *Adjectives.* **substantial,** material, corporeal, bodily, hypostatic *or* hypostatical; actual, true, real, positive, existent, concrete, absolute, tangible, factual; effective, practical, moral, virtual, potential.
essential, indispensable, important, fundamental, basic, substantive, vital, necessary, valuable, consequential.
[*of solid structure or material*] **solid,** strong, stout, firm, stable, massive, bulky, heavy, well-made, lasting, pucka *or pakka* (*Anglo-Indian*).
well-to-do, prosperous, wealthy, rich, propertied, flourishing, influential, commercially sound, responsible.
considerable, large, sizable, goodly, noteworthy, notable, signal, extraordinary (*as, a* substantial *increase*).
IV. *Adverbs.* **substantially,** materially, essentially, etc. (see *adjectives*); in substance, solidly, bodily, corporeally; actually, truly, verily, veritably, really.

See also DENSITY, EXISTENCE, MATERIALITY, SUBJECTIVENESS, TRUTH, WHOLE.—*Antonyms.* See UNSUBSTANTIALITY.

SUBSTITUTE.—I. *Nouns.* **substitute,** proxy, alternate (*as of a delegate to a convention*), deputy, representative, *badli* (*Hind.*), double, dummy, pinch hitter (*colloq.*), understudy; succedaneum, *locum tenens* (*L.*), surrogate; changeling; scapegoat, fall guy (*slang*); change, alternative, *quid pro quo* (*L.*); makeshift, *pis aller* (*F.*), stopgap, temporary expedient, shift, apology; substituent (*chem.*)

II. *Verbs.* **substitute,** exchange, change, interchange, supposite (*rare*), depute, delegate, surrogate (*rare*), subrogate, suffect (*rare*), duplicate, put in the place of; act for, pinch-hit (*colloq.*), replace, supersede, cut out (*colloq.*), supplant, take the place of; commute, redeem, compound for; take the rap (*slang*), be the goat (*slang*).

III. *Adjectives.* **substituted,** exchanged, etc. (see *verbs*); vicarious, vicarial, substitutional, subdititious (*rare*).

substitutive, makeshift *or* makeshifty, temporary, provisional, tentative, experimental; imitative, imitation, imitational, pseudo, counterfeit, resembling, resemblant (*rare*), near (*as,* near *silk*).

IV. *Adverbs.* **instead,** in lieu, in room, in place: *followed by* of.

See also DEPUTY, NEARNESS.

SUBSTITUTION.—*Nouns.* **substitution,** commutation, subrogation (*law*), surrogation (*rare*), exchange, change, supplanting, supersession, supersedure, replacement, novation (*law*), enallage, metonymy, synecdoche; reciprocation, reciprocity, interchange, mutuality.

equivalent, equipollence *or* equipollency, equal, consideration, *quid pro quo* (*L.*); price, worth, exchange value, purchase money, payment, compensation.

See also INTERCHANGE, SUBSTITUTE.

---

subterfuge, *n.* artifice, stratagem, finesse, subtlety. See CUNNING.

subtle, *adj.* crafty, sly, shrewd, artful, wily; clever, expert, ingenious, skillful; ethereal, buoyant, volatile; rare, fine, thin, delicate, tenuous; gossamery, filmy. See CUNNING, SKILL; LEVITY, RARITY, TEXTURE.

suburb, *n.* outskirt, purlieu: *usually in plural.* See ENVIRONMENT, NEARNESS.

subvert, *v.* overturn, overthrow, overwhelm, upset, destroy; pervert, corrupt. See DESTRUCTION, DETERIORATION.

SUCCESS.—I. *Nouns.* **success,** successfulness, favorable issue (*or* result), achievement, attainment, accomplishment, advance, progress, prosperity, luck, good fortune, profit, blessing, godsend, smiles of fortune, bed of roses, fat of the land, prosperous issue.

[*stroke of success*] **masterstroke,** *coup de matre* (*F.*), stroke, *coup* (*F.*), feat, hit, go, ten strike (*U. S. colloq.*), killing (*slang*), prize, trump card, checkmate, half the battle, a feather in one's cap (*colloq.*).

victory, triumph, conquest, palm, ascendancy, walkover (*colloq.*), mastery, advantage, upper hand, whip hand.

victor, victress *or* victrix (*fem.: rare*), conqueror, vanquisher, master, champion, winner; master of the situation (*or* position).

II. *Verbs.* **succeed,** be successful, gain one's end (*or* ends); crown with success; gain (attain, carry, *or* secure) a point *or* an object, win, triumph, be triumphant, gain a victory (*or* an advantage), surpass, distance, get there (*U. S. slang*); manage to, contrive to; accomplish, effect, take (*or* have) effect, prevail, prosper, strike oil (*U. S. slang*), turn to account, make progress, advance, speed, make one's way, make one's fortune, have a run of luck, come off successfully, take (*or* carry) by storm, gain the day (prize, *or* palm), carry all before one, score a success; surmount (*or* overcome) a difficulty, stem the torrent, weather the storm.

defeat, conquer, discomfit, vanquish, overcome, master, overthrow, overpower, overmaster, outwit, outdo, outmaneuver, outgeneral, checkmate, beat, thrash, rout, floor, worst, beat hollow (*colloq.*), lick (*colloq.*), drub, trim (*colloq.*), lick to a frazzle (*colloq.*); settle (*colloq.*), do for (*colloq.*), tread, trample, crush, subjugate, reduce.

quell, silence, put down, suppress, subdue, reduce, repress; confound, nonplus, baffle, circumvent, elude; drive to the wall.

avail, benefit, profit, advantage, suffice, answer, answer the purpose, serve, bestead, assist, help, aid, succour, subserve; do, work well, turn out well, take (*colloq.*), tell, bear fruit.

[*to come after*] **follow,** come next, take the place of, assume the office of, become heir, come into possession (*as, to* succeed *to the throne*); ensue, result, be subsequent to, follow in order (*as, calm* succeeds *the storm*).

III. *Adjectives.* **successful,** prosperous, flourishing, booming, fortunate, lucky, auspicious, happy, felicitous, set up (*colloq.*), triumphant, crowned with success, victorious; unbeaten.
IV. *Adverbs.* **successfully,** prosperously, etc. (see *adjectives*); with flying colors, in triumph, swimmingly.

See also FOLLOWING, POSTERIORITY, PROSPERITY, SEQUENCE.—*Antonyms.* See FAILURE.

---

succession, *n.* lineage, descent; sequence, round, procession, series, rum, cycle, course. See POSTERITY, ROTATION.
successor, *n.* follower, heir. See FOLLOWING.
succinct, *adj.* concise, terse, short, laconic, compact, pithy. See CONCISENESS.
succor, *v.* aid, help, assist, support, relieve, rescue. See RELIEF, SUPPORT.
sudden, *adj.* instant, instantaneous, immediate, unexpected; brief, momentary, abrupt, spasmodic, transient. See EARLINESS, TRANSIENCE.
suddenly, *adv.* forthwith, immediately, at once, plump. See EARLINESS.
sue, *v.* woo, court; prosecute, indict; petition, beg, solicit, claim, demand. See ENDEARMENT, LAWSUIT, REQUEST.
suffer, *v.* feel, endure, undergo; ache, smart, agonize, grieve; permit, let, tolerate. See PAIN, PERMISSION.
sufferer, *n.* victim, prey, martyr. See PAIN.
suffering, *n.* endurance, sufferance; ache, hurt, twinge, pang, discomfort. See FEELING, PAIN.

SUFFICIENCY.—I. *Nouns.* **sufficiency,** adequacy, sufficientness, enough, *quantum sufficit* (*L.*), satisfaction, wherewithal, competence *or* competency, adequate resources.
abundance, plenitude, plenty, copiousness, amplitude, profusion, full measure, "good measure, pressed down, and shaken together, and running over" (*Bible*); repletion, surfeit, satiety, fill; luxuriance, affluence, fat of the land; cornucopia, horn of plenty, horn of Amalthæa.
fitness, competence, ability, efficiency, capability, skill, capacity: *in this sense,* sufficiency *is archaic.*
self-sufficiency, self-confidence, self-content, self-complacency, conceit, self-admiration, self-glorification, overweeningness, toploftiness (*colloq.*).
man of means, man of substance, rich man, moneyed man, plutocrat, millionaire, capitalist, financier, banker.
II. *Verbs.* **suffice,** do, be adequate, avail, answer, serve, content, satisfy, pass muster; have enough, have one's fill.
abound, teem, superabound, exuberate, flow, stream, rain, shower down; pour, pour in; swarm; bristle with.
III. *Adjectives.* **sufficient,** enough, sufficing, adequate, up to the mark, commensurate, satisfactory; ample, full, plenty, plentiful, plenteous, copious, abundant, well-provided, chock-full, lavish, replete; luxuriant, affluent, rich, wantless; unstinted, inexhaustible, exhaustless.
competent, qualified, able, fit, efficient, capable (*in this sense,* sufficient *is archaic.*)
IV. *Adverbs.* **sufficiently,** adequately, etc. (see *adjectives*); in abundance, with no sparing hand, without stint, to one's heart's content, *ad libitum* (*L.*).

See also COMPLETENESS, [2]CONTENT, REDUNDANCE, SATIETY, SERVANT (*suffice*), STORE, WEALTH.—*Antonyms.* See INSUFFICIENCY.

---

suffix, *n.* afflx, postfix, termination, ending. See ADDITION.
suffocate, *v.* stifle, choke, smother, strangle, asphyxiate. See KILLING.
suffocation, *n.* strangulation, smothering, choking, extinguishment. See KILLING.
suffrange, *n.* vote, voice, ballot, franchise. See AFFIRMATION, CHOICE.
sugar, *n.* saccharin, sucrose, dulcin; crystallose, glucose. See SWEETNESS.
suggest, *v.* advice, counsel, recommend; insinuate, intimate, hint; submit, propound, move. See ADVICE, INFORMATION, SUPPOSITION.—**suggest itself,** occur to; absorb, occupy, engross. See THOUGHT.

suggestive, *adj.* remindful, recollective, fresh, vivid; stimulative, allusive. See MEMORY, SUPPOSITION.

suicide, *n.* self-murder, self-destruction, hara-kiri (*Jap.*). See KILLING.

suit, *n.* clothes, dress, costume, habit; courtship, wooing, addresses; case, litigation, petition, prayer, entreaty, supplication, solicitation. See CLOTHING, ENDEARMENT, LAWSUIT, REQUEST.

suit, *v.* please, satisfy, fit, comform; befit, be expedient. See AGREEMENT, EXPEDIENCE.

suitable, *adj.* appropriate, fitting, becoming, proper, meet, congruous; expedient. See AGREEMENT, EXPEDIENCE.

suite, *n.* escort, train, convoy; sequence, progression, round, set, series, chain; set (*of rooms*), apartment; following, bodyguard, staff, court. See ACCOMPANIMENT, CONTINUITY, HABITATION, SERVANT.

suitor, *n.* lover, admirer, wooer, sweetheart; solicitor, applicant, suppliant. See LOVE, PETITIONER.

sulk, *v.* frown, scowl, pout, be sullen. See SULLENNESS.

sulky, *adj.* sullen, morose, grumpy, grouchy, perverse, unsociable. See SULLENNESS.

SULLENNESS.—I. *Nouns.* **sullenness,** moroseness, morosity, melancholy, unsociableness, unsociability, ill temper, spleen, churlishness, irascibility, moodiness, perversity, obstinacy, thornness, spinosity, crabbedness, glumness, sulkiness; sulks, dudgeon, dumps (*usually*, in the dumps), doldrums; black looks, scowl, grouch (*slang*), huff.

II. *Verbs.* **be sullen, sulk, frown, scowl, lower, glower, pout, grouch** (*slang*), have a hang-dog look.

III. *Adjectives.* **sullen,** morose, gloomy, depressing, melancholy; glum, unsociable, sulky, grumpy, grum, grim, grouchy (*slang*), churlish, surly, moody, cantankerous, splenetic, spleenish, spleeny, gruff, scowling, glowering, growling, mumpish, peevish, petulant, fretful, ill-natured, ill-tempered, ill-humored, ill-disposed; crusty, crabbed, sour, sore, cross, cross-grained; perverse, wayward, refractory, restive, ungovernable, cussed (*vulgar or euphemistic*), intractable; spiteful, cynical, malignant.

See also DEJECTION, DISCONTENT, DISCOURTESY, IRASCIBILITY, OBSTINACY, RESENTMENT.—*Antonyms.* Se CHEERFULNESS.

---

sully, *v.* defame, slur, tarnish, stain, blot, smirch, taint; soil, daub, blur. See DISREPUTE, UNCLEANNESS.

sultry, *adj.* close, stifling, stuffy, oppressive, sweltering, humid. See HEAT.

sum, *n.* substance, digest; amount, quantity balance; total, product, example, problem; all, aggregate, entirety. See COMPENDIUM, MONEY, NUMBER, WHOLE.

summary, *n.* abstract, epitone, analysis, brief, *résumé* (*F.*). See COMPENDIUM.

summary, *adj.* short, concise, condensed, laconic, succinct; brief, brisk, quick. See SHORTNESS, TRANSIENCE.

summer, *n.* midsummer; summertime. See HEAT, MORNING.

SUMMIT.—I. *Nouns.* **summit,** top, highest point, *ne plus ultra* (*L.*), vertex (*pl.* vertices), apex, crown, peak, cap, brow, crest, tiptop, tip-crowning point, culmination, capsheaf (*lit. or fig.*), zenith, pinnacle, acme, culmen (*rare or zoöl.*), climax; height, pitch, maximum; goal, consummation; turning point, turn of the tide; fountainhead, watershed.

[*in architecture*] architrave, epistyle, frieze, zoöphorus, cornice, corona; drip, larmier; coping, coping stone, capital, headpiece, capstone, pediment, fastigium, tympanum, entablature; attic, loft, garret; housetop, roof, ceiling.

head, *caput* (*L.; pl. capita: tech.*), pate (*now jocose or derogatory*), noddle (*colloq.*), poll (*in this sense, dial. or jocose*) sconce (*colloq.*), nob *or* knob (*slang*), bean (*slang*), dome (*slang*), skull, cranium (*L. pl.* crania), calvaria *or* calvarium (*anat.*).

II. *Verbs.* **crown, top, cap, crest, head, tip; ride, surmount, overtop; culminate, consummate.**

III. *Adjectives.* topmost, highest, uppermost, culminal (*rare*), culminant (*rare*) top, apical, overmost, tiptop; capital, head, polar; chief, superior, supreme, supernal.
See also COVERING, HEIGHT, SUPERIORITY.—*Antonyms.* See BASE.

---

summon, *v.* cite, bid, call, summons (*colloq.*), subpœna. See COMMAND, LAWSUIT.
summons, *n.* call, subpœna, citation. See COMMAND, LAWSUIT.
sumptuous, *adj.* luxurious, gorgeous, splendid, costly. See OSTENTATION.
sun, *n.* sol, orb, of day, day-star (*poetic*), Helios. See LUMINARY, WORLD.
sunburnt, *adj.* tanned, bronzed, burned. See BROWN.
Sunday, *n.* day of rest, Sabbath, Lord's day. See REPOSE.
Sunday school, Sabbath school, Bible school. See SCHOOL.
sunder, *v.* disjoin, divide, sever, part, separate. See DISJUNCTION, DIVORCE.
sundry, *adj.* several, divers, many, various. See MULTITUDE.
sun god, Helios, Phœbus Apollo, Ra (*Egypt*). See LUMINARY.
sunny, *adj.* cheerful, happy, smiling, optimistic; bright, warm, genial, sunshiny, hot. See CHEERFULNESS, HEAT.
sunrise, *n.* dawn, daybreak, sunup (*colloq.*), cockcrow; the east. See MORNING.
sunset, *n.* nightfall, curfew, dusk, sundown; the west. See EVENING.
superabound, *v.* overabound, swarm, teem. See REDUNDANCE.
superb, *adj.* magnificent, fine, grand, rich, gorgeous. See BEAUTY.
supercilious, *adj.* contemptuous, disdainful, scornful, contumelious; proud, haughty, lofty, lordly, arrogant. See CONTEMPT, PRIDE.
superexcellence, *n.* superiority, supereminence. See GOODNESS.
superficial, *adj.* outer, outermost; frivolous, shallow, shallow-brained, ignorant. See EXTERIORITY, SHALLOWNESS.
superfluous, *adj.* unnecessary, needless, spare, useless, *de trop* (*F.*). See REDUNDANCE.
superheat, *v.* overheat, incandesce. See CALEFACTION.
superintend, *v.* supervise, oversee, administer. See DIRECTION.

SUPERIORITY.—I. *Nouns.* **superiority,** predominance, predominancy, ascendancy, predomination, preëminence, lead, preponderance *or* preponderancy, excellence, greatness, eminence, supereminence, transcendence *or* transcendency, prevalence; vantage ground, advantage, drag (*slang*), pull (*slang*), power, influence, authority, prestige, mana (*New Zealand*); position, rank, nobility.
supremacy, supremeness, paramountcy, primacy, sovereignty, sovranty (*poetic*), scepter *or* sceptre, headship, chieftaincy, captaincy, leadership, maximum, record; highest position, crest, summit, peak; lion's share, Benjamin's mess; majority, bulk, greater part (*or* number), plurality.
superior, chief, chieftain, head, leader, natural leader, captain, ruler, *duce* (*It.*), dux (*L. pl.* duces: *chiefly Scot.*), top sawyer (*colloq.*), swell (*colloq.*), social leader, *nulli secundus* (*L.*), *primus inter pares* (*L.*); suzerain, liege, liege lord, lord paramount, superior being, prince, overman, superman, Triton among the minnows.
superioress (*of a convent*), lady superior, mother superior, domina, abbess, prioress.
II. *Verbs.* **be superior,** exceed, excel, transcend, outdo, outbalance, overbalance, outweigh, outrival, outrank, out-Herod Herod; pass, surpass, overtop, overmatch; cap, beat, cut out (*colloq.*); beat hollow (*colloq.*), outplay, outstrip, eclipse, throw into the shade, take the shine out of, have the upper hand, have the advantage; predominate, prevail; precede, take precedence, come first, rank first, take the cake (*slang*); bear the palm, break the record.
III. *Adjectives.* **superior,** higher, greater, major, upper, over (*used chiefly in composition*), above, ultra, extreme, exceeding; distinguished.
supreme, highest (*as in authority*), greatest, maximal, maximum, utmost, paramount, preëminent, foremost, chief, principal, crowning, excellent, peerless, matchless, unrivaled, unparallelled, unequaled, unapproached, unsurpassed, *facile princeps* (*L.*), dominant, overruling; second to none, *nulli secundus* (*L.*) *sans pareil* (*F.*), sovereign, superlative, incomparable, transcendent.

IV. *Adverbs.* **beyond,** more, over; in addition to, over and above; at its height.
[*in a superior or supreme degree*] **eminently,** preëminently, superlatively, supremely, principally, especially, particularly, peculiarly, notably, surpassingly, *par excellence* (*F.*), *catexochen* (*Gr.* κατ' ἐξοχήν), *a fortiori* (*L.*).

See also AUTHORITY, GREATNESS, HEIGHT, IMPORTANCE, NOBILITY, SUMMIT.—*Antonyms.* See INFERIORITY.

---

supernatural, *adj.* miraculous, superhuman, spiritual, hyperphysical, superphysical. See DEITY.

supersede, *v.* displace, replace, supplant. See SUBSTITUTE.

supervision, *n.* oversight, superintendence, command, control, charge. See DIRECTION.

supine, *adj.* recumbent, prostrate, complanate; listless, inert, sluggish, languid, torpid; leaning backward, inclined. See FLATNESS, INSENSITIVENESS, OBLIQUITY.

supple, *adj.* pliant, flexible, limber, tractable, yielding. See SOFTNESS.

supplement, *n.* appendix (*L. pl.* appendices), addendum (*pl.* addenda), complement, sequel, continuation. See ADDITION, ADJUNCT.

supplicate, *v.* entreat, beseech, plead, implore, pray, petition. See REQUEST.

supply, *v.* furnish, equip, outfit, provide, stock, replenish, refill; accommodate, deliver, render. See PROVISION, SERVANT, STORE.

SUPPORT. I. *Nouns.* [*act of supporting*] **support,** upholding, bearing, maintenance, sustenance, subsistence, sustentation, upkeep, sustainment (*rare*); reënforcement.

advocacy (*of a person or cause*), countenance, favor, help, aid, succor, assistance, encouragement, backing, patronage, championship, defense.

[*that which supports*] **base,** basis, foundation, groundwork; substruction (*arch.*), substructure, underbuilding; stereobate (*arch.*), socle, bed, bedding, underpinning, sill, corner stone, ground, rest, sleeper, tie, grillage (*used in marshy places*), riprap, pierre-perdu (*as for a sea wall*), substratum, ground, *terra firma* (*L.*), bottom; footing, foothold, purchase, hold; rest, resting place, *pou sto* (*Gr.* ποῦ στῶ), fulcrum, *point d'appui* (*F.*); rung, spoke, stave, round, rundle, step, bar.

floor, flooring, deck, pavement, stage, platform, scaffold, dais, rostrum, stand; emplacement (*for a gun*).

shelf, ledge, bracket, console, retable (*eccl.*), gradin, superaltar, predella, *gradino* (*It.*); mantelshelf, mantelpiece.

table, board, stand; trestle, horse, sawhorse, sawbuck (*U. S.*), buck; clotheshorse; desk, teapoy, trivet, taboret, sideboard, dresser, tea wagon; dining table, mahogany; counter.

prop, stay, mainstay, strut, shore, brace, guy, shrouds (*pl.*), buttress; abutment, skid, rib, splint, truss.

staff, stick, rod, walking-stick, cane, Malacca cane, alpenstock, baton, *lathi* (*Hind.*), stump (*cricket*), upright, cowlstaff (*archaic*), crosier, pastoral staff, crook, crutch; caduceus, thyrsus, lituus (*Roman*).

post, pole, shaft, thill, nib (*dial. Eng.*), disselboom (*South Africa*), tongue (*of a vehicle*), neap (*U. S.*), shank, leg; stake, pale, picket, palisade, pile; stanchion, jamb, stile; mullion, pier, pilaster, colonnette, balustrade, banister, baluster, columella (*tech.*), standard, pillar, column, pediment, pedestal; caryatid (*pl.* caryatids *or* caryatides); atlantes (*pl.*), telamones (*pl.*), Atlas.

stalk, stem, pedicel (*tech.*), pedicle, peduncle (*tech.*), caulis (*bot.*), petiole (*bot. and zoöl.*), caudex (*bot.*), caulicle (*bot.*), cauliculus (*arch.*), culm (*bot.*), haulm, spear, spire, stipe (*bot.*), stipes (*pl.* stipites: *zoöl.*).

beam, rafter, joist, girder, lintel, timber, balk, tie, truss, batten, stud, scantling, transom, traverse, trevis (*Scot.*), trave, crossbeam, stringpiece; summer, breastsummer, bressomer (*archaic*), summertree, cantilever.

frame, framework, scaffolding, skeleton, framing, casing, casement, sash, case, rack, yoke, crib, curb; chine (*of an animal*), spine, rachis (*anat.*), ridge, backbone, vertebra (*pl.* vertebræ: *tech.*), spinal column, vertebral column.

arch, cove (*arch.*), fornix (*pl.* fornices: *anat.*), skewback, span, vault, ogive, apse, concha (*pl.* conchæ); keystone.

seat, throne, dais; divan, musnud (*Oriental*), guddee *or* gaddi (*Hind.*), woolsack, ottoman, sofa, *causeuse* (*F.*), *tête-à-tête* (*F.*), davenport, couch, day-bed; stall, *lamba chauki* or *lamba kursi* (*Hind.*), long-sleeve chair (*Anglo-Indian*), chair, wingchair, armchair, *fauteuil* (*F.*), easy-chair, elbow-chair, rocking-chair, rocker, morris chair, settle, settee, *chaise longue* (*F.*), form, bench; saddle, sidesaddle, pillion; aparejo, packsaddle; pommel, horn.
stool, *prie-dieu* (*F.*), hassock, footstool, cricket, camp stool, folding stool.
bed, couch, bedstead, four-poster, pallet, cot; hammock, shakedown; crib, trundle-bed, truckle-bed, cradle, litter, stretcher; bunk, berth, kip (*dial.*), doss (*slang*), roost (*slang*); mattress, paillasse, pallet; mat, rug, cushion; lap, pillow; bedding; litter (*for cattle*).
[*means of sustenance or maintenance*] **maintenance,** necessaries, upkeep, sustenance, keep, provisions, food, victuals, nutriment, bread, stores, stock, living, livelihood, grubstake (*U. S. slang*).
supporter, upholder, maintainer, sustainer, adherent, advocate, patron, stand-by (*colloq.*), defender.
II. *Verbs.* **support,** uphold, sustain, hold up, bolster up, shore up, brace, truss. stay, prop, underprop, underpin, underset, upbear, carry, bear, hold; cradle, pillow; bottom, base, found, bed, embed.
endure, tolerate, bear, undergo, suffer, go through, put up with, abide, submit to.
maintain, sustain, keep, provide for, nourish, nurture, cherish, make up for; relieve, meet (*as a need or deficiency*), fill (*as a vacancy*), carry on.
advocate, vindicate, justify, plead for, shield, protect, defend, champion, patronize, back up, uphold, countenance, back, second.
succor, aid, assist, help, further, forward, befriend, favor; feed, finance, grubstake (*U. S. slang*); strengthen, reënforce, fortify, brace.
verify, substantiate, bear out, confirm, establish, clinch (*colloq.*), accredit, corroborate.
[*in theatrical usage*] **perform,** act, represent, play, sustain, assume (*as, to* support *a character*; support *a star*).
III. *Adjectives.* **supportable,** bearable, endurable, sufferable, abidable, tolerable.
defensible, maintainable, tenable, justifiable, vindicable.
supporting, upholding, sustaining, etc. (see *verbs*); sustentative, sustentacular (*anat.*); fundamental, basic; Atlantean.
See also AGENCY, AID, BASE, EVIDENCE, FEELING, INEXCITABILITY, INFLUENCE, [1]REST, SAFETY.—*Antonyms.* See HINDRANCE, PENDENCY.

SUPPOSITION.—I. *Nouns.* **supposition,** assumption, supposal, postulation (*rare*), presupposition, presumption, condition, hypothesis, postulate, theory. data; thesis, theorem; conjecture, guess, shot (*colloq.*), guesswork, surmise, suspicion, inkling, hint, suggestion, association of ideas; opinion, belief, view; speculation, divination.
theorist, theorizer, speculatist (*rare*), speculator, doctrinaire, doctrinarian (*rare*), hypothesist, notionalist, notionist (*rare*).
II. *Verbs.* **suppose,** assume, presuppose, understand, presume, predicate, hypothesize, posit (*logic*), take for granted; imply, involve.
imagine, believe, think, deem, conjecture, surmise, conclude, judge, guess, regard, view, consider, suspect, dream, fancy, conceive, feel, apprehend; speculate, theorize, doctrinize, divine.
propound, propose, set forth, put forth; put a case, submit; move, make a motion; hazard (*or* put forward) a suggestion (*or* supposition); suggest, intimate, allude to, hint.
III. *Adjectives.* **suppositional,** conjectural, presumptive, suppositive, hypothetical, academic, theoretic, theoretical, speculatory, speculative; assumed, supposed, reputed, putative (*tech.*), imagined, presumptive; gratuitous.
suggestive, stimulative, stimulating; allusive, referential.
supposititious (*now usually employed in its sense of "fraudulently substituted"*), spurious, counterfeit, false, feigned, pretended, sham, pseudo (*used chiefly in composition*), forged, bogus, deceptive.
IV. *Conjunctions.* **if,** provided, if so be, gin (*Scot.*), gif (*Scot. and dial. Eng.*), in the event of, on the supposition that, as if, granting that, supposing that, allowing that, for all one knows; whether, in case.
See also BELIEF, IMAGINATION, PLAN, POSSIBILITY, PROBABILITY, THOUGHT.

suppress, *v.* conceal, hide, stifle, withhold; crush, quash, quell, efface, obliterate; stop, check, restrain, inhibit, subdue. See CONCEALMENT, DESTRUCTION, RESTRAINT.
supremacy, *n.* ascendancy, primacy, preëminence. See SUPERIORITY.
supreme, *adj.* highest, greatest, foremost, principal, dominant. See SUPERIORITY.
sure, *adj.* certain, assured, convinced, confident, positive; reliable, trustworthy, unfailing, fixed, secure. See CERTAINTY, SAFETY.
surface, *n.* exterior, outside, area, superficies, covering, finish. See EXTERIORITY.
surfeit, *n.* oversupply, excess, surplus; satiation. See REDUNDANCE, SATIETY.
surge, *v.* rise, tower; flock, stream; swirl, swell. See ASCENT, ASSEMBLAGE, RIVER.
surly, *adj.* abrupt, discourteous, rude, ill-tempered, snarling, sullen. See DISCOURTESY, SULLENNESS.
surmise, *v.* suppose, guess, consider, suspect, imagine. See SUPPOSITION.
surmount, *v.* climb, scale; exceed, excel, transcend; conquer, overcome; crown, cap, overtop; clear, top, vault. See ASCENT, HEIGHT, SUCCESS, SUMMIT, TAKING.
surpass, *v.* exceed, excel, overtop, surmount; eclipse, overshadow, outshine, outdo, outstrip. See PASSAGE, REPUTE.
surplus, *n.* excess, oversupply, superfluity, overplus. See REDUNDANCE, REMAINDER.
surprise, *v.* startle, stun, astonish, amaze, dumfound, overwhelm, electrify. See NONEXPECTATION, WONDER.
surprise, *n.* nonexpectation, blow, shock, astonishment, amazement. See WONDER.
surrender, *n.* yielding, cession, capitulation (*on certain conditions*), relinquishment. See SUBMISSION.
surrender, *v.* cede, capitulate, yield, relinquish, comply. See SUBMISSION.
surround, *v.* environ, encompass, inclose, encircle, circumscribe. See ENVIRONMENT.
surrounding, *adj.* encompassing, inclosing; suburban, neighboring. See ENVIRONMENT.
survey, *v.* measure, plot, delimit; view, scan, examine, inspect. See MEASUREMENT, VISION.
surveyor, *n.* geodesist, topographer, cartographer. See MEASUREMENT.
survive, *v.* last, endure, remain, abide, continue, persist; subsist, live, outlive. See DURABILITY, PERMANENCE.
susceptibility, *n.* sensibility, impressibility, sentimentality; propensity, predisposition, inclination. See SENSITIVENESS, TENDENCY.
suspect, *v.* imagine, conjecture, surmise, conclude, fancy, judge, guess; doubt, misdoubt, mistrust, distrust, scent, be jealous. See SUPPOSITION, UNBELIEF.
suspend, *v.* interrupt, intermit, arrest, stop; defer, delay, postpone; hang, swing, sling, append. See CESSATION, LATENESS, PENDENCY.
suspense, *n.* stop, pause, abeyance; suspension, continuance (*as of a lawsuit*); hesitation, perplexity, irresolution. See CESSATION, PENDENCY, UNCERTAINTY.
suspicion, *n.* diffidence, dread, apprehension, anxiety; distrust, mistrust, doubt; assumption, conjecture, surmise; dash, hint, suggestion, trace. See FEAR, JEALOUSY, SUPPOSITION, TOUCH.
sustain, *v.* relieve, comfort; uphold, perpetuate, maintain, preserve; confirm, ratify, validate, prove; bear, suffer, endure, brave, undergo; strengthen, support, fortify, reinforce, prop, bolster, hold. See AID, CONTINUANCE, EVIDENCE, FEELING, STRENGTH.
sustenance, *n.* nutrition, nourishment, food, maintenance. See AID.
swagger, *v.* boast, brag, bluster, flourish, strut. See BOASTING.

swagger, *n.* pretentiousness, airs, arrogance, braggadocio. See BOASTING, SIDE.
swallow, *v.* accept, believe; bear, endure, digest, stomach; eat, drink, gulp, ingulf, consume. See CREDULITY, INEXCITABILITY, RECEPTION.
sward, *n.* turf, sod, grass, greensward. See PLAIN.
swarm, *n.* crowd, throng, horde, flock, drove; cloud, hive. See ASSEMBLAGE, MULTITUDE.
swarthy, *adj.* swart, dusky, dark, dark-hued. See BLACKNESS.
swastika, *n.* fylfot, gammadion. See [1]SPELL.
sway, *v.* govern, guide, rule, control, dominate, manage; urge, persuade, bias; fluctuate, rock, vibrate, stagger, totter; incline, lean, lurch, reel, yaw. See INFLUENCE, MOTIVE, OBLIQUITY, OSCILLATION, ROLL.
sway, *n.* swing, wag, wave; ascendancy, control, influence, omnipotence; government, dominion, authority, sovereignty, reign. See OSCILLATION, POWER, RULE.
swear, *v.* affirm, depose, vow, attest; curse, blaspheme. See AFFIRMATION, IMPIETY.
sweep, *v.* brush, whisk; curve, bend, sag; skim, scurry, speed. See CLEANNESS, CURVATURE, VELOCITY.
sweetheart, *n.* suitor, lover, betrothed, *fiancé* (*F.*), *fiancée* (*F.*), See LOVE

SWEETNESS.—I. *Nouns.* sweetness, saccharinity, sugariness, dulcitude (*rare*); agreeableness, pleasantness; fragrance, redolence; melody, harmony, etc. (see *adjectives*).
sugar, saccharin *or* saccharine, sucrose, saccharose, dulcin, crystallose, glucose, dulcite (*all chem.*).
[*in plural*] sweets, confectionery, confections, sweetmeats, comfits, preserves, jam, sugarplum, caramel, lollipop, bonbon, jujube, honey, manna; sirup *or* syrup, treacle, molasses, maple sirup *or* syrup, maple sugar, sugar candy, taffy butterscotch.
pastry, patisserie (*rare*), *pâtisserie* (*F.*); cake, pie, tart, puff, pudding.
[*sweet beverages*] nectar; mead, metheglin, liqueur, sweet wine, cordial.
delights, pleasures, joys, enjoyments, gratifications (*as, the* sweets *of victory*).
II. *Verbs.* sweeten, sugar, saccharize (*tech.*), saccharify (*tech.*), dulcify (*rare in the physical sense*), edulcorate; candy, sirup *or* syrup; mull (*as wine or ale*).
freshen, revive, renew; ventilate, deodorize, disinfect, fumigate, cleanse, purify.
soften, mollify, dulcify, mellow, milden; solace, soothe, relieve.
III. *Adjectives.* sweet, sugary, saccharine, saccharoid, saccharoidal, saccharous (*rare*), sweetened; candied, luscious, cloying, honey-sweet, nectareous, nectarean: *opposite of* sour, bitter.
[*pleasing to the taste*] **fresh,** wholesome, refreshing, sound, pure, flavorous, sapid, delicious; untainted, unsalted: *opposite of* sour, rancid, stale, decayed, etc
[*pleasing to the smell*] **fragrant,** odorous, sweet-smelling, sweet-scented, redolent, perfumed, odoriferous, aromatic, spicy, ambrosial, balmy.
[*pleasing to the ear*] **melodious,** sweet-sounding, mellifluous, mellifluent, smooth, mellow, soft, soothing, dulcet, harmonious, musical, silvery, honeyed *or* honied, Hyblæan (*poetic*).
[*pleasing to the eye*] **fair,** beautiful, comely, shapely, good-looking, attractive, desirable, winsome, charming.
[*pleasing in general*] **pleasant,** agreeable, pleasurable, gratifying, pleasing, delightful, enjoyable, entrancing, exquisite, delightsome, gladsome, joyful, welcome, acceptable, satisfactory.
sweet-tempered, amiable, good-natured, agreeable, charming, gentle, bland, kind, mild, affectionate, lovable, dear, beloved.
[*of land*] fertile, productive, cultivable, cultivatable (*rare*), workable, yielding; warm: *opposite of* sour.
[*of machinery*] smooth, frictionless, noiseless, smooth-running.
IV. *Adverbs.* sweetly, pleasantly, agreeably, etc. (see *adjectives*) smoothly noiselessly (*as a machine*).
See also CLEANNESS, LOVE (*lovable*), MELODY.—*Antonyms.* See SOURNESS.

---

swell, *v.* expand, dilate, distend, bulge, increase: bud, sprout. See EXPANSION

swell, *n.* bulge, swelling, protuberance, excrescency, elevation; volume (*of sound*), peal, boom; billow, surge, undulation; *Colloq.*: dandy, beau; superior. See CONVEXITY, LOUDNESS, RIVER, FOP, NOBILITY, SUPERIORITY.
swelter, *v.* glow, sweat, perspire, pant. See HEAT.
swerve, *v.* diverge, turn, incline, deviate, deflect. See DEVIATION.
swift, *adj.* rapid, speedy, quick, fleet, expeditious. See VELOCITY.
swindle, *v.* cheat, defraud, deceive, trick, hoax, victimize, steal, peculate, embezzle. See DECEPTION, STEALING.
swindler, *n.* cheat, fraud, sharper, trickster, faker (*slang*); peculator, forger, defaulter, embezzler, counterfeiter. See DECEIVER, THIEF.
swine, *n.* pig, hog, boar, sow. See ANIMAL.
swing, *v.* sway, dangle, wave, wag; depend, hang. See OSCILLATION, PENDENCY.
swing, *n.* sway, beat, rhythm. See OSCILLATION.
switch, *n.* shunt (*chiefly Brit.*), by-pass (*elec.*); twig, withe; rod, birch, rattan. See DEVIATION, PART, SCOURGE.
switch, *v.* swish, sweep, swing; sidetrack, shift, divert, shunt (*Brit.*); birch, cane, flog, slash. See AGITATION, DEVIATION, PUNISHMENT.
sword, *n.* blade, saber, rapier, broadsword. See ARMS.
sword-shaped, *adj.* ensate (*bot.*), gladiate (*bot.*), xiphoid (*anat.*). See SHARPNESS.
sycophant, *n.* parasite, fawner, flatterer, cringer. See SERVILITY.
syllable, *n.* phone (*tech.*), monosyllable, particle, affix. See LETTER.
symbol, *n.* sign, token, figure, mark, note, device, emblem. See INDICATION.
symbolize, *v.* typify, signify, emblemize; indicate, show, denote, imply; represent, illustrate. See FIGURE, INDICATION, REPRESENTATION.

SYMMETRY.—I. *Nouns.* **symmetry,** proportion, proportionality, balance, keeping, correspondence, harmony, congruity, conformity, uniformity, regularity, evenness, parallelism, peloria (*pl.* pelories: *bot.*); order, form, shapeliness, finish, beauty, eurythmics *or* eurhythmics.

ramification (*as of a tree or vein*), radiation, arborescence, branching, arbor vitæ (*anat.*), arborization (*tech.*).

II. *Verbs.* **symmetrize,** proportionate, regularize, balance, make symmetrical.

III. *Adjectives.* **symmetrical,** symmetric, regular, balanced, well-balanced, uniform, even, equal, parallel, peloric (*bot.*); coextensive; proportional, proportionate, eurythmic, harmonious, commensurate, corresponding; isobilateral (*bot.*), zygomorphic *or* zygomorphous (*tech.*); well-set, shapely, beautiful, finished; classic, chaste, severe: *opposite of* asymmetric, unsymmetrical.

ramiform (*esp. bot.*), branched, ramrose, ramous, branching, dendriform, tree-shaped, arborescent, arboriform, dendroid *or* dendroidal, arborized, dendritic *or* dendritical; fern-shaped, filiciform, fernlike, filicoid; raylike, radiated, actinoid, actiniform.

See also BEAUTY, EQUALITY, FORM, REGULARITY, UNIFORMITY.—*Antonyms.* See DISTORTION, FORMLESSNESS.

---

sympathizer, *n.* pitier, condoler; friend, well-wisher, advocate, champion, partisan. See PITY.
sympathy, *n.* compassion, commiseration, pity; fellow-feeling, tenderness, affection, tolerance, consideration; harmony, accord. See CONDOLENCE, FEELING, TOUCH.
symptom, *n.* token, sign, denotation, diagnostic. See INDICATION.
synchromism, *n.* coexistence, coincidence, concurrence, synchronization. See SIMULTANEOUSNESS.
syndicate, *n.* board, directorate; alliance, league, union. See COUNCIL, PARTY.
synonym, *n.* equivalent, pœcilonym (*rare*): *opposite of* antonym. See INTERPRETATION.
synonymous, *adj.* equal, equivalent, equipollent, tantamount. See MEANING.

system, *n.* method, organization, regularity, uniformity; scheme, design, arrangement; custom, routine. See ORDER, PLAN, RULE.
systematize, *v.* regulate, classify, methodize, organize, standardize; arrange, systemize. See ORDER, PLAN.

T

table, *n.* synopsis, compendium, file, index, record; plate, tablet, slab; fare, menu *cuisine* (*F.*); stand, desk, board, counter. See ARRANGEMENT, FLATNESS, FOOD, SUPPORT.

TACITURNITY.—I. *Nouns.* **taciturnity,** silence, muteness, pauciloquy, laconism, laconicism, obmutescence (*rare*); uncommunicativeness, reserve, reticence, reticency.
man of few words, man of silence, reticent person, clam (*U. S.*); Spartan, Laconian.
II. *Verbs.* **be taciturn,** keep silence, hold one's tongue, say nothing, remain mum; put a padlock on the lips (*or* mouth), put a bridle on one's tongue, keep one's tongue between one's teeth, not let a word escape one, make no sign, not have a word to say, be mute.
III. *Adjectives.* **taciturn,** silent (*esp. habitually*), mum, mute, still, dumb, word-bound; close, close-mouthed, close-tongued, reserved, reticent, laconic, unsociable, uncommunicative; pauciloquent, concise, sententious, curt, sparing of words.
See also CONCEALMENT, DUMBNESS, SILENCE.—*Antonyms.* See LOQUACITY.

---

tack, *n.* yaw (*naut.*), echelon (*mil.*), zigzag, sidling; path, road, route, course. See DEVIATION, WAY.
tackle, *v.* grapple with, seize (*as in football*); undertake, attempt. See TAKING, UNDERTAKING.
tact, *n.* discernment, insight, penetration; address, discretion, finesse, *savoir-faire* (*F.*). See DISCRIMINATION, SKILL.
tactful, *adj.* diplomatic, conciliatory. See COURTESY.
tag, *n.* tag, pendant; tail, tip, stub; label, slip, ticket; cue, catchword, stock phrase, bob, refrain; appendage, afterpiece; shred, rag. See ADDITION, END, INDICATION, REPETITION, SEQUEL, SMALLNESS.
tail, *n.* rudder; extremity, stub, tag; dock, appendage, cauda (*tech.*), caudal appendage; cue *or* queue, train. See AËRONAUTICS, END, REAR, SEQUEL.
tailor, *n.* garment maker, clothier. See CLOTHING.
taint, *v.* tinge, stain, tint, dye; corrupt, infect, contaminate, defile, vitiate. See COLOR, DETERIORATION.
taint, *n.* pollution, infection, contagion; stain, blot, brand, stigma, defilement; defect, flaw, blemish. See DISEASE, DISREPUTE, IMPERFECTION.
tainted, *adj.* high-flavored, gamy, high; imperfect, defective. See HEIGHT, IMPERFECTION.

TAKING.—I. *Nouns.* **taking,** seizing, seizure, capture, apprehension, arrest, caption (*chiefly Scot. law*), abduction, abstraction, removal, ablation (*chiefly tech.*), appropriation commandeering (*esp. mil.*), assumption, subtraction, subduction (*rare*); acquisition, reception.
dispossession, deprivation, disseizin *or* disseisin (*law*), ademption (*law*), bereavement, disinheritance; attachment, execution, sequestration, confiscation, eviction, ejectment, ejection.
rapacity, greed, graspingness, avidity, avarice, rapaciousness; extortion, bloodsucking, vampirism; theft.
taker, accepter, receiver; captor, capturer; dispossessor, disseizor *or* disseisor (*law*); extortioner *or* extortionist; vampire.
II. *Verbs.* take, grasp, seize, grab, grip, clutch, gripe, hold, snatch, clasp, lay hold of; cull, pluck, gather, pick, draw, crop, reap.

[to get control or possession] **capture,** catch, collar (*colloq.*), seize, tackle (*as in football*), grapple, embrace, bag, net, hook, claw, throttle; get, have, gain, win, pocket, secure, captivate (*archaic in the literal sense*), acquire, attain, procure, entrap, ensnare; take prisoner, arrest, apprehend, lay by the heels, overthrow, conquer, cause to surrender; abstract, take away, take off, run away with, abduct, kidnap; steal upon, pounce (*or* spring) upon, swoop down upon, take by storm (*or* assault).

appropriate, assume, possess oneself of; commandeer (*colloq.*), confiscate, impound, help oneself to, make free with, lay under contribution; intercept, scramble for; deprive of.

dispossess, take from, take away from, tear from, tear away from, wrench (wrest, *or* wring) from, extort; deprive of, bereave; disinherit; oust, evict, eject, divest; levy, distrain (*law*); adeem (*law*), disseize *or* disseise (*law*), sequester, sequestrate, accroach, usurp; despoil, strip, fleece, bleed (*colloq.*).

purchase, buy, procure, coff (*Scot.: archaic*), engage, subscribe for (*as a magazine*); lease, hire, rent (*as, to* take *a house*).

steal, purloin, filch, bone (*slang*), prig (*slang*), pilfer, abstract, plunder, rifle, strip, loot, sack, pillage, swindle; embezzle, misapply, misappropriate.

move, bear, convey, remove, carry, transport, transfer, conduct, lead, escort.

quote, cite, extract, excerpt (*as, to* take *a line from Browning*).

deduce, derive, draw, infer, conclude, interpret; understand, comprehend.

charm, attract, allure, delight, captivate, fascinate, bewitch, engage.

choose, select, adopt, elect; espouse, marry, wed.

receive, accept, admit, entertain; contract, catch (*as a cold*); follow (*as advice*); undergo (*as treatment*), endure, tolerate, put up with.

require, need, necessitate, demand, claim, call for (*as, that* takes *brains*).

use, employ, occupy, consume, expend, use up, swallow up, absorb; avail oneself of, resort to (*as, to* take *a holiday*).

perform, act, do, operate, function, undertake, execute, negotiate.

surmount, clear, leap over, go over, top (*as, to* take *a* hurdle).

regard, look upon, consider, hold, suppose, call, count, esteem, deem (*as, I* took *him for a friend*).

find out, ascertain, determine, discover, decide, fix, settle (*as, to* take *one's bearings*).

feel, experience, conceive, bear, entertain, find (*as, to* take *offense*).

take advantage of, overreach, outwit; make the most of, profit by.—**take back,** retract, recall, revoke, recant, withdraw, retire; abjure, disavow.—**take in, 1,** embrace, encompass, inclose, comprise, include; **2, receive,** admit, get, entertain, accommodate, acquire, let in (*as,* take in *water;* take in *work*); **3, understand,** grasp, apprehend, discern, see, make out, perceive, believe, know, comprehend; **4, lessen,** shorten, diminish, reduce, furl (*a sail*), narrow, contract; **5, deceive,** cheat, defraud, trick, fool, hoax, impose upon.—**take up, 1,** lift, raise, hoist, pick up; gather up, absorb; **2, undertake,** enter upon, attempt, begin, set about, pursue, resume; **3, secure** (*as a dropped stitch*), fasten, fix gather together, catch; **4, engross,** occupy, engage, fill, absorb, immerse, enwrap, monopolize (*as, to* take up *one's time*); **5, collect** (*as a contribution*), send the hat round, gather in, demand, exact; **6, pay** (*as a note or loan*), satisfy, discharge, settle, meet, honor.—**take into custody,** take prisoner, arrest, seize, apprehend.

III. *Adjectives.* **taking,** attractive, pleasing, alluring, captivating, winning, charming, winsome, prepossessing.

catching, infectious, communicable, contagious, epidemic, pandemic; pestiferous, pestilential.

predatory, plundering, pillaging, predacious, raptorial (*zoöl.*), wolfish, rapacious, ravening, ravenous; parasitic.

See also ACQUISITION, BORROWING, DECEPTION, DEDUCTION, PURSUIT, RECEPTION, RETENTION, SKILL, STEALING, UNDERTAKING.—*Antonyms.* See RESTITUTION.

---

tale, *n.* story, yarn, anecdote, fable, narration, recital; tally, numbering, enumeration. See DESCRIPTION, NUMERATION.

talent, *n.* ability, cleverness, faculty, gift, aptitude, genius. See PART, SKILL.

talisman, *n.* amulet, charm, fetish, mascot. See [1]SPELL.

talk, *v.* converse, discuss, consult, chat, gossip; speak, say, utter, tell, declare. See CONVERSATION, SPEECH.

talk, *n.* converse, discourse; gossip, rumor, hearsay, report, scandal; utterance. parlance, address, lecture. See CONVERSATION, NEWS, SPEECH.
talkative, *adj.* loquacious, garrulous, chattering, fluent, glib. See LOQUACITY.
talkativeness, *n.* garrulity, verbosity, volubility, eloquence. See LOQUACITY.
talker, *n.* speaker, conversationalist, orator; chatterer, gossip. See CONVERSATION, LOQUACITY.
tall, *adj.* exaggerated; high, lofty, towering, soaring, delevate; lank. See EXAGGERATION, HEIGHT, LENGTH.
tally, *n.* stub, duplicate, tag, label, badge; score, file, row; tale, roll call, muster. See INDICATION, LIST, NUMERATION.
tally, *v.* agree, match, conform, square. See CORRESPONDENCE.
tame, *adj.* gentle, meek, subdued, submissive, unresisting; feeble, dull, flat, insipid, vapid, jejune. See INEXCITABILITY, MILDNESS.
tame, *v.* domesticate, train, break in; master, subdue. See DOMESTICATION, SUBJECTION.
tamper, *v.* meddle, interfere; alter, vary, diversify; bribe, adulterate, alloy, doctor (*colloq.*): *usually followed by* with. See ACTIVITY, CHANGE, DETERIORATION.
tang, *n.* nip, keenness; relish, smack, flavor, savor. See PUNGENCY, TASTE.
tangible, *adj.* material, embodied, sensible, palpable, evident; real, touchable, tactile; solid, stable, substantial. See MATERIALITY, TOUCH, TRUTH.
tangle, *n.* jumble, snarl, disorder; quandary, dilemma. See DERANGEMENT, UNCERTAINTY.
tantalize, *v.* lure, tempt; tease, torment, disappoint, balk. See DESIRE, DISAPPOINTMENT.
[1]**tap,** *v.* strike, rap, smack, pat; thump, crack. See IMPULSE, SNAR.
[2]**tap,** *v.* draw off, broach; pierce, bore, perforate. See EJECTION, OPENING.
taper, *v.* narrow, diminish, lessen. See NARROWNESS.
tardy, *adj.* late, dilatory, slow, overdue, behindhand. See LATENESS.
tarnish, *v.* dull, discolor, stain; taint, slur, brand, defame; soil, smear, smirch, smudge, sully. See BLEMISH, DISREPUTE, UNCLEANNESS.
tarry, *v.* delay, dally, lag, prolong, protract; wait, linger, loiter; rest, stay, remain. See DURABILITY, LATENESS, PERMANENCE.
tart, *adj.* sarcastic, severe, crusty, crabbed; acrid, sharp, austere, sour, astringent. See DISCOURTESY, ROUGHNESS.
task, *n.* work, toil, job, stint, mission, charge, duty; lesson, assignment, exercise. See BUSINESS, TEACHING.
task, *v.* tax, strain, overwork; put to task. See FATIGUE, USE.

TASTE.—I. *Nouns.* **taste,** flavor, gusto, gust (*archaic*), goût (*F.*), sapidity, savor; relish, piquancy; gustation; tooth (fig.).
[*organ of taste*] **tongue,** lingua (*pl.* linguæ: *tech.*), lingula (*pl.* lingulæ: *tech.*); palate.
touch, smack, tang, twang (*dial. Eng.*), aftertaste, spice, streak, vein, strain, hint, suggestion, dash, shade, thought, *soupçon* (*F.*).
morsel, bit, sample, sip, mouthful, bite, fragment.
[*intellectual relish*] **liking,** fondness, predilection, partiality, appetite, desire (*as, a* taste *for literature*).
discrimination, discernment, acumen, acuteness, penetration, judgment, refinement, distinction, delicacy, fine feeling; good (refined, *or* cultivated) taste, cultivation, culture, grace, polish, elegance, tact, finesse, virtuosity, æstheticism *or* estheticism.
style, manner, *ton* (*F.*), good usage, custom, form, conventionality, the thing, correctness (*as, in good* taste).
science of taste: æsthetics *or* esthetics.
man of taste, connoisseur, judge, critic, *cognoscente* (*It.; pl. cognoscenti*), virtuoso, amateur, dilettante, æsthetician *or* esthetician, purist, precisian; *arbiter elegantiæ* (*L.*), *arbiter elegantiarum* (*L.*); Aristarchus, Corinthian; Aristotle, Stagirite.

II. *Verbs.* **taste,** try the flavor of, partake of, savor, smack, sip, smatch (*dial. Eng.*), flavor, degust, degustate (*rare*), relish; tickle the palate, smack the lips
experience, undergo, assay, feel, perceive, meet, have, encounter.
[*to display taste*] **discriminate,** discern, distinguish, differentiate, judge, criticize.
III. *Adjectives.* **tasteful,** tasty, savory, palatable, tastable, gustable (*rare*), appetizing, toothsome, toothy (*colloq.*), relishable, gustful, gusty (*chiefly Scot.*), gustatory, gustative, sapid, saporous, saporific, delicious, flavorous, flavorsome, flavored, spiced (*as, a* tasty *dish*).
[*in good taste*] **refined,** cultured, elegant, polished, discriminative, æsthetic *or* esthetic, artistic, cultivated, attractive, charming, dainty, tasty (*colloq. or vulgar in this sense*), graceful; unaffected, pure, chaste, classical, Attic; prim, precise, formal; *simplex munditiis* (*L.*).
to one's taste, to one's mind, after one's own heart (*or* fancy), *comme il faut* (*F.*).
IV. *Adverbs.* **tastefully,** refinedly, etc. (see *adjectives*); with quiet elegance, with elegant simplicity; without ostentation.

See also DISCRIMINATION, ELEGANCE, SAVORINESS, TOUCH.—*Antonyms.* See INSIPIDITY, VULGARITY.

---

tasteless, *adj.* flat, insipid, unflavored, watery. See INSIPIDITY.
tattle, *v.* chatter, gossip, prate. See CONVERSATION.
tattler, *n.* chatterer, magpie; gossip, newsmonger, talebearer. See CONVERSATION, NEWS.
taunt, *v.* reproach, deride, twit, jeer at. See ACCUSATION.
tautology, *n.* wordiness, verbosity, redundance. See DIFFUSENESS.
tawdry, *adj.* showy, flashy, loud, gaudy, garish. See VULGARITY.
tax, *n.* impost, duty, toll, tariff, levy, custom, assessment. See DUTY, PRICE.
tax, *v.* charge, accuse, censure; demand, require, exact, impose; overtax, strain; audit; assess, enact; task, put to task. See ACCUSATION, COMMAND, FATIGUE, INQUIRY, PRICE, USE.
taxable, *adj.* assessable, dutiable, ratable. See PRICE.
taxation, *n.* assessment, capitation, exaction, levy. See PRICE.
taxicab, *n.* motor cab, taxi (*colloq.*). See VEHICLE.
taxonomy, *n.* classification, categorization. See ZOÖLOGY.

TEACHER.—*Nouns.* **teacher,** instructor (*masc. or fem.*), instructress (*fem.*), preceptor, preceptress (*fem.*), trainer, master, tutor, schoolmaster, schoolmistress (*fem.*); schoolma'am (*U. S. dial.*), mistress, kindergartner, pupil teacher, governess, dominie (*Scot.*), pedagogue, director, bear leader (*jocose*), dry nurse (*slang*), munshi (*Moham.*), khoja (*Turkish*), usher (*Brit.*), guru (*India*), pædotribe (*gymnastics*), *maestro* (*It.*: *music*), mystagogue (*as in the early Christian church*); educator, principal, professor, lecturer, reader, coryphæus (*Oxford*), don (*University cant*), coach (*colloq.*), crammer (*colloq.*); preacher, pastor, catechist; *privatdocent or docent* (*Ger.; pl. docenten*).
[*collective*] **faculty,** professorate, body of instructors, teaching staff.
guide, counselor, adviser, mentor, pioneer, apostle, missionary, propagandist; example, pattern, model.
instructorship, teachership (*rare*), mastership, preceptorship, tutorship, professorship, chair, fellowship.

See also INTERPRETER, SCHOOL.—*Antonyms.* See LEARNER.

TEACHING.—I. *Nouns.* **teaching,** instruction, education, tuition, tutorship, tutelage; pedagogics, pedagogy, didactics; edification, inculcation, indoctrination, initiation, direction, guidance; doctrine, lore.
preparation, qualification, training, schooling, discipline; drill, practice.
lesson, lecture, recitation, sermon, homily, harangue, prelection *or* prælection, discourse, explanation, interpretation, disquisition; apologue, parable; exercise, task, example (*as in arith.*); assignment, imposition; curriculum, course; Chautauqua, educational entertainment, lyceum, university extension.
II. *Verbs.* **teach,** instruct, educate, edify, school, tutor, cram (*colloq.*), grind (*colloq.*), prime, coach, profess; enlighten, inform, direct, guide, show; give

lessons in; inculcate, infuse, instill, imbue, impregnate, implant; disseminate, propagate; indoctrinate, expound, explain, interpret; lecture, hold forth, preach, sermonize, moralize; sharpen the wits, enlarge the mind, open the eyes, bring forward, "teach the young idea how to shoot" (Thomson).

train, rear, discipline, form, ground, prepare, qualify, drill, exercise, practice, familiarize with, inure, initiate, graduate.

III. *Adjectives.* **educational,** scholastic, academic, disciplinary, instructive, informative, pedagogic *or* pedagogical, didactic, doctrinal, homiletic *or* homiletical, propædeutic *or* propædeutical; coeducational; cultural, humanistic, humane; pragmatic, practical, utilitarian; naturalistic, scientific, psychological, eclectic; prevocational, vocational.

See also INFORMATION, INTERPRETATION.—*Antonyms.* See LEARNING, MISTEACHING.

---

team, *n.* crew, side; pair, span, tandem, rig (*U. S.*). See PARTY, VEHICLE.

tear, *v.* burst, split, slit, rend, rive, sever, lacerate; rave, rage, rant; hasten, run, race, rush, dash, fly. See DISJUNCTION, EXCITABILITY, VELOCITY.

tearful, *adj.* lachrymose, weeping, mournful. See LAMENTING.

tease, *v.* plague, vex, annoy, pester, harass; importune, beg. See PAIN, REQUEST.

technique, *n.* technic, finish, execution. See SKILL.

tedious, *adj.* dull, dry, wearisome, uninteresting. See DRYNESS, WEARINESS.

tediousness, *n.* tedium, dullness, dreariness, wearisomeness. See DRYNESS, WEARINESS.

tedium, *n.* tiresomeness, irksomeness, monotony. See WEARINESS.

teem, *v.* produce, bear, generate, multiply; abound, exuberate. See PRODUCTIVENESS, SUFFICIENCY.

telegram, *n.* telegraphic message, wire (*colloq.*), cablegram, cable (*colloq.*), wireless (*colloq.*), radiotelegram, marconigram. See NEWS.

telegraph, *n.* signal; cable, wire (*colloq.*), wireless (*colloq.*), radio. See INDICATION, MESSENGER.

telepathy, *n.* thought transference, telepathic transmission. See PSYCHICAL RESEARCH.

telephone, *n.* phone (*colloq.*); radiophone, wireless telephone. See MESSENGER.

telescope, *n.* spyglass, field glass; equatorial. See OPTICAL INSTRUMENTS.

tell, *v.* describe, narrate, recount, explain; count, weigh; inform, acquaint, advise; speak, utter, declare, state. See DESCRIPTION, INFLUENCE, INFORMATION, SPEECH.

temerity, *n.* audacity, impetuosity, incautiousness. See RASHNESS.

temper, *v.* harden, anneal, steel; mollify, moderate, soften. See HARDNESS, MODERATION.

temper, *n.* spleen, ill temper; solidity, rigidity, toughness; anger, passion; nature, character, type, quality, structure, disposition, temperament. See DISCOURTESY, HARDNESS, IRASCIBILITY, SUBJECTIVENESS.

temperament, *n.* disposition, make-up; nature, propensity. See SUBJECTIVENESS, TENDENCY.

TEMPERANCE.—1. *Nouns.* **temperance,** moderation, frugality, sobriety, soberness, forbearance, abnegation; self-denial, self-restraint, self-control.

abstinence, abstemiousness, asceticism; vegetarianism; teetotalism, total abstinence, Rechabitism, nephalism (*rare*), prohibition (*when observed*), Encratism (*hist.*); Pythagoreanism, Stoicism.

abstainer, abstinent, ascetic; gymnosophist (*India*), Pythagorean, Stoic; nephalist (*rare*), Rechabite, teetotaler, prohibitionist, dry (*slang*); vegetarian, fruitarian.

II. *Verbs.* **be temperate,** abstain, forbear, refrain, deny oneself, spare, refrain from indulgence; look not upon the wine when it is red; get on the water wagon (*slang*), take the pledge.

III. *Adjectives.* **temperate,** moderate, sober, frugal, sparing; abstemious, abstinent, teetotal; nonalcoholic, nonintoxicating; self-denying, self-controlled, self-restraining, ascetic, austere.
[*of climate or temperature*] **mild,** balmy, clement, cool, calm, moderate.
See also ASCETICISM, MILDNESS, MODERATION, SOBRIETY.—*Antonyms.* See INTEMPERANCE.

---

tempest, *n.* storm, hurricane, blizzard, cyclone, tornado. See AGITATION, WIND.
tempestuous, *adj.* boisterous, turbulent, violent, stormy. See ROUGHNESS.

TEMPLE.—I. *Nouns.* **temple,** fane (*archaic or poetic*), place of worship, sanctuary, house of God, house of prayer; cathedral, *duomo* (*It.; pl. duomi*), minster, church, basilica, kirk (*Scot. and dial. Eng.*), chapel, meeting-house, conventicle, holy place, chantry, oratory.
synagogue, tabernacle; mosque (*Moham.*), masjid (*Moham.*), dewal (*Hindu*), kiack (*Buddhist*), pagoda, Chinese temple, joss house (*colloq.*); pantheon, naos *or* cella (*arch.*), sacellum (*pl.* sacella: *Roman religion, also eccl.*); shrine, delubrum (*pl.* delubra: *Roman*), dagoba (*India*); tope *or* stupa (*Buddhist*).
[*conventual establishment*] **convent** (*for men or women, but usually women*), cloister, nunnery (*for nuns*), monastery, monkery, charterhouse (*Carthusian: archaic*), priory, friary, abbey, cenoby (*rare*), math (*Hindu*), lamasery (*as in Tibet*), khankah (*Moham.*), vihara (*Buddhist or Jain*); preceptory, commandery.
parsonage, rectory, vicarage, manse, deanery, clergy house; bishop's palace; Vatican.
pulpit, desk, ambo (*early Christian*), rostrum, platform; lectern, reading desk.
II. *Adjectives.* **cloistered,** cloistral, claustral, monachal, monastic, monasterial, conventual, abbatial; churchly, ecclesiastical, sacerdotal.
See also CHURCHDOM, CLERGY, RITE.

---

temporal, *adj.* lay, secular, civil, political, profane; short-lived, transient, transitory, temporary, ephemeral. See LAITY, TRANSIENCE.
temporary, *adj.* brief, fleeting; temporal, ephemeral, impermanent. See TRANSIENCE.
tempt, *v.* attract, lure, allure, charm, captivate, fascinate. See DESIRE, MOTIVE.
tempter, *n.* coaxer, prompter, instigator; the Devil. See MOTIVE, SATAN.

TEN.—I. *Nouns.* **ten,** decade, decad (*now rare*), decuple, decapod (*ten-footed animal*), dicker (*as of hides*), decagon (*geom.*), decahedron (*geom.*), decastyle (*arch.*), decasyllable, decathlon (*Olympic games*), decemvir (*as in ancient Rome*), decemvirate; decennium, decennary; Decalogue.
[*metric measures*] decagram *or* decagramme, decaliter *or* decalitre, decare, decameter *or* decametre, decastere; decigram, deciliter, decimeter.
II. *Verbs.* multiply by ten, make tenfold, decuple.
III. *Adjectives.* **tenfold,** denary, decimal, decuple; decagonal, decahedral, decastyle (*arch.*), decasyllabic.

TENACITY.—I. *Nouns.* **tenacity,** toughness, strength, tenaciousness; cohesiveness, cohesion, adhesion; gumminess, glutinousness, stickiness, adhesiveness, viscidity, viscosity.
pertinacity, persistence *or* persistency, perseverance, doggedness, pertinaciousness, firmness, resoluteness, resolution, stubbornness, obstinacy.
[*of memory*] retentiveness, retentivity, retention; recollection, remembrance, readiness.
[*comparisons*] leather; gristle, cartilage; bulldog, leech.
II. *Adjectives.* **tenacious,** cohesive, tough, strong, resisting; adhesive, sticking, clingy, clinging, stringy, viscid, gummy, glutinous, gristly, cartilaginous, leathery, leatherlike, coriaceous; tough as whitleather (*or* white leather).
pertinacious, persistent, persevering, dogged, firm, constant, resolute, stubborn, obstinate, unyielding, unwavering.

[*of memory*] **retentive, retaining, grasping, apt to retain, unforgetting, unforgetful;** reliable, trustworthy.

See also COHERENCE, OBSTINACY, PERSEVERANCE, RESOLUTION, RETENTION.—*Antonyms.* See BRITTLENESS, IRRESOLUTION.

---

tenant, *n.* occupier, occupant, householder, lessee, renter. See INHABITANT, POSSESSOR.

[1]**tend,** *v.* attend, wait upon, take care of; serve, minister to. See AID, SERVANT.

TENDENCY.—I. *Nouns.* **tendency,** inclination, bent, leaning (*with* to *or* towards), affection, disposition, proclivity, bias, set, *penchant* (*F.*), warp, turn, tone, trend, drift, gravitation, aim, scope; aptness, aptitude, proneness, liability, propensity, susceptibility, predisposition, heredity (*biol.*), Mendel's law, Mendelianism *or* Mendelism, matrocliny (*from the mother*), patrocliny (*from the father*); quality, nature, temperament, idiosyncrasy; cast, vein, grain, humor mood; import, purport.

II. *Verbs.* [2]**tend,** incline, trend, gravitate towards, work towards, move towards, lean, warp, turn, bend to; predispose, serve, conduce, lead, promote, be directed to, contribute, influence, dispose, verge, affect; carry, redound to, bid fair to.

III. *Adjectives.* **tending,** conducive, working towards, in a fair way to, likely to, calculated to; subservient, instrumental, useful; subsidiary, accessory; inclining, inclined, apt, liable, prone, disposed, predisposed, matroclinous (*biol.*), patroclinous (*biol.*).

See also DIRECTION, LIABILITY.—*Antonyms.* See CONTRARIETY, REPULSION.

---

tender, *v.* proffer, present; bid, propose, suggest. See OFFER.

tender, *adj.* kind, merciful, humane; delicate, subdued; loving, compassionate, sympathetic; gentle, soft-hearted, courteous; weak, fragile; callow, immature, youthful. See BENEVOLENCE, COLOR, LOVE, SOFTNESS, WEAKNESS, YOUTH.

tenet, *n.* dogma, doctrine, creed. See BELIEF.

tenor, *n.* course, trend, tendency; sense, drift, purport; vocalist, singer; viola, tenor viol; nature, character. See DIRECTION, MEANING, MUSICIAN, MUSICAL INSTRUMENTS, SUBJECTIVENESS.

tense, *adj.* rigid, stiff, taut; intent, rapt. See HARDNESS, THOUGHT.

tent, *n.* canvas, marquee, tepee. See COVERING, HABITATION.

tentative, *adj.* experimental, probationary, makeshift, temporary. See ESSAY.

tenuous, *adj.* thin, rare, subtle, unsubstantial, rarefied. See GASEITY.

tenure, *n.* holding, tenancy, occupation. See POSSESSION.

tepid, *adj.* lukewarm, warm, mild; moderate. See HEAT.

term, *n.* end, bound, boundary post, termination, terminus; expression, locution, word, phrase; period, duration, span, season. See LIMIT, NOMENCLATURE, TIME.

termination, *n.* end, ending, consequence, issue, result, conclusion; boundary, term, terminus, terminal. See EVENT, LIMIT.

terminology, *n.* technical expressions, technology, glossology. See NOMENCLATURE.

terrestrial, *adj.* earthly, worldly, mundane. See LAND.

terrible, *adj.* terrific, terrifying, fearful, appalling, frightful. See FEAR.

terrify, *v.* frighten, startle, alarm, horrify, appall. See FEAR.

territorial, *adj.* regional, sectional, topographical. See REGION.

territory, *n.* state, kingdom, realm; tract, area, district. See PROPERTY, REGION.

terror, *n.* dread, alarm, fright, horror, dismay, panic. See FEAR.

terse, *adj.* concise, brief, short, laconic, crisp, pithy. See CONCISENESS.

test, *n.* trial, attempt, essay, probation, examination, proof. See EXPERIMENT.

Testament, *n.* Old Testament, New Testament. See SCRIPTURES.

testator, *n.* grantor, devisor (*law*), bequeather. See GIVING.

testify, *v.* affirm, avow, support, attest, witness, certify. See EVIDENCE

testimony, *n.* admission, declaration, attestation, affirmation. See EVIDENCE.
tether, *v.* picket, tie, stake, chain, fasten. See JUNCTION, LOCATION, RESTRAINT.
text, *n.* matter, letterpress; subject, theme. See PRINTING, TOPIC.

TEXTURE.—I. *Nouns.* **texture,** arrangement, disposition, contexture, intertexture, constitution, character, structure, make, organization; tissue, grit (*of stone*), grain, fiber *or* fibre, nap, tooth, surface, warp and woof (*or* weft); fineness (*or* coarseness) of grain.
fabric, textile, cloth, stuff, web, tissue, webbing, gossamer; homespun, frieze, linsey-woolsey, fustian; drill, twill, tweed, serge, etc.
[*in biology*] tissue, muscle, cartilage, parenchyma, prosenchyma, tracheal tissue, vascular tissue, fibrous tissue, connective tissue, muscular tissue, adipose tissue, nervous tissue.
II. *Adjectives.* **textural,** textile, woven, textorial (*rare*), textrine (*rare*); coarse-grained, homespun; fine-grained, fine, delicate, subtle, gossamery, filmy; ingrain, ingrained.
See also STRUCTURE.

---

thankful, *adj.* grateful, appreciative. See GRATITUDE.
thankless, *adj.* unthankful, ungrateful, ingrate. See INGRATITUDE.
thanks, *n.* thankfulness, acknowledgment, grace. See GRATITUDE.
thanks! *interj.* thank you! *merci!* (*F.*), gramercy! (*archaic*). See GRATITUDE.
thanksgiving, *n.* giving thanks; grace, praise, laudation. See GRATITUDE, WORSHIP.
thaw, *v.* melt, dissolve, liquefy, run, fuse; unbend, soften. See HEAT, SOFTNESS.
theater, *n.* scene of action, field of operations; playhouse, the drama. See ARENA, DRAMA.
theatrical, *adj.* affected, stilted, unnatural, stagy; dramatic, histrionic; spectacular. See AFFECTATION, DRAMA, OSTENTATION.
theft, *n.* thievery, robbery, swindling, cheating, larceny. See STEALING.
theme, *n.* essay, thesis, treatise; subject, matter, text. See DISSERTATION, TOPIC.
then, *adv.* therefore, wherefore, consequently; at that time, immediately, afterward, later. See REASONING, TIME.

THEOLOGY.—I. *Nouns.* **theology,** science of God, science of religion; theosophy, divine wisdom; divinity, hierology, hogiology, hagiography; monotheism, theism, religion; religious persuasion (sect, denomination, *or* affiliation); creed, articles (declaration, profession, *or* confession) of faith.
theologian, divine, theologist (*now rare*), theologue (*now rare*), theologus (*L. pl.* theologi), theolog (*cant*), theologaster (*a quack in theology: rare*); monotheist, theist; canonist, literalist, textualist, Schoolman, Scholastic, Christian philosopher; the Fathers.
II. *Adjectives.* **theological,** religious, divine, canonical, patristic *or* patristical; denominational, sectarian.
See also BELIEF.

---

theoretic, *adj.* abstract, pure, unapplied; theoretical, speculative. See PURITY, SUPPOSITION.
theorist, *n.* theorizer, speculatist (*rare*), doctrinaire. See SUPPOSITION.
theory, *n.* surmise, conjecture, speculation, principle. See SUPPOSITION.
therefore, *adv.* hence, consequently, accordingly, so. See ATTRIBUTION, REASONING.
thermal unit, calorie, heat unit. See HEAT.

THERMOMETER.—*Nouns.* **thermometer,** mercury, glass (*both popular*); calorimeter, respiration calorimeter, clinical thermometer; thermopile, pyrometer, thermoelectric thermometer; thermometrograph, thermoscope *or* differential thermometer; thermostat *or* thermoregulator, telethermometer; register (*or* self-registering) thermometer; gas (metallic, electric, resistance, *or* platinum) thermometer; Fahrenheit, Centigrade, Reaumur.

thesis, *n.* essay, theme, treatise; proposition. See DISSERTATION, TOPIC.
thicket, *n.* copse, coppice, canebrake, covert, bosk, bosket. See VEGETABLE.

THICKNESS.—I. *Nouns.* **thickness,** density, denseness, solidity, compactness, crowdedness, closeness, heaviness; diameter, bore; coarseness, grossness.
stiffening, spissitude, inspissation, coagulation, solidification, jellification, condensation, concentration; viscosity, stiffness; clot, coagulum.
II. *Verbs.* **thicken,** widen, inspissate; solidify, stiffen, harden, compact, coagulate, clot, curdle, set, jelly, congeal, cake, candy, concrete, petrify; deepen, intensify, darken, becloud, roil, bemire, befoul.
III. *Adjectives.* **thick,** dense, compact, close, solid, bulky; dumpy, squat, squab, thickset, stubby, chunky (*U. S.*), squatty, stumpy (*colloq.*), stocky; gross, coarse, heavy, crass; deep, intense, profound, excessive.
numerous, abundant, frequent, crowded, packed.
[*of fluids*] **dense,** inspissated, coagulated, firm, condensed, evaporated, viscous, viscid; clotted, grumous; sedimental, feculent, roily, roiled, turbid, muddy.
[*of the weather*] **cloudy,** foggy, misty, hazy, murky, vaporous.
[*of the voice*] **inarticulate,** indistinct, obscure, confused, muffled, blurred, indistinguishable.
[*of the mind*] **stupid,** dense, **dull, crass,** obtuse, wooden, unintelligent, stolid, dumb (*colloq.*).
intimate, friendly, familiar, confidential, inseparable, chummy (*colloq.*), thick as thieves: *in this sense,* thick *is colloq.*
IV. *Adverbs.* **thickly,** densely, compactly, etc. (see *adjectives*).
See also ASSEMBLAGE, BREADTH, DENSITY, HEAVINESS, SEMILIQUIDITY, SIZE.—*Antonyms.* See THINNESS.

THIEF.—*Nouns.* **thief,** robber, *homo trium literarum* (*L.*), crook (*slang*), spoiler, depredator, pillager, marauder; harpy, shark (*slang*), land pirate, *chor* (*Hind.*); rustler (*U. S.*), cattle thief; poacher, kidnaper *or* kidnapper; blackmailer, shoplifter, smuggler, contrabandist; filcher, rifler, pilferer, plagiarist; kleptomaniac.
pirate, corsair, viking, buccaneer, privateer, runner (*colloq.*), rum runner, hijacker (*slang*); Paul Jones.
brigand, bandit, filibuster, freebooter, dacoit (*India*), thug, bushranger, mosstrooper (*hist.*), road agent (*Western U. S.*), highwayman, footpad, nighthawk, strong-arm man (*U. S.*), holdup (*U. S. slang*).
Dick Turpin, Claude Duval, Jonathan Wild, Macheath, Nevison.
pickpocket, cutpurse, dip (*slang*), pickpurse (*rare*), gonoph (*Eng. slang*), dipper (*slang*); light-fingered gentry.
Autolycus, Jeremy Diddler, Robert Macaire, Artful Dodger.
swindler, peculator, fleecer, sharper, *chevalier d'industrie* (*F.*), hawk, trickster, welsher (*slang*), defaulter, embezzler, thimblerigger, bunkoman, skin (*slang*), rook (*esp. at dice or cards*), card sharper, card cheat, diddler (*slang*), wrong 'un (*slang*), spieler (*Australia*); forger, coiner, counterfeiter; fence, receiver of stolen goods, swagman (*cant*); swell mob (*generic: slang*), flash gentry (*slang*).
burglar, housebreaker, yeggman *or* yegg (*slang*), cracksman (*slang*), magsman (*slang*), sneak thief; second-story thief; Bill Sikes, Jack Sheppard.
See also STEALING.

---

thievish, *adj.* thieving, larcenous, predatory. See STEALING.
thing, *n.* article, object, something; entity, person, creature, being. See MATERIALITY, SUBSTANTIALITY.
think, *v.* hold, opine, conceive, surmise, presume; understand, reason, reflect, meditate, speculate. See BELIEF, THOUGHT.

THINNESS.—I. *Nouns.* **thinness,** slenderness, fineness, slimness, etc. (see *adjectives*); attenuation, tenuity, emaciation, leanness.
[*comparisons*] lath, shaving, wafer, rail, strip, skeleton, shadow, thread, scrag; mere skin and bone.
II. *Verbs.* **thin,** make (*or* become) thin, reduce, diminish, curtail, remove; prune, thin out, eliminate; attenuate, rarefy; dilute, water, adulterate.
III. *Adjectives.* **thin,** slender, fine, slim, delicate, slight, threadlike, tenuous.
lean, slim, slender; spare, lank, lanky, gaunt, bony, skinny, scrawny, scraggy

emaciated, spare, meager, rawboned, weedy (*colloq.*), spindly (*colloq.*), lathy (*colloq.*); spindle-legged, spindle-shanked, spindling; pinched, starved, shriveled, attenuated; worn to a shadow; "lean as a rake" (*Chaucer*), skeletal, hatchet-faced, lantern-jawed.

[*not dense*] **rare,** rarefied, fine, subtile (*archaic*), subtle, unsubstantial, imponderable, tenuous (*as,* thin *air*).

[*not full or crowded*] **scanty,** inadequate, insufficient, meager, spare, sparse (*as, a* thin *attendance*).

shrill, high-pitched, faint, feeble, weak (*as, a* thin *voice*).

transparent, diaphanous, flimsy, sleazy, sheer, slight, frail, shallow (*as, a* thin *disguise*).

See also FEWNESS, INSUFFICIENCY, RARITY, WEAKNESS.—*Antonyms.* See THICKNESS.

---

thirst, *n.* craving, longing (*as for knowledge or for liquid*). See DESIRE.

thorn, *n.* bramble, brier, spine, prickle; annoyance, pest. See BANE.

thorny, *adj.* vexations, trying, difficult; peevish, bad-tempered; spiny, barbed, prickly. See DIFFICULTY, DISCOURTESY, SHARPNESS.

thorough, *adj.* radical, sweeping, absolute, complete; exhaustive, consummate; regular (*colloq.*), unmitigated; consistent, constant. See COMPLETENESS, COMPLETION, REGULARITY, UNIFORMITY.

thoroughfare, *n.* roadway, highway, street, avenue. See WAY.

THOUGHT.—I. *Nouns.* **thought,** reflection, thoughtfulness, cogitation, consideration, contemplation, rumination, meditation, study, speculation, deliberation, lucubration, mentation, brainwork, cerebration; understanding, perception, consciousness, intellect; current (*or* train) of thought, association of ideas; close study, application.

abstraction, absorption, engrossment; musing, reverie, brown study, self-communing, self-consultation; depth of thought.

second thought (*or* thoughts), reconsideration, reëxamination, review, retrospection, introversion, excogitation, mature thought; afterthought, subsequent reflection.

solicitude, concern, anxiety, care, anxiousness, worry, uneasiness, heed, reck (*poetic*).

little, trifle, mite, shade, somewhat (*as, make it a* thought *larger: colloq.*).

[*that which is thought*] **idea,** notion, conception, fancy, imagining, imagination, opinion, view, belief; intention, design; recollection, memory.

II. *Verbs.* **think,** reflect, cogitate, consider, consult, take into consideration, reason, deliberate, contemplate, meditate, ponder, muse, dream, ruminate, speculate, fancy, trow (*archaic*), suppose, believe, conceive, brood over, mull over (*U. S. colloq.*), sweat over (*colloq.*), con over, study; bend (*or* apply) the mind; digest, discuss, hammer at, hammer out; weigh, realize, appreciate; rack (ransack, beat, *or* cudgel) one's brains, mentalize (*rare*), cerebrate, set one's wits to work.

harbor, cherish, entertain, nurture (*as an idea*), imagine; bear in mind; reconsider, turn over in the mind.

suggest itself, present itself, occur to, come into one's head; strike one, come uppermost; enter (cross, flash across, *or* occupy) the mind; have in one's mind; absorb, occupy, engross, enwrap.

III. *Adjectives.* **thoughtful,** pensive, thinking, meditative, reflective, cogitative, contemplative, deliberative, studious, museful, wistful, introspective, philosophical, speculative, metaphysical, abstract, abstruse; absorbed, rapt, engrossed in, intent, lost in thought, tense.

heedful, careful, attentive, mindful, regardful, watchful, conscientious (*as,* thoughtful *of his duty*).

considerate, concerned, anxious, solicitous, kindly, kind, kind-hearted, friendly neighborly (*as, a* thoughtful *act*): *opposite of* thoughtless.

IV. *Adverbs.* **thoughtfully,** pensively, etc. (see *adjectives*); all things considered; taking everything into consideration (*or* account).

See also ATTENTION, BELIEF, IDEA, IMAGINATION, INQUIRY, INTELLECT, INTELLIGENCE. MEMORY. WISDOM.—*Antonyms.* See VACUITY.

thoughtless, *adj.* inattentive, unheeding, heedless, inconsiderate, careless, neglectful; unthinking, unreasoning, unintellectual. See INATTENTION, VACUITY.

THOUSAND.—*Nouns.* **thousand,** chiliad, milliad (*rare*); millenary, millenium; chiliarch (*commander of 1000 men*); millepede, millipede, *or* milliped (*zoöl.*).
[*metric measures*] milligram *or* milligramme, milliliter *or* millilitre, millimeter *or* millimetre; kilogram *or* kilogramme, kiloliter *or* kilolitre, kilometer *or* kilometre, kilocycle (*ratio*).

---

thrash, *v.* beat, whip, lash, trounce; defeat, conquer. See PUNISHMENT, SUCCESS.

thread, *n.* yarn, twist, linen, cotton. See FILAMENT.

THREAT.—I. *Nouns.* **threat,** menace, intimidation, defiance, abuse, denunciation, commination, fulmination, thunder, thunderbolt; gathering clouds.
II. *Verbs.* **threaten,** menace, threat (*archaic*), alarm, frighten, overawe; snarl, growl, mutter, bully; defy, intimidate, forebode, warn, shake the fist at; thunder, fulminate, bluster, look daggers.
III. *Adjectives.* **threatening,** menacing, forbidding, minatory, minacious, comminatory, black, baneful, sinister, ominous, lowering, lowery *or* loury, imminent, impending, dire, ill-boding; denunciatory, abusive, defiant; *in terrorem* (*L.*); under the ban.
See also BLACKNESS, DANGER, DEFIANCE, FEAR, MALEDICTION, PREDICTION, UGLINESS, WARNING.

THREE.—I. *Nouns.* **three,** triplet, trio, ternion, tenary, trine (*rare*), trey (*cards, dice, or dominoes*), triplet, tierce, leash (*as of hares*); trinomial (*tech.*), trionym (*biol.*), cube, delta, triangle, triskelion *or* triskele, trigon, trinity, triunity trigraph, trilemma (*esp. logic*); trident, tripod, trireme, triumvirate; triality (*rare*), hat trick (*as in cricket*).
II. *Adjectives.* **three,** triform, tertiary, trinomial (*math. and biol.*), triune triple, treble, threefold.
triangular, trigonal, trigonous, triquetral (*rare*), triquetrous (*tech.*), deltoid, delta-shaped.
See also TRIPLICATION, TRISECTION.

---

three-sided, *adj.* trilateral (*geom.*), triquetrous (*tech.*). See SIDE.

threshold, *n.* doorsill, vestibule, entrance, beginning, outset. See EDGE.

thrift, *n.* thriftiness, frugality; growth, vigor (*as of a plant*). See ECONOMY, VEGETATION.

thriftless, *adj.* shiftless, unthrifty, wasteful, prodigal. See NONPREPARATION.

thrill, *n.* excitement, kick (*slang*), flutter, tremor. See FEELING.

thrive, *v.* prosper, flourish, succeed. See PROSPERITY.

throat, *n.* jugular region, gorge, gullet (*a loose use*), jugulum (*pl.* jugula: *zoöl.*); windpipe, weasand (*archaic*). See CHANNEL, OPENING.

throb, *v.* pulsate, beat, palpitate. See AGITATION.

throne, *n.* royal seat, chair of state; sovereign power. See SCEPTER.

throng, *n.* crowd, host, multitude, mob. See ASSEMBLAGE.

throttle, *v.* close, check; choke, strangle, stifle. See CLOSURE, KILLING.

through, *prep.* by, for, *per* (*L.*), by reason of, by way of; during, throughout. See INSTRUMENTALITY, TIME.

throw, *v.* fling, cast, pitch, toss, heave, hurl. See PROPULSION.

thrust, *n.* lunge, pass, jab (*colloq.*), cut; push, shove, start, propel. See ATTACK, IMPULSE.

thump, *v.* strike, hit, knock, beat, whack, pound. See IMPULSE.

thunder, *v.* peal, roar, boom, resound, roll, rumble; crack, crash. See LOUDNESS, RESONANCE, VIOLENCE.

thus, *adv.* in such wise, so, consequently. See CIRCUMSTANCE.

thwart, *v.* oppose, balk, frustrate, defeat, contravene. See HINDRANCE.

ticket, *n.* badge, label, check, notice, certificate; list (*of candidates*). See INDICATION, PLAN.
tickle, *v.* titillate; please, enliven, amuse. See ITCHING, PLEASURABLENESS.
ticklish, *adj.* delicate, critical, unstable, risky; tickly. See DIFFICULTY, ITCHING.
tide, *n.* flow, flood, current, stream. See RIVER.
tidings, *n. pl.* intelligence, information, message. See NEWS.
tidy, *adj.* neat, spruce, trim, trig; methodical, orderly, shipshape; considerable, substantial. See CLEANNESS, ORDER, SIZE.
tidy, *v.* arrange, order; trim, neaten (*rare*). See ARRANGEMENT, CLEANNESS.
tie, *v.* fasten, bind, secure, knot, unite, connect. See JUNCTION.
tie, *n.* necktie, neckerchief, cravat, bow; obligation, allegiance; dead heat, drawn game; link, bond; beam, post, sleeper; fastening, ligature, knot. See CLOTHING, DUTY, EQUALITY, RELATION, SUPPORT, VINCULUM.
tiger, *n.* tigress (*fem.*), cat; wild beast, destroyer; yell, cheer; attendant, groom, bell-boy. See ANIMAL, EVILDOER, REJOICING, SERVANT.
till, *prep.* until, to, up to. See TIME.
till, *v.* cultivate, plow, harrow, hoe, farm. See HUSBANDRY.
tilt, *n.* just *or* joust, bout, conflict; trip, slip, lurch; incline, slant, slope, tip. See CONTENTION, DESCENT, OBLIQUITY.
timber, *n.* wood, lumber, raff (*dial.*), stumpage (*U. S.*), beam; timberland, forest, woods; *Fig.:* material (*as, senatorial* timber). See MATERIALS, VEGETABLE.
timbre, *n.* tone color, quality, clang (*music*). See MELODY.

TIME.—I. *Nouns.* **time,** duration, period, term, tide (*archaic*), instar (*zoöl.*), stage, space, snap, span, spell, lifetime, season, course; present life, date, year, moment, hour; glass of time, ravages of time, whirligig of time, scythe of Time, noiseless foot of Time; the enemy (*colloq.*).
[*available or spare time*] **leisure,** ease, freedom, convenience, opportunity, liberty, chance (*as,* time *for reading*).
[*intermediate time*] **interval,** interim, meantime, while; interlude, recess, pause, interruption, intermission, interregnum; respite.
era, epoch, eon, kalpa (*Hindu*), yuga (*Hindu*), Manvantara (*Hindu*), cycle, age, reign, dynasty, administration.
II. *Verbs.* **continue,** last, endure, stay, go on, remain, persist, abide, run, subsist, dure (*archaic*), extend, prolong, sustain, carry on, stand, stick (*colloq.*), hold out, perpetuate, preserve.
pass time, spend (*or* while away) time, tide over; employ time, fill time, occupy time; consume time; seize an opportunity; linger on, drag on, tarry, waste time, procrastinate.
time, regulate, measure, adjust; keep time, harmonize with.
III. *Adverbs.* **meantime,** meanwhile, in the interim, in the meantime, *ad interim* (*L.*), during the interval, *pedente lite* (*law*); at the same time.
once, formerly, erstwhile (*archaic*); at one time, erst (*archaic or poetic*), once upon a time, one fine morning.
then, at that time (moment, *or* instant), on that occasion; soon afterward, immediately, hereupon, thereupon, whereupon; at another time, again, later.
when, at what time? on what occasion? how long ago? how soon? while, whereas, although; whenever, whensoever, at whatever time, as soon as.
IV. *Prepositions.* **during,** until, pending, in the time of; for the period of, over, through, throughout.
till, until, to, up to, as far as, down to, up to the time of.
V. *Conjunctions.* **until,** till, to the time when.
while, whilst (*esp. Brit.*), as long as, during the time that, whiles (*archaic*), at the same time as; although, whereas.
See also DURABILITY, EARLINESS, FUTURE, INSTANTANEITY, LAPSE, LATENESS, LEISURE, ORDER, PAST, PERIOD, PERPETUITY, [1]PRESENT, TIMELINESS.—*Antonyms* See TIMELESSNESS.

timekeeper, *n.* timepiece, clock, watch, hourglass; time recorder (*esp. for workmen or in sports and games*). See CHRONOMETRY.

TIMELESSNESS.—I. *Nouns.* **timelessness,** interminableness, boundlessness, endlessness, illimitableness, unendingness, eternity; absence of time, no time, *dies non* (*L.*), Greek Calends (*or* Kalends), Tib's eve (*or* St. Tib's eve: *there being no such saint*).

unseasonableness, intempestivity (*rare*), inopportuneness, untimeliness, prematureness: *in this sense,* timelessness *is archaic.*

II. *Adjectives.* **timeless,** interminable, unending, never-ending, eternal, everlasting, sempiternal, endless, boundless, illimitable, immeasurable.

unseasonable, inopportune, intempestive (*rare*), ill-timed, untimely, premature: *in this sense,* timeless *is archaic.*

III. *Adverbs.* **timelessly,** interminably, etc. (see *adjectives*); at no time, at no period, never, ne'er (*poetic*), *ad kalendas Græcas* (*L.*), on (*or* at) the Greek Calends, *jamais de ma vie* (*F.*), nevermore, on no occasion, *sine die* (*L.*).

Antonyms. See TIME, TIMELINESS.

TIMELINESS.—I. *Nouns.* **timeliness,** seasonableness, opportuneness, convenient time, fit (*or* proper) time, suitable time (*or* season), high time, nick of time; chance, opportunity, opening, occasion, show (*U. S. colloq.*), room, scope, space, place; *mollissima fandi tempora* (*L.*); golden opportunity, clear stage, fair field; spare time, leisure, liberty.

crisis, turning point, turn, emergency, juncture, conjuncture, rub, pinch; critical period, climacteric.

II. *Verbs.* **improve the occasion,** seize an opportunity, use (*or* profit by) an opportunity, strike the iron while it is hot, *battre le fer pendant qu'il est chaud* (*F.*), seize the present hour, make hay while the sun shines, take time by the forelock, *prendre la balle au bond* (*F.*).

III. *Adjectives.* **timely,** well-timed, opportune, seasonable, timeous (*rare or Scot.*), convenient (*archaic in this sense*), appropriate, suitable; lucky, providential, fortunate, happy, favorable, propitious, auspicious.

occasional, incidental, casual, accidental, extemporaneous, extemporary; contingent, provisional.

IV. *Adverbs.* **timely,** opportunely, seasonably, acceptably, timeously (*rare*), early, soon; in due time (course, *or* season), in good time, in the nick of time, just in time, at the eleventh hour; now or never.

by the way, by the by, in passing, *en passant* (*F.*), *à propos* (*F.*), *pro re nata* (*L.*), *pro hac vice* (*L.*); *par parenthèse* (*F.*), parenthetically, while on the subject, speaking of, *par exemple* (*F.*), for example; extempore, on the spur of the moment. See also EARLINESS, EXPEDIENCE.—*Antonyms.* See UNTIMELINESS.

---

timepiece, *n.* timekeeper, clock, watch, chronometer. See CHRONOMETRY

timesaver, *n.* temporizer, trimmer, opportunist. See APOSTASY.

timid, *adj.* diffident, timorous, faint-hearted, pusillanimous; nervous, fearful, afraid; weak, pliant, irresolute; shy, bashful, modest, demure, retiring. See FAINTNESS, FEAR, IRRESOLUTION, MODESTY.

tincture, *n.* tint, shade, hue, tone; tinge, touch, dash, smack. See COLOR MIXTURE.

tinder, *n.* spunk, amadou, punk, touchwood. See FUEL.

tinge, *n.* tint, shade, hue, tone; tincture, touch, dash, smack, *soupçon* (*F.*) See COLOR, MIXTURE.

tingle, *v.* thrill, sting, prickle. See ITCHING, PAIN.

tinkle, *v.* chink, clink, jingle. See FAINTNESS, RESONANCE.

tinsel, *n.* pretense, sham; finery, frippery. See DECEPTION, ORNAMENT.

tint, *n.* hue, tone, shade, tinge, tincture. See COLOR.

tiny, *adj.* minute, diminutive, wee, miniature, microscopic. See LITTLENESS.

[1]tip, *n.* point, extremity; top, vertex, apex, pinnacle, peak. See END, SUMMIT.

[2]tip, *n.* gratuity, fee, gift, donation, reward, perquisite; hint, suggestion, pointer (*U. S. colloq.*). See GIVING, INFORMATION.

tire, *v.* fatigue, weary, bother, bore, exhaust. See WEARINESS.

tiresome, *adj.* irksome, wearying, wearisome, monotonous. See WEARINESS.
tissue, *n.* set (*as of lies*), collection; web, network; tissue paper, onionskin, membrane; fabric, parenchyma (*bot.* and *zoöl.*), muscle, cartilage, etc. See ASSEMBLAGE, CROSSING, LAYER, TEXTURE.

TITLE.—I. *Nouns.* title, name, application, appellative, designation, epithet, denomination, style, dignity, honor.
[*personal appellations*] emperor, king, prince, duke, marquis, count, earl, lord, etc.; majesty, highness, excellency, grace, lordship, worship; reverence, reverend; esquire, sir, master, Mr., *monsieur* (*F.*), *signor* (*It.*), *señor* (*Sp.*), *Mein Herr* (*Ger.*), *Mynheer* (*Dutch*); your (*or* his) honor.
empress, queen, princess, duchess, marchioness, countess, lady; madam, *madame* (*F.*), ma'am (*used at the English court in addressing the queen or a royal princess, in general, colloq.*).
decoration, mark of honor; laurel, palm, wreath, garland, bays; medal, ribbon, cordon, cross, crown, coronet, star, garter; epaulet, chevron, *fourragère* (*F.*), colors, cockade; livery; order, arms, coat of arms, shield, escutcheon *or* scutcheon, crest; handle to one's name.
[*of a book, manuscript, etc.*] **name,** designation, leading title (*in the narrowest sense*), title-page; heading, head, caption (*chiefly U. S.*), legend (*as beneath an illustration*), inscription, lemma, division (*as of a statute*).
right, claim, due, part, prerogative, privilege; ownership, possession, possessorship, ground of claim.
II. *Verbs.* **title,** name, call, designate, entitle, term, denominate.
III. *Adjectives.* titled (*having a title*), noble, aristocratic, patrician.
See also MAN, NOBILITY, PROPERTY, RIGHT, RIGHTFULNESS, WOMAN.

---

toady, *n.* cringer, fawner, truckler, sycophant. See FLATTERER.
to and fro, back and forth. See OSCILLATION.
toast, *v.* heat, warm, dry, brown; drink to, honor, propose, pledge. See CALEFACTION, CELEBRATION, REPUTE.
tobacco, *n.* nicotine, smoke, cigar, cigarette, snuff. See PUNGENCY.—**tobacco pipe,** pipe, brier *or* briar, meerschaum, clay (*colloq.*), corncob, hookah. See RECEPTACLE.
together, *adv.* collectively, in a body, conjointly, mutually; simultaneously. See ACCOMPANIMENT, SIMULTANEOUSNESS.
toil, *n.* work, labor, grind, drudgery, exhaustion. See EXERTION, FATIGUE.
toilsome, *adj.* laborious, arduous, wearisome, hard. See PAINFULNESS.
token, *n.* sign, symbol, mark, trait, trace; reminder, memento, keepsake, souvenir. See INDICATION, MEMORY.
toleration, *n.* lenity, clemency, indulgence; tolerance, laxity, sufferance, concession, freedom. See MILDNESS, PERMISSION.
toll, *n.* duty, tax, impost. See PRICE.
tomb, *n.* grave, sepulcher, vault, mausoleum. See INTERMENT.
tomfoolery, *n.* mummery, fooling, escapade, nonsense. See ABSURDITY.
tone, *n.* quality, character, harmony; hue, shade, tint; tonality, intonation, accent, inflection, vibration; tenor, mood, condition. See COLOR, [1]SOUND, STATE.
tongue, *n.* speech, vernacular, dialect, accent, utterance, discourse; pole (*of a wagon*), neap (*U. S.*); lingua (*tech.*), organ of taste (*or* speech). See LANGUAGE, SUPPORT, TASTE.
tonic, *adj.* bracing, invigorating; sonant, voiced. See HEALTHINESS, LETTER.
too, *adv.* also, likewise, additionally. See ADDITION.
tool, *n.* puppet, cat's-paw; device, implement, utensil, machine; medium, vehicle, intermediary. See AUXILIARY, INSTRUMENT, INSTRUMENTALITY.
tooth, *n.* fang, tusk, snag, grinder (*slang*); barb, tine; discriminating taste, liking, fondness. See RETENTION, SHARPNESS, TASTE.
tooth-shaped, *adj.* toothlike, dentiform, odontoid. See SHARPNESS.
top, *n.* vertex, apex, crown, head, peak, tip, crest, acme. See SUMMIT.

TOPIC.—I. *Nouns.* **topic,** subject, matter, subject matter, *motif* (*F.*), theme, leitmotif *or Leitmotiv* (*Ger.: music*), thesis, text, locus (*rare*), business, affair, matter in hand, question, problem, commonplace (*logic*), maxim, theorem, proposition, motion, resolution, case, point; moot point, point at issue, debatable point; subject of thought, material for thought, food for the mind, mental pabulum, field of inquiry.
II. *Adjectives.* **topical,** local, limited, restricted, particular (*as, a* topical *remedy*); of topics, subjective.
[*not demonstrative*] **probable,** likely, presumable, presumptive, inconclusive, possible, on the cards.
III. *Adverbs.* **under consideration,** under advisement; in question, in the mind; at issue, before the house, on foot, on the carpet, on the tapis, *sur le tapis* (*F.*).
See also INQUIRY.

---

topmost, *adj.* highest, uppermost, chief, supreme, head. See SUMMIT.
torch, *n.* firebrand, flambeau, light. See FUEL.
torment, *n.* torture, agony, anguish, distress. See PAIN.
torpid, *adj.* inactive, passive, inert, dull, stupid, apathetic, sleepy, listless, sluggish, dormant. See INACTIVITY, INSENSITIVENESS.
torpor, *n.* inactivity, lethargy, coma, stupor. See INSENSITIVENESS.
torrid, *adj.* hot, tropical, arid, parching, burning. See HEAT.
torture, *n.* cruelty, persecution; torment, agony, anguish, excruciation. See MALEVOLENCE, PAIN.
torture, *v.* pervert, garble, misrepresent, distort, misapply; agonize, torment, rack. See DISTORTION, PUNISHMENT.
toss, *v.* agitate, disturb; tumble, sway, roll, pitch, heave; cast, fling, throw. See AGITATION, OSCILLATION, PROPULSION.
total, *n.* sum, aggregate, amount; all. See NUMBER, WHOLE.
total, *v.* add, sum up, reckon; amount to, come to. See ADDITION, MONEY.
totter, *v.* falter, stagger, sway, wabble; flag, fail. See SLOWNESS, WEAKNESS.

TOUCH.—I. *Nouns.* [*sensation of pressure*] **touch,** contact, taction, tangency, tact (*now rare in this sense*), tactility, palpability, feeling, feel, sensation, impact, attaint (*archaic*); contrectation (*rare, except in law*), handling, palpation (*esp. med.*), manipulation, stereognosis (*tech.*); kneading, rubbing, stroking, massage; licking, lambency; graze, brush, glance, lick, kiss, stroke.
[*organ of touch*] hand, dukes (*pl.: slang*), finger, forefinger, thumb, paw, feeler, palpus (*pl.* palpi: *zoöl.*), antenna (*pl.* antennæ), tongue.
[*close relation*] **harmony,** accord, agreement, accordance, understanding, comprehension, sympathy, correspondence, intercourse, communication, fellowship, *entente* (*F.*).
[*slight amount*] **dash,** trace, tinge, hint, suggestion, suspicion, *soupçon* (*F.*), **little,** grain, smack, taste, sprinkling; twinge (*as of pain*).
imperfection, defect, blemish, taint, fault, flaw, weakness (*as, a* touch *in the brain*).
[*characteristic manner or method*] **execution,** performance, rendition, interpretation, skill, finish, technique (*as, the* touch *of a master*).
II. *Verbs.* **touch,** feel, finger, thumb, paw; fumble, grope, grabble; brush, kiss, graze, lick, sweep, glance; stroke, pass (*or* rub) the fingers over, touch lightly, throw out a feeler; twiddle, tweedle (*Scot. and dial.*); massage, rub, knead, manipulate, palpate, palm, handle, wield; contact (*tech.*), join, adjoin, border, neighbor, meet, hit, come into contact.
concern, regard, relate to, pertain to, bear upon, refer to; treat of (*a subject*).
refer to (*lightly*), allude to, speak of, make reference to, hint at, make allusion to.
reach, come to, arrive at, attain, get to, get at, extend to (*as, to* touch *the goal*).
stop (*as at a port*), call at, stay, halt, tarry, visit.
impair (*as fruit*), injure, blemish, harm, damage, spoil, mar, taint, infect, affect (*as the brain*).
[*to affect the feelings of*] **soften,** melt, move, work upon, affect, mollify.
irritate, ruffle, annoy, nettle, hurt, wound, sting (*as, to* touch *one's pride*).

[*to make an impression on*] impress, affect, act upon; cut, scratch, abrade; modify, change, alter, transform.
taste (*food or drink*), partake of, take, receive.
touch up, improve (*as a drawing or writing*), correct, amend, emend, refine, finish off; strike lightly (*as a horse*), incite, urge on; jog (*the memory*), remind.
III. *Adjectives.* **touchable,** tangible, tactile, palpable, tactual (*tech.*); material, substantial, real.
touching, tangent (*esp. geom.*), stereognostic (*tech.*); lambent, licking; gliding over, skimming; adjacent, abutting, contiguous.
pathetic, moving, affecting, impressive, pitiable, heart-rending.
See also CONTACT, EXCITEMENT, ITCHING, MIXTURE, MOTION, PAINFULNESS, PITY, RELATION, TASTE.—*Antonyms.* See INSENSITIVENESS, NUMBNESS.

---

touchy, *adj.* irritable, cross, petulant, peevish. See IRASCIBILITY.
tough, *adj.* difficult, hard; tenacious, cohesive, strong. See DIFFICULTY, TENACITY.
tour, *n.* expedition, trip, pilgrimage. See JOURNEY.
tourist, *n.* sight-seer, voyager, excursionist. See TRAVELER.
tournament, *n.* tourney, justs *or* jousts (*pl.*), combat; contest (*as at tennis*). See CONTENTION.
tow, *v.* draw, drag, pull, haul, tug. See TRACTION.
tower, *n.* fortress, citadel; column, spire, steeple, campanile, turret, sky-scraper; rock, pillar. See DEFENSE, HEIGHT, STABILITY.
tower, *v.* soar, spire, overtop; loom, transcend. See ASCENT, GREATNESS, HEIGHT.
town, *n.* borough, city. See HABITATION.
toy, *n.* plaything, doll, puppet, bauble, gewgaw. See AMUSEMENT, UNIMPORTANCE.
trace, *v.* scent, probe, sift, detect, solve; track, trail, pursue; draw, sketch, delineate; deduce, etymologize. See DISCOVERY, INQUIRY, REPRESENTATION, WORD (*derive*).
trace, *n.* footprint, track, trail, scent; vestige, sign, relic, token, remains; touch, tinge, hint. See INDICATION, RECORD, SHADE.
track, *n.* footprint, trail, scent, spoor, vestige, trace; path, road, course. See INDICATION, WAY.
[1]**tract,** *n.* thesis, dissertation, treatise, tractate. See ESSAY.
[2]**tract,** *n.* space, area, stretch. See REGION.
tractable, *adj.* manageable, submissive, yielding; tractile, plastic. See FACILITY, SOFTNESS.

TRACTION.—I. *Nouns.* **traction,** drawing, hauling, etc. (see *verbs*); draft *or* draught, pull, haul, tug, yank (*U. S. colloq.*); haulage, towage; contraction (*as of a muscle*).
II. *Verbs.* **draw,** haul, pull, lug, rake, trawl, draggle, drag, snake (*U. S. colloq. or slang*), tug, tow, take in tow, trail, yank (*U. S. colloq.*), jerk, twitch, wrench.
III. *Adjectives.* **tractional,** tractive, pulling, attractive, drawing; tractile, ductile.
See also ATTRACTION.—*Antonyms.* See PROPULSION, REPULSION.

---

trade, *n.* bargaining, exchange, commerce, trading, business. See BARTER.
trader, *n.* dealer, tradesman, shopkeeper, retailer. See MERCHANT.
tradewind, trades (*pl.*), monsoon. See WIND.
tradition, *n.* custom, usage, unwritten law. See OLDNESS.
traduce, *v.* slander, defame, brand, decry, vilify. See DETRACTION.
traffic, *n.* trade, commerce, business; transportation. See BARTER, TRANSFER.
tragic, *adj.* dramatic, buskined; fatal, deadly, disastrous, calamitous, dire. See DRAMA, KILLING, PAINFULNESS.
trail, *n.* track, trace, vestige, footprint, scent, spoor; train, wake. See INDICATION, SEQUEL.

train, *v.* drill, exercise, discipline; instruct, prepare. See FORM, TEACHING.
train, *n.* suite, retinue, wake, trail, rear; succession, series; railroad cars, rolling stock. See FOLLOWING, SEQUEL, SEQUENCE, VEHICLE.
training, *n.* preparation, schooling, discipline, practice. See TEACHING.
trait, *n.* characteristic, feature, peculiarity, particularity. See INDICATION, SPECIALTY.
traitor, *n.* betrayer, conspirator, renegrade, recreant. See KNAVE.
tramp, *v.* walk, march, hike (*colloq.*). See JOURNEY.
tramp, *n.* stroll, ramble, hike (*colloq.*); vagabond, hobo (*U. S.*). See JOURNEY, PEOPLE (*vagrant*).
trance, *n.* catalepsy, coma; hypnosis, ecstasy. See INSENSITIVENESS, PSYCHICAL RESEARCH.
tranquil, *adj.* still, calm, quiet; peaceful, placid. See MODERATION, PEACE.
tranquilize, *v.* calm, quiet, soothe, pacify, compose. See PACIFICATION.
transact, *v.* do, perform, execute, dispatch, negotiate. See CONDUCT.
transaction, *n.* act, deed, affair, business, dealings (*pl.*), proceeding, process. See ACTION, CONDUCT, EVENT.
transcend, *v.* excel, outdo, outrival, outrank, surpass. See SUPERIORITY.
transcribe, *v.* copy, reproduce, decipher, decode. See MANIFESTATION.
transcript, *n.* duplicate, transcription, engrossment, tenor (*law*). See COPY.

TRANSFER.—I. *Nouns.* **transfer,** transference, removal, shift, change, dislodgment, displacement, translocation; relegation, reference (*to an authority*), assignment, submission, commitment (*as to a legislative committee*), committal; transplantation, carrying, conduction (*tech.*), deportation, asportation (*felonious*), amotion (*esp. from office*); metastasis (*tech.*), metathesis (*tech.*), convection (*physics*), transmittal, transmission, transfusion, transposal, transposition, transferal (*rare*); contagion, infection.

transportation, transport, movement, moving, carriage, conveyance, translation, transvection (*rare*); transshipment, shipment, cartage, carting, truckage, portage, carry (*U. S. and Canada*), freight, freightage, telpherage *or* telferage, ferriage, waftage (*rare*); transit, passage, transition.

[*transfer of property or right*] **conveyance,** assignment, alienation, conveyancing, abalienation, enfeoffment; disposal, sale, lease, deed, quitclaim, release, barter, exchange; devise, devisal, bequest, gift, legacy, demise, bequeathal (*rare*); succession, reversion.

[*thing transferred*] **deposit,** alluvion, alluvium, detritus, silt, drift, diluvium (*geol.*), sinter (*geol.*), loess (*geol.*); sublimate (*chem.*), sediment, precipitation.

freight, cargo, lading, load, goods (*Brit.*), baggage, luggage (*Brit.*), mail; traffic.

II. *Verbs.* **transfer,** transport, move, change residence, convey, carry, tote (*U. S.*), bear, waft, float, hand, hand over, pass, forward; shift, remove, relegate change, transpose, displace, dislodge, transplant, translate (*esp. as a bishop*) transfuse; bring, fetch, reach; conduct, convoy.

send, dispatch, transmit, delegate, consign, deliver; ship, freight, embark; mail, post, express (*U. S.*).

[*in law*] **convey** (*as a right or title*), assign, alienate, sequester, enfeoff, grant, cede, pass, consign; will, devise, bequeath, demise, leave, donate, give, mancipate (*Roman law*); sell, lease, rent, let, deed (*U. S.*), negotiate, exchange; hand over, make over, pass on (*or* down), transmit, hand down.

inherit, receive, possess, obtain, acquire, come in for, come to, devolve upon, come into possession of, be heir to, succeed.

disinherit, dispossess, cut off, disown, exheredate (*rare*).

III. *Adjectives.* **transferable,** assignable, alienable, conveyable, negotiable, transmissible, transmissive, transmittible; reversional, bequeathable, devisable; movable, portable; conductible, contagious, catching, infectious, communicable.

See also CHANGE, COPY, DELIVERANCE, DISPLACEMENT, INTERCHANGE.

---

transformation, *n.* metamorphosis, transmutation. See CHANGE.
transgress, *v.* infringe, violate; overstep, trespass, intrude; err, sin. See NONOBSERVANCE, OVERRUNNING, VICE.

transgression, *n.* fault, offense, iniquity, delinquency, sin; encroachment, infraction, infringement. See DEVIATION, OVERRUNNING.

transgressor, *n.* wrongdoer, evildoer, sinner, offender. See BAD MAN, IMPIETY.

TRANSIENCE.—I. *Nouns.* **transcience** *or* transiency, evanescence, impermanence; fugacity, fugaciousness, temporariness, ephemerality, volatility (*rare in this sense*), caducity (*rare*), transitoriness, changeableness, mortality, span, brevity; nine days' wonder, bubble; velocity, swiftness, suddenness, abruptness; temporary arrangement, interregnum.

transient, ephemeron (*pl.* ephemera), ephemeral, ephemerid (*zoöl.*); transient guest, temporary lodger: *in this sense,* transient *is U. S. colloq.*

II. *Verbs.* **be transient,** flit, pass away, fly, gallop, vanish, sink, melt, fade, evaporate; pass away like a cloud (summer cloud, shadow, *or* dream).

III. *Adjectives.* **transient,** transitory, passing, evanescent, fleeting, fugitive, elusive, caducous (*rare*), impermanent, temporal, temporary, provisional, provisory, short-lived, diurnal, monohemerous (*med.*), ephemeral, deciduous, perishable, mortal, precarious,

brief, quick, brisk, fleet, meteoric, volatile, summary, hasty, hurried, cursory, pressed for time, sudden, momentary, spasmodic, instantaneous.

IV. *Adverbs.* **transiently,** transitorily, in passing, *en passant* (*F.*), *in transitu* (*L.*), temporarily, for the moment, *pro tempore* (*L.*), for a time, awhile, briefly, soon; between cup and lip.

See also CHANGEABLENESS, HASTE, INSTANTANEITY, VELOCITY.—*Antonyms.* See DURABILITY, PERMANENCE.

---

transit, *n.* change, passing; transportation, conveyance. See PASSAGE, TRANSFER.

transition, *n.* passage, change, shift. See CONVERSION.

translate, *v.* transform, transmute; interpret, construe, render, decode, decipher; transfer, remove. See CHANGE, INTERPRETATION, TRANSFER.

translation, *n.* rendition, version, key; transference, removal. See INTERPRETATION, TRANSFER.

transmit, *v.* send, dispatch, consign, mail. See TRANSFER.

TRANSPARENCY.—I. *Nouns.* **transparency,** transparence, translucence *or* translucency, diaphaneity, translucidity, diaphanousness; lucidity, limpidity, clearness, pellucidity, cloudlessness; transillumination (*tech.*).

[*transparent medium*] glass, crystal, lymph, water, hyaline (*poetic*).

perspicuity, clearness, plainness, lucidity, lucidness, intelligibility, palpability, perspicuousness.

frankness, openness, ingenuousness, honesty, sincerity, simplicity.

II. *Adjectives.* **transparent,** pellucid, lucid, diaphanous, translucent, transpicuous (*rare*), lucent, limpid, clear, serene, cloudless, crystal, crystal-like, crystalline, vitreous, glassy, hyaline; gauzy, thin, flimsy, easily seen through: *opposite of* opaque.

[*readily understood*] **perspicuous,** clear, plain, unambiguous, unequivocal, explicit, lucid, luminous, clear-cut, distinct, intelligible, unmistakable, apparent, manifest, evident.

[*free from affectation*] **frank,** open, ingenuous, direct, artless, unsophisticated, simple, honest, sincere.

See also ARTLESSNESS, INTELLIGIBILITY, THINNESS.—*Antonyms.* See OPACITY.

---

transport, *n.* ectasy, rapture; transportation, shipment. See PLEASURE, TRANSFER.

transportation, *n.* transport, conveyance, shipment; transit, passage. See TRANSFER.

transpose, *v.* reverse, change, shift. See CONTRARIETY, INTERCHANGE, INVERSION.

transverse, *adj.* oblique, cross, thwart. See CROSSING.

trap, *n.* snare. pitfall, springe, net, ambush. See DECEPTION.

trashy, *adj.* worthless, useless, insignificant, unimportant. See UNMEANINGLESS.

travel, *v.* go, tour, voyage, cruise, peregrinate. See JOURNEY.

TRAVELER.—I. *Nouns.* **traveler,** wayfarer, voyager, journeyer, *voyageur* (*F.*), sailor, trekker (*S. Africa*), globe-trotter (*colloq.*), sight-seer, tourist, excursionist, tripper (*colloq.*); explorer, adventurer, mountaineer, airman, aviator; commuter, passenger.

wanderer, rover, peregrinator (*rare*), itinerant, straggler, rambler, roamer, gadabout (*colloq.*); landlouper, vagrant, loafer, tramp, hobo (*U. S.*), vagabond, Bohemian, gypsy, *zingaro* (*It.; pl. zingari*), camper, nomad, Arab, Wandering Jew; pilgrim, palmer, hadji *or* hajji (*Moham.*); immigrant; emigrant, *émigré* (*F.*).

fugitive, refugee; runaway, renegade, runagate.

courier, messenger, runner, express, postrider, post, dispatch rider (*or* bearer), estafette; Mercury, Iris, Ariel.

pedestrian, walker, foot passenger, hiker (*colloq.*), tramper, peripatetic (*usually jocose*).

rider, horseman, horsewoman (*fem.*), equestrian, equestrienne (*fem.*), cavalier; jockey, trainer, breaker, roughrider; huntsman, whip; postilion, postboy.

driver, coachman, Jehu (*jocose*), dragsman, reinsman (*rare*), charioteer, cabman, cabdriver, *cocher* (*F.*), *cochero* (*P. I.*), *voiturier* (*F.*), *vetturino* (*It.; pl. vetturini*), hackman, cabby (*colloq.*), jarvey (*Eng. slang*), gharry-wallah *or* gari-wala (*India*); carter, wagoner *or* waggoner, drayman, teamster, truckman; mahout (*elephant*); camel driver, cameleer; muleteer.

[*railroad*] engine driver (*Brit.*), engineer (*U. S.*); fireman, stoker; conductor, guard (*Brit.*), motorman.

[*automobile*] driver, chauffeur, chauffeuse (*fem.*), automobilist, motorist; taxi driver, jitneur (*colloq.*).

See also MARINER, REPRESENTATIVE (*salesman*).

---

traverse, *v.* cross, ford, pass, overpass, travel over, range. See CROSSING, MEASUREMENT.

treacherous, *adj.* false, faithless, disloyal, perfidious. See IMPROBITY.

treachery, *n.* double dealing; betrayal, perfidy, treason. See DECEPTION, IMPROBITY.

tread, *v.* dance (*as a minuet*); walk, step, march, pace, tramp, go; trample upon, crush, subdue. See AGITATION, JOURNEY, SUCCESS.

treason, *n.* sedition, *lèse-majesté* (*F.*); treachery, betrayal, perfidy. See DISOBEDIENCE, IMPROBITY.

treasure, *n.* riches, savings, hoard, wealth. See MONEY, STORE.

TREASURER.—I. *Nouns.* **treasurer,** receiver, bursar (*as of a college*), depositary, quæstor (*Roman*), cofferer (*hist.*), purser, banker, financier; steward, trustee, accountant, almoner, paymaster, cashier, teller.

TREASURY.—I. *Nouns.* **treasury,** bank, exchequer, bursary (*of a college or monastery*), fiscus (*Roman*), fisc *or* fisk (*hist. or rare*), state treasury, kutcherry *or* kachahri (*India*); strong box, stronghold, strong room; coffer, chest, safe, depository, cash register, cash box, money-box, till.

purse, moneybag, *portemonnaie* (*F.*), pocketbook, wallet, pouch (*archaic or literary*), gipser *or* gipsire (*worn at the girdle: archaic*), pocket; purse strings.

securities, stocks, shares, scrip; public stocks, (funds, *or* securities); Consols (*Eng.*), *crédit mobilier* (*F.*), debentures, obligations, bonds, government bonds. Liberty bonds (*U. S.*), gilt-edged securities.

---

treat, *v.* negotiate, covenant; entertain, refresh, gartify; doctor (*colloq.*), dose, attend; behave toward, handle, manage. See COMPACT, PLEASURABLENESS, REMEDY, SERVANT, USE.

treatise, *n.* monograph, tract, essay, thesis, study. See BOOK, DISSERTATION.

treatment, *n.* handling, course, manner of dealing; medical care. See CONDUCT, REMEDY.

treaty, *n.* alliance, league, agreement (*esp. between nations*). See COMPACT.

tree, *n.* pedigree, stock, line, lineage, genealogical (*or* family) tree; stand, sapling. See PATERNITY, VEGETABLE.
tree-shaped, *adj.* branched, treelike, dendriform, arborescent. See SYMMETRY.
tremble, *v.* shiver, shudder, quake; totter, shake. See FEAR, WEAKNESS.
tremendous, *adj.* fearful, dreadful, terrible. See FEAR.
tremor, *n.* trembling. shaking, quivering, trepidation. See AGITATION, FEAR.
trench, *n.* fortification, intrenchment, dugout; ditch, gutter. See DEFENSE, FURROW.
trenchant, *adj.* crisp, pointed, sententious; keen, sharp, caustic, biting, pungent. See CONCISENESS, FEELING.
trend, *v.* aim, set, drift, tend toward, gravitate, incline. See DIRECTION.
trepidation, *n.* agitation, fear, perturbation, alarm. See EXCITABILITY.
trespass, *v.* encroach, infringe, intrude; sin, transgress. See OVERRUNNING, VICE.
trial, *n.* misfortune, sorrow, blow, infliction; attempt, essay; test, examination, inspection; hearing (*law*). See ADVERSITY, EXPERIMENT, INQUIRY, LAWSUIT,
triangular, *adj.* deltoid, delta-shaped, trigonal. See THREE.
tribe, *n.* clan, brotherhood, association; family, lineage, house, stock, race. See ASSEMBLAGE, CONSANGUINITY.

TRIBUNAL.—I. *Nouns.* **tribunal,** court, board, bench, judicature, judicatory, forum, court of justice (*or* law), court-martial (*pl.* courts-martial), inquisition, Star Chamber (*hist.*); judgment seat, mercy seat; woolsack (*seat of English Lord Chancellor in House of Lords*), Areopagus; bar, bar of justice; town hall, statehouse (*U. S.*), townhouse, courthouse; sessions (*Eng.*), assizes (*Eng.*); county court, police court, petty sessions (*Eng.*).

[*British courts*] shiremote (*or* -moot), wardmote, burghmote, hallmote *or* court baron, courtleet, court of piepoudre (*or* piepowder), eyre; Curia Regis, Aula Regis: *all historic.*

High Court of Justice, *subdivided into the following divisions:* Chancery, King's Bench (*combining the former* Common Pleas *and* Exchequer), Probate, Divorce. Admiralty.

Supreme Court of Judicature (*combining the* High Court of Justice *and the* Court of Appeal).

[*United States courts*] U. S. Supreme Court, U. S. District Court, U. S. Circuit Court of Appeal; Federal Court of Claims, Court of Private Land Claims; Supreme Court, Superior Court, court of sessions, criminal court, police court, juvenile court.

See also JUDGE, JURISDICTION.

---

tributary, *n.* affluent, feeder, stream. See RIVER.
tribute, *n.* ransom, bribe, reward: contribution. See EXPENDITURE, GIVING.
trick, *n.* prank; artifice, wile, blind; craft, knack, sleight, deftness; peculiarity, mannerism. See CAPRICE, DECEPTION, SKILL, SPECIALTY.
trickster, *n.* cheat, swindler, faker (*slang*), sharper. See DECEIVER.
tricky, *adj.* trickish, wily, foxy, deceptive, shifty. See CUNNING, DECEPTION.
trifle, *n.* fragment, modicum; jot, iota, fig, bagatelle. See SMALLNESS, UNIMPORTANCE.
trifle, *v.* toy, dally; scamp, slur, skim. See ENDEARMENT, NEGLECT.
trifler, *n.* time waster, idler, procrastinator. See NEGLECT.
trifling, *adj.* trivial, unimportant, frivolous, slight, weak, petty. See UNIMPORTANCE.
trill, *v.* quaver, shake, warble. See MUSICIAN, ROLL.
trim, *v.* dodge, hedge, temporize; berate, chastise, trounce; balance, adjust, equalize; decorate, deck, embellish, garnish; cut, clip, lop, shear, mow. See APOSTASY, DISAPPROBATION, EQUALITY, ORNAMENT, SHORTNESS.
trim, *adj.* neat, tidy, spruce, smart, *chic* (*F.*). See BEAUTY.
Trinity, *n.* The Triune God, Triunity. See DEITY.

trip, *v.* stumble, tumble; fail; err, blunder; caper, frisk, cavort; skip, scud. See DESCENT, ERROR, LEAP, VELOCITY.
trip, *n.* stumble, lurch, misstep; mistake, slip, bungle; excursion, expedition, tour. See DESCENT, ERROR, JOURNEY.

TRIPLICATION.—I. *Nouns.* **triplication,** triplicity, trebleness; trine (*esp. astrology*), trigon, triplet, trilogy.
II. *Verbs.* **triplicate,** treble, triple, cube.
III. *Adjectives.* **triplicate,** triple, treble, threefold, three-ply, ternary, tern, ternate, ternal, trinal, trinary (*rare*), triadic, triplex; trilogistic.
IV. *Adverbs.* **triply,** trebly, threefold; thirdly, in the third place; thrice.
See also THREE.—*Antonyms.* See TRISECTION.

TRISECTION.—I. *Nouns.* **trisection,** tripartition, trichotomy; third, third part.
II. *Verbs.* **trisect,** divide into three parts, third; triangulate.
III. *Adjectives.* **trisected,** tripartite, triparted, three-parted, trifid, trichotomous; trifurcate *or* trifurcated, trisulcate, three-forked, trident, tridental, tridentate; three-footed, tripodic, tripodal, tripedal; tripetalous (*bot.*), trimerous (*bot. and zoöl.*), trifoliolate (*bot.*), three-leaved, triarch (*bot.*).
Antonyms See TRIPLICATION.

---

triumph, *v.* exult, crow, gloat; win, surpass, prevail, succeed. See REJOICING, SUCCESS.
triviality, *n.* levity, jest, smallness, nothing. See UNIMPORTANCE.

TROPHY.—*Nouns.* **trophy,** prize, medal, palm, laurel, laurels, bays, crown, chaplet, wreath, garland, civic crown, decoration, citation, war medal; blue ribbon, feather in one's cap; plum (*colloq.*), cup (*sporting*), pot (*slang*), plate; memento, memorial, triumphal arch.
[*educational*] scholarship, studentship (*rare in U. S.*), exhibition (*Eng. universities*), bursary (*Scot.*), fellowship.
See also TITLE (*decoration*), WARFARE (*war medal*).

---

tropical, *adj.* figurative, metaphorical; hot, torrid, fiery, blazing; passionate, fervid. See FIGURE, HEAT.
trouble, *v.* disconcert, perturb, annoy, plague, incommode, disturb, harass. See DERANGEMENT, PAIN.
trouble, *n.* misfortune, affliction, hardship; disturbance, row; riot; pains, duty; wory, distress. See ADVERSITY, DISORDER, EXERTION, PAIN.
troublesome, *adj.* annoying, tiresome, irksome. See PAINFULNESS.
trounce, *v.* beat, flog, drub, lash, whip. See PUNISHMENT.
trousers, *n. pl.* breeches, pants (*colloq.*), pantaloons. See CLOTHING.
truant, *n.* absentee, shirk, quitter; deserter, runaway. See ABSENCE, AVOIDANCE.
truce, *n.* recess, respite, lull; armistice, suspension of arms. See CESSATION, PACIFICATION.
trudge, *v.* plod, lumber, lag, drag, shamble. See SLOWNESS.
true, *adj.* lawful, rightful, legitimate; straight, even, undeviating; real, genuine, correct, authentic, sound, pure, truthful, faithful, loyal. See RIGHT, STRAIGHTNESS, TRUTH.
true, *v.* adjust, regulate, square, set. See TRUTH.
truly, *adv.* verily (*archaic*), indeed, in fact, in reality. See TRUTH.
trumpery, *n.* trash, rubbish, frippery. See UNIMPORTANCE.
trumpet, *n.* horn, bugle, cornet, clarion (*poetic*). See MUSICAL INSTRUMENTS.
trumpet, *v.* proclaim, herald; blow, blare. See PUBLICATION, [1]SOUND.
trundle, *v.* wheel, roll; revolve, spin. See ROTATION.
trunk, *n.* proboscis (*of an elephant*); chest, box; bole, stock, butt. torso. body, main part. See CONVEXITY. RECEPTACLE, WHOLE.

trust, *n.* faith, credit, credence, reliance, confidence, hope; corporation, combination, merger; right, interest, use, benefit. See BELIEF, PARTY, PROPERTY.

trust, *v.* believe; confide in, rely upon. See BELIEF.

trustworthy, *adj.* reliable, dependable; loyal, constant, faithful, stanch, true. See CERTAINTY, PROBITY.

TRUTH.—I. *Nouns.* **truth,** verity, trueness, reality, existence, right, authenticity, actuality, realness, fact, principle; veracity, truthfulness, troth (*archaic*), sooth (*archaic*), gospel; naked truth, *nuda veritas* (*L.*); plain (honest, sober, unalloyed, unvarnished, stern, exact, *or* intrinsic) truth; the truth, the whole truth, and nothing but the truth.

fidelity, faithfulness, constancy, steadfastness, trustiness, devotion, loyalty, fealty, honor; conformity, accordance.

sincerity, honesty, genuineness, singleness, purity, single-mindedness, guilelessness, single-heartedness, integrity, probity.

accuracy, exactitude, exactness, correctness, preciseness, precision, regularity, mathematical precision, nicety; literalism, textualism; *ipsissima verba* (*L.*), the very words; orthology.

[*in literature and art*] **realism,** truth to nature, fidelity, graphicalness, naturalness, naturalism, Zolaism.

II. *Verbs.* **hold true,** stand the test, have the true ring, hold good.

true, adjust, regulate, readjust, square, fix, set, make true (*as, to* true *a wheel*).

III. *Adjectives.* **true,** real, genuine, actual, veritable; authentic, rightful, legitimate, orthodox, canonical, official, sterling, sound, pure, true-blue; unimpeachable, unadulterated, Simon-Pure (*colloq.*), unvarnished, undisguised; veracious, truthful, unimagined, true to life, realistic; certain, true as gospel, true to the facts, factual; unrefuted, unconfuted.

faithful, constant, loyal, steadfast; trustworthy, devoted, stanch *or* staunch, unwavering, unswerving, steady, reliable, true as steel.

sincere, honest, upright, genuine, single-minded, single-hearted, ingenuous, natural, unsophisticated.

exact, accurate, definite, concrete, precise, well-defined, just, right, correct, strict, severe, clean-cut, clear-cut, rigid, rigorous, scrupulous, literal, textual, punctilious, mathematical, scientific, unerring; particular, nice, meticulous, delicate, fine.

valid, well-grounded, well-founded, solid, stable, pucka *or pakka* (*Anglo-Indian*), substantial, tangible.

IV. *Adverbs.* **truly,** verily (*archaic*), actually, veritably, indeed, in reality; in very truth, in fact, as a matter of fact, beyond doubt, beyond question.

exactly, accurately, etc. (see *adjectives*); *ad amussim* (*L.*), verbatim, *verbatim et literatim* (*L.*), word for word, *mot à mot* (*F.*), literally, *au pied de la lettre* (*F.*), to the letter; *sic* (*L.*), *totidem verbis* (*L.*), chapter and verse; *ad unguem* (*L.*), to a nicety, to a hair, to a turn, to a T; neither more nor less, in every respect, in all respects, *sous tous les rapports* (*F.*).

See also CERTAINTY, EXISTENCE, ORTHODOXY, PROBITY, RIGHT, STRAIGHTNESS, VERACITY.—*Antonyms.* See ERROR, FALSEHOOD, IMPROBITY.

---

try, *v.* purify, refine; strive, endeavor, attempt, test, experiment; hear, examine, adjudicate. See CLEANNESS, ESSAY, LAWSUIT.

tube, *n.* pipe, main, hose, tunnel. See OPENING.

tubular, *adj.* fistular, fistulous, tubate. See OPENING.

tuck, *n.* doubling, folding, pleat, plait, lap. See [1]FOLD.

tuft, *n.* clump, tussock, group, cluster; crest, topknot. See ASSEMBLAGE, ROUGHNESS.

tug, *v.* struggle, strive; draw, haul, pull, drag, tow. See EXERTION, TRACTION.

tumble, *v.* trip, pitch, plunge, sprawl, fall. See DESCENT.

tumid, *adj.* swollen, bloated, distended; bombastic, turgid. See CONVEXITY, EXPANSION, ORNAMENT.

tumult, *n.* disquiet, excitement, turbulence, hubbub; turmoil, trouble, commotion, uproar, riot, *mêlée* (*F.*). See AGITATION, DISORDER.

tune, *n.* melody, aria, strain, measure; accord. See AIR, MUSIC, HARMONY.
tunnel, *n.* mine, shaft, adit, gallery. See OPENING.
turbid, *adj.* confused, muddled, disordered; thick, muddy, dirty. See DISORDER, OPACITY.
turbulence, *n.* disorder, agitation, commotion, excitement, tumult. See VIOLENCE.
turbulent, *adj.* restless, disturbed, agitated; violent, stormy, tumultuous, raging, riotous. See EXCITABILITY, VIOLENCE.
turb, *n.* race, course; peat; sward, sod, grass. See ARENA, FUEL, PLAIN.
turgid, *adj.* diffuse, digressive; bloated, inflated, tumid; bombastic, grandioquent. See DIFFUSENESS, REDUNDANCE, EXPANSION, OSTENTATION,
turmoil, *n.* ferment, commotion, disturbance, tumult. See DISORDER.
turn, *v.* shift, veer, swerve, deflect; bend, round, wheel; convert, alter, vary, transform, transmute; reverse, invert, subvert; spin, roll, revolve, rotate; ferment, curdle, acidify. See CHANGE, CIRCUITY, CONVERSION, INVERSION, ROTATION, SOURNESS.
turn, *n.* bend, curve, twist, winding; type, cast, mold, fashion; stroll, ramble, run, drive; ornamental passage (*music*), embellishment; revolution, cycle, round, bout; reel, spin, whirl, twirl, swirl; forte, genius, faculty, aptitude; bent, inclination, tendency. See CURVATURE, FORM, JOURNEY, MUSIC, REGULARITY, ROTATION, SKILL, WILLINGNESS.
turncoat, *n.* opostate, renegade, deserter, backslider. See APOSTASY.
turning point, crisis, juncture, climacteric. See TIMELINESS.
turpitude, *n.* degradation, baseness, depravity. See IMPROBITY.
turret, *n.* tower, cupola tourelle (*arch.*). See HEIGHT.
tutor, *n.* instructor, perceptor, master. See TEACHER.
twaddle, *n.* gibberish drivel, babble. See UNMEANINGNESS.
twang, *n.* nasality. See RESONANCE, STRIDENCY.

TWENTY.—I. *Nouns.* twenty, score.
II. *Adjectives.* twentieth, vicenary, vigesimal; vicennial.

---

twice, *adv.* double, once more, over again. See DUPLICATION.
twice-told tale, old story, chestnut (*slang*). See REPETITION.
twiddle, *v.* twirl, wiggle (*colloq.*), fidget. See UNMEANINGNESS.
twig, *n.* offshoot, sprig, withe, slip, branch. See PART.
twilight, *n.* gloaming, crepuscule, dusk, dawn. See DIMNESS.
twin, *adj.* fellow, duplex; two, twain (*archaic*); double, second; like, alike. See ACCOMPANIMENT, DUALITY, DUPLICATION, SIMILARITY.
twinkle, *v.* glimmer, flicker, sparkle, scintillate, beam. See LIGHT.
twirl, *v.* twist, coil, wind, roll. See CIRCUITY, CONVOLUTION.
twist, *v.* twirl, coil, twine; wind, slue, wheel; distort, contort, writhe, gnarl, knot. See CIRCUITY, DEVIATION, DISTORTION.
twit, *v.* taunt, reproach, blame. See ACCUSATION.
twitter, *v.* chirp, cheep, chirrup, peep, sing. See ULULATION.
two, *n.* deuce, couple, twain (*archaic*), pair. See DUALITY.
two-faced, *adj.* double-faced, double-dealing, hypocritical, deceitful. See FALSEHOOD.
two-sided, *adj.* bilateral, dihedral (*tech.*). See SIDE.
type, *n.* kind, sort, nature, character, style; sign, symbol, cipher, figure; letter (*printing*); model, pattern, standard, example; image, simile, comparison. See CLASS, INDICATION, PRINTING, PROTOTYPE, SIMILARITY.
typesetting, *n.* typography, composing. See COMPOSITION.
typical, *adj.* normal, exemplary, illustrative; characteristic, symbolic, representative, suggestive. See CONFORMITY, INDICATION.
typify, *v.* indicate, signify, symbolize, represent. See INDICATION.
typographic, *adj.* typographical, printed. See PRINTING.

tyranny, *n.* despotism, absolutism, autocracy, cruelty. See ILLEGALITY, SEVERITY.

tyrant, *n.* despot, autocrat, oppressor. See SEVERITY.

tyro, *or* **tiro,** *n.* (*pl.* tyros *or* tiros), beginner, novice. See LEARNER.

U

UGLINESS.—I. *Nouns.* **ugliness,** deformity, inelegance, unsightliness, etc. (see *adjectives*); asymmetry, want of symmetry, distortion; squalor, repulsiveness, hideousness.

eyesore, blemish, disfigurement, defacement, blot on the landscape; object, figure, sight (*colloq.*), fright, scarecrow; hag, crone, harridan, witch; satyr, monster, Caliban.

II. *Verbs.* **deface,** disfigure, deform, distort, blemish, injure, mar, mangle, mutilate, spoil; soil.

III. *Adjectives.* **ugly,** inartistic, unsightly, unseemly, uncomely, unlovely, unbeautiful, coarse, plain, homely; unshapely, shapeless, ill-shaped, ill-made, ill-proportioned, crooked, distorted, misproportioned, monstrous, gross; unprepossessing, hard-favored, hard-featured, ill-favored, ill-looking; haggard, grim, grisly, ghastly, cadaverous, gruesome.

ungainly, uncouth, clumsy, awkward, graceless, inelegant, ungraceful, stiff, rough, gross, rude, gawky, lumbering, unwieldy.

ill-natured, cross-grained, quarrelsome, ill-tempered, ill-humored, surly, churlish, bearish, cantankerous, snappish, grouchy (*slang*), crusty (*as, an* ugly *disposition: U. S. colloq.*).

repellant, forbidding, frightful, hideous, odious, repulsive, squalid, foul, loathsome, revolting, horrid, horrible, shocking.

gaudy, tawdry, showy, gimcrack, trumpery, gingerbread, pretentious, garish.

[*of the weather*] **threatening,** menacing, lowering *or* louring, lowery *or* loury, overcast

See also BLEMISH, DISTORTION.—*Antonyms.* See BEAUTY.

---

ulterior, *adj.* far-off, remote; unavowed, prospective. See DISTANCE, FUTURE.

ultimate, *adj.* farthest, extreme; final, conclusive; elemental. See DISTANCE, END, SIMPLENESS.

ultra, *adj.* extreme, radical, advanced. See REVOLUTION, SUPERIORITY.

ULULATION [animal sounds].—I. *Nouns.* **ululation,** howling, wailing, cry, roar, howl, bark, barking, latration (*rare*), yelp, bowwow, belling; call, note, hoot, woodnote; twittering, drone.

II. *Verbs.* **ululate,** howl, wail, cry, bark, yelp, bay, bay the moon, yap, growl, snarl, howl, whine; grunt, snort, squeak; neigh, bray; mew, purr, caterwaul; bleat, blat (*colloq.*); low, moo; roar, bellow; trumpet (*said of elephants*); crow, screech, croak, caw, coo, gobble, quack, cackle, cluck; chirp, cheep, chirrup, peep, sing, twitter, chatter, hoot; hum, buzz; hiss.

III. *Adjectives.* **ululant,** howling, wailing, crying, blatant, latrant (*used figuratively*), clamorous; deep-mouthed (*as hounds*).

See also CRY.

---

umbrage, *n.* pique, dudgeon, offense. See RESENTMENT.

umbrella, *n.* gamp (*jocose*), sunshade, parasol. See COVERING, SHADE.

umpire, *n.* arbitrator, arbiter, referee. See JUDGE, MODERATION.

unabashed, *adj.* unblushing, barefaced, shameless, brazen. See INSOLENCE.

unable, *adj.* powerless, weak, incapable, incompetent. See IMPOTENCE.

unaccented, *adj.* unemphatic, unemphasized, weak, obscure. See LIGHTNESS.

unacceptable, *adj.* undesirable, uninviting, distasteful, unpleasant. See PAINFULNESS.

unaccommodating, *adj.* unobliging, uncivil, ungracious. See DISAGREEMENT, DISCOURTESY.

unaccompanied, *adj.* alone, solitary, unattended. See UNITY.

unaccountable, *adj.* inexplicable, incomprehensible, mysterious. See UNINTELLIGIBILITY.
unaccustomed, *adj.* unused, unskilled, uninitiated; new, strange, unfamiliar. See DISUSE, UNSKILLFULNESS, NEWNESS.
unacknowledged, *adj.* unavowed, unthanked, unrequited. See INGRATITUDE.
unacquainted, *adj.* uninformed, uninitiated, unknowing. See IGNORANCE.
unadorned, *adj.* plain, unornamented, severe; simple, unembellished, ordinary. See SEVERITY, SIMPLENESS.
unadulterated, *adj.* pure, unmixed; real, true, genuine. See PURITY, TRUTH.
unaffected, *adj.* untouched, unmoved, unimpressed; artless, simple, natural, sincere, ingenuous. See INSENSITIVENESS, SIMPLENESS.
unaided, *adj.* unassisted, single-handed, alone. See UNITY.
unanimity, *n.* unison, accord: *esprit de corps* (*F.*). See ASSENT, COÖPERATION.
unanimous, *adj.* agreeing, consentient, like-minded. See ASSENT.
unanimously, *adv.* consentiently, with one voice. See ASSENT, CONCORD.
unanticipated, *adj.* unexpected, unforeseen, sudden, startling. See NONEXPECTATION.
unappreciated, *adj.* unvalued, unprized, depreciated. See UNDERESTIMATION.
unarmed, *adj.* weaponless, defenseless. See IMPOTENCE, POWERLESSNESS.
unasked, *adj.* voluntary, free, spontaneous. See WILLINGNESS.
unassuming, *adj.* modest, reserved, unobtrusive, unpresumptuous. See MODESTY.
unattainable, *adj.* unachievable, unobtainable, unreachable, insuperable. See IMPOSSIBILITY.
unattractive, *adj.* unalluring, undesired, undesirable. See INDIFFERENCE.
unauthorized, *adj.* unsanctioned, unlawful, illegal, unconstitutional. See RIGHTFULNESS.
unavoidable, *adj.* unpreventable, inevitable, irresistible, necessary. See NECESSITY.
unaware, *adj.* unwarned, nonexpectant, inattentive. See NONEXPECTATION.
unbearable, *adj.* unendurable, insufferable, intolerable. See PAINFULNESS.
unbecoming, *adj.* improper, unfit, unseemly, inappropriate. See RIGHTLESSNESS.

UNBELIEF.—I. *Nouns.* **unbelief,** disbelief, incredulity, infidelity, misbelief, heresy, miscreance (*archaic*), nonconformity, dissent, change of opinion, retractation.
doubt, indecision, uncertainty, skepticism *or* scepticism, misgiving, dubiety, doubtfulness, dubiousness, demur, discredit, distrust, mistrust, misdoubt, suspicion, jealousy, scruple, qualm, hesitation; *onus probandi* (*L.*).
incredibility, incredibleness, unbelievability, inconceivability, inconceivableness.
II. *Verbs.* **disbelieve,** discredit, misbelieve, dissent; refuse to believe.
doubt, distrust, mistrust, question, challenge, dispute, deny, have one's doubts; shake one's faith, stagger one's belief; startle, stagger, perplex, cavil, wrangle; suspect, scent, smell, smell a rat (*colloq.*), harbor suspicions.
demur, scruple, object, take exception, protest, stick at, pause, hesitate, shy at, waver, hesitate, raise objections.
III. *Adjectives.* **unbelievable,** inconceivable, incredible, hard to believe, doubtful, disputable, questionable, suspicious, suspect (*archaic*).
unbelieving, skeptical *or* sceptical, incredulous, disbelieving, distrusting, distrustful of, suspicious of.
IV. *Adverbs.* with caution, with grains of allowance, *cum grano salis* (*L.*).
See also DISSENT, INCREDULITY, IRRELIGION, UNCERTAINTY.—*Antonyms.* See BELIEF.

---

unbeliever, *n.* skeptic, agnostic, infidel, heathen. See INCREDULITY, IRRELIGION.
unbiased, *adj.* unprejudiced, uninfluenced, impartial. See FREEDOM.
unblemished, *adj.* perfect, pure, sound, faultless, flawless. See PERFECTION.

unborn, *adj.* unconceived, unbegotten, uncreated; future. See NONEXISTENCE.
unbounded, *adj.* unrestricted, unrestrained; boundless, unlimited, illimitable, interminable, endless. See FREEDOM, INFINITY.
unbridled, *adj.* reinless, unrestrained, licensed; unruly, ungovernable, intractable. See LAXITY, VIOLENCE.
unbroken, *adj.* uninterrupted, successive, continuous; intact, unimpaired. See CONTINUITY, PRESERVATION.
unburdened, *adj.* unencumbered, unloaded, free. See FACILITY.
uncanny, *adj.* weird, eerie, spooky (*colloq.*), unearthly. See SCEPTER.
unceasing, *adj.* perpetual, endless, eternal, uninterrupted. See PERPETUITY.

UNCERTAINTY.—I. *Nouns.* **uncertainty,** incertitude, indecision, uncertainness, doubt, doubtfulness, dubiousness, hesitation, suspense, perplexity, confusedness, embarrassment, dilemma, Morton's fork (*hist.*), bewilderment; puzzle, quandary; timidity, vacillation, wavering, indetermination, insecurity, precariousness.

vagueness, haze, fog, obscurity, indefiniteness, confusion, ambiguity, open question, blind bargain, pig in a poke, leap in the dark.

fallibility, unreliability, unreliableness, untrustworthiness, errancy.

II. *Verbs.* **be uncertain,** hesitate, falter, stumble, stagger, boggle, flounder; lose the clew (*or* clue), miss one's way, lose oneself, wander aimlessly, beat about, not know which way to turn, float in a sea of doubt, lose one's head.

depend, hang in suspense, hang, hang (*or* tremble) in the balance, rest, hinge, be undecided; be contingent, be dependent (*with* on *or* upon).

render uncertain, perplex, pose, puzzle, embarrass, confuse, confound, bewilder, muddle, rattle (*colloq.*), daze, disconcert, bother, moider (*dial.*), nonplus, throw off the scent.

III. *Adjectives.* **uncertain,** unsure, doubtful, dubious, ambiguous, equivocal; insecure, unstable, indecisive, unsettled, undecided, undetermined, in question, undemonstrated, experimental, tentative; casual, random, aimless.

vague, indefinite, undefined, confused, confusing, perplexing, enigmatic, paradoxical, apocryphal, problematical, mysterious, oracular, cryptic, veiled, obscure, indefinable, undefinable.

fallible, questionable, debatable, untrustworthy, unreliable, unauthentic.

puzzled, perplexed, bewildered; lost, *désorienté* (*F.*), bushed, distracted, distraught.

irresolute, wavering, vacillating, inconstant, changeable, capricious, fickle, variable, unsettled, fitful, unsteady (*as, an* uncertain *person;* uncertain *weather*)

IV. *Adverbs.* **uncertainly,** unsurely, doubtfully, etc. (see *adjectives*); astray, adrift, abroad, at sea, at fault, at a loss, at one's wit's end, in a dilemma, in a maze, out of one's reckoning (*or* bearings), off the track; at random.

See also CHANCE, CHANGEABLENESS, DANGER, DARKNESS, EQUIVOCALNESS, EXPERIMENT, INQUIRY, INVISIBILITY, IRREGULARITY, IRRESOLUTION, SENSITIVENESS, UNBELIEF, UNINTELLIGIBILITY.—*Antonyms.* See CERTAINTY.

---

unchangeable, *adj.* unalterable, immutable, invariable, irrevocable. See STABILITY.
unchaste, *adj.* lewd, indecent, dissolute, immoral. See IMPURITY.
uncivilized, *adj.* barbarous, heathenish, savage. See PEOPLE.

UNCLEANNESS.—I. *Nouns.* **uncleanness,** dirtiness, filthiness, etc. (see *adjectives*); uncleanliness, squalor, squalidness, slovenliness; impurity, defilement, contamination, abomination.

corruption, decay, putridity, putrescence, putrefaction, decomposition, caries (*med.*), cariosity (*med.*), mucor (*rare*); rot, mold *or* mould, must, blight, rust, mildew, dry rot, taint.

pus, matter, suppuration, humor, empyema (*med.*), purulence.

dirt, filth, soil, slop; dust, smoke, soot, smudge, smut, grime; obscenity.

mud, mire, quagmire, slit, slime, slush, sludge, ooze, muck, *moya* (*volcanic mud: South America*), sposh (*U. S. dial.*).

dross, leavings, refuse, recrement, slag, scoria (*pl.* scoriæ), sprue, sullage, cinders, clinker, ashes, residuum, exuviæ (*pl.*), scum, froth; lees, dregs, grounds, sediment,

bottoms, heeltap, taplash (*dial. Eng.*), tartar, sordes, excretion, colluvies (*med.*), sordor (*rare*), offscourings, outscourings (*rare*), garbage, offal, sweepings, brash, chaff, rubbish; dung, ordure, feces *or* fæces, feculence, excrement, excreta (*pl.*).
[*repositories of filth or refuse*] cesspool, drain, sewer, sink, sump, basin, hollow, cloaca (*pl.* cloacæ), cloaca maxima, sough (*dial. Eng.*); midden (*dial.*), dunghill, dungheap, mixen (*archaic or dial.*), dump; dustbin, ash bin, ash pit, ash hole, dust hole; ash can, ash barrel, garbage pail.
[*foul retreat*] pigsty, sty, lair, den, Augean stable, sink of corruption; slum, rookery.
II. *Verbs.* **soil**, dirt, dirty, tarnish, spot, smear; daub, blot, blur, smudge smutch, smoke, smirch; drabble, draggle, daggle, spatter, bemire, clart (*dial.*), besmear, befoul, splash, stain, sully, pollute, defile, debase, corrupt, taint, contaminate.
rot, putrefy, putresce, fester, gather, suppurate. rankle, reek; mold *or* mould, molder *or* moulder, go bad, decay.
III. *Adjectives.* **unclean**, dirty, filthy, grimy, lutose, muddy, miry, grubby, soiled, mussy (*U. S.*), clarty (*dial.*), dusty, smutty, sooty.
uncleanly, slovenly, slatternly, untidy, frowzy, sluttish, unkempt, unwashed, draggle-tailed, drabble-tailed, slammocky *or* slummocky (*dial.*).
offensive, nasty, coarse, squalid, foul, impure, abominable, beastly, reeky, fetid; moldy, musty, rancid, bad, touched, rotten, corrupt, tainted, putrid, putrescent, putrefactive, carious, purulent; morbid, peccant (*esp. med.*), unclean, repulsive; gory, bloody, blood-stained.
[*morally impure*] **indecent**, indelicate, indecorous, immodest, unseemly, gross, vile, obscene, lewd, impure, immoral; smutty, *risqué* (*F.*), off-color, improper.
See also BLACKNESS, FETOR, IMPURITY.—*Antonyms.* See CLEANNESS.

---

uncomfortable, *adj.* uneasy (*mentally or physically*), disquieted, disturbed, restless. See PAIN, POVERTY.

uncommon, *adj.* unexampled, exceptional, uncopied, original; infrequent, unusual, singular, rare, scarce; strange, remarkable, unfamiliar, unconventional. See NONIMITATION, RARITY, UNCONFORMITY.

uncompleted, *adj.* incomplete, unfinished, unaccomplished, inchoate. See NONCOMPLETION.

uncompromising, *adj.* strict, rigid, orthodox, unyielding, inflexible. See CONFORMITY, SEVERITY.

unconcerned, *adj.* uninterested, apathetic, listless, indifferent. See INDIFFERENCE.

unconditional, *adj.* absolute, unqualified, unlimited, free. See COMPLETENESS, FREEDOM.

unconfined, *adj.* free, unhampered, unchecked, unbridled. See FREEDOM.

UNCONFORMITY.—I. *Nouns.* **unconformity**, inconsistency, irregularity, anomaly, anomalousness, anomalism, dissimilarity, aberration, abnormity, teratism (*rare*); exception, rarity, *bizarrerie* (*F.*), oddity, peculiarity, eccentricity, *je ne sais quoi* (*F.*).
nonconformity, nonobservance, noncompliance, disconformity, disagreement, dissent; unconventionality, informality, bohemianism; infraction (breach, violation, *or* infringement) of custom *or* usage.
individuality, character, personality; singularity, originality, idiosyncrasy, mannerism, peculiarity.
original, character (*colloq.*), nonesuch, crank (*colloq.*), monomaniac, queer person, eccentric, bohemian, nondescript (*usually derogatory*), sulphite (*slang*); prodigy, wonder, marvel, miracle; curiosity, freak, oddity; sport (*biol.*), *lusus naturæ* (*L.*), *rara avis* (*L.*).
monster, monstrosity, miscreation, abortion, mooncalf (*archaic*), cacogenesis (*med.*); teratogeny (*med.*).
[*legendary beings*] phœnix, chimera *or* chimæra, hydra, sphinx; manticore, gorgon, minotaur, centaur, sagittary, hippocampus, hircocervus, hippogriff; kraken, cockatrice, basilisk; sea serpent; wivern, roc, dragon, griffin; mermaid, merman; unicorn; ogre, ogress (*fem.*), Cyclops, "men whose heads do grow beneath their shoulders" (*Othello*).

outcast, outlaw, *proscrit* (*F.*), Ishmael, pariah, derelict, man without a country.
II. *Adjectives*. **unconformable**, exceptional, abnormal, unnatural, teratoid, teratogenetic *or* teratogenic (*tech.*), monstrous; heterogeneous, amorphous, anomalous, misplaced, out of order, irregular, arbitrary, lawless; informal, stray, eccentric, peculiar, exclusive, egregious; out of the beaten track, out of the common (*or* common run).
unusual, unaccustomed, uncustomary, unwonted, uncommon, rare, singular, unique, curious, odd, extraordinary, strange, wonderful, remarkable, noteworthy; queer, quaint, nondescript, *sui generis* (*L.*), original; unorthodox, unconventional, bohemian; unprecedented, unparalleled, unexampled, unheard of; fantastic, newfangled, eccentric, grotesque, bizarre, *outré* (*F.*); unfamiliar, outlandish, exotic, preternatural, *tombé des nues* (*F.*).
hybrid, crossbred, mixed, mongrel, crossed, hermaphrodite, hermaphroditic, androgynous, androgynal, monoclinous (*bot.*), bisexual, gyandrous (*bot.*), epicene.
intractable, perverse, obstinate, refractory, noncompliant, unyielding, stubborn, headstrong, unmanageable, ungovernable, obdurate, immovable, incoercible; inadaptable, inharmonious.
III. *Adverbs*. **unconformably**, exceptionally, etc. (see *adjectives*).
IV. *Prepositions*. **except**, excepting, save, saving, bating (*now rare*), barring, but, unless (*archaic as prep.*).
See also DISAGREEMENT, DISTORTION, DIVERSITY, MIXTURE, NOMINITATION, WONDER.—*Antonyms*. See CONFORMITY.

---

uncongenial, *adj.* incompatible, mismatched, displeasing. See DISAGREEMENT.
unconnected, *adj.* separate, disjoint; unrelated, irrelevant; illogical, inconsequent. See DISJUNCTION, IRRELATION, SOPHISTRY.
unconquerable, *adj.* resistless, irresistible, invincible, impregnable. See STRENGTH.
unconscious, *adj.* unaware, uninformed; insensitive, insensible. See IGNORANCE, INSENSITIVENESS.
unconventional, *adj.* informal, unfashionable, unorthodox. See DISUSE, UNCONFORMITY.
uncouth, *adj.* ungainly, clumsy, awkward, rough, rude; unpolished, unrefined. See UGLINESS, VULGARITY.
uncover, *v.* disclose, discover, unfold; divest, denude, bare, doff, open, unclose, unseal, unveil, reveal, expose. See DISCLOSURE, DIVESTMENT, OPENING.
unction, *n.* fervor, gusto; unguent, ointment. See FEELING, UNCTUOUSNESS.

UNCTUOUSNESS.—I. *Nouns*. **unctuousness**, oiliness, oleaginousness, etc (see *adjectives*); unctuosity, lubrication.
unguent, ointment, unction, anointment, balm, nard, salve, cerate; lubricant.
suavity (*esp. excessive or insincere*), blandness, urbanity, pleasingness, complaisance, courtesy; gushingness, gush, fervor (*affected*).
II. *Verbs*. **anoint**, oil, salve, oint (*archaic or dial. Eng.*), anele (*archaic*), chrism (*rare*), balsam; smear (*archaic or contemptuous in this sense*), lard, grease, lubricate.
III. *Adjectives*. **unctuous**, oily, oleaginous, adipose, sebaceous, unguinous, smegmatic (*tech.*), fat, fatty, greasy; waxy, soapy, saponaceous, pinguid, lardaceous, buttery, butyraceous; slimy, sliddery (*dial.*), slithery (*dial.*), slippery, lubricous.
suave (*esp. without sincerity*), bland, smooth-spoken, complaisant, soft-spoken, smooth-tongued, oily, glib, fawning, fervid, gushing.
See also COURTESY, FLATTERY, IMPIETY, LUBRICATION, OIL.—*Antonyms*. See ARTLESSNESS, PULPINESS.

---

uncultivated, *adj.* illiterate, untaught, unread; unprepared, unready, unfit; uncultured, unrefined. See IGNORANCE, NONPREPARATION, VULGARITY.
undaunted, *adj.* fearless, dauntless, intrepid, plucky, bold. See COURAGE.
undeceive, *v.* correct, disabuse, set right. See INFORMATION.
undecided, *adj.* doubtful, uncertain, problematical, tentative. See UNCERTAINTY.

undemonstrative, *adj.* placid, tranquil, calm, reserved. See INEXCITABILITY.
undeniable, *adj.* conclusive, unquestionable, irrefutable, indisputable. See CERTAINTY.
under, *adv.* below, underneath, in a lower position. See LOWNESS, SUBJECTION.
—**under way,** on the move, on the march; under sail, afloat. See MOTION, NAVIGATION.
underbrush, *n.* undergrowth, scrub, brush, brushwood. See VEGETABLE.
underclothing, *n.* underwear, undergarments, *lingerie* (*F.*). See CLOTHING.

UNDERESTIMATION.—I. *Nouns.* **underestimation,** undervaluation, underestimate, depreciation; inappreciation, inappreciativeness; self-detraction, self-depreciation, modesty, belittling, belittlement, understatement, meiosis (*rhet.*), litotes (*rhet.*); pessimism, malism, miserabilism.
pessimist, malist, cynic, miserabilist, crape-hanger (*slang*), depreciator, knocker (*slang: opposite of* optimist).
II. *Verbs.* **underestimate,** undervalue, underrate, underprize (*rare*), misprize. disprize; belittle, run down (*colloq.*), knock (*slang*), slam (*slang*), traduce, defame, asperse, derogate, depreciate, disparage, detract, decry, ridicule, deride, slight, neglect; slur over; make light (*or* little) of, minimize, set no store by, set at naught, disregard.
III. *Adjectives.* **depreciative,** depreciatory, derogatory, disparaging, injurious, detractive; pessimistic, cynical, malistic.
inappreciative, unappreciative, unappreciating, unapplausive (*rare*), unresponsive, uninterested, indifferent.
unappreciated, unvalued, unprized, depreciated.

See also CONTEMPT, DETRACTION, MODESTY, NEGLECT.—*Antonyms.* See OVER ESTIMATION.

---

undergo, *v.* experience, bear, endure, sustain, suffer; pass, pass through, spend. See EVENT, RECEIVING, SERVANT.
underhand, *adj.* devious, tricky, deceitful, crooked. See LATENCY, OBLIQUITY.
underhand, *adv.* stealthily, slyly, surreptitiously; unfairly. See CONCEALMENT.
undermine, *v.* mine, excavate, tunnel; thwart, frustrate, foil; weaken, demoralize. See CONCAVITY, HINERANCE, IMPOTENCE.
underrate, *v.* underestimate, undervalue, belittle, decry. See UNDERESTIMATION.
undersized, *adj.* diminutive, dwarfish, undergrown, scrub. See SHORTNESS.
understand, *v.* perceive, sense (*colloq.*), learn apprehend, grasp, discern, comprehend, see, know; assume. See INTELLIGIBILITY, RECEIVING, SUPPOSITION, TAKING (*take in*).
understanding, *n.* compact, adjustment; insight, perception, intellectuality comprehension, penetration, discernment. See AGREEMENT, INTELLECT, INTELLIGENCE, KNOWLEDGE.
undertaker, *n.* mortician, funeral director. See INTERMENT.

UNDERTAKING.—I. *Nouns.* **undertaking,** enterprise, emprise (*archaic or poetic*), endeavor, venture, attempt, task, essay, move, adventure, business, work, project, affair.
promise, pledge, assurance, stipulation, guarantee, guaranty, warranty (*law*), engagement, contract, covenant, compact, obligation, agreement.
II. *Verbs.* **undertake,** engage in, embark in, launch (*or* plunge) into, volunteer, devote oneself to, take up, take on, accept, take in hand, tackle (*colloq.*), set about; go about, launch forth, attempt, betake oneself to, turn one's hand to, have in hand, be in for (*colloq.*), enter upon, assume, begin, broach, institute; put one's shoulder to the wheel, put one's hand to the plow (*or* plough).
promise, pledge, stipulate, contract, engage covenant, agree, guarantee.
III. *Adjectives.* **undertaking** (*rare*), enterprising, adventurous, venturesome, energetic, pushing, pushful, active, industrious, resourceful.

See also ACTION, BEGINNING, BUSINESS, COMPACT, ESSAY, PROMISE, RESOLUTION, TAKING (*take up*).—*Antonyms.* See AVOIDANCE, INACTION.

undesirable, *adj.* disliked, unacceptable; inexpeident, inadvisable, unsatisfactory; distasteful, unwelcome, unpleasant. See DISLIKE, INEXPEDIENCE, PAINFULNESS.

undetermined, *adj.* undecided, indecisive, problematical, irresolute, uncertain. See INQUIRY, IRRESOLUTION.

undignified, *adj.* unbefitting, indecorous, ungentlemanly, ill-bred. See DISCOURTESY, VULGARITY.

undiscordant, *adj.* concordant, congenial; euphonious, harmonious. See HARMONY, PURITY (*of sounds*).

undisguised, *adj.* real, pure, true, genuine, unadulterated. See TRUTH.

undisputed, *adj.* conclusive, undeniable, indisputable, unquestioned. See CERTAINTY.

undissolved, *adj.* unmelted, unliquified, unthawed. See DENSITY.

undisturbed, *adj.* unagitated, unruffled, motionless, resting. See [1]REST.

undivided, *adj.* entire, whole, complete, intact. See COMPLETENESS.

undo, *v.* cancel, offset, neutralize; overturn, destroy, crush, ruin; untie, unfasten, unravel; unmake. See COUNTERACTION, DESTRUCTION, DISJUNCTION, INACTION.

undone, *adj.* lost, ruined, overwhelmed. See FAILURE.

undress, *v.* disrobe, dismantle, strip, denude. See DIVESTMENT.

undue, *adj.* excessive, extreme, inordinate; illegal, unlawful, unsanctioned. See GREATNESS, RIGHTLESSNESS.

undulate, *v.* wave, swell, billow, vibrate. See ROLL.

undutiful, *adj.* disobedient, unsubmissive, disrespectful, unworthy. See DISOBEDIENCE, VICE.

unearth, *v.* discover, uncover, expose; uproot, eradicate, extirpate; disinter, exhume. See DISCOVERY, EJECTION, INTERMENT.

uneasy, *adj.* uncomfortable, disquieted, disturbed, worried; ill at ease. See PAIN.

uneatable, *adj.* inedible, unpalatable, unappetizing. See DISLIKE.

uneducated, *adj.* illiterate, unschooled, untaught, untrained, uninstructed. See IGNORANCE, NONPREPARATION.

unemotional, *adj.* inexcitable, phlegmatic, unfeeling, cold. See INSENSITIVENESS.

unemployed, *adj.* unapplied, unexercised; idle, disengaged, loafing, resting. See DISUSE, INACTION.

unenlightened, *adj.* ignorant, unlettered, untaught, benighted; unintelligent. See DARKNESS, IMBECILITY.

unequal, *adj.* uneven, disparate; irregular, rough. See INEQUALITY, IRREGULARITY.

unequaled, *adj.* unmatched, unparalleled, inimitable, incomparable, unique. See INEQUALITY, SUPERIORITY.

unessential, *adj.* irrelevant, inapposite, unrelated; secondary, nonessential, accessory; unimportant, immaterial. See IRRELATION, OBJECTIVENESS, UNIMPORTANCE.

uneven, *adj.* variegated, motley; unequal, disparate, unbalanced; rough, unlevel, rugged, broken. See DIVERSITY, INEQUALITY, IRREGULARITY.

unexpected, *adj.* unanticipated, unforseen, sudden. See NONEXPECTATION.

unfair, *adj.* one-sided, dishonest, unjust, partial. See IMPROBITY, WRONG.

unfaithful, *adj.* disloyal, false, faithless, untrue. See IMPROBITY, UNTRUTH.

unfamiliar, *adj.* unheard of, strange, newfangled. See UNCONFORMITY.

unfashionable, *adj.* out of fashion, unmodish, unconventional; antiquated, out-of-date. See DISUSE, OLDNESS.

unfasten, *v.* loose, disjoin, disconnect, untie, liberate. See DISJUNCTION, LIBERATION.

unfathomable, *adj.* fathomless, soundless; unintelligible, inexplicable. See DEPTH, UNINTELLIGIBILITY.

unfavorable, *adj.* inclement, foul (*as weather*); sinister, adverse, contrary; disadvantageous, unfortunate; untimely, inopportune. See CONTRARIETY, LOWNESS, POVERTY, UNTIMELINESS.

unfeeling, *adj.* insensible, senseless, numb, unconscious; passionless, soulless, insensitive; inconsiderate, hard, cruel, insensate. See INSENSIBILITY, INSENSITIVENESS, ROUGHNESS.

unfetter, *v.* untie, loose, unbind, disengage, extricate. See LIBERATION.

unfinished, *adj.* incomplete, uncompleted, imperfect, unaccomplished. See INCOMPLETENESS, NONCOMPLETION.

unfit, *adj.* unfitted, inefficient, unqualified; unready, incomplete, unripe; unbefitting, unseemly, unsuitable; unskilled, inexpert, incompetent; objectionable, improper. See IMPOTENCE, NONPREPARATION, RIGHTLESSNESS, UNSKILLFULNESS, WRONG.

unfitness, *n.* inaptitude, impropriety, unsuitability, irrelevancy. See DISAGREEMENT.

UNFOLDMENT.—I. *Nouns.* **unfoldment,** unfolding, expansion, growth, development, maturation, elaboration, evolvement, evolution; inversion.

[*in biology*] ontogeny *or* ontogenesis (*evolution of an individual organism*), phylogeny *or* phylogenesis (*evolution of a race or group*), physiogeny *or* physiogenesis (*development of vital activities*); Lamarckism, Darwinism, Neo-Lamarckism (*heredity: opposite of* Neo-Darwinism *and* Weismannism), pangenesis (*Darwin's theory of heredity: opposite of* blastogenesis), evolutionism: *opposite of* spontaneous generation *or* abiogenesis.

II. *Verbs.* **unfold,** unroll, unwind, uncoil, untwist, unfurl, untwine, unravel disentangle, open, expand, evolve, develop, ripen, mature; spread out, reveal, disclose, display, make known.

III. *Adjectives.* **evolutional,** evolutionary, evolutive, ontogenic *or* ontogenetic (*biol.*), phylogenic *or* phylogenetic (*biol.*).

See also PRODUCTION.—*Antonyms.* See DESTRUCTION, ROTATION.

---

unforeseen, *adj.* unexpected, unanticipated. See NONEXPECTATION.

unforgiving, *adj.* unrelenting, relentless, implacable. See REVENGE.

unfortunate, *adj.* unhappy, unprosperous; unfavorable, inexpedient. See ADVERSITY, UNTIMELINESS.

unfounded, *adj.* groundless, erroneous, untrue, false, fictitious. See ERROR, UNTRUTH.

unfriendly, *adj.* hostile, adverse, antagonistic, inimical. See ENMITY.

unfruitful, *adj.* unproductive, unyielding, sterile, barren. See UNPRODUCTIVENESS.

ungainly, *adj.* ungraceful, uncouth, clumsy, awkward. See INEXPEDIENCE, UGLINESS.

ungenerous, *adj.* illiberal, close, stingy, miserly, mean. See PARSIMONY, SELFISHNESS.

ungovernable, *adj.* headstrong, unruly, unbridled, irrepressible. See VIOLENCE.

ungraceful, *adj.* graceless, ungainly, awkward, clumsy. See UGLINESS.

ungracious, *adj.* uncivil, discourteous, ungallant, unmannerly, rude. See DISCOURTESY.

ungrammatical, *adj.* improper, incorrect, faulty, unidiomatic. See SOLECISM.

ungrateful, *adj.* unthankful, thankless, ingrate. See INGRATITUDE.

unguent, *n.* unction, ointment. See UNCTUOUSNESS.

unhappy, *adj.* unfortunate, unlucky, unblest, unprosperous; wretched, miserable, sad, comfortless, dejected. See ADVERSITY, PAIN.

UNHEALTHINESS.—I. *Nouns.* **unhealthiness,** insalubrity, insalubriousness, unsoundness (*moral or spiritual*), unwholesomeness, etc. (see *adjectives*); contagion, toxicity, poisonousness.

unhealth, ill health, sickness, infirmity, indisposition, illness, feebleness, valetudinarianism, unsoundness, disease, morbidity.

II. *Adjectives.* **unhealthy,** insalubrious, unwholesome, unhealthful, unsound, healthless, insanitary, injurious, harmful, deleterious, pernicious, noisome, noxious, morbific, morbiferous, pestiferous, pestilential; virulent, venomous, poisonous, septic, toxic, toxiferous, azotic (*rare*), nitrogenous, deadly.
catching, infectious, contagious, communicable, taking, inoculable, epidemic, pandemic, pestilential, pestiferous, endemic (*opposite of* epidemic *and* sporadic), zymotic, (*obsolescent*) epizoötic (*of animals*).
[*not enjoying health*] **unwell,** ailing, indisposed, sick, sickly, seedy (*colloq.*), weak, feeble, delicate, poorly (*colloq.*), out of sorts (*colloq.*), laid up, infirm; diseased, morbid.
innutritious, indigestible, innutrient (*rare*), unnutritious (*rare*), undigestible (*rare*), not nourishing: *opposite of* nutritious.
See also DISEASE.—*Antonyms.* See HEALTH, HEALTHINESS.

---

unheard-of, *adj.* unknown, concealed, hidden; improbable, inconceivable, unbelievable; unprecedented, unparalleled, unexampled. See IGNORANCE, IMPROBABILITY, UNCONFORMITY.
unhinge, *v.* derange, unsettle, upset, unbalance. See DERANGEMENT.
unholy, *adj.* unhallowed, unsanctified, ungodly. See IRRELIGION.

UNIFORMITY.—I. *Nouns.* **uniformity,** homogeneity, consonance *or* consonancy, consistency, accordance, unity, unanimity, agreement; constancy, regularity, evenness, sameness, uniformness, stability, continuity, permanence; routine, monotony, even tenor.
II. *Verbs.* **be uniform,** accord with, conform to.
render uniform, level, smooth, even, dress, grade, symmetrize; make like (to *or* with), assimilate, harmonize.
III. *Adjectives.* **uniform,** homogeneous, of a piece, consistent, correspondent, symmetrical; undeviating, invariable, unvaried, undiversified, unvarying, regular, even, smooth, level, flat, dead, unbroken, equal, equable, constant; singsong, monotonous, dreary, drearisome.
IV. *Adverbs.* **uniformly,** consistently, etc. (see *adjectives*); in a rut.
always, ever, evermore, perpetually, forever, eternally, everlastingly, invariably.
See also AGREEMENT, CONFORMITY, DEATH, RULE, SYMMETRY.—*Antonyms.* See DIVERSITY.

---

unimitated, *adj.* uncopied, original, unique, inimitable. See NONIMITATION.

UNIMPORTANCE.—I. *Nouns.* **unimportance,** insignificance *or* insignificancy, inconsiderableness, nothingness, immateriality.
triviality, levity, frivolity, paltriness, smallness, matter of indifference; nothing, small (*or* trifling) matter; joke, jest, snap of the fingers, fudge, fiddlestick, flimflam, falderal *or* folderol, incident, *peu de chose* (*F.*), mere nothing; nine days' wonder, *ridiculus mus* (*L.*), flash in the pan, much ado about nothing, tempest in a teapot, storm in a teacup.
trifle, bagatelle, fico (*archaic*), fig, jot, iota, peppercorn, mote, old song, straw, pin, button, halfpenny, bawbee (*Scot.*), doit, rap, farthing, brass farthing, cent, red cent (*U. S. colloq.*), picayune (*colloq.*), damn, tinker's dam (*or* damn), continental (*U. S.*), feather; "trifles light as air" (*Othello*).
toy, plaything, gewgaw, bauble, trinket, kickshaw, knickknack, whimwham.
trumpery, trash, rubbish, stuff, frippery, *fatras* (*F.*), balderdash, chaff, dross, froth, scum, bubble, smoke; weed; refuse, litter.
[*insignificant person*] **nonentity,** nobody, cipher, insignificancy, whiffet (*colloq.*), whippersnapper, two spot (*slang*), jackstraw, man of straw; small fry (*pl.*).
II. *Verbs.* **be important,** not matter, matter (*or* signify) little, not matter a straw; make light of.
III. *Adjectives.* **unimportant,** immaterial, nonessential, unessential, irrelevant; indifferent, mediocre, passable, fair, soso *or* so-so, tolerable, commonplace; mere, common, ordinary, insignificant, nugatory, inappreciable, inconsequential (*rare in this sense*).
triffling, trivial, slight, slender, light, airy, flimsy, idle, frivolous, shallow, weak, powerlessi petty, niggling, piddling, peddling, fribble, fribbling, finical.
paltry, trashy, rubbishy, worthless, scrubby, scurvy, mean, scrannel (*archaic*).

poor, pitiful, contemptible, puerile; sorry, meager, shabby, miserable, wretched, vile, niggardly, beggarly, two-by-four (*U. S. colloq.*), cheap, catchpenny, gimcrack, trumpery, inferior, second-rate, one-horse (*U. S. colloq.*), twopenny-halfpenny.
of no importance, not worth mentioning (speaking of, a thought, *or* while), beneath contempt, beneath consideration; not worth a rap (hair, straw, curse, etc.); of no consequence.
IV. *Adverbs.* **slightly**, somewhat, in a small degree, but little, rather, fairly, indifferently, tolerably, passably.
V. *Interjections.* **no matter!** never mind! *n'importe!* (*F.*), what matter! what signifies! what of that! what's the odds! pish! tush! tut! pshaw! pugh! pooh! pooh-pooh! bosh! fudge! humbug! fiddlesticks! stuff! nonsense! stuff and nonsense!

See also IMMATERIALITY, IMPOTENCE, INDIFFERENCE, INUTILITY, LIGHTNESS, SIMPLENESS, SMALLNESS, UNMEANINGNESS.—*Antonyms.* See IMPORTANCE.

---

uninhabited, *adj.* unoccupied, untenanted, abandoned, deserted. See SECLUSION.

uninjured, *adj.* unscathed, unharmed; unimpaired, unbroken. See HEALTH, PRESERVATION.

unintelligent, *adj.* unintellectual. unenlightened, unteachable. See IGNORANCE, IMBECILITY.

UNINTELLIGIBILITY.—I. *Nouns.* **unintelligibility,** incomprehensibility, imperspicuity (*rare*), impenetrableness, impenetrability, unfathomableness, inscrutability, inconceivableness, vagueness, obscurity, *obscurum per obscurius* (*L.*), ambiguity, confusion; mystification, enigma, riddle, mystery, sealed book; jargon, gibberish.
II. *Verbs.* **render unintelligible,** conceal, veil, darken, confuse, obscure, mystify, perplex, bewilder.
III. *Adjectives.* **unintelligible,** incomprehensible, indecipherable, undecipherable, illegible, undiscoverable, incognizable, inextricable, unaccountable, unfathomable, inexplicable, inscrutable, insoluble, impenetrable; puzzling, enigmatic *or* enigmatical, crabbed, intricate.
obscure, dark, muddy, dim, nebulous, mysterious, hidden, latent, occult, apocalyptic *or* apocalyptical, mystic, mystical, acroamatic *or* acroamatical, recondite, abstruse; indefinite, vague, loose, inexact, ambiguous.
inexpressible, unspeakable, indescribable, incommunicable, unutterable, ineffable, undefinable.

See also CONCEALMENT, DARKNESS, DIMNESS, EQUIVOCALNESS, LATENCY, OBSCURITY, OPACITY, UNCERTAINTY.—*Antonyms.* See INTELLIGIBILITY.

---

unintentional, *adj.* unpremeditated, accidental; involuntary, unthinking. See CHANCE, NECESSITY.

uninteresting, *adj.* flat, dull, tame, monotonous, wearying, dry. See FLATNESS, WEARINESS.

uninterrupted, *adj.* continuous, constant, unbroken; unceasing. See CONTINUITY, PERPETUITY.

uninvited, *adj.* unwelcome; unbidden, unasked. See EXCLUSION.

uninvolved, *adj.* uncomplicated, unelaborate, clear, intelligible. See SIMPLENESS.

union, *n.* harmony, concord, unanimity, unity; alliance, association, league, guild, club; connection, meeting, joining, marriage. See AGREEMENT, COMBINATION, JUNCTION.

unionize, *v.* federate, amalgamate, organize. See COMBINATION.

unique, *adj.* unparalleled, unequalled, unsurpassed; unusual, uncommon, rare, singular, unprecedented; one, sole, lone, single. See INEQUALITY, UNCONFORMITY, UNITY.

unison, *n.* agreement, accord, harmony, union, unanimity. See AGREEMENT.

UNITY.—I. *Nouns.* **unity,** oneness, individuality; undividedness, singleness, selfsameness, identity, compaction (*rare*), compages (*sing. and pl.*), consistency, solidarity; coherence, interconnection (*of parts*), integral, integrality, organic totality, systematic whole; unification, conflation (*esp. of variant readings*), amalgamation, synthesis, coalescence, fusion, centralization, union; junction, coadunation; completeness, completion.

concord, harmony, uniformity, agreement, sameness, coincidence, accordance, unanimity.

[*in law*] joint tenancy; joint possession (*by one person of different rights*).

unit, one, ace, monad (*tech.*), monas (*pl.* monades: *rare*), integer, individual, entity; standard, norm.

II. *Verbs.* **unite,** join, combine, connect, couple; merge, fuse, conflate (*as two variant readings*), coalesce, blend, merge, cement, weld; centralize, consolidate, solidify, coadunate, unify, concentrate; harmonize, reconcile; federate, ally, confederate, league, associate, band together, conjoin, amalgamate, incorporate.

III. *Adjectives.* **one,** sole, lone, single, odd, azygous (*esp. anat.*), individual, monadic, singular, unique.

alone, solitary, isolated, insulated, insular, *solus* (*L.*), unattended, unaccompanied, detached, separate, lonely; lonesome; single-handed, unassisted, unaided.

united, joined, combined, etc. (see *adjectives*); undivided, unitary, indiscrete, homogeneous, coadunate, conjoint, conjunctive, conjugate (*tech.*), related, allied, cognate, connate; confederate, confederated, leagued, federal, amalgamated, consolidated, unified, corporate, incorporated.

harmonious, concordant, in accord, agreeing, unanimous, friendly, fraternal.

uniting, unitive, unific, unifying, combinative, combinatory, connectional, connective, connecting, conjunctival, conjunctive, coalescent; confederative, federative, incorporative.

IV. *Adverbs.* **singly,** individually, severally, particularly; by itself, *per se* (*L.*), apart, independently, separately, one by one, one at a time.

solely, simply, barely, merely, purely, scarcely, alone, exclusively.

unitedly, jointly, conjointly, concordantly, harmoniously, as one man.

See also AGREEMENT, ASSEMBLAGE, COHERENCE, COMBINATION, COMPLETENESS, CONCORD, CONCURRENCE, CONVERGENCE, IDENTITY, JUNCTION, MIXTURE, PARTY, SECLUSION, UNIFORMITY.—*Antonyms.* See ACCOMPANIMENT, DISCORD, DISJUNCTION.

---

universal, *adj.* total, entire, complete; general, catholic, ecumenical, worldwide; cosmic. See COMPLETENESS, GENERALITY, WORLD.—**universal language,** pasigraphy, Volapük, Esperanto, Ido. See LANGUAGE.

universe, *n.* creation, nature, cosmos. See WORLD.

unjust, *adj.* wrongful, unfair, inequitable, partial; injurious. See WRONG.

unjustifiable, *adj.* indefensible, inexcusable; unreasonable, unwarrantable. See VICE, WRONG.

unkind, *adj.* cruel, harsh, unsympathetic, brutal, merciless, heartless, pitiless. See MALEVOLENCE, PITILESSNESS.

unknown, *adj.* unrecognized, unheralded, ignored; unperceived, concealed. See DARKNESS, IGNORANCE.

unlawful, *adj.* illegal, illegitimate, illicit, unconstitutional, prohibited; spurious, usurped, misbegotten. See ILLEGALITY, RIGHTLESSNESS.

unlearned, *adj.* thickheaded, stupid; illiterate, uninstructed, uneducated, ignorant. See IGNORAMUS, IGNORANCE.

unlike, *adj.* dissimilar, different, diversified, heterogeneous. See DISSIMILARITY.

unlimited, *adj.* limitless, unbounded, unrestricted, full, absolute; immeasurable, interminable, infinite. See FREEDOM, GREATNESS.

unload, *v.* empty, discharge; transfer; disburden, unlade, unship; sell, dump. See DISPLACEMENT, EJECTION, SALE.

unloved, *adj.* unbeloved, uncared for, unvalued, disliked. See HATE.

unlucky, *adj.* unfortunate, unprosperous; baleful, hopeless, disastrous;

untimely, unseasonable, inopportune, unpropitious. See ADVERSITY, PAINFULNESS, UNTIMELINESS.

unman, *v.* unnerve, devitalize, emasculate. See IMPOTENCE.

unmanly, *adj.* craven, cowardly; ignoble, inglorious; womanish, effeminate. See COWARDICE, IMPROBITY, WOMAN.

unmannerly, *adj.* ill-mannered, impolite, discourteous, uncivil, ill-bred. See DISCOURTESY, VULGARITY.

unmarried, *adj.* celibate, unwedded, virgin. See CELIBACY.—**unmarried man,** bachelor, misogamist; monk, celibate. See CELIBACY.—**unmarried woman,** maiden, virgin, spinster; nun, *religieuse* (*F.*). See CELIBACY.

UNMEANINGNESS.—I. *Nouns.* **unmeaningness,** senselessness, meaninglessness, nonsensicalness, empty sound, *vox ed præterea nihil* (*L.*), "sounding brass and a tinkling cymbal" (*Bible*); "a tale told by an idiot, full of sound and fury, signifying nothing" (*Macbeth*); ambiguity, vagueness, unintelligibleness; scrabble, scribble, scrawl.

nonsense, jargon, gibberish, drivel, twaddle, tosh (*slang*), jabber, babble, *bavardage* (*F.*), *baragouin* (*F.*), mere words, rant, bombast, fustian, flummery, flapdoodle (*colloq.*), poppy-cock (*U. S. colloq.*), bosh (*colloq.*), moonshine (*dry variety*), wish-wash (*slang*), balderdash, trash, rubbish; absurdity, imbecility, folly, silliness, *niaiserie* (*F.*), inanity, blah (*slang*).

II. *Verbs.* **be unmeaning,** etc. (*see adjectives*); mean nothing, gibber, jabber, twaddle, babble, gabble, rant.

scribble, scrawl, scratch, scrabble.

twiddle (*as one's thumbs*), twirl, twist, fiddle, wiggle (*colloq.*), fidget, fidge, trifle, toy (*or* play) with.

III. *Adjectives.* **unmeaning,** meaningless, senseless, nonsensical; inexpressive, vague, blank, expressionless.

trashy, worthless, rubbishy, twaddling, washy, wishy-washy (*colloq.*), inane, trumpery, trivial, insignificant.

See also ABSURDITY, FOLLY, IMBECILITY, UNINTELLIGIBILITY.—*Antonyms.* See MEANING.

---

unmerciful, *adj.* merciless, unpitying, unfeeling, cruel. See PITILESSNESS.

unmistakable, *adj.* certain, sure, positive, clear. See CERTAINTY, MANIFESTATION.

unnatural, *adj.* affected, insincere, self-conscious; merciless, heartless, cold; unconformable, exceptional, abnormal; counternatural, irregular. See AFFECTATION, MALEVOLENCE, UNCONFORMITY, VIOLENCE.

unnecessary, *adj.* useless, superfluous, needless, uncalled for. See INUTILITY, REDUNDANCE.

unoccupied, *adj.* vacant, empty, untenanted, abandoned, deserted; unemployed, idle, loafing, resting. See ABSENCE, INACTION.

unpack, *v.* disburden, unload, remove. See EJECTION.

unpaid, *adj.* owing, due, unsettled, unliquidated, outstanding. See DEBT.

unpalatable, *adj.* distasteful, disagreeable, unpleasant; unsavory. See PAINFULNESS, UNSAVORINESS.

unparalleled, *adj.* peerless, unequaled, unrivaled, inimitable, unique. See INEQUALITY, SUPERIORITY.

unpleasant, *adj.* unpleasing, displeasing, distasteful, offensive. See PAINFULNESS.

unpopular, *adj.* unacceptable, unapproved, out of favor, disliked (*esp. by the public*). See DISLIKE.

unprejudiced, *adj.* unbiased, impartial, uninfluenced, judicial. See FREEDOM.

unpremeditated, *adj.* undesigned, unintentional; improvised, spontaneous. See CHANCE, IMPULSE.

unprepared, *adj.* unready, unfit, unqualified, incomplete. See NONPREPARATION.

unprepossessing, *adj.* ugly, uncomely, unattractive. See INDIFFERENCE, UGLINESS.

unprincipled, *adj.* unscrupulous. knavish; wicked, evil, sinful. See IMPROBITY, VICE.

UNPRODUCTIVENESS.—I. *Nouns.* **unproductiveness,** unproductivity, infertility, sterility, barrenness, unfruitfulness, infecundity, impotence; unprofitableness.

waste, desert, Sahara, wild, wilderness, howling wilderness, barren.

II. *Verbs.* **be unproductive,** hang fire, flash in the pan, come to nothing.

render unproductive, sterilize (*biol.*), make sterile, Tyndallize (*tech.*), Pasteurize (*as milk*); incapacitate.

III. *Adjectives.* **unproductive,** unyielding, infertile, unfertile, arid, sterile, barren, unprolific, infecund (*rare*); issueless, *sine prole* (*L.*); infructuose (*rare*), acarpous, unfruitful, fruitless, useless, fallow; unprofitable, unsuccessful, vain, void, nugatory, null, dead, lifeless, inoperative, ineffectual, inefficacious, inefficient, impotent, useless.

See also IMPOTENCE, INUTILITY.—*Antonyms.* See PRODUCTIVENESS.

---

unprofitable, *adj.* inexpedient, unwise; unproductive, profitless, useless. See INEXPEDIENCE, INUTILITY.

unpropitious, *adj.* adverse, unpromising, unfavorable, inauspicious, ill-omened, sinister, minatory, untimely. See ADVERSITY, HOPELESSNESS, UNTIMELINESS.

unprovided, *adj.* unsupplied, unfurnished; unequipped. See INSUFFICIENCY, NONPREPARATION.

unpurified, *adj.* uncleansed, defiled, unhallowed, unsanctified. See IMPURITY.

unqualified, *adj.* certain, unmistakable; unconditional, unmitigated, consummate; unadapted, unfitted, unsuited; disqualified. See CERTAINTY, COMPLETENESS, NONPREPARATION, RIGHTLESSNESS.

unquestionable, *adj.* undeniable, conclusive, irrefutable, indisputable. See CERTAINTY.

unquiet, *adj.* disturbed, agitated, restless, fidgety. See AGITATION, EXCITEMENT.

unravel, *v.* disentangle, card; decipher, interpret, solve; unfold, evolve, disclose. See ARRANGEMENT, INTERPRETATION, UNFOLDMENT.

unreal, *adj.* fanciful, chimerical, imaginary, unsubstantial, shadowy, nebulous, vaporous, flimsy. See IMAGINATION, NONEXISTENCE, UNSUBSTANTIALITY, VAPORIZATION.

unreasonable, *adj.* immoderate, exorbitant, vast; absurd, unlikely. irrational, impractical; obstinate, stubborn, bigoted; unjustifiable; unwarrantable. See GREATNESS, IMPOSSIBILITY, MISJUDGMENT, WRONG.

unrefined, *adj.* unpolished, rough, coarse, rude, uncultivated. See ROUGHNESS, VULGARITY.

unrelated, *adj.* irrelative, unallied, unconnected, heterogeneous, unessential, extraneous, foreign. See IRRELATION.

unrelenting, *adj.* unforgiving, vindictive, rancorous, revengeful. See REVENGE.

unreliable, *adj.* irresponsible, unstable, fickle; untrustworthy. See IRRESOLUTION, UNCERTAINTY.

unreserved, *adj.* unrestrained, emotional, ingenuous, communicative; frank, plain-spoken, open, candid. See DEMONSTRATION, VERACITY.

unresisting, *adj.* passive, yielding, obedient, compliant. See SUBMISSION.

unrespected, *adj.* unregarded, unhonored, ignored. See DISRESPECT.

unrest, *n.* restlessness, disquietude, uneasiness. See CHANGEABLENESS.

unrestrained, *adj.* unreserved, coarse, outspoken; unfettered, unobstructed, free. See BREADTH, FREEDOM.

unrestricted, *adj.* unlimited, unqualified, unconditioned. See FREEDOM.

unripe, *adj.* premature, immature; hard, green, sour. See NONPREPARATION, SOURNESS.
unruffled, *adj.* calm, tranquil, serene, undisturbed, still. See SMOOTHNESS.
unruly, *adj.* ungovernable, unmanageable, obstinate, stubborn. See DISOBEDIENCE.
unsafe, *adj.* dangerous, perilous, unprotected, insecure. See DANGER.
unsalable, *adj.* unmarketable, unmerchantable, unpurchased. See SALE.
unsatisfactory, *adj.* imperfect, defective, faulty, unsuitable. See BADNESS.

UNSAVORINESS.—I. *Nouns.* **unsavoriness,** tastelessness, insipidity; unpalatableness, distastefulness, roughness, acridity, acridness, acerbity, sourness; offensiveness, etc. (see *adjectives*); Marah, gall and wormwood.
II. *Verbs.* **be unsavory,** be unpalatable; sicken, disgust, nauseate, pall, turn the stomach.
III. *Adjectives.* **unsavory,** insipid, tasteless; unpalatable, ill-flavored, distasteful, harsh, rough, bitter, acrid, acrimonious.
offensive, repulsive, repugnant, obnoxious, unpleasant, objectionable, disagreeable, uninviting, nasty, sickening, nauseous, loathsome, disgusting, revolting.
See also DISLIKE, INSIPIDITY, SOURNESS.—*Antonyms.* See SAVORINESS.

---

unscrupulous, *adj.* unconscientious, dishonest, unprincipled. See IMPROBITY, SHARPNESS.
unseasonable, *adj.* inopportune, ill-timed, untimely. See TIMELESSNESS, UNTIMELINESS.
unseemly, *adj.* improper, unsuitable; uncomely, unsightly. See INEXPEDIENCE, RIGHTLESSNESS, UGLINESS.
unseen, *adj.* invisible, imperceptible, undiscerned. See INVISIBILITY, LATENCY.

UNSELFISHNESS.—I. *Nouns.* **unselfishness,** self-forgetfulness, disinterestedness, generosity, large-heartedness, liberality, altruism, benevolence, loftiness of purpose, exaltation, magnanimity; honor, chivalry, heroism, bravery, valor, sublimity.
self-denial, self-restraint, self-control, stoicism, asceticism; devotion, labor of love, self-renunciation, self-abnegation, self-devotion, self-devotedness, self-sacrifice, self-immolation, martyrdom, suttee, kenosis (*theol.*); Good Shepherd, Good Samaritan.
III. *Adjectives.* **unselfish,** self-denying, self-forgetful, devoted, self-sacrificing, altruistic; unbiased, unprejudiced, impartial, fair, just, dispassionate, disinterested, impersonal.
magnanimous, high-minded; princely, great, high, elevated, lofty, exalted, great-hearted, large-hearted, beneficent, generous, liberal; courageous, honorable, chivalrous, heroic, noble, sublime.
See also BENEVOLENCE.—*Antonyms.* See SELFISHNESS.

---

unsettle, *v.* disarrange, convulse, trouble, confound; unhinge, unbalance. See DERANGEMENT.
unsettled, *adj.* inconstant, unsteady, restless, transient; unplaced, homeless, unestablished; undecided, pending; unfixed, adrift; experimental, tentative. See CHANGEABLENESS, DISPLACEMENT, OPENING, SHIP, UNCERTAINTY.

UNSKILLFULNESS.—I. *Nouns.* **unskillfulness** *or* unskilfulness, inexpertness, want of skill, incompetence, inability, clumsiness, inaptitude, inexperience, disqualification.
mismanagement, misconduct, misguidance, misdirection, misapplication; bad policy, impolicy; maladministration, misrule, misgovernment.
blunder, mistake, bungle, botch, *gaucherie* (*F.*), *étourderie* (*F.*), botchery, *balourdise* (*F.*); bad job, sad work, act of folly.
II. *Verbs.* **bungle,** blunder, botch, muff (*esp. baseball*), fumble, boggle, make a mess of (*colloq.*), make a hash of (*colloq.*), mar, spoil, flounder, stumble, trip; **mismanage,** misdirect, misapply, act foolishly.

mistake, err, slip, misapprehend, take the shadow for the substance, bark up the wrong tree; be in the wrong box (*colloq.*); lose one's way, miss one's way; fall into a trap, catch a Tartar: misidentify.

III. *Adjectives.* **unskillful** *or* **unskilful,** unskilled, inexpert, bungling, awkward, clumsy, gawky, unhandy, maladroit, *gauche* (*F.*), lubberly; inapt, unteachable, intractable; stupid, ill-qualified, incompetent, unfit: *opposite of* skillful.

unaccustomed, unused, strange, unfamiliar, untrained, uninitiated, inexperienced, raw, green, unconversant; rusty, out of practice; shiftless, unpractical, impractical (*rare*), unbusinesslike, unstatesmanlike.

ill-advised, injudicious, misadvised; ill-devised, ill-judged, ill-contrived, ill-conducted; misguided, unwise, foolish, infelicitous, unfortunate, wild; penny wise and pound foolish.

See also BUNGLER, ERROR, FOLLY, INATTENTION.—*Antonyms.* See SKILL.

---

unsociability, *n.* unsociableness, inhospitality, self-sufficiency. See SECLUSION.

unsociable, *adj.* unsocial, inhospitable; reserved, stand-offish. See SECLUSION.

unsophisticated, *adj.* natural, unstudied, ingenuous, naïve, simple. See SIMPLENESS.

unsound, *adj.* false, illogical; imperfect, impaired; fallacious, invalid, untenable, unreasonable; decayed, wasted. See ERROR, IMPERFECTION, SOPHISTRY, WEAKNESS.

unspeakable, *adj.* unutterable, indescribable, ineffable, inexpressible. See GREATNESS, WONDER.

unspoken, *adj.* unuttered, unexpressed; implied, tacit. See SILENCE.

unspotted, *adj.* spotless, clean, pure, immaculate, stainless, perfect. See BEAUTY, CLEANNESS.

unstable, *adj.* inconstant, changeful, uncertain, variable, unsteady, unfixed; shaky, tottery, insecure; irresolute, wavering. See CHANGEABLENESS, DANGER, IRRESOLUTION.

unsteady, *adj.* unstable, unsettled, inconstant; shaky, insecure. See CHANGEABLENESS, DANGER.

UNSUBSTANTIALITY.—I. *Nouns.* **unsubstantiality,** immateriality, incorporeity, insubstantiality, imponderability, visionariness, unreality, nonentity, nonexistence, nullity, nihility, nothingness, blank, void, hollowness; "such stuff as dreams are made on" (*Tempest*); "baseless fabric of a vision" (*Tempest*).

phantom, apparition, specter, phantasm, phantasma (*pl.* phantasmata), phasm (*archaic*), illusion, shadow, dream, vision, will-o'-the-wisp, *ignis fatuus* (*L.*).

nothing, naught *or* nought (*archaic, except in arith.*), *nil* (*L.*), zero, cipher, nix (*slang*).

[*in games, "no score"*] duck, duck egg, goose egg; love (*tennis, etc.*), pair of spectacles (*cricket*), pair, spectacles: *all slang except "love."*

II. *Verbs.* **vanish,** disappear, fade, sink, fly, dissolve, evaporate, pass away, melt away, die away, die out.

III. *Adjectives.* **unsubstantial,** visionary, imaginary, immaterial, spectral, apparitional, dreamy, dreamlike, illusory, unreal, cloud-built, gossamery, shadowy, ethereal, airy, gaseous, vaporous, insubstantial, imponderable, tenuous, vague; flimsy, groundless, baseless, ungrounded, without foundation.

vacant, vacuous, empty, void, blank, hollow.

See also ERROR, IMAGINATION, IMMATERIALITY, NONEXISTENCE, WEAKNESS.—*Antonyms.* See SUBSTANTIALITY.

---

unsuccessful, *adj.* unprosperous, luckless, unfortunate; fruitless, ineffectual. See FAILURE, POVERTY.

unsuitable, *adj.* inappropriate, inapplicable, unbecoming, inexpedient, unsatisfactory. See DISAGREEMENT, INEXPEDIENCE.

unsullied, *adj.* unsoiled, untainted, immaculate, stainless, pure. See CLEANNESS, PROBITY.

unsuspicious, *adj.* confiding, childlike; trustful, credulous, gullible; unsuspecting, fearless. See ARTLESSNESS, BELIEF, HOPE.

unsweet, *adj.* bitter, tart, acid, acidulous, unsweetened, dry (*as wines, etc.*), not fruity. See DRYNESS.

unsymmetrical, *adj.* asymmetric, irregular, unbalanced, amorphous. See FORMLESSNESS.

unsympathetic, *adj.* uncongenial, mismatched; unfeeling, hard. See DISAGREEMENT, HARDNESS.

untaught, *adj.* illiterate, uneducated, unlettered, unread. See IGNORANCE, NONPREPARATION.

untenable, *adj.* unsound, illogical, inconsistent, indefensible, insupportable. See SOPHISTRY, SUBMISSION.

unthinkable, *adj.* inconceivable, unimaginable, impossible, improbable. See IMPOSSIBILITY.

untidy, *adj.* careless, slovenly, slatternly, unkempt. See DISORDER, UNCLEANNESS.

untie, *v.* unfetter, loose, free. See LIBERATION.

until, *prep.* till, to, up to, up to the time of. See TIME.

UNTIMELINESS.—I. *Nouns.* **untimeliness,** unseasonableness, inopportuneness, inopportunity, intempestivity (*rare*), prematureness, unsuitable time, improper time; intrusion.

hitch, impediment, *contretemps* (*F.*), check, obstacle, difficulty, mischance, mishap, accident, misadventure, misventure (*archaic*), misfortune.

II. *Verbs.* **be ill-timed,** mistime, intrude, come amiss, break in upon; be busy, be occupied, be engaged.

lose an opportunity, neglect an opportunity; allow (*or* suffer) the opportunity to pass (slip, go by, *or* escape), waste time, procrastinate, postpone, delay, linger, let slip through the fingers.

III. *Adjectives.* **untimely,** unseasonable, inopportune, inconvenient, intempestive (*rare*), *mal à propos* (*F.*), malapropos, ill-timed, untoward, mistimed, ill-fated, ill-omened, ill-starred, unfavorable, unlucky, inauspicious, unpropitious, unfortunate, unsuited, inexpedient, premature, immature; late, unpunctual, tardy, dilatory.

IV. *Adverbs.* **untimely,** unseasonably, inopportunely, etc. (see *adjectives*); out of season; in an evil hour.

See also ANACHRONISM, EARLINESS, INEXPEDIENCE, LATENESS.—*Antonyms.* See TIMELINESS.

---

untiring, *adj.* unflagging, persevering, steadfast, indefatigable. See PERSEVERANCE.

untoward, *adj.* adverse, unfortunate; perverse, stubborn; ill-timed, inconvenient. See ADVERSITY, OBSTINACY, UNTIMELINESS.

untrained, *adj.* untaught, unskilled, inexperienced. See NONPREPARATION, UNSKILLFULNESS.

untrustworthy, *adj.* illusive, deceptive; inaccurate, unreliable; false, unfaithful, disloyal; fallible, questionable. See ERROR, FALSEHOOD, IMPROBITY, UNCERTAINTY.

UNTRUTH.—I. *Nouns.* **untruth,** falseness, incorrectness, error; inveracity, falsity, faithlessness, infidelity, disloyalty, treachery.

falsehood, lie, story (*euphemistic*), fib, whopper (*colloq.*), crammer (*slang*) tarradiddle *or* taradiddle (*colloq.*).

fabrication, forgery, invention; misstatement, misrepresentation, perversion, falsification, gloss, *suggestio falsi* (*L.*), false coloring, exaggeration, bounce, bouncer (*colloq.*); concoction, imagination, fiction; fable, nursery tale, fairy tale, romance, extravaganza; yarn (*colloq.*), fish story (*colloq.*), bedtime story traveler's tale, cock-and-bull story, myth, moonshine. bosh (*colloq.*), canard, hoax, sell (*colloq.*), hum (*slang*).

half truth, white lie, pious fraud, equivocation, mental reservation, suppression; irony, sarcasm.
pretense, pretext, subterfuge, evasion, shift, shuffle, make-believe, sham, simulation, assumption, affectation, false show, artifice, disguise, profession, Judas kiss, cajolery, flattery.
untruthfulness, inveracity, lying, fibbery, unveracity, mendacity, mendaciousness, falsity, deceit, deceitfulness.
II. *Verbs.* **pretend,** profess, simulate, feign, make-believe, assume, affect, sham, counterfeit; lie, misrepresent.
III. *Adjectives.* **untrue** (*not true*), false, trumped up, fictitious, fabulous, fabricated, fraudulent, forged, counterfeit, fictive, sham; unfounded, invented, *ben trovato* (*It.*), supposititious.
incorrect, inaccurate, wrong, faulty, erroneous, defective, imperfect, inexact.
unfaithful, disloyal, perfidious, faithless, treacherous, false, recreant.
untruthful (*not truthful*), unveracious, lying, mendacious, deceitful, inveracious; evasive.
See also CONCEALMENT, DECEPTION, ERROR, EXAGGERATION, FALSEHOOD.—*Antonyms.* See VERACITY.

---

unusual, *adj.* extraordinary, extreme; uncustomary, rare, uncommon. See HEAVINESS, UNCONFORMITY.
unutterable, *adj.* indescribable, unspeakable, inexpressible, ineffable. See GREATNESS, WONDER.
unveil, *v.* disclose, unmask, uncover, reveal, expose. See DISCLOSURE.
unwary, *adj.* unguarded, remiss, reckless, heedless. See NEGLECT.
unweakened, *adj.* unworn, unexhausted, unspent, unwithered. See STRENGTH.
unwell, *adj.* ailing, indisposed, sick, delicate. See UNHEALTHINESS.
unwholesome, *adj.* unhealthful, insalubrious, injurious, unsound. See UNHEALTHINESS.
unwieldy, *adj.* cumbersome, burdensome, massy, heavy; clumsy, awkward, ungainly; hulky, lubberly. See GRAVITY, INEXPEDIENCE, SIZE.

UNWILLINGNESS.—I. *Nouns.* **unwillingness,** indisposition, disinclination, aversion, averseness, reluctance, nolition (*opposite of* volition: *rare*), nolleity (*rare*), renitency, recalcitrance *or* recalcitrancy, noncompliance, obstinacy; indifference, backwardness, slowness.
scruple, hesitation, hesitance *or* hesitancy, indecision, qualm, scrupulosity, scrupulousness, delicacy, fastidiousness, punctiliousness, shrinking, recoil.
II. *Verbs.* **be unwilling,** nill (*archaic*), hesitate, scruple, stickle, demur, dislike, stick at, hang fire, shirk, slack, recoil, shrink, avoid, oppose, dissent, refuse, shy at, fight shy of, duck (*slang*).
III. *Adjectives.* **unwilling,** disinclined, indisposed, averse, reluctant, loath *or* loth, renitent, recalcitrant, opposed, adverse, laggard, backward, remiss, slack, indifferent, scrupulous, fastidious, squeamish; repugnant, restive; grudging, forced.
IV. *Adverbs.* **unwillingly,** grudgingly, with an ill grace; against one's will, *nolens volens* (*L.*), *invita Minerva* (*L.; connoting lack of inspiration*); against the grain, *à contre cœur* (*F.*), *malgré soi* (*F.*), in spite of oneself, with a heavy heart, with a bad (*or* ill) grace, under compulsion, under protest.
See also COMPULSION, DISLIKE, FASTIDIOUSNESS, INDIFFERENCE, NECESSITY, REFUSAL, SLOWNESS.—*Antonyms.* See WILLINGNESS.

---

unwise, *adj.* impolitic, imprudent, ill-advised, injudicious. See FOLLY.
unworthy, *adj.* unbecoming, derogatory; discreditable, blameworthy, reprehensible. See DISREPUTE, VICE.
unyielding, *adj.* rigid, solid, implastic; firm, inflexible, uncompromising; severe, stern, immovable; pertinacious, resolute, unwavering, tenacious; perverse, intractable; self-willed, headstrong. See HARDNESS, RESISTENCE, SEVERITY, TENACITY, UNCONFORMITY, WILL.
up, *adv.* upward, aloft, skyward, above, overhead. See ASCENT, HEIGHT.

upbraid, *v.* scold, reprove, denounce, accuse, revile. See DISAPPROBATION.
upheaval, *n.* raising, upthrow, cataclysm, eruption, rebellion, uprising. See ELEVATION, REVOLUTION.
uphill, *adj.* laborious, toilsome, strenuous; precipitious. See EXERTION, OBLIQUITY.
uphold, *v.* maintain, support, advocate, sustain, vindicate, champion. See DEFENSE.
upholder, *n.* seconder, backer, supporter, advocate, champion. See AUXILIARY.
uplift, *v.* raise, upraise, lift, elevate; refine, inspire, animate. See ELEVATION, IMPROVEMENT.
upper, *adj.* higher, superior; supernal. See HEIGHT.—**upper house,** first chamber, Senate, House of Lords. See COUNCIL.
upright, *adj.* honest, honorable, square, just, incorruptible, pure, straightforward; vertical, perpendicular, erect. See STRAIGHTNESS, VERTICALITY.
uproar, *n.* turmoil, tumult, riot, pandemonium; noise, hubbub, clangor, clamor, clatter. See DISORDER, LOUDNESS.
uproot, *v.* root up, pull up, eradicate, extirpate, stub. See EXTRACTION.
upset, *v.* overturn, overthrow, overwhelm; disturb, disconcert, confound, embarrass; overbalance, upturn, capsize. See DESTRUCTION, DISREPUTE. INVERSION.
upshot, *n.* result, end, outcome, consummation, conclusion, effect. See SEQUEL.
upstart, *n.* parvenu, *nouveau riche* (*F.*). See NEWNESS, PEOPLE, PROSPERITY.
upturned, *adj.* turned up, elevated, raised, uplifted. See ASCENT.
urban, *adj.* town, civic, metropolitan; suburban. See HABITATION.
urbane, *adj.* polite, courteous, civil, mannerly. See COURTESY.
urge, *v.* quicken, hurry; spur, goad, drive, impel; entreat, implore, press, tease, importune. See HASTE, IMPULSE, REQUEST.
urgent, *adj.* pressing, critical, crucial, exigent; solicitous, importunate, instant, insistent. See IMPORTANCE, REQUEST, REQUIREMENT.

USE.—I. *Nouns.* use, employment, exercise, application (*to a purpose*), adhibition, appliance; disposal, consumption; recourse, resort; usefulness, utility, usableness, availability, suitableness, adaptability, convenience.
[*conversion to use*] utilization, service, wear.
[*repeated practice*] usage, custom, habit, wont, familiarity, practice, mode, method, treatment, way; manner of working (*or* operating), *modus operandi* (*L.*), procedure; ritual, liturgy.
need, necessity, want, occasion, requisiteness, exigency, urgency, indispensableness: *often with* for.
[*in law*] **benefit,** profit, behalf, advantage, avail; enjoyment of property, right of using, usufruct, user (*a different word from* user, "*one who uses*").
user, consumer, purchaser, enjoyer, absorber; purchasing (*or* buying) public, demand, popular demand, market: *opposite of* producer.
II. *Verbs.* **use,** make use of, employ, utilize, occupy, turn to account (*or* use), put to use, apply, put in action, put into operation, set in motion, set to work, task, tax, put to task; adhibit, administer, bring into play, operate, ply, work, wield, handle, manipulate; exert, exercise, practice, avail oneself of, exploit, profit by; resort to, have recourse to, recur to, take up, try; devote, dedicate, consecrate.
habituate, accustom, familiarize, harden, inure (*as, he is not* used *to hardship*).
treat, behave toward, deal with, handle, manage, act toward (*as, to* use *a horse cruelly*).
use up, consume, exhaust, swallow up, devour, absorb, expend, wear, wear out (*as with overwork*).
III. *Adjectives.* **useful,** serviceable, helpful, valuable, invaluable, beneficial, salutary, profitable, advantageous, gainful, remunerative; favorable, good, commodious, convenient, suitable, fit, suited, adapted; contributive, conducive, subservient, instrumental; utilitarian, practical, pragmatic.

effective, efficient, capable, competent, active, operative, causative; adequate, effectual, availing, sufficient, efficacious.
IV. *Adverbs.* **usefully**, serviceably, helpfully, etc. (see *adjectives*); in a useful manner.
See also AGENCY, HABIT, INSTRUMENTALITY, TAKING, UTILITY.—*Antonyms.* See DISUSE, MISUSE.

---

useless, *adj.* futile, unavailing, ineffectual; fruitless, unproductive. See INUTILITY, UNPRODUCTIVENESS.
usher, *v.* precede, forerun; herald, announce; introduce: *usually followed by* in. See BEGINNING, PREDICTION, RECEPTION.
usual, *adj.* ordinary, common, customary, regular, habitual. See GENERALITY, HABIT.
usurpation, *n.* assumption, seizure, dispossession. See RIGHTLESSNESS.
usurper, *n.* pretender, impostor, wrongful possessor. See RIGHTLESSNESS.

UTILITY.—I. *Nouns.* **utility**, usefulness, profitableness, serviceableness, advantageousness, helpfulness, applicability, subservience, efficacy, efficiency, adequacy; service, use, help, aid, benefit, profit, avail, advantage, value, worth, productiveness; step in the right direction.
[*in ethics*] **happiness**, well-being, public good, public welfare, commonweal *or* common weal (*archaic*), the greatest happiness of the greatest number, utilitarianism.
II. *Verbs.* **utilize**, make use of, put to use, turn to account, use, make useful.
avail, serve, conduce, tend, answer (*or* serve) one's turn; benefit, bestead, stand one in good stead, be the making of, bear fruit, profit, remunerate, bring grist to the mill.
act a part, discharge a function, render a service, render yeoman's service, help, aid, assist.
III. *Adjectives.* **utilizable**, available, usable, ready, handy, at hand, tangible, applicable, adaptable, disposable, accessible, obtainable.
See also AID, BUSINESS, GOODNESS, INSTRUMENTALITY, PHILANTHROPY, PRODUCTIVENESS, USE.—*Antonyms.* See INUTILITY.

---

utter, *adj.* absolute, downright, entire, total. See PERFECTION.
utter, *v.* speak, enunciate, express; divulge, reveal, tell; emit, articulate, voice, announce; issue, circulate; pronounce, pass (*as judgment*); publish, disclose; talk, say, declare. See DELIVERANCE, DISCLOSURE, GIVING, MONEY, PASSAGE, PUBLICATION, SPEECH.
utterly, *adv.* quite, completely, wholly, totally, altogether. See COMPLETENESS.

V

vacancy, *n.* vacating, opening, opportunity; void, emptiness, vacuum, unintelligence, inanity. See AVOIDANCE, VACUITY.
vacant, *adj.* untenanted, unoccupied; unemployed, free; empty, blank, hollow; unfilled, depleted, exhausted. See ABSENCE, INACTION, UNSUBSTANTIALITY, VACUITY.
vacate, *v.* quit, depart; resign, relinquish, abandon, desert, evacuate. See DISPLACEMENT, RESIGNATION.
vacillation, *n.* irresolution, indecision, faltering, hesitation. See OSCILLATION.

VACUITY.—I. *Nouns.* **vacuity**, emptiness, void, vacuum; unintelligence, incognitance *or* incognitancy, thoughtlessness, vacancy, poverty of intellect, inanity, fatuity, expressionlessness.
II. *Verbs.* **be vacuous**, put away thought, relax (*or* divert) the mind, make the mind a blank, let the mind lie fallow; indulge in reverie.
III. *Adjectives.* **vacuous**, empty, void, vacant, unfilled, unoccupied, idle, blank, depleted, exhausted.

inane, unintellectual, stupid, expressionless, dull, inexpressive, unintelligent, incogitant, thoughtless, incogitative, unthinking, irrational, unreasoning, inattentive, diverted.

See also ABSENCE, IMBECILITY, INATTENTION, UNSUBSTANTIALITY.—*Antonyms.* See THOUGHT.

---

vagrant, *adj.* unsettled, erratic, wandering, roving, itinerant. See CHANGEABLENESS, JOURNEY.

vagrant, *n.* vagabond, wanderer, tramp, beggar. See PEOPLE, TRAVELER.

vague, *adj.* obscure, ill-defined, ambiguous; indefinite, confused, cryptic. See OBSCURITY, UNCERTAINTY.

vagueness, *n.* indefiniteness, inexactness, mystery, ambiguity. See GENERALITY, OBSCURITY, UNCERTAINTY.

vain, *adj.* worthless, inane, empty, trivial, useless, unavailing. See INUTILITY, VANITY.

vale, *n.* valley, dale, glen. See CONCAVITY.

valediction, *n.* farewell, adieu, good-by. See DEPARTURE.

valet, *n.* man, manservant, *valet de chambre* (*F.*). See SERVANT.

valiant, *adj.* brave, valorous, intrepid, undaunted. See COURAGE.

valid, *adj.* cogent, powerful; well-grounded, solid, substantial. See POWER, TRUTH.

valley, *n.* dale, glen, vale (*poetic*). See CONCAVITY.

valor, *n.* bravery, boldness, daring, heroism, prowess, intrepidity. See COURAGE.

valuable, *adj.* useful, profitable, advantageous, admirable, estimable. See GOOD, USE.

value, *n.* tone, tint, tinge, shade; merit, worth, excellence; estimation, valuation, profit; avail, advantage, usefulness. See COLOR, GOODNESS, PRICE, UTILITY.

value, *v.* treasure, prize, appreciate; assess, appraise, rate. See IMPORTANCE, MEASUREMENT.

vampire, *n.* temptress, vamp (*slang*); ghoul. See MOTIVE, MYTHICAL BEINGS.

[1]van, *n.* head, vanguard, front rank. See FRONT.

[2]van, *n.* wagon, dray, truck, motor truck, car. See VEHICLE.

vanish, *v.* disappear, fade, sink, fly, dissolve, die. See UNSUBSTANTIALITY.

VANITY.—I. *Nouns.* **vanity,** emptiness, unsubstantiality, falsity, unreality; empty pride, vainglory, vaingloriousness, conceit, conceitedness, self-conceit, self-sufficiency, self-praise, self-glorification, self-applause, self-laudation, self-love, self-esteem, *amour propre* (*F.*), self-admiration, selfishness.

pretension, pretentiousness, airs, affected manner, mannerism; egoism, egotism, priggishness, priggism, arrogance, pride, ostentation, ostentatious display.

II. *Verbs.* **be vain,** pique oneself, have too high an opinion of oneself, strut, put oneself forward; give oneself airs, boast.

render vain, inflate, puff up, swell, turn one's head.

III. *Adjectives.* **vain,** empty, unsubstantial, void, idle, unsatisfying, trivial, worthless, unprofitable; foolish, futile, ineffectual, unavailing, useless.

conceited, overweening, forward, vainglorious, showy, high-flown, ostentatious, puffed up, inflated, flushed, elate; assured, self-possessed, self-complacent, self-satisfied, complacent, self-confident, self-sufficient, self-admiring, pretentious, priggish, affected, egotistic *or* egotistical, boastful, arrogant, *entêté* (*F.*); vain as a peacock; unabashed, unblushing, unconstrained.

See also AFFECTATION, FOP, INSOLENCE, INUTILITY, OSTENTATION, PRIDE, SELFISHNESS.—*Antonyms.* See MODESTY.

---

vanquish, *v.* defeat, conquer, overcome, overpower, outwit. See SUCCESS.

vapid, *adj.* feeble, insipid, flat, spiritless, lifeless, dull, dry, jejune. See FEEBLENESS, INSIPIDITY, WATER.

VAPORIZATION.—I. *Nouns.* **vaporization,** volatilization, vaporescence, atomization, evaporation, gasification, cohobation (*chem.*), distillation, sublimation; fumigation, steaming.
vaporizer, atomizer, spray, evaporator, still, retort.
II. *Verbs.* **vaporize,** atomize, spray; distill, finestill, sublimate, evaporate, volatilize, gasify, exhale, emit vapor; fumigate; fume, smoke, reek, steam.
III. *Adjectives.* **vaporific,** vaporescent, volatile, volatilized, vaporiferous, vaporable, vaporizable, evaporable.
vaporous, vapory, vaporish, gaseous, halituous, steamy, fumy, fumous (*rare*), reeking, exhalant; flatulent, windy.
unreal, unsubstantial, imaginary, illusory, illusive, illusionary, flimsy, vain.
See also GASEITY.—*Antonyms.* See LIQUEFACTION.

---

variance, *n.* disagreement, difference, dissension, incompatibility. See DISCORD.

VARIATION.—I. *Nouns.* **variation,** alteration, change, mutation, modification, deviation, divergence *or* divergency, difference, deflection, aberration, disagreement, discrepancy, diversity, discordance, contrariety; innovation, departure; interchange, rotation, alternation.
II. *Verbs.* **vary,** change, alter, differ, modify, variate, diversity, variegate; deviate, veer, fluctuate, diverge, swerve, depart; alternate, vary by turns, interchange, rotate.
III. *Adjectives.* **variable,** changeable, mutable, mobile, altering, alterable, modifiable, variant, aberrant (*biol.*); unsteady, changeful, protean, changing, fickle, fitful, inconstant: *opposite of* invariable.
varied, altered, changed, modified; diversified, diverse, various; checkered, dædal (*poetic*), variegated, dissimilar, multiform: *opposite of* unvaried, uniform.
See also CHANGE, DEVIATION, DIFFERENCE, DISSIMILARITY, DIVERGENCE, DIVERSITY.—*Antonyms.* See PERMANENCE, UNIFORMITY.

VARIEGATION.—I. *Nouns.* **variegation,** diversification, spottiness, maculation, striation, streakiness, marbling; iridization, iridescence, irisation, opalescence, play of colors; pleochroism *or* pleochromatism (*including* dichroism *and* trichroism: *a property of some crystals*).
check, plaid, tartan, patchwork; marquetry, parquet, parquetry, mosaic, checkerwork; chessboard, checkers *or* chequers.
streak, stripe, stria (*pl.* striæ: *tech.*), vein, line, thread, fleck.
[*comparisons*] spectrum, rainbow, iris, tulip, peacock, chameleon, butterfly, zebra, leopard, ocelot, cheetah; mother-of-pearl, nacre, tortoise shell, opal, marble; mackerel, mackerel sky; Joseph's coat; harlequin.
II. *Verbs.* **variegate,** checker *or* chequer, diversify, stripe, striate, streak, fleck, polychromatize (*rare*), iridize, iris, opalesce, marble, marbleize, speckle, besprinkle, sprinkle, stipple, dot, spot, bespot, maculate, mottle, tattoo, inlay, tessellate; damascene (*as steel*), water; lace, fret, interlace, embroider, quilt.
III. *Adjectives.* **variegated,** diversified, multicolor, many-colored, many-hued, divers-colored, varicolored, versicolor, party-colored, dædal (*poetic*), polychromatic, kaleidoscopic, pleochroic (*tech.*).
iridescent, irised, irisated, rainbowlike, rainbowy, pavonine, opaline, opalescent, prismatic, pearly, nacreous, *gorge-de-pigeon* (*F.*), chatoyant, cymophanous, *nacré* (*F.*), nacred, shot, tortoise-shell.
mottled, pied, piebald, skewbald, motley; marbled, marmoraceous, marmoreal, marmorean; pepper-and-salt, dappled, clouded, watered.
spotted, spotty, punctate *or* punctated (*rare*), flecked, nævose *or* nevose, freckled, speckled, flecky, fleckered, powdered, flea-bitten, studded.
banded, striped, barred, belted, lined, veined; brinded, brindled, tabby; streaked, striate *or* striated, strigose (*zoöl.*), fasciate *or* fasciated (*tech.*).
checkered *or* chequered, checked, checky (*heraldry*), mosaic, tessellated; plaid tartan.
See also COLOR, VARIATION.—*Antonyms.* See UNIFORMITY.

---

variety, *n.* dissimilarity, diversity, variance, variation; kind, sort, species, genus, class, type, brand. See DIFFERENCE, FORM.

various, *adj.* different, diverse, diversified; several, many, manifold. See DIFFERENCE, MULTITUDE.

varnish, *n.* stain, enamel; lac, shellac, lacquer; gloss, extenuation. See COVERING, RESIN, VINDICATION.

vase, *n.* urn, jar, amphora, *tazza* (*It.*). See RECEPTACLE.

vassal, *n.* subject, liegeman, bondman, thrall. See SERVANT.

vast, *adj.* immense, enormous, great, infinite, boundless. See GREATNESS, SIZE, SPACE.

vault, *n.* arch, dome, span; mausoleum, sepulcher; crypt, dungeon. See CONVEXITY, INTERMENT, LOWNESS.

vaunt, *v.* boast, brag, blow (*colloq.*). See BOASTING.

veer, *v.* shift, turn, swerve, gybe (*naut.*), deviate, diverge. See CHANGE.

VEGETABLE.—I. *Nouns.* **vegetable kingdom,** flora, plants (*collectively*).

vegetable (*in the broad sense*), plant, organism, vegetal, herb; shrub, frutex (*bot.*), bush, tod (*archaic*), scrog (*Scot. and dial. Eng.*), bushlet, bushling; creeper, vine, perennial, annual; exotic, native; grass, herbage (*collective*), turf, cereal, grain (*collective*), vetch, drawk, weed; fog, eddish (*dial.*), aftermath, rowen; moss bryophyte (*bot.*), lichen, liverwort, hepatic (*bot.*); bulb, bud (*subterranean*), tuber, corm, chive, clove, bulblet.

food plants, legumes, peas, beans, lentils, pulse, greens, truck (*U. S.*), produce; potatoes, cabbages, turnips, etc.; fruit, fruitage.

tree, stand, cordon (*hort.*), pollard, rampick *or* rampike (*dial.*), espalier (*hort.*), arbor (*L. pl.* arbores: *bot.*), arbuscle *or* arbuscula, Yggdrasill (*Norse myth.*); sapling, seedling; fruit tree, timber tree, oak, elm, beech, birch, pine, maple, etc.

woodland, timberland, forest, virgin forest, wood, greenwood, wildwood; grove, copse, coppice, spinney (*Eng.*), thicket, canebrake, covert, bosk, bosket *or* bosquet, shrubbery, plantation, holt (*poetic or dial.*), hurst (*wooded eminence*), shaw (*dial.*), frith (*poetic or dial.*), hanger (*wooded slope*), tope (*India*), clump, wood lot, timber; bush, jungle, chaparral, chamisal (*California*); ceja (*Texas*); park, paradise (*Oriental*), chase (*Eng.*).

underbrush, undergrowth, underwood, brush, brushwood, scrub, brake, rice (*Scot. and dial Eng.*), boscage, *bocage* (*F.*), heath, heather, fern, bracken, furze, gorse, whin, broom, sedge, carex (*pl.* carices: *bot.*), rush, rash (*Scot. and dial Eng.*), bulrush.

seaweed, wrack, kelp, ware (*dial.*), fucus (*pl.* fuci: *bot.*), fucoid, rockweed, tangle, tang (*dial.*), dulse (*edible*), alga (*pl.* algæ), sea lettuce; sea lentil, gulfweed, sargasso, sargassum (*as in the Sargasso Sea*).

leafage, foliage, leaves (*collectively*), frondescence (*rare*), verdure, foliation; vernation (*bot.*), prefoliation (*bot.*).

leaf, foliage leaf, frond, petal, needle (*as of the pine*), bract; bractlet, bracteole (*bot.*); phyllome (*bot.*), pad (*U. S.*), flag; leaflet, foliole (*bot.*); blade, lamina (*bot.*); stem, caulis (*pl.* caules: *bot.*), stalk, leafstalk, petiole (*bot.*), phyllode (*bot.*) stipe; stipule (*leaflike appendage: bot.*), seed stalk, funicle (*bot.*); seed leaf cotyledon (*bot.*); calyx leaf, sepal (*bot.*); caulome (*bot.*), stem formation.

branch, shoot, limb, bough, offshoot, rame (*rare*), phylloclade (*bot.*); twig, sprig, spray, branchlet, ramulus (*pl.* ramuli: *bot.*), ramule, runner, tendril; ramage (*collective*).

flower, blossom, bloom, blow, floscule (*rare*), floret, bud, floweret, flowering plant; flower stalk, peduncle (*bot.*), pedicel (*bot.*), pedicle; inflorescence, flowering, flowerage, florescence, blossoming, florification; full bloom, anthesis (*bot.*).

II. *Adjectives.* **vegetable,** vegetative, vegetal (*rare*), olitory (*rare*), vegetarian; leguminous, herbaceous, herblike, herbal, botanic *or* botanical; arboreous, arboreal, silvan *or* sylvan; ligneous, lignose (*rare*), xyloid, woody, wooden; bosky, copsy; mossy, turfy, grassy, verdant, verdurous.

flowery, blossomy, bloomy, floral, flosculous (*bot.*), discoid (*tech.*), florescent, floriated (*decorative art*).

native, domestic, native-grown, home-grown, indigenous, autochthonous: *opposite of* exotic.

See also BOTANY, VEGETATION.—*Antonyms.* See ANIMAL.

VEGETATION.—I. *Nouns.* **vegetation,** vegetable life, vegetable growth, plant life, thrift, vigor, growth, herbage, flowerage, plants (*collectively*); vegetable nature, vegetality, vegetability (*rare*); inert existence, vegetativeness, stagnation, unprogressiveness.
II. *Verbs.* vegetate, germinate, sprout, grow, shoot up, live, develop, increase, luxuriate, grow rank, fungate (*med.*), flourish; flower, blossom, bloom, bud.
become inactive, idle, bask, lead a passive existence, live a monotonous life, become rooted (*or* plantlike).
III. *Adjectives.* **vegetative, vegetal, vegetable;** growing, vigorous, thrifty; blooming, bloomy, blossoming, flowering.
luxuriant, rank, dense, exuberant, excessive, prolific, lush, wild.
inert, passive, inactive, sluggish, stagnant, dull, dead, unprogressive, stick-in-the-mud (*colloq.*).
See also INACTION.

---

vehement, *adj.* wild, hot-headed, violent, passionate, ardent, fiery, impetuous, forcible. See EXCITABILITY, HEAT, STRENGTH, VIGOR.

VEHICLE.—I. *Nouns.* **vehicle,** conveyance, carriage, *voiture* (*F.*), chariot (*poetic or hist.*), rig, equipage, turn-out (*colloq.*); wagonette, break. char-à-bancs (*pl.* chars-à-bancs) brougham, landau, sociable, *vis-à-vis* (*F.*), victoria, barouche, calash, *calèche* (*F.; as used on the Continent*), chariotee, berlin, *dormeuse* (*F.*), surrey, stanhope, coupé, phaëton, clarence, britzka, buggy, rockaway, buckboard, Concord buggy, runabout; wheel chair, Bath chair; baby carriage, perambulator, gocart.
coach, caroche, drag, tallyho, stagecoach, stage, diligence, mail stage, post chaise; omnibus, bus (*colloq.*).
cab, hackney, hack, growler (*Eng. slang*), fly (*Eng.*), four-wheeler. hansom *or* hansom cab, *fiacre* (*F.*), droshky *or* drosky (*as used in Russia*), gharry *or* gari (*India*), *vettura* (*It.*).
[*two-wheelers*] curricle, chaise, shay (*dial.*), cabriolet, hansom, *calèche* (*F.; as used in Quebec*), gig, tilbury, dogcart, trap (*colloq.*), carriole, road cart, carromata (*Philippines*), sulky, tonga (*India*), Cape cart (*South Africa*), ekka (*India*), shandrydan *or* shandradan (*Scot. and Irish*), jaunting car (*Ireland*); jinrikisha *or* jinricksha (*Japan*), ricksha (*colloq.*).
wagon or waggon (*Brit.*), wain (*archaic*), lorry, truck; Conestoga wagon (*or* wain), prairie schooner (*U. S.*); araba (*Oriental*), telega (*Russia*); ammunition wagon, *fourgon* (*F.*); van, caravan, car, gondola car *or* gondola (*U. S.*); patrol wagon, police van, black Maria (*U. S. colloq.*).
cart, dray, Whitechapel cart, *charrette* (*F.*), bullock cart, hackery (*India*), tumbrel *or* tumbril, dump cart, tipcart; handcart, pushcart, barrow, wheelbarrow, handbarrow.
team, rig (*U. S.*), pair, span, tandem; spike team (*U. S.*), unicorn; four-in-hand.
sled, sledge, sleigh, jumper, bob, bobsled (*U. S.*), doublerunner (*U. S.*), toboggan; pung (*U. S.*), train (*Canada*), cutter; ski (*pl.* ski *or* skis), snowshoes, skates
litter, portacle couch, stretcher, palanquin *or* palankeen, polki (*India*), munchil (*India*), doolie (*India*), dandy *or* dandi (*India*), jampan (*India*), sedan chair, sedan, tonjon (*Ceylon*), norimon (*Jap.*), lectica (*ancient Rome*); kajawah (*Oriental*), camel litter, *cacolet* (*F.*), brancard; ambulance.
cycle, bicycle, machine (*colloq.*), wheel (*colloq.*), tricycle, tandem, motor cycle; velocipede, hobbyhorse.
automobile, motor car, auto (*colloq.*), motor (*colloq.*), car, machine (*colloq.*), auto car, limousine, sedan, coach, berlin, brougham, touring car, victoria, speedster, cloverleaf, roadster, coupé, steamer, electric, runabout, coupelet, cabriolet, landaulet; motor cab, taxicab, taxi (*colloq.*), flivver (*slang*), jitney (*colloq.*), autobus, motor bus, electrobus (*colloq.*), autotruck, automobile truck; tractor, caterpillar tractor, caterpillar.
[*allied terms*] tonneau, chassis, radiator, fan, engine, motor, cylinder, manifold, carburetor, intake, exhaust, muffler, throttle, gear, gear shift, clutch, differential, transmission, universal joint, crank shaft, brake drum, steering wheel; hood, top, ignition, spark plug, generator, distributor, magneto, self-starter, ammeter, speedometer, oil gauge, tire, shoe, rim; gasoline *or* gasolene, gas (*colloq.*), petrol (*Brit.*): filling station, gasoline station, garage.

train, railroad train, express, mail, special, limited, corridor train, passenger train, freight (*U. S.*), goods train (*Brit.*), accommodation train (*U. S.*), parliamentary train (*Brit.*), rolling stock; sleeping car, palace car, Pullman car, Pullman, sleeper (*U. S. colloq.*); parlor car, drawing-room car; smoking car, smoker; car, coach, day coach, carriage (*Brit.*), compartment; baggage car, luggage van (*Brit.*), trolley *or* trolley car (*U. S. and Canada*), electric car, electric (*colloq*); trailer.

medium, agency, instrumentality, interagency, intermedium, intermediary, instrument of conveyance; liquid medium, menstruum, excipient (*pharm.*).

II. *Adjectives.* **vehicular,** vehiculary (*rare*), vehiculatory (*rare*), curricular (*rare*): *opposite of* pedestrian.

See also INSTRUMENTALITY, TRAVELER.—*Antonyms.* See SHIP.

---

veil, *v.* conceal, hide, cover, screen, cloak, mask, curtain. See CONCEALMENT, SHADE.

vein, *n.* blood vessel, vena (*L. pl.* venæ: *tech.*), veinlet, nerve (*bot.*); humor, mood; shade, strain, tinge, dash; lode, bed (*as of coal*); streak, stripe. See CHANNEL, DISPOSITION, MIXTURE, STORE, VARIEGATION.

VELOCITY.—I. *Nouns.* **velocity,** speed, celerity, swiftness, quickness, rapidity, expedition, haste, acceleration.

spurt, burst, sprint, rush, dash, race, round pace, clip (*colloq.*); swoop, descent, tantivy (*archaic*); flight, scamper, scuttle, scurry.

pace, gallop, canter, trot, round trot, run, hand gallop.

[*comparisons*] lightning, greased lightning (*slang*), flash, light, electricity, wind, hurricane, cyclone, torrent; cannon ball, bullet, rocket, arrow, dart, quicksilver; telegraph, radio, thought, split second.

eagle, antelope, courser, race horse, gazelle, ostrich, greyhound, hare, doe, squirrel, swallow; scorcher (*automobile slang*), speed maniac, companion of the wind; Mercury, Ariel, Puck, Camilla (*Æneid*).

[*measurement of velocity*] velocimeter, speedometer; **log** (*naut.*), log line, patent log, traffrail log.

II. *Verbs.* speed, hie, hasten, spurt, sprint, trip, post, scud, whiz, run, dart, swoop, fly, race, shoot, tear, whisk, sweep, skim, scorch (*colloq.*), rush, dash, bolt, scurry, scamper, scuttle, skedaddle (*colloq.*), run like mad (*colloq.*), run away, ride hard, hurry, hasten, haste, accelerate, quicken; carry sail, crowd sail; burn up the road (*automobile cant*), wing one's way, outstrip the wind, make forced marches (*mil.*).

III. *Adjectives.* **swift,** rapid, fast, speedy, quick, fleet; nimble, agile, expeditious, express; active, brisk, light-footed, nimble-footed; winged, eagle-winged.

IV. *Adverbs.* **swiftly,** rapidly, etc. (see *adjectives*); space, at full speed, full gallop, posthaste, in double-quick time, whip and spur, tantivy (*fox hunting*); *ventre à terre* (*F.*), with rapid strides, by leaps and bounds, *à pas de géant* (*F.*), in seven-league boots; *remis velisque* (*L.*), in full sail, under press of sail (*or* canvas).

See also ACTIVITY, HASTE, VIOLENCE.—*Antonyms.* See SLOWNESS.

---

venal, *adj.* corrupt; mercenary, sordid, mean. See IMPROBITY, PARSIMONY.

veneer, *n.* facing, scale, layer; paint, enamel, plaster; gloss, outward show. See COVERING, LAYER, OSTENTATION.

venerable, *adj.* aged, patriarchal; revered, time-honored. See AGE, SAGE.

veneration, *n.* reverence, devotion, worship; admiration, esteem. See PIETY, RESPECT.

vengeance, *n.* revengefulness, vindictiveness, retaliation. See REVENGE.

venomous, *adj.* malicious, malignant, caustic, envenomed, spiteful; virulent, poisonous, septic, toxic, deadly. See MALEVOLENCE, UNHEALTHINESS.

vent, *n.* utterance, expression; outlet, passage, spout, tap, faucet; venthole, airhole, blowhole. See DISCLOSURE, EGRESS, OPENING.

ventilate, *v.* freshen, oxygenate, purify; discuss, review, comment; vent, utter, publish. See AIR, DISSERTATION, PUBLICATION.

ventilator, *n.* funnel, flue, louver, transom, fan. See AIR, WIND.

venture, *n.* gamble, risk, hazard, speculation; business, work, enterprise, project, essay. See CHANCE, UNDERTAKING.
venture, *v.* risk, hazard, dare, undertake; try, test, experiment, speculate; advance, put forward. See DANGER, ESSAY, PROBABILITY.
venturesome, *adj.* rash, bold, reckless; adventurous, enterprising. See RASHNESS, UNDERTAKING.

VERACITY.—I. *Nouns.* **veracity,** truthfulness, frankness, truth, veridicality, sincerity, candor, probity, honesty, fidelity, love of truth; correctness, exactitude, trueness.
II. *Verbs.* **be veracious,** speak the truth, tell the truth; speak on oath; speak without equivocation (*or* mental reservation), make a clean breast, disclose, speak one's mind; show in its true colors, undeceive, debunk (*slang*).
III. *Adjectives.* **veracious,** truthful, truth-telling, honest, reliable, trustworthy, scrupulous, punctilious, sincere, candid, frank, open, outspoken, straightforward, unreserved, guileless, pure, true, faithful, genuine, soothfast (*archaic*), truth-loving, true-blue, as good as one's word; unfeigned, ingenuous.
IV. *Adverbs.* **veraciously,** truthfully, etc. (see *adjectives*); truly, in plain words, honor bright (*colloq.*), soothfast (*archaic*), *bona fide* (*L.*), in fact, in sooth, in earnest, unfeignedly, from the bottom of one's heart; openly, straightforwardly, *cartes sur table* (*F.*), *in foro conscientiæ* (*L.*).
See also ARTLESSNESS, PROBITY, TRUTH.—*Antonyms.* See FALSEHOOD.

---

veranda, *n.* portico, piazza, porch. See RECEPTACLE.
verbal, *adj.* literal, verbatim, textual; oral, spoken. See WORD.
verbiage, *n.* verbosity, wordiness, prolixity. See DIFFUSENESS, WORD.
verdant, *adj.* verdurous; fresh, raw, inexperienced, unsophisticated. See GREEN.
verdure, *n.* greenness, vegetation, greenery. See GREEN.
verge, *n.* brink, brow, brim, border, rim; end, extreme. See EDGE, LIMIT.
verge, *v.* border (*on*), skirt; incline, tend, trend. See EDGE, TENDENCY.
verify, *v.* prove, establish, identify; substantiate, confirm. See DISCOVERY, EVIDENCE, SUPPORT.
verily, *adv.* truly, indeed, really: *archaic.* See TRUTH.
vermin, *n.* lice, fleas, flies, bugs, mice, etc. See ANIMAL.
versatile, *adj.* kaleidoscopic, protean; many-sided. See CHANGEABLENESS.
verse, *n.* metrical line, rime *or* rhyme, stanza, stave; metrical composition, versification. See POETRY.
versification, *n.* riming, prosody; scansion. See POETRY.

VERTICALLY.—I. *Nouns.* verticality, perpendicularity, erectness, uprightness, plumbness, *aplomb* (*F.*); elevation, erection; normal (*geom.*), right angle; azimuth circle, ventrical circle.
cliff, steep, crag, bluff, precipice, wall, scar *or* scaur, krantz (*South Africa*), palisades (*as along a river*).
II. *Verbs.* **be vertical,** stand erect (*or* upright), stand on end, stick up, cock up. **render vertical,** set up, raise up, erect, rear, raise, pitch, uprear, upraise, uplift, upend, upheave.
III. *Adjectives.* **vertical,** upright, erect, perpendicular, sheer, steep. plumb, bolt upright, stand-up (*as a lunch: colloq.*); normal (*geom.*), rectangular, orthogonal, right-angled; rampant (*esp. heraldry*); longitudinal.
IV. *Adverbs.* **vertically,** uprightly, etc. (see *adjectives*); on end, endwise, *à plomb* (*F.*), at right angles.
See also ELEVATION, STRAIGHTNESS.—*Antonyms.* See HORIZONTALITY.

---

vertigo, *n.* dizziness, giddiness. See INSANITY.
very, *adv.* extremely, exceedingly; absolutely. See GREATNESS.
vesper, *adj.* vespertine, nocturnal, nightly. See EVENING.
vessel, *n.* utensil, jar, vase, bowl, etc.; sailing vessel, steamship, craft. See RECEPTACLE, SHIP.

vested, *adj.* clothed, robed; authorized, legalized, fixed. See CLOTHING, LEGALITY, STABILITY.

vestige, *n.* remains, trace, relic. See RECORD.

VESTMENTS.—*Nouns.* vestments, canonicals, Eucharistic vestments; *pontificalia* (*L.; pl.*), pontificals; robe, gown, Geneva cloak (*or* gown), surplice, cassock, alb, scapular, dalmatic, cope, stole, maniple; pallium, pall; girdle, scarf, tunicle, tunic, chasuble, mantelletta; chimer *or* chimere, rochet (*worn by bishops*); cowl, hood, amice; bands, apron, biretta, miter *or* mitre (*worn by bishops*); tiara, triple crown (*worn by the Pope*).

See also CLOTHING.

VETERAN.—I. *Nouns.* **veteran,** old man, patriarch, grisard (*rare*), graybeard, gaffer (*esp. an aged rustic*), oldster (*rare*), old timer (*colloq.*), antediluvian, old fogy (*colloq.*); old stager, old soldier (*opposite of* recruit); dean (*as of a diplomatic corps*), *doyen* (*F.*); sexagenarian, octogenarian, nonagenarian, centenarian; preadamite, Methuselah, Nestor.

grandfather, grandsire (*archaic*), grandparent, granddad (*childish or affectionate*), grandpa *or* grandpapa (*familiar*), gramfer (*dial.*), granther (*dial.*).

grandmother, grandam *or* grandame (*archaic*), grandparent, grandma *or* grandmamma (*familiar*), granny (*familiar, affectionate, or sometimes disrespectful*), grannam (*dial.*), beldam *or* beldame (*archaic in this sense; in modern usage, it denotes* hag *or* virago).

[*old loving couple*] Darby and Joan, Philemon and Baucis (*classical instance revived in Gounod's opera of this name*).

old woman (*used also disparagingly of men*), crone, hag (*both contemptuous*); dowager (*colloq.*), granny (*a loose usage*), old lady.

forefathers, forbears *or* forebears, ancestors, progenitors, forerunners, predecessors, fathers, ancients.

II. *Adjectives.* **verteran,** old, aged, grayheaded; experienced, practiced, seasoned, salted (*slang*); warworn, *aguerri* (*F.*), disciplined.

See also AGE, EXPERT, YOUTH.—*Antonyms.* See INFANT, LEARNER.

---

veterinarian, *n.* veterinary surgeon, horse doctor, vet (*colloq.*). See DOMESTICATION.

veto, *n.* forbiddance, prevention, restriction, interdiction. See PROHIBITION.

vex, *v.* irritate, ruffle, roil, annoy, displease, anger. See HATE, PAIN.

vexation, *n.* annoyance, irritation, chagrin, pique, mortification. See PAINFULNESS, RESENTMENT.

vibrate, *v.* fluctuate, waver, vary; wave, oscillate, pulsate, sway. See OSCILLATION.

VICE.—I. *Nouns.* vice, evildoing, wrongdoing, perversity, wickedness, corruption, depravation, depravity, demoralization, profligacy, flagrancy, excess, enormity, atrocity, brutality, infamy, knavery, obliquity, backsliding, recidivism (*tech.*), degradation, viciousness, iniquity, sin, the old Adam; immorality, debauchery, unchastity, impurity, laxity, looseness, immoral conduct, immoral habits, want of principle, unnatural desires.

defect (*as of character, style, etc.*), fault, blemish, failing, imperfection, weakness, flaw, shortcoming, demerit, deficiency, lack, want, inadequacy, weak point, foible, frailty, error, besetting sin, failure, infirmity.

[*resorts*] **den,** haunt, joint (*slang*), dive (*U. S.*), gambling house, opium den; disorderly house; house of ill fame (*or* repute), brothel, bagnio, lupanar, bawdyhouse, stew (*usually in pl.: archaic*); red-light district, Yoshiwara (*Jap.*).

II. *Verbs.* **be vicious,** sin, commit sin, err, transgress; misconduct oneself, misbehave; fall, lapse, slip, trip, offend, trespass, go astray, stray, deviate from the line of duty (*or* path of virtue); sow one's wild oats.

render vicious, demoralize, brutalize, corrupt, degrade, debase, vitiate, contaminate.

III. *Adjectives.* **vicious,** iniquitous, immoral, unrighteous, wicked, evil, sinful, unprincipled, wrong, bad, naughty (*archaic or euphemistic in this sense*), criminal, lawless, disorderly, recreant, demoralized, corrupt, depraved, degenerate,

evil-minded, heartless, graceless, shameless, abandoned, steeped (*or* sunk) in iniquity, accursed.
base, ignoble, infamous, sinister, foul, gross, vile, black, felonious, nefarious, shameful, scurvy, opprobrious, scandalous, villainous, flagitious, heinous, flagrant, atrocious, monstrous.
diabolic *or* diabolical, devilish, fiendish, fiendlike, Mephistophelian, satanic, hellish, infernal, hellborn, demoniacal.
incorrigible, irreclaimable, recidivous, irreformable, obdurate, reprobate; refractory, unruly, unmanageable (*as, a* vicious *horse*).
unjustifiable, indefensible, inexcusable, inexpiable, unpardonable.
discreditable, disreputable, disgraceful, culpable, blamable, reprehensible, censurable, unworthy, blameworthy, undutiful.
weak, pliable, frail, lax, infirm, spineless, invertebrate, irresolute, unstable.
[*of language, reasoning, etc.*] **defective,** faulty, incorrect, imperfect, corrupt, improper, unsound, illogical.
spiteful, malicious, malignant, venomous, ill-disposed, mischievous, bitter, unfriendly, inimical (*as,* vicious *criticism*).

See also DRUNKENNESS, EVIL, IMPROBITY, IMPURITY, LIBERTINE, MALEVOLENCE.—*Antonyms.* See VIRTUE.

---

vicinity, *n.* neighborhood, environs, vicinage, purlieus. See ENVIRONMENT, NEARNESS.
vicious, *adj.* corrupt, faulty, unsound; spiteful, malevolent; wicked, immoral, depraved. See IMPERFECTION, MALEVOLENCE, VICE.
vicissitude, *n.* fluctuation, change, mutation. See CHANGEABLENESS.
victim, *n.* gull, puppet, cat's-paw; sufferer, prey, martyr; malefactor, culprit, *condamné* (*F.*). See DUPE, PAIN, SCOURGE.
victimize, *v.* trick, hoax, dupe, bamboozle (*colloq.*), cheat. See DECEPTION.
victor, *n.* conqueror, master, champion, winner. See SUCCESS.
victory, *n.* triumph, conquest, palm, mastery. See SUCCESS.
victuals, *n. pl.* eatables, viands, comestibles. See FOOD.
vie, *v.* contend, strive, emulate, rival. See GOOD.
view, *n.* sight, show; scene, prospect, landscape, seascape, panorama; opinion, theory, impression, conception, judgment; look, regard, survey, inspection, observation. See APPEARANCE, FINE ARTS, IDEA, VISION.
view, *v.* attend, watch, observe, see, look, eye, survey, scan, inspect. See ATTENTION, VISION.
viewpoint, *n.* standpoint, angle, aspect, point of view. See IDEA, VISION.
vigilance, *n.* watchfulness, wakefulness, alertness, caution, circumspection. See ACTIVITY, CARE.
vigilant, *adj.* cautious, heedful, chary, prudent, alert, attentive, wary, circumspect. See CAUTION, SHARPNESS.

VIGOR.—I. *Nouns.* **vigor,** strength, power, potency, efficacy, force, might, vitality, sap, pith, stamina, lustihood (*archaic*), robustness, soundness, sturdiness, vital force, health, energy, physical strength; spirit, vim (*colloq.*), pep (*slang*), punch (*slang*), vigorousness, virility.
[*intellectual force*] **mentality,** mental power, mental endowment, intellectuality, keenness, penetration, forcibleness, effectiveness, cogency, forcefulness, boldness, trechancy, incisiveness, pointedness, point, acumen; animation, ardor, enthusiasm, verve, glow, fire, warmth; liveliness, sprightliness, raciness, piquancy, pungency; impressiveness, gravity, weight, pithiness, sententiousness; "thoughts that breathe and words that burn" (Gray, *The Progress of Poesy*).
eloquence, oratory, facundity (*archaic*), command of words (*or* language), rhetoric, spellbinding, impassioned utterance, fluency; loftiness, elevation, grandeur, sublimity.
II. *Adjectives.* **vigorous,** strong, lusty, robust, hale, sturdy, pithsome (*rare*), virile, masculine, sinewy, muscular, sound, brisk, alert.
forcible, effective, cogent, telling, irresistible, energetic, active, strenuous, potent, powerful, mettlesome; nervous (*said of literary style*), spirited, lively,

glowing, sparkling, racy, bold, slashing, forceful, trenchant, mordant, incisive, biting, pungent, piquant, full of point, pointed, pithy, marrowy, meaty; graphic, vivid, picturesque, striking, emphatic, terse, sententious.
lofty, exalted, elevated, sublime, majestic, poetic, grand, impressive, weighty, ponderous; eloquent.
vehement, passionate, violent, impassioned, ardent, fervent, burning, on fire, eager, zealous.
III. *Adverbs.* **vigorously**, lustily, forcibly, etc. (see *adjectives*); in glowing terms, in good set terms, in no measured terms.

See also ENERGY, GREEN, HEALTH, LIFE, POWER, RESOLUTION, SNAP, STRENGTH.—*Antonyms.* See FEEBLENESS.

---

vile, *adj.* disgusting, repulsive, odious; low, common, mean, base, ignoble, contemptible; foul, gross, evil. See BADNESS, IMPROBITY, VICE.
vilify, *v.* belittle, brand, asperse, malign, libel, traduce. See DETRACTION.
village, *n.* hamlet, settlement, thorp. See HABITATION.
villian, *n.* heavy (*theatrical cant*); rascal, knave, miscreant, scoundrel. See DRAMA, EVILDOER.
villainous, *adj.* base, vicious, unprincipled, corrupt, depraved. See EVIL.
vim, *n.* energy, vigor, briskness, liveliness, spirit, force (*colloq.*). See ENERGY.

VINCULUM.—*Nouns.* **vinculum** (*connecting medium; pl.* vincula), bond, tie, link, nexus, connection, connective (*esp. tech.*), interconnection, bond of union, copula (*tech.*); couple, yoke, union; bonder (*masonry*), bondstone, binding stone; bridge, stepping-stone; neck, isthmus, jugulum (*zoöl.*); ridge, fol, frænum *or* frenum (*anat.*), ligation.
[*in writing and printing*] brace, bracket, ligature, tie, hyphen.
cord, ligature, tendon (*anat.*), leader, sinew, thew (*usually in pl.*), ligament; string, twist, funicle, funiculus (*tech.*), sennit (*naut.*); rope, line, cable, painter (*of a boat*), hawser; chain, catena; lace, lacing.
cordage (*collective*), cording, rigging, tackle, service (*naut.*), ropework, roping.
band, binder, fillet, snood, braid, bandage, strap, brace, couple, leash, thong; cincture, girdle, girth, cinch (*U. S.*), belly band, surcingle, belt, sash, cummerbund (*Anglo-Indian*), cestus (*Roman*), zoster (*Greek*), zone.
noose, loop, lariat, lasso, cabestro (*Southwestern U. S.*), hitch (*naut.*), knot, slipknot, running knot, halter.
fastening, fastener, clip, clinch, clamp, holdfast, rivet, staple, ring, larigo (*Sp. Amer.*), catch, clasp, buckle, hook, hook and eye, latch, latchet, bolt, bar, lock, padlock, link, shackle, coupler, coupling; tack, brad, thumb tack, drawing pin (*Eng.*); nail, pin, dowel, thole, tholepin, peg, spike, treenail *or* trenail, toggle (*naut.*), duledge (*as of a gun carriage*), kevel (*naut.*), cleat, bollard.
cement, glue, gum, paste, size, wafer, solder, lute, luting, lime, putty; birdlime, viscum; mortar, plaster, stucco, grout.

See also INTERJACENCE, JUNCTION, RESTRAINT.—*Antonyms.* See DISJUNCTION.

VINDICATION.—I. *Nouns.* **vindication,** justification, right, sanction, authorization, warrant; exoneration, exculpation, acquittal; whitewashing, extenuation, palliation, softening, mitigation; apology, acknowledgment, explanation, gloss, varnish, extenuating, circumstances, allowance.
answer, reply, response, rejoinder, plea (*law*), defense *or* defence, statement of defense (*law*), excuse, denial, objection, demurrer (*law*), rebutter (*law*); recrimination, retort, countercharge.
vindicator, justifier, apologist, defender, advocate; avenger.
II. *Verbs.* **vindicate,** justify, maintain, claim, assert; support, defend, plead; advicate, plead one's cause, speak for, stand up for, stick up for (*colloq.*), contend for, say in defense, bear out, keep in countenance, bolster up; right, warrant, clear, exculpate, exonerate, acquit; avenge, retaliate, requite, revenge.
extenuate, palliate, excuse, absolve, pardon, forgive, apologize for, soften, gloss over, varnish, whitewash, gloze, smooth over, make allowance for, give the Devil his due.

III. *Adjectives.* **vindicative,** vindicatory, vindicating, justificatory, palliative, extenuating, exculpatory, apologetic.
excusable, defensible, allowable, permissible, pardonable, venial, justifiable; plausible, specious.
See also ACQUITTAL, PLEA.—*Antonyms.* See ACCUSATION.

---

vindictive, *adj.* revengeful, resentful, avenging, retaliative. See REVENGE.
violate, *v.* infringe, transgress, abuse, disregard; desecrate, outrage; ravish, rape; arrogate, usurp. See DERELICTION, ILLEGALITY, IMPIETY, IMPURITY, RIGHTLESSNESS.

VIOLENCE.—I. *Nouns.* **violence,** vehemence, might, force, brute force; brunt, strain, shock; impetuosity, ferocity, rage, fury, eagerness, fierceness, severity, exacerbation (*esp. med.*), irritation, exasperation, acuteness, intensity, sharpness, poignancy, furiousness, *acharnement* (*F.*), ferociousness, malignity.
turbulence, disorder, commotion, ebullition, excitement, disturbance, boisterousness, bluster, tumult, rioting, tumultuousness, uproar, riot, row (*colloq.*), rumpus (*colloq.*).
outrage, violation, infraction, infringement, transgression, ravishment, profanation; attack, assault.
paroxysm, spasm, convulsion, fit, ictus (*med.*), throe, passion, frenzy, agitation, orgasm, erethism (*med.*), entasia (*med.*), attack, access (*as of illness or emotion*), epitasis (*med.*); hysterics.
outbreak, outburst, eruption, disruption, debacle, discharge, volley, explosion, blast, blow-up, detonation, crash, roar, quake, temblor, earthquake; thunderstorm, storm, squall, line squall (*a line of squalls and thunderstorms advancing broadside over the country: meteorol.*).
[*violent person*] spitfire, fire eater (*colloq.*), hotspur; berserk *or* berserker, demon, fiend, hellhound, wild beast, tiger, dragon; fury (*esp. a woman*), termagant, virago, vixen, hell-cat; Fury (*classical myth.*), Erinys (*pl.* Erinyes), Eumenides (Tisiphone, Megæra, Alecto); Diræ (*L.; pl.*).
II. *Verbs.* **be violent,** ferment, effervesce, boil, boil over, fume, foam, rampage, run wild, run amuck, rage, roar, riot, storm; ride roughshod, out-Herod Herod.
explode, go off, detonate, fulminate, let off, let fly, discharge, blow up, flash, fulgurate, flare, deflagrate (*chem.*), burst, crack, crash, thunder.
render violent, stir up, quicken, excite, incite, urge, lash, stimulate; irritate, inflame, kindle, foment, exasperate, exacerbate, convulse, infuriate, madden, lash into fury, add fuel to the flame, *oleum addere camino* (*L.*).
III. *Adjectives.* **violent,** vehement, acute, extreme, intense, severe, sharp; rough, tough (*colloq.*), rude, bluff, brusque, abrupt; wild, impetuous, rampant, unrestrained, savage, fierce, ferocious, merciless, cruel.
turbulent, tumultuous, disorderly, raging, stormy, restless, disturbed, troublous, riotous, obstreperous, refractory, boisterous, uproarious; frenzied, mad, insane; rash, passionate, desperate, infuriate, furious, fuming, rabid, frantic, outrageous.
fiery, flaming, scorching, hot, red-hot, ardent, inflamed.
headstrong, ungovernable, uncontrollable, unruly, unbridled, stubborn, intractable, unrestrainable, irrestrainable, obdurate, irrepressible.
convulsive, convulsionary, spasmodic, paroxysmal, paroxysmic (*rare*), spastic (*med.*); explosive, volcanic.
[*not natural*] **unnatural,** counternatural, contranatural (*rare*), abnormal, irregular, unexpected, accidental; murderous, bloody, homicidal, suicidal (*as, a* violent *death*).
IV. *Adverbs.* **violently,** vehemently, etc. (see *adjectives*); by violence, by force, forcibly, by storm, by main force, *vi et armis* (*L.*), amain, with might and main, tooth and nail, at the point of the sword (*or* bayonet), at one fell swoop, with a vengeance, in desperation, to the death, *à outrance* (*F.*); headlong, headfirst, headforemost, precipitately.
See also AGITATION, DISORDER, EXCITABILITY, GREATNESS, INSANITY, RASHNESS, STRENGTH.—*Antonyms.* See MODERATION.

---

violin, *n.* fiddle (*colloq. or depreciatory*); Stradivarius. Strad (*colloq.*). See MUSICAL INSTRUMENTS.
violinist, *n.* fiddler (*colloq.* or *derogatory*). See MUSICIAN.

virgin, *n.* maid, maiden, vestal, spinster, celibate. See CELIBACY, PURITY.
virile, *adj.* adult, masculine, manly, manlike; potent, masterful. See MAN, STRENGTH.
virtual, *adj.* substantial, practical, tantamount to; potential. See SUBSTANTIALITY.

VIRTUE.—I. *Nouns.* **virtue,** morality, rectitude, uprightness, integrity, moral excellence, morals, moral practice, probity, honor, nobleness, goodness, well-doing, good actions, good behavior, self-control, self-denial, well-spent life, duty, cardinal virtues (*the four "natural virtues,"* justice, prudence, temperance, fortitude, *and the three "theological virtues,"* faith, hope, charity); innocence, purity, chastity.
merit, worth, desert, excellence, quality, value, worthiness, credit.
[*inherent power*] **efficacy,** potency, strength, power, energy, force, efficiency *or* efficience, effectiveness, efficaciousness, effectuality, potentiality.
II. *Verbs.* **be virtuous,** practice virtue, do (fulfill, perform, *or* discharge) one's duty, fight the good fight; acquit oneself well, keep in the right path, set a good example.
III. *Adjectives.* **virtuous,** moral, morally excellent, righteous, right, good, sterling, noble, right-minded, whole-souled, meritorious, deserving, worthy, dutiful, duteous; creditable, laudable, commendable, praiseworthy, exemplary, matchless, peerless; saintly, saintlike, angelic, godlike.
chaste, pure, innocent, continent, undefiled, honest (*archaic in this sense*), spotless, immaculate, unsullied, virgin: *in this sense,* virtuous *is now applied esp. to women.*
See also DUTY, GOOD, GOODNESS, INNOCENCE, POWER, PROBITY, PURITY, REPUTE, TEMPERANCE.—*Antonyms.* See VICE.

---

virulent, *adj.* poisonous, venomous, deadly; malignant, caustic. See BADNESS, RESENTMENT.
visage, *n.* face, countenance; aspect, guise, likeness, semblance. See APPEARANCE.
visceral, *adj.* splanchnic (*tech.*), intestinal, ventral. See INTERIORITY.
viscid, *adj* sticky, glutinous, viscous, mucilaginous. See SEMILIQUIDITY.

VISIBILITY.—I. *Nouns.* **visibility,** perceptibility, perceivability, visuality, atmospheric transparency (*in a horizontal direction; as, good* visibility: *aëro. and meteorol.*), discernibleness, manifestation, appearance, apparentness, apparency exposure, ocular demonstration; clearness, conspicuousness, distinctness, definition (*of outline*), precision.
II. *Verbs.* **become visible,** appear, materialize, rise, loom, emerge, arise, issue, spring, come in sight, peer (*archaic in this sense*), show, come into view, attract the attention, burst upon the view, catch the eye, open to the view, peep out, peer out, present (show, manifest, reveal, expose, *or* betray) itself, stand forth, stare, be conspicuous, stand out, gleam, glimmer, glitter, glow, glare, burst forth, start up, spring up, heave in sight (*naut. or colloq.*), come out, come forth, come forward, reappear.
III. *Adjectives.* **visible,** perceptible, perceivable, seeable, visual, discernible, apparent, unhidden, discoverable; open, revealed, manifest, observable, noticeable; in view, in full view, in sight, exposed to view, *en évidence* (*F.*).
distinct, plain, clear, definite, well-defined, in focus, well-marked, unclouded, obvious, recognizable; glaring, palpable, patent, evident, staring, noticeable, salient, conspicuous; macroscopic (*opposite of* microscopic), megascopic (*tech.*) in bold (strong, *or* high) relief.
IV. *Adverbs.* **visibly,** perceptibly, distinctly, etc. (see *adjectives*); in sight of, before one's eyes, *à vue d'œil* (*F.*), under one's very nose; *veluti in speculum* (*L.*).
See also APPEARANCE, MANIFESTATION, VISION.—*Antonyms.* See INVISIBILITY.

VISION.—I. *Nouns.* **vision,** sight, eyesight, seeing, light (*poetic*), perception, discernment; optics, macrography (*study with the naked eye*).
look, glance, *coup d'œil* (*F.*), ken, glimpse, glint, blink, peep, peek; gaze, stare, leer; contemplation, regard, survey, inspection, view, observation, reconnaissance

ocular inspection, ocular view, autopsy (*esp. med.*); espionage, *espionnage* (*F.*); watch, lookout; sight-seeing.
viewpoint, standpoint, point of view: *chiefly figurative.*
lookout (*the place*), post of observation, beacon, tower, watchtower, crow's-nest (*naut.*), belvedere, observatory, gazebo; sighthole, loophole, peephole.
field of view, field of observation, field of vision (*psychol.*), field of regard (*psychol.*), theater *or* theatre, amphitheater, arena; panoramic view, bird's-eye view; vista, view, prospect, perspective, horizon.
[*organ of vision*] **eye**, visual organ, oculus (*pl.* oculi: *tech.*), optic (*now usually jocose*), orb (*poetic*), peeper (*colloq.*), ocular (*jocose*), glim (*slang*), lamps (*pl.: slang*); naked eye, unassisted eye, unaided eye; eagle (piercing, *or* penetrating) eye, clear (sharp, *or* quick) sight.
[*comparisons*] eagle, hawk; cat, lynx, Argus.
[*that which is seen*] **sight**, spectacle, view, exhibition, show; object; form, thing, phenomenon.
[*mental vision*] **imagination**, imaginativeness, conception, mental image, creation, fancy, notion, thought, belief, idea; fantasy, dream, daydream, air castle, hope; prospect, foresight, forelook (*U. S.*), anticipation, forward view.
apparition, phantom, appearance, specter *or* spectre, ghost, revenant, illusion, chimera *or* chimæra, hallucination, image, phantasm, phantasma (*pl.* phantasmata); prophetic sight, supernatural appearance.
visionary, dreamer, castle-builder, daydreamer, idealist, utopian, optimist, visionist (*rare*), fantast, Laputan.
II. *Verbs.* **vision**, see (*as in a vision*), imagine, fancy, fantasy (*archaic*), dream, believe, conceive, create, visualize, envisage.
see, behold, discern, read, perceive, descry, sight, ken (*archaic*), make out, discover, distinguish, recognize, spy, espy, catch a glimpse of, command a view of; witness, attend, notice, observe, contemplate, look on, see at a glance.
look, view, eye, survey, scan, inspect, reconnoiter; glance, peep, peek, peer, pry, squint, watch, keep watch, watch for; stare, goggle, glare, gaze, look intently, strain one's eyes, rivet the eyes upon, pore over; gloat over; leer, ogle, cock the eye, look askance *or* askant.
III. *Adjectives.* **ocular**, visual, optic *or* optical; ophthalmic.
clear-sighted, clear-eyed, farsighted, sharp-sighted, keen-eyed, gimlet-eyed, eagle-eyed, hawk-eyed, lynx-eyed; Argus-eyed.
visionary, imaginary, dreamy, utopian, Laputan, impractical, unpractical, quixotic, chimerical, air-built, fantastic, fanciful, vain, delusive, unreal, ideal, unsubstantial, unfounded, wild, illusory, romantic, visioned.
IV. *Adverbs.* **at sight**, at first sight, at a glance, at the first blush, *prima facie* (*L.*), at first view, on presentation (*as of a draft*).
See also IMAGINATION, NONEXISTENCE, OPTICAL INSTRUMENTS, SPECTER, UNSUBSTANTIALITY, VISIBILITY.—*Antonyms.* See BLINDNESS.

---

visit, *v.* arrive, drop in, call upon; stop, tarry, stay. See ARRIVAL, SOCIALITY, TOUCH.
visit, *n.* call, interview, appointment, visitation. See SOCIALITY.
visitant, *n.* visitor, guest. See ARRIVAL.
visitation, *n.* misfortune, infliction, blow, trial, sorrow; seizure, attack, paroxysm, stroke; official visit. See ADVERSITY, DISEASE, SOCIALITY.
visitor, *n.* visitant, guest, newcomer; frequenter, habitué. See ARRIVAL, FRIEND.
visualize, *v.* envisage, objectify. See EXTERIORITY.
vital, *adj.* essential, radical, cardinal; living, existing, vivifying. See IMPORTANCE, LIFE.
vitality, *n.* vital power, virility, vigor. See LIFE, STABILITY.
vitiate, *v.* invalidate, impair; debase, corrupt, contaminate. See DESTRUCTION, DETERIORATION.
vivacious, *adj.* sprightly, animated, lively, gay, brisk, light-hearted. See ACTIVITY, AIR, CHEERFULNESS, LIFE, SENSITIVENESS.
vivacity, *n.* animation, energy, liveliness, sprightliness. See LIFE.
vivid, *adj.* bright, brilliant, gay, intense; graphic, striking, telling, expressive

lively, vigorous; radiant, resplendent. See COLOR, INTELLIGIBILITY, LIGHT.

vividness, *n.* sharpness, definition, distinction, prominence. See RELIEF.

vivification, *n.* vitalization, revival. See LIFE.

vocabulary, *n.* dictionary, lexicon, glossary, wordbook; range of language. See LIST, WORD.

vocal, *adj.* choral, lyric; voiced, sonant. See MUSIC, VOICE.

vocalist, *n.* singer, chanter, caroler, vocal musician: *distinguished from* instrumentalist. See MUSICIAN.

vocation, *n.* calling, occupation, profession. See BUSINESS, PURSUIT.

vociferate, *v.* shout, roar, bawl, yell. See CRY.

vogue, *n.* style, mode, custom, usage. See FASHION, HABIT.

VOICE.—I. *Nouns.* **voice,** articulate sound, utterance, speech, tongue, tone, *vox* (*L.*), intonation, modulation, enunciation, articulation, vocalization, ecphonesis (*rhet.*), exclamation, expletive, ejaculation, vociferation, cry; delivery, attack.

accent, accentuation, emphasis, stress; rhythmical stress, ictus (*tech.*); pronunciation, orthoëpy.

admonition, warning, caution, exhortation, direction, instruction (*as, the* voice *of conscience*).

choice, option, preference, say (*colloq.*), wish, opinion; vote, suffrage.

II. *Verbs.* **voice,** utter, express, announce, divulge, proclaim, rumor; **tune** (*as an organ: music*); make sonant (*phonetics*).

speak, utter, sound, breathe, say, use; talk, converse; ejaculate, rap out; articulate, enunciate, modulate, vocalize, pronounce, accentuate; whisper, murmur, pipe, shout, cry; emit, deliver, discourse, hold forth, orate; publish, proclaim.

III. *Adjectives.* **vocal,** phonetic, oral, uttered, modulated, spoken, voiced, ejaculatory, articulate, distinct, euphonious, melodious, sonorous, sounding, voiceful (*poetic*).

[*in phonetics*] **voiced,** sonant, phthongal, vocalized, intonated, tonic, vocal: *opposite of* voiceless.

See also AFFIRMATION, CHOICE, CRY, FLATNESS, JUDGMENT, LETTER (*phonetics*), MELODY, PHRASE, [1]SOUND, SPEECH.—*Antonyms.* See DUMBNESS.

---

voiceless, *adj.* speechless; nonvocal, surd (*phonetics*), hard. See DUMBNESS, HARDNESS, LETTER.

void, *adj.* empty, vacant, untenanted, unoccupied, vacuous, blank, hollow. See ABSENCE, UNSUBSTANTIALITY.

volatile, *adj.* changeable, capricious, inconstant; gaseous, vaporous; lively, light, buoyant, airy; vaporific, evaporable. See CHANGEABLENESS, GASEITY, LEVITY, VAPORIZATION.

volitional, *adj.* free-willed, volitionary, voluntary, optional. See WILL.

volley, *n.* fusillade, shooting; report, salvo, discharge. See ATTACK, SNAP.

voluble, *adj.* talkative, fluent, glib, loquacious. See LOQUACITY.

volume, *n.* tome; vastness, size, bulk, mass, quantity. See BOOK, GREATNESS.

voluminous, *adj.* great, big, bulky, ample, copious. See GREATNESS, SIZE.

voluntarily, *adv.* spontaneously, freely, deliberately, purposely. See WILL.

voluntary, *adj.* spontaneous, free, gratuitous, unasked, unbidden, intentional. See WILLINGNESS.

volunteer, *n.* free-will worker; territorial (*Brit.*), national guardsman (*U. S.*): *opposite of* conscript. See WILLINGNESS.

volunteer, *v.* proffer, tender, come forward. See OFFER, WILLINGNESS.

voluptuous, *adj.* sensual, carnal, fleshly; sensuous, luxurious. See INTEMPERANCE, PLEASURABLENESS.

vomit, *v.* spew, cast up, disgorge, belch forth. See EJECTION.

voracious, *adj.* greedy, ravenous, gluttonous, edacious. See GLUTTONY.

votary, *n.* devotee, zealot, enthusiast, adherent. See DESIRE.

vote, *n.* voice, choice, judgment, election, poll, ballot, plebiscite, suffrage, franchise. See AFFIRMATION, CHOICE.

voter, *n.* elector, constituent, balloter; electorate (*collective*). See CHOICE.
vouch, *v.* avouch, answer for, certify, warrant, attest: *often with* for. See AFFIRMATION, DEBT, EVIDENCE.
voucher, *n.* receipt, certificate, verification, authentication. See SECURITY.
vow, *v.* vouch, certify, affirm, asseverate. See AFFIRMATION.
voyage, *n.* cruise, sail, passage; crossing, route. See NAVIGATION, PASSAGE.

VULGARITY.—I. *Nouns.* **vulgarity,** commonness, plebeianism, ill-breeding, *mauvais ton* (*F.*), bad taste, *mauvais goût* (*F.*), ungentlemanliness, boorishness, clownishness, awkwardness, *gaucherie* (*F.*), want of tact, indecorum, misbehavior; loudness (*colloq.*), ostentation; vulgarism, barbarism, Vandalism.
lowness, coarseness, grossness, low life, brutality, blackguardism, rowdyism, ruffianism; ribaldry, obscenity, indecency, smuttiness; ribald jest.
[*excess of ornament*] **tawdriness,** gaudiness, flashiness, trumpery, frippery, trickery, tinsel, clinquant, gingerbread.
the vulgar (*collective*), the common people, plebs, plebeians, populace, *hoi polloi* (*Gr.*), the masses.
vulgarian, vulgar person (*esp. a rich one*), parvenu, upstart, *nouveau riche* (*F., pl. nouveaux riches; fem. pl. nouvelles riches*), *novus homo* (*L.*), snob, cad, bounder (*Eng. slang*); Goth, Vandal, barbarian, Bœotian, clown; rough diamond; cub (*jocose or contemptuous*), unlicked cub.
II. *Verbs.* **be vulgar,** misbehave, misconduct oneself, behave improperly, show a want of consideration; be a vulgarian.
vulgarize, make vulgar, make common, plebeianize, plebify (*rare*), coarsen.
III. *Adjectives.* **vulgar,** plebeian, common, popular, ordinary, general, public; vernacular, national (*as, the* vulgar *tongue*).
ill-bred, ill-mannered, underbred, uncivil, unmannerly, discourteous, rude, impolite, disrespectful, carlish, ungentlemanly, uncourtly, unladylike, *contra bonos mores* (*L.*), snobbish, caddish; undignified, unseemly, indecorous, unbecoming, unbeseeming, ungracious.
unrefined, uncultivated, unpolished, uncultured, inelegant, in bad taste; uncouth, unkempt, homely, homespun, rustic, countrified, provincial, rough, awkward, clownish, boorish; savage, brutish, wild, barbarous, barbaric, outlandish, rowdy, rowdyish.
coarse, gross, low, raffish, vile, base, ribald, obscene, smutty, indecent, offensive, scurrilous, foul-mouthed, foul-spoken, blackguardly, blackguard, abusive.
tawdy, gaudy, meretricious, obtrusive, flaunting, loud, crass, showy, flashy, brummagem (*slang*), garish, cheap, gimcrack, trumpery, tinsel, Bowery (*U. S.*).
See also DISCOURTESY, INELEGANCE, PEOPLE.—*Antonyms.* See COURTESY, TASTE.

---

vulnerable, *adj.* exposed, defenseless, accessible, assailable. See DANGER, WEAKNESS.

W

wabble, *v.* sway, swerve, stagger; vacillate, waver. See OSCILLATION.
wag, *v.* waggle, oscillate, shake, wigwag. See AGITATION, OSCILLATION.
wag, *n.* joker, jester, wit; swing, sway, shake. See HUMORIST, OSCILLATION.
wager, *v.* stake, bet, back, gamble, punt. See CHANCE.
wages, *n. pl.* earnings, salary, pay, remuneration, stipend. See ACQUISITION, REWARD.
wagon, *n.* lorry, truck, wain (*archaic*), van. See VEHICLE.
wail, *v.* mourn, lament, bewail, bemoan; howl, cry. See LAMENTATION, ULULATION.
wait, *v.* linger, tarry, stay, bide; attend (*upon*), serve. See LATENESS, SERVANT.
waiter, *n.* tray, salver; waitress (*fem.*), steward, stewardess (*fem.*), *garçon* (*F.*), attendant. See RECEPTACLE, SERVANT.
[1]**wake,** *n.* train, trail, track, path, trace. See REAR, SEQUEL.

[2]**wake,** *n.* vigil, watch (*esp. of a corpse before burial, often attended with merry-making: an Irish custom*). See INTERMENT.
wakeful, *adj.* sleepless, restless; watchful, vigilant, alert. See ACTIVITY, CARE.
walk, *v.* step, tread, march, pace, tramp. See JOURNEY.
walk, *n.* sphere, province, department; behavior, procedure; promenade, stroll, saunter, ramble; walking, amble. See BUSINESS, CONDUCT, JOURNEY, SLOWNESS.
walker, *n.* pedestrian, foot passenger, tramper, hiker. See TRAVELER.
walking-stick, *n.* cane, stick, staff. See SUPPORT.
wall, *n.* rampart, parapet; fence; partition, bulkhead; cliff, bluff, precipice. See DEFENSE, INCLOSURE, INTERJACENCE, VERTICALITY.
wallet, *n.* purse, roll, wad (*slang*); bag. sack, pouch, pocketbook. See MONEY, RECEPTACLE.
wallow, *v.* grovel, welter, flounder, roll, toss. See LOWNESS, PLUNGE.
wampum, *n.* wampumpeag, seawan. See MONEY.
wan, *adj.* pale, pallid, bloodless, colorless. See COLORLESSNESS.
wand, *n.* rod, staff, baton; caduceus, divining rod. See SCEPTER, [1]SPELL.
wander, *v.* deviate, stray, digress; dote, rave, ramble; roam, rove, range, prowl; move, flow, drift. See DEVIATION, INSANITY, JOURNEY, MOTION.
wanderer, *n.* rover, itinerant, straggler, rambler. See TRAVELER.
wandering, *adj.* vagrant, roving, straying. See CIRCUIT.
wane, *v.* decrease, decline, abate, subside, ebb, fail. See CONTRACTION, DETERIORATION.
want, *n.* lack, need, requirement; poverty, privation, necessity, exigency, starvation, famine, dearth. See ABSENCE, INSUFFICIENCY.
want, *v.* wish for, crave, cover; lack, need, require; fall short, not reach. See DESIRE, INSUFFICIENCY, SHORTCOMING.
wanton, *adj.* capricious, wayward, froward, perverse; light, loose, unchaste, immoral. See CAPRICE, LIGHTNESS.
ward, *n.* care, protection, charge, custody, guardianship; room (*as in a hospital*); district, division, precinct; dependent, *protégé* (*F.*). See DEFENSE, RECEPTACLE, REGION, SERVANT.
warden, *n.* churchwarden; custodian, guardian, jailer; gamekeeper, ranger. See CLERGY, KEEPER, MASTER, SAFETY.
warder, *n.* guard, jailer, turnkey. See KEEPER, SAFETY.
wardhouse, *n.* storehouse, depot, repository, magazine *entrepôt* (*F.*). See MART.

WARFARE.—I. *Nouns.* **warfare,** fighting, military operations, hostilities, war, bloodshed, arms, the sword, appeal to arms (*or* the sword), arbitrament of the sword, *ultima ratio regum* (*L.*), ordeal (*or* wager) of battle, declaration of war; mobilization, battle array, order of battle; campaign, crusade, jihad *or* jehad (*Moham.*), expedition; warpath, service, campaigning, active service, tented field; war to the death (*or* knife), *guerre à mort* (*F.*), *guerre à outrance* (*F.*), Titanomachy, gigantomachy (*classical myth.*); Ares (*Gr.*), Mars (*Roman*), Bellona (*Roman goddess of war*).
art of war, military art, rules of war, the war game, tactics, strategy, generalship, soldiership, castramentation, attack, defense.
battle, conflict, fight, encounter, combat, contest, fray, affray, engagement, action, struggle; brush, dog fight (*aëro. slang*), skirmish; Armageddon.
war medal, military medal, medal of honor; distinguished service medal (*U. S.*), distinguished service cross (*U. S.*), Congressional Medal; Victoria Cross *or* V. C. (*Eng.*), Distinguished Service Order *or* D. S. O. (*Eng.*), Order of Merit *or* O. M. (*Eng.*); *croix de guerre* (*F.*), *médaille militaire* (*F.*); iron cross (*Ger.*).
II. *Verbs.* **war,** make war, go to war, declare war, wage war, arm, take up (*or* appeal to) arms; "let slip the dogs of war" (*Julius Cæsar*); take the field, give battle, engage, fight, combat, contend, battle with; carry on war (*or* hostilities).
serve, enroll, enlist; see service, be on service (*or* active service), shoulder a

musket, wield the sword, campaign; smell powder, be under fire; be on the warpath, keep the field; take by storm; go over the top (*colloq.*); sell one's life dearly.

III. *Adjectives.* **armed,** in (*or* under) arms, armed to the teeth (*or* cap-a-pie), sword in hand; in battle array, embattled, in the field.

warlike, belligerent, armigerous, hostile, combative, bellicose; martial, military, militant; soldierly, chivalrous; civil, internecine; irregular, guerrilla.

IV. *Adverbs.* in the thick of the fray, *flagrante bello* (*L.*), in the cannon's mouth; at the sword's point, at the point of the bayonet.

V. *Interjections.* **to arms!** *aux armes!* (*F.*); to your tents, O Israel! *væ victis!* (*L.*); "Charge, Chester, charge! On, Stanley, on!" (*Scott*); "Up, Guards, and at 'em!" (*traditional order given by Wellington at Waterloo*); "Fire when ready, Gridley!" (*Dewey at Manila Bay*).

See also ARENA, ARMS, COMBATANT, CONTENTION, KILLING.—*Antonyms.* See PACIFICATION, PEACE.

---

warm *adj.* flushed, feverish, excited; cordial, fervent, ardent; mild, genial, tepid; quick, hasty; hot, glowing, deep, passionate. See EXCITEMENT, FEELING, HEAT, IRASCIBILITY, ORANGE, STRENGTH (*intense*).

warm, *v.* chafe, foment; tepefy, make hot, heat. See CALEFACTION.

war medal, military medal, medal of honor. See WARFARE.

warmth, *n.* fervor, fervency, fire, hotness, glow, flush, fever. See HEAT, VIGOR.

WARNING.—I. *Nouns.* **warning,** caution, notice, caveat, admonition, notification, monition, intimation, calling, summons; forewarning, premonishment (*rare*), premonition, prediction, token, indication, sign, symptom; lesson, example, ensample (*archaic*); handwriting on the wall, *tekel upharsin* (*Daniel* v. 25); monitor, warning voice; Mother Cary's chickens, stormy petrel, bird of ill omen; gathering clouds.

sentinel, sentry, watch, watchman, nightwatchman, guard, watch and ward; patrol, picket, vedette (*mil.*), scout, spy, lookout, flagman, signalman; watchdog, bandog.

II. *Verbs.* **warn,** caution; forewarn, prewarn (*rare*), admonish, forebode, give warning, notify, inform, advise, approse, make aware, put on one's guard; picket, guard, patrol; sound the alarm.

beware, take care, take warning, look out, avoid, shun.

III. *Adjectives.* **warning,** cautionary, precautionary, premonitory, admonitory, monitory, admonitive (*rare*); sematic (*biol.*), symptomatic *or* symptomatical, indicative; threatening, ominous, menacing, minatory, lowering, significant.

IV. *Adverbs.* **warningly,** premonitorily, admonitorily; after due warning, with one's eyes open; on guard, with alarm.

V. *Interjections.* **beware!** ware! take care! mind! look out! watch your step! mind your eye! (*slang*).

See also ALARM, CARE, DISSUASION, OMEN, PREDICTION, SAFETY, THREAT.

---

warp, *v.* swerve, deviate, pervert; distort, twist; bias, prejudice, influence; trend, incline. See CHANGE, DISTORTION, MISJUDGMENT, TENDENCY.

warp, *n.* variation, deflection; bias, one-sidedness; proclivity, drift, trend. See DEVIATION, MISJUDGMENT, TENDENCY.

warrant, *n.* summons, subpœna; permit, pass, passport; authentication, verification. See COMMAND, PERMISSION, SECURITY.

warrant, *v.* vouch, certify, assure; uphold, sustain; license, authorize, sanction, justify; guarantee, attest. See AFFIRMATION, EVIDENCE, PERMISSION, PROMISE.

warrior, *n.* soldier, brave, man at arms: *rhetorical or poetic.* See COMBATANT.

warship, *n.* man-of-war, battleship, war vessel, cruiser. See COMBATANT.

wary, *adj.* cautious, shy, guarded, vigilant, heedful, chary. See CAUTION.

wash, *v.* cleanse, swab, scrub, lave, launder, purge; paint, stain. See CLEANNESS, COLOR.

washing, *n.* coat (*as metal with silver*), coating; ablution, bathing, bath, immersion; wash. See COVERING, WATER.

WASTE.—I. *Nouns.* **waste,** desert, Sahara, barren, wilderness, solitude, wild, deserted region, dreary void (*or* expanse).
[*act of wasting*] **consumption** (*esp. useless*), destruction, dissipation, dispersion, expenditure, loss, decrement, diminution, exhaustion, wear and tear, detriment, damage, injury, misuse, decay, devastation, ruin, estrepement (*law*), ravage, havoc, desolation; ineconomy (*rare*), prodigality, extravagance, lavishness, squandering, wastefulness.
[*that which is wasted*] wastage, refuse, offal, waste material, chaff, husks, scraps, remnants, shreds, loss, leakage; dross, culm, detritus, alluvium (*L. pl.* alluvia), debris, wreckage, spilth, rubbish, junk, slops, wash, overflow.
II. *Verbs.* **waste,** lay waste, devastate, desolate, ravage, pillage, plunder, spoil, strip, sack, scour, harry, despoil, destroy, sack, demolish, ruin.
consume (*unprofitably*), use up, spend, expend, swallow up, devour, absorb, engulf: exhaust, drain, empty, deplete; spill, squander, disperse, dissipate, burn up, lavish, misspend, prodigalize; cast away, throw away, fritter away; burn the candle at both ends, wear out.
labor in vain, "waste its sweetness on the desert air" (*Gray*); cast pearls before swine; waste powder and shot.
run to waste, ebb, leak, melt away, disappear, vanish, evaporate, run dry, dry up; run to seed.
III. *Adjectives.* **waste,** desert, barren, desolate, wild, uninhabited, unoccupied, uncultivated, untilled, abandoned; void, empty; bare, devastated, cheerless, gloomy, dismal, forlorn, dreary, monotonous.
worthless, valueless, useless, refuse, losel (*dial.*), unserviceable, unprofitable, unproductive, superfluous (*as,* waste *products;* waste *paper*).
wasteful, extravagant, lavish, prodigal, thriftless, improvident, profuse, squandering; ruinous, destructive.
See also DECREASE, DECREMENT, DESTRUCTION, DETERIORATION, DISPERSION, INUTILITY, LOSS, PRODIGALITY, SPACE, UNPRODUCTIVENESS.—*Antonyms.* See ECONOMY, PROVISION, UTILITY.

---

watch, *v.* attend, observe, see, mark, regard, listen; take care, be cautious, mind, tend, chaperon; patrol, scout, picket; gaze, stare. See ATTENTION, CARE, SAFETY, VISION.
watchdog, *n.* bandog, bloodhound, cerberus; guard, warder, sentinel. See SAFETY, STOPPER.
watcher, *n.* watchman, lookout, picket, detective, watchdog. See CARE.
watchful, *adj.* wakeful, vigilant, prudent, wary, circumspect, cautious, surefooted. See CARE.
watchman, *n.* watch, sentry, policeman. See SAFETY, WARNING.
watchtower, *n.* observation post, turret, beacon. See VISION (*lookout*).
watchword, *n.* password, catchword. See INDICATION.

WATER.—I. *Nouns.* **water,** lymph (*poetic*), crystal (*poetic*), Adam's ale (*jocose*), *aqua* (*L.*), *eau* (*F.*), *pani* (*Hind.*); fluid, diluent, rheum (*med.*); body of water, sea, lake, stream, etc.
washing, ablution, lavation, lavage (*esp. med.*), lavabo (*R. C. Ch.*), elution (*chem.*); bathing, bath, immersion, dipping, dip (*colloq.*), tub (*colloq.*), tubbing; humectation, affusion, balneation (*rare*).
sprinkler, sprayer, spray, atomizer, aspergillum (*R. C. Ch.*), sparger; shower, shower bath, needle bath, douche; syringe, fountain syringe; nozzle, rose, rosehead, sprinkling can, watering can, watering pot, *jet d'eau* (*F.; pl. jets d'eau*).
watering, sprinkling, wetting, moistening, drenching, submersion; dilution, infiltration, irrigation.
II. *Verbs.* **water,** wet, moisten, damp, drench, steep, soak, macerate; slosh, douse *or* dowse, souse, dip, baptize, immerse, submerge, duck, drown; wash, lave, bathe, dabble, paddle, splash, spatter, sparge, sprinkle, asperge, besprinkle; inject, syringe, gargle, irrigate, infiltrate, percolate, seep (*dial. and U. S.*); flush, flood, deluge, inundate.
dilute, attenuate, weaken, thin, adulterate, add water to (*as, to* water *milk*); dilute capital (*as, to* water *stock: finance*).
calender (*as silk*), tabby, cloud, moiré.

III. *Adjectives.* **watery,** aqueous, overmoist, wet, humid, moist, liquid, lymphatic; sodden, soggy; seepy, infiltrative; tearful, lachrymose.
[*of liquids*] **weak,** diluted, thin, transparent, pale, waterish, insipid, tasteless, flat.
[*of style, speech, etc.*] **vapid,** spiritless, dull, feeble, uninteresting, tame, jejune, dry, unanimated.

See also FLUIDITY, GULF, LAKE, MOISTURE, OCEAN, RIVER, STREAM, VAPORIZATION. —*Antonyms.* See AIR, DRYNESS.

---

watercourse, *n.* waterway, stream, run, canal. See CHANNEL.
water drinker, prohibitionist, abstainer, teetotaler, dry (*slang*). See SOBRIETY.
waterfall, *n.* fall, cascade, cataract, Niagara. See RIVER.
wave, *v.* signal, beckon; oscillate, undulate, vibrate, flutter. See INDICATION, OSCILLATION.
wave, *n.* winding, coil, roll, curl; undulation, swell, billow, comber; tide (*as of enthusiasm*), flood. See CONVOLUTION, RIVER.
waver, *v.* sway, totter, vibrate, undulate; vacillate, fluctuate, falter. See AGITATION, IRRESOLUTION.
waverer, *n.* trimmer, timeserver, opportunist. See IRRESOLUTION.
wavy, *adj.* undulating, undulate, undulatory, ripply, waved, curly. See CONVOLUTION.

WAY.—I. *Nouns.* **way,** road, route, path, beat, tack, walk, footpath, berm (*fortification*), ledge, pathway, towpath, track, trail, beaten track, lane, cut, alley, artery, channel, avenue, fairway, airway, air route, waterway; wireway, wire ropeway, ropeway, rope railway; trajectory, orbit, direction, course, bearing, trend, progression, journey, transit.
roadway, thoroughfare; highway, turnpike, state road, King's (*or* Queen's) highway, street, parkway, boulevard, speedway; by-road, crossroad, *carrefour* (*F.*); crossway; railroad (*in U. S. and Canadian usage, a steam road*), railway (*in British usage, a "railroad"; also in the U. S., a tramway or electric road*), line, track, street, railway, trolley track, tramway; viaduct, bridge, drawbridge, footbridge, pontoon bridge; overpass, underpass.
pavement, pave (*archaic*), sidewalk, *pavé* (*F.*), *trottoir* (*F.*), flags, flagstones, flagging, causeway *or* causey, dike, cobbles.
approach, access, passage, passageway; secret passage, covert way; cloister, covered way, window, aisle, lobby, hall, entrance, gateway, gate, door.
distance, interspace, interval, space, stretch, extent, remoteness, traveling distance (*as, a long* way *off*).
method, manner, wise (*rare, except in phrases*), form, mode, style, fashion, guise, mien, practice, habit; custom, conduct, behavior (*as, his* way *of speaking*).
procedure, proceeding, step, course, *modus operandi* (*L.*), device, plan, scheme (*as, the* way *to succeed*).
respect, point, particular, detail, aspect, feature, point of view (*as, in every* way).
II. *Adverbs.* **anyhow,** in any way, anywise, anyway, in any event, at any rate, in any case, nevertheless, however.
how, in what way, in what manner, by what mode, by what means (*or* process); to what extent, in what condition, for what reason, why, by what name, to what effect, at what price.

See also CONDUCT, HABIT, OPENING, PASSAGE, PLAN.

---

wayfarer, *n.* journeyer, walker, traveler, rambler, voyager. See JOURNEY.
wayward, *adj.* capricious, fluctuating, changeable, wanton; stubborn, perverse, froward. See CAPRICE, OBSTINACY.
weak-kneed, *adj.* irresolute, wavering, fickle, undecided, changeable. See WEAKNESS.
weak-minded, *adj.* feeble-minded, foolish, shallow, witless. See WEAKNESS.

WEAKNESS.—I. *Nouns.* **weakness,** debility, feebleness, languor, infirmity, infirmness, enervation, debilitation, impotence, decrepitude, atony (*tech.*), loss of strength, asthenia (*med.*), neurasthenia (*med.*), adynamia (*med.*), adynamy (*rare*), cachexia *or* cachexy (*med.*), malnutrition, attenuation; anæmia, bloodless-

ness, poverty of blood; invalidism, invalidity, delicacy, fragility, faintness, prostration; effeminacy, feminality, femininity.
[*comparisons*] reed, thread, rope of sand, house of cards, house built on sand; child, baby, chicken, kitten, cat, rat; water, gruel, milk and water, cambric tea.
irresolution, indecision, vacillation, instability, irresoluteness, unstableness, changeability, wavering, fickleness, inconstancy.
vulnerability, vulnerableness, exposedness, accessibility, assailableness; susceptibility, susceptibleness.
[*weak point*] failing, frailty, foible, imperfection, deficiency, defect, fault, lapse; liking for, inclination for, leaning, propensity.
weakling, feeble creature, invertebrate, jellyfish (*fig.*), weathercock (*fig.*); mollycoddle, sissy (*colloq.*), tenderling (*rare*).
II. *Verbs.* **be weak,** drop, crumble, give way; totter, dodder; tremble, shake; halt, limp; fade, languish, faint, decline, flag, fail.
weaken, enfeeble, debilitate, relax, enervate, unnerve, deprive of strength, invalidate, undermine, sap, impair, reduce, effeminize, devitalize, exhaust, incapacitate, emasculate, unman, cripple, cramp, rick (*chiefly Brit.*), wrench, sprain, strain, impoverish.
dilute, thin, diminish, attenuate, water, reduce in strength, reduce the strength of; *mettre de l'eau dans son vin* (*F.*).
III. *Adjectives.* **weak,** feeble, infirm; debilitated, asthenic (*med.*), enfeebled, enervated, unnerved, unstrung, relaxed, limp, flaccid, languid, sluggish, dull, slack, languishing, faint, sickly, weakly, exhausted, unsteady, groggy (*esp. pugilistic cant*), spent, wasted, strengthless, sapless, powerless, helpless, impotent, decrepit, laid low.
soft, effeminate, milky, timorous, womanish, unmanly, spineless, invertebrate.
frail, fragile frangible, shattery, brittle, breakable, flimsy, slimsy (*U. S. colloq.*), delicate, tender, sleazy, papery, unsubstantial, gimcrack, kutcha *or kachcha* (*Anglo-Indian*), jerry-built, broken, lame, shattered, shaken, crazy, shaky, cranky, rickety, tumbledown.
unsound, decayed, rotten, worn, seedy (*colloq.*), withered, wasted, effete, deteriorated, used up, forworn (*archaic*), the worse for wear; on its last legs.
vulnerable, exposed, unprotected, accessible, assailable, unguarded, woundable (*as, a* weak *position*).
ineffective, inefficient, inefficacious, impotent, useless, futile, ineffectual, unavailing, fruitless, vain, lame, unsatisfactory, illogical, inconclusive, unsustained, unconvincing (*as, a* weak *argument*).
weak-kneed, irresolute, wavering, vacillating, unstable, inconstant, fickle, undecided, undetermined, changeable; pliable, easily led.
weak-minded, feeble-minded, foolish, weak-headed, shallow, witless.
[*of mixed liquid or solution*] **thin,** diluted, small (*as beer*), light, watery, attenuated, vapid, insipid.
[*of style*] **diffuse,** prolix, verbose, slipshod, pointless, loosely knit, not nervous.
[*of sound*] **faint,** low, feeble, gentle, small, indistinct, murmurous.
[*in phonetics*] **light,** soft, unstressed, unaccented: *opposite of* strong.
See also DISEASE, FAINTNESS, IMPOTENCE, INFANT, INSIPIDITY, IRRESOLUTION, LAXITY, LETTER (*voiced*), LOWNESS, SMALLNESS, SOPHISTRY, VICE, WATER.—*Antonyms.* See STRENGTH.

WEALTH.—I. *Nouns.* **wealth,** riches, gold, fortune, opulence, affluence; wealthiness, richness, abundance; independence, competence; easy circumstances.
capital, money, great wealth, gold, capital stock (*or* fund), accumulated wealth, treasure, mint of money, mine of wealth; bonanza, El Dorado, Golconda; Pactolus, Pactolian sands; Philosopher's Stone; the Golden Touch; purse of Fortunatus; *embarras de richesse* (*F.*).
pelf, mammon (*Biblical*), lucre, filthy lucre, ill-gotten gain; fleshpots of Egypt, loaves and fishes.
means (*pl.*), resources, substance, command of money; property, income, revenue; livelihood, living, subsistence, sustenance, maintenance.
rich man, moneyed man, man of substance, moneybags, profiteer, milord *or milor* (*French term for wealthy Englishman*), capitalist, millionaire, multimillionaire, billionaire, plutocrat; nabob, Crœsus, Midas, Plutus, Dives.
science of wealth: plutology, economics, political economy.

II. *Verbs.* **be wealthy,** be rich, roll (*or* wallow) in wealth, have money to burn (*colloq.*); afford, well afford, command money.
become wealthy, get rich, make money, richen (*rare*), fill one's pocket, feather one's nest, make a fortune, make a killing (*slang*); worship Mammon, worship the golden calf.
make wealthy, make rich, etc. (see *adjectives*); enrich, endow, millionize.
III. *Adjectives.* **wealthy,** rich, affluent, opulent, moneyed, well-to-do, independent, well off, rolling in riches, flush; golden, Pactolian; capitalistic.
abundant, ample, full, plentiful, copious, bountiful, bounteous, lavish, thick, prolific, teeming, rife, superabundant, profuse, exuberant.

See also ACQUISITION, MONEY, PROPERTY, SUFFICIENCY, TREASURY.—*Antonyms.* See POVERTY.

---

weapon, *n.* sword, spear, club, bow, firearms, etc. See ARMS.
wear, *v.* don, put on, carry; waste, dwindle, diminish, consume, impair; gybe, yaw, sheer, tack (*all naut.*); weary, tire, exhaust, bore, annoy. See CLOTHING, DECREASE, DEVIATION, WEARINESS.
wear, *n.* wear and tear, impairment, disrepair, disintegration; service. See DETERIORATION, USE.

WEARINESS.—I. *Nouns.* **weariness,** fatigue, tiredness, lassitude, wearisomeness, tedium tediousness, languor, drowsiness, ennui, boredom, monotony, sameness; heavy hours, dull work.
disgust, nausea, loathing, sickness, *tædium vitæ* (*L.*); satiety, repletion.
bore, annoyance, pest, plague, nuisance; buttonholer, proser, twaddler, dry-as-dust, fossil (*colloq.*), wet blanket.
II. *Verbs.* **weary,** tire, fatigue, fag, jade, exhaust, wear, wear out; irk (*archaic*), bore, buttonhole, annoy, harp on the same string.
disgust, nauseate, sicken, revolt, pall, surfeit, glut, cloy.
III. *Adjectives.* **wearisome,** tiresome, irksome, tedious, weariful, prolix, wearing, tiring, wearying, toilsome, laborious; borish, slow, dull, uninteresting, stupid, bald, monotonous, dry, arid, humdrum, flat, prosy, prosaic, prosing; soporific, somniferous.
weary, tired, aweary (*poetic*), fatigued, drowsy, sleepy; flagging, used up (*colloq.*), worn-out, exhausted, dispirited, grieved, sad, careworn, life-weary, sick of, *blasé* (*F.*), impatient of, uninterested, *ennuyé* (*F.*), ennuied.
IV. *Adverbs.* **wearily,** tiredly, etc. (see *adjectives*); *usque ad nauseam* (*L.*).

See also DEJECTION, FATIGUE, INACTIVITY, PAINFULNESS, SLOWNESS.—*Antonyms.* See AMUSEMENT, ENERGY, NEWNESS.

---

wearisome, *adj.* toilsome, burdensome, arduous, laborious, difficult; slow, tedious, irksome, stupid. See EXERTION, PAINFULNESS, SLOWNESS.
weather, *n.* atmospheric conditions, climate. See AIR.—**weather prophet,** weather forecaster, weather man (*colloq.*). See ORACLE.
weathervane, *n.* weathercock, cock, vane. See AIR.
weave, *v.* fabricate, compose, construct, form, make; lace, interlace, interweave, intertwine. See COMPOSITION, CROSSING.
wed, *v.* marry, espouse, join, couple. See MARRIAGE.
wedding, *n.* nuptials, bridal, marriage ceremony. See MARRIAGE.
wedge, *n.* chock, shim, quoin, keystone, cleat. See INSTRUMENT.
wedlock, *n.* matrimony, nuptial tie. See MARRIAGE.
weed, *v.* clear of weeds, root up. See EJECTION.—**weed out,** separate, segregate, eliminate, remove. See EJECTION, EXCLUSION.
weep, *v.* cry, sob, blubber, shed tears, greet (*Scot.*). See LAMENTATION.
weeping, *n.* sobbing, crying. See LAMENTATION.
weigh, *v.* load, press, cumber; balance, poise; carry weight, tell, count; consider, estimate, realize. See GRAVITY, INFLUENCE, THOUGHT.
weight, *n.* heaviness, pressure, load, burden; consequence, prominence, value; power, ascendancy, favor; impressiveness. See GRAVITY, IMPORTANCE, INFLUENCE, VIGOR.

weighty, *adj.* determinative, confirmatory, significant, heavy, massive, unwieldy; considerable, ponderous. See EVIDENCE, GRAVITY, IMPORTANCE.
weird, *adj.* uncanny, eerie, spooky (*colloq.*), spectral. See SPECTER.
welcome, *adj.* cordial, genial, agreeable, acceptable. See PLEASURABLENESS.
welcome, *n.* entertainment; greeting, salutation, *bienvenue* (*F.*). See RECEPTION, SOCIALITY.
welcome, *v.* greet, hail, receive, bid welcome. See COURTESY.
welfare, *n.* well-being, thrift, affluence, happiness. See PROSPERITY.
well, *n.* source, spring, font, fountain, reservoir, wellspring; pit, shaft, hole. See CAUSE, LAKE; DEPTH.
well, *v.* flow, issue, spring, jet, spout, gush, pour. See RIVER.
well, *adv.* favorably, rightly, worthily, excellently; abundantly; quite. See GOOD.
well, *adj.* sound, strong, robust, healthy. See HEALTH.
well-behaved, *adj.* well-mannered, orderly, decorous, well-bred, courteous. See COURTESY, GOOD.
well-being, *n.* welfare, weal (*archaic*), good, happiness. See PLEASURE, PROSPERITY.
well-bred, *adj.* refined, cultivated, courteous, well-born, thoroughbred. See COURTESY, FASHION.
well-defined, *adj.* sharp-cut, clear-cut, clear, distinct. See SHARPNESS.
well-known, *adj.* known, recognized, renowned, famous; proverbial, familiar. See KNOWLEDGE.
well-laid, *adj.* prearranged, deliberate, well-devised. See PREDETERMINATION.
well-to-do, *adj.* well off, prosperous, rich, wealthy, propertied, influential. See PROSPERITY, SUBSTANTIALITY.
welter, *v.* wallow, roll, toss, tumble about. See PLUNGE.
werewolf, *n.* *loup-garou* (*F.*). See MYTHICAL BEINGS (*changeling*).
western, *adj.* west, westward, occidental: *opposite of* eastern. See SIDE.
wet, *adj.* opposed to prohibition (*as, a* wet *State*: *U. S. slang*); moist, damp, humid, rainy. See DRUNKENNESS, MOISTURE.
wet, *n.* antiprohibitionist (*opposite of* dry: *U. S. slang*); wetness, moistness, water, liquid; rain, damp. See DRUNKENNESS, MOISTURE, RIVER.
whale, *n.* cetacean, finback, sperm whale, etc. See ANIMAL.
wharf, *n.* pier, quay, landing, dock. See EDGE, HABITATION.
wheedle, *v.* flatter, cajole, humor, coax, lure. See FLATTERY, MOTIVE.
wheel, *v.* wind, twist, turn aside; veer, double, countermarch; rotate, revolve, turn, turn around. See DEVIATION, REGRESSION, ROTATION.
wheel, *n.* disk, circle; turn, revolution; bicycle. See CIRCULATORY, ROTATION, VEHICLE.—**wheel and axle,** revolving lever, simple machine. See INSTRUMENT.
when, *adv.* at what time? how long ago? how soon? while, whereas, whenever, as soon as. See TIME.
whet, *v.* stimulate, rouse, awaken, inspire, excite; incite, provoke, instigate; sharpen. See EXCITEMENT, MOTIVE, SHARPNESS.
whether, *conj.* in case, if. See SUPPOSITION.
while, *conj.* whilst (*esp. Brit.*), as long as, at the same time as; although, whereas. See TIME.
whim, *n.* fancy, humor, notion; wish, inclination, bent; fantasy, vagary. See CAPRICE, DESIRE, IMAGINATION.
whimsical, *adj.* capricious, erratic, freakish; grotesque, outlandish, quaint, fanciful. See CAPRICE, RIDICULOUSNESS.
whine, *v.* whimper, wail, bewail, bemoan, cry. See LAMENTATION.
whip, *v.* hurry, impel, urge, flog, goad, lash, strike, smite, scourge. See HASTE, MOTIVE, PUNISHMENT.
whirl, *n.* flutter, flurry, spin, twirl, swirl, gyration. See EXCITABILITY, ROTATION.

whirling, *adj.* revolving, gyral, vortical, circumgyratory. See ROTATION.
whirlpool, *n.* vortex, eddy, swirl, surge, maelstrom. See GULF, PITFALL, RIVER, ROTATION.
whirlwind, *n.* windstorm, cyclone, tornado, typhoon. See AGITATION, WIND.
whisker, *n.* beard, goatee, imperial, Vandyke; bristle, vibrissa (*pl.* vibrissæ: *tech.*), feeler: *usually in pl.* See ROUGHNESS.
whisper, *v.* divulge, reveal, utter; breathe, murmur; sigh. See DISCLOSURE, FAINTNESS, WIND.
whistle, *v.* pipe, flute; wheeze, sibilate; howl, wail. See MUSICIAN, SIBILATION, WIND.

WHITENESS.—I. *Nouns.* **whiteness,** hoariness, frostiness, milkiness, lactescence, canescence, whitishness, paleness, colorlessness; argent (*heraldry*); blink (*tech.*), ice blink.
[*comparisons*] snow, driven snow, sheet, paper, milk, lily, ivory, silver, alabaster
whitening, blanching, bleaching, albescence, albication, albification (*rare*), dealbation, etiolation (*as of plants*), leucoderma *or* leucodermia (*med.*); albinism, albinoism, leucopathy, absence of pigmentation.
whiting, whitewash, whitening, calcimine, white lime.
purity, cleanness, spotlessness, immaculateness, immaculacy, chasteness.
II. *Verbs.* **whiten,** bleach, blanch, silver, frost, white, white out (*printing*), grizzle, pale, etiolate (*tech.*), albify (*rare*), dealbate (*rare*).
whitewash, calcimine, white; gloze (*fig.*), gloss over, extenuate, varnish, palliate.
III. *Adjectives.* **white,** snow-white, snowy, niveous, frosted, hoar, hoary, candid (*archaic*), candent, canescent; milky, milk-white, lactescent; chalky, cretaceous; silver, silvery, argentine, argent, bright, shining (*as burnished steel*) marmoreal *or* marmorean; colorless, transparent, blank (*as in printing*).
whitish, creamy, pearly, ivory, fair, blond, ash-blond; blanched, light, gray *or* grey, wan, pale, ashen, light-colored, fair-skinned; albescent, albicant, albificative (*rare*), albinistic (*tech.*), etiolated (*as plants grown in darkness*).
pure, spotless, stainless, immaculate, clean, clear, chaste, unblemished, unstained, unsullied, innocent.
honorable, upright, just, straightforward, fair, genuine, trustworthy, trusty (*as, a* white *man: colloq.*).

See also COLORLESSNESS, GRAY.—*Antonyms.* See BLACKNESS.

---

whitewash, *v.* calcimine, white; gloze over, palliate. See COVERING, WHITENESS; VINDICATION.

WHOLE.—I. *Nouns.* **whole,** totality, integrity, integrality, allness, omnitude (*rare*), wholeness, *ensemble* (*F.*), *tout ensemble* (*F.*), entirety, completeness, collectiveness, complex, complexus (*L. pl.* complexus), assemblage; undividedness, universality, intactness, indivisibility, indiscerptibility; integration (*tech.*), organic unity, compages (*sing. and pl.*), compaction (*rare*); complete unity, integer, integral (*esp. math.*).
all, the whole, general (*archaic*), everything, everybody; total, aggregate, sum, sum total, gross amount; length and breadth of, Alpha and Omega, be-all, "the be-all and the end-all" (*Macbeth*).
bulk, mass, lump, tissue, staple, body, gross; major (greater, best, principal, *or* main) part, lion's share, Benjamin's mess, almost all.
trunk, bole, butt, stock, bouk (*Scot. and dial. Eng.*), torso, body, main part, caudex (*pl.* caudices: *bot.*), axis (*pl.* axes: *bot.*), stem, shaft, *tige* (*F.*), scape (*tech.*).
II. *Verbs.* **form a whole,** constitute a whole, aggregate, assemble, amass, agglomerate, integrate; total, amount to, come to.
III. *Adjectives.* **whole,** entire, complete, total, gross, integral, integrate; unbroken, undivided, unsevered, uncut, unshorn, unimpaired, uninjured, undiminished, intact, indiscrete, perfect.
indivisible, undividable, inseparable, indiscerptible, indissoluble, indissolvable.
healthy, hale, well, sound, in good health; healed, restored: *in this sense,* whole *is archaic.*
wholesale, sweeping, extensive, widespread, indiscriminate, comprehensive; done on a large scale, dealing in large quantities.

IV. *Adverbs.* wholly, altogether, totally, completely, entirely, perfectly, fully, *in extenso* (*L.*), as a whole, all, all in all, in a body, collectively, in the main (mass, lump, gross, *or* aggregate), *en masse* (*F.*), *en bloc* (*F.*), on the whole, bodily, substantially.

See also ASSEMBLAGE, COMPLETENESS, GREATNESS, UNITY.—*Antonyms.* See PART.

---

wholesale, *adj.* sweeping, extensive, widespread, comprehensive; in bulk. See WHOLE.

wholesome, *adj.* healthy, healthful, salubrious; sane, rational. See HEALTHINESS, SANITY.

why? *adv.* wherefore? whence? how so? See ATTRIBUTION.

wicked, *adj.* vicious, iniquitous, unrighteous, evil, sinful. See VICE.

wickedness, *n.* depravity, sin, iniquity, unrighteousness, immorality. See EVIL, VICE.

wide, *adj.* broad, ample, vast, spacious, large, roomy; extensive, comprehensive, general. See BREADTH, SPACE.

wide-awake, *adj.* alert, keen, shrewd, astute, knowing. See KNOWLEDGE.

widen, *v.* expand, spread, stretch, amplify. See BREADTH.

WIDOWHOOD.—I. *Nouns.* **widowhood,** viduation (*rare*), viduage (*rare*), viduity (*rare*); weeds.

widow, relict (*as in the legal phrase, "his relict" or "relict of"*), dowager (*widow endowed with title or property*), jointress, jointuress (*rare*); widower (*masc.*).

grass widow, widow bewitched (*colloq.*); grass widower (*masc.*).

II. *Verbs.* **widow,** bereave, deprive of mate, make desolate (*poetic*).

III. *Adjectives.* **widowed** (*as, a* widowed *mother*), bereaved, husbandless, vidual (*rare*), viduous (*rare*).

See also DIVORCE.—*Antonyms.* See MARRIAGE.

---

width, *n.* broadness, wideness, span, beam. See BREADTH.

wield, *v.* flourish, brandish, shake; control, manage, sway; manipulate, handle; employ, utilize, ply, work. See AGITATION, INFLUENCE, TOUCH, USE.

wife, *n.* married woman, helpmeet, spouse, matron. See MARRIAGE.

wig, *n.* peruke, periwig, toupee. See CLOTHING (*headdress*).

wild, *adj.* frantic, raving, mad; flighty, distracted, bewildered; self-indulgent, dissipated, fast; daring, reckless; ill-advised, unwise, crazy, foolish; rank, dense, luxuriant; fierce, savage, violent; barbarous, outlandish. See EXCITEMENT, INSANITY, INTEMPERANCE, RASHNESS, UNSKILLFULNESS, VEGETATION, VIOLENCE, VULGARITY.—**wild beast,** savage beast, ferine (*rare*); tiger, leopard, panther, etc. See ANIMAL, EVILDOER.

wile, *n.* trick, trickery, plot, stratagem, dodge. See CUNNING.

WILL.—I. *Nouns.* **will,** volition, conation (*psychol.*), volitiency, voluntarism (*philos.*), voluntariness, spontaneity, spontaneousness, velleity, originality; free will, power of choosing, unhampered choice, freedom, discretion; choice, option, preference, purpose, intent, intention.

wish, desire, pleasure, inclination, mind, disposition, longing, craving, yearning.

determination, resolution, will power, force of will, resoluteness, decision, will of one's own, grit (*colloq.*), strength of character; energy of intention, self-control, moral courage.

[*what is wished by another*] **request,** requirement, demand, order, direction, command, decree, behest; testament (*law*), last will and testament.

II. *Verbs.* **will,** desire, want, wish for, long for, prefer, incline to, list (*archaic*) wish (*as, what* wilt *thou?*): *in this sense,* will *is archaic.*

determine, decide, resolve, intend, see fit, choose, think fit, do what one chooses, have one's own way (*or* will), use one's discretion; enjoin, direct, impel, dominate; order, command, ordain, decree; bequeath, devise.

III. *Adjectives.* **willed,** inclined, disposed, having a will: *used chiefly in composition; as, self-*willed.

volitional, volitionary, volitive, volitient, free-willed, free, unconstrained, voluntary, spontaneous; optional, discretionary, discretional, facultative.
determined, decided, resolute, resolved, set, bent, strong-willed, purposeful; autocratic, arbitrary, despotic, bossy (*U. S. colloq.*), domineering, dictatorial.
willful *or* wilful, intentional, deliberate, intended, designed, contemplated, purposed, premeditated, studied, planned.
self-willed, obstinate, unyielding, stubborn, perverse, headstrong.
IV. *Adverbs.* **at will,** at pleasure, *à volonté* (*F.*), *à discrétion* (*F.*), as one thinks fit (*or* proper), *al piacere* (*It.*), *ad libitum* (*L.*), *ad arbitrium* (*L.*), *a beneplacito* (*It.*).
voluntarily, of one's own accord, spontaneously, freely, intentionally, deliberately, purposely, by choice, of one's own free will, *proprio motu* (*L.*), *ex mero motu* (*L.*), on one's own responsibility.

See also CHOICE, FREEDOM, INTENTION, OBSTINACY, PLEASURE, PREDETERMINATION, RESOLUTION, WILLINGNESS.—*Antonyms.* See NECESSITY.

WILLINGNESS.—I. *Nouns.* **willingness,** voluntariness, desire, readiness, promptness, eagerness, alacrity, zeal, enthusiasm, earnestness; cordiality, geniality, good nature, good will, heartiness, assent, compliance, acquiescence.
propensity, disposition, inclination, leaning, tendency, proclivity, proneness, bent, *penchant* (*F.*), liking, turn, frame of mind, humor, mood, vein, aptitude.
labor of love, unrewarded effort, self-appointed task, unpaid (*or* gratuitous) service, voluntary labor, voluntary (*rare*).
volunteer, unpaid worker, free-will worker, amateur, nonprofessional; national guardsman (*U. S.*), territorial (*Brit.*): *opposite of* conscript.
II. *Verbs.* **be willing,** incline, lean to, mind, hold to, cling to, desire; acquiesce, assent, comply with; nibble at the bait, gorge the hook; swallow bait, hook, and sinker; jump at, catch at; take up, plunge into, have a go at (*colloq.*), go in for (*colloq.*).
volunteer, offer, proffer, undertake, bestow voluntarily, offer one's services.
III. *Adjectives.* **willing,** ready, prompt, forward, earnest, eager, zealous, enthusiastic, bent upon, desirous, fain, minded, disposed, inclined, well-disposed, favorably inclined, lief (*archaic*), content, favorable, willing-hearted.
persuasible, persuadable, amenable, easily persuaded, easy, compliant, manageable, susceptible, ductile, facile, docile, easy-going, tractable, genial, gracious, cordial.
voluntary, gratuitous, spontaneous, unasked, unforced, unbidden, unimpelled, unconstrained, free, deliberate, intentional, intended, purposed.
IV. *Adverbs.* **willingly,** readily, freely, gladly, cheerfully, lief (*as in "I would as* lief"), fain (*used with* would), with pleasure, of one's own accord, voluntarily, with all one's heart, *con amore* (*It.*), *ex animo* (*L.*), with good will, *de bonne volonté* (*F.*); graciously, with a good grace, without demur.

See also ASSENT, CONSENT, DESIRE, OFFER, WILL.—*Antonyms.* See UNWILLINGNESS.

---

will-o'-the-wisp, *n. ignis fatuus* (*L.*), jack-o'-lantern, Sr. Elmo's fire; shadow, dream, vision. See LUMINARY, UNSUBSTANTIALITY.
wily, *adj.* crafty, artful, sly, subtle. See CUNNING.
win, *v.* acquire, get, gain, earn, obtain, procure; attain, triumph, surpass. See ACQUISITION, SUCCESS.—**win over,** convince, convert, wean; sway, influence, persuade, prevail on. See BELIEF, MOTIVE, SALE.
wince, *v.* flinch, shrink, shy, quail, blench. See FEAR, PAIN.
wind, *v.* coil, twine, reel, curl, roll, entwine, infold; wreathe, loop, meander, twist. See CIRCUITY, CONVOLUTION.

WIND.—I. *Nouns.* **wind** (*air in motion*), air, draft *or* draught, breath, flatus, afflatus (*usually in sense of "inspiration"*), puff, whiff, whiffet, stream, current, breeze, zephyr; indraft *or* indraught (*as of air against the propeller blades of an airplane*), inflow, inrush; emanation, aura (*tech.*).
[*in classical mythology*] Æolus *or* Eolus, cave of Æolus; Boreas (*north wind*), Eurus (*east wind*), Zephyrus *or* Favonius (*west wind*), Notus (*south wind*), Caurus *or* Corus (*northwest wind*), Vulturnus *or* Volturnus (*southwest wind*), Afer (*southwest wind*).

gust, blast, squall, flaw, flurry, capful of wind, fresh breeze, half a gale.
trade wind, trades (*pl.*), monsoon; anti-trade.
windstorm, storm, tempest, blow, gale, blizzard, hurricane, whirlwind, cyclone, typhoon, baguio (*Philippines*), tornado, twister (*U. S.*), samiel *or* simoom (*as in Asia Minor*), harmattan (*W. coast of Africa*), sirocco (*as in W. Africa, Texas, and Kansas*), khamsin (*Egypt*), levanter, Euroclydon, mistral (*Mediterranean*), *bise* (*F.*), foehn, chinook, willy-nilly (*Australia*); norther (*as in Texas, Florida, and the Gulf of Mexico*), northeaster, northeast gale.
wind gauge, anemometer, ventometer, anemograph, anemoscope; weathercock, weathervane, vane.
science of wind: anemology, anemography, aërodynamics, aërology, aërography, aërometry, pneumatics.
ventilator, aërator (*rare*), louver (*as on a roof or on the sides of an automobile hood*), transom, airpipe, funnel.
fan, palm leaf, punkah *or* punka (*India*), electric fan, flabellum, thermantidote (*India*); fanner, fan blower, blower, winnower, van (*dial*), colmar (*fashionable in Queen Anne's reign*).
breathing, respiration, eupnœa (*opposite of* dyspnœa: *med.*), inspiration, inhalation, expiration, exhalation; blowing, fanning, inflation.
[*respiratory organ*] **lung,** *pulmo* (*L.*), bellows (*pl.*), lights (*pl.; of sheep, pigs, oxen, etc.*), gill (*of fishes*), ctenidium (*pl.* ctenidia: *zoöl.*), branchia (*pl.* branchiæ: *zoöl.*).
flatulence *or* flatulency, windiness, gas; borborygmus (*med.*), eructation, belch.
empty talk, idle words, mere talk, babble, twaddle, fustian, bombast, claptrap, humbug hot air (*slang*), windbag eloquence, gas, boasting, bull (*slang*).
II. *Verbs.* **wind,** blow (*as a horn*), sound, toot, tootle, bugle, peal forth.
breathe, respire; inhale, inspire; exhale, expire (*from the lungs*); puff, pant, blow gasp, wheeze; sough, sigh, whisper, murmur, sob (*as the wind*); snuff, snuffle sniff, sniffle; sneeze, cough, hiccup *or* hiccough.
inflate, blow up, pump, aërate, distend, swell, expand, sufflate (*rare*).
fan, blow, ventilate, cool, refresh; winnow, clean; stimulate (*fig.*).
howl (*as the wind*), wail, moan, groan, growl, roar, scream, whistle, sing, pipe, sing in the shrouds.
blow, move (*as air*), breeze, breeze up (*naut.*), bluster, flaw (*rare*), squall; puff, whiff, whiffle; waft, float.
III. *Adjectives.* **windy,** breezy, blowy, gusty, blasty, flawy, dirty, foul, blustery, blusterous, blustering, squally; wind-swept, exposed, bleak, raw.
stormy, tempestuous, boisterous, violent, raging, turbulent; cyclonic, typhonic.
wordy, verbose, prolix, garrulous, diffuse, long-winded, empty.
See also AIR, HEAT (*hot wind*).

---

wind gauge, anemometer, weathercock, weathervane. See WIND.
winding, *n.* tortuosity, involution, circuit, meandering. See CONVOLUTION.
windlass, *n.* capstan, winch. See ELEVATION.
window, *n.* casement, lattice, skylight, porthole. See OPENING.
windpipe, *n.* trachea, weasand (*archaic*). See AIR PIPE.
windstorm, *n.* storm, tempest, gale, blizzard, hurricane, cyclone. See WIND.
wing, *n.* adjunct, ell, extension, ramification; supporting surface (*as of an airplane*); flight, flying, volitation; left *or* right (*as of an army*); off stage, side of stage, side scenery; pinion, arm, sail (*of a windmill*), ala (*pl.* alæ: *tech.*); flank. See ADDITION, AËRONAUTICS, COMBATANT, DRAMA, PART, SIDE.
wink, *v.* blink, squint, nictate, nictitate. See DIM-SIGHTEDNESS.—**wink at,** excuse, overlook, condone, pass over, ignore, connive at, favor, humor. See FORGIVENESS, NEGLECT, PERMISSION.
winnow, *v.* select, cull, glean; sift, fan, separate. See CHOICE, CLEANNESS, SIMPLENESS.
winsome, *adj.* pleasant, cheerful, bonny, lovable, winning, charming, captivating. See CHEERFULNESS, LOVE, PLEASURABLENESS.
winter, *n.* cold season, *hiems* (*L.*); old age. See COLD, EVENING.
wintry, *adj.* arctic, hiemal, boreal, winterly, brumal. See COLD, EVENING.
wipe, *v.* clean, rub, mop; dry. See CLEANNESS, DRYNESS.

wire, *n.* metal thread; telegraph, cable, telephone. See FILAMENT, MESSENGER, NEWS.

wireless, *n.* marconigram, radiotelegram, radiogram, radio (*colloq.*). See MESSENGER, NEWS.

wiry, *adj.* filamentous, filiform; strong, sinewy, tough. See FILAMENT, STRENGTH.

WISDOM.—I. *Nouns.* **wisdom,** sagacity, wiseness, sapience, sense, common sense, horse sense (*U. S. colloq.*), clear thinking, rationality, reason, judgment, discernment; solidity, depth, profundity, caliber *or* calibre.

prudence, circumspection, discretion, tact, discreetness, policy, expediency, advisability; carefulness, vigilance, foresight; self-possession, *aplomb* (*F.*), poise, balance, sobriety, ballast, stability.

learning, erudition, scholarship, knowledge, enlightenment, lore.

II. *Adjectives.* **wise,** sage, sagacious, sapient (*often ironical or jocose*), sensible, rational, reasonable, sound, strong-minded; profound; wise as Solomon (Solon, Nestor, *or* Mentor).

knowing, informed, learned, erudite, scholarly, accomplished, lettered; skillful, dexterous, skilled; sophisticated, worldly-wise.

prudent, circumspect, politic, discerning, wary, discreet, cautious, tactful, careful, vigilant, watchful, prepared, provident; sober, staid, solid.

[*applied to actions*] **judicious,** discreet, sensible, well-advised, prudent, well-judged, rational, sound; politic, diplomatic, expedient.

See also CARE, CAUTION, FORESIGHT, INTELLIGENCE, PREPARATION, SAGE.—*Antonyms.* See FOLLY, RASHNESS.

---

wise man, authority, mentor; thinker, philosopher. See ORACLE, SAGE.

wish, *n.* longing, yearning, craving, hunger, inclination. See DESIRE, WILL.

wishbone, *n.* merrythought, furcula (*pl.* furculæ: *tech.*). See [1]SPELL.

wistful, *adj.* desirous, wishful, longing; earnest, pensive. See DESIRE, FEELING.

WIT.—I. *Nouns.* **wit,** intelligence, understanding, mind, intellect, sense, gumption, perception, nous (*colloq.*), ready wit.

wittiness, cleverness, brightness, sparklingness, smartness, Attic salt, Atticism; salt, *esprit* (*F.*), piquancy, point, fancy, whim, humor.

banter, raillery, chaff, joshing (*slang*), *badinage* (*F.*), persiflage, airy nothings, *nugæ canoræ* (*L.*), pleasantry, repartee, retort, *quid pro quo* (*L.*).

buffoonery, fooling, harlequinade, clownery, tomfoolery, farce, broad farce, fun.

jocularity, jocoseness, facetiousness waggishness, *espièglerie* (*F.*), drollery, jesting, jocosity, merriment, comicality.

witticism, smart saying, sally, wise crack (*slang*), gag (*slang*), flash, scintillation, flash of wit, *jeu d'esprit* (*F.*); *mot pour rire* (*F.*), jest, joke, epigram, *bon mot* (*F.*), mot, quirk, quip, quiddity, *plaisanterie* (*F.*), *concetto* (*It.*), conceit "quips and cranks" (*Milton*).

wordplay, play upon words, *jeu de mots* (*F.*), pun, quibble, quillet (*archaic*), equivoque *or* equivoke, *double-entendre* (*or entente: F.*), *calembour* (*F.*), paronomasia, carriwitchet *or* carwitchet (*rare*), riddle, conundrum.

II. *Verbs.* **be witty,** etc. (see *adjectives*); scintillate, flash, flash back, retort, *ridentem dicere verum* (*L.*); joke, jest, cut jokes, crack a joke, pun, set the table in a roar.

banter, rally, chaff, josh (*slang*), jolly (*colloq.*), rag (*Eng. slang*), guy (*U. S. colloq.*), roast (*colloq.*), kid (*slang*), persiflate (*rare*), badinage, make merry with.

III. *Adjectives.* **witty,** clever, keen, keen-witted, brilliant, pungent, quick-witted, nimble-witted, smart, jocular, jocose, funny, waggish, facetious, comic, laughable, paronomastic, whimsical, humorous, sprightly, *ben trovato* (*It.*), sparkling, epigrammatic.

See also HUMORIST, INTELLECT, INTELLIGENCE, RIDICULE, RIDICULOUSNESS.—*Antonyms.* See DULLNESS.

---

witch, *n.* enchantress, fascinator; sorceress, pythoness; hag, crone. See BEAUTY, SORCERER, UGLINESS.

with, *prep.* despite, notwithstanding; among, in the company of, amidst; beside. See COMPENSATION, MIXTURE.
withdraw, *v.* retreat, retire, depart, vacate, recede, regress; retract, recall; resign, relinquish, abdicate, desert. See ABSENCE, REGRESSION; ANNULMENT, RESIGNATION.
wither, *v.* contract, shrivel, waste, wane, decline, wilt, droop, fade, decay. See CONTRACTION, DETERIORATION.
withering, *adj.* scornful, disdainful, arrogant; shriveling, marcescent (*bot.*), cynical, cutting, severe, trenchant. See CONTEMPT, CONTRACTION, DISAPPROBATION.
withhold, *v.* reserve, conceal, keep from; check, restrain, hinder, hold back, prohibit, restrict. See CONCEALMENT, RESTRAINT.
within, *adv.* inside, interiorly, internally, inwardly; indoors. See INTERIORITY.
within, *prep.* inside of, in, inclosed by; not beyond, not exceeding; in the reach of. See INTERIORITY.
without, *adv.* outside, outdoors; outwardly, externally. See EXTERIORITY.
without, *prep.* in the absence of, in default of, beyond, free from, less; outside of. See ABSENCE.
withstand, *v.* resist, confront, face, defy, oppose. See OPPOSITION, RESISTANCE.
witness, *n.* testifier, deponent; beholder, eyewitness, observer, onlooker. See EVIDENCE, SPECTATOR.
witticism, *n.* flash of wit, sally, smart saying, *jeu d'esprit* (*F.*). See WIT.
witty, *adj.* clever, smart, humorous, facetious, sparkling. See WIT.
woeful, *adj.* wretched, deplorable, lamentable, mournful, sad. See BADNESS, PAINFULNESS.

WOMAN.—I. *Nouns.* **woman,** female, *femme* (*F.*), petticoat (*fig.*), she (*rare as a noun*), weaker vessel (*usually jocose*), skirt (*slang*), fair (*archaic*), belle, dona (*slang*), dame (*archaic or specific*), goodwife (*archaic*), wife, mother, goody (*archaic*), matron, frow, *Frau* (*Ger.*), *Vrouw* (*Dutch*), madam, mistress, Mrs., *madame* (*F.; pl. mesdames*), *signora* (*It.*), *señora* (*Sp.*), *senhora* (*Pg.*), memsahib (*Anglo-Indian*); lady, *doña* (*Sp.*), *dona* (*Pg.*) *donna* (*It.*), *domina* (*L.*), **dowager** (*specific or colloq.*), *bibi* (*Hind.*), *sahibab* (*Hind.*); squaw (*Amer. Indian*).
[*unmarried woman*] **spinster,** maid, maiden, damsel, damosel (*archaic*), **virgin,** nymph, colleen (*Irish*), girl, flapper (*slang*), miss, *mademoiselle* (*F.; pl. mesdemoiselles*), *Fraulein* (*Ger.*), *signorina* (*It.*), *señorita* (*Sp.*), *senhorita* (*Pg.*); old maid, bachelor girl, celibate, new woman.
womankind, womanhood, femininity, feminie (*archaic*), muliebrity, **womenfolk** (*colloq.*), the distaff (*symbolic*), the sex, fair sex, eternal feminine (*usually jocose*), female sex, world (*or* realm) of women; matronage, matronhood.
harem *or* haram (*Moham*), seraglio (*It. pl.* seragli), serai (*Oriental*), **zenana** (*India*), purdah (*India*), gynæceum (*pl.* gynæcea: *classical*).
[*effeminate person*] **molly,** mollycoddle, sissy, milksop, betty, muff, old woman, tame cat (*all contemptuous and used esp. of men*).
[*female animal*] hen; bitch, slut, brach (*hound*), brachet; cow, mare, ewe, gimmer (*dial.*), sow, doe, hind, roe; she-goat, nanny-goat (*colloq.*), nanny (*colloq.*); lioness, tigress; vixen.
[*political*] **woman's rights** (*or* women's rights, *if regarded as of women individually instead of collectively or in the abstract*), rights of women, feminism; female suffrage, woman suffrage, suffragettism.
feminist, suffragist, woman-suffragist (*colloq.*), suffragette (*colloq. or cant*).
II. *Adjectives.* **womanish** (*not becoming a man: contemptuous*), effeminate, soft, weak, unmanly.
womanly (*not masculine or girlish*), feminine, gynecic *or* gynæcic, female (*opposite of* male), womanlike (*opposite of* manlike), tender, sympathetic, gentle; motherly matronlike, matronly; feministic.
maidenly, maidenlike, girlish, artless, modest, virginal, virgin, vestal, chaste pure, unsullied.
See also ADOLESCENCE, MARRIAGE.—*Antonyms.* See MAN.

woman hater, misogynist, misogyne (*rare*). See MISANTHROPY.
woman-hating, *adj.* misogynic, misogynous. See MISANTHROPY.
womb, *n.* uterus: *also fig.; as, the* womb *of time.* See CAUSE, INTERIORITY.
women, government by, gynecocracy; metrocracy, matriarchy; petticoat rule. See AUTHORITY.

WONDER.—I. *Nouns.* **wonder,** astonishment, amazedness, wondering, amazement, surprise, wonderment, bewilderment, admiration (*archaic in this sense*), fascination, awe; stupor, stupefaction.
marvel, prodigy, miracle, wonderwork, portent, phenomenon; *rara avis* (*L.*), rarity, curiosity.
II. *Verbs.* **be wonderful,** etc. (see *adjectives*); beggar (*or* baffle), description, stagger belief.
II. *Verbs.* **wonder,** marvel, admire (*archaic in this sense*), feel surprise, be amazed, be surprised, start, stare; gape, hold one's breath, stand aghast, be taken aback.
astonish, surprise, amaze, astound, dumfound, dumfounder, startle, dazzle, daze, strike, electrify, stun, stupefy, petrify, confound, bewilder, flabbergast (*colloq.*), stagger, fascinate, take away one's breath, strike dumb.
[*to be curious to know*] **speculate,** conjecture, meditate, ponder, theorize, query, question, surmise, imagine, suspect, fancy, suppose.
III. *Adjectives.* **wonderful,** wondrous, surprising, striking, marvelous, miraculous, unexpected, mysterious, monstrous, prodigious, stupendous, inconceivable, incredible, strange, extraordinary, astonishing, amazing, remarkable, unprecedented, singular, signal, unwonted, unusual.
astonished, surprised, aghast, breathless, agape, open-mouthed, thunderstruck, spellbound; lost in amazement, lost in wonder (*or* astonishment), confused, confounded, blank, dazed, awestruck, struck all of a heap (*colloq.*), wonderstruck.
wonder-working, thaumaturgic, mirific *or* mirifical (*rare*), miraculous, working wonders.
IV. *Adverbs.* **wonderfully,** wondrously, etc. (see *adjectives*); fearfully; for a wonder, strange to say (*or* relate), *mirabile dictu* (*L.*) *mirabile visu* (*L.*), to one's great surprise.
See also NONEXPECTATION, PRODIGY.—*Antonyms.* See CONFORMITY, EXPECTANCE.

---

wonder-working, *adj.* miraculous, thaumaturgic. See WONDER.
wont, *adj.* accustomed, habituated, used to, given to. See HABIT.
woo, *v.* solicit, court, importune, address, sue; seek, pursue. See DESIRE, ENDEARMENT, PURSUIT.
wood, *n.* timber, forest, grove, coppice, copse. See VEGETABLE.
woodland, *n.* timberland, wood, forest, grove. See VEGETABLE.
woody, *adj.* ligneous, xyloid. See VEGETABLE.
woolly, *adj.* flocculent, lanate; fleecy, downy. See ROUGHNESS, SOFTNESS.

WORD.—I. *Nouns.* **word,** term, vocable, name, phrase, remark, expression, utterance, ideophone, root, derivative; part of speech, unit of discourse.
promise, pledge, agreement, plight (*archaic*), undertaking, engagement, parole, plighted faith, affiance, word of honor; statement, declaration, avowal, assurance, affirmation.
news, intelligence, information, report, tidings, account, advice, message (*as, to send* word).
command, order, bidding, behest, injunction, direction, mandate, decree, fiat, precept (*as, his* word *is law*).
password, watchword, countersign, *mot de passe* (*F.*), *mot d'ordre* (*F.*).
dictionary, lexicon, vocabulary, wordbook, *Wörterbuch* (*Ger.*), gradus (*prosody*), gloss, glossary, thesaurus.
science of language: glossology, glottology, linguistics, philology, comparative philology, etymology, terminology; pronunciation, orthoëpy, orismology (*scientific terms*), glossography, lexicology, lexigraphy (*rare*), lexicography.
lexicographer, lexicologist, glossologist, glottologist, glossographer, glossarist, orismologist (*rare*), vocabulist; "a writer of dictionaries; a harmless drudge" (*Dr. Johnson's famous definition*).

verbiage, verbosity, wordiness, prolixity, diffuseness, loquacity, verbalism.
the Word, God's Word, the Word of God, the Scriptures, the Bible; the Logos.
[*in plural*] **words**, speech, language, discourse, conversation, talk, converse (*archaic*), intercourse, parley, chat (*as, a man of few* words).
dispute, wrangle, contention, altercation, bickering, argument, jangle, wrangling, quarrel (*as, high* words).
II. *Verbs.* **word**, phrase, express, voice, put into words, give expression to clothe in words.
derive, trace, deduce; etymologize, philologize.
III. *Adjectives.* **wordy**, verbose, prolix, wordish (*rare*), diffuse, discursive, digressive, rambling, long-winded, lengthy, loquacious, periphrastic, ambagious, circumlocutory: *opposite of* concise.
verbal, literal, word for word, *mot à mot* (*F.*), verbatim, textual, lexical; **oral**, spoken, unwritten.
[*similarly derived*] **conjugate**, paronymous, allied, related, akin, coderived.
See also COMMAND, DIFFUSENESS, GRAMMAR, LANGUAGE, NEOLOGY, NEWS, PHRASE, PROMISE, STYLE, WIND.

---

wordplay, *n.* riddle, conundrum, pun, quibble, *jeu de mots* (*F.*). See WIT.
work, *n.* task, employment, occupation; function, office, business; production, performance, handiwork; toil, drudgery, grind; book, publication, production. See ACTION, AGENCY, EFFECT, EXERTION, WRITING.
work, *v.* labor, practice, carry on, do; toil, drudge, slave, grind; ferment, leaven, raise; ply, wield, operate, manipulate. See ACTION, EXERTION, LEVITY, USE.
worker, *n.* doer, performer, operator; laborer, toiler. See AGENT, EXERTION.
workman, *n.* artisan, craftsman, mechanic, workingman. See AGENT.
workmanship, *n.* craftsmanship, handiwork, work, achievement, manufacture. See ACTION, PRODUCTION.

WORKSHOP.—*Nouns.* **workshop,** laboratory, manufactory, establishment, plant, works, mill, factory, studio, *atelier* (*F.*), workroom; hive, hive of industry, beehive; bindery; yard, railroad yard, dock, dockyard, navy yard, slip, wharf: foundry, forge, furnace; armory, arsenal.
melting pot, crucible, caldron *or* cauldron, mortar, alembic.

---

workwoman, *n.* female operative; seamstress, laundress, charwoman. See AGENT.

WORLD.—I. *Nouns.* **world,** creation, nature, universe; earth, *terra* (*L.; used esp. in phrases*), terrene (*rare*), globe, sphere, terrestrial globe, terraqueous globe, wide world; cosmos, macrocosm, megascosm (*rare*); Midgard (*myth.*).
heavens, sky, ceiling (*aëro.*), welkin (*archaic*), empyrean, starry cope, starry host, firmament, vault (*or* canopy) of heaven, celestial spaces.
heavenly bodies, celestial bodies, luminaries, stars, asteroids, planetoids; Galaxy, Milky Way, *Via Lactea* (*L.*), galactic circle; constellations, planets, satellites; comet, meteor, falling (*or* shooting) star, meteoroid, aërolite, meteorite; meteor trail, meteoric trail; meteor dust, cosmic dust; solar system; inferior planets (Mercury, Venus), superior planets (Mars, Jupiter, Saturn, Uranus, Neptune, Pluto).
sun, orb of day, day-star (*poetic*); sun god, Sol (*Roman*), Hyperion (*Gr.*), Helios (*Gr.*), Phœbus *or* Phœbus Apollo (*Gr.*), Phaëthon (*Gr.*), Ra (*Egyptian*), Shamash (*Assyrian*).
moon, satellite (*esp. the earth's*), secondary planet; new moon, crescent, increscent moon, increscent (*esp. heraldry*); decrescent moon, decrescent (*esp. heraldry*); half moon, demilune; full moon, plenilune (*poetic*), harvest moon, hunter's moon; silver-footed queen, Queen of Night, moon goddess, Luna (*Roman*), Diana, Phœbe, Cynthia, Artemis, Hecate *or* Hekate, Selene (*Gr.*), Astarte (*Phœnician*).
science of heavenly bodies: astronomy, astrology (*formerly synonymous with* astronomy), astrography, uranography, uranology, uranometry, astrognosy, astrochemistry, astrophysics, astrophotography, astrophotometry.

cosmology, cosmography, cosmogony; cosmic philosophy, cosmism, cosmic evolution.
astronomer, stargazer (*jocose*), astrophysicist, astrochemist, uranologist.
astrologer, astromancer, astroalchemist, Chaldean, soothsayer.
cosmologist, cosmogonist, cosmographer, cosmographist; geographer, geodesist.
[*inhabitants of the earth*] **mankind,** humanity, humankind, men, people, inhabitants; the public.
human affairs, material interests (*as opposed to* spiritual), secular affairs, worldly aims, mundane interests, active life, social intercourse, social life.
[*individual experience*] **life,** experience, career, course of life, pilgrimage, journey (*fig.*), current of events, course of human affairs.
division, part, section, group, class, system; domain (*as of letters*), region, realm, kingdom, sphere, department.
the world, society, *le monde* (*F.*), fashionable society, the great world, *le beau monde* (*F.*), worldly people.
II. *Adjectives.* **worldly,** earthly, terrestrial, terrene, terraqueous, telluric, sublunar *or* sublunary, subastral, mundane; temporal: *opposite of* heavenly, spiritual.
cosmic, universal, cosmogonal, cosmogonic *or* cosmogonical, cosmographic *or* cosmographical; extraterrene, extraterrestrial.
[*of the visible heavens*] **empyrean,** empyreal, celestial, heavenly, uranic, astronomical; starry, stellar, stellary, astral, sidereal, sideral (*esp. astrology*), planetary; solar, heliac *or* heliacal; lunar, Cynthian (*poetic*), lunate, crescent-shaped; planetesimal, planetoidal, asteroidal, nebular; interstellar, intersidereal.
worldly-minded, unspiritual, pleasure-loving, carnal, fleshly, secular, money-grubbing, money-making, unsanctified, ungodly.
III. *Adverbs.* **in all creation, on the face of the globe, here below, under the sun.**
See also EVENT, FASHION, IRRELIGION, MANKIND, SELFISHNESS, SPACE.

---

worldly, *adj.* earthly, mundane, carnal, unspiritual. See IRRELIGION, SELFISHNESS.
worldly-minded, *adj.* unspiritual, pleasure-loving, worldly. See SELFISHNESS, WORLD.
worldly wisdom, discretion, prudence, tact, strategy. See CAUTION, SKILL.
world-wide, *adj.* widespread, universal, far-reaching. See GREATNESS.
worn, *adj.* worn-out, exhausted; shabby, threadbare. See FATIGUE, WEAKNESS.
worn-out, *adj.* dilapidated, used up (*colloq.*), decrepit, broken-down, effete. See DETERIORATION, WEARINESS.
worry, *v.* molest, harry, persecute, harass, fret, grieve. See MALEVOLENCE, PAIN.
worry, *n.* care, anxiety, solicitude, concern. See PAIN.

WORSHIP.—I. *Nouns.* **worship,** adoration, devotion, aspiration, heavenly-mindedness, spiritual-mindedness, vow, homage, service, cult (*as of Apollo*), cultus (*sing. and pl.*); latria (*R. C. Ch.*), dulia (*to saints: R. C. Ch.*), hyperdulia (*to the Virgin Mary: R. C. Ch.*); kneeling, genuflection, prostration.
prayer, invocation, supplication, intercession, orison (*archaic*), petition; collect, miserere, rogation, litany, Lord's prayer, paternoster; Ave, Ave Maria, Hail, Mary; complin *or* compline.
praise, laudation, exaltation, magnification, glorification, pæan, benediction, grace, thanksgiving, *non nobis Domine* (*L.*), doxology, hosanna, hallelujah, alleluia, *Te Deum* (*L.*), Magnificat, *Gloria* (*L.*); psalm, hymn, chant; response, anthem, motet, antiphon, antiphony.
offering, oblation, sacrifice, incense, libation; offertory, collection.
divine service, religious service, office, duty; exercises; Mass, Eucharist, Lord's Supper, Holy Communion, Communion; matins, morning prayer; prayer meeting, camp meeting, revival; evensong, evening prayer, vespers, vigils, lauds (*pl.*).
honor, respect, reverence, esteem, repute, dignity, deference, estimation, idolization, admiration (*as, an object of* worship; *the* worship *of intellect*).
worshiper *or* worshipper, adorer; communicant, celebrant; congregation (*collective*).
idolater, idolatress (*fem.*), **idolist** (*rare*), **iconolater, iconodulist** (*hist.*), **fetishist, pagan, idolizer; admirer.**

II. *Verbs.* worship, adore, reverence, venerate, revere, lift up the heart, aspire; do service, pay homage, offer one's vows, vow; bow down and worship; attend public worship.

pray, invoke, supplicate, beseech, entreat, implore, crave, beg; commune with God, offer up prayers, say one's prayers; tell one's beads, recite the rosary.

praise, laud, glorify, magnify, exalt, celebrate, extol; sing praises, chant, sing, hymn, doxologize; hallow, bless, give thanks, return thanks, say grace.

idolize, idolatrize, deify, adore; honor, admire (*extravagantly*), love, dote upon, make an idol of.

III. *Adjectives.* **worshipful,** honorable, estimable, esteemed, worthy, respected: *a term of respect, as used of certain magistrates and corporate bodies and of the master of a Masonic lodge; sometimes, a term of ironical respect.*

worshiping *or* worshipping, adoring, etc. (see *verbs*); devout, devotional, reverent, solemn, fervent, prayerful, holy, religious, heavenly-minded, spiritual-minded.

IV. *Interjections.* **hallelujah! alleluia! hosanna! praise ye the Lord! glory be to** God! *sursum corda!* (*L.*).

See also IDOLATRY, PIETY, RESPECT, RITE.—*Antonyms.* See IRRELIGION.

---

worth, *n.* estimation, valuation; benefit, avail, advantage; importance, merit, desert, worthiness. See PRICE, UTILITY, VIRTUE.

worthless, *adj.* empty, inane; meritless, valueless, useless, unsalable, unproductive. See INUTILITY, WASTE.

worthy, *adj.* reputable, estimable, honorable; meritorious, deserving, fit. See REPUTE, VIRTUE.

wound, *n.* gash, stab, cut, laceration; injury, mishap, blow. See EVIL, PAINFULNESS.

wound, *v.* lacerate, pierce, stab, cut, hurt. See PAIN, RESENTMENT.

wrangle, *n.* altercate, bicker, brawl, contend, dispute, argue. See DISCORD, REASONING.

wrap, *v.* envelop, cloak, hide; inclose, wind, swathe. See COVERING, ROLL.

wrap, *n.* blanket, quilt, coverlet; shawl, overcoat, etc. See CALEFACTION, CLOTHING.

wrath, *n.* fury, rage, ire, passion. See RESENTMENT.

wreath, *n.* festoon, garland, chaplet. See ORNAMENT.

wreck, *n.* shipwreck; crash, smash, ruin; ruins. See DESTRUCTION, FAILURE, REMAINDER.

wrench, *v.* wrest, wring, twist, distort, pervert; extract, extort, wring from; sprain, strain. See DISTORTION, EXTRACTION, WEAKNESS.

wrestle, *v.* grapple, contend, contest, strive, struggle. See CONTENTION.

wrestling, *n.* throwing, grappling. See CONTENTION.

wretch, *n.* miscreant, rogue, knave; sufferer, victim, martyr: *often a term of playful abuse.* See BAD MAN, PAIN.

wretched, *adj.* sad, unfortunate, pitiable, unhappy, miserable, infelicitous; shabby, beggarly, mean, contemptible. See BADNESS, PAIN, UNIMPORTANCE.

wring, *v.* contort, twist; hurt, torment, oppress, rack, torture. See CONVOLUTION, PAINFULNESS.

wrinkle, *v.* crinkle, cockle, pucker, crumple, rumple. See [1]FOLD.

writhe, *v.* twist, distort, contort. See DISTORTION, PAIN.

WRITING.—I. *Nouns.* **writing,** chirography, handwriting, scription (*rare*), longhand, hand, fist (*colloq.*), calligraphy, pencraft, penmanship, quilldriving (*jocose*), lexigraphy (*as Chinese*), cerography (*on wax*), stylography; uncial writing, cuneiform, hieroglyphics, Ogham, runes; macrography (*large*), micrography (*minute*); **engrossment, inscription, stroke** (*or* **dash**) **of the pen,** ***coup de plume*** (*F.*); penscript; typewriting, typescript; character, letter.

manuscript (*abbr.* MS., *pl.* MSS.), original, author's copy, copy; document; deed, instrument, holograph, script. *litteræ scriptæ* (*L.*); codex (*as of the Scrip-*

tures), opisthograph (*on both sides*), palimpsest, *codex rescriptus* (*L.*); **these** presents (*law*).
[*good writing*] **calligraphy**, flowing hand, Spencerian hand, elegant penmanship.
[*bad writing*] **cacography**, scrawling, scrawl, scribble, *griffonage* (*F.*), *barbouillage* (*F.*), cramped (crabbed, *or* illegible) hand, fly tracks, *pattes de mouche* (*F.*).
composition, lucubration, production, work, book, authorship, inditement (*rare*); novel, play, textbook, conflation (*fusion of variant readings*), screed, article, paper, essay, theme, thesis; poem, book of poems (*or* verse).
itch for writing, *cacoëthes scribendi* (*L.*), graphomania, creative urge.
shorthand, stenography, phonography, brachygraphy (*esp. disused systems*), tachygraphy (*esp. Greek and Roman*), pasigraphy (*representing ideas and not words*), logography (*a form of reporting speeches in longhand*), speed writing.
[*secret writing*] **cryptography**, cipher, steganography, code.
writer, scribe, scrivener (*hist.*), penman, quill driver (*jocose*), pen (*fig.*), penner, calligraphist, chirographer, yeoman (*U. S. Navy*), clerk, scriptor (*rare*); copyist, transcriber, amanuensis, secretary, stenographer, shorthand writer, phonographer; typewriter, typist; author, scribbler.

II. *Verbs.* **write**, pen, scribble, scrawl, scrabble, scratch, inscribe, record, scriven (*archaic*), set down, set forth, write down, note, note down; copy, transcribe, engross, address, superscribe; take pen in hand, take up the pen, shed (*or* spill) ink; typewrite, type (*colloq.*).
compose, indite, draw up, draft, formulate, dictate; dash off, spoil paper (*jocose*), turn out.

III. *Adjectives.* **written**, in writing, in black and white, recorded, scriptory (*as wills: rare*), literal (*as a contract*): *opposite of* oral, printed.
shorthand, stenographic, phonographic, stenographical; verbatim.

See also BOOK, COMPOSITION, CORRESPONDENCE, LETTER, RECORD.—*Antonyms.* See PRINTING.

WRONG.—I. *Nouns.* **wrong**, iniquity, wickedness, unrighteousness, improbity, wrongdoing, evil, sin, guilt, shame, disobedience, misdoing, delinquency, malpractice, obliquity; grievance, tort (*law*), injury, offense, *malum in se* (*L.*), transgression, crime, villainy; falsity, error.
injustice, unfairness, unjustness, inequity, hardship, imposition, oppression, foul play; partiality, leaning, bias, prejudice, prepossession, nepotism, favor, favoritism, partisanship; undueness, unlawfulness, illegality.

II. *Verbs.* **do wrong**, be inequitable, show partiality, favor, lean towards; encroach; impose upon; reap where one has not sown.
wrong, injure, harm, damage, hurt, serve ill, misserve, disserve, do injury to, maltreat, abuse, cheat, defraud, treat unjustly; dishonor, disgrace.

III. *Adjectives.* **wrong**, wrongful, iniquitous, bad, wicked, reprehensible, sinful, immoral, evil, blameworthy; injurious, detrimental, hurtful, harmful, baneful, deleterious, noxious, pernicious.
unjust, unfair, inequitable, unequal, partial, one-sided.
unjustifiable, unreasonable, unwarrantable, objectionable, inexcusable, unauthorizable, unjustified; unlawful, illegal, immoral, criminal.
[*out of order*] **disordered**, deranged, amiss, faulty, out of kilter (*U. S. colloq.*), disarranged, disturbed, out of gear, crank, cranky, shaky, in bad condition.
erroneous, inaccurate, incorrect, faulty, inexact, unsound, illogical, mistaken, false, untrue, wide of the mark (*as, a* wrong *conclusion*).
improper, unfit, inappropriate, unsuitable, inapposite, inapt, incongruous.

IV. *Adverbs.* **wrong**, amiss, wrongly, erroneously, inaccurately, incorrectly, falsely, improperly.
wrongfully, unjustly, unfairly, inequitably, injuriously, banefully, etc. (see *adjectives*).

See also BADNESS, EVIL, ILLEGALITY, IMPROPRIETY, MALEVOLENCE, VICE.—*Antonyms.* See RIGHT.

---

wry, *adj.* twisted, contorted, distorted, crooked, awry, askew. See DISTORTION, OBLIQUITY.

X

xiphoid, *adj.* sword-shaped, ensiform, gladiate (*bot.*). See SHARPNESS.
X-ray photograph, radiograph, X-ray (*colloq.*). See REPRESENTATION.
X-rays, *n. pl.* Röntgen rays. See LIGHT.
x-shaped, *adj.* decussate (*esp. tech.*), crossed. See CROSSING.
xyloid, *adj.* woody, ligneous, lignose (*rare*). See VEGETABLE.

Y

yacht, *n.* sloop, boat, vessel, pleasure boat, racing vessel. See SHIP.
yard, *n.* courtyard, curtilage, court, close, garth, compound (*Oriental*), barnyard; railroad yard, navy yard, etc. See INCLOSURE, WORKSHOP.
yarn, *n.* story, tale, anecdote; fish story (*colloq.*), boasting; spun wool; fabrication, perversion. See DESCRIPTION, EXAGGERATION, FILAMENT, UNTRUTH.
yawn, *v.* gape, oscitate (*rare*), open wide. See FATIGUE, OPENING.
year, *n.* twelvemonth, cycle (*of seasons*); astronomical (*or* solar) year, lunar year, calendar (civil, *or* legal) year. See PERIOD, TIME.
years, *n. pl.* old age; time of life (*as, young for his* years). See AGE.
yearn, *v.* long, covet, crave, hanker: *with* for *or* after. See DESIRE, PAIN.
yearning, *n.* longing, hankering, hungering; tender passion. See DESIRE, LOVE.
yeast, *n.* leaven, barm, ferment, zyme. See LEVITY.
yell, *v.* shout, halloo, bellow, hoot, scream, shriek, squall. See CRY.

YELLOW.—I. *Nouns.* **yellow, gold,** etc. (see *adjectives*); or (*heraldry*), **jonquil;** yellowness, xanthoderma *or* xanthochroia (*med.*), xanthrophyll (*as in autumn leaves*), saffron.

[*comparisons*] saffron, crocus, buttercup, primrose; quince; **gold, guinea, topaz,** *giallo antico* (*It.*); London fog.

[*pigments*] gamboge, yellow ocher (*or* ochre), fustic, massicot, aureolin, cadmium yellow; chrome yellow, Paris yellow; Indian yellow, euxanthin, purree; king's yellow, orpiment; lemon yellow, barium chromate (*or* chrome), barium yellow, baryta yellow, permanent yellow; xanthin, xanthein (*extracted from yellow flowers*).

[*in plural*] **yellows** (*archaic*), jaundice, icterus (*med.*); jealousy.

II. *Verbs.* **yellow, make yellow, gild,** golden (*rare*), begild, engild; **jaundice,** turn yellow.

III. *Adjectives.* **yellow,** aureate, golden, gold, gilt, aurated, gilded, gold-colored; lemon, citreous, citrine, citron-colored, lemon-colored, luteous, xanthic (*tech.*), xanthous (*ethnol.*), xanthochroid (*ethnol.*), saffron, croconic (*tech.*), fallow; sallow, icteroid, icteritious *or* icteritous, xanthocroous (*med.*), jaundiced; fulvous, fulvescent, cream-colored, cream, creamy; straw-colored, stramineous, festucine, flaxen, yellowish, icterine, amber-colored, amber, primrose, primrose yellow, buff, écru; tawny, ocherous *or* ochreous, ochery *or* ochry, gambogian; auricomous, golden-haired.

[*of feelings, mood, etc.*] **jealous,** envious, covetous, jaundiced (*fig.*), prejudiced, suspicious, distrustful; melancholic, melancholy.

[*expressing sensationalism*] **sensational,** lurid, exciting, emotional, melodramatic, stirring, thrilling, chauvinistic, jingo, jingoish, jingoistic, hysterical (*as, the* yellow *press*).

[*expressing cowardice*] **cowardly,** craven, white-livered, lily-livered, afraid, unmanly, pusillanimous; contemptible, despicable, dishonorable (*as, he showed a* yellow *streak: slang*).

See also COWARDICE, EXCITEMENT, JEALOUSY, ORANGE.

---

yelp, *v.* cry; bark, yap. See LAMENTATION, ULULATION.

yeoman, *n.* beefeater (*Eng.*), yeoman of the guard; farmer, small landowner, agriculturist; commoner; freeholder, laird (*Scot.*), duniwassal (*Scot.*); attendant, retainer (*hist.*); clerk (*U. S. Navy*). See COMBATANT, HUSBANDRY, PEOPLE, POSSESSOR, SERVANT, WRITING.

yes, *adv.* yea, aye *or* ay, true, granted, it is so. See ASSENT.

yield, *v.* concede, allow, acknowledge; fetch, sell for, return, bring in; bear, produce, furnish, bring forth; relinquish, surrender, cede; bend, give, relent; obey, submit, give in, capitulate. See CONSENT, PRODUCTION, RECEIPT, RELINQUISHMENT, SOFTNESS, SUBMISSION.

yielding, *adj.* manageable, tractable, submissive, compliant, obedient; soft, ductile, plastic, pliant; fertile, productive. See FACILITY, SOFTNESS, SWEETNESS (*of land*).

yoke, *n.* couple, pair (*of oxen*), match; bondage, enslavement, servitude; bond, tie, link, union. See DUALITY, SUBJECTION, VINCULUM.

yoke, *v.* join, link, couple, bracket; marry. See JUNCTION.

young, *adj.* youthful, juvenile, childlike, immature, inexperienced. See YOUTH.

youngster, *n.* child, stripling, lad, adolescent. See YOUTH.

YOUTH.—I. *Nouns.* **youth,** youthfulness, juvenility, youthhead (*archaic*), Juventas (*Roman myth.*), Hebe (*Gr. myth.*), juvenescence, youthiness (*Scot.*); boyism, boyishness, girlishness; juniority, adolescence, boyhood, girlhood, childhood, incunabula (*pl.*), infancy, babyhood, cradle, nursery; immaturity, teens, minority, wardship, pupilage, nonage, youthhood, tender age, bloom; pucilage (*rare*), virginity, puberty; leading strings.

flower of life, flower of youth, springtide of life, seedtime of life, golden season of life; heyday of youth, school days.

[*young person*] **youngster,** youngling (*also a young animal or plant*), child, younker (*archaic or colloq.*), stripling, strip (*rare*), adolescent, scion, slip, sprig (*usually disparaging*); lad, boy, cub, callant (*Scot.*), laddie (*chiefly Scot.*), buckeen (*Anglo-Irish*), gossoon (*Anglo-Irish*), whipster (*rare*), whippersnapper (*colloq.*), springal or springald (*archaic*), hobbledehoy (*colloq.*), hopeful, cadet, minor, boykin; rising generation (*collective*).

[*second youth*] **rejuvenescence,** rejuvenation, rejuvenization, reinvigoration renewal of youth.

II. *Verbs.* **make youthful,** make young, juvenilify, juvenilize (*rare*); rejuvenesce, rejuvenate, reinvigorate.

III. *Adjectives.* **youthful,** young, juvenescent, juvenile, immature, callow, green, unripe, tender, under age, in one's teens, *in statu pupillari* (*L.*), budding, beardless, newfledged, unfledged, boyish, boylike, puerile, childlike.

junior (*abbr.* Jr. *or* jr.), younger, puisne (*law*), lower (*as in rank*), subordinate, inferior, later, more recent, more modern; *opposite of* senior.

fresh, blooming, vigorous, active, keen, enthusiastic, buoyant, light-hearted (*as,* youthful *energy or spirits*).

See also ADOLESCENCE, INFANT.—*Antonyms.* See AGE.

Z

zany, *n.* buffoon, clown, merry-andrew; simpleton, half-wit. See FOOL.

zeal, *n.* eagerness, ardor, fervor, enthusiasm, alacrity. See ACTIVITY, WILLINGNESS.

zealot, *n.* enthusiast, fanatic, partisan, bigot. See CERTAINTY, OBSTINACY.

zealous, *adj.* earnest, ardent, willing, ready, eager, enthusiastic. See FEELING, WILLINGNESS.

zenith, *n.* summit, acme, pinnacle, culmination, climax. See HEIGHT.

zephyr, *n.* west wind, soft breeze. See WIND.

ZERO.—*Nouns.* **zero,** cipher, nothing, naught, nought, none, nil, nix (*slang*), duck *or* duck's egg (*in games: slang*), goose egg (*U. S. slang*); point of commencement (*as on a thermometer*), lowest point, nadir, nothingness, nullity.

See also UNSUBSTANTIALITY.—*Antonyms.* See MULTITUDE, PLURALITY, SUBSTANTIALITY.

---

zest, *n.* exhilaration, enjoyment, gusto, thrill, kick (*slang*); relish, flavor, tang, piquancy. See PLEASURE, SAVORINESS.

zigzag, *adj.* staggered, angled, sinuous, like a worm (*or* Virginia) fence. See ANGULARITY, DEVIATION, OBLIQUITY.

zone, *n.* band, girdle, belt, zonule, circuit; beltlike region (*or* area). See CIRCULARITY, OUTLINE, REGION.

zoo, *n.* zoölogical garden, menagerie, vivarium (*colloq.*). See DOMESTICATION.

ZOÖLOGY.—I. *Nouns.* **zoölogy,** science of animals, natural history of animals: *correlative of* botany *or* phytology.

[*form and structure*] **morphology,** morphography (*descriptive*); anatomy, comparative anatomy, zoötomy; histology (*microscopic anatomy*), cytology (*cells*), embryology; plasmology; paleontology *or* palæontology.

[*functions and phenomena*] **animal physiology,** zoöphysiology, biodynamics, zoödynamics; zoöphysics, zoöchemistry (*distinguished from* biochemistry), zoöpsychology; comparative physiology.

[*development*] **ætiology** *or* etiology, ontogeny (*of an individual organism*), phylogeny (*of a race or group*), evolution, Darwinism, natural selection, Lamarckism, Neo-Darwinism (*opposed to* Neo-Lamarckism), Weismannism.

[*habits, environment, etc.*] **bionomics,** ecology, bionomy (*rare*), zoönomy (*rare*), thremmatology (*breeding*), zoötechnics (*scientific breeding and domestication*), teleology (*organic adaptations*); zoögeography (*distribution*), zoögraphy (*descriptive zoölogy*).

[*classification*] **taxonomy,** systematic zoölogy; categories: phylum (*pl.* phyla), class, order, family, genus (*pl.* genera), species, subspecies (*or* variety).

mammalogy (*mammals*), mastology, therology (*rare*); anthropology, anthropography, anthropometry, ethnography, anthropogeography; ornithology (*birds*), entomology (*insects*), herpetology (*reptiles*), ophiology (*snakes*), helminthology (*worms*), ichthyology (*fishes*), cetology (*whales*), malacology (*mollusks*), conchology (*shells or mollusks*), carcinology *or* crustaceology (*crustaceans*); zoöphyte.

zoölogist, zoögrapher, zoögraphist, naturalist; morphologist, zoötomist, histologist, etc. (see *nouns*).

II. *Verbs.* **zoölogize,** study zoölogy, collect zoölogical specimens.

III. *Adjectives.* **zoölogical,** zoölogic, zoögraphical; morphological, morphographical, etc. (see *nouns*).

See also ANIMAL, DOMESTICATION.

---

zymotic, *adj.* fermentative, bacterial: *said of infectious and contagious diseases, such as typhoid fever and smallpox, regarded as developed by a process analogous to fermentation: obsolescent medical term.* See UNHEALTHINESS.

FOREIGN WORDS AND EXPRESSIONS

FOREIGN WORDS AND EXPRESSIONS

OCCURRING IN LITERATURE AND IN COLLOQUIAL USE

including all such terms embodied in this work

TRANSLATED INTO ENGLISH

à bas (*F.*), down with! away with! off with!
abattoir (*F.*), a public slaughterhouse.
abbé (*F.*), abbot; a title of respect in France given to a man entitled to wear ecclesiastical dress, esp. without official duties.
a beneplacito (*It.*), at pleasure.
Aberglaube (*G.*), excessive belief; superstition.
ab extra (*L.*), from without.
ab incunabilis (*L.*), from the cradle; from childhood.
ab initio (*L.*), from the beginning.
ab intra (*L.*), from within.
à bon droit (*F.*), with good reason; with justice.
à bon marché (*F.*), at a good bargain; cheap.
ab origine (*L.*), from the origin (*or* beginning).
ab ovo (*L.*), from the egg; from the beginning.
ab ovo usque ad mala (*L.*), lit., from the egg to the apples; from beginning to end (*of a dinner*).
à bras ouverts (*F.*), with open arms.
abrégé (*F.*), abridged; short; summary.
abri (*F.*), shelter; protection.
absit invidia (*L.*), let there be no ill will; envy apart.
ab uno disce omnes (*L.*), from one learn all.
ab urbe condita (*L.*), from the founding of the city [Rome, founded about 753 B.C.]: *abbr.* A.U.C.
a capite ad calcem (*L.*), from head to heel.
acciaccatura (*It.*), a short grace note, one half step below a principal note: *music.*
accouchement (*F.*), delivery in childbed; confinement.
accueil (*F.*), reception; welcome.
acharné (*F.*), infuriated; rabid.
acharnement (*F.*), blind fury; ferocity; bloodthirstiness.
à cheval (*F.*), on horseback; astride.
à compte (*F.*), on account.
à contre cœur (*F.*), reluctantly; against the grain.
à corps perdu (*F.*), lit., with lost body; impetuously; headlong.
à coup sûr (*F.*), with sure stroke; surely.
à couvert (*F.*), under cover; sheltered; secure.
actus (*L.*), an act; hence, realization; actuality; in philosophy, equivalent to ἐνέργεια (energy, activity) as used by Aristotle.
ad amussim (*L.*), according to a rule or level; accurately; exactly.
ad arbitrium (*L.*), at will; at pleasure.
ad captandum (*L.*), for the sake of pleasing: *said of an argument or appeal.*
ad captandum vulgus (*L.*), to catch (*or* attract) the crowd.
addio! (*It.*), adieu!
ad eundem (gradum) (*L.*), to the same (degree or standing).
adeus! (*Pg.*), adieu!
à deux (*F.*), for two; between two.
ad finem (*L.*), to the end; at the end: *abbr.* ad fin.
ad hoc (*L.*), for this (particular purpose); special.
ad hominem (*L.*), to the man; i.e., to his interests and prejudices.
ad infinitum (*L.*), to infinity; without limit; forever.
ad instar (*L.*), after the fashion of; like.
ad interim (*L.*), in (*or* for) the meantime; meanwhile; temporary: *abbr.* ad int.
adios! (*Sp.*), adieu!
à discrétion (*F.*), at discretion; at will.
ad kalendas Græcas (*L.*), at the Greek calends; i.e., never [the Greeks had no calends].
ad libitum (*L.*), at pleasure; as one wishes; to any extent: *abbr.* ad lib.
ad nauseam (*L.*), to nausea; to the point of disgust or satiety.
adorer le veau d'or (*F.*), to worship the golden calf (i.e., riches).
ad quem (*L.*), at (*or* to) which: *opposite of* a quo.
ad referendum (*L.*), for reference; for further consideration.
ad rem (*L.*), to the purpose; to the point.
à droite (*F.*), to the right; on the right.
adsum (*L.*), I am present; here!
ad unguem (*L.*), to a finger nail; to a nicety.
ad valorem (*L.*), according to the value: *abbr.* ad val.
ad verbum (*L.*), to a word; literally; word for word.
ad vitam aut culpam (*L.*), for life or until misbehavior; during good behavior.
advocatus diaboli (*L.*), Devil's advocate; a person chosen to dispute before the papal court the claims of a candidate for canonization.
ægrescitque medendo (*L.*), and he (*or* it) grows worse with the treatment.
ægri somnia (*L.*), a sick man's dreams.
æquo animo (*L.*), with an equal mind; with equanimity.
ære perennius (*L.*), more lasting than brass (*or* bronze).
affaire d'amour (*F.*), a love affair.
affaire de cœur (*F.*), an affair of the heart; a love affair.
affaire d'honneur (*F.*), an affair of honor; a duel.
affiche (*F.*), poster; placard.
à fond (*F.*), to the bottom; thoroughly.
a fortiori (*L.*), with stronger reason; more conclusively.
à gauche (*F.*), to the left; on the left.
age quod agis (*L.*), do what you are doing; attend to the work you have in hand.
à grands frais (*F.*), at great expense.
aguerri (*F.*), inured to war; disciplined.
à haute voix (*F.*), in a loud voice; loudly; aloud.
à huis clos (*F.*), with closed doors.
aide-toi, le ciel t'aidera (*F.*), help yourself, (and) heaven will help you.
aimer éperdument (*F.*), to love passionately.
à la (*F.*), after the manner of.
à la belle étoile (*F.*), under the stars; in the open air (at night).
à la bonne heure (*F.*), in good time; very well; excellent.
à la carte (*F.*), according to the bill of fare: *distinguished from* table d'hôte.
à la dérobée (*F.*), by stealth; privately.
à la française (*F.*), in the French style (*or* fashion).
à la guerre comme à la guerre (*F.*), in war as in war; i.e., one must take things as they come.
à la lanterne! (*F.*), to the lamp-post with him! lynch him!
à la mode (*F.*), according to the fashion (*or* prevailing mode); fashionably; fashionable.
à l'anglaise (*F.*), in the English style (*or* fashion).
à la sourdine (*F.*), secretly; on the sly.
à la Tartuffe (*F.*), in the style of (*or* like) Tartuffe; hypocritically.

albergo (*It.*), inn.
alentours (*F.*), surroundings; environs; also, associates.
al fresco (*It.*), in the open air; open air.
aliéné (*F.*), deranged; mad.
alieni appetens (*L.*), eager for another's property; covetous.
à l'improviste (*F.*), on a sudden; unexpectedly; unawares.
aliquando bonus dormitat Homerus (*L.*), sometimes even the good Homer nods; i.e., the greatest are sometimes caught napping.
aljibar (*Sp. Amer.*), a cistern.
allégresse (*F.*), mirth; joy; sprightliness.
allegretto (*It.*), somewhat briskly: *music.*
allegro (*It.*), lively; brisk: *music.*
aller à tâtons (*F.*), to grope along; feel one's way.
allez-vous-en! (*F.*), be off! begone!
al piacere (*It.*), at pleasure.
alter ego (*L.*), one's other self; bosom friend.
alto-rilievo (*It.*), high relief; *sculp.*
amantium iræ (*L.*), lovers' quarrels.
âme damnée (*F.*), lit., a damned (*or* lost) soul; devoted adherent; willing slave; tool.
amende honorable (*F.*), satisfactory apology; reparation.
a mensa et thoro (*L.*), lit., from table and board; from bed and board: *law.*
à merveille (*F.*), admirably; marvelously.
amicus curiæ (*L.*), a friend of the court; disinterested adviser.
amicus humani generis (*L.*), a friend of the human race.
amicus usque ad aras (*L.*), a friend as far as to the altars; i.e., in everything but what is contrary to one's religion.
à moi! (*F.*), help! here!
amor nummi (*L.*), love of money.
amoroso (*It.; pl.* amorosi), a lover.
amor patriæ (*L.*), love of one's country.
amour propre (*F.*), self-esteem; vanity.
ancien régime (*F.*), the ancient régime; time before the French Revolution of 1789.
ancilla theologiæ (*L.*), the handmaid of theology; i.e., philosophy.
andante (*It.*), moderately slow: *music.*
andantino (*It.*), rather quicker (*originally,* slower) than *andante: music.*
Anglice (*NL.*), in English; in English form.
anguis in herba (*L.*), a snake in the grass; an unsuspected danger.
anima bruta (*L.*), the brute soul; vital principle.
anima divina (*L.*), the divine soul.
anima mundi (*L.*), the soul (*or* vital essence) of the world.
anno ætatis suæ (*L.*), in the — year of his (*or* her) age.
anno Domini (*L.*), in the year of our Lord: *abbr.* A.D.
anno regni (*L.*), in the year of the reign: *abbr.* A.R.
anno urbis conditæ (*L.*), in the year (*or* from the time) of the founded city [Rome, founded about 753 B.C.]: *abbr.* A.U.C.
annus mirabilis (*L.*), wonderful year.
ante bellum (*L.*), before the war.
ante Christum (*L.*), before Christ: *abbr.* A.C.
ante meridiem (*L.*), before noon: *abbr.* A.M.
antonyme (*F.*), antonym.
à outrance (*F.*), to the utmost; to the death.
apage Satanas! (*L.*), get thee hence, Satan!
à pas de géant (*F.*), with a giant's stride.
aperçu (*F.*), rapid view; glance; sketch; conspectus.
apéritif (*F.*), appetizer.
à perte de vue (*F.*), beyond one's view; as far as the eye can reach; hence, at random.
à peu près (*F.*), nearly; almost.
à pied (*F.*), on foot.
à plomb (*F.*), plumb; perpendicularly; hence, with assurance.
aplomb (*F.*), perpendicularity; hence, self-possession; assurance.
a posteriori (*L.*), (reasoning) from effect to cause; inductive; empirical.
appliqué (*F.*), applied ornament.
appoggiatura (*It.*), an added note of embellishment; a grace note: *music.*
après moi (*or* **nous**) **le déluge** (*F.*), after me (*or* us) the deluge; a remark attributed to Louis XV.
a priori (*L.*), (reasoning) from cause to effect; deductive or deductively; presumptive.
à propos (*F.*), to the purpose; opportunely or opportune.
à propos de bottes (*F.*), lit., apropos of boots; foreign to the subject; about nothing.
à propos de rien (*F.*), apropos of nothing; irrelevant.
aqua (*L.*), water.
aquila (*L.*), eagle.
a quo (*L.*), from which: *opposite of* ad quem.
arbiter elegantiæ *or* **elegantiarum** (*L.*), a judge of elegance; a supreme authority in matters of taste.
Arcades ambo (*L.*), Arcadians both; i.e., skilled in pastoral music; hence, two persons of similar, esp. simple, tastes; ironically, two simpletons.
arcana imperii (*L.*), state secrets.
à rebours (*F.*), against the grain; the wrong way.
à reculons (*F.*), backward.
arête (*F.*), lit., fish bone; sharp ascending ridge of mountains.
argumentum ad crumenam (*L.*), an argument to the purse; an appeal to one's interests.
argumentum ad hominem (*L.*), lit., an argument to the man; an evasive argument that seeks to discredit an opponent by attacking his character and inconsistencies or by appealing to his interests and prejudices.
argumentum ad ignorantiam (*L.*), an argument (*or* appeal) to ignorance, i.e., to an opponent's ignorance of the facts; in logic, the fallacy of basing one's argument upon the impossibility of proving the opposite.
argumentum ad misericordiam (*L.*), an argument (*or* appeal) to pity.
argumentum ad populum (*L.*), an argument (*or* appeal) to the people, i.e., to their passions and prejudices rather than to their intellect.
argumentum ad verecundiam (*L.*), lit., an argument (*or* appeal) to modesty; an attempt to settle an issue by appealing to the respect for some great authority, without independently considering the arguments for or against the question.
argumentum baculinum (*NL.*), an appeal to the rod (i.e., to force).
ariston metron (*Gr.* ἄριστον μέτρον), due measure is best; moderation is best.
a rivederci! (*It.*), au revoir!
arme blanche (*F.*), lit., white arm; cavalry sword or lance.
arpeggio (*It.*), production of the tones in a chord in rapid succession instead of simultaneously: *music.*
arrectis auribus (*L.*), with ears pricked up.
arrière-pensée (*F.*), mental reservation; ulterior motive.
arrondissement (*F.*), district; administrative subdivision of a French department.
ars artium (*L.*), lit., art of arts; logic.
ars artium omnium conservatrix (*L.*), the art preservative of all arts; printing.
ars est celare artem (*L.*), (true) art is to conceal art.
ars longa, vita brevis (*L.*), art is long, life is short.
artiste (*F.*), artist; professional singer, dancer, etc.
Art Nouveau (*F.*), New Art: a form of decorative design introduced about 1895.
assistant (*F.*), bystander; onlooker.
assister (*F.*) to assist; attend.
atelier (*F.*), workshop; studio.
à tort et à travers (*F.*), at random.

à toute force (*F.*), lit., with all force; by every means.
à toute outrance (*F.*), beyond measure.
aubade (*F.*), morning serenade or concert.
auberge (*F.*), inn; tavern.
au bout de son latin (*F.*), at the end of his Latin; at his wits' end.
au bout du compte (*F.*), lit., at the end of the account; when all is said and done; after all.
au contraire (*F.*), on the contrary.
au courant (*F.*), fully acquainted with; well-informed; up to date.
au désespoir (*F.*), in despair.
audi alteram partem (*L.*), hear the other side.
au fait (*F.*), conversant; expert; well-instructed.
Aufklärung (*G.*), enlightenment; an empirical movement of the 18th century: *philos.*
au fond (*F.*), at bottom; in the main; fundamentally.
auf wiedersehen! (*G.*), lit., to the seeing again; au revoir!
au grand sérieux (*F.*), in all seriousness.
au gratin (*F.*), with a brown crust or crisp surface of buttered crumbs.
au naturel (*F.*), naturally; to the life; *Cookery:* (cooked) simply; plain.
au pied de la lettre (*F.*), lit., to the foot of the letter; literally; exactly.
au pis aller (*F.*), at worst; as a last resort.
aura popularis (*L.*), the popular breeze; popular favor.
aurea mediocritas (*L.*), the golden mean.
au reste (*F.*), for the rest; besides.
au revoir! (*F.*), (good-by) till we meet again!
auri sacra fames (*L.*), accursed craving for gold.
aurora australis (*L.*), luminous phenomena radiating from the southern magnetic pole.
aurora borealis (*L.*), northern lights.
au secours! (*F.*), to the rescue! help!
autant d'hommes, autant d'avis (*F.*), so many men, so many minds (*or* opinions).
aut Cæsar aut nullus *or* **aut nihil** (*L.*), either a Cæsar or nobody (*or* nothing); either the first place or nowhere.
auto-da-fé (*Pg.; pl.* autos-da-fé), lit., act of the faith; sentence of the Inquisition; burning of a heretic.
auto-de-fe (*Sp.; pl.* autos-de-fe), same as AUTO-DA-FÉ.
autres temps, autres mœurs (*F.*), other times, other manners (*or* customs).
aux abois (*F.*), at bay; at one's wits' end.
aux aguets (*F.*), on the watch.
aux armes! (*F.*), to arms!
avaler des couleuvres (*F.*), lit., to swallow snakes; to pocket affronts.
avant-coureur *or* **avant-courrier** (*F.*), a forerunner; precursor; harbinger.
avant-propos (*F.*), preliminary matter; preface.
ave! (*L.*), hail! farewell!
avec permission (*F.*), with permission.
avec plaisir (*F.*), with pleasure.
a verbis ad verbera (*L.*), from words to blows.
aviatik (*G.*), a German airplane, having twin propellers.
a vinculo matrimonii (*It.*), from the bond of marriage.
avion (*F.*), aëroplane.
avoir le diable au corps (*F.*), to have the devil in one.
à volonté (*F.*), at will; at pleasure.
à votre santé! (*F.*), to your health!
à vue d'œil (*F.*), by the eye; visibly.

B

badaud (*F.*), a credulous idler.
badinage (*F.*), light raillery; chaff.
badli (*Hind.*), a substitute.
baignoire (*F.*), lit., bathtub; a theater box on a level with the stalls.
bain-marie (*F.*), a double-boiler; hence, **cuire au bain-marie,** to cook in a double-boiler.
ballerina (*It.; pl.* ballerine), ballet girl; danseuse.
ballon d'essai (*F.*), a trial balloon; a device to test opinion.
bal masqué (*F.*), masked ball.
balourdise (*F.*), gross blunder; stupidity.
bambino (*It.*), a baby; an image of the infant Jesus.
banlieue (*F.*), suburbs; outskirts.
baragouin (*F.*), gibberish.
bara khana (*Hind.*), lit., a big dinner; banquet.
barbouillage (*F.*), scribble; scrawl; also, twaddle.
bari (*or, popularly,* **bara**) **hazri** (*Hind.*), lit., large breakfast; déjeuner. Cf. CHOTA HAZRI.
bas bleu (*F.*), a bluestocking; literary woman.
basso (*It.*), bass: *music.*
basso profondo (*It.*), a deep bass.
basso-rilievo (*It.*), bas-relief; low relief: *sculp.*
batterie de cuisine (*F.*), kitchen utensils.
battre la campagne (*F.*), to beat (*or* scour) th country; hence, to beat about the bush divagate.
battre la générale (*F.*), beat the general (*mil.*) sound a general assembly.
battre le fer pendant qu'il est chaud (*F.*) to strike the iron while it is hot.
battue (*F.*), beating for game; beat.
bavardage (*F.*), babbling; cackle.
beatæ memoriæ (*L.*), of blessed memory.
beau idéal (*F.*), lit., the ideal Beautiful; the ideal of consummate beauty or of perfection.
beau monde (*F.*), the world of fashion; fashionable society.
beau sabreur (*F.*), dashing cavalryman, esp. an officer.
beaux yeux (*F.*), fine eyes; good looks.
bel esprit (*F.; pl.* beaux esprits), a man of wit; a wit; a brilliant mind.
belles-lettres (*F.*), polite or elegant literature; writings of a purely literary kind.
belle tournure (*F.*), fine figure.
ben trovato (*It.*), well found; well invented; characteristic if not true.
berceuse (*F.*), a cradle song; lullaby; lullaby music.
berloque (*F.*), a drumbeat used as a signal for meals, etc.; a barrack call: *mil.*
bersaglieri (*It.; pl.*), Italian sharpshooters.
bête noire (*F.*), lit., black beast; a bugbear; special aversion.
bêtise (*F.*), silliness; absurdity; an ill-timed remark or action.
bibi (*Hind.*), a lady.
bibliothécaire (*F.*), librarian.
bibliothèque (*F.*), library.
bien cuit (*F.*), well cooked.
bien entendu (*F.*), well understood; of course.
bien obligé (*F.*), much obliged.
bienséance (*F.*), decorum; propriety.
bienvenue (*F.*), welcome.
bijou (*F.; pl.* bijoux), jewel; trinket.
bijouterie (*F.*), jewelry; trinkets.
billet-doux (*F.; pl.* billets-doux), love letter.
bis dat qui cito dat (*L.*), he gives twice who gives quickly.
bise (*F.*), a cold north wind of southern Europe.
bizarrerie (*F.*), caprice; whim; eccentricity.
blague (*F.*), humbug; pretentiousness; brag.
blasé (*F.*), surfeited with pleasure; cloyed; used up.
Blut und Eisen (*G.*), blood and iron.
bocage (*F.*), boscage; coppice.
bona fide (*L.*), in good faith; genuine *or* genuinely: *opposite of* mala fide.
bona fides (*L.*), good faith; honest intention: *opposite of* mala fides.
bon ami (*F.; fem.* bonne amie), good friend; also, sweetheart.
bona roba (*It.*), a courtesan.
bon enfant (*F.*), lit., good child; good fellow.
bon gré, mal gré (*F.*), (with) good grace (or) ill grace; voluntarily or against one's will.
bon jour (*F.*), good day; good morning.

bon marché (*F.*), bargain; cheapness.
bon mot (*F.; pl.* bons mots), a witty saying or repartee; witticism.
bon naturel (*F.*), good nature.
bonne (*F.*), nursemaid; maid.
bonne bouche (*F.*), choice morsel; titbit, esp. to finish with.
bon soir (*F.*), good evening.
bon ton (*F.*), good breeding; good style; fashionable society.
bon vivant (*F.; pl.* bons vivants; *fem.* bonne vivante, *pl.* bonnes vivantes), a lover of good living; gourmet.
bon voyage! (*F.*), a good voyage (*or* journey) to you!
borné (*F.*), limited; narrow; of limited ideas; narrow-minded.
bouilli (*F.*), boiled or stewed meat.
bouillon (*F.*), broth; soup.
bouleversé (*F.*), overthrown; upset (*fig.*); distracted.
bouleversement (*F.*), overthrow; convulsion; confusion; disorder.
bouleverser (*F.*), to overthrow; upset; unsettle.
bourgeois (*F.; fem.* bourgeoise), *n.* citizen of the shopkeeping class; commoner.
bourgeois (*F.; fem.* bourgeoise), *adj.* middle-class; ordinary; humdrum; Philistine.
bourgeois gentilhomme (*F.*), the shopkeeper turned gentleman: from the title of Molière's comedy, "Le Bourgeois Gentilhomme."
bourgeoisie (*F.*), the middle class.
boutade (*F.*), caprice; frolic.
boutique (*F.*), shop.
boutonnière (*F.*), a buttonhole bouquet; buttonhole (*colloq.*).
boyau (*F.*), a winding or zigzag trench: *mil.*
brio (*It.*), vivacity; spirit; animation.
brouillerie (*F.*), misunderstanding; discord.
brouillon (*F.*), rough draft.
brusquerie (*F.*), brusqueness; bluntness.
brutum fulmen (*L.*), a harmless thunderbolt; vain display of force; empty threat.
Bund (*G.*), league; confederacy.

C

cacoëthes loquendi (*L.*), mania for talking.
cacoëthes scribendi (*L.*), itch for writing; scribbling mania.
cacolet (*F.*), mule litter.
cadre (*F.*), framework; scheme; permanent establishment of a military unit, forming a nucleus for expansion.
calèche (*F.*), barouche; calash; in Quebec, a two-wheeled carriage with a folding hood.
calembour (*F.*), a pun.
camaraderie (*F.*), comradeship; good-fellowship; party spirit.
campo santo (*It.*), lit., holy field; a cemetery.
Campus Martius (*L.*), the field of Mars.
canaille (*F.*), rabble.
canapé (*F.*), sofa or divan; *Cookery:* a piece of bread fried in butter and covered with anchovies, cheese, etc.
candida Pax (*L.*), white-robed Peace.
canis in præsepi (*L.*), dog in the manger.
cantatrice (*It. or F.; It. pl.* cantatrici), a female professional singer.
cantus firmus (*NL.*), lit., fixed song; Gregorian melody.
cantus planus (*NL.*), plain song; Gregorian chant.
canzone (*It.; pl.* canzoni), a song; ballad; lyric.
capriccio (*It.*), caper; freak; fancy; in music, a caprice.
caput (*L.; pl.* capita), head.
caput mortuum (*L.*), lit., dead head; worthless residue; in old chemistry, the residuum after distillation or sublimation.
caqueterie (*F.*), cackling; gossiping.
cara sposa (*It.*), dear wife.
caro sposo (*It.*), dear husband.
carpe diem (*L.*), enjoy (*or* make use of) the present day; seize the opportunity.
carrefour (*F.*), crossroad; intersection of streets.
carte blanche (*F.*), lit., white paper; unlimited authority; full discretionary power.
carte du pays (*F.*), map of the country; lie of the land.
cartes sur table (*F.*), cards on the table; aboveboard.
casus belli (*L.*), an act justifying war.
casus fœderis (*L.*), lit., a case of the treaty; a case within the provisions of a treaty.
catalogue raisonné (F.), a catalogue arranged according to subjects.
catexochen (*Gr.* κατ' ἐξοχήν), preëminently; par excellence.
cause célèbre (*F.; pl.* causes célèbres), a celebrated case; a lawsuit that excites much attention.
causerie (*F.*), chat; informal talk; also, a chatty newspaper article, esp. on literary subjects.
causeuse (*F.*), a settee for two.
cavalier (*or* **cavaliere**) **servente** (*It.*), lit., a serving cavalier; a gallant or lover of a married woman.
caveat emptor (*L.*), let the purchaser beware (i.e., he buys at his own risk): *law.*
cave canem (*L.*), beware of the dog.
cavendo tutus (*L.*), safe by taking heed.
cavo-rilievo (*It.*), hollow relief: *sculp.*
cedant arma togæ (*L.*), let arms yield to the gown (i.e., military to civil power).
cela va sans dire (*F.*), that goes without saying; that is a matter of course.
cénacle (*F.*), a group with common interests, in allusion to the Last Supper; a literary coterie.
c'est-à-dire (*F.*), that is to say.
c'est autre chose (*F.*), that is another (*or* a different) thing.
c'est égal (*F.*), it is all one.
c'est la guerre (*F.*), that is war.
cetera desunt (*L.*), the rest are wanting.
ceteris paribus (*L.*), other things being equal.
chacun à son goût (*F.*), every one to his taste.
chaise longue (*F.*), lit., long chair; a long seat or couch, usually with an end support for the back.
Champ de Mars (*F.*), lit., Field of Mars; an open space on the left bank of the Seine in Paris.
champlevé (*F.*), a form of enamel work in which depressions or cells are cut in the metal, into which the enamel is laid and fused.
Champs Élysées (*F.*), Elysian Fields: name of an avenue in Paris.
chanson (*F.*), a song.
chantage (*F.*), extortion of hush money; blackmail.
chant du cygne (*F.*), swan song.
chaparajos *or* **chapareras** (*Mexican Sp.*), leather or sheepskin overalls, as worn by cowboys; chaps (*colloq.*).
chapeau (*F.*), hat.
chargé *or* **chargé d'affaires** (*F.; pl.* chargés), deputy ambassador; envoy at a minor court.
charmeuse (*F.*), enchantress; bewitching woman.
charrette (*F.*), cart.
château en Espagne (*F.*), a castle in Spain; castle in the air.
chaudron (*F.*), kettle; also, a copperish red.
chaussure (*F.*), footgear; boots, shoes, etc.
chef *or* **chef de cuisine** (*F.*), head cook (*male*); master cook.
chef-d'œuvre (*F.; pl.* chefs-d'œuvres), a masterpiece.
chemin de fer (*F.*), lit., iron road; railroad.
chemin faisant (*F.*), on the way.
cher ami (*F.; fem.* chère amie), dear friend.
cherchez la femme (*F.*), look for the woman.
che sarà, sarà (*It.*), what will be, will be.
cheval de bataille (*F.*), a war horse; charger; also, a strong point; bobby.

chevalier d'industrie (*F.*), one who lives by his wits; sharper; swindler.
chevalier sans peur et sans reproche (*F.*), fearless and stainless knight; Bayard.
chevaux-de-frise (*F.; pl.*), iron spikes set in timber to repel cavalry; spikes set on the top of a paling.
chiaroscuro (*It.*), lit., bright dark; black and white; light and shade, as in painting.
chic (*F.*), stylish; smart.
chor (*Hind.*), thief.
chose jugée (*F.*), thing already settled and profitless to discuss; closed chapter.
chota hazri (*Hind.*), lit., small breakfast; a light meal, usually of tea, toast, and fruit, in the very early morning.
chronique scandaleuse (*F.*), scandalous reports; unsavory gossip.
chup! (*Hind.*), silence! quiet!
chup raho! (*Hind.*), remain silent! be quiet! hold your tongue!
cicisbeo (*It.; pl.* cicisbei), recognized gallant of a married woman.
ci-devant (*F.*), former; late; ex-.
cierge (*F.*), taper; church candle.
ci-gît (*F.*), here lies; hic jacet.
circa *or* **circiter** (*L.*), about.
circulus in probando (*L.*), lit., a circle in the proof; reasoning in a circle: *logic.*
claqueur (*F.*), hired applauder; claquer.
clavis (*L.; pl.* claves), a key; glossary.
cliché (*F.*), stereotyped expression; hackneyed phrase.
cloisonné (*F.*), inlaid between partitions: said of enamel in which thin metal strips are bent to the outline of the design.
clôture (*F.*), closure; a method of ending debate by a vote that "the question be now put."
cocher (*F.*), coachman; cabman.
cochero (*Sp.*), a hackney driver: *Philippines.*
cocotte (*F.*), a woman of light character; courtesan.
codex rescriptus (*L.*), palimpsest.
cogito ergo sum (*L.*), I think, therefore I am (*or* exist): *Descartes.*
cognoscente (*It.; pl.* cognoscenti), connoisseur.
coiffeur (*F.*), hairdresser.
coiffure (*F.*), headdress; style of arranging the hair.
col (*F.*), neck; a depression in a mountain chain.
coloratura (*It.*), runs, trills, and other embellishments in vocal music; coloratura.
comme ci comme ça (*F.*), so-so; middling.
comme deux gouttes d'eau (*F.*), lit., as two drops of water; (as like) as two peas.
comme il faut (*F.*), as it should be; proper; in good form; well-bred.
commencement de la fin (*F.*), beginning of the end.
commis-voyageur (*F.*), commercial traveler; traveling salesman.
communibus annis (*L.*), in common (*or* average) years.
communi consensu (*L.*), by common consent.
communiqué (*F.*), official communication.
compagnon de voyage (*F.*), traveling companion.
compos mentis (*L.*), sane in mind; in one's right mind.
compte rendu (*F.*), an account rendered; a report.
con amore (*It.*), with love; earnestly; zealously.
concerto (*It.*), a composition written for one (or sometimes two or three) principal instruments, with orchestral accompaniment: *music.*
concetto (*It.; pl.* concetti), a conceit; flash of wit.
concierge (*F.*), doorkeeper; janitor.
conciliatrix (*L.*), a procuress.
concordia discors (*L.*), discordant harmony.
condamné (*F.*), condemned man; convict.
confrère (*F.*), colleague; fellow member.
congé (*F.*), unceremonious dismissal: discharge; also, a kind of molding.
congé d'élire (*F.*), lit., leave to elect; royal permission to elect a bishop.
consommé (*F.*), strong clear soup made from meat or from meat and vegetables.
contadino (*It.; pl.* contadini; *fem.* contadina, *pl.* contadine), Italian peasant.
conte à dormir debout (*F.*), old wives' tale; tedious nonsense.
contra bonos mores (*L.*), against good manners (*or* morals).
contrecoup (*F.*), counterblow; rebound; consequence; result.
contretemps (*F.*), an unlucky accident; a vexatious happening; hitch.
conversazione (*It.; pl.* conversazioni), lit., conversation; an evening assembly for conversation or discussion.
copia verborum (*L.*), abundance of words.
coquillage (*F.*), shellwork.
coram (*L.*), in the presence of; before.
coram judice (*L.*), before a judge.
coram populo (*L.*), publicly; in public.
corbeau (*F.*), crow; raven; also, a very dark shade of green.
cordon bleu (*F.*), formerly, the blue ribbon worn by Knights of the Holy Ghost; hence, a person of distinction; jocularly, a first-rate cook.
cordon sanitaire (*F.*), sanitary cordon; a line of guards stationed between infected and uninfected districts.
corona lucis (*L.*), lit., crown of light; a circular chandelier hung from the roof of a church; a corona.
corps de réserve (*F.*), a body of reserve: *mil.*
corpus (*L.; pl.* corpora), body; collection of writings.
corpus delicti (*L.*), the body of the crime; the substance or fundamental facts of a crime or of an offense.
corpus juris (*L.*), a body of law; collection of the law of a country or jurisdiction.
cortège (*F.*), train of attendants; retinue; procession.
cortile (*It.; pl.* cortili), an inclosed courtyard.
coryphée (*F.*), leading ballet dancer.
cotillon (*F.*), originally, a French quadrille; in the U.S., a german; also, the music for these.
couci-couci (*F.*), so-so; indifferently.
coulée (*F.*), bed of a deep stream, having inclined sides.
couleur de rose (*F.*), rose color; rose-colored (*fig.*); roseate.
couloir (*F.*), steep gorge; Alpine gully.
coup (*F.*), a stroke; blow.
coup de grâce (*F.*), lit., a stroke of mercy; finishing stroke.
coup de main (*F.*), a sudden vigorous attack; bold stroke.
coup de maître (*F.*), a master stroke.
coup de pied (*F.*), a kick.
coup de plume (*F.*), a literary attack.
coup de soleil (*F.*), sunstroke.
coup d'essai (*F.*), a first attempt.
coup d'état (*F.*), a stroke of state (*or* policy); a violent overthrow of the existing government.
coup de théâtre (*F.*), a sudden and sensational turn or action in, or as in, a play; theatrical effect; stage trick.
coup d'œil (*F.*), a comprehensive glance; general view.
coûte que coûte (*F.*), cost what it may; at any price.
couturière (*F.*) dressmaker, seamstress.
crambe repetita (*L.*), warmed-over cabbage; tedious repetition; an old story.
credat Judæus Apella (*L.*), let Apella the Jew (i.e., a credulous person) believe it (I won't).
crédit mobilier (*F.*), a loan upon movables or personal property.
crème de la crème (*F.*) cream of the cream; the very choicest.
crème de menthe (*F.*) lit. cream of mint; peppermint liqueur, green in color.

croix de guerre (*F.*), the French war cross, awarded for bravery under fire.
crux criticorum (*L.*), the crux (*or* puzzle) of critics.
cui bono? (*L.*), who benefits by it?
cuisine (*F.*), kitchen arrangements; style of cooking.
culbute (*F.*), somersault; fall; failure.
culbuter (*F.*), to upset; overthrow; ruin.
cul-de-lampe (*F.; pl.* culs-de-lampe), a bracket or pendant suggestive of the bottom of an ancient church lamp: *arch.*
cul-de-sac (*F.; pl.* culs-de-sacs), lit., bottom of a bag; a blind alley: *often used figuratively.*
cum grano salis (*L.*), with a grain of salt; with reserve or precaution.
cum multis aliis (*L.*), with many others.
curé (*F.*), parish priest.
curiosa felicitas (*L.*), nice felicity of expression.
currente calamo (*L.*), with a running pen; offhand.
custos morum (*L.*), the guardian of morals (*or* manners).
custos rotulorum (*L.*), keeper of the rolls.
cygne noir (*F.*), black swan; extreme rarity.
cyma recta (*L.*), a cornice molding forming a double curve, concave above and convex below: *arch.*
cyma reversa (*L.*), a cyma in which the curve is convex above and concave below: *arch.*

D

da capo (*It.*), from the beginning: *music.*
d'accord (*F.*), in accord; in agreement; agreed.
damnosa hereditas (*L.*), lit., a damaging inheritance, i.e., one that brings more burden than profit.
danke *or* **danke schön!** (*G.*), thanks! thanks very much!
danseuse (*F.*), ballet girl; ballet dancer; figurante.
débâcle (*F.*), the break-up of ice in a river; hence, a confused rush; stampede.
de bon augure (*F.*), of good omen.
de bonne grâce (*F.*), with good grace; willingly.
de bonne volonté (*F.*), with good will; willingly.
débris (*F.*), scattered fragments; remains; rubbish.
début (*F.*), first appearance before the public; entrance into society; coming out (*colloq.*).
débutant (*F.; fem.* débutante), one appearing before the public or in society for the first time.
décalage (*F.*), lit., unwedging; the difference in inclination between the upper and lower wings of a biplane; in a monoplane, the angle between the chord of the wings and that of the stabilizers.
deceptio visus (*L.*), optical illusion.
décolleté (*F.; fem.* décolletée), low-necked (*said of a dress*); wearing low-necked dress.
de die in diem (*L.*), from day to day: *abbr.* d. d. in d.
de facto (*L.*), in fact; actual or actually: *distinguished from* de jure.
de fide (*L.*), lit., of the faith; required to be held as an article of faith.
de fond en comble (*F.*), from the foundations to the roof; from top to bottom; wholly.
dégagé (*F.; fem.* dégagée), easy; unconstrained.
de gustibus non est disputandum (*L.*), there is no disputing about tastes.
de haut en bas (*F.*), from top to bottom; from head to foot; hence, scornfully; in a superior manner.
Dei gratia (*L.*), by the grace of God.
de integro (*L.*), afresh; anew.
déjeuner (*F.*), breakfast; lunch.
déjeuner à la fourchette (*F.*), lit., breakfast with the fork; meat breakfast; luncheon.
de jure (*L.*), by right; by law; rightful or rightfully: *distinguished from* de facto.
délabrement (*F.*), ruin; decay; dilapidation.
de lana caprina (*L.*), lit., about goat's wool (*a thing not existing, as goats have hair*); hence, about any worthless object.
delenda est Carthago (*L.*), Carthage must be destroyed.
deliciæ humani generis (*L.*), the delight of mankind: appellation of the Emperor Titus.
démêlé (*F.*), altercation; quarrel.
démenti (*F.*), contradiction; official denial.
dementia a potu (*L.*), dementia from drinking; delirium tremens.
de mortuis nil nisi bonum (*L.*), of the dead (say) nothing but good.
de nihilo nihil (*L.*), from nothing nothing (can come).
dénouement (*F.*), the unraveling (*or* end) of a plot; issue; catastrophe; final solution.
de novo (*L.*), anew; afresh.
Deo gratias (*L.*), thanks to God.
Deo volente (*L.*), God willing: *abbr.* D. V.
de profundis (*L.*), out of the depths (*Psalm* cxxx.1).
de règle (*F.*), customary; proper.
de rigueur (*F.*), obligatory; indispensable; required by etiquette.
dernier cri (*F.*), the last cry; latest thing; the rage.
dernier ressort (*F.*), a last resort; desperate expedient.
désagrément (*F.*), something disagreeable; unpleasantness.
desipere in loco (*L.*), to indulge in trifling at the proper time.
désobligeant (*F.*), disobliging; unkind.
désœuvré (*F.*), unoccupied; idle.
désolé (*F.*), disconsolate; broken-hearted.
désorienté (*F.*), having lost one's bearings; astray; bewildered.
détenu (*F.; fem.* détenue), a detained person, prisoner.
détour (*F.*), deviation; circuitous route.
de trop (*F.*), too much (*or* too many); unwanted; in the way; unwelcome.
deus ex machina (*L.*), a god from a machine (alluding to the practice in the ancient theater of bringing on a god to solve superhuman difficulties); providential intervention, esp. in a play or novel.
Deus vult (*L.*), God wills (it): rallying cry of the First Crusade.
devoir (*F.*), duty; task; courteous attentions: *usually in pl.*
diable (*F.*), devil; the Devil.
diable à quatre (*F.*), the devil to pay.
diablerie (*F.*), devilry; witchcraft.
Diabolus (*L.*), the Devil.
dies faustus (*L.*), a lucky day.
dies infaustus (*L.*), an unlucky day.
dies iræ (*L.*), day of wrath; Day of Judgment.
dies non (*L.; short for* **dies non juridicus,** nonjudicial day), a day on which the business of the courts cannot legally be carried on; hence, a day that does not count.
Dieu défend le droit (*F.*), God defends the right.
Dieu et mon droit (*F.*), God and my right: motto in British royal arms.
Dieu vous garde (*F.*), God guard you.
difficile (*F.*), difficult; trying; unaccommodating; hard to please.
dignus vindice nodus (*L.*), a knot worthy of (such) a liberator.
di grado in grado (*It.*), by degrees; gradually.
di majores (*L.*), the greater gods; fig., men of outstanding eminence.
di minores (*L.*), the lesser gods; fig., men of lesser merit.
dis aliter visum (*L.*), to the gods it has seemed otherwise.
disjecta membra (*L.*), scattered remains (*or* parts).
disjecti membra poetæ (*L.*), limbs of the dismembered poet.
distingué (*F.; fem.* distinguée), distinguished; of aristocratic air or bearing.

distrait (*F.*), absent-minded; abstracted.
diva (*It.; pl.* dive), prima donna.
divertissement (*F.*), entertainment; diversion (as between the acts of a play).
divide et impera (*L.*), divide and rule.
divorcé (*F.; fem.* divorcée), a person divorced; divorcee.
dixi (*L.*), I have said (all that I am going to).
docendo discimus (*L.*), we learn by teaching.
dolce far niente (*It.*), sweet doing nothing; pleasant idleness.
domina (*L.; pl.* dominæ), lady.
Domine dirige nos (*L.*), Lord, direct us.
Dominus vobiscum (*L.*), the Lord (be) with you.
dona (*Pg.*), **doña** (*Sp.*), *or* **donna** (*It.*), lady; mistress; madam: when capitalized, a title of respect prefixed to the Christian name of a lady.
dormeuse (*F.*), a traveling carriage adaptable for sleeping.
double entente *or, esp. in English,* **double entendre** (*F.*), an ambiguous expression; indelicate play upon words.
douceur (*F.*), lit., sweetness; a gratuity; tip.
doyen (*F.*), dean; senior member of a group.
dramatis personæ (*L.*), the characters in a play.
drap d'or (*F.*), cloth of gold.
droit des gens (*F.*), the law of nations; international law.
drôle de corps (*F.*) a queer fellow; an odd character.
duce (*It.*), leader; commander.
du fort au faible (*F.*), lit., from the strong to the weak; one thing with another; on an average.
dulce "Domum" (*L.*), sweet "Home" (*or* "Homeward"): from the song sung by students of Winchester College and other English schools at the close of the term.
dum spiro, spero (*L.*), while I breathe, I hope.
dum vivimus, vivamus (*L.*), while we live, let us live.
duo (*It.*), duet, esp. an instrumental duet: *music.*
duomo (*It.; pl.* duomi), Italian cathedral.

E

eau (*F.*), water.
eau de Cologne (*F.*), perfumed toilet water made at Cologne; cologne.
ébauche (*F.*), rough draft; outline of the main features.
éboulement (*F.*), falling down, as of a rampart; landslip.
Ecce Homo (*L.*), behold the man (*John* xix.5): a representation of Christ crowned with thorns.
ecce signum (*L.*), behold the sign; look to the proof.
écervelé (*F.*), hare-brained; rash.
échafaudage (*F.*), scaffolding; great preparations; display.
échapper belle (*F.*), to have a narrow escape.
éclaircissement (*F.*), clearing up; elucidation; explanation.
écorcher les oreilles (*F.*), to grate on one's ears.
édition de luxe (*F.*), a sumptuous edition.
editio princeps (*L.*), the first printed edition of a book.
effleurer (*F.*), to graze; skim over; glance at; touch but slightly.
égards (*F.*), regards; respects.
ejectamenta (*L.; pl.*), ejecta; ejected matter.
élan (*F.*), vivacity; dash; rush.
élève (*F.*), pupil; student.
élite (*F.*), choice; pick; flower; select few.
elixir vitæ (*L.*), elixir of life.
éloge (*F.*), eulogium; panegyric; funeral oration.
embarras de choix (*F.*), embarrassment of choice.
embarras de richesses (*F.*), an embarrassment of riches.
embonpoint (*F.*), plumpness; stoutness.
émeute (*F.*), riot; outbreak; popular rising.
émigré (*F.*), emigrant; esp., a Royalist fugitive at the time of the French Revolution.
empressement (*F.*), eagerness; demonstrativeness; excessive cordiality.
en avant (*F.*), forward; onward.
en bloc (*F.*), in a lump; as a whole; wholesale.
enceinte (*F.*), *adj.* pregnant; with child.
enceinte (*F.*), *n.* inclosure (as within a town walls); precincts; main inclosure of a fortress.
en déshabille (*F.*), in undress.
endimanché (*F.*), dressed in Sunday clothes.
en effet (*F.*), in effect; in reality; substantially; really.
en évidence (*F.*), in evidence.
en famille (*F.*), in (*or* with) one's family; among oneselves; informally.
enfant (*F.*), child.
enfant gâté (*F.*), a spoiled child.
enfant perdu (*F.; pl.* enfants perdus), lit., a lost child; a soldier sent to a dangerous post; *pl.*, a forlorn hope.
enfant terrible (*F.*), lit., terrible child; a child who makes disconcerting remarks.
enfant trouvé (*F.*), a foundling.
enfin (*F.*), in fine; in short; at last.
en foule (*F.*), in a crowd.
en grande tenue (*F.*), in full dress or uniform.
en grande toilette (*F.*), in full dress.
en grand seigneur (*F.*), as a great lord; in lordly style.
en masse (*F.*), in a mass; in a body; all together.
ennuyé (*F.; fem.* ennuyée), mentally wearied; bored; ennuied.
en passant (*F.*), in passing; by the way.
en plein jour (*F.*), in broad daylight.
en rapport (*F.*), in accord; in sympathy.
en règle (*F.*), according to rule; in due form; in order.
en revanche (*F.*), in requital; in return.
en route (*F.*), on the way.
ens (*L.*), lit., a thing; being, in the abstract sense: *philos.*
ensemble (*F.*), the whole; general effect.
Ens Entium (*L.*), Being of Beings; the Supreme Being.
ens rationis (*L.*), a creature of the reason; a product of mental action.
en suite (*F.*), in company; in a series or set.
en tapinois (*F.*), stealthily; slyly.
entente (*F.*), an understanding; agreement.
entente cordiale (*F.*), friendly understanding, esp. between two countries.
entêté (*F.*), headstrong; stubborn; self-willed.
entourage (*F.*), surroundings; attendant persons; associates (*collectively*); circle.
en-tout-cas (*F.*), umbrella-sunshade.
entr'acte (*F.*), interval between two acts; interlude.
entre chien et loup (*F.*), lit., between dog and wolf; in the dusk or twilight.
entre deux âges (*F.*), lit., between two ages; middle-aged.
entremets (*F.*), side dish (*or* side dishes).
entremetteuse (*F.*), go-between; procuress.
entre nous (*F.*), between ourselves.
entrepôt (*F.*), warehouse; temporary storehouse; mart; commercial center.
entrepreneur (*F.*), enterpriser; organizer, esp. of musical entertainments.
en vérité (*F.*), in truth; truly.
épanchement (*F.*), outpouring; effusion.
éperdu (*F.*), distracted; bewildered.
e pluribus unum (*L.*), one out of many: motto of the United States.
éprouvette (*F.*), an apparatus for testing gunpowder; in assaying, a small spoon for fluxes.
ergo (*L.*), therefore; hence.
errare est humanum (*L.*), to err is human.
escadrille (*F.*), naval or aviation squadron; as, the Lafayette *escadrille.*
espièglerie (*F.*), roguish trick; waggishness.
espionnage (*F.*), spying; use of spies; espionage.
espressivo (*It.*), with expression: *music.*

esprit (*F.*), spirit; wit; sprightliness.
esprit de corps (*F.*), the animating spirit of a collective body and regard for the honor and interests of such body.
esprit fort (*F.*), lit., a strong spirit; freethinker; strong-minded person.
esse (*L.*), existence; being.
estaminet (*F.*), a café in which smoking is allowed.
estancia (*Sp. Amer.*). cattle ranch.
est modus in rebus (*L.*), there is a medium (*or* due measure) in all things.
esto perpetua! (*L.*), be thou perpetual! may she (*or* it) be everlasting.
étagère (*F.*), a whatnot.
étalage (*F.*), exposing for sale; ostentatious display; show.
étape (*F.*), public storehouse; halting place (*mil.*); stage.
état-major (*F.*), staff; staff office: *mil.*
et hoc (*or* **id**) **genus omne** (*L.*), and everything of this kind.
Ètoile du Nord (*F.*), star of the North; North Star.
étourderie (*F.*), thoughtless act; heedlessness; thoughtlessness.
et tu, Brute (*L.*), and thou also, Brutus! (implying betrayal by a friend).
evviva! (*It.*), hurrah!
Ewigkeit (*G.*), eternity.
Ewig-Weibliche (*G.*), (the) eternal feminine: part of the line from Goethe's *Faust*, "Das Ewig-Weibliche zieht uns hinan," the eternal feminine doth draw us on.
ex abundante cautela (*L.*), from excessive precaution.
ex abundantia (*L.*), out of the abundance.
exalté (*F.*), enthusiast; fanatic.
ex animo (*L.*), from the heart; heartily; sincerely.
ex cathedra (*L.*), from the chair; authoritatively.
exceptis excipiendis (*L.*), the due exceptions being made.
escerpta (*L.; pl.*), excerpts; clippings.
ex concesso (*L.*), from what has been conceded.
ex curia (*LL.*), out of court.
ex dono (*L.*), by the gift; as a present.
exempli gratia (*L.*), for the sake of example; for example: *abbr.* e.g.
exeunt (*L.*), they go out (*or* leave the stage).
exeunt omnes (*L.*), all go out (*or* retire); all leave the stage.
ex hypothesi (*L.*), by hypothesis.
exigeant (*F.; fem.* exigeante), exacting; hard to please.
exit (*L.*), he goes out (*or* goes off the stage).
ex libris (*L.*), lit., from the books (of); an inscription used, with the owner's name, in a book; a bookplate.
ex mero motu (*L.*), out of mere impulse; of one's own accord.
ex more (*L.*), according to custom.
ex necessitate rei (*L.*), from the necessity of the case.
ex nihilo nihil fit (*L.*), from nothing, nothing is made; nothing produces nothing.
ex officio (*L.*), in virtue of one's office.
ex parte (*L.*), from one party (*or* side); in the interests of one side only.
ex pede Herculem (*L.*), from the foot (we may judge of) Hercules; from a part we may divine the whole.
experimentum crucis (*L.*), a crucial experiment (*or* test).
experto credite (*L.*), believe one who knows by experience.
exposé (*F.*), exposure (of something discreditable); showing up; statement of facts.
ex post facto (*L.*), after the deed is done; retrospective.
extincteur (*F.*), fire extinguisher.
extra muros (*L.*), beyond the walls.
ex uno disce omnes (*L.*), from one learn all; from one judge of the rest.
ex voto (*L.*), according to (*or* in pursuance of) one's vow.

F

facile princeps (*L.*), easily chief (*or* first).
facilis descensus Averno *or* **Averni** (*L.*), the descent to Avernus (*or* hell) is easy.
façon de parler (*F.*), way of speaking.
facta non verba (*L.*), deeds, not words.
facteur (*F.*), postman; letter carrier.
fade (*F.*), insipid; pointless; stale; flat.
fæx populi (*L.*), dregs of the people; the rabble.
fainéant (*F.*), *adj.* idle; inactive; slothful.
fainéant (*F.*), *n.* idler; do-nothing; sluggard.
faire antichambre (*F.*), to dance attendance.
faire l'amende honorable (*F.*), to make amends; apologize.
faire le diable à quatre (*F.*), to play the devil.
faire les yeux doux (*F.*), to cast loving glances (at).
faire pattes de velours (*F.*), to draw in its claws; hence, to cajole; flatter.
fait accompli (*F.*), an accomplished fact; a thing already done.
fait à peindre (*F.*), extremely well-made; very handsome.
fallacia consequentis (*L.*), fallacy of the consequent; non sequitur: *logic.*
falsi crimen (*L.*), the crime of falsifying.
farceur (*F.*), joker; wag; also, a farce writer or player.
fare fac (*L.*), say, do.
fasti (*L.; pl.*), calendar of events; annals.
Fata obstant (*L.*), the Fates oppose.
fatras (*F.*), medley; jumble; trash.
faubourg (*F.*), suburb; outskirt.
faute de mieux (*F.*), for want of better.
fauteuil (*F.*), armchair; theater stall.
faux pas (*F.*), a false step; slip in behavior; social indiscretion.
fecit (*L.*), lit., he (*or* she) made (it): appended to artist's name on a picture: *abbr.* fec.
femme (*F.*), woman; female; wife.
femme de chambre (*F.*), a lady's maid; chambermaid.
feræ naturæ (*L.*), of a wild nature; not domesticated.
festina lente (*L.*), make haste slowly.
fête champêtre (*F.*), a rural festival; an outdoor fête.
feu de joie (*F.*), lit., fire of joy; a firing of guns at a time of public rejoicing; bonfire.
feu d'enfer (*F.*), a scathing fire.
feuilleton (*F.*), a ruled-off section at the foot of a French newspaper, devoted to fiction, criticism, etc.
fiacre (*F.*), hackney coach; cab.
fiancé (*F.; fem.* fiancée), a betrothed.
fiat justitia, ruat cælum (*L.*), let justice be done though the heavens fall.
fiat lux (*L.*), let there be light.
fidei defensor (*L.*), defender of the faith: *abbr.* F.D.
fides Punica (*L.*), Punic faith; treachery.
fidus Achates (*L.*), faithful Achates; a trusty friend; devoted follower.
fieri facias (*L.*), lit., cause it to be done; a writ commanding the sheriff to execute judgment: *abbr.* fi. fa.
fille (.*F*), daughter; girl.
fille de chambre (*F.*), chambermaid.
fille de joie (*F.*), courtesan; prostitute.
fils (*F.*), son: often used after French surname to distinguish son from father. Cf. PÈRE.
finale (*It.*), close of drama, etc.; catastrophe; last movement of a musical composition; closing piece in any act of an opera.
fin de siècle (*F.*), lit., end of century; characteristic of the close of the nineteenth century; modern; advanced: *used adjectivally.*
finis coronat opus (*L.*), the end crowns the work.

fioritura (*It.; pl.* fioriture), embellishment; florid ornament (*pl.*): *music.*
flagrante bello (*L.*), lit., while the war is blazing; during actual hostilities.
flagrante delicto (*L.*), lit., while the crime is blazing; in the very act; red-handed.
flambé (*F.*), singed; ruined; done for.
flânerie (*F.*), lounging; idling; aimlessness.
flâneur (*F.*), lounger; idler.
flèche (*F.*), lit., arrow; slender spire, esp. at the intersection of the nave and transepts of a church.
flux de bouche (*F.*), salivation; also, flow of words.
flux de mots *or* **paroles** (*F.*), flow of words.
folâtre (*F.*), frolicsome; playful.
fondre en larmes (*F.*), to burst into tears.
fons et origo (*L.*), the source and origin.
forçat (*F.*), a convict sentenced to imprisonment with hard labor; galley slave.
force majeure (*F.*), superior force; irresistible compulsion.
fortiter in re, suaviter in modo (*L.*), strongly in deed, gently in manner.
fourgon (*F.*), baggage or ammunition wagon: *mil.*
fourragère (*F.*), an ornamental braided cord looped under the left arm and attached to the shoulder of the uniform: *mil.*
frater (*L.; pl.* fratres), brother.
Frau (*G.; pl.* Frauen), woman; wife; a title of respect equivalent to *Mrs., Madam.*
Fräulein (*G.; sing. and pl.*), unmarried woman; a title of respect or address equivalent to *Miss.*
frondeur (*F.*), lit., slinger; faultfinder; in French history, a member of the Fronde; hence, a malcontent; rebel.
front à front (*F.*), face to face.
fruges consumere nati (*L.*), born to consume the fruits of the earth.
fugit hora (*L.*), the hour flies.
fuit Ilium (*L.*), Troy has been (i.e., exists no longer).
furor loquendi (*L.*), a rage for speaking.
furor poeticus (*L.*), poetic frenzy.
furor scribendi (*L.*), a range for writing.

G

gaieté de cœur (*F.*), gayety of heart.
galantuomo (*It.*), man of honor; gentleman.
galbe (*F.*), outline; outward form; conformation: *art.*
Gallice (*L.*), lit., in Gaulish; in French.
garçon (*F.*), boy; fellow; waiter.
Gasthof (*G.*), hotel; inn.
gauche (*F.*), lit., left-handed; clumsy; awkward, esp. in society; tactless.
gaucherie (*F.*), awkwardness; want of ease or grace; tactlessness.
gaudeamus igitur (*L.*), let us then be joyful.
gendarme (*F.*), a soldier employed as a policeman, esp. in France.
genius loci (*L.*), the genius (*or* presiding deity) of a place.
genre (*F.*), kind; sort; species; style; *Fine Arts:* portrayal of scenes from everyday life.
gens d'armes (*F.*), men at arms.
gens de guerre (*F.*), military men; soldiery.
gens de même famille (*F.*), birds of a feather.
gentilhomme (*F.*), nobleman; gentleman.
genus irritabile vatum (*L.*), the irritable (*or* sensitive) race of poets.
Germanice (*NL.*), in German.
Gesundheit! (*G.*), (to your) health!
geta (*Jap.*), a wooden sandal, mounted on two high crosspieces, used by the Japanese in muddy weather.
giallo antico (*It.*), lit., ancient yellow; a rich yellow marble found among Italian ruins.
gibier de potence (*F.*), a gallows bird.
glacé (*F.*), smooth; polished; highly polished; *of fruits, cake, etc.*, iced; glazed; frosted.
Gloria (*L.*), glory; short for *Gloria in Excelsis, Gloria Patri,* or *Gloria Tibi: eccl.*
Gloria in Excelsis (Deo) (*L.*), Glory (to God) on high (*Luke* ii. 14): the "greater doxology."
Gloria Patri (*L.*), Glory be to the Father: the "lesser doxology."
Gloria Tibi, Domine (*L.*), Glory be to thee, O Lord.
glückliche Reise! (*G.*), a prosperous journey! bon voyage!
gnothi seauton (*Gr.* γνῶθι σεαυτόν), know thyself; inscribed on the temple of Apollo at Delphi.
gorge-de-pigeon (*F.*), iridescent; shot.
gourmet (*F.*), connoisseur of table delicacies.
goût (*F.*), taste; relish.
grâce à Dieu (*F.*), thanks to God.
gradino (*It.*), an altar shelf; a gradin: *eccl.*
Græculus esuriens (*L.*), hungry Greekling; parasite.
grande passion (*F.*), great passion; love; passionate love affair.
grande toilette (*F.*), ceremonial dress (*or* costume).
grand seigneur (*F.*), a great noble; a man of eminence.
gratis dictum (*L.*), a mere assertion.
grazie! (*It.*), thanks!
grenat (*F.*), garnet.
griffonage (*F.*), scrawl; scribble.
guerre à mort (*F.*), war to the death.
guerre à outrance (*F.*), war to the uttermost (*or* death).
guerre de plume (*F.*), paper warfare.
Gymnasium (*G.*), German classical school; grammar school (in the English sense.).

H

habeas corpus (*L.*), lit., you must have the body; a write requiring a person to be brought into court, to investigate the lawfulness of his restraint: *law.*
habet! (*L.*), he has it! he is hit! *See* HOC HABET.
haud passibus æquis (*L.*), not with equal steps.
hauteur (*F.*), haughtiness; arrogance; loftiness.
haut goût (*F.*), high flavor; high seasoning; slight taint.
haut monde (*F.*), high society.
haut ton (*F.*), high tone; high fashion; high social standing.
Heimweh (*G.*), homesickness.
helluo librorum (*L.*), a devourer of books; bookworm.
Herr (*G.; pl.* Herren), lord; master; gentleman; a title of respect equivalent to *Mr., Sir.*
hesterni quirites (*L.*), Roman citizens of yesterday (i.e., slaves recently set free).
hiatus valde deflendus (*L.*), a gap (*or* deficiency) greatly to be deplored: used to mark a blank in a work, also used of persons whose achievements fall short of their promises.
hic et ubique (*L.*), here and everywhere.
hic jacet (*L.*), here lies: used in epitaphs.
hiems (*L.*), winter.
hinc illæ lacrimæ (*L.*), hence these tears.
hoc genus omne (*L.*), all of this class (*or* sort).
hoc habet! (*L.*), he has it! he is hit! (the cry of the spectators at a gladiatorial combat).
hoc opus hic labor est (*L.*), this is the task, this the toil; this is the real difficulty; there's the rub.
hodie mihi, cras tibi (*L.*), today for me, tomorrow for thee; my turn today, yours tomorrow.
hoi polloi (*Gr.* οἱ πολλοί), the many; the multitude; the masses.
homme de court (*F.*), a man of the court; courtier.
homme d'esprit (*F.*), a man of wit.
homo (*L.*), man.
homo multarum literarum (*L.*), lit., a man of many letters; a man of great learning.
Homo sapiens (*L.*), lit., wise (*or* reasoning) man; the single human species of the genus *Homo.*

homo trium literarum (*L.*), a man of three letters (i.e., *f u r*, the Latin for thief); a thief.
honi soit! (*F.*), an abbreviated form of **honi soit qui mal y pense**, shamed be he who thinks evil of it: motto of the Order of the Garter.
hôpital (*F.*), hospital.
horresco referens (*L.*), I shudder to relate (it).
horribile dictu (*L.*), horrible to relate.
hors concours (*F.*), not competing for prize: said of a picture in an exhibition.
hors de combat (*F.*), out of the combat; disabled.
hors d'œuvre (*F.*), a side dish; relish.
hortus siccus (*L.*), lit., a dry garden; herbarium.
Hôtel des Invalides (*F.*), a hospital in Paris, founded by Louis XIV, for aged and infirm soldiers.
hôtel de ville (*F.*), town hall.
hôtel Dieu (*F.*), a hospital.
hukm (*Hind.*), an order; a command.
humanum est errare (*L.*), to err is human.
hurler avec les loups (*F.*), lit., to howl with the wolves; do as others do.

I

ibidem (*L.*), in the same place (in a book): *abbr.* ib., ibid.
ich dien (*G.*), I serve: motto of Prince of Wales.
ici on parle français (*F.*), French is spoken here.
idée fixe (*F.*), fixed idea; monomania.
idem (*L.*), the same; the same as above: *abbr.* id.
idem quod (*L.*), the same as.
id est (*L.*), that is; that is to say: *abbr.* i.e.
ignis fatuus (*L.; pl.* ignes fatui), will-o'-the-wisp; delusive hope.
ignobile vulgus (*L.*), the baseborn multitude.
ignorance crasse (*F.*), gross ignorance.
ignoratio elenchi (*L.*), ignorance of the point in dispute; fallacy of appearing to refute an opponent by arguing a point not raised by him: *logic.*
ignotum per ignotius (*L.*), the unknown (explained) by the still more unknown.
Ilias malorum (*L.*), an Iliad of woes; a series of calamities.
il n'a pas inventé la poudre (*F.*), lit., he has not invented powder; he will never set the Thames on fire.
il n'y a pas de quoi (*F.*), there is no occasion for it; don't mention it.
il n'y a que le premier pas qui coûte (*F.*), it is only the first step that costs.
il penseroso (*Old It.*), the pensive (*or* melancholy) man.
ils ne passeront pas! (*F.*), they shall not pass!
immedicabile vulnus (*L.*), an incurable wound.
impasse (*F.*), blind alley; inextricable difficulty; dilemma.
impayable (*F.*), invaluable; matchless; priceless; unheard of.
imperium in imperio (*L.*), a sovereignty within a sovereignty; an absolute authority within the jurisdiction of another.
imprimis (*L.*), in the first place.
improvvisatore (*It.; fem.* improvvisatrice), an improviser; one who composes extempore.
in æternum (*L.*), forever; everlastingly.
in articulo mortis (*L*), at the point (*or* in the instant) of death.
in camera (*L.*), in a chamber; in private.
incipit (*L.*), (here) begins (book, poem, etc.).
Index Expurgatorius (*L.*), a list of books from which condemned passages must be expunged before the books may be read by Catholics: *R.C.Ch.*
Index Librorum Prohibitorum (*L.*), a catalogue of prohibited books: *R.C.Ch.*
in equilibrio (*L.*), in equilibrium.
in esse (*L.*), in being; in actual existence: *contrasted with* in posse.
in extenso (*L.*), at full length.
in extremis (*L.*), in the last extremity; at the point of death.
infandum renovare dolorem (*L.*), to renew an unspeakable grief.
in flagrante delicto (*L.*), lit., while the crime is blazing; in the very act.
in forma pauperis (*L.*), in the form of a pauper; as a poor man; not liable to costs: *law.*
in foro conscientiæ (*L.*), in the court (*or* before the tribunal) of conscience.
infra dignitatem (*L.*), beneath one's dignity; unbecoming: *abbr.* infra dig.
ingénue (*F.*), artless girl or young woman: an actress representing such a type.
in hoc signo vinces (*L.*), in (*or* by) this sign [the Cross] thou shalt conquer.
in limine (*L.*), on the threshold; at the beginning: *abbr.* in lim.
in loco (*L.*), in the (proper or natural) place.
in loco parentis (*L.*), in the place of a parent.
in medias res (*L.*), into the midst of things.
in memoriam (*L.*), in memory of.
in nomine (*L.*), in the name of.
in nubibus (*L.*), in the clouds.
in omnia paratus (*L.*), ready (*or* prepared) for all things.
in ovo (*L.*), in the egg; undeveloped.
in petto (*It.*), in the breast; secretly; in contemplation.
in posse (*LL.*), potentially; in possibility: *contrasted with* in esse.
in præsenti (*L.*), at the present moment.
in propria persona (*L.*), in one's own person (*or* character).
in puris naturalibus (*L.*), stark-naked.
in re (*L.*), in the matter of; concerning.
in rerum natura (*L.*), in the nature of things.
in sæcula sæculorum (*L.*), for ages of ages; forever.
insculpsit (*L.*), he (*or* she) engraved it.
in situ (*L.*), in its (original) place.
insouciance (*F.*), indifference; listlessness; unconcernedness.
instar omnium (*L.*), worth all of them.
in statu pupillari (*L.*), in a state of pupillage.
in statu quo (*L.*), in the same state as formerly.
insulaire (*F.*), islander.
intaglio rilevato (*It.*), hollow relief; cœlanaglyphic sculpture.
inter alia (*L.*), among other things.
inter alios (*L.*), among other persons.
inter nos (*L.*), between ourselves.
in terrorem (*L.*), as a warning.
inter se (*L.*), between (*or* among) themselves.
in totidem verbis (*L.*), in so many words.
in toto (*L.*), in the whole; entirely.
intra muros (*L.*), within the walls (esp. city walls).
intransigeant (*F.*), ultraradical; irreconcilable; Red.
in transitu (*L.*), in course of transit.
in utrumque paratus (*L.*), prepared for either (event).
in vacuo (*L.*), in a vacuum.
in vino veritas (*L.*), in wine there is truth; truth is told under influence of intoxicants.
invita Minerva (*L.*), Minerva being unwilling; artistic or literary inspiration being lacking.
ipse dixit (*L.*), lit., he himself said it; a dogmatic statement supported by bare authority; dictum.
ipsissima verba (*L.*), the very words.
ipso facto (*L.*), by that very fact.
ipso jure (*L.*), by the law itself.

J

Jacquerie (*F.*), a revolt of French peasants in 1358; hence, any peasant uprising.
jaldi karo (*Hind.*), make haste.
jalousie (*F.*), Venetian blind; latticed shutter.
jamais de ma vie (*F.*), never in my life; never, never.
jam satis (*L.*), already enough.
januis clausis (*L.*), with closed doors.
jardin (*F.*), garden.

jardinière (*F.*), ornamental flower stand.
je ne sais quoi (*F.*), I know not what; an indescribable something.
jet d'eau (*F.; pl.* jets d'eau), an ornamental jet of water; a fountain.
jeter de la poudre aux yeux (*F.*), to throw dust in the eyes; mislead.
jeter le manche après la cognée (*F.*), to throw the helve after the hatchet; to give a thing up in despair.
jeu de mots (*F.*), a play on words; pun.
jeu d'esprit (*F.*), a witticism; a witty or humorous (literary) trifle.
jeu de théâtre (*F.*), stage trick; claptrap.
jeune premier (*F.; fem.* jeune première), lit., first young (person); an actor or actress who takes lovers' parts; juvenile lead.
jeunesse dorée (*F.*), gilded youth; rich and fashionable young men.
joie de vivre (*F.*), joy of living.
jour maigre (*F.*), lit., a lean day; fish day.
journal intime (*F.*), private diary.
Jubilate Deo (*L.*), rejoice in God; be joyful in the Lord.
Judenhetze (*G.*), Jew baiting; persecution of Jews.
julienne (*F.*), a clear soup made of chopped vegetables cooked in meat broth.
jurare in verba magistri (*L.*), to swear in the words of the master.
jure divino (*L.*), by divine right (*or* law).
jure humano (*L.*), by human law.
jus civile (*L.*), civil law.
jus divinum (*L.*), divine law (*or* right).
jus et norma loquendi (*L.*), the law and rule of speech.
jus gentium (*L.*), the law of nations; international law.
jus gladii (*L.*), the right of the sword; supreme jurisdiction.
juste-milieu (*F.*), the just (*or* golden) mean.
j'y suis, j'y reste (*F.*), here I am, here I remain.

K

kala admi (*Hind.*), black man.
kala jagah (*Hind.*), lit., a black place; a shady nook or retreat.
kama rupa (*Skr.*), the desire form or body; astral body: *theos.*
Kapelle (*G.*), lit., chapel; hence, a private choir or orchestra.
Kapellmeister (*G.*), orchestra conductor or choir leader.
Klangfarbe (*G.*), clang tint; tone color.
Kultur (*G.*), culture; civilization; esp. the striving for efficiency and progress as exemplified by Germany before the World War.
kushti (*Hind.*), Hindu wrestling.
kutcha *or* **kachcha** (*Anglo-Indian*), unripe; raw; crude; makeshift: *opposite of* pucka.

L

laborare est orare (*L.*), to work is to pray; work is worship.
labor omnia vincit (*L.*), labor conquers all things.
laisser-aller (*F.*), lit., a letting go; unconstraint; unlimited freedom.
laisser-faire (*F.*), let alone; noninterference, esp. by government in commerce and individual action generally.
l'allegro (*It.*), the cheerful (*or* merry) man.
lamba chauki *or* **kursi** (*Hind.*), a long chair: a kind of easy chair with extended arms that serve as a leg rest.
lapsus calami (*L.*), a slip of the pen.
lapsus linguæ (*L.*), a slip of the tongue.
lapsus memoriæ (*L.*), a slip of the memory.
lar (*L.; pl.* lares), tutelary deity; beneficent ancestral spirit.
lares et penates (*L.*), household gods; the home.
lar familiaris (*L.*), household tutelary.
larghetto (*It.*), somewhat slow or slowly; between *adagio* and *largo*: *music.*
largo (*It.*), slow or slowly; also, a largo movement or piece: *music.*
lasciate ogni speranza voi ch'entrate (*It.*), all hope abandon, ye who enter here: inscription on the entrance to the hell of Dante's *Inferno.*
latet anguis in herba (*L.*), a snake lies hid in the grass.
lathi (*Hind.*), a club; stick; quarterstaff.
laudari a laudato viro (*L.*), to be praised by a man (who is himself) praised.
laudator temporis acti (*L.*), a praiser of times past; a preferrer of the good old days.
laus Deo (*L.*), praise to God.
l'avenir (*F.*), the future.
laver la tête (*F.*), to berate; blow up.
le beau monde (*F.*), the fashionable world.
lebewohl! (*G.*), farewell!
le dessous des cartes (*F.*), the under side of the cards; (to be in) the secret; behind the scenes.
le Diable (*F.*), the Devil.
le droit du plus fort (*F.*), the right of the strongest.
legato (*It.*), smoothly; without breaks: *music.*
légèreté (*F.*), lightness; fickleness; levity.
le grand Monarque (*F.*), the Great Monarch (i.e., Louis XIV).
Leitmotiv (*G.*), theme associated throughout the piece with some person, idea, or situation: *music.*
le monde (*F.*), the fashionable world; society.
le pas (*F.*), lit., the step; precedence; preeminence.
le premier pas (*F.*), the first step.
le roi est mort, vive le roi! (*F.*), the king is dead, long live the king!
le roi le veut (*F.*), the king wills it: formula of royal assent. In Norman French, the form is *le roy le veult.*
le roi s'avisera (*F.*), the king will consider: formula of royal veto formerly used.
les bras croisés (*F.*), the arms folded; doing nothing; idle.
lèse-majesté (*F.*), high treason.
les larmes aux yeux (*F.*), tears in one's (*or* the) eyes.
le style, c'est l'homme (*F.*), the style is the man.
l'état, c'est moi (*F.*), the state, it is I; I myself am the state: a saying formerly attributed to Louis XIV.
le tout ensemble (*F.*), the whole (taken) together.
lettre de cachet (*F.*), a sealed letter, esp. one from the sovereign; royal warrant.
lettre de créance (*F.*), letter of credit.
levée en masse (*F.*), a gathering (*or* rising) in a body.
lever de rideau (*F.*), curtain raiser.
le véritable Amphitryon est l'Amphitryon où l'on dine (*F.*), the true Amphitryon is the Amphitryon where one dines; i.e., the person who provides the feast (whether known or not) is the real host.
lex loci (*L.*), the law of the place.
lex mercatorium *or* **mercatoria** (*L.*), mercantile law; law merchant.
lex non scripta (*L.*), unwritten law; the common law.
lex scripta (*L.*), written law; statute law.
lex talionis (*L.*), the law of retaliation.
l'homme propose, et Dieu dispose (*F.*), man proposes, and God disposes.
liaison (*F.*), connection; intimacy, esp. an illicit one; in military usage, the communication established between units; a linking of operations.
liberum arbitrium (*L.*), free will or choice.
librairie (*F.*), bookshop; publishing house.
licentia vatum (*L.*), the license of the poets; poetic license.
Lied (*G.; pl.* Lieder), a song; ballad; a German lyric.

Liederkranz (*G.*), lit., wreath of songs; German vocal club for men.
limæ labor et mora (*L.*), the labor and delay of the file; the laborious polishing a a literary composition.
l'inconnu (*F.*), the unknown.
linga sharira (*Skr.*), the etheric double: *theos.*
lingerie (*F.*), linen articles, esp. women's underwear.
literati (*L.; pl.*) men of letters; the learned class.
literatim (*L.*), letter for letter; literally.
litteræ humaniores (*L.*), the humanities; polite letters; ancient classics: *abbr.* Lit. Hum.
litteræ scriptæ (*L.*), written letters; manuscript.
littera scripta manet (*L.*), the written letter remains.
littérateur (*F.*), literary man; man of letters.
livraison (*F.*), a part or number (*of a book published in parts*).
livre jaune (*F.*), yellow book; in France, a yellow-bound governmental publication.
loco citato (*L.*), in the place cited; in the passage already quoted: *abbr.* loc. cit. *or* l.c.
locum tenens (*L.*), a substitute or deputy, esp. for a clergyman or physician.
locus classicus (*L.*), a classical passage; a standard or authoritative passage on a word or subject.
locus pœnitentiæ (*L.*), opportunity for repentance.
locus sigilli (*L.*), the place of the seal: *abbr.* L.S.
locus standi (*L.*), a place of standing; recognized position; right to be heard.
l'œil du maître (*F.*), the eye of the master.
longéron (*F.*), a longitudinal member of a fuselage; *aëro.*
longo intervallo (*L.*), by (*or* at) a long interval.
loquitur (*L.*), he (*or* she) speaks: *stage direction.*
l'ordre du jour (*F.*), order of the day: *mil.*
lorette (Z.), a courtesan of a class formerly living near the church of Notre Dame de Lorette in Paris.
lorgnon (*F.*), eyeglass or eyeglasses; pince-nez.
loup-garou (*F.*), werewolf; bugbear.
lucidus ordo (*L.*), clear (*or* perspicuous) arrangement.
lucus a non lucendo (*L.*), lit., a grove from not being light (a fanciful derivation of *lucus.* grove, from *lucere,* to shine); hence, any paradoxical or absurd derivation; explanation by contraries.
lumen naturale (*L.*), natural insight (*or* wisdom).
l'usage du monde (*F.*), the way of the world.
lusus naturæ (*L.*), a freak of nature; a sport.
lycée (*F.*), lyceum; government high school.

M

mabap (*Hind.*), lit., mother-father; parents: often used by Hindus in expressing obligation to a benefactor; as, *sahib mabap hai,* "the sahib is my father and my mother."
ma chère (*F.; fem.*), my dear. Cf. MON CHER.
Macht ist Recht (*G.*), might is right.
macte virtute (*L.*), persevere in virtue; go on and prosper.
madame (*F.; pl.* mesdames), my lady; married woman; a title or form of address equivalent to *Mrs., Madam.*
mademoiselle (*F.; pl.* mesdemoiselles), a girl or unmarried woman; a title of respect or address equivalent to *Miss., abbr.* Mlle.
maestoso (*It.*), majestically: *music.*
maestro (*It.; pl.* maestri), eminent musical composer, teacher, or conductor.
ma foi! (*F.*), my faith! upon my word! indeed!
magasin (*F.*), store; emporium; warehouse.
magna civitas, magna solitudo (*L.*), a great city (is) a great solitude.
magna est veritas et prævalebit (*L.*), truth is mighty and will prevail.
magnifique et pas cher (*F.*), magnificent and not dear.
magni nominis, umbra (*L.*), the shadow of a great name.
magnum opus (*L.*), a great work; esp. a great literary undertaking.
magnus Apollo (*L.*), great Apollo.
maiden (*Anglo-Indian*), a plain; an open grassy tract; a common.
maison (*F.*), house; establishment; firm.
maison de santé (*F.*), private hospital or asylum.
maître d'hôtel (*F.*), house steward; hotel landlord.
malade imaginaire (*F.*), imaginary invalid.
maladie du pays (*F.*), homesickness; nostalgia.
mala fide (*L.*), in bad faith: treacherously; *opposite of* bona fide.
mala fides (*L.*), bad faith: *opposite of* bona fides.
mal à propos (*F.*), ill-timed; out of place; malapropos.
mal de mer (*F.*), seasickness.
mal du pays (*F.*), homesickness.
mal entendu (*F.*), ill-conceived; ill-managed.
malentendu (*F.*), *n.* a misunderstanding; misconception.
malgré nous (*F.*), in spite of us.
malgré soi (*F.*), in spite of oneself.
malum in se (*L.; pl.* mala in se), a thing evil in itself; a thing unlawful in itself, irrespective of statute.
malum prohibitum (*L.; pl.* mala prohibita), a prohibited wrong; an act that is unlawful because forbidden by law.
mañana (*Sp.*), tomorrow.
manger son blé en herbe (*F.*), to eat one's corn in the blade; spend one's money before one has it.
mania a potu (*L.*), mania from drinking delirium tremens.
manibus pedibusque (*L.*), with hands and feet; with might and main.
maniéré (*F.*), affected; unnatural; mannered.
manu forti (*L.*), with a strong hand.
maquereau (*F.; fem.* maquerelle), lit., mackerel; a pander; procurer: *slang.*
Märchen (*G.; sing. and pl.*), folk tale; fairy story.
mare clausum (*L.*) closed sea; a sea within the jurisdiction of a particular country.
mariage de convenance (*F.*), marriage of convenience; a marriage contracted from motives of interest.
matelot (*F.*), sailor; seaman.
materfamilias (*L.*), mother of a family (or household).
matériel (*F.*), materials; material supplies and equipment; baggage and munitions of an army: *distinguished from* personnel.
mauvaise honte (*F.*), false shame; diffidence; bashfulness.
mauvais goût (*F.*), bad taste.
mauvais quart d'heure (*F.*), bad quarter of an hour; a brief but unpleasant experience.
mauvais sujet (*F.*), lit., a bad subject; a worthless scamp; black sheep.
mauvais ton (*F.*), bad taste; ill breeding; vulgarity.
mea culpa (*L.*), my fault; by my fault.
médaille militaire (*F.*), French military medal, awarded for gallantry in action.
médecine expectante (*F.*), expectant medicine or treatment.
meden agan (*Gr.* μηδὲν ἄγαν), nothing too much, no excess.
medio tutissimus ibis (*L.*), in the middle course you will go most safely.
mehr Licht! (*G.*). more light! (*Goethe's last words*).
Mein Herr (*G.*), a title of respect or address equivalent to *Sir, Mr.*
me judice (*L.*), I being judge; in my opinion.

mélange (*F.*), mixture; medley; miscellany.
melée (*F.*), fray; fight; skirmish; squabble; clash.
memento mori (*L.*), remember you must die; an object (such as a skull) serving as a reminder of death.
memoria in æterna (*L.*), in everlasting remembrance.
memoria technica (*L.*), artificial memory; a mnemonical system or contrivance.
memoriter (*L.*), by (*or* from) memory; by heart.
mens sana in corpore sano (*L.*), a sound mind in a sound body.
mens sibi conscia recti (*L.*), a mind conscious to itself of rectitude; a good conscience.
menteur à triple étage (*F.*), a consummate liar.
meo periculo (*L.*), at my own risk.
merci! (*F.*), thanks! thank you!
mésalliance (*F.*), a misalliance; marriage with one of lower rank.
métayage (*F.*), a system of share rent by which the tenant gives half the produce to the owner, who supplies stock, tools, and seed.
métier (*F.*), calling; profession; line.
mettre de l'eau dans son vin (*F.*), lit., to put water in one's wine; lower one's pretensions.
meum et tuum (*L.*), mine and thine: used to express rights of property.
mezzo-rilievo (*It.*), half relief: *sculp.*
mezzo termine (*It.*), a middle term or course.
milieu (*F.*), middle; medium; environment; sphere.
minauderie (*F.*), lackadaisicalness; simpering; mincing manners; affectation.
mirabile dictu (*L.*), wonderful to relate.
mirabile visu (*L.*), wonderful to see.
mise en scène (*F.*), stage setting; surroundings of an event.
modiste (*F.*), a dressmaker or milliner.
modus operandi (*L.*), manner of operating (*or* working).
modus vivendi (*L.*), manner of living; a temporary working agreement between disputants.
mollissima fandi tempora (*L.*), the most favorable times for speaking.
mon ami (*F.; fem.* mon amie), my friend.
mon cher (*F.; masc.*), my dear. Cf. MA CHÈRE.
monde (*F.*), the world of fashion; society; one's set or coterie.
monocoque (*F.*), lit., single shell; an airplane having a fuselage reinforced by strips of veneer wrapped around formers.
monsieur (*F.; pl.* messieurs), lit., my lord; sir; a title of respect or address equivalent to *Mr.*; *abbr.* M.; in *pl.* MM. *or* Messrs.
mont-de-piété (*F.; pl.* monts-de-piété), a public or municipal pawnshop.
monumentum ære perennius (*L.*), a monument more lasting than brass.
morceau (*F.*), a piece; morsel; esp., a short musical or literary piece.
more majorum (*L.*), after the manner of one's ancestors.
more suo (*L.*), in his own way; in his usual manner.
morgue (*F.*), haughtiness; hauteur.
morgue littéraire (*F.*), literary self-sufficiency.
morituri te salutamus (*L.*), we (who are) about to die salute thee: cry of the gladiators to the Roman emperor.
mot à mot (*F.*), word for word; verbatim.
mot de l'énigme (*F.*), the answer to the riddle; key to the mystery.
mot de passe (*F.*), password.
mot d'ordre (*F.*), watchword; password.
mot du guet (*F.*), watchword; password.
motif (*F.*), in artistic composition, salient feature; dominant idea.
mot pour rire (*F.*), jest; joke.
motu proprio (*L.*), by one's own motion; of one's own impulse or accord.
mouchard (*F.*), a police spy.
mouillé (*F.*), lit., wet; softened in sound, as *ill* in *fille* (pronounced fē'y').
moulin à paroles (*F.*), chatterbox.
mousseux (*F.*), foaming; sparkling (*as wine*).
moyen âge (*F.*), Middle Ages.
multum in parvo (*L.*), much in little (*or* in small compass).
mutatis mutandis (*L.*), necessary changes being made; with due alteration of details.
mutato nomine (*L.*), the name being changed.
Mynheer (*Dutch*), a title of respect or address equivalent to *Mr.* or *Sir;* hence, **mynheer,** a Dutchman.

N

nacré (*F.*), nacreous; pearly.
nager entre deux eaux (*F.*), to waver between two parties; trim.
naïve (*F.*), artless; unaffected.
naïveté (*F.*), native simplicity; ingenuousness: naturalness.
natura non facit saltum (*L.*), nature makes no leap.
n'avoir pas le sou (*F.*), not to have a sou; to be penniless.
née (*F.*), born; used in adding the maiden name of a married woman.
négligé (*F.*), easy or unceremonious attire.
nemine contradicente (*L.*), no one contradicting; unanimously; *abbr.* nem. con.
nemine dissentiente (*L.*), no one dissenting: *abbr.* nem. diss.
nemo me impune lacessit (*L.*), no one assails me with impunity: motto of Scotland.
ne plus ultra (*L.*), not more beyond; the uttermost point attained or attainable; acme; culmination.
ne quid nimis (*L.*), not anything too much: avoid excess.
nescio quid (*L.*), I know not what.
n'est-ce pas? (*F.*), isn't that so?
névé (*F.*), expanse of granular snow at the upper end of a glacier, firn.
niaiserie (*F.*), silliness; trifling; foolery; a silly trifle.
nicht wahr? (*G.*), isn't that so?
nihil (*L.*), nothing.
nihil ad rem (*L.*), nothing to the point; irrelevant.
nil (*L.*), nothing; no number or amount.
nil admirari (*L.*), to be astonished at nothing.
nil conscire sibi (*L.*), to be conscious of nothing (wrong).
nil desperandum (*L.*), nothing must be despaired of; never despair.
n'importe (*F.*), it's no matter.
nisi Dominus, frustra (*L.*), except the Lord (build the house, they labor) in vain: motto of Edinburgh.
noblesse (*F.*), nobility; rank; the nobility.
noblesse oblige (*F.*), rank imposes obligation.
Noël (*F.*), Christmas; yuletide.
nolens volens (*L.*), unwilling (*or*) willing; willy-nilly; perforce.
noli me tangere (*L.*), touch me not.
nolle prosequi (*L.*,) to be unwilling to prosecute: an entry on the court record denoting discontinuance or stay of proceedings: *abbr.* nol. pros.
nolo episcopari (*L.*), I do not wish to be made a bishop: a phrase expressing refusal of a responsible office.
nom de guerre (*F.*), lit., war name; a pseudonym; assumed name.
nom de plume (*pseudo French*), a pen name.
nom de théâtre (*F.*), stage name.
nominis umbra (*L.*), the shadow of a name.
non compos (mentis) (*L.*), not of sound mind.
non ego (*L.*), lit., not I; the external world or object; *opposed to* ego.
non esse (*L.*), nonbeing; nonexistence.
non est (*L.*), he (*or* it) is not.
non est inventus (*L.*), he has not been found: *law*

non libet (*L.*), it does not please me.
non liquet (*L.*), it (i.e., the case) is not clear: *law.*
non multa, sed multum (*L.*), not many things, but much.
non nobis Domine (*L.*), not unto us, O Lord (*Psalm* cxv. 1).
non nobis solum (*L.*), not for ourselves alone.
non obstante (*L.*), notwithstanding.
non omnis moriar (*L.*), I shall not wholly die.
non passibus æquis (*L.*), not with equal steps.
non possumus (*L.*), lit., we cannot: a statement expressing inability to act or move in a matter.
non sequitur (*L.*), it does not follow; illogical inference.
nosce te ipsum (*L.*), know thyself.
nota bene (*L.*), note well; take notice: *abbr.* N.B.
Notre Dame (*F.*), Our Lady; the Virgin Mary.
nous avons changé tout cela (*F.*), we have changed all that.
nous verrons (*F.*), we shall see.
nouveau riche (*F.; pl.* nouveaux riches), a person newly become rich; an upstart.
novena (*L.; pl.* novenæ), a nine days' devotion: *R. C. Ch.*
novus homo (*L.*), a new man; a man newly risen from obscurity.
noyade (*F.*), wholesale execution by drowning, as in France during the Reign of Terror (1793-1794).
nuance (*F.*), shade; tint; subtle distinction or difference, as in meaning, color, etc.
nuda veritas (*L.*), naked (*or* undisguised) truth.
nugæ (*L.; pl.*), trifles; unprofitable minutiæ.
nugæ canoræ (*L.*), melodious trifles (*or* nonsense).
nulla dies sine linea (*L.*), no day without a line; no day without something done.
nulli secundus (*L.*), second to none.
nunc aut nunquam (*L.*), now or never.
Nunc Dimittis (*L.*), the canticle "Lord, now lettest thou (thy servant) depart"; hence, willingness (*or* permission) to depart; departure.

O

obiit (*L.*), he (*or* she) died.
obiter dictum (*L.; pl.* obiter dicta), an unofficial expression of opinion; a thing said by the way; incidental remark.
objet d'art (*F.; pl.* objets d'art), an object of artistic value.
obscurum per obscurius (*L.*), (explaining) an obscurity by something more obscure.
octroi (*F.*), grant; concession; toll; duty, esp. on commodities entering a town.
odi profanum vulgus et arceo (*L.*), I hate the profane (*or* uninitiated) rabble and keep them far from me.
odium theologicum (*L.*), the hatred of (rival) theologians.
œil-de-bœuf (*F.; pl.* œils-de-bœuf), lit., eye of an ox; a round or oval window.
œuvre (*F.*), a work, esp. of art or literature.
ohne Hast, ohne Rast (*G.*), without haste, without rest: motto of Goethe.
oleum (*L.*), oil.
oleum addere camino (*L.*), to pour oil upon the fire; aggravate an evil.
omnia mutantur, nos et mutamur in illis (*L.*), all things are changing, and we are changing with them.
omnia suspendens naso (*L.*), turning up his nose at everything.
omnia vincit amor (*L.*), love conquers all things.
on dit (*F.*), they say; it is said; hence, **on-dit,** a piece of hearsay; rumor.
onus probandi (*L.*), the burden of proof.
opéra bouffe (*F.*), opera of farcical character.
operæ pretium est (*L.*), it is worth while.
opere citato (*L.*), in the work cited: *abbr.* **op. cit.**
opiniâtre (*F.*), opinionated; stubborn.
opus (*L.; pl.* opera), a work; musical composition.
ora et labora (*L.*), pray and work.
ora pro nobis (*L*), pray for us.
orator fit, poeta nascitur (*L.*), the orator is made, the poet is born.
ore rotundo (*L.*), with round full voice; with well-turned speech.
O si sic omnia (*L.*), oh, if all things (were) thus! oh, that he had always done or spoken thus!
O tempora! O mores! (*L.*), alas for the times! alas for the manners!
otiosa sedulitas (*L.*), idle assiduity; leisurely industry.
otium cum dignitate (*L.*), ease with dignity; dignified leisure.
ouï-dire (*F.*), hearsay.
outré (*F.*), outside the bounds of propriety; indecorous; eccentric; bizarre.
outre mer (*F.*), beyond the sea.
ouvrage de longue haleine (*F.*), lit., a work of long breath; a work which lasts or is long.
ovis (*L.*), sheep.

P

pace (*L.*), by leave of; with all deference to.
pace tanti viri (*L.*), by the favor (*or* leave) of so great a man; if so great a man will forgive me.
pace tua (*L.*), by your leave.
padrone (*It.; pl.* padroni), master; the master of a Mediterranean coaster; Italian employment agent.
palafitte (*F.*), lake dwelling.
palmam qui meruit ferat (*L.*), let him bear the palm who has deserved it.
pani (*Hind.*), water.
paralysis agitans (*L.*), shaking palsy: *med.*
parc (*F.*), park.
parcere subjectis (*L.*), to spare the conquered.
pardonnez-moi (*F.*), pardon me; I beg your pardon.
par excellence (*F.*), preëminently; above all.
par exemple (*F.*), for example.
par hasard (*F.*), by chance.
pari mutuel (*F.; pl.* paris mutuels), lit., mutual stake; a form of betting in which those who have backed the winner divide the stakes on the rest, less a small percentage.
pari passu (*L.*), with (*or* at) equal pace; equally and simultaneously.
parlementaire (*F.*), bearer of a flag of truce.
parler à tort et à travers (*F.*), to speak at random or thoughtlessly.
par nobile fratrum (*L.*), a noble pair of brothers; two just alike.
parole d'honneur (*F.*), word of honor: *esp. mil.*
par parenthèse (*F.*), by way of parenthesis; by the way.
Parthis mendacior (*L.*), more mendacious than the Parthians.
particeps criminis (*L.*), an accomplice in a crime.
partie carrée (*F.*), lit., square party; a pleasure party of two men and two women.
parti pris (*F.*), preconceived opinion.
parturiunt montes; nascetur ridiculus mus (*L.*), the mountains are in labor; an absurd little mouse will be brought forth.
parva componere magnis (*L.*), to compare small things with great.
pas (*F.*), a step; precedence.
passage d'armes (*F.*), passage of arms.
passé (*F.; fem.* passée), past; past one's prime; esp., past the period of a woman's greatest beauty; faded; antiquated; behind the times.
passe-partout (*F.*), a master key; pass-key; also, a cut-out mount used in framing a photograph, etc.
passetemps (*F.*), pastime.
pas si bête (*F.*), not such a fool; not so green.

passim (*L.*), everywhere; scatteredly: said of allusions, expressions, etc., found in all parts of a particular book or used by a given author.
pasticcio (*It.; pl.* pasticci), medley; hodgepodge; potpourri.
pastiche (*F.*), medley; imitation (*of an author or artist*); pasticcio.
pastorale (*It.; pl.* pastorali), a piece of music of an idyllic or rustic character; a pastoral.
pâté (*F.*), a pie; pasty; patty.
pâté de foie gras (*F.*), goose-liver pie.
paterfamilias (*L.*), father of a family; head of a household.
pater patriæ (*L.*), father of his country.
patio (*Sp.*), a court or courtyard; esp., an inner court open to the sky in a Spanish or Spanish American house.
pâtisserie (*F.*), pastry.
patte (*F.*), paw (*of animals*); foot (*of birds and in heraldry*); leg (*of an insect*).
pattes de mouche (*F.*), fly tracks; scrawl.
paucis verbis (*L.*), in (*or* with) few words.
pauvre diable (*F.*), poor devil; poor wretch.
pavé (*F.*), pavement; also, a setting of jewels in which the stones are placed close together.
pax (*L.*), peace.
pax in bello (*L.*), peace in war.
pax vobiscum (*L.*), peace be with you.
paysage (*F.*), landscape; landscape painting.
peccavi (*L.*), I have sinned (*or* been to blame); hence, (*n.*) a confession of guilt.
peignoir (*F.*), woman's loose dressing gown; wrapper.
peine forte et dure (*F.*), strong and severe punishment: a form of judicial torture by pressing under heavy weights.
pelure (*F.*), lit., peel; rind; a hard, thin paper, as sometimes used for postage stamps.
penchant (*F.*) inclination; liking (for).
pendeloque (*F.*), pendant; eardrop.
pendente lite (*L.*), pending the suit.
penetralia mentis (*L.*), the secret recesses of the mind.
pensée (*F.*), a thought; maxim.
pensionnat (*F.*), boarding school.
per (*L.*), through; by means of; by; for; for each.
per annum (*L.*), by the year; annually.
per capita (*L.*), lit., by heads; for each individual.
per contra (*L.*), on the contrary; on the other side (*as of an account*).
per diem (*L.*), (so much) by the day; daily.
perdre son latin (*F.*), lit., to lose his Latin; to be unable to make anything (of it); rack one's brains in vain.
père (*F.*), father: often used after French surname to distinguish father from son. Cf. FILS.
per fas et nefas (*L.*), through right and wrong.
perfervidum ingenium (*L.*), ardent temper (*or* disposition).
per incuriam (*L.*), through carelessness.
per mensem (*L.*), (so much) by the month; monthly.
per procurationem (*L.*), by proxy; by the action of: *abbr.* p.p. *or* per pro.
per saltum (*L.*), by a leap; at a single bound.
per se (*L.*), by (*or* in) itself; extrinsically.
persifleur (*F.*), a banterer; quiz.
persona grata (*L.*), an acceptable person.
persona non grata (*L.*), an unacceptable person.
petite (*F.; fem.*), small; little; trim.
petite dame (*F.*), little lady; also, a gay woman.
petite noblesse (*F.*), the petty nobility.
petitio principii (*L.*), begging of the question.
petit maître (*F.*), dandy; coxcomb.
petit souper (*F.*), little supper; an informal supper for a few intimate friends.
petits soins (*F.*), little attentions.
petit verre (*F.*), a little glass, esp. of liqueur.
pétroleur (*F.; fem.* pétroleuse), an incendiary who uses petroleum.
peu à peu (*F.*), little by little.
peu de chose (*F.*), a trifle.
Pfahlbauten (*G.; pl.*), lake dwellings.
piazza (*It.*), place; square; market place.
Pickelhaube (*G.*), spiked helmet.
pièce de résistance (*F.*), lit., piece of resistance; the main dish of a meal: *also used figuratively.*
pièce justificative (*F.*), voucher.
pied (*F.*), foot.
pied-à-terre (*F.*), a resting place; temporary lodging.
Pietà (*It.*), a representation of the Virgin Mary holding the dead body of Christ on her lap.
pince-nez (*F.; sing. and pl.*), eyeglasses with a spring to grip the nose.
pincette (*F.*), tweezers; small pincers; forceps.
pinxit (*L.*), lit., he (*or* she) painted (it): appended to artist's name on a picture: *abbr.* pinx.
pis aller (*F.*), lit., to go worst; last resource.
pisces (*L.; pl.*), fishes.
pisces natare docere (*L.*), to teach fishes to swim; do what is superfluous.
piste (*F.*), trace; track; scent.
place (*F.*), place; room; square.
place aux dames (*F.*), make room (*or* way) for the ladies; ladies first.
plaisanterie (*F.*), pleasantry; jesting; jest; joke.
plat (*F.*), a dish of food.
plaza (*Sp.*), public square; market place.
plus royaliste que le roi (*F.*), more royalist than the king.
poco a poco (*It.*), little by little.
pogrom (*Russ.*), organized massacre.
poilu (*F.*), lit., hairy one; French soldier in field service: *slang.*
point d'appui (*F.*), point of support; basis.
point de réunion (*F.*), place of meeting; rendezvous.
poisson d'avril (*F.*), lit., fish of April; mackerel: April-fool joke.
polisson (*F.*), blackguard; low fellow.
pons asinorum (*L.*), the bridge of asses: the fifth proposition of the first book of Euclid; hence, anything difficult to beginners.
pontificalia (*L.; pl.*), vestments and insignia of a bishop; pontificals.
porte-cochère (*F.*), carriage entrance; courtyard gateway; erroneously, carriage porch.
portefeuille (*F.*), portfolio.
portemonnaie (*F.*), small flat purse or pocketbook.
portière (*F.*), curtain hung over door or doorway.
posada (*Sp.*), an inn; hotel.
poseur (*F.; fem.* poseuse), an affected person; prig.
posse comitatus (*L.*), the power of the county; a body of men who may be summoned by the sheriff to assist in preserving the public peace; popularly, a posse.
poste restante (*F.*), lit., remaining post; to be held in the post office until called for: used in addressing letters.
post hoc ergo propter hoc (*L.*), after this, therefore on account of this: an illogical way of reasoning.
post meridiem (*L.*), after midday: *abbr.* **P.M.** *or* p.m.
post mortem (*L.*), after death.
post obitum (*L.*), after death.
potage (*F.*), soup.
pourboire (*F.*), gratuity; tip.
pour faire rire (*F.*), to excite laughter.
pourparler (*F.*), an informal preliminary discussion; parley; conference.
pour passer le temps (*F.*), to pass away the time.
pour prendre congé (*F.*), to take leave: *abbr.* p.p.c.
pour rire (*F.*), in jest; for fun.
pousse-café (*F.*), a liqueur after coffee; esp., a particolored drink of various liqueurs appearing in layers.
pou sto (*Gr.* ποῦ στῶ), lit., where I may stand; standing place; basis for operation.

précieuse (*F.; fem.*), precious; overnice; affectedly refined.
précieuse ridicule (*F.*), ridiculous précieuse: from the title of Molière's play, "Les Précieuses Ridicules," satirizing the affected purism of the literary women of the day.
précis (*F.; sing. and pl.*), summary; abstract.
première (*F.*), leading woman (*as in a play*); also, first performance; first night.
première danseuse (*F.*), first or leading dancer (*fem.*).
prendre la balle au bond (*F.*), to take the ball at the rebound; take time by the forelock.
prendre la lune avec les dents (*F.*), lit., to seize the moon with the teeth; aim at impossibilities.
prendre le mors aux dents (*F.*), to take the bit in the teeth; fly into a passion; apply oneself unrestrainedly; buckle to.
prenez garde (*F.*), take care; beware.
prestance (*F.*), commanding appearance; bearing presence.
preux chevalier (*F.*), a gallant knight.
prévenance (*F.*), kind attention; obliging manner.
prie-dieu (*F.*), prayer desk; kneeling desk.
prima facie (*L.*), at first view; (based) on the first impression.
primeur (*F.*), first of the season (*said of fruit, flowers, etc.*); hence, early news.
primo (*L.*), in the first place.
primum mobile (*L.*), lit., the first moving thing; in the Ptolemaic system, the outermost sphere, carrying with it the contained spheres in its daily revolution; hence, the prime source of motion; mainspring.
primus inter pares (*L.*), the first among equals.
principia, non homines (*L.*), principles, not men.
principiis obsta (*L.*), resist the beginnings (*as of evil*).
privatdocent *or* **privatdozent** (*G.; pl.* privatdocenten), in German universities, a private teacher recognized by the university.
pro aris et focis (*L.*), for our altars and our hearths; for civil and religious liberty.
pro bono publico (*L.*), for the public good (*or* weal).
procès-verbal (*F.; pl.* procès-verbaux), official report; minutes; in French law, an authenticated statement of fact in support of a charge.
pro et contra (*L.*), for and against.
profanum vulgus (*L.*), the profane herd; unhallowed multitude.
pro forma (*L.*), for the sake of form; as a matter of form.
pro hac vice (*L.*), for this occasion only.
prôneur (*F.; fem.* prôneuse), puffer, eulogist.
pro patria (*L.*), for one's country.
proprio motu (*L.*), by one's own motion or initiative; spontaneously.
propter hoc (*L.*), on this account.
pro rata (*L.*), according to rate (*or* proportion); proportional or proportionally.
pro re nata (*L.*), for an occasion as it arises; for a special emergency.
proscrit (*F.*), outcast; outlaw.
prosit! (*L.*), lit., may it do you good; your health!
pro tanto (*L.*), for so much; to that extent; so far.
protégé (*F.; fem.* protégée), one under the protection or patronage of another.
pro tempore (*L.*), for the time being; temporarily; *abbr.* pro tem.
proxime accessit (*L.*), he (*or* she) came very near (*the winner of a prize, etc.*).
proximo (*L.*), in the next month after the present one; *abbr.* prox.
pucka, pukka, *or* **pakka** (*Anglo-Indian*), lit., ripe; cooked; thorough; hence, permanent; solid; well-built; genuine: *opposite of* kutcha.
pugnis et calcibus (*L.*), with fists and heels; with all one's might.
pulmo (*L. pl.* pulmones), lung.
Punica fides (*L.*), Punic faith; treachery.
purée (*F.*), thick soup of vegetables, fish, etc., boiled to a pulp and put through a sieve.
pur et simple (*F.*), pure and simple; absolute; unconditional.
pur sang (*F.*), pur blood; aristocratic birth or descent.

Q

quære (*L.*), inquire; question: *abbr.* qu.
qualis ab incepto (*L.*), such as from the beginning.
qualis rex, talis grex (*L.*), like king, like people.
quamdiu se bene gesserit (*L.*), so long as he behaves himself well; during good behavior.
quand même (*F.*), even though; whatever may happen; all the same.
quantum libet (*L.*), as much as you please: *abbr.* q.l. *or* q. lib. (*in prescriptions*).
quantum mutatus ab illo! (*L.*), how changed from what he once was!
quantum placet (*L.*), as much as you please: *abbr.* q.p. *or* q. pl. (*in prescriptions*).
quantum sufficit (*L.*), as much as suffices; a sufficient quantity: *abbr.* q.s. *or* quant. suff. (*in prescriptions*).
quantum vis (*L.*), as much as you will: *abbr.* q.v.
quasi (*L.*), as if; as it were; in a manner; seeming; seemingly: used with noun, adjective, or adverb.
quelque chose (*F.*), something; a trifle.
que docet discit (*L.*), he who teaches learns.
quid pro quo (*L.*), something in return; equivalent; compensation; consideration.
quid times? (*L.*), what do you fear?
quién sabe? (*Sp.*), who knows?
quieta non movere (*L.*), not to move quiet things; don't stir things at rest.
quis custodiet ipsos custodes? (*L.*), who shall guard the guards themselves?
qui s'excuse s'accuse (*F.*), who excuses himself accuses himself.
quis separabit? (*L.*), who shall separate?
qui va là? (*F.*), who goes there?
qui vive? (*F.*), who goes there?—**on the qui vive,** on the alert.
quoad (*L.*), as to; as regards.
quoad hoc (*L.*), in this respect; as to this; as far as this goes.
quo animo? (*L.*), with what intention?
quod erat demonstrandum (*L.*), which was to be demonstrated: *abbr.* Q.E.D.
quod erat faciendum (*L.*), which was to be done; *abbr.* Q.E.F.
quodlibet (*L.*), lit., what you please; a debatable point; a subtlety.
quod vide (*L.*), which see: *abbr.* q.v.
quo jure? (*L.*), by what right?
quondam (*L.*), formerly.
quorum pars magna fui (*L.*), of which things I was an important part.
quot homines, tot sententiæ (*L.*), as many men, so many minds (*or* opinions).

R

raconteur (*F.; fem.* raconteuse), a teller of anecdotes; story-teller; narrator.
rafale (*F.*), squall; hence, a violent fusillade; barrage (*mil.*).
raison d'état (*F.*), reason of state.
raison d'être (*F.*), reason for existence; the reason or purpose that justifies or causes a thing's existence.
râle (*F.*), a diagnostic sound accompanying that of respiration: *med.*
rallentando (*It.*), gradually slower: *music.*
ranz des vaches (*Swiss dial.*), a characteristic melody played on the alpenhorn by Swiss herdsmen.
rapprochement (*F.*), the act of bringing (*or* coming) together; reëstablishment of cordial relations, esp. between countries.

rara avis (*L.*), a rare bird; rarity.
rari nantes (*L.*), swimming here and there (*or* one here and another there).
Realschule (*G.; pl.* Realschulen), a nonclassical secondary school.
réchauffé (*F.*), something warmed over; a warmed-up dish; rehash (*lit. and fig.*).
recherché (*F.*), sought out with care; choice; exquisite; rare; far-fetched.
réclame (*F.*), the securing of notoriety; newspaper puff; press-agenting.
rectus in curia (*L.*), upright in the court; with clean hands.
reculer pour mieux sauter (*F.*), lit., to go back in order to leap better; to await a better opportunity.
reductio ad absurdum (*L.*), reduction to absurdity; proof of the falsity of a conclusion or principle by reducing it to absurdity.
regarder de haut en bas (*F.*), lit., to look at from top to bottom (*or* from head to foot); regard scornfully.
Regina Cœli (*L.*), Queen of Heaven; the Virgin Mary.
règlement (*F.*), a regulation; rule.
regnant populi (*L.*), the people rule.
re infecta (*L.*), the business being unfinished.
religieuse (*F.*), a nun.
religio loci (*L.*), the religious sanctity of a place.
remis velisque (*L.*), with oars and sails; with all one's might.
rencontre (*F.*), an encounter; a hostile meeting; also, a casual meeting; rencounter.
rente (*F.*), yearly income, esp. from annuities and dividends.
rentier (*F.*), one who has a fixed income; stockholder; annuitant; imdependent gentleman.
répondez, s'il vous plaît (*F.*), answer, if you please: *abbr*. R.S.V.P.
répondre en Normand (*F.*), to reply like a Norman; give an evasive answer.
repoussage (*F.*), the art or process of hammering out metal on the reverse side, as in repoussé work.
repoussé (*F.*), formed in relief: said of ornamental metal work hammered on the reverse side.
requiescat in pace (*L.*), may he (*or* she) rest in peace: *abbr*. R.I.P.
res adjudicata *or* **res judicata** (*L.*), a thing or matter already settled.
res angusta domi (*L.*), straitened circumstances at home; poverty.
réséda (*F.*), a grayish green color, like that of mignonette.
res gestæ (*L.*), things done; deeds; transactions; exploits.
respice finem (*L.*), look to the end.
respublica (*L.*), commonwealth; republic.
restaurateur (*F.*), restaurant keeper.
résumé (*F.*), summary; abstract.
resurgam (*L.*), I shall rise again.
retenue (*F.*), reserve; discretion; self-control.
retroussé (*F.*), turned up (*esp. of the nose*).
revanche (*F.*), revenge; retaliation.
revenons à nos moutons (*F.*), let us return to our sheep; let us return to our subject.
revue (*F.*), review; inspection; survey.
rez de chaussée (*F.*), ground floor.
rhythmus (*L.*), measured motion; rhythm.
ridentem dicere verum (*L.*), to speak the truth, even while laughing.
ridiculus mus (*L.*), a ridiculous (*or* absurd little) mouse. See PARTURIUNT MONTES.
ridotto (*It.*), a public entertainment, with music and dancing; a dancing party, often in masquerade.
rifacimento (*It.; pl.* rifacimenti), a remaking; recasting; esp., a remodeled form of a literary work or musical composition.
rigor mortis (*L.*), lit., rigor of death; the stiffening of the body after death.
rilievo (*It.*), relief: *sculp.*
risqué (*F.*), risky; improper; suggestive.
ritardando (*It.*), retarding; slower: *music.*
ritornello (*It.*), ritornelle: *music.*
rituale (*L.*), a manual for priests; ritual *R. C. Ch.*
rose du Barry (*F.*), a rose tint used in Sèvres porcelain.
rôti (*F.*), a roast; roast meat.
roturier (*F.; fem.* roturière), plebeian; commoner.
roué (*F.*),, debauchee; rake.
ruat cælum (*L.*), though the heavens fall; let the heavens fall!
rucksack (*G.*), knapsack, as carried by hikers and mountain climbers.
rudis indigestaque moles (*L.*), a rude and undigested mass.
rusé (*F.; fem.* rusée), given to ruses; artful; sly; cunning.
ruse de guerre (*F.*), a stratagem of war.
rus in urbe (*L.*), the country in a city.

S

sabot (*F.*), wooden shoe; clog.
sabreur (*F.*), cavalryman; swordsman, dashing cavalry officer.
sabr karo (*Hind.*), have patience; wait a little.
sagouin (*F.; fem.* sagouine), sloven.
sahibah (*Hind. and Ar.*), a lady.
saignant (*F.*), underdone: said of meat.
salle à manger (*F.*), dining room.
salle d'attente (*F.*), waiting room.
salon (*F.*), reception room; fashionable assemblage in the reception room of a lady of fashion; hence, the Salon, annual Parisian exhibition of paintings, sculpture, etc., by living artists.
saman (*Hind.*), furniture; equipment; gear.
sanctum sanctorum (*L.*), holy of holies; holy place; hence, study; den.
sang-de-bœuf (*F.*), lit., ox's blood; a deep red color found on old Chinese porcelain.
sang-froid (*F.*), coolness; composure.
sans cérémonie (*F.*), without ceremony; unceremonially.
sans Dieu rien (*F.*), nothing without God.
sans doute (*F.*), without doubt; doubtless.
sans façon (*F.*), without ceremony; unceremoniously; outspokenly.
sans-gêne (*F.*), absence of constraint; offhandedness; familiarity; coolness.
sans le sou (*F.*), without a sou; penniless.
sans pareil (*F.*), without equal; matchless.
sans peur et sans reproche (*F.*), without fear and without reproach; chivalrous.
sans phrase (*F.*), without circumlocution; in a word.
sans souci (*F.*), without care; happy-go-luckyism.
sans tache (*F.*), without spot (*or* blemish).
sartor resartus (*L.*), the tailor retailored; the patcher repatched.
satis superque (*L.*), enough and too much (*or* more than enough).
satis verborum (*L.*), enough of words.
Saturnia regna (*L.*), the reign of Saturn; the golden age.
sauté (*F.*), quickly fried with a small quantity of fat.
sauvage (*F.*), savage; untamed; unsociable.
sauve qui peut (*F.*), save (himself)who can.—**sauve-qui-peut**, precipitate flight; complete rout.
savant (*F.*), *adj.* learned; erudite.
savant (*F.; fem.* savante), *n.* man of learning; scholar; scientist.
savoir-faire (*F.*), lit., a knowing how to do; readiness in doing the right thing; tact; address.
savoir gré (*F.*), to be grateful; appreciate.
savoir-vivre (*F.*), lit., a knowing how to live; being at one's ease in society; good breeding.
sayonara! (*Jap.*), lit., if that be so (we shall meet again), good-by!

scandalum magnatum (*L.*), lit., scandal of magnates; defamation of a peer or high official of the realm.
scherzando (*It.*), in a playful manner: *music.*
scripsit (*L.*), he (*or* she) wrote (it).
sculpsit (*L.*), he (*or* she) carved or engraved (this work): *abbr.* sc. *or* sculp. (*usually following artist's name*).
se battre contre des moulins (*F.*), to fight with windmills.
secrétaire (*F.*), an escritoire; secretary.
secundum artem (*L.*), according to art (*or* rule); scientifically; also, artificially.
secundum naturam (*L.*), according to nature; naturally; not artificially.
secundum quid (*L.*), lit., according to something; in some respect only; with limitations.
selon les règles (*F.*), according to rule.
semper eadem (*L.*), always the same (*fem.*).
semper et ubique (*L.*), always and everywhere.
semper fidelis (*L.*), always faithful.
semper idem (*L.*), always the same (*masc. and neuter*).
semper paratus (*L.*), always ready.
semplice (*It.*), simple; without embellishments: *music.*
senatus consultum (*L.*), decree of the senate.
senatus populusque Romanus (*L.*), the senate and people of Rome: *abbr.* S.P.Q.R.
senhor (*Pg.*) *or* **señor** (*Sp.*), a title of respect or address equivalent to *Mr.*, *Sir;* also, a gentleman.
senhora (*Pg.*) *or* **señora** (*Sp.*), a title of respect or address equivalent to *Mrs.*, *Madam;* also, a lady.
senhorita (*Pg.*) *or* **señorita** (*Sp.*), a title of respect or address equivalent to *Miss;* also, a young lady.
seniores priores (*L.*), elders first.
sens dessus dessous (*F.*), upside down; topsy-turvy.
sensu malo (*L.*), in a bad sense.
separatio a mensa et thoro (*L.*), separation from bed and board; legal separation.
separatio a vinculo matrimonii (*L.*), separation from the bond of marriage; divorce.
sérac (*Swiss F.*), a pinnacle of ice, formed by the crossing of crevasses in a glacier.
serein (*F.*), evening mist or fine rain.
seriatim (*NL.*), in a series; serially.
sesquipedalia verba (*L.*), words a foot and a half long; very long words.
sforzando (*It.*), with sudden emphasis: *music.*
sfumato (*It.*), lit., smoked; with indistinct outlines: said of a painting.
sgraffito (*It.; pl.* sgraffiti), decoration by scratches showing a different-colored ground; graffito: *art.*
sic (*L.*), thus: put in brackets after a word or expression in a quoted passage to indicate that the peculiarity or misspelling is the same in the original.
sic itur ad astra (*L.*), such is the way to the stars (i.e., to immortality).
sic passim (*L.*), so everywhere; so here and there throughout.
sic transit gloria mundi (*L.*), so passes away the glory of the world.
sicut ante (*L.*), as before.
sic volo sic jubeo (*L.*), thus I will, thus I command.
sic vos non vobis (*L.*), thus (do) ye, (but) not for yourselves: used of work where the credit and reward fall not to the doer but to another.
signor (*It.*), man of rank; gentleman; a title of respect or address equivalent to *Mr.:* used before a man's name.
signora (*It.; pl.* signore), a title of respect or address equivalent to *Mrs.*, *Madam.*
signore (*It.; pl.* signori), Sir, Mr.; a title of respect or address: not used before the name.
signorina (*It.; pl.* signorine), a title of respect or address equivalent to *Miss.*
signorino (*It.; pl.* signorini), young gentleman; master.
silent leges inter arma (*L.*), the laws are silent in time of war.
s'il vous plaît (*F.*), if you please.
similia similibus curantur (*L.*), like cures like.
simpatico (*It.*), sympathetic; congenial.
simplex munditiis (*L.*), plain in (thy) neatness; elegant in simplicity.
sine cura (*L.*), without charge (*or* care).
sine die (*L.*), without date; without a day being appointed (i.e., indefinitely adjourned): *abbr.* s.d.
sine ictu (*L.*), without a blow.
sine prole (*L.*), without issue (*or* offspring).
sine qua non (*L.*), lit., without which not; an indispensable condition; a necessity.
siste, viator (*L.*), stop, traveler.
sit tibi terra levis (*L.*), may the earth lie lightly upon thee.
sobriquet (*F.*), nickname; assumed name.
socius criminis (*L.*), an associate in crime.
soi-disant (*F.*), self-styled; pretended; would-be.
solus (*L.; fem.* sola), alone: used in stage directions.
sordamente (*It.*), in a muffled manner; softly: *music.*
sordino (*It.*), a mute (*as for a violin*).
sordo (*It.*), muted; muffled: *music.*
soror (*L.; pl.* sorores), sister.
sortes Vergilianæ (*L.*), divination by the random selection of passages from Vergil.
sostenuto (*It.*), in a sustained manner: *music.*
sotto voce (*It.*), in an undertone.
soufflé (*F.*), made light and frothy by beating; as, omelet *soufflé;* also, a delicate dish treated in this manner.
soupçon (*F.*), a suspicion; a very small quantity; a dash; a taste.
soupe-maigre (*F.*), a thin soup made chiefly of vegetables.
sous tous les rapports (*F.*), in all respects.
spargere voces in vulgum ambiguas (*L.*), to spread doubtful words (*or* hints) among the people.
spero meliora (*L.*), I hope for better things.
spiritoso (*It.*), spiritedly; with spirit: *music.*
spiritus (*L.*), spirit; a breathing; aspirate.
spiritus asper (*L.*), rough breathing: *Gr. gram.*
spiritus lenis (*L.*), smooth breathing: *Gr. gram.*
splendide mendax (*L.*), nobly mendacious; untruthful for a good object.
spolia opima (*L.*), the richest spoils; spoils of honor; the arms stripped from a defeated enemy; hence, supreme achievement.
spretæ injuria formæ (*L.*), the offense of slighting (*or* despising) her beauty.
stare super antiquas vias (*L.*), to stand on the old paths.
status quo (*L.*), the state in which (anything is); existing condition.
status quo ante bellum (*L.*), the state existing before the war.
stiacciato (*It.*), very low relief, as on coins: *sculp.*
storge (*Gr.* (στοργή), parental affection.
strictum jus (*L.*), strict law; the strict letter of the law.
Sturm und Drang (*G.*), storm and stress.
sua cuique voluptas (*L.*), every one has his own pleasure.
suaviter in modo, fortiter in re (*L.*), gently in manner, strongly in deed.
subaudi (*L.*), supply (implied word or words) by means of subaudition; read between the lines.
sub dio *or* **divo** (*L.*), under the open sky; in the open air.
sub Jove (*L.*), lit., under Jupiter; in the open air.
sub judice (*L.*) before the judge (*or* court); under judicial consideration.
sub rosa (*L.*), under the rose; confidentially.
sub silentio (*L.*), in silence; privately.

sub specie (*L.*), under the appearance of.
sub voce (*L.*), under the word (*in reference to dictionaries, etc.*): *abbr.* s.v.
succès d'estime (*F.*), lit., success of esteem; indifferent or partial success, as of a play.
suggestio falsi (*L.*), suggestion of a falsehood; misrepresentation.
sui generis (*L.*), of its own kind; in a class by itself; unique.
summum bonum (*L.*), the supreme good.
summum jus (*L.*), the highest law, i.e., strict law as distinguished from equity.
suo jure (*L.*), in one's own right.
suo loco (*L.*), in its proper place.
suo Marte (*L.*), by one's own exertions.
suo periculo (*L.*), at his (*or* one's) own risk.
suppressio veri (*L.*), a suppression of the truth; concealment of facts.
sur le tapis (*F.*), on the tapis; under discussion or consideration.
sursum corda (*L.*), lift up your hearts.
suum cuique (*L.*), to each his own.

T

tableau vivant (*F.; pl.* **tableaux vivants**), living picture; tableau.
table d'hôte (*F.*), a common table for guests at a hotel; an ordinary; a meal at a fixed hour and price: *distinguished from* à la carte.
tabula rasa (*L.*), an erased (*or* blank) tablet; *fig.*, the mind at birth.
tædium vitæ (*L.*), weariness of life.
tailleur (*F.; fem.* tailleuse), tailor; cutter.
tais-toi! (*F.*), hold your tongue! be silent!
tangere ulcus (*L.*), to touch a sore; renew one's grief.
tantæne animis cælestibus iræ? (*L.*), can such anger (*or* resentment) dwell in heavenly minds?
tantas componere lites (*L.*), to settle so great a dispute.
tante (*F.*), aunt; also, pawnbroker or "uncle."
tant mieux (*F.*), so much the better.
tant pis (*F.*), so much the worse.
tant s'en faut (*F.*), lit., so much is wanting; far from it.
ant soit peu (*F.*), ever so little.
ardamente (*It.*), slowly: *music.*
auben-post (*G.*), pigeon post.
azza (*It.*), a large saucer-shaped cup or vase, resting on a pedestal.
Te Deum laudamus (*L.*), we praise thee, O God.
te judice (*L.*), you being the judge; in your judgment.
tekel upharsin (*Heb.*), part of the writing on the wall of Belshazzar's banqueting hall. (*Daniel* v. 25) and translated, "Thou art weighed in the balances and art found wanting; thy kingdom is divided."
telum imbelle sine ictu (*L.*), a feeble dart thrown without effect.
tempus fugit (*L.*), time flies.
tenax propositi (*L.*), tenacious of purpose.
tente d'abri (*F.*), shelter tent.
teres atque rotundus (*L.*), smooth and round; polished and complete: said of a wise man.
terminus ad quem (*L.*), the end (*or* limit) to which; terminating point.
terminus a quo (*L.*), the end (*or* limit) from which; starting point.
terra (*L.*), the earth; earth.
terræ filius (*L.; pl.* terræ filii), son of the soil; lowly born person.
terra firma (*L.*), solid earth; dry land; a secure foothold.
terra incognita (*L.*), an unknown region.
tertium quid (*L.*), a third something; something intermediate, as between mind and matter.
tête-à-tête (*F.*), lit., head to head; private; confidential; a private conversation or interview; also, a settee for two.
tête baissée (*F.*), headlong.
thé dansant (*F.*), a tea at which there is dancing.
Tiergarten (*G.*), game preserve; zoölogical garden.
tiers état (*F.*), the third estate; the commonalty or bourgeoisie, as distinguished from the nobles and clergy in France before the Revolution.
tige (*F.*), shaft of column (*arch.*); stalk or stem (*bot.*).
timeo Danaos et dona ferentes (*L.*), I fear the Greeks even (when they are) bringing gifts.
tirer le diable par le queue (*F.*), lit., to pull the devil by the tail; lead a struggling existence.
toccata (*It.*), a brilliant piece or prelude for the organ or harpsichord.
toga virilis (*L.*), the manly toga; the dress of manhood.
to kalon (*Gr.* τὸ καλόν), the beautiful.
tombé des nues (*F.*), fallen from the clouds.
ton (*F.*), tone; style; fashion; vogue.
to prepon (*Gr.* τὸ πρέπον), that which is becoming or proper.
totidem verbis (*L.*), in so many words; in these very words.
toties quoties (*L.*), as often as; on each occasion; repeatedly.
totis viribus (*L.*), with all one's might.
toto cælo (*L.*), lit., by the whole heaven; by an immense distance; diametrically opposed.
toujours perdrix (*F.*), lit., always partridge; too much of a good thing.
tour de force (*F.*), a feat of strength (*or* skill).
tourner casaque (*F.*), to turn one's coat; change sides.
tournure (*F.*), figure; shape; outline.
tous frais faits (*F.*), all expense defrayed.
tout à fait (*F.*), entirely; wholly; quite.
tout à l'heure (*F.*), presently; in a moment; also, just now; only a moment ago.
tout au contraire (*F.*), quite to the contrary.
tout à vous (*F.*), wholly yours.
tout comprendre, c'est tout pardonner (*F.*), to understand all is to pardon all.
tout court (*F.*), quite short; (of name, etc.) without addition; only that and no more.
tout de suite (*F.*), immediately.
tout ensemble (*F.*), the whole taken together; general effect.
tout le monde (*F.*), all the world; everybody.
traiter de haut en bas (*F.*), to treat with contempt.
transi de froid (*F.*), chilled with cold.
Trinkgeld (*G.*), lit., drink money; a gratuity; tip.
trottoir (*F.*), side pavement; sidewalk.
trou-de-loup (*F.; pl.* trous-de-loup), lit., wolf hole; a V-shaped pit with a pointed stake in the middle; a traphole: *mil.*
tulipe noir (*F.*), black tulip; a rarity.
tu quoque (*L.*), thou also; you too; you're another.
tutamen (*L.; pl.* **tutamina**), protection; protective part.

U

uberrima fides (*L.*), superabounding faith: the most perfect good faith.
ubi supra (*L.*), lit., where above; in the place (in book, etc.) above mentioned.
ultima ratio regum (*L.*), last argument of kings; resort to arms; war.
ultima Thule (*L.*), farthest Thule; utmost limit.
ultimo (*L.*), in the month preceding the present one: *abbr.* ult.
ultra vires (*L.*), beyond one's power; transcending authority conferred by law.
umbra (*L.*), shade; shadow; hence, uninvited guest brought by a guest.
una voce (*L.*), with one voice; unanimously.
und so weiter (*G.*), and so forth; et cetera: *abbr.* u.s.w.
unguibus et rostro (*L.*), with claws and beak; tooth and nail.

uno animo (*L.*), with one mind; unanimously.
uno saltu (*L.*), in one leap; at a single bound.
un sot à triple étage (*F.*), lit., a fool to the third degree; consummate blockhead.
urbi et orbi (*L.*), to the city and to the world.
usque ad nauseam (*L.*), even to nausea; even so far as to disgust.
usus loquendi (*L.*), usage in speaking.
utile dulci (*L.*), the useful with the agreeable.
ut infra (*L.*), as (shown or stated) below: *abbr.* u.i.
uti possidetis (*L.*), lit., as you possess; with the possessions you at present hold.
ut supra (*L.*), as (shown or stated) above: *abbr.* u.s.

V

vade in pace (*L.*), go in peace.
vadium mortuum (*L.*), a mortgage: *law.*
væ victis (*L.*), woe to the vanquished.
vale! (*L.*), farewell!
valeat quantum valere potest (*L.*), let it pass for what it is worth.
valet (*F.*), footman; valet; in card playing, knave or jack.
valet de chambre (*F.*), a valet; body servant.
valet de place (*F.*), a valet who attends on transients and who often acts as courier.
valete et plaudite (*L.*), farewell and applaud: said by Roman actors at the end of a piece.
vaquero (*Sp.*), herdsman; cowboy.
varia lectio (*L.; pl.* variæ lectiones), variant reading.
variorum notæ (*L.*), notes of various commentators.
va-t'en! (*F.*), go away! be off!
vega (*Sp. Am. and P. I.*), a low moist track of land; a plain; Cuban tobacco field.
veilleuse (*F.*), shaded night lamp.
veloce (*It.*), with great rapidity: *music.*
veluti in speculum (*L.*), even as in a mirror.
veni, vidi, vici (*L.*), I came, I saw, I conquered: Cæsar's message to the senate announcing his defeat of Pharnaces, king of Pontus, 47 B. C.
ventre à terre (*F.*), lit., belly to ground; at full speed.
verbatim et literatim (*L.*), word for word and letter for letter.
verbum (sat) sapienti (*L.*), a word to the wise (is enough): *abbr.* verb. sap.
Verein (*G.*), union; association; club.
verre (*F.*), glass; tumbler.
vers libre (*F.*), free verse.
versus (*L.*), against; opposed to: *abbr.* v. *or* vs.
vesica piscis (*L.*), lit., fish bladder; an oval auriole surrounding the figure of a saint or deity: *eccl. art.*
vettura (*It.; pl.* vetture), hackney coach.
vetturino (*It.; pl.* vetturini), a hackney driver; proprietor or driver of a hackney coach (*vettura*).
vexata quæstio (*L.*), a vexed question.
Via Lactea (*L.*), the Milky Way.
via media (*L.*), a middle way (*or* course).
via trita, via tuta (*L.*), the beaten path (is) the safe path.
vice versa (*L.*), the order being changed; conversely: *abbr.* V.V.
vide ante (*L.*), see before.
vide infra (*L.*), see below: *abbr.* v.i.
videlicet (*L.*), lit., one may see; namely; in other words; to wit: *abbr.* viz.
vide post (*L.*), see after this.
vide supra (*L.*), see above: *abbr.* v.s.
vide ut supra (*L.*), see as above; see above statement.
vi et armis (*L.*), by force and arms; by main force.
vigoroso (*It.*), with vigor: *music.*
vigueur de dessus (*F.*), strength from on high.
villeggiatura (*It.*), sojourn (*or* retirement) in the country.
vincit qui patitur (*L.*), he conquers who endures.
vincit qui se vincit (*L.*), he conquers who conquers himself.
vinculum matrimonii (*L.*), the bond of marriage
vin ordinaire (*F.*), a cheap dinner claret; red ink (*slang*).
virginibus puerisque (*L.*), for girls and boys.
vis a tergo (*L.*), a force from behind.
vis-à-vis (*F.*), *adv.* face to face; opposite.
vis-à-vis (*F.*), *n.* an open four-wheeled carriage, with seats facing each other.
vis comica (*L.*), comic power or talent.
vis conservatrix (*L.*), the preservative power.
vis inertiæ (*L.*), the power of inertia; resistance to force applied.
vis medicatrix naturæ (*NL.*), the healing power of nature.
vis mortua (*L.*), dead force; force that does no work.
vis vitæ (*L.*), vital force.
vis viva (*L.*), living force; kinetic energy.
vitam impendere vero (*L.*), to devote one's life to the truth.
viva (*It.*), long live; hurrah: a cry or salute.
vivace (*It.*), in a lively manner; with spirit *music.*
vivandier (*F.; fem.* vivandière), in Continental armies, a sutler.
vivat regina! (*L.*), long live the queen!
vivat rex! (*L.*), long live the king!
viva voce (*L.*), by the living voice; oral or orally.
vive *or* **vivat!** (*F.*), hurrah! huzza!
vive la bagatelle! (*F.*), long live trifles (*or* frivolity)!
vive le roi! (*F.*), long live the king!
vive valeque! (*L.*), long life to you and farewell.
voce di testa (*It.*), head voice.
vogue la galère! (*F.*), lit., row the galley! come what may! here goes!
voilà! (*F.*), behold! look! there! there it is! here you are!
voilà tout (*F.*), that is all.
voir le dessous des cartes (*F.*), to see the under side of the cards; be in the secret.
voiture (*F.*), carriage; vehicle.
voiturier (*F.*), carrier; wagoner; driver.
volte-face (*F.*), complete change of front; a facing about.
Vorspiel (*G.*), prelude; overture: *music.*
vouloir prendre la lune avec les dents (*F.*), to wish to seize the moon with the teeth; aim at impossibilities.
vox (*L.; pl.* voces), voice.
vox et præterea nihil (*L.*), a voice and nothing more; sound without sense.
vox populi, vox Dei (*L.*), the voice of the people (is) the voice of God.
voyageur (*F.*), a traveler; Canadian boatman trapper.
vraisemblance (*F.*), verisimilitude.
vrouw (*Dutch*), a woman; housewife; frow.
vulgo (*L.*), commonly.
vultus est index animi (*L.*), the face is the index of the soul (*or* mind).

W

Wanderjahr (*G.*), year of wandering.
Wanderlust (*G.*), passion for traveling (*or* wandering).
Weltanschauung (*G.*), lit., world view; conception of life or of the world in all its aspects: world philosophy.
Weltschmerz (*G.*), world sadness; vague discontent with the constitution of things; pessimistic melancholy.
Wirtshaus (*G.*), inn; tavern.
Wörterbuch (*G.*), dictionary; wordbook.

Z

Zeitgeist (*G.*), the spirit of the age; trend of thought and feeling in any particular period.
zingaro (*It.; pl.* zingari), a gypsy.
Zollverein (*G.*), customs union.
zum Beispiel (*G.*), for example; *abbr.* z.B.
zwischen uns sei Wahrheit (*G.*), truth b between us.